1 MONTH OF
FREE
READING

at

www.ForgottenBooks.com

By purchasing this book you are eligible for one month membership to ForgottenBooks.com, giving you unlimited access to our entire collection of over 1,000,000 titles via our web site and mobile apps.

To claim your free month visit:

www.forgottenbooks.com/free1295471

ISBN 978-0-483-13892-6
PIBN 11295471

Ward 1—Precinct 1

CITY OF BOSTON

LIST OF RESIDENTS
20 YEARS OF AGE AND OVER

(NON-CITIZENS INDICATED BY ASTERISK)
(FEMALES INDICATED BY DAGGER)

AS OF

JANUARY 1, 1945

THOMAS F. SULLIVAN, *Chairman*
FREDERIC E. DOWLING, *Secretary*
WILLIAM A. MOTLEY, JR.
FRANCIS B. McKINNEY
EVERETT R. PROUT

Listing Board.

CITY OF BOSTON ⬭ PRINTING DEPARTMENT

Page.	Letter.	FULL NAME.	Residence, Jan. 1, 1945.	Occupation.	Supposed Age.	Reported Residence, Jan. 1, 1944. Street and Number.

Bennington Street

K	Sevier Lucy—†	15	housewife	41	here
L	Sevier Thomas F	15	chauffeur	45	"
O	Schraffa Louis E	19	physician	42	"
P	Schraffa Joseph J	19	custodian	43	"
R	Schraffa Thomasina M—†	19	housewife	39	"
S	Grandi Eleanor—†	21	secretary	43	15 Bennington
T	Ferrino Julia—†	21	housewife	30	here
U	Ferrino Peter J	21	physician	30	
V	Keating Dorothy—†	21	operator	25	194 Falcon
W	McLaughlin Charles	21	shipfitter	52	194 "
X	McLaughlin Louise—†	21	operator	48	194 "
Y	Massa Antonio	23	physician	57	here
	2					
B	Conlin Nellie E—†	25	housekeeper	78	"
C	Whalen Margaret—†	25	"	76	..
D	Whalen Mary—†	25	"	63	
E	Becker Ludivine—†	25	"	55	
H	Ruggiero Fannie—†	29A	housewife	47	"
K	Ruggiero Joseph	29A	U S M C	21	"
L	Ruggiero Michael	29A	painter	47	
M	Ruggiero Ralph	29A	U S N	20	"
O	Ritchie Arline—†	35	housewife	44	15 Saratoga
P	Ritchie Harry	35	painter	55	15 "
R	Mennella Charles M	35	watchmaker	48	here
S	Mennella Edith B—†	35	housewife	40	"
T	Mennella James C	35	painter	22	"
U	Mennella Phyllis E—†	35	stenographer	20	"
V	Carney George	35	U S M C	21	"
W	Carney John J	35	watchman	52	"
X	Carney John J, jr	35	U S A	29	
Y	Carney Margaret—†	35	housewife	-51	"
Z	Carney Rita M—†	35	inspector	23	"
	3					
A	Carney William M	35	U S A	25	
B	Little Alice—†	37	housewife	35	"
C	Little John	37	longshoreman	37	"
D	McGrath Margaret—†	37	housewife	75	"
E	McGrath William	37	retired	82	"
F	Driscoll Hannah—†	37	housewife	75	"
G	Driscoll Michael A	37	social worker	79	"

K	Sylvester Gertrude—†	41	housewife	31	here
L	Sylvester Santo	41	brazier	35	"
M	Wessling Annie—†	41	housewife	61	"
N	Wessling Herman	41	mechanic	36	"
O	Wessling John	41	cutter	60	"
R	Brossene Albert	43	U S C G	22	Ohio
S	Brossene Jean—†	43	candymaker	22	here
T	LaMonica Connie—†	43	housewife	43	"
U	LaMonica Helen—†	43	inspector	20	"
V	LaMonica Joseph	43	blacksmith	49	"
Y	Goveia Frank P	45	rigger	53	
Z	Goveia Manuel P	45	U S A	20	
	4				
A	*Goveia Mary—†	45	housewife	44	"
C	Hickey Eleanor J—†	47	operator	20	"
D	Hickey Mary F—†	47	housewife	61	"
E	Aguetta Margaret—†	47	housekeeper	50	"
F	Miemoni Carmine	47	U S A	22	"
H	Kent Anthony F	49	U S M C	29	"
K	Matthews Alfred J	49	janitor	39	
L	Matthews Katherine M—†	49	housewife	38	"
M	Sparaco Mary—†	49	"	33	989 Bennington
N	Sparaco Sabato	49	chauffeur	30	989 "
O	Frongello Dorothy—†	51	housewife	23	here
P	Frongello John	51	coppersmith	24	"
R	Rose Albert	51	U S N	44	"
S	Rose Naomi—†	51	saleswoman	43	"
U	Marotta Alfonso	53	baker	57	"
V	Marotta Frank	53	"	23	"
W	Marotta Vincenza—†	53	housewife	51	"
X	*Palazzo Stella—†	53	housekeeper	67	"
Y	Landolfi Domenic	53	U S A	25	
Z	Landolfi Mary—†	53	housewife	23	"
	5				
A	Fazio Mariano J	57	laborer	41	Pennsylvania
B	Fazio Mildred—†	57	housewife	36	"
C	Taurasi Carolina—†	57	"	32	here
D	Taurasi Frank	57	pipefitter	34	"
E	Emma Rose—†	57	clerk	38	"
F	Emma Salvatore	57	shoemaker	40	"
G	Tracia Mary—†	57	housewife	23	"

Page	Letter	Full Name.	Residence, Jan. 1, 1945.	Occupation.	Supposed Age.	Reported Residence, Jan. 1, 1944. Street and Number.

Bennington Street—Continued

	H	Wall Elizabeth—†	57	housekeeper	48	here
	K	Acone Mary—†	59	housewife	24	121 Havre
	L	Acone Modestino	59	barber	23	121 "
	M	Barbiero Antonio	59	laborer	58	here
	N	DiBenedetto Alfred	59	chromeplater	56	"
	O	DiBenedetto Josephine—†	59	housewife	56	"
	P	Fiandaca Fred	59	carpenter	78	"
	R	Celestra Angela—†	59	trimmer	24	"
	S	Celestra Jennie—†	59	stitcher	22	"
	T	Papia Josephine—†	59	housewife	52	"
	U	Papia Rosario	59	weaver	53	
	V	Rondino Anthony	59	U S A	28	
	W	Rondino Benedict	59	U S N	23	
	X	Rondino Vincenzo	59	tailor	57	
	Z	DiGregorio Antonetta—†	61	stitcher	34	"

6

	A	DiGregorio Carmella—†	61	housewife	61	"
	B	DiGregorio Victor	61	U S A	23	"
	C	Fariole Lawrence	61	fireman	29	67 Bennington
	D	Fariole Margaret—†	61	housewife	29	67 "
	E	Lavoie Della—†	67	housekeeper	66	114 "
	F	Turco Evelyn—†	67	housewife	26	here
	G	Turco Mario	67	U S A	26	"
	K	Standrick Julia—†	69	saleswoman	48	55 White
	L	McDougall Elizabeth—†	69	housekeeper	45	here
	M	Georgopoulous Bertha—†	71	housewife	44	"
	O	Georgopoulous Peter	71	storekeeper	45	"
	N	Georgopoulous Charles	71	U S A	21	"
	P	Georgopoulous Priscilla—†	71	clerk	22	

Border Street

	S	Magliocca Victoria—†	65	teacher	20	here
	T	*Charron Albert	65	retired	79	348 Saratoga
	U	*LaPage Anna—†	65	at home	48	348 "
	V	Mullen Esther S—†	65	housewife	46	348 "
	W	Mullen Francis R	65	rodman	53	348 "
	X	Triant Christ	65	laborer	43	here
	Y	Triant Helen—†	65	housewife	27	"
	Z	Triant Nicholas	65	machinist	40	"

7

	A	Lindstrom Dorothy—†	67	housewife	38	"

Border Street—Continued

	Letter	Full Name	Residence, Jan. 1, 1945.	Occupation	Supposed Age	Reported Residence, Jan. 1, 1944.
	B	Lindstrom Frederick	67	fisherman	46	here
	c	*Lindstrom Walter	67	laborer	34	"
	E	Petrakes Daniel	67	"	26	"
	F	Petrakes Leo	67	U S A	22	
	G	*Petrakes Mary—†	67	housewife	61	"
	H	Petrakes Nicholas	67	machinist	30	"
	K	Petrakes Sotero	67	U S A	31	
	L	Manuel Alida—†	69	housewife	21	"
	M	Manuel Francis	69	U S A	25	
	N	*Chagas Joseph	69	fisherman	44	"
	o	Jerome John R	69	"	45	"
	P	*Leao Docelina—†	69	housewife	57	"
	R	*Leao Luiz M	69	longshoreman	64	"
	s	Reis Francisco	69	fisherman	46	"
	T	Remei Edward	71	storekeeper	71	"
	u	Rodriguez Anthony	75	U S A	27	"
	v	Rodriguez Mabel—†	75	clerk	25	
	w	Rodriguez Manuel F	75	U S A	39	"
	x	*Rodriguez Mary—†	75	housewife	62	"
	Y	Franco Alda—†	75	packer	21	
	z	*Franco John	75	laborer	48	
8						
	c	*Maurici Angelina—†	77	housewife	53	"
	D	Maurici Placido	77	laborer	63	
	F	Curto Frank	79	roofer	28	
	G	Curto Rose—†	79	housewife	35	"

10   Decatur Street

	Letter	Full Name	Residence, Jan. 1, 1945.	Occupation	Supposed Age	Reported Residence, Jan. 1, 1944.
	H	White Bernadetta—†	20	housewife	33	here
	K	White James V	20	painter	35	"
	L	Sbordoni Madeline—†	20	housewife	37	"
	M	Sbordoni Ralph	20	shipfitter	36	"
	N	Sbordoni Carmella—†	20	housewife	65	"
	o	Sbordoni Giuseppe	20	retired	73	
	P	Sbordoni Joan—†	20	dressmaker	27	"
	R	Sbordoni Nunzio	20	U S A	25	
	s	Salvi Alfonso	22	laborer	59	
	T	Salvi Angelina—†	22	housewife	52	"
	u	Salvi Charles	22	clerk	21	"
	v	*Materazzo Nancy—†	22	floorwalker	62	"

Page.	Letter.	FULL NAME.	Residence, Jan. 1, 1945.	Occupation.	Supposed Age.	Reported Residence, Jan. 1, 1944. Street and Number.

Decatur Street—Continued

Page.	Letter.	FULL NAME.	Residence, Jan. 1, 1945.	Occupation.	Supposed Age.	Reported Residence, Jan. 1, 1944. Street and Number.
	w	*Materazzo Pasquale	22	chef	65	here
	x	Greco Esther—†	22	stitcher	30	"
	y	Greco Joseph	22	U S N	32	"
	z	DellOrfano Alberto A	24	"	22	
11						
	A	DellOrfano Arsilio M	24	U S A	25	
	B	DellOrfano Florence—†	24	packer	20	"
	C	DellOrfano Julia—†	24	nurse	22	
	D	DellOrfano Michael	24	watchman	67	"
	E	DellOrfano Richard	24	electrician	26	"
	F	DellOrfano Rosa—†	24	housewife	25	"
	G	DellOrfano Anthony	24	technician	34	"
	H	DellOrfano Maria—†	24	housewife	32	"
	K	O'Neil Olive M—†	25	"	43	
	L	*Italiano Benjamin	25	plumber	59	"
	M	Italiano Pietro	25	U S A	26	
	N	*Ingala Lena—†	25	housewife	40	"
	O	*Ingala Philip	25	retired	49	
	P	Ingala Ralph	25	U S N	20	
	R	Palermo Concetta—†	26	housewife	29	"
	S	Palermo Dominic	26	laborer	31	"
	T	Giovanniello Madeline—†	26	machinist	21	4 Liverpool av
	U	LaConte Filomena—†	26	housewife	31	here
	V	LaConte Joseph	26	laborer	33	"
	w	Rossetti Angela—†	26	housewife	35	"
	x	Rossetti Stephen	26	chauffeur	35	"
	Y	Morgardo John	27	custodian	28	2 Liverpool av
	z	Morgardo Rose—†	27	housewife	27	55 Havre
12						
	A	*Tirone Angelina—†	27	"	58	here
	B	Tirone Jennie—†	27	stitcher	20	"
	C	Tirone Joseph	27	U S A	23	"
	D	Tirone Paul	27	fireman	60	"
	E	Tirone Theresa—†	27	stitcher	24	"
	G	DiClerico Cesira—†	28	"	45	"
	H	DeVito Andrew	28	laborer	56	
	K	*DeVito Concetta—†	28	housewife	65	"
	M	Penta George	29	U S A	32	"
	N	Penta John	29	retired	80	
	O	Penta Marguerite—†	29	factoryhand	29	"
	T	Lopes Manuel	30	machinist	51	"

6

Page.	Letter.	FULL NAME.	Residence, Jan. 1, 1945.	Occupation.	Supposed Age.	Reported Residence, Jan. 1, 1944. Street and Number.

Decatur Street—Continued

u	Virga Antoinetta—†	30	housewife	55	here
v	Virga Vincent	30	U S A	28	"
w	Noonan Mary—†	30	housewife	64	"
x	*Vega Nicholas	32	barber	62	
y	*Vega Rose—†	32	housewife	59	"
z	*Allescia Angela—†	32	"	57	"

13

a	*Allescia Peter	32	laborer	62	"
b	Carsto James	32	foreman	47	Somerville
c	Carsto Mary—†	32	housewife	38	"
d	Marley Annie E—†	34	"	81	here
e	Marley Frank	34	electrician	45	42 Chestnut
f	Marley Harry	34	guard	52	here
g	Marley Agnes—†	34	housewife	34	"
h	Marley Walter	34	letter carrier	39	"
l	Bognanno Anthony	36	storekeeper	24	"
m	Bognanno Frank	36	"	55	"
n	Bognanno Rose—†	36	housewife	49	"
o	Saporito Fannie—†	36	"	30	
p	Saporito Rocco	36	mechanic	32	"
r	*Vella Angelina—†.	36	housewife	60	"
t	DeLorenzo Frank	38	salesman	39	3 Saratoga pl
u	DeLorenzo Sarah—†	38	housewife	36	3 "
v	LaGrasso Elizabeth—†	38	laundrywkr	42	191 Chelsea
w	Quito John	38	laborer	53	Maine
x	Cascio Carmella—†	40	housewife	26	Fitchburg
y	Cascio Joseph S	40	laborer	32	"
z	Canzano Joseph	40	U S A	30	here

14

a	*Pisano Anna—†	40	housewife	63	"
b	Pisano John J	40	U S N	23	"
c	Pisano Rose—†	40	clerk	20	"
d	DellOrfano Annie—†	40	housewife	23	Somerville
e	DellOrfano Henry	40	seaman	24	"

Grady Court

f	Paulson John A	1	U S N	41	here
g	Paulson Laura R—†	1	housewife	41	"
h	Erwin Haskell A	1	U S N	31	"
k	Erwin Mildred—†	1	housewife	27	"

Page.	Letter.	Full Name.	Residence, Jan. 1, 1945.	Occupation.	Supposed Age.	Reported Residence, Jan. 1, 1944. Street and Number.

Grady Court—Continued

L	Rose John E	1	rigger	34	here
M	Rose Josephine—†	1	housewife	29	"
N	Wiggins James O	1	U S C G	24	"
O	Sweeney C Marjorie—†	1	housewife	33	"
P	Sweeney John P	1	toolmaker	34	"
R	Schoppmeyer Leo J	1	U S N	24	1 Fairfield pl
S	Schoppmeyer Nellie—†	1	housewife	23	1 "
T	Darcy Elsie—†	1	"	38	here
U	Darcy Richard	1	draftsman	37	"
V	McGuire Elizabeth—†	1	housekeeper	41	"
W	Brinson Ernest	1	U S N	36	
X	Brinson Margaret—†	1	housewife	27	"
Y	Metcalf Helen—†	1	packer	36	Somerville
Z	Lanning Hannah—†	1	cleaner	63	here
	15				
A	Lanning Julia—†	1	clerk	26	
B	Hartwell Henry E	1	shipfitter	50	"
C	Hartwell John W	1	U S N	20	
D	Hartwell Mary—†	1	housewife	46	"
E	D'Amico Alfonse	1	packer	32	264 Webster
F	D'Amico Minnie—†	1	housewife	30	264 "
G	Runfola Bella L—†	17	"	32	here
H	Runfola Joseph	17	U S N	43	"
K	Coolidge Roscoe	17	brazier	33	"
L	Coolidge Sarah—†	17	housewife	27	"
M	Dutra Diana—†	17	"	29	
N	Dutra Norman	17	metalworker	34	"
O	Smith Catherine L—†	17	housewife	29	"
P	Smith Sidney A	17	laborer	42	"
R	Proulx Hector	17	welder	27	
S	Proulx Rita—†	17	housewife	24	"
T	Cheverie Catherine—†	17	"	36	"
U	Cheverie Percy	17	fisherman	36	
V	Campbell Agnes—†	17	housewife	30	98 Bayswater
W	Campbell Frank J	17	U S N	35	98 "
X	Foley Clara—†	17	housewife	44	here
Y	Foley Thomas J	17	machinist	43	"
Z	Peterson Albert E	17	U S N	69	66 Sumner
	16				
A	Peterson Amanda—†	17	housewife	59	66 "
B	Peterson Arline—†	17	WAVE	21	here

Grady Court—Continued

		FULL NAME.	Residence, Jan. 1, 1945.	Occupation.	Supposed Age.	Reported Residence, Jan. 1, 1944. Street and Number.
	c	Normand Lillian—†	17	housewife	31	here
	d	Normand Lionel	17	welder	32	"
	e	Blundo Josephine—†	17	housewife	25	252 Paris
	f	Blundo Nicholas	17	U S A	26	252 "
	g	Provenzano Joseph	17	shipfitter	38	here
	h	Provenzano Rosalie—†	17	housewife	33	"
	k	Paulsen Hans	25	radioman	36	"
	l	Paulsen Meredith—†	25	housewife	40	"
	m	Milliken Mary—†	25	"	27	
	n	Milliken Paul	25	U S N	31	
	o	Jodoin Alice—†	25	housewife	35	"
	p	Jodoin Sylvio	25	welder	37	
	r	Cravotta Charles	25	U S N	26	..
	s	Cravotta Josephine—†	25	housewife	23	"
	u	Thompson Helen M—†	25	operator	31	41 St Edward rd
	v	Clark Caroline—†	25	housewife	44	here
	w	Clark Frederick	25	U S N	20	"
	x	Clark Thomas	25	longshoreman	45	"
	y	*Lafferty Edith—†	25	housekeeper	77	"
	z	Lafferty Margaret—†	25	forewoman	41	"
17						
	a	Butterfield Edith—†	25	housewife	26	"
	b	Butterfield William E	25	U S N	26	"
	c	Bradley Manassah	25	"	44	
	d	Bradley Mary—†	25	housewife	42	"
	e	Stabler Eugene L	25	U S N	30	58 Horan way
	f	Stabler Helen—†	25	housewife	29	58 "
	g	Quigg Helen—†	25	"	44	here
	h	Quigg Walter	25	U S N	21	"
	k	Quigg William	25	chauffeur	45	"
	l	Joyce Annie—†	25	housewife	75	"
	m	Joyce Jeffery	25	retired	76	
	n	Greer Jeannette M—†	41	housewife	45	"
	o	Greer John J	41	U S A	22	
	p	Barry Glenda C—†	41	housewife	26	"
	r	Barry Walter B	41	welder	32	"
	s	Marineau Gerard	41	"	28	
	t	Marineau Margaret—†	41	housewife	25	"
	u	Perrier Charles E	41	rigger	34	
	v	Perrier Ida B—†	41	housewife	33	"
	w	*Barresa Judith—†	41	"	29	Canada

Page.	Letter.	FULL NAME.	Residence, Jan. 1, 1945.	Occupation.	Supposed Age.	Reported Residence, Jan. 1, 1944. Street and Number.

Grady Court—Continued

	x	Barresa William	41	mechanic	23	Canada
	y	Foresteire Adeline E—†	41	housewife	31	here
	z	Foresteire Phillip J	41	molder	30	"
18						
	a	Gagnon Alphonse	41	welder	34	
	b	Gagnon Marie A—†	41	housewife	33	"
	c	Lewis Emmet R	41	printer	34	
	d	Lewis Marie—†	41	housewife	28	"
	e	White Frank S	41	storekeeper	62	"
	f	White Ida B—†	41	clerk	60	"
	g	Payne Arthur	41	pipefitter	38	"
	h	Payne Eva—†	41	housewife	40	"
	k	Leary Ada B—†	41	"	41	
	l	Leary Edward J	41	machinist	46	"
	m	Bevins Marcelle—†	41	nurse	40	
	n	Fitzgibbons John J	41	laborer	48	
	o	Fitzgibbons Mary F—†	41	housewife	38	"
	p	York Donald P	49	shipfitter	37	"
	r	York Pearl S—†	49	housewife	33	"
	s	McDonough Bertha C—†	49	"	30	
	t	McDonough Joseph M	49	shipfitter	34	"
	u	McDonald Ann E—†	49	housewife	29	"
	v	McDonald Wilfred L	49	electrician	32	"
	w	Baker Harold	49	welder	37	
	x	Hunt Gerald F	49	painter	37	
	y	Hunt Laura G—†	49	housewife	29	"
	z	Hollis Jean—†	49	"	37	
19						
	a	Hollis Melvin C	49	U S N	41	
	b	Forrestall Gladys—†	49	housewife	40	"
	c	Forrestall Wilfred	49	manager	39	"
	d	Burnett James	49	seaman	26	53 Beachview rd
	e	Burnett Lorraine—†	49	housewife	22	53 "
	f	Healy John	49	salesman	43	here
	g	Healy Sylvia—†	49	housewife	39	"
	h	Daddario Elda—†	49	"	25	65 Grady ct
	k	Daddario Matthew	49	electrician	27	65 "
	l	Morano Mary—†	49	housewife	23	here
	m	Morano Richard V	49	seaman	26	"
	n	Retzsch Margaret T—†	49	U S M C	24	"
	o	Toolin Margaret A—†	49	housewife	66	"

Grady Court—Continued

P	Mesita Patrick	65	welder	32	here
R	Mesita Sylvia—†	65	housewife	33	"
S	DeLuca Mary—†	65	operator	23	Chelsea
T	Parziale Adolphe	65	machinist	36	17 New
U	Parziale Anna—†	65	housewife	28	17 "
V	Segal Edith—†	65	"	26	here
W	Segal Max	65	laborer	27	"
X	Scarpato Joseph	65	candymaker	41	"
Y	Scarpato Rose—†	65	housewife	36	"
Z	Surette John	65	U S N	23	292 Princeton

20

A	Surette Mary—†	65	housewife	20	292 "
B	Carroll Agnes—†	65	"	35	here
C	Carroll Joseph	65	chauffeur	38	"
D	Denisov Gabriel V	65	U S C G	38	"
E	Denisov Mary L—†	65	housewife	36	"
F	Hussey John	65	laborer	47	
G	*Hussey Nora—†	65	housewife	44	"
H	Jarvis Ann E—†	65	"	30	
K	Jarvis Joseph T	65	U S N	30	
L	Radzik Edward T	65	U S A	29	
M	Thompson Abraham D	65	mechanic	35	"
N	Thompson Angela M—†	65	housewife	34	"
O	Pugliese Norman	65	U S N	35	
P	Pugliese Ruby—†	65	housewife	24	"
R	Olsen Anders	65	shipfitter	56	"
S	Olsen Jennie—†	65	housewife	56	"
T	Johnson Hilding E	66	inspector	35	"
U	Johnson Louise M—†	66	housewife	36	"
V	Herman Joseph E	66	U S N	35	Florida
W	Herman Theresa M—†	66	housewife	27	"
X	McCarthy Charles	66	chauffeur	36	here
Y	McCarthy Mabel—†	66	housewife	35	"

21

A	Bruso Beatrice—†	66	"	44	"
B	Bruso Florence—†	66	maid	21	Vermont
C	Bruso William	66	machinist	42	here
D	Odell Dorothy—†	66	housewife	26	Vermont
E	Griffin George	66	printer	53	here
F	Griffin Josephine—†	66	housewife	52	"
G	Ennis Blanche—†	66	"	36	"

Grady Court—Continued

H	Ennis Fred	66	machinist	35	here
K	Ulwick Greta—†	66	housewife	28	127 Wordsworth
L	Ulwick Walter	66	U S C G	31	127 `"`
M	Walsh Margaret A—†	66	housewife	29	here
N	Walsh Patrick J	66	clerk	31	"
O	McCready Maude—†	66	housewife	28	Maine
P	McCready Robert	66	mechanic	30	"
R	Harney Genevieve N—†	66	housewife	36	here
S	Harney John F	66	painter	41	"
T	Egan Helen—†	66	factoryhand	50	"
U	Burke John F	73	retired	77	
V	O'Connor Gertrude—†	73	housewife	39	"
W	O'Connor James T	73	U S N	23	
X	O'Connor Joseph T	73	"	21	
Y	O'Connor Thomas	73	pipecoverer	46	"
Z	Gallo Marie—†	73	housewife	34	325 Warren
	22				
A	Gallo Vincent C	73	U S A	33	325 "
B	Thomas Dorothy K—†	73	housewife	38	here
C	Thomas William J	73	U S N	46	"
D	Messer Charles	73	U S A	37	474 Saratoga
E	Messer Regina—†	73	housewife	32	474 "
F	Doherty Francis G	73	attorney	42	Hull
G	Doherty Lillian B—†	73	housewife	42	"
H	Lococo Alfred	73	U S A	32	here
K	Lococo Josephine—†	73	clerk	30	"
L	Arnold Margaret E—†	73	housewife	25	South Dakota
M	Arnold Robert R	73	U S C G	30	"
N	Garrett George	73	pipefitter	40	38 Paris
O	Garrett Mary—†	73	housewife	31	38 "
P	Duckworth Arthur F	73	U S A	26	here
R	Duckworth Arthur H	73	retired	—69	"
S	Duckworth Mary E—†	73	housewife	68	"
T	Duckworth Mary H—†	73	W A C	23	"
U	Kennedy Cecile—†	73	housewife	38	Florida
V	Kennedy David R	73	longshoreman	38	"
W	Smith Samson	73	guard	35	here
X	Smith Veronica—†	73	housewife	36	"
Y	Graziano Antoinette—†	73	"	34	149 Bennington
Z	Graziano Paul	73	mechanic	32	149 "

23
Grady Court—Continued

A	Morrison Georgianna—†	74	housewife	21	66 Grady ct
B	Morrison Joseph D	74	painter	30	here
C	Goundry Arline—†	74	housewife	28	Georgia
D	Theberge Eva—†	74	"	51	here
E	Theberge Jeannette—†	74	photographer	24	"
F	Theberge Ludger	74	machinist	53	"
G	Dorfman Hyman	74	U S A	28	..
H	Dorfman Nettie—†	74	housewife	26	"
K	Cahill Elizabeth G—†	74	"	42	"
L	Cahill William J	74	shipfitter	50	"
M	Hayes Yvette—†	74	housewife	41	"
N	Dunn Charles P	74	operator	31	"
O	Dunn Margaret—†	74	housewife	25	"
P	Rudinsky Marion L—†	74	"	30	
R	Rudinsky Peter	74	shipfitter	34	"
S	Fleming Gertrude—†	74	housewife	35	"
T	Fleming James	74	welder	34	
V	Hunt Alice M—†	74	housewife	48	"
W	Hunt DeForest R	74	brazier	49	..
X	Hunt Kenneth W	74	U S A	23	
Y	Hunt Richard E	74	"	27	

24

A	Hunt Robert V	74	U S N	25	
B	Hunt Stephen F	74	shipfitter	20	"
C	Adams John	74	driller	28	
D	Adams Ruby—†	74	housewife	26	"
E	Tuck Lillian—†	74	"	32	
F	Tuck Raymond	74	U S C G	35	"
G	McKenna Dorothea L—†	89	housewife	36	25 Bennington
H	McKenna George W	89	engineer	36	25 "
K	Buckley John	89	clerk	43	195 Webster
L	Buckley Margaret—†	89	housewife	40	195 "
M	Griffin Lena T—†	89	"	50	here
N	Griffin Louise—†	89	clerk	47	"
O	Griffin Mary F—†	89	operator	53	"
P	Clark Bernard	89	carpenter	40	"
R	Clark Rita—†	89	housewife	39	"
S	Wilson Ashley	89	shipfitter	50	"
T	Wilson Elizabeth—†	89	housewife	58	"

Page.	Letter.	FULL NAME.	Residence, Jan. 1, 1945.	Occupation.	Supposed Age.	Reported Residence, Jan. 1, 1944. Street and Number.

Grady Court—Continued

	u	Brosnahan Alice—†	89	operator	35	here
	v	Crowley William	89	retired	74	"
	w	Reno Catherine—†	89	housewife	23	"
	x	Reno Elwood	89	U S C G	25	"
	y	Savoie Elizabeth—†	89	housewife	41	"
	z	Savoie George	89	electrician	44	
25						
	a	Fitzmeyer Mabel	89	housewife	66	"
	b	Fitzmeyer Mabel—†	89	operator	30	"
	c	Hunt Amelia—†	89	housewife	38	"
	d	Hunt Philip	89	carpenter	43	"
	e	White Peter J	89	inspector	34	"
	f	White Rita M—†	89	housewife	28	"
	g	Salvatore Catherine—†	89	"	37	
	h	Salvatore John	89	butcher	42	"
	k	Downie Helen—†	90	housewife	28	"
	l	Downie William	90	U S N	36	"
	m	D'Addario Adele—†	90	housewife	20	65 Webster
	n	D'Addario Vincent	90	meatcutter	24	82 Chelsea
	o	Govostes Rose—†	90	housewife	39	here
	p	Govostes Theodore	90	chauffeur	36	"
	r	O'Leary Hannah—†	90	waitress	59	98 Sumner
	s	O'Leary Timothy F	90	U S A	24	98 "
	t	Grady George J	90	U S N	45	Lynn
	u	Grady George J, Jr	90	"	22	"
	v	Grady Louise M—†	90	housewife	40	"
	w	Coughlin James	90	U S A	23	139 High
	x	Coughlin May—†	90	housewife	22	139 "
	y	Petrie John	90	laborer	38	here
	z	*Petrie Margaret—†	90	housewife	35	"
26						
	a	Hull Robert W	90	mechanic	27	Maine
	b	Hull Ruth E—†	90	housewife	26	"
	c	Young Mabel—†	90	"	31	18 Grady ct
	d	Young Malcolm	90	machinist	33	18 "
	e	Bossler Frederick	90	mechanic	32	here
	f	Bossler Helen—†	90	housewife	30	"
	g	Flaherty Agnes E—†	90	"	45	"
	h	Flaherty Stephen M	90	U S A	47	Maine
	k	DeIorio Charles	90	"	27	Somerville
	l	DeIorio Elizabeth—†	90	housewife	26	Winthrop

14

Liverpool Avenue

n *Cologero Amico	2	laborer	63	here
o *Margardo Josephine—†	2	housewife	61	"
p Santosuosso Louise—†	2	"	64	"
s *Amico Mary—†	3	housekeeper	88	"
t Cordaro Frances—†	3	"	65	"
u Giovaniello Mary—†	4	housewife	50	"
v Giovaniello Rocco	4	laborer	55	
w Giovaneillo John	4	U S N	28	
x Giovaniello Michael	4	U S A	25	
y Giovaniello Virginia—†	4	clerk	20	
z Caristinos Amelia—†	6	housewife	30	"
27				
a Caristinos Mithel	6	machinist	41	"
b *Marshall Mary—†	6	housekeeper	66	"

Liverpool Street

c Gregorio Josephine—†	52	clerk	26	here
d Gregorio R Joseph	52	U S N	22	"
e Gregorio Ralph	52	U S A	24	"
f *Gregorio Theresa—†	52	housewife	50	"
g McDonald John	52	cook	52	
h McDonald Murdock	52	blacksmith	86	"
k Pallidino Anne—†	52	housewife	46	"
l Pallidino Ella—†	52	clerk	26	"
m Johnson Edward W	53	U S A	23	
n Malloy Mary C—†	53	housewife	44	"
o Amerault Edward J	53	seaman	44	"
p Amerault Madeline—†	53	housewife	42	"
r Pechigallo Rosina—†	54	"	68	
s *Pechigallo Vasilio	54	painter	65	
t Sardina Marcelino	54	engineer	55	"
u Sardino Maria A—†	54	housewife	55	"
v Belt Laura—†	56	housekeeper	68	29 Decatur
w Paglucca Angelina—†	56	clerk	24	here
x Paglucca Julia—†	56	"	23	"
y *Paglucca Maria—†	56	housewife	52	"
z Paglucca Michael	56	laborer	59	
28				
a Paglucca Michael, Jr	56	"	20	
b Paglucca Vincenza—†	56	clerk	21	

Liverpool Street—Continued

c	Mariano John	58	seaman	51	here
d	Perry Clara—†	58	housekeeper	54	"
e	Catalanotto Leonardo	58	laborer	47	"
f	*Catalanotto Vincenza—†	58	housewife	43	"
g	Briana Charles W	58	creamery wkr	33	"
h	Briana Louise—†	58	housewife	34	"
k	Cuddi Anthony	60	U S A	27	
l	Cuddi Charles	60	painter	22	"
m	Cuddi Josephine—†	60	housewife	60	"
n	Flaherty Evelyn—†	60	"	42	
o	Flaherty John J	60	electrician	36	"
p	Cuddi Clementina—†	60	housewife	29	"
r	Cuddi Louis	60	guard	32	
s	Buccelli Edmund	62	U S A	28	
t	Buccelli Victoria—†	62	housewife	28	"
u	Falzarano Anthony	62	U S M C	20	"
v	Falzarano Rose—†	62	stitcher	22	"
w	*Falzarano Stephen	62	laborer	58	
x	Miraglia Biagio	62	U S A	20	
y	*Miraglia Nancy—†	62	housewife	60	"
z	Miraglia Salvatore	62	laborer	66	
	29				
a	Vella Frances—†	62	housewife	31	"
b	Vella Joseph	62	barber	37	
c	Rizzo Ardella—†	62	housewife	66	"
d	Rizzo Pelligrino	62	retired	66	"
¹d	Rizzo Carmella—†	62	candymaker	36	"
e	Rizzo Ernest	62	painter	34	
f	Rizzo Filomena—†	62	clerk	33	
g	Rizzo Mary—†	62	"	26	
h	LaMarco Ida—†	71	housewife	32	"
k	LaMarco Orlando	71	tailor	35	"
l	Fatalo Emilio	71	U S A	23	
m	Fatalo Grace—†	71	housewife	62	"
n	Fatalo Grace—†	71	stitcher	23	"
o	Fatalo Jennie—†	71	"	31	
p	Fatalo Sylvia—†	71	"	26	
r	*Brogna Angelina—†	71	housewife	65	"
s	*Brogna Pasquale	71	fireman	67	"
t	Romano Louis	71	U S A	25	
u	Romano Marie—†	71	housewife	25	"

v	Bruno Andrew	72	laborer	24	here
w	Bruno Mary—†	72	housewife	62	"
x	Lauria Anthony	72	laborer	25	"
y	Lauria Joseph	72	pressman	23	"
z	Lauria Nellie—†	72	operator	27	
	30				
a	Sala Girolamo	72	laborer	70	
b	Sala Josephine—†	72	clerk	28	
c	Sala Mary—†	72	"	30	
d	Cusimano Anthony	73	U S N	21	
e	Cusimano Casimiro	73	barber	63	
f	Cusimano James	73	U S A	24	"
g	Cusimano Joseph	73	"	24	
h	*Cusimano Josephine—†	73	housewife	62	"
k	Cusimano Theresa—†	73	at home	33	
l	Guarino Annette—†	73	proofreader	24	"
m	Guarino Lilly—†	73	housewife	54	"
n	Guarino Richard	73	engineer	59	
o	Tollis Angelo	73	laborer	54	
p	Tollis Francesca—†	73	housewife	49	"
r	Robinson Catherine—†	74	"	30	
s	Robinson John H	74	clerk	38	
t	Chiampa Fred	74	U S A	23	
u	Chiampa Louise—†	74	housewife	56	"
v	Chiampa Mary—†	74	stitcher	32	
w	Capone Carmen	74	chauffeur	38	"
x	Capone Frances—†	74	housewife	40	"
y	Durante Adelaide—†	75	"	32	
z	Durante Carlo	75	chauffeur	29	"
	31				
a	*Dorso Angelina—†	75	housewife	60	"
b	Dorso Frank	75	fisherman	33	"
c	Dorso Michael	75	"	35	
f	Laiacona Florence—†	85	housewife	34	"
g	Laiacona James	85	lumber dealer	36	"
h	*Tucci Mary—†	85	housewife	39	"
k	Tucci Nicholas	85	electrician	42	"
l	Tricardi Anthony	89	laborer	27	
m	Tricardi Joseph	89	"	55	
n	Aleo Alexander	89	"	57	
o	Aleo Alfonso	89	"	23	

1—1

Page.	Letter.	FULL NAME.	Residence, Jan. 1, 1945.	Occupation.	Supposed Age.	Reported Residence, Jan. 1, 1944. Street and Number.

Liverpool Street—Continued

P	Aleo Catherine—†	89	stitcher	21	here
R	Aleo Dorothy—†	89	housewife	54	"
S	Festa William	89	U S A	23	"
T	Poccio Antoinette—†	89	stitcher	20	"
U	*Poccio Enrico	89	laborer	49	
V	Poccio Peter	89	U S A	23	
W	*Poccio Sebastiana—†	89	housewife	48	"
X	Greco Antonio	93	tailor	45	
Y	*Voci Gregorio	93	laborer	62	
Z	*Voci Maria—†	93	housewife	61	"

32

A	Pisano Albert	93	laborer	32	
B	Pisano Anna—†	93	at home	28	"
C	Pisano Carmine	93	laborer	59	
D	*Pisano Christina—†	93	housewife	57	"
E	Pisano Fred	93	U S A	26	
F	Pisano Theresa—†	93	seamstress	20	"
G	DeFino Constance—†	93	clerk	24	
H	DeFino Stefano	93	plasterer	54	"
K	Gallo Mary—†	93	housekeeper	35	"
O	Burke Helen—†	97	housewife	47	"
P	Burke Thomas	97	laborer	45	
X	Amorotis Anthony	103	fishcutter	40	" .
Y	Amorotis Michael	103	fireman	49	13 Winthrop
Z	Amorotis William	103	laborer	38	here

33

A	Recupero Paul	103	pedler	37	
B	Recupero Rose—†	103	housewife	34	"
D	Rota Phyllis—†	105	"	25	
E	Rota Victor	105	meatcutter	25	"
F	Celestina Catino	105	storekeeper	62	"
G	Celestina Jennie—†	105	stitcher	23	"
H	Celestina Josephine—†	105	forewoman	27	"
K	Celestina Rose—†	105	housewife	55	"
L	Caggiano Fiore	105	storekeeper	30	"
M	Caggiano Grace—†	105	housewife	29	"
N	Masucci John	107	shipfitter	37	"
O	Masucci Mary—†	107	housewife	32	"
P	DeAngelis Antonio	107	machinist	60	"
R	*DeAngelis Elvira—†	107	housewife	55	"
S	DeAngelis John	107	U S A	20	

Liverpool Street—Continued

T	DeAngelis Ralph	107	retired	23	here
U	DeAngelis William	107	U S A	27	"
X	Caponigro Andrew	109	welder	25	"
Y	*Caponigro Angelina—†	109	housewife	55	"
Z	Caponigro Serafino	109	guard	58	"
	34				
A	Caponigro Angelo	109	carpenter	34	"
B	Caponigro Rose—†	109	housewife	28	"
G	Hafey James	160	watchman	61	"
H	DeVito Louis	162	merchant	50	" "

London Street

K	Biancucci Vincenzo	50	laborer	67	here
L	Canio Lucente	50	"	55	"
M	DiGianvittorio Anthony	50	U S N	20	185 Maverick
N	DiGianvittorio Egidio	50	tailor	61	185 "
O	*DiGianvittorio Lena—†	50	housewife	57	185 "
P	Golisano Grace—†	50	"	45	here
R	Golisano Guy	50	laborer	53	"
S	Golisano Guy, jr	50	"	21	"
T	Golisano Joseph	50	U S A	26	"
V	Colombo Antonio	52	presser	66	
W	Colombo Concetta—†	52	stitcher	25	"
X	Colombo Guy	52	U S A	28	
Y	Colombo Marion—†	52	housewife	60	"
Z	Petrella Guy	52	brazier	27	
	35				
A	*Petrella Rose—†	52	housewife	57	"
B	Petrella Rose—†	52	stitcher	23	"
C	*Petrella Saverio	52	retired	62	
D	Petrella Saverio	52	U S A	33	
E	Schmahl Gertrude—†	54	housewife	36	"
F	Schmahl Karl	54	pipefitter	42	"
G	Chifellie Anna—†	54	saleswoman	48	Maine
H	Lamole Angie—†	54	housekeeper	47	"
K	*Vitolo Emilio	54	shoemaker	76	here
L	*Vitolo Letizia—†	54	housewife	70	"
M	Doody Francis	56	U S N	27	Medford
N	Doody Hannah—†	56	housewife	72	"
O	Doody Joseph	56	laborer	42	"

London Street—Continued

P	Doody Thomas F	56	U S N	40	Medford	
R	*Fruscione Matteo	56	painter	59	46 Everett	
S	*Fruscione Nancy—†	56	housewife	71	46 "	
T	*Zarro John	56	laborer	59	46 "	
U	Diaz Joseph	56	fireman	58	76 Porter	
V	Diaz Joseph, jr	56	U S N	23	76 "	
W	*Diaz Josephine—†	56	housewife	48	76 "	
X	Diaz Mary—†	56	packer	20	76 "	
Y	Amico George	58	U S N	23	here	
Z	Amico Pasquale	58	painter	53	"	

36

A	Bringolo Carmela—†	58	housewife	25	"	
B	Bringolo Thomas	58	pipefitter	39	"	
C	Vella Joseph	58	laborer	43		
D	Vella Josephine—†	58	housewife	39	"	
F	Chellemi Frances—†	60	"	40		
G	DiLorenzo Michelina—†	60	"	29		
H	Carroll Agatha—†	62	"	27		
K	Carroll Robert	62	U S N	27		
L	Sousa Laura—†	62	housewife	28	"	
M	Sousa William	62	laborer	30		
N	Meli Flora—†	62	housewife	39	"	
O	Meli Joseph P	62	welder	44		
P	Vito Marco	64	laborer	61	"	
R	Fleming Hannah—†	64	housewife	66		
S	McKillop Catherine—†	64	"	68	319 Meridian	
T	Carlson Martha—†	66	"	78	here	
U	Incrovato James	66	U S A	34	"	
V	Incrovato Vivian—†	66	housewife	34	"	
W	Marino Margaret—†	66	"	30		
X	Marino Peter	66	laborer	34		
Y	Bannon Sarah G—†	68	housewife	75	"	
Z	McQuillen Catherine—†	68	"	67	24 Maverick	

37

A	Gallagher Margaret—†	68	"	59	here	
B	Dionizio Maria—†	70	housekeeper	59	10 Winthrop	
C	Colombo Ernest	70	realtor	62	here	
D	Murphy Frances—†	70	housewife	68	"	
E	Taiani Carlo	72	painter	62	"	
F	*Taiani Nicholas	72	laborer	54	"	
G	Poto Edward	72	manager	30	"	

H	Poto Ida—†	72	housewife	29	here
K	Scannapieco Amelia—†	72	"	55	"
L	Scannapieco Antoinetta-†	72	stitcher	24	"
M	Scannapieco John	72	retired	70	"
N	Scannapieco John, jr	72	U S A	21	"
O	Bonelli Catherine—†	74	housewife	23	New York
P	Bonelli Joseph	74	counterman	35	"
R	Milito Anna—†	74	housewife	41	here
S	Milito Joseph	74	welder	45	"
T	Cirrone Margaret—†	74	housewife	48	"
U	Caristo Albert	76	U S N	23	"
V	Caristo Mary—†	76	operator	22	"
W	Caristo Rose—†	76	housewife	56	"
X	Lopez Elvira—†	76	"	45	"
Y	Lopez Frank	76	rigger	49	"
Z	Miano Albert	76	foreman	37	99 London

38

A	Miano Elizabeth—†	76	housewife	35	99 "
C	*Fidalgo John	78	baker	39	76 Havre
D	*Fidalgo Regina—†	78	housewife	31	76 "
F	Laserra Nicholas	80	laborer	55	Somerville
G	*Marino Gaetana—†	80	housewife	67	here
H	Marino Nicola	80	laborer	65	"
K	Polio Jennie—†	80	housewife	45	"
L	Polio Joseph	80	U S A	23	
M	Polio Paul	80	laborer	68	
N	Woodford Mary—†	82	housewife	63	"
O	Woodford William	82	welder	33	"
P	Ventresca Anthony	82	electrician	42	36 Paris
R	Ventresca Beatrice—†	82	housewife	33	36 "
S	Pistone Joseph	82	machinist	50	here
T	Pistone Mary—†	82	housewife	38	"
U	DeBonis Vincent	84	chipper	35	"
V	DeBonis Virginia—†	84	housewife	29	"
W	DellaIacono Clara—†	84	nurse	22	
X	DellaIacono Lena—†	84	machinist	23	"
Y	DellaIacono Pasquale D	84	carpenter	59	"
Z	DellaIacono Virginia—†	84	housewife	53	"

39

A	DePalma Mary—†	99	"	35	
B	DePalma Nicholas	99	shipworker	37	"

21

Page.	Letter.	FULL NAME.	Residence, Jan. 1, 1945.	Occupation.	Supposed Age.	Reported Residence, Jan. 1, 1944. Street and Number.

London Street—Continued

c	DellaRusso Louis	99	laborer	40	Chelsea
d	DellaRusso Louise—†	99	housewife	38	"
e	Chintos Florence—†	99	"	42	here
f	Chintos Nicholas	99	fireman	51	"
g	Rossano Catherine—†	101	housewife	53	"
h	Rossano Thomas	101	painter	53	
k	Caponigro Armando	101	cabinetmaker	23	"
l	*Caponigro Madeline—†	101	housewife	52	"
m	Siracusa Mary—†	101	operator	33	"
n	Lanza Irene—†	102	housewife	36	"
o	Lanza James	102	salesman	36	"
p	Cioffi Anna—†	102	housewife	32	"
r	Lanza Angelina—†	102	"	59	
s	Lanza Frank	102	presser	65	
t	Lanza Joseph	102	U S A	21	
u	Miano Louis	102	custodian	48	"
v	Miano Mary—†	102	housewife	46	"

40

a	Belt Helen—†	104	"	34	
b	Sasso Anthony	104	clerk	33	
c	Sasso Emily—†	104	housewife	31	"
d	Maurici Salvatore	104	presser	41	
e	Maurici Vincenza—†	104	housewife	36	"
f	Giordano Charles	106	laborer	52	
g	Giordano Fannie—†	106	housewife	45	"
h	Giordano Rose—†	106	riveter	24	
k	Giacobbo Joseph	106	laborer	74	"
l	Giacobbo Margaret—†	106	stitcher	34	"
m	Armenguali Manuel	106	laborer	48	"
n	Armenguali Mary—†	106	housewife	54	"
o	Franco James	108	laborer	55	141 Chelsea
p	Franco Salvatrice—†	108	housewife	55	141 "
r	Saldi Angelo	108	U S A	24	here
s	Saldi Antoinette—†	108	housewife	45	"
t	Saldi Frank	108	laborer	54	"
u	Pucillo Albert	108	U S A	30	
v	Pucillo Nicola	108	laborer	66	"
w	Pucillo Rose—†	108	housewife	70	"
x	Pucillo Samuel	108	U S A	28	
y	Locke Alice—†	110	housewife	31	"
z	Locke George	110	laborer	44	

Page.	Letter.	FULL NAME.	Residence, Jan. 1, 1945.	Occupation.	Supposed Age.	Reported Residence, Jan. 1, 1944. Street and Number.

London Street—Continued

A	Morris Isabel—†	110	housewife	34	25 Morris
B	Morris James	110	laborer	35	25 "
C	Altieri Frank	110	salesman	48	here
D	Altieri Philomena—†	110	housewife	51	"
E	Lamie David J	112	engineer	57	"
F	Lamie William	112	laborer	51	"
G	Partee Althea—†	112	housewife	33	118 London
H	Partee Henry	112	operator	37	118 "
K	Little Frances—†	112	housewife	24	here
L	Little Valentine	112	chauffeur	30	"
M	DiLorenzo Maria S—†	114	housewife	35	"
N	DiLorenzo William	114	plumber	37	"
O	DeSantis Anthony	114	musician	42	"
P	DeSantis Mary—†	114	at home	60	"
R	DeSantis Rose—†	114	housewife	35	"
S	Drakoulas Elefthereos	114	restaurateur	49	"
T	Casato John J	114	foreman	39	"
U	Casato Madeline F—†	114	operator	39	"
V	Ruggiero Eleanor M—†	114	housewife	20	"
W	Ruggiero Joseph A	114	U S M C	21	"
Y	Leavitt Genevieve—†	116	housewife	31	"
Z	Leavitt Newton A	116	traffic officer	39	"

A	Ranelli Jean—†	116	housewife	31	"
B	Ranelli Vincent	116	inspector	30	"
C	Spadorcia Fiore	116	retired	79	
D	Dixon Anna T—†	118	housekeeper	62	"
E	Doyle Arthur	118	fisherman	55	93 Princeton
F	Galloway Dorothea—†	118	at home	33	here
G	Jay William	118	laborer	31	Quincy
H	Kelly James	118	porter	45	here
K	Kelly Thomas	118	laborer	47	"
L	Lascalla Amadeo A	118	clerk	25	23 Lexington
M	Ruby William H	118	molder	52	Everett
N	Ruggiero Dominic	118	barber	45	here
O	Russo Salvatore	118	cabinetmaker	58	"
P	Vallee Ulric A	118	weaver	52	"
R	Broussard Edward F	120	welder	33	35 Princeton
S	Lockhart Charles	120	chauffeur	35	102 Belvidere
T	McKay Robert	120	fishcutter	55	here

London Street—Continued

u	McTighe Eleanor S—†	120	at home	59	here
v	Oliver Anthony	120	salesman	56	"
w	Reveri John	120	carpenter	60	New York
x	Rock Mary M—†	120	housewife	66	here
y	Rock Timothy J	120	retired	69	"
z	Ryan James J	120	fisherman	30	"

43

a	Smiley Harold	120	engineer	50	New York
b	Titus Herman	120	yardmaster	58	here
c	Colbert Patrick J	122	shipworker	60	"
d	Dunn John J	122	fisherman	55	"
e	*Fagerquist Arvid	122	molder	46	
f	Hoffman Elizabeth—†	122	housekeeper	67	"
g	Insana Giuseppe	122	barber	48	
h	*Martin Patrick	122	fisherman	44	"
k	Matarazzo Aurelio	122	shoecutter	43	"
l	McDonald Robert H	122	retired	75	
m	Mitts Joseph	122	operator	57	"
n	Norris George	122	fisherman	43	"
o	Ryan Richard A	122	"	46	
p	Scarpas Thomas	122	restaurateur	47	"
r	Brady Dorothy B—†	124	clerk	38	"
s	Brady Margaret—†	124	housewife	65	"
t	Colbourne Andrew	124	janitor	62	"
u	DeFeo Frank	124	guard	21	221 Trenton
v	Dioguardi George	124	chauffeur	25	here
w	Dioguardi Nicholas	124	attendant	36	"
x	Hearn Robert	124	machinist	53	"
y	Lessy Thomas	124	welder	35	
z	Lyons Horace W	124	retired	77	"

44

a	Pero James N	124	chauffeur	54	"
b	Powers John	124	watchman	66	"
c	Nicosia Charles	128	electrician	34	"
d	Nicosia Susan—†	128	housewife	32	"
f	Bonfiglio Mary—†	128	electrician	28	"
g	Edmands Hattie A—†	128½	cleaner	64	
h	*Reitano Monica—†	138	housewife	46	"
k	Reitano Robert J	138	U S A	24	"
l	*Reitano Sylvester	138	wireworker	47	"
m	Barbanti Mary—†	138	candyworker	60	"

N	Barbanti Rose—†	138	shoeworker	27	here
O	Lazzaro Joseph	140	"	33	"
P	Lazzaro Mary—†	140	housewife	32	"
R	Ciampolillo John	140	restaurateur	47	24 Trenton
S	Ciampolillo Sarah—†	140	"	43	24 "
T	Ricciardelli Antonio	140	laborer	36	here
U	*Ricciardelli Benedetto	140	retired	79	"
V	Ricciardelli Elvira—†	140	housewife	31	"
W	McCarthy Helen B—†	142	tel operator	44	"
X	McGinn Charles W	142	U S A	22	"
Y	McGinn James F	142	"	23	
Z	McGrane Helen B—†	142	clerk	30	

45

A	McGrane Mary E—†	142	housewife	72	"
B	McGrane Thomas J	142	retired	69	
D	Marashka John	144	painter	33	
E	Marashka Josephine—†	144	housewife	32	"
F	Tipping Joseph	144	longshoreman	30	"
G	Tipping Violet—†	144	housewife	31	"
H	Miller Edward	144	U S N	32	"
K	Miller Emma—†	144	at home	74	"
L	Leonard Gilda—†	146	housewife	24	"
M	Leonard James	146·	longshoreman	26	"
N	Kelly Agnes M—†	146	housewife	52	"
O	Kelly Catherine T—†	146	at home	75	"
P	Kelly John F	146	attendant	44	"
R	Sarro Edward	146	manager	39	"
S	Sarro Jennie—†	146	housewife	40	"
T	Pacci Mary—†	148	"	30	··
U	Pacci Salvatore	148	electrician	30	"
V	Augusta Biagio	148	bartender	33	"
W	*Augusta Madeline—†	148	housewife	62	"
X	Augusta Pasquale	148	laborer	64	
Y	Camarra Clement	148	machinist	28	"
Z	Camarra Mary—†	148	housewife	28	"

46

A	Augusta Anthony	150	chipper	39	
B	Augusta Celia—†	150	housewife	33	"
C	Nappa Carmine	150	bartender	60	"
D	Nappa Michele	150	U S A	32	
E	*Nappa Petronilla—†	150	housewife	66	"

Page.	Letter.	FULL NAME.	Residence, Jan. 1, 1945.	Occupation.	Supposed Age.	Reported Residence, Jan. 1, 1944. Street and Number.

	F	Amico Josephine—†	150	housewife	37	here
	G	Amico Phillip	150	beautician	37	"
	H	Penta Josephine—†	152	housewife	27	"
	K	Penta Salvatore	152	chipper	30	"
	L	Penta Arthur	152	clerk	26	
	M	Penta Sabina—†	152	housewife	54	"
	N	Penta Samuel	152	U S A	28	
	O	Penta Saverio	152	candymaker	55	"
	P	Capozzi Carmella—†	152	housewife	32	"
	R	*Capozzi Peter	152	laborer	33	
	S	Pizzo Concetta—†	158	housewife	55	"
	T	Pizzo Paul	158	laborer	62	
	U	Marino Alfonse	158	machinist	25	"
	V	Marino Cecelia—†	158	packer	23	
	W	Marino Nicholas	158	laborer	59	
	X	Marino Rafaella—†	158	housewife	44	"
	Y	Marino Theresa—†	158	inspector	26	"
	Z	Cardinale Benedetto	158	fisherman	29	67 Maverick sq
47						
	A	Coggia Anna—†	160	housewife	38	here
	B	Coggia Jerome	160	painter	38	"
	C	Celata Frederick J	160	manager	48	"
	D	Celata Frederick J, jr	160	U S A	24	
	E	Celata Lena—†	160	housewife	45	"
	F	Scrima Frank P	160	retired	70	"
	G	*Scrima Mary—†	160	housewife	69	"
	L	Shea Mary A—†	172	"	74	
	M	Shea Michael J	172	retired	75	
	N	Buckley Anna L—†	172	housewife	71	"
	O	Buckley John H	172	foreman	73	"
	P	Harding Anna—†	172	at home	71	"
	R	Nugent Ellen J—†	174	housewife	59	"
	S	Nugent Mary A—†	174	secretary	25	"
	T	Nugent Richard J	174	retired	65	"
	U	Coughlin John J	174	engineer	67	"
	V	Donahue Mary—†	174	houseworker	63	"
	W	Dalessio Gaetano	180	oil dealer	64	"
	X	Orlandino Edmund	180	chauffeur	33	"
	Y	Orlandino Margaret—†	180	housewife	24	"
	Z	DiFraia Joseph	180	chauffeur	28	"

48
London Street--Continued

		FULL NAME	Res.	Occupation	Age	Residence
A		DiFraia Josephine T—†	180	housewife	28	here
B		McCarthy Rose—†	182	clerk	75	"
C		LaMonica Samuel	184	painter	31	"
D		Lenarduzzi Fermino	184	"	42	
E	*Lenarduzzi Mary—†	184	housewife	36	"
F		Caccanesi Charles	184	cobbler	34	
G		Caccanesi Josephine—†	184	housewife	35	"
H		DeSimone Josephine—†	186	"	29	145 Havre
K		DeSimone Milinino	186	candyworker	33	145 "
L		Campano Mary—†	186	housewife	29	Malden
M		Campano Pasquale	186	meatcutter	28	"
N		Tamagna Andrean—†	186	at home	27	here
O		Tamagna Angelina—†	186	"	35	"
P	*Tamagna Gaetano	186	foreman	44	"
R		Tamagna Rose—†	186	at home	27	"
S		Tamagna Victor S	186	U S A	30	"
T		Tamagna Vincent	186	candymaker	40	"
U		Sordillo Angela—†	188	stitcher	25	"
V		Sordillo Arthur C	188	U S A	28	"
W		Sordillo Carmella S—†	188	milliner	23	"
X		Sordillo Julia T—†	188	housewife	47	"
Y		Sordillo Norma F—†	188	shipper	21	"
Z		Sordillo Ralph C	188	candymaker	55	"

49

		FULL NAME	Res.	Occupation	Age	Residence
A	*Ramos Carl	190	millhand	43	"
B	*Ramos Ondina M—†	190	housewife	38	"
D	*Lottero Joseph	194	shoeworker	65	"
E		Lottero Michael	194	clerk	32	
F		Lottero Rose—†	194	housewife	62	"
G		Lottero Albert	194	U S A	27	
H		Lottero Evelyn M—†	194	housewife	25	"
K		Lottero Joseph E	194	draftsman	24	"
L		Shea Ambrose F	196	U S A	20	
M		Shea Ambrose V	196	carpenter	56	"
N		Shea Anthony	196	U S A	26	
O		Shea Joseph E	196	"	23	
P		Shea Mary—†	196	housewife	44	"
R		DiBerto Mary L—†	198	"	30	
S		DiBerto Romeo G	198	butcher	33	"

Page.	Letter.	FULL NAME.	Residence, Jan. 1, 1945.	Occupation.	Supposed Age.	Reported Residence, Jan. 1, 1944. Street and Number.

London Street—Continued

T	Barnes Charles E	198	mechanic	32	here
U	Barnes Francis	198	U S A	20	"
V	Barnes Josephine T—†	198	at home	58	"
W	Barnes William C	198	U S A	26	
X	Imprescia Joseph F	198	electrician	29	"
Y	Imprescia Phyllis L—†	198	housewife	26	"
Z	*DiDonato Alfonso	200	retired	61	

50

A	DiDonato Helen—†	200	assembler	28	"
B	LaConti Viola—†	200	houseworker	35	"
C	DeChristoforo Amelia—†	200	housewife	30	"
D	DeChristoforo Flaviano	200	pipefitter	34	"
E	Viola Joseph	200	candyworker	37	"
F	Viola Phyllis—†	200	housewife	31	"
G	Bruttaniti Evelyn E—†	202	"	23	
H	Bruttaniti Joseph	202	calker	24	
K	Morello Ida—†	202	housewife	35	"
L	Morello Salvatore	202	hairdresser	41	"
M	Cali Anthony	202	machinist	29	"
N	Cali Virginia J—†	202	housewife	28	"

Maverick Street

O	Goddard Floyd E	1	carpenter	42	here
P	Goddard Leona M—†	1	housewife	44	"
R	Qualey Marie—†	1	"	30	"
S	Qualey Thomas	1	U S N	30	"
T	Dionne John	1	metalworker	35	64 Stoughton av
U	Dionne Theresa—†	1	housewife	36	64 "
V	Rose Jessie—†	1	inspector	23	here
W	Rose Thomas C	1	U S N	24	"
X	*Sinatra Gertrude—†	1	housewife	38	"
Y	Sinatra Vincent	1	clerk	38	
Z	MacInnis Beulah M—†	1	housewife	34	"

51

A	MacInnis John W	1	painter	40	"
B	Breault Edna A—†	1	housewife	32	"
C	Breault Joseph H	1	U S N	34	"
D	Reynolds Michael F	1	laundryworker	57	"
E	Whelpley Margaret—†	1	housewife	27	41 Newcastle rd

28

Page.	Letter.	Full Name.	Residence, Jan. 1, 1945.	Occupation.	Supposed Age.	Reported Residence, Jan. 1, 1944. Street and Number.

Maverick Street—Continued

F	Whelpley Stewart	1	U S A	27	41 Newcastle rd
G	Dalton Edward F	1	longshoreman	20	here
H	Dalton Margaret A—†	1	housewife	39	"
K	Dalton Walter J	1	stevedore	37	"
L	Reidy John E	1	laborer	29	"
M	Ashman Francis	1	seaman	33	"
N	Ashman Helen E—†	1	housewife	34	"
O	Alimonti Andrew E	1	U S A	20	"
P	Alimonti Mary—†	1	housewife	41	"
R	Giacchetti Jennie—†	1	stitcher	37	15 Frankfort
S	Bucci Marcella—†	17	housewife	21	122 Havre
T	Bucci Vincent	17	seaman	25	122 "
U	Andrews Henry E	17	U S N	37	111 St Alphons's
V	Andrews Marie C—†	17	housewife	35	111 "
W	Lyons Mary A—†	17	"	35	here
X	Lyons William	17	retired	34	"
Y	Johnson Lillian—†	17	housewife	28	9 Pond
Z	Johnson Robert	17	fireman	34	9 "
	52				
A	Desrosiers Kenneth	17	U S N	24	here
B	Desrosiers Mary—†	17	housewife	25	"
C	Berry Albertine—†	17	"	34	"
D	Berry Louis H	17	trackman	34	"
E	Massina Joseph	17	pipefitter	31	"
F	Massina Mary—†	17	housewife	31	"
G	Wynters John W	17	U S N	43	
H	Wynters Matilda—†	17	housewife	42	"
K	Carter George W	17	U S N	28	
L	Carter Mary—†	17	housewife	65	"
M	Giordano Ciro	17	laborer	50	
N	Giordano Gloria—†	17	clerk	20	
O	O'Neill Francis	17	laborer	28	
P	O'Neill Marie—†	17	housewife	27	"
R	O'Connell Arthur L	17	welder	31	Stoneham
S	O'Connell Katherine L—†	17	housewife	28	"
W	Apicco Angelina—†	22	"	51	here
X	Apicco James	22	shoeworker	54	"
Y	Apicco Michael	22	U S A	29	"
U	Lovering Leon	22	seaman	33	"
V	Lovering Mary—†	22	housewife	28	67 Border

Maverick Street—Continued

z	Richards Emilie S—†	24	housewife	66	here
53					
A	Richards Ernest W	24	vulcanizer	45	"
B	Richards Noel E	24	retired	76	
C	Hart Catherine—†	24	at home	63	"
D	Mack James	24	sorter	67	
E	*Mack Mary—†	24	housewife	66	"
F	Deasley Elizabeth J—†	25	"	26	
G	Deasley James A	25	riveter	34	
H	Cottle George	25	machinist	51	"
K	Cottle Mary—†	25	housewife	49	"
L	Maynard Evelyn—†	25	"	27	
M	Desharnais Eva—†	25	"	37	
N	Desharnais Walter	25	shipfitter	34	"
O	Morris Charles G	25	boilermaker	33	"
P	Morris Elsie I—†	25	housewife	32	"
R	Hoffman Margaret—†	25	housekeeper	70	"
S	Young Margaret—†	25	housewife	38	"
T	Young Walter F	25	U S A	20	
U	Venable Vera L—†	25	housekeeper	31	"
V	Kelly Charles E	25	longshoreman	39	"
W	Kelly Mary E—†	25	housewife	38	"
X	Vaillancort Albert J	25	rigger	22	N Hampshire
Y	Vaillancort Dorothy—†	25	housewife	22	"
z	Galvin Pearl—†	25	housekeeper	35	Watertown
54					
A	Cordeau Arthur A	25	guard	40	here
B	Cordeau Pearl W—†	25	housewife	35	"
C	Morris Frank	25	guard	39	"
D	Morris Mary—†	25	housewife	42	"
E	LaHar Florence—†	25	"	36	"
F	LaHar Norman F	25	machinist	38	"
G	*Caruso Josephine—†	26	housewife	40	"
H	Caruso Matteo	26	storekeeper	55	"
K	Danplo Anthony	26	U S A	21	"
L	Nucci Antoinette—†	26	housewife	23	"
M	DeLuca Anthony	26	brazier	39	Chelsea
N	DeLuca Helen—†	26	housewife	43	"
O	Fowler Edwin, jr	28	chauffeur	37	66 Grady ct
P	Fowler Mary—†	28	housewife	37	66 "
R	Buckley John	28	U S N	20	here

s	Buckley Margaret—†	28	housewife	42	here
t	Buckley William	28	printer	49	"
u	Johnson Arthur	28	U S A	30	"
v	Johnson, Helen—†	28	operator	23	Somerville
w	Fowler Edward	30	storekeeper	64	here
x	Fowler Ella—†	30	waitress	57	"
y	Mess Charles W	30	foreman	47	26 Maverick
z	Mess Helen E—†	30	housewife	50	26 "

55

a	Acenoulos Alex	42	fireman	57	here
b	*Firistra Antoni	42	"	65	"
c	*Mathiudakis George J	42	retired	63	"
d	*Melos Theodore	42	fireman	54	New York
e	Senoglos Peter	42	chef	50	here
f	Flaherty Rose—†	44	housekeeper	73	"
g	*Pettipas Marion—†	44	housewife	70	"
h	Pettipas Stanley	44	U S A	25	
k	*Bongivani Giuseppe	46	laborer	58	
l	Bongivani Nancy—†	46	housewife	51	"
m	*DeMonte Elvira—†	46	"	50	"
n	DeMonte Matteo	46	chauffeur	22	"
o	*DeMonte Ralph	46	laborer	57	"
p	Lombardo Anna—†	46	housewife	42	"
r	Lombardo Joseph	46	machinist	50	"
s	*Morello Angelo	48	retired	73	
t	*Morello Concetta—†	48	housewife	63	"
u	Morello James	48	U S N	25	
v	Piazza Alexander	48	pipecoverer	46	"
w	Piazza Louis	48	machinist	20	"
x	Piazza Rose—†	48	housewife	38	"
y	Marsiglia Anthony	48	U S A	32	
z	Marsiglia Grace—†	48	housewife	27	"

56

b	Cali Antonio	50	shoemaker	65	"
c	*Cali Marie—†	50	housewife	58	"
d	Michalis Dennis	50	fireman	58	"
e	Michalis Sophia—†	50	housewife	50	"
f	Gualtieri Carmella—†	54	dressmaker	27	"
g	Gualtieri Domenic	54	laborer	54	
h	Gualtieri Louise—†	54	housewife	50	"
k	Gualtieri Bruno	54	barber	29	39 Clark

Page.	Letter.	FULL NAME.	Residence, Jan. 1, 1945.	Occupation.	Supposed Age.	Reported Residence, Jan. 1, 1944. Street and Number.

Maverick Street—Continued

	L	Gualtieri Carrie—†	54	housewife	29	39 Clark
	M	Belmonte Alexander	54	operator	28	50 London
	N	Belmonte Marie—†	54	housewife	66	50 "
	O	Belmonte Phyllis—†	54	decorator	35	50 "
	P	Zichella Amedeo	58	shoeworker	35	here
	R	Zichella Rose—†	58	housewife	30	"
	U	Naso Josephine—†	60	housekeeper	23	"
	V	Naso Maria—†	60	housewife	50	"
	W	Naso Nicholas	60	chauffeur	51	"
	X	Logiudice Frances—†	60	typist	22	"
	Y	Logiudice Rocco	60	carpenter	53	"
	Z	Logiudice Rose—†	60	housewife	41	"

57   Meridian Street

	B	Avallone Nunziante	86	barber	54	here
	C	Lariviere Eugene A	86	millhand	60	"
	D	Lariviere Lydia—†	86	housewife	53	"
	G	Lenoci Domenic	92	laborer	58	
	H	Lenoci Nancy—†	92	housewife	53	"
	K	Socci Anthony	92	U S N	22	
	L	Socci Carmen	92	"	30	"
	M	*Socci Lucy—†	92	housewife	57	"
	N	Socci Stephen	92	laborer	58	
	U	Hollingsworth Mary—†	102A	clerk	60	
	V	Hollingsworth Sarah—†	102A	"	55	
	W	Wilson Margaret E—†	102A	housewife	50	"
	X	Wilson Robert L	102A	stevedore	59	"
	Y	Cohen Eva—†	108	secretary	36	"
	Z	Cohen Helen—†	108	housewife	36	"
		58				
	A	Cohen Louis	108	physician	44	"
	B	Cowin Maurice	108	optician	33	"
	C	Novakoff Goldie—†	108	housewife	45	"
	D	Novakoff Joel	108	retired	51	
	E	Novakoff Leatrice—†	108	clerk	20	"
	H	Czarnetzki Florence—†	122	housewife	52	281 Meridian
	K	Czarnetzki Fred J	122	janitor	46	281 "
	L	Gillis Alexander	122	machinist	53	here
	M	*Gillis John D	122	hipfitter	21	"

Page.	Letter.	FULL NAME.	Residence, Jan. 1, 1945.	Occupation.	Supposed Age.	Reported Residence, Jan. 1, 1944. Street and Number.

Meridian Street—Continued

	N	Gillis Laura—†	122	operator	44	here
	R	*Vallen Catherine—†	126	housewife	38	"
	S	Vallen Daniel E	126	guard	46	"
	T	*Deveau Margaret—†	126	housewife	33	"
	U	Deveau Patrick	126	carpenter	42	"
	V	Head Jesse J	126	U S N	23	Georgia
	W	*Melanson Fannie—†	126	housewife	51	here
	X	Melanson Frank	126	U S A	27	"
	Y	Melanson Raymond	126	"	22	"
	Z	Poirier Wilfred	126	laborer	42	
59						
	C	Nigro Gerald	130	salesman	29	"
	B	Nigro Gilda—†	130	housewife	27	"
	D	Centofanti Vincent	130	machinist	22	"
	E	Iorio Clorinda—†	130	housewife	41	"
	F	Iorio John	130	carpenter	48	"
	G	Iorio Victor	130	U S A	21	
	H	Testa Anthony	130	"	24	
	K	Testa Christina—†	130	housewife	49	"
	L	Testa Joseph	130	tailor	53	
	N	Santangelo Charles	134	chauffeur	32	"
	O	Santangelo Ida—†	134	housewife	22	"
	P	*Nigro Eupremio	134	laborer	53	
	R	*Nigro Filomena—†	134	housewife	54	"
	S	Nigro Marie M—†	134	stitcher	25	"
	T	Centofanti Alfred	134	tool grinder	25	"
	U	Centofanti Lucy—†	134	housewife	20	"
	W	Maloney Earl	138	U S A	23	
	X	Maloney Margaret—†	138	housewife	44	"
	Y	Maloney Marguerite—†	138	operator	20	"
	Z	Maloney Thomas	138	carpenter	53	"
60						
	C	Farmer Elizabeth—†	141	housewife	67	"
	D	Farmer Mary—†	141	boxmaker	46	"
	E	*Dwyer Andrew	141	foreman	36	"
	F	Dwyer Lillian—†	141	housewife	33	"
	G	Joy Catherine—†	143	"	63	
	H	Joy James	143	retired	69	
	K	*Bishop Bernard	143	laborer	53	
	L	Bishop Florence—†	143	clerk	20	
	M	Bishop Janet—†	143	typist	21	

1—1

Page.	Letter.	FULL NAME.	Residence, Jan. 1, 1945.	Occupation.	Supposed Age.	Reported Residence, Jan. 1, 1944. Street and Number.

Meridian Street—Continued

N	*Bishop Maude—†	143	housewife	50	here
o	Bishop Paul	143	U S N	24	"
P	Lawrence Helen—†	143	clerk	23	"
R	Lawrence Leo	143	U S A	26	
U	Bishop Aiden C	149	"	26	
V	*Bishop Cecelia—†	149	housewife	65	"
W	Bishop Geraldine M—†	149	attendant	33	"
X	Bishop Harold J	149	U S A	32	
Y	Critch Catherine A—†	149	WAVE	23	"
Z	Critch Mildred—†	149	engraver	21	"

61

A	Dobbins Catherine—†	149	housewife	57	"
B	Dobbins David J	149	retired	68	"
C	Ivy Frank	149	U S A	24	Florida
D	Ivy Lucille—†	149	sorter	21	"
E	McMullen Helen—†	149	"	32	here
F	Doran Loretta—†	151	brazier	23	Malden
G	Fagan Peter	151	fisherman	45	here
H	Maloney Catherine—†	151	operator	24	"
K	Maloney James	151	rigger	52	"
L	Maloney Jerome	151	U S A	22	"
M	Maloney Sadie—†	151	housewife	54	"
N	Chefaro Helen—†	151	at home	29	"
O	Vaccari Andrew	151	steelworker	43	"
P	Vaccari Margaret—†	151	housewife	30	"
R	Burge Josephine—†	157	laundress	34	"
S	Donovan Cornelius	157	shipwright	58	"
T	Donovan Cornelius J	157	"	37	"
U	Willis James A	157	bartender	58	"
V	Willis Stella—†	157	housewife	40	"
W	Ford Harry	157	U S A	23	"
X	Morey Robert	157	rigger	41	
Y	Perry Jennie—†	157	housewife	41	"

62   New Street

C	Rossner Edward A	9	student	25	here
D	Rossner Esther—†	9	housewife	23	"
E	Coughlin Joseph D	9	plumber	34	"
F	Coughlin Rena—†	9	housewife	31	"
G	Sullivan Helen—†	9	operator	34	"

New Street—Continued

H	DeSousa Joseph	9	painter	43	here
K	DeSousa Mary—†	9	housewife	35	"
L	Fitzgerald Anastasia—†	9	"	70	Winthrop
M	Fitzgerald Joseph	9	boilermaker	39	"
N	Phillips Harold F	9	U S A	33	here
O	Phillips Mary L—†	9	housewife	30	"
P	Barthelemy Charles H	9	laborer	47	"
R	Williams Lorraine J—†	9	housewife	20	"
S	Williams Richard J	9	U S C G	24	"
T	Burke Mary E—†	9	housewife	35	"
U	Burke William J	9	U S A	36	"
V	Santilli Anthony	9	"	29	131 Orleans
W	Santilli Marian—†	9	housewife	23	131 "
X	Connolly John P	9	clerk	30	here
Y	Connolly Lucy D—†	9	housewife	30	"
Z	Burlacqua Gina—†	9	at home	51	258 Everett
	63				
A	Todisco Albert	9	U S A	28	258 "
B	Todisco Lena—†	9	housewife	29	258 "
C	Meehan Joseph	9	waiter	40	here
D	*Meehan Margaret—†	9	housewife	40	"
F	O'Neill Anna—†	17	"	45	Cambridge
G	O'Neill Willard	17	painter	44	"
H	Gillis William	17	factoryhand	22	203 Falcon
K	Brueggeman Eileen—†	17	electrician	28	here
L	Coyne Elizabeth—†	17	housewife	62	"
M	Coyne Thomas	17	U S N	62	"
N	McLaughlin Burleigh	17	cabinetmaker	28	Maine
O	McLaughlin Wilma—†	17	housewife	23	"
P	Menzies Edythe—†	17	"	26	here
R	Menzies Norman M	17	steamfitter	54	"
S	Menzies Norman M, jr	17	"	33	"
T	Colbert Jean—†	17	housewife	29	Maryland
U	Colbert Lanscott	17	U S N	31	"
V	Baldassare Frances—†	17	housewife	23	here
W	Baldassare Pasquale	17	rigger	28	"
X	Brewster Geneva—†	17	houseworker	33	Vermont
Y	Sanborn Dorothy—†	17	housewife	22	here
Z	Sanborn Irwin	17	U S A	25	"
	64				
A	Burns Herbert A	17	U S N	43	

Page.	Letter.	FULL NAME.	Residence, Jan. 1, 1945.	Occupation.	Supposed Age.	Reported Residence, Jan. 1, 1944. Street and Number.

New Street—Continued

	B	Burns Irene G—†	17	housewife	39	here
	D	Hughes Victor H	17	U S C G	34	"
	C	Hughes Winifred E—†	17	housewife	29	"
	E	Silver Lillian—†	17	"	29	
	F	Silver Maurice	17	carpenter	30	"
	G	Bent Francis J	17	U S A	28	Lynn
	H	Bent Margaret F—†	17	housewife	24	11 Trenton
	K	Flanagan Agnes E—†	17	winder	22	10 Princeton
	L	Flanagan Helen D—†	17	receptionist	26	10 "
	P	Atkinson Norma—†	33	housewife	27	here
	R	Atkinson William	33	seaman	40	"
	S	Leuchte Frances M—†	33	housewife	27	"
	T	Leuchte Paul A	33	welder	30	
	U	Walter Emma A—†	33	at home	80	"
	V	Walter Mary R—†	33	factoryhand	56	"
	W	Olsen Bertha—†	33	housewife	35	107 Park
	X	Kincaid Marion—†	33	"	27	here
	Y	Kincaid Miller	33	U S N	38	"
	Z	Delaney Leo T	33	shipfitter	47	"

65

	A	Delaney Marion M—†	33	housewife	42	"
	B	Strehlow Fern C—†	33	"	30	
	C	Strehlow Lyle F	33	U S N	32	
	D	Prevost Mary—†	33	housewife	44	"
	E	Vivert John	33	U S M C	21	"
	F	Arvin Clara—†	33	housewife	35	"
	G	Arvin Samuel	33	U S N	25	
	H	Lanza Caroline—†	33	housewife	33	"
	K	Lanza Vincent	33	shipper	36	"
	L	Healey Daniel F	33	inspector	66	"
	M	Healey Mary E—†	33	housewife	55	"
	N	Downey Charles F	33	U S A	26	
	O	Downey Helen E—†	33	housewife	44	"
	P	Downey Joseph C	33	operator	46	"

66 Porter Street

	A	Laggaro Gaetano	22	butcher	60	here
	B	Laggaro Rosaria—†	22	housewife	54	"
	C	Minichiello Angelina—†	24	"	53	"
	D	Minichiello Antoinetta—†	24	forewoman	21	"

Page.	Letter.	FULL NAME.	Residence, Jan. 1, 1945.	Occupation.	Supposed Age.	Reported Residence, Jan. 1, 1944. Street and Number.

Porter Street—Continued

E	Minichiello Antonio	24	machinist	51	here
G	Caggiano John A	26	laborer	61	"
H	DeVingo Edward J	26	operator	36	"
K	DeVingo Josephine M—†	26	housewife	27	"
M	Marrama Hugo	28	mechanic	40	"
N	Marrama Lena—†	28	operator	28	"
O	Lozzi Joseph	28	tailor.	45	
P	Lozzi Theresa—†	28	housewife	39	"
R	*Dinubla Paul	30	shoemaker	55	"
S	Santiano Anthony	30	U S A	30	
T	Santiano Dominic	30	"	26	"
U	Santiano John	30	"	24	
V	*Santiano Lena—†	30	housewife	67	"
W	*Santiano Louis	30	retired	76	
X	Caruso Philomena—†	30	housewife	35	"

Sumner Street

Z	Goodwin Beatrice—†	34	housewife	31	here
	67				
A	Goodwin James	34	U S N	39	"
B	Knox Charles	34	longshoreman	33	"
C	Knox Helen—†	34	housewife	31	"
D	LaChance Amelia—†	34	"	43	
E	LaChance Raoul	34	shipwright	43	"
F,	LaChance Robert G	34	U S A	21	"
G	Barillaro Christine—†	34	housewife	24	"
H	Barillaro Joseph C	34	U S C G	23	"
K	Swenson Emil R	34	guard	42	
L	Swenson Genevieve—†	34	housewife	42	"
M	Cournoyer Dorilla—†	34	"	49	
N	Cournoyer Joseph P	34	U S N	20	
O	Cournoyer Philip	34	shipfitter	55	"
P	Culber Frank J	34	engineer	28	"
R	Culber Mary E—†	34	metalworker	23	"
S	Degnan Alice G—†	34	housewife	60	Winthrop
T	Degnan Francis M	34	machinist	63	"
U	Tramonte Leonard	34	barber	45	here
V	Tramonte Mary—†	34	housewife	32	"
W	Lothrop Mary—†	34	"	43	20 King
X	Nowell Lawrence	34	U S A	29	20 "

Page	Letter	Full Name	Residence, Jan. 1, 1945.	Occupation	Supposed Age	Reported Residence, Jan. 1, 1944. Street and Number.

Sumner Street—Continued

	Y	Foresta Marie—†	34	housewife	25	here
	Z	Foresta Victor A	34	U S M C	26	"
68						
	A	Geary Marie E—†	34	housewife	44	61 St Andrew rd
	B	Bouve Franklin T	42	technician	39	Maine
	C	Bouve Geraldine—†	42	housewife	27	"
	D	Fitch Edward A	42	calker	56	here
	E	Fitch Ruby—†	42	housewife	56	"
	F	Marshall Walter	42	U S A	23	"
	G	Ingersoll Charles	42	machinist	34	61 St Andrew rd
	H	Ingersoll Claire—†	42	housewife	33	61 "
	K	Remillard Cecelia—†	42	"	29	17 New
	L	Remillard Cyril	42	retired	69	Connecticut
	M	Remillard Ulysses C	42	shipfitter	38	17 New
	N	Marshall Catherine—†	42	housewife	23	here
	O	Marshall George W	42	radioman	27	"
	P	Casey Caroline—†	42	housewife	35	"
	R	Casey Edwin T	42	shipfitter	28	"
	S	Mills Elizabeth—†	42	housewife	34	"
	T	Mills Norman	42	engineer	36	"
	U	Cibello Edith—†	42	housewife	34	"
	V	Cibello Louis	42	machinist	39	"
	W	*Nelson Hilda—†	42	housewife	50	"
	X	Nelson John I	42	metalworker	57	"
	Y	Parker James T	42	U S N	31	
	Z	Parker Margaret—†	42	housewife	28	"
69						
	A	Forti Paul	42	painter	36	"
	B	Forti Theresa—†	42	housewife	24	"
	C	Byrne Esther—†	42	"	41	
	D	Byrne William J	42	metalworker	38	"

William J. Kelly Square

	E	Barrasso Anthony	6	welder	27	here
	F	Ferrarra Thomas	6	chef	69	"
	G	Modugno Salvatore	6	carpenter	52	"
	H	Orlandi Pasquale	6	stonecutter	56	"
	K	Palazzo James	6	weaver	54	
	L	Palma Helen—†	6	housekeeper	35	"
	M	Palma William	6	painter	38	"

38

N	Pasquarelli Vincent	6	carpenter	54	here
O	Bonner Bernard F	7	"	45	"
P	Bonner Margaret F—†	7	housewife	45	"
R	Dietrich Ernest	7	asbestos wkr	60	"
S	Riley Mildred—†	7	laundress	25	"
T	Simonson Margaret F—†	7	at home	23	"
X	Geiss Edith—†	13	welder	26	130 Webster
Y	Nevola Fred	13	machinist	31	here
Z	Nevola Mary—†	13	housewife	26	"
	70				
A	Rizzo Angelina—†	13	"	50	"
B	Rizzo Michael	13	laborer	46	"
C	Carney John	13	retired	82	
D	Ciccarelli Cesare	13	printer	46	"
E	Sicuranza Angelo	13	welder	35	124 Chelsea
G	Pina Antonio	14	U S A	23	75 Saratoga
H	Pina Joseph	14	"	25	75 "
K	Vass Frank	14	machinist	52	75 "
L	Vass Sarah—†	14	operator	49	75 "
M	Morelli Nita—†	14	shoeworker	33	here
N	Valiante Alfred	14	U S A	30	"
O	Valiante Edith—†	14	stitcher	33	"
P	Valiante Peter	14	machinist	39	"
R	Valiante Robert	14	U S A	28	
S	Valiante Rose—†	14	cook	57	"
U	Conway Philip	17	longshoreman	70	23 Princeton
V	Fazio Salvatore	17	retired	57	here
W	Langwasser Ruth—†	17	at home	22	"
X	Shiveree John	17	clerk	20	"
Y	Shiveree Mary C—†	17	housewife	48	"
Z	Sprague Rhodella H—†	17	at home	68	"
	71				
A	Wahoai Joseph K	17	steward	58	"
C	Stanley Charles A	64	U S A	27	
D	Stanley Jane E—†	64	housewife	53	"
E	Stanley Martin K	64	operator	52	"
F	Stanley Martin K, jr	64	U S A	29	"

Ward 1–Precinct 2

CITY OF BOSTON

LIST OF RESIDENTS
20 YEARS OF AGE AND OVER

(NON-CITIZENS INDICATED BY ASTERISK)
(FEMALES INDICATED BY DAGGER)

AS OF

JANUARY 1, 1945

THOMAS F. SULLIVAN, *Chairman*
FREDERIC E. DOWLING, *Secretary*
WILLIAM A. MOTLEY, JR.
FRANCIS B. McKINNEY
EVERETT R. PROUT

Listing Board.

CITY OF BOSTON PRINTING DEPARTMENT

200

Alna Place

A	McVey Elizabeth—†	1	housewife	30	85 Everett
B	McVey Gerald	1	machinist	34	85 "

Brigham Street

c	Menard Alfred	1	longshoreman	38	here
D	Menard Amelia—†	1	housewife	35	"
E	Stevens Margaret—†	1	welder	40	Brockton
F	Cunningham Lillian—†	1	housewife	25	here
G	Disario Angelina—†	1	shoeworker	54	"
H	Disario Emilio F	1	sculptor	56	"
K	Disario Emilio F, jr	1	U S A	20	
M	Centeio Antonio	2	seaman	24	"
N	Monteiro Anthony	2	"	30	
O	Monteiro Frank	2	"	21	
P	Monteiro John	2	U S N	22	
R	Monteiro Joseph	2	seaman	28	"
S	Monteiro Louise—†	2	housewife	30	"
T	Monteiro Theodore	2	U S A	25	
U	Monteiro William	2	seaman	27	"
W	Fleming Agnes—†	3	bookkeeper	35	Gloucester
Y	Muise Eugene	4	U S A	33	"
Z	Muise Idamae—†	4	waitress	32	"

201

A	Cadden Bernard	4	retired	64	1 Brigham
B	Cadden Bridget—†	4	housewife	45	1 "
c	Cadden Patrick	4	U S A	20	here
F	Ferrara John	6	"	27	"
G*| Ferrara Joseph	6	retired	69	"
H	Ferrara Joseph, jr	6	longshoreman	33	"
K	Ferrara Louisa—†	6	cashier	35	"
L	Ferrara Mary—†	6	clerk	22	
M	Ferrara Rose—†	6	housewife	65	"
P	Johnson Catherine—†	10	forewoman	32	"
R	Johnson Margaret—†	10	inspector	26	"
S	Johnson Martha—†	10	factoryhand	21	"
T	Johnson Nellie—†	10	housewife	63	"
U*| Johnson William	10	longshoreman	65	"
V	Gasparelli Nicholas	10	retired	65	194 Marginal
W	Icona Gaspar	10	U S A	25	here

2

Brigham Street—Continued

x	*Siriano Michael	10	retired	76	here
y	Siriano Michael A	10	U S A	22	"
z	*Siriano Rose—†	10	housewife	63	"
	202				
a	Stornainolo Albert	10	U S N	20	
b	Stornainolo Carmine	10	painter	41	
c	*Stornainolo Jennie—†	10	housewife	46	"
d	Stornainolo Lena—†	10	operator	23	"
e	McCarthy John J	18	longshoreman	36	"
f	*McCarthy Mabel—†	18	housewife	37	"
g	*Barone Louis	20	retired	53	
h	McCarthy Alice—†	21	housewife	35	"
k	McCarthy Daniel	21	U S A	31	
l	McCarthy Edward	21	"	26	
m	McCarthy Joseph	21	longshoreman	38	"
n	McCarthy Martha—†	21	housewife	22	2 Brigham
o	Sweeney Annie G—†	22	"	73	here
p	*Sweeney William G	22	retired	73	"

Cottage Street

t	Caruso Edith—†	10	housewife	30	here
u	Caruso Felico A	10	chauffeur	29	"
v	Cocchi Joseph	10	U S A	23	"
w	*Cocchi Lena—†	10	housewife	58	"
x	Cocchi Paul	10	laborer	59	
y	Cocchi Virginia—†	10	welder	26	"
z	Cocchi Yolando E—†	10	"	21	
	203				
a	Chiamca Josephine L—†	10	housewife	23	"
b	Chiamca Louis Q	10	clerk	29	"
c	DeRosa Anna M—†	12	housewife	36	"
d	DeRosa Carmine A	12	welder	35	"
e	DeSimone Anthony	12	carpenter	45	"
f	DeSimone Mary—†	12	candymaker	48	"
g	Sweeney Eleanor—†	12	housewife	33	"
h	Sweeney William Q	12	painter	37	"
k	Tiso Anna M—†	14	housewife	26	77 Cottage
l	Tiso Patrick P	14	U S N	28	77 "
m	Aceto Antonio V	14	electrician	30	72 Webster
n	Aceto Lena M—†	14	housewife	27	72 "

Page.	Letter.	FULL NAME.	Residence, Jan. 1, 1945.	Occupation.	Supposed Age.	Reported Residence, Jan. 1, 1944. Street and Number.

Cottage Street—Continued

	P	Guarino Antonette—†	15	housewife	38	here
	R	Guarino Michael	15	pipefitter	39	"
	S	*Conti Anthony	15	trackman	60	"
	T	Conti Gloria M—†	15	boxmaker	21	"
	U	Conti Helen M—†	15	stitcher	23	"
	V	Conti Rose J—†	15	housekeeper	26	"
	W	Conti Sadie A—†	15	stitcher	29	"
	X	Salvo Joseph A	15	painter	31	
	Y	Salvo Theresa R—†	15	housewife	31	"
	Z	Curto Catherine A—†	16	"	22	

204

	A	Curto Vincent S	16	electrician	23	"
	B	Gravallese Josephine M-†	16	housewife	30	"
	C	Gravallese Michael	16	foreman	31	"
	D	Gravallese Pasquale	16	shoeworker	45	"
	E	McKenna Catherine E—†	17	housewife	23	"
	F	McKenna Edward J	17	U S N	24	
	H	McKenna Jeremiah	17	"	23	
	K	McKenna Nora—†	17	housewife	60	"
	L	McKenna William	17	watchman	62	"
	M	Venelli Columbia—†	18	candymaker	51	"
	N	Venelli Mary—†	18	housewife	31	"
	O	Venelli Ubaldo	18	barber	53	"
	P	Goddard Albert E	18	longshoreman	49	146 Webster
	R	Goddard Jennie—†	18	housewife	42	146 "
	S	St John Mary R—†	18	"	27	146 "
	Y	Bellio Mary M—†	33	"	36	here
	Z	Bellio Silvio A	33	painter	48	"

205

	A	*Carine Adeline—†	33	housewife	59	"
	B	Carine John F	33	U S A	21	
	C	*Carine Joseph	33	laborer	71	"
	D	Carine Joseph, jr	33	painter	29	"
	E	Carine Louise—†	33	dressmaker	27	"
	F	Lombardi Ida—†	34	housewife	37	"
	G	Lombardi Jennie—†	34	winder	40	
	H	*Lombardi Mary—†	34	at home	86	"
	K	Lombardi Michael J	34	ironworker	38	"
	L	Stasio Amelia T—†	34	housewife	42	"
	M	Stasio John B	34	installer	47	"
	N	Stasio Emilio H	34	technician	42	"

Cottage Street—Continued

o	Stasio Rose S—†	34	housewife	38	here
p	Stasio Vincent P	34	U S N	20	"
s	Martel Ernest	36	laborer	70	"
t	Martel Rose—†	36	housewife	65	"
u	DeFilippo Maria S—†	36	at home	56	"
v	Mendolia Diejo J	36	U S A	20	
w	Mendolia Marianna—†	36	candymaker	42	"
x	Malafronte Nicola	36	machinist	59	"
y	*Malafronte Olga—†	36	housewife	55	"
z	Murphy Charles J	36	U S N	29	
	206				
a	Murphy Theresa E—†	36	clerk	23	
d	Maffei Romano J	38	pipecoverer	62	"
e	Maffei Silvia C—†	38	housewife	62	"
f	Zenkin Anna—†	38	stitcher	31	
g	Zenkin Walter S	38	upholsterer	45	"
h	Mazzotta Frank	38	U S A	21	
k	Mazzotta Gregory	38	janitor	57	
l	Mazzotta Marianna—†	38	housewife	50	"
m	Belger Mary—†	39	saleswoman	57	"
n	Malerba Anna—†	41	housewife	27	"
o	Malerba Dominic	41	painter	30	"
p	Porcaro John S	41	"	24	156 Webster
r	Porcaro Rose M—†	41	housewife	23	156 "
s	Collizzi Christopher	41	U S N	21	here
t	*Triperi Alphonzina—†	41	housekeeper	47	"
u	Cammerano Nancy F—†	42	at home	22	"
v	Luporto Catherine J—†	42	welder	26	"
w	*Luporto Ignazio	42	retired	59	
x	Luporto Joseph I	42	longshoreman	28	"
y	DiChiara Angelio A	42	mason	28	
z	DiChiara Dorothy—†	42	housewife	25	"
	207				
a	Amato John	42	carpenter	50	"
b	*Donnaruma Anna—†	42	housewife	44	8 Sumner pl
c	*Donnaruma Cono	42	retired	69	11 Wiggin
d	Donnaruma Sabatino	42	laborer	43	8 Sumner pl
g	DiChiara Frank J	43	U S A	20	here
h	DiChiara Olga—†	43	housewife	45	"
k	DiChiara Ralph	43	ironworker	49	"
l	Guanciali Anthony	43	welder	34	

Page:	Letter.	FULL NAME.	Residence, Jan. 1, 1945.	Occupation.	Supposed Age.	Reported Residence, Jan. 1, 1944. Street and Number.

Cottage Street—Continued

M	Guanciali Mary—†	43	housewife	31	here
N	Milo Lena—†	44	stitcher	39	"
O	Milo Leonard	44	barber	44	"
P	Chin Daney	47	laundryman	41	"
R	George Fred D	49	chauffeur	32	41 Rossmore rd
S	George Jennie B—†	49	housewife	25	41 "
T	Ragusa Dorothy—†	49	stitcher	30	2 Webster av
U	Ragusa James	49	U S A	35	2 "
X	Lemire Wilfred	54	U S N	20	here
Y	Lemire William	54	shipfitter	55	"
Z	Lemire William G	54	clerk	25	"
	208				
B	Corso Florence P—†	54	housewife	30	"
C	Corso Frank M	54	chauffeur	36	"
D	Vocino Imbriani D	54	longshoreman	48	"

Cottage Street Place

E	Runney Arlene—†	2	manager	52	here
F	Runney Georgianna—†	2	housewife	91	"
H	Serino Antonio	2	shipfitter	49	98 Everett
K	Serino Joseph	2	U S A	23	98 "
L	Serino Victoria—†	2	housewife	45	98 "
M	Amico Giovannina—†	2	"	57	here
N	Amico Luciano	2	machinist	62	"
O	Ritchie Harry W	2	U S C G	24	Virginia
P	Ritchie Mary L—†	2	housewife	21	here
R	Polignone Anthony	4	retired	57	"
S	Polignone Frank	4	U S A	20	"
T	Polignone Josephine—†	4	laundress	25	"
U	Polignone Michael	4	U S N	22	
V	*Polignone Michelina—†	4	housewife	52	"
W	Polignone Tina—†	4	shoeworker	21	"
X	Carraggi Ida—†	4	housewife	59	"
Y	Carraggi Joseph	4	laborer	60	
Z	Carraggi Stephen	4	metalworker	21	"

209   Haynes Street

B	Mascis Frank	2	laborer	30	here
C	Mascis Ruby—†	2	housewife	29	"

Page.	Letter.	FULL NAME.	Residence, Jan. 1, 1945.	Occupation.	Supposed Age.	Reported Residence, Jan. 1, 1944. Street and Number.

Haynes Street—Continued

	D	Loviso Joseph	2	plasterer	61	here
	E	Loviso Sabina—†	2	housewife	58	"
	F	Porrazzo James	2	chauffeur	36	84 Everett
	G	Porrazzo Mary—†	2˙	housewife	31	84 "
	M	Ranese Antoinette—†	6	"	34	here
	N	Ranese Joseph	ˏ6	laborer	55	"
	O	Ranese Josephine—†	6	stitcher	20	"
	P	Forgione Anthony	6	U S A	25	
	R	*Forgione Joseph	6	laborer ·	55	
	S	Forgione Joseph, jr	6	U S A	20	
	T	Forgione Martin	6	"	23	
	U	*Forgione Mary—†	6	housewife	50	"
	V	*Cozzino Joseph	7	carpenter	57	"
	W	Cusinotto Lillian—†	7	housekeeper	65	"
	Y	*Delspero Carmen	7	oiler	65	..
	Z	Delspero Mary—†	7	housewife	37	"
	210					
	A	Botte Fred	8	laborer	50	6 Haynes
	B	Cioffi Anthony	8	U S A	26	here
	C	Cioffi Benjamin	8	"	22	"
	D	Cioffi Enrico	8	tailor	54	"
	E	Cioffi Enrico, jr	8	U S N	24	
	F	Cioffi Jennie—†	8	housewife	54	"
	G	Cioffi Jennie—†	8	stitcher	24	"
	H	Cioffi Margaret—†	8	"	20	"
	K	Parisi Pasquale	9	laborer	67	
	L	Moran Margaret—†	9	housewife	56	"
	M	Powers James J	9	painter	22	
	N	Powers Margaret M—†	9	boxmaker	25	"
	O	*Sorrentino Louis	9	laborer	48	"
	P	Sorrentino Virginia—†	9	housewife	37	..
	R	Bruno Ralph ·	10	U S A	31	
	S	Bruno Virginia—†	10	operator	29	"
	T	DiGregorio Felice—†	10	housewife	59	"
	U	DiGregorio Michael	10	laborer	70	
	V	DiGregorio Vincent	10	U˙ S A	21	
	Z	O'Leary Daniel J	13	longshoreman	68	"
	211					
	A	O'Leary Margaret—†	13	inspector	34	"
	B	O'Leary Mary—†	13	housewife	70	"
	C	O'Leary William F	13	watchman	31	"

Haynes Street—Continued

D	Galucci Michael	14	laborer	64	here
E	Memmolo Josephine—†	14	housewife	23	"
F	Memmolo Rocco	14	packer	24	"
G	*Montalto Joseph	14	shoeworker	63	"
H	*Montalto Josephine—†	14	housewife	60	"
K	Montalto Louis J	14	U S A	23	
L	Hanson Catherine—†	15	housewife	63	"
M	Hanson John	15	supervisor	71	"
N	Rossi Gerome	16	laborer	52	"
O	*Bellino Grace—†	16	housewife	67	"
P	Bellino James	16	laborer	41	"
R	*Indorato Anna—†	16	housewife	53	"
S	Indorato Anna M—†	16	machinist	24	"
T	Indorato Louis	16	longshoreman	55	"
U	Malagrifa Louis J	17	U S N	21	
V	Malagrifa Theresa—†	17	housewife	46	"
W	Barbetta Elizabeth—†	18	operator	26	"
X	Barbetta Lillian—†	18	"	23	
Y	Barbetta Rose—†	18	housewife	58	"
Z	Barbetta Santo	18	painter	28	"

212

C	*Kirby Catherine—†	19	housewife	68	"
D	*Kirby James J	19	retired	71	"
E	Kirby Thomas F	19	longshoreman	20	"
F	*Malerba Mary—†	20	housewife	59	"
G	*Malerba Michael	20	laborer	66	
H	Petrillo Jennie—†	20	housewife	39	"
K	Petrillo Pasquali	20	janitor	49	
L	Malerba Anthony	20	longshoreman	33	"
M	Malerba Rose—†	20	housewife	28	"
N	Peterson Albert E	21	U S N	38	
O	Peterson Ruth I—†	21	housewife	36	"
P	Stasi Anthony	22	retired	73	
R	*Stasi Lucy—†	22	housewife	74	"
U	Russo Carman	22	U S A	23	
V	Russo Mary—†	22	housekeeper	50	"
W	Barbetta Anthony	23	welder	38	"
X	Barbetta Charlotte—†	23	housewife	34	"
Y	Modica Anthony	24	laborer	60	"
Z	Modica Josephine—†	24	housewife	54	"

213

Haynes Street—Continued

A	Modica Peter	24	U S A	26	here
B	Modica Michael	24	watchman	33	"
C	Modica Rose—†	24	housewife	25	"
D	Cintolo Alex	24	longshoreman	30	"
E	Cintolo Ethel—†	24	housewife	24	"
F	Sullivan Catherine—†	26	teacher	66	"
G	Cappucci Anthony	28	U S A	28	
H	Cappucci Daniel	28	proprietor	67	"
K	Cappucci Louis	28	U S A	30	
L	Cappucci Mary—†	28	housewife	56	"
M	Cappuci Robert	28	welder	32	
N	Cappucci Rocco	28	U S N	21	
O	Cappucci Stanley	28	U S A	26	"
P	D'Avolio Rosaria	30	tailor	54	
R	Paglucia Frank	30	U S A	26	
S	*Paglucia Louise—†	30	housewife	65	"
T	Paglucia Mary—†	30	painter	22	"
V	O'Neil Arthur F	31	laborer	32	"
W	O'Neil Lena—†	31	housewife	26	"
X	Centato Carmen	31	U S A	22	
Y	Centato Francis	31	salesman	38	"
Z	Centato Margaret—†	31	stitcher	26	

214

A	Centato Michael	31	retired	69	"
B	Cenato Susie—†	31	housewife	63	"
C	Materazzo Armando	31	U S A	31	"
D	Materazzo Jennie—†	31	stitcher	26	"
E	Materazzo Letitia—†	31	housewife	28	"
F	Materazzo Margaret—†	31	bookbinder	33	"
G	Harnish Lottie—†	32	housekeeper	51	"
H	McCashion Joseph P	32	laborer	58	"
K	McCashion Sara A—†	32	housewife	58	"
L	Costello Mary—†	32	"	33	
M	Costello William J	32	longshoreman	41	"
N	Gardner Joseph	32	laborer	29	38 Decatur
O	Gardner Rita—†	32	housewife	29	38 "
R	Ciampa Antonio	33	retired	67	here
S	Ciampa Antonio, jr	33	U S A	34	"
T	Ciampa Carmela—†	33	packer	30	"

Page	Letter	FULL NAME.	Residence, Jan. 1, 1945.	Occupation.	Supposed Age.	Reported Residence, Jan. 1, 1944. Street and Number.

Haynes Street—Continued

	Letter	FULL NAME.	Residence	Occupation	Age	Reported Residence
	u	Ciampa Carmen C	33	U S N	23	here
	v	Ciampa Charles	33	chef	37	"
	w	Ciampa Concetta—†	33	housewife	27	"
	x	Ciampa Elizabeth—†	33	packer	25	
	y	*Seracusa Joseph	34	retired	65	"
215						
	a	Matanza Santa—†	34	housewife	37	"
	b	Matanza Sebastian	34	shipper	37	"
	c	*Paglucca Michael	35	laborer	62	
	d	*Paglucca Rena—†	35	housewife	71	"
	e	*Cordova Charles	35	retired	71	
	h	Nazzaro Ellen—†	36	housewife	39	"
	k	Olivieri Agnes—†	36	stitcher	21	"
	l	Olivieri Luigi	36	painter	53	
	m	Olivieri Nunzia—†	36	housewife	50	"
	o	*Pagliuca Maria—†	37	"	47	
	p	Pagliuca Nicholas	37	laborer	47	
	s	Voto Antoinette—†	39	housewife	60	"
	t	Voto Antonio	39	laborer	62	"
	u	Voto Josephine—†	39	clerk	20	"
	v	LaRosa Jennie—†	39	housewife	35	"
	w	LaRosa Phillip	39	machinist	39	"
	x	Ruggerio Angelo	39	U S N	22	36 Haynes
	y	Ruggerio Antoinette—†	39	bagmaker	20	36 "
	z	*Landrigan Nora—†	41	housekeeper	65	here
216						
	a	Galliazzo Nicholas	41	laborer	61	
	b	Guerreri Florence—†	41	welder	23	"
	c	*Guerreri Mary—†	41	housewife	39	"
	d	Guerreri Salvatore	41	laborer	55	
	e	Brogioni Ernest	43	maintenance	57	"
	f	Agreste Mary—†	44	candymaker	34	"
	g	Muise Dorothy—†	44	housewife	31	"
	h	Muise Vincent	44	U S N	33	
	k	*Giammatteo Andrea	45	laborer	63	
	l	*Martino Anthony	45	"	63	
	m	Casey Hugh	47	watchman	65	"
	n	Costello Ellen—†	47	housekeeper	65	"
	o	Costello Ellen B—†	47	stenographer	28	"
	p	McKenna Isabel—†	47	housewife	30	"
	r	McKenna Thomas	47	longshoreman	30	"

Haynes Street—Continued

s	Cammarano Anthony	48	fireman	32	here
t	Cammarano Ernestine—†	48	housewife	32	"
u	Cammarano Domenic	48	foreman	62	"
v*| Cammarano Mary—†	48	housewife	60	"
w	Cammarano Pasquali	48	U S A	27	"
x	Cammarano Vincent	48	longshoreman	59	"
y	Gill Helen M—†	49	housewife	44	"
z	Gill Henry M	49	watchman	54	"

217

a	Callahan Charles T	49	U S A	33	
b	Callahan John B	49	U S N	35	
c	Callahan John J	49	laborer	62	
d	Callahan Mary—†	49	housewife	63	"
e	Dennehy Helen—†	49	cook	60	"
f	Dorazio Eileen A—†	49	housewife	32	"
g	Dorazio John J	49	U S A	30	
h	Shine Hannah—†	49	cook	61	
k	Shine Mary P—†	49	nurse	29	
l	Driscoll Julia E—†	52	housekeeper	72	"
m	McCarthy Dennis	52	watchman	62	"
n*| D'Amore Anna—†	62	housewife	54	"
o	D'Amore Dominic	62	U S A	21	
p	D'Amore Gennaro	62	laborer	50	
r	D'Amore Samuel	62	U S N	23	
s	O'Leary Harold	62	longshoreman	32	"
t	O'Leary Sara—†	62	housewife	26	"
u	Cogliani Jennie—†	62	"	28	"
v	Cogliani Louis	62	laborer	31	"

Marginal Street

y	Linvill Bessie—†	72	social worker	25	here
z	Linvill William	72	teacher	25	"

218

a	Munsterburg Elizabeth—†	72	social worker	25	"
d	Lanza Frank J	90	factoryhand	29	"
e	Davenport Anna—†	90	housewife	21	"
f	Davenport Loren C	90	U S C G	23	"
g	Lanza Biagio	90	U S A	33	
h*| Lanza Venera—†	90	housewife	64	"
k	Santa Maria Pasqualina—†	91	"	63	

Page.	Letter.	Full Name.	Residence, Jan. 1, 1945.	Occupation.	Supposed Age.	Reported Residence, Jan. 1, 1944. Street and Number.

Marginal Street—Continued

	Letter	Full Name	Res.	Occupation	Age	Reported Residence
	L	Waters Antonetta—†	91	housewife	33	here
	M	Waters Edmond	91	longshoreman	35	"
	N	Gigliello John	92	"	34	"
	O	Gigliello Theresa—†	92	housewife	33	"
	R	Gigliello Florence—†	100	"	28	
	S	Gigliello Michael	100	carpenter	65	"
	T	Gigliello Nicholas	100	longshoreman	33	"
	U	DeSpirito James	100	U S A	26	
·	V	*Mascis Frank	102	retired	72	
	W	Mascis Louis	102	U S A	28	
	X	*Mascis Michelena—†	102	housewife	58	"
	Y	Marchi Mary—†	106	"	25	
	Z	Marchi Richard	106	salesman	29	"
219						
	A	Voto Alma—†	106	housewife	35	"
	B	Voto Angello R	106	painter	37	
	C	Manganelli Antoinette–†	110	laboratory	23	"
	D	Manganelli Frank	110	salesman	64	"
	E	Manganelli Rose—†	110	housewife	55	"
	F	Reidy Mary C—†	110	"	28	..
	G	Reidy Michael L	110	painter	31	
	H	Smith Nanthaniel	112	longshoreman	55	"
	K	Fahey Bridget—†	112	housewife	69	"
	L	Fahey Catherine—†	112	assembler	35	"
	M	Fahey David	112	retired	74	..
	N	Fahey Leo D	112	U S N	29	
	O	Fahey Mary M—†	112	collector	37	"
	P	O'Brien John T	112	checker	50	"
	T	Quilty Florence—†	116	fishcutter	20	"
	U	Quilty Jessie—†	116	"	20	..
	V	Hanlon John J	116	longshoreman	44	"
	W	Hanlon Rita—†	116	housewife	37	"
	X	Chiango Carmen	118	metalworker	30	"
	Y	Chiango Grace—†	118	housewife	26	"
	Z	Chiango Elia—†	118	"	33	..
220						
	A	Chiango Frank	118	painter	35	"
	C	Aceto Beatrice—†	126	housewife	67	.. "
	D	Aceto Simone	126	retired	66	
	E	Whalen Elizabeth—†	126	stitcher	61	"
	F	Whalen Helen—†	126	housewife	65	"

12

Page.	Letter.	FULL NAME.	Residence, Jan. 1, 1945.	Occupation.	Supposed Age.	Reported Residence, Jan. 1, 1944. Street and Number.

Marginal Street—Continued

	G	Whalen William J	126	shipper	59	here
	H	Crowley Catherine—†	126	housewife	48	"
	K	Crowley Daniel J	126	longshoreman	50	"
	M	Schipani Mary—†	128	housewife	36	"
	N	Schipani Thomas	128	cobbler	42	"
	O	Kennedy Mary—†	128	housewife	30	"
	P	Kennedy William J	128	pipefitter	39	"
	R	Ulisi Ugo	132	welder	48	..
	S	Terenzi Anna—†	132	packer	20	"
	T	*Terenzi Emilia—†	132	housewife	51	"
	U	Terenzi Marino	132	U S A	22	"
	V	Terenzi Martha—†	132	packer	25	
	W	*Terenzi Ornaldo	132	tailor	57	..
	X	Terenzi Thomas	132	U S A	28	
	Y	King Edmund N	136	"	26	"
	Z	King Irene H—†	136	clerk	28	
221						
	A	Porter Joseph R	136	fireman	45	"
	B	Porter Margaret I—†	136	housewife	52	"
	C	Vallen John	136	laborer	53	
	D	Vallen Lillian—†	136	housewife	57	"
	E	Goggin Anna F—†	136	domestic	31	"
	F	Goggin Edward P	136	longshoreman	39	"
	G	Goggin Helen M—†	136	houseworker	40	"
	H	Goggin Mary A—†	136	"	45	
	K	Goggin Thomas C	136	longshoreman	34	"
	L	Morcaldi Gabriel	138	U S A	23	
	M	*Morcaldi Raffaele	138	retired	76	
	N	Santagata Silvestra	138	U S A	24	"
	O	Kirby Catherine—†	138	housewife	27	116 Marginal
	P	Kirby Paul	138	longshoreman	29	116 "
	T	Ratta Celia—†	140	housewife	41	here
	U	Ratta Onofrio	140	laborer	46	"
	V	Amorosa Catherine—†	140	candymaker	38	7 Henchman
	W	Lomanno Joseph	140	packer	38	here
	X	Lomanno Mary—†	140	housewife	33	"
	Y	Siciliano Antonio	142	proprietor	53	"
	Z	Siciliano Leo	142	shipfitter	28	"
222						
	A	Siciliano Maria—†	142	housewife	50	"
	B	Siracusa Catherine—†	142	"	20	

13

Marginal Street—Continued

c	Siracusa Joseph	142	U S A	22	here
e	Silva Barbara—†	184	at home	20	Gloucester
f	Meninno Geraldine—†	184	housewife	20	4 Brigham
g	Meninno Michael	184	U S N	24	4 "
k	*Russo Aniello	188	laborer	49	here
l	Russo Charlotte—†	188	housewife	28	"
m	Grifoni Giocondo	194	laborer	53	"
n	Grifoni Nancy—†	194	clerk	26	
o	Grifoni Nicoletta—†	194	WAC	20	"
p	Grifoni Pasquale	194	U S A	21	
r	*Grifoni Vincenza—†	194	housewife	46	"
s	Lowry Ernest	194	fireman	39	..
t	Twitchell Frank	194	painter	40	
u	Twitchell Gladys—†	194	housewife	39	"
w	Hagan Elizabeth M—†	198	"	72	
x	Hagan Henry J	198	janitor	41	
y	DiFiore Frances—†	210	WAC	21	
z	DiFiore Gertrude—†	210	stitcher	25	"

223

a	DiFiore Mary—†	210	welder	20	
b	*DiFiore Michelina—†	210	housewife	50	"
f	Carigano Angelina–† rear	216	"	35	"
g	Carigano Genaro "	216	chauffeur	36	"
h	Carigano Alexander "	216	U S A	21	
k	*Carigano Frank "	216	laborer	65	
l	*Carigano Josephine–† "	216	housewife	61	"
m	Carigano Josephine–† "	216	clerk	21	
n	Foster Angelina—† "	216	housewife	26	"
o	Foster Herbert "	216	U S A	31	

Murray Court

w	Coviello Anthony	1	electrician	40	here
x	Coviello Antoinette—†	1	housewife	45	"
y	Garofalo Carmela—†	1	at home	25	"
z	Garofalo Frank	1	retired	64	

224

a	Garofalo Frank	1	U S A	23	"
b	Garofalo Michael	1	longshoreman	21	"
c	*Garofalo Raffaela—†	1	housewife	58	"
d	DeRocco Dominic	1	foreman	47	"

14

Murray Court—Continued

E	DeRocco Grace—†	1	housewife	37	here
F	*Bozza Chester	2	painter	59	"
G	Bozza Elena—†	2	housewife	42	"
H	*Bozza Emilio	2	foundryman	46	"
K	Esposito Mary—†	2	housewife	23	"
L	Esposito Michael	2	U S C G	23	"
M	Indorato Anna—†	2	housewife	48	"
N	Indorato Josephine—†	2	stamper	24	"
O	Indorato Albina—†	2	housewife	22	"
P	Indorato Joseph	2	longshoreman	27	"
R	Cameron William	3	"	52	
S	Cameron Winifred—†	3	housewife	51	"
T	*McDonald Alice—†	3	"	72	
U	McDonald John	3	warehouse	38	"
V	*McDonald Richard	3	longshoreman	66	"
W	McDonald William	3	shipworker	36	"
X	Campagnoni Florence—†	3	saleswoman	20	"
Y	Campagnoni Frank	3	mechanic	49	"
Z	Campagnoni Jenny—†	3	housewife	44	"
	225				
A	Campagnoni Olga—†	3	secretary	21	"
B	Ciano Caroline—†	4	at home	23	"
C	Ciano Michael	4	laborer	68	
D	Pedalino Charles J	4	chauffeur	49	"
E	Pedalino Joan—†	4	saleswoman	22	"
F	Pedalino Mary—†	4	stitcher	26	"
G	Pedalino Rose—†	4	stamper	29	"
H	Pedalino Teresa—†	4	housewife	50	"
K	DeAngelis Ernest	4	machinist	31	"
L	DeAngelis Mildred—†	4	housewife	32	"
M	Frabizzo Pasquale	5	laborer	55	
N	Giello John	5	shipworker	46	"
O	Giello Michael	5	laborer	41	
P	*Giello Rose—†	5	at home	76	"
R	Disario Celestine—†	9	factoryhand	35	"
S	Disario Mary—†	9	housewife	77	"
T	Limongiello Gabriel	9	machinist	43	"
U	Limongiello Mary—†	9	housewife	40	"
V	Cardello Joseph	9	carpenter	47	"
W	Cardello Rose—†	9	housewife	38	"
Z	O'Brien Isabel—†	15	"	27	New York

Murray Court—Continued

A	O'Brien William	15	welder	35	New York
B	Fagone Aggrippino	15	laborer	54	here
C	Fagone Josephine—†	15	housewife	53	"
D	Fagone Rose—†	15	technician	20	"
E	Parziale John	15	pipefitter	38	"
F	Parziale Mary—†	15	housewife	31	"
G	McDonald Leo	16	painter	42	
H	McDonald Ruth—†	16	housewife	31	"
K	Ciano Carmella—†	17	"	28	"
L	Ciano Pasquale	17	plumber	32	"
M	Valerio Frank	17	shipworker	44	"
N	Valerio Nancy—†	17	operator	35	"
O	Chiampa Albert	17	chauffeur	39	"
P	Chiampa Mary—†	17	housewife	31	"
R	Buono Emma—†	19	"	34	
S	Buono Leo	19	bartender	34	"
T	Chiampa Frank	19	U S N	32	
U	Chiampa James	19	jeweler	36	
V	Triulzi Edith—†	19	stenographer	26	"
W	Triulzi Erminio	19	jeweler	62	"
X	*Triulzi Rosina—†	19	housewife	62	"
Y	Repucci George	22	U S A	34	"
Z	*Repucci Maria—†	22	housewife	67	"

A	Repucci Philomena—†	22	saleswoman	35	"
B	Repucci Pellegrino	22	laborer	65	
C	*Ianconelli Marie—†	22	housewife	33	"
D	*Ianconelli Nicholas	22	machinist	32	"

Orleans Street

F	Scaramella Albert C	39	mortician	44	here
G	Scaramella Madeline—†	39	at home	84	"
H	Scaramella Rose L—†	39	housewife	33	"
K	Scaramella Flora B—†	39	"	47	
L	Scaramella Ralph	39	longshoreman	21	"
M	Scaramella Vincent	39	salesman	56	"
O	Scannelli Anthony	41	chauffeur	23	365 Sumner
P	Scannelli Carmen—†	41	housewife	23	365 "
R	DePietro Americo	41	pipefitter	36	here

Orleans Street—Continued

	s	DePietro Bessie B—†	41	housewife	31	here
	T	Grugnale Maria—†	43	operator	59	"
	U	Caserta Anna—†	43	housewife	49	"
	V	Caserta Carmen	43	tinsmith	63	"
	W	Picardi Carmen	43	U S A	21	
	X	Picardi Grace—†	43	housewife	24	"
	Y	Simoli Agrippino	43	laborer	62	
	Z	Simoli Joseph	43	U S N	23	
228						
	A	Simoli Mary—†	43	housewife	52	"
	B	Simoli Mary—†	43	operator	32	"
	D	Fredericks Alvin J	45	U S N	31	
	E	Fredericks Edythe—†	45	housewife	28	"
	F	Katz David	45	U S A	23	
	G	Katz Louis	45	"	26	"
	H	Katz Mollie—†	45	housewife	60	"
	K	Katz Samuel	45	proprietor	62	"
	L	Larsen Donald F	45	U S A	21	
	M	Larsen George E	45	"	25	
	N	Larsen James P	45	seaman	58	..
	O	Larsen Mary A—†	45	housewife	52	"
	P	Larsen Mary C—†	45	clerk	20	..
	R	Milgram David	45	U S A	36	
	S	Milgram Rose—†	45	housewife	30	"

Sumner Street

	U	Indelicato Antoinetta—†	265	stitcher	20	here
	V	Indelicato Rosaria—†	265	"	28	"
	W	Indelicato Salvatore	265	meatcutter	28	"
	X	Picardi Carmella M—†	265	housewife	50	"
	Y	Picardi Joseph A	265	machinist	25	"
	Z	Picardi Michael	265	proprietor	50	"
229						
	A	Caliendo Anne—†	269	housewife	46	"
	B	Caliendo Raymond	269	barber	52	
	C	Luciano Enrico	269	riveter	49	
	D	Luciano Joseph	269	longshoreman	20	"
	E	Luciano Margaret—†	269	housewife	40	"
	F	Martucci Augustino A	269	chauffeur	29	"
	G	Martucci Margaret R—†	269	housewife	27	"

Page	Letter	FULL NAME.	Residence, Jan. 1, 1945.	Occupation.	Supposed Age.	Reported Residence, Jan. 1, 1944. Street and Number.

Sumner Street—Continued

	Letter	FULL NAME.	Residence	Occupation	Age	Reported Residence
	H	Addivinola Carmela—†	271	housewife	25	here
	K	Addivinola Joseph L	271	welder	27	"
	M	Addivinola John	271	electrician	62	"
	N	Addivinola Lawrence A	271	U S N	24	
	O	Addivinola Raffaela—†	271	at home	49	"
	P	Addivinola Yolando—†	271	stitcher	22	"
	R	*Amabile Raffaele A	273	salesman	66	"
	S	*Gallo Mary—†	273	housewife	40	"
	T	Quartaro Josephine—†	273	stitcher	39	"
	U	Picardi Dominic	275	chauffeur	22	"
	V	Picardi Vincenza M—†	275	housewife	20	"
	W	Simonelli Angelo A	275	machinist	32	"
	X	Simonelli Mary L—†	275	stitcher	29	"
	Y	Catena Frank	275	rigger	40	
	Z	Catena Rose—†	275	at home	37	"

230

	Letter	FULL NAME.	Residence	Occupation	Age	Reported Residence
	A	*Gugliecelo Celesta—†	279	housewife	73	"
	B	*Gugliecelo Vito	279	retired	79	
	C	Cornetta John	279	finisher	50	
	D	Cornetta Mary R—†	279	candymaker	40	"
	E	*Cornetta Raffaela—†	279	housewife	84	"
	F	Cornetta Phyllis—†	279	clerk	36	
	G	Cornetta Rosario	279	shoemaker	44	"
	K	*Velestrino Luigi	281	retired	72	
	L	Velestrino Sofia—†	281	housewife	64	"
	M	Yanelli Albert M	281	machinist	34	52 Everett
	N	Yanelli Anna E—†	281	housewife	35	52 "
	O	Boeri John	281	laborer	29	here
	P	Boeri Louise E—†	281	housewife	21	"
	R	Lupoli Nicola	283	proprietor	60	"
	S	Lupoli Nicola G	283	U S A	21	
	T	*Lupoli Silvia—†	283	housewife	64	"
	U	*Matarese Clara—†	283	"	42	
	V	Matarese Concetta L—†	283	inspector	20	"
	W	Matarese James G	283	tailor	44	"
	X	Matarese Vito	283	barber	46	
	Y	Belsito Alfred A	285	U S A	23	"
	Z	Belsito Jerry	285	chauffeur	52	"

231

	Letter	FULL NAME.	Residence	Occupation	Age	Reported Residence
	A	Belsito Josephine—†	285	at home	48	"
	B	Belsito Rita E—†	285	packer	20	"
	C	*Bruno Mary—†	285	at home	82	"

18

Page.	Letter.	FULL NAME.	Residence, Jan. 1, 1945.	Occupation.	Supposed Age.	Reported Residence, Jan. 1, 1944. Street and Number.

Sumner Street—Continued

D	Fagone Vincenza—†	285	at home	21	here
E	Petrucelli Daniel E	287	shoemaker	42	"
F	*Sousa Manuel	287	baker	44	94 Chelsea
G	*Gulinello Josephine—†	287	housewife	66	here
H	*Gulinello Salvatore	287	laborer	66	"
K	Enos Bessie—†	287	at home	87	"
L	Ladorella Anthony	289	molder	52	"
M	Ladorella Susie—†	289	housewife	45	"
N	Goldsworthy Dora—†	289	at home	21	"
O	Pardi Anthony A	289	U S A	23	
P	Pardi Concetta—†	289	housewife	48	"
R	Pardi Louis	289	laborer	48	"
S	Pace Albert N	289	timekeeper	30	"
T	Pace Alfred J	289	U S A	25	"
U	Pace Edmund C	289	"	29	
V	Pace Helen L—†	289	operator	27	"
W	Pace Pacifio	289	shoemaker	56	"
X	Pace Theresa—†	289	housewife	55	"

232

A	Hrono Mary—†	291	"	31	"
B	Fazio Charles D	291	barber	54	208 Webster
C	Fazio Emilio M—†	291	housewife	35	208 "
D	*Armeta Mary—†	291	"	32	here
E	Armeta William	291	shoemaker	38	"
F	Dalelio Dominic A	rear 291	finisher	41	"
G	Dalelio James	" 291	retired	71	"
K	Coscia Anne M—†	293	housewife	44	144 Everett
L	Coscia Helen—†	293	trimmer	24	144 "
M	Coscia Louise—†	293	dressmaker	27	144 "
N	Coscia William	293	carpenter	52	144 "
O	*Amiro James	293	engineer	49	here
P	*Amiro Oscar	293	fisherman	52	"
R	*Belliveau Mary—†	293	at home	63	"
S	Gurski Edward	293	laborer	25	Chelsea
T	Gurski Marguerite—†	293	housewife	26	here
W	Jorgensen Arthur	295	laborer	26	"
X	Jorgensen Esther—†	295	housewife	50	"
Y	Jorgensen Jofgen P	295	steward	53	"
Z	Gasbarro Adeline—†	295	housewife	30	15 Everett

233

A	Gasbarro Vincent	295	machinist	40	117 Maverick
B	Barney Willard	295	U S C G	24	108 Webster

Sumner Street—Continued

c	Nelson Frederick	295	rigger	65	108 Webster
d	Constantino Joseph B	297	electrician	39	here
e	Constantino Rose—†	297	housewife	32	"
f	Jenkins Julia—†	297	matron	64	"
g	Yocum Ernest L	297	retired	74	"
h	Constantino George	297	"	66	
k	DeLisa Eva—†	299	housewife	50	"
l	*DeLisa Frank	299	laborer	55	
m	DeLisa Michael I	299	U S N	21	"
n	Bottaro Anthony G	299	U S A	28	
o	Bottaro Mary—†	299	housewife	27	"
p	Doria Anna—†	299	"	30	
r	Doria Vito	299	shoeworker	34	"
s	*Manzo Ralph	299	janitor	69	
t	Manzo Virginia—†	299	operator	24	"
u	Gianbrone Frank	299	U S A	26	"
v	Gianbrone Joseph	299	laborer	29	
w	Giambrone Louis	299	U S A	20	"
x	Gianbrone Michael	299	"	23	
y	Marino Anthony	299	laborer	60	"
z	Marino Frances—†	299	housewife	57	"
	234				
b	Todisco Emma—†	305	leatherworker	30	"
c	Todisco Generoso P	305	U S A	27	
d	Todisco Louise—†	305	at home	31	"
e	Todisco Mildred—†	305	housewife	53	"
f	Todisco Vincent	305	shoemaker	66	"
g	Grana Leonard	305	U S A	35	
h	Grana Mary L—†	305	housewife	35	"
k	Wolfram Jenny—†	305	"	27	"
l	Wolfram Raymond	305	U S N	24	
n	Crocetti Alfred A	307	U S A	26	"
o	Crocetti Valerie—†	307	housewife	26	"
p	Gualtieri Catherine—†	307	"	40	
r	Gualtieri Salvatore	307	clerk	47	
s	Gualtieri Theresa L—†	307	WAC	22	
u	Milazzo Luigi	rear 309	pedler	62	
w	Ventresca Demetro	" 309	U S A	23	
x	Ventresca Guiseppe	" 309	rigger	58	
	235				
b	Scavo Antonio	315	baker	51	

Sumner Street—Continued

c	Scavo Joseph	315	U S A	21	here
d	*Scavo Josephine—†	315	housewife	46	"
e	Falanga Joseph	315	electrician	31	"
f	Falanga Rose—†	315	housewife	30	"
k	Venuti Antonio	315	shipfitter	48	"
l	*Venuti Concetta—†	315	housewife	48	"
p	Fagone Clara—†	317	"	31	245 Webster
r	Fagone Frank	317	driller	25	245 "
s	Cantalupo Anthony	317	U S A	24	here
t	*Cantalupo Josephine—†	317	housewife	60	"
u	*Cantalupo Louis	317	retired	64	"
v	Cantalupo Mildred—†	317	stenographer	20	"
w	*Fabello Enrico rear	317	porter	62	
x	Fabello Palmer—† "	317	housewife	60	"
y	*Abruzzese Adele—† "	317	"	38	
z	*Abruzzeso Generoso "	317	tailor	41	
236						
b	Campo Angelina—†	319	housewife	49	"
c	Campo Paul	319	storekeeper	55	"
d	Campo Stephen	319	U S A	22	"
e	DiNatale Joseph	319	"	24	37 Havre
f	DiNatale Sara—†	319	housewife	24	here
g	Scimone Gaspar	319	collector	26	"
h	Sciomòne Louise—†	319	housewife	28	"
k	*Massullo Madaline—† rear	319	at home	78	"
l	DiPietro Joseph "	319	clerk	46	"
m	Pelosi Agnes—† "	319	housewife	42	"
n	Pelosi Michael "	319	shoeworker	50	"
r	Arciero Peter	327	bartender	46	Sudbury
s	Tarquinio Sabatino C.	327	proprietor	54	here
t	DePasquale Antonio	329	baker	30	"
u	DePasquale Theresa—†	329	housewife	28	"
z	Murphy Margaret—†	343	at home	64	"
237						
a	O'Connell John	343	waiter	60	"
b	O'Connell Mary—†	343	housewife	60	"
d	Albano Alfred	345	U S A	20	
e	Albano Anna—†	345	housewife	59	"
f	Albano Concetta—†	345	"	22	
g	Albano Fred	345	baker	39	
h	Albano Gaetano	345	storekeeper	38	"

Page.	Letter.	Full Name.	Residence, Jan. 1, 1945.	Occupation.	Supposed Age.	Reported Residence, Jan. 1, 1944. Street and Number.

Sumner Street—Continued

	K	Albano Joseph	345	storekeeper	26	here
	L	Connell John	347	counterman	58	"
	M	Connell Mary—†	347	housewife	58	"
	N	Murphy Margaret H—†	347	housekeeper	65	"
	O	Walsh Margaret M—†	349	"	65	"
	P	Walsh Patrick T	349	retired	72	"
	R	Creio Caesar	349	welder	40	Rhode Island
	S	Creio Priscilla—†	349	housewife	31	"
	T	Cecca Carmella—†	349	"	49	here
	U	Cecca Enrico	349	pipecoverer	53	"
	V	Cecca Louis	349	director	23	"
	W	Cecca Salvatore	349	U S N	21	"

Webster Avenue

	Z	*Rozzi Petronella—†	4	at home	80	here
		238				
	A	Rozzi Thomas	4	mechanic	40	"
	B	Vanuti Angela—†	6	at home	34	"
	C	Vanuti Armando	6	U S A	20	
	D	Vanuti Attilio	6	"	25	
	E	*Vanuti Carmela—†	6	housewife	57	"
	F	Vanuti Henry	6	U S N	22	"
	G	Vanuti John	6	laborer	60	
	H	Vanuti Michael	6	U S A	23	
	K	DeGregorio Antonio	8	retired	72	
	L	DeGregorio Christopher	8	"	42	
	M	DeGregorio Michael	8	U S A	34	"
	N	DeGregorio Phyllis—†	8	housewife	33	"
	O	*Allisica Frank	10	dishwasher	60	"
	P	*Rosa Rose—†	10	housewife	42	"
	R	Rosa Vincent	10	laborer	47	
	S	Orsini Angelina—†	12	housewife	54	"
	T	Orsini Annette—†	12	stitcher	20	"
	U	Orsini Dante	12	shipworker	33	"
	V	Orsini Henry	12	shoeworker	54	"

Webster Street

	W	Infantino Joseph	55	laborer	60	here
	X	Infantino Joseph, jr	55	U S A	20	"

Page.	Letter.	FULL NAME.	Residence, Jan. 1, 1945.	Occupation.	Supposed Age.	Reported Residence, Jan. 1, 1944. Street and Number.

Webster Street—Continued

Y	Infantino Rose—†	55	housewife	51	here
z	Infantino Salvatore	55	machinist	23	"
	239				
A	Marannano Mario	55	laborer	35	
B	Baglio Carmela—†	55	housewife	48	"
c	Baglio Eugene	55	U S A	22	
D	Baglio John	55	candymaker	55	"
E	Baglio Tina—†	55	factoryhand	21	"
F	*DeFlorio Maria F—†	57	housewife	80	"
G	DeFlorio Sarah—†	57	tailor	43	
H	Sansoucy Alfred	57	laborer	25	"
K	Sansoucy Bertha—†	57	housewife	23	"
L	McPhee George	57	stevedore	48	40 Webster
M	McPhee Helen—†	57	housewife	47	40 "
N	McPhee Joseph	57	seaman	23	40 "
o	McPhee Thomas	57	U S A	26	40 "
R	Bickford Charles L	59	laborer	45	22 Haynes
s	Bickford Victoria—†	59	housewife	39	22 "
T	Morrissey John M	59	painter	31	238 Everett
U	Morrissey Rose—†	59	housewife	33	238 "
v	Indorato Josephine—†	59	"	49	here
w	Indorato Ottavio	59	clerk	28	"
x	Indorato Salvatore	59	laborer	60	"
Y	Indorato Santina—†	59	factoryhand	23	"
z	Indorato Sebastiano	59	U S N	25	
	240				
A	Sanno Anna—†	59	housewife	21	"
B	Sanno Ferdinando	59	U S A	23	
c	Mina Joseph	59	factoryhand	50	"
D	Lanzilli Albert L	60	chauffeur	38	"
E	Lanzilli Cornelia—†	60	housewife	33	"
F	Pizzano Andrew	60	machinist	40	"
G	Pizzano Mildred—†	60	housewife	36	"
H	Liberatore Anna—†	60	"	46	..
K	Liberatore Maria—†	60	factoryhand	44	"
L	Liberatore Mary—†	60	"	21	
M	Liberatore Peter	60	candymaker	45	"
N	Liberatore Stanley	60	factoryhand	47	"
P	LaGambina Joseph	61	U S N	21	
R	LaGambina Rosaria—†	61	housewife	43	"
s	LaGambina Sebastiano	61	factoryhand	52	"

Webster Street—Continued

v	DeAngelis Antonio	62	foreman	52	here
w	DeAngelis Margaret—†	62	housewife	54	"
x	DeAngelis Speranza—†	62	factoryhand	21	"
y	Gianvittorio Fiorindo	62	U S N	25	
z	Gianvittorio Helen—†	62	housewife	23	"

241

A	DeSavino Frances—†	62	"	49	
B	DeSavino Michael	62	laborer	50	"
c	DeSavino Samuel	62	U S N	21	"
D	DeAgostino Angelo	63	"	31	"
E	DeAgostino Mary—†	63	housewife	29	"
F	Franco Mafalda—†	63	"	26	
G	Franco Vincent	63	U S N	25	
H	Giordano Pasquale	63	guard	28	
K	Giordano Theresa—†	63	housewife	28	"
L	Manno Gennaro	64	laborer	50	
N	*Lombardo Anthony	65	fisherman	61	"
O	Lombardo Rose—†	65	factoryhand	21	"
P	*Lombardo Sebastiana—†	65	housewife	53	"
R	Brissitte James	65	molder	29	"..
s	Brissitte Mary—†	65	housewife	26	"
T	Incagnoli Assunta—†	65	"	62	
U	Incagnoli Augustus	65	merchant	62	"
v	Incagnoli Joseph	65	U S A	27	
w	Grana Maria—†	66	housewife	63	"
x	Grana Vincenzo	66	carpenter	70	"
y	Cogliana Helen—†	67	housewife	30	"
z	Cogliana Salvatore	67	chauffeur	29	"

242

A	Capraro Joseph	67	painter	24	
B	Capraro Louise—†	67	housewife	21	"
c	Vocino Joseph	67	mechanic	27	"
D	Vocino Martha—†	67	dressmaker	24	"
E	Vocino Mateo	67	clerk	59	
F	Vocino Raymo	67	factoryhand	23	"
G	Vocino Theresa—†	67	housewife	57	"
H	Murray Helen—†	68	"	33	
K	Murray John W	68	U S N	29	
L	Anderson Charles	68	stevedore	31	"
M	Anderson Marie G—†	68	housewife	25	"
N	Todesco Albert C	68	U S A	27	

Webster Street—Continued

Page.	Letter.	Full Name.	Residence, Jan. 1, 1945.	Occupation.	Supposed Age.	Reported Residence, Jan. 1, 1944. Street and Number.
	o	Todesco Jennie—†	68	waitress	49	here
	p	DiDio Lucy—†	68	housewife	33	"
	r	DiDio Salvatore	68	factoryhand	52	"
	s	Pelargonio Assunta—†	69	housewife	48	"
	t	Pelargonio Carmina—†	69	factoryhand	22	"
	u	Romano Costanino	69	laborer	72	"
	v	Romano Virginia—†	69	housewife	67	"
	w	Amico Joseph A	69	bookbinder	42	"
	x	Amico Mary C—†	69	housewife	35	"
	y	DiMinico Grace—†	70	factoryhand	37	"
	z	DiMinico Joseph	70	mason	37	
243						
	a	Giadone John	70	U S M C	23	"
	b	Giadone Josephine—†	70	dressmaker	28	"
	c*	Giadone Lucy—†	70	housewife	53	"
	d*	Giadone Phillip	70	laborer	59	"
	e	Giadone Phillip, jr	70	U S A	21	..
	f	Panarello Fannie—†	70	housewife	48	"
	g	Panarello Joseph	70	laborer	61	"
	h	DeBello Elizabeth—†	71	housewife	75	"
	k	DeBello John	71	laborer	50	"
	l	Siracuso Francesca—†	71	housewife	63	"
	m*	Siracuso Nicola	71	laborer	60	"
	n	Siracuso Rosina—†	71	secretary	21	"
	o	Formicula Frank	71	barber	55	
	p	Formicula Micholina—†	71	housewife	49	"
	r	Stella Benjamin	71	machinist	26	"
	s	Stella Mary—†	71	housewife	26	"
	t	Salvo Anthony T	73	machinist	27	"
		Salvo Emma J—†	73	housewife	22	"
	v	Carbone Jennie—†	73	"	29	
	w	Carbone John	73	painter	27	"
	x	Carbone Alfred	73	factoryhand	54	"
	y	Carbone Amelia—†	73	housewife	52	"
	z	DeAmore Rose—†	73	bookkeeper	30	"
244						
	a	Bertolino Frank	74	fisherman	27	"
	b	Bertolino Mary—†	74	housewife	24	"
	c	Mottola Fiore	74	seaman	30	..
	d	Mottola Stefana—†	74	housewife	67	"
	e	Mottola Vincenzo	74	laborer	68	

Page.	Letter.	FULL NAME.	Residence, Jan. 1, 1945.	Occupation.	Supposed Age.	Reported Residence, Jan. 1, 1944. Street and Number.

Webster Street—Continued

	F	Mottola Amato—†	74	carpenter	40	here
	G	Mottola Michelina—†	74	housewife	39	"
	H	Corbin Esther—†	75	"	22	"
	K	Corbin John ,	75	U S M C	25	"
	L	Cavignaro Genaro	75	laborer	57	
	M	Cavignaro Helen—†	75	factoryhand	24	"
	N	Cavignaro Joseph	75	seaman	26	"
	O	Cavignaro Michael	75	U S A	31	
	P	Cavignaro Filomena—†	75	housewife	55	"
	R	Cavignaro Rose—†	75	clerk	21	
	S	DiGirolamo Alfred	75	U S A	24	
	T	DiGirolamo Alverio—†	75	factoryhand	35	"
	U	DiGirolamo Francesco	75	laborer	69	
	V	DiGirolamo Henry	75	U S N	21	
	W	DiGirolamo Nicolina—†	75	housewife	67	"
	X	Goggin Florence—†	76	"	24	
	Y	Goggin James	76	operator	39	"
	Z	Carcerano Antonetta—†	76	housewife	28	"

245

	A	Carcerano Salvatore	76	pipefitter	33	"
	B	Matolla Margaret—†	76	housewife	38	"
	C	Matolla Michael	76	laborer	39	
	D	Mazzola Michelina—†	77	housewife	44	"
	E	Mazzola Philip	77	U S N	23	
	F	Mazzola Sebastian	77	laborer	48	
	G	Turner Yolanda—†	77	stitcher	21	"
	H	Varone Reggerio	77	U S A	25	
	K	Varone Severo	77	boilermaker	60	"
	L	Mazzola Joseph C	77	machinist	25	"
	M	Mazzola Phyllis—†	77	housewife	21	"
	N	Vardaro Julia—†	79	"	36	
	O	Vardaro Lewis	79	stevedore	41	"
	P	Lightbody Carmels—†	79	housewife	29	"
	R	Lightbody William C	79	stevedore	29	"
	S	Carapezza Joseph R	79	electrician	32	"
	T	Carapezza Sarah—†	79	housewife	32	"
	U	Bozzo Zaccaria	80	clerk	83	
	V	Bozzo Aurora—†	80	housewife	32	"
	W	Bozza Filomena—†	80	"	58	
	X	Bozzo Mary—†	80	bookkeeper	30	"
	Y	Bozzo Settimio	80	barber	62	"

Page.	Letter.	FULL NAME.	Residence, Jan. 1, 1945.	Occupation.	Supposed Age.	Reported Residence, Jan. 1, 1944. Street and Number.

Webster Street—Continued

z	Nocito Antonette—†	80	housewife	26	here
246						
A	Nocito Joseph	80	painter	28	
B	Sears Angelia—†	81	housewife	31	"
C	Sears Luther	81	U S N	33	
D	Pagliuca James	81	shipper	40	"
E	Pagliuca Lucy—†	81	housewife	35	"
F	Calvino Charles	81	U S N	24	
G	Calvino Gaetano	81	laborer	61	"
H	Calvino John H	81	U S N	22	"
K	Calvino Lucy—†	81	housewife	51	"
L	DiBenedetta Angelo	82	steamfitter	52	"
M	DiBenedetto Madaline—†	82	housewife	32	"
N	Nocito Carmella—†	82	"	32	"
O	Cocito Michael	82	salesman	44	"
P	Nocito Elizabeth—†	82	housewife	52	"
R	Nocito Michael	82	U S A	22	"
S	Fabiano Julia—†	83	housewife	21	"
T	Fabiano Nickolas	83	laborer	32	
U	Febbi Nancy—†	83	glassmaker	39	"
V	Mezetti Frances—†	83	housewife	21	"
W	Mezetti Herbert	83	U S A	24	"
X	*DiApuzzo Angelina—†	84	housewife	62	"
Y	*DiApuzzo Nicola	84	tailor	66	
Z	Vaccaro Carmella—†	84	housewife	42	"
247						
A	Vaccaro John	84	laborer	53	
B	Ferrara Girolamo	84	tailor	72	"
C	Ferrara Victoria—†	84	housewife	64	"
D	Angello Ida—†	85	"	48	
E	Angello Joseph	85	laborer	59	"
F	Dimino Catherine—†	85	welder	20	64 Webster
G	Dimino Lillian—†	85	housewife	42	64 "
H	Dimino Salvatore	85	fisherman	53	64 "
K	Rossi Anthony	85	laundrywkr	62	here
L	Rossi Frances—†	85	stitcher	21	"
M	Rossi Pellegrino	85	U S N	23	"
N	Rossi Raffaela—†	85	at home	28	"
O	Rossi Ralph	85	stevedore	25	"
P	Christina Lillian—†	87	housewife	27	"
R	Christina Louis	87	shipper	28	"

Page.	Letter.	FULL NAME.	Residence, Jan. 1, 1945.	Occupation.	Supposed Age.	Reported Residence, Jan. 1, 1944. Street and Number.

Webster Street—Continued

	s	Cotte Adelaide—†	87	assembler	24	here
	t	Cotte Helen—†	87	typist	21	"
	u	Cotte Margaret—†	87	dipper	50	"
	v	Cotte Nunzio	87	stevedore	31	"
	w	Cotte Olga—†	87	housewife	29	"
	x	Pisiello George	88	laborer	39	
	y	Pisiello Mary—†	88	housewife	37	"
	z	DiAngelis Archangelo	88	laborer	63	
248						
	a	DiAngelis Maria—†	88	housewife	68	"
	b	Scire Theresa—†	88	housekeeper	38	..
	c	Marmorale Anthony	88	painter	49	
	d	Marmorale Caroline—†	88	housewife	41	"
	e	Marmorale Edmund	88	U S A	21	
	f	Marotte Louise—†	89	housewife	35	"
	g	Marotte Philip	89	stevedore	35	"
	h	Espersito Phyllis—†	89	stitcher	23	"
	k	Zeoli Ernest	89	retired	55	
	l	Zeoli Josephine—†	89	dressmaker	55	"
	m	Prisco Quinta—†	89	housekeeper	34	"
	n	Haggstrom Emilia A—†	90	housewife	62	"
	o	Haggstrom Olga A—†	90	packer	30	
	p	Haggstrom Otto H	90	fireman	74	"
	r	Vacirca Michael	90	laborer	27	30 Orleans
	s	Vacirca Stella—†	90	housewife	26	30 "
	t	Bottaro Beatrice—†	90	"	26	108 London
	u	Bottaro Nicolas	90	salesman	26	108 "
	v	Varssallo Angelina—†	91	housewife	38	here
	w	Varssallo James	91	factoryhand	43	"
	x	DeChristofore Dominick	91A	carpenter	67	"
	y	DeChristofore Palmira—†	91A	housewife	64	"
	z	Pessia Elvira—†	91A	housekeeper	57	"
249						
	a	Pessia Gilda—†	91A	factoryhand	22	"
	b	Pessia Lareto	91A	U S A	28	
	c	Pessia Mary—†	91A	social worker	23	"
	d	Pessia Theresa—†	91A	factoryhand	31	"
	e	Esposito Eugene	92	U S A	22	
	f	Esposito Gaetano	92	laborer	53	
	g	Esposito Josephine—†	92	housewife	48	"
	h	Criseoli Anthony	92	factoryhand	52	"

Webster Street—Continued

K	Criseoli Jennie—†	92	stitcher	45	here
L	*Santillo Antonio	92	retired	65	"
M	*Santillo Julia—†	92	housewife	55	"
N	Santillo Michael	92	shipfitter	20	"
O	Santillo Philip	92	U S A	25	
P	Santillo Ralph	92	"	22	"
R	Bonnell Eugene	93	tinsmith	38	34 Dwight
S	DeGloria Esther—†	93	housewife	28	Haverhill
T	DeGloria Rosario	93	factoryhand	39	Medford
U	Pasco Jeannette—†	93A	clerk	20	here
V	Pasco Margaret—†	93A	housewife	39	"
W	Pasco Nickolas	93A	shipfitter	46	"
X	Sistilio Antonetta—†	93A	housewife	45	"
Y	Sistilio Frank	93A	tinsmith	57	"
Z	Sistilio Peter	93A	pipefitter	21	"
	250				
A	Astucci James	94	laborer	26	
B	Astucci Lucy—†	94	packer	22	
C	*Astucci Mary—†	94	housewife	52	"
D	*Astucci Michael	94	stevedore	54	"
E	*Vacirca Agripina—†	94	housewife	50	"
F	Vacirca Joseph	94	welder	29	"
G	Vacirca Mary—†	94	domestic	23	"
K	Cristoforo Charles	95	chauffeur	48	"
L	Cristoforo Marie A—†	95	candymaker	32	"
M	Cristoforo Maurice	95	U S A	32	
N	Houghton Agnes B—†	95	housekeeper	50	"
O	Piccardi Anna R—†	96	factoryhand	20	"
P	Piccardi Hugo	96	pipefitter	48	"
R	Piccardi Theresa—†	96	housewife	40	"
S	Iasbarrone Donato	96	welder	45	
T	Iasbarrone Louise—†	96	housewife	33	"
U	*Squadrito Jerome	96	fisherman	51	"
V	Squadrito Martha—†	96	housewife	38	"
W	Distaso Joseph	97	U S A	26	
X	Distaso Marie—†	97	housewife	55	"
Y	Distaso Santo	97	clerk	28	
Z	Cesero Ernest	97	"	48	
	251				
A	Cesero Florence—†	97	saleswoman	22	"
B	Cesero Lucy—†	97	housewife	43	"

Page.	Letter.	Full Name.	Residence, Jan. 1, 1945.	Occupation.	Supposed Age.	Reported Residence, Jan. 1, 1944. Street and Number.

Webster Street—Continued

	c	Grallo Germano	98	machinist	30	here
	d	Grallo Mary—†	98	housewife	29	"
	e	Bozza Anna—†	98	"	37	118 Bremen
	f	Bozza Samuel	98	packer	37	118 "
	g	Bruno Louise—†	98	housewife	44	here
	h	Bruno Michael	98	laborer	51	"
	k	Rongone Alfred	99	engineer	40	"
	l	Rongone Susan—†	99	housewife	37	"
	m	Roach Allen	100	electrician	45	"
	n	Roach Margaret—†	100	housewife	45	"
	o	Gagliardi Angelo	100	U S A	20	
	p	Gagliardi Anthony	100	"	24	"
	r	Gagliardi Frank	100	"	23	
	s	Gagliardi Rose—†	100	housewife	48	"
	t	Gagliardi Sabina	100	laborer	48	
	u	DiBello James	100	brakeman	40	"
	v	DiBello Jennie—†	100	housewife	40	"
	w	*Costello Bridget—†	101	"	64	
	x	Costello Michael	101	U S A	39	
	y	Costello Mildred—†	101	stitcher	35	"
	z	*Walsh William	101	stevedore	58	"
	252					
	a	Kennedy Albert F	101	U S N	26	
	b	Kennedy David J	101	retired	72	
	c	Kennedy Elizabeth A—†	101	at home	40	"
	d	Kennedy Ernest E	101	U S N	27	
	e	Kennedy Martin A	101	U S A	35	
	f	Kennedy Mary F—†	101	at home	36	"
	g	DiBello Anna—†	102	packer	28	
	h	*DiBello Josephine—†	102	housewife	75	"
	k	Pasto Alba—†	102	"	49	
	l	Pasto Elizabeth—†	102	secretary	22	"
	m	Pasto Mario	102	U S N	21	
	n	Pasto Salvatore G	102	"	24	
	o	*Pilegi Catherine—†	102	housewife	84	"
	p	Pantano Nozarina—†	102	"	48	
	r	Pantano Rose—†	102	factoryhand	22	"
	s	Pantano Santo	102	laborer	51	
	t	DiRago Pasquale	rear 102	"	59	
	u	Giello Florence—†	103	typist	37	
	v	Giello Joseph M	103	retired	79	

Webster Street—Continued

w	Giello Lillian C—†	103	typist	25	here
x	Giello Rose M—†	103	housewife	67	"
y	Simione Joseph	106	salesman	46	"
z	Simione Mary—†	106	housewife	45	"
	253				
A	Letty Edith—†	108	"	25	Medford
B	Letty Frank	108	welder	30	"
c	Karavos May—†	108	operator	46	here
D	Magliano Antonette—†	110	housewife	29	"
E	Magliano John	110	stevedore	31	"
G	Morgan Edward W	112	painter	38	
H	Morgan Helen M—†	112	housewife	38	"
N	Goggin Helen E—†	115	"	31	
o	Goggin Joseph P	115	shipper	36	
P	Goggin John J	115	retired	73	"
R	Goggin Josephine—†	115	housewife	70	"
s	Gillen James	116	stevedore	46	"
T	Gillen Margaret—†	116	stenographer	28	"
U	Gillen May—†	116	housewife	38	"
v	Marino Accurzio	116	buyer	36	
w	Marino Rose—†	116	housewife	34	"
x	Piscitelli Angelina—†	116	"	45	
Y	Piscitelli Joseph	116	laborer	44	
z	O'Leary Jessie A—†	117	housewife	35	"
	254				
A	O'Leary John J	117	stevedore	46	"
B	Sheehan Mary—†	117	housekeeper	60	"
c	Johnson Andrew B	117	retired	68	"
D	Sallemi Domnick	117	salesman	62	"
E	Albano Carman	118	chauffeur	34	"
F	Albano Mary—†	118	housewife	30	"
G	Rauseo Carmella—†	118	stenographer	21	"
H	Rauseo Domenick	118	presser	30	"
K	Rauseo Mary—†	118	stenographer	22	"
L	*Rauseo Michelena—†	118	housewife	52	"
M	Rauseo Rocco	118	U S N	33	
N	Rauseo Vito	118	U S A	28	
o	Albano James	118	guard	36	
P	Albano Theresa—†	118	housewife	34	"
R	Goggin Catherine—†	119	"	38	
s	Goggin Richard J	119	foreman	40	"

Webster Street—Continued

T	Salini Julius	119	baker	38	here
U	Salini Phyllis—†	119	housewife	28	"
V	Bagnera Anthony	119	shipfitter	36	"
W	Bagnera Viola—†	119	housewife	29	"
X	Tarquinio George	120	operator	26	198 Orient av
Y	Filippone Henry F	120	U S M C	32	Salem
Z	Filippone Margaret—†	120	housewife	30	"
	255				
A	Calabrese Fanny—†	120	"	25	49 Cottage
B	Calabrese Nello	120	machinist	28	49 "
C	Teso Anthony	120	stevedore	30	41 Orleans
D	Teso Madeline—†	120	housewife	26	41 "
E	Uccello Concetto	122	merchant	54	here
F	Uccello Filomena—†	122	housewife	48	"
G	Uccello Rose—†	122	saleswoman	23	"
H	Adamo Concetta—†	122	housewife	29	"
K	Adamo Frank	122	ropemaker	28	"
L	Marciano Angina—†	123	clerk	20	
M	Marciano Anthony	123	U S A	31	
N	Marciano Giuseppe	123	merchant	56	"
O	Marciano Grace—†	123	housewife	57	"
P	Falla Anna—†	123	"	61	..
R	Falla Mary—†	123	operator	26	"
S	Falla Ralph	123	janitor	67	
T	Morgante Albert	123	guard	53	"
U	Morgante Felicia—†	123	housewife	51	"
V	Morgante Pasquale	123	laborer	48	
X	Barrasso Carmela—†	125	housewife	28	"
Y	Barrasso Jeremiah	125	clerk	35	"
Z	Henebury Ellen—†	125	housewife	28	"
	256				
A	Henebury John R	125	foreman	32	"
B	Walsh Mary J—†	125	housewife	69	"
C	Walsh William J	125	watchman	68	"
D	*Picardi Esther—†	126	housewife	44	"
E	Picardi Ralph	126	laborer	46	
F	*Ambrosino Michael	126	retired	81	
G	Ambrosino Rose—†	126	factoryhand	35	"
H	DiBlasi Charles	126	U S N	22	
K	DiBlasi Louise—†	126	housewife	32	"
L	DiBlasi Salvatore	126	stevedore	49	"

Webster Street—Continued

M	Gaeta Carmen	127	chauffeur	25	207 Saratoga
N	Gaeta Mary—†	127	housewife	23	207 "
O	Parise Alvina—†	127	"	27	here
P	Parise Anthony	127	shoeworker	30	"
R	*Parise Michele	127	"	63	"
S	Crocette Carl	127	merchant	59	"
T	Crocette Jennie—†	127	housewife	53	"
U	Zirpolo Angelina—†	128	"	41	
V	Zirpolo Michael	128	stevedore	50	"
W	Zirpolo Michael	128	U S N	20	
X	Chiarella Mildred—†	128	housewife	31	"
Y	Chiarella Vincent	128	electrician	30	"
Z	Chiuchiolo Angie—†	128	housewife	27	"

257

A	Chiuchiolo John	128	laborer	29	"
B	*Chiuchiolo Joseph	128	candymaker	58	"
C	Chiuchiolo Louise—†	128	operator	23	"
D	Chiuchiolo Rose—†	128	housewife	25	"
E	Chiuchiolo Theresa—†	128	factoryhand	21	"
F	Racana Alfred A	129	electrician	20	"
G	Racana Anthony A	129	machinist	22	"
H	Racana John	129	bricklayer	66	"
K	Racana Louise—†	129	housewife	58	"
L	Racana Olga—†	129	candymaker	30	"
M	Iannarone Agnes—†	129	housewife	34	"
N	Iannarone Leonard	129	metalworker	34	"
O	Racana Helena—†	129	housewife	30	"
P	Racana Rocco	129	shipfitter	33	"
R	Curzi John	130	rigger	41	"
S	Varone Grace—†	130	housewife	33	"
T	Varone Salvatore	130	machinist	34	"
U	DiBiasio Angelina—†	130	housewife	36	"
V	DiBiasio Emilio C	130	carpenter	36	"
W	Rigano Margaret—†	130	cigarmaker	52	"
X	Liberti Ettore	131	retired	58	"
Y	Liberti Ferminia—†	131	typist	33	
Z	Liberti Galdino	131	U S N	20	"

258

A	Liberti Prasside—†	131	housewife	57	"
B	Liberti Sabatino	131	U S N	32	
C	Liberti Ugo	131	U S A	22	

Page.	Letter.	Full Name.	Residence, Jan. 1, 1945.	Occupation.	Supposed Age.	Reported Residence, Jan. 1, 1944. Street and Number.

Webster Street—Continued

	Letter	Full Name	Res.	Occupation	Age	Reported Residence
	D	Liberti Vera—†	131	beautician	24	here
	E	LaMar Carmela—†	135	at home	23	460 Sumner
	F	Sarro Anthony	135	laborer	56	460 "
	G	Sarro Catherine—†	135	cutter	31	460 "
	H	Sarro Jennie—†	135	housewife	53	460 "
		Sarro Josephine—†	135	fishcutter	30	here
		Tosi Helen—†	136	housewife	51	"
		Neri Angelo	136	chauffeur	38	138 Webster
		Neri Lena—†	136	housewife	35	138 "
	N	Hanlon Bernard	136	stevedore	40	1 Alna pl
	P	Snow Elizabeth—†	136	domestic	28	1 "
	R	*Arciuoli Alvira—†	136	housewife	61	here
	S	Arciuoli John	136	laborer	64	"
	T	Arciuoli Joseph	136	U S A	24	"
	U	Digan Anna W—†	137	at home	60	"
	V	Digan Arthur E	137	attorney	54	"
	W	Digan Carrie L—†	137	saleswoman	58	"
	X	Digan Lucy E—†	137	at home	56	"
	Y	Colagiovanni Anna—†	138	housewife	22	166 Putnam
	Z	Colagiovanni Donato	138	machinist	22	166 "

259

	Letter	Full Name	Res.	Occupation	Age	Reported Residence
	A	Borrelli Antonetta—†	138	housewife	53	here
	B	Borrelli Michael	138	machinist	60	"
	C	Ewton Concetta R—†	138	housewife	23	"
	D	Ewton John C	138	U S A	30	"
	E	Kella Mildred—†	138	clerk	30	Medford
	F	Kella William	138	welder	33	Missouri
	G	Velardo John	138	machinist	32	here
	H	Velardo Nicolette—†	138	housewife	28	"
	L	Burno Josephine—†	141	at home	25	41 Orleans
	M	Burno Nicholas M	141	clerk	28	320 Saratoga
	N	Guida Gennaro	141	chipper	34	here
	O	Guida Vincenza—†	141	housewife	27	"
	P	Solemina James P	143	shoeworker	22	Revere
	R	*Carangelo Carmella—†	143	housewife	53	here
	S	Carangelo Nickolas	143	laborer	53	"
	T	Chierus Francis W	143	electrician	22	Cambridge
	U	Chierus Helen G—†	143	housewife	21	60 Bremen
	V	Mortissi Concetta—†	147	factoryhand	20	here
	W	Petrillo Anthony	147	laborer	54	"
	X	Petrillo Mary—†	147	housewife	57	"

34

Webster Street—Continued

Y	Petrillo Peter	147	U S N	23	here
Z	Salamanca Manuel	147	U S A	28	154 Webster
260					
A	Salamanca Rafflia—†	147	housewife	25	154 "
B	DiRenzo Anna—†	147	"	70	here
C	DiRenzo Gaetano	147	retired	73	"
D	Andriotti George	149	U S N	24	"
E	Andriotti Mary—†	149	housewife	63	"
F	Gallo Yolanda—†	149	stitcher	27	"
G	Ciampa Aurora—†	149	housewife	39	"
H	Ciampa Nickolas	149	shipper	38	
K	Musi Evelyn—†	149	housewife	41	"
L	Musi Michael	149	engineer	40	"
M	Rotigliano Michael	155	shoemaker	67	"
N	Aronson Aaron	155	merchant	46	"
O	Aronson Goldie—†	155	housewife	44	"
P	Rotigliano Joseph	155	machinist	30	"
R	Rotigliano Mary—†	155	housewife	28	"
S	Howe Frances—†	177	"	40	
T	Howe Lawrence P	177	manager	39	"
U	Phelps Dorothy L—†	179	social worker	38	72 Marginal
V	Serino Angelina—†	181	housewife	55	here
W	Serino Domenic	181	shoemaker	57	"
X	Serino Nancy—†	181	cutter	22	"
Y	Pelosi Achille	181	tailor	47	"
Z	Pelosi Mary—†	181	housewife	45	"
261					
A	Cerullo Louis	181	engineer	40	"
B	Cerullo Mary—†	181	housewife	28	"
C	Vardaro Anthony	181	carpenter	36	"
D	*Vardaro Mary—†	181	housewife	75	"
F	Clay Arline—†	183	"	21	..
G	Clay Bernard	183	U S A	23	"
H	Santilli Angelina—†	183	housewife	35	"
K	Santilli Pasquale	183	chauffeur	30	"
N	Lamarca Catherine—†	185	housewife	58	"
O	Lamarca Catherine—†	185	tailor	38	
P	Lamarca Josephine—†	185	stitcher	29	"
R	Frasca Mary—†	185	housekeeper	34	"
S	Manzo Mary—†	185	housewife	31	"
T	Manzo Peter	185	shipper	40	..

Page.	Letter.	Full Name.	Residence, Jan. 1, 1945.	Occupation.	Supposed Age.	Reported Residence, Jan. 1, 1944. Street and Number.

Webster Street—Continued

	U	Pierce James F	187	custodian	62	here
	V	Pierce Mary A—†	187	housewife	60	"
	W	Pierce Mary G—†	187	clerk	26	"
	X	Pierce William J	187	U S A	37	
	Y	Davies Elizabeth D—†	187	housewife	40	"
	Z	Davies Joseph F	187	salesman	43	"
262						
	A	Anderson Annice A—†	189	teacher	59	
	B	Hennessy Mary E—†	189	housewife	27	"
	C	Watt Helen E—†	189	at home	70	"
	D	McLean Grace—†	189	housekeeper	58	"
	E	Couch Phyllis—†	191	"	20	..
	F	Melito Domenic	191	U S A	22	
	G	Melito Palmie—†	191	housewife	41	"
	H	Melito Vito	191	laborer	42	"
	K	Varone Mario	191	shipfitter	23	77 Webster
	L	Catero Anthony	191	bartender	43	here
	M	Catero Carmella—†	191	housewife	37	"
	N	Healy William C	193	clerk	71	"
	O	Leonard Elizabeth F—†	193	housewife.	68	"
	P	Leonard William L	193	clerk	59	
	R	Marotta Celia—†	195	beautician	36	"
	S	Hicks Howard L	195	chauffeur	43	Chelsea
	T	Hicks Theresa—†	195	housewife	37	"
	Y	Barry William J	199	clergyman	71	here
	Z	Burke Ellen—†	199	housekeeper	65	"
263						
	A	Sweeney George B	199	clergyman	32	"
	B	Matarazzo Alfred	201	brushmaker	32	"
	C	Matarazzo Susan—†	201	housewife	33	"
	D	Tringali Carmelo	201	retired	78	
	E	Tringali Domenic	201	boatbuilder	30	"
	F	Tringali Domenica—†	201	at home	33	"
	G	Sirianni Eleanor—†	201	factoryhand	20	"
	H	Sirianni Jennie—†	201	at home	42	"
	K	Vozella Rose—†	201	clerk	23	
	L	Indorato James	205	stevedore	28	"
	M	Indorato Mary—†	205	stitcher	26	"
	N	Torti Louise—†	205	tailor	44	
	O	Torti Zeno	205	"	46	

Page.	Letter.	FULL NAME.	Residence, Jan. 1, 1945.	Occupation.	Supposed Age.	Reported Residence, Jan. 1, 1944. Street and Number.

Webster Street—Continued

	P	Manganielli Joseph	205	printer	54	here
	R	Pollini Dominick	205	cutter	59	"
	S	Pollini Frances—†	205	housewife	56	"
	T	Pollini Rita—†	205	stenographer	20	"
	U	Dowd Mary A—†	207	at home	75	"
	V	Dowd Mary C—†	207	secretary	39	"
	W	Finn Sarah G—†	207	clerk	45	"
	X	Usseglio Aurelia—†	211	at home	70	"
	Y	Usseglio Mary—†	211	clerk	47	
	Z	Muldoon Joseph J	211	lineman	54	"
264						
	A	Muldoon Margaret—†	211	operator	20	"
	B	Muldoon Mary—†	211	inspector	23	"
	C	Muldoon Mary A—†	211	housewife	48	"
	D	Lowden Catherine—†	213	"	27	141 Webster
	E	Lowden Leslie	213	U S N	30	141 "
	F	Usseglio Charles	213	pipefitter	39	here
	G	Usseglio Helen—†	213	housewife	35	"
	H	Faiello Anna—†	215	housekeeper	31	"
	K	Ventresca Adele—†	215	nurse	28	
	L	Ventresca Anna—†	215	operator	20	"
	M	Ventresca Anthony	215	painter	26	"
	N	Ventresca Lino	215	U S A	24	
	O	Ventresca Maria—†	215	housewife	50	"
	P	Ventresca Olga—†	215	chauffeur	21	"
	R	Ventresca Viola—†	215	assembler	28	"
	S	Hoitt Charles	215	chauffeur	26	"
	T	Hoitt Dorothy—†	215	housewife	25	"
	U	Baker Theresa—†	217	"	24	30 Moore
	V	DeMarco Frank	217	laborer	49	here
	W	DeMarco Frank	217	clerk	21	"
	X	DeMarco Jennie—†	217	housewife	48	"
	Y	Mumofo Ida—†	217	"	35	
	Z	Mumofo Ignazio	217	stevedore	45	"
265						
	B	Taylor Mary E—†	221	housewife	38	Winthrop
	C	Taylor Richard	221	clerk	46	"
	E	Crowley John J	223	stevedore	46	here
	F	Knowles Catherine M—†	223	housewife	54	"
	G	Knowles Catherine M—†	223	operator	27	"

Page.	Letter.	FULL NAME.	Residence, Jan. 1, 1945.	Occupation.	Supposed Age.	Reported Residence, Jan. 1, 1944. Street and Number.

Webster Street—Continued

H	Knowles James E	223	operator	56	here
K	Gay Dorothy M—†	223	clerk	21	"
L	Gay Ernest W	223	guard	57	"
M	Gay Ernest W, jr	223	U S A	25	
N	Gay Francis R	223	"	23	
O	Gay Veronica E—†	223	housewife	49	"
P	Burke Mary E—†	225	housekeeper	63	"
R	Leahy Helen—†	225	clerk	34	"
S	Knowles Inez—†	225	housewife	27	"
T	Knowles James E, jr	225	manager	31	"
U	Kelley Annie—†	225	housewife	41	"
V	Kelley Jerome	225	chef	44	"
W	Pfeifer Helen—†	227	housewife	40	"
X	Pfeifer John	227	stevedore	37	"
Y	Blake Lillian—†	227	housewife	45	"
Z	Smiddy Joseph P	227	stevedore	54	"
	266				
A	Duane Mary L—†	227	housekeeper	81	"
B	Lambert Alexander P	227	steamfitter	72	"

Wilbur Court

C	Rehn Albert	1	U S N	20	here
D	Rehn John	1	pipefitter	52	"
F	Donatelli Lucrezia—†	2	housewife	32	"
G	Donatelli Luigi	2	electrician	28	"
H	Kirkorian Haigis P	2	U S N	34	100 Marginal
K	Kirkorian Louise L—†	2	housewife	30	100 "
M	Evangelista John	3	laborer	42	here
N	Evangelista Marie T—†	3	housewife	38	"
O	Augusta Louise—†	3	stenographer	35	"
P*	Augusta Rose—†	3	housewife	77	"
R	D'Ambrosio Ernest A	3	brazier	28	
S	D'Ambrosio Mildred—†	3	housewife	27	"
T	Martella Ernest	4	U S A	35	
U	Martella Henry	4	"	38	
W	Sartori John	4	chipper	40	"
X	Sartori Mollie—†	4	housewife	36	"
Z	Corrado Lucy—†	5	"	45	

Wilbur Court—Continued

A	Corrado Ralph	5	carpenter	49	here
B	Morello Carmen	5	boilermaker	24	73 Cottage
C	Morello Mary—†	5	housewife	22	73 "
E	Dinolfo Vincenzo	6	porter	60	here
F	Drago Giovanni	6	salesman	60	"
G	Martignetti Antonio	6	laborer	53	"
H	Martignetti Olympia—†	6	housewife	51	"

Ward 1–Precinct 3

CITY OF BOSTON

LIST OF RESIDENTS
20 YEARS OF AGE AND OVER

(NON-CITIZENS INDICATED BY ASTERISK)
(FEMALES INDICATED BY DAGGER)

AS OF

JANUARY 1, 1945

THOMAS F. SULLIVAN, *Chairman*
FREDERIC E. DOWLING, *Secretary*
WILLIAM A. MOTLEY, JR.
FRANCIS B. McKINNEY
EVERETT R. PROUT

Listing Board.

CITY OF BOSTON PRINTING DEPARTMENT

Page	Letter	Full Name.	Residence, Jan. 1, 1945.	Occupation.	Supposed Age.	Reported Residence, Jan. 1, 1944. Street and Number.

300

Airport Street

	o	Ambrasino John	5	laborer	40	here
	p	*Merullo Angelo	5	mechanic	52	"
	r	Salemi Joseph	5	laborer	52	"
	s	Salemi Mary—†	5	housewife	52	"

Ardee Street

	w	Pace Frank	3	laborer	26	here
	x	Pace Pantaleone	3	"	50	"
	y	*Bonavista Catherine—†	3	housewife	59	"
	z	*Bonavista James	3	laborer	61	

301

	a	Bonavista Rose M—†	3	operator	23	"
	c	Cinelli James A	5	U S A	24	184 Marginal
	d	*Cinelli Nancy—†	5	housewife	61	184 "
	e	Mercurio Charles F	5	mechanic	42	here
	f	Mercurio Margaret—†	5	housewife	40	"
	g	Salemi Josephine—†	5	"	54	"
	h	Salemi Sebastian	5	millhand	53	"
	k	Pagnani Gino	5	pipecoverer	22	"
	l	Pagnani Hugo	5	laborer	54	

Deer Island

	m	Bancroft Warren		herdsman	40	72 Peterboro
	n	Connelly Joseph T		guard	53	here
	o	Cronin Frederick J		"	48	"
	p	Devine Joseph A		"	51	"
	r	Doyle John P		supt	43	
	s	Doyle Mary E—†		at home	75	"
	t	Doyle Mary E—†		housewife	38	"
	u	Drewes Henry F		supervisor	49	"
	v	Finnerty James F		guard	67	"
	w	Ford Daniel F		"	50	
	x	Gallagher Francis W		"	51	
	y	Gilbert Clifford M		"	47	
	z	Gilbert Lela F—†		housewife	31	"

302

	a	Grappi Louis		guard	46	
	b	Keefe Daniel J		"	49	
	c	Luciano Frank J		"	42	"

2

Page	Letter	Full Name.	Residence, Jan. 1, 1945.	Occupation.	Supposed Age.	Reported Residence, Jan. 1, 1944. Street and Number.

Deer Island—Continued

	Letter	Full Name	Residence	Occupation	Age	Reported Residence
	D	Lucy Joseph R		guard	53	here
	E	Macke Robert F		"	53	"
	F	Martin Coleman F		"	62	"
	G	McCarthy Andrew H		"	55	
	H	McCarthy Margaret A—†		housewife	53	"
	K	McKenna Edson L		guard	53	
	L	McMullan Peter A		clerk	42	
	M	Moore Leo		guard	45	"
	N	Morrison William K		"	58	"
	O	Moylette William J		"	56	
	P	O'Brien John J			53	
	R	O'Halloran George		"	43	
	S	O'Neil Francis P		retired	74	
	T	O'Neil Helen M—†		housewife	73	"
	U	Teevens Patrick H		guard	59	
	V	Walters Stephen J		"	45	
	W	Yirrell Frederick W		"	44	

Everett Court

	Letter	Full Name	Residence	Occupation	Age	Reported Residence
	Y	Salamone Giuseppe	2	laborer	59	here
	Z	*Salamone Stella—†	2	housewife	95	"
303						
	A	*Cavola Angelo	3	laborer	65	"
	B	Lavoie Beatrice—†	3	housewife	35	244 Everett
	C	Lavoie George	3	salesman	44	244 "
	D	Coviello Phyllis—†	4	packer	38	here
	E	Coviello Prisco	4	shoeworker	40	"
	F	LaPia Antoinette—†	4	stitcher	30	"
	G	LaPia Genaro	4	laborer	56	
	H	LaPia Jennie—†	4	housewife	50	"
	K	LaPia Jennie—·†	4	stitcher	20	"
	L	LaPia Michael	4	U S A	29	
	M	Cinelli Domenic	5	"	28	
	N	Cinelli Evangeline—†	5	housewife	26	"
	O	Costopoulos Antonio	5	rigger	23	
	P	Costopoulos Christopher	5	U S A	25	
	R	*Costopoulos John	5	laborer	52	"
	S	Costopoulos Olga—†	5	housewife	47	"
	T	Mancuso Joseph	6	seaman	24	"
	U	Mancuso Olga—†	6	housewife	23	"

Page.	Letter.	FULL NAME.	Residence, Jan. 1, 1945.	Occupation.	Supposed Age.	Reported Residence, Jan. 1, 1944. Street and Number.

Everett Place

	w	Clex Charles	2	laborer	52	here
	x	Keohane James	2	"	22	"
	y	Keohane Josephine—†	2	housewife	21	"
	z	Mucci Anna—†	4	"	33	
304						
	a	Mucci Camillo	4	U S A	35	
	b	Mucci John	4	laborer	69	
	c	Todd Susan—†	4	housewife	22	"
	f	Todesco Rocco	7	laborer	38	
	g	Todesco Violet—†	7	stitcher	29	"

Everett Street

	k	Patti Pasquale	185	painter	21	here
	h	Patti Pauline—†	185	housewife	25	"
	l	Patti Mary—†	185	"	40	"
	m	Cifuni Alfred	187	metalworker	22	"
	n	Cifuni Amelia—†	187	assembler	28	"
	o	Cifuni Charles	187	machinist	34	"
	p	Cifuni Edith—†	187	stitcher	23	"
	r	*Cifuni Gennaro	187	retired	63	
	s	*Cifuni Maria—†	187	housewife	59	"
	t	Lomanno Salvatore	189	tinsmith	43	"
	u	Lomanno Victoria—†	189	housewife	21	"
	v	Screnci Cornelia—†	189	"	22	
	w	Screnci Thomas	189	U S C G	24	"
	x	Albanese Giuseppina—†	191	stitcher	56	"
	y	Albanese Michael	191	laborer	66	"
	z	Mangone Pearl—†	191	housewife	38	146 Everett
305						
	a	Mangone Thomas	191	clerk	41	146 "
	b	Albanese Francis	191	U S A	25	here
	c	Albanese Madeline—†	191	housewife	25	"
	e	Sasso Carmella—†	192	"	24	"
	f	Sasso Michael	192	U S N	24	
	g	Liguri Augustine	192	salesman	23	"
	h	Liguri Frank	192	machinist	65	"
	k	*Liguri Josephine—†	192	housewife	60	"
	l	Liguri Louis	192	U S A	25	"
	m	D'Amato Frances—†	193	housewife	30	216 Everett
	n	D'Amato Fred	193	laborer	44	216 "

Everett Street—Continued

o	D'Amato Jerry	193	U S A	23	216 Everett
R	Hogan Anastasia—†	193	housewife	50	here
s	Hogan Thomas	193	watchman	55	"
T	Juliano Rosario	195	metalworker	34	"
U	Juliano Rose—†	195	housewife	31	"
v	Lauletta Angelina—†	195	clerk	47	
w	Lauletta Antonio	195	baker	51	
x	Lauletta Mary—†	195	welder	20	
Y	Lauletta Vincent	195	U S N	21	
z	Cifuni Mary—†	195	housewife	29	"

306

A	Cifuni Salvatore	195	fishcutter	30	"
B	Lacey Alice—†	196	stitcher	27	"
c	Sullivan Nora—†	196	at home	58	"
D	Small Annie M—†	198	housewife	59	"
F	Screnci Peter C	200	U S N	20	
G	Screnci Saverina—†	200	housewife	55	"
H	Screnci Thomas	200	broker	53	
K	Festa Angelina—†	206	housewife	30	"
L	Festa Nicholas	206	clerk	36	"
M	Cooke Claude	206	welder	32	
N	Cooke Inez—†	206	housewife	30	"
o	Prezioso Ovedio	206	machinist	28	"
P	Costa Salvatore	206	electrician	23	191 Everett
R	Cifelli Genaro	210	watchman	53	here
s	*Cifelli Rosa—†	210	housewife	60	"
T	Porzio Gino	210	U S A	22	"
U	Porzio Guido	210	laborer	20	
v	Porzio Nicholas	210	pipefitter	49	"
w	Porzio Nora—†	210	housewife	45	"
x	*Licciardi Antonetta—†	210	"	31	
Y	Licciardi Paul	210	machinist	36	"
z	Pugliese Antonio	214	laborer	56	

307

A	Pugliese Concetta—†	214	housewife	49	"
B	Pugliese Mary F—†	214	clerk	20	"
c	Pugliese Saverio	214	laborer	24	
D	Pugliese Seraphina—†	214	clerk	22	"
E	Burnside Mary—†	216	at home	44	237 Everett
F	*Piazza Antonetta—†	216	housewife	25	218 "
G	Piazza Benadetto	216	U S A	29	218 "

Everett Street—Continued

H	Ferranti Anthony	216	laborer	59	here
K	*Ferranti Carmella—†	216	housewife	56	"
L	*Correale Minagala—†	218	at home	75	"
M	Salemi Agrippino	218	retired	74	"
N	Salemi Maria—†	218	at home	82	"
O	Marinelli Carmella—†	218	housewife	36	"
P	Marinelli John	218	laborer	47	
R	Masciulli Lucy—†	221	housewife	61	"
S	Pepe Eleanor—†	221	operator	26	"
T	Pepe Vincént	221	packer	23	"
U	Masciulli Ralph	221	stripper	20	"
W	Pasquariello Theresa—†	222	housewife	38	"
X	Pasquariello Vincent	222	bricklayer	47	"
Z	Prizioso Antonette—†	223	housewife	34	"
	308				
A	Prizioso Edward A	223	laborer	34	"
B	Perosino Genaro	223	tailor	51	
C	Perosino Raffina—†	223	housewife	50.	"
D	Signorelli Alfred A	223	U S N	26	
E	Signorelli Julia A—†	223	housewife	26	"
F	Squillacioti Alfonse S	223	laborer	47	
G	Squillacioti Victoria—†	223	housewife	41	"
H	Grady Albert	224	mechanic	34	233 Everett
K	Grady Ruth—†	224	housewife	29	233 "
M	Mennino Dorothy—†	224	waitress	37	5 Ardee
S	Macchia Alfonso	226	clerk	28	here
T	Macchia Ernestine—†	226	"	22	"
U	Macchia Leo	226	shoeworker	65	"
V	*Macchia Mary—†	226	housewife	61	"
W	Macchia Peter	226	U S A	32	"
X	Bagnera Joseph	226	clerk	35	249 Everett
Y	Bagnera Mary—†	226	housewife	29	249 "
Z	*Pereira Anna—†	227	"	47	here
	309				
A	DeMartinis Amelia—†	227	"	47	
C	Gravallese Giuseppe	228	retired	75	
D	Gravallese Lucia—†	228	housewife	74	"
E	Gerosa Frances—†	228	"	44	
F	Gerosa Joseph	228	clerk	21	"
G	Carangelo Domenic	228	laborer	27	504 Summer
H	Carangelo Dorothy—†	228	housewife	25	504 "

Page.	Letter.	Full Name.	Residence, Jan. 1, 1945.	Occupation.	Supposed Age.	Reported Residence, Jan. 1, 1944. Street and Number.

Everett Street—Continued

	N	Gizzi Adeline—†	230	stitcher	20	here
	O	Gizzi Angelina—†	230	housewife	56	"
	P	Gizzi Mary—†	230	clerk	22	"
	R	Gizzi Thomas	230	retired	69	"
	S	Todesco Angelina—†	234	stitcher	22	"
	T	Todesco Aurilla—†	234	housewife	51	"
	U	Todesco Carlo	234	tailor	21	..
	V	Todesco Carmen	234	"	53	"
	W	Todesco Celeste—†	234	stitcher	24	"
	X	Celannino Anthony A	235	welder	30	
	Y	Celannino Maria C—†	235	housewife	30	"
	Z	Tringale Antonio J	235	boatbuilder	48	"
310						
	A	Tringale Mary G—†	235	housewife	43	"
	B	Gallagher Ellen J—†	237	"	60	
	C	Gallagher Hugh B	237	boilermaker	59	"
	D	Donahue Hugh F	237	"	34	
	E	Donahue Mary M—†	237	housewife	32	"
	F	Zichello Alexander	237	student	25	"
	G	Zichello Michael	237	laborer	58	
	H	Zichello Nicholas H	237	U S A	27	..
	K	Zichello Vincenza—†	237	housewife	47	"
	M	DeLuca Joseph	238	laborer	21	366 Bremen
	N	Scarpone Anna—†	238	housewife	48	366 "
	O	Scarpone Nicholas	238	laborer	44	366 "
	P	Fay Angelina D—†	239	housewife	20	here
	R	Fay John J	239	welder	21	"
	S	Carbone Jennie—†	239	housewife	36	"
	T	Carbone Ralph M	239	painter	38	"
	U	Driscoll Daniel J	239	U S A	38	..
	V	Driscoll Marie A—†	239	clerk	40	"
	W	Autillo Humbert	241	chauffeur	30	"
	X	Autillo Mary—†	241	housewife	25	"
	Y	Gesa Adeline—†	241	"	27	
	Z	Gesa William V	241	clerk	31	..
311						
	A*	Baldassarre Carmella—†	241	housewife	56	"
	B	Baldassarre Joseph F	241	laborer	63	
	C	DiSessa Charles	242	"	30	"
	D	DiSessa Kathryn—†	242	housewife	25	176 Chelsea
	E	DiSessa Samuel	242	barber	72	here

Everett Street—Continued

	F	DiSessa Sarah—†	242	housewife	64	here
	H	Bona Elizabeth—†	243	machinist	49	"
	K	Bona Helen—†	243	clerk	26	"
	M	Larsen Arthur	244	U S N	24	245 Everett
	N	Larsen Blanche—†	244	housewife	21	245 "
	O	Larsen Clarence	244	U S A	26	245 "
	P	Larsen Lillian—†	244	housewife	25	245 "
	R	Smith Thomas	244	rigger	60	245 "
	V	Stuffle Mildred—†	246	housewife	29	here
	W	Stuffle William	246	laborer	37	"
	X	*Brogna Antonetta—†	246	housewife	60	"
	Y	Brogna Antonio	246	laborer	55	
	Z	Brogna Dominic	246	brazier	33	
312						
		Brogna Michael	246	painter	28	
		Joslin Sally—†	247	housewife	30	"
		Milano Louis	247	U S A	35	
		Milano Rosalie—†	247	housewife	31	"
		Caruso Alice—†	247	stitcher	20	"
	B	Caruso Anita—†	247	housewife	49	"
	G	Caruso Anthony	247	clerk	52	
	H	Caruso Mary—†	247	waitress	23	"
	K	DiTomasso Antonio	247	U S A	27	
	L	DiTomasso Dominic	247	"	24	
	M	DiTomasso Frances—†	247	seamstress	29	"
	N	*DiTomasso Justino	247	laborer	65	
	O	*DiTomasso Mary—†	247	housewife	55	"
	P	DiTomasso Peter	247	laborer	22	
	R	DiTomasso Phyllis—†	247	machinist	20	"
	S	DiTomasso Santo	247	U S A	31	"
	T	Federico Herman	249	rigger	28	158 Cottage
	U	Federico Pearl—†	249	housewife	23	158 "
	V	*Cinelli Bridget—†	249	"	45	6 Everett ct
	W	Cinelli Helen—†	249	machinist	20	6 "
	X	Cinelli James	249	U S A	23	6 "
	Y	Cinelli Rocco	249	laborer	53	6 "
	Z	Piazza Angelina—†	249	housewife	55	here
313						
	A	Piazza Benedetta—†	249	stitcher	25	"
	B	Piazza John	249	U S A	27	
	C	Piazza Joseph	249	"	22	

Everett Street—Continued

D	Piazza Luigi	249	laborer	62	here
E	Loglio Giuseppe	250	"	55	"
F	Rindone Anthony	250	U S A	26	"
G	Rindone Giuseppe	250	"	22	
H	*Rindone Lena—†	250	housewife	57	"
K	Rindone Michael	250	U S A	24	
L	*Rindone Vincenzo	250	retired	64	"
M	Green John	254	chauffeur	30	4 Appian pl
N	Fullerton Clarence	254	painter	48	here
O	Fullerton Emma—†	254	housewife	30	"
P	Nardone Joseph	255–257	retired	64-	"
R	Nardone Joseph F	255–257	salesman	39	"
S	Nardone Pasqualina–†255–257		housewife	63	"
T	Nardone Vito	255–257	U S A	21	
U	Coviello Geraldine—†	256	housewife	34	"
V	Coviello John	256	salesman	30	"
W	Bickford Arthur	256	shipper	35	"
X	Bickford Elvira—†	256	at home	79	"
Y	Morelli Michael	258	brazier	20	201 London
Z	Haseman Anna—†	258	housewife	47	here
	314				
A	Haseman Phillip	258	electrician	48	"
B	Fay George E	258	U S A	23	259 Everett
C	Fay Helen G—†	258	at home	48	259 "
E	Giannasoli Ricardo	259	shipfitter	27	here
F	Nardone Emilio P	259	longshoreman	49	261 Everett
K	Trainor Catherine—†	260	housewife	29	here
L	Trainor William F	260	longshoreman	33	"
M	O'Brien James W	260	U S C G	22	"
N	O'Brien Lillian—†	260	housewife	48	"
O	Mucci Domenic	261	U S A	26	
P	Mucci Michelina—†	261	housewife	28	"
S	Cinelli Florinda—†	261	"	38	
T	Cinelli Giuseppe	261	operator	50	"
U	Cinelli James	261	shipfitter	21	"
W	Bruno Frank	263	U S A	24	
X	Bruno John	263	laborer	54	
Y	Bruno Lillian—†	263	housewife	48	"
Z	Gaito Anthony	263	U S A	27	"
	315				
A	Gaito Mary—†	263	housewife	27	"

Page.	Letter.	Full Name:	Residence, Jan. 1, 1945.	Occupation:	Supposed Age.	Reported Residence, Jan. 1, 1944. Street and Number:

Ipswich Place

	c	DiNicolantonio Consezio	1	retired	65	here
	d	DiNicolantonio Geneva—†	1	stitcher	27	"
	e	DiNicolantonio Ralph	1	pipefitter	30	"
	f	DiNicolantonio Romeo	1	U S A	25	"
	g	Romano Marie—†	1	housewife	24	"
	h	*Murphy Patrick	1	retired	78	"
	k	Volta Helen—†	1	housewife	35	"
	l	Taromano Joseph	1	laborer	42	
	m	Taromano Louise—†	1	housewife	35	"

Jeffries Street

	s	Burrows Elizabeth M—†	4	housewife	44	here
	t	Burrows Joseph J	4	laborer	21	"
	u	Muise John D	4	fishcutter	39	"
	v	*Muise Lawrence W	4	"	47	
	w	*Muise Mary—†	4	housewife	78	"
	x	Muise Philip G	4	U S A	22	
	y	*Muise William H	4	janitor	76	
	z	Larsen Carl J	4	painter	27	
316						
	a	Larsen Charles J	4	"	51	"
	b	Larsen Francis H	4	U S A	23	
	c	Larsen Mary B—†	4	housewife	51	"
	e	Cecchinelli Mary—†	6	"	21	549 Summer
	f	Fay Isabella E—†	6	"	53	549 "
	g	Fay Joseph J	6	operator	54	549 "
	h	Fay Herbert C	6	painter	39	259 Everett
	k	Fay Josephine M—†	6	housewife	39	259 "
	l	Lombardi Jennie M—†	7	"	36	here
	m	Lombardi Michael P	7	welder	36	"
	n	Lombardi Nicholas L	7	U S A	25	"
	o	Lombardi Victoria B—†	7	housewife	22	"
	r	Rock Gilbert J	8	mechanic	44	"
	s	Rock Rose M—†	8	housewife	28	"
	t	Gonsalves Anthony A	8	laborer	58	"
	u	*Gonsalves Mary—†	8	housewife	55	"
	v	Bona Dorothy M—†	9	"	25	258 Everett
	w	Bona Joseph H	9	rigger	25	258 "
	x	Dorato Carmine	9	laborer	24	here
	y	Dorato Vincenza—†	9	housewife	37	"

10

317
Jeffries Street—Continued

A	Etheridge Margaret—†	10	housewife	26	Connecticut
B	Newbury Harry N	10	cutter	37	here
c	*Newbury Sadie M—†	10	housewife	39	"
D	Ascolillo Amerigo	10	shoeworker	41	"
E	Ascolillo Rose J—†	10	housewife	35	"
G	Eisenburg Mary—†	12	"	37	"
H	Eisenburg William C	12	U S N	44	
K	Costa Margaret—†	12	houseworker	38	"
L	*Costa Virginia—†	12	housewife	63	"
M	Rondina Alice C—†	12	supervisor	27	"
N	Jacobs Aagot—†	23	housewife	66	"
O	Jacobs John G	23	machinist	69	"
P	Anderson George C	25	"	28	
R	Keohane Rita R—†	25	saleswoman	25	"
S	Vitale Domenic A	25	salesman	30	"
T	Vitale Joseph A	25	bricklayer	54	"
U	Vitale Mary S—†	25	housewife	27	"
V	Morrissey Helen E—†	27	"	49	"
W	Morrissey Joseph P	27	laborer	47	"
X	Morrissey Joseph W	27	U S A	22	"
Y	Heil Margaret—†	27	housewife	34	"
Z	Heil William J	27	longshoreman	36	"

318

A	Fay Richard N	27	deckhand	34	"
B	Fay William M	27	longshoreman	37	"
C	Ferriera Elizabeth M—†	29	housewife	67	"
E	Nigrelli John	29	laborer	62	
F	Nigrelli Marie—†	29	housewife	54	"
H	DiStasio Anna M—†	40	clerk	38	"
K	DiStasio Joseph	40	"	40	
L	DeGrigorio Eileen—†	40	waitress	28	"
M	DeGrigorio Robert	40	U S A	34	
N	Rhodes Lillian—†	40	housewife	44	"
O	Periello Caroline—†	42	"	64	"
P	Frazier Helen M—†	42	clerk	48	
R	Frazier Joseph P	42	fishcutter	61	"
S	Barron Leo F	42	riveter	42	
T	Barron Violet M—†	42	housewife	39	"
U	Barron Warren F	42	U S N	20	
V	Nigrelli Cosmo	44	U S A	26	"

Jeffries Street—Continued

w	Nigrelli Marie—†	44	housewife	24	here
x	Jackson Gilbert C	44	weigher	47	"
y	Jackson Margaret H—†	44	housewife	42	"
	319				
b	Innes Arthur N	45	printer	51	
c	Innes Ruth L—†	45	housewife	54	"
d	Finn Evelyn—†	45	leatherworker	45	130 Sumner
e	Shaughnessy Edward L	45	U S A	25	here
f	Hankard Esther A—†	46	skiver	58	"
g	Hankard Ruth C—†	46	stenographer	32	"
h	MacDonald George A	46	aviator	43	"
k	MacDonald Hazel M—†	46	housewife	31	"
l	Campbell Anna C—†	46	"	62	
m	Campbell Archibald F	46	storekeeper	67	"
n	Campbell Francis N	46	operator	41	"
o	Moran Clara V—†	47	housewife	68	"
p	Moran Michael L	47	retired	74	
r	Dermody Margaret I—†	47	clerk	25	
s	Dermody Robert E	47	U S N	22	
t	Moran Agnes F—†	47	clerk	32	
u	Moran Francis W	47	draftsman	34	"
w	Judge Christine L—†	48	housewife	44	"
x	Judge Francis P	48	lineman	46	"
z	Driscoll John H	49	longshoreman	49	11 Hooten ct
	320				
a	Porcaro Fiorello	49	painter	34	here
b	Porcaro Francesco	49	retired	72	"
c*	Porcaro Rose—†	49	housewife	66	"
d	Anoelli Domenic	49	carpenter	33	22 Oneida
e	Anoelli Sarah—†	49	housewife	33	22 "
g	Hanton George J	50	seaman	45	here
h	Hanton James H	50	U S N	21	"
k	Hanton Julia T—†	50	clerk	42	"
l*	Penney Elizabeth—†	50	houseworker	67	Medford
m	Woodside Albert D	50	welder	31	here
n	Woodside Beatrice S—†	50	housewife	27	"
s	Milano Antonetta—†	52	"	59	"
t	Milano James	52	U S N	25	"
u	Milano Luigi	52	machinist	70	"
v	Milano Richard	52	U S N	27	
w	Milano Alfred	52	U S A	23	

Page.	Letter.	FULL NAME.	Residence, Jan. 1, 1945.	Occupation.	Supposed Age.	Reported Residence, Jan. 1, 1944. Street and Number.

Jeffries Street—Continued

x	Milano John	52	U S A	20	here
y	Masello Carmen M	52	rigger	38	"
z	Masello Christine M—†	52	housewife	35	"
	321				
a	Riley Joseph F	53	chauffeur	27	"
b	Riley Mafalda F—†	53	housewife	27	"
c	Tulipani Rosina—†	53	"	60	
d	Tulipani Salvatore	53	musician	35	"
e	Tulipani Louis G	53	guard	41	"
f	Tulipani Nellie—†	53	housewife	39	"
g	Cuzzi Carmine	54	retired	70	"
h	Cuzzi Daniel	54	U S A	26	
k	Cuzzi Marie—†	54	housewife	65	"
l	Giampietro John	54	laborer	52	"
m	Giampietro John, jr	54	U S N	20	
n	Giampietro Philomena—†	54	packer	49	
o	Ciavola Richard N	54	U S A	30	
p	Gianfelice Gaetano	54	laborer	50	
r	Gianfelice Theresa—†	54	operator	37	"
s	Fontenot Caroline E—†	56	housewife	24	"
t	Fontenot Iway J	56	U S A	27	"
u	DelBene Elena J—†	56	stitcher	20	"
v	DelBene Julio	56	laborer	52	
w	DelBene Michelena—†	56	housewife	57	"
x	Lombardi Paul J	56	engineer	29	"
y	Lombardi Theresa—†	56	housewife	26	"

Lamson Street

z	Powell Elizabeth R—†	1	housekeeper	52	here
	322				
a	Powell Joseph M	1	retired	68	
b	Powell Sarah A—†	1	housewife	54	"
c	McDonald Gertrude L—†	1	"	52	
d	McDonald Warren F	1	storekeeper	51	"
e	Adams Nellie—†	2	clerk	32	"
f	Riley Harriet—†	2	housewife	76	"
g	Riley Regina M—†	2	clerk	51	
h	Curll Ellen M—†	2	housekeeper	75	"
k	McLaughlin James A	2	retired	72	"
l	Storlazzi Alfred	3	inspector	33	"

Lamson Street—Continued

M	Storlazzi Gertrude—†	3	housewife	32	here	
N	DiPietro Irene—†	3	"	31	"	
O	DiPietro Pasquale	3	laborer	38	"	
P	Storlazzi Adolph	3	tailor	56		
R	Storlazzi Ann—†	3	saleswoman	25	"	
S	Storlazzi Anthony	3	U S A	30	"	
T	Storlazzi Cesira—†	3	housewife	57	"	
U	Storlazzi Enes—†	3	clerk	35	"	
V	Storlazzi Ernani	3	U S N	31	"	
W	Storlazzi Gloria—†	3	clerk	22	"	
X	Cioffi Joseph N	3	stitcher	29	"	
Y	Cioffi Mary—†	3	housewife	26	"	
Z	Caparro Rose—†	4	clerk	25		
	323					
A	D'Olympia Anthony	4	laborer	46		
B	*D'Olympia Lawrence	4		73		
C	*D'Olympia Mary—†	4	housewife	75	"	
D	Caparro Annette—†	4	clerk	28	346 North	
E	Caparro Frances—†	4	marker	21	346 "	
F	*Caparro Pauline—†	4	housewife	55	346 "	
G	Caggiano Antoinette—†	4	housekeeper	31	here	
H	Faugano Carmella—†	4	housewife	43	"	
K	Faugano Jerry	4	U S A	20	"	
L	*Greco Alphonso	5	laborer	52	"	
M	*Greco Philomena—†	5	housewife	62	"	
N	Marino Frank	5	janitor	42		
O	Marino James	5	"	30	"	
P	Natalucci Rose—†	5	housewife	37	109 Eutaw	
R	Natalucci Vincent	5	shipper	40	109 "	
S	*Carlucci Joseph	5	retired	74	here	
T	Carlucci Joseph, jr	5	electrician	36	"	
U	Carlucci Mildred—†	5	housewife	27	"	
V	Larson George	5	longshoreman	45	"	

Long Island

W	Bailey James		supervisor	54	here	
X	Berry Katherine L—†		nurse	44	"	
Y	Blanchette Albert J		clerk	42	"	
Z	Boyle Gertrude F—†		technician	42	"	

14

Page.	Letter.	Full Name.	Residence, Jan. 1, 1945.	Occupation:	Supposed Age.	Reported Residence, Jan. 1, 1944. Street and Number.

Long Island—Continued

A	Brady Christopher G	clerk	57	here
B	Brady Elizabeth C—†	nurse	39	"
C	Broderick Margaret M—†	maid	67	"
D	Brown Mary A—†	nurse	50	
E	Browne Ethel C—†	"	39	
K	Carey George F	porter	58	
F	Cochran Lillian M—†	nurse	46	
G	Connelly Mary F—†	housekeeper	40	"
H	Connors Elizabeth A—†	dietitian	38	"
L	Curran James W	watchman	64	"
M	Dalton Margaret M—†	clerk	38	
N	Dauley Ruth—†	cook	47	"
O	Dawson Agnes M—†	matron	60	
P	DiPietro Anthony	teamster	34	"
R	Dodd Anne—†	attendant	60	"
S	Dodd Katherine I—†	maid	62	
T	Donikian Antrian L—†	nurse	53	
U	Donnelly Rita P—†	social worker	26	"
V	Dwyer Rose P—†	laundress	60	"
W	Finnerty Walter F	laborer	44	"
X	Gallagher Daniel J	oiler	63	"
Y	*Goldner Jacques W	pathologist	50	Brookline
Z	Greene Mabel B—†	nurse	50	here

A	Hackett Mary J—†	laundress	51	"
B	Harrington Marion H—†	"	59	"
C	Hickey Annie M—†	nurse	42	
D	Hopkins Elizabeth G—†	"	48	"
E	Joyce Peter	watchman	58	18A River
F	Kearns Alice R—†	maid	49	5 Rollins
G	Keating John M	electrician	41	here
H	Kelley James J	foreman	58	124 Fisher av
K	Kelly Elizabeth G—†	dietitian	22	409 Hunt'n av
L	Kingman Albert P	laborer	56	here
M	Kinneen John B	clergyman	35	"
N	Knox Agnes M—†	organist	60	"
O	Larkin Robert A	painter	63	"
P	Leear Frank H	laundrywkr	52	673 Mass av
R	Lehan Stella L—†	maid	49	here
S	Long Edmund J	caretaker	56	"

Long Island—Continued

T	Lyman Richard		plumber	70	here
U	Lynch Hannah—†		attendant	39	"
V	Maguire George F		cook	65	"
W	Major Emil		physician	54	"
X	Maloney John J		porter	50	
Y	McAuliffe Thomas H		electrician	49	"
Z	McCormick Frances C—†		physioth'r'pist	50	"

326

A	McGillivray Florence—†		laundress	50	"
B	McGrath Mary A—†		maid	47	
C	McNamara Catherine F—†		matron	60	" .
D	Moran Mary E—†		laundress	31	18 Grady ct
E	Morrill Marion R—†		matron	62	here
F	Morris Mark		choreman	57	"
G	Nutter Doris O—†		nurse	35	"
H	O'Neill Theresa B—†		seamstress	61	"
K	Padian Henry J		cook	53	
L	Riley Helena J—†		nurse	38	
M	Roach Arthur		laundrywkr	62	"
N	Sarna Edna A—†		technician	24	"
O	Scheeler Mary J—†		housekeeper	50	"
P	Shaffer Edith B—†		stenographer	47	"
R	Sheehy John F		attendant	39	"
S	Smith Mary B—†		"	43	
T	Stewart Gertrude L—†		"	60	
U	Strain Margaret M—†		technician	29	"
V	Stratton Mary E—†		seamstress	48	"
W	Tobin Patrick F		choreman	69	"
X	Woods Edward P		attendant	24	"

327   **Marginal Street**

B	Rolfe Arthur	286	technician	37	here
C	Rolfe Josephine—†	286	housewife	29	"
E	Dalton Florence—†	288	"	36	"
F	Dalton James J	288	foreman	37	"
G	Dalton Joseph L	288	U S A	27	
P	*Scolastico Angelina—†	294	housewife	77	"
R	Scolastico Jean—†	294	"	37	
S	Scolastico Michael	294	laborer	46	
T	DeFelice Domenic	294	"	49	

U	DeFelice Joseph	294	retired	86	here
V	DeFelice Rosalie—†	294	housewife	83	"
X	Sandstrom Theodora—†	300	housekeeper	60	"
Y	Hansjon Henry	300	painter	47	"
Z	Hansjon Henry N	300	U S N	23	

328

A	Hansjon Nora C—†	300	housewife	45	"
B	Otterson Ann C—†	300	"	71	
C	Otterson Harry	300	retired	73	
D	Buckley Beda—†	300	housewife	60	"
E	Buckley Edward	300	painter	56	
F	Neth Dorothy—†	300	housewife	25	"

Maverick Street

G	Annese Anthony	333	U S A	22	here
H	Annese Dominic	333	laborer	42	"
K	Annese Ida—†	333	housewife	23	"
L	Annese Marie—†	333	"	40	
M	Annese Orlando	333	machinist	21	"
N	Costanzo Concetta—†	333	stitcher	24	
P	Costanzo Leo	333	electrician	23	"
O	Costanzo Lucy—†	333	housewife	44	"
R	Costanzo Nicholas	333	rigger	49	
S	Dzedulonus James	333	fishcutter	32	"
T	Dzedulonus Rosalie—†	333	housewife	29	"
U	Dalimonte George	335	janitor	33	
V	Dalimonte Rachael—†	335	housewife	32	"
W	Pizzi Benjamin	335	laborer	28	
X	Pizzi Phyllis—†	335	housewife	24	"
Y	Lettieri Matilda—†	335	"	36	
Z	Lettieri Samuel	335	cleanser	32	

329

A	Leccese Dominic	337	laborer	30	
B	Leccese Theresa—†	337	housewife	29	"
C	Scandone Albert	337	mechanic	23	"
D	Scandone Eleanor—†	337	housewife	28	"
E	Scandone Elvira—†	337	at home	26	
F	Scandone Madeline—†	337	housewife	30	"
G	Scandone Nellie—†	337	"	50	
H	Scandone Peter	337	guard	54	

Maverick Street—Continued

L	Durante Catherine—†	343	housewife	28	here
M	Durante John	343	metalworker	33	"
N	*Bonavita Angelina—†	343	housewife	58	"
O	Bonavita Anthony	343	welder	26	
P	Bonavita Carmen	343	machinist	22	"
R	Bonavita Frank	343	rigger	58	
S	Bonavita Nicholas	343	U S A	30	
T	Bonavita Sophie—†	343	saleswoman	24	"
U	Mulawka Mildred—†	343	clerk	28	
V	Perosino Gerald	343	U S N	25	
W	Perosino Ruth—†	343	housewife	25	"
X	Jones Margaret—†	345	packer	37	"
Y	DiRienzo Agostino	345	U S A	28	
Z	DiRienzo Anthony	345	U S N	26	
	330				
A	DiRienzo Carmella—†	345	stitcher	30	"
B	DiRienzo Edith—†	345	forewoman	23	"
C	DiRienzo Frank	345	U S A	42	
D	*DiRienzo Rose—†	345	housewife	62	"
E	DiRienzo Susie—†	345	packer	27	
F	Faiella Jennie—†	345	housewife	29	"
G	Faiella Joseph	345	poultryman	31	"
H	Rizzo Angelo	347	clerk	35	
K	Rizzo Edith—†	347	housewife	34	"
L	Rizzo Catherine—†	347	"	61	
M	Rizzo Michael	347	laborer	62	
N	Rizzo Marciano	347	oiler	39	
O	Rizzo Mary—†	347	housewife	38	"
P	Lauletta Grace—†	363	"	38	
R	Lauletta Vincent	363	laborer	43	..
S	*Dellacrossa Vincent	363	retired	66	
T	Larido Anthony	363	chauffeur	54	"
U	Larido Josephine—†	363	packer	36	"
V	Carabott Albert	367	cook	65	"
W	Carabott Concetta—†	367	operator	21	"
X	Carabott Rose—†	367	housewife	25	"
Y	Tancredi Anna—†	367	inspector	23	"
Z	Tancredi Dante	367	U S N	28	
	331				
A	Annese Albert	367	"	21	
B	Annese Dominic	367	laborer	62	"

Maverick Street—Continued

c	Annese Lucy—†	367	operator	31	here
D	*Annese Theresa—†	367	housewife	57	"
E	Capezza Vincent	367	retired	75	"
F	Communale James	369	electrician	32	
G	Fletcher Pearl—†	369	stitcher	30	140 Everett
H	Small Eleanor—†	369	housewife	28	here
K	Small Samuel L	369	seaman	28	"
L	Emmett Helen C—†	369	shoeworker	57	"
M	Emmett Oliver R	369	U S A	33	
N	Hancock John H	369	welder	53	"
o	Amadeo Jean—†	371	housewife	23	"
P	Amadeo Peter	371	U S A	29	
R	Lombardi Anthony	371	"	31	
s	Lombardi Eleanor—†	371	bookkeeper	27	"
T	Lombardi Rose—†	371	finisher	27	"
v	*Ventresca Dolores—†	375	housewife	59	"
w	Ventresca Lucy—†	375	stitcher	25	"
x	D'Eramo Andrew	375	laborer	40	
y	D'Eramo Rose—†	375	housewife	35	"
z	*Tuttisanti Jennie—†	377	"	59	"

332

A	Tuttisanti Luigi	377	laborer	61	
B	Tuttisanti Carmen	377	fireman	40	
c	Tuttisanti Fannie—†	377	packer	36	
E	Correale Frederick	379	painter	22	"
F	*Correale James	379	laborer	44	"
G	*Correale Rose—†	379	housewife	42	"
H	Correale Vincent	379	U S A	22	
K	Pepe Annetta—†	381	operator	21	"
L	Pepe Mary—†	381	packer	42	"
M	Grasso Josephine—†	381	housewife	43	"
N	Grasso Nicolo	381	laborer	49	
o	Materia Natalie—†	381	stitcher	21	"
P	Gaito Carmen	381	U S M C	20	"
R	Gaito Dominic	381	U S A	24	
s	*Gaito Theresa—†	381	housewife	47	"
T	Nardone Charles	383	engineer	32	"
u	Nardone Mary—†	383	housewife	32	"
v	Coviello Angelina—†	383	stitcher	20	"
w	Goglia Amodeo	383	chauffeur	47	"
x	Goglia Mary—†	383	housewife	40	"

Maverick Street—Continued

Y	Belmonte Agostino	383	cutter	52	here	
Z	Belmonte Agostino	383	U S A	25	"	
	333					
A	Belmonte Clarinda—†	383	housewife	48	"	
B	Belmonte Mary—†	383	stitcher	23	"	

McCormick Square

E	Tranfaglia George	1	watchman	41	here	
F	Tranfaglia Jennie—†	1	housewife	29	"	
G	Tranfaglia Lenore—†	1	stitcher	24	"	
H	Tranfaglia Orlando	1	U S A	38		
K	Tranfaglia Pasquale	1	pipefitter	40	"	
L	Tranfaglia Ursula—†	1	housewife	60	"	
M	Tranfaglia Victoria—†	1	"	31		
N	Angrisano George	1	barber	40	"	
O	Angrisano Josephine—†	1	housewife	39	"	
P	Rowan Catherine—†	3	"	55		
R	Rowan Edward J	3	repairman	51	"	
S	Rowan John E	3	U S A	24		
T	Ciampa Carmine	3	metalworker	54	"	
U	Ciampa Fred	3	U S A	23		
V	Ciampa John	3	"	24	"	
W	Ciampa Mary—†	3	housewife	50	"	
X	Ciampa Ralph	3	U S A	23		
Y	Ciampa Theresa—†	3	clerk	20		
Z	Sharp Allan	3	meter reader	60	"	
	334					
A	Sharp Mary—†	3	housewife	58	"	

Spectacle Island

C	Lowther George P		watchman	64	here	
D	McNamee Laurence T		janitor	34	Connecticut	
E	McNamee Mary—†		housewife	42	"	
F	Rudnicki Martin		laborer	70	here	
G	Timmons Annie A—†		housewife	55	"	
H	Timmons Marion E—†		nurse	24	34 Old Harbor	
K	Timmons Warren A		painter	56	here	
L	Wander Mary F—†		housewife	28	Virginia	
M	Wyatt Benjamin		U S A	26	here	

20

Page	Letter	Full Name.	Residence, Jan. 1, 1945.	Occupation.	Supposed Age.	Reported Residence, Jan. 1, 1944. Street and Number.

Spectacle Island—Continued

	N	Wyatt Elsie M—†		housewife	52	here
	O	Wyatt Roy E		supt	54	"

Sumner Street

	P	Screti Antonelle—†	460	operator	20	134 Everett
	R	Screti John	460	shipworker	48	134 "
	S	Screti Mary—†	460	housewife	43	134 "
	T	Arzai Carmella—†	461	"	48	here
	U	*Arzai Felizia—†	461	candymaker	52	"
	V	Chiuli Anthony	461	U S A	21	"
	W	Chiuli Mary—†	461	housewife	48	"
	X	Chiuli Sabatino	461	laborer	54	
	Y	Mottole Adaline—†	461	housewife	29	"
	Z	Mottole Attore	461	machinist	29	"
335						
	A	Correale Josephine—†	462	housewife	24	"
	B	Correale Vincent	462	painter	26	
	C	Ambrosino Alfred	462	metalworker	39	"
	D	Ambrosino Carmella—†	462	housewife	32	"
	E	Alabiso Angelo	462	barber	59	"
	F	Alabiso Fannie—†	462	dressmaker	21	"
	G	*Alabiso Sarah—†	462	housewife	55	"
	H	*DiDonata Nicoletta—†	463	"	57	158 London
	K	DiDonata Vincenzo	463	pedler	52	158 . "
	L	DeLuca Lucia—†	463	housewife	61	here
	M	DeLuca Romeo	463	U S N	34	"
	N	Maglio Anthony F	463	U S A	29	"
	O	Maglio Elena—†	463	housewife	32	"
	P	Bossi Charles	463	shipfitter	33	"
	R	Bossi Clara—†	463	housewife	33	"
	S	Porzio Carmella—†	463	at home	73	"
	T	Tentindo Louise—†	464	housewife	25	1 Venice
	U	Tentindo Salvatore	464	millhand	· 27	1 "
	V	Mariano Joseph	464	checker	25	183 Webster
	W	Mariano Louis G	464	laborer	49	183 "
	X	Mariano Olympia—†	464	housewife	50	183 "
	Y	Zecchino Frank	464	musician	24	here
	Z	Zecchino Mary—†	464	housewife	48	"
336						
	A	Zecchino Ralph	464	shoeworker	48	"

21

Sumner Street—Continued

B	Natale Maria—†	465	stenographer	21	here
C	Natale Nicholas	465	machinist	65	"
D	Natale Stella—†	465	housewife	45	"
E	Duffy Emma—†	465	clerk	40	
F	Flood John H	466	laborer	52	
G	Smith S Catherine—†	466	teacher	65	"
H	McColgan Helen T—†	467	clerk	21	
K	McColgan John C	467	janitor	62	"
L	McColgan Julia T—†	467	housewife	61	"
M	McColgan Mary E—†	467	secretary	23	"
N	McColgan Thomas J	467	U S N	24	..
O	Murphy Charles J	468	"	28	"
P	Murphy Margaret—†	468	housewife	63	"
R	Phelan Mary A—†	468	"	59	"
S	Phelan Michael J	468	guard	51	"
T	Scarfo Celia—†	469	housewife	30	"
U	Scarfo Joseph	469	shipworker	30	"
V	Zambella Andrew	469	machinist	58	"
W	Zambella Emma—†	469	dressmaker	28	"
X	Zambella Lucy—†	469	housewife	52	"
Y	Sarpi Betty—†	470	"	20	
Z	Sarpi John	470	machinist	23	"
	337				
A	*Sarpi Ambrose	470	laborer	50	"
B	Sarpi Helen—†	470	operator	25	"
C	Sarpi Josephine—†	470	housewife	46	"
D	Georgione Marie—†	470	"	29	
E	Georgione Silvio	470	collector	30	"
F	Lopilato Edith—†	472	WAVE	30	
G	Lopilato Vincenzo	472	storekeeper	59	"
H	Catania Santa—†	472	housewife	28	"
K	Catania William	472	operator	31	"
L	Clark Annette—†	472	housewife	32	"
M	Clark William	472	clerk	38	'
N	DeLuca Gemma—†	473	factoryhand	29	"
O	*DeLuca Incoronata—†	473	housewife	49	"
P	DeLuca Mary—†	473	factoryhand	28	"
R	DellaCroce Anthony	473	mechanic	24	"
S	DellaCroce Yolanda—†	473	housewife	27	"
T	Ford Theresa—†	474	waitress	55	"
U	Sherwin Albert	474	U S A	26	

Page.	Letter.	FULL NAME.	Residence, Jan. 1, 1945.	Occupation.	Supposed Age.	Reported Residence, Jan. 1, 1944. Street and Number.

Sumner Street—Continued

	v	Sherwin John	474	U S A	28	here
	w	Sherwin Katherine—†	474	housewife	58	"
	x	Sherwin Richard	474	U S A	21	"
	y	Sherwin Rosemary—†	474	beautician	29	"
338						
	a	Blades Betty—†	475	housekeeper	68	"
	b	Bussey Jacob	475	retired	84	"
	c	Grasso Carmella—†	477	housewife	50	"
	d	Grasso Margaret—†	477	stitcher	21	"
	e	Grasso Ralph	477	shoeworker	50	"
	f	Vitals Anna—†	477	housewife	27	"
	g	Vitals Michael	477	watchman	24	"
	h	Lee Bertha C—†	477	cook	52	"
	k	*Nilsen Hans C	477	machinist	62	18 Paris
	l	DeMarco Alfred	477	U S A	29	here
	m	DeMarco Virginia—†	477	housewife	32	"
	n	Zambella Bruna—†	479	"	42	"
	o	Zambella Emilio	479	U S A	20	
	p	Zambella Vincent	479	barber	51	
	r	Caccanio Anthony	479	roofer	28	
	s	Caccanio Carmella—†	479	housewife	24	"
	t	Correnti Angelo	479	presser	48	
	u	Correnti Jennie—†	479	housewife	43	"
	v	Rosa Bianca—†	481	"	24	
	x	Rosa Frederick	481	U S A	24	
	w	Rosa Frederick	481	carpenter	56	"
	y	Rosa Gaetana—†	481	housewife	58	"
	z	Salamone Benedetto	481	laborer	31	"
339						
	a	Salamone Elvira—†	481	housewife	26	"
	b	DiBerto Emelia—†	483	dressmaker	48	"
	c	Barbere Frank	483	steamfitter	50	"
	d	Barbere Theresa—†	483	housewife	46	"
	e	Barbere Alfred G	483	U S A	22	"
	f	Kenney Alice—†	488	housekeeper	56	"
	g	*Melanson Priscilla—†	488	leatherworker	63	"
	h	Frevold Clarence	488	U S A	35	"
	k	Frevold Margaret—†	488	operator	37	"
	l	Frevold Olivia—†	488	housewife	66	"
	m	Hockney Edna—†	488	shipper	26	"
	n	Westad Herman	488	engineer	60	"

Page.	Letter.	FULL NAME.	Residence, Jan. 1, 1945.	Occupation.	Supposed Age.	Reported Residence, Jan. 1, 1944. Street and Number.

Sumner Street—Continued

	o	Harkins Mary E—†	490	clerk	51	here
	p	Long Margaret—†	490	tel operator	37	"
	r	Kilduff Nellie—†	490	packer	42	"
	s	Chiochetti Edmond	492	stitcher	46	"
	t	Chiochetti Theresa—†	492	housewife	44	"
	u	Penta John	492	U S A	21	"
	v	Penta Mary—†	492	housewife	45	"
	w	Penta Michael	492	agent	45	
	x	Mercandante Elsie—†	492	housewife	32	"
	y	Mercandante Joseph	492	rigger	32	"
	z	*Mercandante Vincent	492	retired	69	
340						
	a	Bertolino Anthony	494	fisherman	30	254 Meridian
	b	Bertolino Antonetta—†	494	saleswoman	28	470 Sumner
	c	Bartolo Andrew	494	U S A	29	here
	d	Bartolo Biagio	494	machinist	60	"
	e	Bartolo Mary—†	494	housewife	63	"
	f	Farrell John	494	U S N	29	3 Monmouth
	g	Farrell Phyllis—†	494	housewife	28	3 "
	h	Doherty Francis	496	electrician	38	here
	k	Doherty Rita—†	496	housewife	28	"
	l	Sasso Anthony	496	painter	26	"
	m	*Sasso Isabelle—†	496	housewife	54	"
	n	Sasso Joseph	496	U S N	28	
	o	Sasso Rose—†	496	housewife	22	"
	p	DeAngelis Frances—†	496	"	28	"
	r	DeAngelis Joseph	496	machinist	31	"
	s	Murgolo Joseph	497	laborer	48	New York
	t	Murgolo Sadie—†	497	housewife	49	"
	u	Capone Concetta—†	497	"	36	here
	v	Capone John L	497	rigger	37	"
	w	Stoddard Anna—†	497	housewife	30	"
	x	Stoddard John	497	fishcutter	31	"
	y	Humphrey Mary T—†	498	housewife	47	"
	z	Humphrey Oliver	498	longshoreman	53	"
341						
	a	Mahoney Marie T—†	498	inspector	24	"
	b	Jacobs Helen—†	498	housewife	33	"
	c	Jacobs John	498	machinist	33	"
	d	Pezzella Henry	498	U S A	25	"
	e	Mirasolo Frank	498	milkman	31	"

24

Sumner Street—Continued

F	Mirasolo Leona—†	498	housewife	24	here
G	Saponaro Evelyn—†	499	"	25	"
H	Saponaro Joseph	499	barber	28	"
K	Belmonte Anita—†	499	packer	30	
L	Belmonte Salvatore	499	electrician	30	"
M	Woodside Edward A	499	painter	41	
N	Woodside Josephine—†	499	housewife	39	"
O	Catalano Catherine—†	500	"	21	
P	Catalano Manuel	500	welder	25	"
R	Catalano Angelo	500	pedler	53	"
S	Catalano Joseph	500	U S A	24	"
T	Catalano Mary—†	500	clerk	22	
U	Catalano Philomena—†	500	housewife	41	"
V	Catalano Philomena—†	500	checker	21	"
W	Valentine Louis	500	rigger	37	
X	Valentine Theresa—†	500	housewife	32	"
Y	Abate Ferdinand	502	U S A	33	
Z	Abate Grace—†	502	factoryhand	33	"

342

A	*Capone Antonetta—†	502	housewife	57	"
B	Capone Charlie	502	freighthandler	62	"
C	Capone George	502	U S A	21	
D	Caprini Emilia—†	502	housewife	25	"
E	Caprini Stanley	502	welder	29	"
F	Marrozzo Agostino	502	painter	40	
G	Marrozzo Rose—†	502	stitcher	31	"
H	Cirone Guerino	504	pipefitter	46	186 Webster
K	Cirone Settimia—†	504	dressmaker	38	186 "
L	Crocker Nellie—†	504	housewife	66	here
M	Hoppe Edith—†	504	clerk	43	"
N	*Mirasolo Joseph	506	carpenter	58	"
O	Mirasolo Pasqualina—†	506	housewife	20	"
P	Mirasolo Rose—†	506	"	22	
R	*Dipietro Marie—†	506	"	65	
S	*Dipietro Pasquale	506	janitor	78	
T	Dipietro Phyllis—†	506	presser	22	
U	Dipietro Rocco	506	tailor	33	
V	Ulwick Cecelia—†	506	housewife	27	"
W	Ulwick Donald	506	painter	28	"
X	Pistone Frank	508	designer	25	"
Y	Pistone Joseph	508	laborer	60	"

Sumner Street—Continued

z	Casiello Elvira M—†	508	housewife	32	here

343

A	Casiello Joseph	508	painter	37	
B	Vernucci Anthony	508	U S A	27	
C	Vernucci James	508	U S N	25	
D	*Vernucci Josephine—†	508	housewife	63	"
E	Vernucci Nicholas	508	tailor	61	
F	*Terenzio Ralph	510	retired	81	"
G	Micciche Antonette—†	510	housewife	39	"
H	Micciche Joseph	510	machinist	44	"
M	Brogna Joseph	512	guard	34	49 Bennington
N	Brogna Rose—†	512	housewife	27	49 "
O	Carangelo Angelina—†	512	"	57	here
P	Carangelo Antonio	512	U S N	23	"
R	Carangelo Cosimo	512	rigger	55	"
S	Carangelo John	512	U S A	25	
T	Carangelo Vincenzo	512	"	24	
V	Saponaro Emma—†	514	clerk	22	
W	Saponaro Anna—†	514	housewife	48	"
X	Saponaro Romaine—†	514	tel operator	21	"
Y	Saponaro Edith—†	514	saleswoman	25	"
z	Saponaro William	514	U S N	24	"

344

B	Ciampa Armando	516	carpenter	27	310 Sumner
C	Ciampa Lucy—†	516	housewife	24	310 "
E	Micciche Lena—†	516	"	23	91 Cottage
F	Micciche Paul	516	machinist	24	91 "
G	McCormick Anna F—†	518	stenographer	33	here
H	McCormick Annie—†	518	housewife	70	"
K	Hallahan Rita—†	518	at home	21	"
L	Treiber Frederick	518	U S N	26	
M	Treiber Rosanna—†	518	housewife	60	"
N	Treiber Ruth—†	518	welder	23	
O	Sheremeta Frances—†	518	housewife	27	"
P	Sheremeta Vladimir	518	machinist	31	"
R	Platt Ellen M—†	520	housewife	34	"
S	Platt Ernest	520	guard	37	
T	Heil Elizabeth—†	520	housewife	41	"
U	Heil John L	520	painter	44	
V	Reidy James	520	student	23	"

Page.	Letter.	FULL NAME.	Residence, Jan. 1, 1945.	Occupation.	Supposed Age.	Reported Residence, Jan. 1, 1944. Street and Number.

	w	Jameson Isabella—†	520	housewife	51	here
	x	Jameson Walter	520	U S C G	26	"
	y	Visca Carlo	522	tailor	55	"
	z	*Visca Valentino	522	laborer	58	
345						
	b	Angell Edward	522	painter	38	"
	c	Angell Harold	522	U S A	28	..
	d	Angell Helen—†	522	housewife	63	"
	e	Catalano Antonette—†	524	"	47	
	f	Catalano Josephine R—†	524	operator	21	"
	g	Catalano Mario	524	U S C G	24	"
	h	Catalano Pasquale	524	tavernkeeper	54	"
	k	Trainor Dorothy M—†	524	housewife	31	"
	l	Trainor Edward J	524	longshoreman	31	"
	n	Smith Arthur J	535	chauffeur	37	"
	o	Smith Catherine E—†	535	housewife	33	"
	r	Clark Clara—†	535	factoryhand	51	"
	s	Clark Sarah—†	535	"	55	
	t	Crowley Edward A	537	policeman	60	"
	u	Crowley Elsie—†	537	housewife	56	"
	v	Lagariello Carlo	537	U S A	24	"
	w	Lagariello Catherina—†	537	factoryhand	22	"
	x	Lagariello Isabelle—†	537	housewife	48	"
	y	Lagariello Leonardo	537	shipworker	44	"
	z	Warner Alfonsine—†	537	housewife	21	"
346						
	a	Warner Edward	537	shipworker	23	"
	b	Botting William	539	laborer	65	"
	c	Gladney Elaine—†	539	housewife	42	725 E Sixth
	d	Gladney Leo F	539	U S A	21	here
	e	Smith Anne—†	539	housekeeper	69	"
	f	Fay Eleanor—†	541	housewife	23	"
	g	DePalma Joseph	541	laborer	59	
	h	*DePalma Olympia—†	541	housewife	52	"
	k	Boy Catherine—†	541	"	30	
	l	Boy Domenic	541	driller	33	
	m	Popeo Esther—†	545	housewife	42	"
	n	Popeo Vincent	545	agent	48	
	s	Pelusi Elena—†	551	housewife	43	"
	t	Pelusi Luigi	551	laborer	53	

u	Pelusi Joseph	551	clerk	25	here
v	Pelusi Theresa—†	551	housewife	24	"
w	Bibo Phyllis—†	551	"	21	"
x	Bibo Ralph	551	U S A	22	"
y	Pelusi Frank	551	U S N	24	"
z	Pelusi Mary—†	551	housewife	22	"

347   Thompson's Island

A	Albee Clifton E	director	38	here
B	Baird Mark C	instructor	45	"
c	Baird Zella M—†	"	41	"
D	Buttles Madeline S—†	teacher	28	"
E	Coffill Henrietta—†	instructor	58	"
F	Fullum Gracia—†	teacher	55	Halifax
G	Fullum Harry E	herdsman	57	"
H	Hamilton Ruth L—†	instructor	38	Maine
K	Jardine James H	U S A	35	here
L	Jones Jeanette A—†	instructor	31	"
M	Jones Robert C	U S A	31	"
N	Jones Ronald P	instructor	33	"
o	Kihlstrom Bror Y	"	61	
P	Kitching Robert R	"	61	"
R	Lawrence Miriam B—†	dietitian	54	Hyannis
s	Matteson Abijah	engineer	73	here
T	Meacham Rena M—†	housewife	48	"
U	Meacham William M	teacher	48	"
v	Meacham William M, jr	U S A	21	"
w	Opsahl Christopher A	boatman	62	3 Penfield
x	Parker Lena B—†	instructor	56	here
y	Pickard Arthur H	U S A	28	"
z	Thomas Raymond	supervisor	34	"

348

A	Thomas Wilhelmina B-†	secretary	32	"

Webster Place

B	Cicero Bartolo	1	laborer	52	here
c	Cicero Emanuela—†	1	housewife	44	"
D	Cicero Joseph	1	pressman	20	"

Webster Street

F	Faiella Antonio	208	laborer	24	here
G	Faiella Lena—†	208	housewife	30	"
K	Hennessey Marie—†	210	clerk	50	"
H	Hennessey Mary—†	210	housekeeper	55	"
L	Stafford Charles A	212	retired	79	
M	Stafford Mary E—†	212	housewife	72	"
N	Welch Eleanor K—†	212	"	34	
O	Ruggiero Michael	216	examiner	29	"
P	Ruggiero Theresa—†	216	housewife	27	"
R	DioGuardi Assunta—†	216	WAC	21	"
S	DioGuardi Elvira—†	216	housewife	55	"
T	DioGuardi Joseph	216	U S A	29	
U	DioGuardi Maria A—†	216	clerk	27	
V	DioGuardi Vincenzo	216	shoeworker	59	"
W	Leblanc Gilda—†	216	housewife	24	"
X	Leblanc Lawrence	216	U S N	28	Fitchburg
Y	Catrone Jennie—†	218	at home	75	here
Z	Russo Margaret—†	218	housewife	49	"
	349				
A	Russo Modestino	218	laborer	56	
B	Maiola Anthony	218	mason	50	
C	Maiola Jeannette—†	218	clerk	20	
D	Maiola Susan—†	218	housewife	57	"
F	Campanaro Donato	228	shipwright	49	"
G	Campanaro Florence—†	228	housewife	45	"
H	Coscia Anthony F	228	U S A	24	249 Webster
K	Coscia Carolina—†	228	housewife	55	249 "
L	Coscia Michael	228	cobbler	56	249 "
M	Coscia Vincenza J—†	228	secretary	33	249 "
N	Cericola Armand	228	laborer	25	here
O	Cericola Rita—†	228	housewife	22	"
P	Younie Beatrice—†	233	"	43	"
R	Younie Edward	233	machinist	47	"
S	Younie William	233	retired	90	"
U	Morrissey Sylvester	234	"	40	10 Lamson ct
V	Stack Helen—‡	234	housewife	34	10 "
W	Stack Lawrence	234	longshoreman	33	10 "
X	Johns Edward	234	painter	42	414 Sumner
Y	Johns Theresa—†	234	housewife	42	414 "
	350				
B	Buchanan Mildred M—†	235	welder	37	463 '

Webster Street—Continued

c	Buchanan William E	235	U S N	38	463 Sumner
d	Walker Daniel P	235	rigger	45	463 "
e	Domegan James P	235	longshoreman	33	here
f	Domegan Mary C—†	235	housewife	30	"
g	Rossi Francis	236	machinist	37	"
h	Rossi Louise—†	236	housewife	31	"
k	Dermody Anna T—†	236	"	37	
l	Dermody George	236	steamfitter	47	"
m	Dermody James	236	painter	20	
n	Donovan Dorothy—†	236	clerk	34	"
o	Donovan Frank	236	longshoreman	46	"
p	Donovan Margaret—†	236	tel operator	32	"
r	Donovan Mary—†	236	housekeeper	70	"
s	Brogna Achille	237	boilermaker	62	"
t	Brogna Anna—†	237	housewife	52	"
u	Bowen Eleanor—†	237	"	24	Florida
v	Bowen Rupert C	237	U S N	25	here
w	Lombardi Ethel—†	237	housewife	26	"
x	Lombardi Vincent	237	shipfitter	28	"
y	Bosco Antonetta—†	238	at home	80	"
z	Tarquini Christina—†	238	housewife	47	"
	351				
a	Tarquini Ralph	238	laborer	48	"
b	DeLucca John	238	retired	72	
c*	Marotta Charles	238	sausagemaker	58	"
d*	Marotta Gemma—†	238	housewife	48	"
e	Marotta Jennie—†	238	stitcher	20	"
f	Marotta Josephine—†	238	dressmaker	24	"
g	Marotta Marie—†	238	at home	23	"
h	Marotta Mario	238	U S A	25	
k	Grana James M	238	B F D	33	
l	Grana Marion E—†	238	housewife	31	"
m	Sweeney Mary E—†	239	"	58	"
n	Winchenback Gertude—†	239	"	34	"
o	Winchenback Lester F	239	mechanic	41	"
p	Higginbottom Alice—†	239	housewife	85	"
r	Higginbottom John	239	plumber	55	"
s	McDonald Mary C—†	239	housewife	49	"
t	O'Keefe John F	239	U S A	22	"
u	Barker Gilda A—†	241	housewife	27	"
v	Barker James E	241	longshoreman	36	"

Page.	Letter.	FULL NAME.	Residence, Jan. 1, 1945.	Occupation.	Supposed Age.	Reported Residence, Jan. 1, 1944. Street and Number.

Webster Street—Continued

	w	DiSalvo Carmella M—†	241	housewife	67	here
	x	DiSalvo Yolanda C—†	241	dressmaker	24	"
	y	DiTroia Mario F	241	attorney	46	"
	z	DiTroia Rose M—†	241	housewife	42	"
352						
	a	DiSalvo Anthony	241	painter	38	
	b	DiSalvo Frances—†	241	housewife	34	"
	c	DeBenedetto Agostino	242	springmaker	39	"
	d	DeBenedetto Mary—†	242	housewife	37	"
	e	Sacco Anthony	242	U S N	28	..
	f	*Sacco Ciriaco	242	coremaker	59	"
	g	*Sacco Josephine—†	242	housewife	62	"
	h	Barnetti Antonetta—†	242	"	31	
	k	Barnetti Raymond	242	U S A	25	
	l	Sinagra Joseph	244	watchman	35	"
	m	Sinagra Luigi	244	retired	62	"
	n	Sinagra Nancy—†	244	housewife	34	"
	o	Spinney Charles	245	laborer	38	..
	p	Spinney Jane—†	245	housewife	65	"
	r	Garofalo Mary—†	245	"	54	"
	s	DeLeonardis Umberta	245	machinist	63	"
	t	DeLeonardis Vincenza–†	245	housewife	59	"
	u	Larsen Herbert	246	U S A	31	
	v	Larsen Mary—†	246	housewife	30	"
	w	Penny Joseph	246	U S A	22	
	x	Fagone Joseph	246	cutter	59	
	y	Fagone Josephine—†	246	clerk	26	
	z	Fagone Lucy—†	246	at home	21	"
353						
	a	Fagone Philip	246	U S M C	24	"
	b	Fagone Rose—†	246	housewife	57	"
	c	Millerick Elizabeth A—†	247	"	75	
	d	Millerick Elizabeth A—†	247	teacher	45	"
	e	Millerick Helen E—†	247	housewife	32	"
	f	Millerick Thomas J	247	pilot	34	
	g	Jensen Arne	248	rigger	47	
	h	Nelsen Magda—†	248	housekeeper	55	"
	k	Mastrangelo Frank	249	laborer	44	..
	l	Mastrangelo Mary—†	249	housewife	39	"
	m	Fagioli Amarosa—†	249	"	39	
	n	Fagioli Amedino	249	laborer	42	

Webster Street—Continued

o	Perna Helen—†	249	housewife	34	114 Everett
p	Perna Raymond	249	pipefitter	40	114 "
r	Barbere Anthony	250	operator	25	here
s	Barbere Florence—†	250	housewife	21	"
t	Cirone Elisa—†	250	"	50	"
u	Cirone Ricardo	250	bricklayer	58	"
v	Cirone Rita—†	250	dressmaker	25	"
w	Coscia Nunziatta—†	250	housewife	43	"
x	Coscia Pasquale	250	shoeworker	55	"
y	Stibolt Eugene	251	retired	72	
z	Stibolt Frank L	251	rigger	38	
	354				
a	Stibolt Mary M—†	251	housewife	32	"
b	Stibolt Mina J—†	251	"	70	
c	Gilmore Emaline E—†	251	factoryhand	48	"
d	Johnson Adolf S	251	carpenter	35	"
e	Johnson Florence W—†	251	housewife	29	"
f	Sharkey James P	252	checker	74	"
g	Sharkey Julia—†	252	housekeeper	40	"
k	Petrucelli Frank	254	machinist	26	"
l	Petrucelli Jennie—†	254	housewife	25	"
m	Landolfi Domenic	254	tailor	51	
n	Landolfi Geneva—†	254	at home	21	"
o	Landolfi Michael J	254	U S A	20	
p	Landolfi Virginia—†	254	housewife	44	"
r	Faiello Felix	254	machinist	22	"
s	Faiello Olga—†	254	housewife	22	"
t	Gleason Dorothy—†	255	factoryhand	24	"
u	Gleason Joseph	255	U S A	23	"
v	Tipping Charles	255	laborer	58	"
w	Tipping Dorothy—†	255	tel operator	20	"
x	Tipping Helen—†	255	cashier	24	
y	Tipping Margaret—†	255	factoryhand	24	"
z	Tipping Nettie—†	255	housewife	58	"
	355				
a	Ranieri Fred	256	U S A	24	
b	Ranieri Fulvio	256	U S N	23	
c	Ranieri Natalina—†	256	housewife	54	"
d	Ranieri Antonio	256	machinist	27	"
e	Ranieri Gladys—†	256	housewife	25	"
f	Palmieri Edward	256	barber	36	

Page.	Letter.	FULL NAME.	Residence, Jan. 1, 1945.	Occupation.	Supposed Age.	Reported Residence, Jan. 1, 1944. Street and Number.

Webster Street—Continued

	G	Palmieri Josephine—†	256	housewife	36	here
	H	Eskedahl Carl	257	laborer	58	"
	K	Polvin Priscilla—†	257	housewife	27	Somerville
	L	Polvin William H	257	shoeworker	38	"
	M	Porzio Alfonso	257	factoryhand	51	here
	N	Porzio Louis G	257	U S A	24	"
	O	Porzio Raffaela—†	257	housewife	44	"
	P	Farren Frances K—†	257	"	43	
	R	Farren James J	257	boilermaker	48	"
	S	Leone Alfred F	258	electrician	30	39 Lamson
	T	Leone Anna L—†	258	housewife	28	345 Sumner
	U	Frazier Feliksia—†	258	"	28	here
	V	Frazier William H	258	painter	28	"
	W	Tringali Clara—†	258	housewife	44	"
	X	Tringali Grace—†	258	technician	23	"
	Y	Tringali Marian—†	258	colorist	20	
	Z	Tringali Sebastian	258	boatbuilder	51	"
		356				
	A	Tringali Theodora—†	258	nurse	22	
	B	Discenza Antonetta—†	259	clerk	26	
	C	Discenza Carmen A	259	tailor	69	
	D	Discenza Rose—†	259	housewife	64	"
	E	Ottoson Carl O	259	rigger	47	
	F	Ottoson Frances M—†	259	housewife	39	"
	G	Gleason Elizabeth P—†	259	"	46	
	H	Gleason George L	259	U S A	21	
	K	Gleason Joseph E	259	laborer	48	
	L	Andriotti Anna—†	261	housewife	32	"
	M	Andriotti Michael	261	oiler	33	
	N	DiMaio Concetta—†	261	housewife	48	"
	O	DiMaio Mary—†	261	machinist	26	"
	P	Paolina Salvatore	261	shoemaker	69	"
	R*	Paolina Virginia—†	261	housewife	62	"
	S	Galvin Estelle—†	263	"	55	
	T	Galvin William	263	laborer	56	
	U	Morelli Margaret—†	263	housewife	38	"
	V	Morelli Nicholas	263	shoemaker	41	"
	W	Ferrara Alfred	263	U S A	26	"
	X	Ferrara Joseph	263	buffer	29	"
	Y	Ferrara Nancy—†	263	housewife	67	"
	Z	LaConca John B	264	laborer	49	"

1—3

33

357

Webster Street—Continued

A	LaConca Louisa—†	264	housewife	44	here
B	LaConca Vincent	264	U S A	22	"
C	Iannarone Grace—†	264	housekeeper	55	"
D	Iannarone Lillian—†	264	seamstress	34	"
E	Iannarone Olga—†	264	"	30	
F	Pizzi Daniel	264	shoeworker	37	"
G	Pizzi Rose—†	264	operator	24	"
H	Gallo Carmen	265	U S N	20	
K	*Gallo Elizabeth—†	265	housewife	49	"
L	Gallo Frank	265	U S A	27	
M	Gallo John	265	"	24	
N	Gallo Rose—†	265	dressmaker	23	"
O	Tauilla Helen—†	265	"	30	
P	Marino Dominic	265	welder	20	
R	*Marino Louise—†	265	housewife	48	"
T	Aliprandi Dominic	269	grocer	68	"
U	Aliprandi Frances—†	269	housewife	51	"
V	Aliprandi Louise—†	269	teacher	23	
W	Aliprandi Mary—†	269	beautician	21	"

358

A	McNeil Albert	271	painter	37	
B	McNeil Bridget—†	271	housewife	71	"
C	Kindrick Clifford	271	U S N	43	"
D	Kindrick Ellen—†	271	housewife	43	"
E	Simpson David P	271	longshoreman	67	275 Webster
F	Simpson Margaret—†	271	housewife	64	275
G	Sullivan Rose M—†	273	tel operator	41	here
H	Sullivan Timothy F	273	retired	75	"
K	Gallagher Mary—†	273	tel operator	38	"
L	McLaughlin Elizabeth—†	273	clerk	48	
M	McLaughlin Mary A—†	273	saleswoman	46	"
N	McLaughlin William S	273	clerk	46	"
O	Bowman Jane A—†	275	housewife	75	127 Webster
P	Bowman Jane A—†	275	clerk	42	127 "
R	Cashman Charlotte F—†	275	"	50	here
S	Cashman Mary P—†	275	"	21	273 Webster
T	Cashman Ona M—†	275	"	23	273 "
U	Maramaldi Evelyn—†	275	stitcher	20	here
V	Maramaldi Fidele	275	shipfitter	53	"
W	Maramaldi Raffaella—†	275	clerk	25	"

Webster Street—Continued

X	Maramaldi Theresa—†	275	housewife	45	here
Y	Donohue Agnes F—†	277	at home	69	"
Z	Donohue Arthur J	277	motorman	36	"

359

A	Donohue Margaret M—†	277	housewife	33	"
B	Barry Florence M—†	277	clerk	26	
C	Barry Mary E—†	277	"	50	
D	Volpini Angelo	277	bookbinder	56	"
E	Volpini Elvira—†	277	operator	25	"
F	Volpini Gabriel	277	welder	20	
G	Volpini Josephine—†	277	housewife	52	"
H	Millerick Edward C	279	chauffeur	42	"
K	Millerick Imelda—†	279	housewife	35	"
L	Cullen Elizabeth A—†	279	"	48	
M	Cullen James H	279	watchman	51	"
N	Matera Dominic	279	barber	54	
O	Matera Eugene	279	laborer	48	
P	*Matera Joseph	279	retired	85	"
R	Matera Joseph	279	U S N	23	
S	*Matera Margaret—†	279	housewife	44	"
T	Matera Victor	279	inspector	21	"
U	Long Annie T—†	281	housewife	85	"
V	Crescenzi Angelina—†	281	"	42	
W	Crescenzi Carmen	281	laborer	46	"
X	Crescenzi Matthew	281	U S N	22	"
Y	Grillo Arthur	281	"	28	
Z	Grillo Yolanda—†	281	housewife	25	"

360

A	Bell Julian	283	painter	37	"
B	Bell Ruth—†	283	housewife	34	"
C	DiPierro Antoinette—†	283	"	28	
D	DiPierro Antonio	283	U S N	26	"
E	DiPierro Donato	283	welder	31	
F	Finno Alfred	283	U S A	23	"
G	Voto Lydia—†	283	housewife	30	"
H	Voto Salvatore	283	guard	32	
K	DiDonato Lucille—†	285	housewife	36	"
L	DiDonato Philip	285	welder	31	"
M	*Cundari Joseph	285	U S A	26	"
N	*Cundari Marie—†	285	housewife	60	"
O	Florentine Dorothy—†	285	"	27	

Page.	Letter.	FULL NAME.	Residence, Jan. 1, 1945.	Occupation.	Supposed Age.	Reported Residence, Jan. 1, 1944. Street and Number.

Webster Street—Continued

P	Florentine Frank	285	laborer	29	here
R	Hanson Christian G	285	"	45	"
S	McLaughlin Elizabeth T–†	285	housewife	50	"
T	Howland Catherine—†	291	clerk	36	
U	Howland James	291	laborer	68	"
V	Howland Margaret—†	291	clerk	38	
W	Heil Joseph	291	B F D	44	
X	Heil Otto	291	painter	50	
Y	Heil Rita F—†	291	housewife	44	"
Z	McDonough Helen—†	291	"	29	
	361					
A	McDonough Thomas C	291	bartender	33	"
C	Lindergreen Elizabeth–†	293	housewife	55	"
D	Lindergreen Rudolph	293	longshoreman	61	"
E	O'Brien Mary J—†	293	housewife	61	"
F	O'Brien Patrick J	293	retired	58	"
G	Sorensen Lars	295	rigger	58	"
H	Sorensen Nancy—†	295	housewife	56	"

Ward 1–Precinct 4

CITY OF BOSTON

LIST OF RESIDENTS
20 YEARS OF AGE AND OVER

(NON-CITIZENS INDICATED BY ASTERISK)
(FEMALES INDICATED BY DAGGER)

AS OF

JANUARY 1, 1945

THOMAS F. SULLIVAN, *Chairman*
FREDERIC E. DOWLING, *Secretary*
WILLIAM A. MOTLEY, Jr.
FRANCIS B. McKINNEY
EVERETT R. PROUT
Listing Board.

CITY OF BOSTON PRINTING DEPARTMENT

400
Bremen Place

A	Zanfani Domenica—†	4	waitress	24	here
B	Emmett Mary—†	4	"	27	227 London
c	*Vasques Anna—†	4	housewife	44	here
D	Vasques Frances—†	4	nurse	23	"
E	Vasques Joseph	4	U S N	21	"
F	Vasques Sebastian	4	bricklayer	47	"

Bremen Street

G	Luke Frederick B	6	watchman	49	here
H	*Luke Olive A—†	6	housewife	50	"
M	Campbell Alice—†	8	"	70	79 Brooks
N	Campbell Edward	8	longshoreman	63	79 "
P	Minichiello Albert	12	U S A	25	here
R	Minichiello Antonio	12	painter	23	"
S	Russo Adeline—†	12	housewife	36	"
T	Russo Anthony	12	laborer	35	
U	Minichiello Frank P	12	cutter	40	"
V	*Minichiello Josephine—†	12	housewife	36	"
W	Giglio James	14	shipper	28	"
X	Giglio Marie—†	14	housewife	30	"
Y	DeSimone Angelina—†	14	"	42	
Z	DeSimone Emidio	14	laborer	42	
	401				
A	DeSimone Henry	14	clerk	20	
B	D'Argenio Alfred	16	U S A	25	
C	D'Argenio Antonio	16	motorman	51	"
D	D'Argenio Mary—†	16	housewife	48	"
E	D'Argenio Rose—†	16	stitcher	24	"
F	Giordano Antonette—†	16½	housewife	21	"
G	Giordano Italo	16½	electrician	26	"
H	*Merata Jennie—†	16½	housekeeper	64	"
K	Merata Pino	16½	welder	40	"
L	Burnash Camille—†	16½	housewife	45	"
M	D'Argenio Beatrice—† rear	16½	"	22	
N	D'Argenio Vincent "	16½	U S A	24	
O	Azzatto Emma—†	18	housewife	38	"
P	Azzatto Thomas J	18	mechanic	42	"
R	Rizzutti Dorothy—†	18	housewife	34	"
S	Rizzutti John	18	shipfitter	35	"

Bremen Street—Continued

T	Lovarro John	18	bartender	51	here
U	Lovarro John, jr	18	U S A	20	"
V	Lovarro Mary J—†	18	housewife	45	"
W	Lovarro Tina—†	18	stitcher	23	"
X	*Ippolito Marie—†	20	housewife	68	"
Y	*Ippolito Thomas	20	retired	75	"
Z	Sacco Concetta—†	20	welder	27	

402

A	Sacco Joseph	20	plumber	36	"
B	Costa Filippo N	20	retired	69	"
C	Costa Nunzia—†	20	housewife	68	"
D	Mastrogiovanni Josephine—†	22	"	26	
E	Mastrogiovanni Silvio	22	metalworker	27	"
F	DeFronzo Anthony T	22	"	29	"
G	DeFronzo Josephine—†	22	housewife	25	"
H	DeFronzo John F	22	U S N	31	"
K	*DeFronzo Maria C—†	22	housewife	67	"
L	Grandolfi Alfred	24	musician	28	"
M	Grandolfi George	24	retired	73	
N	Grandolfi Giovanna—†	24	housewife	69	"
O	*Fradestefano Domenic	24	retired	76	"
P	Fradestefano Joseph	24	artist	44	"
R	Giglio John	24	U S A	24	"
S	*Giglio Josephine—†	24	housewife	53	"
T	*Giglio Mario	24	laborer	54	"
U	Deveau David	26	retired	82	
V	Deveau Emily—†	26	housewife	76	"
W	Aquaviva Caroline—†	26	"	52	"
X	Aquaviva Gerald	26	U S N	20	
Y	Aquaviva Rose—†	26	clerk	22	"
Z	Caporello Carmen	26	mechanic	56	"

403

A	*Ciani Anna—†	26	housewife	54	"
B	*Ciani Vincenzo	26	laborer	62	"
D	*Amore Angelina—†	28	housekeeper	53	"
E	*Amore Theresa—†	28	housewife	82	"
G	Chiampa Anthony	28	mechanic	42	"
H	Chiampa Mary—†	28	housewife	30	"
L	Spino Anna—†	30	"	35	
M	Spino Patrick	30	laborer	51	
N	Malacaso James V	30	U S A	21	

Page.	Letter.	Full Name.	Residence, Jan. 1, 1945.	Occupation.	Supposed Age.	Reported Residence, Jan. 1, 1944. Street and Number.

Bremen Street—Continued

o	Malacaso Phyllis—†	30	packer	25	here
p	Malacasso Rose—†	30	stitcher	29	"
r	Cataruzolo Antonio	32	electrician	29	"
s	Cataruzolo Mildred—†	32	housewife	27	"
t	Giardina Fannie—†	32	stitcher	24	"
u	Giardina Guy	32	shoecutter	24	"
v	Gentile Joseph	32	laborer	20	
w	*Gentile Mary—†	32	housewife	60	"
x	Surette Arthur	32	U S N	23	
y	Surette Theresa—†	32	housewife	23	"

404   Decatur Street

k	Cave Frances—†	35	housewife	28	here
l	Cave Thomas R	35	seaman	28	"
m	Giordano Catherine—†	37	housewife	25	"
n	Giordano Dominic	37	U S A	26	
o	*Didio Angelo	37	retired	77	
p	*Didio Josephine—†	37	housewife	67	"
r	Giambusso Angelo	37	U S A	21	
s	Giambusso Frank	37	tailor	54	"
t	Giambusso Salvatore	37	U S A	23	"
u	Giambusso Sarah—†	37	housewife	45	"
v	Guerra Joseph	37	welder	35	
w	Guerra Theresa—†	37	housewife	28	"
x	Cammarata Charles	37	shipper	28	
y	Cammarata Sarah—†	37	housewife	25	"
z	Gallo Dante	37	presser	23	

405

a	Gallo Rose—†	37	housewife	22	"
c	Fairani Anthony	39	finisher	48	"
d	*Fairani Helen—†	39	housewife	35	"
e	*Gardella John	39	laborer	55	"
f	*Cammorata Catherine—†	39	housewife	48	"
g	Cammarata Katie—†	39	laundress	24	"
h	Cammarata Salvatore	39	welder	21	
p	DeMarco Mary—†	43	dressmaker	23	"
r	*DeMarco Salvatore	43	retired	70	"
s	Cardosi Edith—†	43	housewife	52	"
t	Cardosi John	43	U S A	20	
u	Cardosi Joseph	43	roofer	53	

Decatur Street—Continued

v	Cardosi Robert	43	U S A	23	here
x	Catavolo George	45	laborer	25	"
y	Catavolo Mary—†	45	housewife	57	"
z	Catavolo Mary—†	45	dressmaker	29	"
	406				
A	Dodge Rita A—†	45	packer	22	"
B	Gutro Elizabeth—†	45	housewife	61	"

Grady Court

c	Tebbetts Doris G—†	2	housewife	25	89 Edgewater Drive
D	Tebbetts Harry E	2	U S A	32	89 "
E	Stoney Lena—†	2	packer	34	here
F	Stoney Walter	2	foreman	39	"
G	Milan Adeline—†	2	housewife	34	22 Chelsea
H	Milan Edward H	2	mechanic	22	Newton
K	Joyce Andrew	2	longshoreman	37	here
L	Joyce Anne—†	2	housewife	29	"
M	Tamasiunas Anita—†	2	"	31	Hudson
N	Tamasiunas John	2	toolmaker	27	"
o	Nazzaro Carl	2	barber	35	18 Havre
P	Nazzaro Grace—†	2	housewife	35	18 "
R	Leonard Gertrude—†	2	clerk	31	here
s	Leonard Mary F—†	2	housewife	62	"
T	Russell Hardy F	2	riveter	51	"
U	Russell Lena—†	2	housewife	47	"
v	Hogle Mary—†	2	"	52	
w	Hogle Reginald	2	shipfitter	45	"
x	Muollo Helen—†	2	waitress	34	"
y	Monahan Alice—†	2	housewife	25	Illinois
z	Monahan Edward T	2	U S A	26	"
	407				
A	Mercurio Christopher	2	machinist	45	Revere
B	Mercurio Pauline—†	2	housewife	36	here
c	Palmisano Augustine	2	retired	68	"
D	Gravallese Carmella—†	18	housewife	36	"
E	Gravallese John	18	machinist	35	"
F	*Gravallese Rose—†	18	housewife	66	"
G	Sawyer Geneveive L—†	18	housekeeper	59	26 Grady ct
H	Wininger Harriet—†	18	housewife	25	26 "
K	Wininger Max	18	U S N	27	26 "

Page.	Letter.	FULL NAME.	Residence. Jan. 1, 1945.	Occupation.	Supposed Age.	Reported Residence, Jan. 1, 1944. Street and Number.

Grady Court—Continued

	L	Reidy Margaret—†	18	housewife	36	here
	M	Reidy Patrick J	18	maintenance	39	"
	N	Pascale Helen—†	18	housewife	27	"
	O	Pascale William	18	U S N	32	
	P	Guevin Clara—†	18	housewife	44	"
	R	Guevin Ernest	18	steamfitter	43	"
	S	Bernier Mary L—†	18	housewife	34	"
	T	Bernier Raymond J	18	U S N	32	
	U	Horn Arthur F	18	longshoreman	40	"
	V	Horn Elizabeth—†	18	housewife	38	"
	W	Beaton Imelda—†	18	"	23	"
	X	Beaton John H	18	U S C G	24	"
	Y	Culbert Sarah—†	18	housekeeper	57	"
	Z	Moores Anne F—†	18	housewife	35	"
		408				
	A	Moores John C	18	machinist	45	"
	B	Land John	18	U S M C	37	"
	C	Land Katherine—†	18	housewife	36	"
	D	French Bessie—†	18	"	51	
	E	French Clifford	18	U S A	22	
	F	McGeorge Elizabeth M–†	18	housewife	27	"
	G	McGeorge Eugene H	18	electrician	29	"
	H	King Gertrude—†	26	housekeeper	61	345 Border
	K	MacCallum Elizabeth—†	26	at home	23	345 "
	L	Terry Arline—†	26	housewife	27	here
	M	Terry George	26	pipefitter	35	"
	N	Frye James E	26	pilot	36	"
	O	Frye Winifred—†	26	housewife	35	"
	P	Santaniello John	26	chauffeur	44	122 Sumner
	R	Santaniello Rose—†	26	housewife	36	122 "
	S	Saunders Robert	26	electrician	30	here
	T	Saunders Ruth—†	26	housewife	27	"
	U	Tribuna Angelo	26	chipper	40	"
	V	Tribuna Edith—†	26	housewife	35	"
	W	Bader James	26	U S N	24	Michigan
	X	Bader Margaret—†	26	housewife	23	"
	Y	Bent Doris—†	26	"	25	here
	Z	Bent John J	26	shipfitter	28	"
		409				
	A	Trask Fred G	26	retired	77	Winthrop
	B	Buontempo Anna—†	26	housewife	39	23 Monmouth

6

Page.	Letter.	FULL NAME.	Residence, Jan. 1, 1945.	Occupation.	Supposed Age.	Reported Residence, Jan. 1, 1944. Street and Number.

Grady Court—Continued

	c	Buontempo Patrick	26	guard	42	23 Monmouth
	d	Williams Clara—†	26	housewife	38	Maine
	e	Williams Roger F	26	engineer	34	"
	f	Bell Anne M—†	26	welder	39	Lowell
	g	Bell Charles H	26	"	31	"

Havre Street

	h	Bergin Daniel J	3	retired	75	here
	k	Hill Edna M—†	3	operator	36	"
	l	McCarthy Patrick H	3	retired	80	Winthrop
	m	Sanfilippo Charles	3	U S N	37	here
	n	Carlson Hjalmar W	3	watchman	43	"
	o	DeZenzo Arthur	5	carpenter	32	"
	p	DeZenzo Mary—†	5	housewife	27	"
	r	Coutinho Emelia—†	5	"	63	
	s	Coutinho Manuel	5	oiler	61	"
	t	Silva Alice—†	5	housewife	44	"
	u	Silva Anselmo	5	engineer	43	"
	v	Piazza Louis	7	tailor	31	
	w	Piazza Mary—†	7	housewife	24	"
	x	Celeste Angelo	7	U S A	26	
	y	Celeste James	7	U S N	20	"
	z	Celeste Joseph	7	"	29	"
410						
	a	*Celeste Josephine—†	7	housewife	48	"
	b	Celeste Philip	7	candymaker	58	"
	c	McArdle Albert	9	policeman	48	"
	d	McArdle Margaret A—†	9	housewife	45	"
	e	McArdle Monica—†	9	operator	22	"
	f	Vecchione Elizabeth A—†	9	housewife	21	"
	g	Vecchione Vincent P	9	U S A	23	
	h	DeCola Joseph	10	laborer	33	
	k	DeCola Mary—†	10	housewife	32	"
	l	Landry Edgar J	10	pipefitter	42	"
	m	Landry Mary E—†	10	housewife	32	"
	n	Keith Donald F	10	electrician	34	"
	o	Keith Kathleen M—†	10	housewife	30	"
	p	Frasier Helen—†	10	"	37	172 Boylston
	r	Frasier Joseph	10	U S A	37	172 "
	s	Bozzi John A	10	pipefitter	36	here

Havre Street—Continued

T	Bozzi Roxe M—†	10	housewife	33	here	
U	Hennington Hazel M—†	10	"	31	"	
V	Conville Francis	10	laborer	21	"	
W	*Conville Mary T—†	10	housewife	49	"	
X	Conville Thomas J	10	laborer	49		
Y	Conville William	10	U S N	23		
Z	*Micalchuk Frances—†	10	housewife	23	"	

411

A	Micalchuk Michael	10	U S C G	25	"	
B	Colarusso Anna—†	10	housewife	29	"	
C	Colarusso Fioranti	10	electrician	33	"	
D	Fisher Lorraine—†	10	housewife	25	Winchester	
E	Fisher Robert	10	operator	34	"	
F	Saunders Albert W	10	electrician	37	here	
G	Saunders Alice G—†	10	housewife	35	"	
H	Darley Florence—†	10	actress	29	Lexington	
K	Darley Ralston	10	U S A	27	"	
L	Villar Joseph	11	laborer	31	here	
M	Villar Julia—†	11	housewife	27	"	
N	Furlong James P	11	retired	63	"	
O	Murray Annie—†	11	housewife	69	"	
P	Murray John J	11	fisherman	39	"	
R	Villar Joseph	11	laborer	59		
S	*Villar Maria—†	11	housewife	60	"	
T	Limbo Adeline—†	13	"	36		
U	Limbo Genara	13	guard	36	"	
V	Limbo Anthony	13	laborer	26		
W	Limbo Carmella—†	13	dressmaker	31	"	
X	*Limbo Filomena—†	13	housewife	62	"	
Y	*Limbo Michael	13	dairyman	64	"	
Z	Limbo Nancy—†	13	stitcher	28	"	

412

A	Rotundo Blanche—†	15	housewife	55	"	
B	Rotundo Carmine	15	driller	53	"	
C	Feneck Alice—†	15	housewife	27	"	
D	Feneck Joseph	15	welder	28	Hanson	
E	Hauser Michael A	15	shipper	22	11 Emerald	
F	*Hauser Ignacy	15	rabbi	63	11 "	
H	*Mauriello Angelina—†	17	housewife	56	here	
K	Mauriello Carmella—†	17	bookkeeper	22	"	
L	Mauriello Concetta—†	17	stitcher	28	"	

Page.	Letter.	FULL NAME.	Residence, Jan. 1, 1945.	Occupation.	Supposed Age.	Reported Residence, Jan. 1, 1944. Street and Number.

Havre Street—Continued

	M	Mauriello Joseph	17	retired	54	here
	N	Mauriello Louis	17	U S N	24	"
	O	Mauriello Mary—†	17	stitcher	21	"
	P	Mauriello Nancy—†	17	bookkeeper	20	"
	R	Mauriello Pasquale	17	U S A	27	"
	S	Tambouro Antonio	17	tailor	43	
	T	Tambouro Julia—†	17	housewife	69	"
	U	Iacona Francis M	17	operator	28	"
	V	Iacona Josephine—†	17	housewife	63	"
	W	Iacona Lydia R—†	17	student	21	"
	X	Iacona Pia—†	17	clerk	30	
	Y	Brown George	18	electrician	29	"
	Z	Brown Mary—†	18	housewife	29	"
413						
	A	Pardy Claire—†	18	"	33	"
	B	Pardy John E	18	machinist	37	"
	C	Brooks Gertrude—†	18	housewife	44	"
	D	Brooks Joseph	18	electrician	44	"
	E	Brooks Lorraine—†	18	operator	23	"
	F	DiCarlo Mary—†	18	housewife	32	"
	G	DiCarlo Thomas	18	U S A	35	
	H	Holcomb Dorothy—†	18	housewife	34	"
	K	Holcomb Mark C	18	U S N	44	
	L	*Amirault Frances—†	18	housewife	44	"
	M	Amirault Peter H	18	carpenter	46	"
	N	Maloney Louise—†	18	housewife	22	"
	O	Maloney Roland T	18	toolmaker	24	"
	P	Goodwin Douglas A	18	engineer	28	226 Lexington
	R	Goodwin Katherine M—†	18	housewife	26	226 "
	S	Collins Dorothy—†	18	supervisor	30	here
	T	Collins Henry	18	machinist	65	Saugus
	U	Collins Russell	18	U S A	35	here
	V	Aylward Catherine—†	18	clerk	37	"
	W	Aylward Phillip	18	U S A	33	"
	X	Brothers Cecelia—†	18	machinist	31	"
	Y	Dalton Isabella—†	18	housewife	59	"
	Z	Belli Nicholas	18	U S N	33	1084 Saratoga
414						
	A	Belli Rose—†	18	housewife	33	1084 "
	B	DiMarzo Anita—†	18	"	35	here
	C	DiMarzo Salvatore	18	laborer	37	"

9

Page.	Letter.	FULL NAME.	Residence, Jan. 1, 1945.	Occupation.	Supposed Age.	Reported Residence, Jan. 1, 1944. Street and Number.

Havre Street—Continued

	E	Amato Amelio	19	electrician	46	here
	F	Paterno Angela—†	19	housewife	48	"
	G	Belmonte Angelina—†	19	"	35	"
	H	Belmonte John	19	pressman	39	"
	K	Baldwin Arthur	19	U S C G	48	"
	L	Baldwin Irene—†	19	housewife	38	"
	M	Lambert Andrew	21	sexton	66	
	N	Angell Catherine—†	21	at home	79	"
	O	Cordeau Catherine—†	21	housewife	58	"
	P	Cordeau Walter	21	rigger	62	"
	R	*Ward William	23	retired	85	"
	S	Andersen Anton	23	clerk	69	
	T	Andersen Edith—†	23	teacher	31	
	U	*Andersen Olga—†	23	housewife	58	"
	V	Paolillo Andrew	27	U S A	20	
	W	Paolillo Carmen	27	laborer	58	
	X	Paolillo Jennie—†	27	housewife	48	"
	Y	Paolillo Jennie—†	27	stitcher	24	"
	Z	*Benvenuto Antonina—†	27	housewife	50	"

415

	A	Benvenuto Antonina—†	27	operator	25	"
	B	*Benvenuto Nunzio	27	fisherman	60	"
	C	Chichetti August	27	knitter	44	
	D	Chichetti Edith—†	27	housewife	31	"
	E	Romano Anthony	29	chauffeur	37	"
	F	Romano Mary—†	29	housewife	36	"
	G	Gallo Baldassario	29	shoeworker	50	"
	H	Gallo Bernadette—†	29	housewife	35	"
	O	Guarante Gaetano	29	carpenter	53	"
	P	Guarante Gregorio	29	machinist	23	"
	R	Guarante Josephine—†	29	housewife	54	"
	S	Brogna Albert	31	driller	32	"
	T	Brogna Angela—†	31	housewife	28	"
	U	Spattaro Filomena—†	31	"	30	"
	V	Spattaro Salvatore	31	seaman	30	
	W	*Giangregorio Antonia—†	31	housewife	63	"
	X	*Giangregorio Antonio	31	retired	83	
	Y	Giangregorio Enrico	31	U S A	24	
	Z	Giangregorio Louis	31	shipfitter	41	"

416

	A	Meola Anthony	33	driller	29	

10

Havre Street—Continued

	Letter	FULL NAME	Residence	Occupation	Age	Reported Residence
	B	Meola Frances—†	33	housewife	28	here
	C	Meola Americo	33	machinist	22	"
	D	Meola John	33	retired	73	"
	E	Meola Lucy—†	33	housewife	68	"
	F	Meola Orlando	33	rigger	20	"
	G	Mendolia Christine—†	33	housewife	23	134 Saratoga
	H	Mendolia Joseph	33	U S A	23	134 "
	L	Muro Beatrice—†	34	housewife	52	here
	M	Doran Joseph A	34	U S M C	22	"
	N	Doran Mary J—†	34	housewife	50	"
	O	Braccia Joseph	34	U S A	37	
	P	Braccia Valentina—†	34	housewife	32	"
	R	DiBello Edward S	34	U S A	27	Wisconsin
	S	DiBello Florence—†	34	housewife	22	"
	T	Casella Francis	34	laborer	38	here
	U	Casella Pauline—†	34	housewife	58	"
	V	Hudson Elizabeth—†	34	"	59	"
	W	Hudson Howard	34	U S N	20	"
	X	*Potherier Anne—†	34	housewife	42	"
	Y	Potherier Lawrence	34	rigger	45	
	Z	Wingren Anna L—†	34	housewife	28	"
417						
	A	Wingren Carl A	34	U S N	28	"
	B	Heatley Albert F	34	guard	54	
	C	Heatley Eva M—†	34	housewife	51	"
	D	Heatley Gerald M	34	U S A	21	
	E	*Gurevich Freda—†	34	housewife	25	"
	F	Gurevich Ralph	34	machinist	29	"
	G	Turco Rose—†	34	housewife	42	"
	H	Turco Salvatore	34	welder	20	
	K	Jenkins Ethel—†	34	housewife	31	"
	L	Jenkins William J	34	U S C G	28	"
	M	Alfresco Joseph	35	U S A	26	
	N	Alfresco Mary—†	35	stenographer	26	"
	O	Castiglione Catherine—†	35	clerk	33	"
	P	Ferrario Aldo	35	U S A	30	"
	R	Ferrario Rose—†	35	housewife	29	"
	S	*Fresco Grace—†	35	at home	60	"
	T	Fresco Pasquale	35	U S N	30	"
	U	Cincotti Jennie—†	37	housewife	33	"
	V	Cincotti Philip	37	U S A	39	

Havre Street—Continued

w	DiNatale Joseph	37	U S A	25	here
x	*DiNatale Josephine—†	37	housewife	63	"
y	DiNatale Vincent	37	U S A	20	"
z	DiNatale Vincenzo	37	barber	68	"
	418				
a	Carvotta Joseph	37	foreman	44	"
b	Carvotta Rosemary—†	37	housewife	34	"
c	Moscillo Joseph	51	U S A	38	"
d	Moscillo Mary—†	51	housewife	62	"
e	Moscillo Rose—†	51	"	20	
f	Pasqualino Angelina—†	51	"	24	
g	Pasqualino Salvatore	51	tailor	23	
h	Moscillo Frank	51	operator	25	"
k	Moscillo Lillian—†	51	housewife	26	"
l	*Mazzola Sebastiana—†	53	"	88	
m	DellaPola Joseph	53	rigger	56	
n	Gaeta Anthony	53	carpenter	60	"
o	Gaeta Lucy—†	53	housewife	51	"
p	DiMartino Giovanna—†	53	"	76	
r	DiMartino Margaret—†	53	operator	34	"
s	*Todesco Angelo	55	laborer	60	"
t	*Todesco Nellie—†	55	housewife	60	"
u	*Colatrella Anna—†	55	"	56	"
v	Colatrella John	55	U S N	23	
w	*Crocci Domenic	55	storekeeper	54	"
x	DeSimone Alfred	55	laborer	26	"
y	Barry Rita E—†	56	teacher	27	"
z	Bergazzi Mary—†	56	"	31	"
	419				
a	Bishop Helen—†	56	housekeeper	55	Cambridge
b	Caron Anna—†	56	"	61	here
c	Crowley Mary—†	56	teacher	45	"
d	Dailey Mary—†	56	"	29	"
e	Devine Helen—†	56	"	52	"
f	Devlin Margaret—†	56	"	61	
g	Donovan Mary—†	56		36	
h	Hemkampe Edith—†	56	"	44	
k	Huban Priscilla—†	56		36	
l	Kennedy Marion—†	56	"	34	"
m	Lamond Teresa—†	56		32	
n	Lynch Margaret—†	56	"	59	

Havre Street—Continued

o	Moriarty Anna—†	56	teacher	36	here
p	*Morrissey Mary—†	56	housekeeper	65	"
R	O'Brien Teresa—†	56	teacher	38	"
s	Payne Doris M—†	56	"	21	Waltham
T	Powers Norine M—†	56	"	21	"
u	Quinn Helen—†	56	...	35	here
v	Reid Esther—†	56		50	"
w	Scannell Alice—†	56		32	"
x	Scollard Mary W—†	56	"	45	
Y	Sexton Helen—†	56	"	25	
z	Shea Geraldine—†	56		39	
	420				
A	Sugrue Mary J—†	56		21	
B	Timiny Mary—†	56	"	51	
c	Atwood Earl R	57	engineer	50	"
D	DiSpirito Edward	57	rigger	27	
E	DiSpirito Esther—†	57	waitress	47	"
F	Powers Grace A—†	57	clerk	37	
G	Powers John P	57	policeman	51	"
H	Powers Patrick F	57	guard	58	
K	Reichart Anna—†	57	housewife	48	"
L	O'Brien Catherine—†	57	"	56	
M	O'Brien Mary—†	57	cutter	29	
N	O'Brien Patrick	57	painter	59	
o	Sinnott Edward	57	rigger	44	
p	Widdleton Anna F—†	57	saleswoman	24	"
R	Widdleton Frederick	57	U S C G	23	"
s	Livanos Nicholas	59	laborer	50	164 Paris
T	DiNubla Mary—†	61	housewife	53	here
u	DiNubla Rocco	61	foreman	52	"
v	DiGregorio Andrew	61	porter	34	"
w	DiGregorio Catherine—†	61	bookkeeper	21	"
x	DiGregorio Michael A	61	U S A	36	"
Y	DiGregorio Paul	61	laborer	59	"
z	DiGregorio Pauline—†	61	housewife	32	"
	421				
A	DiGregorio Salvatore	61	U S A	23	"
B	*Murphy Anna—†	63	operator	56	"
c	Murphy Bridget—†	63	inspector	62	"
D	Murphy Elizabeth—†	63	stitcher	70	"
E	Rapa Joseph	63	shoeworker	63	"

Page.	Letter.	FULL NAME.	Residence, Jan. 1, 1945.	Occupation.	Supposed Age.	Reported Residence, Jan. 1, 1944. Street and Number.

Havre Street—Continued

	F	Cardinale Andrew	76	U S A	29	92 Lexington
	G	Cardinale Josephine—†	76	housewife	23	92 "
	H	Luisa Angeline—†	76	"	55	here
	K	Luisa Angelo	76	laborer	63	"
	L	Cardinale Anna—†	76	housewife	44	"
	M	Cardinale Cosimo	76	U S N	21	
	N	Cardinale Frank	76	fisherman	53	"
	O	Cardinale Luigi	76	U S A	22	
	P	Cardinale Pauline—†	76	clerk	20	
	R	Volta Joseph	78	mechanic	37	"
	S	Volta Rose—†	78	housewife	34	"
	T	Nickerson Allston	78	U S N	31	
	U	Nickerson Marie—†	78	clerk	31	"
	V	Volta Anna—†	78	machinist	29	"
	W	Volta Carmen	78	laborer	42	
	X	Volta Cosimo	78	U S A	34	"
	Y	Volta Elizabeth—†	78	operator	27	"
	Z	Volta Mary—†	78	machinist	28	"

422

	A	Volta Minnie—†	78	at home	40	"
	B	*Turnbell Amy—†	80	housewife	32	"
	C	Turnbell Grant	80	laborer	35	"
	D	Lesser Dorothy—†	80	housewife	36	"
	E	Lesser Louis	80	clerk	35	"
	C	Casaletto Frank	80	plumber	39	"
	G	Casaletto Lena—†	80	housewife	35	"
	H	Icabucci Angelina—†	82	"	46	
	K	Icabucci Leo	82	U S A	25	
	L	*DePaolo Frances—†	82	housewife	49	"
	M	DePaolo John	82	U S N	22	"
	N	DePaolo Louise—†	82	clerk	24	"
	O	Ardagna Bart	82	painter	47	"
	P	Ardagna Carmela—†	82	housewife	31	"
	R	Maurello Patrick	84	U S A	26	17 Havre
	S	Maurello Ruth B—†	84	housewife	23	136 Marginal
	T	Terilli Albert	84	U S A	26	here
	U	Terilli Mary—†	84	at home	23	"
	V	Terilli Raymond	84	chauffeur	55	"
	W	Giagonelli Jenny—†	84	stitcher	22	10 Salutation
	X	Giagonelli Pasquale	84	salesman	22	10 "
	Y	Faretra Caroline—†	86	clerk	29	here
	Z	Faretra Charles	86	painter	26	"

14

Page.	Letter.	FULL NAME.	Residence, Jan. 1, 1945.	Occupation.	Supposed Age.	Reported Residence, Jan. 1, 1944. Street and Number.

Havre Street—Continued

A	Faretra Pasquale	86	U S A	21	here
B	Faretra Thomas	86	laborer	23	"
C	*Rotondo Rose M—†	86	housewife	44	"
D	Rotondo Roy	86	baker	45	
E	Santarpio Arnold	86	clerk	32	
F	Santarpio Teresa—†	86	housewife	30	"
G	Faretra Ida—†	88	at home	28	"
H	Faretra Immaculate—†	88	housewife	56	"
K	Faretra Pasquale	88	carpenter	58	"
L	DiGiovanni John	88	salesman	38	"
M	DiGiovanni Rose—†	88	housewife	33	"
N	Caso Elena—†	88	"	24	"
O	Caso Thomas	88	welder	26	"
P	Cimeno Carmela—†	90	housewife	31	"
R	DeGregorio Frances—†	90	stitcher	32	"
S	DeGregorio Michael A	90	U S A	22	
T	LaMonica Joseph	90	"	22	"
U	LaMonica Josephine—†	90	stitcher	33	"
V	*LaMonica Louis	90	retired	81	"
W	LaMonica Michelina—†	90	stitcher	29	"
X	LaMonica Philip	90	retired	76	"
Y	*LaMonica Rose—†	90	housewife	58	"
Z	LaMonica Carmella—†	90	stitcher	22	"

A	LaMonica Gaetano	90	retired	71	"
B	LaMonica Jennie—†	90	stitcher	26	"
C	*LaMonica Josephine—†	90	at home	55	"
D	LaMonica Michelina—†	90	saleswoman	21	"
E	LaMonica Rosario	90	mechanic	24	"
F	LaMonica Vincent	90	millhand	29	"
G	Keefe Esther—†	94	housewife	53	"
H	Keefe Grace—†	94	inspector	22	"
K	Keefe Thomas, jr	94	U S A	27	27 Wordsworth
L	Pettingill Frank	94	jeweler	45	Reading
M	Story Cora—†	94	inspector	34	here
N	Story Durwood	94	seaman	34	"

Henry Street

R	Cataldo Florence—†	10	housewife	45	44 Charter
S	Cataldo Joseph	10	machinist	53	44 "

Henry Street—Continued

T	Carabello Angelo	10	laborer	25	here
U	*Carabello Agrippino	10	baker	63	"
V	Carabello Concetta—†	10	stitcher	28	"
W	*Carabello Louise—†	10	housewife	57	"
X	Carabello Nancy—†	10	packer	31	"
Y	Sennato Concetta—†	10	"	46	
Z	Sennato Paul	10	painter	49	
	425				
A	Micciche Helen—†	10	housewife	27	"
B	Micciche Michael	10	U S A	29	"
C	Anello Enrico G	11	fireman	34	89 Orleans
D	D'Avella Frederick	11	watchman	32	here
E	Kitchell George W	11	retired	93	"
F	Larson Oscar E	11	engineer	62	"
G	O'Neil Joseph	11	laborer	42	27 Taylor
H	Perry Joseph R	11	fisherman	58	157 Meridian
K	Silva Norbert C	11	watchman	25	Provincetown
L	Treanor George A	11	mechanic	50	Cambridge
M	Zedalis John P	11	laborer	39	N Hampshire
N	*Greco Isabella—†	12	housewife	35	here
O	Greco Pasquale	12	bricklayer	39	"
P	Viola Anthony	12	weaver	45	"
R	*Viola Constanza—†	12	housewife	70	"
S	Viola Joseph	12	U S A	29	"
T	Zalandi Edith—†	12	dyer	26	60 Phillips
U	Zalandi George	12	cutter	26	178 Havré
V	*Incovato Anna—†	12	housewife	71	here
W	Mauriello Helen—†	12	"	28	"
X	Ranalli Sylvester	12	laborer	47	"
Y	DeFilippo Angelo	16	U S C G	21	"
Z	*DeFilippo Luigi	16	weaver	54	"
	426				
A	*DeFilippo Rose—†	16	housewife	50	"
B	DeFilippo Theresa—†	16	stitcher	29	"
C	Pettito Joseph	16	tinsmith	54	"
D	Pettito Mary—†	16	packer	50	
E	Capeszza Isabella—†	16	stitcher	23	"
F	*Capeszza Josephine—†	16	at home	75	"
G	*Crovatta Mary—†	16	clerk	54	

Page.	Letter.	FULL NAME.	Residence, Jan. 1, 1945.	Occupation.	Supposed Age.	Reported Residence, Jan. 1, 1944. Street and Number.

Lewis Street

	H	Juliano John	3	rigger	46	here
	K	Juliano Margaret—†	3	inspector	20	"
	L	Juliano Philomena—†	3	housewife	44	"
	M	Juliano Rosario	3	U S N	23	
	N	Kramer Jacob	3	storekeeper	76	"
	O	*Lynch Frederick	3	retired	79	
	P	Lynch Frederick F	3	U S C G	34	"
	R	Lynch Ida M—†	3	bookkeeper	39	"
	S	Lynch John	3	U S C G	22	"
	T	*Lynch Margaret—†	3	housewife	66	"

427   London Street

	D	Bayers Sydney	65	clergyman	34	here
	E	Diomizio Maria—†	65	cook	60	"
	F	Kavaney Catherine—†	65	housekeeper	50	"
	G	McMahon John	65	clergyman	59	"
	H	Seckel Theodore J	65	"	38	
	L	Albanese Edith—†	75	housewife	23	"
	M	Albanese Francis	75	chauffeur	34	"
	N	Zagarella Frances—†	75	packer	29	
	O	Zagarella Josephine—†	75	stitcher	24	"
	P	*Zagarella Maria—†	75	housewife	68	"
	R	Zagarella Peter	75	retired	70	
	S	*Carvotta Josephine—†	77	at home	77	"
	T	Amato Phillipa—†	77	"	40	
	U	Micciche Frank	77	U S A	27	
	V	Micciche Giuseppe	77	laborer	63	
	W	*Micciche Stella—†	77	housewife	62	"
	X	Micciche Stella T—†	77	packer	36	"
	Y	Micciche Vincent	77	U S A	22	
	Z	Gibbons Helen L—†	79	housewife	33	"

428

	A	Gibbons William H	79	retired	65	
	B	Gibbons William H, jr	79	cleaner	41	
	C	Bevilacqua Joseph	81	operator	48	"
	D	*Bevilacqua Vincenza—†	81	at home	42	"
	E	Salvo Mary—†	81	stitcher	25	"
	F	Salvo Richard	81	operator	26	"

Page.	Letter.	FULL NAME.	Residence, Jan. 1, 1945.	Occupation.	Supposed Age.	Reported Residence, Jan. 1, 1944.
						Street and Number.

London Street—Continued

	G	Tortorce Angelo	81	shoemaker	60	here
	H	Tortorce Josephine—†	81	hairdresser	20	"
	K	Tortorce Rosalia—†	81	stitcher	50	"
	M	Sansone Andrew	83	retired	70	58 Everett
	N	Sansone Joseph	83	clerk	26	58 "
	O	Sansone Silvia—†	83	at home	67	58 "
	P	Tripi Giacomo	83	laborer	44	here
	R	Tripi Rose—†	83	operator	20	"
	S	Tripi Vincenza—†	83	housewife	39	"
	T	*Costa Salvatore	85	laborer	64	
	U	*Costa Vincenza—†	85	housewife	61	"
	V	Lanovaro Rose—†	85	"	29	
	W	Lanovaro Stephen	85	chipper	29	"
	X	DiPerri John	85	brazier	31	
	Y	DiPerri Lucy—†	85	housewife	28	"
	Z	Salerno Carmella—†	87	"	57	
429						
	A	*Salerno Michael	87	retired	72	"
	B	DeBenedictis Edward S	87	milkman	33	"
	C	DeBenedictis Mary—†	87	stitcher	36	"
	D	Salerno Elizabeth—†	87	housewife	33	"
	E	Salerno Joseph	87	draftsman	35	"
	F	Colacchio Anthony	89	welder	39	"
	G	Colacchio Josephine—†	89	housewife	34	"
	H	*Ferrara Frances—†	89	at home	54	"
	K	Ferrara Josephine—†	89	stitcher	22	"
	M	Schifano Antonio	91	laborer	65	
	N	*Schifano Maria—†	91	housewife	57	"
	O	Amico Catherine—†	91	stitcher	35	"
	P	Amico Grace—†	91	housewife	57	"
	R	Amico Peter	91	U S A	30	"
	S	Pagliuca Achille	91	painter	58	25 Gove
	T	Pagliuca Francis	91	laborer	32	25 "
	U	Pegliuca Michael	91	"	26	25 "
	V	*Pagliuca Theresa M—†	91	housewife	56	25 "
	X	Cavaleri Eva—†	93	"	23	here
	Y	Cavaleri Louis	93	chauffeur	20	"
	Z	Rizza Edith—†	93	housewife	27	25 Morris
430						
	A	Rizza Salvatore	93	rigger	31	25 "
	B	Fitzgerald Blanche—†	93	housewife	20	California

Page.	Letter.	FULL NAME.	Residence, Jan. 1, 1945.	Occupation.	Supposed Age.	Reported Residence, Jan. 1, 1944. Street and Number.

London Street—Continued

c	Fitzgerald Lester	93	U S N	22	California
d	Phillips Blanche—†	93	welder	40	here
e	Pasqualetto Catherina—†	95	housewife	46	"
f	Pasqualetto Gasper	95	tailor	55	"
g	Pasqualetto Josephine—†	95	dressmaker	22	"
h	Vasapolli Frances—†	95	housewife	21	"
k	Vasapolli Philip	95	U S A	24	

Maverick Square

n	Rago Charles	3	U S N	34	here
o	Rago Josephine—†	3	housewife	30	"
p	Campbell Elizabeth—†	3	housekeeper	65	"
r	Fraser Thomas	3	retired	70	"
s	Hogan Daniel	3	longshoreman	50	195 Sumner
t	Ippolito Frederick	3	laborer	52	here
u	Spain Daniel J	3	operator	53	"
v	Wise John P	3	retired	72	"
z	Thompson George E	7	U S N	49	
	431				
a	Thompson Josephine C—†	7	housewife	43	"
b	Thompson Josephine J—†	7	operator	21	"
c	Farmer John W	7	machinist	47	"
d	Farmer Mary E—†	7	housewife	37	"
h	Zellen Helen—†	11	"	28	2 Elbow
k	Zellen Robert	11	longshoreman	31	2 "
l	Guidiciana John	11	"	33	here
m	White Dennis	11	retired	71	"
n	White Emma—†	11	housewife	74	"
o	White Ernest	11	longshoreman	31	"
t	Lelos Margaret—†	15	housekeeper	48	"
u	Rosario Francis	15	clerk	23	"
v	Layhe Francis	15	brazier	38	
w	Layhe Sarah—†	15	housewife	32	"
	432				
b	*Franca Joseph V	21	longshoreman	46	"
c	Franca Manuel	21	U S A	21	"
d	Franca Rose—†	21	housewife	39	"
e	DelloRusso Frederick U	21	shipfitter	34	"
f	DelloRusso Genevieve—†	21	housewife	33	"
g	DelloRusso Joseph A	21	machinist	36	"

Maverick Square—Continued

	Letter	FULL NAME	Residence	Occupation	Age	Reported Residence
	H	DelloRusso Mary A—†	21	housewife	34	here
	K	Cipriano Louise—†	21	"	21	256 Sumner
	L	Cipriano Pasquale	21	laborer	23	256 "
	M	Ristaino Concetta—†	21	housewife	62	here
	N	Ristaino Jennie—†	21	fishcutter	24	"
	O	Ristaino Joseph	21	laborer	62	"
	S	Carrozza Amelia—†	27	stitcher	23	"
	T	Carrozza Bridget—†	27	operator	21	"
	U	Carrozza David	27	bricklayer	66	"
	V	Carrozza Elio	27	longshoreman	27	"
	W	Carrozza Enrico	27	"	33	
	X	Carrozza Frances—†	27	housewife	59	"
	Y	Carrozza John	27	U S A	37	
	Z	Carrozza Lesandrina—†	27	inspector	34	"

433

	Letter	FULL NAME	Residence	Occupation	Age	Reported Residence
	A	Carrozza Ralph	27	laborer	25	"
	B	Carrozza Themistocle	27	bricklayer	39	"
	C	Barresi Anthony	27	chauffeur	27	"
	D	Barresi Carlo	27	welder	22	
	E	Barresi Joseph	27	U S A	31	
	F	Barresi Josephine—†	27	shoeworker	39	"
	G	Barresi Virginia—†	27	housewife	59	"
	H	Barresi Virginia—†	27	stitcher	28	"
	K	Giaquinto Angelo	27	shoe dealer	56	"
	L	Giaquinto Jennie—†	27	housewife	39	"
	M	*DiCiccio Anna—†	29	"	50	
	N	DiCiccio Antonio	29	laborer	24	
	O	DiCiccio Pasquale	29	"	54	
	P	Nardizzi Eleanor—†	29	housewife	29	"
	R	Nardizzi Vincent R	29	U S N	35	
	S	Palladino Patrick	29	"	22	"
	T	*Hlabanis Filomena—†	29	housewife	44	"
	U	*Hlabanis George	29	painter	46	"
	V	Nocito Rita—†	29	housewife	22	"
	Y	Frazier Clarence	33	carpenter	65	"
	Z	Clark John J	33	U S N	27	

434

	Letter	FULL NAME	Residence	Occupation	Age	Reported Residence
	A	Clark William D	33	"	29	
	B	Gorman Mary M—†	33	housewife	27	"
	C	Gorman Richard F	33	U S A	27	
	D	Walsh John J	33	longshoreman	63	"

Page:	Letter.	FULL NAME.	Residence, Jan. 1, 1945.	Occupation.	Supposed Age.	Reported Residence, Jan. 1, 1944. Street and Number.

Maverick Square—Continued

E	Walsh John J	33	U S A	28	here
F	Walsh Marie F—†	33	housewife	61	"
G	Gonsalves Henry	33	clerk	62	4 Paris ct
H	Cyr Eva—†	33	housewife	49	here
K	Cyr Joseph J	33	fisherman	52	"
P	Bertolino Antonio A	39	U S N	23	"
R	*Bertolino Carmela—†	39	housewife	47	"
S	*Bertolino Peter	39	fisherman	48	"
U	Monaco Anthony	41	laborer	48	
V	Monaco Concetta—†	41	housewife	45	"
W	Monaco Grace—†	41	WAVE	22	
X	Scopa Dominic	41	welder	34	
Y	Scopa Louise M—†	41	housewife	34	"

435

E	Trevisonne Clementina—†	47	"	47	"
F	Trevisonne Louis	47	shipfitter	62	"
G	Trevisonne Olivio	47	U S A	23	"
H	*Signorino Jennie—†	47	housewife	49	1429 River
K	Signorino Lena J—†	47	cleaner	20	1429 "
L	Signorino Leo	47	pressman	22	1429 "
M	Signorino Mary L—†	47	stitcher	25	1429 "
P	Stott Gertrude—†	51	matron	40	here
S	*LoMio Louis	55	bootblack	45	"
T	Bocchetti Carmelo	55	barber	58	"
U	Bocchetti Concetta M—†	55	welder	28	
V	Bocchetti Eleanor A—†	55	waitress	23	"
W	Bocchetti Louise—†	55	housewife	49	"
X	Bocchetti Michael	55	laborer	21	"
Y	Bocchetti Orlando	55	longshoreman	20	"

436

A	LaFratta Mary F—†	59	stitcher	22	"
B	Spitaleri Anna M—†	59	housewife	25	"
C	Spitaleri Michael A	59	U S A	26	
D	Palmeira Edward	59	U S N	22	
E	Palmeira George	59	U S A	27	
F	*Palmeira Joseph	59	retired	62	
G	*Palmeira Mary—†	59	housewife	59	"
H	Zinna Agrippino	59	painter	50	"
K	Zinna Frances—†	59	bus girl	20	"
L	*Zinna Santa—†	59	housewife	39	"
S	Carlson Frances C—†	67	"	56	

21

Maverick Square—Continued

	T	Carlson Olaf	67	retired	71	here
	U	Sparvieri Michael	67	ironworker	62	"
	V	DeStefano Arthur	67	laborer	31	"
	W	DeStefano Louise—†	67	at home	67	"
	X	DeStefano Peter	67	hatter	71	
	Y	Vernacchio Mildred M—†	67	housewife	41	"
	Z	Vernacchio Philip J	67	mechanic	41	"
437						
	A	Kines Ethel—†	67	clerk	23	
	B	Kuhn Emily M—†	67	bus girl	46	··
	E	DiMuro Leonardo	73	dentist	55	
	F	Salvatore Angelina R—†	73	housewife	49	"
	G	Salvatore Anna A—†	73	clerk	25	
	H	Salvatore Louis W, jr	73	U S N	22	
	K	Salvatore Stanley L	73	"	23	

Maverick Street

	N	Reppucci Philomena—†	rear 49	housewife	38	here
	O	Sullivan Bertha F—†	" 49	waitress	39	"
	P	Sullivan John J	" 49	foreman	40	"
	R	Costello Mary—†	" 49	waitress	37	"
	S	Costello Michael F	" 49	longshoreman	39	"
	T	Crowell Raymond V	" 49	mover	40	
	U	Crowell Ruth M—†	" 49	housewife	38	"
	V	Moore Charles V	" 49	painter	34	122 Falcon
	W	Moore Ruth M—†	" 49	housewife	31	122 "
	X	Pointer Louise—†	" 49	machinist	20	here
	Y	Sasso Caroline—†	" 49	assembler	39	"
	Z	Sasso John	" 49	painter	40	"
438						
	A	Costello Albert J	65	roofer	37	"
	B	Costello Isabelle A—†	65	housewife	34	·"
	C	O'Leary Lillian E—†	65	"	35	117 Brighton
	D	*Barnes Margaret R—†	65	"	27	here
	E	Barnes Russell P	65	longshoreman	30	"
	F	Vieira Frank	65	laborer	57	"
	G	Vieira Mary R—†	65	housewife	34	"
	H	Laliberte Louise—†	65	"	31	
	K	Laliberte Noel	65	welder	36	··
	L	Monahan Alphonsus G	65	painter	46	

Page	Letter	Full Name.	Residence, Jan. 1, 1945.	Occupation.	Supposed Age.	Reported Residence, Jan. 1, 1944. Street and Number.

Maverick Street—Continued

	Letter	Full Name	Residence	Occupation	Age	Reported Residence
	M	Monahan Mary R—†.	65	housewife	39	here
	N	Belanger Frances L—†	65	"	28	34 Sumner
	O	Belanger Lucian A	65	U S C G	27	34 "
	P	Cook Gladys F—†	65	housewife	46	Georgetown
	S	Garofalo Concetta—†	65	"	30	here
	R	Garofalo Dominic F	65	U S C G	34	"
	T	Ippolito Anthony	65	retired	68	"
	U	DeMarco Mae—†	65	housewife	39	"
	V	DeMarco William F	65	U S N	20	
	W	Altri John E	65	longshoreman	36	"
	X	Altri Laura M—†	65	operator	34	"
	Y	Warner James J	65	student	20	"
	Z	Whiting Joseph R	65	longshoreman	42	"

439

	Letter	Full Name	Residence	Occupation	Age	Reported Residence
	A	Corbett Emily—†	65	boxmaker	26	"
	B	Sullivan Ethel E—†·	65	housewife	31	"
	C	Sullivan John M	65	foreman	32	"
	D	Overlan Josephine G—†	73	housewife	30	"
	E	Overlan Peter W	73	machinist	31	"
	F	Williamson Marietta A—†	73	housewife	22	"
	G	Williamson Theodore W	73	U S N	26	"
	H	Murphy Marguerite D—†	73	housewife	35	Ipswich
	K	Murphy Thomas F	73	rigger	35	"
	L	Dixon Andrew A	73	salesman	59	Brookline
	M	Dixon Julia J—†	73	housewife	56	"
	N	Doody James A	73	decorator	37	here
	O	Doody Julia L—†	73	housewife	38	"
	P	Stowe Lillian A—†	73	"	24	"
	R	Stowe Ray F	73	U S N	28	
	S	Hildreth John E	73	guard	39	
	T	Hildreth Marion J—†	73	housewife	37	"
	U	King Genevieve F—†	73	"	27	237 Lexington
	V	King Horace W	73	U S A	30	237 "
	W	Menz George J	73	inspector	35	65 Maverick
	X	Menz Marion F—†	73	housewife	28	65 "
	Y	McColgan Beatrice E—†	73	"	30	here
	Z	McColgan Elmer F	73	electrician	31	"

440

	Letter	Full Name	Residence	Occupation	Age	Reported Residence
	A	Vitale James	73	machinist	37	"
	B	*Vitale Sarah M—†	73	housewife	36	"
	C	Donahue Irene—†	73	"	27	35 Eutaw

23

Page	Letter	Full Name.	Residence, Jan. 1, 1945.	Occupation.	Supposed Age.	Reported Residence, Jan. 1, 1944. Street and Number.

Maverick Street—Continued

	Letter	Full Name.	Res.	Occupation.	Age	Reported Residence
	D	Donahue John J	73	U S N	31	35 Eutaw
	E	Sullivan John J	81	laborer	64	here
	F	Sullivan Mary F—†	81	laundress	57	"
	G	Santagati Ethel F—†	81	housewife	30	"
	H	Santagati Joseph J	81	chipper	31	"
	K	Matthews Clarence J	81	rigger	40	
	L	Matthews Evelyn R—†	81	housewife	29	"
	M	*McMullin Barbara E—†	81	"	37	
	N	McMullin Philip W	81	U S A	38	..
	O	Sawyer Bernard G	81	machinist	36	"
	P	Sawyer Susan L—†	81	housewife	35	"
	R	Quinlan Ruth J—†	81	"	37	"
	S	Heichman Ida—†	81	"	25	73 Maverick
	T	Heichman Max J	81	welder	26	73 "
	U	*Feudo Julia—†	81	housewife	36	97 Princeton
	V	Feudo Salvatore	81	retired	48	97 "
	W	Bailey Helen I—†	81	housewife	39	here
	X	Bailey Niles E	81	retired	47	"
	Y	Grover Charles L, jr	81	technician	29	"
	Z	Grover Norma G—†	81	teacher	29	..
441						
	A	Rahilly Joseph P	81	chauffeur	32	"
	B	Rahilly Virginia C—†	81	housewife	28	"
	C	Cavaleri Joseph	81	machinist	54	"
	D	Cavaleri Mary P—†	81	housewife	42	"
	F	*Ruggiero Mary—†	86	"	65	
	G	Scopa Angelina—†	86	"	27	
	H	Scopa Pasquale	86	shipworker	30	"
	K	Columbus Angela—†	86	packer	34	
	L	Graziano Louise—†	86	tailor	53	
	M	*Benjamin John E	88	weaver	60	"
	N	Crowley John	88	mason	60	"
	O	Jeffery Alice M—†	88	housewife	65	"
	P	Mahoney Richard	88	retired	71	"
	R	Seeger Emma—†	88	houseworker	48	"
	S	Montesano Josephine—†	89	welder	34	
	T	O'Brion Harry L	89	machinist	57	"
	U	O'Brion Laura B—†	89	housewife	45	"
	X	Fatalo Joseph	91	retired	76	..
	Y	Fatalo Rose—†	91	housewife	72	"
	Z	Ruggiero Anthony	91	assembler	37	"

24

442

Maverick Street—Continued

A	Ruggiero Julia—†	91	housewife	37	here
B	Ravagno Angelo	91	coppersmith	31	"
C	Ravagno Tomasina—†	91	housewife	30	"
D	*Scaffeo Alphonzo	92	retired	82	
E	*Scaffeo Angelina—†	92	housewife	76	"
F	Bonasoro John	92	machinist	30	"
G	Bonasoro Josephine—†	92	housewife	25	"
H	DiFronzo Alphonse	92	longshoreman	30	"
K	DiFronzo Josephine—†	92	housewife	30	"
L	DiStefano Mary—†	92	stitcher	21	63 Salem
M	Riley John J	95	clerk	60	here
N	Riley Lillian C—†	95	housewife	60	"
O	Gregory Anthony	95	finisher	47	"
P	Gregory Rose—†	95	housewife	39	"
R	Mangiafico Lena—†	95	"	40	"
S	Mangiafico Paul	95	laborer	44	"
T	Marmorale Beatrice—†	95	hairdresser	20	"
V	McDonald Rose—†	97	housewife	52	"
W	McDonald Thomas	97	longshoreman	42	"
X	Jeffery Dwight	97	welder	40	"
Y	Dunn Edith—†	97	housewife	30	"
Z	Dunn Edward	97	machinist	32	"

443

A	Barletta Grace—†	98	housewife	28	"
B	Barletta James V	98	shipfitter	31	"
C	Celona Lena—†	98	housewife	34	"
D	Celona Nicholas	98	brazier	33	"
F	Goldenberg Meyer	100	U S A	21	
G	Goldenberg Rose—†	100	stenographer	24	"
H	Goldenberg Sarah—†	100	housewife	49	"
K	Goldenberg William	100	merchant	49	"
L	Zaltzberg Edward	100	U S A	20	
M	Zaltzberg Irving	100	merchant	25	"
N	Zaltzberg Samuel	100	"	59	
O	Zaltzberg Sarah—†	100	housewife	54	"
P	Latour Nellie—†	101	"	66	
R	Latour William	101	retired	69	"
S	McCormack Helen F—†	101	housewife	32	224 W Sixth
T	McCormack Peter F	101	policeman	4?	224 "
V	Baker Cyril	103	brazier	38	here

Maverick Street—Continued

w	Bollard Stephen	103	rigger	48	here
x	Burch George	103	brazier	38	56 Bennington
y	Cantagna Christos	103	laborer	60	New Jersey
z	Frine Anthony	103	machinist	49	here

444

a	Kershari John E	103	carpenter	48	40 Prince
b	Marci John	103	"	55	here
c	Spagiani Dominic	103	laborer	50	New Jersey
d	Spina Nicholas	103	foreman	58	New York
e	Trifari Joseph	103	shipworker	45	New Jersey
g	Cady Clara—†	106	at home	46	here
h	Nardo Antonio	106	retired	65	"
k	Zirk Karl	106	longshoreman	63	"
m	Shaw Chin Chung	108	laundryman	63	"
n	Shaw Chin Guan—†	108	housewife	53	"
o	Wong Anna—†	108	laundress	23	"
p	Wong Helen—†	108	"	20	"
r	Dotlow Joseph A	109	boilermaker	56	Brockton
s	Goffe Elizabeth V—†	109	housewife	54	Chelsea
t	McKinnon William B	109	machinist	55	"
u	McLeod Sarah—†	111	houseworker	70	here
v	Wheaton Annie—†	111	housewife	65	"
w	Wheaton Charles E	111	laborer	50	"
x	Miller Bridget—†	111	housewife	80	"
z	Laurino Rocco M	117	tailor	59	

445

a	DiLorenzo Beatrice—†	117	factoryhand	30	"
b	Palladino Jennie—†	117	housewife	39	"
c	Palladino Joseph	117	chauffeur	45	"
d	Scarpelli Frank	117	printer	21	"
e	Scarpelli Mary—†	117	houseworker	46	"
f	DelPrato Nicolo	119	shoemaker	51	"
g	Leonardo Angelo	119	laborer	46	"
h	*DeFronzo Constantino	119	presser	62	"
k	DeFronzo Wanda—†	119	seamstress	37	"
n	Gueli John	125	U S A	23	
o	Gueli Rocco	125	manager	55	"
p	Gueli Theresa—†	125	housewife	42	"
r	Liggiero Fiore	125	welder	23	
s	*Liggiero Michelina—†	125	housewife	55	"
t	*Cerasuolo Theresa—†	125	"	75	

v	Corey Nellie—†	127	houseworker	74	here
w	Lynch Timothy	127	boilermaker	54	"
u	Olders Frank	127	longshoreman	50	"
x	Whalen Elizabeth—†	127	at home	80	"

446

b	Saracino Anna—†	147	housewife	39	"
c	Saracino Emilio	147	shoemaker	41	"
d	Scifo Alfonsa—†	149	housewife	72	150 Webster
e	DiMarzo Michael	149	laborer	38	here
f	DiMarzo Rose—†	149	housewife	62	"
g	Murphy Francis J	151	operator	61	34 Bremen
h	Murphy Helen—†	151	housewife	58	34 "
k	Abruzzese Mary—†	151	WAC	24	here
l	Christina Albert W	153	musician	37	"
m	*Christina Santa—†	153	housewife	64	"
n	Scifo Joseph	153	cableworker	42	Revere
o	Scifo Mary—†	153	housewife	38	"
r	Alberti Germano	157	boilermaker	45	264 Sumner
s	Alberti Mary—†	157	housewife	40	264 "
t	Cambria Charles	157	clerk	30	227 Saratoga
u	Rich Clyde	157	U S N	22	here
v	Rich Filomena—†	157	housewife	22	"
w	Spano Leo	157	lather	47	"
x	Spano Sarah—†	157	housewife	42	"

447   Meridian Street

e	Sheffield William	62	calker	67	here
f	Panteluff Nicholas	62	laborer	68	"
g	Chase Margaret—†	62	housewife	55	"
h	Chase Ray	62	plumber	59	"
k	Hagerty Catherine—†	62	at home	60	"
l	Meaney Edward	62	painter	55	
w	DeBenedictis Elvira—†	78	at home	69	"

Orleans Street

y	Citron Elliot	28	U S A	36	here
z	Citron Joseph H	28	clerk	65	"
¹z	Citron Robert I	28	U S M C	36	"

27

Orleans Street—Continued

Page.	Letter.	Full Name.	Residence, Jan. 1, 1945.	Occupation.	Supposed Age.	Reported Residence, Jan. 1, 1944. Street and Number.
	A	Citron Rose I—†	28	housewife	57	here
	B	*DeAngelis Archangelo	28	barber	59	"
	C	DeAngelis Eleanora—†	28	operator	23	"
	D	DeAngelis Harry	28	musician	35	"
	E	DeAngelis Nicoletta—†	28	housewife	54	"
	G	*Scannelli Joseph	30	painter	60	
	H	*Scannelli Josephine—†	30	housewife	59	"
	K	*Petrizzo Mary—†	30	"	76	
	L	*Petrizzo Nicholas	30	retired	79	
	M	*Briana Frank	32	"	75	
	N	*Briana Mary—†	32	housewife	69	"
	O	Petrilli Alfredo	32	machinist	60	"
	P	Petrilli Anna—†	32	housewife	48	"
	R	*Vandaro Antonio	32	plasterer	69	82 Gladstone

Paris Street

Page.	Letter.	Full Name.	Residence, Jan. 1, 1945.	Occupation.	Supposed Age.	Reported Residence, Jan. 1, 1944. Street and Number.
	S	Bringola Lucy—†	6	housewife	72	here
	T	Dorso Margaret—†	6	"	63	"
	U	Antico Dominic	6	confectioner	49	"
	V	Hutchins George W	8	longshoreman	63	Revere
	W	Boyle Mary C—†	8	housewife	50	34 Havre
	X	Disusa Manuel	8	watchman	50	here
	Y	Borrows Margaret A—†	10	housewife	46	"
	Z	Borrows Robert	10	cook	64	"
		449				
	A	DeFilippo Angelo	11	U S C G	21	"
	B	*DeFilippo Luigi	11	millhand	54	"
	C	*DeFilippo Rose—†	11	housewife	50	"
	D	DeFilippo Theresa—†	11	clerk	29	
	E	DeCicco Anna A—†	11	domestic	20	"
	F	DeCicco Dionigna A—†	11	housewife	46	"
	G	DeCicco Joseph	11	plasterer	49	"
	H	Peredne Margaret—†	11	operator	36	57 Dudley
	K	Signorino Ida—†	11	welder	21	7 Worcester sq
	L	*Signorino James	11	electrician	40	7 "
	M	Melchionda Gaetano	12	maintenance	33	here
	N	Melchionda Jennie—†	12	housewife	31	"
	O	Mechetti Egisto	12	printer	32	233 Saratoga
	P	Mechetti Sarah N—†	12	housewife	31	233 "

Paris Street—Continued

R	*Vitagliano Paolo	12	printer	68	233 Saratoga
S	DiPerri Joseph	12	laborer	62	here
T	DiPerri Phyllis—†	12	housewife	55	"
U	Cibello Anthony M	14	laborer	40	"
V	Cibello Isabelle C—†	14	housewife	31	"
W	Perillo Elizabeth B—†	14	"	41	
X	Perillo Frederick A	14	shoeworker	20	"
Y	Perillo Gustave	14	"	46	"
Z	*Cibello Marie—†	14	housewife	72	"

450

A	*Imbrici Raffaela—†	16	"	68	
B	Imbrici Rose—†	16	stitcher	33	"
C	Imbrici Sabino	16	retired	69	
D	Imbrici Salvatore	16	U S A	22	
E	*Degno Sabino	16	laborer	68	"
F	Procaccini Joseph	16	"	44	71 Lubec
G	Procaccini Mary—†	16	housewife	36	71 "
H	Holmberg Emma—†	18	"	70	here
K	*Holmberg Gustave	18	machinist	59	"
L	Bedard Xavier	18	carpenter	55	N Hampshire
M	Dinan William	18	freighthandler	65	here
N	DiPaola Raphael	18	mason	60	"
O	Marineau Joseph	18	carpenter	40	N Hampshire
P	Salvatore Ippolite	18	welder	54	here
R	Scire Francis R	18	engineer	42	California
S	Callando Thomas J	20	shipfitter	35	Bridgewater
T	Deveau Archibald	20	carpenter	50	New Bedford
U	Francis Fred	20	retired	70	here
V	Jeffrie Alice M—†	20	housekeeper	65	"
W	Kimball Flora—†	20	housewife	22	56 Trenton
X	Kimball Raymond	20	laborer	30	56 "
Y	Mallowney James J	20	fisherman	58	here
Z	Merchant Peter	20	retired	84	"

451

A	Rice John	20	laborer	65	"
B	Tripolitis Peter	20	fireman	45	"
C	Wood Rose—†	20	housewife	43	"
D	Wood Rupert	20	shipfitter	48	"
E	Anderson Catherine M—†	22	housewife	66	"
F	Anderson Hans P	22	laborer	59	
G	Anderson Lillian P—†	22	secretary	25	"

Paris Street—Continued

H	Anderson Mary C—†	22	typist	29	here
K	Anderson Paul J	22	operator	27	"
L	Anderson William C	22	U S A	28	"
M	Fitzgerald Mary G—†	22	cleaner	70	
N	Fryduland Valdemar	22	fisherman	60	"
O	Guarante Angelo	24	retired	75	10 Allen
P	Lanning Cornelius M	24	U S A	34	here
R	Lanning Ellen M—†	24	housewife	66	"
S	Lanning Julia A—†	24	secretary	31	"
T	Lanning Michael C	24	retired	75	"
U	Meuros Louis D	24	seaman	63	New Bedford
V	Trainor Ellen M—†	24	housewife	26	here
X	Logan Addie F—†	32	housekeeper	67	"
Y	Foster Mary M—†	32	housewife	80	30 Lexington
Z	Foster Melvin H	32	cook	57	30 "
	452				
A	*Bellveau Gustave	34	calker	60	here
B	Boudreau Stephen	34	freighthandler	48	"
C	Careau Richard	34	laborer	59	"
D	Cronin William J	34	retired	70	"
E	Flynn Harry	34	welder	63	"
F	Ganhusky John	34	laborer	38	317 Lexington
G	Kingsbury Harold	34	"	58	103 Maverick
H	McArdle Thomas	34	retired	56	here
K	Meers John	34	cook	50	"
L	Owens Fred	34	retired	69	"
M	Rubino Michael	34	longshoreman	50	"
N	Davis Ellis	36	U S C G	22	18 Henry
O	Davis Elvira J—†	36	housewife	24	18 "
P	Mecrones, Mary—†	36	"	38	here
R	Mecrones Spero	36	chef	45	"
S	Gutchi John	36	packer	60	36 Bremen
T	Callan Joseph	38	painter	32	3 Lexington av
U	Callan Louise—†	38	housewife	32	3 "
V	Cosgrove Marie—†	38	waitress	34	20 Paris
W	Crandall Harold F	38	longshoreman	50	here
X	*Dooling Elizabeth—†	38	operator	36	"
Y	Frisco Ralph	38	laborer	52	212 Bremen
Z	MacIndewar William	38	shipfitter	44	Medford
	453				
A	Matera Fred	38	painter	44	here

Page:	Letter.	Full Name.	Residence, Jan. 1, 1945.	Occupation.	Supposed Age.	Reported Residence, Jan. 1, 1944. Street and Number.

Paris Street—Continued

B	Stassan Nicholas	38	rigger	25	here
C	Willis Andrew	38	laborer	59	"
D	Villa Geno A	46	welder	31	98 Harvard
E	Villa Josephine M—†	46	housewife	29	98 "
F	DiGiovanni Joseph	46	rigger	42	136 Webster
G	DiGiovanni Raffaela—†	46	housewife	38	136 "
H	Elia Anthony	46	retired	75	136 "
K	Rosato Rachela—†	48	housewife	59	here
L	Rosato Thomas A	48	plasterer	61	"
M	Lopilato Louis A	48	manager	39	"
N	Lopilato Mary C—†	48	housewife	37	"

Sumner Street

R	Cotreau Lennie—†	66	housekeeper	47	here
S	McManus Rachel—†	66	housewife	29	"
T	McManus Roger	66	welder	29	"
U	Pigeon A Standish	66	supervisor ·	36	"
V	Pigeon Mary B—†	66	housewife	36	"
W	Kaczmarcyk Edith—†	66	"	32	
X	Kaczmarcyk Martin	66	U S N	39	
Y	Dailey Rose—†	66	housewife	28	"
Z	Dailey William R	66	metalworker	30	"
	454				
A	Dearborn Edith—†	66	housekeeper	62	N Hampshire
B	Orr Frances—†	66	housewife	30	Connecticut
C	Orr Jordan	66	U S C G	34	"
D	Holder Elsie—†	66	housewife	40	here
E	Holder Nelson	66	draftsman	39	"
F	Nauman Barbara—†	66	housewife	21	"
G	Nauman Fred	66	U S A	22	"
H	Barney Elmer	66	"	41	1 Maverick
K	Barney Evelyn—†	66	housewife	30	1 "
L	Gould Gordon D	66	rigger	40	here
M	Gould Helen R—†	66	housewife	42	"
N	Johnson Frank M	66	U S N	33	"
O	Johnson Luella—†	66	housewife	32	"
P	Minahan John	66	U S N	43	"
R	Minahan Olga—†	66	housewife	40	"
	455				
E	Begin Bella—†	90	"	32	

Sumner Street—Continued

F	Begin Henry J	90	plumber	34	here
G	Walsh John F	90	U S N	29	89 London
H	Walsh Leonilda—†	90	housewife	29	89 "
K	Bowser Alice M—†	90	operator	35	here
L	Adamson Joseph, jr	90	U S C G	25	"
M	Adamson Mary A—†	90	housewife	21	"
N	Gillogly Mildred B—†	90	"	45	49 Eutaw
O	Gillogly William	90	electrician	52	49 "
P	McDonell Richard	90	retired	76	49 "
R	Williams George	90	electrician	31	1086 Dor av
S	Williams Mary—†	90	housewife	29	1086 "
T	Lowney Helen F—†	90	housekeeper	46	here
V	DeGruttola Joseph	90	merchant	45	"
W	DeGruttola Lucy—†	90	housewife	49	"
X	Montefusco Mario	90	U S C G	21	"
Y	Montefusco Rose—†	90	housewife	22	"
Z	Gitner Samuel	90	coppersmith	24	1 Grady ct
	456				
A	Gitner Sylvia—†	90	housewife	22	1 "
B	Bettano Dori—†	90	housekeeper	39	here
C	Spolsino Alfred	90	mechanic	23	232 Havre
D	Spolsino Concetta—†	90	housewife	22	232 "
E	Day Robert E	98	mechanic	23	New York
F	Day Rose—†	98	housewife	21	Vermont
G	O'Leary Daniel V	98	shipfitter	26	here
H	O'Leary Mildred B—†	98	housewife	22	"
K	Holden Violet—†	98	clerk	26	"
L	Luce Arthur	98	electrician	50	"
M	Luce Arthur R, jr	98	U S N	22	
N	Luce Mary—†	98	housewife	51	"
O	Capodilupo Angelina—†	98	"	36	"
P	Capodilupo Anthony	98	chef	42	"
R	Capobianco Angelo	98	machinist	32	"
S	Capobianco Erica—†	98	housewife	28	"
T	Sheffield Catherine R—†	98	student	22	"
U	Sheffield Thomas J	98	electrician	55	"
V	Bissett Mary—†	98	supervisor	37	"
W	Laurano Emilio	98	chauffeur	39	"
X	Laurano Florence—†	98	housewife	30	"
Y	McClellan Clara—†	98	"	26	303 Lexington
Z	McClellan Henry P	98	U S A	25	303 "

Page.	Letter.	FULL NAME.	Residence, Jan. 1, 1945.	Occupation.	Supposed Age.	Reported Residence, Jan. 1, 1944. Street and Number.

457
Sumner Street—Continued

	A	Walsh Julia—†	98	housewife	43	here
	B	Walsh Michael J	98	carpenter	49	"
	C	Sandstrom Deborah—†	98	housewife	31	6 Vernon pl
	D	Sandstrom Fred	98	U S N	33	6 "
	E	Bergen Catherine—†	98	housewife	26	7½ Caldwell
	F	Bergen Francis	98	guard	42	7½ "
	H	McKillop Alice G—†	122	housewife	46	here
	K	McKillop William G	122	fireman	46	319 Meridian
	M	Prenont Archibald J	122	U S N	28	here
	N	Prenont Esther—†	122	housewife	25	"
	O	Myers Hazel M—†	122	"	30	"
	P	Myers Robert A	122	electrician	32	"
	R	Carbone Antoinette M–†	122	housewife	36	"
	S	Carbone Vincent M	122	contractor	36	"
	T	Brownlow Charlotte A–†	122	housewife	33	"
	U	Brownlow Eugene	122	U S N	29	
	V	Coppell Camilla D—†	122	housewife	26	"
	W	Coppell William A	122	rigger	30	
	X	StFrancis Ernest B	122	electrician	36	"
	Y	StFrancis Madeline K—†	122	housewife	32	"
	Z	*Dattoli Grace M—†	122	"	33	

458

	A	Dattoli Vincent	122	barber	48	"
	B	O'Brien Harold J	122	machinist	27	Everett
	C	O'Brien Rebecca A—†	122	housewife	26	"
	D	Rose Mary—†	122	"	32	here
	E	Rose Ronald J	122	pipefitter	35	"
	F	Bennett Arthur	122	U S N	29	"
	G	Bennett Mary J—†	122	housewife	67	"
	H	Kelly Ernest C	130	U S N	38	315 Sumner
	K	Kelly Mary R—†	130	housewife	28	315 "
	L	Levasseur Lillian G—†	130	"	24	2 Grady ct
	M	Levasseur Norman V	130	seaman	29	2 "
	N	Filoso Anthony G	130	laborer	30	here
	O	Filoso Palma—†	130	housewife	27	"
	P	Francis Antoinette—†	130	"	26	"
	R	Francis Joseph	130	U S N	29	
	S	Jeskey Anthony	130	shipfitter	29	"
	T	Jeskey Edna—†	130	housewife	28	"
	U	Cooney Lawrence A	130	U S A	36	71 Homer

1—4

Sumner Street—Continued

v	Cooney Mary A—†	130	housewife	35	71 Homer
w	Katz Bertha—†	130	"	27	here
x	Katz Israel	130	chauffeur	27	"
y	DeAngelis Amelia—†	130	housewife	31	"
z	Mudge James	130	shipfitter	41	"
	459				
A	Mudge Mary—†	130	clerk	36	
B	Malone John F	130	dispatcher	40	"
C	Malone Mary E—†	130	housewife	40	"
D	Rosato John	130	machinist	36	"
E	Rosato Rose—†	130	housewife	35	"
F	Belmonte Anthony	130	machinist	31	"
G	Belmonte Lillian—†	130	housewife	31	"
H	Berner Joseph	130	maintenance	56	"
o	Ching Chung	154	laundryman	65	"
P	Melody Alonzo	154½	laborer	52	300 Paris
R	Willneff Annie—†	154½	housekeeper	66	300 "
S	Fradna Catherine V—†	154½	housewife	52	here
T	Fradna Cristobal	154½	oiler	59	11 Henry
U	Merchant Ellen V—†	154½	hostess	22	here
V	Sullivan John H	154½	foreman	62	25 Chaucer
W	Sullivan Joseph A	154½	engineer	55	Winthrop
Y	*Flynn Benjamin	158	retired	63	here
z	Forrey Lillian R—†	158	housewife	44	"
	460				
A	Forrey Patrick L	158	proprietor	44	"
B	*French Silas	158	retired	83	
C	Hart George W	158	"	73	
D	*Leary Thomas J	158	laborer	45	"
E	Mullaney James P	158	blueprints	52	"
F	*Pandelis Demetrios	158	retired	63	"
G	Miller Barbara E—†	160	at home	22	"
H	Miller Clyde J	160	U S A	28	"
K	Miller Elizabeth—†	160	operator	59	"
L	Miller James W	160	retired	64	"
M	Nicholas Anastasios	160	fireman	48	
N	Riley Matthew	160	laborer	55	"
T	Bonney Frances—†	166	housekeeper	62	68 Marion
U	*Ciccarello Mary—†	166	housewife	59	56 Liverpool
V	*Ciccarello Serafino	166	proprietor	60	56 "
W	Cook Florence—†	166	at home	29	68 Marion

Sumner Street—Continued

	Letter	Full Name	Residence	Occupation	Age	Reported Residence
	x	Worth Gladys—†	166	electrician	30	68 Marion
	y	Diaz Eugenio O	168	oiler	50	here
	z	Franceskos Irene—†	168	operator	44	"
461						
	A	Garvey Arthur	168	U S A	21	
	B	Garvey Joseph	168	shipfitter	42	"
	c	Garvey Margaret—†	168	housewife	42	"
	D	McClellan Rosanna—†	168	electrician	42	" .
	E	Papafotis Alexander	168	U S A	28	
	F	Chacos George	172	retired	71	"
	G	Lemanis John	172	seaman	63	190 Sumner
	H	*Tsolakis Anestos	172	"	55	here
	K	Cornetta Benjamin, jr	172	"	20	"
	L	Cornetta Mary—†	172	clerk	49	"
	P	Baren Lawrence	184	fisherman	50	"
	R	Cardoza Antonio R	184	laborer	45	110 Trenton
	s	Delespro Michael H	184	"	39	here
	T	*DiGianvittorio Caesar	184	carpenter	67	"
	U	*Gunnarson Gustaf	184	fireman	52	"
	v	Johnson Astrid—†	184	housekeeper	39	"
	w	Lynch Edward	184	laborer	50	259 Meridian
	x	Margiotte Antonio	184	retired	78	here
	Y	Mullaney Peter	184	longshoreman	65	"
	z	Nielsen Arnold	184	retired	67	"
462						
	A	*Patti Giuseppe	184	laborer	55	"
	B	*Swanson Eric	184	machinist	55	Topsfield
	c	Youngquist Elizabeth—†	184	housekeeper	70	here
	D	Boudreau Charles	184½	cleaner	43	"
	E	Cameron John J	184½	retired	72	"
	H	Jensen Oscar	184½	laborer	63	
	F	Johnson John	184½	retired	67	
	G	*Jorgerson Waldemar	184½	painter	72	
	K	Quinn Bridget—†	184½	housewife	66	"
	L	Quinn Hugh G	184½	retired	46	
	M	Riley Melvin	184½	laborer	30	
	N	Riley Thomas	184½	fisherman	58	"
	O	*Walsh James J	184½	freighthandler	67	"
	s	Dilboy Evangelios	190	fireman	47	13 Winthrop
	T	*Koutsoulis Demitrios	190	"	46	here
	U	*Sirigos Costas	190	"	51	"

Sumner Street—Continued

v *Tsatsaronis Theodore	190	fireman	53	172 Sumner
w Carlson Elsie—†	190½	housewife	40	here
x Carlson Ingvald	190½	painter	45	"
Y *Erickson Ernest	190½	fireman	64	"
z Erickson Ralph	190½	longshoreman	25	"
463				
A Gilbert Theodore	190½	fireman	74	
B *Olsen Harold	190½	seaman	39	
c Arciero Alfred	191	"	20	
D Arciero Angelina—†	191	housewife	47	"
E Arciero Carlo	191	seaman	22	
F Arciero Christopher	191	chauffeur	49	"
H Aldus Mary—†	193	housekeeper	44	"
K Clemens George	193	retired	51	13 Winthrop
L Curran Nicholas	193	"	68	here
M Kilroy William	193	electrician	34	Chelsea
N *LeBlanc Edward	193	fishcutter	47	here
o *Marafino Pasquale	193	plumber	45	"
P *Marques Alfredo	193	laborer	55	New York
R McAteer John	193	stevedore	50	7 Lewis
s *Santonio Julio	193	laborer	70	here
T *Svendsen Olaf	193	seaman	26	New York
u *Jensen Martin	195	fireman	49	here
v Kline George	195	dishwasher	57	780 Saratoga
w *Kramp Peter	195	laborer	69	here
x Murphy Joseph	195	"	58	7 Lewis
Y *Nuno John	195	"	55	New York
z Puluco Enrico	195	pedler	60	7 Lewis
464				
A Sheehan Timothy	195	fisherman	55	here
B Walsh Patrick	195	"	36	"
N Fontana Domenic	228	U S A	21	"
o Fontana Libra—†	228	operator	22	"
P Fontana Maria—†	228	housewife	55	"
R Fontana Mary—†	228	stitcher	25	"
s *Fontana Michael	228	machinist	55	"
u *Panto Bernardina—†	230	housewife	53	"
v Panto Frances—†	230	stitcher	25	"
w Panto Frank	230	fisherman	23	"
x Panto Joseph	230	electrician	20	"
Y Panto Peter	230	mason	63	

Page.	Letter.	FULL NAME.	Residence, Jan. 1, 1945.	Occupation.	Supposed Age.	Reported Residence, Jan. 1, 1944. Street and Number.

Sumner Street—Continued

	z	LaMarca Alfonso	230	retired	75	here
465						
	A	LaMarca Anthony	230	U S A	27	
	B	LaMarca Clorina—†	230	housewife	64	"

Webster Street

	G	Riley Annie B—†	42	housewife	75	here

Winthrop Street

	L	Clifford William F	4	machinist	44	Somerville
	M	God Samuel	4	laborer	65	N Hampshire
	N	Layhe Elizabeth C—†	4	housewife	63	here
	O	Layhe George R	4	clerk	34	"
	P	Layhe Margaret—†	4	at home	25	"
	R	McDonnell John J	4	machinist	60	"
	S	Olsen Hans P	4	fisherman	59	"
	T	*Giangregorio Carmella—†	6	cutter	69	
	U	Giangregorio Raffaele	6	laborer	51	
	V	Belmonte Frances—†	6	clerk	20	
	W	Belmonte Giovanna—†	6	at home	55	"
	X	Belmonte Giuseppe	6	U S A	24	
	Y	Gardino Stefano	6	"	23	
	Z	Gardino Virginia—†	6	shoeworker	21	"
466						
	A	Mercurio Carmella—†	6	stitcher	29	"
	B	Mercurio Pasquale	6	U S A	28	
	C	Pucillo Sabato	6	laborer	45	
	D	Melito Filomena—†	6	housewife	27	"
	E	Melito Ralph	6	chauffeur	25	"
	F	Bando Thomas	8	laborer	59	
	G	Ezekiel Michael	8	retired	73	"
	H	Fay Andrew	8	shipfitter	46	"
	K	Halsall Henry	8	retired	73	
	L	Smith William J	8	roofer	72	"
	M	Armstrong James	9	retired	78	89 Maverick
	N	Donahue William	9	laborer	45	New Bedford
	O	Murray William	9	longshoreman	55	here
	P	Savage Bertram E	9	laborer	55	Newbury
	R	*Sinclair Alice—†	9	at home	78	here

37

Page.	Letter.	FULL NAME.	Residence, Jan. 1, 1945.	Occupation.	Supposed Age.	Reported Residence, Jan. 1, 1944. Street and Number.

Winthrop Street—Continued

s	Williams Walter A	9	boilermaker	43	69 Saratoga
t	Silva John	10	chauffeur	27	38 Paris
u	Silva Vera—†	10	housewife	23	38 "
v	Falzone Michael ,	10	electrician	51	"
w	Falzone Santa—†	10	seamstress	41	"
x	Amico Cologero	10	laborer	60	"
y	Amico Gaspara L—†	10	housewife	55	"
z	Vasapolli Joseph	10	carpenter	29	"
	467				
a	Vasapolli Phyllis—†	10	housewife	24	"
b	*Aleto Angelo	11	laborer	60	"
c	Barry Catherine—†	11	cook	44	Cambridge
d	Green Anthony	11	U S N	25	New Jersey
e	Haverly Josephine—†	11	at home	77	here
f	Maskevij Frank	11	bartender	30	New York
g	*Rodney Joseph	11	millhand	49	here
h	*Sanimarco Antonio	11	retired	75	Medford
k	Sorndino Pasquale	11	laborer	36	here
l	Stone Edna—†	11	waitress	30	"
m	Anderson Christopher	13	longshoreman	53	193 Sumner
n	*Bennett Minnie—†	13	housekeeper	58	here
o	Dapkas Ray P	13	riveter	50	267 E
p	Day James	13	porter	30	4 Winthrop
r	Irving William W	13	retired ·	70	166 Marion
s	Pappas Andrew	13	rigger	50	Woburn
t	Sullivan John	13	laborer	54	91 Liverpool
u	Vaskesky John	13	"	29	here

Ward 1–Precinct 5

CITY OF BOSTON

LIST OF RESIDENTS
20 YEARS OF AGE AND OVER

(NON-CITIZENS INDICATED BY ASTERISK)
(FEMALES INDICATED BY DAGGER)

AS OF

JANUARY 1, 1945

THOMAS F. SULLIVAN, *Chairman*
FREDERIC E. DOWLING, *Secretary*
WILLIAM A. MOTLEY, Jr.
FRANCIS B. McKINNEY
EVERETT R. PROUT

Listing Board.

CITY OF BOSTON PRINTING DEPARTMENT

500
Bremen Street

B	Montalto Joseph P	56	mechanic	46	here
C	Montalto Josephine—†	56	housewife	38	"
D	Chisari Mary—†	56	clerk	21	"
E	Piscetti Nancy—†	56	housekeeper	62	"
F	Farro Evelyn—†	58	housewife	27	"
G	Farro Frank	58	rigger	27	
H	DellaRusso Arthur	58	florist	32	
K	DellaRusso Carlo	58	"	68	
L	DellaRusso Carlo, jr	58	U S N	21	
M	DellaRusso James	58	"	28	
N	DellaRusso Rose—†	58	at home	25	"
O	*Palumbo Antoinetta A—†	60	housewife	50	"
P	Palumbo Edward	60	U S A	27	
R	Palumbo Marie—†	60	factoryhand	24	"
S	Palumbo Palmarino	60	U S A	23	..
T	*Palumbo Pasquale	60	laborer	57	"
U	McIntyre John J	62	longshoreman	30	276 Prescott
V	McIntyre Nora G—†	62	housewife	53	276 "
W	Sullivan James	62	longshoreman	54	here
X	Sullivan Margaret—†	62	housewife	40	"
Y	Doherty Mary E—†	62	at home	71	27 Iffley rd

501

A	Porcaro Agnes—†	64	operator	27	here
B	Porcaro George	64	barber	58	"
C	Porcaro John	64	U S A	20	"
D	Porcaro Marie—†	64	housewife	53	"
E	Porcaro Rose—†	64	packer	30	
F	Porcaro Anthony	64	shipper	25	"
G	Porcaro Mary—†	64	housewife	23	"
H	Grosso Jennie—†	66	inspector	20	"
K	Grosso Mary—†	66	housewife	41	"
L	Grosso Saverio	66	laborer	48	"
M	Gallagher Helen—†	66	wrapper	36	"
N	Gallagher Mary—†	66	inspector	66	"
O	McMullen George	66	U S N	49	
P	McMullen Marie—†	66	housewife	47	"
T	Ventola Dominic	82	stockman	34	276 Maverick
U	Ventola Jennie—†	82	housewife	25	188 "
V	Rossi Antoinetta—†	82	stitcher	21	here
W	Rossi Concetta—†	82	housewife	46	"

Bremen Street—Continued

	Letter	Full Name	Res.	Occupation	Age	Reported Residence
	x	Rossi Elvira—†	82	packer	22	here
	y	Rossi Joseph	82	laborer	56	"
	z	Costanzo Frank	82	retired	74	"
502						
	a	Spinazzola Marie J—†	84	housewife	28	"
	b	Spinazzola Pasquale	84	factoryhand	30	"
	c	Conti Blanche—†	84	housewife	50	"
	d	Conti Carmelo	84	retired	50	"
	e	Leone Emilio	84	laborer	44	190 Cottage
	f	Leone Peter	84	"	40	190 "
	g	Simione Nicholas	86	retired	73	here
	h	Leone Leo	86	U S A	34	"
	k	Leone Mildred—†	86	housewife	35	"
	l	Grieco Carmela—†	86	at home	56	"
	m	Portrait Alice—†	86	housewife	33	"
	n	Portrait George	86	operator	32	"
	p	Bono James	88	rigger	41	15 Norman
	r	Bono Marion—†	88	housewife	28	36 Paris
	s	Fiorenti Mary—†	88	at home	21	9 Eaton
	t	Charlone Stella—†	88	"	72	here
	w	DeFalco Anna—†	92	housewife	61	"
	x	DeFalco Savino	92	baker	63	"
	y	Samnarco Carmelo	92	boilermaker	33	"
	z	Samnarco Mary—†	92	housewife	32	"
503						
	a	*Fabio Frank	92	retired	78	
	b	Paltrone Vincenzo	92	laborer	65	

Chelsea Place

	Letter	Full Name	Res.	Occupation	Age	Reported Residence
	c	Corelli Alphonse	5	retired	52	here
	r	*Corelli Concetta—†	5	housewife	54	"
	e	Frinquelli Nicola	5	factoryhand	61	"
	f	*Cucugliata Rosario	5	retired	64	
	h	Fiore Filomena—†	6	at home	74	"
	l	Tracia Louise—†	7	housekeeper	62	"
	m	O'Brien Joseph J	7	pressman	35	210 Lexington
	n	O'Brien Mabel—†	7	housewife	33	210 "
	o	DeBenedetto Louis	7	retired	34	Winthrop
	p	DeBenedetto Vaerie—†	7	housewife	29	"
	r	Tuscano Frank	8	retired	74	here

Page.	Letter.	FULL NAME.	Residence, Jan. 1, 1945.	Occupation.	Supposed Age.	Reported Residence, Jan. 1, 1944. Street and Number.

Chelsea Place—Continued

T	*Amato Frank	8	factoryhand	50	80 Porter
V	Epolitto Antoinette—†	10	housewife	33	here
W	Epolitto Frances—†	10	factoryhand	24	"
X	Epolitto Rose—†	10	"	26	"
Y	Ferrare Joseph	10	laborer	42	
Z	Ferrare Margaret—†	10	housewife	38	"

504 Chelsea Street

H	Miramantes Joseph	5	fireman	43	New York
K	Miramantes Josephine—†	5	housewife	33	"
L	Presti Frank	5	molder	34	here
M	Presti Natalie—†	5	housewife	31	"
N	Aprea Gilda—†	5	"	36	"
O	Aprea Orlando	5	molder	42	
P	Torriero Angelo	6	laborer	50	
R	Torriero Mary—†	6	housewife	49	"
S	Nordstrom Carl	6	U S C G	39	37 Haynes
T	Nordstrom Santa—†	6	housewife	27	37 "
W	Sarro Ann—†	7	"	20	here
X	Sarro Carmen	7	chauffeur	20	"
Y	Pastone Mary—†	7	housewife	40	"
Z	Pastone Michael	7	florist	35	"
	505				
A	Renna Angelina—†	7	housewife	30	"
B	Renna Joseph	7	chauffeur	30	"
D	Barrone Luida—†	8	housewife	21	"
E	Barrone Pasquale	8	barber	65	
F	*Appignani Celeste—†	8	housewife	54	"
G	Appignani Frank	8	cabinetmaker	56	"
H	Appignani Ida—†	8	bookkeeper	21	"
K	Appignani Tina—†	8	tailor	20	"
M	Rapino Michelina—†	9	housewife	49	"
N	Rapino Pasquale	9	mortician	54	"
S	Clark Rufus	10	pilot	52	
T	Cunningham Jeremiah J	10	shipfitter	52	"
U	Gibbons George	10	clerk	47	
V	Bonito Edith—†	11	operator	24	"
W	*Bonito Leah—†	11	packer	54	
X	Caliguri Elizabeth—†	11	tailor	46	
Y	Caliguri Sadie—†	11	operator	26	"

Chelsea Street—Continued

z	Nardone Adrian	11	machinist	30	here	
	506					
A	Nardone Mary—†	11	housewife	22	"	
c	DiMarzo Domenick	12	metalworker	29	"	
D	DiMarzo Lena—†	12	housewife	29	"	
E	Drago Joseph	12	metalworker	21	"	
H	Caggiano Louis P	13	salesman	36	"	
K	Guarini Evelyn G—†	13	housewife	33	"	
L	Guarini Peter R	13	engineer	36	"	
M	DeLong Alfred	13	brakeman	26	95 Cottage	
N	DeLong Mary—†	13	housewife	28	95 "	
o	Rotigliano Amelia M—†	14	stitcher	22	62 Webster	
P	Rotigliano Michael A	14	machinist	25	155 "	
R	Milano Peter	14	chauffeur	48	here	
s	Milano Phyllis—†	14	housewife	41	"	
T	Marello Anthony	14	chauffeur	45	"	
U	Milano Antoinette—†	14	inspector	33	"	
V	Milano Daniel	14	U S N	36		
w	Milano Joseph	14	watchman	42	"	
x	Milano Patrick	14	chauffeur	54	"	
Y	Luisi Pasquale	15	retired	71		
z	Luisi Philomena—†	15	housewife	67	"	
	507					
A	Morena Andrew	15	carpenter	45	"	
B	Morena Mary—†	15	housewife	35	"	
c	*Bellone Amelia—†	15	"	42		
D	*Bellone Ciro	15	shoemaker	54	"	
F	Basillio Concetta—†	16	housewife	28	"	
G	Basillio Gregory	16	rigger	28	"	
H	Cardillo Antoinetta—†	16	housewife	49	188 Maverick	
K	Cardillo Salvatore	16	laborer	57	188 "	
N	Nargi Joseph	18	longshoreman	20	here	
o	Nargi Rachel—†	18	packer	41	"	
P	Nargi Salvatore	18	U S A	21	"	
R	Aiello Helen—†	19	housewife	29		
s	Aiello Leonard	19	painter	33		
T	Trapeno Charles	19	barber	33		
U	Trapeno Mary—†	19	housewife	29	"	
V	Iengo Dominic	19	machinist	29	104 Havre	
w	Iengo Tina—†	19	clerk	24	104 "	
x	*Speciale Ida—†	19	at home	60	here	

5

Chelsea Street—Continued

Y	Speciale Virginia—†	19	operator	25	here
	508				
A	Benninati Blanche—†	20	furrier	33	
B	Benninati Frank	20	steamfitter	34	"
C	Laurano Annie—†	20	housewife	52	Revere
D	Laurano Anthony	20	U S A	28	here
E	Laurano Caterina—†	20	at home	84	"
F	Laurano Frank	20	U S N	44	"
G	Laurano Michael A	20	agent	60	Revere
H	Pisano Domenick	20	tailor	61	here
K	Pisano John	20	U S A	26	"
L	Pisano Pasqualena—†	20	housewife	51	"
M	Francis Alice—†	20	tailor	22	
N	Francis Anthony	20	electrician	21	"
O	Francis Joseph	20	plumber	24	"
P	Francis Mary—†	20	tailor	27	
R	Davis Charles	21	machinist	35	"
S	Davis Libra—†	21	housewife	32	"
T	Bellone Gaetano	21	pipefitter	30	"
U	Bellone Ida—†	21	housewife	30	"
V	DiCorato Frances—†	21	"	33	
W	DiCorato Rocco	21	barber	33	
X	Vigliaroli Jennie—†	21	housewife	27	"
Y	Vigliaroli Michael	21	welder	28	''
	509				
A	Cardillo Carmella—†	22	at home	73	"
B	Rafaniello Adeline L—†	22	housewife	38	"
C	Rafaniello Joseph J	22	steamfitter	40	"
D	Marani Frances—†	22	factoryhand	27	95 Cottage
E	Marani Joseph	22	plasterer	67	95 "
F	Marani Rachel—†	22	housewife	58	95 "
G	*DiGirolamo Restituto	22	shoemaker	69	Medford
H	Picardi Carmino F	22	salesman	39	here
K	Picardi Emma M—†	22	housewife	36	"
L	Conalucci Anna—†	23	"	25	"
M	Conalucci Armando	23	U S N	28	
N	Pantano Mary—†	23	dressmaker	21	"
O	Pantano Michelina—†	23	housewife	49	"
P	Pantano Salvatore	23	U S A	23	"
R	Pantano Santo	23	retired	56	
S	Chiampa Henry	23	machinist	30	"

6

Page.	Letter.	Full Name.	Residence, Jan. 1, 1945.	Occupation.	Supposed Age.	Reported Residence, Jan. 1, 1944. Street and Number.

Chelsea Street—Continued

	T	Chiampa Marie—†	23	housewife	29	here
	U	Popolo Ralph	23	retired	67	"
	w	*Esposito Mary—†	24	housewife	34	"
	X	Esposito William	24	plumber	34	"
	Y	Termini Charles	24	U S A	25	
	Z	Termini Joseph	24	"	29	
510						
	A	Termini Lena—†	24	stitcher	22	"
	B	Termini Louis	24	U S A	34	
	C	Spampinato Carmella—†	24	packer	49	
	D	Spampinato Rosario	24	laborer	49	"
	E	Rossetti Antoinetta—†	25	housewife	22	56 Bremen
	F	Rossetti Philip	25	painter	31	28 Chelsea
	G	Fuimara Frances—†	25	stitcher	34	here
	H	Fuimara Josephine—†	25	housewife	44	"
	K	Fuimara Mary—†	25	bookkeeper	24	"
	L	Fuimara Salavatore	25	storekeeper	55	"
	M	*DaMore Louise—†	25	at home	66	"
	N	Ciampi Louis	25	storekeeper	37	"
	O	Ciampi Susie—†	25	housewife	32	"
	P	Bruno Jennie—†	26	"	29	
	R	Bruno Vincent	26	welder	31	
	S	Cardinale Domenic	26	mechanic	29	"
	T	Cardinale Lydia—†	26	housewife	37	"
	U	DeVito A Frank	26	U S N	21	
	V	DeVito Elvira—†	26	housewife	56	"
	W	DeVito Joseph	26	U S A	24	
	X	DeVito Salvatore	26	laborer	54	"
	Z	Grasse Anthony	27	factoryhand	50	7 Lewis
511						
	A	Czerwinski Joseph	27	laborer	36	21 Eutaw
	B	Czerwinski Mary—†	27	housewife	37	21 "
	C	Brunco Esther—†	27	"	37	here
	D	Brunco Joseph	27	electrician	49	"
	F	Nicosia Grace—†	28	clerk	35	"
	G	Nicosia Salvatore	28	baker	44	
	H	Umbro Concetta—†	28	housewife	45	"
	K	Umbro Joseph	28	laborer	52	
	L	Umbro Rocco	28	welder	21	
	M	Rossetti Agostino	28	boxmaker	33	"
	N	Rossetti Louisa—†	28	packer	22	

Chelsea Street—Continued

	o	Rossetti Maria—†	28	at home	29	here
	p	*Rossetti Raffaele	28	laborer	55	"
	r	*Rossetti Teresa—†	28	housewife	53	"
	s	Rossetti Virginia—†	28	factoryhand	27	"
	t	Bragaglia Vincenzo	29	laborer	57	
	u	McCormick Isabella—†	29	at home	64	"
	v	McCormick John	29	painter	43	"
	w	McCormick Lawrence	29	U S A	36	
	x	Giello Mildred—†	29	tailor	24	
	y	*Grano Josephine—†	29	"	59	
	z	Stacey Leon	29	U S A	28	"

512

	a	Stacey Lillian—†	29	housewife	28	"
	b	Basilio Alexander	31	laborer	54	
	c	Basilio Rose—†	31	housewife	50	"
	d	Foti Antonio	31	pedler	65	"
	e	Capafato Marianne—†	31	at home	59	"
	f	Shonis Christopher	31	guard	28	239 Broadway
	g	Shonis Phyllis—†	31	housewife	21	here
	h	Mollica Antonio	31	retired	74	33 Havre
	k	Fiore James	31	brazier	23	286 Lexington
	l	Fiore Lena—†	31	housewife	20	181 Webster
	m	Scoffi Alfonso	33	storekeeper	32	here
	n	Scoffi Mary—†	33	housewife	34	"
	o	LaMarco Armando	33	boilermaker	31	"
	p	LaMarco Viola—†	33	operator	29	"
	r	LeDuc Nicoletta—†	33	"	26	34 Havre
	s	Strangie Grace—†	33	housewife	21	34 "
	t	*Strangie Pasquale	33	machinist	22	968 Saratoga
	u	*Lanciotti Cesira—†	33	tailor	62	here
	v	*Lanciotti Victor	33	U S A	26	"
	w	Basilio Gregory	35	"	23	"
	x	Basilio Rachel—†	35	housewife	21	"
	z	*Gianpapa Charles	35	painter	51	"

513

	a	*Gianpapa Connie—†	35	housewife	43	"
	b	Gianpapa Josephine—†	35	clerk	24	"
	c	Basilio Mary—†	35	housewife	21	89 Webster
	d	Basilio Michael	35	chauffeur	21	31 Chelsea
	e	Gucciardi Concetta—†	35	housewife	41	here
	f	Gucciardi Setimo	35	laborer	58	"

Chelsea Street—Continued

G	Ruggerio Laura—†	37	housewife	34	here
H	Ruggerio Ralph	37	painter	50	"
K	*Sposito Joseph	37	retired	75	"
L	Caponi Mary—†	37	housewife	27	"
M	Caponi Pellegrino	37	carpenter	28	"
N	Morano Anthony	37	U S N	22	
O	*Morano Catherine—†	37	housewife	59	"
P	Morano Helen—†	37	saleswoman	20	"
R	Morano Mary—†	37	typist	23	
S	Esposito Anthony	39	brazier	22	
T	*Esposito Frances—†	39	housewife	59	"
U	*Esposito Frank	39	janitor	62	
V	Esposito Joseph	39	factoryhand	21	"
W	Esposito Anna—†	39	housewife	27	"
X	Esposito Thomas	39	carpenter	32	"
Y	Miola Helen—†	39	housekeeper	27	"
Z	Fagione Lucille—†	39	housewife	24	"

514

A	Fagione Vincent	39	U S A	24	
B	Dahringer Herman	40	fireman	77	"
C	Lizine Amelia—†	40	housewife	40	"
D	Lizine Edgar	40	engineer	42	"
E	*D'Amico Fiore	40	cook	63	
F	D'Amico Hugo J	40	reporter	25	"
G	D'Amico Olga—†	40	at home	20	"
H	*D'Amico Peter	40	shipper	66	"
K	Dulcetta Joseph	40	U S A	26	186 Havre
L	Dulcetta Michelena—†	40	at home	22	here
M	Galante Silvio	40	bartender	61	"
N	Femino Nancy—†	40	housewife	70	"
O	Femino Santo	40	retired	72	
P	Femino Stella S—†	40	stitcher	31	"
R	Maggerra Benedetto	40	U S A	33	
S	Maggerra Teresa—†	40	stitcher	38	"
T	Palladino Emily—†	41	factoryhand	28	"
U	Palladino Salvatore	41	U S A	30	"
V	Pratola Anthony	41	factoryhand	42	"
W	Pratola Irene—†	41	bookkeeper	21	"
X	Pratola Mary—†	41	factoryhand	40	"
Y	Piazza John	41	laborer	50	
Z	Morrelli Joseph	41	"	58	

515

Chelsea Street—Continued

A	DeFranzo Isobel—†	42	housewife	41	here
B	DeFranzo Michael	42	collector	43	"
C	Femino Andrew	42	factoryhand	46	"
D	Femino Margaret—†	42	packer	43	
E	*Lazzaro Anna—†	42	housewife	48	"
F	Lazzaro Lena—†	42	factoryhand	21	"
G	Lazzaro Phillip	42	laborer	54	
H	Rotondo Samuel	42	chauffeur	49	"
K	Rallo Leonarda—†	43	housewife	34	"
L	Rallo Vito	43	fisherman	44	"
M	Rigione Anna—†	43	housewife	40	"
N	Rigione Dominic	43	laborer	52	
O	Casaletta Linda—†	43	housewife	40	"
P	Casaletta Michael	43	shipbuilder	41	"
R	Febbi Anthony	43	machinist	21	"
S	Vecchione Marie—†	45	housewife	30	Revere
T	Vecchione William	45	metalworker	37	"
U	Mazziotta Mary—†	45	housewife	56	here
V	Mazziotta Rosario	45	ironworker	64	"
W	DiMarzo Antoinetta—†	45	housewife	30	"
X	DiMarzo Raymond	45	machinist	32	"
Y	Tutella Anthony	45	laborer	23	"
Z	Tutella Michael	45	"	21	"

516

A	Tutella Pasqualina—†	45	housewife	53	"
B	Iacuzio Gennaro	46	bartender	28	"
C	Iacuzio Mary—†	46	housewife	28	"
D	Modica Antoinetta—†	46	operator	20	"
E	*Modica Maria—†	46	housewife	49	"
F	Modica Mario	46	operator	58	"
G	Siracusa Albert	46	U S N	23	"
H	Siracusa Angelina—†	46	stitcher	22	"
K	Porrveccio John	47	retired	70	"
L	Gueli Helen—†	47	housewife	25	36 Frankfort
M	Gueli Joseph	47	policeman	28	36 "
N	LaConti Nicholas	47	laborer	39	here
O	LaConti Rose—†	47	housewife	36	"
R	Forti Rose M—†	48	"	23	49 Leyden
S	Forti Vincent	48	U S N	25	49 "
T	Langone Cecile—†	48	clerk	21	here

Page.	Letter.	FULL NAME.	Residence, Jan. 1, 1945.	Occupation.	Supposed Age.	Reported Residence, Jan. 1, 1944. Street and Number.

Chelsea Street—Continued

u	Langone Florence M—†	48	housewife	45	here
v	Langone James F	48	seaman	49	"
w	*DiVincenzo Diana—†	48	housewife	55	"
x	DiVincenzo John	48	U S N	20	"
y	DiVincenzo Philip	48	"	23	
z	DiVincenzo Thomas	48	laborer	55	..

517

a	Mazzio Antonio	49	"	51	
b	Mazzio Josephine—†	49	housewife	50	"
c	Mazzio Angelo	49	machinist	22	"
d	Mazzio Maria—†	49	factoryhand	21	"
e	DeSciscio Angelo	49	"	40	
f	DeSciscio Yolanda—†	49	housewife	39	"
g	Fase Amanda—†	49	waitress	26	62 Gove
h	Lepore Marian—†	49	operator	21	62 "
k	Giaquinto Andrew	50	longshoreman	36	here
l	Giaquinto Theresa—†	50	housewife	35	"
m	Panzini Bernadetto	50	painter	37	302 Saratoga
n	Panzini Grace—†	50	housewife	38	302 "
o	Coppney Charles	50	laborer	32	here
p	Coppney Jennie—†	50	housewife	32	"
r	Annunziata Frank W	51	U S A	30	"
s	Annunziata Santa—†	51	housewife	31	"
t	Bragiforti Phillip	51	laborer	44	
u	Bragiforti Phyllis—†	51	housewife	32	"
v	Amoroso Arcangelo	51	U S A	27	
w	Amoroso Rosaria—†	51	housekeeper	51	"
y	Pisello Elizabeth—†	52	housewife	47	"
z	Pisello Joseph	52	roofer	46	

518

a	Collins Mary J—†	52	at home	65	90 Bremen
b	Severino Arthur	52	painter	35	here
c	Severino Concetta—†	52	housewife	32	"
d	Gentile Francesco	53	artist	40	"
e	Gentile Vera—†	53	housewife	34	"
f	*Gentile Dominic	53	printer	74	
g	Gentile Marsalle	53	"	28	
h	Amoroso Jennie—†	53	housekeeper	58	"
k	Festa Henry	53	operator	49	"
l	Festa Jennie—†	53	housewife	44	"
m	Festa Frank	53	U S A	23	

Page	Letter	FULL NAME.	Residence, Jan. 1, 1945.	Occupation.	Supposed Age.	Reported Residence, Jan. 1, 1944. Street and Number.

Chelsea Street—Continued

	N	Festa Josephine—†	53	saleswoman	21	here
	o	Messina Antonino	53	fisherman	65	"
	P	Messina Dominic	53	laborer	21	"
	R	Messina Grazia—†	53	housewife	63	"
	s	Maienzo Rocco	53	cook	33	"
	T*	Provenzano Joseph	53	laborer	50	"
	w	Lana Antonio	54	factoryhand	59	"
	x	Mazzola Catherine—†	54	housewife	49	"
	Y	Mazzola Philip	54	storekeeper	59	"
	z	Olina Diane—†	54	at home	54	"

519

	A	Olina Leo	54	U S C G	24	"
	B	Olina Mary—†	54	stitcher	22	"
	c	Olina Ranzo	54	U S A	20	
	E	Farina Irene—†	58	housewife	33	"
	F	Farina Joseph	58	painter	32	
	G	Quattrocchi Rose—†	58	stitcher	37	"
	H	Tango Michael	58	painter	53	"
	K	Macaluso Biaggio	58	clerk	25	
	L	Macaluso Marie—†	58	at home	71	"
	M	DeMonte Grace—†	60	housewife	20	"
	N	DeMonte Ralph	60	machinist	30	"
	o	Fiarino Emanuel	60	presser	59	
	P	Fiarino Mary—†	60	housewife	49	"
	R	Fiarino Salvatore	60	U S A	27	
	s*	Forgione Antoinette—†	60	housewife	38	"
	T	Forgione Salvatore	60	laborer	45	
	U	LaCourt Peter W	62	guard	61	"
	v	Cardinale Florence—†	62	housewife	32	135 Orleans
	w	Cardinale Michael	62	metalworker	35	135 "
	x	Astuccio Frances—†	62	boxmaker	33	here
	Y	Brucato Pietro	64	retired	82	"
	z*	Brucato Vincenza—†	64	housewife	72	"

520

	A	Kincaid Lorraine—†	64	"	23	Winthrop
	B	Kincaid William	64	U S A	25	"
	c	LaMonica Mildred—†	64	housewife	41	here
	D	LaMonica Salvatore	64	casketmaker	42	"
	E	Prisco Alphonse	66	expressman	59	"
	F	LaMonica Andolfo	66	baker	25	"

Chelsea Street—Continued

	G	*LaMonica Calogera—†	66	housewife	58	here
	H	LaMonica Carmella—†	66	"	22	"
	K	LaMonica Santo	66	laborer	60	"
	L	LaMonica Clara—†	66	housewife	26	"
	M	LaMonica Phillip	66	clerk	32	
	N	DiFiore Fred	68	shoeworker	50	"
	O	DiFiore Fred W, jr	68	U S A	23	
	P	DiFiore Pasquale	68	shoeworker	21	"
	R	DiFiore Pauline—†	68	housewife	38	"
	S	*Martello Michelena—†	68	tailor	43	
	T	Martello Nicola	68	"	48	
	U	*Paradiso Giulia—†	68	at home	71	"
	V	Paradiso Leonardo	68	retired	71	"
	W	Capone Emilio	68	U S A	23	"
	X	*Colangelo Harry	68	janitor	49	"
	Y	Colangelo Jennie—†	68	housewife	44	"
	Z	Fiore Antonio	68	laborer	53	
521						
	A	Fiore Lena—†	68	housewife	43	"
	B	Fiore Mary—†	68	stitcher	24	"
	C	Fiore Olympia—†	68	at home	20	"
	D	Fiore Theresa—†	68	metalworker	22	"
	E	Altieri Adeline—†	70	housewife	40	10 Chelsea
	F	Altieri Carlo	70	upholsterer	43	10 "
	G	Altieri Louis C	70	metalworker	20	10 "
	H	DiMonte Angelo	70	laborer	55	here
	K	DiMonte Gina—†	70	entertainer.	21	"
	L	DiMonte Rose—†	70	housewife	43	"
	M	D'Apolito Carmine	70	U S A	21	
	N	D'Apolito Pasquale	70	machinist	33	"
	O	D'Apolito Rocco	70	retired	56	"
	P	D'Apolito Rose—†	70	housewife	54	"
	R	*Mellone Anthony	70	laborer	59	
	S	Mellone Josephine—†	70	housewife	43	"
	T	Albano Anthony	72	laborer	24	
	U	Albano Gilda—†	72	housewife	21	"
	V	*Galindo Benjamin	72	laborer	47	"
	W	Galindo Theresa—†	72	housewife	48	"
	X	Gugliemo Pasquale	72	meatcutter	40	"
	Y	Lauria Henry	72	shipfitter	33	"

Page.	Letter.	Full Name.	Residence, Jan. 1, 1945.	Occupation.	Supposed Age.	Reported Residence, Jan. 1, 1944. Street and Number.

Chelsea Street—Continued

	z	Lauria Josephine—†	72	housewife	28	here
		522				
	A	Iarossi Antonette—†	74	"	22	
	B	Iarossi Pasquale	74	pipefitter	33	"
	c	Fasano John	74	retired	77	"
	D	Indorato Lena—†	74	factoryhand	53	"
	E	Indorato Mario	74	tailor	57	"
	F	O'Halloran Ada—†	74	housewife	31	1224 Com av
	G	O'Halloran Thomas	74	clerk	38	1224 "
	H	Olivolo Anthony	74	shipfitter	26	here
	K	Olivolo Emma—†	74	housewife	21	"
	L	Indorato Salvatore	74	pipefitter	33	"
	M	Indorato Viola—†	74	housewife	30	"
	N	Crisafulli Filomena—†	76	"	60	
	o	Crisafulli John	76	U S A	24	
	P	Crisafulli Rose—†	76	clerk	22	
	R	Crisafulli Yolanda—†	76	stitcher	20	"
	s	Amico Lena I—†	76	housewife	25	63 Neptune rd
	T	Amico Salvatore F	76	engineer	31	63 "
	U	*Baldini Assunta—†	76	housewife	59	here
	v	Baldini Carlo	76	U S A	30	"
	w	Baldini Clara—†	76	dressmaker	25	"
	x	Magnifico Anna—†	78	housewife	56	"
	Y	Magnifico John	78	barber	57	
	z	Magnifico Phillip	78	U S A	27	
		523				
	A	Glufling Frances—†	78	housewife	32	"
	B	Glufling James	78	U S N	33	
	c	Hurley Margaret—†	78	factoryhand	34	"
	D	Puzzo Lena—†	78	stitcher	34	"
	E	Puzzo Salvatore	78	laborer	42	"
	F	Scudieri Vincenzo	80	engineer	64	"
	G	*Montivano Rose—†	80	housewife	55	"
	H	DiMaio Mary—†	80	"	26	"
	K	Faldetta Camilla—†	80	"	47	
	L	Faldetta Frank	80	printer	21	
	M	Faldetta Helen—†	80	operator	24	"
	N	Faldetta Salvatore	80	longshoreman	52	"
	P	D'Addario Armando	82	U S A	22	
	R	D'Addario Camilla—†	82	operator	26	"
	s	D'Addario Carmen	82	clerk	23	

14

Page.	Letter.	Full Name.	Residence, Jan. 1, 1945.	Occupation.	Supposed Age.	Reported Residence, Jan. 1, 1944. Street and Number.

Chelsea Street—Continued

	T	D'Addario Ginditta—†	82	housewife	49	here
	U	D'Addario Orlando	82	U S A	20	"
	V	D'Addario Salvatore	82	retired	55	"
	W	Bertolino Anthony	82	U S A	23	
	X	Bertolino Carlo	82	retired	61	
	Y	Bertolino Catherine—†	82	housewife	58	"
	Z	Bertolino Paul F	82	U S A	33	"

524

	A	Bertolino Salvatore	82	U S N	21	
	D	Paone Ada—†	84	housewife	28	"
	E	Paone Armando	84	chauffeur	28	"
	F	*Vanni Ancieto	84	plasterer	69	"
	G	*Vanni Mary—†	84	housewife	52	"
	H	Vanni Rennet	84	U S A	22	"
	K	Vanni Walter	84	plasterer	25	"
	M	Grillo Giuseppe	86	retired	75	
	N	Maggio Marian—†	86	housewife	25	"
	O	*Maggio Salvatore	86	barber	35	"
	P	Liberatore Anthony	86	clerk	26	89 E Canton
	R	Liberatore Grace—†	86	housewife	22	89 "
	S	Kirkpatrick Beatrice—†	86	stitcher	20	here
	T	LaGrassa Lena—†	86	housewife	42	"
	U	LaGrassa Vincenzo	86	laborer	52	"
	W	Aloi Maria—†	88	finisher	60	
	X	*Perrotti Dominic	88	operator	64	"
	Y	Perrotti Giaconda—†	88	factoryhand	27	"
	Z	Perrotti Rita—†	88	"	23	

525

	A	Perrotti Salvatore	88	U S N	30	
	B	*Perrotti Vera—†	88	housewife	50	"
	C	Ferrera Alice—†	88	"	23	
	D	Ferrera Natale	88	laborer	26	
	E	Cinseruli Ella—†	90	housewife	41	"
	F	Cinseruli Matthew	90	chauffeur	20	"
	G	Cinseruli Vincent	90	bartender	47	"
	H	Cinseruli Vincent, jr	90	U S N	22	
	K	Basillio Carmen	90	U S A	23	
	L	Basillio Josephine—†	90	housewife	50	"
	M	Pugliese Mary—†	90	dressmaker	24	"
	N	Pugliese Sabatino	90	U S N	26	
	O	Genovese Carmella—†	92	housewife	68	"

Chelsea Street—Continued

P	Genovese Donato	92	laborer	67	here
R	Genovese Giuseppe	92	newsdealer	33	"
S	Pistone Marie—†	92	housewife	54	"
T	Pistone Paul	92	retired	64	"
U	Grimaldi Angelo	92	U S A	27	180 Paris
V	Grimaldi Giuseppe	92	laborer	55	180 "
W	*Grimaldi Mary—†	92	housewife	54	180 "
X	Fera Martin	94	factoryhand	33	here
Y	Fera Raffaela—†	94	housewife	32	"
Z	Parziale Carmen	94	metalworker	41	"

526

A	Parziale Maria C—†	94	housewife	37	"
B	Fiorino Josephine—†	94	"	41	
C	Fiorino Vincenzo	94	baker	46	"
E	Pirrello Josephine—†	96	housewife	41	278 Chelsea
F	Pirrello Michael A	96	U S N	20	278 "
G	Pirrello Philip J	96	machinist	22	278 "
H	Famiglietti Gennaro P	96	bricklayer	49	here
K	Famiglietti Joseph	96	machinist	27	"
L	Currzi Biagio	98	laborer	50	"
M	Currzi Emilio	98	U S N	22	
N	Currzi Santa—†	98	housewife	45	"
O	Gagliardi Albert	98	chauffeur	29	19 Cotting
P	Gagliardi Antoinetta—†	98	housewife	64	19 "
R	Gagliardi Nicholas	98	U S A	32	19 "
S	Gagliardi Phyllis—†	98	stitcher	21	19 "
T	Gagliardi Theresa—†	98	at home	23	19 "
U	DeMarino Josephine—†	102	housewife	31	here
V	DeMarino Phillip	102	electrician	32	"
W	Coia Pietro	102	laborer	57	"
X	Coia Sebastian	102	"	21	"
Y	Freni Mary—†	102	housewife	50	"
Z	Freni Pauline—†	102	clerk	24	

527

A	Cocozziello Ceasare	102	laborer	47	81 E Lenox
B	Cravotta Joseph	102	"	56	here
C	Cravotta Marie—†	102	housewife	45	"
D	Cravotta Marie—†	102	stitcher	21	"
E	Cravotta Phillip	102	U S A	22	
F	*Melino Concetta—†	102	housewife	55	"
G	Melino Frank	102	laborer	60	

16

Chelsea Street—Continued

H	Pisapia Caroline—†	104	stitcher	23	here
K	*Pisapia Grace—†	104	housewife	45	"
L	Pisapia Luigi	104	baker	50	"
M	Pisapia Orazio	104	U S N	22	
O	Gomes Anthony	104	"	28	
P	Gomes Julia—†	104	housewife	26	"
R	Ricciardi James	104	machinist	36	'
S	Ricciardi Palma—†	104	housewife	27	"
T	Piazza Catherine—†	104	"	44	
U	Piazza Catherine—†	104	operator	23	"
V	Piazza Joseph	104	laborer	52	"
W	DePietro Anthony	104	machinist	31	23 Margaret
X	DePietro Rose—†	104	housewife	21	23 "
Y	Minichello Albert	106	seaman	31	here
Z	*Minichello Amelia—†	106	housewife	59	"
	528				
A	Minichello Arthur	106	U S A	28	
B	Minichello Generoso	106	laborer	64	
C	*Scimone Charles	106	retired	84	
D	*Scimone Jennie—†	106	housewife	71	"
E	Bartolo Constance—†	106	"	28	
F	Bartolo Frank	106	laborer	27	
G	*Rodrigues Alida—†	106	housewife	36	"
H	*Rodrigues Jose	106	mechanic	41	"
K	*Tarsi Ardella—†	106	housewife	74	"
L	Tarsi Mary—†	106	stitcher	36	"
M	*Tarsi Peter	106	retired	74	"
N	DeNisi Josephine—†	106	housewife	24	231 Chelsea
O	DeNisi Nicholas	106	presser	32	231 "
P	Lombardo Joseph	108	cutter	51	here
R	Saldi Margaret—†	108	housewife	21	"
S	Saldi Salvatore	108	U S A	23	"
T	Ferrera Salvatore	108	brazier	27	
U	Ferrera Stella—†	108	housewife	27	"
V	Balba Agrippina—†	108	"	60	
W	Balba Santa—†	108	stitcher	25	"
X	Barone Christopher	108	U S A	46	
Y	Barone Mary—†	108	housewife	39	"
Z	Cammarita Cologero	108	laborer	59	
	529				
A	*Cammarita Frances—†	108	housewife	58	"

1—5   17

Chelsea Street—Continued

B	Siciliano Phillipa—†	110	housewife	55	here
C	Siciliáno Rocco	110	millhand	65	"
D	LaTorraca Domenic	110	carpenter	47	"
E	LaTorraca Enrichetta—†	110	housewife	49	"

Drake Place

H	Addario Anthony C	1	U S A	21	here
K	*Addario Antoinetta—†	1	housewife	64	"
L	Addario Nicolo	1	janitor	67	"
M	Scrima Frank A	1	shipper	30	
N	Scrima Helen—†	1	housewife	26	"
O	Giuggio Antonio	1	restaurateur	40	"
P	Locigno Michaela—†	1	housekeeper	67	"
R	*Galati Catherine—†	1	housewife	61	"
S	Galati Joseph	1	fireman	54	"
T	Lagrotteria Rocco	1	retired	56	"
U	Coluccino John C	2	metalworker	28	236 Princeton
V	Coluccino Theresa—†	2	housewife	25	236 "
W	*Lopilato Anthony	2	retired	86	here
X	*Lopilato Lena—†	2	housewife	59	"
Y	Lopilato Manuel	2	U S A	28	"
Z	Lopilato Sabastian	2	laborer	63	
	530				
A	Mirabella Emilio	2	clerk	43	"
B	*DiPrimio Anna—†	3	housewife	56	96 Chelsea
C	DiPrimio Anthony	3	operator	51	96 "
D	DiPrimio Elvira—†	3	stitcher	22	96 "
E	Avola Calagero	4	laborer	65	here
F	Avola Rose—†	4	housewife	48	"
G	Albanese Angelina—†	4	"	48	"
H	Albanese Gaetano	4	U S A	26	"
K	Albanese Joseph A	4	U S C G	22	"
L	Albanese Maria—†	4	stitcher	24	"
M	Albanese Saverino	4	laborer	49	"
N	Delosio Alfred	5	U S A	34	
O	*Delosio Angelina—†	5	housewife	64	"
P	Delosio Ernest	5	U S A	24	
R	Delosio Eugene	5	welder	23	
S	Delosio Ralph	5	laborer	60	"
T	Laiacone Frank	5	U S A	30	140 Everett

Drake Place—Continued

u	Laiacone Marlene—†	5	housewife	28	here
v	Riccio Anthony	5	laborer	37	"
w	Riccio Mary—†	5	housewife	33	"
x	*Daloisio Maria—†	6	housekeeper	60	"
y	Montalto John P	6	chauffeur	30	164 Cottage
z	Montalto Josephine—†	6	housewife	25	164 "
	531				
a	*Carnabuci Josephine—†	7	housekeeper	60	Brockton
b	DeRuosi Dominica—†	7	housewife	49	here
c	DéRuosi Sylvester	7	brazier	49	"
d	DiSousa Helen—†	8	housewife	26	"
e	DiSousa Joseph	8	laborer	29	
f	*Grasso Amelio	8	teamster	55	"
g	Grasso Frabonia—†	8	housewife	55	"
h	Grasso Joseph	8	U S A	21	"
k	Modica John	8	"	20	

Elbow Street

l	Brown Frances L—†	2	housewife	43	62 Bremen
m	Brown Ralph L	2	janitor	51	62 "
n	DeMarco Vincent	2	longshoreman	49	here
o	Hayes Annie E—†	2	housekeeper	47	25 Grady ct
p	Norcott Patrick	2	retired	75	25 "
r	Bianchei Angelo	4	U S A	22	here
s	*Bianchei Fidelia—†	4	housewife	51	"
t	Bianchei Frank	4	U S A	23	"
u	*Bianchei Michael	4	storekeeper	62	"
v	Buonopane Anthony	4	rigger	32	
w	Buonopane Margaret—†	4	housewife	29	"
x	Iacobacci Peter	4	shipfitter	49	"
y	*Iacobacci Winifred—†	4	housewife	48	"

Emmons Street

z	D'Agostino Adeline—†	1	inspector	20	here
	532				
a	D'Agostino Anthony	1	tailor	54	
b	D'Agostino Virginia—†	1	housewife	42	"
c	Imperato Louis	3	shoeworker	36	"
d	Viscinti David M	5	U S N	20	

19

Emmons Street—Continued

	Letter	Full Name	Res.	Occupation	Age	Reported Residence
	E	Viscinti Michael	5	painter	43	here
	F	Viscinti Mildred—†	5	housewife	40	"
	G*	DePietro Elizabeth—†	7	"	67	"
	H	DePietro John	7	machinist	31	"
	K	DePietro Livia—†	7	housewife	32	34 Clark
	L	Barrasso Eleanor—†	8	stitcher	25	68 Chelsea
	M	Barrasso Julia—†	8	housekeeper	60	68 "
	N	Bucci Anna—†	8	housewife	58	here
	O	Bucci Grace—†	8	stenographer	20	"
	P	Bucci James	8	retired	56	"
	R	Verro Louise—†	8	housewife	28	"
	S	Verro Pasquale	8	laborer	30	
	T	Williams Earl C	8	mechanic	27	"
	U	Williams Mary—†	8	housewife	22	"
	V	Angelo Frances—†	9	stitcher	26	"
	W*	Angelo Sarah—†	9	housewife	61	"
	X	Calabrese Alfred	9	sorter	40	··
	Y	Rosato Anthony	10	laborer	32	
	Z	Rosato Josephine—†	10	housewife	31	"
		533				
	A	Diaz Jean—†	10	"	41	
	B	Diaz Jose	10	rigger	42	
	C	Thirens Ethel—†	10	housewife	39	"
	D	Thirens George	10	painter	49	
	E	Messina Emma—†	10	saleswoman	25	"
	F	Messina Lucy—†	10	housewife	53	"
	G	Messina Nicholas	10	laborer	55	
	H	Famigletti Anthony	11	"	23	··
	K	Famigletti John	11	"	48	
	L	Famigletti Mary—†	11	housewife	39	"
	M	Garllo Vincent	11	laborer	24	
	N	Perez Camilla—†	11	housewife	52	"
	O	Perez Manuel	11	longshoreman	52	"
	P	Scanlon Anna—†	12	housewife	26	"
	R	Scanlon James	12	U S A	32	"
	S	Sorrentino Anthony	12	barber	28	
	T	Sorrentino Rose—†	12	operator	26	"
	U	Maggio Andrew	12	photographer	45	"
	V	Scopa Albert	12	bartender	32	"
	W	Scopa Mary—†	12	housewife	32	"
	X	Leotta Louis	12	machinist	32	Revere

Page.	Letter.	FULL NAME.	Residence, Jan. 1, 1945.	Occupation.	Supposed Age.	Reported Residence, Jan. 1, 1944. Street and Number.

Emmons Street—Continued

Y	Leotta Mary—†	12	housewife	32	Revere
z	Liuzza Mary—†	12	stitcher	26	here
	534				
A	Liuzza Michael	12	shoeworker	64	"
B	Liuzza Sara—†	12	stitcher	59	"
c	Schraffa Mildred—†	12	housewife	35	"
D	Schraffa Vito	12	U S N	32	
E	Vozzelle Mary—†	12	housewife	40	"
F	Vozzelle Ralph	12	printer	39	
G*	Gobbe Camilla—†	13	housewife	39	"
H*	Gobbe Frank	13	laborer	56	"
K	Lento Pasquale	13	"	73	4 F

Gove Street

N	Smith Concetta—†	11	housewife	24	Chelsea
o	Wilson Lena—†	11	"	36	here
P	Wilson Joseph	11	machinist	55	"
T*	Canatella Mary—†	21	housewife	57	"
U*	Canatella Salvatore	21	pedler	56	
v	Boudreau Antoinette—†	21	housewife	29	"
w	Boudreau Herbert	21	laborer	32	
x	Bua Anthony	25	U S N	25	"
Y*	Bua Michelina—†	25	housewife	60	"
z*	Ferrario John B	25	baker	55	
	535				
A*	Ferrario Louise M—†	25	housewife	54	"
B	Columbo Fred	25	laborer	62	
c	Columbo Joseph	25	U S A	24	
D*	Columbo Rose—†	25	housewife	62	"
F*	DiDonato Carmella—†	36	"	57	
G	DiDonato Joseph	36	painter	57	
H	DiDonato Lucy—†	36	clerk	23	
K	DiDonato Margaret—†	36	"	25	
M	Mottola Agnes—†	36	housewife	33	"
N	Mottola Joseph	36	painter	33	
o	Noto Nancy—†	38	housewife	52	"
P	Noto Salvatore	38	laborer	62	
R	Belino Antonia—†	38	housewife	51	"
s	Belino Salvatore	38	U S A	29	
T	Carabella Catherine—†	38	housewife	51	"

Page.	Letter.	FULL NAME.	Residence, Jan. 1, 1945.	Occupation.	Supposed Age.	Reported Residence, Jan. 1, 1944. Street and Number.

Gove Street—Continued

u*	Carabella Joseph	38	baker	55	here
v	Simmons Abel	40	U S N	37	"
w	Simmons Paulmina—†	40	housewife	30	"
x	Simonelli Jessie—†.	40	"	34	
y	Simonelli Salvatore	40	shipfitter	34	"
z*	Capobianco Jessie—†	40	housewife	60	"

536

a	Capobianco Joseph	40	U S A	24	..
b	Capobianco Pasquale	40	laborer	64	..
c	Capobianco Rose—†	40	stitcher	22	"
d	Coleman Henry	42	retired	72	34 Bremen
e	Madden Josephine—†	42	housewife	33	here
f	Madden Warren J	42	plumber	46	"
g	Paglieroni Ersilio T	42	U S A	21	"
h*	Paglieroni Josephine—†	42	housewife	48	"
k*	Paglieroni Julio	42	machinist	48	"
l	Anzalone Eleanor—†	43	housewife	28	"
m	Anzalone Pasquale	43	U S A	29	
n*	Nazzaro Marie—†	43	housewife	65	"
o	Fuccillo Anna—†	43	"	47	
p	Fuccillo Florence—†	43	clerk	22	
r	Fuccillo Lillian—†	43	stitcher	26	"
s	Fuccillo Massimino	43	laborer	52	
t	Fuccillo Olympia—†	43	entertainer	25	"
u	D'Apice Carmen	43	chauffeur	39	"
v	D'Apice Edith—†	43	housewife	38	"
w	Collura Rosario	44	retired	70	
x	Collura Grace—†	44	housewife	35	"
y	Collura Vincent	44	painter	40	
z	Biancucci Anthony	44	laborer	30	..

537

a	Biancucci Pauline—†	44	housewife	25	"
c	Waddingham Arthur	59	carpenter	39	"
d	Waddingham Sadie—†	59	housewife	50	"
e*	Fanzone Anna—†	59	"	59	
f	Fanzone Jerry	59	laborer	25	
g*	Jacinto Adriana A—†	61	housewife	71	"
h*	Jacinto Emanuel	61	fireman	52	..
k*	Catalfano Carmella—†	61	housewife	63	"
l*	Catalfano Phillip	61	laborer	63	

Page.	Letter.	FULL NAME.	Residence, Jan. 1, 1945.	Occupation.	Supposed Age.	Reported Residence, Jan. 1, 1944. Street and Number.

Gove Street—Continued

	M	Salamone Angelo	61	laborer	57	here
	N	Salamone Catherine—†	61	stitcher	21	"
	O	Salamone Vincenza—†	61	housewife	53	"
	P	Catillo Louis	63	retired	70	333 Paris
	R	Rizza Angelina—†	63	housewife	69	here
	S	Rizza Salvatore	63	retired	69	"

Havre Street

	X	*Massina Jennie—†	110	housewife	45	here.
	Y	Massina Mariono	110	storekeeper	55	"
	Z	*Petronio Catherine—†	112	housewife	75	"
		538				
	A	*Petronio Gregorio	112	retired	79	
	C	Barbetta Dorothy—†	112	housewife	24	"
	D	Barbetta Michael	112	painter	35	"
	E	Nigri Arminio	113	lather	52	"
	F	Nigri Carmela—†	113	housewife	46	"
	G	Giordano Angelo	113	factoryhand	34	"
	H	Giordano Josephine—†	113	housewife	30	"
	K	Lacorazza Carmella—†	113	"	26	"
	L	Lacorazza Daniel	113	mechanic	28	"
	M	Caroniti Rose—† rear	113	housewife	32	"
	N	Caroniti Saverio "	113	laborer	46	
	O	Provenzano Margaret —†	113	housewife	54	"
	P	Provenzano Michael S "	113	U S N	20	
	R	Provenzano Salvatore "	113	laborer	53	
	S	Lussier Nora A—†	114	clerk	35	"
	T	Wellings Francis J	114	manager	75	"
	U	Wellings Nora A—†	114	housewife	75	"
	V	Guzzo Angelina—†	115	"	36	Chelsea
	W	Guzzo Joseph	115	laborer	52	"
	X	Tomasello Josephine—†	115	housewife	51	here
	Y	Tomasello Luigi	115	laborer	59	"
	Z	Tomasello Santa—†	115	operator	27	"
		539				
	A	Lalicata Angelo	115	retired	56	
	B	Lalicata Concetta—†	115	housewife	57	"
	C	Lalicata Guy	115	machinist	23	"
	D	*Palermo Maria—† 1st r	115	housewife	45	"
	E	*Palermo Salvatore 1st "	115	baker	55	

Havre Street—Continued

F	*Testa Anna—†	1st r 115	housewife	62	here
G	Testa Mary—†	1st " 115	dressmaker	28	"
H	Testa Mary—†	1st " 115	housewife	50	"
K	*Testa Calogero	1st " 115	retired	68	
L	Repicci Anna—†	2d " 115	housewife	37	"
M	Repicci Charles	2d " 115	baker	42	
N	Abruzzese Generoso	2d " 115	U S N	33	
O	Abruzzese Marie—†	2d " 115	housewife	33	"
P	Mazzone Anthony	2d " 115	shipfitter	26	205 E Eagle
R	Mazzone Josephine—†	2d " 115	housewife	28	205 "
S	Gulli Joseph	116	laborer	41	here
T	Lynch Jessie—†	116	housekeeper	56	"
U	Murphy Frederick J	116	clerk	56	"
V	Neville Frank	116	fireman	55	"
W	Giordano Caroline—†	117	housewife	69	"
X	Giordano Phillip	117	retired	75	
Y	Caprera Grace—†	117	packer	22	
Z	Caprera Josephine—†	117	stitcher	23	"

540

A	Caprera Mario	117	machinist	50	"
B	*Caprera Mary—†	117	housewife	42	"
C	Caprera Peter	117	U S A	50	"
D	Cappiello Chester	117	machinist	29	210 Bennington
E	Cappiello Frances—†	117	housewife	29	210 "
F	Miles Henry	118	laborer	51	here
G	Goglia Agnes—†	119	housewife	30	"
H	Goglia Vincent	119	rigger	30	"
K	Bruno Mary—†	119	housekeeper	52	"
L	Bruno Nicholas	119	candymaker	59	"
M	Steele Anna—†	119	clerk	28	Everett
N	Bruno Lucy A—†	119	"	34	here
O	Bruno Michael	119	retired	67	"
R	Camerlengo Alfonso	120	painter	36 ·	"
S	Camerlengo Clementina-†	120	housewife	32	"
T	DiCarolis Amato	120	laborer	62	
U	*DiCarolis Concetta—†	120	housewife	52	"
V	DiCarolis Ralph	120	U S N	23	"
W	Pastore Anna—†	120	housewife	29	"
X	Freda Margaret—†	121	"	27	
Y	Freda Pasquale	121	painter	29	"
Z	Stocco Charles	121	electrician	43	"

24

Page.	Letter.	FULL NAME.	Residence, Jan. 1, 1945.	Occupation.	Supposed Age.	Reported Residence, Jan. 1, 1944. Street and Number.

541

Havre Street—Continued

	Letter	FULL NAME	Res.	Occupation	Age	Reported Residence
	A	Stocco Concetta—†	121	housewife	37	here
	B	Camerlengo Angelina—†	121	housekeeper	66	"
	c	Camerlengo Arthur	121	U S N	22	"
	D	Camerlengo Benjamin	121	longshoreman	43	"
	E	Blades Gertrude—†	122	operator	34	32 Langdon
	F	Hanafin Carmella—†	122	housewife	26	here
	G	*Petagno Raymond	122	shoemaker	35	"
	H	Carney Francis	122	seaman	24	Somerville
	L	DeBono Mary—†	126	housewife	28	here
	M	DeBono Pasquale	126	laborer	30	"
	N	Poglia Albert	126	U S A	31	"
	O	Poglia Barbereno	126	retired	61	
	P	Poglia Mario	126	musician	32	"
	R	Poglia Sandra—†	126	clerk	35	"
	T	Lopresti Adeline—†	128	housewife	30	"
	U	Lopresti Anthony	128	shipfitter	32	"
	V	Giordano Lillian—†	128	housewife	25	"
	W	Giordano Vincent	128	U S N	27	
	X	*Lopresti Frances—†	128	housewife	55	"
	Y	Lopresti Frank	128	barber	67	
	Z	Lopresti Lillian—†	128	operator	34	"

542

	Letter	FULL NAME	Res.	Occupation	Age	Reported Residence
	A	*Modica Angelina—†	131	housekeeper	70	"
	B	*Modica Joseph	131	retired	72	"
	E	Seracuse Alice—†	132	housewife	29	"
	F	Seracuse Joseph	132	painter	29	"
	G	Spina Luciano	132	U S N	24	
	H	Spina Mary—†	132	housewife	24	"
	K	Poscucci Anna—†	132	tailor	21	"
	L	Poscucci Antonio	132	U S A	23	
	M	Poscucci Joseph	132	electrician	48	"
	N	Poscucci Olympia—†	132	housewife	48	"
	O	DiFilippo Anthony	133	U S A	28	"
	P	DiFilippo Carmela—†	133	housewife	25	124 Everett
	R	Ventresca John	133	mechanic	33	309 Sumner
	S	Ventresca Marie—†	133	housewife	22	21 Everett
	T	Caruso Carmela—†	133	U S A	21	here
	U	Caruso Catherine—†	133	housewife	57	"
	V	Caruso Natale	133	pressman	55	"
	W	Caruso Rose—†	133	clerk	23	

25

Havre Street—Continued

x	DeCarlo Elizabeth—†	134	housewife	49	here
y	*Bard Sylvia—†	134	"	26	"
z	Bard Thomas	134	longshoreman	29	"
	543				
a	Spina Carolina—†	134	housewife	51	"
b	Spina Gaetano	134	pedler	55	"
c	Cavino Anthony	135	painter	42	110 Paris
d	Cavino Rose—†	135	housewife	35	110 "
e	Lewis Arthur	135	chef	46	here
f	Lewis Josephine—†	135	housewife	45	"
g	DiPerri Alfred	135	shoeworker	20	"
h	DiPerri Palma—†	135	housewife	61	"
k	DiPerri Salvatore	135	retired	64	
l	Mancuso Constance—†	136	housewife	23	"
m	Mancuso Fedele	136	painter	25	
n	Mancuso Anthony	136	U S N	23	
o	Mancuso Gabriel	136	U S A	26	
p	Mancuso Mary—†	136	housewife	45	"
r	Mancuso Salvatore	136	solecutter	56	"
s	Marciello Domenic	136	shipper	29	"
t	Marciello Grace—†	136	housewife	26	"
u	Sartori Joseph	137	longshoreman	37	376 Sumner
v	Pasqualino Angelo	137	laborer	61	here
w	Pasqualino Francisca—†	137	housewife	52	"
x	Pasqualino Ida—†	137	stitcher	21	"
y	Leonardo Salvaggio	137	candymaker	45	"
z	Tedesco Mollie—†	138	housewife	35	"
	544				
a	Kanelakos Arthur	138	merchant	57	"
b	Kanelakos George	138	"	55	
c	Amato Josephine—†	138	coil winder	20	"
d	D'Angelo Margaret—†	138	housewife	26	"
e	D'Angelo Patrick	138	shipfitter	31	"
f	Uva Helen—†	139	housewife	28	"
g	Uva Peter	139	factoryhand	27	"
h	*Chiango Jennie—†	139	housewife	69	"
k	Chiango Agostino	139	retired	69	"
l	Barrett Mary C—†	139	housewife	56	21 Eutaw
m	Lacovino Dominic	140	U S N	20	here
n	Lacovino Frank	140	machinist	46	"
o	Lacovino Josephine—†	140	housewife	38	"

Havre Street—Continued

P	Scorzelloa Elvira—†	140	housewife	25	here	
R	Scorzelloa Joseph	140	electrician	29	"	
S	Pitari Agrippina—†	141	housewife	50	"	
T	Pitari Agrippino	141	bartender	52	"	
U	Cavagnaro Joseph A	141	chauffeur	35	"	
V	Cavagnaro Marie—†	141	housewife	28	"	
W	Scaduto Agrippina—†	141	"	31		
X	Scaduto Salvatore	141	rigger	35	"	
Y	DelVento Incoronata—†	142	housewife	45	"	
Z	DelVentò Nicolo	142	pipefitter	52	"	
	545					
A	Leandro Giuseppe	142	"	53		
B	Leandro Immaculata—†	142	housewife	40	"	
C	Leandro Rose—†	142	dressmaker	20	"	
D	Leandro Sabina—†	142	clerk	21		
E	Valiante George	143	chauffeur	37	"	
F	Valiante Nina—†	143	housewife	31	"	
G	Tomei Mary—†	143	factoryhand	49	"	
H	Napolitano Ralph	143	laborer	29	"	
K	Napolitano Vincenza—†	143	housewife	29	"	
L	*Cataldo Maria—†	144	"	60		
M	Norcia Mae E—†	144	stitcher	32	"	
N	Norcia Ralph	144	clerk	52		
O	Norcia Silvio	144	U S A	43	"	
P	Ward John E	145	laborer	28	64 Everett	
R	Ward Rita L—†	145	housewife	24	64 "	
S	Pisano Julia—†	145	"	50	134 Bremen	
T	Coco John	145	U S A	23	here	
U	Coco Mary—†	145	clerk	24	"	
V	Jozaitis Helen—†	145	assembler	26	"	
W	Jozaitis Vincent	145	U S A	29		
X	Saldi Angelo	147	rigger	24		
Y	Saldi Mary—†	147	housewife	23	"	
Z	*Rosa Grace—†	147	"	36		
	546					
A	Rosa Anthony	147	tailor	43		
B	Cali Frank	147	operator	21	"	
C	Cali Rose—†	147	housewife	44	"	
D	Cali Vincent	147	chef	47	"	
E	Dorais Aurora—†	148	housewife	41	N Hampshire	
F	Dorais William	148	metalworker	41	"	

Page	Letter	Full Name.	Residence, Jan. 1, 1945.	Occupation.	Supposed Age.	Reported Residence, Jan. 1, 1944. Street and Number.

Havre Street—Continued

	Letter	Full Name.	Res.	Occupation.	Age	Reported Residence
	G	Briana Caroline—†	148	housewife	49	here
	H	Briana William	148	operator	53	"
	K	*Recupio Frank	149	pedler	58	"
	L	*Recupio Laura—†	149	housewife	61	"
	M	Nelson Pearl—†	149	factoryhand	40	"
	N	*Mischio Antonetta—†	149	housewife	55	"
	O	*Mischio Michele	149	laborer	59	..
	P	Mischio Philomena—†	149	driller	29	"
	R	DeVincentis Frank	153	painter	40	
	S	DeVincentis Phyllis—†	153	housewife	31	"
	T	*Cucinotta Mary—†	153	housekeeper	58	"
	U	MacDougall Sally—†	153	housewife	30	"
	V	Iozzo Joseph	153	chauffeur	29	"
	W	Iozzo Mary—†	153	housewife	25	"
	X	Meloni Fred	155	machinist	32	"
	Y	Meloni Phyllis—†	155	housewife	34	"
	Z	Santora Arthur	155	machinist	32	"
		547				
	A	Santora Gilda—†	155	housewife	33	"
	B	Capone Anthony	155	mechanic	40	"
	C	Capone Mary—†	155	housewife	40	"
	D	DeAngelo Lucy—†	157	"	21	278 Havre
	E	DeAngelo Nicholas	157	U S A	29	278 "
	F	*Valletto Frank	157	pedler	55	here
	G	Valletto James	157	machinist	22	"
	H	*Valletto Mary—†	157	housewife	55	"
	K	*Pucillo James	157	operator	61	"
	L	*Pucillo Vincenzo	157	laborer	59	
	M	*Zaccaria Maria G—†	157	housekeeper	50	"
	N	Ricupori Joseph	159	laborer	51	"
	O	Grasso Angelina—†	159	housewife	51	"
	P	Grasso Felix	159	barber	60	"
	R	Grasso Mary—†	159	driller	20	"
	S	Grasso Salvatore	159	U S A	26	
	T	DiStefano Joseph	159	laborer	56	
	U	*DiStefano Liboria—†	159	housewife	46	"
	V	Coco Antonio	161	laborer	26	
	W	Coco Aratiso	161	machinist	21	"
	X	Coco Carmella—†	161	housewife	46	"
	Y	Coco Carmella—†	161	dressmaker	22	"
	Z	Coco Charles	161	machinist	23	"

Page	Letter	Full Name.	Residence, Jan. 1, 1945.	Occupation.	Supposed Age.	Reported Residence, Jan. 1, 1944. Street and Number.

548

Havre Street—Continued

A	Coco Joseph	161	clerk	20	here
B	Coco Mario	161	retired	54	"
C	Auteltoni Vincenza—†	161	housewife	65	79 Chelsea
D	Auteltoni Julia—†	161	housekeeper	27	79 "

London Street

F	Burke Gladys F—†	119	housewife	42	here
G	Burke Joseph I	119	repairman	41	"
H	Golden Estelle—†	119	housewife	43	"
K	Baudanza Manuel	119	chef	60	"
L	Baudanza Mary—†	119	housewife	32	"
O	Montalto Camille	125	U S A	35	
P	Montalto Jean—†	125	housewife	30	"
R	Mason Charles	125	presser	28	
S	Donnelly Julia—†	125	housewife	51	"
T	Donnelly William J	125	fireman	64	"
U	Monaco Americo	125	seaman	29	
V	Monaco Frances—†	125	housewife	31	"
w*	Frank Aida—†	127	"	70	
X	Frank Harry	127	retired	75	
Y	Frank Marion—†	127	WAVE	27	
Z	Hurwitz Doris—†	127	housewife	35	"

549

A	Hurwitz Edward	127	attorney	40	"
B	Frank David	127	storekeeper	45	"
C	Frank Lena—†	127	housewife	41	"
D	Carnabuci Gora—†	127	"	23	
E	Carnabuci Leo	127	foreman	32	"
G	DiRocco Concetta—†	131	housewife	39	"
H	DiRocco Gaetano	131	machinist	42	"
K	DiRocco Mary—†	131	housewife	41	"
L	DiRocco Peter	131	carpenter	46	"
M	Martinelli Henry	131	clerk	49	"
N	Martinelli Henry, jr	131	U S A	21	
O	Martinelli Margaret—†	131	housewife	47	"
P	Callahan Laura—†	133	"	52	
R	Doyle Susan—†	133	clerk	55	
S	McGrane Thomas	133	pipefitter	50	"
T	Zuffante Anna—†	133	housewife	22	"

London Street—Continued

u	Zuffante Charles	133	U S A	22	here
v	Scott Agnes G—†	133	housewife	40	"
w	Scott Rufus	133	chauffeur	53	" .
x	Scott William J	133	U S A	24	
y	Dooley Catherine L—†	135	housewife	75	"
z	McDonough Catherine T—†	135	"	79	
	550				
a	Morris Annie F—†	135	"	80	
b	White Ellen C—†	135	"	36	
c	White John T	135	mortician	35	"
d	Ramirez Lillian—†	137	housewife	50	"
e	Ramirez Mary—†	137	at home	26	"
f	Ramirez Rosario	137	finisher	56	
g	*Reitano Jennie—†	137	housewife	75	"
h	Reitano Pauline—†	137	clerk	35	
k	Bourgoin Arthur	137	seaman	45	..
l	Bourgoin Emma—†	137	housewife	50	"
n	Livolsi Andrew	139	barber	50	
o	Livolsi Frances—†	139	welder	22	"
p	Livolsi Josephine—†	139	housewife	46	"
r	*Anastasio Anna—†	139	at home	73	"
s	Anastasio Anna—†	139	clerk	25	..
t	Anastasio Theresa—†	139	housewife	47	"
u	Anastasio Vincent	139	laborer	48	"
v	DePula Joseph	139	chauffeur	45	"
w	DePula Josephine—†	139	clerk	20	
x	DePula Mary—†	139	housewife	41	"
y	Murphy Rose—†	141	"	38	Everett
z	Murphy William	141	shipfitter	43	"
	551				
a	Troy Rose—†	141	housewife	47	here
b	Maloney John	141	retired	84	"
c	Maloney Mary—†	141	housewife	75	"
d	LaSalla Bridget—†	143	"	51	"
e	LaSalla Joseph	143	driller	27	"
f	LaSalla Louis	143	laborer	55	
g	*Cennamo Ida—†	143	housewife	52	"
h	Cennamo Ida—†	143	factoryhand	23	"
k	Cennamo Lucy—†	143	at home	21	"
l	Cennamo Mary—†	143	factoryhand	27	"
m	Cennamo Salvatore	143	"	58	

Page.	Letter.	Full Name.	Residence, Jan. 1, 1945.	Occupation.	Supposed Age.	Reported Residence, Jan. 1, 1944. Street and Number.

London Street—Continued

| | N | Iannaccone Mary—† | 143 | housewife | 41 | here |
| | O | Iannaccone Michael | 143 | chauffeur | 49 | " |

Maverick Street

	W	Magaletta Frank	144	proprietor	53	here
	X	Magaletta Josephine—†	144	housewife	48	"
	Y	Freese Henry	146	foreman	50	"
	Z	Amato Peter	146	carpenter	48	"
552						
	A	Iaccarone Alfredo	146	shoemaker	60	"
	B	Ratti Ugo	146	chef	62	
	C	Napolitano Achille	146	tailor	65	
	E	Previti Catherine—†	148	hairdresser	24	"
	F	Previti Grace—†	148	housewife	52	"
	G	Previti Jeannette—†	148	secretary	22	"
	H	Previti John J	148	storekeeper	57	"
	K	Previti Joseph	148	U S A	26	"
	L	Previti Matthew	148	manager	29	"

Meridian Street

	O	Packard Elma A—†	1A	housekeeper	70	here
	P	Tubin Bessie—†	1A	storekeeper	48	"
553						
	B	Wright Christina S—†	11	housewife	55	"
	C	Wright John F	11	clerk	57	
	D	Beaton Lillian H—†	11	housewife	26	"
	E	Beaton Melvin E	11	U S A	27	"
	F	Curran Catherine A—†	11	packer	53	"
	H	Raimo Anthony	13A	printer	59	
	K	Raimo Anthony	13A	U S A	22	
	L	Raimo Mary—†	13A	housewife	54	"
	M	Viscione Jerry L	13A	butcher	23	"
	N	Viscione Josephine V—†	13A	housewife	28	"
	R	Samuels Philip	20	attorney	63	"
	W	Forrest John J	49	retired	84	
	X	Sullivan Christina—†	49	clerk	44	
	Y	Morin Joseph F	49	"	51	"
	Z	Morin Marie V—†	49	housewife	50	"

31

554

Meridian Street—Continued

K	Sullivan Mary E—†	65	housewife	49	here
L	Sullivan John P	65	engineer	52	"
M	Burke Thomas J	65	seaman	41	131 Eutaw
N	Lightbody Charles A	65	engineer	57	131 "
O	Lightbody Edith M—†	65	housewife	56	131 "
R	LaRosa Lillian D—†	67	"	31	here
T	Pitts Charlotte B—†	71	"	32	27 Eutaw
U	Pitts Frank J	71	rigger	39	27 "
V	Hovsepian Ella M—†	71	manager	36	here
W	Hovsepian Harry H	71	machinist	39	"
Z	Roysten Anne A—†	77	housewife	32	"

555

A	Roysten Eugene E	77	bartender	32	"
B	Maher Anne M—†	77	housewife	63	"
C	Maher Daniel J	77	seaman	62	
D	Maher William F	77	U S A	25	
E	Lanovara Joseph	77	chipper	27	"
F	Lanovara Rita—†	77	housewife	26	"
N*	McCue Norman J	95	fisherman	33	"
O	Powers James A	95	laborer	62	
P	Powers James J	95	seaman	30	"
R	Powers Loretta E—†	95	housewife	33	"
S	Powers William E	95	clerk	35	
T*	Rogers John	95	longshoreman	64	"
U	Rogers Michael E	95	"	29	"
V	Cullen John E	97	fireman	41	
W	Fracasso Frank	97	tailor	52	
X	Heveran John	97	laborer	43	
Y	Hunter James	97	pile driver	68	"
Z	Vandola Alphonse	97	tailor	50	

556

B	Farrell Minnie—†	101	housewife	50	"
H	Amirault Reuben	109	fishcutter	57	"
K	Boland Jeremiah	109	fisherman	55	"
L	Cagliano Alfonso	109	laborer	48	
M	Considine John	109	mechanic	38	"
N	Cunningham John J	109	proprietor	52	"
O	Dillis Arthur W	109	fishcutter	46	"
P	Fothergill John W	109	watchman	61	50 Lexington
R	Gillespie Arthur	109	laborer	44	here
S	Jensen Carl	109	foreman	41	"

Page.	Letter.	Full Name.	Residence, Jan. 1, 1945.	Occupation.	Supposed Age.	Reported Residence, Jan. 1, 1944. Street and Number.

Meridian Street—Continued

	T	Pepe Antonio	109	laborer	64	here
	v	Petracone Modestina—†	111	operator	22	Barre
	w	Sinyard Michael F	111	rigger	33	24 Princeton
	x	Diaz Leo	111	U S A	25	46 Paris
	y	Diaz Mary—†	111	housewife	54	46 "
	z	Kassinger Luther V	111	U S A	29	13 Adams
557						
	A	Kassinger Rita E—†	111	housewife	24	13 "

Model Place

	E	*Guarini Vincent	3	pedler	64	here
	F	*Quadara John	3	painter	55	"
	K	Hitchcock John	4	rigger	52	"
	L	*Woodger Susan—†	4	housekeeper	50	"

Paris Court

	M	Lespasio Dominic	2	U S A	28	5 Gould's ct
	N	Lespasio Ralph	2	retired	71	5 "
	o	Lespasio Thomas	2	U S A	26	5 "
	P	Sawyer Marie—†	2	housekeeper	42	here

Paris Place

	u	*Barile Biagio	1	laborer	65	here
	v	Farago Antonio	1	"	45	"
	w	*Silver Alice—†	1	housewife	40	"
	x	*Silver Manuel	1	ironworker	52	"
	y	Silver Manuel, jr	1	U S N	20	
558						
	A	Howard Fred	3	chef	65	107 Meridian
	B	Goodwin Dexter	3	laborer	38	214 E Eagle
	c	Goodwin Eva—†	3	housewife	59	here
	D	Goodwin Inez—†	3	at home	25	"
	E	Kennedy Anna—†	3	"	23	"
	F	Young Jennie M—†	3	"	66	"
	G	Paine Frank W	5	retired	73	11 Winthrop
	H	Willis Andrew J	5	bartender	56	148 Border
	K	D'India Mildred—†	5	housewife	33	here
	L	D'India Ralph	5	welder	36	"

1—5   33

Paris Place—Continued

M	Pohl Charles	5	U S N	22	New York
N	Lunetta Salvatore	6	retired	78	here
P	Costanza Joseph	6	machinist	47	38 Monmouth
R	Sullivan Eugene	6	laborer	33	5 Saratoga pl
S	*Carabianos Constance—†	7	housewife	37	3 Paris pl
T	Carabianos George	7	engineer	58	3 "
U	*Shepard Robert J	7	carpenter	65	here
V	Usher Mary—†	7	at home	41	"

Paris Street

Y	Perez Clara—†	78	housewife	25	here
Z	Perez Donald	78	longshoreman	25	"
	559				
A	Allatte Angelina—†	78	housewife	53	"
B	Allatte Joseph	78	storekeeper	66	"
G	Ciampa Alfonse	83	welder	30	
H	Ciampa Lucy—†	83	housewife	28	"
K	*DeStefano Angelina—†	83	"	53	
L	DeStefano Clara—†	83	factoryhand	21	"
M	*DeStefano John	83	"	52	"
N	DeStefano Louise—†	83	operator	24	"
O	DeStefano Ortino	83	U S A	22	
P	Napoleon Bessie—†	83	housewife	28	"
R	Napoleon Nicholas	83	painter	52	
S	Spataro Jennie—†	84	stitcher	36	"
U	Akerberg Edwin C	85	machinist	36	"
V	Akerberg Mary—†	85	housewife	36	"
Y	Faldetta Edward	87	janitor	60	
Z	Faldetta Grace—†	87	clerk	25	
	560				
A	Faldetta Maria—†	87	housewife	50	"
B	Riley Mary A—†	87	at home	68	"
C	Bernardinelli Nellie—†	98	housewife	41	"
D	Bernardinelli Pasquale	98	machinist	44	"
E	Reppucci Angelina—†	98	housewife	64	"
F	Reppucci Herbert	98	U S A	31	
G	Reppucci Joseph	98	candymaker	64	"
H	Reppucci Lydia—†	98	at home	95	"
K	Reppucci Lydia—†	98	teacher	29	
L	Reppucci Michael	98	candymaker	52	"

Page	Letter	Full Name	Residence, Jan. 1, 1945.	Occupation	Supposed Age	Reported Residence, Jan. 1, 1944. Street and Number.

Paris Street—Continued

	M	Russo Lena—†	98	housewife	36	here
	N	Russo Sebastian	98	chauffeur	38	"
	O	Catinezzo Adeline—†	100	stitcher	25	"
	P	Catinezzo Mafelda—†	100	at home	23	"
	R	*Catinezzo Nicholas	100	retired	62	
	S	Iacuzio Jennie—†	100	housewife	32	"
	T	Iacuzio Nicholas	100	baker	33	
	U	Fewer Mary—†	100	housewife	53	"
	V	Fewer James	100	laborer	55	
	W	Barrasso Antonio	102	U S A	22	
	X	Barrasso Frank	102	shoemaker	55	"
	Y	*Barrasso Manuela—†	102	housewife	50	"
	Z	Barrasso Michael	102	shoemaker	25	"
		561				
	A	Barrasso Rosario	102	laborer	27	
	B	*Ciaburri Carmella—†	102	housewife	53	"
	C	Ciaburri Mary—†	102	stitcher	24	"
	D	Ciaburri Raffaele	102	glassmaker	59	"
	E	Ciaburri Rose—†	102	stitcher	22	"
	F	*Bellone Fannie—†	102	housewife	50	"
	G	Bellone Joseph	102	laborer	60	"
	H	Savoia Frank	104	"	39	
	K	Savoia Miranda—†	104	housewife	35	"
	L	DellOrfano Evelyn—†	104	hairdresser	32	"
	M	DellOrfano Luigi	104	engineer	61	"
	N	DellOrfano Maria—†	104	housewife	60	"
	O	Petzke Henry	104	shipwright	32	"
	P	Petzke Hilda—†	104	housewife	31	"
	R	Vozzella Nancy—†	106	"	26	"
	S	Vozzella Theodore	106	carpenter	27	"
	T	Minichiello Antoinetta—†	106	housewife	51	"
	U	Minichiello Nunziante	106	plumber	53	"
	V	Rossi Olga—†	106	housewife	24	"
	W	Rossi Ralph	106	U S A	24	
	X	Vozella Anthony	106	U S N	22	
	Y	Zappulla Salvatore	106	shipfitter	31	"
	Z	Zappulla Viola—†	106	cutter	27	
		562				
	A	Stocco Frank	108	laborer	44	83 London
	B	Stocco Tina—†	108	housewife	32	83 "
	C	Abbate Albert	108	U S A	30	here

Paris Street—Continued

D	Abbate Alfred	108	U S A	24	here
E	Abbate Enes—†	108	stitcher	21	"
F	Abbate Esther—†	108	housewife	52	"
G	Abbate Joseph	108	barber	61	
H	Leonardi Ida—†	108	housewife	27	"
K	Leonardi Nicholas	108	shipfitter	35	"
P	Amato Mary T—†	127	housewife	33	"
R	Amato Salvatore	127	letter carrier	48	"
S	Morelli Antonio	127	laborer	54	
T	*Ritso Gustave	127	chef	52	"
V	Gagan Josephine—†	127	saleswoman	29	"
W	Rotondo Charles W	127	U S N	20	
X	Rotondo Concetta—†	127	saleswoman	31	"
Y	Rotondo Frank	127	U S A	22	
Z	Rotondo Mary—†	127	housewife	59	"
	563				
A	Rotondo Philip	127	chauffeur	62	"
B	*DuLuca Charles	rear 127	retired	60	
C	DuLuca Joseph	" 127	brazier	35	
D	Amato Albina—†	" 127	housewife	45	"
E	Amato Andrew	" 127	cutter	50	"
F	DiSilvestro Joseph	" 127	U S N	34	41 Morris
G	DiSilvestro Theresa L—†	" 127	housewife	29	41 "
H	Imbornone Dominic	132	chauffeur	34	Somerville
K	Imbornone Mary—†	132	housewife	29	"
L	Marcotullio Albert	132	shipfitter	35	here
M	Marcotullio Beatrice—†	132	housewife	34	"
N	Phillips Bessie—†	132	"	54	"
O	Phillips Lydia—†	132	"	21	
P	Phillips Stanley D	132	chauffeur	23	"
R	Giordano Concetta G—†	133	housewife	23	"
S	Giordano Salvatore	133	carpenter	27	"
T	Giordano Charles	133	laborer	57	"
U	Giordano Jennie—†	133	stitcher	29	"
V	Giordano Mary S—†	133	housewife	52	"
W	Giordano Vincent	133	U S N	22	
X	Buttleri Mary—†	133	finisher	62	
Y	Megna Joseph	133	U S A	31	
Z	Megna Rose—†	133	housewife	30	"
	564				
A	Pilcher Emma—†	134	"	24	

36

Paris Street—Continued

B	Pilcher Stephen H	134	painter	22	here
C	Guarino Louis	134	U S N	24	"
D	Guarino Nicholas	134	retired	69	"
E	Rotondo Caroline—†	134	housewife	34	"
F	Rotondo Michael	134	barber	36	
G	Danna James	134	electrician	33	"
H	Danna Josephine—†	134	housewife	28	"
K	Bethune Frederic M	135	U S N	29	
L	Bethune Lena V—†	135	housewife	29	"
M	Megna John M	135	chauffeur	38	"
N	Megna Lena V—†	135	housewife	36	"
P	Megna Anthony E	135	U S M C	23	"
O	Megna Antonio	135	barber	56	,,
R	Megna Mildred—†	135	housewife	36	"
S	Vella Joseph	136	janitor	73	"
T	Vella Josephine—†	136	housewife	60	"
U	Vella Luigi	136	shipfitter	34	"
V	Gassiraro Benjamin	136	laborer	54	
W	Gassiraro Elsie—†	136	stitcher	20	"
X	Gassiraro Frank	136	U S A	22	
Y	Gassiraro Marie—†	136	housewife	45	"
Z	Ciarcia Eleanor—†	136	cashier	23	76 Chelsea
	565				
A	Ciarcia Paul	136	tailor	53	76 '
B	Ciarcia Yolanda—†	136	stitcher	20	76 "
C	Odice Vincerca—†	136	housekeeper	64	76 "
D	LaSala Henry	137	barber	43	here
E	LaSala Mary C—†	137	housewife	42	"
F	Spitaleri Concetta—†	137	forewoman	29	"
G	*Spitaleri Nancy—†	137	housewife	62	"
H	Barrasso Joseph	137	U S A	20	
K	Barrasso Mary—†	137	at home	45	"
L	Barrasso Nicholas	137	U S A	21	
M	Barrasso Rose—†	137	dressmaker	29	"
N	*DePalma Theresa—†	137A	housekeeper	67	"
O	Vasapolli Joseph	137A	mattressmkr	52	"
P	*Vasapolli Mary—†	137A	housewife	41	"
R	*Zappulla Rose—†	137A	"	34	
S	Zappulla Vincent	137A	rubberworker	46	"
T	D'Annolfo Carl	138	tailor	40	
U	D'Annolfo Theresa—†	138	housewife	39	"

Page	Letter	Full Name.	Residence, Jan. 1, 1945.	Occupation.	Supposed Age.	Reported Residence, Jan. 1, 1944. Street and Number.

Paris Street—Continued

	v	Lavorgna Anthony	138	chauffeur	33	here
	w	Lavorgna Mary—†	138	housewife	62	"
	x	Montuori Aniello	138	pipefitter	51	"
	y	Monturoi Rose—†	138	housewife	38	"
	z	Verrazzani Josephine—†	138	stitcher	42	"
566						
	a	Verrazzani Lorenzo	138	candymaker	46	"
	b	*Capobianco Josephine—†	139	at home	76	"
	c	Capobianco Michael	139	boxmaker	48	"
	d	Anzalone Anthony	139	U S C G	30	"
	e	Anzalone Josephine—†	139	housewife	38	"
	f	*Tibaudo Antoinetta—†	139	"	59	
	g	Tibaudo Frank	139	shoemaker	46	"
	h	*Petrozzello Maria—†	140	housewife	73	"
	k	*Petrozzello Pasquale	140	retired	75	
	l	Pergola Petrina—†	140	housewife	46	"
	m	Pergola Phillip	140	shipfitter	57	"
	n	LaSale Amelia—†	140	at home	28	"
	o	Petrozzelli Annie—†	140	housewife	39	"
	p	Petrozzelli Lawrence	140	weaver	44	
	r	Pupolo Alfred	141	U S A	22	
	s	Pupolo Angelo	141	retired	65	
	t	Pupolo Carmella—†	141	housewife	63	"
	u	DeFeo Costanza—†	141	"	55	
	v	DeFeo Sabina—†	141	stitcher	21	"
	w	Moscone Eleanor—†	141	housewife	20	113 Trenton
	x	Moscone John	141	operator	22	113 "
	y	Ippolito Josephine—†	142	housewife	26	here
	z	Ippolito Rocco	142	shipfitter	35	"
567						
	a	Capprini Josephine—†	142	housewife	27	"
	b	Capprini Leo	142	welder	30	"
	c	Petrucelli Joseph	142	baker	67	"
	d	Ferrante Charles	142	janitor	49	"
	e	Ferrante Filomena—†	142	housewife	41	"
	f	Ferrante Maria—†	142	electrician	24	"
	g	Ferrante Richard J	142	U S A	20	
	h	DeVingo Marie—†	143	stitcher	20	"
	k	DeVingo Philomena—†	143	housewife	55	"
	l	Zirpolo Angelina—†	143	"	36	
	m	Zirpolo John	143	fireman	41	"

Page.	Letter.	Full Name.	Residence, Jan. 1, 1945.	Occupation.	Supposed Age.	Reported Residence, Jan. 1, 1944. Street and Number.

Paris Street—Continued

	o	Wade Grace—†	144	housewife	24	Lynn
	p	Wade John R	144	sprayer	27	"
	r	Micciche Joseph	144	laborer	73	here
	s	Micciche Joseph, jr	144	U S A	34	"
	t	Vitale Joseph	144	U S N	20	"
	u	Vitale Mary—†	144	housewife	41	"
	v	Vitale Rocco	144	shoemaker	48	"
	w	Carrabino Angelo	146	chauffeur	37	"
	x	Carrabino Angela—†	146	housewife	39	"
	y	Scorzella Angelina—†	146	"	70	
	z	Scorzella Joseph	146	retired	77	

568

	a	Scorzella Louis	146	plumber	36	4 Shelby
	b	Aste Florence—†	146	stitcher	25	here
	c	Conti Joseph	149	blacksmith	56	"
	d	Conti Rose—†	149	candymaker	60	"
	e	*Todisco Celesta—†	149	at home	84	"
	f	Todisco Celesta—†	149	dressmaker	20	"
	g	Todisco Joseph	149	constable	56	"
	h	Todisco Mary—†	149	housewife	47	"
	k	Todisco Michael	149	storekeeper	62	"
	l	Todisco Virginio J	149	U S A	24	"
	m	Russo James	149	laborer	32	143 Paris
	n	Russo Josephine—†	149	housewife	31	143 "
	p	Beggelman Abraham	153	junk dealer	65	here
	r	Beggelman Eva—†	153	bookkeeper	33	"
	s	Beggelman Israel	153	U S A	25	"
	t	Beggelman Rubin	153	"	29	
	u	*Beggelman Sarah—†	153	housewife	60	"

Porter Street

	v	Sorrentini Erminia—†	87	housewife	58	here
	w	DiNapoli Anthony	87	U S A	24	"
	x	DiNapoli Archangela—†	87	housewife	58	"
	y	DiNapoli Joseph	87	retired	65	
	z	DiNapoli Mary—†	87	stitcher	31	"

569

	b	Borisowsky Abraham S	103	engineer	42	"
	c	Borisowsky Israel	103	retired	71	
	d	Borisowsky Lena—†	103	housewife	72	"

Porter Street—Continued

E	*Rotondo Angelina—†	103	housewife	48	here
F	Rotondo Antonio	103	fireman	53	"
G	Rotondo Guido	103	U S A	24	"
M	Caruso Samuel	109	storekeeper	56	"
S	Garry Evelyn—†	117	housekeeper	25	"
T	Garry Marie—†	117	housewife	48	"
U	Tuberosa Joseph .	117	machinist	34	"
V	Tuberosa Margaret—†	117	housewife	33	"
W	Boncore Salvatore	117	presser	46	47 Chelsea
X	Gelardi Jean—†	117	stitcher	22	here
Y	Gelardi Theresa—†	117	housewife	23	"

Ward 1–Precinct 6

CITY OF BOSTON

LIST OF RESIDENTS
20 YEARS OF AGE AND OVER

(NON-CITIZENS INDICATED BY ASTERISK)
(FEMALES INDICATED BY DAGGER)

AS OF

JANUARY 1, 1945

THOMAS F. SULLIVAN, *Chairman*
FREDERIC E. DOWLING, *Secretary*
WILLIAM A. MOTLEY, JR.
FRANCIS B. McKINNEY
EVERETT R. PROUT

Listing Board.

CITY OF BOSTON PRINTING DEPARTMENT

Page.	Letter.	FULL NAME:	Residence, Jan. 1, 1945.	Occupation:	Supposed Age.	Reported Residence, Jan. 1, 1944. Street and Number.

600
Bennington Street

H	*Cohen Esther—†	34	housewife	60	here
K	Cohen Ethel—†	34	housekeeper	37	"
L	*Cohen Max	34	proprietor	60	"
M	Glick Anna—†	34	"	39	
N	*Mason Fannie—†	34	at home	78	"
O	Nicoletti Alice—†	34	housewife	38	"
P	Nicoletti Salvatore	34	painter	40	
Y	Brown Joseph C	56	realtor	37	"
Z	Maze George	56	pipefitter	40	9 Temple

601

A	Gardas Catherine E—†	56	housewife	51	here
B	Gardas William	56	U S C G	22	"
C	Gardas William H	56	fireman	52	"
D	Pero Charles	56	shipfitter	56	"
E	Pero Henry	56	U S A	35	
F	Hall Alma—†	56	bookkeeper	27	"
G	Hewitt Fannie L—†	56	housekeeper	72	"
H	McShane Bertha F—†	56	housewife	51	"
K	McShane Thomas	56	shoemaker	55	"
L	DiPietro Domenic	58	laborer	39	
M	DiPietro Josephine—†	58	housewife	36	"
N	*Nicosia Josephine—†	58	"	60	
O	Nicosia Rose—†	58	painter	37	"
P	Kopaczynski Joseph W	58	U S N	33	Chelsea
R	Kopaczynski Sophie M—†	58	clerk	30	"
S	Constantino John D	60	U S A	21	193 Summer
T	Constantino Richard	60	"	25	193 "
U	O'Connell Agatha—†	60	housewife	56	193 "
V	O'Connell Richard	60	clerk	56	193 "
W	Schiff Bessie—†	60	housewife	64	here
X	Schiff Jacob	60	retired	67	"
Z	Constantino Nicholas	62	electrician	37	"

602

A	Constantino Ruth—†	62	housewife	27	"
B	DiGregorio Angelo	62	U S A	20	"
C	DiGregorio Anthony	62	cutter	51	
D	DiGregorio Celia—†	62	housewife	41	"
E	Scala Angelina—†	64	"	60	"
F	Scala John	64	retired	68	"
G	Scala John, jr	64	U S A	29	

2

Bennington Street—Continued

H	Scala Anthony R	64	technician	26	here
K	Scala Rita—†	64	housewife	22	N Hampshire
L	Goshgarian Ardemis—†	64	factoryhand	40	here
M	Goshgarian Serop	64	operator	55	"
O	Hong Joseph	68	laundryman	41	"
R	Marotta Charles	70	U S N	36	"
S	Marotta Damiano	70	retired	69	
T	Marotta Hilda—†	70	timekeeper	24	"
U	Marotta Michael	70	machinist	33	"
V	Marotta Phyllis—†	70	dressmaker	31	"
W	Marotta Rose—†	70	clerk	22	
X	Marotta Salvatore	70	U S A	27	"
Y	Preshong Albert W	70	laborer	75	
Z	Preshong Joseph	70	seaman	38	"

603

A	Preshong Josephine—†	70	housewife	65	"
B	Preshong Mary—†	70	at home	35	"
D	Carolan Elizabeth—†	72	welder	34	
E	Hogan Joseph T	72	U S A	26	
F	Hogan Sarah—†	72	housewife	66	"
G	Hogan Thomas	72	carpenter	68	"
H	Keating Charlotte N—†	72	housewife	70	"
K	Keating Michael E	72	retired	70	
L	Bonia Mary—†	74	housewife	51	"
M	Bonia Michael J	74	timekeeper	49	"
N	Coppola Josephine—†	74	at home	28	"
O	Paldo Carolina—†	74	clerk	35	"
P	Paldo Domenic	74	laborer	55	
R	Paldo Florence—†	74	housewife	55	"
S	Glennan Joseph H	76	clerk	55	113 Brooks
T	Dagenais Alfred	76	seaman	34	here
U	*Dagenais Emilia—†	76	housewife	54	"
W	Merigan Catherine M—†	78	"	65	"
X	*Shelton Elizabeth—†	78	housekeeper	74	60 Bennington
Z	Festa Arthur R	80	fireman	29	here

604

A	Festa Emily—†	80	housewife	62	"
B	Festa Modestino	80	retired	67	
C	*Enos Joseph	80	"	76	
D	Miglionico Joseph	80	longshoreman	38	"
E	Miglionico Mary L—†	80	housewife	50	"

Bennington Street—Continued

F	Burge Agnes—†	82	inspector	25	here
G	Burge Walter	82	U S N	25	"
H	Plante Lucy—†	82	cutter	41	"
K	Plante Wilfred	82	inspector	47	"

Border Street

M	Stearns Benjamin	219	retired	80	here
P	Buccheri Attelia—†	221	housewife	26	"
R	Buccheri Samuel	221	welder	29	"
S	Buccheri Joseph	221	pipefitter	31	"
T	Buccheri Mildred—†	221	leatherworker	26	"
U	Buccheri Paul	221	blacksmith	66	"
V	*Buccheri Pauline—†	221	housewife	54	"
W	Buccheri Santo	221	U S A	25	
X	Buccheri Victor	221	"	28	
Y	Donnaruma Antonio	223	shipwright	25	"
Z	Donnaruma Bessie—†	223	housewife	23	"

605

A	Fortini Jennie—†	223	housekeeper	30	"
B	Fortini Joseph	223	laborer	57	"
C	Fortini Maria—†	223	stitcher	54	"
D	Fortini Paul	223	U S A	21	"
E	McCormack Caroline A—†	223	housewife	36	5 Saratoga pl
F	McCormack William H	223	shipfitter	35	5 "
G	Falzarano Christopher	225	cement worker	31	here
H	Falzarano Margaret—†	225	housewife	24	"
K	Falzarano Antoinette—†	225	"	25	"
L	Falzarano Salvatore	225	welder	25	"
M	Volo Michelina—†	225	housewife	30	"
N	Volo Vincenzo	225	rigger	31	"
O	Pereria Frances—†	227	housewife	21	148 Havre
P	Letteriello Adolf	227	laborer	34	here
R	Letteriello Louise—†	227	housewife	35	"
S	Letteriello Isabella—†	227	"	31	"
T	Letteriello Ralph	227	laborer	36	"
U	Barrett James	255	longshoreman	43	"
V	Chaffee Mary—†	255	housewife	23	"
W	McPhee Elizabeth—†	255	housekeeper	71	"
X	Mulkern Daniel	255	fisherman	46	"
Y	Mulkern Mary—†	255	machinist	22	"

Border Street—Continued

z	Starke Lorraine—†	255	housewife	20	here
606						
A	Wilkie Helen—†	255	machinist	26	"
B	*Faschi Anna—†	257	housekeeper	62	6 Paris pl
c	*Molfesis Constantino	257	fireman	48	6 " '
D	Galbo Philomena—†	257	housekeeper	74	here
E	Sawtelle Herbert	257	pressman	36	Chelsea
F	Sawtelle Madeline—†	257	housewife	37	"
G	Fendo Florence—†	259	"	25	here
H	Fendo Peter M	259	laborer	25	"
K	*Pietro Felippa—†	259	housekeeper	67	"
L	Fendo Angelina—†	259	housewife	44	"
M	Fendo Christopher	259	U S A	21	
N	Fendo Vincenzo	259	laborer	52	
O	Ferullo Gloria F—†	259	housewife	23	"
P	Ferullo Pasquale	259	longshoreman	23	"
R	McVey Mary—†	261	cook	64	
S	McVey James	261	cleaner	38	"
T	McVey Margaret—†	261	housewife	30	"
V	Stewart Leo L	263	U S A	39	
W	Stewart Rose—†	263	housewife	32	"
X	Spada Alfred	263	U S A	22	
Y	Spada Catina—†	263	housewife	48	"
z	Spada Leo	263	laborer	54	
607						
A	*Buttigliere Mary—†	263	housewife	44	"
B	Buttigliere Rocco	263	laborer	52	
c	O'Donnell Arthur	265	laundryman	49	"
D	O'Donnell Arthur, jr	265	U S A	21	
E	O'Donnell Mary—†	265	housewife	49	"
F	Anthony John L	265	fisherman	46	65 Marion
G	Thomas Elizabeth—†	265	factoryhand	39	80 Eutaw
H	Ervin Norma—†	265	housewife	24	364 Meridian
K	Ervin Sylvan	265	U S N	24	364 "

Brooks Street

L	Ramirez Leonard	100	U S N	33	here
M	Ramirez Rose—†	100	housewife	33	"
N	DiPietro Claude	100	U S A	24	"
O	DiPietro Leonard	100	"	26	"

Brooks Street—Continued

P	DiPietro Lucy—†	100	housewife	62	here
R	DiPietro Rocco	100	chairmaker	63	"
S	DiPietro William	100	salesman	28	"
T	St George Alice—†	102	housewife	45	140 Bennington
U	St George Joseph	102	longshoreman	58	140 "
V	Hilton Annie—†	104	housewife	65	234 "
W	Hilton George	104	laborer	63	Chelsea
X	McCormack Anne—†	104	housewife	58	here
Y	McCormack John	104	ironworker	63	"
Z	McCormack Leonard	104	U S A	32	"

608

A	McCormack Loretta—†	104	stenographer	23	"
B	McCormack Mary—†	104	inspector	22	"
C	Kelly Helen—†	106	housewife	49	"
D	Kelly Helen E—†	106	inspector	22	"
E	Kelly John J	106	fisherman	54	"
F	Muse Anthony	106	laborer	47	
G	Muse Mary—†	106	housewife	44	"
H	Stanley Harriet E—†	106	"	60	"
K	Stanley Joseph S	106	fireman	59	..
L	Cipriani Tullio	108	leatherworker	43	"
M	Cali Phyllis—†	108	housewife	31	"
N	Cali Rocco	108	counterman	37	"
O	Drago Frank	108	laborer	60	"
P	Drago Theresa—†	108	housewife	60	"

Lexington Avenue

R	Pedersen Essadora D—†	1	at home	55	New York
S	Pedersen Peter D	1	operator	58	"
T	Callari Joseph	1	shipfitter	32	here
U	*Callari Josephine—†	1	housewife	54	"
V	Callari Louise—†	1	weaver	32	225 Condor
W	Callari Phillip, jr	1	U S A	28	here
X	Callari Phillipo	1	laborer	58	"
Y	Coolin Edward J	2	wool handler	60	45 Middle
Z	Coolin Gertrude—†	2	housewife	50	149 Chelsea

609

A	Preshong Louise—†	2	waitress	67	here
B	Cook Helen—†	3	at home	67	8 Paris
C	Cook Wallace W	3	painter	22	8 "
D	*Haddock Agnes K—†	3	housewife	37	here

6

Page.	Letter.	FULL NAME.	Residence, Jan. 1, 1945.	Occupation.	Supposed Age.	Reported Residence, Jan. 1, 1944. Street and Number.

Lexington Avenue—Continued

	E	Haddock Walter	3	boilermaker	39	here
	F	Fothergill Mary J—†	4	housewife	54	"
	G*	McMillan Allan J	4	calker	64	"
	H	Brennan Catherine M—†	4	housewife	40	"
	K	Brennan Frederick A	4	electrician	43	"
	L	Brennan John W	4	U S N	20	"
	N	DiPerri Charles	5	laundrywkr	29	"
	O	DiPerri Lorenzo	5	laborer	63	
	P	DiPerri Louis	5	U S A	30	
	R*	DiPerri Mary—†	5	housewife	48	"
	S	DiPerri Michael	5	U S A	22	
	T	DiPerri Phillip	5	"	21	
	U	DiPerri Salvatore J	5	"	26	
	W	Brennen Albert F	6	cleaner	30	
	X	Brennen Blanche M—†	6	housewife	68	"
	Y	Atkinson Herbert	7	rigger	50	308 Meridian
	Z	Atkinson Lavinia—†	7	housewife	37	Maine
610						
	A	Coco Anthony J	7	welder	28	10 Lexington av
	B	Coco Filippa M—†	7	housewife	25	10 "
	C	Crowell Charlotte E—†	8	"	70	here
	D*	Crowell Ernest M	8	fireman	58	"
	E*	Baglio Lillian—†	8	housewife	44	"
	F	Baglio Louis	8	seaman	49	"
	G	Baglio Rocco	8	U S A	21	"
	H	Preshong Mabel L—†	9	laundrywkr	54	"
	K	Polito Devigia—†	9	housewife	40	"
	L	Polito Joseph	9	U S A	43	"
	M	Siravo Enrico H	9	U S N	36	"
	N	Carter Clarence A	10	fisherman	45	94 Lexington
	O	Carter Rose C—†	10	housewife	27	94 "
	P*	Cara Maria—†	10	at home	75	here
	R	Vitale John	10	presser	49	"
	S	Vitale Mary—†	10	housewife	00	"
	T	Vitale Phillip J	10	chauffeur	21	"
	U	Vitale Ralph	10	welder	20	

Lexington Place

	V	Huddleston Emma E—†	1	housewife	27	Illinois
	W	Huddleston Robert L	1	U S C G	28	"
	X	Rubio Antonio A	1	U S N	25	Texas

Lexington Place—Continued

y	Rubio Audelia—†	1	housewife	22	Texas
z	Minichello Anthony J	2	foreman	34	59 Bennington
611					
A	Minichello Emily G—†	2	housewife	33	59 "
B	Minichello Marie A—†	2	clerk	36	here
C	Minichello Michael A	2	retired	65	"
D	Vitale Mary R—†	2	housewife	34	"
E	Vitale Michael F	2	boilermaker	44	"
F	Tate Eugene T	3	U S A	45	
G	Tate Mary A—†	3	housewife	37	"
H	Hirtle Ethel I—†	3	"	40	Revere
K	Hirtle Frank W	3	carpenter	51	Malden
L	Goodwin Mary—†	4	housewife	23	297 Meridian
M	Goodwin William	4	welder	27	297 "
N	Hardin James E	4	U S A	22	Tennessee
O	Hardin Mildred V—†	4	housewife	21	"
P	Ryan Alfred T	4	blacksmith	53	here
R	Ryan Mildred E—†	4	housewife	53	"
S	Noone Helen I—†	5	"	39	"
T	Noone John T	5	bartender	41	"
U	Quinn Phyllis E—†	5	housewife	25	Missouri
V	Quinn William E, jr	5	U S N	26	"
X	LeGallo John H	6	fisherman	28	Revere
Y	Mikkelsen Mary A—†	6	housewife	31	here
Z	Mikkelsen Sverre M	6	seaman	31	"
612					
A	Johnson Elizabeth—†	6	housewife	44	"
B	Johnson Herbert W	6	laundrywkr	49	"
D	Arsenault Emma R—†	7	housewife	28	339 Border
E	Arsenault Philip J	7	chauffeur	38	339 "
F	Lambert Bessie A—†	7	at home	21	6 Lexington pl
G	Lambert Margaret J	7	housewife	45	6 "

Lexington Street

H	Rumney Sarah—†	21	at home	83	here
K	Tyler John P	21	retired	66	"
L	Alfamo Antonio F	21	cook	60	"
M	Alfamo Mary—†	21	housewife	52	"
N	Beacham Ernest	21	U S A	22	"
O	Beacham Helen—†	21	operator	46	"

Lexington Street—Continued

	R	Amico Joseph	23	U S N	24	here
	S	Amico Philip	23	retired	67	"
	T	Swett Charles W	23	machinist	74	"
	U	Swett Elizabeth M—†	23	housewife	61	"
	V	Gargoulo William	23	painter	57	82 Trenton
	X	Vecchia Christopher	27	chef	31	here
	Y	Vecchia Rose—†	27	housewife	28	"
	Z	Caruso Frederick	27	shoeworker	54	"
613						
	A	Caruso Maria—†	27	housewife	45	"
	B	Cinelli Catherine—†	27	operator	26	"
	C	Lomas Josephine—†	27	housewife	22	"
	D	Scioscia Camile—†	27	stitcher	34	"
	E	Hemingway Nathan	29	retired	70	
	F	Britten Eleanor—†	29	factoryhand	22	"
	G	Flaherty Edith—†	29	housewife	23	"
	H	Flaherty Thomas J	29	U S A	39	
	K	Sharp Albert	29	machinist	35	"
	L	Sharp Hugh	29	conductor	55	"
	M	Allen Leo E	31	foreman	50	N Hampshire
	N	Arey Joseph N	31	fisherman	46	here
	O	Brown John	31	laborer	46	New York
	P	DeCoste Harry	31	machinist	42	here
	R	Donohue Thomas P	31	guard	46	"
	S	Ezekiel Theresa—†	31	at home	65	"
	T	Fitzgerald William	31	machinist	70	"
	U	Hancock Deborah—†	31	housewife	57	"
	V	Hancock Joseph	31	carpenter	63	"
	W	Hancock Mary—†	31	operator	30	"
	X	Masco Leo	31	stevedore	28	163 Falcon
	Y	McComiskey Emma—†	31	housewife	59	here
	Z	McComiskey William	31	machinist	60	"
614						
	A	San Joseph	31	carpenter	45	"
	B	Martell Leo	31A	brushmaker	62	"
	C	Nolan John F	31A	printer	57	
	D	Nolan Victoria—†	31A	housewife	56	"
	E	Regan James J	31A	plumber	39	"
	F	Regan Margaret M—†	31A	bookkeeper	32	"
	G	Cannon Julia F—†	33	housewife	68	"
	H	Fraser Helen—†	33	"	31	

Lexington Street—Continued

K	Fraser William	33	seaman	43	here
L	Olsen John	33	operator	57	New York
M	Boudreau Daniel	33	carpenter	54	391 Meridian
N	Dunbar Margaret—†	33	maid	38	164 Falcon
O	Rose Helen—†	33	housewife	27	Winthrop
P	Rose William	33	foreman	26	"
R	Torri Silva—†	33	nurse	36	here
S	Riccobene Angelo	45	retired	72	"
T	Riccobene Concetta—†	45	housewife	62	"
U	*Marabella Assunta—†	45	"	52	
V	Marabella Joseph	45	retired	64	"
W	Fay Marie—†	45	saleswoman	22	214 E Eagle
X	Nickerson Lester	47	laborer	34	here
Y	*Russo Bridget—†	47	housewife	60	"
Z	Russo Ciriaco	47	retired	75	"

615

A	Fiorito Filomena—†	47	housewife	39	"
B	Fiorito Leonard	47	welder	44	..
C	*Parsons Robert	49	rigger	54	
D	*Parsons Violet—†	49	housewife	47	"
E	Roach Adeline—†	49	"	26	
F	Roach Bernard	49	U S N	26	..
G	Fitzpatrick Edward	49	U S A	28	
H	Fitzpatrick Hazel—†	49	housewife	22	"
K	Keefe Lillian—†	51	operator	49	24 Eutaw
L	Thibeau Accurzia—†	51	housewife	28	here
M	Thibeau George	51	laborer	35	"
N	Knapp Marjory—†	51	housewife	22	"
O	Knapp William	51	U S N	28	
P	Hardy James	53	cook	59	
R	Hardy Virginia—†	53	housewife	50	"
S	Hardy William	53	seaman	21	"
T	Jones Frederick	53	electroplater	37	"
U	Jones Ruth—†	53	housewife	32	"
V	Salerno Dorothy—†	53	"	26	
W	Salerno Michael	53	rigger	28	..
X	Scarfo Pearl—†	61	housewife	22	"
Y	Scarfo Phillip	61	mechanic	28	"
Z	Fariole Edward	61	laborer	24	192 London

616

A	Fariole Lucy—†	61	housewife	24	3 Davis ct

Page.	Letter.	Full Name.	Residence, Jan. 1, 1945.	Occupation.	Supposed Age.	Reported Residence, Jan. 1, 1944. Street and Number.

Lexington Street—Continued

	B	Zaccaria Anthony	61	laborer	55	here
	c	Zaccaria Leo	61	U S A	24	"
	D	Zaccaria Mary—†	61	housewife	48	"
	F	Cheffi Celia—†	63	"	27	
	G	Cheffi Saverio	63	welder	30	
	H	Gordon Clifford	63	engineer	50	"
	K	Gordon Elizabeth—†	63	housewife	47	"
	L	Psychogies James	63	welder	20	
	M	Psychogies Mary—†	63	housewife	48	"
	N	Psychogies Peter	63	painter	56	
	E	Tedescucci Gaetano	65	shoeworker	50	"
	O	Tedescucci Rose—†	65	housewife	42	"
	P	Magnasco Anna—†	65	"	30	"
	R	Magnasco Gismondo	65	electrician	38	"
	S	Mannetta Carlo	65	laborer	65	"
	T	Mannetta George	65	U S N	28	"
	U	Mannetta John	65	chauffeur	34	"
	V	Mannetta Lena—†	65	housewife	60	"
	W	Mannetta Olivia—†	65	beautician	26	"
	X	Pericola Eve—†	67	housewife	29	"
	Y	Pericola Virginio	67	guard	28	
	Z	DiNatale Emma—†	67	housewife	37	"

617

	A	DiNatale Michael	67	machinist	35	"
	B	Covino Angelo	67	barber	45	
	c	Covino Carmella—†	67	shoeworker	33	"
	D	McDonald Daniel J	69	operator	54	"
	E	McDonald Eugenia—†	69	clerk	24	
	F	McDonald Joseph	69	U S A	23	
	G	McDonald Mary E—†	69	housewife	52	"
	H	McDonald Stephen A	69	carpenter	48	"
	K	Ferreira Cleo—†	71	housewife	36	"
	L	Ferreira John	71	engineer	38	"

Marion Street

	N	Giordano Antonette—†	103	housewife	31	here
	O	Giordano Wilfred	103	carpenter	32	"
	P	Giordano Joseph J	103	stockman	27	"
	R	Giordano Rose—†	103	housewife	23	"
	S	Mingora Giuseppe	103	laborer	54	

Marion Street—Continued

T Mingora Philipena—†	103	housewife	54	here
U Tuberosa Ernest	105	agent	29	"
V Tuberosa Raphaella—†	105	housewife	26	"
W Chieppo Anthony	105	carpenter	63	"
X *Chieppo Theresa—†	105	stitcher	60	"
Y Savino Charles	105	painter	39	
Z Savino Rose—†	105	housewife	32	"
618				
A Bozzi Helen—†	107	"	29	
B Bozzi John	107	cutter	33	
C Gibson John	107	U S A	25	"
D Gibson Josephine—†	107	U S M C	29	"
E Kelly Agnes B—†	107	housewife	50	"
F Kelly Lawrence J	107	U S M C	24	"
G Kelly Lorraine—†	107	clerk	20	
H Murphy Thomas	107	fireman	66	"
K Iantosea Consolita—†	107	housewife	44	"
L Iantosea Felice	107	operator	45	"
M Iantosea Philip	107	factoryhand	60	"
O Tarbi Charles	126	reporter	30	"
P Tarbi Frank	126	U S A	26	
R Tarbi Mary—†	126	housewife	37	"
S Tarbi Rosaria—†	126	"	59	
T Tarbi Rosaria—†	126	saleswoman	31	"
U Tarbi Salvatore	126	U S A	24	
X Amirault Leslie	130	"	37	
Y Amirault Tessie—†	130	inspector	28	"
Z LeBlanc Margaret—†	130	housewife	35	"
619				
A LeBlanc Simon	130	fisherman	40	"
B Burrage Emma—†	130	housewife	67	"
C *Burrage Henry	130	carpenter	73	"
D Gallagher Clara—†	130	saleswoman	30	"
E DeVeau Charles E	130	U S A	24	"
F DeVeau Daisy—†	130	housewife	41	"
G DeVeau Frank	130	carpenter	49	"
H Lombard Marie—†	130	clerk	23	"
K Elwell James	132	laborer	40	
L Elwell Josephine—†	132	housewife	42	"
N McGowie Frances—†	132	operator	30	"
O McGowie Paul	132	U S N	32	"

Page.	Letter.	FULL NAME.	Residence, Jan. 1, 1945.	Occupation.	Supposed Age.	Reported Residence, Jan. 1, 1944. Street and Number.

Marion Street—Continued

	P	Driscoll Agnes A—†	134	housewife	32	here
	R	Driscoll Julia M—†	134	clerk	40	"
	s	Driscoll Margaret J—†	134	"	39	"
	T	Tirone Carl C	134	U S A	23	
	U	Tirone Gracinta—†	134	housewife	47	"
	V	Tirone Lewis	134	U S A	22	
	W	Tirone Marco	134	laborer	56	
	X	Tirone Margaret S—†	134	inspector	26	"
620						
	c	O'Donnell John	151	longshoreman	35	"
	D	O'Donnell Mary—†	151	housewife	35	"
	E	Magee Mary—†	151.	"	42	
	F	Magee Richard	151	fishcutter	40	"
	H	Silva Albert	153	laborer	66	
	K	*Silva Annie—†	153	housewife	51	"
	L	Silva Warren B	153	deckhand	25	"
	M	Scofield Charles	153	guard	22	
	N	Scofield Margaret—†	153	housewife	50	"
	o	Glock John	153	retired	69	
	P	Glock Mary—†	153	housewife	54	"
	R	Vicini Anthony	155	machinist	30	"
	s	Vicini Enrico	155	retired	72	
	T	Vicini Frances—†	155	housewife	70	"
	U	Uva Theresa—†	155	"	55	309 E Eagle
	V	*Mascis Anthony	155	retired	74	here
	W	*Mascis Margherita—†	155	housewife	76	"
	X	Adelizzi Catherine—†	157	cementer	30	"
	Y	DelSardo Anna—†	157	stitcher	27	"
	z	DelSardo Antonio	157	retired	66	
621						
	A	*DelSardo Josephine—†	157	housewife	60	"
	B	Catalano Fioreno	157	manager	22.	"
	c	Catalano Geraldine—†	157	housewife	69	"
	D	Barbacano Gaetano	157	U S A	22	
	E	Barbacano Pauline—†	157	stitcher	20	"
	F	*Barbacano Zupito	157	laborer	54	
	G	Scali Anna—†	159	housewife	28	"
	H	Scali John	159	laborer	30	"
	K	Zerole Antonio	159	shoeworker	55	"
	L	Zerole Frank	159	U S N	24	"
	M	Zerole Ida—†	159	clerk	23	

Marion Street—Continued

N	Zerole Mafaleda—†	159	stitcher	26	here
o	Zerole Mary—†	159	housewife	52	"
P	Casiello Louise—†	159	"	41	"
R	Casiello Samuel	159	painter	41	

Meridian Street

T	Boudreau Anna—†	234	housewife	64	here
U	Boudreau William R	234	retired	67	"
V	Cecchinelli Frank	234	laborer	27	"
W	Cecchinelli Tullio	234	machinist	21	"
X	Salerno Clara—†	234	housewife	44	"
Y	Salerno Edward	234	carpenter	41	"
Z	Bell Francis C	236	proprietor	66	"
	622				
A	*St Croix Elizabeth M—†	236	housekeeper	20	"
B	*Aitken Florence—†	236	at home	70	"
C	Aitken Harold	236	U S A	35	
D	Aitken Joseph	236	"	36	
H	Grant Alice—†	242	housewife	40	"
K	Lee George	244	laundryman	68	"
L	Lee James	244	student	20	"
M	Lee William	244	U S A	22	
N	Lee Wong—†	244	housewife	48	"
O	Butts Vincent	244	physician	55	"
P	Roccuzzo Alfio	244	bottler	49	
R	Roccuzzo Gioacchino	244	cobbler	50	
S	O'Brien Dennis	244	foreman	42	"
T	O'Brien Laura—†	244	housewife	40	"
W	Dargenio Alfred	249	plater	33	
X	Dargenio Anthony	249	machinist	25	"
Y	Dargenio Edward	249	U S M C	23	"
Z	*Gerollo Sally—†	249	housewife	60	"
	623				
A	*Gerollo Vincent	249	barber	66	
C	Gurevich Gertrude—†	251	housewife	58	"
D	Gurevich Harry	251	proprietor	60	"
E	Gurevich Herbert	251	U S A	26	..
F	Shatz Charles	251	"	31	
G	Shatz Ida—†	251	typist	30	
K	Mariani Filomena—†	257	housewife	46	"

Page.	Letter.	FULL NAME.	Residence, Jan. 1, 1945.	Occupation.	Supposed Age.	Reported Residence, Jan. 1, 1944. Street and Number.

Meridian Street-- Continued

	L	Mariani Peter	257	machinist	55	here
	M	Pansera Frank	257	retired	75	"
	N	Farrara Antonina—†	257	packer	31	"
	O	Farrara Mary S—†	257	dressmaker	25	"
	P	Farrara Peter E	257	U S A	27	
	R	*Cancara George	257	millhand	57	"
	S	*Cancara Phoebe—†	257	"	54	
	T	*Capodilupo Anthony	259	proprietor	41	"
	U	Capodilupo Concetta—†	259	housewife	34	"
	V	*Caporale Angelo	259	retired	70	
	W	*Caporale Carmella—†	259	housewife	64	"
	X	LoCoco Luigi	259	retired	65	
	Y	Pinkham Edward	259	cleaner	66	
	Z	Pinkham Helen—†	259	housewife	60	"
624						
	A	Zuccoli Domenic	259	retired	78	427 Meridian
	E	Barcellas Edward	265	"	75	here
	F	Candeliere Ettore	265	machinist	28	"
	G	Candeliere Frances—†	265	housewife	20	"
	H	*Nicoletta Angelo	265	retired	70	
	K	*Rowe Elizabeth—†	265	housewife	39	"
	L	*Rowe Henry	265	fisherman	42	"
	M	Waldron Lucy—†	265	at home	84	"
	P	Donovan Helen—†	269	housewife	43	"
	R	Nickerson Clara—†	269	at home	60	"
	V	Greenwood Edna A—†	274	"	72	
	W	Greenwood Lester M	274	pilot	37	
	X	Greenwood Reginald A	274	engineer	43	"
	Y	Greenwood Valetta—†	274	at home	41	"
	Z	Swinn Marguerite C—†	274	operator	41	"
625						
	A	Nickerson Alberta—†	274	"	33	
	B	Nickerson Benjamin L	274	janitor	64	
	C	Nickerson Elsie M—†	274	supervisor	35	"
	D	Nickerson Rose A—†	274	at home	65	"
	E	Payne Frederick	274	pipefitter	31	"
	F	Payne Mildred—†	274	packer	30	"
	H	Donahue Ruth—†	277	housewife	43	Billerica
	N	Adams Hazel—†	284	bookbinder	30	here
	O	Brooks Herbert	284	watchman	66	"
	P	Brown Anna F—†	284	housewife	50	"

15

Meridian Street—Continued

R	Brown Frank E	284	director	67	here
S	Conary Lillian—†	284	laundrywkr	50	219 Saratoga
T	Kavijian Andrew	284	finisher	32	here
U	Newsome Anna—†	284	housewife	26	Virginia
V	Newsome Lee	284	U S N	28	"
W	Osborne Edith—†	284	bookbinder	32	here
X	Surette Margaret—†	285	waitress	30	45 Union pk
Y	Weiner Rueben	285	riveter	51	here
Z	Wilder Sadie—†	285	housekeeper	27	"
	626				
A	Littlefield Harold	285	cook	57	
B	Littlefield Lena—†	285	housewife	39	"
E	Bertolino Angelo	287A	U S N	24	
F	*Bertolino Antonetta—†	287A	housewife	56	"
G	*Bertolino Baldassare	287A	retired	63	..
H	Bertolino Lawrence	287A	U S A	28	"
K	Bertolino Pauline—†	287A	candymaker	26	"
L	Bertolino Rose—†	287A	stitcher	31	Everett
M	Bertolino Vito	287A	U S N	21	here
N	Dean Benjamin	288	welder	34	"
O	Dean Mildred—†	288	housewife	32	"
P	Driscoll Evelyn—†	288	at home	30	"
R	*Burke Mary—†	288	driller	42	
S	Curtis Francis	288	fisherman	45	"
T	Dwyer Lena—†	288	housewife	33	"
U	*Poirier Francis	288	fisherman	38	"
V	Poirier Hubert	288	U S A	36	
W	Dean Edith M—†	288	housewife	48	"
X	Dean Joseph	288	inspector	51	"
	627				
A	McGinnis Hazel B—†	290	housewife	36	"
B	McGinnis John	290	guard	50	"
C	Poulen Walter	290	cleaner	50	Lawrence
D	Goldberg Harry	291	pipefitter	51	here
E	Morse Ammi L	291	salesman	55	"
F	Pierce Joseph F	291	janitor	73	"
G	Sanford William E	291	engineer	49	"
H	Smith Sarah—†	291	housekeeper	67	"
M	Marden Clayton I	293	U S A	30	..
N	Marden Mary E—†	293	housewife	58	"
O	Marden Valerie H—†	293	technician	25	"

Meridian Street—Continued

P	Nickerson Ralph	293	cutter	33	here
R	Nickerson Violet B—†	293	technician	33	"
S	Giuditta Frank	294	cobbler	53	"
T	Giuditta Maria—†	294	housewife	52	"
U	Weidman Jennie—†	294	at home	27	"
V	Weidman Leslie	294	brakeman	26	"
W	Barnes Blanche—†	294	housewife	70	"
X	*Barnes George	294	retired	73	"
Y	Jensen Miller	294	watchman	58	23 Eutaw
Z	Birkeland Sverre B	295	laborer	45	New York
	628				
A	Tessa Frank	295	shoecutter	38	227 Princeton
B	Gannon Catherine E—†	296	clerk	35	here
C	Gannon May M—†	296	housewife	73	"
D	Gannon Timothy	296	florist	79	"
F	Faraci Joseph	297	painter	28	"
G	Hollen William	297	U S N	25	Ohio
K	Duffy Francis J	298	cashier	50	here
L	Noonan Dorothy—†	298	housewife	33	"
M	Noonan William	298	warehouse	37	"
R	*Martin Moses	299	carpenter	67	"
S	*Martin Sarah—†	299	housewife	61	"
N	Popeo Aida—†	299	typist	24	
O	Popeo Frank	299	musician	51	"
P	Popeo Matilda—†	299	housewife	56	"
T	Parker Linden E	300	undertaker	40	"
U	Rollins Emma C—†	300	at home	75	"
V	Murphy Charles C	300	machinist	52	"
W	Parsons Lillian M—†	300	at home	44	"
X	Parsons William S	300	machinist	52	16 Princeton
Y	Welsh Harry T	300	bartender	58	here

Morton Place

Z	*Muise John Z	1	retired	82	here
	629				
A	*Muise Lucien	1	painter	44	
B	Davis Catherine—†	1	at home	76	"
C	*Edmonds Sadie—†	2	housewife	52	"
D	*Edmonds William	2	laborer	60	
E	Carey Ellen—†	2	housewife	61	"

Morton Place—Continued

	F	Carey Norman P	2	U S A	26	here
	G	Carey Peter	2	machinist	67	"
	H	Peterson Mary—†	3	at home	77	"
	K	Francis Mary—†	3	"	77	

Princeton Street

	L	Barbanti Anna—†	4	operator	44	277 Meridian
	M	Harloff Nellie—†	4	waitress	39	here
	N	Harloff William	4	fisherman	33	"
	O	Comeau Arthur	7	carpenter	44	"
	P	Comeau Constance—†	7	housewife	35	"
	R*	Comeau Helen—†	7	"	40	"
	S	Comeau Wallace	7	fishcutter	40	6 Winthrop
	T	McCluskey Harold	7	boxmaker	31	here
	U	Norwell Sylvester	7	fishcutter	45	6 Winthrop
	V	Oxley Frank	7	watchman	65	Somerville
	W	Rutsky Abraham	7	pipefitter	45	here
	X	Rutsky Thomas	7	"	55	"
	Y	Vitilia Anthony	7	bartender	38	"
	Z	Bona Simon	9	fisherman	60	"
630						
	A	Doyle Robert	9	longshoreman	60	"
	B	Driscoll Frances—†	9	housewife	37	"
	C	Driscoll John	9	longshoreman	42	"
	D	Luther William	9	inspector	55	Rhode Island
	E	Wilkie William	9	shipfitter	42	here
	F	Burke John	10	retired	77	"
	G	Burke Sabina—†	10	housewife	75	"
	H	Synnott William H	10	retired	47	284 Meridian
	K	Courier Edward E	10	chauffeur	37	here
	L	Courier Elizabeth—†	10	housewife	35	"
	M	Pope George	11	U S A	24	141 Saratoga
	N	Pope Mary J—†	11	housewife	60	141 "
	O	Pope Thomas	11	U S A	30	141 "
	P	Gowdy George F	11	metalworker	41	here
	R	Gowdy Sarah M—†	11	housewife	59	"
	S	Robertson Ellen E—†	12	"	73	118 Princeton
	T	Crumley Anna—†	12	"	52	here
	U	Crumley Francis	12	shipfitter	22	"
	V	Crumley Leonard	12	U S A	23	"

Princeton Street—Continued

w	Clancy Edward A	12	longshoreman	37	here
x	Clancy Helen R—†	12	housewife	32	"
y	*Amero Lena—†	13	"	36	"
z	Amero William	13	carpenter	49	"
	631				
a	Iovanna Carmen	14	U S A	22	
b	Iovanna Charles	14	bartender	53	"
c	Waters Jennie R—†	14	housewife	62	"
d	Richard Ethel—†	14	"	32	"
e	Richard Harold	14	welder	33	
f	Gunning Catherine—†	15	housewife	63	"
g	Gunning Robert W	15	engineer	65	"
h	Muccio Lena—†	15	housewife	61	"
k	Muccio Salvatore	15	retired	68	
l	Cox John E	16	laborer	42	
m	Parsons William I	16	retired	83	
n	Goggin Adele—†	16	packer	34	
o	McCarthy Frances E—†	16	at home	49	"
p	Ambrose Olive—†	17	housewife	59	"
r	Lavoie John	17	machinist	61	"
s	Reardon Lawrence K	17	fireman	32	"
t	Sullivan Samuel	17	reporter	64	"
u	Barnacle Edward A	17	shipfitter	48	"
v	Barnacle Henry A	17	musician	38	"
w	Schwartz Annie—†	19	housewife	74	"
x	Schwartz George H	19	physician	52	"
y	O'Keefe Mary—†	19	housewife	38	"
z	O'Keefe Maurice J	19	policeman	47	"
	632				
a	Fitzpatrick Peter	19	fisherman	51	"
b	Hines Ashton	19	"	51	
c	*Hines Evangeline—†	19	housewife	40	"
d	*Nickerson Florence—†	19	at home	62	"
e	Fagan Bernard	19A	fisherman	63	"
f	St Croix Andrew	19A	rigger	59	
g	St Croix Elizabeth A—†	19A	housewife	53	"
h	Campbell Evelyn M—†	19A	"	47	
k	Campbell John W	19A	policeman	53	"
l	Campbell John W, jr	19A	U S A	29	
m	*Bennett Henry	19A	millhand	46	"
n	Ford Daniel	19A	carpenter	54	"

Page	Letter	Full Name	Residence, Jan. 1, 1945.	Occupation	Supposed Age.	Reported Residence, Jan. 1, 1944. Street and Number.

Princeton Street—Continued

Letter	Full Name	Residence, Jan. 1, 1945.	Occupation	Supposed Age.	Reported Residence, Jan. 1, 1944.
o	Ford Joseph L	19A	U S A	26	here
p	*Ford Mary E—†	19A	housewife	56	"
r	Powers Maurice F	20	electrician	43	"
s	Walker Arthur J	20	shoemaker	63	"
t	Walker Mary—†	20	housewife	66	"
u	Ewing Harriet—†	20	"	31	
v	Ewing Ronald	20	seaman	31	"
w	Avila Camillo	21	presser	50	
x	Avila Ida—†	21	clerk	23	
y	Avila Rose—†	21	housewife	47	"
z	Avila Rose—†	21	clerk	26	
	633				
a	Avila Samuel P	21	U S A	24	
b	Campagna Alfred	21	clerk	30	
c	Campagna Marie C—†	21	housewife	27	"
d	Briand Floretta—†	22	factoryhand	50	"
e	*Briand Joseph	22	fishcutter	60	"
f	Drake Albert J	22	"	61	
g	Drake Annie M—†	22	housewife	56	"
h	Drake Phillip J	22	seaman	25	"
k	Gillespie Mary—†	22	waitress	22	50 Prescott
l	Monihan Hannah—†	22	housewife	85	here
m	Smith John	22	fisherman	40	"
n	Snowdon Clarence V	22	guard	67	340 Meridian
o	Adams Willie S	23	lumberman	23	Maine
p	Camara Edward	23	machinist	30	New Bedford
r	Clouter George	23	retired	72	here
s	Cote Rene	23	seaman	29	"
t	Folden Walter E	23	cook	38	"
u	Hallett William E	23	laborer	20	Maine
v	O'Reilly John V	23	U S A	33	here
w	Russell Harold	23	seaman	40	New York
x	Solem Hans A	23	"	41	here
y	Walsh Thomas W	23	engineer	31	Wakefield
z	*White Margaret—†	23	housewife	53	here
	634				
a	Donnelly Joseph	24	foreman	50	Cambridge
b	LaMaroco Guy	24	retired	68	here
c	Malloy Harry	24	"	67	"
d	Maupas John	24	rigger	38	"
e	Maupas Phyllis—†	24	housewife	30	"

Page.	Letter.	FULL NAME.	Residence, Jan. 1, 1945.	Occupation.	Supposed Age.	Reported Residence, Jan. 1, 1944. Street and Number.

Princeton Street—Continued

	F	Richards Louis	24	laborer	25	here
	G	Smart Thomas	24	engineer	58	"
	H	Turco Mario	24	presser	41	"
	K	Delaney Elizabeth J—†	25	electrician	43	"
	L	Delaney Frank L	25	U S A	22	"
	M	Gardiner Edward	25	chauffeur	38	"
	N	Gardiner Jane E—†	25	housewife	80	"
	O	Gardiner Jefferson D	25	laborer	50	
	P	Gardiner John G	25	steamfitter	46	"
	R	Cann Jesse C	25	U S A	31	
	S	Cann Joseph S	25	steward	61	"
	T	Cann Sarepta—†	25	housewife	64	"
	U	DellaGrotta Albert	26	U S A	26	
	V	*DellaGrotta Josephine—†	26	housewife	73	"
	W	Mangenelli Mary—†	26	factoryhand	36	"
	X	Condakes George	26	U S A	21	
	Y	Condakes John	26	"	24	
	Z	Condakes Leo	26	salesman	20	"

635

	A	Condakes Nicholas	26	proprietor	57	"
	B	Condakes Pauline—†	26	bookkeeper	22	"
	C	Condakes Peter	26	merchant	62	"
	D	Condakes Stella—†	26	housewife	48	"
	E	Mazzarino Frances—†	26	finisher	54	"
	F	Mazzarino Joseph	26	teacher	31	"
	G	Mazzarino Pasquale	26	presser	57	
	H	Beninati Antonette—†	27	housewife	45	"
	K	Beninati Joseph	27	metalworker	58	"
	L	Beninati Mary—†	27	stitcher	26	"
	M	Beninati Rose—†	27	machinist	21	"
	N	Michaels Dorothy T—†	27	welder	24	Norwood
	O	Michaels George S	27	seaman	25	"
	P	Mondello James F	27	U S A	27	"
	R	Mondello Joan A—†	27	welder	22	"
	S	Cleary James	27	janitor	60	here
	T	Cleary Sadie—†	28	housewife	67	"
	U	King John	28	laborer	45	"
	V	King Margaret—†	28	housewife	43	"
	W	Connors Mary—†	28	"	42	
	X	Connors Stephen	28	chauffeur	45	"
	Z	Frizzell Helen—†	29	housewife	57	"

21

636
Princeton Street—Continued

A	Celano John	29	cabinetmaker	50	here
B	Celano Joseph	29	machinist	21	"
C	*Armstrong Ellen—†	29	housewife	38	"
D	Armstrong William P	29	rigger	42	"
E	Ferrera Eleanor—†	30	housewife	28	"
F	Ferrera Frank	30	carpenter	30	"
G	*Indingaro Rachel—†	30	housewife	58	"
H	Indingaro Samuel	30	hat cleaner	58	"
K	White Everett	31	carpenter	40	"
L	White Rose—†	31	housewife	28	"
M	Doucette Bertha L—†	31	"	54	
N	Doucette Dorothy A—†	31	clerk	23	
O	Doucette Edward C	31	laborer	21	"
P	Doucette Frederick M	31	woodworker	54	"
R	Doucette Frederick M, jr	31	U S A	27	"
S	Beninati Matti—†	32	housewife	36	"
T	Beninati Rocco	32	tailor	42	
U	Cimino Dominick	32	welder	27	
V	Cimino Georgiana—†	32	housewife	25	"
W	Kapolis Mary—†	32	factoryhand	20	103 Shawmut av
X	Andrews Thomas	33	baker	66	here
Y	Caruso Adam E	33	pipefitter	52	"
Z	Caruso Margaret T—†	33	housewife	46	"

637

A	*Dobrokhotoff Nicholas	33	baker	50	"
B	Masselli Frank	33	fishcutter	28	61 Everett
C	Tacelli Benjamin	33	retired	70	here
D	Fagot Frederick	33	U S C G	23	"
E	Dunn Ann—†	34	housewife	22	Somerville
F	Dunn Luke	34	U S A	27	"
G	McGrath Bridget—†	34	factoryhand	25	28 Princeton
H	McGrath William	34	U S A	31	Medford
K	Walsh Elias W	34	operator	20	28 Princeton
L	*Walsh Margaret—†	34	housewife	47	28 "
M	Tobin Martin L	34	rigger	43	here
N	Tobin Mary E—†	34	housewife	41	"
O	Askins Leo E	35	carpenter	65	"
P	Askins Margaret J—†	35	housewife	64	"
R	Beaulieu Raymond	35	machinist	54	"
S	Clark Mary—†	35	at home	65	"

22

T	*Clark Stella—†	35	at home	63	here
U	DeMasellis James	35	tailor	53	"
V	Gallagher Thomas	35	operator	56	"
W	Kelleher Cornelius	35	plumber	61	"
X	McCarthy Charles	35	engineer	33	"
Y	Pelosi Julio	35	machinist	30	"
Z	Reddy Edward	35	fisherman	59	"

638

A	Rotinno Victor	35	waiter	27	
B	Schwarz Clara—†	36	shipfitter	30	"
C	Schwarz William	36	supt	32	Winthrop
D	*Costigan Nora—†	36	housewife	46	here
E	Costigan Patrick	36	fisherman	47	"
F	Coombs Alexander	36	U S A	33	"
G	Coombs Mary—†	36	housewife	22	"
H	Braff Jacob	37	paper dealer	59	"
K	Hewey Leon N	37	guard	59	
L	Hewey Mildred H—†	37	housewife	54	"
M	Swimm Amaryllis—†	37	"	41	"
N	Swimm Herbert J	37	shipper	53	
O	Corrado Amelia—†	38	housewife	42	"
P	Corrado John	38	tree surgeon	48	"
R	Corrado Mary—†	38	packer	21	"
S	Hamilton Anna E—†	38	factoryhand	39	423 Saratoga
T	Hamilton Peter C	38	chauffeur	41	423 ".
U	*Maloney Christine—†	38	housewife	34	here
V	Maloney Patrick	38	fisherman	32	"
W	*Indica Carmello	39	shoemaker	51	13 Morris
X	Indica Josephine—†	39	stitcher	20	13 "
Y	*Indica Teresa—†	39	housewife	41	13 "
Z	Davidson Alma E—†	40	saleswoman	29	here

639

A	Davidson John J	40	pipefitter	38	"
B	Phillips Kate E—†	40	waitress	31	"
C	Spagnuolo Constantino	40	candymaker	50	"
D	Spagnuolo Evelyn—†	40	stitcher	23	565 Adams
E	Spagnuolo Olympia—†	40	housewife	53	here
F	Spagnuolo Quirino	40	U S A	25	"
F	Spagnuolo Carmen	40	carpenter	31	"
H	Spagnuolo Louise—†	40	housewife	27	"
K	Stevenson Estelle—†	41	at home	80	"

Princeton Street—Continued

	L	Stevenson Helen—†	41	at home	78	here
	M	Donaldson Albert	44	machinist	38	"
	N	Donaldson Mary—†	44	housewife	35	"
	O	Benner George F	46	retired	85	
	P	Greene Thomas	46	fisherman	42	"
	R	Karaglanes Nicholas	46	laborer	55	
	S	*Karasen Peter W	46	"	22	
	T	Lyons Reginald S	46	cook	60	"
	U	Staples George F	46	retired	84	117 Lexington
	V	Pearson Alfred	48	shipfitter	31	23 Eutaw
	W	Pearson Alice—†	48	housewife	30	23 "
	X	Indigaro Gabriel	48	carpenter	30	here
	Y	Indigaro Vera—†	48	housewife	28	"
	Z	Montague Laura J—†	48	caterer	65	"
640						
	A	Bradley Emily—†	50	housewife	45	"
	B	Bradley Frederick	50	electrician	45	"
	C	Bradley James	50	laborer	60	"
	D	Fielding Eileen—†	50	housewife	22	"
	E	Fielding Joseph	50	student	25	Everett
	F	Haynes Annie—†	50	housewife	48	Alabama
	G	Haynes Daniel C	50	engineer	43	"
	H	Crowell Arnold	54	seaman	43	here
	K	Crowell Mary—†	54	housewife	50	"
	L	McKinnon Sadie—†	54	waitress	60	"
	M	Melcher Florence—†	54	saleswoman	55	"
	N	Bergstrom Annie—†	56	housewife	55	"
	O	Bergstrom Harold N	56	electrician	40	"
	P	Bergstrom Regina V—†	56	factoryhand	28	"
	R	Brown Albert M	56	painter	40	30 Lexington
	S	Carroll John	56	machinist	60	here
	T	Haggert Paul	56	fisherman	59	"
	U	Nichols Earl	56	machinist	50	"
	V	Trunkett Gilbert	56	timekeeper	48	Lawrence
	W	*Trunkett Iva—†	56	saleswoman	34	"
	X	Ruddick Clarence P	58	shipwright	41	here
	Y	Ruddick Ethel—†	58	housewife	33	"
	Z	Marino Albert	58	fishcutter	24	"
641						
	A	*Marino Mary—†	58	housewife	67	"
	B	Arnoldson Madeline—†	60	nurse	33	

Page.	Letter.	FULL NAME.	Residence, Jan. 1, 1945.	Occupation.	Supposed Age.	Reported Residence, Jan. 1, 1944. Street and Number.

Princeton Street—Continued

c	Cavanaugh Elizabeth—†	60	housewife	58	here
d	Cavanaugh Mary—†	60	stenographer	20	"
e	Cavanaugh Patrick	60	rigger	62	"
f	Connors Ann—†	60	factoryhand	48	"
h	Faraci Charles	62	presser	29	"
k	Faraci Josephine—†	62	housewife	26	"
l	Faraci Angela—†	62	"	48	
m	Faraci James V	62	musician	22	"
n	Faraci Joseph	62	presser	55	··
o	*Caristo Assunta A—†	77	at home	70	"
p	*Giglio Carmella—†	77	housewife	59	38 Decatur
r	Giglio Charles P	77	U S A	24	38 "
s	*Giglio Frank	77	retired	70	38 "
t	Giglio Patrick	77	cutter	28	38 "
u	Theriault Joseph W	79	carpenter	40	here
v	Theriault Lena—†	79	housewife	38	"
w	Nicosia Arthur	81	shoeworker	23	341 Border
x	Nicosia Dorothy—†	81	housewife	25	341 "
y	Pasquariello Adeline—†	81	"	56	here
z	Pasquariello Olympia—†	81	bookkeeper	21	"
	642				
a	Agostino John	81	U S A	21	
b	Agostino Margaret—†	81	housewife	42	"
c	Agostino Nicholas	81	tailor	47	
d	Matheson Anna M—†	83	housewife	29	"
e	Matheson Neil E	83	foreman	38	"
f	Impemba Immaculata—†	83	housewife	45	"
g	Impemba John	83	shoemaker	47	"
h	Impemba Martin	83	U S A	21	
k	Precopio Catherine—†	87	housewife	22	"
l	Precopio Concetta—†	87	cook	36	
m	Precopio Frank	87	salesman	41	"
n	*Precopio Leo	87	retired	72	
o	Precopio Mario	87	electrician	38	"
p	Precopio Natale	87	foreman	29	"
r	Precopio Philomena—†	87	winder	39	"
s	Precopio Rocco	87	U S A	27	"
t	Precopio Vito	87	"	22	"
u	Freni Louis	89	pressman	29	14 Monmouth
v	Freni Mary—†	89	housewife	30	14 "
w	Calla Edith—†	89	"	25	Revere

Page	Letter	Full Name.	Residence, Jan. 1, 1945.	Occupation.	Supposed Age.	Reported Residence, Jan. 1, 1944. Street and Number.

Princeton Street—Continued

	x	Calla Orlando	89	welder	31	here
	y	Scarfo Geraldine—†	89	housewife	46	"
	z	Scarfo Nicolas	89	tailor	67	"
643						
	A	Giansircusa Nicola	91	laborer	45	
	B	*Giansircusa Paulina—†	91	housewife	76	"
	c	*Britton Minnie—†	93	at home	47	",
	D	Poirier Mary—†	93	housewife	61	"
	E	Poirier Wallace J	93	rigger	63	
	F	Pignato Dominic	93	laborer	62	
	G	*Pignato Josephine—†	93	housewife	55	"
	H	DeRosa James	93	chauffeur	28	"
	K	DeRosa Susan—†	93	housewife	28	"
	L	Danna Anna	rear 93	stitcher	34	"
	M	*Danna Grace—†	" 93	housewife	55	"
	N	Danna Josephine—†	" 93	shoeworker	22	"
	o	Danna Salvatore	" 93	U S A	25	"
	P	Danna Sebastian	" 93	"	31	
	R	*Alvarez Rose—†	95	stitcher	51	..
	s	Cointi Frank	95	U S A	30	..
	T	Cionti Josephine—†	95	housewife	54	"
	U	Cionti Mary—†	95	stitcher	20	"
	v	DiGirolamo Antonette—†	95	housewife	27	"
	w	DiGirolamo Joseph, jr	95	laborer	29	261 Border
	x	LaPorta Antonio	97	"	41	here
	y	LaPorta Louise C—†	97	housewife	38	"
	z	*LaPorta Pasquale	97	laborer	59	"
644						
	A	White Yolanda M—†	97	welder	29	54 Princeton
	B	Aiello Ignazea	101	laborer	50	here
	c	*Benvissuto Theresa—†	101	housewife	75	"
	D	Benvissuto Viola—†	101	"	29	"
	E	Benvissuto William T	101	machinist	31	"
	F	Pesaturo Angelina—†	103	housewife	50	"
	G	Pesaturo Emma—†	103	stitcher	30	"
	H	Pesaturo John	103	shoeworker	52	"
	K	Taurasi Agnes—†	103	stitcher	32	"
	L	*Taurasi Assunta—†	103	housewife	66	"
	M	Taurasi Malvina—†	103	stitcher	30	"
	N	Beath James A	105	machinist	59	"
	o	Willis Andrew	105	manager	38	"

Letter	Full Name	Residence, Jan. 1, 1945.	Occupation	Supposed Age	Reported Residence, Jan. 1, 1944. Street and Number.
P	Willis Christine—†	105	housewife	36	here
R	Brown Beverley J—†	105	SPAR	22	"
S	Brown Ethel M—†	105	housewife	52	"
T	Brown Harold R	105	seaman	57	"
U	Brown Harold R	105	U S A	27	
V	Brown Robert N	105	U S N	20	
W	*Tacelli Carmela—†	107	housewife	77	"
X	Tacelli Edith—†	107	clerk	34	
Y	Tacelli Joseph	107	machinist	74	"
Z	Tacelli William J	107	clerk	39	

645

Letter	Full Name	Residence, Jan. 1, 1945.	Occupation	Supposed Age	Reported Residence, Jan. 1, 1944. Street and Number.
A	Tacelli Arthur	107	"	40	
B	Tacelli Grace M—†	107	housewife	28	"
C	Tacelli Stella M—†	107	"	41	
D	Butler Alice—†	109	waitress	23	"
E	Butler Margaret—†	109	housewife	66	"
F	Butler Thomas	109	U S N	27	"
G	Chaoes Hester—†	109	candymaker	65	Somerville
H	Carney William	109	laborer	50	here
K	*Jackman Gerald	109	fisherman	42	"
L	*Ryan Lawrence	109	"	50	190 Sumner
M	*Toomey William	109	"	43	here
N	Randall Margaret—†	109	machinist	24	"
O	Randall Robert	109	U S N	27	Greenfield
P	Serra Joseph P	111	carpenter	31	here
R	Serra Mary O—†	111	housewife	32	"
S	Preziosi Americo	111	meatcutter	25	"
T	Preziosi Andrew	111	"	32	
U	Preziosi Angelo	111	"	57	
V	Preziosi Columbia—†	111	housewife	52	"
W	Preziosi John J	111	meatcutter	27	"
X	Barranco Agostino	113	laborer	64	
Y	Barranco Charles	113	U S N	26	
Z	*Barranco Sadie—†	113	housewife	55	"

646

Letter	Full Name	Residence, Jan. 1, 1945.	Occupation	Supposed Age	Reported Residence, Jan. 1, 1944. Street and Number.
A	Barranco Samuel	113	mechanic	25	"
B	Barranco Frank	113	U S N	32	"
C	Barranco Mary—†	113	housewife	35	"
D	DeSantis Ida—†	113	teacher	28	
E	DeSantis Vito	113	pressman	66	"
F	Carrozza James G	115	U S A	22	

27

Princeton Street—Continued

G	Carrozza John A	115	U S N	21	here
H	Carrozza Philip	115	mason	55	"
K	Carrozza Philomena—†	115	housewife	54	"
L	D'Alto Josephine C—†	115	"	29	
M	D'Alto Sabino	115	electrician	30	"
N	Hunter Lettie—†	117	clerk	50	
O	D'Alto Dominic	117	machinist	31	"
P	D'Alto Rose M—†	117	housewife	30	"
R	Bickley Alma M—†	117	"	49	
S	Bickley Joseph W	117	engineer	45	"
T	Goglia Anna—†	119	housewife	22	"
U	Goglia Julian	119	U S N	23	
V	Ventie Mary—†	119	housewife	36	"
W	Ventie Rocco	119	caretaker	41	"
X	Pelrine Agnes T—†	121	housewife	54	"
Y	Pelrine Edward M	121	laborer	59	"
Z	Pelrine Eleanor R—†	121	operator	24	"
	647				
A	Pelrine Genevieve—†	121	saleswoman	20	"
B	Pelrine Theresa M—†	121	operator	22	"
C	Delehanty Annie—†	121	at home	78	"
D	Delehanty John	121	clerk	54	
E	Frevold Eleanor M—†	123	housewife	30	"
F	Frevold Stanley O	123	painter	30	
G	Maglio Ermenia—†	123	housewife	50	"
H	Maglio Frank	123	shoeworker	48	"
K	Maglio Mary C—†	123	clerk	24	
L	Maglio Michael	123	U S A	23	
M	Paglialonga Domenico	123	laborer	49	"
N	Rotondo Anna—†	125	stitcher	43	"
O*	Rotondo Calogera—†	125	housewife	69	"
P	Rotondo Nellie—†	125	stitcher	31	"
R	Rotondo Rosario	125	retired	74	"
S	Hanel Mary—†	125	housewife	27	67 W Eagle
T	Hanel Roland H	125	fireman	27	67 "
U	Abramo Louis	125	U S A	25	here
V	Abramo Mary—†	125	housewife	22	"
W	Castone Florence—†	125	"	26	"
X	Patti Andrew	125	mechanic	24	"
Y*	Patti Rose—†	125	housewife	47	"
Z	Driscoll Patrick	127	retired	65	

Page	Letter	Full Name.	Residence, Jan. 1, 1945.	Occupation.	Supposed Age.	Reported Residence, Jan. 1, 1944. Street and Number.

648

Princeton Street—Continued

	A	Pecora Antonetta—†	127	housewife	24	here
	B	Pecora Joseph	127	U S A	27	"
	C	Pecora William	127	U S N	22	"
	D	Rubbico Silvio	127	manager	28	
	E*	Rubbico Theresa—†	127	housewife	55	"
	F	Heeck Margaret—†	127	at home	72	"
	G	Schroeder Mary—†	127	"	69	
	H	Moore Jennie—†	131	"	69	"
	K	DelCore Alice †—†	131	WAVE	29	
	L	DelCore Bettina—†	131	housewife	56	"
	M	DelCore Pasqulido E	131	U S A	31	"
	N	Murray Mary A—†	133	at home	78	"
	O	DeDeo Gwemma—†	133	clerk	34	"
	P	DeDeo el Leonard	133	retired	70	"
	R	DeDeo rg Violet—†	133	stenographer	37	"

Saratoga Place

	T	DeSc	1	longshoreman	38	here
	U*	DeS breza Louis	1	housewife	35	"
	V	Lop oreza Mary—†	1	"	25	"

649

Saratoga Street

	K	Ma N	9	housewife	37	here
	L	Ma Vlone Helen—†	9	operator	46	"
	M	Car A lone Thomas J	9	janitor	63	"
	N	Day ter Samuel	9	stenographer	24	"
	O	Day Jo Edith A—†	9	waitress	58	"
	P	Mat Jol Jennie—†	9	presser	23	4 Trenton
	R	Mat ose arese Anthony	9	U S A	25	4 "
	S*	Matiky arese James	9	housewife	52	4 "
	T	Matiky arese Jennie—†	9	U S A	21	4 "
	U	Muisd V arese Vito	11	laborer	20	45 Saratoga
	V	Muisd We Kenneth L	11	housewife	40	45 "
	W	Muisohn e Margaret—†	11	cook	43	45 "
	X	Barryson e Raymond J	13	housewife	43	here
	Y	Barry Mari Adelaide—†	13	boilermaker	49	"
	Z	Bois Ma Joseph X Beatrice A—†	13	cashier	44	"

29

650

Saratoga Street—Continued

A	Bois John	13	custodian	47	here
B	Crochetiere Alice—†	13	at home	69	"
C	August Albina—†	15	housewife	49	Chelsea
D	August Anna C—†	15	operator	25	"
E	August Joseph	15	accountant	54	"
F	Goff Jane—†	15	housewist	50	here
G	Goff Leo	15	cashier	50	"
H	Goff Leo, jr	15	U S A	28	"
K	Ferriani Dante	17	machinist	34	"
L	Ferriani Eva—†	17	housewife	23	"
M	Ricci Anna P—†	17	sorter	3	"
N	Ricci Anthony	17	laborer		
O	Ricci Josephine—†	17	housewife	5	"
P	Ricci Mary—†	17	hairdresser	24	"
R	Ricci Michael	17	U S A	27	
S	Langone Joseph	19	guard	31	
T	Langone Margaret—†	19	housewife	31	
U	DiCocco Angelina—†	19	inspector	23	
V	DiCocco Anthony	19	welder	24	
W	DiCocco Joseph	19	chipper	57	"
X	DiCocco Loretta—†	19	cementer	29	"
Y	DiCocco Rita—†	19	housewife	46	"
Z	Irvin Mary E—†	20	at home	69	35 W J Kelly sq

651

A	*Burke Georgiana—†	20	housewife	45	her
B	Burke James D	20	laborer	45	"
C	Bennett Mary—†	20	at home	74	1 Mmouth
D	Cooper Morris A	21	pipefitter	31	340 eridian
E	Cooper Philomena—†	21	housewife	25	340
F	Bonafine Sandra—†	21	at home	25	her
G	Lovetere John	21	baker	51	"
H	Lovetere Josephine—†	21	housewife	37	"
K	Iverstrom Freda—†	22	"	66	
L	Iverstrom Frithof	22	engineer	75	
M	Alexander Maude—†	22	housewife	71	
N	Fougere Cornelius	22	cleaner	38	
O	Fougere Lena—†	22	housewife	55	
R	Lowell Alice M—†	25	operator	37	
S	Lowell Bridget—†	25	housewife	60	
T	Lowell Harold J	25	U S A	24	

Saratoga Street—Continued

	U	Lowell James R	25	U S A	39	here
	V	O'Brien Edward A	25	retired	65	"
	W	O'Brien Herbert J	25	U S A	25	"
	X	Cardullo Margaret—†	26	housewife	37	"
	Y	Cardullo Thomas	26	warehouse	40	"
	Z	Marino Adele—†	26	clerk	29	
652						
	A	*Marino Amedeo	26	retired	63	
	B	Marino Anthony	26	U S A	33	
	C	*Marino Jennie—†	26	housewife	64	"
	D	Marino Josephine—†	26	"	25	"
	F	Carrado Carl	27	chauffeur	31	"
	G	Carrado Eleanor—†	27	housewife	31	"
	H	Keough Edward W	28	U S A	33	..
	K	Keough Helen G—†	28	housewife	55	"
	L	Kratenberg George	28	porter	50	
	M	Lingren Carl	28	engineer	63	"
	N	Massa Joseph	28	mechanic	55	"
	O	Volkman Berthold	28	toolmaker	56	"
	P	Winston James F	28	U S A	48	
	R	Guarini Anthony	30	engineer	33	"
	S	Guarini Vincenza—†	30	housewife	30	"
	T	Ferro Carmela—†	30	"	44	..
	U	Ferro Carmela—†	30	operator	23	"
	V	Ferro Frances—†	30	"	27	
	W	Ferro John	30	painter	50	"
	X	Ferro Nancy—†	30	operator	24	"
	Y	Ferro Vincent	30	U S A	21	
	Z	Lasco Anna—†	31	housewife	36	"
653						
	A	Lasco Joseph	31	barber	38	"
	B	Souza John	32	shipfitter	37	11 Princeton
	C	Shea Joseph P	32	orderly	45	New York
	D	Tekulsky Anna H—†	34	housewife	38	here
	E	Tekulsky Jacob	34	agent	40	"
	G	Barnard Verna—†	36	housewife	54	32 Saratoga
	H	Barnard William	36	watchman	44	32 "
	K	Moss John	36	laborer	38	32 "
	L	Henderson Stella—†	36	housekeeper	65	701 Mass av
	M	Holm Marie—†	38	housewife	50	here
	N	Graves Mabel F—†	41	at home	52	"

Saratoga Street—Continued

o	Grattage Edith—†	41	operator	31	Rhode Island
p	Grattage Wilbur	41	U S N	29	23 Follen
r	Hayes Edna—†	41	housewife	29	226 Saratoga
s	Bugely Doris—†	42	social worker	24	Connecticut
t	Hepburn Helen—†	42	"	33	Medford
u	Bickford Edwin	43	custodian	69	here
v	Bickford Lillian—†	43	at home	62	"
w	Bickford Mabel—†	43	"	56	"
x	Cerrone Antonio	43	painter	59	
y	Cerrone Eleanor—†	43	clerk	20	"
z	Cerrone Frances—†	43	housewife	58	"
	654				
a	Cerrone Prudence—†	43	dressmaker	31	"
b	Cerrone Joseph C	43	U S N	29	
c	Cerrone Mary—†	43	operator	27	"
d	Cerrone Phyllis—†	43	stenographer	24	"
e	McCarthy Ellen L—† rear	43	at home	75	"
f	Sullivan Mary T—† "	43	housekeeper	55	"
g	McGrath Mabel—† "	43	waitress	52	"
h	Mullen Francis "	43	U S A	26	
k	Salerno Louis	44	physician	55	"
l	Salerno Pasqualina—†	44	housewife	73	"
m	Martell Florence J—†	44	"	50	
n	Martell Howard D	44	watchman	55	"
o	D'India Albert	45	machinist	29	"
p	D'India Margaret—†	45	housewife	28	"
r	Francis Ellen—†	45	"	30	260 Paris
s	Francis George	45	gaugemaker	29	260 "
t	Staropoli Joseph	45	laborer	51	here
u	Staropoli Josephine—†	45	housewife	41	"
v	Staropoli Michael	45	U S N	22	"
w	Nicastro Anna—†	46	clerk	32	
x	Nicastro Mary—†	46	housewife	54	"
y	Nicastro Michael	46	machinist	58	"
z	Nicastro Michael, jr	46	U S A	20	
	655				
a	Nicastro Rocco	46	..	27	
b	Nicastro Samuel	46	"	24	
c	Goudet Eli	46	fisherman	53	"
d	Jones Clara—†	46	cook	53	
e	Jones Thomas	46	U S A	28	

32

Page.	Letter.	FULL NAME.	Residence, Jan. 1, 1945.	Occupation.	Supposed Age.	Reported Residence, Jan. 1, 1944. Street and Number.

Saratoga Street--Continued

F	DeRuosi Joseph	47	clerk	29	here
G	DeRuosi Mary—†	47	housewife	28	"
H	Catizone Alfred	47	machinist	25	"
K	Catizone Jennie—†	47	housewife	24	"
L	Principe Albert	47	machinist	54	"
M	Principe Celia—†	47	housewife	47	"
N	Principe Frank	47	U S A	20	
O	Boland Celia—†	48	housewife	54	"
P	Boland John	48	laborer	59	
R	Boland John, jr	48	U S A	24	..
S	Boland Stephen	48	"	27	
T	Hearn Ronald	48	"	40	..
U	Faretra Ann—†	49	housewife	29	"
V	Faretra Thomas	49	machinist	31	"
W	Mallett Jeremiah	49A	carpenter	70	"
X	Mallett Josephine—†	49A	housewife	63	"
Y	Mallett Robert	49A	carpenter	37	"
Z	Mallett Yvonne—†	49A	clerk	21	

656

C	Alves Gertrude I—†	49A	at hone	24	"
D	Alves Jesse J	49A	chauffeur	48	"
E	Alves John J	49A	U S A	28	
A	D'Eon Nathan	49A	fishcutter	36	"
B	D'Eon Pauline—†	49A	housewife	29	"
F	Burke Elizabeth I—†	51	"	39	
G	Burke George R	51	chauffeur	42	"
H	Rampon John	51	pipefitter	33	"
K	Rampon Lydia A—†	51	housewife	25	"
L	O'Connell Anna—†	52	"	27	83 Morris
M	O'Connell Paul	52	pipefitter	27	83 "
N	Ciampa Filomena—†	52	housewife	34	here
O	Ciampa Joseph	52	manufacturer	35	"
P	Miller Catherine H—†	56	housewife	50	"
R	Miller Eileen M—†	56	clerk	24	
S	Miller Harry	56	laborer	54	"
T	Miller Lorraine R—†	56	saleswoman	22	"
U	Gonis Peter	56	proprietor	46	"
V	*Gonis Rose—†	56	housewife	42	"
W	Famiglietti Alfred R	56	U S A	29	
X	Famiglietti Antonetta—†	56	housewife	54	"
Y	Famiglietti Joseph A	56	U S A	32	

1—6

Saratoga Street—Continued

z	Famiglietti Mary H—†	56	secretary	31	here
	657				
A	Famiglietti Raffael	56	proprietor	64	"
B	Murphy John F	57	fisherman	39	"
C	Murphy Rita J—†	57	housewife	52	"
D	Luongo Angelina C—†	57	"	57	
E	Luongo Jennie—†	57	clerk	21	"
F	Luongo Michael A	57	painter	55	
G	Luongo Pasquale A	57	"	33	
H	Martella Rose—†	59	at home	24	"
K	Martella Vincenzo	59	candymaker	62	"
L	Italiano Ida—-†	59	housewife	28	"
M	Italiano Salvatore V	59	pipefitter	29	"
N	Pearson Alfred E	59	policeman	54	"
O	Pearson Edward J	59	metalworker	27	"
P	Pearson Josephine—†	59	housewife	49	"
R	Giangregorio Anthony	61	chauffeur	27	Chelsea
S	Giangregorio Lillian—†	61	housewife	27	"
T	Giangregorio Carmela—†	61	"	54	"
U	Giangregorio Dante	61	agent	64	
V	Giangregorio Laurence V	61	clerk	32	
W	Giangregorio Luigi	61	U S A	20	"
X	Manning Alice G—†	63	factoryhand	28	here
Y	Manning Blanche G—†	63	"	48	"
Z	Miraglia Ruth M—†	63	housewife	25	"
	658				
A	West Albert	65	attorney	35	"
B	West Ann F—†	65	housewife	58	"
C	Reddy Joanna M—†	65	"	71	
D	Blake Nora A—†	67	cleaner	64	
E	Flanagan Estelle M—†	67	housewife	26	"
F	Martin Edward T	67	U S M C	25	"
G	Martin Mary A—†	67	housewife	63	"
H	Martin Mary A—†	67	secretary	28	"
K	Martin Thomas	67	engineer	66	"
L	Martin William J	67	U S N	22	
M	Apenas Christopher	69	ironworker	52	"
N	Hogan Eugene	69	retired	71	"
O	Jarvis Charles H	69	guard	63	166 Brooks
P	Peretti Ottino	69	painter	64	here
R	Walsh John	69	retired	72	"

s	Whitton Alfred J	69	carpenter	51	Clinton
t	Whitton Annie—†	69	housewife	41	"
u	Whitton Harriet—†	69	"	69	here
v	Whitton William I	69	guard	71	"
w	Cooper Joseph	71	pipefitter	28	"
x	Cooper Sara—†	71	housewife	23	"
y	Carnavale Edna—†	71	factoryhand	38	"
z	*Carnavale Frank	71	barber	40	

659

a	*Carnavale Salvatore	71	shoeworker	52	"
b	Mazzie Anthony	71	laborer	50	"
c	Mazzie Eleanor T—†	71	factoryhand	22	"
d	*Mazzie Rose S—†	71	housewife	48	"
f	Doucette Joseph G	75	longshoreman	36	426 Chelsea
g	Doucette Mildred V—†	75	housewife	33	426 "
l	Young Elizabeth—†	102	at home	21	226 Lexington
m	Young Margaret—†	102	housewife	44	226 "
n	Young Stanley	102	cleaner	48	226 "
o	Young Wilfred	102	U S A	23	226 "
p	Burke Arthur P	102	"	27	here
r	Burke Clarence	102	laborer	43	"
s	Burke Elmer	102	U S A	34	"
t	Burke Florence—†	102	at home	26	"
u	Burke Isabella S—†	102	housewife	67	"
v	Burke Marion—†	102	packer	31	"
w	Derome Annie—†	104	housewife	52	"
x	Derome Arthur L	104	painter	51	
y	Derome Arthur P	104	U S A	24	
z	Picco Celia—†	106	housewife	29	"

660

a	Picco Harold	106	fisherman	42	"
b	Walsh Mary—†	106	housewife	21	"
c	Walsh Patrick J	106	U S A	29	
d	Cerundolo Mary—†	106	housewife	43	"
e	Cerundolo Salvatore	106	laborer	48	
f	Morrissey Catherine—†	110	at home	38	"
g	Moriarty Edward	110	U S A	20	
h	Moriarty Gertrude—†	110	typist	23	
k	Moriarty Julia—†	110	"	29	
l	Moriarty Mary—†	110	housewife	58	"
m	Moriarty William	110	U S N	27	

Page.	Letter.	FULL NAME.	Residence, Jan. 1, 1945.	Occupation.	Supposed Age.	Reported Residence, Jan. 1, 1944. Street and Number.
	N	Barcardax Peter	114	fisherman	49	here
	O	Brennan Catherine A—†	114	housekeeper	71	"
	P	Donovan Peter	114	letter carrier	51	109 Maverick
	R	Greenbaum Joseph G	114	engineer	51	here
	S	Jackson William	114	cutter	63	"
	T	Smith Louis F	114	chauffeur	41	"
	U	Smith Mary C—†	114	housewife	37	"
	V	Viola Albert	114	machinist	46	"
	W	*Pate Lucy—†	116	housewife	44	Canada
	X	Pate Malcolm H	116	fisherman	39	49A Saratoga
	Y	Mann Elizabeth—†	116	clerk	40	here
	Z	Mann Henry C	116	proprietor	76	"
661						
	A	Mann Minna G—†	116	housewife	70	"
	B	Cardinale James	120	chauffeur	32	"
	C	Cardinale Mary—†	120	housewife	32	"
	D	Leventhal Jacob	120	proprietor	57	"
	E	*Leventhal Sarah—†	120	housewife	56	"
	F	Halloran Ambrose	122	longshoreman	63	"
	G	Halloran Mary—†	122	housewife	63	"
	H	Lavell Anna J—†	122	clerk	33	
	K	Lee Thomas	122	fishhandler	62	"
	L	Reagan John	122	laborer	45	
	M	Bruno Marlin—†	126	housewife	30	"
	N	Bruno Philip	126	auditor	31	"
	O	Matson Gustaf	126	retired	68	"
	P	Barone John	130	rubberworker	34	"
	R	Barone Rose—†	130	housewife	31	"
	S	D'Amico Louise—†	130	"	41	
	T	D'Amico William	130	U S A	22	"
	U	Casey Albert P	130	"	24	21 Saratoga
	V	Casey Marie—†	130	housewife	22	21 "
	W	Paolini Anthony	134	chauffeur	36	here
	X	Paolini Mildred—†	134	housewife	28	"
	Y	Placet Adeline—†	134	stitcher	37	"
	Z	Placet Armand	134	molder	37	
662						
	A	Cardoza Ferdinand	134	foreman	44	73 Morris
	B	Cardoza Helen—†	134	housewife	40	73 "
	C	Giusti Grace—†	136	bookkeeper	21	here

36

Saratoga Street—Continued

D	Giusti Jennie—†	136	housewife	44	here
E	Giusti Joseph	136	pedler	51	"
F	Russo Anthony	136	U S A	29	"
G	Russo Jennie—†	136	housewife	23	"
H	Harris Frances—†	136	"	43	
K	Harris Richard	136	U S A	21	
L	Harris Timothy	136	machinist	42	"
M	Lerro Anna—†	136	housewife	53	"
N	Lerro Josephine—†	136	clerk	30	
O	Lerro Philip	136	U S A	20	
P	Lerro Vito	136	machinist	51	"
R	Heard Celestine—†	140	operator	31	"
S	Russo Gaetano	140	cutter	61	
T	Russo Jennie—†	140	chipper	33	"
U	Russo Stefana—†	140	housewife	60	"
V	Lino Frances—†	140	"	28	
W	Lino Louis	140	mechanic	30	"
X	Catanese Mary—†	140	housewife	29	Medford
Y	Catanese Peter	140	presser	30	"
Z	Gianurio Gabriel	144	cook	39	here
	663				
A	Gianurio Mary—†	144	housewife	34	"
B	Dantona Francis	144	chipper	38	"
C	*Dantona Maria—†	144	at home	70	"
D	Dantona Mary—†	144	housewife	36	"
F	DiCocco Adelcho	146	welder	27	146 Trenton
G	DiCocco Rita—†	146	housewife	22	146 "
H	Romano Anna S—†	146	shoeworker	20	127 Princeton
K	Romano Felice	146	cutter	25	12 Lewis
L	Dugas Concetta—†	146	housewife	42	here
M	Dugas Walter E	146	carpenter	44	"
N	Zuccala Angelina—†	148	housewife	30	14 Pompeii
O	Zuccala Michael	148	mechanic	30	14 "
P	Altri Frank	148	metalworker	37	166 Bennington
R	Altri Rose—†	148	housewife	32	166 "
S	LaRosa Rosàrio	150	retired	71	here
V	Davis Betty—†	156	stitcher	34	"
W	Davis Claude	156	U S N	30	Illinois
X	*Moggi Umberto	156	laborer	65	here
Y	Gontodonato Alfred	158	shipper	20	"

Saratoga Street—Continued

z		Gontodonato Camille—†	158	housewife	57	here
	664					
A		Gontodonato Eleanor—†	158	operator	21	"
B		Gontodonato Luigi	158	maintenance	61	"
C		Gontodonato Maria—†	158	secretary	26	"
D		Gontodonato Joseph	158	estimator	35	"
E		Gontodonato Louise—†	158	housewife	32	"
F		Cannon Cornelius S	160	chauffeur	56	"
G		Cannon John J	160	manager	61	"
H		Cannon Mary E—†	160	at home	69	"
K		Todisco Mildred—†	162	housewife	39	203 Saratoga
L		Todisco Pasquale	162	supervisor	38	203 "
M		Winston Thomas P	162	chauffeur	42	203 "
O		Carberry Irene—†	174	housewife	41	here
P		Carberry Patrick	174	U S N	38	"
R		Hartnett Mary—†	174	at home	60	300 Beacon
S		Cobb Mabel—†	174	"	62	here

William J Kelly Square

Y		McCormack Winifred—†	27	at home	73	here
z		Flynn Helen—†	27	waitress	41	"
	665					
A		Flynn Helen—†	27	saleswoman	22	"
B		Flynn William W	27	U S A	23	"
D		McKay Mary C—†	27	at home	48	"
E		Deering John	27	laborer	42	"
F		Deering Katherine—†	27	housewife	75	"
G		Deering Michael	27	laborer	37	"
N		Cleary John	35	retired	79	Long Island
O		Desmond Edward	35	bartender	55	here
P		Gardner Edward	35	retired	51	"
R		Gorman James	35	"	65	443 Meridian
S		Hall John	35	machinist	52	here
T		Harkins John	35	calker	50	"
U		Harkins Margaret—†	35	housewife	47	"
V		Lawlor Edward	35	painter	35	
W		MacDonald Lena—†	35	waitress	30	"
X		McCormack Walter	35	painter	42	"
Y		Nazzaro James	35	"	42	"
z		Thomas William	35	retired	81	23 Saratoga

Ward 1–Precinct 7

CITY OF BOSTON

LIST OF RESIDENTS
20 YEARS OF AGE AND OVER

(NON-CITIZENS INDICATED BY ASTERISK)
(FEMALES INDICATED BY DAGGER)

AS OF

JANUARY 1, 1945

THOMAS F. SULLIVAN, *Chairman*
FREDERIC E. DOWLING, *Secretary*
WILLIAM A. MOTLEY, JR.
FRANCIS B. McKINNEY
EVERETT R. PROUT
Listing Board.

CITY OF BOSTON PRINTING DEPARTMENT

700
Border Street

A	Sousa Mary—†	275	housewife	43	here
B	Sousa Peter	275	laborer	50	"
C	Aia Mary—†	275	housewife	50	"
D	Aia Michael	275	laundryman	08	"
E	Dickinson John E	305	machinist	57	"
G	Hazelton Harry	319	"	61	26 Concord sq
H	Walker Edna L—†	319	waitress	49	26 "
K	King Clifford	319	U S A	20	here
L	King Florence—†	319	housewife	42	"
M	King John	319	chauffeur	42	"
N	King John, jr	319	U S N	22	"
O	Zimmer Ernest	319	laborer	29	373 Border
P	Broomstein Minnie—†	321	at home	25	Framingham
R	Davenport Carmella—†	321	housewife	25	here
S	Lehman Theresa—†	321	"	22	"
T	Adams Dorothy—†	321	",	28	"
U	Adams Gerald	321	U S A	30	
V	Oxley Edith—†	321	housewife	57	"
W	Oxley Lloyd N	321	U S A	26	
X	Oxley Marie—†	321	examiner	22	"
Y	Oxley Ralph A	321	engineer	55	"
Z	Imparato Ciro	321	machinist	51	"

701

A	Imparato Mary—†	321	housewife	43	"
B	DeSenza Doris—†	323	"	25	497 Sumner
C	DeSenza Nicholas	323	U S N	34	497 "
D	Duffy Francis	323	U S A	22	here
E	Duffy Maude—†	323	housewife	49	"
F	Duffy William P	323	steamfitter	51	"
G	Duffy William P, jr	323	U S A	25	
H	Burns Gerald F	323	motorman	47	"
K	Burns Lillian M—†	323	housewife	46	"
L	White Marion—†	323	"	22	"

Brooks Street

M	Carmen Israel	116	storekeeper	51	here
N	Carmen Sarah—†	116	housewife	45	"
O	Sampson Alfred N	116	engineer	70	168 Princeton
P	Sampson Francis	116	electrician	20	168 "

2

Brooks Street—Continued

R	Sampson Mary—†	116	housewife	57	168 Princeton
S	DeDonato Arthur	118	U S A	20	here
T	DeDonato Joseph	118	machinist	46	"
U	DeDonato Mary—†	118	housewife	46	"
V	*Capozzi James	120	retired	77	
W	D'Apice Ciriaco	120	laborer	61	
X	D'Apice Jeanette—†	120	operator	31	"
Y	*D'Apice Mary—†	120	housewife	55	"
Z	Hulke Benjamin, jr	122	policeman	48	"

702

A	Hulke Donald B	122	U S A	20	"
B	Hulke Florence—†	122	housewife	42	"
C	Campbell Clinton D	126	seaman	54	
D	Campbell Savilla J—†	126	housewife	52	"
E	Keane Mary F—†	127	housekeeper	60	"
F	McDonnell Alfonso J	127	pipefitter	38	"
G	McDonnell Mary H—†	127	housewife	34	"
H	Peterson Marion—†	127	clerk	40	"
K	Splaine John	128	laborer	58	
L	Splaine Mary—†	128	housewife	59	"
N	Sorenson Andrew	129	fisherman	56	"
O	Sorenson Arnold S	129	U S A	25	
P	Sorenson Arthur	129	laborer	22	
R	Sorenson Bernt	129	U S A	24	..
S	Murphy Elizabeth D—†	130	at home	78	"
U	DiYoung Louise—†	131	"	76	..
V	Tripe Felice—†	131	housewife	40	"
W	Tripe Joseph	131	laborer	50	.
X	Tripe Phyllis—†	131	operator	22	"
Y	Tripe Virginia—†	131	"	20	
Z	Piscone Rose—†	131	at home	23	"

703

A	DiGirolamo Dorothy—†	133	dressmaker	30	"
B	DiGirolamo Erminio	133	tailor	59	
C	*DiGirolamo Mary—†	133	housewife	68	"
D	LaMotta Leonardi	133	stevedore	44	"
E	LaMotta Michael	133	"	46	"
F	Leonard Alice—†	135	housewife	32	174 Princeton
G	Leonard Frank E	135	U S A	34	174 "
H	Fogg Lena—†	135	housewife	92	here
K	Cardinale Florence—†	137	at home	82	60 Lubec

Brooks Street—Continued

L	Rabasco Ann—†	137	saleswoman	23	here
M	Rabasco Canio	137	retired	27	"
N	Rabasco Josephine—†	137	housewife	45	"
O	Rabasco Pasquale	137	machinist	56	"
P	Faber Andrew J	139	shipfitter	65	"
R	Faber John A	139	joiner	29	
S	Faber John T	139	machinist	60	"
T	Faber Mary—†	139	housewife	60	"
U	Bonzey Charles H	140	laborer	68	N Hampshire
V	Bonzey Charles M	140	baker	49	here
W	Bonzey Theresa M—†	140	housewife	47	"
X	Huggan Mary R—†	144	at home	55	"
Y	Ryder Grace M—†	144	organist	59	"
Z	Smith Lillian A—†	144	housewife	53	"
	704				
A	Swett Robert W	144	technician	63	"
B	Sirignano Arthur	146	chauffeur	23	"
C	*Sirignano Frances—†	146	housewife	23	"
D	Vitale Joseph	146	barber	56	
E	*Vitale Rose—†	146	housewife	45	"
F	Keough Anita—†	146	"	23	
G	Keough Charles	146	U S N	26	
H	Hyslop James	147	laborer	74	
K	*Hyslop Serena—†	147	housewife	70	"
L	Beattie Ruth—†	147	inspector	21	"
M	Beattie Theresa—†	147	stitcher	50	"
N	Hyslop Caroline—†	147	housewife	49	"
O	Hyslop Harold J	147	laborer	50	"
P	Anderson Hans	148	fisherman	50	"
R	Bergh Axel	148	clergyman	70	"
S	Bergh Inga—†	148	housewife	68	"
T	Baker Frederick	149	clerk	73	
U	Ring Nora T—†	149	housekeeper	65	"
V	Driscoll Catherine—†	149	housewife	77	"
W	Hodgens Francis	149	welder	31	
X	Hodgens Mary K—†	149	housewife	35	"
Y	*Chapman Fannie—†	151	storekeeper	48	"
Z	Freda Charles	151	chauffeur	31	"
	705				
A	Freda Ethel—†	151	housewife	32	"
B	D'Avolio Michael	153	painter	51	33 Chelsea

Page.	Letter.	FULL NAME.	Residence, Jan. 1, 1945.	Occupation.	Supposed Age.	Reported Residence, Jan. 1, 1944. Street and Number.

Brooks Street—Continued

	c	D'Avolio Michael, jr	153	U S A	23	33 Chelsea
	d	D'Avolio Sylvia—†	153	housewife	43	33 "
	e	Villanucci Anna—†	153	clerk	21	Lynn

Eutaw Street

	f	Lyon Arnold	19	electrician	34	here
	g	*Lyon Evanell—†	19	housewife	35	"
	h	McGray Agnes—†	19	clerk	31	90 Lexington
	k	McGray Charles	19	fireman	53	90 "
	l	McGray Dorcas—†	19	housewife	52	90 "
	m	McGray Herbert R	19	engineer	34	90 "
	n	Arena Josephine—†	19	at home	62	223 Havre
	o	Cestone Theresa—†	21	clerk	30	164 Bennington
	p	Tarr Augusta—†	21	"	27	here
	r	Tarr Jennie—†	21	housewife	59	"
	s	Martin Frank	21	mechanic	39	"
	t	Nickerson Harriet—†	23	clerk	37	"
	u	Nickerson Maud—†	23	at home	68	Canada
	v	Rossetti Albert	23	foreman	41	here
	w	Rossetti Rose—†	23	housewife	40	"
	x	Conte Frank	23	joiner	42	"
	y	Conte Mary—†	23	housewife	39	"
	z	Leary James	25	fireman	32	"

706

	a	Leary Margaret—†	25	housewife	30	"
	b	DiFeo Guido	25	clerk	25	"
	c	DiFeo Vincenza—†	25	"	29	
	d	Siraco Anthony R	25	U S A	25	"
	e	Siraco Domenic	25	clerk	22	
	f	Siraco John	25	tilesetter	55	"
	g	Siraco Lucy—†	25	housewife	50	"
	h	Siraco Mary—†	25	at home	33	"
	k	Siraco Anthony	25	diesetter	62	"
	l	Siraco Carmillo	25	ironworker	27	"
	m	Siraco Vincenza—†	25	housewife	59	"
	n	Dalton Eleanor F—†	27	"	30	12 Princeton
	o	Dalton Mark F	27	longshoreman	32	12 "
	p	Carino Joseph A	27	tailor	60	here
	r	Carino Reynold A	27	U S A	25	"
	s	Carino Walter L	27	"	25	"

Page	Letter	Full Name	Residence, Jan. 1, 1945.	Occupation.	Supposed Age.	Reported Residence, Jan. 1, 1944. Street and Number.

Eutaw Street—Continued

	Letter	Full Name	Res.	Occupation	Age	Reported Residence
	T	Bagley Mary—†	29	housewife	34	28 Eutaw
	V	Giangrasso Elvira—†	29	clerk	24	here
	W	Pierro Albert	29	"	26	"
	X	Pierro Arthur	29	U S N	22	"
	Y	Pierro Carmen	29	butcher	53	"
	Z*	Pierro Eleanor—†	29	housewife	48	"
707						
	A	Indresano Albert	31	electrician	37	"
	B	Indresano Leonora—†	31	housewife	35	"
	C*	Indresano Tomasina—†	31	confectioner	60	"
	D	Flynn Mary R—†	33	waitress	34	Watertown
	E	Gannon Sarah J—†	33	houseworker	55	187 Brooks
	F	Hoey Albert F	33	seaman	33	187 "
	G	Hoey Evelyn G—†	33	housewife	34	187 "
	H	Dennis Mildred A—†	33	"	63	122 Meridian
	K	Nickerson Frederick L	33	shipfitter	21	219 Border
	L	Nickerson Helen M—†	33	clerk	24	122 Meridian
	M	Jewkes Anna L—†	35	housewife	33	here
	N	Donahue Ellen—†	35	at home	56	"
	O	Gawlinski Grace E—†	35	secretary	24	"
	P	McCallum Henry	35	metalworker	26	"
	R	McCallum Margaret G—†	35	housewife	21	"
	S	Tozza Dorothy—†	35	clerk	25	
	T	Bevilaqua Dorothea E—†	37	housewife	26	"
	U	Bevilaqua James E	37	U S A	26	
	V	Facchino Angelo	37	presser	55	"
	W	Facchino Maria—†	37	stitcher	51	"
	X	Bevilaqua Anthony	37	U S A	30	
	Y	Bevilaqua Rose—†	37	clerk	24	

708   Lexington Street

	Letter	Full Name	Res.	Occupation	Age	Reported Residence
	B	Roche Frank A	20	supervisor	50	40 Lexington
	C	Roche Gertrude—†	20	housewife	50	40 "
	D	Addonizio Arcangelo	26	storekeeper	27	here
	E	Long Bernard	26	retired	70	"
	F	Perry Joseph D	26	seaman	43	Medford
	H	Robinson Augustine	26	electrician	43	here
	G	Sullivan Catherine—†	26	cook	44	"
	K	DiNicola Elena—†	28	housewife	34	Billerica
	L	DiNicola Rocco	28	tailor	44	"

Lexington Street—Continued

N	Olsen Frank	30	watchman	56	here
O	Thompson John	30	retired	64	"
P	Vierra James	30	laborer	43	21 Princeton
R	Wilcox Benjamin	30	watchman	64	6 Central sq
S	Wilcox James	30	U S A	25	6 "
T	Wilcox Marie—†	30	housewife	28	286 Meridian
U	Grandile Mary—†	30	"	20	286 "
V	Grandile Raymond	30	mechanic	22	Medford
W	Clark George F	34	janitor	63	here
X	Clark Mabel V—†	34	housewife	44	"
Y	Peterson Mary—†	34	at home	65	"
Z	Rodrigues Antonio	34	shipfitter	43	"

709

A	Rodrigues Emma L—†	34	stitcher	21	"
B	*Rodrigues Mary—†	34	housewife	44	"
C	Chiampa Louise—†	36	"	40	
D	Chiampa Joseph	36	shoemaker	50	"
E	*Vezza Ralph	36	laborer	63	
F	Tirone Caroline—†	36	stitcher	27	"
G	Troiano Columbia—†	36	dressmaker	55	"
H	Troiano Theresa—†	36	stitcher	23	"
K	Vozzella Joseph	36	laborer	64	"
L	Landry Arthur E	38	seaman	29	Stoughton
M	Landry Thelma I—†	38	housewife	28	"
N	McEachern James W	38	U S A	26	here
O	McEachern John F	38	"	24	"
R	McEachern Joseph	38	"	31	"
P	McEachern Joseph A	38	painter	56	
S	McEachern Leonard	38	U S A	23	
T	McEachern Rita A—†	38	housewife	48	"
V	Bromfield Jennie M—†	40	"	62	
W	Bromfield John F	40	foreman	54	"
X	Symons Annette M—†	40	dressmaker	37	38 Lexington
Y	Symons John J	40	cleaner	38	38 "
Z	Roche Charles G	42	manager	41	40 "

710

A	Roche Gladys M—†	42	bookkeeper	33	here
B	Kiernan Harry	42	electrician	63	"
C	Cotta Albert E	42	U S A	26	"
D	Cucinotta Flavia—†	42	housekeeper	67	"
E	Carson John M	44	shipfitter	24	Maine

Page.	Letter.	Full Name.	Residence, Jan. 1, 1945.	Occupation.	Supposed Age.	Reported Residence, Jan. 1, 1944. Street and Number.

Lexington Street—Continued

	F	Chase Nellie F—†	44	at home	85	here
	G	Dempsey Helen—†	44	waitress	48	"
	H	Ford Harold E	44	shipfitter	56	57 Bennington
	K	Ford Mabel E—†	44	housewife	49	57 "
	L*	Lynch Michael	44	fisherman	51	here
	M	MacFarrell Gertrude—†	44	housewife	32	"
	N	MacFarrell James	44	ironworker	32	"
	O*	Ryder William	44	seaman	73	"
	P	Sanders Hermon D	44	retired	70	
	R	Stewart Annie E—†	44	housekeeper	45	"
	S	Wilson Alfreda—†	44	clerk	28	"
	T	Wilson Laura—†	44	"	50	"
	U	Buonopane Dolores—†	46	housewife	40	"
	V	Buonopane Ralph	46	clerk	43	
	W	Buonopane John	46	"	39	"
	X	Buonopane Mary—†	46	candymaker	35	"
	Y*	Buonopane Lena—†	46	housekeeper	72	"
	Z	Buonopane Phyllis—†	46	operator	35	"
711						
	B	Testa Amadeo	70	machinist	34	"
	C	Testa Jennie—†	70	housewife	29	"
	D	Testa Eugenio	70	printer	32	
	E	Testa Josephine—†	70	housewife	30	"
	F	Testa Anna—†	70	candyworker	28	"
	G	Testa Assunta—†	70	housewife	69	"
	H	Testa Carmine	70	chauffeur	40	"
	K	Testa Felix	70	retired	69	
	L	Barrett Mildred—†	72	housewife	52	"
	M	Barrett Peter	72	machinist	67	"
	N	Belino John	72	barber	42	
	O	Belino Mary—†	72	housewife	38	"
	S	Belino Agrippino	72	laborer	69	"
	P	Belino Anna—†	72	teacher	23	"
	R*	Belino Jennie—†	72	housewife	66	"
	T	Belino Theresa—†	72	instructor	20	"
	U	Surrette Adolph	74	counterman	42	"
	V	Surrette Louise—†	74	housewife	47	"
	W	Surrette James	74	retired	69	"
	X	Beach Edward D	78	machinist	60	"
	Y	Hager Elson K—†	78	fisherman	54	"
	Z	McLeish Charlotte—†	78	housekeeper	58	"

8

712
Lexington Street—Continued

A	Lee Joseph F, jr	78	agent	39	here
B	Lee Thelma M—†	78	housewife	31	"
C	Bailey Walter L	78	stevedore	52	"
D	Lindell Elina—†	78	housewife	55	"
E	Lindell John	78	welder	57	"
F	Tibbett Edith—†	78	clerk	25	96 Byron
H	Alonzo Nicolo	81	laborer	43	here
K	Comeau Albert	81	carpenter	53	"
L*	Comeau Mary—†	81	housekeeper	60	"
M*	Crowell Ivan	81	fisherman	42	"
N	DeFlumari Ralph	81	laborer	30	
O	Madaeo Louis	81	"	66	"
P	Vincenzo John	81	retired	64	
R	DiBiccaro Edith—†	83	clerk	27	
S	DiBiccaro Frank	83	operator	27	"
T	Pastore Anthony	83	carpenter	47	"
U	Pastore Rose—†	83	housewife	39	"
V	Baccardax Juanita—†	85	"	45	92 Trenton
W	Baccardax Warren C	85	U S N	21	92 "
X	Daley Edward	85	U S A	39	here
Y	Daley Mary—†	85	timekeeper	38	"
Z	Monson Albertine A—†	85	bookkeeper	43	"

713

A	Monson Henry	85	rigger	49	"
B	Roy Armadine—†	85	housekeeper	50	"
C	Roy Elias	85	chef	74	"
D	Kerr Derana—†	85½	hairdresser	41	Reading
E	Staffier Jennie—†	85½	housewife	24	here
F	Nicholsen Evelyn—†	86	"	37	"
G*	Nicholsen John H	86	seaman	42	"
H*	Page Gladys E—†	86	housewife	27	"
K	Page Lawrence S	86	seaman	31	"
L	Chiampa Anthony	86	mechanic	46	186 London
M	Chiampa Marion—†	86	housewife	48	186 "
N	Russo Joseph	86	plumber	45	186 "
O	Saunier Anna V—†	88	housewife	50	here
P	Saunier Daniel E	88	machinist	24	"
R	Saunier Melvin E	88	retired	51	"
S	Conrad Ralph	88	millwright	50	11 Bowdoin
T	Swindell Jane—†	88	presser	58	here

9

Page.	Letter.	FULL NAME.	Residence, Jan. 1, 1945.	Occupation.	Supposed Age.	Reported Residence, Jan. 1, 1944. Street and Number.

Lexington Street—Continued

	Letter	Full Name	Residence	Occupation	Age	Reported Residence
	U	Swindell Samuel	88	cleaner	65	here
	V	Molloy Sarah—†	89	housewife	47	"
	W	Molloy Thomas	89	rigger	44	"
	X	Arcari Anthony	89	electrician	46	"
	Y	Arcari Christine—†	89	housewife	34	"
	Z	Lanni Angelo	89	shoeworker	53	"
714						
	A	Lanni Nancy—†	89	housewife	53	"
	B	Fabiano Anna—†	90	saleswoman	42	"
	C	Fabiano Joseph	90	chef	40	
	D	Pedalino Edward	90	U S A	35	"
	E	Sullivan Ethel—†	90	housewife	26	265 Border
	F	Sullivan Robert	90	seaman	27	265 "
	G	Kempton Anna—†	90	saleswoman	50	here
	H	Kempton Frederick	90	U S N	24	"
	K	Long Irene M—†	92	housewife	25	44 Water
	L	Long Norman	92	machinist	33	44 "
	M	Giglio Edith A—†	92	housewife	27	here
	N	Giglio Joseph J	92	accountant	27	"
	O	Mento Charles	92	chauffeur	36	"
	P	Mento Michalina—†	92	saleswoman	30	"
	R	Lofgren Frederick W	93	bookkeeper	49	"
	S	Lofgren Gladys—†	93	housewife	37	"
	T	Pierce Ernest	93	engineer	54	"
	U	Iapicca Esther—†	93	operator	30	"
	V	Iapicca Felix	93	U S A	26	
	W	Paolini Donato A	93	dairyman	60	"
	X	Paolini Emma—†	93	stitcher	35	"
	Y	Paolini Linda—†	93	operator	25	"
	Z*	Paolini Lucy—†	93	housewife	60	"
715						
	A	Paolini Mario	93	U S N	22	
	B	Paolini Renato	93	"	23	"
	C	Morrow Helen F—†	94	dressmaker	25	44 Lexington
	D	Morrow Irving A	94	U S A	37	44 "
	E	Kruger Lena—†	94	housekeeper	37	here
	F	Martucci Anthony	94	painter	47	"
	G*	Cuozzo Anthony	94	shoemaker	33	"
	H	Cuozzo Florence—†	94	housewife	30	"
	K	Melanson Daniel	95	carpenter	53	21 Marion
	L	Melanson Rebecca—†	95	housewife	46	21 "

Lexington Street—Continued

M	Olson Bonoria—†	95	at home	65	here
N	Whitten Eileen—†	95	housewife	34	"
O	Whitten Woodrow	95	chauffeur	32	"
P	Lynch James E	96	retired	72	
R	Morgan Anna—†	96	at home	76	"
S	O'Hara Ronald F	96	chauffeur	27	"
T	Borick Frances J—†	96	housekeeper	52	"
U	French John	96	retired	75	..
V	Lang Edward	96	boilermaker	62	"
W	Lang Edward J	96	U S A	25	"
X	Liacho Pandy	96	storekeeper	50	"
Y	*Romeraldò Alfred	96	laborer	50	88 Bennington
Z	Clark James W	96	steward	45	180 "
	716				
A	Clark Margaret A—†	96	housewife	36	180 "
B	*Shaughnessey Augustus	96	fisherman	40	180 "
C	Gross Calvin S	97	salesman	49	here
D	McGloan Frederick A	97	retired	74	"
E	McGloan Martha J—†	97	housewife	57	"
F	Foster Hattie L—†	97	"	59	
G	Foster Thomas E	97	cutter	30	"
H	Foster William L	97	fireman	60	"
K	Puzzo Anna—†	98	stitcher	37	"
L	Puzzo Vincent J	98	laborer	45	"
M	Licari Giacomina—†	98	housewife	53	"
N	Reed Gertrude E—†	99	at home	70	"
O	Guerrero Jennie—†	100	housewife	49	"
P	Guerrero Louis	100	U S A	22	
R	Guerrero Phyllis—†	100	U S M C	21	"
S	Guerrero Ralph	100	chauffeur	53	"
T	Nickerson Frank G	103	U S A	22	
U	Nickerson Gardner A	103	"	20	
V	Nickerson Gardner H	103	repairman	51	"
W	Nickerson Marion A—†	103	housewife	51	"
X	Penta George A	104	shipfitter	37	"
Y	Penta Viola—†	104	shoeworker	35	"
Z	Pizzuto Frank L	105	clergyman	48	"
	717				
A	Pizzuto Santina—†	105	housewife	39	"
B	Dingley Albert F	107	seaman	55	"
C	Ferrari Joseph	107	stevedore	35	"

Page.	Letter.	FULL NAME.	Residence, Jan. 1, 1945.	Occupation.	Supposed Age.	Reported Residence, Jan. 1, 1944. Street and Number.

	D	Hallohan Mary—†	107	operator	37	here
	E	Hunt Fitzherbert L	107	retired	71	"
	F	Hunt Rosamond T—†	107	housewife	71	"
	G	Rebboli James	107	guard	68	
	H	O'Brien Edward J	108	retired	80	
	K	O'Brien Mary A—†	108	secretary	52	"
	L	Bowman Carl V	109	U S A	43	
	M	Gage Gertrude—†	109	at home	70	"
	N	Hawkins James	109	student	24	Maine
	O	McCarthy Patrick M	109	guard	50	here
	P	Roberts Vlenchard	109	janitor	69	"
	R	Liberatore Louis	110	U S N	26	16 Frankfort
	S	Liberatore Mary J—†	110	housewife	24	16 "
	T	Manzo Annie A—†	110	"	43	337 Maverick
	U	Manzo Louis R	110	chauffeur	45	337 "
	V	Day Bert	111	engineer	55	372 Sumner
	W	Madison Edward	111	rigger	41	35 Falcon
	X	McAlpine Effie—†	111	at home	76	here
	Y	Yeaton Clinton G	111	U S N	24	"
	Z	Yeaton Josephine—†	111	housewife	43	"
718						
	A	Penny Martha—†	114	"	48	
	B	Penny Vincent	114	welder	48	
	C	Crozier Charlotte—†	116	teacher	36	"
	D	Crozier Grace E—†	116	housewife	61	"
	E	DeSimone Angelina—†	117	stitcher	27	"
	F	DeSimone Joseph	117	seaman	31	
	G	*DeSimone Pasqualina—†	117	housewife	55	"
	H	DeSimone Sadie—†	117	welder	23	
	K	DeSimone Sophie—†	117	stitcher	25	"
	L	DeSimone Violandi—†	117	"	21	
	M	Monaco Anthony	117	laborer	35	
	N	Monaco Marie—†	117	housewife	30	"
	O	Warren Elsie—†	117	"	50	
	P	Warren Harold	117	boilermaker	51	"
	R	McEwen Allen W	118	retired	79	
	S	Nichols Emma J—†	118	housekeeper	71	"
	T	Comeau Eva—†	119	housewife	42	"
	U	Comeau Leo	119	carpenter	40	"
	V	Thibodeau Charles	119	rigger	38	
	W	Thibodeau Elizabeth—†	119	operator	30	"

Lexington Street—Continued

x	Thibodeau Henry	119	rigger	67	here
y	Thibodeau Hilda—†	119	at home	27	"
z	Thibodeau Mary A—†	119	housewife	68	"

719

a	*Pepi Antonetta—†	119	"	54	
b	Pepi John	119	clerk	24	
c	Pepi Joseph	119	U S A	33	
d	Pepi Michael	119	cleaner	55	
e	Cote Dorothy—†	119	housewife	36	"
f	Cote Paul	119	chef	39	"
g	Crouse Edward	119	seaman	47	93 Faywood av
h	Beranger Vivian—†	119	operator	30	here
k	Raab Blanche—†	119	at home	24	"
l	Raab Paul	119	U S N	33	"
m	Albano Anne—†	119	housewife	25	188 Cottage
n	Albano Anthony	119	driller	28	188 "
o	Augo Frank	123	retired	72	166 Princeton
p	Iacobbo Pasquale	123	shoeworker	56	137 Cottage
r	Walsh Joseph J	123	retired	65	here
s	Woods Fred E	123	"	79	"
t	Woods Isabel M—†	123	housewife	72	"
u	Hargrave Cora M—†	124	at home	72	"
v	McCallum Malcolm M	124	secretary	38	"
w	McCallum Minnie B—†	124	at home	78	"
x	Small Henrietta—†	124	"	79	
y	D'Entremont Annie M—†	125	housewife	45	"
z	D'Entremont Edward J	125	accountant	49	"

720

a	Amirault Anna—†	125	housekeeper	46	"
b	Nutter Caroline E—†	125	at home	83	"
c	Alves Mary M—†	126	"	76	
d	Forster Barbara D—†	126	forewoman	52	"
e	Forster Eugenia—†	126	W A V E	20	"
f	Forster Gertrude L—†	126	housewife	48	"
g	Forster Mary—†	126	clerk	22	..
h	Forster Mary A—†	126	at home	77	"
k	Forster William J	126	B F D	50	
l	Kamholz Rita—†	126	clerk	28	
m	Kamholz William R	126	U S A	30	"
o	Rich Evelyn—†	127	housewife	22	· Medford
p	Rich Herbert	127	operator	28	366 Princeton

Lexington Street—Continued

R	Surette Augustine	127	welder	35	here
S	Surette Louise—†	127	housewife	33	"
T	Boudreau Simon A	128	retired	67	"
U	Cunningham Walter	128	U S N	27	
V	Edmunds Alvin E	128	fisherman	45	"
W	Edmunds Marie—†	128	housewife	40	"
X	Kelley Francis W	128	U S A	21	
Y	Kelley Louise—†	128	housewife	20	"
Z	Lee Dolores L—†	128	"	42	"

721

A	Lee Robert J	128	seaman	55	"
B	Lee Robert J, jr	128	U S N	24	"
C	Richards Charles P	128	fisherman	56	"
D	Honduis Mary S—†	129	at home	58	"
E	Consilvio Anna H—†	129	housewife	25	"
F	Consilvio Francis T	129	U S A	34	153 Saratoga
G	Hughes Dorothy—†	129	housewife	27	here
H	Hughes Mary—†	129	"	50	"
K	Hughes Thomas A	129	steamfitter	53	"
L	Hughes Thomas J	129	carpenter	28	"
M	Guarente Daniel	136	U S A	29	
N	*Guarente Enrico	136	storekeeper	60	"
O	Guarente Enrico	136	U S N	22	"
P	*Guarente Florence—†	136	housewife	55	"
R	Guarente Margaret—†	136	stitcher	24	"
S	Donaldson Ernest	136	butcher	45	"
T	Nocera Angelo	138	shoemaker	42	"
U	Nocera Elvira—†	138	shoeworker	33	"
V	Impeduglia Lawrence	138	operator	32	"
W	Impeduglia Lillian—†	138	housewife	30	"
X	Amico Anna—†	138	"	50	
Y	Amico Pietro	138	retired	65	"
Z	Frost Catherine—†	140	housewife	31	156 Lexington

722

A	Frost Hervey A	140	bartender	34	42 Upton
B	*Surette Clifford	140	brazier	36	here
C	*Surette Margaret—†	140	housewife	32	"
D	*DesRoaches Charles	140	fisherman	36	"
E	DesRoaches Mildred—†	140	housewife	29	"
F	Maurano Mary—†	141	artist	25	304 Saratoga
G	Gavaghan Francis J	141	chauffeur	46	here

Lexington Street—Continued

H	Gavaghan Julia—†	141	housewife	42	here
K	Gavaghan Paul	141	U S A	20	"
L	Matarazzo Carmella—†	142	housewife	25	25 Gladstone
M	Minichillo Anthony	142	operator	68	here
N	Minichillo Elizabeth—†	142	checker	23	"
O	Minichillo Rosalie—†	142	housewife	65	"
R	Gallinaro Salvatore	142	laborer	32	"
P	Gallinaro Sylvia—†	142	housewife	32	"
S	*Letteriello Anna—†	143	finisher	53	"
T	Letteriello Joseph	143	barber	57	
U	Letteriello Nora—†	143	stitcher	33	"
V	Bartolo Tina—†	143	housewife	59	"
W	*DiGiocomo Santo	143	pedler	60	
X	Falzone Ellen—†	144	housewife	30	"
Y	Falzone Salvatore	144	chauffeur	30	"
Z	Marino Catherine—†	144	housewife	24	"
	723				
A	Marino Leo J	144	motorman	26	"
B	DiGianvittio Dino	144	musician	27	"
C	DiGianvittio Jennie—†	144	housewife	28	"
D	*Maurano Caroline—†	145	"	76	
E	Maurano Peter	145	chauffeur	38	"
F	Laura Dominic	145	welder	41	
G	Laura Emma—†	145	housewife	41	"
H	Nantia Josephine—†	145	shoeworker	48	"
K	Ulm Nettie—†	146	housekeeper	32	81 Brooks
M	Doucette Edna—†	146	housewife	36	here
N	Doucette George	146	fishcutter	37	"
O	*Nadile Mary—†	147	at home	74	"
P	Schiappa Joseph	147	bartender	54	"
R	Jones Edmund D	148	shipfitter	50	"
S	Jones Elsie J—†	148	housewife	43	"
T	Jones George	148	operator	29	"
U	Jones Rose—†	148	housewife	37	"
V	Jones Mary D—†	148	housekeeper	57	"
W	Zeuli Adolph	149	barber	55	"
X	Zeuli Frank	149	packer	21	"
Y	Zeuli Mary—†	149	inspector	20	"
Z	*Zeuli Philomena—†	149	stitcher	55	"
	724				
A	Carrozza Alva—†	149	housewife	21	180 Marion

Lexington Street—Continued

B	Carrozza George	149	machinist	25	115 Princeton
C	Heighton Lillian—†	150	housewife	23	here
D	*VanBuskirk Albert	150	retired	52	"
E	*VanBuskirk Elizabeth—†	150	housewife	55	"
F	VanBuskirk Gordon	150	U S N	20	
G	Dodge Marguerite—†	150	housewife	50	"
H	Schraffa Florence—†	150	"	37	
K	Schraffa Thomas	150	painter	37	"
L	Jault Beryl—†	152	presser	31	N Hampshire
M	Prejean Albert W	152	baker	36	24 Cedar
N	Prejean Theresa E—†	152	housewife	29	24 "
P	Picardi Mary—†	154	"	35	"
R	Picardi Massimino	154	photographer	36	"
S	Balcheck Ruth—†	154	typist	20	"
T	Balcheck Stephen	154	U S N	21	Wisconsin
U	Nunes Harold	154	"	44	here
V	Nunes Rose—†	154	housewife	41	"
W	Nichols George	154	retired	75	"
X	Nichols Mary—†	154	housekeeper	69	"
Y	Chetwynd Ida—†	156	clerk	30	"
Z	Chetwynd Samuel	156	fisherman	56	"
	725				
A	*Goodwin Mildred—†	156	housekeeper	44	"
B	Anderson Alice—†	156	housewife	48	"
C	Anderson Oscar	156	carpenter	50	"
D	Gannon George	156	U S N	24	"
E	O'Meara Hattie—†	156	housewife	46	"
F	O'Meara Michael H	156	pipefitter	47	"
G	Rollins Charles A	156	retired	83	
H	Fitzpatrick James F rear	156	"	70	
K	Cottreau Joshua	157	laborer	42	
L	Mulcahy Elmer	157	U S A	20	
M	Mulcahy Francis	157	machinist	23	"
N	*Mulcahy Mary E—†	157	at home	63	"
O	Sorensen Christian	157	engineer	52	"
P	*Valenti Bartolomeo	157	"	46	Italy
R	Ramirez Leo	158	floorlayer	67	here
S	Ramirez Lina—†	158	housewife	67	"
T	Ramirez Sally—†	158	clerk	40	"
U	Rizzo Joseph	158	cleaner	30	Medford
V	Rizzo Victoria—†	158	presser	27	"

Lexington Street—Continued

w	DeSimone Florence E—†	159	operator	22	here
x	DeSimone Joseph	159	electrician	53	"
y	DeSimone Mary J—†	159	housewife	53	"
z	Falsini Arthur	162	oiler·	32	86 Putnam

726

A	Falsini Maria—†	162	housewife	28	86 "
B	Pignotti John	162	tailor	54	here
C	Pignotti Louis	162	retired	60	"
D	Pignotti Olympia—†	162	housewife	46	"
E	Valenti Antonetta—†	162	shoeworker	22	194 Lexington
F	Valenti George	162	candymaker	23	194 "
G	Nordia Angelo	163	laborer	55	here
H	Nordia Josephine—†	163	housewife	53	"
K	Nordia Josephine—†	163	clerk	21	"
L	Nordia Peter	163	U S A	26	
M	Nordia Thomas	163	weigher	23	"
P	D'Entermont Elie A—†	163	fishcutter	46	"
R	D'Entremont Exilda—†	163	housewife	40	"
S	D'Entremont Richard	163	U S C G	20	"
N	Doucette Jeannette—†	163·	housewife	35	"
O	Doucette Joseph	163.	fisherman	33	"
T	Larkin Helen—†	164	housewife	47	"
U	Bosco Edith--†	164	"	40	
V	Bosco Elio	164	agent	21	
W	Bosco Lincoln	164	U S N	22	"
X	Schraffa Joseph	164	operator	36	61 Princeton
Y	Schraffa Rose—†	164	housewife	35	61 "
z	Brown Edna—†	165	stenographer	45	here

727

A	Brown Sabina—†	165	at home	71	"
B	Oxley Emma—†	165	housekeeper	58	"
C	Lawler Harold	165	grinder	30	"
D	Lawler Marion—†	165	housewife	24	"
F	Salviati Joseph	167	U S A	23	
G	*Salviati Leo	167	shoemaker	66	"
H	*Salviati Rose—†	167	housewife	61	"
K	Paro Joseph	170	chauffeur	41	"
L	Paro Mary—†	170	housewife	31	"
M	Lightbody Frederick F	170	U S N	26	
N	Lightbody Mary—†	170	clerk	24	"
O	Brugioni Frank	170	laborer	47	44 Lexington

1—7

Page.	Letter.	FULL NAME.	Residence, Jan. 1, 1945.	Occupation.	Supposed Age.	Reported Residence, Jan. 1, 1944. Street and Number.

Lexington Street—Continued

	R	Ferrara Anthony	170	operator	43	here
	T	Ferrara Joseph	170	"	43	"
	U	Ferrara Rosinà—†	170	housewife	72	"
	P	Ferrara Annie—†	170	operator	33	"
	S	Ferrara Benjamin	170	repairman	39	"
	V	Buckley Dennis	171	clerk	70	"
	W	Buckley Denns A	171	U S A	28	
	X	Buckley John L	171	watchman	32	"
	Y	O'Connell James J	171	agent	41	"
	Z	O'Connell Margaret—†	171	housewife	38	"
728						
	A	*Covil Katherine—†	173	"	31	
	B	Covil Pasquale	173	laborer	41	"
	C	Gregory Isabel—†	173	housewife	24	"
	D	Mirabello Anthony	173	shipper	28	"
	E	Mirabello Antonio	173	laborer	54	"
	F	*Mirabello Gasperina—†	173	housewife	50	"
	G	Anthes Naomi A—†	174	"	43	
	H	Anthes Philip E	174	clergyman	44	"
	K	Spack David	174	storekeeper	59	"
	L	Spack Ida—†	174	housewife	54	"
	M	Lopardi Angeline—†	174	"	40	
	N	Lopardi Anthony	174	painter	46	"
	O	Lopardi Louis	174	machinist	21	"
	P	Hamilton Charles R	176	U S N	26	
	R	Hamilton Edith—†	176	housewife	55	"
	S	Hamilton Robert	176	stevedore	56	"
	T	Joyce Anthony C ·	176	U S A	34	"
	U	Joyce Edith—†	176	typist	32	
	V	Smith William C	177	banker	67	
	W	Hansen Henry K	178	U S A	23	"
	X	Hansen Neils A	178	guard	64	"
	Y	Hansen Norris O	178	research wkr	25	Stoneham
	Z	Hansen Olga—†	178	housewife	52	here
729						
	A	Hansen Priscilla M—†	178	"	23	Stoneham
	B	Memmolo Dante	179	U S A	27	here
	C	Memmolo Mary—†	179	housewife	25	"
	D	Beamish Florence—†	179	seamstress	40	"
	E	Murphy Bertha—†	179	housewife	63	"
	F	Murphy George F	179	retired	72	

18

Lexington Street—Continued

G	Laurano Anthony	179	student	20	here
H	Laurano Edna—†	179	clerk	21	"
K	Laurano Eleanor—†	179	at home	23	"
L	Laurano Rita—†	179	housewife	51	"
M	Chiaramonte Carmello	180	renderer	32	"
N	Chiaramonte Mary—†	180	housewife	32	"
O*	Cipriano Rose—†	180	at home	67	"
P	O'Donnell Catherine E-†	182	housewife	32	"
R	O'Donnell William J	182	electrician	35	"
S	Trahan Angelina—†	184	housewife	50	"
T	Trahan John	184	shipwright	46	"
U*	Trahan Marie A—†	184	domestic	42	"
V	Melchionda Josephine—†	185	housewife	27	278 E Eagle
W	Melchionda Michael C	185	welder	31	278 "
X	Alvino Florence—†	185	"	22	here
Y	Alvino Joseph	185	U S A	23	"
Z	Melchionda Angelo	185	shoecutter	51	"
	730				
A	Melchionda John	185	U S A	24	
B	Melchionda Louise—†	185	housewife	48	"
C	Spina Anthony	186	locksmith	26	"
D	Spina Margaret—†	186	housewife	23	"
E	Scimone Carmela—†	186	"	57	
F	Scimone Frank	186	U S N	33	"
G	Scimone James V	186	"	21	"
H	Scimone Joseph	186	grinder	61	"
K	Hoffmann John M	187	engineer	60	"
L	Swansburg Alfred I	187	guard	44	
M	Swansburg Dora G—†	187	at home	63	"
N	Swansburg Dwight K	187	carpenter	59	"
O	Swansburg Edna J—†	187	clerk	49	"
P	Distaso Guy	188	foreman	20	97 Webster
R	Peraino Margaret—†	188	stitcher	57	here
S	Sozio Josephine—†	188	housewife	37	"
T	Sozio Louis	188	clerk	42	"
W	Vega Antoinette—†	190	housewife	52	"
X	Vega Clarinda—†	190	secretary	23	"
Y	Vega Josephine—†	190	at home	20	"
Z	Vega Pasquale	190	watchman	55	"
	731				
A	Massio Delores—†	191	nurse	38	

Page	Letter	FULL NAME.	Residence, Jan. 1, 1945.	Occupation.	Supposed Age.	Reported Residence, Jan. 1, 1944. Street and Number.

Lexington Street—Continued

	B	Masucci Frances—†	191	housewife	72	here
	C	Masucci Fred	191	laborer	29	"
	D	Masucci Guido	191	cutter	40	"
	E	Masucci Leonida—†	191	at home	36	"
	F	Stefano Ethel—†	191	housewife	33	"
	G	Stefano Fred	191	clerk	35	"
	H	Pompeo Elia—†	192	housekeeper	21	117 Falcon
	K	Carlo Emma—†	192	stitcher	23	here
	L	Carlo Nicholas	192	pipefitter	45	"
	M	Carlo Rose—†	192	operator	21	"
	N	Carlo Rose M—†	192	housewife	39	"
	P	Contino Anna R—†	193	"	20	134 Morton
	R	Contino Michael	193	butcher	23	134 "
	S	Paladino Jennie—†	193	stitcher	46	here
	T	Paladino Victor	193	barber	43	"
	U	Cosato Christi	194	"	58	"
	V	*Cosato Lucy—†	194	housewife	55	"
	W	Luciano Anthony	194	tailor	48	
	X	Luciano Anthony, jr	194	musician	21	"
	Y	Luciano Helen—†	194	housewife	44	"

732   Marion Street

	C	*Cochrane Catherine—†	53	housewife	49	119 Eutaw
	D	Cochrane Frank	53	laborer	43	119 "
	E	*McKay Anna—†	53	housekeeper	47	here
	F	McKay Melvin T	53	U S A	30	"
	G	McKillop William	53	longshoreman	57	"
	H	Dexter Evelyn—†	55	at home	78	"
	K	Dexter Myrtle—†	55	housekeeper	52	"
	M	Terry Anna—†	55	housewife	37	"
	N	Terry Seraphine	55	clerk	37	
	O	Merlino Mary C—†	57	housekeeper	44	"
	P	*Arnone Joseph	57	paperhanger	61	"
	R	Arnone Josephine—†	57	clerk	28	
	S	*Arnone Lydia—†	57	housewife	51	"
	T	Arnone Paul	57	mechanic	31	"
	U	*Rispoli Angelina—†	57	at home	63	"
	V	Morton Archie F	59	U S A	30	
	W	Morton Fannie M—†	59	housewife	30	"
	X	Canney Helen M—†	59	"	34	

Marion Street—Continued

Page.	Letter.	FULL NAME.	Residence, Jan. 1, 1945.	Occupation.	Supposed Age.	Reported Residence, Jan. 1, 1944. Street and Number.
	y	Curtin Anne M—†	59	clerk	32	here
	z	Curtin James	59	U S A	32	"
733						
	a	*Renberg John	59	retired	64	
	b	Renberg John D	59	U S A	27	
	c	Renberg Lillian M—†	59	U S M C	20	"
	d	Renberg Margaret—†	59	secretary	25	"
	e	Renberg Olga M—†	59	housewife	63	"
	f	Pellegrino Anna—†	61	"	23	
	g	Pellegrino Joseph	61	shoeworker	24	"
	h	Pellegrino Bernardino	61	"	49	
	k	Pellegrino Frances—†	61	housewife	45	"
	l	Ahern Christine—†	61	"	26	
	m	Ahern Edgar	61	U S A	30	
	n	DeStefano Joseph	63	plumber	40	"
	o	DiGiacomo Louis	63	U S N	24	
	p	Maffeo Antonio	63	retired	70	
	r	Maffeo Mary—†	63	housewife	58	"
	t	Thornhill Clinton L	63	seaman	32	
	s	Thornhill Kathleen M—†	63	housewife	35	"
	u	Flynn Anne—†	65	"	71	
	v	Flynn William H	65	brazier	35	
	w	*Calla Diana—†	65	housewife	59	"
	x	Calla Domenic	65	salesman	27	"
	y	Calla Ernest	65	machinist	33	"
	z	Calla Phyllis—†	65	housewife	32	"
734						
	a	Toy Gladys—†	67	"	34	
	b	Toy Raymond	67	chef	36	
	c	O'Neil Edna—†	67	housewife	51	"
	d	O'Neil Joseph	67	seaman	31	"
	e	O'Neil Warren	67	laborer	25	"
	f	Dwyer James	67	"	38	
	g	Dwyer Madeline—†	67	housewife	36	"
	h	Bibby Lillian—†	69	housekeeper	35	"
	k	Porcelli Elizabeth—†	69	housewife	39	"
	l	Porcelli John	69	U S A	20	
	m	Rose Mary—†	69	housekeeper	32	"
	n	Boudreau Adeline—†	71	housewife	33	"
	o	Boudreau John R	71	shipfitter	37	"
	p	McMillan Edith—†	71	WAC	37	

Marion Street—Continued

R	Ferrara Carmen	71	storekeeper	50	here
S	Ferrara Concetta—†	71	clerk	21	"
T	Ferrara Lucy—†	71	housewife	44	"
U	Walsh Anne M—†	75	at home	81	"
V	Walsh Mary A—†	75	housewife	74	"
W	Walsh William F	75	bookbinder	39	"
X	Creamer Jeremiah	75	engineer	48	"
Y	Creamer Mary—†	75	housewife	42	"

735

A	Martin Catherine—†	77	housekeeper	67	"
B	D'Orlando Albert	79	clergyman	29	Revere
C	D'Orlando Pauline—†	79	teacher	28	"
D	Cacciatore Grace—†	80	housewife	26	here
E	Cacciatore Stephen	80	millwright	31	"
F	Thornton Henry F	80	boilermaker	48	"
G	Thornton Mary—†	80	housewife	43	"
H	Candelire Lillian—†	82	"	38	
K	Candelire Pasquale	82	chauffeur	41	"
L	Candelire Arthur F	82	laborer	36	"
M	Candelire Sarah—†	82	housekeeper	63	"
O	Calla Albert	87	salesman	34	"
P	*Calla Angelina—†	87	housewife	58	"
R	Calla Emma—†	87	clerk	36	
S	*Calla John	87	retired	75	"
T	Landry Edna—†	90	stitcher	40	"
U	Landry Peter	90	machinist	42	"
V	Thorstensen Anna—†	90	waitress	40	"
W	Osterle Bertha L—†	98	housewife	66	"
X	Osterle Frank J	98	butcher	67	"
Y	Halliday Ida E—†	98	at home	84	"

736

A	Moritz Elsie—†	100	housewife	36	"
B	Moritz Robert	100	chauffeur	37	"
C	*Cohen Rose—†	100	housekeeper	70	"
D	*Mori Mary—†	102	"	65	"
E	Terrone Angelina—†	102	housewife	55	"
F	Terrone Louis	102	retired	55	
G	Femino Assilia—†	102	housewife	26	"
H	DiBartolo Giuseppe	104	presser	46	157 Lexington
K	*Pellegrini Mary—†	104	saleswoman	31	157 "
L	Censullo Joseph	104	U S N	25	here

Page	Letter	Full Name	Residence, Jan. 1, 1945.	Occupation	Supposed Age	Reported Residence, Jan. 1, 1944. Street and Number.

Marion Street—Continued

	M	Censullo Peter	104	U S A	23	here
	N	Censullo Rose—†	104	housewife	53	"
	O	Censullo Dorothea—†	104	"	23	"
	P	Censullo Frank	104	chauffeur	27	"
	R	DeRose Joseph A	106	U S A	20	
	S	DeRose Mary A—†	106	housewife	39	"
	T	DeRose Rocco A	106	rigger	40	
	U	McArdle James	110	longshoreman	52	"
	V	McArdle Mary—†	110	housewife	48	"
	W	DeCristoforo Adeline—†	110	"	33	
	X	DeCristoforo Americo	110	clerk	33	
	Y	Fitzpatrick Phyllis—†	110	housewife	26	"
	Z	Fitzpatrick William	110	laborer	30	
737						
	A	Irwin James	112	"	55	
	B	Murray Arthur J	112	guard	28	
	C	Murray John J	112	retired	71	
	D	Murray John L	112	longshoreman	42	"
	E	Murray Hannah—†	112	housewife	65	"
	F	Damelgo Frank	112	pipefitter	36	"
	G	Damelgo Josephine—†	112	housekeeper	55	"
	H	Shelley Henry J	112	janitor	58	"
	K	Goldberg Frank	112	realtor	47	..
	L	Goldberg Sarah S—†	112	housewife	54	"
	M	Wiseman Isadore	112	laborer	32	

Meridian Street

	O	Amato Sebastian	306	tailor	50	here
	P	Carlson Charles	306	longshoreman	73	"
	R	Moore Catherine—†	306	operator	50	84 Eutaw
	S	Peacock William	306	bartender	51	here
	T	Robicheau Zacharie	306	watchman	52	"
	U	Walker Helen N—†	308	housewife	50	"
	V	Walker John J	308	carpenter	54	"
	W	Eide George	308	U S N	22	"
	X	Eide Mary E—†	308	housewife	21	"
	Z	Ferri Ernest	309A	plumber	46	"
738						
	A	Ferri Jennie—†	309A	housewife	46	"
	B	Ferri Richard E	309A	U S C G	23	"

23

Meridian Street—Continued

c	*Reppucci Concetta—†	309A	housewife	68	here
d	Reppucci Eleanor—†	309A	shoeworker	26	"
e	Reppucci George	309A	U S A	36	"
f	Banks John C	310	"	23	"
g	Banks Virginia—†	310	housewife	22	"
h	Hammond Lottie—†	310	"	61	
k	Burke Augustus	310	retired	70	
l	Burke Barbara R—†	310	operator	21	"
m	Burke Mary B—†	310	housewife	67	"
n	White Lillian R—†	310	operator	37	Revere
o	Cowhig William	311	laundrywkr	46	here
p	Depore Theodore	311	laborer	35	Dedham
r	Feeley Alfred	311	longshoreman	38	here
s	Feeley Caroline—†	311	housewife	74	"
t	Feeley Elizabeth—†	311	clerk	38	"
u	Iverson Thomas	311	seaman	38	306 Meridian
v	Quinlan Sophie—†	311	housekeeper	77	here
w	Swan Arthur H	312	seaman	28	"
x	Swan Catherine—†	312	housewife	28	"
y	Swan Edwin A	312	chauffeur	36	"
	739				
a	Coleman John G	313A	"	47	Newton
b	Lovett Eva F—†	313A	at home	47	here
c	Lovett Sarah A—†	313A	"	83	"
d	McLaughlin James	313A	butcher	48	"
e	*Palermo Mildred S—†	314	housewife	29	"
f	Campbell Susan—†	314	"	64	
g	LaCortiglia Frank	314	welder	26	
h	LaCortiglia Gertrude M—†	314	housewife	25	"
k	Adams Ethel M—†	315	"	21	
l	Adams Pleasant A	315	U S N	34	
m	Collins Mary E—†	315	housewife	62	"
n	Collins William G	315	U S N	23	"
o	Symons Arthur A	315	U S A	28	"
r	Fife Frances R—†	317	housewife	60	"
s	Fife John W	317	guard	62	"
t	Heeck Bina—†	319	housewife	60	116 Bennington
v	Garron Austin	323	fisherman	58	here
w	Harper Eleanor V—†	323	waitress	20	"
x	Lacey Evelyn G—†	323	housekeeper	22	"
y	Sampson Catherine C—†	323	housewife	43	"

Page.	Letter.	FULL NAME.	Residence, Jan. 1, 1945.	Occupation.	Supposed Age.	Reported Residence, Jan. 1, 1944. Street and Number.

Meridian Street—Continued

	z	Sampson Clarence D	323	rigger	50	here
740						
	B	D'Angelo Amadeo	326	laborer	54	
	c	D'Angelo Mary—†	326	housewife	29	"
	D	Marsh Joan—†	326	secretary	26	Florida
	E	Tino Domenic	326	chef	27	here
	F	Tino Frank	326	operator	62	"
	G	Tino Mary A—†	326	housewife	65	"
	H	Tino Anthony	326	chef	36	"
	K	Tino Virginia—†	326	dressmaker	36	"
	M	DePalma Michael	328	pipefitter	23	"
	N	DePalma Yolanda—†	328	housewife	20	"
	o	Shanahan John F	328	longshoreman	20	56 Trenton
	P	Shanahan Viola H—†	328	housewife	21	36 Falcon
	R	Chiarello Antonina—†	328	"	62	347 Meridian
	s	Chiarello Peter	328	shipfitter	64	347 "
	T	Pagliarulo Marion—†	328	operator	22	347 "
	U	Pagliarulo Michael	328	U S A	29	347 "
	V	Ford Percy	330	counterman	48	here
	w	Joyce Sophie—†	330	waitress	48	"
	x	Vick Pauline V—†	330	housewife	24	Maine
	Y	Vick Willard D	330	seaman	23	N Carolina
	z	Cameron David E	330	laborer	38	here
741						
	A	Cameron John W	330	"	41	
	B	Sinclair Susie—†	330	housewife	69	"
	c	Sinclair Whit T	330	retired	82	"
	D	McCarty Delle W	330	engineer	56	20 Rutland sq
	E	McCarty Jennie M—†	330	housewife	56	20 "
	F	Penney Edward	330	U S A	28	here
	G	Penney Eileen—†	330	waitress	25	"
	H	Pedro George	332	U S N	20	"
	K	Pedro Lillian—†	332	housewife	52	"
	L	Pedro Manuel	332	laborer	42	"
	M	Censullo James	332	U S A	22	"
	N	Censullo Jennie—†	332	housewife	45	"
	o	Censullo Peter	332	chauffeur	57	"
	P	Torgersen Mary M—†	332	housewife	33	"
	R	*Torgersen Trygve O	332	steward	34	"
	s	Murphy John F	333	U S A	37	
	T	Simonian Agnes K—†	333	housewife	58	"

Meridian Street—Continued

U	Simonian Kane	333	U S A	32	here
V	Simonian Mabel—†	333	stenographer	25	"
W	Simonian Whynott A	333	clerk	34	"
X	Muise Dorothy G—†	334	housewife	32	"
Y	Muise Lester W	334	cleaner	41	"
Z	Bois Dorothy—†	334	packer	22	"

742

A	Bois Eugene	334	spinner	52	"
B	Bois Margaret—†	334	housewife	59	"
C	Bois Ruth—†	334	stenographer	20	"
D	Porras Perfecto	334	machinist	56	"
E	Porras Ralph	334	U S A	23	
F	Rizzuto Marguerite—†	334	housewife	78	"
K	Krafve Genevieve A—†	336	operator	32	"
L	Krafve William A	336	machinist	42	"
M*	Robicheau Anna M—†	336	housewife	60	"
N*	Cardone Carmelia—†	336	"	45	44 White
O	Cardone Gabriel	336	janitor	46	44 "
P	Soriano Patrick	336	U S N	20	44 "
R	Soriano Rose—†	336	stenographer	22	44 "
S	Botchie Carmen—†	336	housewife	34	347 Meridian
T	Botchie Paul R	336	U S C G	33	347 "
U	Bogosian Armen	337	U S A	35	here
V	Bogosian Mary—†	337	housewife	57	"
W	Bogosian Mary—†	337	clerk	34	"
X	Bogosian Paul K	337	tailor	69	
Y	Marcella James A	338	laborer	37	"
Z	Marcella Theresa—†	338	housewife	37	"

743

A	Domegan Mary—†	338	welder	44	"
B	Domegan Thomas	338	fishcutter	41	"
C	Domegan Winifred—†	338	at home	69	"
D*	LaSalle Isabella—†	338	housewife	30	"
E	McDonald Andrew	338	U S A	32	
F	McDonald Luke	338	steamfitter	33	"
G	Guppy Laura A—†	339	laundrywkr	59	"
H	Huey Mary A—†	339	at home	82	"
K	Brown Margaret J—†	339	"	75	
L	McCormick Anna M—†	339	housewife	45	"
M	McCormick Joseph M	339	laborer	55	"
N	Grant Mary—†	340	housewife	42	28 Lexington

Page.	Letter.	FULL NAME.	Residence, Jan. 1, 1945.	Occupation.	Supposed Age.	Reported Residence, Jan. 1, 1944. Street and Number.

Meridian Street—Continued

O	Grant Nathan S	340	chauffeur	39	28 Lexington
P	Mombourquette Anna—†	340	housewife	41	here
R	Mombourquette Charles	340	fisherman	44	"
S	Connell Dennis	340	checker	48	"
T	Connell Sarah—†	340	housewife	29	"
V	Forti James	342	longshoreman	33	"
W	Forti Jennie—†	342	housewife	69	"
X	Forti Michael	342	U S A	30	
Y	Delehanty James M	342	laborer	50	"
Z	Delehanty Theresa L—†	342	operator	46	"
	744				
A	Bryant Gertrude R—†	342	housewife	32	"
B	Bryant William C	342	operator	35	"
C	McCluskey Malcolm F	342	U S A	22	
D	Peterson Emery R	345	coppersmith	44	"
E	Peterson Phyllis—†	345	cook	43	
F	Ranahan Anna M—†	345	housewife	48	"
G	Ranahan William S	345	checker	47	"
H	Finch Carlton	347	U S N	25	Ohio
K	Finch Lucille—†	347	housewife	23	"
L	Cavalieri Frank	347	printer	26	here
M	Cavalieri Joseph	347	laborer	56	"
N	Cavalieri Rose—†	347	housewife	44	"
O	Cavalieri Rose M—†	347	bookkeeper	23	"
P	Cunningham Rita—†	347	operator	26	236 Princeton
R	Flaherty Catherine—†	347	housewife	25	236 "
S	Flaherty Joseph	347	U S A	30	236 "
T	Lavangie Charles A	349	shipper	59	here
U	Lavangie Mary H—†	349	housewife	65	"
V	Magnusson Eleanor—†	349	operator	25	"
W	Magnusson William	349	U S A	26	
X	Verbal Herman G	349½	rigger	43	"
Y	Verbal Lucy A—†	349½	housewife	37	"
Z	Flaherty Martin J	349½	retired	56	
	745				
A	Pendleton Alice E—†	349½	factoryhand	27	"
B	Pendleton Clarissa—†	349½	operator	54	"
C	Crescey Catherine A—†	351	housewife	34	"
D	Crescey Herbert N	351	seaman	42	
E	Campbell Helen A—†	351	housewife	41	"
F	Campbell Robert L	351	carpenter	47	"

Page	Letter	Full Name.	Residence, Jan. 1, 1945.	Occupation.	Supposed Age.	Reported Residence, Jan. 1, 1944. Street and Number.

Princeton Street

	Letter	Full Name.	Res.	Occupation.	Age	Reported Residence
	H	Guarente John	80	U S N	28	here
	K	Guarente Mary—†	80	housewife	29	"
	L	Pignato Margaret—†	80	"	33	89 Liverpool
	M	Pignato Patrick	80	foreman	32	89 "
	N	Woods Adeline—†	80	housewife	26	10 Henry
	O	Woods Glen	80	U S N	28	10 "
	P	Gallant Augustine G	90	U S A	26	Andover
	R	Gallant Frances—†	90	housewife	20	here
	T	Graff Edward	90	fireman	46	"
	S	Graff Mary—†	90	at home	39	"
	U	Cashman Laura—†	94	housewife	55	"
	V	Tedford Minnie—†	96	"	67	
	W	Ciarcia Anna—†	98	"	30	
	X	Ciarcia Anthony	98	shipfitter	30	"
	Y	Turner George	98	pipefitter	56	"
	Z	Turner Ruth—†	98	housewife	53	"
746						
	A	Boynton Walter	98	welder	32	Chelsea
	F	Fossett John F	102	fireman	28	here
	G	Fossett Marion—†	102	housewife	26	"
	H	Loperfido Alphonso	102	U S A	20	"
	K	Loperfido Emanuel	102	U S N	24	
	C	Serrapica Celia—†	102	housewife	50	"
	D	Serrapica Gloria—†	102	stitcher	20	"
	E	Serrapica Sebastian	102	merchant	62	"
	L	Asci Philipo	104	laborer	46	
	M	*Balestriere Antonina—†	104	housekeeper	77	"
	N	Danca Frank	104	barber	42	"
	O	Danca Santina—†	104	housewife	37	"
	P	Spencer Gertrude—†	104	"	59	
	R	McCaul Dorothy—†	106	"	39	
	S	McCaul William	106	laborer	39	"
	T	Pesaturo Marietta—†	106	housewife	28	"
	U	Pesaturo Salvatore	106	printer	28	"
	V	Emmons Anna—†	108	housewife	28	"
	W	Emmons Howard	108	laborer	26	"
	X	Colburn Mary—†	108	housewife	23	Florida
	Y	Scandura John	108	laborer	60	125 Princeton
	Z	Scandura Mary—†	108	housewife	50	125 "
747						
	A	Vitale Mildred—†	108	saleswoman	30	here

Princeton Street—Continued

	Letter	Full Name	Residence	Occupation	Age	Reported Residence
	B	Asci Diomira—†	110	housewife	43	here
	C	Asci Edmund	110	U S N	21	"
	D	Asci Gaetano	110	engineer	54	"
	E	Castrucci Biagio	110	laborer	56	
	F	DelCore Luigi	110	"	57	
	G	*Andrea Andrew	110	"	51	
	H	*Andrea Olympia—†	110	housewife	49	"
	K	Catino Prescenzo	110	laborer	49	
	L	Sofia Ernest	110	U S A	30	"
	M	Sofia Louis	110	laborer	27	"
	N	*Nickerson Eva—†	112	housewife	46	"
	O	*Nickerson Louise—†	112	clerk	24	"
	P	*Nickerson Wallace	112	cooper	55	"
	R	Harding Gertrude—†	112	housewife	33	"
	S	Harding Gustave	112	rigger	34	
	T	Bassett Arthur	114	electrician	26	"
	U	Bassett Florence—†	114	housewife	58	"
	V	Bassett Herbert	114	clerk	60	
	W	Bassett Merrill	114	accountant	29	"
	X	Hart Arline—†	114	housewife	21	"
	Y	Hannon Edmund	116	U S A	27	
	Z	Hannon Thelma—†	116	housewife	27	"
748						
	A	Hannon Edward	116	stevedore	51	"
	B	Hannon Gertrude—†	116	housewife	46	"
	C	Hannon Helen—†	116	stenographer	20	"
	D	Hannon John	116	U S A	24	
	E	Hannon Robert	116	"	26	
	F	Hannon Ruth—†	116	housewife	27	"
	G	Nardo Annette—†	118	"	33	
	H	Nardo Frank	118	laborer	35	
	K	*Ulogiares Fannie—†	118	housewife	51	"
	L	*Ulogiares George	118	laborer	54	
	M	Ulogiares Joan—†	118	clerk	21	
	N	DeSanctis Josephine—†	118	housewife	20	"
	O	DeSanctis Wilson	118	laborer	27	
	P	DiBenedetto Rachel—†	120	housewife	35	"
	R	DiBenedetto Vincent	120	carpenter	42	"
	S	Ficcaglia Laura—†	120	housewife	26	262 Maverick
	T	Ficcaglia Vincent	120	foreman	32	262 "
	U	O'Brien Inez—†	124	housewife	28	here

Page.	Letter.	FULL NAME.	Residence, Jan. 1, 1945.	Occupation.	Supposed Age.	Reported Residence, Jan. 1, 1944. Street and Number.

Princeton Street—Continued

v	O'Brien William	124	shipfitter	29	here
w	Quindley Andrew	124	engineer	45	"
x	Quindley Marion—†	124	housewife	45	"
¹x	Scaramella Geralamo	126	laborer	64	"
y	Tritto Erasmo	126	U S M C	21	"
z	Tritto Frank	126	machinist	54	"

749

A	Tritto Marie—†	126	housewife	44	"
c	Moscatelli Olga—†	126	"	39	
D	Moscatelli Sabino	126	tailor	42	
E	Hunt James	128	painter	64	"
F	*Martin Mary—†	128	housewife	71	"
G	Powell Robert S	128	shipfitter	79	"
K	*Chevarier Dominic	130	electrician	25	"
L	*Chevarier Grace—†	130	housewife	27	"
M	*Zucco Julia—†	130	housekeeper	62	"
N	Ciampi Anna—†	130	welder	21	
o	Ciampi Emilio	130	U S A	26	
P	*Ciampi Fiore	130	laborer	57	"
R	Ciampi Louis	130	rigger	24	
s	*Ciampi Mary—†	130	housewife	51	"
T	Ciampi Mildred—†	130	cashier	25	"
U	Garvey Caroline—†	130	housewife	28	96 Brooks
w	Gushue Anna—†	142	secretary	20	here
x	Gushue Bridget—†	142	housewife	52	"
Y	Gushue Eleanor—†	142	secretary	22	"
z	Gushue Madeline—†	142	"	24	"

750

B	Landry Mary I—†	144	housewife	41	"
A	Landry Wilfred	144	engineer	42	"
c	Boudreau Joseph B	146	inspector	47	"
D	Boudreau Mary A—†	146	housewife	45	"
E	Sampson Blanche—†	146	SPAR	24	
F	Sampson Edith—†	146	housewife	45	"
G	Sampson Leo	146	machinist	54	"
H	Driscoll John J	148	retired	66	
K	Driscoll Margaret E—†	148	at home	55	"
L	Russo Anna—†	150	housewife	30	"
M	Russo James	150	operator	62	"
N	Russo John B	150	U S N	20	
o	Russo Thomas L	150	electrician	32	"

Princeton Street—Continued

P	Camuso James A	150	tailor	30	here
R	Curcio Henry	150	mechanic	43	"
S	Giannattasio Angelina—†	150	housewife	48	"
T	Giannattasio Antonio	150	upholsterer	53	"
U	Giannattasio Michael	150	U S N	21	"
V	Rubbico Joseph	154	mechanic	33	"
W	Rubbico Rose—†	154	housewife	32	"
X	Bosco Caroline—†	154	"	38	"
Y	Bosco John	154	machinist	43	"
Z	*Teza Giacomina—†	154	housewife	54	223 Havre
	751				
A	Teza Sebastiano	154	carpenter	59	223 "
B	Castelluccio Michael	158	chauffeur	45	here
C	Castelluccio Rosemarie—†	158	housewife	48	"
D	Bishop Madeline—†	158	operator	36	"
E	Boudreau Anna—†	158	candymaker	41	"
F	*Boudreau Emma M—†	158	at home	74	"
G	Bluhm Minna—†	160	housewife	73	"
H	Bluhm Morris	160	mechanic	68	"
K	*Cheivars Helen—†	166	clerk	28	
L	Cheivars Margaret—†	166	housewife	75	"
M	Cheivars Nicholas J	166	retired	75	"
N	Bruno Lucy—†	166	housewife	60	320 Saratoga
O	Bruno Ralph	166	U S A	26	320 "
P	Bruno Riccardo	166	cabinetmaker	58	320 "
R	Bruno Richard	166	U S A	22	320 '
S	Picarello Anthony	166	U S N	31	320 "
T	Picarello Rose—†	166	housewife	31	320 "
U	Bruno Frank P	166	librarian	31	138 Webster
V	Bruno Mary J—†	166	housewife	22	138 "
W	Bozza Josephine—†	168	"	38	162 Lexington
X	Bozza Michael	168	barber	43	162 "
Y	Bage Frederick	168	cutter	34	here
Z	Bage Thora A—†	168	housewife	29	"
	752				
A	Lochiatto Alfonso	168	laborer	39	"
B	Lochiatto Philomena—†	168	housewife	33	"
C	Erskine Harry T	172	bookkeeper	25	"
D	Erskine Irene L—†	172	"	20	"
E	Erskine Thelma—†	172	housewife	52	"
F	Erskine Walter T	172	engineer	52	"

31

Princeton Street—Continued

G	Ekman Carl	172	fisherman	52	here
H	Magnusson John	172	"	52	"
K	Filler Anna—†	172	housewife	25	New York
L	Filler Frank	172	U S N	27	"
M	Hemenway Annie—†	172	operator	54	here
N	Poto John	172	radioman	42	"
O	Benda Arcangela—†	174	welder	24	120 Eutaw
P	Benda Charles	174	shipfitter	33	89 Burrell
R	Raeke Charles J	174	starter	41	here
S	Racke John F	174	chauffeur	43	"
T	Riggs Helen M—†	174	clerk	38	"
U	Pessia Aurelio D	176	operator	27	"
V	Pessia Carpinella—†	176	housewife	24	"
W	Contini Jennie—†	176	"	57	
X	Contini Louis	176	U S A	27	..
Y	Contini Michael	176	carpenter	65	"
Z	Ficaro Frank	176	barber	65	
	753				
A	DiNunzio Amelia—†	178	housewife	30	"
B	DiNunzio Clement	178	laborer	35	
C	Blasi Angelina—†	178	housewife	75	"
D	Blasi Michael	178	retired	76	
E	Nappi Armando	178	welder	39	
F	Nappi John	178	U S N	20	
G	Nappi Mary—†	178	housewife	38	"
H	Katz Abraham	180	fireman	31	..
K	*Katz Annie—†	180	housewife	65	"
L	Katz Lillian—†	180	operator	35	"
M	Katz Max	180	retired	65	"
N	Katz Sally—†	180	clerk	33	"
O	Correnti Angelina—†	180	operator	23	"
P	Correnti Anthony	180	U S A	22	"
R	Correnti Joseph	180	barber	50	
S	Correnti Mary—†	180	candymaker	42	"
T	DeFilippo Carmella—†	182	stitcher	20	"
U	DeFilippo Joseph	182	stonecutter	49	"
V	DeFilippo Rita—†	182	housewife	45	"
W	Aleo Joseph	182	U S A	28	
X	Aleo Mary—†	182	packer	22	
Y	DeBiccari Arline—†	184	housewife	31	"
Z	DeBiccari Lewis	184	chauffeur	32	"

754
Princeton Street—Continued

A	Salza Concordia—†	184	housewife	58	here
B	Salza John	184	U S A	28	"
C	Salza Lewis	184	"	24	"
D	Salza Nicholas	184	laborer	64	
E	Salza Ponzi	184	U S A	23	
F	Babine Margaret—†	186	housewife	35	"
G	Babine Robert	186	U S A	36	"
H	Babine Samuel	186	shipper	34	"
K	Caplan Abraham	186	physician	42	"
L	Stone Daniel	186	chauffeur	28	"
M	Babine Lewis	190	fisherman	53	"
N	Boudreau Adesse—†	190	housewife	67	"
O	Boudreau Mary E—†	190	secretary	37	"

Putnam Street

U	*Interbartolo Anna—†	87	housewife	38	here
P	Interbartolo Charles	87	chauffeur	40	"
R	Fernandes John	87	longshoreman	63	"
S	*Fernandes Marie—†	87	housewife	62	"
T	Fernandes Marie—†	87	saleswoman	38	"
V	Flot Lillian—†	87	housewife	48	"
W	Flot Louis	87	welder	45	
X	Robicheau David	87	painter	39	"
Y	Fernandes John	89	laborer	33	
Z	Fernandes Lucy—†	89	housewife	30	"

755

A	Mason Ruth—†	89	"	30	
B	Salerno Albert	89	laborer	41	"
C	Salerno Frank	89	"	80	"
D	*Salerno Marie—†	89	housewife	75	"
E	Giardina Gaetano	91	U S A	22	"
F	Giardina Jennie—†	91	housewife	21	294 Sumner
G	Giardina Michelina—†	91	"	40	here
H	Giardina Vincent	91	laborer	54	"
K	Sozio George	107	machinist	28	"
L	Sozio Letitia—†	107	housewife	25	"
M	Banks Ellen P—†	107	"	80	
N	Banks Ellen V—†	107	secretary	54	"
O	Duca Ida—†	109	housewife	37	"

1—7   33

Putnam Street—Continued

P	Duca Joseph	109	painter	39	here
R	*Carlson Mary—†	111	housekeeper	64	"
S	Denehy Alice—†	111	housewife	36	"
T	Denehy Henry J	111	machinist	38	"

Trenton Street

U	LaVirtue Augusta A	3	U S A	28	here
W	LaVirtue George A	3	machinist	57	"
X	LaVirtue Matilda—†	3	housewife	51	"
V	LaVirtue Vernon	3	U S N	22	"
Y	*Langone Caroline—†	4	housewife	61	"
Z	Langone Jerry	4	U S A	21	
	756				
A	*Langone Joseph	4	laborer	64	
B	Langone Lucy—†	4	stitcher	24	"
C	Langone Mildred—†	4	clerk	27	
D	Drew Ora—†	4	housewife	54	"
E	Greco Vincenzo	4	mason	64	
F	McRoberts Robert	4	machinist	45	"
G	Baxter Edward	4	laborer	45	
H	Baxter Hazel—†	4	housewife	39	"
K	Newhall Desmond	4	U S C G	20	"
L	Santiano Grace—†	6	housewife	38	"
M	Santiano Joseph	6	printer	42	
N	Cuzzi Anthony	6	cutter	35	
O	Cuzzi Lucy—†	6	housewife	35	"
P	Rizzo Adele—†	6	"	30	
R	Rizzo George	6	pressman	33	"
T	Coombs Bridget M—†	7	housewife	67	"
U	Coombs Eli	7	retired	73	
V	Coombs William J	7	laborer	30	
W	Costigan Bernard	7	longshoreman	52	"
X	Costigan Elizabeth—†	7	operator	21	"
Y	Costigan Mary—†	7	housewife	49	"
Z	Hickey John	9	retired	80	
	757				
A	Hickey Mary J—†	9	housewife	70	"
B	Trocano Domenic	9	laborer	48	
C	*Trocano Grace—†	9	housewife	57	"
D	Trocano Rosario	9	U S A	25	

Trenton Street—Continued

E	Ahern James	9	laborer	31	here
F	St John James F	9	ironworker	51	"
G	St John Mary—†	9	housewife	54	"
K	*Muise Elizabeth—†	11	housekeeper	20	"
L	Muise John I	11	chef	46	"
M	Muise Loretta—†	11	housewife	47	"
N	Fawcett Elizabeth—†	12	"	67	
O	Fawcett Patrick A	12	brazier	30	
P	Fawcett Richard W	12	retired	70	
S	Barry John	14	electrician	35	"
T	Barry Julia—†	14	housekeeper	53	104 Marion
U	Gioscio Dominic	14	U S A	28	196 Brooks
V	Gioscio Gladys—†	14	housewife	28	196 "
W	*Whitten Louise—†	14	at home	70	196 "
X	Simms Mary E—†	15	nurse	60	here
Y	Fougere Grace M—†	15	packer	34	"
Z	Bailey Elizabeth—†	17	housewife	65	"
	758				
A	Bailey Harry C	17	clerk	68	
B	Bailey Harry C, jr	17	U S A	27	
C	McWeeny Ella E—†	18	housewife	69	"
D	Hezlitt Alice—†	18	"	32	
E	Hezlitt Edgar	18	U S A	33	
F	Recupero Carmello	18	laborer	26	"
G	Constantino Joseph	19	cabinetmaker	31	"
H	Constantino Mildred—†	19	housewife	28	"
K	Bowden Edward L	19	fitter	57	
L	Bowden Hannah—†	19	housewife	50	"
M	Lovett John W	19	seaman	61	"
N	D'Erico Anna—†	20	housewife	22	"
O	D'Erico Vincent	20	U S A	23	
P	Kirby Helen—†	20	inspector	33	"
R	Caristo Myrtle—†	20	housewife	20	"
S	Caristo Richard	20	pipefitter	25	"
T	Carino Rose—†	21	housewife	33	"
U	Carino William	21	U S A	29	"
V	Constantino Concetta—†	21	housewife	59	"
W	Constantino Frank	21	retired	65	"
X	Constantino John	21	U S A	20	"
Y	Constantino Mary—†	21	stitcher	21	"
Z	Constantino Matthew	21	U S A	29	

Trenton Street—Continued

Page.	Letter.	Full Name.	Residence, Jan. 1, 1945.	Occupation.	Supposed Age.	Reported Residence, Jan. 1, 1944. Street and Number.
	A	Coombs Edward V	22	seaman	29	Wilmington
	B	Coombs Eleanor—†	22	housewife	24	"
	C	DeSisto Edward	22	clerk	28	here
	D	DeSisto Mary—†	22	housewife	26	"
	E	Imbriano Pasquale	22	U S N	22	"
	F	*Imbriano Pasqualina—†	22	housewife	59	"
	G	Imbriano Helen—†	22	"	27	
	H	Imbriano Ralph	22	machinist	28	"
	L	Ferrara Leonard D	24	brazier	25	"
	K	Ferrara Leonora—†	24	housewife	26	"
	M	Banks Joseph	24	engineer	29	210 E Eagle
	N	Banks Virginia—†	24	housewife	26	210 "
	O	Morani Marion—†	24	"	25	345 Border
	P	Morani Thomas	24	laborer	30	345 "
	R	Vega Caroline—†	26	housewife	45	125 Eutaw
	S	Vega Dominic	26	retired	50	125 "
	T	Saggese Adelina—†	26	housewife	60	276 Princeton
	U	Saggese Amando	26	U S N	21	276 "
	V	Saggese Joseph	26	laborer	66	276 "
	W	Mantica Anna—†	26	housewife	25	Chelsea
	X	Mantica Augustino	26	fisherman	27	"
	Y	Doble Henry	28	electrician	51	here
	Z	Doble Henry, jr	28	student	20	"
760						
	A	Doble Paul	28	U S N	24	··
	B	Schepici Rose—†	28	housewife	28	"
	C	Schepici Salvatore	28	foreman	32	"
	D	Howe Arthur V	28	U S N	21	
	E	Howe Emma I—†	28	housewife	58	"
	F	Howe Grace—†	28	clerk	20	
	G	Howe Harry R	28	blacksmith	60	"
	H	Kelly Ellen—†	30	housewife	25	"
	K	Kelly Mark	30	clerk	30	··
	L	Coppola Peter	30	chauffeur	39	"
	M	Coppola Philomena—†	30	housewife	36	"
	N	DiMauro Joseph	30	barber	38	
	O	DiMauro Santa—†	30	housewife	34	"
	P	Gifford Mary E—†	32	at home	76	"
	R	Guarino Anna—†	32	housewife	46	"
	S	Guarino Ida—†	32	clerk	23	"

Trenton Street—Continued

T	Guarino Joseph	32	sausagemaker	50	here
U	Guarino Michelina—†	32	stitcher	22	"
V	Magnasco Anna—†	34	housewife	31	"
W	Magnasco Emilio	34	riveter	32	
X	Lorizio Anthony	34	U S A	33	"
Y	Lorizio Emma—†	34	housewife	57	"
Z	Lorizio Joseph	34	U S A	28	

761

A	Lorizio Pasquale	34	chauffeur	33	"
B	Lorizio Vincent	34	manager	56	"
C	Lorizio Vito	34	bartender	34	"
D	Curro Angelina—†	34	housewife	29	"
E	Curro Peter	34	cleaner	31	
F	Petre Alfonso	36	retired	66	
G	Petre Fred	36	barber	27	
H	Petre Mary—†	36	housewife	24	"
K	Petre Rose—†	36	"	59	
L	D'Eon Albert	36	painter	42	"
M	D'Eon Ida—†	36	housewife	41	"
O	DelleGrotto Emilie—†	57	"	53	
P	DelleGrotto Peter	57	painter	50	"
R	Santoro Camilla—†	57	housewife	66	"
S	Santoro John	57	attorney	44	"
T	Santoro Joseph	57	retired	72	"
U	Santoro Thomasina—†	57	teacher	41	
V	Picardi Amorino	61	welder	42	
W	Picardi Eva—†	61	housewife	40	"
Y	Parziale Lillian—†	61	instructor	44	"
Z	Parziale Josephine—†	61	housewife	72	"
X	Parziale Lillian—†	61	at home	42	"

762

C	Richard Goldie—†	75	housewife	52	"
D	Richard Maurice	75	grocer	54	
E	Richard Stanley	75	U S A	28	
F	Moore Esther C—†	77	housewife	27	"
G	Moore William E	77	rigger	28	
H	*Thibodeau Edward	77	retired	74	"
K	Thibodeau Joseph	77	U S A	35	
L	Thibodeau Lillian—†	77	housewife	32	"
M	*Thibodeau Nelsie—†	77	"	74	
N	Beattie Margaret I—†	77	"	75	"

Page.	Letter.	FULL NAME.	Residence, Jan. 1, 1945.	Occupation.	Supposed Age.	Reported Residence, Jan. 1, 1944. Street and Number.

Trenton Street—Continued

	o	Vitale Angela—†	81	clerk	20	151 Saratoga
	p	Vitale Giuseppe	81	laborer	52	151 "
	r	Vitale Nicolina—†	81	housewife	45	151 "
	s	Cadigan Anna M—†	85	"	38	here
	t	Cadigan John F	85	operator	46	"
	u	*Cole Annie—†	85	housewife	59	"
	v	Cole William J	85	fisherman	58	"
	w	Bellino Agrippino	85	retired	79	
	x	Giarratana John	85	tailor	45	
	y	Giarratana Josephine—†	85	housewife	45	"
763						
	a	DeLuccia Eleanora—†	87	stitcher	24	"
	b	DeLuccia Grace—†	87	housewife	53	"
	c	DeLuccia Mary—†	87	packer	30	"
	¹c	Grasso Josephine—†	87	saleswoman	28	"
	d	Tibbetts Orlando L—†	87	clergyman	25	"
	e	Tibbetts Phyllis J—†	87	housewife	25	"
	f	*Ricci May—†	87	"	50	
	g	Ricci Theodore	87	fireman	48	"
	h	Ricci Theodore, jr	87	teacher	24	"
	k	Spada Bartholomew	89	U S A	28	"
	l	Spada Catherine R—†	89	housewife	52	"
	m	Spada Frank	89	carpenter	58	"
	n	Spada Leo	89	U S A	23	
	o	Lynch Gerald	89	"	35	"
	p	Lynch Phyllis—†	89	housewife	36	"
	r	Celona Leila—†	89	"	25	72 Frankfort
	s	Celona Stephen	89	machinist	30	72 "
	t	Beranger Charles	91	cook	71	38 Princeton
	u	*Beranger Lillian—†	91	housewife	65	38 "
	v	Kyle Lucy P—†	91	"	27	Virginia
	w	Kyle Robert	91	U S N	34	"
	x	Cobb Mary—†	91	waitress	30	here
	y	McEachern Allan	91	mover	26	"
	z	McEachern Elizabeth—†	91	housewife	52	"
764						
	a	McEachern Ronald	91	fireman	52	"
	b	Barletta Rose—†	91	stitcher	27	"
	c	DiGiorgio Mildred—†	91	housewife	25	"
	d	DiGiorgio Vitale	91	machinist	26	"
	e	Greer Alice H—†	93	housewife	58	"

38

Trenton Street—Continued

F	Flynn Catherine—†	93	clerk	60	here
G	Larkin Cecil	95	fisherman	43	"
H	*Nickerson Bradford	95	cutter	39	"
K	Nickerson Mary—†	95	housewife	33	"
L	Carlton Angela—†	95	"	20	254 Bremen
M	Carlton Ernest	95	U S N	22	254 "
N	Siracusa Anthony	95	laborer	50	here
O	Siracusa Joseph	95	toolmaker	30	"
P	*Siracusa Josephine—†	95	housewife	48	"
R	Lavin James	97	janitor	40	Winthrop
S	Lavin Lillian—†	97	housewife	35	134 Marion
T	Connolly Phyllis M—†	97	"	37	here
U	Connolly Thomas F	97	boilermaker	38	"
V	Wellings Agnes G—†	97	operator	54	"
W	Lotti Anna—†	99	housewife	20	"
X	Lotti Deofrasio	99	U S N	23	
Y	Letterie Florence—†	99	housewife	48	"
Z	Letterie Frank	99	U S A	22	
	765				
A	Letterie Pasquale	99	"	25	
B	Letterie Vincenzo	99	operator	56	"
C	Szymanski Joseph	99	U S A	28	
D	Szymanski Nora—†	99	housewife	28	"
E	Giovinio Anna—†	101	"	34	
F	Giovinio Edward	101	plumber	38	"
G	Fortenberry Charlotte L—†	101	housewife	25	14 Trenton
H	Fortenberry Walter I	101	seaman	26	14 "
K	Labouras Charles A	101	waiter	32	here
L	Labouras Rose—†	101	housewife	30	"
M	Giovino Concetta—†	103	"	31	"
N	Giovino Edmund	103	musician	33	"
O	Pagliaro Anthony	103	counterman	38	"
P	*Pagliaro Carmelo	103	retired	74	
R	Pagliaro Rose—†	103	housewife	65	"
S	*Vadala Fortunata—†	103	"	43	
T	DiPietro Josephine—†	103	"	40	
V	Lewis Evelyn—†	107	stenographer	30	"
W	Lewis George A	107	salesman	60	"
X	Lewis Gertrude M—†	107	housewife	57	"
Y	Lewis Sidney L	107	U S A	22	"
Z	Salerno Helen—†	107	housewife	25	153 Marion

Page.	Letter.	FULL NAME.	Residence, Jan. 1, 1945.	Occupation.	Supposed Age.	Reported Residence, Jan. 1, 1944. Street and Number.

766
Trenton Street—Continued

	Letter	FULL NAME	Res.	Occupation	Age	Reported Residence
	A	Slofsky Catherine—†	107	housewife	27	here
	B	Slofsky Samuel	107	rigger	31	"
	C	Viola Anthony	109	welder	33	"
	D	Viola Louise—†	109	housewife	31	"
	E	Viola Mary—†	109	stitcher	52	"
	F	Viola Mary P—†	109	"	24	"
	G	Brown Arthur R	111	U S N	23	139 Condor
	H	Brown May B—†	111	secretary	20	here
	K	McCallum Dorothy A—†	111	"	23	"
	L	McCallum John E	111	painter	49	"
	M	McCallum Josephine—†	111	housewife	46	"
	N	Logan Julia A—†	111	housekeeper	74	"
	O	Camplese Frances—†	113	stitcher	26	"
	P	Camplese Ugo	113	shoemaker	30	"
	R	Crandall Josephine—†	113	stitcher	22	"
	S	Crandall Mark	113	U S A	23	
	T	*Saporito Concetta—†	113	housewife	52	"
	U	Saporito Rocco	113	laborer	57	"
	V	Palermo Jane S—†	115	stitcher	24	"
	W	Palermo Joseph	115	janitor	55	..
	X	Palermo Josephine—†	115	housewife	49	"
	Y	Palermo Paul A	115	machinist	23	"
	Z	Analoro Joseph	115	baker	52	"

767

	Letter	FULL NAME	Res.	Occupation	Age	Reported Residence
	A	Analoro Lena—†	115	operator	24	"
	B	Analoro Theresa—†	115	stitcher	44	"
	C	Laurano Felicia—†	115	assembler	38	"
	D	Sannella Frank J	115	U S A	20	"
	E	Sannella Ralph	115	laborer	55	"
	F	Sannella Thomasa—†	115	stitcher	42	"
	G	Meuse John J	117	fishcutter	36	"
	H	Meuse Loretta B—†	117	housewife	44	"
	K	Sabin Esther M—†	117	"	37	
	L	Sabin Linus	117	fisherman	41	"
	M	Davidson Ellen M—†	117	housewife	42	"
	N	Davidson Joseph J	117	metalworker	38	"
	O	Davidson Mary I—†	117	operator	22	"
	P	O'Meara Thomas H	117	draftsman	37	"
	R	Tarsi Carmella—†	119	housewife	29	"
	S	Tarsi John J	119	operator	39	"

Trenton Street—Continued

	T	Chaffee Della—†	119	housewife	70	here
	U	Chaffee Dora L—†	119	housekeeper	42	"
	V	Chaffee Frederick W	119	retired	71	"
	W	Govoni Carmella O—†	119	housewife	44	94 Trenton
	X	Govoni John E	119	B F D	49	94 "
	Y	McConnell Robert W	121	U S N	20	380 Lovell
	Z	McDonald Eugene	121	"	22	here
768						
	A	McDonald George L	121	foreman	62	"
	B	*McDonald Margaret—†	121	operator	21	"
	C	*LeBlanc Eve P	121	carpenter	61	"
	D	*LeBlanc Naomi M—†	121	housewife	61	"
	E	Schaffer Charles A	121	U S A	31	New Jersey
	F	*Schaffer Flora M—†	121	housewife	22	here
	G	*King Estelle—†	121	"	75	"
	H	King James F	121	fisherman	64	"
	K	Wilson Nora—†	121	operator	23	"
	L	*Ferrante Fred	123	actor	45	"
	M	Ferrante Jeanne—†	123	housewife	45	"
	N	Ferri Albertine L—†	123	"	26	
	O	Ferri Carl P	123	machinist	35	"
	P	Fera Elizabeth—†	123	housewife	65	"
	R	Fera Firavanti	123	laborer	64	
	S	*Palano Joseph	125	storekeeper	24	"
	T	Palano Rose—†	125	housewife	21	"
	U	Figliolini Frank A	125	cutter	26	
	V	Figliolini Maria F—†	125	housewife	25	"
	W	*Sbrigilo Concetta—†	125	"	54	
	X	Sbrigilo Paul	125	laborer	63	
	Y	Russo Ignatius	129	rigger	42	"
	Z	Russo Marie—†	129	housewife	69	"
769						
	A	Lawton John J	129	carpenter	29	"
	B	*Lawton Marie V—†	129	housewife	29	"
	C	Gammon Leonard J	129	U S N	28	"
	D	Gammon Rose E—†	129	housewife	27	"
	E	*Morrow Nina J—†	131	"	62	38 White
	F	Morrow William R	131	U S A	20	38 "
	G	Deveau Edward W	131	carpenter	24	here
	H	*Deveau Fannie—†	131	housewife	55	"
	K	Deveau Rita E—†	131	welder	20	"

Page.	Letter.	FULL NAME.	Residence, Jan. 1, 1945.	Occupation.	Supposed Age.	Reported Residence, Jan. 1, 1944. Street and Number.

Trenton Street—Continued

L	Tanner Margaret L—†	131	housewife	24	here
M	Tanner William E	131	U S A	26	"
N	Surette Jane E—†	133	housewife	39	"
O	Surette Sylvester J	133	mechanic	38	"
R	Ventre Charles	139	leatherwkr	41	"
S	Ventre Lillian—†	139	housewife	36	"
T	Ventre Anthony	139	U S A	21	
U	*Ventre Carmella—†	139	housewife	65	"
V	*Ventre Massimino	139	retired	71	
W	Ventre Peter	139	mechanic	32	"
X	Chillemi John J	139	tailor	38	
Y	Chillemi Josephine—†	139	stitcher	38	"
Z	Russo Joseph J	141	chauffeur	45	"
	770				
A	Russo Mary—†	141	housewife	38	"
B	Taurase Katherine—†	141	"	40	
C	Taurase Peter	141	metalworker	46	"
D	Connor Frank J	141	foreman	57	"
E	Connor Palmina L—†	141	housewife	39	"
F	Myett Francis A	143	timekeeper	41	"
G	Myett Margaret B—†	143	housewife	40	"
H	Sheffield James A	143	pipecoverer	58	"
K	Sheffield Pauline F—†	143	housekeeper	37	"
L	Dow Nettie—†	143	housewife	83	"
M	Dow Winthrop	143	toolmaker	44	"
N	Peranio Jemma P—†	145	housewife	33	"
O	Peranio John B	145	boxmaker	36	"
P	Layne Elizabeth—†	145	housewife	22	"
R	Mackey Elizabeth F—†	145	"	46	
S	Mackey Madeline F—†	145	clerk	20	
T	Mackey Richard F	145	rigger	48	
U	Mackey Thomas F	145	U S A	23	
V	Vitale Felix	145	pedler	58	"
W	Vitale Joseph F	145	clerk	22	
X	Vitale Josephine—†	145	housewife	52	"
Y	Vitale Salvatore A	145	cleaner	20	"
Z	Baracchini Charles W	147	coppersmith	41	561 Saratoga
	771				
A	Baracchini Charlotte—†	147	housewife	75	561 "
B	Vars Clara—†	147A	"	30	here
C	Baracchini Harold S	147A	U S N	33	"

Trenton Street—Continued

		FULL NAME.	Residence Jan. 1, 1945.	Occupation.	Age.	Reported Residence
G		DeGrace Gina—†	149	stitcher	37	here
E	*	DiBicari Leonora—†	149	housewife	58	"
F		DiBicari Lillian—†	149	stitcher	25	"
H	*	D'Entremont Edgar	151	cutter	41	
K	*	D'Entremont George	151	retired	77	
L		Surette Damien	151	cutter	50	"
M	*	Surette Rose—†	151	housewife	45	"
N		Daley Clement J	151	fisherman	37	237 Chelsea
O	*	Daley Gertrude A—†	151	housewife	42	237 "
P	*	Abreau Anna—†	151	"	65	here
R	*	Abreau John	151	retired	69	"
S	*	Abreau John, jr	151	textilewkr	40	"
T		Leahey Hugh F	153	clerk	52	"
U		Leahey Sarah A—†	153	housewife	48	"
V		Linehan Elizabeth A—†	153	"	69	
W		Mealey Madeline M—†	153	"	31	
X		Mealey Thomas H	153	clerk	39	
Y		Sacco Mary—†	153	housewife	32	"
Z		Sacco Peter J	153	welder	37	

772

		FULL NAME.	Residence Jan. 1, 1945.	Occupation.	Age.	Reported Residence
A		Piacenza Carlo	153	machinist	55	"
B		Piacenza Josephine—†	153	operator	50	"
C		D'Entremont Edmond V	155	ironworker	57	"
D		D'Entremont Rose I—†	155	housewife	56	"
E		Romano Pauline—†	155	"	28	
F		Romano Principio	155	barber	32	
G		Spinazzola Caroline—†	155	dressmaker	29	"
H		Spinazzola Josephine—†	155	housewife	63	"
K		Spinazzola Pasquale	155	cleaner	64	
L		Salamone Evelyn—†	157	housewife	44	"
M		Salamone Phyllis A—†	157	stenographer	20	"
N		Salamone Vincent	157	metalworker	44	"
O		Catino Camella—†	157	housewife	39	65 Putnam
P		Catino Charles	157	U S A	20	65 "
R		Laterva Theresa—†	157	housewife	67	65 "
S		Figliolini Rose E—†	157A	"	28	here
T		Figliolini Sylvestro	157A	welder	32	"

7

Ward 1–Precinct 8

CITY OF BOSTON

LIST OF RESIDENTS
20 YEARS OF AGE AND OVER

(NON-CITIZENS INDICATED BY ASTERISK)
(FEMALES INDICATED BY DAGGER)

AS OF

JANUARY 1, 1945

THOMAS F. SULLIVAN, *Chairman*
FREDERIC E. DOWLING, *Secretary*
WILLIAM A. MOTLEY, JR.
FRANCIS B. McKINNEY
EVERETT R. PROUT

Listing Board.

CITY OF BOSTON PRINTING DEPARTMENT

800
Border Street

F	Mascis Domenico	325	barber	49	here
G	Mascis Katherine—†	325	housewife	48	"
H	Adwan Nicqueta—†	325	"	30	"
K	Adwan Philip	325	U S A	30	
L	Smith Josephine—†	325	factoryhand	54	"
M	Gambino Joseph	327	pipefitter	45	"
N	Gambino Pauline—†	327	housewife	37	"
O	Caruso Enis—†	329	"	34	"
P*	Caruso Maria—†	329	"	70	"
R	Caruso Stephen	329	mechanic	34	"
T	Capanelli George	329	welder	31	
U	Capanelli Mary—†	329	housewife	28	"
Y	Doyle Mary—†	339	waitress	41	"
Z	Doyle Phyllis—†	339	housekeeper	21	"

801

A	Thornell Blanche—†	339	housewife	40	"
B	Thornell James	339	cable splicer	42	"
F	Monaco Frances—†	343	housekeeper	27	"
G	Monaco Ralph	343	metalworker	26	"
H	Moran Thomas	343	tinsmith	56	"
K	Avilli Louis	343	retired	77	"
L	Culkeen Agnes—†	343	housewife	29	"
M	Culkeen Joseph	343	laborer	42	
N	Garron Clayton	343	"	53	
O	Myers Agnes—†	345	housewife	37	"
P	Myers Edward	345	shipfitter	34	"
R	King Anna—†	345	factoryhand	53	"
T	Caizzi Antonette—†	347	housewife	27	"
U	Caizzi Attilio	347	U S N	26	
V	Denti Christopher	347	laborer	30	
W	Denti Joseph	347	"	50	
X	Denti Madeline—†	347	stitcher	22	"
Y	Denti Mary—†	347	housewife	47	"
Z	Denti Nicholas	347	tailor	24	

802

A	Famiano Joseph	347	shoe worker	39	"
B	Famiano Minnie—†	347	"	36	
H	Grifone John	366	laborer	45	
K	Grifone Lulu—†	366	housewife	61	"
L	Hassen Joseph	366	fireman	51	

Border Street—Continued

M	Hassen Mary E—†	366	housewife	61	here
N	Richards Hannah—†	366	housekeeper	82	"
O	Ferri Pasquale	367	laborer	77	"
V	Nelson Charlotte—†	369	housewife	52	"
W	Nelson Henry A	369	laborer	53	"
X	Donatelli Frederico	369	welder	31	
Y	Donatelli Louisa—†	369	housewife	33	"
Z	Cototreau Adeline—†	369	"	39	

803

A	Cototreau Charles	369	boilermaker	45	"
E	Zimmer Albert	373	guard	38	..
F	Zimmer Chester	373	U S A	23	
G	Zimmer Elmer	373	"	27	"
H	Zimmer George, jr	373	laborer	36	"
K	Zimmer George W	373	potter	62	"
L	Zimmer Sarah L—†	373	housewife	60	"

Brooks Street

T	Powell Elizabeth—†	166	housekeeper	52	140 Bennington
U	Powell Frank	166	shipper	23	140 "
V	Powell William	166	U S A	20	140 "
W	Dellaria John	168	welder	35	here
X	Dellaria Rita—†	168	housewife	30	"
Y	Morrison Edna—†	168	"	62	"
Z	Morrison William	168	finisher	64	"

804

A	Buonopane Nicholas	169	janitor	46	
B	Buonopane Philomena—†	169	housewife	38	"
C*	Doucette Loretta—†	169	housekeeper	45	"
D	Folsom Irene—†	169	housewife	20	"
E	Folsom James	169	U S A	23	
F	Pellegrini Armando	169	"	24	
G	Pellegrini Carmen	169	"	27	
H	Pellegrini Enrico	169	U S N	22	
K	Pellegrini Laura—†	169	housewife	47	"
L	Messina John	170	machinist	36	"
M	Messina Nancy—†	170	housewife	32	"
N	Budowicz Geraldine—†	170	"	23	Saugus
O	Budowicz Peter	170	U S A	30	"
P	Raddin Everett	170	laborer	52	here

3

Brooks Street—Continued

R	Raddin Lillian—†	170	housewife	49	here
s	Kerr Joseph	171	restaurateur	36	Reading
T	Staffier Domenic	171	upholsterer	33	here
U	Staffier Emilio	171	tailor	54	"
v	*Staffier Louise—†	171	housewife	53	"
w	Staffier Angelo	171	U S A	31	
x	Staffier Ralph	171	"	28	"
y	Staffier Vito	171	letter carrier	21	"

805

A	DuMoulin Harold	174	machinist	32	"
B	DuMoulin Margaret L—†	174	housewife	39	"
C	Zaffiro Anthony	174	mechanic	33	169 Princeton
D	Zaffiro Carmela—†	174	housewife	31	169 "
E	Fererra Carmen	174	mechanic	22	here
F	Ferarra Frank	174	storekeeper	48	"
G	*Ferarra Pellegrina—†	174	housewife	48	"
K	Collucci Arthur	176	laborer	27	"
L	Collucci Santa—†	176	housewife	26	"
M	Giorgio Albert	176	shipfitter	20	"
N	Giorgio Anthony	176	brazier	22	"
o	Giorgio Charles	176	U S A	24	
P	Giorgio Joseph	176	"	30	
R	Giorgio Mary—†	176	housewife	51	"
s	Giorgio Mildred—†	176	clerk	25	
T	Giorgio Raffaele	176	janitor	61	"
U	Ohlson James H	176	fireman	42	"
v	Ohlson Margaret—†	176	housewife	36	"
x	Graziano Josephine—†	178	"	27	
y	Graziano Thomas	178	welder	32	
z	Belliveau Frances—†	178	housewife	39	"

806

A	Belliveau Frank	178	foreman	39	"
B	Tagariello Catherine—†	178	secretary	20	"
C	Tagariello Joseph	178	finisher	57	"
D	Tagariello Lucy—†	178	teacher	20	"
E	Tagariello Mary—†	178	housewife	46	"
F	Burgess Katherine—†	188	at home	69	190 Brooks
G	Welch Edward R	188	instructor	36	here
H	Welch Loretta J—†	188	housewife	38	"
K	Pomeroy Arthur F	190	welder	23	"
L	Pomeroy Bridget M—†	190	housewife	66	"

Page	Letter	Full Name.	Residence, Jan. 1, 1945.	Occupation.	Supposed Age.	Reported Residence, Jan. 1, 1944. Street and Number.

Brooks Street—Continued

	M	Pomeroy Joseph E	190	U S A	32	here
	N	Mulieri Alfred	192	U S N	27	"
	O	Mulieri Edith—†	192	operator	23	"
	P	Mulieri Ernest	192	U S N	25	"
	R	Phelan George R.	192	rigger	38	Medford
	S	Phelan Josephine M—†	192	housewife	29	"
	U	Ricardo Anthony	194	machinist	32	here
	V	Ricardo Antoinette—†	194	housewife	30	"
	W	Bonaiuto Annette—†	194	housekeeper	61	"
	X	Lembo Mary—†	194	housewife	34	"
	Y	Lembo Michael	194	electrician	45	"
	Z	Duthie Bessie—†	196	housekeeper	78	59 White
807						
	A	Catoggio Antoinette—†	196	housewife	33	here
	B	Catoggio Nicholas	196	shoeworker	39	"
	C	Catoggio Mary—†	196	housekeeper	59	"
	D	Lanieri Carl	198	physician	32	"
	E	Lanieri Phyllis—†	198	housewife	28	"
	F	Ceruolo Angelina—†	198	housekeeper	37	"
	G	Bennett Eugene	198	shoeworker	50	"
	H	Bennett Margaret—†	198	housewife	60	"
	K	Bennett William	198	shoeworker	62	"
	L	Diorio Domenic	200	painter	56	..
	M	Diorio Susie—†	200	housewife	55	"
	N	Daddico Patrick	200	laborer	41	167 Lexington
	O	Daddico Santa—†	200	housewife	30	167 "
	P	Keough Louise—†	200	housekeeper	45	here

Eutaw Place

	R	Crouse James E	1	carpenter	62	here
	S	Crouse Lillian—†	1	housewife	66	"
	V	Fabiano Anna—†	3	"	28	"
	W	Fabiano Joseph	3	laborer	38	
	X	Grasso Josephine—†	3	at home	29	"
	Y	Violetto Concetta—†	3	housewife	55	"
	Z	Violetto Joseph	3	inspector	25	"
808						
	A	Violetto Mary—†	3	saleswoman	24	"
	B	Pisano Antonio	3	laborer	52	
	C	Pisano Frank	3	U S A	21	

5

Page.	Letter.	FULL NAME.	Residence, Jan. 1, 1945.	Occupation.	Supposed Age.	Reported Residence, Jan. 1, 1944. Street and Number.

Eutaw Place—Continued

	D	Pisano Lena—†	3	housewife	32	here
	E	*Pisano Mary—†	3	"	53	"
	F	Pisano Mary—†	3	stitcher	25	"
	G	Norcott Maude—†	4	housewife	40	"
	H	Norcott William	4	rigger	34	"
	K	Escher Rose—†	5	housewife	22	California
	L	Escher Rudolph	5	U S N	26	"
	M	Stella Charles	5	laborer	34	here
	N	Stella John	5	"	63	"
	O	Stella Lucy—†	5	housewife	50	"
	P	Stella Samuel	5	laborer	20	"
	R	Mattina Margaret—†	6	housewife	26	"
	S	Mattina Peter	6	welder	29	
	T	Mattina John	6	laborer	55	
	U	Gallagher James L	7	retired	75	"
	V	Trott Andrew	7	laborer	35	Chelsea
	W	Barry Augustine W	7	retired	78	here
	X	Lewis Alfred	8	salesman	40	"
	Y	Lewis Anna—†	8	housewife	36	"

Eutaw Street

	Z	Schultz Mildred E—†	6	housewife	32	here
		809				
	A	Schultz William	6	laborer	30	177 Everett
	B	Beck Dorothy—†	20	bookkeeper	39	here
	C	Beck Nathan	20	shoe dealer	71	"
	D	Beck Rosalind—†	20	clerk	25	"
	E	Beck Rose—†	20	housewife	61	"
	F	Kenney Geneva N—†	20	janitress	56	"
	G	Kenney Minnie M—†	20	welder	24	
	H	Kenney Solomon M	20	boatbuilder	60	"
	K	Brown Amy E—†	20	housewife	58	"
	L	Brown Clare F—†	20	houseworker	21	"
	M	Brown Creta L—†	20	"	24	New Mexico
	N	Brown Edward C	20	U S A	33	here
	O	Brown George A	20	"	25	"
	P	Brown Robert R	20	clerk	23	"
	S	Dunbar Charles H	24	seaman	54	Rhode Island
	T	Dunbar Christina L—†	24	housewife	56	"
	U	Tallman Ethel F—†	24	"	55	here

Page.	Letter.	FULL NAME.	Residence, Jan. 1, 1945.	Occupation.	Supposed Age.	Reported Residence, Jan. 1, 1944. Street and Number.

Eutaw Street—Continued

v	Tallman Harry T	24	clerk	60	here
w	Tallman Leon D	24	seaman	25	"
x	Ciulla Margaret—†	26	housewife	25	"
y	Ciulla Stephen	26	fishcutter	25	"
z	Grover Harold L	26	rigger	43	

810

a	Grover Josephine B—†	26	housewife	44	"
b	Madison Herbert H	26	U S A	30	
c	Gentile M Grace—†	26	housewife	43	"
d	Gentile R Armando	26	shoeworker	52	"
e	Murphy Frederick J	28	machinist	39	"
f	Perry George T	28	retired	72	
g	Perry George T, jr	28	U S A	23	
h	Perry Margaret A—†	28	housewife	60	"
k	King Elmer A	30	chauffeur	51	212 E Eagle
l	King Elmer A, jr	30	U S N	24	212 "
m	King Grace M—†	30	housewife	50	212 "
n	Cresey Edna—†	32	at home	52	here
o	Crescy Lottie—†	32	"	82	"
p	McAuley Bertha—†	32	housewife	45	"
r	McAuley Lawrence	32	guard	45	
s	*Cerrato Elizabeth—†	34	housewife	51	"
t	Cerrato Francis	34	shoemaker	28	"
u	*Cerrato Pasquale	34	shoecutter	55	"
v	Cuscianotto Anthony	34	shoemaker	31	"
w	Cuscianotto Theresa—†	34	candymaker	30	"
x	Harrigan Edwin C	34	scaler	59	9 Bulfinch
y	Marchesi Felix	36	chauffeur	53	here
z	Marchesi Margaret—†	36	housewife	47	"

811

a	*Maggio Angelina—†	38	"	69	
b	*Maggio Michael	38	laborer	67	
c	Marchesi Dominic	38	carpenter	46	"
d	Dunbar Edward	40	U S A	20	
e	Dunbar Myron	40	laborer	46	
f	Dunbar Thelma—†	40	housewife	42	"
g	Winer Frances—†	42	"	33	"
h	Winer George E	42	welder	35	"
k	LaVoie Alice N—†	44	housewife	50	"
l	LaVoie Alice N—†	44	waitress	21	"
m	LaVoie Frances—†	44	WAVE	24	"

Page.	Letter.	FULL NAME.	Residence, Jan. 1, 1945.	Occupation.	Supposed Age.	Reported Residence, Jan. 1, 1944. Street and Number.

	N	LaVoie Norbert	44	shipfitter	47	here
	O	LaVoie Norbert L	44	brazier	26	60 Gladstone
	R	Clipp Marjorie A—†	48	nurse	37	here
	S	Winsor Frank	48	carpenter	68	"
	T	Winsor Rebecca—†	48	housewife	57	"
	V	Piretti Elizabeth G—†	49	"	38	
	W	Piretti Raymond E	49	painter	40	"
	X	DiIeso Ellen—†	49	housewife	26	"
	Y	DiIeso Paul	49	repairman	29	"
	Z	Hunter James	50	machinist	28	"
		812				
	A	Hunter Jean—†	50	housewife	26	"
	B	Keenan Margaret—†	50	"	62	"
	C	Keenan Walter F	50	electrician	64	"
	D	Keenan Walter F, jr	50	U S C G	24	"
	E	Marks Evelyn M—†	50	housewife	26	Texas
	F	O'Brien Agnes G—†	50	at home	72	here
	G	Crotty Andrew J	51	installer	45	"
	H	Crotty Evelyn I—†	51	housewife	44	"
	K	Crotty James E	51	U S A	20	
	L	Hickey Evelyn M—†	51	secretary	22	"
	M	Hickey George B	51	U S A	24	47 Bennington
	N	Salerno Antoinette—†	52	stitcher	22	here
	O	Salerno Florence—†	52	housewife	55	"
	P	Salerno Nicholas	52	chipper	58	"
	R	Salerno Samuel	52	seaman	26	"
	S	Mancini Alma—†	52	housewife	31	"
	T	Mancini Armando J	52	painter	28	"
	W	Magnell Hilma—†	56	housewife	47	"
	X	Magnell Joseph	56	U S C G	23	"
	Y	Magnell Joseph N	56	printer	47	"
	Z	Magnell Mary H—†	56	artist	20	"
		813				
	A	Magnell Wallace	56	U S N	21	
	B	Bianco Catherine—†	58	housewife	54	"
	C	Bianco Nicholas	58	U S C G	23	"
	D	Ciampa Katherine—†	58	housewife	29	"
	E	Walsh Joseph	58	fisherman	38	"
	F	Walsh Mary—†	58	housewife	37	"
	G	Staretz Leah—†	60	"	38	"
	H	Staretz Samuel	60	plumber	40	"

K	Adelman David	60	U S M C	29	here
L	Adelman Henry	60	physician	33	Charlton
M	Adelman Max H	60	carpenter	64	here
N	Adelman Sarah D—†	60	housewife	58	"
O	Rogers Anna—†	60	stitcher	50	"
P	Jacobs Jacob	62	tailor	68	
R	Jacobs Mary M—†	62	at home	36	"
S	D'Amato Alfred W	62	chauffeur	38	"
T	D'Amato Elizabeth—†	62	housewife	28	"
U	D'Amato Vincent	62	laborer	30	
V	Bonta Carmelo	62	painter	41	
W	Bonta Rosaria—†	62	housewife	38	"
X	Bailey Dorothea—†	64	"	52	
Y	Bailey John P	64	blacksmith	55	"
Z	Orlando Attilio	64	U S A	24	

814

A	Orlando Carmella—†	64	housewife	21	"
B	Cimo Jennie—†	64A	"	57	
C	Cimo Salvatore	64A	storekeeper	54	"
D	Tarquinio Mario	64A	dishwasher	27	"
E	Latson Mary O—†	66	typist	25	
F	Latson Timothy C	66	U S A	25	
G	*Cima Ottorino	66	laborer	46	
H	Re Angela—†	66	clerk	35	
K	Re Celso	66	bartender	66	"
L	Re Elvira—†	66	clerk	38	
M	*Re Mary—†	66	housewife	62	"
N	Tomasso Frank D	66	laborer	46	
O	Alexander Maria R—†	68	teacher	41	
P	Alexander Robert	68	supt	38	
R	Merces Joseph A	70	cook	69	
S	*Pina Carlotta—†	70	housewife	58	"
T	Pina Jennie—†	70	stitcher	28	
U	Almeida Anthony L	70	deckhand	45	"
V	Almeida Mary E—†	70	housewife	39	"
W	McFarland Margaret—†	70	clerk	29	
X	*Sousa Anthony	71	laborer	65	
Y	Sousa John	71	U S A	24	"
Z	Sousa Joseph	71	"	22	

815

A	Sousa Mary—†	71	housewife	57	"

Eutaw Street—Continued

	b	*Pedro Anna F—†	71	housewife	54	here
	c	Pedro Anna M—†	71	"	25	"
	d	Pedro Annabelle—†	71	factoryhand	21	"
	e	*Pedro Anthony	71	laborer	70	"
	f	Pedro Joseph A	71	"	31	"
	g	Perry John	71	clerk	44	
	h	Spolsino Emily—†	71	factoryhand	27	"
	k	Iantosca Angelo	72	U S A	34	
	l	Iantosca Maritta—†	72	housewife	33	"
	m	LoVetere Rose—†	72	"	63	
	n	Eaton Mary—†	72	"	27	
	o	Eaton Walter	72	U S A	32	
	p	Crotty Anna J—†	73	stenographer	36	"
	r	Crotty Mary E—†	73	at home	72	"
	s	Crotty Mary H—†	73	teacher	38	"
	t	Nihan Margaret—†	73	seamstress	73	"
	u	Maggio Mario	74	salesman	47	2 Montmorenci av
	v	*Barranco Angelo	74	retired	80	here
	w	*Barranco Josephine—†	74	housewife	75	"
	x	Barranco Salvatore	74	painter	40	"
	y	Christopher Ann—†	74	housewife	29	"
	z	Christopher John	74	musician	33	"
816						
	a	Neilson Charles	75	U S A	26	
	b	Neilson Matilda—†	75	housewife	25	"
	c	Cotecchia Rose—†	75	"	30	
	d	Cotecchia Warren	75	machinist	27	"
	e	Bernardi Alfred	75	guard	37	
	f	Bernardi Mary—†	75	housewife	36	"
	g	Langone Jennie—†	76	"	34	89 Princeton
	h	Langone John	76	motorman	33	89 "
	k	Bellabona Joseph	76	carpenter	33	74 Trenton
	l	Bellabona Olympia N—†	76	housewife	31	74 "
	m	Crawford Myron E	77	motorman	48	here
	n	Crawford Ralph M	77	U S A	23	"
	o	Crawford Ruth—†	77	housewife	47	"
	p	Rubino Angela—†	77	at home	30	"
	r	Rubino Jennie—†	77	housewife	56	"
	s	Rubino Luigi	77	shipper	60	"
	t	Rubino Mary—†	77	clerk	32	
	u	*Kelly Bertha—†	79	housewife	46	"

10

Page.	Letter.	Full Name.	Residence, Jan. 1, 1945.	Occupation.	Supposed Age.	Reported Residence, Jan. 1, 1944. Street and Number.

Eutaw Street—Continued

	v	Kelly James L	79	U S C G	40	here
	w	Levy William H	79	U S N	22	"
	x	Neill Ruby—†	79	inspector	25	"
	y	Curcio Amelio	79	engineer	50	"
	z	Curcio Carmella—†	79	housewife	48	"
817						
	A	Curcio Catherine—†	79	stenographer	22	"
	B	Curcio Emilio	79	repairman	57	"
	c	DiMartino Catherine—†	79	housewife	36	"
	D	DiMartino Joseph A	79	machinist	40	"
	E	Meuse Antoinette—†	80	housewife	40	"
	F	Meuse John S	80	metalworker	46	"
	G	Thomas Beatrice—†	80	housewife	29	"
	H	Thomas Joseph W	80	rigger	31	"
	K	Regan Anne M—†	81	housewife	36	"
	L	Regan Daniel	81	asbestoswkr	36	"
	M	Kallas George	81	textilewkr	62	"
	N	Snowdon Emma M—†	81	housewife	58	"
	o	Snowdon Wallace E	81	operator	68	"
	P	Elkins Eva—†	82	waitress	49	"
	R	Fahey Gladys—†	83	housewife	36	"
	s	Fahey James F	83	machinist	36	"
	T	Albino Edith—†	83	operator	40	"
	U	Albino George	83	shoemaker	52	"
	v	Albino James	83	baker	26	
	w	Clair John	83	fishcutter	65	"
	x	Milia Andrew	84	cook	59	115½ Havre
	y	*Milia Carmela—†	84	housewife	49	115½ "
	z	Elvey Estelle E—†	84	"	44	here
818						
	A	Elvey Milton H	84	treasurer	46	"
	B	Orlando John	84	printer	33	
	c	Orlando Victoria—†	84	housewife	28	"
	D	Yetman Mary—†	85	"	54	
	E	Yetman Robert	85	retired	62	
	c	Cacciatore Angelina—†	85	housewife	50	"
	G	Cacciatore Angelo	85	U S A	25	
	H	Cacciatore Domenic	85	"	20	··
	K	Cacciatore Giacomo	85	. "	29	
	L	Cacciatore Raymond	85	clerk	62	
	M	Stasio Mary—†	86	housewife	52	"

Eutaw Street—Continued

	N	Stasio Ralph	86	treasurer	55	here
	O	DeSantis John	86	laborer	41	"
	P	DeSantis Michelina—†	86	housewife	40	"
	R	Markis Charles	86	laborer	47	
	S	Markis Mary—†	86	housewife	43	"
	T	Markis Milton	86	U S A	20	"
	U	Nardi Agazio	87	candymaker	59	"
	V	Nardi Mary—†	87	housewife	48	"
	W	Nardi Victor	87	U S A	25	
	X	Bickford Mildred—†	87	guard	45	
	Y	Bickford Mildred—†	87	housewife	40	"
	Z	Cataldo Ida—†	87	operator	28	"

819

	A	Nicosia James	88	U S A	20	
	B	Russo Dominic	88	machinist	63	"
	C	Russo Sarah—†	88	housewife	63	"
	D	Marotta Albert	88	barber	45	
	E	Marotta Mary A—†	88	housewife	36	"
	F	Russo Margaret—†	88	painter	30	"
	G	Santoro Eleanor—†	90	housewife	29	"
	H	Santoro Salvatore	90	U S A	31	
	K	Day Louise H—†	90	housewife	30	"
	L	Day Walter I	90	chauffeur	33	"
	M	Alba Andrew	90	repairman	66	"
	N	Alba Marie—†	90	candymaker	25	"
	O	Alba Mary—†	90	housewife	57	"
	P	Christiansen Carl	92	machinist	43	"
	R	Christiansen Harold	92	longshoreman	40	"
	S	Christiansen Sophia—†	92	housewife	76	"
	T	MacDonald Cathrine—†	96	"	60	"
	U	MacDonald David T	96	U S N	26	"
	W*	McLellan Jennie—†	105	housewife	65	85 Lexington
	X	McLellan William	105	bottler	62	85 "
	Y	Doucette Norman J	105	calker	47	here
	Z	Pusatere James	105	chauffeur	29	"

820

	A	Pusatere Lola—†	105	housewife	22	"
	B	Abbott Clarence M	107	baker	27	
	C	Abbott Irene—†	107	housewife	24	"
	D	Schettino Antoinetta—†	107	"	49	
	E	Schettino Michael	107	shoemaker	52	"

Page.	Letter.	Full Name.	Residence, Jan. 1, 1945.	Occupation.	Supposed Age.	Reported Residence, Jan. 1, 1944. Street and Number.

Eutaw Street—Continued

	F	Ford George E	107	longshoreman	36	here
	G	Ford Thetka C—†	107	housewife	33	"
	D	DePalma Albert	109	seaman	25	"
	K	DePalma Mary—†	109	housewife	52	"
	L	DePalma Virginia—†	109	stitcher	22	"
	M	Bethune Frances G—†	109	housewife	21	329 W Eagle
	N	Bethune Thomas M	109	U S N	26	329 "
	O	Rich Elizabeth M—†	109	housewife	57	366 Princeton
	P	Rich Julius	109	molder	60	366 "
	R	Rich William G	109	U S A	32	366 "
	S	DeLaria Mary—†	109	housewife	28	here
	T	DeLaria Vincent J	109	designer	27	"
	U	Gentuso Ignazio	111	storekeeper	63	"
	V	Gentuso Rose—†	111	housewife	59	"
	W	Juliana Joseph	111	U S M C	22	"
	X	Juliana Maria—†	111	stitcher	45	"
	Y	Grosso Joan—†	111	housewife	28	"
	Z	Grosso Joseph	111	chauffeur	28	"

821

	A	Macrina Louise—†	111	operator	23	"
	B	Caristo Ottavina—†	113	housewife	30	"
	C	Caristo Salvatore	113	tailor	38	
	D	Camerlengo Louise—†	113	housewife	50	"
	E	Camerlengo Philip	113	assessor	51	"
	F	Lippens Peter J	113	U S C G	27	"
	G	Lippens Rita—†	113	housewife	23	"
	H	Daley John B	113	bookbinder	52	"
	K	Daley Mary E—†	113	housewife	52	"
	L	Chadwick Milton R	115	machinist	26	"
	M	Chadwick Nancy G—†	115	housewife	25	"
	N	Gallagher Sarah A—†	115	housekeeper	78	"
	O	O'Brien Frederick L	115	prob'n officer	60	"
	P	Salamone Josephine—†	117	housewife	25	"
	R	Salamone Rocco	117	cable splicer	26	"
	S	D'Errico Anna—†	117	clerk	20	"
	T	D'Errico Antonetta—†	117	housewife	52	"
	U	D'Errico Savino	117	storekeeper	61	"
	V	Marchionda Louise—†	117	stitcher	22	"
	W	Lalli Joseph	117	painter	52	
	X	Lalli Josephine—†	117	housewife	39	"
	Y	Lalli Nancy—†	117	clerk	20	

Eutaw Street—Continued

z	D'Errico Christina—†	119	housewife	30	here
	822					
A	D'Errico Michael	119	welder	31	
c	Cravotta Elizabeth—†	119	housewife	22	"
D	Cravotta Salvatore	119	machinist	23	"
E	White Isabelle—†	121	housewife	35	"
F	Miraglia Ida—†	121	at home	24	"
G	Miraglia Louis	121	student	21	"
H	Miraglia Mary—†	121	saleswoman	23	"
K	Lagammo Joseph	121	shoeworker	37	"
L	Lagammo Theresa—†	121	housewife	34	"
M	Surette Joseph	123	shipfitter	42	"
N	Surette Margarette—†	123	housewife	37	"
O	Clancy Gladys—†	123	"	30	"
P	Clancy Peter	123	welder	32	"
R	Myers Edward	123	guard	61	"
S	Myers George	123	laborer	24	"
T	Myers Georgianna—†	123	housewife	61	"
U	Myers Marion—†	123	factoryhand	21	"
V	Myers William	123	U S A	23	"
W	Bottaglia Frank	125	retired	68	135 Eutaw
X	Bottaglia Samuel	125	salesman	32	135 "
Y	Lewis Albert	125	engineer	29	here
z	Lewis Kathleen—†	125	housewife	24	"
	823					
A	Comunale Antoinette—†	125	"	41	
B	Comunale Joseph	125	millhand	50	"
c	Comunale Rose—†	125	clerk	20	
D	Comunale Vincent	125	U S A	21	
E	Comunale Rose—†	127	housewife	70	"
F	Comunale Vincent	127	retired	70	"
G	Foster Adeline—†	127	housewife	44	33 Eutaw
H	DeFeo Gaetano	127	chauffeur	24	188 Falcon
K	DeFeo Sarah—†	127	housewife	23	188 "
M	Carroll David	129	U S A	28	here
N	Carroll James	129	mechanic	25	"
O	Carroll Mary—†	129	housewife	50	"
P	Carroll Mary—†	129	"	29	
R	Carroll Norma—†	129	at home	20	"
S	Barbere Angelo	129	longshoreman	32	"
T	Barbere Theresa—†	129	housewife	31	"

u	Amoroso Bernice—†	131	housewife	30	here
v	Amoroso Joseph	131	mechanic	50	"
w	Amoroso Joseph	131	laborer	24	"
x	*Amoroso Salvatore	131	"	20	
y	Manucci Cosmos	131	"	66	
z	Manucci Dominic	131		36	
	824				
a	*Manucci Mary—†	131	housewife	69	"
b	Zavarelli Frances—†	131	"	33	105 Eutaw
c	Zavarelli Phillip	131	U S N	31	105 "
d	Taurasi Salvatore	133	shoeworker	63	here
e	Taurasi Virginia—†	133	housewife	55	"
f	Warner Leonard	133	U S N	29	"
g	Warner Mildred—†	133	housewife	30	"
h	Gaeta Edwin L	133	U S A	26	204 Saratoga
k	Gaeta Irene—†	133	housewife	21	204 "
l	Surette Mary M—†	133	"	41	204 "
m	*Perrisco Anna—†	135	"	52	here
n	Perrisco Michael	135	laborer	52	"
p	Battaglia Dominic	135	U S A	26	"
r	Battaglia Edna—†	135	housewife	21	"
s	Waters Joseph	135	pedler	49	
t	Waters Mary—†	135	housewife	39	"
u	*Lucca Antonio	137	barber	51	"
v	Lucca Frances—†	137	housewife	53	"
w	Votta Antonio	137	watchman	61	"
x	Votta Carmella—†	137	stitcher	21	
y	Votta Frances—†	137	"	20	
z	Votta Rose—†	137	housewife	49	"
	825				
a	Petraglia Albert	137	laborer	35	92 Putnam
b	Patraglia Angelina—†	137	housewife	31	92 "
c	McDonald Eleanor—†	139	tel operator	28	here
d	McDonald John W	139	fireman	52	"
e	McDonald William	139	U S N	27	"
f	Smith Augusta—†	141	clerk	33	
g	Smith Gladys—†	141	housewife	52	"
h	Smith Louis	141	U S N	28	"
k	Smith Ross	141	fishcutter	57	"
l	Scoffi Alphonse	143	storekeeper	32	"
m	Scoffi John	143	"	54	"

Page.	Letter.	FULL NAME.	Residence, Jan. 1, 1945.	Occupation.	Supposed Age.	Reported Residence, Jan. 1, 1944. Street and Number.

Eutaw Street—Continued

	N	*Scoffi Louise—†	143	housewife	48	here
	O	Scoffi Salvatore	143	electrician	30	"
	P	Dion Antonio	145	brakeman	26	53 W Eagle
	R	Rodriguez Juanita—†	145	housewife	36	59 "

Marion Street

	U	Brown Alec	3	U S N	20	here
	V	Brown Frederick	3	storekeeper	42	"
	W	Brown Sophie—†	3	housewife	46	"
	X	*MacLean Jeanette—†	5	"	37	
	Y	*MacLean John	5	chauffeur	42	"
	Z	Cotreau Frederick	5	engineer	42	"
826						
	A	Cotreau Rita—†	5	housewife	36	"
	B	Smith Edward G	5	salesman	41	"
	C	*Smith Ethel—†	5	housewife	41	"
	D	Flaherty Lavinia—†	9	"	56	
	E	Flaherty William H	9	watchman	62	"
	F	Grace Edith H—†	11	clerk	20	
	G	Grace Gerald A	11	operator	46	"
	H	Grace Mildred P—†	11	housewife	41	"
	K	Verdy Charlisina—†	11	"	66	..
	L	Verdy Edward	11	court officer	65	"
	M	Verdy George	11	U S A	35	
	N	Cox Joseph F	12	watchman	64	"
	O	Cox Vincenza—†	12	housewife	56	"
	P	Keenan Edna V—†	12	"	53	
	R	Keenan William E	12	bartender	52	"
	S	Morrison Doris A—†	13	housewife	41	63 W Eagle
	T	Morrison William, jr	13	pipefitter	35	63 "
	U	Witter Andrew	14	baker	44	111 Meridian
	V	Witter Nellie—†	14	housewife	27	111 ✎
	W	Farioli Clara—†	14	"	57	here
	X	Farioli William	14	U S A	39	"
	Y	Moriarty Elizabeth—†	14	housewife	72	"
	Z	Anderson Marion L—†	15	"	24	77 Monument
827						
	A	Anderson William J	15	painter	32	77 "
	B	Brown Eileen—†	15	housewife	22	here
	C	Brown Raymond H	15	mechanic	23	"

16

Page.	Letter.	Full Name.	Residence, Jan. 1, 1945.	Occupation.	Supposed Age.	Reported Residence, Jan. 1, 1944. Street and Number.

Marion Street—Continued

	D	Nagle Ruth—†	16	accountant	26	here
	E	Nagle Timothy	16	printer	36	Milton
	F	Webb Marie—†	16	housewife	57	here
	G	Webb Patrick X	16	cook	64	"
	H	Doran John	17	rigger	37	"
	K	Doran Julia—†	17	housewife	35	"
	L	Joyce George	17	steamfitter	39	"
	M	Joyce Marie—†	17	housewife	35	"
	N	LeBlanc Blanche—†	17	"	62	..
	O	LeBlanc Gordon	17	U S A	33	
	P	LeBlanc Louis C	17	chef	68	
	R	LeBlanc Ralph	17	U S A	24	..
	S	Gray David	18	cobbler	73	"
	T	Smith Edith—†	18	housewife	42	"
	U	Smith Paul	18	physician	48	"
	V	Pearson Rita—†	19	housewife	26	"
	W	Pearson Walter	19	foreman	29	"
	X	Rizzuto Joseph	19	laborer	35	"
	Y	White Ellen—†	19	housewife	58	"
	Z	Ducharme Leo	20	metalworker	27	14 Monmouth
828						
	A	Ducharme Rose—†	20	housewife	26	14 "
	B	Loverro Felix	20	U S N	27	here
	C	Loverro Margaret—†	20	housewife	27	"
	D	Ducharme Elric	20	fisherman	58	27 White
	E	Germano Charles C	21	operator	33	260 Maverick
	F	Germano Josephine—†	21	housewife	30	260 "
	G	Cross Josephine—†	21	"	21	here
	H	Cross Lawrence	21	U S A	23	"
	K	Richards Charles	21	U S N	29	"
	L	Richards Mary—†	21	housewife	23	"
	M	DeNaro Constance—†	21	"	31	"
	N	DeNaro Michael	21	rigger	31	
	O	Keyes Bertha—†	22	housewife	78	"
	P	Keyes Chester A	22	engineer	53	"
	R	Keyes Edith—†	22	housewife	50	"
	S	Fraccastoro Americo	24	inspector	25	"
	T	Fraccastoro Concetta—†	24	housewife	26	"
	U	Villani Joseph	24	retired	51	
	V	Tedeschi Joseph	24	cabinetmaker	56	" .
	W	Tedeschi Matilda—†	24	housewife	50	"

1—8   17

Page.	Letter.	FULL NAME.	Residence, Jan. 1, 1945.	Occupation.	Supposed Age.	Reported Residence, Jan. 1, 1944. Street and Number.

Marion Street—Continued

	x	Tacelli Albert S	24	foreman	37	here
	y	Tacelli Melinda—†	24	housewife	29	"
	z	Gannon Augustine S	26	florist	49	"
829						
	a	Gannon Augustine S, jr	26	U S N	22	"
	b	Gannon Helen E—†	26	housewife	46	"
	c	Gannon Mary E—†	26	secretary	20	"
	d	Holland Jennie G—†	37	housewife	54	"
	e	Sullivan Katherine E—†	39	"	56	
	f	Sullivan William J	39	shipper	61	"
	g	Montello Frances—†	40	housewife	50	"
	h	Montello Francisco	40	laborer	50	"
	k	Adami Edgar	40	machinist	37	"
	l	Adami Eleanor—†	40	housewife	29	"
	m	Giardiello Fannie—†	40	"	53	
	n	Giardiello George	40	U S A	20	"
	o	Giardiello Michael	40	tailor	53	"
	p	Giardiello Roger	40	U S C G	23	"
	r	McDonald Margaret D—†	41	housewife	74	"
	s	Lewis Frederick M	43	shipper	66	"
	t	Lewis Mary E—†	43	housewife	55	"
	u	O'Hara Margaret C—†	43	stenographer	23	"
	v	Lentini Louise—†	44	housewife	38	"
	w	Lentini Samuel	44	electrician	38	"
	x	Dichiara Alphonzo	44	U S A	22	
	y	Dichiara Angelo	44	"	23	
	z	Dichiara Matteo	44	mason	21	
830						
	a	Dichiara Nicholas	44	"	48	
	b	Tsolakis Lucas	44	seaman	60	"
	c	Zambrinos Anna—†	44	housewife	46	"
	d	Zambrinos William	44	watchman	66	236 Princeton
	e	Carbonaro Joseph	48	laborer	59	here
	f	*Carbonaro Santa—†	48	housewife	59	"
	g	*Capocci Ernest	48	chef	36	"
	h	*Capocci Mary—†	48	housewife	29	"
	k	Terry Florence—†	48	wrapper	23	275 Havre
	l	*DiChiara Delores—†	48	housewife	48	here
	m	DiChiara Nicolas	48	U S N	20	"
	n	DiChiara Ralph	48	laborer	54	"
	o	Murphy Emma—†	48	clerk	23	"

Page	Letter	Full Name.	Residence, Jan. 1, 1945.	Occupation.	Supposed Age.	Reported Residence, Jan. 1, 1944. Street and Number.

Marion Street—Continued

	P	Souza Carmella—†	48	packer	24	here
	R	Fagone John S	52	chauffeur	29	"
	S	Fagone Marcella—†	52	housewife	26	"
	T	Carso Louis	52	mechanic	40	7 Lexington av
	U	*Carso Phyllis—†	52	housewife	50	7 "
	V	Peracola Carmella—†	52	packer	20	7 "
	W	Peracola Mario	52	U S A	22	7 "
	X	Delia Antonio	52	"	22	here
	Y	Delia Mary—†	52	clerk	20	"
	Z	Delia Michael	52	laborer	49	"
831						
	A	Delia Philomena—†	52	housewife	43	"
	B	DePaolis Alexander	52A	storekeeper	25	"
	C	DePaolis Catherine—†	52A	stitcher	21	"
	D	DePaolis Hugo	52A	mechanic	50	"
	E	DePaolis Lena—†	52A	housewife	51	"
	F	DePaolis Louis	52A	U S A	27	
	G	Gullas Gina—†	52A	housewife	28	"
	H	Gulla Leo	52A	boilermaker	27	"
	K	Lima Elsie—†	54	housewife	35	"
	L	Lima John	54	machinist	39	187 London
	M	Cerulli Nancy—†	56	housewife	38	here
	N	Cerulli Thomas	56	engineer	38	"
	O	Maffeo Annette R—†	58	housewife	25	"
	P	Mangone Anna C—†	58	"	37	
	R	*Maffie Alphonse	58	retired	79	"
	S	Maffie Anthony	58	U S A	20	"
	T	Maffie Joseph L	58	"	26	
	U	Maffie Mildred—†	58	packer	24	
	V	Maffie Mildred C—†	58	housewife	52	"
	W	Maffie Peter	58	laborer	53	"
	X	Repucci Anthony	60	student	28	"
	Y	Repucci Carlo	60	salesman	58	"
	Z	Repucci Carmella—†	60	clerk	26	
832						
	A	Repucci Lucy—†	60	"	22	
	B	Repucci Marie—†	60	housewife	60	"
	C	Repucci Joan—†	60	"	25	181 Marion
	D	*Evans James J	68	fisherman	60	Chelsea
	E	*Smallcomb Bernard L	68	"	55	"
	F	Smallcomb Mary M—†	68	housewife	59	"

Meridian Street

K	Benziger Irene—†	358	operator	36	here
L	Cooke Claude F	358	retired	62	"
M	Cooke George	358	U S A	34	"
N	Cooke Julia L—†	358	housewife	61	"
O	Oldanie Anthony J	358	U S M C	42	"
P	Oldanie Celia--†	358	housewife	38	"
R	Ross Edna M—†	358	clerk	23	"
S	Ross Howard M	358	foreman	46	"
T	Ross Myrtle—†	358	housewife	50	"
U	Donohue John H	358	plumber	40	"
V	Donohue Madeline R—†	358	housewife	38	"
X	Hamilton Christina—†	359A	"	74	"
Y	Hamilton James H	359A	laborer	38	
Z	Hackett Joanna—†	359A	housekeeper	80	"
	833				
A	Garron Florence—†	359A	packer	40	
B	Garron Gertrude—†	359A	at home	26	"
C	Garron Ida—†	359A	housewife	62	"
D	Garron Kenneth	359A	operator	36	"
E	Garron Stanley	359A	welder	21	"
F	Garron Walter	359A	laborer	30	
H	Cole Jennie—†	361	housekeeper	78	"
K	Weiner Celia—†·	361	housewife	65	"
L	Weiner Myer	361	retired	70	"
M	Walsh Mary—†	361	housewife	48	153 Bennington
N	Walsh Michael	361	shoeworker	46	153 "
O	Nolan Florence—†	362	housewife	29	here
P	Nolan Francis W	362	machinist	29	"
R	Wilson John H	362	shipper	40	"
S	Wilson John R	362	retired	74	
T	Wilson Susan—†	362	housewife	66	"
U	Gunning Margaret—†	362	packer	44	
V	Gunning Robert	362	seaman	46	
W	Gunning Walter	362	U S A	24	
X	Smith Mary—†	362	housewife	38	"
Y	Smith Raymond R	362	engineer	38	"
Z	Scott Annie L—†	362	at home	80	"
	834				
A	Huey Murray C	363	painter	48	"
B	Huey Victoria—†	363	cook	31	"
C	Nazzaro Antonio	363	U S A	30	140 Lexington

Meridian Street—Continued

D	Nazzaro Charlotte—†	363	housewife	30	140 Lexington
E	Aiello Generosa—†	364	"	32	here
F	Aiello Peter	364	salesman	34	"
G	Thibodeau Augustine	364	painter	43	91 Trenton
H	*Thibodeau Mary—†	364	housewife	43	91 "
K	Aiello Frances—†	364	"	60	here
L	Aiello Lorenzo	364	pressman	59	"
M	Aiello Nina—†	364	clerk	24	"
N	Amerena Maude E—†	365	housewife	52	"
O	Amerena Vincent J	365	pipefitter	49	"
P	McCoy Agnes J—†	365	housewife	56	"
R	McCoy John E	365	U S N	32	
S	McCoy Lawrence J	365	clerk	29	"
T	McCoy Rose—†	365	"	24	"
U	McCoy Thomas	365	U S N	28	
V	Maiolino Florence A—†	365	housewife	49	"
W	Maioline Joseph M	365	U S A	23	"
X	Maiolino Mary R—†	365	welder	26	"
Y	Masoli Salvatore F	365	retired	60	
Z	Donohue David	366	tavernkeeper	72	"

835

A	Malfy Frederick	366A	operator	58	"
B	Malfy Frederick, jr	366A	U S A	27	
C	Malfy Henry G	366A	"	20	"
D	Malfy Mabel—†	366A	housewife	52	"
E	Almond Doris—†	366A	saleswoman	20	"
F	Almond Jennie—†	366A	factoryhand	53	"
G	Almond Norma—†	366A	operator	28	"
H	Almond Peter	366A	blacksmith	67	"
K	Rock Helen—†	368	housewife	37	"
L	Rock Timothy	368	painter	37	
M	Lurvey Albert	368A	coppersmith	28	"
N	Lurvey Ellen—†	368A	housewife	61	"
O	Lurvey Helen—†	368A	bookkeeper	32	"
P	Lurvey John	368A	U S N	25	"
R	Lurvey Mary—†	368A	tel worker	30	"
S	Lurvey Reginald	368A	engineer	55	"
T	McCarthy Ruth—†	368A	housewife	37	"
U	Christopher Dorothy—†	368A	factoryhand	27	"
V	Christopher Joseph	368A	bartender	32	"
W	Rose Elizabeth—†	368A	housewife	66	"

Page.	Letter.	FULL NAME.	Residence, Jan. 1, 1945.	Occupation.	Supposed Age.	Reported Residence, Jan. 1, 1944. Street and Number.

Meridian Street—Continued

x	Rose Harold	368A	U S N	23	here
y	Rose Patrick	368A	carpenter	66	"
z	Rose William	368A	clerk	35	"
	836				
a	Enos John R	369	shipper	58	"
b	Enos Mary—†	369	housewife	55	"
c	Denning June—†	-369	"	56	
d	Denning Thomas F	369	laborer	64	
e	Golding Frank T	369	chauffeur	37	"
f	Smith Leonard M	369	U S N	20	
g	Smith Velma—†	369	housewife	39	"
h	Deering Annie C—†	370	teacher	65	
k	Josselyn Mabel L—†	370	at home	68	"
l	Atwood Nancy—†	370	housekeeper	78	"
m	Bethel Hilton	370	seaman	54	"
n	MacDonald Jennie—†	370	at home	67	"
o	Tallman Daniel	370	retired	70	"
p	Thompson Ruth H—†	370	accountant	44	77 Marion
r	Cameron Alice H—†	370	housekeeper	64	here
s	Hunter Cora E—†	370	broker	67	"
t	Nocito Clara—†	371	housewife	43	"
u	Nocito Helen—†	371	at home	21	62 Lubec
v	Nocito Joseph	371	painter	49	here
w	Aida Anna—†	371	housewife	21	"
x	Aida John	371	operator	24	"
y	McCormack John	372	shipbuilder	62	"
z	McCormack John	372	U S A	26	
	837				
a	McCormack Mary—†	372	housewife	24	"
b	McCormack Thomas	372	U S N	24	"
c	Clauss Mary—†	372	housewife	32	"
d	Clauss Paul	372	shipfitter	35	"
e	Cunningham Helen E-†	372	WAVE	27	"
f	Cunningham Helen N—†	372	housewife	41	"
g	Cunningham Thomas H	372	clerk	49	"
h	Reardon William	372	printer	46	Cambridge
k	Olsen Carl	373	asbestoswkr	58	here
l	Olsen Elsie—†	373	housewife	42	"
m	Brittaniti Frances—†	379	"	29	"
n	Brittaniti Samuel	379	foreman	31	"
o	Jenricks Elizabeth—†	379	waitress	64	117 Chandler

Meridian Street—Continued

P	Shaw Clarence	379	retired	70	here
R	Shaw Delia—†	379	housewife	70	"
S	DiBenedetto Mary L—†	379	"	31	"
T	DiBenedetto Vincent	379	chef	49	
U	DiBenedetto Clara—†	379	saleswoman	24	"
V	DiBenedetto Mary T—†	379	housewife	45	"
W	DiBenedetto Ralph	379	tailor	52	
X	Palmer John	379	laborer	54	
Y	*Palmer Mary—†	379	housewife	54	"
Z	Palmer Mary—†	379	at home	25	"
	838				
A	Palmer Vincent	379	U S A	20	"
B	Leone Bridget T—†	381	stitcher	20	96 Chelsea
C	Leone Joseph	381	U S A	21	134 Everett
D	Bonfiglio Louise—†	381	housewife	30	179 Trenton
E	Bonfiglio William	381	electrician	34	206 Maverick
F	Bevilacqua Mary—†	381	housewife	43	22 Monmouth
G	Bevilacqua Salvatore	381'	factoryhand	50	22 "
H	*Cattinazzo Louis	383	shoeworker	38	here
K	Cattinazzo Margaret—†	383	housewife	39	"
L	Blase Anthony	383	operator	28	"
M	Blase Mildred—†	383	housewife	27	"
N	Pestone Fannie—†	383	clerk	21	69 Bennington
O	Pestone Rosario	383	laborer	55	69 "
R	Browne John B	385	storekeeper	42	here
S	Browne Mary—†	385	housewife	37	"
T	Landers John	385	deckhand	48	"
U	Landers Norah—†	385	housewife	45	"
V	Consolo Felice	387	woodworker	30	"
W	Consolo Rose—†	387	housewife	26	"
X	Fazio Aurelio	387	shoemaker	59	"
Y	Fazio Josephine—†	387	housewife	52	"
Z	LeBlanc Josephine—†	387	clerk	22	"
	839				
A	LeBlanc Thomas	387	U S A	25	
B	Perna Ignazio	387	mechanic	24	"
C	Perna Josephine—†	387	housewife	53	"
D	Perna Nicolo	387	plasterer	57	"
E	Perna Rose—†	387	housewife	25	"
F	Graves Janet—†	388	secretary	52	"
G	Graves Jennie—†	388	housekeeper	69	"

Meridian Street—Continued

H	Kieling John	388	custodian	68	here
K	Kieling Lillian E—†	388	housewife	61	"
M	Aitken Catherine E—†	389	"	41	"
N	Aitken Florence H—†	389	clerk	21	"
O	Aitken Francis D	389	machinist	43	"
P	Aitken Lorraine F—†	389	manager	20	"
R	Goldenberg Edward	389	"	55	
S	Goldenberg Lillian—†	389	housewife	54	"
T	Goldenberg Regina—†	389	secretary	23	"
U	Dillon John F	389	printer	28	"
V	Dillon Josephine F—†	389	housewife	26	"
W	Wellington Alfred	390	retired	71	
X	Ahearn Malcolm	391	fisherman	37	"
Y	Canty Frederick	391	longshoreman	54	"
Z	Greene Edward P	391	retired	71	
	840				
A	Hines Florence—†	391	at home	33	"
B	Merchant Agnes—†	391	housewife	41	"
C	Merchant Edward C	391	chauffeur	48	"
D	Merchant Edward T	391	U S N	21	
E	Horne Marie—†	393	saleswoman	40	"
F	Horne Walter	393	boilermaker	42	"
G	Langewald Mariah S—†	393A	attorney	70	"
H	Whippen Marion E—†	393A	housewife	27	"
K	Whippen William	393A	operator	31	"
L	Safrin Annie M—†	393A	housewife	60	"
M	Safrin Francis A	393A	decorator	63	"
N	Safrin Francis E	393A	welder	43	
O	DiPlacido Frank	394	operator	59	"
P	DiPlacido Mary—†	394	housewife	35	"
R	Benoit Arthur	394	rigger	39	
S	Benoit Victoria—†	394	housewife	31	"
T	Flynn Ethel—†	394	"	55	
U	Flynn Grace—†	394	clerk	26	"
W	Marie Frank	395	fishcutter	38	1 Maverick
X	*Marie Helen—†	395	housewife	33	1 "
Y	*Muise Natalie—†	395	"	42	here
Z	Porter Clarence J	395	deckhand	33	"
	841				
A	Hartigan Richard	396	retired	75	
B	Sloane Margaret—†	396	clerk	66	"
C	Burns Daniel F	396	laborer	40	

Meridian Street—Continued

D	Stokes Ellen T—†	396	housewife	42	here
E	Stokes Frank J	396	laborer	42	"
F	Stokes Jennie—†	396	housewife	72	"
G	Stokes Walter A	396	U S N	38	"
H	Brown Willis S	398	retired	81	"
K	Davis Louise L—†	398	housewife	58	"
L	Davis Sumner C	398	druggist	57	"
M	McElman Annabelle—†	398	housewife	31	"
N	McElman John A	398	welder	31	"
O	Dotoli Louise—†	398	housewife	47	96 Falcon
P	Dotoli Ralph	398	engineer	45	96 "
R	Richard John J	398	U S N	21	96 "
S	*Martinez Andres	401	fireman	39	6 Moon
T	Martinez Maria—†	401	housewife	26	Everett
U	Porcaro Edward	401	barber	57	here
V	Porcaro Elena—†	401	stitcher	26	"
W	Porcaro Ermine—†	401	"	28	"
X	Porcaro Fiorinda—†	401	housewife	52	"
Y	Porcaro Frances—†	401	stitcher	29	"
Z	Porcaro Mary—†	401	shoeworker	30	"

842

A	Porcaro Ralph	401	U S A	20	
B	Porcaro Yolando—†	401	shoeworker	26	"
C	Barbarisi Antoinetta—†	401	candyworker	25	"
E	Bordonaro Constance—†	402	clerk	24	
F	Bordonaro Felicia—†	402	housewife	53	"
G	Bordonaro Joseph	402	janitor	58	
H	Bordonaro Josephine—†	402	telegrapher	20	"
K	Bordonaro Peter	402	U S A	29	"
L	Bordonaro Tina—†	402	stitcher	32	"
M	Trodella Anthony	402	U S N	25	"
N	Trodella Phyllis—†	402	housewife	27	"
O	Zagarella Joseph L	402	machinist	26	"
P	Zagarella Marion R—†	402	housewife	24	"
R	Belmonte Frank	402	machinist	34	"
S	Belmonte Helen—†	402	housewife	33	"
U	Montesanti Joseph	403A	U S A	28	
V	Montesanti Rose—†	403A	housewife	26	"
W	Vitello Joseph	403A	presser	60	
X	Vitello Mary—†	403A	housewife	56	"
Y	Gray LeForest	404	retired	79	
Z	McLaren Charlotte P—†	404	housewife	40	"

843
Meridian Street—Continued

A	McLaren Felton C	404	musician	59	here
B	Allen Edward	404	fishcutter	61	"
C	Allen Olive—†	404	housewife	44	"
D	Santaniello Concetta—†	404	"	46	
E	Santaniello Michael	404	storekeeper	55	"
F	Almeida Frederick	404	policeman	47	"
G	Almeida Isabelle—†	404	housewife	44	"
H	Almeida Walter	404	U S A	24	"
K	Kergald Alice H—†	404	clerk	26	
L	Kergald George C	404	electrician	57	"
M	Silva Anthony	404	clerk	40	
N	Silva Julia—†	404	housewife	35	"
R	Orr Marie—†	406	"	62	"
S	Orr Mary C—†	406	social worker	33	"
T	Abric Grace—†	407	housewife	36	"
U	*Abric Louis	407	fishcutter	42	"
V	Sullivan Joseph I	407	rigger	47	

Monmouth Square

Y	Brownell Eleanor—†	1	at home	82	12 Hemenway
Z	Burgess Sarah—†	1	"	72	123 Charles

844

A	DeFeo Catherine—†	1	inspector	25	284 Lexington
B	DeSpirito Michael	1	retired	56	here
C	Dole Margaret—†	1	at home	55	50 Newton
D	Lang Patrick	1	retired	77	14 Falcon
E	Leighton Arthur	1	"	48	13 Marion
F	Malone Ellen—†	1	at home	75	141 London
G	McConlogue Eunice—†	1	"	64	7 Elm
H	Narroway Rose—†	1	"	83	here
K	O'Brien Elizabeth—†	1	"	70	193 Brooks
L	O'Brien Patrick	1	retired	68	193 "
M	Strong James H	1	physician	73	here
N	Strong Mary L—†	1	nurse	37	"

Monmouth Street

O	DeSisto Angelina—†	1	shoeworker	25	here
P	*DeSisto Michelena—†.	1	housewife	54	"

26

Monmouth Street—Continued

R	DeSisto Raffaele	1	rubberwkr	21	here
S*| DeSisto Thomas	1	"	48	"
T	Tarr Beatrice—†	1	housewife	36	Everett
U	Tarr Herman	1	chauffeur	36	"
V	LeBlanc Willis	1	proprietor	55	here
W	Surette Howard	1	fisherman	48	"
X	Surette Lennie—†	1	waitress	46	"
Y	Fahey David	3	checker	40	112 Marginal
Z*| Fahey Mary—†	3	housewife	37	Brookline

845

A	Smith Dorothy—†	3	"	27	here
B	Smith Elwin E	3	chemist	31	"
C	Leman Arthur A	3	manufacturer	74	"
D	Leman Maude L—†	3	housewife	64	"
E*| Berinato Annie—†	5	"	55	"
F	Berinato Anthony, jr	5	printer	31	"
G*| Berinato Antonio	5	finisher	65	"
H	Berinato Carrie—†	5	operator	24	"
K	Drane Edward	5	seaman	31	Quincy
L	Drane Helen—†	5	housewife	34	"
M	Johnson Clifford	5	mechanic	27	here
N	Johnson Dorothy—†	5	at home	30	"
O*| Johnson Jennie—†	5	"	61	"
P	Machado Ruth—†	5	"	22	Pennsylvania
R	Quirk James W	7	retired	72	here
S	Quirk Mary E—†	7	housewife	75	"
T	Lawless Agnes G—†	7	at home	60	"
U	Lawless John	7	laborer	53	
X	Yeo Jennie M—†	9	at home	65	"
Y	Cancian Charles	9	custodian	39	88 Cottage
Z	Cancian Edith—†	9	clerk	34	88 "

846

A	Martell Helen—†	10	housewife	66	here
B	Martell William	10	shipworker	35	"
C	Bertucelli George	10	baker	37	"
D	Bertucelli Mary A—†	10	housewife	43	"
E*| Smith John	10	retired	76	Malden
F	DeAngelis Dominic	11	U S A	29	here
G	DeAngelis Jennie—†	11	housewife	28	"
H	Natola Eleanor—†	11	at home	26	"
K	Natola Generoso	11	U S A	25	

Page.	Letter.	FULL NAME.	Residence, Jan. 1, 1945.	Occupation.	Supposed Age.	Reported Residence, Jan. 1, 1944. Street and Number.

Monmouth Street—Continued

L	Cotillo Adeline—†	11	housewife	53	here
M	Cotillo Olga—†	11	at home	22	"
N	Cotillo Raffaele	11	barber	53	"
O	Finney Charles B	11	foreman	66	"
P	Finney Clarinda—†	11	housewife	70	"
R	Antonelli Edith—†	12	inspector	38	"
S	Kendall Irene—†	12	housewife	42	"
T	Kendall Louis W	12	U S N	44	
U	Melisi Bridget—†	12	housewife	39	"
V	Melisi Thomas	12	machinist	42	"
W	Sullivan Frank L	13	U S N	55	
X	Sullivan Laura B—†	13	matron	51	
Y	Greenwood Margaret P-†	13	housekeeper	60	"
Z	Varner Alfred F	13	retired	57	"
	847				
A	Varner Alfred F, jr	13	U S N	23	
B	Varner Arnold M	13	U S A	21	
C	Varner Bertha A—†	13	WAC	49	
D	Coffin Ellen—†	13	at home	74	"
E	Proffitt Frazier	13	rigger	29	
F	Proffitt Margaret E—†	13	cashier	34	"
G	Fullerton Doris I—†	14	housewife	32	Beverly
H	Fullerton Frederick D	14	fisherman	38	"
K	McCormick Alexander	14	roofer	47	here
L	McCormick Florence G-†	14	brazier	37	"
M	*McQuaide Catherine—†	15	housewife	73	"
N	McQuaide Henry M	15	retired	75	"
O	Hubbard Donald T	15	U S N	23	
P	*Kenney Earl E	15	chauffeur	42	"
R	*Kenney Marie B—†	15	housewife	41	"
S	*Melanson Rose A—†	15	at home	37	"
U	Reed Annie V—†	17	housewife	71	"
V	Reed Gilbert C	17	retired	72	"
W	Bolan Catherine—†	17	housewife	55	"
X	Bolan Lawrence	17	fisherman	62	"
Y	Bolan Lawrence, jr	17	rigger	24	
Z	Dean George R	17	U S A	29	"
	848				
A	Dean Rita—†	17	housewife	28	"
B	Zaino Angela—†	21	"	62	
C	Zaino Francesco	21	laborer	65	"

28

Monmouth Street—Continued

	D	Collins Harley L	21	U S C G	37	here
	E	Collins Marion F—†	21	nurse	29	"
	F	O'Connell Cornelius F	21	guard	36	35 White
	G	O'Connell Marjorie V—†	21	waitress	33	35 "
	H	D'Addieco Louis	22	presser	31	here
	K	D'Addieco Mary—†	22	housewife	29	"
	L	Cucchiara Gaetano	22	presser	62	"
	M	Cucchiara Paul	22	U S A	33	
	N	Cucchiara Rose—†	22	housewife	53	"
	O	Kruger James R	23	laborer	48	46 Adams
	P	Bernardinelli Liberus—†	23	housewife	29	here
	R	Bernardinelli Salvatore	23	salesman	31	"
	S	*Cassaro Diego	23	carpenter	63	"
	T	Cassaro Michael	23	garageman	32	"
	U	*Cassaro Rose—†	23	dressmaker	52	"
	V	Pisano Josephine—†	23	clerk	28	"
	W	Guide Frank	23	tailor	28	Revere
	X	Guide Mary—†	23	housewife	28	57 Webster
	Y	Bulens Harry	25	machinist	40	here
	Z	Bulens Nellie C—†	25	housewife	37	"

849

	A	Chase Mary L—†	25	at home	79	"
	B	Hamilton Jeannette—†	26	housewife	50	"
	C	Hamilton Linwood	26	seaman	50	"
	D	Justman Amy—†	26	housewife	35	California
	E	Justman Robert	26	U S C G	32	"
	F	Sullivan Frank E	26	retired	64	here
	G	O'Brien Elizabeth A—†	27	housewife	44	"
	H	O'Brien Francis F	27	U S N	23	"
	K	O'Brien Thomas F	27	garageman	46	"
	L	Maggio Maria—†	28	housewife	50	"
	M	Maggio Michael	28	carpenter	57	"
	N	Kamin Edward O	28	engineer	47	"
	O	Kamin Mary G—†	28	housewife	46	"
	P	MacPhee William A	28	seaman	20	"
	R	Sullivan Francis	28	"	44	
	S	Sullivan Violet—†	28	housewife	34	"
	T	Miller Elizabeth—†	29	clerk	32	"
	U	Miller George W	29	student	21	"
	V	Miller John	29	shipfitter	60	"
	W	Miller Priscilla S—†	29	housewife	66	"

Monmouth Street—Continued

	x	Miller Sarah I—†	29	clerk	30	here
	y	Coffin Seymour	29	retired	79	"
	z	Coffin Susanna P—†	29	housewife	74	"
850						
	b	Comeau George	30	pipefitter	35	"
	c	Comeau Verna—†	30	housewife	32	"
	a	Doucette Lawrence	30	painter	20	Cambridge
	d	Nostro Frank	30	clerk	42	here
	e	Nostro Josephine—†	30	housewife	37	"
	f	Sherzi Mary—†	30	"	45	"
	g	Sherzi Mary H—†	30	stenographer	22	"
	h	Sherzi Vincent	30	plasterer	52	"
	k	*Ryan Renee Y—†	31	housewife	41	"
	l	Ryan Thomas S	31	longshoreman	39	"
	m	*LePeron Henrietta—†	31	at home	67	"
	n	Capezzuto Beatrice—†	32	shoeworker	34	214 Maverick
	o	Scopa Joseph, jr	32	U S A	39	here
	p	Scopa Joseph A	32	metalworker	65	"
	r	Scopa Lucy—†	32	milliner	33	"
	s	Scopa Mary—†	32	housewife	31	"
	t	Scopa Michael	32	U S A	25	"
	u	Staffieri Annette—†	32	housewife	27	"
	v	Staffieri Samuel	32	U S N	32	
	w	Ballam Bernard F, jr	33	"	21	
	x	Ballam Gertrude B—†	33	clerk	32	"
	y	Ballam Joseph M	33	operator	39	"
	z	Ballam Mary G—†	33	housekeeper	71	"
851						
	a	O'Brien Concetta—†	34	housewife	33	"
	b	O'Brien Cyril	34	clerk	34	
	c	*Prisco Clara—†	34	housewife	59	"
	d	Prisco Francesco	34	waiter	65	
	e	Prisco Letizia—†	34	stitcher	28	"
	f	Guarnera Anthony	36	U S N	23	
	g	Guarnera Carmella—†	36	stitcher	28	"
	h	Guarnera Carmelo	36	mason	64	"
	k	Guarnera Catherine—†	36	housewife	62	"
	l	Guarnera Eleanor—†	36	stitcher	26	"
	m	Guarnera Salvatore	36	U S A	22	"
	n	Guarnera Gaetano	36	machinist	34	"
	o	Guarnera Josephine—†	36	housewife	27	"

Monmouth Street—Continued

P	Geradell Herbert	36	physician	40	here
R	Geradell Marie—†	36	stitcher	35	"
S	Wessling Frank A	37	laborer	49	"
T	Wessling Margaret M—†	37	housewife	54	"
U	Kennedy Annie—†	37	"	73	"
V	Kennedy Bernard F	37	retired	75	
W	Kennedy William J	37	U S A	33	
X	Morella Anthony C	38	mortician	40	"
Y	Morella Laura—†	38	housewife	37	"
	852				
A	Francis Blanche—† rear	38	"	31	"
B	*Francis Manuel V "	38	laborer	59	"
C	Francis Manuel V, jr "	38	riveter	22	
D	*Amirault Elisa—†	39	housewife	42	"
E	Amirault Leslie	39	engineer	42	"
F	Crowley Edward P	39	U S A	24	
G	Crowley Mary Y—†	39	housewife	24	"
H	Doucette Genevieve—†	39	operator	26	"
K	Doucette Margaret—†	39	housewife	49	"
L	Doucette Phillip	39	fishcutter	52	"
M	Maginn Edward	39	machinist	72	"
N	Pascucci Mario A	40	laborer	32	
O	Pascucci Mary M—†	40	housewife	33	"
P	Pascucci Amerino P	40	U S N	24	
R	Pascucci Madeline C—†	40	operator	22	"
S	Pascucci Nicoletta—†	40	housewife	58	"
T	Pascucci Sabino	40	cleaner	61	
U	Lane Anthony	41	packer	38	
V	Lane Rose—†	41	housewife	38	"
W	Boland Julia—†	41	"	47	
X	Boland Vincent	41	seaman	45	
Z	Maginn Charles	42	patternmaker	66	"
	853				
A	McCarthy Elizabeth B—†	43	housewife	44	"
B	McCarthy Genevieve O—†	43	nurse	22	"
C	McCarthy James B	43	B F D	47	
D	Burr Elizabeth K—†	43	electrolysist	70	"
E	*Hessler Charles	44	fisherman	56	"
F	Schluter Doris W—†	44	housewife	32	Cambridge
G	Schluter Harold	44	U S N	43	"
H	Tracy Ethel V—†	44	nurse	36	here

31

Page	Letter	Full Name	Residence, Jan. 1, 1945.	Occupation	Supposed Age	Reported Residence, Jan. 1, 1944. Street and Number.

Monmouth Street—Continued

	K	Tracy May E—†	44	housewife	64	here
	L	Tracy Paul D	44	machinist	66	"
	M	Crocker Carlton W	45	druggist	71	"
	N	Crocker Caroline M—†	45	housewife	29	"
	O	Crocker Harvey J	45	U S N	27	
	P	Crocker Kimball T	45	manager	25	"
	R	Lister Jean—†	45	housewife	29	"
	S	Lister Lloyd	45	U S A	31	
	T	Murphy Edward	45	machinist	45	"
	U	McCarthy Edward J	46	teacher	51	..
	V	McCarthy Mary—†	46	housewife	78	"
	W	McCarthy William	46	teacher	39	
	X	*Penta Rose—†	47	at home	69	"
	Y	Gallagher Elizabeth—†	47	"	59	
	Z	Todd George W	47	U S A	27	

854

	A	Todd Mary—†	47	housewife	23	"
	B	Indingaro Anthony	47	clerk	29	
	C	Indingaro Louise—†	47	housewife	29	"
	D	Mercer Augustus	48	laborer	47	
	E	Mercer Helen—†	48	attendant	46	"
	F	Power Stephen	48	retired	70	
	G	Power Susan—†	48	housewife	65	"
	H	Grimshaw Irene E—†	49	clerk	20	"
	K	Grimshaw James	49	U S A	20	10 Gladstone
	L	Norman Edith T—†	49	at home	50	here
	M	Thivierge William A	49	painter	52	"
	N	Campbell Joseph A	49	B F D	47	"
	O	Campbell Margaret A—†	49	housewife	47	"
	P	Campbell Norman	49	electrician	22	"
	R	Lombard Eileen—†	50	housewife	29	"
	S	Lombard Robert	50	attorney	28	"
	T	Centracchio Nicholas	50	guard	45	"
	U	Ferris Antone L	50	"	65	
	X	Lombard Frances—†	50	housewife	48	"
	V	McInerney Alice—†	50	"	60	
	W	McInerney Clementina—†	50	operator	29	"
	Y	Forrest Elizabeth—†	51	at home	75	"
	Z	Forrest Maude—†	51	bowmaker	47	"

855

	A	Clohesy Thomas J	51	U S A	25	"

Page	Letter	Full Name.	Residence, Jan. 1, 1945.	Occupation.	Supposed Age.	Reported Residence, Jan. 1, 1944. Street and Number.

Monmouth Street—Continued

B	Nazzaro Elizabeth—†	51	housewife	44	here
C	Nazzaro Robert	51	electrician	43	"
D	Mazzarella Angelo	51	laborer	38	"
E	Mazzarella Yolanda E—†	51	housewife	29	"
G	O'Brien Alice—†	53	secretary	54	"
H	Sorensen George	55	U S N	30	..
K	Sorensen Olive—†	55	housewife	55	"
L	Sorensen Theodore	55	machinist	56	"
M	Sorensen Walter	55	U S A	24	"
R	Sullivan Thomas C	57	painter	65	
N	Wellings John S	57	policeman	51	"
O	Wellings Loretta M—†	57	teacher	31	"
P	Wellings Mary A—†	57	housewife	50	"
S	Warren Fred L	59	salesman	49	"
T	Warren George W	59	clergyman	84	"
U	Warren Marjory C—†	59	social worker	52	"
V	Guide Mildred—†	61	housewife	30	"
W	Guide Thomas J	61	adjuster	29	"
X	LaMotta Grace—†	61	housewife	38	"
Y	LaMotta Harold	61	longshoreman	37	"
Z	Guide Joseph A	61	barber	32	

856

A	Guide Rose M—†	61	stenographer	32	"
B	Pisello Carmen	63	foreman	48	"
C	Pisello Maria—†	63	housewife	40	"
D	Pisello Robert N	63	U S A	20	
E	Repucci Edith—†	63	housewife	29	"
F	Repucci Edward	63	chauffeur	34	"
G	*Repucci Joseph	63	retired	77	
H	Repucci Alfred	63	custodian	42	"
K	Repucci Caroline—†	63	housewife	40	"
L	Repucci John	63	chauffeur	45	"
M	Repucci Rose—†	63	housewife	37	"

Putnam Street

N	*Morella Marino	65	retired	79	here
O	Gambardella Theresa—†	65	housewife	31	Maine
P	Gambardella Vincent	65	welder	32	"
R	Lepore Anthony	67	operator	45	here
S	*Lepore Concetta—†	67	housewife	33	"

1—8

Putnam Street—Continued

T	Lepore Geraldine—†	67	stitcher	24	here
U	Marenza Frank	69	salesman	31	"
V	Marenza Mary—†	69	housewife	28	"
W	Mareschi Lena—†	69	"	50	"
X	Mareschi Ralph	69	laborer	54	"
Y	Silva Elsie—†	69	housewife	26	56 Putnam
Z	Silva Richard	69	laborer	25	56 "

857

A	Gallo Joseph B	71	clerk	41	here
B	*Gallo Mary—†	71	housewife	33	"
C	Capararello Frank W	71	silversmith	22	"
D	Capararello Marie A—†	71	housewife	44	"
E	Capararello Thomas	71	candymaker	45	"
F	Young Mary—†	71	housewife	35	"
G	Young Richard	71	laborer	40	"
H	Orlando Carmella—†	73	housewife	56	"
K	Orlando Dominic	73	retired	56	
L	Orlando Lillian—†	73	operator	25	"
M	Bertino Anthony	75	storekeeper	26	"
N	*Bertino Antoinette—†	75	housewife	53	"
O	Bertino Catherine—†	75	teacher	21	"
P	Bertino Carmelo	75	conductor	25	"
R	Bertino Mary—†	75	housewife	26	"

Trenton Street

T	Dagle Margaret—†	56	housewife	23	Maine
U	Dagle Russell	56	seaman	25	Rhode Island
V	Shanahan John	56	laborer	20	here
W	Shanahan Rose G—†	56	housewife	57	"
X	Conners John O	56	laborer	47	Maine
Y	DeLeo Joseph	56	"	20	Rhode Island
Z	Ford Daniel	56	"	39	here

858

A	Ford Julia—†	56	housewife	66	"
B	Ford Michael	56	longshoreman	66	"
C	Fitzgerald Ann—†	58	clerk	34	35 Eutaw
D	Fitzgerald Bridget—†	58	housewife	72	35 "
E	Giovino Alfred	58	pipefitter	30	here
F	*Giovino Carmino	58	retired	75	"

Page.	Letter.	FULL NAME.	Residence, Jan. 1, 1945.	Occupation.	Supposed Age.	Reported Residence, Jan. 1, 1944. Street and Number.

Trenton Street—Continued

G	*Giovino Jennie—†	58	housewife	70	here	
H	Giovino Louis	58	U S A	35	"	
K	Faldetta John	60	machinist	29	"	
L	Faldetta Julia—†	60	housewife	21	"	
M	Walters Alfred	60	shipfitter	24	283 K	
N	Walters Josephine—†	60	housewife	20	283 "	
O	Ferrino Antonetta—†	60	stitcher	24	here	
P	Ferrino Enrico	60	laborer	60	"	
R	*Ferrino Josephine—†	60	housewife	58	"	
S	Alves Caroline—†	62	"	28		
T	Alves Napoleon	62	seaman	30	"	
U	Stacey Bessie C—†	62	housewife	50	"	
V	Stacey Howard	62	laborer	20		
W	Stacey Hubbard F	62	machinist	58	"	
X	Marascia Concetta—†	62	housewife	25	"	
Y	Marascia John	62	sailmaker	27	"	
Z	McKee John	rear 62	salesman	38	149 Princeton	

859

A	McKee Pauline—†	" 62	housewife	25	149 "	
B	Penney Mary—†	64	"	69	here	
C	Penney William	64	fisherman	65	"	
D	Campagna Adelaide—†	64	clerk	42	"	
E	Iocco Flora M—†	64	typist	21		
F	Iocco Joseph A	64	U S A	22	"	
G	Iocco Rocco	64	millman	50	"	
H	Iocco Theresa M—†	64	housewife	54	"	
K	Almeida Possidonio B	66	longshoreman	47	"	
L	Thomas Maria P—†	66	housekeeper	58	"	
M	Neves Alfred	66	laborer	20	"	
N	Neves Anna—†	66	housewife	48	"	
O	Neves Josephine—†	66	seamstress	22	"	
P	Neves Lawrence	66	millworker	56	"	
R	Ramos Joseph	66	laborer	49	"	
S	Santos Manuel	66	"	60		
T	Spencer August	66	"	60	"	
U	Martin Alice D—†	68	housewife	20	284 Chelsea	
V	Martin Jesse	68	galvanizer	23	284 "	
W	Swan Edward A	68	cleaner	69	312 Meridian	
X	Pegran Laura—†	68	brazier	26	Revere	
Y	Uccelli Carmella—†	68	housewife	40	"	

35

Trenton Street—Continued

z	Uccelli Pasquale	68	baker	52	here
	860				
A	Leone Giacomo	68	laborer	64	
B	Leone Guido	68	retired	69	"
C	DeLucci Ada—†	70	housewife	26	173 Trenton
D	DeLucci Benjamin	70	laborer	31	173 "
E	DiNicola Albert	70	U S A	27	here
F	Mariani Carina—†	70	housewife	50	"
G	Mariani Dante	70	U S A	21	"
H	Mariani Dominic	70	laborer	31	
K	Mariani Sabatino	70	"	66	
L	Mariani Samuel	70	U S A	27	"
M	Ciandella John	72	finisher	41	..
N	Ciandella Purina—†	72	housewife	38	"
O	LaBella Charles	72	salesman	38	"
P	LaBella Margaret—†	72	housewife	30	"
R	Avola Adeline—†	74	"	30	7 Lexington av
S	Avola Frank	74	brazier	29	7 "
T	Saggese Anthony	74	barber	35	here
U	Saggese Sestina—†	74	housewife	32	"
V	Catania Alberta—†	74	"	32	"
W	Catania Joseph	74	machinist	29	"
Y	DeAvolio Carmen	76	lather	48	here
Z	DeAvolio Margaret—†	76	housewife	47	"
	861				
A	DeAvolio Helen—†	78	"	26	
B	DeAvolio Michael	78	driller	27	
C	Staffier Anthony	78	welder	25	"
D	Staffier Mary—†	78	housewife	24	"
E	McBride Julia E—†	80	"	79	
F	McBride William H	80	retired	84	
G	Doucette Levi	80	fishcutter	57	"
H	Harrison Anne F—†	80	housekeeper	60	"
K	Riggs Anna K—†	80	waitress	37	"
L	Waters Herbert	80	carpenter	57	"
M	Packard William	82	U S C G	21	"
N	*Pina Labina—†	82	housekeeper	63	"
O	Scott Anthony L	82	seaman	48	"
P	Scott Anthony L, jr	82	U S A	24	
R	Scott Doris—†	82	clerk	21	
S	Scott Eugene	82	U S M C	20	"

Page.	Letter.	FULL NAME.	Residence, Jan. 1, 1945.	Occupation.	Supposed Age.	Reported Residence, Jan. 1, 1944. Street and Number.

Trenton Street—Continued

	T	Scott Marie—†	82	housewife	40	here
	U	Scott Walter E	82	U S M C	23	"
	V	Meuse Mary C—†	82	housewife	39	"
	W	Meuse Peter B	82	laborer	44	"
	X	Deleaco Henry	82	draftsman	37	"
	Y	Deleaco Velia—†	82	housewife	33	"
	Z	Formicola Caroline—†	82	stitcher	22	"
862						
	A	*Formicola Mary—†	82	housekeeper	55	"
	B	Snider Almond	82	U S N	24	New York
	C	Snider Lucy—†	82	housewife	24	here
	D	*Ducey Catherine—†	86	"	40	"
	E	Ducey Thomas	86	carpenter	50	"
	F	Martino Angelina—†	86	housewife	40	"
	G	Martino Peter	86	barber	46	"
	H	DeBillio Gaetano	86	retired	62	"
	K	*DeBillio Maria C—†	86	housewife	52	"
	L	Rasetta Luigi	88	engineer	48	"
	M	Rasetta Mary—†	88	housewife	47	"
	N	LaBella Antonio	88	barber	60	"
	O	LaBella Erminia—†	88	housewife	60	"
	P	LaBella Lauretta—†	88	candyworker	22	"
	R	Martin Gloria—†	90	housekeeper	60	140 Chelsea
	S	Tortora Leo	90	laborer	25	Chelsea
	T	Tortora Phoebe—†	90	housewife	22	140 Chelsea
	U	Buono Antonio	90	laborer	51	here
	V	Buono Constantino	90	U S N	21	"
	W	Buono Maria—†	90	housewife	48	"
	X	DeMato Josephine—†	92	housekeeper	67	53 Marion
	Y	Lamberti Mary—†	92	housewife	45	here
	Z	Lamberti Nicholas	92	U S A	24	"
863						
	A	Lamberti Philip	92	millworker	59	"
	B	Lamberti Ralph	92	U S A	22	"
	C	Duann Arthur J	94	carpenter	36	162 Lexington
	D	Duann Marie L—†	94	housewife	31	162 "
	E	Puorro Filomena—†	94	tailoress	43	here
	F	Puorro Rose S—†	94	operator	21	"
	K	Coelho John P	96	laborer	32	"
	L	Coelho Lucille—†	96	housewife	30	"
	M	Grasso Consolino	96	pilot	30	Turners Falls

Page.	Letter.	FULL NAME.	Residence, Jan. 1, 1945.	Occupation.	Supposed Age.	Reported Residence, Jan. 1, 1944. Street and Number.

Trenton Street—Continued

N	Grasso Mary—†	96	housewife	28	Turner Falls
O	Pericola Flora—†	96	"	25	here
P	Pericola Peter	96	packer	25	"
R	Hardy Charles O	98	foreman	50	"
S	Hardy Francis	98	U S N	20	"
T	Hardy Lillian—†	98	housewife	49	"
U	Thompson Anne L—†	100	"	70	
V	Thompson Helen I—†	100	teacher	34	
W	Ford John C	102	mechanic	51	"
X	Macciche Blanche—†	102	housewife	23	"
Y	Macciche Michael	102	U S A	22	
Z	Wennerberg Emil	102	retired	77	"
	864				
C	Silva Antonio	110	U S A	20	
D	Silva Gertrude—†	110	housewife	49	"
E	Silva Julietta—†	110	clerk	22	
F	Silva Manuel D	110	retired	67	
G	Sulkey Evelyn—†	110	housewife	43	"
H	Sulkey William	110	U S N	46	
K	Falco Ralph	112	pipefitter	56	"
L	Tuttle Anna—†	112	housewife	40	"
M	Tuttle Dorothy—†	112	packer	20	
N	Tuttle Harold	112	pipefitter	50	"
O	Gates Anna G—†	112	housewife	33	"
P	Gates Edward P	112	laborer	63	
R	Petrillo Joseph	114	shipfitter	25	"
S	Petrillo Sarah—†	114	housewife	21	"
T	Pugliese Albert	114	U S A	23	
U	*Pugliese Andrew	114	retired	67	
V	Pugliese John	114	U S A	28	
W	Pugliese Joseph	114	laborer	61	
X	Pugliese Josephine—†	114	clerk	24	"
Y	*Pugliese Julia—†	114	housewife	53	"
Z	Benvissuto Alfred	116	shipfitter	38	"
	865				
A	Benvissuto Serafina—†	116	housewife	34	"
B	*Connors David	116	fisherman	36	"
C	*Connors Lucy—†	116	housewife	32	"
D	Whalen Alexander	116	retired	72	
E	Lewis Gordon	116	fisherman	34	"

Trenton Street—Continued

F	Lewis Mary—†	116	housewife	33	here
G	Pacella Frank	118	U S A	33	87 Eutaw
H	*Pacella Marie—†	118	housewife	61	87 "
K	*Pacella Rocco	118	retired	63	87 "
L	StCroix Henry	118	laborer	29	here
M	StCroix Ruth—†	118	housewife	28	"
N	Greeley Elizabeth—†	118	"	24	214 Brooks
O	Greeley Thomas	118	U S A	26	214 "
P	Connors Irene—†	120	housewife	37	166 "
R	*Connors Joseph	120	shipper	45	166 "
S	Donahue Frances—†	120	secretary	20	166 "
T	Morgan Gertrude—†	120	candymaker	48	here
U	Morgan Joseph	120	welder	46	"
V	*Ristaino Antonio	120	longshoreman	52	"
W	*Ristaino Carmella—†	120	housewife	49	"
X	Ristaino Lena—†	120	clerk	22	
Y	Ristaino Louis	120	pipefitter	20	"

866

A	Whiteway Arthur E	122	retired	75	
B	Whiteway Martha—†	122	housewife	75	"
C	French Frank	124	painter	39	
D	*French Jennie—†	124	housewife	66	"
E	Gannon Joseph P	124	U S N	24	"
F	Gannon Mary—†	124	housewife	24	"
G	Santangelo Victoria—†	124	"	65	
H	Driver Arthur	124	sorter	33	
K	Driver Mildred—†	124	housewife	32	"
L	Uva Anna—†	126	"	61	
M	Uva Michael	126	laborer	60	
N	Muise Bertha—†	126	housewife	43	"
O	Muise George E	126	fishcutter	44	"
P	Gall Charles	126	millworker	49	"
R	*Gall Olga—†	126	housewife	56	"
S	Pergola Lena—†	128	"	26	"
T	Pergola Michael	128	machinist	29	"
U	Dantona Grace—†	128	housewife	46	"
V	Dantona Joseph	128	candymaker	52	"
W	Dantona Leo R	128	U S N	23	"
X	Avila Isabelle—†	128	housewife	22	21 Princeton
Y	Murray Isabelle E—†	128	"	49	here

Page.	Letter.	FULL NAME.	Residence, Jan. 1, 1945.	Occupation.	Supposed Age.	Reported Residence, Jan. 1, 1944. Street and Number.

Trenton Street—Continued

	z	Murray John F	128	boilermaker	49	here
867						
	A	Murray Lillian M—†	128	typist	25	
	B	Enos Mary C—†	130	housewife	52	"
	c	Enos Paulmeda—†	130	boxmaker	48	"
	D	Enos Virginia C—†	130	housewife	78	"
	E	Enos William	130	electrician	39	"
	F	McGillivray Alexander J	130	foreman	61	"
	G	McGillivray Stella—†	130	housewife	60	"
	H	Ward Bertha—†	130	"	64	"
	K	Ward John E	130	blacksmith	62	"
	L	O'Connell Josephine—†	132	housewife	30	"
	M	O'Connell Thomas	132	U S A	34	
	N	Musto Angelo, jr	132	social worker	27	"
	o	Musto Dolores—†	132	housewife	26	"
	P	Basile Anna—†	132	"	32	
	R	Basile Salvatore	132	clerk	31	
	s	Buontempo Michael	134	metalworker	47	"
	T	Buontempo Rose—†	134	housewife	43	"
	U	Capolupo Emanuella—†	134	"	44	
	v	Capolupo Vincent	134	laborer	46	..
	w	Hawes Anna—†	134	laundrywkr	63	"
	X	McNamee Elizabeth—†	134	clerk	60	
	Y	*Sauchella Giovino	136	retired	60	
	z	Sauchella Parillo	136	clerk	38	
868						
	A	*Sauchella Pasqualina—†	136	housewife	60	"
	B	Sauchella Sunta—†	136	houseworker	25	"
	c	Amenta Lucy—†	136	stitcher	30	"
	D	Amenta Mary—†	136	clerk	24	
	E	Amenta Michelina—†	136	housewife	67	"
	F	Caputo Josephine—†	136	"	32	"
	G	Caputo Paul	136	welder	36	
	H	Moralis John	138	janitor	57	"
	K	Moralis Sebastiano—†	138	housewife	57	"
	L	Battaglia Joseph	138	salesman	38	"
	M	Battaglia Julia—†	138	housewife	34	"
	N	Bertino Andrew	138	manager	30	"
	o	Bertino Mary—†	138	housewife	28	"
	P	DiMaura Antonia—†	140	"	65	
	R	DiMaura Sebastian	140	laborer	68	

Trenton Street—Continued

s	Cadotte Margaret—†	140	domestic	28	here
t	Dwyer Mary—†	140	housewife	55	"
u	Visico Florence—†	140	"	27	"
v	Jardin Joseph	140	deckhand	21	"
w	*Jardin Julia—†	140	housewife	45	"
x	Jardin Julio	140	weaver	44	"
y	Dunning Agnes—†	142	housewife	29	"
z	Dunning Harry P	142	chauffeur	36	"
	869				
a	Francis Esther—†	142	housewife	70	"
b	Francis Joseph	142	retired	69	
c	Susan Leo	142	clerk	65	
d	Susan Robert	142	chipper	61	"
e	Susan Samuel	142	salesman	63	"
f	LaVacca Assunta—†	144	housewife	25	"
g	LaVacca Rocco	144	laborer	25	
h	Rinaldi Louise—†	144	housewife	24	"
k	Rinaldi Rocco	144	accountant	24	"
l	Fiorentino Angelo	144	bartender	48	"
m	Fiorentino Mary—†	144	housewife	43	"
n	Taurasi Anthony	146	clerk	23	108 Bennington
o	Ferraro John	146	welder	23	Beachmont
p	Ferraro Thomasina—†	146	housewife	22	"
r	Penta Concetta—†	146	"	24	here
s	Penta Edward L	146	U S A	27	Winthrop
t	D'Entremont Cecile—†	148	housewife	30	19 Mt Vernon
u	D'Entremont William	148	leverman	32	New York
v	LaBlanc George H	148	calker	60	here
w	LaBlanc James E	148	U S A	26	"
x	LaBlanc Joseph E	148	"	30	"
y	LaBlanc Mary—†	148	housewife	54	"
z	LaBlanc Melvin P	148	U S A	24	
	870				
a	Godbold Caroline A—†	150	housewife	73	"
b	Smith Harold K	150	U S A	37	
d	Damass Rose—†	152	clerk	45	
c	Dellapino Florence—†	152	"	21	
e	Orfao John G	152	millworker	47	"
f	Silva Manuel J	152	deckhand	50	"
g	Silva Maria J—†	152	housewife	46	"
h	Testa Myrtle L—†	154	"	48	

1—8

Page.	Letter.	FULL NAME.	Residence, Jan. 1, 1945.	Occupation.	Supposed Age.	Reported Residence, Jan. 1, 1944. Street and Number.

Trenton Street—Continued

	K	Testa Robert F	154	grocer	52	here
	L	Testa Phyllis—†	154	housewife	23	"
	M	Testa Robert F, jr	154	grocer	27	".
	N	Lake Harry	156	engineer	60	"
	O	Lake Marion—†	156	housewife	49	"

White Street

	R	Hipwell Gertrude—†	1	housewife	44	here
	S	Hipwell Joseph F	1	laborer	43	"
	T	Sullivan Daniel	1	seaman	65	381 Meridian
	U	Sullivan Margaret—†	1	housewife	25	382 "
	V	Costigan John	1	longshoreman	65	here
	W	Fitzpatrick Thomas M	17	clerk	59	"
	X	Herman Helen F—†	17	at home	69	"
	Y	Brannan Amy L—†	17	housewife	38	"
	Z	Brannan Winston C	17	deckhand	43	"
871						
	A	Atkinson Olive—†	19	domestic	38	"
	B	Isaacs Thomas	19	fisherman	46	"
	C	Frank John C	19	machinist	46	"
	D	LeBlanc Cora M—†	19	housewife	31	"
	E	LeBlanc Joseph A	19	mariner	34	"
	F	Zaverlli Antonio	21	retired	69	5 Lexington
	G	Zavarelli Frank	21	U S N	31	5 "
	H	Zavarelli Paneilio	21	laborer	22	5 "
	K	Swim Harriet F—†	21	housewife	40	here
	L	Foster Emmaline L—†	21	at home	40	"
	M	Evans Liston C	23	cook	48	"
	N	Evans Nettie—†	23	at home	65	"
	O	Crouse Sophia—†	23	"	87	21 White
	P	Conrad Florence—†	23	housewife	72	Malden
	R	*Conrad Howard	23	carpenter	68	226 Saratoga
	S	Ruggireo Anna V—†	25	machinist	29	here
	T	Ruggireo Anthony A	25	U S A	32	"
	U	Joyce Charles H	25	fireman	31	"
	V	Joyce Frederick J	25	engineer	58	"
	W	Joyce Matilda A—†	25	housewife	54	"
	X	McGrath John F	25	U S A	26	
	Y	McGrath Marion G—†	25	machinist	24	"

42

White Street—Continued

	z	McGurin Harold A	27	shipfitter	51	48 Saratoga
872						
	A	McGurin Helen M--†	27	housewife	47	48 "
	B	Grace George	27	shipfitter	39	here
	C	Grace Joseph A	27	U S A	29	"
	D	Grace William	27	"	36	"
	E	Pickles Mary E—†	29	domestic	52	5 Eutaw pl
	F	Waltman Blanche M--†	29	housewife	47	here
	G	Waltman Carl E	29	machinist	44	"
	H	Boudreau Harold T	29	attendant	26	. "
	K	Boudreau Mary R—†	29	housewife	24	"
	L	Shea James F	31	engineer	69	"
	M	Shea Jeremiah L	31	clerk	59	"
	N	Shea Thomas J	31	electrician	64	"
	O	Dooley Margaret—†	33	housewife	22	"
	P	Dooley Michael F	33	stevedore	29	"
	R	Fullerton David F	33	fisherman	47	"
	S	Fullerton Mary A—†	33	housewife	38	"
	T	Stones Amanda—†	33	"	49	
	U	Stones Harry S	33	machinist	52	"
	V	Joyce John F, jr	35	electrician	27	73 Horace
	W	Joyce Rita F—†	35	housewife	24	145 Trenton
	X	Coyle Frances—†	35	inspector	24	here
	Y	Coyle Joseph A	35	retired	73	"
	z	Coyle Joseph A, jr	35	U S A	35	"
873						
	A	Coyle Mary E—†	35	housewife	63	"
	B	Cayon Angelina—†	37	accountant	23	"
	C	Cayon Mary—†	37	secretary	21	"
	D	Cayon Rosalie—†	37	housewife	53	"
	E	Cayon Roy G	37	chef	60	"
	F	Doucette Annie E—†	39	housewife	67	4 White pl
	G*	Doucette Arthur	39	carpenter	60	4 "
	H	Doucette John E	39	U S A	23	4 "
	K	Bohn Susanna—†	41	domestic	65	here
	L	Salomen Arthur A	41	U S N	35	"
	M	Davis David	41	shoeworker	63	"
	N*	Davis Rose—†	41	housewife	62	"
	O	Healy John	41	retired	71	
	R	Carnevale Esther—†	87	housewife	53	"
	S	Carnevale Walter	87	U S A	23	

White Street—Continued

T	Carnevale William	87	U S A	21	here
U	Carnevale Zefferino	87	tailor	62	"
V	Anzalone Phyllis—†	89	housewife	44	"
W	*Piccerela Costabile	89	retired	79	
X	Vincola Rose—†	89	housewife	26	"
Y	Morelli Anna—†	91	"	40	
Z	Morelli Joseph	91	longshoreman	45	"

Ward 1–Precinct 9

LIST OF RESIDENTS
20 YEARS OF AGE AND OVER

(NON-CITIZENS INDICATED BY ASTERISK)
(FEMALES INDICATED BY DAGGER)

AS OF

JANUARY 1, 1945

THOMAS F. SULLIVAN, *Chairman*
FREDERIC E. DOWLING, *Secretary*
WILLIAM A. MOTLEY, JR.
FRANCIS B. McKINNEY
EVERETT R. PROUT

Listing Board.

900

Bennet Place

A	Caton Bertha M—†	1	at home	64	here
B	Morrison Helen J—†	1	housewife	42	"
C	Morrison John R	1	laborer	42	"
D	Hodgkins Carrie—†	2	housewife	34	"
E	Hodgkins Rupert	2	machinist	42	"
F	McInnis James J	3	supervisor	39	"
G	McInnis Mary G—†	3	housewife	38	"
H	Downing Eugene	4	U S N	21	Cambridge
K	Ford Daniel G	4	"	30	here
L	Kennedy Alphonsus	4	rigger	60	"
M	Kennedy Joseph E	4	U S A	21	"

Border Street

P	Bates Wilfred D	443	laborer	71	here

Brooks Street

T	Vargus Harold	185	U S A	25	here
U	Vargus Helen—†	185	housewife	23	"
V	Hancock Anna—†	185	"	36	285 Lexington
W	Hancock Reuben	185	boilermaker	38	285 "
	901				
B	McGuire Alice—†	191	housewife	81	here
C	McGuire William	191	retired	87	"
E	Gartland Gertrude—†	193	housewife	23	105 Trenton
F	Gartland Joseph	193	U S A	25	105 "
G	Sousa Frederick M	193	"	28	here
H	Sousa Manuel M	193	retired	68	"
K	DiGiovanni Anthony	195	chauffeur	43	"
L	DiGiovanni Mary—†	195	housewife	43	"
M	DiGiovanni Nicholas	195	pedler	21	"
N	Sousa John A	195	fireman	31	"
O	Sousa Mary T—†	195	housewife	27	"
P	Baker Josephine—†	195	"	53	
R	Mooney Arthur J	195	janitor	40	
S	Mooney Claire E—†	195	housewife	35	"
T	Gonzales Francis L	214	engineer	56	"
U	*Lopez Carmen	214	housewife	49	"
V	Lopez Josephine—†	214	operator	26	"

2

Brooks Street—Continued

	w	Otero John	214	engineer	53	here
	x	Rose James A	214	U S A	24	"
	y	Rose Lorina—†	214	operator	25	"
	z	Lanieri Annetta—†	214	housewife	50	"
902						
	a	Lanieri Filipina—†	214	operator	22	"
	b	Lanieri Gloria—†	214	clerk	20	
	c	Lanieri Jean—†	214	"	32	
	d	Lanieri Joan—†	214	"	27	
	e	Lanieri Rinaldo	214	upholsterer	56	"
	f	Bruno John	214	foreman	53	"
	g	Bruno Louise—†	214	operator	27	"
	h	Bruno Victoria—†	214	housewife	53	"
	k	Annese Anthony	216	manufacturer	36	"
	l	Annese Celia—†	216	housewife	38	"
	m	Forgione Frank	216	shipper	37	
	n	Forgione Mary—†	216	housewife	38	"
	o	Harding Walter	218	deckhand	47	"
	p	Safrine Diana—†	218	housewife	53	"
	r	Thibodeau Alcide J	218	carpenter	53	"
	s	Silva Edith—†	218	housewife	37	"
	t	Silva Joseph	218	laundryman	41	"
	u	Joyce Dorothy F—†	220	operator	21	"
	v	Laracy Frederick J	220	pipefitter	42	"
	w	Laracy Mary F—†	220	housewife	44	"
	x	Connelly Mary—†	220	WAC	26	"
	y	Connelly Patrick	220	U S A	35	"
	z	Capolupo Anthony	220	shoeworker	52	"
903						
	a	Capolupo Anthony	220	U S A	21	"
	b	Capolupo Philomena—†	220	housewife	42	"
	c	Lehtola Armas	224	pipefitter	37	41 White
	d	Hill Amanda—†	224	housewife	50	here
	e	Hill Toivo F	224	U S A	27	"
	f	*Selin Hulda K—†	rear 224	housewife	56	"
	g	*Selin Urho	" 224	retired	55	

Condor Street

	h	Lavalle Annie—†	5	at home	64	here
	k	*Boudreau Elias	5	retired	72	"

3

Page.	Letter.	Full Name.	Residence, Jan. 1, 1945.	Occupation.	Supposed Age.	Reported Residence, Jan. 1, 1944. Street and Number.

Condor Street—Continued

	L	Boudreau Evelyn—†	5	operator	25	here
	M	*Boudreau Virginia—†	5	at home	67	"
	N	O'Brien Albert	5	U S N	33	"
	O	O'Brien Ethel V—†	5	operator	33	"
	P	Gallagher Catherine—†	5	at home	72	"
	R	Tedford Althea—†	5	housewife	42	"
	S	Tedford Eileen—†	5	clerk	20	
	T	Tedford George	5	machinist	42	"
	U	Magee Florence—†	7	at home	67	"
	V	Riley William E	7	shipper	64	"
	W	Hoy James D	7	custodian	58	135 Condor
	X	Hoy Margaret—†	7	housewife	54	135 "
	Y	Hoy William	7	clerk	21	135 "
	Z	Chamness Ambrozine—†	9	waitress	47	here
904						
	A	Chamness Wilbur	9	U S N	21	"
	B	Garcia Ambrozine—†	9	at home	77	"
	C	McCauley Ambrozine—†	9	operator	20	"
	D	Finn Lawrence	11	welder	26	
	E	Finn Maryba—†	11	clerk	56	"
	F	Finn William	11	U S A	31	"
	M	Heeck Cornelius R	15	printer	72	"
	N	Heeck Florence L—†	15	housewife	61	"
	O	Kelleher Lawrence F	15	machinist	29	"
	P	Kelleher Margaret M—†	15	housewife	56	"
	R	Kelleher Paul R	15	electrician	21	"
	S	Kelleher Pauline R—†	15	operator	21	"
	T	Hebert Adeline A—†	21	housewife	20	"
	U	Whitehead James E	21	seaman	44	"
	V	Whitehead Rose F—†	21	housewife	40	"
	X	Mahoney Julia M—†	30	"	41	
	Y	Mahoney Timothy J	30	laborer	48	
	Z	Murphy Daniel F	30	retired	80	
905						
	A	Murphy Mary—†	30	housewife	72	"
	B	Murphy Antonina N—†	32	"	47	
	C	Murphy William F	32	chauffeur	46	"
	D	Burke John	33	carpenter	64	"
	E	Coogan Laurence	33	machinist	65	"
	F	Coogan Mary—†	33	housewife	63	"

Condor Street—Continued

	G	Kane Emma—†	33	housewife	47	here
	H	Kane Joseph A	33	engineer	47	"
	K	Leary Florence E—†	33	housewife	56	"
	L	Leary Lewis B	33	sign writer	60	"
	M	McGillivray Arlene P—†	33	clerk	29	..
	N	McGillivray William B	33	U S N	29	
	O	Scandone Joseph	34	ironworker	45	"
	P	Scandone Lillian—†	34	housewife	53	"
	R	Smith Ernest	34	U S A	22	
	S	Fortier Charles	36	chauffeur	28	"
	T	Fortier Martha—†	36	housewife	28	"
	U	Melville Hazel—†	37	"	55	"
	V	Melville James	37	machinist	55	"
	W	Ellis Frank	37	clerk	55	
	X	Ellis Marion—†	37	"	50	
	Y	Smith Ella—†	37	at home	76	"
	Z	Smith Nema—†	37	houseworker	49	"
		906				
	A	Hickey Frederick	38	welder	30	"
	B	Hickey Mary C—†	38	matron	48	"
	C	Hickey Peter A	38	U S C G	26	"
	D	Hickey Richard F	38	welder	28	
	E	Siraco Joseph A	40	shipper	31	"
	F	Siraco Rose—†	40	housewife	31	"
	G	Rizzo Michael	41	shipper	45	..
	H	Rizzo Rita—†	41	housewife	30	"
	K	Cataldo Enrico	41	cleaner	50	..
	L	Cataldo Tina—†	41	housewife	40	"
	M	Rizzo Emma—†	41	at home	29	"
	N	Rizzo Gennaro	41	retired	69	
	O	Rizzo Louise—†	41	packer	30	
	P	Rizzo Mary—†	41	clerk	28	
	R	Thornton Charles R	42	U S A	26	"
	S	Thornton Elizabeth—†	42	housewife	67	"
	T	Thornton James	42	fireman	69	"
	U	Bright Phyllis A—†	44	clerk	21	..
	V	O'Brien Albert F	44	U S N	28	
	W	O'Brien Matthew M	44	steelworker	49	"
	X	O'Brien Sarah A—†	44	housewife	49	"
	Y	O'Brien Thomas G	44	U S N	23	

5

z	Groom Helena—†	46	housewife	41	here
	907				
A	Groom Robert J	46	agent	53	
B	Groom Robert W	46	U S M C	20	"
C	Hulke William A	46	assembler	53	"
D	Fraser Mary—†	47	at home	59	237 Condor
E	Pitts Charlotte—†	47	"	58	237 "
F	Bruce Harold	47A	painter	36	here
G	Bruce Mary—†	47A	housewife	45	"
H	Cunningham Franklin L	47A	U S M C	23	"
K	Cunningham Henry D	47A	U S A	25	..
L	Cunningham Walter A	47A	U S N	26	
M	Melanson Edward	47B	machinist	45	"
N	Melanson Emily—†	47B	housewife	41	"
O	Thornton Patrick T	48	engineer	41	"
P	Johnson Mary—†	49	at home	60	N Hampshire
R	Johnson Walter G	49	U S N	26	"
S	Sanford E Grace—†	51	housewife	53	here
T	Sanford William E	51	supt	62	"
U	DiVito Edna—†	57	clerk	26	"
V	DiVito Thomas	57	U S A	29	"
W	Hall Edward	57	fireman	62	..
X	Hall Olivia—†	57	housewife	58	"
Y	O'Keefe Lawrence	57	electrician	25	"
z	O'Keefe Mary—†	57	housewife	24	"
	908				
A	Ryan Mary—†	61	at home	65	"
B	Baker Loa—†	61	housekeeper	24	Michigan
C	Gayhart George	61	U S A	26	464 Meridian
D	Gayhart John	61	U S N	22	464 "
E	Gayhart Mary—†	61	housewife	53	464 "
F	Whitmarsh Frederick	61	blockmaker	61	here
G	Whitmarsh Mabel—†	61	housewife	59	"
K	Lindsey Mary—†	63	"	38	Ipswich
L	Lindsey Robert	63	chauffeur	30	"
M	Recupero Rosalie—†	63	at home	30	here
N	Johnson William	63	seaman	69	"
P	Platt Mary—†	65	at home	66	5 Paris pl
R	Bosley Lemuel	65	laborer	41	Vermont
S	Coley Myrtle—†	65	housekeeper	35	"
T	Berry George E	65	U S A	28	here

Page.	Letter.	FULL NAME.	Residence, Jan. 1, 1945.	Occupation.	Supposed Age.	Reported Residence, Jan. 1, 1944. Street and Number.

Condor Street—Continued

	U	Berry Ida—†	65	at home	52	here
	V	Berry Rosella—†	65	"	23	"
	W	Amirault Eleanor—†	67	housewife	28	"
	X	Amirault Frank E	67	U S A	24	
	Y	Surette Marion—†	67	housewife	34	"
	Z	Surette Pierre	67	laborer	36	
		909				
	A	Dow Hazel—†	67	housekeeper	62	"
	B	Dana Doris—†	75	clerk	24	
	C	Peterson Emma R—†	75	housewife	70	"
	D	Peterson John T	75	repairman	72	"
	E	Peterson Alice—†	77	housewife	33	"
	F	Peterson John	77	machinist	35	"
	G	Hagerty Edith—†	79	housewife	67	"
	H	Hagerty Edward	79	expressman	64	"
	K	Lane Margaret—†	79	housekeeper	29	"
	M	Coombs Celia—†	79½	housewife	44	224 E Eagle
	N	Coombs Henry	79½	laborer	46	224 "
	O	Coombs Margaret—†	79½	at home	20	224 "
	R	Petito Eugene	81	guard	46	here
	S	Clark Frank L	81	clerk	65	"
	T	Napier Paul	81	cutter	25	"
	U	Napier Rita A—†	81	at home	30	"
	V	Nimblett Ann—†	81	tester	27	Maine
	W	Pethoud Cynthia—†	81	"	22	here
	X	West Catherine—†	81	housewife	55	"
	Y	West James H	81	engineer	54	"
	Z	Miller Florence—†	85	housewife	50	"
		910				
	A	Miller James	85	foreman	52	"
	B	Miller Loretta—†	85	at home	20	"
	C	Miller William	85	U S A	22	
	D	Dooley John W	85	"	38	
	E	Whalen John A	85	seaman	24	
	F	Whalen Mary J—†	85	at home	53	"
	G	McDermott Katherine—†	87	housewife	34	"
	H	McDermott Mary A—†	87	at home	66	"
	K	Wilson James P	87	welder	34	
	L	Corbett George	89	cutter	63	
	M	Corbett George T	89	machinist	33	"
	N	Corbett Margaret—†	89	housewife	30	Missouri

Condor Street—Continued

o	Corbett Mary E—†	89	housewife	56	here
p	Corbett William G	89	carpenter	29	Missouri
r	Cordona Ann C—†	91	housewife	22	155 Chelsea
s	Cordona Libby	91	machinist	22	New York
t	Flammia Michael	91	"	47	here
u	Flammia Virginia—†	91	housewife	45	"
v	DeFeo Caroline—†	93	"	43	"
w	DeFeo Pasquale	93	laborer	50	"
y	Cardinale Domenic	97	longshoreman	23	Chelsea
z	Cardinale Joseph	97	porter	53	"

911

a	Story Oliver	97	musician	58	"
b	Wright Elsia—†	97	waitress	45	"

Eutaw Street

d	Froio Louis P	104	mechanic	27	here
e	Froio Vera M—†	104	housewife	30	"
f	*Froio John	106	finisher	60	"
g	*Froio Rose M—†	106	housewife	59	"
h	Froio Theresa M—†	106	packer	31	
n	Cordeau Ada E—†	108	housewife	39	"
o	Cordeau Arthur B	108	ironworker	46	"
k	LaBrie Georgena—†	108	operator	64	"
l	McLean Catherine A—†	108	dressmaker	66	"
m	McNeil Emily F—†	108	housekeeper	55	"
p	McLaughlin Aloysius L	112	letter carrier	50	"
r	McLaughlin Margaret T—†	112	housewife	49	"
s	Shea Ellen C—†	112	"	51	"
t	Shea Helen T—†	112	boxmaker	47	"
u	Shea Mary L—†	112	supervisor	54	"
v	Shea Timothy J	112	watchman	46	"
w	DiFiore Nicholas	116	artist	30	127 Eutaw
x	DiFiore Vincenza—†	116	housewife	29	127 "
y	DelCore Cecelia—†	118	"	28	here
z	DelCore Guido A	118	operator	28	"

912

a	Stacey Evelyn A—†	120	bookkeeper	30	"
b	Stacey Roland F	120	clerk	30	"
c	Fallavollita Adeline A—†	120	assembler	22	"
d	Fallavollita Angelina—†	120	housewife	53	"

8

Page.	Letter.	FULL NAME.	Residence, Jan. 1, 1945.	Occupation.	Supposed Age.	Reported Residence, Jan. 1, 1944. Street and Number.

Eutaw Street—Continued

	E	Fallavollita Antonio P	120	electrician	32	here
	F	Fallavollita Serfino H	120	chauffeur	20	"
	G	*Buonagurio Julia—†	122	housewife	60	"
	H	Buonagurio Stanley W	122	U S N	23	
	K	Rotondi Julia—†	122	bookkeeper	32	"
	L	King Louis E	124	machinist	44	"
	M	King Violet F—†	124	housewife	36	"

Falcon Street

	N	Bragdon Clifford	5	retired	74	here
	O	Bragdon Sarah—†	5	housewife	69	"
	P	Gibbons John F	5	proprietor	31	"
	R	Gibbons Mary—†	5	housewife	28	"
	S	D'Entremont Charles	7	mechanic	46	"
	T	D'Entremont Domitille—†	7	housewife	45	"
	U	McIntyre Bernice—†	9	clerk	20	
	V	McIntyre Clarence T	9	steamfitter	43	"
	W	McIntyre Eva M—†	9	housewife	43	"
	Y	King Anna—†	14	at home	67	"
	Z	Lang Beatrice—†	14	housewife	45	"
913						
	A	Lang Doris—†	14	student	20	"
	B	Lang Edward	14	inspector	49	"
	C	Iannelli Charles	2	U S A	35	
	D	Iannelli Evelyn—†	2	at home	33	"
	E	Iannelli John		U S A	24	"
	F	Iannelli Louise—†		at home	56	"
	G	Iannelli Silvio		barber	60	"
	H	Iannelli Anne—†		housewife	24	22 Trenton
	K	Iannelli Ugo	22	bartender	26	22 "
	L	Danner Edward		seaman	57	here
	M	Danner Joseph		U S C G	26	"
	N	Danner Nina—†	22	housewife	45	"
	O	Danner William		U S N	25	"
	P	Wall Chester		"	27	
	R	Wall Marie—†	22	housewife	27	"
	S	*Grifone Annibal	24	tailor	76	"
	T	Grifone Carlo	24	pressman	37	"
	U	Grifone Emma—†	24	forewoman	41	"
	V	Grifone Jennie—†	24	stitcher	44	"

9

Page.	Letter.	FULL NAME.	Residence, Jan. 1, 1945.	Occupation.	Supposed Age.	Reported Residence, Jan. 1, 1944. Street and Number.

Falcon Street—Continued

w	*Grifone Madeline—†	24	at home	28	here
x	McPhee Charles D	25	pressman	54	"
y	McPhee Charles S	25	U S M C	25	"
z	McPhee Irvin F	25	rigger	30	Chelsea

914

A	McPhee Kathleen A—†	25	electrician	21	here
B	McPhee Mary J—†	25	housewife	53	"
c	McPhee Melvin J	25	operator	32	"
D	Ryan Margaret E—†	25	at home	75	"
E	Healey Monica J—†	25	housewife	38	"
F	Healey Phillip J	25	longshoreman	42	"
G	Batson Edward M	25	laborer	56	227 Brooks
H	Batson Lena—†	25	housewife	51	227 "
K	Hefferon Catherine—†	25	housekeeper	75	227 "
L	McKinnon Catherine—†	26	at home	65	here
M	McKinnon Herbert	26	U S A	24	"
N	McKinnon Lena—†	26	at home	34	"
o	*McKinnon Stephen	26	fisherman	63	"
P	McKinnon Stephen	26	U S A	29	"
R	Ellis Herbert A	27	U S N	58	2 Cedarwood rd
s	LaBohn Willard J	27	inspector	56	here
T	Guardabassio Mary—†	27	sorter	29	15 Boardman
U	Sfarzo Angela R—†	27	housewife	53	here
v	Sfarzo Anna—†	27	sorter	24	"
w	Sfarzo Carmen	27	fireman	62	"
x	Sfarzo Frank	27	U S A	27	"
y	Sfarzo Helen—†	27	spinner	34	
z	Sfarzo Marino	27	U S N	22	

915

A	Donahue Coleman B	27	dispatcher	36	"
B	Donahue Helen E—†	27	tel operator	35	"
c	Nelson August E	27	clerk	60	
D	Nelson Helen M—†	27	housewife	60	"
E	Nelson Robert A	27	U S N	22	"
F	Nelson Warren F	27	U S A	29	
G	Peterson Alvera M—†	27	winder	26	"
H	Cutcliffe Charles	28	boilermaker	45	"
K	Cutcliffe Mary—†	28	at home	39	"
L	Hansen Barbara—†	28	"	58	
M	Hansen Haakon	28	seaman	30	
N	Hansen John	28	painter	64	"

10

Falcon Street—Continued

	o	Hansen Ruth—†	28	bookkeeper	29	here
	p	Fanara Anthony	29	electrician	27	"
	r	Fanara Carmella—†	29	housewife	23	"
	s	Delcore Elvira—†	29	"	34	
	t	Delcore John	29	welder	38	"
	w	Johnson Dorothy—†	30	clerk	21	
	x	Johnson Theresa—†	30	packer	44	"
	u	Parker Charles	30	proprietor	72	"
	v	Parker Grace—†	30	housewife	69	"
	y	Shea Dorothy—†	30	clerk	38	
	z	Shea John	30	"	40	

916

		Litchfield Katherine—†	31	nurse	54	"
	B	Litchfield Laurence	31	brakeman	32	"
	c	Litchfield Muriel—†	31	housewife	27	"
	d	McBournie John W	31	watchman	77	"
	e	McBournie Margaret—†	31	housewife	77	"
	c	McBournie Walter S	31	U S A	41	
	g	McBournie William	31	clerk	48	
	h	McRae Ira	31	millwright	52	"
	k	McRae Jessie—†	31	housewife	44	"
	l	*Ciani Elizabeth—†	32	at home	90	"
	n	DeRienzo Angelo	32	U S A	22	
	m	DeRienzo Cetira—†	32	housewife	44	"
	o	DeRienzo Frank	32	pressman	44	"
	p	DeRienzo Vincenzo	32	U S M C	20	"
	r	Clarke Christine—†	33	housewife	37	"
	s	Clarke George	33	welder	38	
	t	McCormack Ella W—†	33	housewife	59	"
	u	McCormack Helen M—†	33	teacher	33	"
	v	McCormack Norma E—†	33	"	29	
	w	McCormack Ralph E	33	U S A	21	
	x	McCormack Wilton M	33	"	24	
	y	Elliott Jennie E—†	33	housewife	52	"
	z	Elliott Robert A	33	motorman	54	"

917

	a	Wall Amy J—†	34	WAC	29	
	b	Wall Constance W—†	34	waitress	63	"
	c	Wall Mary E—†	34	operator	38	"
	d	Cooper Daniel	34	seaman	63	
	e	Cooper Jessie—†	34	housewife	63	"

Falcon Street—Continued

	Letter	FULL NAME	Residence	Occupation	Age	Reported Residence
	F	Morse Mabel—†	34	at home	52	here
	G	Morse Richard	34	shipfitter	25	"
	H	Bonner Edward L	35	guard	58	"
	K	Bonner Ella A—†	35	housewife	53	"
	L	Scharaffa Elvira—†	35	"	26	207 Lexington
	M	Scharaffa Frank	35	machinist	25	207 "
	N	DelloRusso Lucy—†	35	housewife	31	217 Havre
	O	DelloRusso Orlando	35	printer	42	217 "
	P	Borsi Helen—†	36	saleswoman	34	here
	R	Borsi Vincent	36	cleaner	28	"
	S	Johnson Clara—†	36	at home	72	"
	T	Johnson Harry	36	cleaner	48	
	U	McAlbee Helen—†	36	housewife	24	"
	V	McAlbee Mack	36	U S A	31	
	W	Sullivan Joseph	36	seaman	50	
	X	Sullivan Stella—†	36	housewife	52	"
	Y	McGurin John	37	retired	72	"
	Z	McGurin Leo W	37	"	46	"
918						
	A	McGurin Sarah—†	37	housewife	42	"
	B	Noyes Vera L—†	37	"	47	
	C	McElman Allen B	37	machinist	62	"
	D	McElman James H	37	chauffeur	24	"
	E	McElman Nellie J—†	37	housewife	61	"
	F	Gage Laura—†	38	bookkeeper	52	"
	G	Gage Winthrop	38	salesman	52	"
	H	Logan Blanche—†	38	clerk	49	
	K	Logan Julia M—†	38	housewife	46	"
	L	Logan Leslie D	38	grocer	51	
	M	Denehy Alice E—†	39	clerk	39	"
	N	Denehy Edward J	39	fish dealer	37	"
	O	Denehy Louise—†	39	housewife	44	"
	P	D'Entremont Albert	40	inspector	38	"
	R	D'Entremont Margaret—†	40	housewife	35	"
	S	Kane Addie—†	40	"	58	··
	T	Kane Thomas	40	laborer	61	
	U	*Scopa Jennie—†	40	housewife	56	"
	V	Scopa Salvatore	40	U S A	21	"
	W	*Belliveau Charles J	41	shipfitter	40	Wilmington
	X	*Belliveau Mary E—†	41	housewife	41	"
	Y	Clemens Edward J	41	foreman	45	here

Falcon Street—Continued

z	Clemens Helen—†	41	housewife	42	here	
	919					
A	*Alves Antonio	42	retired	75	"	
B	Alves Leo	42	toolmaker	43	"	
c	*Alves Virginia—†	42	housewife	74	"	
D	Finney Arthur	42	retired	64	"	
E	Finney Ethel M—†	42	housewife	62	"	
F	Finney Warren	42	steamfitter	36	"	
G	Finney William	42	U S N	44	··	
H	Lombardi Anne—†	42	housewife	35	"	
K	Lombardi Humbert	42	laborer	35		
L	Della Russo Ettore	44	painter	37	"	
M	Della Russo Lena—†	44	housewife	30	"	
N	LeMoure Abigail—†	44	"	54		
o	LeMoure Francis	44	U S A	30		
P	LeMoure Joseph	44	"	32		
R	LeMoure Richard	44	"	22		
s	LeMoure Thomas	44	fishcutter	28	"	
T	Eldridge Arthur	44	machinist	29	"	
U	Eldridge Mary—†	44	housewife	26	"	
V	Gallagher Rose—†	44	matron	50		
w	Marini Alice—†	47	housewife	44	"	
x	Marini Catherine—†	47	typist	21		
Y	Marini John	47	machinist	56	"	
z	Marini John, jr	47	U S A	23		
	920					
A	Marini Ralph	47	U S C G	25	"	
B	Nickerson Catherine—†	48	decorator	43	"	
c	Nickerson Ivan	48	chauffeur	43	"	
D	*Nickerson Mary E—†	48	at home	67	"	
E	Nickerson Nellie—†	48	dairyworker	36	"	
F	Crosby Frederick	48	retired	74	"	
G	Crosby Lillian M—†	48	housewife	77	"	
H	Guarino Angelo	48	cobbler	41	"	
K	Guarino Mary—†	48	housewife	38	"	
L	Fobert Angelica—†	49	typist	21		
M	Fobert Jennie M—†	49	housewife	50	"	
N	Fobert Victoria—†	49	clerk	25	··	
o	O'Connor Josephine—†	49	housewife	27	"	
P	*Hirtle Florence—†	50	"	51		
R	*Hirtle Louis	50	carpenter	56	"	

s	Baptista Adeline—†	50	housewife	50	here
t	Baptista Adeline—†	50	stylist	28	"
u	Baptista Edward J	50	U S A	22	"
v*	Baptista John E	50	supervisor	55	"
w	Bettano Anthony	51	bartender	41	198 Maverick
x	Bettano Helen—†	51	housewife	42	198 "
y	Labella Giro	52	guard	33	120 Trenton
z	Labella Louise—†	52	housewife	30	120 "

921

a	DeMattia Alfred	53	U S A	26	here
b*	DeMattia Anna—†	53	operator	46	"
c	DeMattia Stanley	53	U S A	24	"
d	Martino Florence—†	53	housewife	22	"
e	Martino William F	53	U S A	23	"
f	Stapleton Edna—†	54	housewife	39	"
g	Stapleton Leo J	54	U S N	44	
h	Stapleton Virginia—†	54	packer	20	
k	Curran Julia E—†	55	at home	84	"
l	Halstead Charles A	55	guard	47	
m	Halstead Edith J—†	55	housewife	46	"
n	Halstead Etta M—†	55	at home	25	"
o	Halstead Bertha M—†	55	housewife	70	"
p	Halstead William F	55	seaman	77	"
r	Amodeo John	56	electrician	38	196 Bennington
s	Amodeo Sadie—†	56	housewife	37	here
t	Virginio Leo	56	pipefitter	55	"
u	DiPaolo Rosalie—†	57	housewife	22	"
v	DiPaolo Samuel	57	U S A	23	
w	Macauley Franklin	57	U S N	41	
x	Macauley Verna—†	57	housewife	42	"
y	Hamel Angela—†	57	"	44	
z	Hamel Donald	57	pipefitter	44	"

922

a	Hamel Donald	57	U S A	23	"
b	Gubitose Guy	58	machinist	35	"
c	Gubitose Theresa—†	58	housewife	33	"
d	Addy John A	60	U S C G	24	"
e	Addy Veronica F—†	60	housewife	22	"
f	Calsimitto Louise—†	60	cleaner	62	
g	LaVita Anthony	60	pipecoverer	41	"
h	LaVita Mary—†	60	housewife	38	"

Falcon Street—Continued

Letter	Full Name	Residence	Occupation	Age	Reported Residence
K	Laskey Daisy—†	60	housewife	27	here
L	Laskey Herbert	60	chauffeur	31	"
M	Verbanas Caroline—†	60	cleaner	41	"
N	Verbanas John	60	waiter	53	
O	Verbanas Paul	60	U S A	20	
P	St John Catherine—†	62	housewife	22	"
R	St John Walter	62	longshoreman	24	"
S	Fiore Lillian—†	62	toolmaker	24	"
T	Fiore Mario	62	longshoreman	25	"
U	Mitchell Lillian—†	62	housewife	46	"
V	*Mitchell Percy R	62	galvanizer	58	"
W	Mitchell Thomas	62	U S A	29	
X	Mitchell William	62	U S N	21	
Y	Preston Blanche L—†	63	housewife	31	"
Z	Preston Michael J	63	laborer	35	..

923

Letter	Full Name	Residence	Occupation	Age	Reported Residence
A	Preston Frances A—†	63	housewife	27	"
B	Preston John F	63	U S A	29	
C	Preston Mary E—†	63	housewife	55	"
D	Ryan Charles J	63	chauffeur	44	"
E	Ryan Rose A—†	63	housewife	44	"
F	Condon Richard	64	laborer	45	"
G	Tobin Nora—†	64	housewife	58	"
H	Tobin Patrick	64	laborer	60	
K	Eldridge Alice—†	64	housewife	54	"
L	Eldridge John	64	blacksmith	56	"
M	Catone Arthur	64	clerk	20	
N	Catone Clara—†	64	housewife	47	"
O	Catone Elda—†	64	WAVE	25	
P	Catone Gaetano	64	laborer	59	
R	Catone Gaetano, jr	64	U S N	23	"
S	Catone Michael	64	U S A	28	
T	Catone Orlando	64	"	23	"
U	Buontempo Edward	66	chauffeur	30	75 White
V	Buontempo Grace—†	66	housewife	27	75 "
W	Merchant Helen—†	66	"	31	here
X	Merchant James	66	foreman	34	"
Y	Pagano Charles	66	laborer	36	"
Z	Pagano Esther—†	66	housewife	31	"

924

Letter	Full Name	Residence	Occupation	Age	Reported Residence
A	Eldridge George	68	metalworker	21	65 Chandler

Falcon Street—Continued

B	Mangone Augustine	68	U S A	38	here
c	*Mangone Biggi	68	retired	69	"
D	*Mangone Francesca—†	68	housewife	69	"
E	Cerrone Angelina—†	68	"	36	
F	Cerrone Carlo	68	laborer	29	
G	Hicks Alice M—†	69	housewife	34	"
H	Hicks James P	69	machinist	37	"
K	Patz Clara—†	69	housewife	46	"
L	Patz George	69	U S A	24	"
M	Patz John	69	mason	54	
N	Hodgkins Louise M—†	69	housewife	49	"
O	Hodgkins Paul A	69	U S A	24	
P	Hodgkins Robert W	69	"	23	
R	Hodgkins William F	69	engineer	53	"
S	Hodgkins Wilma—†	69	operator	26	"
U	Maceiras Felicia—†	71	housewife	50	"
V	Maceiras Juan	71	engineer	49	"
W	Noguerol Jose	71	carpenter	51	"
X	Nigro Angelina—†	71	housewife	46	"
Y	Nigro Ciro	71	clerk	23	"
Z	Nigro Ermino	71	U S A	21	"
	925				
A	Nigro Joseph	71	laborer	55	
B	Nigro Marion—†	71	nurse	29	
C	Cleary Christopher	71	longshoreman	44	"
D	Cleary Jeannette—†	71	housewife	39	"
F	Whitten Margaret M—†	71	"	70	"
G	Johnson Carl	74	seaman	62	Concord
H	Kristoffersen Agnes—†	74	housewife	55	here
K	Khristoffersen Mathias	74	fireman	62	"
L	Murphy John	74	seaman	50	"
M	Malacaso Charles J	77	boilermaker	27	"
N	Malacaso Mary A—†	77	housewife	23	"
O	Blowers Anna E—†	77	"	33	
P	Blowers Reginald	77	machinist	42	"
R	Mahan Frances—†	77	housewife	20	Lynn
S	Gillen Margaret—†	77	stenographer	33	119 Webster
T	Gillen Martin	77	longshoreman	38	here
U	Gillen Mary—†	77	housewife	35	"
V	*Atkins Annie—†	78	"	78	"
W	*Atkins James A	78	retired	79	

Falcon Street—Continued

x*Johnson Barbara—†	78	housewife	21	here
y Johnson Vernon	78	U S C G	26	"
z Butler Leslie I	78	guard	47	"

926

A Butler Viola—†	78	housewife	49	"
B Albanese Ida—†	79	"	26	"
C Albanese Michael	79	U S A	31	
D D'Addieco Alfred	79	student	21	"
E D'Addieco Michael	79	pressman	61	"
F D'Addieco Susan—†	79	housewife	52	"
G Millar John L	79	U S N	20	
H Millar Nellie—†	79	housewife	59	"
K Millar Thomas P	79	shipfitter	30	"
L Millar William J	79	seaman	24	
M Reed George S	81	machinist	29	"
N Reed Helen M—†	81	housewife	25	"
O LaBella Gerardo	87	fireman	30	"
P LaBella Marie—†	87	housewife	29	"
R Duke James	87	rigger	56	
S Duke Mary—†	87	housewife	52	"
T LaTorre Josephine—†	87	"	40	
U LaTorre Salvatore	87	baker	47	"
V Cianciarulo Gerardo	89	teacher	41	"
W Cianciarulo Maria—†	89	housewife	40	"
X Cianciarulo Rafaella—†	89	at home	67	"
Y Repetto Florence E—†	89	operator	27	"
Z Repetto Nicholas A	89	B F D	31	"

927

A Repetto Anna—†	89	W A C	28	
B*Borghero Francesco	89	retired	69	
C Repetto John B	89	machinist	59	"
D Repetto Salvatore	89	U S A	22	
E Maher Elsie—†	93	housewife	35	"
F Maher Michael	93	rigger	39	
G Dalton Elizabeth—†	93	nurse	63	
H Heffron Elizabeth C—†	93	inspector	24	"
K Heffron Fred L	93	collector	60	"
L Heffron Margaret E—†	93	housewife	54	"
M Heffron Margaret M—†	93	secretary	23	"
N Heffron William	93	laborer	69	"

o	Heino Aino—†	95	laundress	50	here
p	Heino Anne—†	95	WAVE	24	"
r	Heino Reino	95	seaman	26	"
s	Irving Herbert E	95A	retired	70	
t	Irving Viola P—†	95A	housewife	69	"
u	Bailey Benjamin	97	machinist	60	"
v	Bailey Benjamin A	97	clerk	34	
w	Bailey Elizabeth—†	97	housewife	58	"
x	Bailey Lawrence	97	clerk	30	
z	McBournie Ina B—†	99	"	49	

928

a	Robicheau Edith M—†	99	housewife	32	"
b	Robicheau Joseph B	99	shipwright	38	"
c	McCabe Bernard	101	chauffeur	33	"
d	McCabe Dorothy—†	101	housewife	31	"
e	Mills Lawrence	101	U S A	24	"
f	Jaczkowski Isabella—†	101	brazier	25	Chelsea
g	Jaczkowski Walter J	101	U S N	28	"
h	Long Alice—†	101	housewife	60	here
k	Long Thomas G	101	U S A	27	"
l	Long William C	101	operator	57	"
m	Collins Frances B—†	103	at home	64	"
n	O'Rourke Helen—†	103	operator	30	"
o	Turpin Ella J—†	103	housewife	54	"
p	Turpin John E	103	engineer	57	"
r	Grady Alice P—†	103	housewife	47	"
s	Grady Pauline—†	103	operator	26	"
t	Grady William F	103	metalworker	53	"
u	Broussard James E	105	salesman	45	"
v	Broussard Mary E—†	105	housewife	41	"
w	White William H	105	guard	54	
x	Keough Annie F—†	105	housewife	66	"
y	Keough William F	105	watchman	67	"
z	Hancock James	105	pipefitter	45	"

929

a	Hancock Victoria—†	105	operator	43	"
b	Martinez Domingo	107	machinist	59	"
c	Martinez Manuela—†	107	housewife	46	"
d	Fernandez Jose	107	machinist	58	"
e	Fernandez Virginia—†	107	housewife	52	"

18

Falcon Street—Continued

F	Amico Luciano	109	rigger	34	here
G	Amico Teresa—†	109	housewife	31	"
H	Renzi Constantino	109	driller	33	"
K	Renzi Diamond—†	109	housewife	34	"
L	Vellotti Pelligrino	109	U S A	28	
M	Sullivan John J	111	B F D	48	
N	Sullivan John J, jr	111	U S C G	24	"
O	Sullivan Lorraine A—†	111	operator	26	"
P	Sullivan Robert F	111	U S N	20	
R	Sullivan Ruth—†	111	housewife	44	"
S	Benson Charles	111	retired	81	
T	Benson Herbert B	111	shipwright	47	"
U	Benson Olive E—†	111	secretary	20	"
V	Benson Signe R—†	111	housewife	39	"
W	Borghi Abbie—†	117	"	50	
X	Borghi Florence—†	117	clerk ·	20	..
Y	Borghi Harold	117	U S A	25	
Z	Borghi Raymond	117	pipefitter	53	"
	930				
A	Enos Deolda—†	117	housewife	44	"
B	Enos John	117	fireman	48	"
C	Enos Joseph M	117	U S N	20	"
D	Piva Geraldine—†	117	housewife	30	95 Homer
E	Piva Joseph S	117	welder	43	95 "
F	Kimball Anna T—†	119	housewife	28	here
G	Kimball Arthur K	119	metalworker	35	"
H	Mattera Cesare	119	longshoreman	57	"
K	Mattera Eva C—†	119	operator	23	"
L	Mattera Jennie—†	119	typist	28	
M	Mattera Joseph N	119	U S N	26	..
N	Mattera Josephine—†	119	housewife	56	"
O	Mattera Louise J—†	119	clerk	24	
P	Mattera Mary—†	119	packer	36	
R	*Doucette Francis	119	engineer	57	"
S	Doucette James W	119	U S N	23	
T	*Doucette Mary—†	119	housewife	53	"
V	Garofano Frank	121	chauffeur	46	"
W	Garofano Mary—†	121	housewife	38	"
X	Fulginiti Christine—†	121	"	44	"
Y	Fulginiti James D	121	plasterer	54	"

Page.	Letter.	FULL NAME.	Residence, Jan. 1, 1945.	Occupation.	Supposed Age.	Reported Residence, Jan. 1, 1944. Street and Number.

Falcon Street—Continued

z	Page Emil	121	U S A	28	here	
931						
A	Pagliarulo Adelaide—†	121	housewife	62	"	
B	Pagliarulo Anthony	121	retired	71	"	
C	Pagliarulo Eleanor—†	121	clerk	20	"	
D	Pagliarulo Florence—†	121	accountant	21	"	
E	Pagliarulo George	121	agent	34	"	
F	Pagliarulo Henry	121	U S N	22		
G	Pagliarulo John	121	U S A	23		
H	Pagliarulo Joseph	121	engineer	42	"	
K	Pagliarulo Michael	121	U S A	29		
L	McGuin Frederick D	129	retired	53		
M	McGuin Frederick J	129	U S A	24	"	
N	McGuin Josephine M—†	129	housewife	51	"	
O	*Molloy Clara—†	129A	"	43		
P	Molloy George J	129A	rigger	43		
R	Gray Joseph	131	retired	73		
S	Norris Anna—†	131	housewife	42	"	
T	Norris Michael J	131	guard	42		
U	Norcutt Lorna—†	131A	housewife	27	"	
V	Norcutt Peter	131A	fisherman	34	"	
W	McLaughlin Alice R—†	133	housewife	44	"	
X	McLaughlin Charles E	133	pedler	49		
Y	Capithorne Charlotte M–†	133A	housewife	35	"	
z	Capithorne Richard J	133A	meter reader	38	"	
932						
A	Boyer Francis	135	rigger	38	"	
B	Boyer Mary—†	135	housewife	37	"	
C	Deveau Edward	135A	U S A	24		
D	*Deveau Irene	135A	carpenter	53	"	
E	*Deveau Lucy—†	135A	housewife	46	"	

Meridian Street

F	Dorazio John J	414	riveter	53	here	
G	Dorazio Philomena—†	414	WAC	23	"	
H	Dorazio Rose M—†	414	housewife	55	"	
K	Dorazio Rose M—†	414	clerk	21	"	
L	Dorazio Victor F	414	U S N	24	"	
M	Kovacev Anthony	414	meatcutter	31	416 Meridian	
N	Kovacev Maria—†	414	housewife	29	416 "	

20

Meridian Street—Continued

o	Hardy Barbara V—†	414	housewife	20	here
p	Hardy William C	414	machinist	28	"
r	DeRota Ettore	416	pipefitter	62	"
s	DeRota Lydia—†	416	waitress	21	"
t	*DeRota Rachel—†	416	housewife	54	"
u	DeRota Ralph	416	U S N	24	
v	DeRota Victoria—†	416	packer	26	"
w	Cornetta Benedetto	416	guard	57	1073 Saratoga
x	Pastore James	416	bartender	34	here
y	Pastore Sarah—†	416	housewife	27	"
z	Haberlin Geraldine—†	416	"	21	7 Bruce

933

a	Haberlin James T	416	machinist	24	7 "
b	Nicastro Cosimo	417	attorney	49	here
c	Nicastro Esther F—†	417	housewife	44	"
d	Orr Donald L	418	shipper	43	"
e	Orr Irene V—†	418	housewife	41	"
f	Sacco Biagio	418	bartender	33	43 Burbank
g	Sacco Violet E—†	418	housewife	23	43 "
h	Persson Edith V—†	418	"	66	here
k	Reed Frank R	418	operator	37	"
l	Marcucella Anthony	419	clerk	31	"
m	Marcucella Joseph	419	storekeeper	67	"
n	Marcucella Theresa—†	419	housewife	27	"
o	Marcucella Clara—†	419	"	27	
p	Marcucella James	419	bartender	32	"
r	O'Rourke Catherine—†	421	housewife	51	"
s	O'Rourke Mary—†	421	attendant	55	"
t	O'Rourke Patrick J	421	policeman	49	"
u	Pastore Carmen	421	shoecutter	41	"
v	Pastore John	421	carpenter	39	"
w	Pastore Yolanda—†	421	housewife	35	"
x	Ferrara Angelina—†	421	"	31	
y	Ferrara Joseph	421	salesman	39	"
z	Ferrara Francesco	421	retired	70	

934

a	Pastore Helen—†	421	housewife	41	"
b	*Kovacev Angelina C—†	422	"	55	
c	Kovacev John	422	butcher	24	"
d	Vitkovich Anna C—†	422	housewife	32	New York
e	Vitkovich John J	422	carpenter	36	"

F	Kovacev Natale	422	butcher	29	here
G	Kovacev Patria F—†	422	housewife	27	"
H	*Bracciotti Anna K—†	422	"	73	"
K	Bracciotti Lamberto	422	retired	78	"
L	Bracciotti Nello A	422	clerk	33	"
M	Nunes Emery	423	manager	24	"
N	Nunes Frank	423	U S N	33	
O	*Nunes Minnie—†	423	housewife	60	"
P	Warchol Edward	423	U S N	23	
R	Warchol Yvonne—†	423	factoryhand	21	"
S	Dugan Charles	423	U S A	25	
T	Dugan Marianna—†	423	housewife	25	"
U	Maragioglia Gasperina-†	423	"	54	
V	Maragioglia Stephano	423	factoryhand	61	"
W	Gislason Caroline E—†	423	housewife	32	"
X	Gislason Oscar	423	U S A	43	
Y	Youngberg George	423	U S N	42	"

935

A	Carco Marie—†	425	housewife	26	"
B	Carco Sebastian	425	merchant	25	"
C	McNear Georgianna—†	425	dressmaker	65	"
D	Panarese John	426	laborer	50	
E	Panarese Mary—†	426	housewife	38	"
F	Caper Roy	426	chauffeur	41	Somerville
G	Deininger Caroline—†	426	housekeeper	56	10 Goodrich rd
H	Sherman Loretta M—†	426	housewife	32	here
K	Sherman Norman F	426	electrician	32	"
L	Day Emma F—†	427	housewife	72	"
M	Johnson Ruth M—†	427	secretary	31	"
N	Moon Mary E—†	427	housewife	75	"
O	Rollins Lendall P	427	guard	68	
P	Ryan Edward L	427	laborer	60	
R	McInnis Beatrice—†	427	inspector	25	"
S	McInnis Francis	427	U S A	26	"
T	McInnis Gertrude—†	427	clerk	22	
U	McInnis Helen—†	427	housewife	57	"
V	McInnis Helen—†	427	clerk	21	
W	McInnis Lillian—†	427	factoryhand	32	"
X	Curran Emma M—†	427	housewife	58	"
Y	Curran Henry P	427	mechanic	60	"
Z	Riley Emily—†	427	housewife	72	"

936
Meridian Street—Continued

A	Smith Lillian A—†	428	mechanic	32	here
B	Smith Lillian M—†	428	teacher	49	"
C	Libby Mary J—†	428	saleswoman	50	"
D	Williamson Caroline—†	428	housewife	40	"
E	Williamson William	428	nurse	42	Fall River
F	Hoffman Barbara—†	428	operator	47	here
G	Hoffman Christie—†	428	at home	78	"
H	Hoffman Donald	428	motorman	42	"
K	Hoffman Lucy—†	428	at home	35	"
L	Hoffman Sadie—†	428	clerk	39	"
M	MacDonald Christie—†	428	"	49	
N	Grant Margaret B—†	430	matron	56	"
O	Kerr Catherine L—†	430	at home	86	"
P	Kerr Edmund H	430	investigator	52	"
R	Kerr Mary L—†	430	clerk	54	"
S	Riley Elizabeth K—†	432	housewife	54	"
T	Riley Frederick	432	guard	56	
U	Riley Jean M—†	432	WAVE	22	"
V	Dolly William	432	laborer	52	
W	McKeogh Cecelia—†	432	at home	80	"
X	McKeogh Josephine—†	432	operator	52	"
Y	McKeogh Margaret—†	432	at home	50	"
Z	Greenwood Anna E—†	432	housewife	44	"

937

A	Greenwood John W	432	metalworker	44	"
B	Greenwood Robert W	432	U S A	21	"
C*	Grifone Anthony	434	butcher	45	52 Marion
D	Grifone Lucy—†	434	housewife	38	52 "
E	Bostrom Helen—†	436	clerk	22	here
F	Olsson Charles R	436	technician	48	"
G	Olsson Francis R	436	U S A	20	"
H	Olsson Margaret A—†	436	U S M C	21	"
K	Olsson Ruth—†	436	housewife	27	"
L	Barrett John	436	machinist	45	"
M	Barrett Margaret—†	436	housewife	72	"
N	Barrett Margaret—†	436	bookkeeper	32	"
O	Barrett Robert	436	retired	74	"
P	Phillips Daniel	437	policeman	47	"
R	Phillips Ethel—†	437	housewife	41	"
S	Payne Catherine—†	437	"	25	

Meridian Street—Continued

T	Payne Charles	437	foreman	50	here
U	Memmolo Helen—†	437	housewife	25	"
V	Memmolo Pasquale	437	boilermaker	28	"
W	DeAngelis Amelia—†	438	housewife	47	"-
X	DeAngelis Florence—†	438	operator	23	"
Y	DeAngelis Henry	438	cutter	50	"
Z	DeAngelis Joseph	438	U S N	24	
	938				
A	DeAngelis Robert	438	"	21	
B	Mulone Anna—†	438	housewife	31	"
C	Mulone Anthony	438	U S A	32	
D	Colantuono Edith—†	438	stitcher	40	"
E	Boyle Margaret—†	439	cook	54	74 W Eagle
F	Powers Margaret L—†	439	housewife	47	74 "
G	Powers Marie L—†	439	tel operator	22	74 "
H	Powers Robert E	439	U S M C	24	74 "
K	Powers Robert J	439	clerk	47	74 "
L	Mullane Daniel F	439	laborer	27	here
M	Mullane Jeremiah	439	rigger	29	"
N	Mullane Michael J	439	laborer	33	"
O	*Mullane Thomas	439	retired	71	
P	Hollohan Augustine	439	U S A	20	
R	Hollohan Michael	439	machinist	52	"
S	Hollohan Monica—†	439	housewife	44	"
T	Freethy Isabelle—†	440	"	50	
U	Freethy Roy H	440	engineer	59	"
V	Hunter Virginia—†	440	housewife	27	"
W	Hunter William S	440	U S A	26	"
X	Lafferty Florence E—†	440	housewife	65	"
Y	Lafferty William F	440	retired	67	
Z	Bremer Adele J—†	440	manager	53	"
	939				
A	May Mary E—†	440	housewife	64	"
B	May William J	440	retired	71	..
C	Lipson William	440	polisher	44	"
D	McCarthy Charles J	440	clerk	63	
E	McCarthy Mabel C—†	440	housewife	64	"
F	Silva Clara H—†	440	laundress	55	Chelsea
G	Mattola Lena—†	441	shoeworker	27	here
H	Tufo Anthony	441	U S A	24	"
K	Tufo Edward	441	chauffeur	26	"

Meridian Street—Continued

L	Tufo Josephine—†	441	housewife	43	here
.	Tufo Umberto	441	barber	46	"
	Barrasso Thomasina—†	441	stitcher	31	"
	Mascetta Ambrose	441	machinist	25	"
	Mascetta Elizabeth—†	441	stitcher	26	"
	Mascetta Ferdinand	441	tailor	60	
	Mascetta Josephine—†	441	housewife	29	"
M	Mascetta Phyllis—†	441	stitcher	32	"
U	Mascetta Remigio	441	cutter	29	
C	Mascetta Rolmilda—†	441	housewife	57	"
W	DiFrancesco Angelo	441	machinist	20	"
X	DiFrancesco Frances—†	441	binder	24	"
Y	DiFrancesco Joseph	441	factoryhand	59	"
Z	DiFrancesco Stephen	441	U S A	22	"
	940				
A	DiFrancesco Teresa—†	441	housewife	57	"
B	DiFrancesco Thomas	441	U S A	22	"
D	Moore Arthur E	443	"	36	
E	Moore Charles V	443	retired	74	
F	Moore Lillian E—†	443	housewife	73	"
G	*Comeau Leo	443	carpenter	65	"
H	*Comeau Leonie—†	443	housewife	75	"
K	Richard George P	443	fisherman	38	"
L	Flaherty Bertha—†	445	tel operator	41	"
M	Keating Beverly C—†	445	secretary	32	"
N	Tierney Irene—†	445	housewife	43	"
O	Tierney William J	445	B F D	51	
P	Woods Esther C—†	445	at home	65	"
R	Mann Bertha L—†	445	housewife	68	"
S	Mann Diedrich H	445	grocer	71	
T	Wiegand Louise A—†	445	stenographer	35	"
U	Curry George L	445	clerk	44	"
V	Curry Mary M—†	445	tel operator	46	"
W	Gallo Annie—†	447	housewife	53	"
X	Gallo Jennie—†	447	typist	22	
Y	Gallo Ralph	447	merchant	53	"
Z	Veje Andrew	447	seaman	47	
	941				
A	Veje Elsie—†	447	secretary	21	"
B	Veje Evelyn—†	447	housewife	46	"
C	DiAngelis John	451	pharmacist	30	"

D	DiAngelis Margaret—†	451	housewife	26	here
E	Coffey Edna—†	451	"	35	"
F	Coffey James S	451	executive	45	"
G	Coffey Joseph	451	welder	36	"
H	Coffey Mary E—†	451	housewife	71	"
K	Coffey Mary G—†	451	"	44	
L	Coffey Thomas	451	retired	72	
M	Coffey Thomas F	451	U S A	21	
N	Johnson Robert	451	U S N	25	
O	Johnson William	451	"	26	"
P	LaVoie Mary—†	451	housewife	23	60 Gladstone
R	Nolan Esther H—†	451	"	46	here
S	Nolan John	451	optician	50	"
T	Sullivan Mary C—†	451	housewife	70	"
U	Dermody Patrick	451	seaman	45	"
V	McKenna Annie—†	451	housewife	65	"
W	McKenna Edward	451	longshoreman	58	"
X	Moss Catherine—†	451	factoryhand	22	"
Y	Moss Charles	451	U S N	22	793 Bennington
Z	Dalaher Frederick	452	B F D	60	here

942

B	Cooney William L	452	starter	52	"
C	Cronin Elizabeth—†	452	boxmaker	54	"
A	Dalaher Jennie—†	452	housewife	61	"
D	Keyes Clement R	453	motorman	50	"
E	Keyes Melvin C	453	U S A	25	
F	Keyes Winifred—†	453	housewife	48	"
G	Ranelli Antoinette—†	453	chemist	31	"
H	Ranelli Dominic	453	U S A	24	
K	Ranelli Eliza—†	453	housewife	60	"
L	Ranelli Enrico	453	merchant	63	"
M	Ranelli Theresa—†	453	stitcher	22	"
N	Crosby Frank M	453	printer	53	"
O	Crosby Josephine—†	453	housewife	47	"
P	Crosby Rita—†	453	clerk	22	
R	Hamilton Phillip	453	boilermaker	45	"
S	Kincade Richard	453	clerk	27	
T	Lang Patrick	454	plumber	77	"
U	DeVeau Joseph C	455	metalworker	45	348 Saratoga
V	Saulnier Lawrence	455	carpenter	49	348 "
W	*Saulnier Martha—†	455	housewife	82	348 "

Meridian Street—Continued

x	Saulnier Mary E—†	455	housewife	41	348 Saratoga
y	McGrath John J	455	fisherman	51	here
z	McGrath Joseph	455	U S A	23	"

943

A	McGrath Ralph	455	"	21	
B	McGrath Theresa—†	455	housewife	48	"
C	Bartolo Julia—†	456	"	28	
D	Bartolo Michael	456	toolmaker	31	"
E	Butler Margarette—†	456	housekeeper	72	"
F	Cannon Gertrude—†	456	technician	44	"
G	Cannon Mary L—†	456	WAVE	24	"
H	Sheridan Jane—†	456	at home	70	442 Meridian
K	Cordeau Albert	458	longshoreman	29	here
L	Cordeau Alfreida—†	458	housewife	28	"
M	Palmieri Anthony	458	painter	53	"
N	Palmieri Cecelia—†	458	clerk	23	"
O	Palmieri Edward	458	U S N	21	
P	Palmieri Louise—†	458	housewife	47	"
R	Dean Matilda—†	459	"	52	
S	Dean Norman R	459	painter	54	
T	Trevor Edward	459	pipefitter	45	"
U	Trevor Lorraine—†	459	instructor	20	"
V	Trevor Margaret—†	459	housewife	43	"
W	Burke Catherine—†	459	"	52	"
X	Burke James R	459	seaman	23	
Y	Burke John W	459	U S A	21	
Z	Burke Joseph P	459	pipefitter	50	"

944

A	Burke Joseph P	459	U S A	26	
B	Worthy Alice M—†	460	housewife	30	"
C	Worthy Edward S	460	inspector	35	"
D	Mitchell Joseph E	460	laborer	52	
E	Mitchell Mary C—†	460	housewife	47	"
F	Perry Hattie B—†	460	"	44	
G	Perry Ivan M	460	seaman	40	"
K	Lane Evelyn—†	462	housewife	25	264 Meridian
L	Lane Maxwell	462	U S A	23	264 "
M	Hoy Mary E—†	462	housewife	28	here
N	Hoy Walter J	462	rigger	30	"
O	Powers Catherine—†	463	WAC	25	"
P	Powers Edward	463	printer	29	

27

Page	Letter	Full Name.	Residence, Jan. 1, 1945.	Occupation.	Supposed Age.	Reported Residence, Jan. 1, 1944. Street and Number.

Meridian Street—Continued

	Letter	Full Name.	Res.	Occupation.	Age	Reported Residence
	R	Powers Loretta—†	463	stenographer	26	here
	S	Powers Nicholas	463	welder	50	"
	T	Powers Rose—†	463	housewife	51	"
	U	Powers Rosemarie—†	463	checker	23	"
	V	Randall Ann—†	463	stenographer	50	"
	W	Randall Joseph	463	U S A	27	"
	X	Rogers Dorothy—†	463	housewife	27	"
	Y	Rogers William	463	longshoreman	35	"
945						
	A	*Banks Elsie—†	464	housekeeper	49	69 Marion
	B	Doucette Frank B	464	brazier	26	here
	C	Doucette Lydia A—†	464	housewife	25	"
	D	Foote Charles	465	seaman	51	"
	E	Frasier Maud—†	465	housewife	66	"
	F	Fortier Eliza—†	465	"	82	2 Eutaw pl
	H	Hegner Andrew G	469	laborer	58	37 W Eagle
	K	Hegner Francis L	469	policeman	27	37 "
	L	Hegner Harold E	469	U S A	21	37 "
	M	Hegner Ruth—†	469	WAVE	23	37 "
	N	Hegner Sarah J—†	469	housewife	55	37 "
	O	Flynn Ellen F—†	469	"	60	here
	P	Flynn Joseph B	469	U S A	24	"
	R	Flynn Joseph P	469	machinist	65	"
	S	Flynn Rose—†	469	bookkeeper	22	"
	T	Gangemi Anthony	469	laborer	52	
	U	Gangemi Elizabeth—†	469	housewife	43	"
	V	Gangemi Joseph	469	U S N	23	
	Y	Hayden Alice—†	473	housewife	60	"
	Z	Hayden Patrick	473	mechanic	65	"
946						
	A	Tomaselli Joseph F	473	U S M C	27	Lawrence
	B	Lane Albert	475	machinist	28	here
	C	Lane Florence—†	475	housewife	25	"
	D	Lane Anna J—†	475	waitress	26	"
	E	Lane Helen F—†	475	clerk	20	
	F	Lane Helen T—†	475	housewife	53	"
	G	Lane Samuel	475	U S A	22	
	H	Hunt Daniel	477	watchman	51	"
	K	Hunt Ethel—†	477	factoryhand	46	"
	L	Barrasso Carmella—†	477	laundrywkr	27	192 Marion
	M	Barrasso Helen—†	477	tel operator	25	192 "

Page.	Letter.	FULL NAME.	Residence, Jan. 1, 1945.	Occupation.	Supposed Age.	Reported Residence, Jan. 1, 1944. Street and Number.

Meridian Street—Continued

	N	Barrasso Mary—†	477	housewife	60	192 Marion
	O	Barrasso Nicholas	477	chauffeur	55	192 "
	P	Barrasso Nicholas	477	U S A	23	192 "
	R	Connolly Catherine—†	477	factoryhand	23	here
	S	Connolly Catherine C—†	477	housewife	50	"
	T	Connolly John	477	engineer	53	"
	U	Connolly Martha—†	477	student	21	"

947   West Eagle Street

	B	McIver James	2	retired	73	here
	C	Newbury Etta—†	2	housekeeper	70	"
	D	Coffin Arma—†	2	clerk	23	"
	E	Coffin Beatrice—†	2	housewife	49	"
	F	Coffin Bernadette—†	2	WAVE	21	
	G	Coffin William	2	shipfitter	49	"
	H	Shipp George	4	molder	31	
	K	Shipp Iva—†	4	housewife	23	"
	L	Capobianco Jennie—†	4	"	43	
	M	Capobianco Thomas	4	clerk	42	
	N	Jacobson John J	6	rigger	60	
	O	Pedersen Elizabeth—†	6	housewife	49	"
	P	Pedersen Thomas E	6	machinist	57	"
	R	St Croix Thelma—†	6	housewife	25	"
	S	Buontempo Albert	6	shipper	31	
	T	Buontempo Mary—†	6	housewife	28	"
	U	Scali Dante	6	clerk	23	"
	V	Scali Joseph	6	tailor	58	
	W	Scali Theresa—†	6	housewife	45	"
	X	McInnis John	8	electrician	34	140 Falcon
	Y	McInnis Mary—†	8	housewife	33	140 "
	Z	Kelly Earl	8	engineer	57	here

948

	A	Kelly Hilda—†	8	housewife	58	"
	B	Sullivan Helen—†	8	"	24	"
	C	Sullivan Leo	8	fishcutter	30	"
	D	Meyer Frances M—†	23	housewife	34	58 Bennington
	E	Meyer Paul H	23	painter	35	58 "
	F	Alfoma Frank	23	U S N	20	here
	G	*Alfoma Mary L—†	23	housewife	53	"
	H	*Alfoma Lottie—†	23	clerk	23	"

29

K	Baker Florence—†	23	packer	25	here
L	Morrisroe Bertha—†	26	housekeeper	65	"
M	Bagley Edward J	27	longshoreman	46	"
N	Bagley Elizabeth F—†	27	housewife	76	"
O	Bagley Michael F	27	seaman	42	"
P	Cocorochio Louis	28	welder	41	
R	Quigley Antoinette—†	28	housewife	32	"
S	Quigley William	28	rigger	36	
T	Quigley Louise—†	28	clerk	41	
U	Quigley Mary—†	28	inspector	38	"
V	Tanner Ernest	29	pipefitter	32	"
W	Tanner George	29	U S A	24	
X	Tanner Hattie—†	29	housewife	56	"
Y	Tanner Louis	29	U S A	30	
Z	Tanner Mildred—†	29	clerk	26	

949

A	Caddigan Mary—†	30	housekeeper	51	"
B	Collins John	30	splicer	39	"
C	Collins Lillian—†	30	housewife	40	"
D	DeCristoforo Cecelia—†	30	"	42	
E	DeCristoforo Paul	30	teacher	39	
F	Dolan Mary E—†	31	tel operator	32	"
G	Lang Anna G—†	31	accountant	52	"
H	Millar Eleanor J—†	31	housewife	25	"
K	Millar William J	31	shipfitter	25	"
L	Dingwell Chester N	31	expressman	45	"
M	Dingwell Harold C	31	"	42	
N	Dingwell Mary E—†	31	housewife	40	"
O	Takach Eugene J	31	agent	32	"
P	Takach Florence A—†	31	housewife	29	"
R	Rizzo John	32	chauffeur	43	"
S	Rizzo Theresa—†	32	housewife	34	"
T	Bonnano Louise—†	32	shoeworker	37	"
U	Cannariato Anna—†	32	housewife	45	"
V	Cannariato George	32	shoeworker	48	"
W	Cannariato Josephine—†	32	housewife	53	"
X	Lottero Louis	32	foreman	30	
Y	Lottero Vincenza—†	32	housewife	26	"
Z	Baptista Alice—†	33	"	32	

950

A	Baptista Manuel	33	seaman	48	

West Eagle Street—Continued

B	Morgera Charles	33	retired	59	118 Chelsea
C	Morgera Dominic	33	locksmith	30	here
D	Morgera Mary—†	33	housewife	30	"
E	Ciampi Armando	34	welder	33	"
F	Ciampi Boniface	34	shipfitter	28	"
G	Ciampi Ersilia G—†	34	secretary	25	"
H	Ciampi Patrick	34	U S A	30	"
K	Mannetta John	34	foreman	65	"
L	Massaro Henry	34	tileworker	36	"
M	Massaro Louise—†	34	housewife	34	"
N	Stella Esther—†	34	saleswoman	36	"
O	Denehy Daniel	35	U S C G	21	"
P	Denehy Daniel A	35	shipwright	49	"
R	Denehy Josephine—†	35	housewife	45	"
S	Denehy Mary L—†	35	clerk	34	
T	Hines Albert L	35	fisherman	63	"
U	Hines Albert L, jr	35	U S A	34	
V	Hines Annie B—†	35	housewife	60	"
W	Hines Arnold L	35	foreman	39	"
X	Hines Wilfred H	35	U S C G	38	"
Y	Maguire Jennie A—†	35	housewife	31	"
Z	Gibbons Catherine—†	35	"	78	

951

A	Gibbons Hazel M—†	35	clerk	52	
B	Gibbons John J	35	shipfitter	54	"
C	Gibbons Morgan	35	retired	80	
D	Massaro Carmella—†	36	housewife	33	"
E	Massaro Herman J	36	technician	38	"
F	DeStefano Josephine—†	36	housewife	41	"
G	DeStefano Ralph	36	barber	42	
H	Festa Dora—†	36	housewife	33	"
K	Festa Louis	36	welder	34	
L	Bruno James	37	laborer	21	
M	Bruno Mary—†	37	housewife	53	"
N	Bruno Peter	37	laborer	54	"
O	Harvey Albert F	37	machinist	28	46 White
P	Harvey Gertrude G—†	37	housewife	35	46 "
R	Faretra Anne—†	37	"	30	55 Marion
S	Faretra Armando	37	laborer	34	55 "
T	Cotreau Andrew	38	carpenter	56	here
U	Cotreau Andrew, jr	38	U S N	28	"

Page.	Letter.	FULL NAME.	Residence, Jan. 1, 1945.	Occupation.	Supposed Age.	Reported Residence, Jan. 1, 1944. Street and Number.

West Eagle Street—Continued

	v	Cotreau Edward	38	clerk	24	here
	w	Cotreau Lucy—†	38	housewife	59	"
	x	Cotreau Paul	38	U S N	22	"
	z*	O'Hanley Agnes M—†	39	housewife	41	"
952						
	A	O'Hanley Roy F	39	brazier	36	
	B	Rankin Mary A—†	39	domestic	42	"
	c	Johnson Albert J	39	rubberworker	26	"
	D	Johnson Christopher W	39	U S A	23	"
	E	Johnson Mary—†	39	housewife	49	"
	F	Johnson Norman	39	U S A	22	
	G	Giangrasso Lillian—†	39	housewife	24	"
	H	Souza John	39	laborer	22	
	K	Souza Joseph	39	boilermaker	36	"
	L	Souza Mary—†	39	housewife	55	"
	M	Souza Matilda—†	39	clerk	34	
	N	Barbarossa Louis	40	retired	75	"
	o	Barbarossa Louis, jr	40	carpenter	39	"
	P	Barbarossa Mary—†	40	housewife	62	"
	R	Barranco Delphine—†	40	"	34	"
	s	Barranco John	40	foreman	34	"
	T	Hembrough Evelyn—†	40	housewife	35	"
	U	Hembrough Frederick	40	operator	30	"
	v	McNeil Mabel L—†	41	housewife	38	"
	w	McNeil Milton J	41	foreman	40	"
	x	Wyse David J	41	seaman	54	
	Y	Wyse Elizabeth M—†	41	housewife	49	"
	z	Tedesco Frances—†	41	"	64	
953						
	A	Tedesco Joseph	41	cabinetmaker	66	"
	B	Trafton Lillian—†	42	housekeeper	65	"
	c	Erickson Arthur	42	pipefitter	33	Reading
	D	Erickson Emma—†	42	housewife	29	"
	E	Cafano Alice—†	42	"	30	51 W Eagle
	F	Cafano Gus	42	U S A	30	here
	G	White James F	43	B F D	43	"
	H	White John F	43	U S A	20	"
	K	White Marguerite—†	43	housewife	40	"
	L	Culkeen Elizabeth E—†	43	houseworker	26	"
	M	Culkeen Joseph L	43	U S N	27	
	N	McArdle Andrew P	43	inspector	46	"

West Eagle Street—Continued

	Letter	Full Name	Residence	Occupation	Age	Reported Residence
	o	McArdle Irene G—†	43	housewife	44	here
	p	McArdle John P	43	welder	21	"
	r	Murphy Helen B—†	43	clerk	24	"
	s	Ohlson Alexander	44	chauffeur	29	"
	t	Ohlson Evelyn—†	44	housewife	25	"
	u	Ziniti Emma—†	44	"	49	38 Harvard av
	v	Ziniti John	44	clerk	49	38 "
	w	Hough Clara—†	44	operator	49	here
	x	Hopkins Effie G—†	49	at home	37	"
	y	Snow Leonard N	49	engineer	52	"
	z	Snow Mildred—†	49	housewife	46	"
954						
	a	Roche Anna M—†	49	"	82	
	b	Roche Helen T—†	49	stitcher	36	"
	c	Roche James E	49	calker	47	
	d	Danielson Esther—†	49	bookkeeper	26	"
	e	Danielson Helen—†	49	"	30	
	f	Danielson John	49	architect	34	"
	g	Danielson Kavark M	49	merchant	66	"
	h	Danielson Yeranoohi—†	49	housewife	53	"
	k	*Nalbandian Bagdasar	49	merchant	76	"
	l	Stefano Henry	51	U S N	30	
	m	Stefano Mildred—†	51	housewife	26	"
	n	Viggiano Carmela—†	51	"	66	
	o	Viggiano Joseph	51	retired	74	
	p	Stevens Ernest	51	instructor	36	"
	r	Stevens Rose M—†	51	housewife	36	"
	s	Bucca Frank	51	mechanic	45	"
	t	Bucca Jennie—†	51	housewife	43	"
	u	Bona Daniel	52	machinist	45	"
	v	German Blanche—†	52A	clerk	20	"
	w	German Hermeline—†	52A	housewife	47	53 White
	x	German Thomas	52A	laborer	53	53 "
	y	German Thomas, jr	52A	U S N	21	53 "
	z	Surrett Hector	52A	machinist	20	53 "
955						
	a	Austin Esther M—†	52A	housewife	50	here
	b	Austin William J	52A	foreman	55	"
	c	Austin William J, jr	52A	U S N	22	"
	d	Crupi Angelina—†	53	at home	64	"
	e	Scarcella Anthony	53	laborer	67	

F	Blowers Eliza J—†	53	housewife	76	here
G	Blowers James E	53	U S A	35	"
K	Munroe Frederick	54	clerk	44	"
L	Munroe Marcella—†	54	welder	20	"
M	Munroe Margaret—†	54	housewife	43	"
N	Beekman Dorothy—†	54A	clerk	25	
O	Hermand Rita—†	54A	"	23	
P	O'Neil Mary A—†	54A	housewife	57	"
R	O'Neil William P	54A	laborer	67	
S	Botto Mary—†	54A	housewife	55	"
T	Botto Michael	54A	laborer	57	"
U	Sheehan Anna L—†	55	housewife	60	116 Brooks
V	Sheehan Anna L—†	55	bookkeeper	20	116 "
W	Sheehan Daniel J	55	blacksmith	60	116 "
X	Dunbar Florence C—†	55	housewife	29	here
Y	Dunbar Ralph S	55	chauffeur	30	"
Z	Hoy Bertha M—†	55	welder	29	Reading
	956				
A	Hoy Charles H	55	longshoreman	28	"
B	Doyle Lucy—†	56	housewife	35	here
C	Doyle Martin L	56	longshoreman	39	"
D	Kehoe Julia—†	56	clerk	28	"
E	McRae Mary—†	56	housewife	54	"
F	McRae William	56	mechanic	56	"
G	Costa Marie—†	56	operator	21	"
H	Dacosta Marie P—†	56	housewife	46	"
K	Dacosta Paulino J	56	supt	59	
L	Dobbins Leo F	57	U S A	33	
M	Dobbins Marie—†	57	housewife	33	"
N	Gatti Almo	57	pipefitter	40	"
O	Gatti Lena—†	57	housewife	43	"
P	Gatti Peter	57	pipefitter	20	"
R	Austin Emily M—†	57	housewife	26	52 W Eagle
S	Austin Thomas M	57	weaver	26	52 "
T	Menezes John	58	U S A	23	here
U	Menezes Luiz	58	longshoreman	63	"
V	Menezes Lorenzia—†	58	housewife	47	"
W	Romano Assunta—†	58	"	36	
X	Romano Giacomo	58	laborer	40	
Y	Cabral Filomena—†	58	housewife	27	"
Z	Cabral James	58	operator	45	"

Page.	Letter.	Full Name.	Residence, Jan. 1, 1945.	Occupation.	Supposed Age.	Reported Residence, Jan. 1, 1944. Street and Number.

West Eagle Street—Continued

	B	Del Vecchio Flora—†	59	housewife	36	here
	C	Del Vecchio Joseph	59	welder	47	"
	D	Amari Alba D—†	59	dressmaker	22	"
	E	Amari Joseph	59	stevedore	55	"
	F	Amari Mary S—†	59	dressmaker	24	"
	G	*Amari Peter	59	retired	87	
	H	Amari Rose—†	59	housewife	50	"
	K	Luzinski Frank	60	policeman	46	"
	L	Luzinski Frank H	60	U S A	20	"
	M	Luzinski Henrietta—†	60	housewife	40	"
	N	Sheets Ervis D	61	machinist	34	"
	O	Sheets Harriet E—†	61	saleswoman	29	"
	P	Meyer Melvin	61	assembler	30	"
	R	Meyer Rachel—†	61	housewife	31	"
	S	Leno Henry	61	machinist	36	"
	T	Leno Mary—†	61	housewife	38	"
	U	Clifford Sadie—†	62	housekeeper	80	"
	V	Simington Charles	62	laborer	40	"
	Z	Visco Jennie—†	64	housewife	42	358 Princeton

	A	Visco Joseph	64	plumber	46	358 "
	B	Visco Dominica—†	64	housewife	42	here
	C	Visco Francis	64	tailor	51	"
	E	Rich John J	65	shipper	34	"
	F	Rich Peter	65	retired	58	
	G	Zagarella Anna M—†	65	housewife	30	"
	H	Zagarella James V	65	presser	32	
	K	Dantona Frances—†	65	housewife	48	"
	L	Dantona Liborio	65	coppersmith	54	"
	M	D'Entremont Bernard	66	carpenter	39	"
	N	D'Entremont Irene—†	66	housewife	39	"
	O	*D'Eon Emeline—†	66	housekeeper	72	"
	P	Carusone George	66	seaman	25	"
	R	Carusone Irma—†	66	housewife	24	"
	S	Constantina Alice—†	66	"	54	
	T	Constantina Edward	66	U S N	23	"
	U	Constantina Inez—†	66	shipfitter	21	"
	V	Constantina Pasquale	66	laborer	55	
	W	Ross Charles	66	"	38	
	X	Ross Emma—†	66	housewife	37	"

Page.	Letter.	FULL NAME.	Residence, Jan. 1, 1945.	Occupation.	Supposed Age.	Reported Residence, Jan. 1, 1944. Street and Number.

West Eagle Street—Continued

	Y	Modica Carmella—†	67	housewife	37	Florida
	z	Modica Guiseppi	67	U S A	20	"
959						
	A	Modica Joseph	67	"	42	"
	B	Lopez Elizabeth—†	67	housewife	21	Cambridge
	C	Lopez Frank	67	U S C G	23	214 Brooks
	D	Asaro Iolanda—†	67	housewife	22	here
	E	Asaro Joseph	67	U S A	26	"
	F	Burone Charles	67	painter	60	"
	G	Burone Josephine—†	67	housewife	55	"
	H	Souza Fredericko	67	U S A	27	
	K	Souza Mary—†	67	housewife	28	"
	L	Parsons Marion L—†	69	"	23	
	M	Parsons Robert W, jr	69	U S A	23	
	N	Carusone John	69	retired	70	
	O	Carusone John, jr	69	U S A	23	"
	P	Carusone Josephine—†	69	housewife	55	"
	R	Carusone Josephine—†	69	saleswoman	21	"
	S	Noble Mary M—†	69	inspector	20	11 Saratoga
	T	Winn Doris E—†	69	housewife	30	here
	U	Winn Harold E	69	shipfitter	36	"
	V	Robinson Ethel—†	70	housewife	27	"
	W	Robinson Ralph	70	chauffeur	31	"
	X	Poirier Ina—†	70	housekeeper	49	"
	Y	Des Jardins Joseph	70	fireman	49	"
	z	Des Jardins Nellie—†	70	housewife	38	"
960						
	A	Des Jardins Oscar	70	fireman	45	"
	B	Clements Cerita—†	71	housewife	53	"
	C	Clements Raymond	71	U S A	24	
	D	Clements Richard	71	"	29	"
	E	Clements Robert	71	millhand	23	"
	F	Clements William	71	"	66	"
	G	Vitello Francis	72	painter	39	"
	H	Vitello Theresa—†	72	housewife	35	"
	K	Leville Frederick	72	U S A	25	"
	L	Leville Mary—†	72	housewife	56	"
	M	Leville Paul	72	U S C G	22	"
	N	Leville Virginia—†	72	operator	20	"
	O	Leville William H	72	dyesetter	56	"
	P	Jaakola Arthur	72	rigger	51	

36

West Eagle Street—Continued

R	Jaakola Elina—†	72	housewife	53	here
S	Iaderosa Andrew C	73	U S A	27	"
T	Iaderosa Louise—†	73	clerk	21	"
U	Iaderosa Mary—†	73	housewife	47	"
V	Morante Anna—†	73	clerk	31	"
X	McIntyre Daniel	75	carpenter	42	"
Y	McIntyre Edgar	75	dispatcher	38	"
Z	McIntyre Herbert	75	conductor	34	"

961

A	McIntyre Mary—†	75	operator	29	"
B	McIntyre Rhoda—†	75	housewife	35	"
C	Shapiro Anna—†	76	"	43	
D	Shapiro Joseph	76	chauffer	46	"
E	Ciliberto Edith—†	77	shoeworker	23	464 Sumner
F	Ciliberto Frank G	77	"	23	118 Falcon
G	Goglia Agnes G—†	77	lithographer	27	here
H	Goglia James J	77	U S M C	28	"
K	Larson Anne—†	77	housekeeper	43	Somerville
L	LaRaia Annie—†	77	housewife	56	here
M	LaRaia Isabel—†	77	waitress	24	"
N	LaRaia Joseph	77	U S A	25	"
O	LaRaia Nicholas	77	U S C G	22	"
P	Nolan Louis F	81	guard	52	
R	Nolan Mary E—†	81	housewife	59	"
S	Hemeon Calvin H	81	U S A	22	"
T	Hemeon Edith—†	81	housewife	59	"
U	Hemeon Edward	81	guard	62	"
V	*Couzo John	82	maintenance	49	77 W Eagle
W	Diaz Anne—†	82	housewife	28	77 "
X	Diaz Richard	82	machinist	30	77 "
Y	McPhee Mary—†	82	housewife	28	here
Z	McPhee Robert	82	rigger	31	"

962

A	Brazil Gertrude—†	84	waitress	39	37 Prescott
B	Brazil John	84	U S N	20	37 "
C	Corby Mary—†	84	waitress	32	here
D	Moynihan Catherine—†	84	brushmaker	23	"
E	Moynihan Gerald	84	U S N	23	"
F	Walker Catherine—†	84	housewife	57	"
G	Walker John	84	cleaner	56	"
H	Walker Mark	84	U S A	27	

K	Bryson William	84	machinist	22	Billerica
L	Farnkoff George H	84	chauffeur	41	here
M	Farnkoff Josephine M—†	84	housewife	40	"
N	Nickerson John A	86	teller	41	"
O	Nickerson Mildred—†	86	housewife	40	"
P	Stone Samuel	86	druggist	44	"
R	Amirault Edgar	86	fishcutter	43	"
s*	Amirault Mary—†	86	housewife	41	"

White Street

U	Murphy Florence—†	24	clerk	36	414 Meridian
V	Murphy James	24	U S N	39	414 "
W	Goldberg Bertha—†	24	housewife	50	here
X	Goldberg Joseph	24	physician	54	"
Y	Goldberg Ruth—†	24	technician	30	"
Z	Goldberg Sophia—†	24	secretary	25	"
	963				
A	Costigan Albert E	26	fishcutter	28	"
B	Costigan James J	26	longshoreman	58	"
C	Costigan Margaret—†	26	housewife	53	"
E	LeBlanc Frank	28	carpenter	37	"
F	LeBlanc Regina M—†	28	housewife	32	"
G	O'Driscoll Edward T	28	U S A	33	"
H	O'Driscoll George	28	"	27	"
K	O'Driscoll Mary—†	28	housewife	65	"
L	O'Driscoll Mary E—†	28	inspector	44	"
M	O'Driscoll Thomas W	28	U S A	30	"
N	Fubel Carl H	32	seaman	22	76 Grover av
O	Fubel Nellie F—†	32	packer	22	34 White
P	Larsen Isabel M—†	32	housewife	29	here
R	Larsen William A	32	engineer	31	"
S	Comeau Joseph E	32	clerk	37	"
T	Comeau Leander	32	carpenter	69	"
U	Comeau Marie L—†	32	housewife	38	"
V	Comeau Philomena—†	32	"	70	
W	Doyle Marion B—†	32	"	27	
X	Doyle Ralph T	32	U S C G	31	"
Y	D'Entremont Joseph R	34	rigger	40	"
Z	D'Entremont Theresa A-†	34	housewife	40	"

Page.	Letter.	FULL NAME.	Residence, Jan. 1, 1945.	Occupation.	Supposed Age.	Reported Residence, Jan. 1, 1944. Street and Number.

964
White Street—Continued

A	*Hansen Anna—†	34	housewife	82	here
B	Mullen Arthur R	34	chauffeur	41	"
C	Mullen Sadie H—†	34	housewife	41	"
D	Vaccaro Angelina—†	34	"	47	
E	Vaccaro Frank	34	mason	56	
F	Cahalane Catherine—†	36	housewife	75	"
G	Cahalane Helen L—†	36	"	33	
H	Cahalane Robert J	36	chauffeur	38	"
K	McLaughlin Evangeline A—†	36	tel operator	37	19 Princeton
L	*Marinello Francesco	38	laborer	35	here
M	Carson Clara—†	38	housewife	54	"
N	Carson Dorothy—†	38	"	25	"
O	Carson Robert	38	chauffeur	31	"
P	Stanley Margaret—†	38	secretary	35	343 Maverick
R	Panzina Barbara—†	42	housewife	37	here
S	Panzina John	42	operator	42	"
T	Grasso John	42	U S A	25	"
U	Grasso Martin	42	laborer	69	"
V	*Grasso Sophia—†	42	housewife	59	"
X	Vaccaro Anthony	44	U S M C	20	"
Y	Vaccaro Luigi	44	laborer	54	
Z	*Vaccaro Michelina—†	44	housewife	52	"
	965				
A	Donnelly Dorothy—†	44	operator	46	"
B	Murray Homer	46	U S C G	41	"
C	Murray Marguerite—†	46	bus girl	33	"
D	Amenta Anthony	46	machinist	28	"
E	Amenta Mary A—†	46	housewife	33	"
F	Vaiarella Italia—†	46	"	23	224 Chelsea
G	Vaiarella Salvatore	46	fisherman	23	224 "
H	O'Keefe Dorothy—†	48	housewife	27	here
K	O'Keefe John	48	fireman	35	"
L	Marmand Emma M—†	48	housewife	29	"
M	Marmand Joseph C	48	watchman	34	"
N	White James E	48	electrician	21	"
O	Basile Anna C—†	48	clerk	21	
P	Basile Anthony L	48	U S A	33	
R	Basile Carmela—†	48	housewife	60	"
S	Basile Vincent	48	U S M C	24	"
T	Basile Vincenzo	48	laborer	64	

Page	Letter	Full Name	Residence, Jan. 1, 1945.	Occupation	Supposed Age	Reported Residence, Jan. 1, 1944. Street and Number.

White Street—Continued

	U	Rauseo John	48	U S A	⌒30	here
	V	Rauseo Mary—†	48	housewife	28	"
	W	Brown Marcella—†	52	"	47	"
	X	Brown Raymond	52	chauffeur	42	139 Condor
	Y	Carey Charles	52	laborer	55	here
	Z	Dame William	52	foreman	52	"
966						
	A	Ebanks Wesley	52	seaman	41	
	B	Gorman Frank	52	operator	50	"
	C	Joyce William	52	painter	65	
	D	McAuliff Denis	52	operator	47	"
	E	Melanson George	52	calker	50	
	F	Ranahan William	52	longshoreman	49	"
	G	Sheridan Frank	52	guard	49	"
	H	Vitale Louis	52	merchant	44	"
	K	Hegner Annie M—†	53	housewife	55	"
	L	Hegner Arthur J	53	clerk	23	
	M	Hegner Joseph F	53	U S A	26	
	N	Hegner Mary C—†	53	WAC	21	
	O	Hegner Walter G	53	chauffeur	53	"
	P	Mazzarino Adeline—†	53	operator	28	"
	R	Mazzarino Rosalie—†	53	dressmaker	53	"
	S	Pingiaro Ann—†	53	housewife	23	. "
	T	Pingiaro John	53	U S N	24	"
	U	Aleo Alexander	53	salesman	22	"
	V	Aleo Anthony	53	U S A	20	
	W	Aleo Joseph	53	barber	50	
	X	Aleo Josephine—†	53	housewife	50	"
	Y	Aleo Peter	53	U S A	24	"
	Z	Fossett George M	53	"	24	"
967						
	A	Fossett Mary—†	53	housewife	25	"
	B	McLaughlin Hildred L—†	55	"	25	Maine
	C	McLaughlin James P	55	tinsmith	28	New York
	D	Murray Edward H	55	ironworker	62	here
	E	Murray Helen E—†	55	housewife	49	"
	F	D'Amico Albert	55	shipper	26	40 Chelsea
	G	D'Amico Annette N—†	55	housewife	25	40 "
	H	Garcia Eugenia—†	57	"	32	here
	K	Perez John G	57	fireman	40	"
	L	Barros John	57	"	53	"
	M	Barros Mary—†	57	housewife	43	"

40

White Street—Continued

N	*Sanchez Joseph	57	carpenter	42	here
O	*Souza Mary—†	57	at home	60	"
P	Pigeon Elizabeth W—†	58	housewife	68	"
R	Pigeon Fred L	58	merchant	69	"
S	Sandquist Dorothy—†	59	housewife	26	"
T	Sandquist Eric J	59	pressman	30	"
U	Sandquist Catherine L—†	59	housewife	45	"
V	Sandquist Eric T	59	clerk	52	
W	Fagone Joseph	60	proprietor	32	"
X	Fagone Phyllis—†	60	housewife	30	"
Y	Blanciforte Frank	60	seaman	25	"
Z	Carney Helen—†	60	housewife	26	"
	968				
A	Carney John J	60	U S A	30	"
B	*Vetere Antonetta—†	60	housewife	52	"
C	Fagone Angelina—†	60	"	29	"
D	Fagone Charles	60	proprietor	34	"
E	Swam Edna—†	61	housewife	40	New York
F	Swam Frank	61	U S A	29	"
G	Zimmer Harold	61	U S N	25	here
H	Zimmer Ruth—†	61	housewife	22	"
K	Tribuna Antoinette—†	61	at home	74	"
L	Cheek Margaret M—†	63	housewife	31	Illinois
M	Cheek Raymond E	63	finisher	31	"
O	Dalton Grace M—†	68	clerk	61	here
P	Dalton Joseph H	68	"	38	"
R	Lipinsky Fannie—†	68	housewife	54	"
S	Lipinsky Samuel	68	conductor	61	"
T	Sherr Charles	68	shipfitter	20	Canton
U	Wenesky Herbert	68	"	46	here
V	Corrado Anna L—†	68	housewife	39	"
W	Fenton Ellen—†	68	"	78	"
Z	Alves Joseph	75	seaman	20	63 White
	969				
A	Gill Albert	75	carpenter	39	63 "
B	Gill Martin M	75	U S A	37	here
C	Hawes Margaret J—†	75	housewife	44	63 White
D	Hawes Stephen P	75	laborer	48	63 "
E	Monkewicz Antonina—†	76	housewife	55	here
F	*Monkewicz Constantin	76	gaugemaker	63	"
G	Monkewicz William B	76	laborer	21	"
H	Covino Joseph	76	U S A	24	"

White Street—Continued

k	Grosso Vincenzo	76	shoemaker	67	here
l	Zollo Anthony F	76	U S M C	20	"
m	Zollo Carmen F	76	"	21	"
n	Zollo Fedele	76	laborer	47	..
o	Zollo Malvina—†	76	forewoman	44	"
p	*Hughes Willa—†	76	housewife	27	"
r	Hughes William	76	foreman	38	"
s	Pagliccia Emidio	77	laborer	48	
t	Flaherty Hannah—†	77	at home	74	"
u	Kelleher Mary—†	77	"	75	
v	Casella Frances—†	78	housewife	36	"
w	Casella Joseph W	78	chauffeur	38	..
y	D'Alessandro Biagio	79	tailor	44	
z	D'Alessandro Eleanor—†	79	housewife	44	"

970

a	Cappuccio Ann—†	80	stitcher	25	"
b	Cappuccio Thomas	80	U S A	29	"
c	Licciardi Laura—†	80	housewife	34	"
d	Licciardi Oscar	80	machinist	34	"
g	Flynn Elizabeth—†	82	housewife	22	"
h	Flynn William	82	longshoreman	25	"
k	Gaeta Anna—†	82	housewife	38	"
l	Gaeta Dante	82	blacksmith	48	"
m	Nuzzola Charles	82	painter	43	
n	Nuzzola Josephine—†	82	candymaker	32	"
o	*Severino Allessandra—†	82	housewife	76	"
p	Severino Erminia—†	82	dressmaker	30	"
s	Cavino Frank	85	chauffeur	43	"
t	Cavino Mary—†	85	housewife	36	"
u	Mario Antonetta—†	85	"	39	
v	Mario Carmen	85	baker	40	

White Street Place

w	Surette Mary L—†	1	housewife	42	here
x	Surette Basil	1	maintenance	51	"
y	Deveau Alphie	2	U S A	25	"
z	Deveau Enos	2	retired	69	

971

a	Piccinolo Louis	4	carpenter	31	26 Trenton
b	Piccinolo Mildred R—†	4	housewife	30	26 "

Ward 1–Precinct 10

CITY OF BOSTON

LIST OF RESIDENTS
20 YEARS OF AGE AND OVER

(NON-CITIZENS INDICATED BY ASTERISK)
(FEMALES INDICATED BY DAGGER)

AS OF

JANUARY 1, 1945

THOMAS F. SULLIVAN, *Chairman*
FREDERIC E. DOWLING, *Secretary*
WILLIAM A. MOTLEY, JR.
FRANCIS B. McKINNEY
EVERETT R. PROUT

Listing Board.

CITY OF BOSTON PRINTING DEPARTMENT

Page.	Letter.	Full Name.	Residence, Jan. 1, 1945.	Occupation.	Supposed Age.	Reported Residence, Jan. 1, 1944. Street and Number.

1000

Brooks Street

	B	Salmi Aino—†	223	housewife	47	here
	C	Salmi Amiel	223	longshoreman	49	"
	D	Godlewski Ruth—†	225	clerk	35	Texas
	E	MacNeil Annie E—†	225	housekeeper	72	61 Beachcroft
	F	Towlson Charles A	225	chauffeur	60	here
	G	Towlson Stella M—†	225	housewife	51	"
	H	Bent Anna—†	227	"	38	Chelsea
	K	Bent James	227	chauffeur	36	"

Condor Street

	P	King Margaret F—†	121	housewife	40	here
	R	King Mary F—†	121	"	64	"
	S	King William C	121	machinist	43	"
	T	King William F	121	foreman	64	"
	V	Weeks Frederick A	133	retired	84	455 Meridian
	W	Weeks Margaret M—†	133	housewife	59	455 "
	X	Gillis John A	133A	machinist	39	here
	Y	Gillis Lillian—†	133A	housewife	31	"
	Z	Gillis Margaret—†	133A	"	75	"

1001

	A	McCarthy James H	133A	U S A	22	
	B	McCarthy John F	133A	"	24	"
	C	McCarthy William J	133A	student	20	Worcester
	D	Engley Mary F—†	135	at home	65	here
	E	Wainwright Doris M—†	135A	clerk	20	"
	F	Wainwright Lottie K—†	135A	housewife	65	"
	K	*Sturrock Jessie—†	137A	"	52	"
	L	*Sturrock Martin G	137A	machinist	53	"
	M	Duffy Annie N—†	137A	housewife	44	"
	N	Duffy Patrick J	137A	machinist	50	"
	O	Brown Alice M—†	139	housekeeper	66	"
	P	Merigan Mary—†	139A	housewife	29	"
	R	Merigan Thomas	139A	reporter	33	"
	S	Holt Isabelle—†	139A	housewife	21	"
	T	Holt Richard	139A	clerk	30	"
	V	O'Brien John	155	U S A	23	205 Falcon
	W	O'Brien Ruth—†	155	housewife	22	N Hampshire
	X	Antonucci Corinna—†	157	"	43	here
	Y	Antonucci Giacinto	157	bricklayer	54	"

2

Page	Letter	Full Name.	Residence, Jan. 1, 1945.	Occupation.	Supposed Age.	Reported Residence, Jan. 1, 1944. Street and Number.

Condor Street—Continued

	z	Antonucci Angela R—†	157	clerk	20	here
		1002				
	A	Orr Alfred J	163	brazier	39	"
	B	Orr Mabel E—†	163	housewife	37	"
	C	Thibeau Frederick J	165	machinist	31	Maine
	D	Thibeau Gertrude—†	165	housewife	32	"
	E	Damigella Joseph	167	U S N	27	here
	F	Damigella Regina—†	167	housewife	35	"
	G	DiMarco Angelina—†	169	"	22	"
	H	DiMarco Anna—†	169	clerk	40	
	K	DiMarco John	169	U S N	24	"
	L	Nolfo Giuseppe	169	laborer	63	"
	M	Nolfo Josephine—†	169	housewife	60	"
	N	Marshall Henry	171	longshoreman	48	"
	O	Marshall Julia—†	171	housewife	49	"
	P	Albargo Angela—†	173	"	57	
	R	Albargo Philip	173	pedler	64	"
	S	Riley Helen B—†	175	tel operator	40	"
	P	Montalto Jennie—†	177	housewife	31	67 White
	U	Montalto Joseph	177	coppersmith	37	67 Webster
	V	Lally Mary A—†	179	stitcher	45	361 Meridian
	W	O'Donnell Frances E—†	179	housewife	25	361 "
	X	O'Donnell James J	179	U S A	26	361 "
	Y	Cunningham Rose—†	181	at home	70	here
	z	McNeil Francis	181	clerk	36	"
		1003				
	A	McNeil Margaret R—†	181	housewife	37	"
	B	Phillips Mary F—†	181	clerk	39	"
	E	Rawlins Earle R	195	operator	34	"
	F	Rawlins Hazel E—†	195	housewife	30	"
	G	Correia Matilda—†	195	housekeeper	65	"
	H	Adams Albert A	197	electrician	43	"
	K	Adams Alice M—†	197	housewife	36	"
	M	Goodwin Esther—†	203	clerk	21	
	N	Goodwin Isaac B	203	laborer	62	
	O	Goodwin Lillian—†	203	housewife	56	"
	P	Goodwin Ruth—†	203	clerk	21	
	R	Anderson Andrew	203	proprietor	69	"
	S	Anderson Jennie C—†	203	housewife	70	"
	U	Adams Madeline G—†	213	housekeeper	62	61 Putnam
	V	*Margotti Carmela—†	213	housewife	69	here

Condor Street—Continued

w	*Margotti Frank	213	laborer	56	here
x	*Margotti Rose—†	213	housekeeper	75	"
z	Flammia Antonio	225	salesman	39	"

1004

A	Flammia Frances—†	225	housewife	36	"
B	Flammia William A	225	machinist	35	"
C	Gimilaro Alice—†	225	housewife	43	"
L	*Candido Ignazia—†	243	"	65	
M	Candido Salvatore	243	salesman	61	"
N	DeLuca Pauline—†	243	clerk	29	,,
P	Pizzi Daniel	243	welder	33	,,
R	Pizzi Grace—†	243	housewife	24	"

East Eagle Street

v	Ferullo Alfred	202	shipper	35	here
w	Ferullo Elizabeth—†	202	housewife	32	"
x	Zaccaro Frank	202	painter	34	48 Putnam
y	Zaccaro Rose—†	202	housewife	32	48 "
z	Kenney Bertha—†	204	"	21	here

1005

A	*Kenney Everett	204	carpenter	22	"
B	Piretti Louis	204	clerk	36	
C	Piretti Mary—†	204	housewife	36	"
D	Catanese Domenic	204	U S A	30	
E	Catanese Mary—†	204	housewife	31	"
G	Melchionda Alfred S	205	welder	27	
H	Melchionda Lillian—†	205	housewife	27	"
K	Casucci Albert	205	U S A	23	"
L	*Casucci Cesare	205	carpenter	59	"
M	*Casucci Rose—†	205	housewife	56	"
N	Carson Natalie—†	206	"	29	129 Trenton
O	Carson Oscar	206	brazier	31	129 "
P	DiLorenzo Frederick	206	carpenter	68	here
R	DiLorenzo Girardo	206	presser	22	"
S	DiLorenzo Jennie—†	206	stitcher	29	"
T	DiLorenzo Josephine—†	206	housekeeper	32	"
U	DiLorenzo Rocco	206	U S A	26	,,
V	Marolda Daniel	206	machinist	36	"
W	Marolda Rose—†	206	housewife	36	"
X	DeSisto Marie—†	207	"	25	

East Eagle Street—Continued

Y	DeSisto Phillip	207	U S A	25	here	
z	Rocco Marie—†	207	housewife	58	"	
	1006					
A	Rocco Vincenzo	207	laborer	50		
B	Maniaci Marie—†	207	housewife	30	"	
C	Maniaci Salvatore	207	ironworker	31	"	
D	Berardi Angela—†	207	housewife	34	"	
E	Berardi Frank	207	rubberworker	40	"	
F	Berardi Galdini—†	207	housekeeper	61	"	
G	*McCormack Ellen B—†	208	housewife	52	"	
H	McCormack Patrick	208	machinist	48	"	
K	Zeringis Alice—†	208	housewife	34	"	
L	Zeringis Anthony	208	tubemaker	32	"	
M	Casucci Augusto	208	machinist	34	"	
N	Casucci Louise—†	208	housewife	29	"	
O	Zeuli Henry R	211	barber	50		
P	Zeuli Rose M—†	211	housewife	37	"	
R	Adelizzi Eugene	211	machinist	28	31 Wordsworth	
S	Adelizzi Florence—†	211	housewife	23	31 "	
T	McCormick Agatha—†	211	operator	20	here	
U	McCormick Annie—†	211	housewife	54	"	
V	McCormick James	211	seaman	31	"	
W	Staff Anna—†	213	housewife	35	"	
X	Staff Leonard	213	operator	35	"	
Y	DeLuca Ettore	213	tailor	60		
z	DeLuca Florence—†	213	operator	21	"	
	1007					
A	DeLuca Lucy—†	213	housewife	54	"	
B	Faraci Eleanor—†	213	"	29	California	
C	Faraci Louis	213	U S A	35	"	
D	Franklin Emanuel	213	poultryman	36	"	
E	Franklin Patricia—†	213	housewife	31	"	
F	Cameron Dorothy—†	214	waitress	24	here	
G	Cameron Edward J	214	laborer	20	"	
H	Cameron Eustace R	214	U S A	26	"	
K	Cameron Florence—†	214	housewife	50	"	
L	Cameron Roderick	214	carpenter	64	"	
M	*DeCoste Caroline—†	214	at home	84	"	
N	Vinesky Patricia—†	214	waitress	33	Chelsea	
O	Goodwin Gladys—†	214	operator	31	here	
S	Keller Catherine—†	216	housewife	30	164 Falcon	

East Eagle Street—Continued

T	Keller Eugene	216	U S N	37	164 Falcon
U	Lugrin Bertrand F	217	guard	70	here
V	Lugrin Elizabeth—†	217	housewife	70	"
W	Lugrin Frederick W	217	retired	48	"
X	Santirocco George	217	engineer	50	"
Y	Santirocco Theresa—†	217	housewife	29	"
Z	Stankes Alfred J	217	U S M C	27	213 Condor

1008

A	Stankes Sophie—†	217	housewife	26	213 "
B	Breda Joseph	217	photographer	60	here
C	Breda Mary—†	217	housewife	64	"
D	Giancristiano Lillian—†	218	"	50	"
E	Giancristiano Nicholas	218	retired	49	
F	Primavera Frances—†	218	stitcher	42	"
G	Primavera Pasquale	218	laborer	50	"
H	Aldrich Leslie	218	U S N	30	Dedham
K	Aldrich Margaret—†	218	housewife	27	"
L	Nadeau Edgar N	220	rigger	33	here
M	Nadeau Frances—†	220	housewife	28	"
N	Chiulli Anthony	220	U S A	26	"
O	Chiulli Elizabeth—†	220	operator	29	"
P	Chiulli Liberato	220	laborer	63	"
R	*DeSanctis Assunta—†	220	housewife	54	"
S	DeSanctis Frank	220	carpenter	55	"
T	DeSanctis Louis	220	U S N	30	"
U	DeSanctis Vera—†	220	bookkeeper	32	"
V	Bevere Marion—†	221	candymaker	33	"
W	Melchiano Alphonse	221	fruit	41	
X	Melchiano Fannie—†	221	housewife	40	"
Y	Lerra Gaetano	221	laborer	35	198 Chelsea
Z	Lerra Mary—†	221	housewife	31	198 "

1009

A	DeStefano Margaret—†	221	"	30	here
B	DeStefano Peter	221	mechanic	32	"
C	Anzalone Edward	222	carpenter	35	"
D	*Anzalone Philomena—†	222	at home	59	"
E	Anzalone Rose—†	222	housewife	34	"
F	Anzalone Ernestine—†	222	"	31	
G	Anzalone Joseph	222	agent	37	
H	DeLellis Amelia—†	222	clerk	22	
K	DeLellis Michael	222	tailor	51	"

East Eagle Street—Continued

L	Marasca Anthony	223	U S A	31	here
M	Marasca Christine—†	223	housewife	69	"
N	Marasca Ferdinand	223	machinist	45	"
O	Mercurio Adelaide—†	223	housewife	43	"
P	Mercurio Louis	223	U S N	20	
R	Mercurio Mary—†	223	dressmaker	23	"
S	Mercurio Michael	223	boilermaker	46	"
T	Marasco Louis	223	diemaker	45	"
U	Marasco Margaret—†	223	housewife	37	"
V	Marasco Vincent A	223	U S N	20	
W	Pastore Angelina—†	224	housewife	38	"
X	Pastore Lorenzo	224	driller	52	"
Y	Del'Signore Clara—†	224	housewife	28	940 Hyde Park av
Z	Del'Signore Oliver	224	pipefitter	33	940 "
	1010				
A	Ciliberto Anthony	224	electrician	32	118 Falcon
B	Ciliberto Henrietta—†	224	housekeeper	39	118 "
C	Ciliberto Mary—†	224	bookkeeper	21	118 "
D	Curigga James	224	barber	57	118 "
E	Sinopoli Gerardo	224	driller	49	118 "
F	Debilio Carmelo	225	longshoreman	38	here
G	Debilio Mary—†	225	housewife	37	"
H	Debilio Mary—†	225	"	37	"
K	Debilio Phillip	225	machinist	41	"
L	DeSanctis Frank	230	tailor	49	
M	DeSanctis Leo	230	cutter	20	
N	DeSanctis Raymond	230	"	20	
O	DeSanctis Santine—†	230	housewife	49	"
P	Mezzone Eugene	235	molder	57	
R	Mezzone Mary—†	235	housewife	54	"
S	Mezzone Theodore	235	U S A	24	"
T	Pepicelli Josephine—†	235	housekeeper	20	"
U	Rosaldi Antoinette—†	235	housewife	32	"
V	Rosaldi Louis	235	painter	34	
W	Vena Constance—†	235	housewife	34	"
X	Vena Louis	235	retired	36	
Y	Viscione Frank	235	meatcutter	26	"
Z	Viscione Nell—†	235	housewife	26	"
	1011				
A	Stanton George	242	welder	30	Watertown
B	Stanton Josephine—†	242	housewife	31	"

East Eagle Street—Continued

c	Nelchionda Ida—†	242	housewife	29	here
d	Nelchionda William	242	laborer	36	"
e	Johnson Nils	242	steamfitter	47	"
f	Johnson Victoria—†	242	housewife	33	"
g	Trocano Alice—†	250	"	22	85 Neponset av
h	Trocano Peter	250	chauffeur	22	9 Trenton
k	Chaput Joseph O	250	machinist	55	24 Princeton
l	Chaput Mary A—†	250	housewife	32	N Hampshire
m	Guilemette Adaline—†	250	"	71	"
n	Guilemette Joseph	250	retired	78	"
o	Cunha Alice—†	252	housekeeper	27	here
p	Cunha George	252	U S M C	22	"
r	*Cunha Mary—†	252	housewife	58	"
s	Scorzello Mary—†	252	"	23	227 Trenton
t	Scorzello Michael	252	manager	30	227 "
u	Murphy Anna—†	252	housewife	33	here
v	Murphy Paul	252	chauffeur	37	"
w	Magaletta Albert Y	254	retired	48	"
x	Magaletta Mary R—†	254	typist	22	"
y	Magaletta Michael A	254	U S A	21	
z	Magaletta Rose—†	254	housewife	47	"
	1012				
a	Salerno Joseph	254	tailor	44	
b	Salerno Mary—†	254	housewife	41	"
c	DeFlumeri Jean—†	254	"	35	
d	DeFlumeri Joseph	254	brazier	34	
e	Ricupero Irene—†	258	housewife	30	"
f	Ricupero Richard S	258	oil dealer	31	"
g	Milano Joseph	258	U S A	23	
h	Vasquez Alphonse	258	U S N	31	"
k	Vasquez Augusta—†	258	housewife	28	"
l	Deraedt Edmond R	258	mechanic	36	"
m	Deraedt Rose M—†	258	housewife	30	"
n	Cardinale Josephine C—†	262	"	29	"
o	Cardinale Pasquale	262	welder	29	"
p	Consolo Felice	262	presser	30	
r	Consolo Mary—†	262	housewife	29	"
s	Mozzetta Albert	262	painter	46	"
t	Mozzetta Dena—†	262	housewife	38	"
u	Cashman Catherine M—†	264	machinist	33	"
v	Cashman Michael J	264	electrician	63	"

Page.	Letter.	Full Name.	Residence, Jan. 1, 1945.	Occupation.	Supposed Age.	Reported Residence, Jan. 1, 1944. Street and Number.

	w	Cashman Richard J	264	U S A	30.	here
	x	Downing Marita L—†	264	housewife	30	"
	y	Bruce Edward F	266	U S A	21	Colorado
	z	Bruce Josephine—†	266	housewife	21	"
1013						
	a	Healy Henry G	266	shipfitter	45	250 E Eagle
	b	Healy Henry G, jr	266	U S A	22	250 "
	c	Healy Sarah C—†	266	housewife	46	250 "
	d	Gilbrook Marion—†	268	"	25	here
	e	Gilbrook Ralph	268	U S N	26	"
	f	Lauber William	268	laborer	50	"
	g	Emmons Frederick J	270	salesman	55	7 Condor
	h	Emmons Muriel J—†	270	housewife	46	7 "
	k	Emmons Ruth E—†	270	inspector	24	7 "
	l	Favale Giuseppe	272	carpenter	61	here
	m	Favale Joseph V	272	plumber	23	"
	n	Favale Rosina—†	272	housewife	50	"
	o	LoConte John B	272	shipfitter	36	"
	p	LoConte Lena—†	272	housewife	36	"
	r	Rao Daniel	272	U S A	29	
	s	Consolo Fannie—†	272	housewife	50	"
	t	Consolo Joseph	272	barber	55	"
	u	DiPerri Richard	274	U S A	25	
	v	DiPerri Rosalie—†	274	housewife	24	"
	w	Sciortino Rose—†	274	stitcher	44	"
	x	Sciortino Joseph	274	electrician	31	"
	y	Sciortino Mary—†	274	housewife	28	"
	z	DeFeo John P	274	welder	22	
1014						
	a	DeFeo Vincenza—†	274	housewife	22	"
	b	Sciortino Christine—†	274	stitcher	50	"
	c	Sciortino Gaetano	274	waiter	55	"
	d	Spencer Joseph E	278	finisher	30	"
	e	Spencer Martha E—†	278	housewife	29	"
	f	Buttiglieri Millie—†	278	"	37	"
	g	Buttiglieri Rocco	278	machinist	42	"
	h	Cohane John	278	U S A	27	229 Lexington
	k	Cohane Mary—†	278	housewife	27	229 "
	l	DeSanctis Emma—†	280	"	24	here
	m	DeSanctis Joseph	280	shipfitter	27	"
	n	Canha Frank F	280	longshoreman	57	"

East Eagle Street—Continued

o	Canha Mary F—†	280	housewife	47	here
p	Silva Joseph	280	U S A	23	"
r	Silva Mary—†	280	housewife	21	"
s	Manfredonia Grace—†	280	"	31	
t	Manfredonia Ralph	280	machinist	33	"
u	Magner Emily F—†	291	housekeeper	54	"
v	Magner Thomas G	291	U S A	21	..
w	Elo John	291	retired	55	
x	Elo Rosa—†	291	housewife	51	"
y	McCormack Allen J	291	retired	79	
z	McCormack Flora—†	291	housewife	69	"
	1015				
A	McCormack Sarah—†	291	candy packer	40	"
B	DeAngelis Arthur	297	cutter	20	"
c	DeAngelis Margaret—†	297	housewife	38	"
D	Coilty Evelyn—†	297	"	29	
E	Coilty George W	297	U S N	35	
F	Beach Jacob B	297	carpenter	68	"
G	Crowell Susan—†	297	housekeeper	66	"
H	Boyle Adelaide C—†	301	housewife	24	"
K	Boyle James J	301	U S N	23	
L	Sodergrin Anna—†	303	housewife	60	"
M	Sodergrin Henry	303	shipfitter	40	"
N	Sodergrin John	303	retired	67	"
o	Sodergrin Kathleen—†	303	housewife	37	"
P	Mahoney Anne J—†	305	"	73	..
R	Mahoney Michael F	305	retired	71	"
s	Cleary George	305	laborer	46	"
T	Cleary George H	305	U S A	20	"
u	Grande Ernestina—†	307	housewife	43	"
v	Grande Gaetano	307	U S N	20	
w	Grande Raffaele	307	engineer	49	"
x	Scoppetuolo Carmen	309	laborer	41	
y	Scoppetuolo Josephine—†	309	housewife	36	"
	1016				
D	Day Winfield S	315	machinist	63	"
E	Simonson Cecelia—†	315	housekeeper	70	"
F	Doren Elizabeth R—†	317	housewife	43	"
G	Doren William J	317	laborer	54	
H	McGlinchey Catherine E-†	317	housewife	74	"
K	McGlinchey William F	317	machinist	40	"

Falcon Street

M	Goodwin George	84	clerk	27	here
N	Goodwin Irene—†	84	housewife	25	"
O	Hayden Charles F	84	machinist	57	"
P	Hayden Clifford	84	U S A	27	"
R	Hayden John	84	"	31	"
S	Hayden Lillian—†	84	housewife	59	"
T	Ewing Edna—†	84	"	50	
U	Ewing Keith	84	U S N	23	
V	Ewing Robert	84	fireman	51	
W	Meuse Reuben	84	deckhand	78	"
X	Weeks Robert	84	U S C G	29	"
Y	Weeks Ruby—†	84	housewife	29	"
Z	Korsvik Hans	86	seaman	56	
	1017				
A	Korsvik Ralph	86	U S A	21	"
B	Korsvik Sonia—†	86	housewife	56	"
C	Midgett Cecil	86A	machinist	55	"
D	Midgett Ernest	86A	"	25	
E	Midgett Gladys—†	86A	housewife	50	"
F	Midgett John R—†	86A	U S N	22	
G	Midgett Marjorie—†	86A	clerk	23	"
H	Gillis Helen—†	88	waitress	26	Winthrop
K	Gillis John J	88	bartender	28	"
L	Gillis Virginia—†	88	housewife	27	"
M	Knox Albert	88A	painter	49	here
	Knox Margaret M—†	88A	housewife	47	"
	Knox Margaret T—†	88A	operator	26	"
N	Callahan Isabelle—†	90	housewife	31	17 St Marks rd
R	Callahan John F	90	driller	35	17 "
S	Nelson Francis	90½	U S A	30	here
T	Nelson John	90½	"	26	"
U	Nelson Joseph	90½	B F D	61	"
V	Nelson M Margaret—†	90½	WAVE	22	"
W	Nelson Mary A—†	90½	housewife	61	"
X	Moraitopoulos George C	92	counterman	51	"
Y	Moraitopoulos Lovonia—†	92	housewife	43	"
Z	Whitman Margaret—†	92	"	65	
	1018				
A	*DeMeo Florence—†	92A	"	63	"
B	Fringuelli Arpino	92A	mechanic	32	"
C	Fringuelli Mary—†	92A	housewife	28	"

Falcon Street—Continued

D	Smith Enos C	94	machinist	44	here
E	Enos Lela—†	94	housewife	42	"
F	Bonner Joseph	94	laborer	41	"
G	Bonner Joseph	94	U S A	23	"
H	Bonner Leo	94	"	21	
K	Bonner Lillian—†	94	housewife	43	"
L	Manganiello Joseph	96	foreman	32	"
M	Manganiello Marie A—†	96	housewife	36	"
N	Herlihy Helen M—†	96	"	28	Cambridge
O	Herlihy James T	96	U S N	27	"
R	Riley Marjorie—†	98	U S M C	24	here
S	Riley Mary C—†	98	houseworker	22	"
T	Riley Thomas J	98	retired	56	"
U	LaBella Domenic	102	foreman	37	"
V	LaBella Esther—†	102	housewife	36	"
W	Fariole Alfred	104	electrician	37	"
X	Fariole Louise—†	104	housewife	41	"
Y	Manganiello Catherine–†	104	student	23	"
Z	*Sozio Anna—†	104	housewife	62	"

1019

A	Sozio Carl	104	mechanic	33	"
B	Sozio Gerardo	104	candymaker	64	"
C	Sozio Santa—†	104	housewife	33	"
D	Bompane Bruno	106	U S A	31	
E	Sharib Samuel	106	"	34	
F	Sharib Viola—†	106	housewife	33	"
G	Ventola Arthur	106	U S A	28	
H	Ventola Rita—†	106	operator	25	"
K	Possehl Fred W	108	machinist	50	"
L	Possehl Vivian—†	108	housewife	45	"
M	Possehl William F	108	U S A	24	"
N	Rogers William E	108	cook	64	
O	DiCicco Angelo	112	patternmaker	58	"
P	Mattson Gertrude E—†	112	nurse	36	"
R	Mattson John P	112	patternmaker	43	"
S	Mattson Mary M—†	112	housewife	65	"
T	Goglia Angi—†	112	"	24	
U	Goglia Anthony	112	U S A	20	
V	Goglia James	112	U S M C	27	"
W	Goglia Julian	112	candymaker	52	"
X	Goglia Julian, jr	112	U S N	23	

12

Falcon Street—Continued

Y	Goglia Mary L—†	112	housewife	50	here
Z	Goglia Vincent	112	rigger	30	"
1020						
A	Marino Augustine	112	clerk	25	
B	Marino Josephine—†	112	stitcher	28	"
C	*Marino Mary—†	112	housewife	67	"
D	Marino Nicolas	112	U S A	23	"
E	Marino Rose—†	112	houseworker	33	"
F	Marino Vincent	112	laborer	67	"
G	Gioioso Domenico	114	"	52	
H	Gioioso Rose—†	114	housewife	47	"
K	MacKenzie Colin	114	carpenter	60	"
L	MacKenzie Susan—†	114	housewife	55	"
M	MacKenzie Warren	114	U S A	24	"
N	MacKenzie William	114	U S N	23	
O	Joy Annie—†	114	housewife	61	"
P	Joy William	114	shipper	65	"
R	Amodeo Amelia—†	116	housewife	58	"
S	Amodeo Miranda—†	116	attorney	32	"
T	Amodeo Nicholas	116	barber	58	"
U	Colarossi Nicola	116	letter carrier	47	"
V	Colarossi Robert	116	U S A	20	"
W	Colarossi Vanda—†	116	housewife	44	"
X	*Bettencourt Olympia—†	116	tailor	58	168 Putnam
Y	Mancino Frank J	116	clerk	29	540 Saratoga
Z	Mancino Natalie—†	116	housewife	29	251 Chelsea
1021						
A	Grady Daniel	118	assembler	70	61 Condor
B	Grady Effie—†	118	inspector	21	61 "
C	Grady Jessie—†	118	housewife	52	61 "
D	Murphy Catherine—†	118	"	28	61 "
E	Murphy John J	118	U S N	31	61 "
F	Sullivan Alice—†	118	assembler	23	61 "
G	Sullivan John T	118	U S N	23	61 "
H	Eccleston Laura—†	118	housewife	51	here
K	Galvai Anna—†	118	"	41	"
L	Galvia Frank	118	bricklayer	55	"
M	Gaffney Mildred M—†	120	housewife	27	"
N	Gaffney Robert A	120	U S A	32	"
O	Hudson John M	120	"	47	"
P	Hudson Lillian—†	120	housewife	50	"

13

Page.	Letter.	Full Name.	Residence, Jan. 1, 1945.	Occupation.	Supposed Age.	Reported Residence, Jan. 1, 1944. Street and Number.

Falcon Street—Continued

	R	Melling Margaret—†	120	operator	34	here
	S	Cruise William A	120	retired	75	"
	T	Miller Ellen J—†	120	housewife	74	"
	U	Miller Gladys—†	120	clerk	32	
	W	Ferris Nellie—†	122	housewife	63	"
	X	Tedeschi Gaetano	124	carpenter	32	"
	Y	Tedeschi Helen—†	124	housewife	28	"
	Z	Marasca Albert	124	machinist	28	"
		1022				
	A	Marasca Diana—†	124	housewife	24	"
	B	Morrocco Catherine E—†	124	"	24	Salem
	C	Morrocco John J	124	attendant	27	207 E Eagle
	D	Brazzo Anthony	126	laborer	20	here
	E	Brazzo Charles	126	foundryman	47	"
	F	*Brazzo Fannie—†	126	housewife	38	"
	G	Banks Audrey—†	126	nurse	20	
	H	Banks Blanche—†	126	governess	21	"
	K	Banks Esmeralda—†	126	housewife	40	"
	L	*Banks James A	126	fishcutter	41	"
	M	Boudreau Edward	128	U S N	35	
	N	Boudreau Hattie—†	128	housewife	33	"
	O	*Surette James	128	fisherman	49	Maine
	P	*Todd Augustis	128	"	60	here
	R	*Todd John W	128	deckhand	64	"
	S	Todd Joseph L	128	U S A	29	"
	T	*Todd Mary A—†	128	housewife	64	"
	U	Costa Domenic	128	U S N	24	
	V	Costa Joseph	128	laborer	58	
	W	Costa Lawrence	128	U S N	26	
	X	Costa Martha—†	128	housewife	49	"
	Y	Costa Mary—†	128	stenographer	20	"
	Z	Costa Nancy—†	128	housewife	28	"
		1023				
	A	Costa Nicolas	128	U S N	30	"
	B	Stubbs Anna—†	130	housewife	38	"
	C	Stubbs Lewis	130	lineman	37	"
	D	Caristo Mary—†	130	housewife	40	"
	E	Caristo Salvatore	130	shoemaker	42	"
	F	Brutus Adolph E	134	shipwright	62	237 Condor
	G	Brutus Annie M—†	134	housewife	62	237 "
	H	Sullivan James M	134	operator	37	237 "

14

Falcon Street—Continued

K	Breen Andrew J	134	buyer	35	here
L	Breen Hilda—†	134	housewife	37	"
M	Butler Philip	136	shipper	52	"
N	Butler Raymond	136	U S N	23	
O	Butler William R	136	U S C G	21	"
P	Folger Ethel M—†	136	housewife	61	"
R	Folger Gladys C—†	136	operator	53	"
S	Folger Eben	136	clerk	68	
T	Folger Esther—†	136	housewife	54	"
U	Sturrock Doris—†	137	"	26	
V	Sturrock Peter K	137	U S N	26	
W	Baxter Mary—†	137	at home	82	"
X	Sciortino Elizabeth—†	137	housewife	44	"
Y	Sciortino Guy	137	rubberworker	46	"
Z	Gallagher Irene H—†	138	housewife	35	"
	1024				
A	Gallagher John A	138	motorman	36	"
B	Overland Frank	138	salesman	50	"
C	Bostrom Lillian M—†	138	housewife	21	"
D	Bostrom Walter N	138	U S N	24	
E	Anderson Annie—†	139	housewife	34	"
F	Anderson Arthur R	139	letter carrier	43	"
G	Anderson Alfred	139	retired	79	
H	Anderson Alfred H	139	laborer	34	
K	Reekast August	140	fisherman	49	"
L	Reekast Grace L—†	140	housewife	49	"
M	McLaughlin Charles	140	laborer	65	
N	McLaughlin Eva—†	140	housewife	61	"
G	Manning Charles	140	U S A	38	
P	Manning Isabelle—†	140	housewife	50	"
R	Manning Ruth—†	140	packer	20	
S	*Pentilo Hilma—†	140	housewife	54	"
T	Pentilo Isaac	140	chipper	59	"
U	Doig Alice L—†	141	housewife	32	Somerville
V	Doig William E	141	expressman	33	"
W	Anderson Ellen V—†	141	housewife	54	here
X	Anderson John N	141	asbestos wkr	56	"
Y	Driver George R	142	printer	34	"
Z	Driver Sylvia H—†	142	housewife	29	"
	1025				
A	Houlihan Edna—†	142	"	36	

Falcon Street—Continued

B	Houlihan Thomas	142	laborer	38	here
C	Heino Impi—†	142	housekeeper	53	"
D	Leinz Francis	142	U S A	30	"
E	Leinz Martha—†	142	housewife	26	"
F	Marks Frances O—†	143	matron	62	"
G	Patz Edward M	143	U S A	25	"
H	Patz Geraldine E—†	143	housewife	23	"
K	Teevens Eugene S	144	salesman	47	"
L	Teevens Margaret L—†	144	housewife	44	"
M	Mangin Ernest	144	glazier	52	
N	Mangin Mary—†	144	housewife	53	"
O	Moore Alfred	144	U S A	32	
P	Moore Veronica—†	144	housewife	25	"
R	Paul Marie—†	144	"	31	
S	Paul Nathan	144	U S A	26	"
T	Hartman Eliza—†	145	clerk	56	
U	Hartman James F	145	grocer	73	
V	Smithson Samuel	145	janitor	59	
W	Bielakiewicz Mary—†	145	housewife	55	"
X	Bielakiewicz Stanley F	145	painter	60	"
Y	*Elixson Gusti	145	carpenter	62	"
Z	*Elixson Mandy—†	145	housewife	56	"

1026

A	Crowell Dorothy—†	146	clerk	26	
B	Crowell Thelma—†	146	"	30	
C	Ivany Althea—†	146	housewife	59	"
D	Ivany Gladys—†	146	clerk	22	"
E	Ivany Harry	146	laborer	59	
F	Ivany Jessie—†	146	clerk	25	
G	Murphy Maurice	148	timekeeper	40	"
H	Murphy Mildred—†	148	housewife	41	"
K	Stanton William	148	retired	58	
L	McGuire Susie—†	148	housekeeper	59	"
M	Mastrogiovanni Carmine	149	laborer	67	"
N	Mastrogiovanni Margaret—†	149	housewife	60	"
O	McAdams Charles	150	laborer	45	
P	McAdams Elizabeth M—†	150	housekeeper	38	"
R	McAdams Emma E—†	150	"	78	"
S	McAdams Thomas A	150	dairyman	39	"
T	Vranken Impi—†	151	housewife	54	"
U	Vranken John F	151	chef	52	"

Falcon Street—Continued

v	LoConte Luigi	152	laborer	54	here
w	LoConte Mary—†	152	clerk	27	"
x	LoConte Philomena—†	152	housewife	54	"
y	Tarentino Ambrose	152	postal clerk	32	"
z	Tarentino Ida—†	152	housewife	30	"
	1027				
a	Balboni William F	153	laborer	43	
b	Lopez Evelyn—†	153	housewife	24	"
c	Lopez Thomas R	153	U S N	27	
d	Iacoviello Maria—†	153	housewife	35	"
e	Iacoviello Nicholas	153	rigger	40	
f	*O'Brien Catherine—†	154	housewife	58	"
g	O'Brien Catherine—†	154	waitress	26	"
h	O'Brien Charles	154	fishcutter	21	"
k	*O'Brien Michael	154	fish handler	58	"
l	O'Brien Thomas	154	U S A	23	
m	O'Brien William	154	"	23	
n	Thurman Earl	154	U S N	31	"
o	Thurman Mary—†	154	housewife	25	"
p	Brennan Lawrence H	154	foreman	45	"
r	Brennan Ragnhild C—†	154	housewife	46	"
s	Rajewski John F	154	U S N	25	"
u	Stoddard Florence—†	156	housewife	30	63 W Eagle
v	Stoddard Reginald	156	laborer	34	63 "
y	Giles George	158	machinist	46	here
z	Giles Margaret—†	158	housewife	45	"
	1028				
a	DeNietolis Carmella—†	158	"	42	
b	DeNietolis Nicholas	158	plumber	42	"
c	Bithell Doris—†	159	housewife	22	"
d	Bithell William G	159	engineer	34	"
e	Bithell Evelyn M—†	159	housewife	38	"
f	Bithell William P	159	retired	62	
g	Donegan Dorothea—†	160	housewife	37	"
h	Donegan John	160	agent	32	
k	McGray Avard T	160	seaman	29	
l	McGray Mary L—†	160	housewife	29	"
m	O'Brien Edward J	160	guard	52	
n	·O'Brien James F	160	retired	66	"
o	*Sawyer Vassie D—†	160	housewife	39	Foxboro
p	Trahan Anna—†	162	"	32	here

Page.	Letter.	FULL NAME.	Residence, Jan. 1, 1945.	Occupation.	Supposed Age.	Reported Residence, Jan. 1, 1944. Street and Number.

Falcon Street—Continued

	R	*Trahan Clarence	162	seaman	34	here
	T	*Mosca Leonardo	163	mechanic	59	"
	U	Mosca Leonardo, jr	163	longshoreman	30	"
	V	Mosca Mary—†	163	packer	26	
	S	Mosca Philomena—†	163	housewife	50	"
	W	Toft Henry	163A	fishcutter	41	49 Condor
	X	Toft Irene—†	163A	waitress	33	49 "
	Y	Mosca Alfred	163A	longshoreman	28	15 Frankfort
	Z	Mosca Josephine—†	163A	housewife	24	15 "

1029

	A	Hancock Helen C—†	164	housekeeper	37	here
	B	Murphy Catherine—†	164	"	63	"
	C	Murphy John	164	fishcutter	34	"
	D	Perry Elizabeth—†	166	housewife	62	"
	E	Perry Oliver J	166	machinist	70	"
	F	*D'Amico Nancy—†	167	housewife	60	"
	G	*D'Amico Sebastiano	167	millhand	69	"
	H	D'Amico Angelina—†	167A	housewife	36	"
	K	D'Amico Charles	167A	metalworker	36	"
	L	Dolan Norma—†	167A	housewife	20	N Hampshire
	M	Dolan Robert	167A	U S M C	21	here
	N	Masculi Josephine—†	167A	housewife	39	"
	O	Masculi Nunzio	167A	laborer	33	"
	P	Perry Bessie—†	168	housekeeper	40	"
	R	*Hudson Elizabeth—†	170	housewife	69	"
	S	Hudson William	170	rigger	72	
	T	D'Eon Adelbert	171	inspector	38	"
	U	D'Eon Lora—†	171	housewife	38	"
	V	Cole Florence—†	171A	"	28	
	W	Cole John	171A	shipper	32	
	X	Paige Helen—†	171A	operator	49	"
	Y	Hamilton Charles	171A	U S A	27	
	Z	Hamilton Charlotte—†	171A	housewife	24	"

1030

	A	Harney Edward	171A	painter	46	
	B	Harney Edward	171A	U S A	27	
	C	Harney Elizabeth—†	171A	operator	45	"
	D	Harney Phyllis—†	171A	secretary	23	"
	E	Gallagher James F	172	rigger	33	
	F	Gallagher Margaret—†	172	housekeeper	71	"
	G	Gallagher Rita C—†	172	housewife	31	"

18

Falcon Street—Continued

H	Lewis Herbert H	174	laborer	50	here
K	Lewis Margaret—†	174	housekeeper	81	"
L	Walker George V	174	U S N	25	"
M	Walker Harry B	174	bricklayer	54	"
N	Walker Ida A—†	174	housewife	54	"
O	Walker John L	174	U S N	21	
P	D'Entremont Arthur	175	seaman	41	"
R	D'Entremont Mildred—†	175	packer	40	"
S	Murphy Marie—†	175A	clerk	23	"
T	Murphy Wilhelmina—†	175A	housewife	44	"
V	Williams Anna P—†	176	"	45	"
W	Williams Charles A	176	fireman	51	"
X	Williams Charles A, jr	176	U S A	22	
Y	Gregorio Anthony D	178	fireman	51	"
Z	Gregorio Dorothea C—†	178	secretary	21	"
	1031				
A	Gregorio Mary D—†	178	housewife	42	"
B	Stapleton Nellie—†	180	housekeeper	64	"
C	Whitman Agnes—†	180	housewife	41	"
D	Whitman Ernest	180	carpenter	43	"
E	*Santos Carmelita—†	182	housewife	52	"
F	*Santos Joseph	182	laborer	53	"
G	Joachim Mary—†	182	clerk	21	
H	Verbanas Jennie—†	182	housewife	22	"
K	Verbanas Julio	182	laborer	24	
L	Macrina Frank	188	painter	23	"
M	Ciampi Catherine—†	188	housewife	28	"
N	Ciampi Charles	188	chauffeur	32	"
P	Nickinello Anthony	188	pipefitter	28	"
R	Nickinello Mary—†	188	housewife	28	"
S	Bergh Alice—†	191	"	30	
T	Bergh Herbert	191	brazier	32	
U	Tammict Agnes—†	191	operator	25	"
V	Dove Lempi—†	191	housewife	41	"
W	Dove Matti	191	ironworker	54	"
X	McCoy Alberta—†	192	housewife	25	"
Y	McCoy Joseph	192	U S A	30	"
Z	Edison Josephine—†	192	housewife	37	"
	1032				
A	Edison Thomas	192	engineer	41	"
B	Johnson Mary—†	192	housewife	24	"

19

Falcon Street—Continued

c	Johnson Paul	192	longshoreman	31	here
d	Keating Ruth—†	194	housekeeper	27	195 Falcon
e	Enos John	194	U S A	27	here
f	Enos Mario	194	repairman	54	"
g	Enos Virginia—†	194	housewife	44	"
h	O'Hanley Cyril	194	welder	32	
k	O'Hanley Margaret—†	194	housewife	32	"
l	Boyle Mary—†	195	"	62	"
m	Mullane Helen—†	195	"	32	127 Lexington
n	Mullane Thomas	195	laborer	31	127 "
o	*Galante Gustina—†	196	housewife	61	here
p	Galante Tito	196	blacksmith	60	"
r	Consalvi Angelina—†	196	housewife	26	"
s	Consalvi Joseph	196	machinist	27	"
t	Curtin John	197	longshoreman	58	"
u	Driscoll Florance	197	laborer	65	"
v	Driscoll Mary—†	197	housewife	59	"
w	Meuse John E	198	retired	78	
x	Thibodeau Edith—†	198	housewife	46	"
y	Thibodeau Joseph W	198	carpenter	48	"
z	Thibodeau Warren J	198	U S A	23	
	1033				
a	Healy Doris—†	198	stenographer	22	"
b	Healy Laura—†	198	housewife	49	"
c	Healy Matthew	198	rigger	54	"
d	Leonard John	199	U S C G	50	"
e	Leonard Katherine—†	199	housewife	43	"
f	McCarthy Margaret—†	199	inspector	30	"
g	Talbot Hilda—†	200	housekeeper	38	"
h	Paquin Joseph E	200	electrician	49	"
k	Paquin Myrtle—†	200	housewife	35	"
l	MacDonald Duncan A	201	motorman	54	"
m	MacDonald Margaret A—†	201	housewife	48	"
n	Keleher Edwin	202	electrician	35	"
o	Keleher Lawrence N	202	seaman	40	"
p	Keleher Susan—†	202	housekeeper	70	"
r	McCabe Francis P	202	B F D	37	"
s	McCabe Loretta C—†	202	housewife	37	"
t	Merluzzi Marina—†	203	tailor	35	32 Frankfort
u	Tiano Helen—†	203	housewife	30	here
v	Tiano John	203	pipefitter	34	"
w	Ferrand John E	204	shipper	34	"

x	Ferrand Margaret M—†	204	housewife	30	here
y	Thibodeau Lorraine M–†	204	"	24	"
z	Thibodeau Paul	204	U S A	25	"
	1034				
	O'Brien Catherine—†	205	housewife	41	"
♭	O'Brien James F	205	U S N	21	
c	O'Brien John J	205	policeman	44	"
d	Gould Arthur	206	storekeeper	70	"
e	Tobe Esther—†	206	housewife	59	"
f	Tobe Lydia—†	206	secretary	24	"
g	Tobe Samuel	206	supt	59	"
h	Bloom Lena—†	206	housekeeper	80	"
k	Olsen Margaret—†	206	housewife	60	"
l	Olsen Ole	206	watchman	60	"
m	Ahern Marie B—†	207	housewife	49	"
n	Ahern William H	207	letter carrier	61	"
o	Healy Mary E—†	207	housewife	82	"

Glendon Street

p	Foster Clarence W	6	engineer	59	here
r	Smith Bertha M—†	6	housekeeper	53	"
s	Harnum Mabel —†	6	housewife	41	"
t	Goggin Mary L—†	6	"	33	
u	O'Keefe Mary—†	6	housekeeper	69	"
v	Preston Michael J	6	maintenance	38	"
w	Cohan Florence B—†	24	housewife	29	"
x	Cohan John T	24	supervisor	30	"
y	Cohan Maurice	24	foreman	54	
z	Cohan Thomas F	24	U S N	21	
	1035				
a	Boczkowski Lydia—†	28	at home	26	
b	Boczkowski Marie—†	28	housewife	56	"
c	Boczkowski Stanley	28	machinist	51	"
d	Kearney James A	28	molder	54	
e	Kearney Josephine—†	28	housewife	51	"

Lexington Square

f	O'Neil Catherine A—†	1	housewife	57	here
g	O'Neil Daniel J	1	clerk	66	"
h	O'Neil Daniel J, jr	1	student	25	"

Page.	Letter.	FULL NAME.	Residence, Jan. 1, 1945.	Occupation.	Supposed Age.	Reported Residence, Jan. 1, 1944. Street and Number.

Lexington Square—Continued

	K	O'Neil Paul J	1	U S N	20	here
	L	O'Neil Pauline A—†	1	stenographer	27	"
	M	O'Neil Robert E	1	U S N	23	"
	N	Wagner Albert F	2	policeman	47	"
	O	Walker Henry W	2	U S N	30	"
	P	Walker Martha L—†	2	housewife	24	"

Lexington Street

	S	Leddy Mildred—†	198	housekeeper	42	here
	U	Belmonte Christine—†	200	housewife	52	"
	V	Belmonte Frank	200	cobbler	51	"
	W	Belmonte Michael	200	U S N	21	
	X	Caprio Frances—†	200	housewife	26	"
	Y	Caprio John	200	U S N	26	"
	Z	Snodgrass June—†	202	housewife	21	463 Meridian
		1036				
	A	Snodgrass Robert	202	U S N	24	Texas
	B	Wamness Henry	202	longshoreman	46	463 Meridian
	C	Melanson Mary—†	202	housewife	34	here
	D	Melanson William	202	machinist	43	"
	E	McManus Alice—†	202	housewife	63	"
	F	McManus Alice—†	202	WAVE	22	"
	G	McManus Thomas	202	longshoreman	68	"
	H	Sheehan Francis	202	U S A	30	"
	K	Thibeau Celina—†	204	housekeeper	71	"
	L	McLellen George L	204	U S N	38	"
	M	McLellen Margaret—†	204	operator	42	"
	N	Tarquinio Frank	204	shipfitter	34	"
	O	Tarquinio Mary—†	204	housewife	28	"
	R	Bowen Martha—†	206	housekeeper	67	"
	S	Scott John H	206	clerk	70	"
	T	Beohner Emma—†	208	housewife	31	"
	U	Beohner Gordon	208	cutter	56	
	V	Beohner Wilfred	208	chauffeur	33	"
	W	Flemings Priscilla—†	208	stenographer	35	Lowell
	X	Kenney Francis	208	U S A	22	here
	Z	Kenney Harold	208	"	24	"
	Y	Kenney Harry	208	pipefitter	45	"
		1037				
	A	Kenney Teresa—†	208	housewife	43	"

22

Lexington Street—Continued

B	Kenney William	208	clerk	21	here
C	Scarpetta Angelina—†	208	"	23	"
D	Scarpetta Antonio	208	U S A	26	"
E	Scarpetta John	208	"	21	
F	Scarpetta Michael	208	laborer	65	
G	Scarpetta Sarah—†	208	housewife	55	"
H	Scarpetta Vincenzo	208	U S A	24	"
K	*Daley Bridget—†	210	housekeeper	79	147 Trenton
L	Senior Charles J	210	fisherman	37	147 "
M	Senior Loretta—†	210	housewife	36	147 "
N	Alves George H	210	leatherworker	76	here
O	Alves Sarah—†	210	housewife	75	"
P	Pelosi Mary—†	210	"	43	260 Lexington
R	Pelosi Theresa—†	210	clerk	21	260 "
S	Pelosi Vito	210	shoemaker	48	260 "
T	Corvi Margaret—†	212	housewife	32	here
U	Corvi Spartico	212	joiner	36	"
V	Pugliese Rose—†	212	stitcher	28	"
W	Corvi Ardrino	212	cabinetmaker	66	"
X	Corvi Emma—†	212	stitcher	29	"
Y	Corvi Iris—†	212	clerk	31	"
Z	Corvi Ivano	212	U S A	27	"

1038

A	Corvi Madeline—†	212	housewife	57	"
B	Dittmer Eleanor—†	212	"	23	215 Havre
C	Dittmer Myron	212	U S N	29	215 "
D	Kaplan Anna—†	218	housewife	47	here
E	Kaplan Harry	218	storekeeper	49	"
F	Doherty Helen—†	218	clerk	26	Winthrop
G	Doherty Paul A	218	U S N	31	"
H	McCarthy Dorothy—†	218	clerk	24	here
K	McCarthy Paul J	218	U S N	28	148 Coleridge
L	McCarthy Sarah F—†	218	housekeeper	61	here
M	Haberlin John T	218	sexton	58	"
N	Haberlin Rita—†	218	clerk	27	"
O	Marino Antonio	220	painter	30	"
P	Marino Augustina—†	220	housewife	27	"
R	Bergamasco Mary—†	220	housekeeper	46	970 Bennington
S	Rondilone Lucy—†	220	housewife	50	here
T	Rondilone Savino	220	laborer	52	"
U	Stoico Anthony	222	painter	32	126 Trenton

Lexington Street—Continued

v	Stoico Theresa—†	222	housewife	36	126 Trenton
w	Dupuis Joseph	222	seaman	40	68 Webster
x	Dupuis Mary—†	222	housewife	27	68 "
y	Vitello Albert	222	shoecutter	30	here
z	Vitello Stella—†	222	housewife	28	"
	1039					
a	Forte Cecelia—†	224	"	28	
b	Forte Ottavio	224	salesman	29	"
c	Lopilato Anthony	224	laborer	32	"
d	Lopilato Mary G—†	224	housewife	32	"
e	Silver Israel	224	U S C G	30	"
f	Silver Jessie—†	224	nurse	24	
g	*Silver Mollie—†	224	housewife	50	"
k	Villani Anna—†	226	"	26	161 Havre
l	Villani Domenic	226	pipefitter	38	161 "
m	Carine Henry W	226	painter	35	6 Woodside av
n	Carine Viola E—†	226	housewife	32	6 "
r	*Doucette Clarisse—† rear	228	housekeeper	63	here
s	Doucette Clifford	" 228	metalworker	40	"
t	Doucette Lucy—†	" 228	housewife	31	"
u	Hawes Evelyn—†	230	"	22	25 Horan way
v	Hawes Richard	230	U S A	23	25 "
w	Pray Delia—†	230	housekeeper	73	here
x	DeLuca Dorothy—†	230	"	30	112 Havre
y	Razza Josephine—†	232	housewife	23	here
z	Razza Samuel	232	chauffeur	29	"
	1040					
a	Minichello Angelo	232	deckhand	37	146 Trenton
b	Minichello Susie—†	232	forewoman	27	146 "
c	Peterson George	234	U S N	32	here
d	Peterson Mary—†	234	housewife	26	"
e	Donnaruma Benjamin	234	laborer	50	"
g	DeAmico Ethel—†	236	housewife	23	242 Saratoga
h	DeAmico Lawrence	236	technician	23	242 "
k	Carbone Alexander	236	U S N	20	here
l	Carbone Marion—†	236	clerk	28	"
m	Carbone Rose—†	236	housewife	50	"
n	Carbone Sabato	236	laborer	55	
o	Siracusa Ann—†	236	housewife	24	"
p	Siracusa Louis	236	clerk	25	
r	Gasbarro Adeline—†	236	housewife	29	"

Lexington Street—Continued

s	Gasbarro Jesse	236	cook	33	here
t	Cultrera Lucy—†	238	housewife	55	"
u	Cultrera Paul	238	shoemaker	69	"
v	Matteo Palange	238	laborer	48	
w*	Matteo Theresa—†	238	housewife	38	"
x	Beatrice Anthony J	238	U S A	25	
y	Beatrice Florence—†	238	housewife	21	"
z	Jones Emma—†	238	"	43	"
	1041				
a	Jones James D	238	painter	42	··
b	Corcio Anna—†	240	housewife	44	"
c	Corcio Ettore	240	pipefitter	42	"
d	White Fergus E	240	fireman	59	··
e	White John M	240	engineer	32	"
f	White Margaret P—†	240	housewife	28	"
g	Gannon Ellen G—†	240	"	57	
h	Gannon Michael J	240	laborer	58	
k	Trainor Ellen G—†	240	housewife	22	"
l	Trainor James E, jr	240	U S N	22	219 Lexington
m	Keller Agnes E—†	242	housewife	49	here
n	Keller James E	242	carpenter	57	"
o	Loring Benjamin F	242	guard	60	"
p	Loring Ethel M—†	242	housewife	38	"
r	Todisco Mario	244	chauffeur	24	"
s	Todisco Mary—†	244	housewife	22	"
t	DeMeo Domenic	244	U S A	29	
u	DeMeo Frances—†	244	housewife	32	"
v	DeMeo George	244	chauffeur	28	"
w	DeMeo Ralph	244	"	34	"
x*	DeMeo Rose—†	244	housewife	66	"
z	Ventresca Anthony	246	salesman	32	"
	1042				
a	Ventresca Dorothy—†	246	packer	26	··
b*	Ventresca Mary—†	246	housewife	69	"
c	Ventresca Nellie—†	246	inspector	28	"
d	Ventresca Philip	246	retired	73	
f	Antonelli Anthony	250	salesman	39	"
g	Antonelli Louisa—†	250	housewife	35	"
h	Miniscalco Annie—†	250	storekeeper	48	"
k	Miniscalco James	250	retired	63	"
l	Thomas Joseph	250	electrician	32	"

Page.	Letter.	Full Name.	Residence, Jan. 1, 1945.	Occupation.	Supposed Age.	Reported Residence, Jan. 1, 1944. Street and Number.

Lexington Street—Continued

	M	Thomas Rose—†	250	bookkeeper	27	here
	N	Dias Joseph	250	U S A	35	221 Princeton
	O	Dias Linda—†	250	defense wkr	29	221 "
	P	Lanciotti Theresa—†	250	housewife	23	33 Chelsea
	R	*Lanciotti Victor	250	U S A	26	33 "
	T	DiBattista Giuseppe	256	marketman	51	222 Princeton
	U	*DiBattista Mary—†	256	housekeeper	48	222 "
	V	Boudreau Eleanor—†	256	"	28	here
	W	Boudreau John	256	fishcutter	29	"
	X	DiBattista Carmella—†	256	housewife	21	222 Princeton
	Y	DiBattista Liberato	256	U S A	24	222 "

1043

	A	Costa Anthony	258	laborer	60	here
	B	Costa Vincent	258	"	58	"
	C	Cullerton Antoinetta—†	258	housewife	31	"
	D	Cullerton Henry	258	chauffeur	29	"
	E	Gardchinsky Joseph	260	toolmaker	28	10 Prescott
	F	*Gardchinsky Mary—†	260	housewife	23	10 "
	G	Pelosi Anthony	260	U S N	20	here
	H	Pelosi John	260	chauffeur	23	"
	K	Pelosi Theresa A—†	260	housewife	41	"
	L	Pelosi Torindo	260	tailor	45	
	M	Lawrence Ernest	262	engineer	52	"
	N	Lawrence Margaret—†	262	housewife	50	"
	O	Welsh Alice L—†	264	"	63	
	P	Welsh John W	264	printer	61	
	R	Brodus Laura—†	266	factoryhand	22	"
	S	Cothran Martha—†	266	candymaker	48	"
	T	Lochiatto Angelo	266	laborer	41	"
	U	Lochiatto Mary—†	266	housewife	40	"
	V	Bickford John H	266	operator	52	"
	W	Walters Amy M—†	266	housewife	60	"
	X	Walters James	266	shipworker	72	"
	Y	Cullen Arthur	270	postal clerk	26	"
	Z	Cullen Ellen—†	270	factoryhand	25	"

1044

	A	McPherson Helen—†	270	inspector	55	"
	B	Deveau Alfred	274	longshoreman	69	"
	C	Deveau Grace—†	274	nurse	39	
	D	Pomeroy Stella—†	274	bookkeeper	32	"
	E	Sharis Bertha—†	274	stitcher	25	"

26

F	Sharis Daniel	274	baker	29	here	
G	*Sharis George	274	retired	64	"	
H	*Sharis Helen—†	274	at home	55	"	
K	Sharis Nellie—†	274	operator	21	"	
L	Sharis Olga—†	274	tester	23		
M	Sharis Peter	274	U S A	26		
N	Sharis Socrates	274	"	28	"	
O	Gilbrook Ida M—†	276	housewife	64	"	
P	Gilbrook Joseph W	276	inspector	61	"	
R	Nickerson Adele A—†	276	secretary	22	"	
S	Nickerson Cecil L	276	U S A	26	"	
T	Roome Annie E—†	276	housewife	50	"	
U	Roome Edna M—†	276	clerk	20		
V	Roome Everett G	276	U S A	24		
W	Roome Frank G	276	machinist	63	"	
X	Surette Dorothy A—†	278	housewife	35	"	
Y	Surette James B	278	carpenter	41	"	
Z	Baker Clarence T	278	watchman	60	"	
	1045					
A	Daly Flora—†	278	housewife	29	"	
B	McDonald Mary A—†	278	clerk	50		
C	Hulke Ivaline—†	280	technician	20	"	
D	Hulke Lawrence J	280	U S A	22		
E	Coulombe Albert	280	shipper	36		
F	Coulombe Eugene	280	spinner	48		
G	*Coulombe Josephine—†	280	cleaner	52		
H	Coulombe Mary—†	280	at home	84	"	
K	Taimi Eino	280	ironworker	53	"	
L	*Taimi Hilda—†	280	housewife	57	"	
M	Tiano Joseph	282	retired	70		
N	Tiano Mary—†	282	housewife	68	"	
O	Bordieri Concetta—†	282	"	54	218 White	
P	Boudreau Edward	282	U S N	21	218 "	
R	Boudreau Josephine—†	282	housewife	20	218 "	
S	Pellegrino Frances—†	282	"	39	here	
T	Pellegrino Joseph	282	electrician	40	"	
U	Bellino James	282A	baker	32	"	
V	Bellino Laura—†	282A	housewife	31	"	
W	La Rosa Jennie—†	282A	"	47		
X	La Rosa Joseph	282A	presser	50	"	
Y	Miranda Arthur A	282A	U S N	23	"	

Lexington Street—Continued

z	Miranda Rosemarie—†	282A	housekeeper	23	here
	1046				
A	Burke John J	282A	laborer	48	"
B	Burke Mary—†	282A	housewife	46	"
C	Burke Mary R—†	282A	candymaker	21	"
E	Thornton Albert	284	U S A	20	
F	Thornton Frederick G	284	letter carrier	46	"
G	Thornton George	284	fishcutter	44	"
H	Thornton Helen G—†	284	housekeeper	53	"
K	Thornton Lawrence	284	R R man	33	"
L	Thornton Margaret--†	284	at home	42	"
M	Reed Earle C	284	rigger	33	California
N	Reed Olga C—†	284	housewife	30	"
O	Fiore Angelina—†	286	"	54	here
P	Fiore Mildred—†	286	at home	27	"
R	Fiora Vincent	286	molder	59	"
S	Paiva Frank T	286	inspector	42	"
T	Paiva Mary—†	286	at home	80	"
U	Paiva Violet M—†	286	housewife	42	"
V	Ferriani Henry	286	assembler	26	"
W	Ferriani John	286	U S A	24	
X	*Ferriani Louis	286	retired	66	
Y	*Ferriani Mary—†	286	housewife	59	"
Z	Hanlon Albert A	288	operator	53	"
	1047				
A	Hanlon Albert A, jr	288	U S A	27	
B	Hanlon Edward U	288	"	21	
C	Hanlon M Virginia—†	288	secretary	25	"
D	Hanlon Mary C—†	288	housewife	53	"
E	Hanlon Paul C	288	U S M C	22	"
F	Dalton John	290	machinist	48	"
G	Flavin Susan C—†	292	housewife	55	"
H	Marmaud Francis B	292	supervisor	48	"
K	Marmaud Rebecca—†	292.	housewife	73	"
L	Bianchino Albert	294	chauffeur	26	239 Trenton
M	Maylor Ernest	294	"	43	here
N	Hawes Maude V—†	296	housewife	35	"
O	Hawes William J	296	inspector	42	"
P	Moscatelli Evelyn—†	298	electrician	20	"
R	Moscatelli Felicia—†	298	housewife	51	"
S	Moscatelli Laura—†	298	electrician	28	"

Lexington Street—Continued

T	Moscatelli Michael	298	laborer	55	here
U	Moscatelli Rita—†	298	candymaker	22	"
V	Moscatelli Rose—†	298	"	26	"
W	DiSalvo Lydia—†	300	housewife	24	108 Princeton
X	DiSalvo Victor F	300	painter	30	108 "
Y	Ridge Anna—†	302	housekeeper	23	here
Z	Ridge Coleman	302	U S N	31	"
	1048				
A	Ridge John	302	longshoreman	25	"
B	Ridge Mary—†	302	housewife	65	"
C	Ridge Michael	302	U S N	27	
D	Ridge Thomas A	302	retired	73	
F	Almeida Anthony	306	merchant	53	"
G	Almeida Rhoda—†	306	housewife	50	"
H	Almeida Roderick	306	U S N	29	
K	Almeida Ruth—†	306	machinist	20	"
L	MacLeod John R	306	retired	87	"
M	Morrison Margaret A—†	306	housewife	36	"
N	Morrison Robert H	306	U S N	39	

Prescott Street

P	Kennedy Catherine—†	3	housewife	48	here
R	Regan Patrick	3	technician	40	"
S	Sheehan Catherine—†	3	clerk	45	"
T	Neal William A	3	U S A	28	"
U	Pacelli Michael	5	salesman	21	36 Leyden
V	Cappuccio Mary—†	5	stitcher	47	here
W	Velona Anna—†	5	"	30	"
X	Velona John	5	U S A	23	"
Y	Dell'Aria Charles	6	shoemaker	45	"
Z	Dell'Aria Sadie—†	6	housewife	47	"
	1049				
A	Zuccala Anna—†	6	"	39	"
B	Zuccala Giacomo	6	mattressmkr	41	"
C	Wilcox Guy	6	assembler	63	"
D	Zimmer Albert	6	machinist	30	"
E	Zimmer Lillian—†	6	housewife	66	"
F	DiGirolamo Elena—†	7	"	44	
G	DiGirolamo Joseph	7	tilesetter	45	"
H	Gerome Steven	7	U S A	22	"

Prescott Street—Continued

	Letter	FULL NAME	Residence	Occupation	Age	Reported Residence
	K	Valenti Antonio	7	foreman	54	here
	L	Valenti Helen—†	7	machinist	28	"
	M	Valenti Margaret—†	7	housewife	48	" .
	N	Valenti Theresa—†	7	machinist	32	"
	O	Good Joseph	8	laborer	34	"
	P	Good Rose—†	8	housewife	35	"
	R	Luongo Alice—†	8	"	33	
	S	Luongo Silvio	8	merchant	33	"
	T	DeFrancesco Eleanor—†	8	housewife	34	"
	U	DeFrancesco Joseph	8	salesman	36	"
	W	Pesiri Antonette—†	10	housewife	35	Medford
	X	Pesiri Rocco	10	machinist	38	"
	Y	Silva Joseph	10	weaver	45	here
	Z	Silva Philomena—†	10	housewife	33	"
		1050				
	A	*Angelini Elena—†	10	driller	38	
	B	Costagliola Josephine—†	10	housewife	31	"
	C	Costagliola Peter	10	operator	33	"

Putnam Street

	Letter	FULL NAME	Residence	Occupation	Age	Reported Residence
	D	Frasier Edward F	2	chauffeur	45	here
	E	Frasier Mary E—†	2	housekeeper	74	"
	F	Purcell Jessie—†	2	clerk	21	"
	G	Purcell Mary—†	2	housewife	49	"
	H	Purcell Thomas	2	clerk	55	
	K	Purcell William	2	U S N	20	
	L	Purcell Winifred—†	2	operator	23	" .
	M	*D'Entremont Catherine—†	7	housewife	33	"
	N	D'Entremont Elmer C	7	machinist	35	"
	O	Beard Curtis	7	"	44	
	P	*Beard Verna—†	7	housewife	35	"
	R	*Crowell Lottie—†	7	"	54	
	S	Crowell Murray	7	stitcher	56	"
	T	Anderson Susie—†	8	housekeeper	72	"
	U	Newman John H	8	machinist	33	283 Princeton
	V	Mastrogiovanni Anthony	10	foreman	32	here
	W	Mastrogiovanni Lena—†	10	housewife	30	"
	X	Adractas Elvira—†	10	"	34	"
	Y	Adractas George D	10	counterman	45	"
	Z	Alberghini Attilio	47	machinist	54	"

Page.	Letter.	FULL NAME.	Residence, Jan. 1, 1945.	Occupation.	Supposed Age.	Reported Residence, Jan. 1, 1944. Street and Number.

1051
Putnam Street—Continued

A	Alberghini Louis	47	U S A	21	here
B	Alberghini Mary—†	47	housewife	53	"
c	*O'Brien Alice R—†	48	housekeeper	24	Chelsea
D	*Gagnon Emma—†	48	housewife	57	here
E	Gagnon Joseph	48	laborer	60	"
F	McLaughlin Jeanette—†	48	clerk	32	"
G	Scala Edward	48	shoeworker	41	"
H	Scala Inez—†	48	housewife	36	"
K	Walker Daniel	49	U S A	22	"
L	Walker Marguerite—†	49	housewife	21	329 Saratoga
M	Lopilato George	49	chauffeur	51	here
N	Lopilato Lillian—†	49	housewife	40	"
O	Vaccaro Charles	50	weaver	34	"
P	Vaccaro Jénnie—†	50	housewife	28	"
R	DiPaolo Carmella—†	50	operator	54	"
S	Olga Gabriel T	50	U S A	32	
T	Asci Catherine—†	50	housewife	34	"
U	Asci Ernest	50	laborer	38	"
V	Brown Mary S—†	51	at home	51	"
W	Sordillo Angelo	52	toolmaker	31	"
X	Sordillo Elizabeth—†	52	housewife	30	"
Y	Romano Albert	52	painter	28	"
Z	Romano Minnie—†	52	housewife	29	"

1052

A	Blasi James	52	mason	54	
B	Blasi Jennie—†	52	housewife	60	"
C	Romano Conchetta—†	52	stitcher	24	"
D	Mancusi Frances—†	53	waitress	27	309 Saratoga
E	Jeffrey Elizabeth—†	53	"	20	323 "
F	Laskey Charles	54	rigger	27	117 Falcon
G	Laskey Helen—†	54	housewife	29	117 "
H	Law Elizabeth L—†	54	"	34	here
K	Law John	54	chauffeur	41	"
L	Curcio Fannie—†	54	housewife	41	"
M	Curcio John	54	tailor	46	
O	Sorrento Joseph	56	stitcher	24	"
P	Sorrento Santina—†	56	housewife	29	"
R	Rizzari Giacomo	56	painter	51	
S	Rizzari Michelina—†	56	housewife	40	"
T	Rizzari Salvatore	56	U S A	22	

Page.	Letter.	FULL NAME.	Residence, Jan. 1, 1945.	Occupation.	Supposed Age.	Reported Residence, Jan. 1, 1944. Street and Number.

Putnam Street—Continued

	U	Rizzari Theresa—†	56	stitcher	23	here
	W	Barry Catherine M—†	58	at home	65	"
	X	Barry Gertrude C—†	58	technician	25	"
	Y	Barry John M	58	U S N	20	
	Z	Barry Josephine—†	58	at home	27	"
1053						
	A	Barry Mary F—†	58	clerk	33	"
	B	Lidback George S	60	custodian	44	"
	C	Lidback Isabel—†	60	housewife	33	"
	D	Stamm Mary E—†	61	at home	65	"
	E	French Harold	61	painter	22	39 Union
	F	French Margaret—†	61	housewife	22	39 "
	H	Burden Florence—†	62	saleswoman	36	here
	G	Burke Katherine A—†	62	housekeeper	65	"
	K	Garrity Lillian—†	63	"	70	"
	L	Garrity Thomas	63	clerk	46	"
	M	Ryan James	63	laborer	59	
	N	Doran Ellen M—†	63	housewife	66	"
	O	Doran William	63	blockmaker	66	"
	R	DeSteffano Joseph	86	U S A	24	Cambridge
	S	DeSteffano Margaret—†	86	housewife	24	"
	T	Umbro Rocco	86	electrician	24	229 London
	U	Umbro Theresa—†	86	housewife	24	229 "
	V	*Falsini Amelia—†	86	"	54	here
	W	Falsini Lena—†	86	operator	21	"
	X	Falsini Louis	86	chipper	56	"
	Y	Forte Arthur	88	U S N	26	
	Z	Forte Phyllis—†	88	housewife	26	"
1054						
	A	*DeGruttola Carmella—†	88	"	66	
	B	DeGruttola Frank	88	bartender	35	"
	C	DeGruttola Joseph	88	U S A	39	
	D	DeGruttola Matilda—†	88	leatherworker	26	"
	E	Colluccini John	88	U S A	22	
	F	Colluccini Josephine—†	88	housewife	40	"
	G	Colluccini Josephine—†	88	clerk	21	
	H	Colluccini Pasquale	88	candymaker	48	"
	K	Kaeneman Mary—†	90	housewife	41	"
	L	Kaeneman Robert H	90	engineer	44	"
	M	Lucido Angeline—†	92	at home	50	"
	N	Vila John	92	fireman	48	"
	O	Vila Vita—†	92	housewife	35	"

Trenton Street

R	Cipriano Elsie—†	159	housewife	28	here
S	Cipriano Joseph A	159	machinist	30	"
T	Cipriano Maria—†	159	housekeeper	66	"
U	Joyce James P	159	longshoreman	54	"
V	Joyce Josephine—†	159	housewife	45	"
W	Joyce William J	159	U S A	26	
Y	Petroni Dorothy—†	159	waitress	25	"
X	Petroni Lawrence	159	U S N	26	
Z	Chiodi Anthony	161	fisherman	42	"

1055

A	Chiodi Rose—†	161	housewife	40	"
B	Corser Elvin	161	U S C G	24	"
C	Corser Evelyn	161	housewife	21	"
D	Edge Edith—†	161	"	25	"
E	Edge Francis	161	machinist	26	"
F	Kavin Catherine—†	163	housekeeper	61	"
G	Kavin William	163	clerk	36	"
H	Campbell Alice—†	163	housewife	34	"
K	Campbell Joseph	163	operator	35	"
L	Guerriero Marie—†	163	housewife	28	"
M	Guerriero Nicholas	163	welder	29	"
N	Lombardi Enrico	165	shoeworker	54	"
O	Lombardi Maria—†	165	housewife	52	"
P	Busheme Anna—†	165	"	29	
R	Busheme Paul	165	mason	31	
S	Lombardi Alberto	165	cutter	28	
T	Lombardi Bessie—†	165	housewife	23	"
U	Anderson Edwin	167	chauffeur	45	"
V	Anderson Eleanor—†	167	bookkeeper	21	"
W	Anderson Helen—†	167	housewife	42	"
X	Azzoli Giovanni	169	painter	58	
Y	Orlandella Ciriaco M	169	shoeworker	29	"
Z	Orlandella Frances—†	169	housewife	27	"

1056

A	Potito Alfio	169	engineer	29	"
B	Potito Eppifano	169	tailor	60	
C	Potito Margaret—†	169	housekeeper	59	"
D	Rubbicco Philip	169	electrician	27	"
E	Rubbicco Stella—†	169	housekeeper	32	"
G	Grinkiewich Victoria—†	171	"	44	
H	Costello Anne—†	171	housewife	54	"
K	Costello John A	171	U S N	28	"

Trenton Street—Continued

L	Costello Mary K—†	171	teacher	22	here
M	Costello Michael	171	mechanic	55	"
N	Costello Robert J	171	student	21	"
O	Reed Charles H	171	retired	67	"
P	Reed Clarabelle I—†	171	housewife	59	"
R	Reed Eloise T—†	171	housekeeper	20	"
S	DiMaggio Antonio	173	laborer	53	
T	DiMaggio Assunta—†	173	factoryhand	40	"
U	Donnaruma Leonardo	173	U S A	21	
V	Donnaruma Pasquale	173	"	20	
W	Ballarino Constance—†	173	housewife	28	"
X	Ballarino Michael	173	presser	30	"
Y	Landano Gerald	173	letter carrier	37	"
Z	Landano Sophia—†	173	housewife	32	"

1057

A	Polimeno Lena—†	175	"	35	
B	Polimeno Matteo	175	tailor	48	
C	Trainito Crocefissa—†	175	factoryhand	21	"
D	Trainito Gaetana—†	175	"	25	
E	Trainito Gasper	175	U S A	22	"
F	Trainito Rose—†	175	housewife	43	"
G	Trainito Stephen	175	machinist	54	"
H	Trainito Cologero	175	pipefitter	45	"
K	Trainito Gasper	175	retired	85	"
L	Trainito Maria—†	175	housewife	32	"
M	Fox Carmella—†	179	"	34	
N	Fox Ernest	179	chauffeur	36	"
O	Longo Angelina—†	179	housewife	55	"
P	Longo Joseph	179	U S M C	21	"
R	Longo Philip	179	laborer	55	
S	Longo Vincent	179	U S N	22	"
T	*DeMattia Joseph	179	painter	44	
U	DeMattia Lerina—†	179	candymaker	40	"
V	Aliberti Angelina—†	189	housewife	55	"
W	Aliberti Eva—†	189	bookkeeper	21	"
X	Aliberti James	189	U S A	26	
Y	Aliberti Jennie—†	189	factoryhand	31	"
Z	Aliberti Luigi	189	U S N	23	
¹z	*Aliberti Rocco	189	laborer	64	"

1058

A	Perella Carmella—†	189	housewife	26	"

Trenton Street—Continued

B	Perella John	189	painter	30	here
C	Siciliano Louis	189	meatcutter	48	"
D	D'Addario Guerino	191	clerk	59	"
E	D'Addario Maria—†	191	housewife	57	"
F	D'Addario Susan—†	191	factoryhand	21	"
G	D'Addario Victor	191	U S A	24	
H	D'Addario Albert	191	chauffeur	27	"
K	D'Addario Lillian—†	191	housewife	23	"
L	DeLuca Carmella—†	193	"	26	
M	DeLuca Ignatius	193	pharmacist	33	"
N	Mancini Alice—†	193	bookkeeper	28	"
O	Mancini Lillian—†	193	beautician	26	"
P	Mancini Palma—†	193	housewife	55	"
R	Mancini Santino	193	tailor	63	
S	Christopher Carmella—†	195	housewife	21	"
T	Christopher Frank	195	shipfitter	27	"
U	Lawson Ella P—†	195	housewife	48	"
V	Lawson Ethel D—†	195	tel operator	20	"
W	Lawson George A	195	carpenter	56	"
X	Lawson Howard C	195	U S A	25	"
Y	Lawson Ralph E	195	manager	27	"
Z	Kanall Marion A—†	196	housewife	24	"
	1059				
A	Kanall Mary A—†	196	"	54	
B	Kanall Paul	196	merchant	54	"
C	Kanall Theodore	196	U S N	25	"
D	Kanellopulos Anargiros	196	merchant	62	"
E	Kanellopulos Stella—†	196	housewife	54	"
F	Kelly Ina—†	196	saleswoman	45	"
G	Capolupo John	196	barber	50	"
H	Capolupo Mary—†	196	housewife	37	"
K	Giordano Angelo	197	shipfitter	30	"
L	Giordano Christine—†	197	housewife	28	"
M	Golden Helen—†	197	"	37	
N	Golden Mitchell	197	carpenter	40	"
O	Young Irvin	197	mechanic	65	"
P	Young Katherine—†	197	housewife	64	"
R	Champa Francis	198	mechanic	37	"
S	Champa Rose—†	198	housewife	34	"
T	Abruzzese Carl	198	laborer	21	
U	Abruzzese James	198	U S A	23	"

Page.	Letter.	FULL NAME.	Residence, Jan. 1, 1945.	Occupation.	Supposed Age.	Reported Residence, Jan. 1, 1944. Street and Number.

Trenton Street—Continued

	v	*Abruzzese Marie—†	198	housewife	59	here
	w	Abruzzese Patrick	198	U S A	27	"
	x	Driscoll Catherine—†	198	housewife	23	"
	y	Driscoll Paul	198	U S A	29	"
	z	Tarquinio Jean—†	199	packer	30	"
1060						
	A	Tyman James E	199	foreman	38	"
	B	Tyman Mary M—†	199	housewife	37	"
	C	Flaherty Anita—†	199	"	35	
	D	Flaherty William S	199	machinist	39	"
	E	McDonald Joseph A	207	electrician	34	"
	F	McDonald Madaline—†	207	housewife	29	"
	G	McDonald George W	207	laborer	33	
	H	McDonald Hannah E—†	207	housewife	70	"
	K	McDonald Joseph A	207	retired	77	"
	L	Jollimore Alma—†	209	housekeeper	40	"
	M	Emmons Harold	209	chemist	25	"
	N	Emmons Hazel—†	209	housewife	24	"
	O	Fenton Edward	209	operator	45	"
	P	Fenton Loretta—†	209	housewife	45	"
	R	Burroughs Adeline—†	211	"	26	"
	S	Burroughs Alden H	211	agent	33	"
	T	Dell'Aria Salvatore	211	U S A	24	"
	U	Barletta Alfonso	211	"	32	"
	V	Barletta Ciriaco	211	laborer	62	
	W	Ruggiero Dominic	211	carpenter	31	"
	X	Ruggiero Helen—†	211	housewife	26	"
	Y	Viscione Anthony	213	clerk	49	
	Z	Viscione Jennie—†	213	housewife	47	"
1061						
	A	Caluccio Emma—†	213	housekeeper	21	"
	B	Caluccio Gabriel	213	U S A	24	"
	E	Park George	217	baker	53	
	F	Park James	217	U S A	22	"
	G	Park Katherine—†	217	housewife	53	"
	H	Clark Florence—†	217	welder	33	400 Saratoga
	K	Curtin John J	217	seaman	53	400 "
	L	Curtin Michael	217	fireman	55	400 "
	P	Costa Margaret—†	221	housewife	27	319 E Eagle
	R	Costa Rocco	221	painter	28	319 "
	S	DeAngelis Achille	221	clerk	35	here

Trenton Street—Continued

T	DeAngelis Salvatrica—†	221	housewife	32	here
U	McCarthy Lena—†	221	"	24	"
V	McCarthy Nicholas	221	shipfitter	39	"
W	Rivers Isabella—†	223	housewife	32	"
X	Rivers Thomas	223	machinist	28	"
Y	O'Brien Marion—†	223	housewife	49	"
Z	Favale Angela—†	227	"	55	

1062

A	Favale Mary—†	227	stitcher	30	"
B	Favale Michael	227	woodcarver	58	"
C	Scorzello Gweneth—†	227	housewife	22	7 Central sq
D	Scorzello Rocco	227	brazier	27	120 London
F	Potenza Antonetta—†	233	housewife	41	here
G	Potenza Peter	233	laborer	50	"
H	Potenza Anthony	233	technician	21	"
K	Walsh William P	235	machinist	49	"
L	Moore Christine L—†	235	teacher	33	252 E Eagle
N	McGregor Alice—†	237	housewife	66	219 Main
O	Ducette Doris—†	237	"	34	here
P	Ducette William	237	cutter	34	"
S	Palmer Annie—†	239	housewife	76	"
T	Held Alfred D	239	U S A	23	
U	Held Herbert B	239	"	20	
V	Held Jessica—†	239	housewife	40	"
W	Bianchino Angelo	239	U S A	28	
X	*Bianchino Florindo	239	laborer	62	
Y	Bianchino Jennie—†	239	housewife	62	"
Z	Bianco Salvatore	239	chemist	37	Cambridge

1063

A	Cann Concetta—†	239	housewife	24	here
C	Simons Alexander D	241	carpenter	81	"
D	Simons Robert	241	retired	44	"
E	Simons Rosella—†	241	housewife	80	"
G	Murphy Arthur	243	clerk	42	
H	Murphy Bridget—†	243	housewife	39	"
K	Marino Albert	243	laborer	28	
L	Marino Theresa—†	243	housewife	26	"
M	Corkum Frances—†	243	"	46	
N	Corkum Lester	243	machinist	51	"
O	Corkum Russell	243	U S N	20	
P	Daley Mary—†	247	housewife	45	"

Trenton Street—Continued

R	Daley Timothy	247	longshoreman	49	here
S	Seppa John	247	accountant	25	"
T	Seppa Oscar	247	engineer	57	"
U	Seppa Riikka—†	247	housewife	60	"
V	Cullinane Helen G—†	247	teacher	30	"
W	Cullinane Jennie—†	247	housewife	51	"
X	Cullinane William	247	retired	57	

White Street

Y	Manning John T	88	U S A	37	here
Z	Manning Mary C—†	88	nurse	26	"
	1064				
A	Ohlson Alexander E	88	operator	51	"
B	Ohlson Elizabeth M—†	88	saleswoman	50	"
C	Randall Alice M—†	88	housewife	23	"
D	Randall Joseph J	88	U S A	27	"
E	Cooper Ellen M—†	rear 88	housekeeper	80	"
F	Langley Capitola—†	" 88	at home	76	"
H	Veader Mary—†	90	housewife	47	179 Condor
K	Veader Perry L	90	seaman	46	179 "
L	Conley Helen—†	92	housewife	50	here
M	Conley James J	92	stevedore	49	"
N	Saggese Alfred	92	U S A	35	"
O	Saggese Dorothy—†	92	milliner	33	"
P	Saggese Mary—†	92	housewife	73	"
R	Saggese Michael	92	painter	52	"
S	Saggese Victoria—†	92	at home	40	"
T	Dalton Mary—†	100	laundress	31	"
U	Nugent Margaret—†	100	housekeeper	61	"
V	Nugent William	100	carpenter	66	"
X	Morani Antonette—†	104	housewife	28	"
Y	Morani Joseph	104	mechanic	30	"
Z	Nazzaro Antonio C	104	janitor	49	"
	1065				
A	Nazzaro Carmella—†	104	housewife	42	"
B	Fuccillo Carlo	106	candymaker	58	"
C	Fuccillo Louise—†	106	secretary	20	"
D	Fuccillo Mary C—†	106	housewife	48	"
E	Ingala Charles	106	U S A	26	
F	Ingala Frances—†	106	housewife	25	"

G	Salierno Josephine—†	106	stitcher	22	here
H	Salierno Louise—†	106	housewife	48	"
K	Salierno Sarino	106	machinist	53	"
N	Nelson Frederika—†	110	student	21	New York
O	Nelson Irene H—†	110	housewife	50	408 Hunt'n av
P	Nelson Samuel M	110	social worker	55	72 Marginal
R	Mortellite Doris—†	112	housewife	25	here
S	Pondrandolfo Frank	112	barber	57	"
T	Pondrandolfo Rose—†	112	housewife	57	"
U	Pitts Florence—†	112	"	42	
V	Pitts George D	112	engineer	45	"
W	Bradley Dennis	112	foreman	43	"
X	Bradley Louise—†	112	housewife	38	"
Y	DiFranza Lewis	114	laborer	30	"
Z	DiFranza Virginia—†	114	housewife	26	"

1066

A	Clemente Angelo	114	repairman	46	"
B	Clemente Nicolina—†	114	housewife	42	"
C	Carvi Anna—†	114	"	27	
D	Carvi Libero	114	salesman	34	"
E	LoConte Anthony	116	welder	26	
F	LoConte Helen—†	116	housewife	27	"
G	Matera Francis	116	lawyer	34	
H	Matera Manda—†	116	housewife	32	"
L	DiLeonardo Rosina—†	116	"	54	
M	DiLeonardo Salvatore	116	operator	55	"
K	Ferrante Augustino	116	candymaker	44	"
S	DiRienza Annette—†	118	beautician	42	"
N	Sacco Augustino	118	plumber	43	"
O	*Sacco Biaggio	118	retired	69	
P	Sacco Helen—†	118	beautician	26	"
R	*Sacco Marie—†	118	housewife	63	"
T	Guerra Helen—†	118	"	30	"
U	Guerra Victor	118	chauffeur	33	"

Ward 1–Precinct 11

CITY OF BOSTON

LIST OF RESIDENTS
20 YEARS OF AGE AND OVER

(NON-CITIZENS INDICATED BY ASTERISK)
(FEMALES INDICATED BY DAGGER)

AS OF

JANUARY 1, 1945

THOMAS F. SULLIVAN, *Chairman*
FREDERIC E. DOWLING, *Secretary*
WILLIAM A. MOTLEY, JR.
FRANCIS B. McKINNEY
EVERETT R. PROUT

Listing Board.

CITY OF BOSTON PRINTING DEPARTMENT

1100
Bennington Street

B	Miller Richard V	194	machinist	68	here
C	Pisani Matthew	194	guard	26	"
D	Pisani Pauline—†	194	housewife	22	"
E	Trocano Flora—†	194	"	35	
F	Trocano Pasquale	194	shipper	39	"
H	Bossone Saverio	196	laborer	62	"
K	Scorzello Ralph	196	"	62	"
L	Griffin Helen E—†	196	housewife	45	325 Paris
M	Griffin Mary E—†	196	stock girl	22	325 "
N	Griffin Thomas J	196	U S N	20	325 "
P	Caporele Carmen	198	laborer	22	here
R	Caporele Dorothy—†	198	housewife	37	"
S	Sargent Betty J—†	198	clerk	20	Revere
T	Mello Agnes C—†	198	gluer	24	here
U	Mello Charles C	198	carpenter	50	"
V	*Mello Ethel C—†	198	housewife	50	"
W	Mello James E	198	U S A	27	"
Y	Scire Carmello	202	storekeeper	59	"
Z	Scire Frank	202	U S A	27	"

1101

A	*Scire Mary—†	202	housewife	56	"
B	DiLorenzo Anna J—†	202	"	27	
C	DiLorenzo Salvatore J	202	carpenter	26	"
D	Sequeira Bernadette—†	202	housewife	25	232 Lexington
E	DiNubile Giuseppe	204	guard	40	here
F	Rozzi Carmen C	204	milkman	21	"
G	Rozzi Edith R—†	204	stitcher	24	"
H	DeFelice Guy F	204	laborer	34	
K	DeFelice Margaret E—†	204	housewife	30	"
M	*Bertini Peter	206	retired	70	
N	Caggiano Ann A—†	206	stitcher	20	"
O	Caggiano Jenny F—†	206	"	23	
P	*Caggiano Marciano	206	laborer	60	
R	*Caggiano Mary—†	206	housewife	60	"
S	*Scanzillo Luigi	206	retired	50	
T	*Scanzillo Mary—†	206	stitcher	44	"
U	Sciaraffa Pasquale	208	retired	70	"
V	Femino Pasquale A	208	shipfitter	24	342 Meridian
W	Femino Santa—†	208	housewife	26	342 "
X	*Mastacusa Filomena—†	208	inspector	63	here

2

Page.	Letter.	Full Name.	Residence, Jan. 1, 1945.	Occupation.	Supposed Age.	Reported Residence, Jan. 1, 1944. Street and Number.

Bennington Street—Continued

	Y	Mastacusa Frank	208	barber	67	here
	z	Collins Anna C—†	210	housewife	58	27 Morris
1102						
	A	Collins William F	210	laborer	58	27 "
	B	Faretra Eva—†	210	housewife	35	here
	c	Faretra Richard	210	laborer	33	"
	D	Canto Angela—†	210	housewife	36	"
	E	Canto Guy	210	pipefitter	32	"
	F	Nazzaro Joseph	212	shoemaker	50	"
	G	Nazzaro Mary E—†	212	packer	50	
	H	Amirault Mary M—†	212	housewife	35	"
	K	Amirault Roy D	212	fishcutter	40	"
	L	Deon Clayton J	212	"	36	"
	M	Manfredonia Florence M-†212		housewife	31	"
	N	Manfredonia Joseph	212	collector	30	"
	o	Coffin Margaret M—†	214	wrapper	59	199 London
	P	Donovan William W	214	longshoreman	43	Wakefield
	R	Hogan Anna F—†	214	U S A	34	here
	s	McCaffrey Arthur S	214	electrician	30	"
	T	McCaffrey Lillian M—†	214	housewife	32	"
	U	Riley Daniel F	214	guard	52	
	v	Riley Daniel F	214	U S A	26	
	w	Riley Mary E—†	214	housewife	56	"
	x	Riley Mary E—†	214	student	20	"
	Y	Pagliarulo Antoinette-†	215	housewife	31	218 Saratoga
	z	Pagliarulo Saverio	215	U S N	31	218 "
1103						
	A	Granese Ernest	215	laborer	28	here
	B	Granese Rose C—†	215	housewife	26	"
	c	McCormick Leo J	215	rigger	29	"
	D	McCormick Winifred—†	215	housewife	27	"
	E	Ferranti Elvira M—†	216	"	25	"
	F	Ferranti Walter G	216	welder	26	
	G	Podeia Assunta—†	216	clerk	21	..
	H	Podeia Frank	216	chipper	51	..
	K	Podeia Mary—†	216	housewife	45	"
	L	Coady Harold F	216	machinist	38	"
	M	Coady Mary—†	216	housewife	34	"
	N	Zevolo James	217	plumber	23	"
	o	Zevolo Phyllis—†	217	housewife	23	"
	P	Rubino Alfred	217	U S A	28	

Bennington Street—Continued

R	Rubino Phyllis—†	217	housewife	27	here
s	Zevolo Michael	217	U S A	25	"
T	Zevolo Pasquale	217	laborer	52	"
U	Zevolo Rose—†	217	packer	28	"
V	Zevolo Thomasina—†	217	housewife	48	"
W	Cuzzo Guy	219	guard	31	"
X	Cuzzo Phyllis—†	219	housewife	35	251 Bennington
Y	Puopolo Alessio	219	reamer	48	here
Z	Puopolo Elizabeth—†	219	clerk	21	"

1104

A	Puopolo Emilio	219	U S N	23	"
B	Puopolo Angelo	219	reamer	38	"
C	Puopolo Mabel—†	219	housewife	42	"
D	Calistro Catherine—†	221	"	26	364 Meridian
E	Calistro Ralph	221	electrician	29	235 Chelsea
F	Guinta Jennie—†	221	mender	25	here
G	Guinta John	221	metalworker	21	"
H	Guinta Luciano	221	laborer	55	"
K	*Guinta Mary—†	221	housewife	53	"
N	Accomando Maria—†	221	"	60	190 Bennington
O	Accomando Nicholas	221	baker	24	190 "
L	Christamano John	221	laborer	22	29 Charles
M	Christamano Lena—†	221	housewife	21	190 Bennington
P	Loscocco Filomena—†	223	"	50	here
R	Loscocco Frances—†	223	stitcher	22	"
s	Loscocco Louis	223	U S A	24	"
T	*Loscocco Manuel	223	laborer	56	
U	Colichio Agnes—†	223	housewife	54	"
V	Colichio Joseph	223	U S A	30	
W	Colichio Nicholas	223	laborer	66	
X	Stranberg Mildred—†	223	housewife	23	"
Y	Stranberg Neil	223	U S A	20	
Z	Pacella Anna—†	223	housewife	36	"

1105

A	Pacella Antonio	223	barber	51	"
B	Giufrida Mary—†	225	housewife	42	"
C	Giufrida Philip	225	U S A	22	
D	Giufrida Sebastian	225	operator	44	"
E	*D'Amico Concetta—†	225	at home	71	"
F	D'Amico Constance—†	225	stitcher	27	"
G	D'Amico Felix	225	carpenter	75	"

Bennington Street—Continued

H	D'Amico Felix	225	U S N	23	here
K	*D'Amico Josephine—†	225	housewife	46	"
L	D'Amico Peter	225	carpenter	49	"
M	D'Amico Sarah—†	225	at home	25	"
N	D'Amico Theresa—†	225	bookkeeper	21	"
O	Zona Anthony	225	U S N	23	"
P	Zona Joseph	225	painter	49	
R	Zona Theresa—†	225	housewife	45	"
S	Alfano Alfonso	226	pressman	56	"
T	Alfano Dominic A	226	U S N	23	
U	Alfano Luigi	226	painter	22	
V	Alfano Rose—†	226	housewife	41	"
W	Carroll Albert	226	laborer	42	"
X	Carroll Edward	226	machinist	48	"
Y	Carroll Sarah J—†	226	housewife	74	"
Z	Shephard Edmund	226	rigger	36	"
	1106				
A	Shephard Lillian—†	226	housewife	33	"
B	Dove Florence B—†	228	"	35	
C	Dove Walter F	228	accountant	42	"
D	Barrett Emma S—†	228	housewife	55	"
E	Miller Mary B—†	228	clerk	37	
F	*Grillo Frances—†	229	housewife	69	"
G	*Grillo John	229	laborer	70	
H	Doble Angelo E	229	cook	44	
K	Doble Antonetta—†	229	housewife	35	"
L	Crocker Catherine—†	229	"	40	
M	Crocker George	229	longshoreman	41	"
O	Shlager Anna—†	230	housewife	47	"
P	Shlager Charles	230	merchant	47	"
R	Campisano Michael	231	butcher	37	"
S	Campisano Rose—†	231	housewife	31	"
T	Frongillo Grace—†	231	clerk	42	
U	Frongillo Henry	231	machinist	46	"
V	Frongillo Louis G	231	U S A	22	..
W	Vitolo Louis	231	retired	72	
X	Vitolo Mary—†	231	housewife	45	"
Y	Mastrocola Frank	231	operator	58	"
Z	Mastrocola Rose—†	231	housewife	50	"
	1107				
A	Moynihan Francis F	232	salesman	36	"

Bennington Street—Continued

B	Moynihan Mary L—†	232	housewife	36	here
C	Berry George F	232	weigher	35	"
D	Berry Mary V—†	232	housewife	36	"
E	Haggett Alice L—†	232	"	38	
F	Haggett Reginald L	232	salesman	37	"
G	Ambrosino Anthony	233	laborer	48	"
H	Ambrosino Mary—†	233	housewife	48	"
K	Driscoll Hannah A—†	233	at home	67	"
L	Willis Frances—†	233	"	65	
M	McGuire John	233	retired	82	"
N	Incerto Lena A—†	234	housewife	31	214 Bennington
O	Incerto Virgilio	234	salesman	35	214 "
P	Mannetta Eugene	234	shipfitter	32	here
R	Mannetta Phyllis—†	234	housewife	31	"
S	Mulholland John J	235	clerk	20	"
T	Mulholland Peter J	235	laborer	61	
U	Mulholland Sarah C—†	235	housewife	50	"
V	Curran John J	235	shipfitter	49	"
W	McKenna Elizabeth—†	235	housewife	44	"
X	McKenna Harry	235	U S N	22	"
Y	Diamond Gertrude M—†	235	at home	27	"
Z	Diamond John T	235	U S N	30	

1108

A	Skane George W	235	clerk	23	
B	Skane Gertrude B—†	235	housewife	51	"
C	Skane John E	235	U S A	30	"
D	Skane Richard	235	laborer	51	
E	Skane Richard F	235	warrant officer	32	"
F	Gracie Julius	236	electrician	62	"
G	Gracie Mary—†	236	housewife	56	"
H	Goglia Edward G	236	U S A	26	
K	Goglia Ernest A	236	U S C G	31	"
L	Goglia Lucy—†	236	housewife	59	"
M	Goglia Mary L—†	236	social worker	31	"
N	Goglia Nicholas	236	watchman	62	"
O	Perez Alice M—†	236	housewife	56	"
P	Perez Frank L	236	U S A	22	
R	Perez Joseph A	236	"	24	
S	Perez Rose M—†	236	glassblower	28	"
T	Lauricella Anthony	237	retired	66	"
U	Lauricella Frances—†	237	housewife	58	"

Page.	Letter.	Full Name.	Residence, Jan. 1, 1945.	Occupation.	Supposed Age.	Reported Residence, Jan. 1, 1944. Street and Number.

Bennington Street—Continued

	v	Lauricella Salvatore	237	chauffeur	24	here
	w	Tringali Frances—†	237	housewife	28	"
	x	Tringali Sebastian	237	U S A	28	"
	y	DiFilici Lenardo	237	barber	75	"
	z	DiFilici Lucy—†	237	housewife	61	"
1109						
	A	Riccioli Domenic	237	beautician	44	"
	B	Riccioli Mary—†	237	housewife	37	"
	c	Carroll Emma F—†	239	at home	77	"
	D	Rich Annie—†	239	"	77	
	E	Rich Margaret—†	239	welder	45	
	F	Rich Webster A	239	carpenter	42	"
	G	Keyes Milton	247	longshoreman	35	"
	H	Keyes Rita—†	247	housewife	29	"
	K	McCormack Archibald	247	laborer	36	
	L	McCormack Lillian—†	247	housewife	31	"
	M	Diaz Mary—†	247	millkeeper	35	"
	N	Bennett Earl	249	laborer	23	
	o	Bennett Nolia—†	249	housewife	67	"
	P	Larken Helen—†	249	"	46	
	R	Larken William	249	laborer	47	
	s	O'Keefe Cornelius	249	longshoreman	49	"
	T	Shephard Mary E—†	249	housewife	53	"
	v	Watts Herbert	251	U S N	23	174 Brooks
	w	Watts Mary—†	251	housewife	27	174 "
	x	Pardi Frank	251	retired	51	here
	y	Pardi Maria—†	251	housewife	50	"
	z	Benoit Augustus	253	seaman	64	"
1110						
	A	Pitts James	253	painter	38	"
	B	Scarpa Joseph	253	operator	24	"
	c	Scarpa Rosario	253	laborer	51	
	D*	Scarpa Rose—†	253	housewife	51	"
	E	Santoro Emily—†	253	stitcher	21	"
	F	Santoro Pasquale	253	laborer	58	
	G	Montana Rose—†	255	at home	63	"
	H	Cirillo Anthony	255	"	25	
	K	Cirillo Emma—†	255	"	24	"
	L	Cirillo Mary—†	255	housewife	48	"
	M	Attignano Josephine—†	255	"	46	"
	N	Attignano Louis	255	laborer	52	

Bennington Street—Continued

P	Simpson Concetta—†	257	housewife	68	335 Meridian
R	Ingersol James	257	mechanic	34	here
S	Ingersol Sarah—†	257	housewife	52	"
U	Antonelli Giuseppi	259	storekeeper	47	120 Princeton

Bremen Street

V	Sabatini Anthony	326	U S A	28	here
W	Sabatini Frances—†	326	housewife	25	"
X	Gaughan Anna—†	326	at home	28	407 Chelsea
Y	Gaughan Robert J	326	U S A	29	407 "
Z	Manfra Edward	326	"	20	here
	1111				
A	Manfra Jeremiah	326	longshoreman	54	407 Chelsea
B	Manfra Rose—†	326	housewife	50	407 "
C	Disario Emma—†	326	"	48	here
D	Disario Emma F—†	326	operator	21	"
E	Disario Gabriel	326	mechanic	53	"
F	Disario Gabriel J	326	U S A	23	
G	Disario George R	326	"	24	
H	Ranahan John J	344	longshoreman	38	"
K	Ranahan Mary A—†	344	cleaner	66	"
L	Ranahan Winifred M—†	344	stenographer	21	"
M	Chiampa James F	350	painter	37	"
N	Chiampa Margaret—†	350	housewife	32	"
O	DeRosa Katherine—†	350	"	28	
P	DeRosa Pasquale	350	painter	29	"
R	Lanney Frank	352	U S A	25	
S	Lanney Gerald	352	U S M C	21	"
T	*Lanney Josephine—†	352	housewife	48	"
U	Launey Michael	352	U S A	22	"
V	Lanney Nicholas	352	pedler	59	

Chelsea Street

W	Raso Palmia—†	303	housewife	32	here
X	Raso Rosolino	303	clerk	34	"
Y	Dadario Antonio	303	seaman	25	"
Z	Dadario Joseph	303	U S N	23	
	1112				
A	Dadario Luigi	303	laborer	62	"

Page.	Letter.	FULL NAME.	Residence, Jan. 1, 1945.	Occupation.	Supposed Age.	Reported Residence, Jan. 1, 1944. Street and Number.

Chelsea Street—Continued

	B	Dadario Secursa—†	303	housewife	59	here
	c	*Guardabosci Assunta—†	303	housekeeper	73	"
	D	Venuti Louisa—†	303	packer	45	"
	E	Venuti Mildred—†	303	operator	23	"
	F	Latorelli John	305	U S A	36	
	G	Latorelli Antonio	305	retired	62	
	H	Latorelli Michelina—†	305	housewife	61	"
	K	Driver Anna—†	305	housekeeper	26	"
	L	Driver John	305	U S N	31	"
	M	Sarro Edward	307	painter	24	"
	N	Sarro Jennie—†	307	housewife	23	"
	o	Bona Catherine—†	307	"	22	
	P	Bona Thomas	307	U S A	29	
	R	Genovitch Charles	307	seaman	21	"
	s	Genovitch John	307	U S A	28	
	T	*Genovitch Mary—†	307	housekeeper	62	"
	U	Speranza Agrippina—†	307	housewife	47	"
	V	Speranza John	307	U S A	23	
	w	Speranza Peter	307	"	21	"
	x	Speranza Santo	307	laborer	58	
	Y	Bishop Charles	309	meatcutter	39	"
	z	Bishop Elizabeth—†	309	housewife	33	"
1113						
	A	McGonagle Agnes J—†	309	tel operator	49	"
	B	McGonagle Ethel—†	309	housewife	33	"
	c	McGonagle Hilary J	309	policeman	37	"
	D	*Bossi Dominic	311	chauffeur	29	"
	E	Bossi Ida—†	311	housewife	29	"
	F	*Bonafina Frank	311	retired	66	
	G	*Bonafina Rosaria—†	311	housewife	62	"
	H	Simili Joseph	311	U S A	25	"
	K	Simili Lorenzo	311	laborer	58	
	L	*Simili Maria—†	311	housewife	52	"
	M	Simili Mary—†	311	candymaker	27	"
	N	Maffeo Christopher	313	shoemaker	42	"
	o	Maffeo Helen—†	313	housekeeper	37	"
	P	Consolo Concetta—†	313	housewife	37	",
	R	Consolo Felice	313	salesman	41	"
	s	Consolo Josephine—†	313	housekeeper	66	"
	T	Occhipinta Emily—†	313	housewife	54	116 Falcon
	U	Occhipinta Joseph	313	carpenter	61	116 "

Page.	Letter.	FULL NAME.	Residence, Jan. 1, 1945.	Occupation.	Supposed Age.	Reported Residence, Jan. 1, 1944. Street and Number.

Chelsea Street—Continued

Y	Frusciante Anthony	320	machinist	37	here
z	Frusciante Carmella—†	320	housewife	33	"
1114					
A	Frusciante Joseph	320	U S A	32	
B	Nuttoli Enrico	320	mechanic	56	"
C	Nuttoli Enrico	320	U S A	23	
D	Nuttoli Lucy—†	320	housewife	55	"
E	Langone Jerry	320	longshoreman	25	"
F	Langone Rockina—†	320	housewife	25	"
G	Grugnale Florence—†	322	"	22	
H	Grugnale William	322	U S A	23	"
K	Giambaresi Angelo	322	shoeworker	40	"
L	*Giambaresi Catherine—†	322	housekeeper	59	"
M	*Giambaresi Joseph	322	laborer	67	"
N	Broomstein Abraham	322	U S A	27	"
O	Wecker Jennie—†	322	housewife	30	"
P	Wecker Julian	322	electrician	34	"
R	*Capello Anna R—†	324	housekeeper	76	"
S	Velona Anna—†	324	"	93	"
T	Velona Anna—†	324	"	31	
U	Velona Antoinette—†	324	shoeworker	26	"
V	Velona Bruno	324	machinist	33	"
W	Velona Dominic	324	carpenter	55	"
X	Velona Hugo	324	U S A	22	"
Y	Velona Mary—†	324	housewife	53	"
z	Caruso Albert	324	U S N	23	
1115					
A	Caruso Alfred	324	"	25	
B	Caruso Elenora—†	324	secretary	28	"
C	Caruso Mary—†	324	operator	21	"
D	Miraglio Mary—†	324	housewife	53	"
E	Miraglio Vincent	324	tailor	57	"
F	*Vincent Bertha—†	326	housewife	56	"
G	*Vincent William	326	rigger	65	"
H	Fagone Ida T—†	326	housewife	45	"
K	Fagone Josephine M—†	326	operator	22	"
L	Fagone Sebastian	326	barber	50	"
M	*Mangino Filomena—†	326	housewife	71	"
N	Mangino Louis	326	retired	73	
O	LoDuca Cosimo	326	U S A	32	
P	*LoDuca Mary—†	326	at home	76	"

Chelsea Street—Continued

R	LoDuca Mary C—†	326	stitcher	35	here
s	DiMarino Anthony P	328	machinist	36	"
T	DiMarino Theresa—†	328	housewife	32	"
U	Coriani Catherine M—†	328	"	31	
V	Coriani Emilio G	328	machinist	36	"
Y	*DiMarino Antoinetta—†	328	housewife	68	"
Z	DiMarino Constanzo	328	retired	73	
W	Fagone Agrippino J	328	pipefitter	33	"
X	Fagone Mary C—†	328	housewife	35	"
	1116				
A	Corbett George P	330	fisherman	52	"
B	Dunbar Charles H	330	U S A	22	
c	Dunbar Mary J—†	330	housewife	51	"
D	Fagone Frank	330	retired	68	"
E	Fagone Georgia C—†	330	housewife	34	"
F	Fagone Louis J	330	meter reader	36	"
G	Fagone Josephine A—†	330	instructor	28	"
H	Fagone Mary—†	330	stitcher	46	"
L	Cioffi Frank	331	U S M C	24	"
M	Cioffi Fred	331	U S N	21	
N	Cioffi Joseph	331	baker	56	
O	Cioffi Rose—†	331	housewife	54	"
P	Cioffi Sigismondi	331	U S A	22	"
R	Crowell Julia M—†	332	housewife	63	"
s	Fielding Annie J—†	332	housekeeper	56	"
T	Fielding Esther T—†	332	toolmaker	48	"
U	Ormond Eizabeth—†	332	at home	68	"
V	Sullivan Frances J—†	332	housewife	65	"
W	Sullivan Mary J—†	332	clerk	27	"
X	Sullivan William L	332	"	65	
Y	Sacco Daniel	333	baker	56	"
Z	Sacco Viola—†	333	housewife	34	"
	1117				
A	*Masciola Mary—†	333	housekeeper	66	"
B	Barron Helen—†	334	housewife	32	"
c	Barron Jacob	334	manager	43	"
D	Baron Bessie R—†	334	packer	37	"
E	*Baron Fanny—†	334	housekeeper	67	"
F	Marino Nelson M	334	laborer	41	"
G	Marino Ralph F	334	U S A	20	
H	Marino Rita M—†	334	housewife	39	"

11

Page.	Letter.	FULL NAME.	Residence, Jan. 1, 1945.	Occupation.	Supposed Age.	Reported Residence, Jan. 1, 1944. Street and Number.

K	Ibabi Adeline—†	335	operator	52	here
L	Riley Gertrude M—†	337	finisher	50	"
N	Minichello Dorothy—†	339	welder	21	"
O	Minichello Elvira—†	339	housewife	49	"
P	Minichello Nicholas	339	U S N	27	
R	Collins Arthur H	339	chauffeur	35	"
S	Collins Margaret H—†	339	housewife	74	"
T	Collins William C	339	policeman	44	"
U	Levee Minnie—†	339	housewife	73	"
V	Coughlin Catherine—†	339	"	76	
W	Coughlin Matthew J	339	machinist	48	"
X	LaBlanc Albert S.	341	cook	59	"
Y	LaBlanc Maude A—†	341	housewife	55	"
Z	Young Elina M—†	341	"	46	
	1118				
A	Young Elmer H	341	painter	48	..
B	Cioffi Olando D	342	welder	29	
C	Cioffi Theresa M—†	342	housewife	29	"
D	Dedulonus Francis J	342	painter	31	..
E	Dedulonus Phyllis L—†	342	housewife	31	"
F	Gravalese Domenica—†	342	"	23	186 Marion
G	Gravalese Victor	342	plumber	26	186 "
H	Casaratano Guy	344	operator	46	here
K	*D'Avella Margaret—†	344	housewife	59	"
L	D'Avella Mario	344	U S A	23	"
M	D'Avella Pasquale	344	laborer	60	
N	Candelora Frank	344	machinist	25	"
O	Candelora Rose—†	344	housewife	25	"
P	Dorso John M	346	rigger	37	"
R	Dorso Leona G—†	346	housewife	43	"
S	Shepard Robert M	346	U S N	37	
T	*Shepard Sadie—†	346	housewife	42	"
U	Doyle Mary L—†	346	"	37	
V	Doyle Paul F	346	operator	41	"
W	Jacobs William R	346	U S A	39	
Z	*DiNatale Catherine—†	352	at home	35	"
	1119				
A	Ruggiero Angelo	352	laborer	25	354 Chelsea
B	Ruggiero Antonio	352	carpenter	55	354 "
C	Ruggiero Jerry	352	U S A	22	354 "
D	Ruggiero Rose—†	352	housewife	53	354 "

Page	Letter	Full Name.	Residence, Jan. 1, 1945.	Occupation.	Supposed Age.	Reported Residence, Jan. 1, 1944. Street and Number.

Chelsea Street—Continued

	Letter	Full Name.	Res.	Occupation.	Age	Reported Residence
	E	Santosuosso Jeremiah	354	fireman	38	here
	F	Santosuosso Josephine—†	354	housewife	36	"
	G	DeMarco Annie—†	354	"	50	356 Chelsea
	H	DeMarco Pasquale	354	candymaker	51	356 "
	L	Gordon Lawrence M	356	laborer	38	here
	M	Mortiner Catherine T—†	356	housewife	46	"
	N	Mortiner Mary A—†	356	clerk	21	"
	O	Amato Patrick	356	electrician	22	54 London
	P	Amato Yolanda—†	356	housewife	20	54 "
	R	Salovsky Jacob	356	electrician	29	Weymouth
	S	Salovsky Muriel J—†	356	housewife	20	"
	T	Fisher Clara E—†	358	waitress	40	here
	U	*Theotakake Pauline—†	358	at home	51	"

Lexington Street

	Letter	Full Name.	Res.	Occupation.	Age	Reported Residence
	X	Marrotta Charles	195	presser	42	here
	Y	Marrotta Mary—†	195	housewife	33	"
	Z	Barbetto Catherina—†	195	"	52	"
		1120				
	A	Barbetto Gilda—†	195	student	20	"
	B	Barbetto James	195	brazier	30	
	C	Barbetto John	195	sausagemaker	58	"
	E	Luti Frank	197	electrician	30	"
	F	Luti Jennie—†	197	housewife	29	"
	G	Malafonte Nicholas	197	laborer	20	
	H	Malafonte Theresa—†	197	seamstress	49	"
	K	*Raimondi Mary—†	199	housewife	42	"
	L	Raimondi Tancredi	199	mason	45	"
	M	Ricciardelli Antonio	199	laborer	53	
	N	Ricciardelli Mary—†	199	housewife	49	"
	O	*Ricciardelli Rachael—†	199	at home	86	"
	R	Powers Mary —†	201	"	76	"
	S	Cronin Jerome	203	chauffeur	27	93 London
	T	Cronin Josephine—†	203	housewife	24	93 "
	U	Bernard Charles	203	U S A	20	here
	V	Bernard Irene—†	203	housewife	44	"
	W	Bernard Joseph I ·	203	shipfitter	45	"
	X	D'Amelio Emma—†	205	housewife	32	"
	Y	D'Amelio Eugene	205	tester	35	
	Z	Fonti Joseph	207	candymaker	42	"

Page.	Letter.	FULL NAME.	Residence, Jan. 1, 1945.	Occupation.	Supposed Age.	Reported Residence, Jan. 1, 1944. Street and Number.

1121

Lexington Street—Continued

A	Fonti Vincenza—†	207	operator	34	here
B	Giangreco Anthony	207	physician	26	"
c	*Giangreco Diega—†	207	housewife	56	"
D	Giangreco Josephine—†	207	operator	30	"
E	Morabito Domenic	207	cutter	56	110 Paris
F	Morabito Michael T	207	U S A	23	110 "
G	Morabito Rose—†	207	housewife	48	110 "
H	Morabito Sadie—†	207	at home	27	110 "
K	Doherty Gertrude—†	209	painter	22	here
L	Doherty John W	209	U S N	27	"
M	*Surette Celina—†	209	housewife	48	"
N	Surette Frances A—†	209	painter	20	
o	Surette William F	209	rigger	50	
P	Giacchetto Ignacio	209	driller	38	"
R	Giacchetto Thomasina—†	209	housewife	34	"
s	Ciasullo Eugene	211	rigger	43	
T	Ciasullo Ida—†	211	housewife	33	"
U	Pagliarulo Emilio	211	retired	69	
v	Camuso Aurora—†	213	bookkeeper	23	"
w	Camuso Elga—†	213	housewife	60	"
x	Camuso Gilda—†	213	bookkeeper	22	"
Y	Camuso Pasquale	213	tailor	60	"
z	Camuso Pasquale G	213	U S N	20	

1122

A	Hutchinson Margaret C-†	213	housewife	31	"
B	Hutchinson Richard J	213	foreman	38	"
c	Barravechio Angelo	213A	mechanic	38	"
D	*Barravechio Giovanna—†	213A	housekeeper	78	"
E	Mercandante Antolnetta—†	215	saleswoman	22	"
F	Mercandante Josephine-†	215	stock girl	21	"
G	Mercandante Michael	215	foreman	44	"
H	Mercandante Theresa—†	215	housewife	46	"
K	Mercandante Anthony	215	shoeworker	67	"
L	Mercandante Antolnetta—†	215	housewife	65	"
M	Mercandante Gaetano	215	millhand	28	"
N	Mercandante Mary—†	215	"	31	
o	Courtoglous Annie—†	215	housewife	52	"
P	Courtoglous Constantine	215	U S A	20	
R	Courtoglous Theodore	215	cook	54	
s	Thompson John F	215	U S A	28	"

14

Lexington Street—Continued

T *D'Agostino Grace—†	217	housewife	65	here
U D'Agostino Rosario	217	foreman	31	"
V D'Agostino Salvatore	217	retired	76	"
W D'Agostino Josephine—†	217	housewife	38	"
X D'Agostino Salvatore	217	plumber	39	"
Y Bonasera Joseph	217	pressman	50	"
Z Bonasera Salvatore	217	student	21	"

1123

A Bonasera Theresa—†	217	housewife	40	"
B Trainor Anna G—†	219	"	41	
C Trainor Frederick J	219	messenger	21	"
D Trainor James E	219	stevedore	45	"
E Cotter Frederick J	219	machinist	69	"
F Cotter Mary J—†	219	at home	66	"
G Lombardi Augustus	219	carpenter	23	195 Marion
H Lombardi Doris—†	219	housewife	20	7 Patterson way
K Burke Felix	221	metalworker	47	here
L Burke Helen—†	221	housewife	42	"
M Brown Lawrence	221	carpenter	39	"
N *Doucette Simon	221	retired	91	
O Geddry Frank	221	carpenter	72	"
P *Geddry Sarah—†	221	housewife	63	"
R Preshong Elizabeth—†	221	supervisor	30	"
S Preshong Zetha—†	221	housewife	57	"
T Thorne Pauline—†	223	"	31	"
U Thorne Richard	223	manager	37	"
V Callahan Catherine F—†	223	at home	55	"
W Callahan Isabell M—†	223	secretary	53	"
X Latteriello Luigi	225	mechanic	35	"
Y Latteriello Rose—†	225	housewife	30	"
Z Duchi Anita—†	225	stitcher	29	"

1124

A Duchi Hugo	225	tailor	57	
B Duchi Julia—†	225	housewife	53	"
C *Ferrara Fidelina—†	225	at home	79	"
D Corbett Elizabeth—†	225	housewife	59	"
E Corbett Henry D	225	painter	55	"
F Corbett Robert	225	chauffeur	31	"
G Delmont Henry	225	"	22	
H DeGregorio Mario	227	shipfitter	37	"
K DeGregorio Olga—†	227	housewife	37	"

Page.	Letter.	Full Name.	Residence, Jan. 1, 1945.	Occupation.	Supposed Age.	Reported Residence, Jan. 1, 1944. Street and Number.

Lexington Street—Continued

	L	Maravas Bessie—†	227	housewife	45	here
	M	Maravas Ethel—†	227	operator	22	"
	N	Maravas George	227	U S M C	20	"
	O	Maravas Michael	227	proprietor	50	"
	P	Maravas Stella—†	227	clerk	23	"
	R	Romano Columbus	235	U S A	23	"
	S	Romano John	235	retired	67	
	T	Romano Joseph	235	U S N	20	
	U	*Romano Nancy—†	235	housewife	61	"
	V	Oricchio Domenic	235	U S A	24	
	W	Oricchio Enrico	235	leatherwkr	58	"
	X	*Oricchio Lena—†	235	spinner	50	"
	Y	*Oricchio Michael	235	weaver	30	
	Z	Oricchio Nicholas	235	U S A	23	
1125						
	A	Sullivan Edward	237	machinist	43	170 Lexington
	B	Sullivan Rose—†	237	operator	33	170 "
	C	Frati Augustine	237	chauffeur	47	83 Brooks
	D	Frati Margaret—†	237	housewife	36	83 "
	E	Mercuri Frank	237	messenger	20	here
	F	Mercuri Mary—†	237	packer	23	"
	G	DiPerri Calogero	239	laborer	58	"
	H	DiPerri Charles	239	U S A	20	
	K	DiPerri John	239	pleater	28	"
	L	DiPerri Vincenza—†	239	housewife	47	"
	M	Abate Alfred	239	U S A	27	
	N	Abate Elvino	239	chef	26	
	O	Abate Mary—†	239	stitcher	21	"
	P	Abate Rose—†	239	clerk	25	
	R	DeLorenzo Frank	239	shipfitter	36	"
	S	DeLorenzo Phyllis—†	239	stitcher	27	"
	T	Mattera Josephine—†	239	housewife	30	"
	U	Mattera Salvatore	239	longshoreman	30	"
	V	Bonugli Frank	241	metalworker	44	90 White
	W	Bonugli Margaret—†	241	housewife	40	90 "
	X	Williams Edward	241	shipfitter	34	90 "
	Y	Perry Frank A	241	"	44	here
	Z	Perry Helen—†	241	housewife	38	"
1126						
	A	Butare Angelo	241	U S A	34	
	B	Burare Antoinette—†	241	packer	31	

16

Lexington Street—Continued

c	Gangi Jean—†	243	housewife	33	here
d	Gangi Sam	243	polisher	34	"
e	Berardino Emilio	243	U S N	29	"
f	Berardino Francesca—†	243	housewife	30	"
g	Ricciardelli Antonio	243	tailor	44	"
h	Ricciardelli Jennie—†	243	housewife	38	"
k	Paterno Anthony	243½	U S A	32	
l	Paterno Theresa—†	243½	stitcher	28	"
m	Tennerini Louise—†	243½	instructor	26	"
n	*Tennerini Maria—†	243½	housewife	54	"
o	Cestone Anthony	245	metalworker	32	"
p	Cestone Daniel J	245	clerk	21	
r	Cestone Pasquale	245	weaver	54	"
s	*Cestone Pauline—†	245	housewife	52	"
t	Montatto Mary A—†	245	dressmaker	25	"
u	Montatto Vincent J	245	cutter	24	"
v	Borden Albert	245	machinist	28	"
w	Borden Celia—†	245	housewife	29	"
x	Daddio Genaro	247	barber	47	
y	Daddio Rose—†	247	candyworker	38	"
z	Cusenza Anna—†	247	housewife	28	"
	1127				
a	Cusenza Joseph	247	machinist	40	"
b	Daddio Josephine—†	247	housewife	37	"
c	Daddio Luigi	247	coppersmith	50	"
d	Dalton Michael L	249	painter	37	"
e	Dalton Phyllis—†	249	housewife	28	"
f	Rios Alfred	249	rigger	27	
g	Rios Beatrice—†	249	housewife	27	"
h	Muratore Sabina—†	249	"	31	
k	Muratore William	249	pipefitter	33	"
l	Amiro Harold	251	engineer	47	"
m	Amiro Julia—†	251	housewife	43	"
n	Caruccio Albert	251	pressman	20	"
o	Caruccio Angelina—†	251	housewife	47	"
p	Caruccio Frank	251	bartender	52	"
r	Caruccio Michael	251	U S A	23	"
s	Ferri Albert	253	packer	51	
t	Ferri Jenny—†	253	stitcher	45	"
u	Sargent Catherine—†	253	housewife	32	"
v	Sargent Joseph	253	fisherman	41	"

Page.	Letter.	Full Name.	Residence, Jan. 1, 1945.	Occupation.	Supposed Age.	Reported Residence, Jan. 1, 1944. Street and Number.

Lexington Street—Continued

	w	Centracchio Dominic	253	retired	78	here
	x	Centracchio Giovanna—†	253	housewife	52	"
	y	Barletta Carmen	263	toolmaker	20	Revere
	z	Barletta Evelyn—†	263	housewife	20	Newton
1128						
	a	Bertulli Alfred	263	riveter	35	here
	b	Bertulli Edith—†	263	housewife	32	"
	c	Fitzgerald Herbert	263	machinist	26	"
	d	Fitzgerald Rose—†	263	housewife	25	"
	f	Smith Catherine—†	265	"	25	
	g	Smith Robert W	265	metalworker	30	"
	h	Maylor Clyde	265	electrician	40	"
	k	Maylor Hilda—†	265	housewife	31	"
	l	Cavagnaro Josephine—†	267	attendant	33	"
	m	Chiarello Guy	267	presser	24	154 Princeton
	n	Chiarello Phyllis—†	267	housewife	23	154 "
	o	Ferrara Margaret E—†	267	"	34	256 Lexington
	p	Ferrara Rocco	267	chauffeur	37	256 "
	s	Galluccio Edward	269	U S A	21	here
	t	Galluccio Egidio	269	laborer	48	"
	r	Galluccio Emelia—†	269	housewife	42	"
	u	Galluccio Gabriel	269	U S A	23	"
	v	Hubbard Earl F	269	U S N	23	6 Brooks
	w	Hubbard Katherine M—†	269	housewife	31	6 "
	x	Galligan Victoria—†	269	"	46	here
	y	Gatchell Hazel M—†	271	waiter	45	"
	z	Crowley Catherine—†	271	housewife	26	"
1129						
	a	Crowley John F	271	fireman	29	"
	b	Danilchuk Joseph	273	U S A	24	
	c	Danilchuk Laura—†	273	housewife	43	"
	d	Houts James	273	U S N	24	California
	e	Houts Lillian—†	273	housewife	20	here
	f	Swindell Cleon	273	U S N	26	"
	g	Swindell Ruth—†	273	housewife	21	"
	h	Serino Fonsina—†	273	stitcher	21	"
	k	*Serino Giovani	273	carpenter	59	"
	l	Serino Joseph	273	U S A	28	
	m	*Serino Locressia—†	273	housewife	55	"
	n	Serino Pompelia—†	273	dressmaker	22	"
	o	Amerena Anna—†	273	housewife	34	"

18

Lexington Street—Continued

P	Amerena Frank	273	carpenter	37	here
R	Wood Charles J	275	inspector	47	"
S	Wood Ethel M—†	275	housewife	42	"
T	Nickerson Elmer	275	chauffeur	45	"
U	Nickerson Mary A—†	275	housewife	40	"
V	Silva Americo	275	machinist	37	"
W	Silva Mary H—†	275	housewife	33	"
X	Porter Mildred—†	279	"	44	
Y	*Porter Raeine	279	laborer	58	"
Z	Bordieri Anna—†	279	stitcher	25	"
	1130				
A	Bordieri Paul	279	mason	54	"
B	Busheme Josephine—†	279	housewife	28	"
C	Poto Antonette—†	279	"	39	
D	Poto John	279	musician	42	"
E	Scapicchio Angelo	279	U S N	23	"
F	Scapicchio Sophie—†	279	housewife	20	"
G	Pelosi Angelo J	281	electrician	26	"
H	Pelosi Catherine—†	281	housewife	22	"
K	Pecorella Angela—†	281	"	36	"
L	*McCue John	281	longshoreman	45	"
M	*McCue Mary—†	281	housewife	42	"
N	Critch Charles W	283	chipper	28	9 Lamont
O	Critch Josephine—†	283	housewife	27	9 "
P	Quigley Helen—†	283	"	38	here
R	Quigley William	283	meat packer	42	"
S	Hilton Elizabeth—†	283	housewife	24	"
T	Hilton Frank J	283	U S N	26	
V	Hughes Kathleen L—†	283	secretary	26	"
U	Hughes Thomas A	283	deckhand	48	"
W	*Ramos Raymond	285	machinist	45	126 Meridian
Y	Henderson Daniel	285	U S A	29	here
Z	Henderson Martha—†	285	housewife	29	"
	1131				
A	Machado John F	287	retired	37	
B	Machado Marie S—†	287	housewife	63	"
C	Machado Rose—†	287	typist	33	
D	Machado Zeferino	287	retired	80	"
E	Musidelli Anthony	289	gardener	58	"
F	Musidelli Marie—†	289	housewife	49	"
G	Rodrigues Anthony	291	laborer	42	

Lexington Street—Continued

H	*Rodrigues Antonette—†	291	housewife	33	here
K	Cristallo Jeremiah	291	baker	40	"
L	Cristallo Lucy—†	291	housewife	35	"
M	O'Keefe Anna E—†	293	"	48	
N	O'Keefe David	293	pumpman	49	"
R	Fiore Anthony J	295	pipefitter	30	"
S	Fiore Rita I—†	295	housewife	30	"
T	Scandurra Jeanette—†	295	"	27	
U	Scandurra Vincent R	295	U S A	25	
V	Gallo Eugene	295	pressman	49	"
W	Gallo Madeline—†	295	packer	20	
X	Gallo Mary—†	295	at home	23	"
Y	*Gallo Rose—†	295	housewife	52	"
Z	Santoro Grace—†	295	presser	32	
	1132				
A	Vaiarella Angelo	297	fishcutter	21	"
B	Vaiarella Mary—†	297	housewife	23	"
D	Mazzone Clara—†	297	"	46	
C	Mazzone Onofrio	297	molder	46	"
E	Polito Charles	297	U S A	31	
F	*Polito Filomena—†	297	housewife	54	"
G	Polito Joseph	297	laborer	55	
H	Polito Peter	297	U S A	22	
K	Polito Vincenzo	297	seaman	21	
L	Ledoux Angelina—†	299	housewife	30	"
M	*Ledoux Rosario U	299	operator	39	"
N	Goulet Leo P	299	welder	27	
O	Goulet Mary—†	299	housewife	25	"
P	Fahey Margaret—†	299	housekeeper	68	"
R	Mietzner Olga S—†	301	housewife	38	"
S	Mietzner William A	301	electrician	42	"
T	Palmunen Maria L—†	301	housewife	72	"
U	Palmunen Otto N	301	foreman	64	"
V	Coady James T	301	operator	60	"
W	Coady Mary L—†	301	housewife	66	"
X	Keough Charles F	303	operator	49	"
Y	Keough Donald P	303	U S N	22	
Z	Keough Marie C—†	303	housewife	45	"
	1133				
A	Greeley Marion—†	305	"	38	"
B	Giangrande Caroline—†	307	"	27	Somerville

Lexington Street—Continued

c	Giangrande Domenic	307	chauffeur	36	Somerville
d	Murray Jennie—†	307	housekeeper	63	here
e	Rothwell Harry	307	laborer	50	"
f	Turco Cynthia—†	307	housewife	36	"
g	Baker Donald A	309	U S N	25	
h	Baker Florence E—†	309	housewife	25	"
k	Malone Adeline—†	309	"	31	
l	Malone Francis	309	chauffeur	40	"
m	Langford Catherine—†	309	cook	41	
n	McGlew Mary—†	309	housekeeper	50	"
o	McGlew William	309	longshoreman	45	"
p	Spencer Ruth—†	309	clerk	23	
r	Kelsen Annie—·†	311	housekeeper	61	"
s	Kelsen Donald	311	U S C G	24	"
t	Russo Louis L	311	rigger	36	
u	Russo Margaret—†	311	housewife	30	"
v	Sleeper Alice—†	311	"	55	
w	Sleeper Frederick W	311	salesman	58	"
x	Britt Mary—†	311	housewife	48	"
y	Britt Michael	311	laborer	50	
z	Arena Antonio	313	U S N	23	

1134

a*	Arena Giuseppina—†	313	housekeeper	53	"
b	Matt Caroline—†	313	housewife	32	"
c	Matt Michael	313	mechanic	33	"
d	Scarpa Alfred	313	U S A	20	
e	Scarpa Ennocene—†	313	housewife	40	"
f	Scarpa Ralph N	313	mechanic	48	"

Prescott Street

g	Baresi Frances—†	31	stitcher	23	here
h	Barresi Ignatius	31	U S N	25	27 Maverick sq
k	Caruso Carmen	31	fireman	56	here
l	Caruso Ignatius	31	engineer	31	"
m	Caruso Lillian—†	31	housewife	49	"
n	Caruso Sylvia—†	31	"	24	
o	Meads Julia—†	33	"	47	
p	Meads Manuel	33	engineer	51	"
r	Mozinski Bernard	35	U S N	24	282 Lexington
s	Mozinski Ruth—†	35	housewife	22	282 "

Prescott Street—Continued

T	Nunes Anna—†	35	inspector	50	282 Lexington
U	Nunes Joseph	35	retired	50	282 "
V	Nunes Joseph E	35	engineer	24	282 "
W	Kerrigan Louis A	35	laborer	54	here
X	Kerrigan Louis J	35	U S N	21	"
Y	Kerrigan Mary—†	35	housewife	51	"
Z	Saulnier Bertha—†	37	saleswoman	22	90 White

1135

A	Saulnier Catherine—†	37	stenographer	20	90 "
B	Saulnier Edmund	37	shipfitter	54	90 "
C	Saulnier Levina—†	37	housewife	45	90 "
D	Saulnier Richard	37	shipper	23	90 "
E	Sequeira Frank	37	seaman	33	here
F	Sequeira Helen—†	37	housewife	28	"
G	Costa Manuel	47	retired	45	"
H	Dagenais George	47	cleaner	36	
K	Fielding Joseph	47	printer	52	"
L	Jones John	47	laborer	50	446 Lubec
M	Keefe John	47	pipefitter	45	here
N	MacDonald John	47	laborer	33	"
O	Oliver George	47	retired	76	"
P	Wilson Archie	47	boilermaker	50	"
R	Murray Anna—†	49	housewife	52	"
S	Murray Arthur	49	shipper	56	"
T	Cobuccio Agnes—†	51	housewife	26	23 Barton
U	Cobuccio Joseph	51	laundrywkr	30	23 "
V	Stoumbelis Catherine—†	77	housewife	30	here
W	Stoumbelis Nicholas	77	storekeeper	41	"
Z	Carroll Agnes—†	79	housewife	69	"

1136

A	Mitchell Anna—†	79	"	76	
B	Cosgrove Alice E—†	81	"	64	
D	Garuti Agnes—†	93	laundrywkr	36	"
E	Lamborghini Arthur	93	U S N	22	"
F	Lamborghini Mary—†	93	housewife	56	"
G	Lamborghini Robert	93	technician	24	"
H	Mondello Ethel—†	95	housewife	45	"
K	Mondello Frank	95	laundrywkr	53	"
L	Boncore Alma—†	97	housewife	24	"
M	Boncore Angelo	97	welder	25	
N	Lamborghini Charles	97	U S A	26	

Prescott Street—Continued

o	Lamborghini Dora—†	97	assembler	24	here
p	Lucci Josephine—†	97	housewife	53	"
r	Lucci Josephine—†	97	checker	23	"
s	Lucci Michael	97	cooper	55	

Princeton Place

t	Gugliucciello Anna—†	1	clerk	30	here
u	Gugliucciello Jessie—†	1	electrician	44	"
v	Gugliucciello Josephine—†	1	clerk	31	"
w	*Gugliucciello Sabato	1	bootblack	75	"

Princeton Street

x	*Tusa Frank	200	retired	70	193 Lexington
y	*Tusa Rosaria—†	200	housewife	67	193 "
z	Balzotti Charles	200	manager	33	here
	1137				
a	Balzotti Nancy—†	200	housewife	34	"
b	Carino Joseph	200	clerk	22	
c	Carino Marita—†	200	housewife	24	"
d	Cotreau Adrian	201	fisherman	51	"
e	Cotreau Bernard	201	fishcutter	45	"
f	Cotreau George	201	fisherman	49	"
g	Cotreau Herman	201	fishcutter	40	"
h	Cotreau Mark	201	fisherman	54	"
k	*Cotreau Mary—†	201	housekeeper	77	"
l	Livingstone Duncan	201	maintenance	59	"
m	Livingstone Francis	201	U S A	24	"
n	Livingstone George—†	201	U S M C	22	"
o	Livingstone John A	201	U S N	27	
p	Livingstone Lawrence R	201	U S A	26	
r	Livingstone Mary A—†	201	housewife	59	"
s	Livingstone Mary A—†	201	saleswoman	32	"
t	Livingstone Robert D	201	U S N	20	
u	Polcari Anthony	201	drawtender	46	"
v	Polcari Louis	201	painter	41	
w	*Polcari Marie—†	201	housekeeper	71	"
x	Barletta Angelina—†	202	housewife	20	"
y	Barletta Angelo	202	U S A	25	
z	*Barletta John	202	retired	69	

23

1138
Princeton Street—Continued

A	Barletta Lawrence	202	machinist	31	here
B	*Barletta Lisandrea—†	202	housewife	64	"
C	Barletta Evelyn—†	202	"	25	"
D	Barletta Geriacco	202	U S N	27	
E	McDonald Josephine R—†	203	housewife	22	"
F	McDonald Lloyd	203	U S N	21	
G	Principato Henrietta—†	203	housewife	50	"
H	Principato Joseph	203	plumber	47	"
K	Flaschner Caroline—†	203	housewife	42	"
L	Flaschner Leo H	203	chauffeur	44	"
M	Giovino Patrick	203	pipefitter	40	"
N	Giovino Rose—†	203	housewife	36	"
O	Serra Carl A	204	electrician	40	"
P	Serra Rose—†	204	housewife	37	"
R	Cleary Dorothy K—†	204	packer	32	"
S	Cleary Herbert C	204	chauffeur	26	"
T	Cleary M Flossie—†	204	at home	24	"
U	Cleary Sarah L—†	204	housekeeper	62	"
V	Lombard Edward P	204	accountant	33	"
W	Rossetti Andrew	204	laborer	24	"
X	Rossetti Antonetta—†	204	housewife	54	"
Y	Rossetti Pasquale	204	laborer	50	
Z	D'Entremont Caroline—†	205	housewife	50	"

1139

A	D'Entremont Joseph	205	fishcuter	53	"
B	Bonanno Anthony	205	U S M C	23	"
C	Bonanno Carmella—†	205	housewife	50	"
D	Bonanno Mary J—†	205	operator	21	"
E	Bonanno Salvatore	205	rubberworker	61	"
F	*Geraci Santa—†	205	housekeeper	87	"
G	Caci Anna—†	205	stitcher	28	
H	Caci Benjamin	205	laborer	62	
K	Caci Joseph	205	U S A	31	
L	Caci Louise—†	205	housewife	61	"
M	Caci Rosalie—†	205	operator	22	"
N	Cornacchia Antonio	206	shipper	26	"
O	Cornacchia Esther—†	206	housewife	27	"
P	Clark Harold	206	U S A	25	
R	Clark Nellie—†	206	housekeeper	55	"
S	DeFraitas John	206	U S A	30	"

24

Princeton Street—Continued

T	LaTorre Liborio	206	tilesetter	63	here
U	*Inserra Angelina—†	207	housewife	56	"
V	Inserra Jennie—†	207	packer	28	"
W	Inserra Luigi	207	retired	62	"
X	Inserra Vito	207	U S A	26	"
Y	Inserra Yolanda—†	207	rubberworker	20	"
Z	*Francis Augusta—†	207	housewife	56	"

1140

A	Francis Edward	207	shipfitter	20	"
B	Francis Edwin L	207	U S A	27	"
C	Francis John L	207	rigger	62	
D	Francis John L, jr	207	U S A	21	
E	Muise Eileen—†	207	housewife	25	"
F	Muise John F	207	freighthandler	28	"
G	Gately Antonette—†	208	housekeeper	29	"
H	Connolly Emilia—†	208	housewife	43	"
K	Connolly Martin	208	laborer	48	
L	Connolly Mary—†	208	at home	62	"
M	Simons Louis	208	tailor	64	
N	Simons Pearl—†	208	housewife	57	"
O	Ribaudo Concetta—†	211	operator	21	"
P	Ribaudo Marie—†	211	housewife	45	"
R	Ribaudo Vincent J	211	U S A	23	"
S	Sapienza Marie—†	211	housewife	25	"
T	Sapienza Peter L	211	U S A	26	Everett
U	Trunfio Anthony	211	U S N	23	here
V	Trunfio Elena—†	211	clerk	20	"
W	Trunfio Paul	211	pipecoverer	52	"
X	Trunfio Philomena—†	211	housewife	46	"
Y	*Scopa Carmella—†	211	"	68	
Z	Scopa Elvira—†	211	packer	28	
¹Z	Scopa Paul	211	laborer	64	"

1141

A	Matthews Catherine—†	212	housewife	46	"
B	Matthews Wallace	212	mechanic	45	"
C	Bickford Leslie	212	longshoreman	45	"
D	Bickford Loretta—†	212	housewife	30	"
E	Lutanno Mary—†	213	"	26	
F	Lutanno Michael	213	pipefitter	29	"
G	Racca Rose—†	213	housewife	47	"
H	Racca Salvatore	213	shoeworker	50	"

Princeton Street—Continued

K	Curry Isabella—†	213	housewife	47	here
L	Curry James L	213	foreman	48	"
M	Hemenway Gerald	214	operator	26	"
N	Hemenway Seraphine—†	214	housewife	26	"
O	Gazziani Anne—†	214	dressmaker	34	"
P	Gazziani Generoso	214	laborer	33	
R	Gazziani Josephine—†	214	housewife	57	"
S	Gazziani Laura—†	214	clerk	20	"
T	Gazziani Mildred—†	214	boxmaker	22	"
U	*Gazziani Opino	214	retired	57	"
V	Barber Josephine—†	214	clerk	21	133 Havre
W	Bentureira Antonio	214	fireman	48	133 "
X	Bentureira Marie A—†	214	housewife	38	133 "
Y	Mazzarella Constance—†	215	"	33	here
Z	Mazzarella Frank	215	shoeworker	36	"
	1142				
A	Coffin Harold	215	welder	20	
B	Coffin Lucy—†	215	housewife	55	"
C	Coffin Mary B—†	215	stitcher	22	"
D	Coffin Melbourne	215	welder	48	
E	Perriello Caroline—†	215	housewife	40	"
F	Perriello Felix	215	painter	41	..
G	Perriello Vincent	215	U S A	20	
H	Castagna Enrico	216	barber	47	
K	Leno Albert	216	laborer	22	
L	Leno Mary—†	216	housewife	55	"
M	Bettini Charles S	216	printer	33	
N	Bettini Etta M—†	216	housewife	28	"
O	Garofolini Lena—†	216	"	43	
P	Garofolini Louis	216	painter	50	
R	Lynch David	217	"	45	
S	*Lynch Marjorie—†	217	housewife	36	"
T	Cassetta Palma—†	217	"	46	
U	Cassetta Salvatore	217	U S C G	48	"
V	Pastore Antonina—†	217	housewife	21	"
W	Pastore Frederick	217	inspector	25	"
X	Ellis Alexander	217	tailor	61	
Y	Ellis Sarah—†	217	housewife	56	"
Z	Ellis Sydney	217	U S A	36	
	1143				
A	Held Eva—†	217	housewife	26	"

Princeton Street—Continued

Page.	Letter.	FULL NAME.	Residence, Jan. 1, 1945.	Occupation.	Supposed Age.	Reported Residence, Jan. 1, 1944. Street and Number.
	B	Held Melvin	217	U S A	26	here
	C	Butari Joseph	218	U S N	29	"
	D	Butari Louise—†	218	housewife	25	"
	E	Hatch Jennie—†	218	"	30	
	F	Hatch Linwood	218	candyworker	33	"
	G	McCallum Archibald	218	U S N	25	
	H	McCallum Rosalie—†	218	housewife	23	"
	K	Lo Sciuto Mary—†	221	"	22	371 Sumner
	L	Lo Sciuto Thomas	221	machinist	29	371 "
	M	Mosca Claire—†	222	housewife	20	213 Trenton
	N	Mosca Nicholas	222	chauffeur	23	213 "
	O	Mosca Carmella—†	222	housewife	47	here
	P	Mosca Peter	222	foreman	51	"
	R	Rowe Frederick	223	fisherman	37	"
	S	Rowe Harriette—†	223	housewife	34	"
	T	Miniscalco Antonio rear	223	laborer	64	
	U	Miniscalco Domenica–† "	223	housewife	62	"
	V	Bellobona Anthony 2d "	223	carpenter	21	"
	W	*Bellobona Clementina—† 2d "	223	housewife	54	"
	X	Bellobona Generoso 2d "	223	carpenter	50	"
	Y	Bellobona Margaret—† 2d "	223	stitcher	25	"
	Z	Bellobona Theresa–† 2d "	223	paperworker	23	"
1144						
	A	Casaletto Augustino	224	plumber	30	181 Princeton
	B	Casaletto Mary—†	224	housewife	28	181 "
	E	Balliro Joseph, jr	226	chipper	27	here
	F	Balliro Vincenza—†	226	housewife	27	"
	G	Poirier Anthony	226	laborer	29	"
	H	Poirier Lena—†	226	housewife	27	"
	K	Lessa Adelaide—†	227	"	63	
	L	Lessa Carlo	227	shoeworker	63	"
	M	Lessa Charles	227	U S A	23	"
	O	Lessa Josephine—†	227	stenographer	28	"
	N	Lessa Mary F—†	227	embroiderer	32	"
	P	Lessa Michael	227	U S A	26	
	R	Lessa Vera F—†	227	clerk	30	"
	S	Hurley Clara—†	227	housewife	29	"
	T	Hurley James J	227	U S N	33	"
	U	Fortier Adelmar	227	shipper	34	"
	V	Fortier Mary—†	227	housewife	32	"
	W	Murley Chester	228	U S A	25	New York

Page.	Letter.	FULL NAME.	Residence, Jan. 1, 1945.	Occupation.	Supposed Age.	Reported Residence, Jan. 1, 1944. Street and Number.

Princeton Street—Continued

x	Murley Grace—†	228	housewife	21	Chelsea
y	Presterone Joseph	228	fireman	41	here
z	Presterone Rita—†	228	housewife	34	"
1145						
a	Smaldone Florence—†	228	"	37	"
b	Smaldone Henry	228	carpenter	40	"
c	Capuzzo Ines—†	229	housewife	35	102 Chelsea
d	Capuzzo Ubaldo	229	painter	41	102 "
e	Faretre Alphonso	229	electrician	28	here
f	Faretre Carman	229	"	29	"
g	Faretre Joseph	229	laborer	62	"
h	Faretre Mary—†	229	housewife	53	"
k	Woodard Edith—†	229	"	21	"
l	Woodard Robert M	229	U S N	24	"
m	Kinnear Esther M—†	231	housewife	70	"
n	Kinnear George E	231	chauffeur	69	"
o	Rogers John P	233	retired	75	
p	Rogers Joseph J	233	U S A	30	
r	Rogers Mary M—†	233	housewife	71	"
s	Miles Louise—†	234	dressmaker	26	"
t	Miles Margaret—†	234	housekeeper	48	"
u	Miles Michael J	234	lawyer	44	"
v	Miles William A	234	painter	46	"
w	Sampson Agnes—†	234	housewife	46	404 Saratoga
x	Sampson William	234	lumper	46	404 "
y	Gamache Clyde	236	U S A	28	8 Shelby
z	Gamache Stella—†	236	housewife	22	8 "
1146						
a	MacKay Hilma—†	236	"	29	317 Paris
b	MacKay James J	236	U S N	28	317 "
d	Sarno Anna E—†	237	housewife	27	here
e	Sarno Carman	237	contractor	30	"
f	Sarno Angelina—†	237	housewife	52	"
g	Sarno Joseph	237	U S M C	22	"
h	Sarno Onofrio	237	finisher	58	
k	Murphy Emilia—†	238	housewife	28	"
l	Murphy Raymond F	238	blacksmith	38	"
m	Feretti Piere—†	238	housekeeper	42	"
n	Geraci Anthony	238	U S A	28	"
o	Geraci Augustino	238	painter	55	"
p	Geraci Jennie—†	238	housewife	48	"

28

Princeton Street—Continued

R	Quinn George E	rear 238	laborer	72	here
s	Quinn Marjorie—†	" 238	housewife	37	"
u	Marley Alice R—†	239	"	41	"
v	Marley Fredérick H	239	B F D	41	"
w	Bossi Guido	240	U S A	27	
x	Bossi Joseph	240	laborer	63	"
y	Bossi Michael	240	"	20	
z	*Bossi Paolina—†	240	housewife	56	"

1147

A	Bossi Sylvia—†	240	"	27	
B	Furtado Concetta—†	240	"	26	
c	Furtado Frank	240	laborer	27	"
D	Morgera Angelina—†	240	housekeeper	38	218 Chelsea
E	Hurley Rita—†	241	housewife	25	15 Story
F	Hurley William L	241	fishcutter	28	15 "
G	Viscione Eugene	241	chauffeur	28	here
H	Viscione Mary A—†	241	housewife	28	"
K	Indingaro Arthur	242	operator	34	"
L	Indingaro Caroline—†	242	housewife	32	"
M	Jesus Alfred	242	laborer	44	"
N	Jesus Mary—†	242	housewife	43	"
o	Furtado Frank M	243	laborer	61	263 Lexington
P	*Furtado Mary E—†	243	housewife	61	263 "
R	Roach Herbert A	243	waiter	29	here
s	Roach Lawrence M	243	newsdealer	38	"
T	Roach Mary J—†	243	inspector	34	"
U	Roach Sarah—†	243	housewife	69	"
v	Babine Edmund	244	fishcutter	73	"
w	Babine Elizabeth—†	244	housewife	62	"
x	Babine Louis	244	U S A	36	"
y	Babine Peter	244	fishcutter	29	"
z	Babine Mary T—†	244	housewife	42	"

1148

A	Babine Simon	244	fishcutter	44	"
c	Ciccone Alexander	246	pipefitter	43	"
D	Ciccone Rose—†	246	housewife	40	"
E	Sarno Anthony L	246	U S A	25	
F	Sarno Christine—†	246	housewife	27	"
G	O'Donnell James H	247	kitchenman	54	"
H	O'Donnell Mary E—†	247	housewife	44	"
K	August Bernadette M—†	247	stenographer	23	"

Princeton Street—Continued

L	August Emanuel J	247	policeman	27	here
M	August Manuel F	247	carpenter	62	"
N	August Sarah F—†	247	housewife	61	"
O	Burnham Earl	247	letter carrier	62	"
P	Burnham Grace—†	247	housewife	55	"
R	Despouy Paul L	248	clergyman	68	"
S	Kelley Henry L	249	B F D	40	
T	Kelley Marie M—†	249	housewife	39	"
U	Pumphret Alice L—†	249	teacher	37	
V	Pumphret Michael J	249	retired	79	
W	Fulchino Ottino	250	clerk	23	
X	Fulchino Rose—†	250	housewife	21	"
Y	Trainor Georgiana—†	250	"	47	"
Z	Trainor John J	250	shipfitter	57	"
	1149				
A	Trainor John L	250	U S A	24	"
B	Trainor Robert L	250	"	23	··
C	*Fulchino Antonio	250	shoeworker	51	"
D	Fulchino Margaret—†	250	housewife	43	"
E	Fulchino Rose—†	250	stitcher	22	"
F	Owens Louise—†	251	teacher	50	
G	Anderson Mary—†	252	clerk	48	
H	Anderson Thomas F	252	U S N	22	"
K	Stevenson Anne—†	252	housekeeper	72	"
L	Borgess Henry L	252	cabinetmaker	56	"
M	Borgess Louise V—†	252	housewife	52	"
N	Shannon Edward P	252	electrician	46	"
O	Shannon Frederick L	252	mechanic	39	"
P	Shannon Mary—†	252	housekeeper	77	"
R	Venuti Florence—†	253	radioworker	29	1201 Benningt'n
S	Venuti Salvatore	253	U S A	30	1201 "
T	Murphy Mary E—†	253	housewife	57	here
U	Murphy Michael	253	laborer	60	"
V	Murphy Rita M—†	253	inspector	24	"
W	Lacurazza Anthony J	253	plater	34	
X	Lacurazza Lena—†	253	housewife	29	"
Y	Riccardi Filipia—†	255	"	26	
Z	DiFranza Americo M	255	U S A	25	··
	1150				
A	DiFranza Florence M—†	255	clerk	20	
B	DiFranza Joseph	255	U S A	28	

Princeton Street—Continued

c	*DiFranza Saveria—†	255	housewife	61	here
d	Malgioglio Joseph	255	presser	38	"
e	Malgioglio Marie T—†	255	housewife	35	"
g	Carco Constantine	262	machinist	43	188 Marion
h	Carco Josephine—†	262	housewife	45	188 "
k	Palange Anthony	262	retired	60	here
l	Palange Josephine—†	262	housewife	59	"
m	Troiano Joseph	262	manager	39	"
n	Troiano Rachael—†	262	housewife	31	"
o	Vena Ella—†	266	"	41	"
p	Vena John	266	chipper	41	"
r	Vena Antonette—†	266	housewife	62	"
s	Vena Pellegrino	266	bootblack	65	"
t	Kelly John L	266	laborer	51	..
u	Kelly John L, jr	266	U S N	27	
v	Kelly Margaret—†	266	housewife	51	"
x	Irwin Cathleen—†	268	"	38	
w	Irwin Edward	268	clerk	41	..
y	Petralia Frances—†	268	housewife	51	"
z	Petralia Sabastian	268	retired	71	

1151

a	Dumas Eugene J	268	millhand	46	"
b	Dumas Simone—†	268	housewife	34	"
c	Toscano Angelo	270	retired	66	
d	Toscano Carmella—†	270	housewife	24	"
e	Toscano Domenic	270	pipefitter	28	"
f	Antonelli Josephine—†	270	operator	31	4 Kearsarge av
g	Antonelli Michael	270	shoeworker	34	4 "
h	*DeMatteo Carmella—†	270	housewife	51	here
k	DeMatteo John	270	U S A	24	"
l	Hellen Emily—†	270	housewife	20	"
m	Nazzaro Caroline—†	270	"	33	
n	Nazzaro Joseph	270	welder	34	
o	DiFuria Angelina—†	272	housewife	56	"
p	DiFuria Carmello	272	laborer	61	
r	DiFuria Diana—†	272	packer	24	
s	DiFuria Lucy—†	272	clerk	28	
t	Contreau Albany	272	bartender	49	"
u	Pothier George	272	seaman	34	
v	Pothier Isadore	272	watchman	63	"
w	Pothier Madeline—†	272	housewife	37	"

Princeton Street—Continued

Page.	Letter.	Full Name.	Residence, Jan. 1, 1945.	Occupation.	Supposed Age.	Reported Residence, Jan. 1, 1944. Street and Number.
	x	Barrasso Armond	272	fireman	39	here
	y	Barrasso Margaret—†	272	housewife	39	"
	z	Nalen Anthony	274	longshoreman	42	"
1152						
	a	Nalen Gertrude M—†	274	housewife	34	"
	b	Currie Harriette—†	274	"	29	
	c	Currie Lawrence	274	boilermaker	29	"
	d	DeLuca Hilda—†	274	housewife	46	"
	e	DeLuca John	274	mechanic	42	"
	f	Saggese Ann—†	276	housewife	23	26 Trenton
	g	Saggese Patrick	276	chauffeur	28	26 "
	h	Chalmers Fred W	276	engineer	46	here
	k	Chalmers Fred W, jr	276	U S A	22	"
	l	Chalmers Mary—†	276	housewife	45	"
	m	Chalmers Melvin	276	U S M C	20	"
	n	Mitchell Elizabeth—†	276	housewife	37	"
	o	Mitchell Frederick	276	rigger	36	..
	p	*Scanlon Elizabeth—†	276	housewife	73	"
	r	*Anttila Carl	278	machinist	49	"
	s	Stenberg Anna—†	278	housewife	79	"
	t	Powers George	rear 278	U S N	30	"
	u	Powers Marjorie—†	" 278	housewife	24	"
	v	Bordieri Jennie—†	284	"	29	
	w	Bordieri Salvatore	284	supervisor	27	"
	x	*Capo Angelina—†	284	housewife	66	"
	y	Capo John B	284	factoryhand	64	"
	z	Messenger Mary—†	286	housewife	80	"
1153						
	b	Baldassaro Louis	286	U S A	32	
	c	Baldassaro Santalina—†	286	dressmaker	30	"
	d	*Hilton Catherine—†	288	housewife	85	"
	e	Hilton Richard F	288	U S A	20	
	f	*Shanahan Anna—†	288	housewife	79	"
	g	Shanahan Leo F	288	stevedore	40	"
	h	Shanahan Lillian F—†	288	housewife	40	"
	k	Shanahan Patrick	288	longshoreman	53	"
	l	Godwin Catherine—†	288	housewife	22	"
	m	Godwin Herman L	288	machinist	40	283 Princeton
	n	Aléxander Ellen—†	292	housewife	46	here
	o	Alexander Ernest L	292	U S N	20	"
	p	Dean Gertrude M—†	294	housewife	44	"

Princeton Street—Continued

R	Dean Ralph M	294	B F D	49	here
s	Donnelly Frances—†	294	housekeeper	80	"
T	Alexander Victor	296	supervisor	45	"
U	Alexander Winifred—†	296	housewife	40	"
v	Peterson Ernest	298	burner	26	
w	Peterson Irene—†	298	housewife	27	"
x	Smith Mary—†	298	housekeeper	55	"
Y	*Rossi Louis	300	laborer	62	"
z	*Rossi Rose—†	300	housewife	57	"
	1154					
A	Brady Frances—†	310	"	23	..
B	Brady Thomas	310	burner	23	
C	Walsh Charles A	310	machinist	30	"
D	Walsh Doris—†	310	housewife	30	"
E	Matt Elizabeth—†	310	"	28	342 Princeton
F	Matt Nicholas	310	shipfitter	35	342 "
K	Fabiano Frank	312	U S N	22	here
L	Fabiano Rocco	312	shipfitter	27	"
M	Fabiano Rose—†	312	housekeeper	50	"
N	Vitale Amalio	312	laborer	42	"
o	*Vitale Dorothy—†	312	housewife	73	"
P	Vitale James H	312	U S N	22	
R	Vitale Mary—†	312	candydipper	42	"
s	Saviano Philip	314	machinist	33	"
T	Saviano Phyllis—†	314	housewife	30	"
U	Simione Alfred	314	laborer	31	"
v	Simione Jennie—†	314	housewife	38	"
w	Albanese Domenic	314	laborer	66	..
x	Albanese Madeline—†	314	housewife	56	"
Y	Albanese Thomas	314	burner	26	
z	Gill Joseph P, jr	316	machinist	33	"
	1155					
A	Gill Phyllis—†	316	housewife	36	"
B	Briano Angelo F	316	rigger	34	
C	Briano Bessie—†	316	housewife	34	"
D	*Gill Gilamena—†	316	"	60	
E	*Gill Joseph P	316	longshoreman	64	"
F	Gill Manuel P	316	molder	25	"
G	Orlando Helen—†	318	housewife	26	"
H	Orlando John	318	carpenter	32	"
K	Siraco Domenic	318	retired	71	

1—11

Page.	Letter.	FULL NAME.	Residence, Jan. 1, 1945.	Occupation.	Supposed Age.	Reported Residence, Jan. 1, 1944. Street and Number.

Princeton Street—Continued

	L	Siraco Frank	318	upholsterer	47	here
	M	*Siraco Mary—†	318	housewife	71	"
	N	Tassa Camella—†	318	welder	20	"
	o	Tassa Mary—†	318	housewife	39	"
	P	Tassa Samuel	318	weaver	48	
	R	Connelly Josephine—†	320	housewife	32	"
	s	Connelly Lawrence P	320	clerk	34	
	T	Siraco Joseph	320	metalworker	41	"
	U	Siraco Mary—†	320	housewife	37	"
	V	Walker Margaret—†	320	"	24	
	w	Walker Ralph P	320	machinist	29	"
	x	Campbell Florence—†	322	housewife	65	"

1156   Putnam Street

	D	Harris George C	106	retired	71	here
	E	Harris Mary—†	106	housewife	69	90 Savin Hill av
	F	Colontino Leo	106	candymaker	64	here
	G	Colontino Mary—†	106	housewife	58	"
	H	Wyse Catherine—†	106	clerk	64	"
	K	Wyse John	106	operator	41	"
	L	Cerrato Carmella—†	108	housewife	36	"
	M	Cerrato Louis	108	pipefitter	41	"
	N	Frisoli Carmela—†	108	bookkeeper	22	"
	o	Frisoli Dominic	108	roaster	57	"
	P	Frisoli Gilda—†	108	housewife	47	"
	R	Frisoli Leonard	108	U S N	20	"
	s	Benvissuto John	108	barber	52	
	T	Benvissuto Mary—†	108	housewife	43	"
	U	*Hollander Emil	110	ironworker	66	"
	V	*Hollander Hilma—†	110	housewife	65	"
	w	Amundsen Andrew	112	painter	59	
	x	Jensen Annie—†	112	housewife	58	"
	Y	Jensen Anton	112	carpenter	64	"
	z	Jensen Ethel—†	112	clerk	24	"
		.1157				
	A	Amoroso Joseph	126	laborer	55	
	B	Amoroso Rose—†	126	housewife	48	"
	C	Amoroso Salvatore	126	U S C G	24	"
	D	Blunda Francesca—†	126	housewife	69	"

Putnam Street—Continued

E	Blunda Francesco	126	laborer	71	here
F	Blunda Ignazio	126	engineer	42	"
G	Blunda Jasper	126	U S A	38	"
H	Blunda Josephine—†	126	bookkeeper	31	"
K	Blunda Mary—†	126	clerk	33	
L	*Interbartolo Joseph	126	retired	82	
M	Matthews Joseph	126	ordnanceman	39	"
N	Matthews Mary—†	126	housewife	37	"
O	Caruso Frank	128	laborer	65	"
P	Ruotolo Angelo	128	pharmacist	25	"
R	Ruotolo Frank	128	laborer	62	
S	*Ruotolo Mary—†	128	housewife	65	"
T	Ruotolo Louis	128	steamfitter	35	"
U	Ruotolo Rose—†	128	housewife	32	"
V	Ruotolo Gerard	128	electrician	38	"
W	Ruotolo Helen—†	128	housewife	36	"
X	Caci Angelo	130	chauffeur	29	"
Y	Caci Petrina—†	130	housewife	27	"
Z	Lamonica Josephine—†	130	stitcher	50	"
	1158				
A	Lamonica Mildred—†	130	clerk	21	
B	Lamonica Santo	130	barber	68	
C	Nolan Catherine—†	130	supervisor	31	"
D	Nolan James R	130	clerk	57	"
E	Nolan Mary M—†	130	housewife	51	"
G	Perricotti Anna—†	140	"	35	
H	Perricotti Peter J	140	painter	40	"
K	*Salino Ralph	140	laborer	63	
L	*Salino Rose—†	140	housewife	61	"
M	Tranquillino Antonio	140	steamfitter	46	"
N	Hopp Alfred	141	electrician	39	111 Eutaw
P	Staffieri Anthony	141	barber	48	here
R	Staffieri Anthony	141	U S A	20	"
S	Staffieri Domenic	141	"	25	"
T	Staffieri Ralph	141	"	21	
U	Staffieri Thomasina—†	141	housewife	28	"
V	Mason Edward	142	retired	71	"
W	*Ardita Antonio	142	"	68	
X	*Ardita Mary—†	142	housewife	65	"
Y	Ardita Michael	142	U S A	27	
Z	Ardita Nicholas	142	U S N	35	

1159

Putnam Street—Continued

A	*Chiampa Nicholas	142	retired	77	here
B	Passariello Margaret—†	143	clerk	27	"
C	Santoro Alesio	143	U S A	29	"
D	Santoro Angelo	143	U S N	24	
E	Santoro Frances—†	143	housewife	53	"
F	*Laurino Grace—†	143	"	45	
G	Laurino Ida—†	143	rubberworker	21	"
H	*Calvano Antonetta—†	143	housewife	52	"
K	Calvano John	143	laborer	56	
L	Lamb Hannah—†	144	housewife	74	"
M	McMillan Joan—†	144	"	71	
N	Medeiros Patricia—†	144	housekeeper	20	"
O	Medeiros Peter D	144	U S A	25	"
P	Regan Helen—†	144	machinist	27	"
R	Puopolo John	145	shipfitter	35	"
S	Puopolo Josephine—†	145	housewife	26	"
T	Puopolo Nicholas	145	retired	78	
U	Flammia Angelina—†	145	housewife	38	"
V	Flammia Joseph	145	driller	42	"
W	Lodise Christine—†	145	housewife	41	"
X	Lodise Joseph	145	driller	46	"
Y	Memondo Pasquale	146	laborer	48	
Z	*Rinaudo Marie J—†	146	housewife	26	"

1160

A	Rinaudo Peter F	146	U S A	26	"
B	Nigro Anthony F	146	"	23	
C	Nigro Josephine—†	146	housewife	21	"
D	Puopolo Jennie—†	147	"	34	
E	Puopolo Ralph	147	merchant	37	"
F	McCarthy Jane—†	147	toolkeeper	49	"
G	Generson Mary—†	148	at home	78	"
H	Martinelli Edith—†	148	housewife	39	"
K	Martinelli James	148	chauffeur	41	"
L	Bartolo Joseph	148	mechanic	39	"
M	Bartolo Lucy—†	148	housewife	32	"
N	Schraffia Angela M—†	149	"	63	
O	Schraffia Francis	149	physician	32	"
P	Schraffia Rocco	149	tailor	36	"
R	Grasso Angelo	149	machinist	44	"
S	Grasso Josephine—†	149	housewife	43	"

Putnam Street—Continued

u	Joyce Andrew	150A U S A	30	here
v	Joyce Elizabeth C—†	150A housewife	69	"
w	Joyce Lawrence	150A shipfitter	40	"
x	Joyce Mary—†	150A saleswoman	37	"
y	Powers Cecil	150A laborer	44	141 Putnam
z	Powers Lillian—†.	150A housewife	33	141 "

1161

a	Goveia Joseph	151 U S A	22	here
b	*Goveia Mary—†	151 housewife	39	"
c	DellAria Giacomo	151 laborer	66	"
d	DellAria Jennie—†	151 housewife	60	"
e	Gomes Aurelia—†	151 "	51	
f	Gomes Eugene	151 seaman	58	
g	Iannuzzi Thomasina—†	152 tailor	49	..
h	Smaldone John C	152 printer	39	
k	Smaldone Mildred—†	152 housewife	38	"
l	Gillespie Mildred—†	152 "	25	
m	Gillespie William J	152 U S A	28	
n	*Abate John	153 storekeeper	62	"
o	*Abate Rosina—†	153 housewife	59	"
p	McDonald Flora—†	153 inspector	20	153 Brooks
r	Smith Cecelia—†	153 "	22	153 "
s	Smith Cecelia M—†	153 waitress	50	153 "
t	Smith Hugh	153 carpenter	49	153 "
u	DeDeo Anthony	154 laborer	46	here
v	DeDeo Jeanette—†	154 housewife	44	"
w	Montecalvo Marciano	154 laborer	36	"
x	Montecalvo Selma—†	154 housewife	33	"
y	Ceraso Camillo	154 expressman	61	"
z	Ceraso Joseph	154 U S A	24	

1162

a	Ceraso Josephine—†	154 housewife	51	"
b	Ceraso Vincenza—†	154 stitcher	21	"
c	Morrissey Mary—†	156 at home	65	"
d	Flaherty Agnes T—†	156 secretary	29	"
e	Flaherty John P	156 U S N	21	..
f	Flaherty Lawrence J	156 "	29	
g	Flaherty Nellie—†	156 at home	60	"
h	Salvo Dominic	156 laborer	54	
k	Salvo Paul	156 U S N	20	
l	*Salvo Rose—†	156 housewife	47	"

Putnam Street—Continued

M	Manfra Anna—†	158	housewife	26	here
N	Manfra Joseph	158	U S A	24	"
O	Iodice Nicholas	158	shoeworker	38	"
P	Iodice Rose—†	158	housewife	35	"
R	Vitello Anna—†	158	clerk	32	
S	Vitello Concetta—†	158	housewife	59	"
T	Vitello Pasquale	158	laborer	61	
U	*Vella Alice—†	160	housewife	31	"
V	Vella Salvatore	160	fishcutter	33	"
W	Coscia Alfonso	160	shoeworker	49	"
X	Coscia Carmella—†	160	housewife	40	"
Y	*Grimaldi Filomena—†	160	at home	84	"
Z	*Masce Angelina—†	160	housewife	46	"

1163

A	Masce Angelo	160	U S A	21	"
B	Masce Antonio	160	candymaker	49	"
C	Cammorato Biagio	162	U S A	24	308 Chelsea
D	Cammorato Grace—†	162	housewife	23	Medford
E	Corvino Josephine—†	162	"	29	here
F	Corvino Vincenzo	162	fishcutter	35	"
G	Agave Attilio E	162	U S N	21	"
H	Agave Domenica—†	162	housewife	46	"
K	Agave Umberto	162	baker	52	"
L	Serio Carmella—†	164	housewife	30	77 Morris
M	Serio Samuel	164	welder	33	77 "
N	Drago Anna M—†	164	housewife	27	here
O	Drago William V	164	metalworker	27	"
P	Scanzillo Louis	164	U S N	28	"
R	Scanzillo Susan—†	164	housewife	28	"
S	Day Albert W	166	retired	69	39 M
T	Day Elizabeth—†	166	housewife	48	39 "
U	Capinelli Lucy—†	166	"	34	here
V	Capinelli Nicholas	166	machinist	33	"
W	*Cornetta Angelo	166	retired	75	"
X	Cornetta Angelo	166	U S A	22	
Y	Cornetta Anthony	166	"	20	..
Z	Cornetta John	166	welder	42	

1164

A	*Cornetta Rose—†	166	at home	78	"
B	Cornetta Rose—†	166	housewife	38	"
C	Sacco Joseph	168	painter	41	8 Shelby

Putnam Street—Continued

D	Oliver Alfred	168	cabinetmaker	31	here
E	Oliver Mary—†	168	housewife	31	"
F	Iavicoli George D	168	welder	35	70 Trenton
G	Iavicoli Rose A—†	168	housewife	29	70 "
H	Manfra Joseph	170	fish handler	29	here
K	Manfra Lucy—†	170	housewife	29	"
L	Locigno Louise—†	170	"	27	"
M	Locigno Rocco	170	chauffeur	26	"
N	Maienza Joseph	170	machinist	23	218 Havre
O	Maienza Rose—†	170	at home	55	218 "
R	Brass Barnett	172	junk dealer	56	here
S	Brass Minnie—†	172	clerk	47	"
T	Brass Rebecca—†	172	"	46	"
U	Miller David	172	merchant	66	"
V	Miller Sarah—†	172	clerk	66	"
W	Marinelli Domenica M–†	172	housewife	28	"
X	Marinelli Dominic	172	machinist	33	"
Y	*Sansivino Carmella—†	172	at home	53	"

1165

B	Ballero Agrippino	198	U S A	21	
C	Ballero Joseph	198	laborer	58	"
D	Malveira Alzira—†	198	housewife	38	Woburn
E	Malveira Joseph A	198	houseman	42	"
F	Paxton William L	198	U S N	21	N Hampshire

Saratoga Street

G	McLaughlin Mary A—†	251	housekeeper	69	here
H	*Brown Sadie G—†	251	"	61	248 Saratoga
K	Sullivan Mary E—†	251	housewife	34	here
L	Sullivan William	251	chauffeur	36	"
M	Indegaro Charles	253	fishcutter	48	"
N	Indegaro Frances—†	253	housewife	33	"
O	Ciampa Charles	253	driller	28	"
P	Ciampa Mildred—†	253	housewife	29	"
R	*Manganella Louise—†	253	housekeeper	65	"
S	Ciampa Angeline—†	253	operator	20	"
T	Ciampa Caroline—†	253	candymaker	25	"
U	Ciampa Luigi	253	"	58	"
V	Ciampa Philomena—†	253	housewife	50	"
W	Guardasso Frank	255	welder	32	

Page.	Letter.	FULL NAME.	Residence, Jan. 1, 1945.	Occupation.	Supposed Age.	Reported Residence, Jan. 1, 1944. Street and Number.

Saratoga Street—Continued

x	Guardasso Margaret—†	255	housewife	33	here
y	Nobile Gerald	255	lawyer	39	"
z	Nobile Raffale M—†	255	housewife	35	"

1166

A	Guardasso Anthony	255	artist	34	"
B	Guardasso John	255	laborer	59	"
C	Guardasso Lena—†	255	housewife	63	"
D	Genvale Ann—†	257	benchworker	32	288 Princeton
E	Guest Eugene	257	U S N	23	here
F	Bossi Carmine	257	laborer	56	"
G	Bossi Caroline—†	257	benchworker	23	"
H	Bossi Theresa—†	257	housewife	54	"
K	Bossi Viola—†	257	boxmaker	26	"
L	DiCrescenzo Mary—†	257	housewife	30	"
M	DiCrescenzo Michael	257	driller	33	
N	Nelson Elsie R—†	259	shoeworker	23	"
O	Nelson Stanley	259	U S A	24	
P	Scaramozzino Anthony	259	U S N	25	
R	Scaramozzino Esther—†	259	housewife	27	"
U	Zambroni Mary—†	301A	dressmaker	40	"
V	Zambroni Roy	301A	shoemaker	45	"
W	Gambino Benjamin	301A	U S A	30	"
X	Gambino Nellie—†	301A	housewife	50	"
Y	Crescenzo Albina—†	302	"	40	
Z	Crescenzo Vincent	302	carpenter	43	"

1167

A	Carrafello Mary—†	302	housewife	49	148 Havre
B	Mascis America—†	303	saleswoman	23	107 Falcon
C	Mascis Michael	303	salesman	29	155 Marion
D	Callahan Anna M—†	303	housewife	23	here
E	Callahan John T	303	policeman	27	"
F	*Asgrezzi Gelsomia—†	303	housewife	58	"
G	Asgrezzi Salvatore	303	contractor	65	"
H	Furtado Antonio	304	fireman	51	1 Paris pl
K	*Furtado Emilia—†	304	housewife	45	1 "
L	Lacedra Barbara—†	304	"	30	91 Putnam
M	Lacedra Patrick	304	photographer	35	91 "
N	Gullifa Grace—†	304	housewife	40	here
O	Gullifa Ludo	304	chauffeur	41	"
P	Barbarisi Ella—†	305	housewife	21	401 Meridian
R	Barbarisi Emilio C	305	painter	27	401 "

40

Page.	Letter.	Full Name.	Residence, Jan. 1, 1945.	Occupation.	Supposed Age.	Reported Residence, Jan. 1, 1944. Street and Number.

Saratoga Street—Continued

	s	DeSousa Abel F	305	laborer	40	1 Saratoga pl
	t	DeSousa Louis F	305	cleaner	39	1 "
	u	DeSousa Maria H—†	305	housewife	29	1 "
	v	DeSousa Maria I—†	305	"	27	1 "
	w	Barletta Agnes—†	305	"	48	here
	x	Barletta Anthony J	305	U S A	23	"
	y	Fiore Philip	306	cleaner	20	168 Paris
	z	Lombardo Florence—†	306	housewife	45	here
1168						
	a	Lombardo Philip	306	janitor	61	
	b	Lombardo Rose—†	306	clerk	20	"
	c	Cresta John	306	U S A	24	Chelsea
	d	Cresta Rose—†	306	housewife	20	"
	e	*DeAngelis Carmella—†	307	"	64	here
	f	DeAngelis Carmine—†	307	laborer	26	"
	g	*DeAngelis Esther—†	307	housewife	38	255 Paris
	h	DeAngelis Patrick	307	U S A	24	here
	k	*DeAngelis Samuel	307	laborer	64	"
	l	DeAngelis Vincent	307	longshoreman	33	"
	m	Petifield Mary P—†	307	housewife	29	"
	n	Petifield Wilbur	307	repairman	39	"
	o	DeAngelis Mary—†	307	housewife	28	"
	p	DeAngelis Michael	307	checker	33	"
	r	*Setapane Domenic	307	retired	71	"
	s	DeFeo Anthony	308	U S A	23	"
	t	DeFeo Rose—†	308	housewife	22	1201 Benningt'n
	u	Lombardo Carmen	308	merchant	26	306 Saratoga
	v	Lombardo Mary—†	308	housewife	24	306 "
	w	O'Brien Mary Z—†	308	"	28	312 "
	x	O'Brien William J	308	sandblaster	29	312 "
	y	Femino Joseph P	309	pipefitter	21	1185 Benningt'n
	z	Femino Rose M—†	309	housewife	21	178 Paris
1169						
	a	Talasforo Joseph	309	retired	67	here
	b	*Talasforo Marie L—†	309	housewife	77	"
	c	Talasforo Pasquale	309	tel operator	45	"
	d	Evans Alice M—†	309	housewife	31	223 Trenton
	e	Evans Bernard C	309	U S A	27	223 "
	f	Fox Amelia—†	310	at home	30	here
	g	Fox Virgil C	310	U S N	31	"
	h	Alfano Antonio	310	cableman	58	"

Page.	Letter.	FULL NAME.	Residence, Jan. 1, 1945.	Occupation.	Supposed Age.	Reported Residence, Jan. 1, 1944. Street and Number.

Saratoga Street—Continued

	K	Alfano Domenic	310	U S A	28	here
	L	Alfano Generoso	310	"	24	"
	M	Alfano Jennie—†	310	housewife	53	"
	N	Alfano Jennie—†	310	stitcher	22	"
	O	Alfano Mario	310	U S A	21	
	P	Alfano Vincent	310	"	25	
	R	Riggillo Rocco	310	foreman	39	"
	S	Riggillo Yolanda—†	310	housewife	29	"
	T	Ricciardelli Joseph	311	grinder	28	"
	U	Ricciardelli Mary S—†	311	housewife	28	"
	V	Grande Anastasia—†	311	"	54	
	W	Grande Angelina M—†	311	stitcher	21	"
	X	Pierro Antonette—†	311	housewife	31	"
	Y	Pierro Joseph	311	printer	33	"
	Z	Colucci Alda—†	312	housewife	20	277 Princeton
1170						
	A	Colucci Edward	312	electrician	22	277 "
	B	Collins Ellen—†	312	at home	75	here
	C	Collins Thomas	312	plumber	40	"
	D	*Colucci Genonia—†	312	housewife	60	"
	E	Colucci Gerard	312	barber	65	
	G	DeFeo Angelina—†	313	housewife	53	"
	H	DeFeo Antonio	313	blacksmith	63	"
	K	DeFeo Jean—†	313	housewife	28	"
	L	DeFeo William	313	U S A	33	
	M	Burditt Edward J	314	metalworker	29	"
	N	Burditt Helen—†	314	housewife	25	"
	O	Clifford Mary J—†	314	"	36	
	P	Waldron Beatrice—†	314	waitress	39	"
	R	Waldron Clark	314	seaman	40	"
	S	Cahill Mildred—†	315	packer	25	Connecticut
	T	Shea Anna G—†	315	housewife	54	here
	U	Shea Richard F	315	retired	67	"
	V	Frontinella Mary—†	315	welder	25	Sharon
	W	Toomey George	315	retired	61	here
	X	Gallo Jennie—†	316	stitcher	42	"
	Y	Gallo John	316	rigger	31	"
	Z	Gallo John	316	retired	52	
1171						
	A	Gallo Michelina—†	316	housewife	29	"
	B	Scott Jean—†	316	at home	24	876 Harris'n av

Saratoga Street—Continued

c	Scott Jose	316	seaman	30	876 Harris'n av
d	Thomas Rita—†	316	housekeeper	33	18 Union pk
e	DiMaio Carmela—†	316	housewife	48	here
f	DiMaio Chester	316	barber	46	"
g	DiMaio Leonardo	316	U S A	21	"
h	Hender Frederick J	316	"	22	
k	Hender Mary E—†	316	housewife	52	"
l	Hender Walter J	316	shipfitter	52	"
m	Hender Walter J	316	U S A	24	
n	Wright Gilbert	316	rigger	37	
o	Wright Winifred—†	316	at home	25	"
p	Ruotolo John	317	U S A	21	"
r	Ruotolo Joseph	317	retired	65	
s	*Ruotolo Rose—†	317	housewife	61	"
t	Stella Angelina—†.	317	"	33	
u	Stella Rinaldo	317	steamfitter	27	"
v	DelVechio Marion—†	317	housewife	63	"
w	DelVechio Octavio	317	candymaker	62	"
x	Laquaglia Antonio	319	tailor	62	
y	Laquaglia Margaret—†	319	dressmaker	32	"
z	Laquaglia Rose—†	319	housewife	60	"
	1172				
a	Laquaglia Theresa—†	319	tailor	35	"
b	Laquaglia Carmine	319	U S N	30	
c	Laquaglia Rocco	319	U S A	29	
d	Laquaglia Frank	319	"	25	"
e	Laquaglia George	319	"	23	"
f	Laquaglia Santo	319	clerk	22	"
g	St Croix Charlotte—†	320	housewife	56	"
h	St Croix Eileen—†	320	operator	20	"
k	St Croix William	320	fisherman	65	"
l	*DiNatale Mary—†	320	housewife	70	305 Saratoga
m	DiNatale Salvatore	320	at home	83	305 "
n	Puzzo Rocca—†	320	dipper	45	265 Havre
o	Puzzo Vito	320	laborer	48	265 "
p	Romano Frances—†	320	stitcher	25	here
r	Romano Jennie—†	320	housewife	48	"
s	Romano Mary—†	320	stitcher	20	"
t	Romano Philip	320	laborer	50	"
u	Romano Rocco	320	U S A	24	"
v	Romano Salvatore	320	clerk	22	

Saratoga Street—Continued

w	Martinelli Peter	321	chauffeur	20	148 Putnam	
x	Pizziano Mary—†	321	housewife	22	here	
y	Pizziano Raymond	321	plumber	26	"	
z	Banks Gertrude—†	322	housewife	33	"	
	1173					
A	Banks John R	322	metalworker	40	"	
B	Jackson Florence—†	322	housewife	30	"	
C	Jackson William	322	brazier	31		
D	Pucciarella Anna—†	322	at home	20	"	
E	Pucciarella Elizabeth—†	322	stenographer	27	"	
F	Pucciarella Lawrence	322	U S A	24	"	
G	Pucciarella Mary—†	322	housewife	51	"	
H	Pucciarella Pasquale	322	foreman	51	"	
K	Jeffrey Florence R—†	323	housewife	46	"	
L	Jeffrey William J	323	U S N	48	"	
M	Nugent Florence—†	323	secretary	22	273 Lovell	
N	Caggiano Nancy—†	324	housewife	28	here	
O	Caggiano Saverio	324	agent	33	"	
P	Grassie Manuel L	324	porter	63	Cohasset	
R	Scaparato Gabriel	324	"	58	here	
S	Caggiano Antoinette—†	324	stitcher	26	"	
T	Caggiano Antonio	324	machinist	62	"	
U	Caggiano Concetta—†	324	clerk	31		
V	Caggiano Eleanor—†	324	"	22	"	
W	Caggiano Frances—†	324	at home	62	"	
X	Caggiano Theresa—†	324	manager	35	"	
Y	Pizzano Antonio	rear 325	retired	72	"	
Z	Pizzano Assunta—†	" 325	candymaker	37	"	
	1174					
A	Pizzano Eleanor—†	" 325	"	26		
B	Pizzano Elvira—†	" 325	housewife	64	"	
C	Pizzano John	" 325	U S A	22	"	
D	Pizzano Vincent J	" 325	painter	24	"	
E	Iannello Gaetana—†	326	stenographer	20	"	
F	Iannello Pasquale	326	shoeworker	42	"	
G	Iannello Sandra—†	326	housewife	39	"	
K	Boyle John	329	retired	69	160 Sumner	
L	Jeffrey John E	329	oiler	44	here	
	Dwyer Margaret L—†	330	bookkeeper	50	"	
	Ahern James J	330	longshoreman	47	"	
N	Ahern William F	330	policeman	51	"	

Page.	Letter.	Full Name.	Residence, Jan. 1, 1945.	Occupation.	Supposed Age.	Reported Residence, Jan. 1, 1944. Street and Number.

	P	Bly Catherine A—†	330	at home	68	here
	R	Donovan George A	330	U S A	38	"
	S	Grant Edward J	330	U S M C	21	"
	T	Grant Josephine M—†	330	clerk	53	
	U	Grant Patrick J	330	policeman	56	"
	W	Keenan Henry P	331	U S A	27	
	X	Keenan Jane F—†	331	tel operator	43	"
	Y	Keenan John	331	retired	72	"
	Z	Keenan John E	331	steamfitter	40	"
		1175				
	A	Keenan Katherine M—†	331	bookkeeper	35	"
	B	Keenan Leo B	331	letter carrier	30	"
	C	Carvalho Clarice—†	333	stitcher	20	Portugal
	D	Carvalho Maria B—†	333	operator	22	"
	E	Garden Clara—†	333	weaver	24	here
	F	Vieira Louise—†	333	housewife	50	"
	G	Vieira Manuel	333	deckhand	44	"
	K	Amico Frances—†	340	housewife	26	"
	L	Amico Michael	340	machinist	34	"
	M	Caliri Joseph	340	patrolman	55	"
	N	Caliri Lucy—†	340	housewife	52	"
	O	Caliri Rosalie—†	340	clerk	23	
	P	Natale Anna—†	340	cashier	21	
	R	Natale Carmela—†	340	at home	46	"
	S	Natale Frances—†	340	secretary	25	"
	T	Hickey Edward B	342	U S A	29	45 Bennington
	U	Hickey Mary—†	342	at home	29	45 "
	V	Rossi Angela—†	342	U S C G	24	here
	W	Rossi Stella—†	342	at home	54	"
	X	Rossi Vito C	342	barber	56	"
	Y	Barrett Mary—†	342	housewife	20	"
	Z	Barrett Thomas	342	U S N	30	
		1176				
	A	Puopolo Anna—†	342	at home	47	"
	B	Puopolo John	342	"	22	"
	C	Puopolo Joseph	342	U S M C	26	"
	D	Alphas Georgia—†	344	lampmaker	27	"
	E	*Alphas Harriet—†	344	at home	49	"
	F	Alphas Mary—†	344	"	25	"
	G	Alphas Sophie—†	344	lampmaker	22	"
	H	Toukalos Kostos	344	baker	36	Chelsea

Page.	Letter.	Full Name.	Residence, Jan. 1, 1945.	Occupation.	Supposed Age.	Reported Residence, Jan. 1, 1944. Street and Number.

Saratoga Street—Continued

N	Acerra Margaret—†	344	at home	58	here
K	Marino Angelina—†	344	housewife	34	"
L	Marino James	344	painter	36	"
O	Marino Anthony	344	"	34	
P	Marino Marie—†	344	housewife	30	"
R	Moseley Lotta—†	346	"	40	
S	Moseley Thomas E	346	clerk	42	"
T	McMahon Frederick	346	U S N	30	294 Paris
U	Todd Alice—†	346	housewife	27	294 "
V	Todd Stanley	346	rigger	31	294 "
w	*Whynot Abbie M—†	346	at home	73	here
X	Whynot Beulah M—†	346	packer	39	"
Y	Whynot Elsie—†	346	"	30	"
Z	Whynot Mae—†	346	"	33	

1177

A	Ciaramella Angelina—†	348	furrier	31	225 Chelsea
B	Ciaramella Christina—†	348	housewife	62	Pennsylvania
C	Ciaramella Helen—†	348	at home	32	"
D	Ciaramella Louis	348	"	66	"
E	Ciaramella Michael	348	U S A	33	
F	Ciaramella Robert	348	"	22	
G	Ciaramella Stella—†	348	bookkeeper	26	"
H	Prudente Anna—†	348	supervisor	38	here
K	*Prudente Florence—†	348	at home	72	"
L	Prudente Josephine—†	348	stenographer	35	"
M	Prudente Julia—†	348	clerk	36	
N	Prudente William	348	engineer	31	"
O	MacDonald Gertrude—†	348	assembler	26	52 Falcon
P	McDonald Roy A	348	U S N	27	386 Princeton
R	O'Leary Cecelia—†	348	housewife	52	52 Falcon
S	O'Leary Dorothea—†	348	assembler	22	52 "
T	O'Leary Gerard	348	shipper	24	52 "
U	O'Leary Richard	348	stevedore	54	52 "
w	DeFreitas John J	400	at home	67	here
X	DeFreitas Julia—†	400	housewife	48	"
Y	Cilibrasi Charles	400	cutter	55	522 Sumner
Z	Cilibrasi Josephine—†	400	operator	49	522 "

1178

A	DiOrio Domenica—†	400	at home	25	60 Lubec
B	DiOrio Joseph A	400	U S A	26	60 "
c	*Cimmino Louis	400	presser	45	here
D	Cimmino Rose—†	400	housewife	37	"

Shelby Street

E	DeGrazia Mariano	5	tester	25	here
F	DeGrazia Rose—†	5	housewife	24	"
G	Correia Jordan	5	molder	43	"
H	Correia Jordan, jr	5	U S N	23	
K	*Correia Josephine—†	5	housewife	39	"
L	Correia Manuel	5	U S N	20	"
M	Costello Arthur T	5	longshoreman	31	"
N	Costello Frances—†	5	housewife	30	"
O	Olsen John J	5	U S A	26	

Ward 1–Precinct 12

CITY OF BOSTON

LIST OF RESIDENTS
20 YEARS OF AGE AND OVER

(NON-CITIZENS INDICATED BY ASTERISK)
(FEMALES INDICATED BY DAGGER)

AS OF

JANUARY 1, 1945

THOMAS F. SULLIVAN, *Chairman*
FREDERIC E. DOWLING, *Secretary*
WILLIAM A. MOTLEY, JR.
FRANCIS B. McKINNEY
EVERETT R. PROUT
Listing Board.

CITY OF BOSTON ⬥ PRINTING DEPARTMENT

1200
Bennington Street

	Letter	Full Name	Res.	Occupation	Age	Reported Residence
A	Stoppolone Angelina—†	149	operator	21	here
B	Stoppolone Joseph	149	proprietor	56	"
C	Stoppolone Mary—†	149	housewife	49	"
D	Tortora Anthony	149	finisher	65	"
E	*Tortora Josephine—†	149	housewife	64	"
G	Flodin Anna—†	151	housekeeper	77	"
H	Flodin Carl	151	machinist	55	"
K	Tisa Joseph	151	retired	76	..
L	*Tisa Philomena—†	151	housewife	69	"
P	Kirk Lillian—†	153	waitress	31	Maine
R	Kirk Winifred—†	153	at home	67	"
S	Pipi Antoinette—†	153	housewife	62	here
T	Pipi Carmella—†	153	at home	25	"
U	Pipi Mary—†	153	"	21	"
V	Pipi Pellegrino	153	electrician	35	"
W	Pipi Philomena—†	153	at home	38	"
X	Stella Anna M—†	154	housewife	35	78 Frankfort
Y	Stella Gaetano	154	laborer	46	78 "
Z	Saulnier George R	154	U S A	21	here

1201

	Letter	Full Name	Res.	Occupation	Age	Reported Residence
A	Saulnier Joseph A	154	carpenter	51	"
B	Saulnier Mary D—†	154	metalworker	20	"
C	Saulnier Mary G—†	154	housewife	46	"
D	Ferrera Angelina—†	154	typist	22	
E	Ferrera Charles	154	physician	26	"
F	Ferrera Grace—†	154	housewife	55	"
G	Ferrera Ignazio	154	meatcutter	59	"
H	Rinella Barbara—†	155	housewife	30	"
K	Rinella Joseph	155	plumber	41	"
L	Rinella Mary—†	155	housewife	37	"
M	Rinella Samuel	155	U S A	31	
N	Cashman Eleanor—†	155	housewife	50	"
O	Cashman Frank	155	laborer	54	
R	Ruggiero Annie—†	156	housekeeper	50	"
S	*Rizzo Carmen	156	laborer	62	"
T	*Rizzo Rose—†	156	housewife	55	"
U	Falzarano Joseph	156	laborer	27	
V	Falzarano Olga—†	156	housewife	25	"
W	Festa Angelina—†	157	operator	21	"
X	Festa Benjamin	157	U S A	28	

2

Page.	Letter.	FULL NAME.	Residence, Jan. 1, 1945.	Occupation.	Supposed Age.	Reported Residence, Jan. 1, 1944. Street and Number.

Bennington Street—Continued

y	Giangrieco Antonio	157	painter	47	here
z	Giangrieco Luigia—†	157	housewife	53	"
1202						
a	Marinelli Albert	157	laborer	65	
b	*Marinelli Columbia—†	157	housewife	56	"
c	Staffiri Domenic	157	U S A	21	
d	Frati James	157	electrician	29	"
e	Frati Philomena—†	157	housewife	26	"
g	Gomes Manuel	158	laborer	57	"
h	Gomes Maria—†	158	housewife	51	"
k	LaMonica Jennie—†	158	"	24	
l	LaMonica Joseph	158	fishcutter	27	"
n	Johnson Frank	159	machinist	52	"
o	Johnson Frederick	159	shipper	58	"
p	Johnson Winthrop	159	laborer	49	"
t	*Clements Martha E—†	160	housewife	67	"
u	Thibault Martha A—†	160	operator	25	"
v	Picariello Jennie—†	160	housewife	35	"
w	Picariello Joseph	160	painter	35	"
x	Pepe Amelia—†	160	housewife	57	"
y	Pepe Enrico A	160	U S A	27	
1203						
a	Maglio Anthony	161	"	20	"
b	Maglio Domenic	161	presser	50	165 Benningt'n
c	*Maglio Raphaela—†	161	housewife	49	165 "
d	Impemba Concetta—†	161	"	25	60 Trenton
e	Impemba Martin	161	millhand	28	60 "
f	Imperioso Annette—†	161	housewife	31	here
g	Imperioso Joseph	161	machinist	28	"
h	Letras Priscilla—†	161	housewife	25	167 Benningt'n
k	Hoey Frederick J	162	U S A	32	here
l	Hoey Ruth E—†	162	clerk	30	"
m	Moynihan Bridget G—†	162	housewife	62	"
n	Moynihan Lillian G—†	162	tel operator	33	"
o	Moynihan Maurice E	162	U S N	42	
p	DiGregorio Michael	163	retired	51	"
r	Bacco Enrico	163	U S A	21	
s	Bacco Guistino	163	smelter	48	"
t	Bacco Lucy—†	163	housewife	42	"
u	Cordone Michael	163	laborer	21	"
v	Massano Georgianna—†	164	at home	70	"

3

Page.	Letter.	FULL NAME.	Residence, Jan. 1, 1945.	Occupation.	Supposed Age.	Reported Residence, Jan. 1, 1944. Street and Number.

Bennington Street—Continued

	w	Marsh Alice S—†	164	housewife	30	Everett
	x	Marsh Charles A	164	laborer	45	"
	y	Turilli Lottie B—†	164	housewife	20	Florida
	z	Turilli Vincent J	164	seaman	31	"
1204						
	a	*Maglio Antoinetta—†	165	housekeeper	58	here
	b	DeCologero Jennie—†	165	housewife	60	"
	c	DeCologero Salvatore	165	musician	27	"
	d	Mastrangelo Beatrice I–†	165	housewife	32	223 Border
	e	Mastrangelo Ralph J	165	U S A	36	223 "
	f	Devine Louis E	166	laborer	37	here
	g	Devine Margaret L—†	166	housewife	26	"
	h	Pagliarulo John	166	laborer	59	"
	k	*Pagliarulo Josephine—†	166	housewife	63	"
	l	Pagliarulo Mary—†	166	stitcher	21	"
	m	Cuozzo Judy—†	166	housewife	22	Everett
	n	Cuozzo Marino	166	U S A	20	"
	p	Coiro Marie—†	167	housewife	48	here
	r	Coiro Patrick	167	mechanic	52	"
	s	Imperioso Arthur	167	U S A	24	"
	t	Imperioso Raymond	167	"	22	..
	u	Minola Ciriaco	167	watchman	68	"
	v	Minola Palmina—†	167	housewife	49	"
	w	Paldo Lena—†	167	"	25	
	x	Paldo Liberato	167	U S A	28	
	y	*Riley Catherine—†	168	housewife	60	"
	z	Riley James J	168	retired	77	
1205						
	a	Riley Rosanna L—†	168	waitress	26	"
	b	Caggiano Antonio	168	metalworker	35	"
	c	Caggiano Mary D—†	168	housewife	33	"
	d	Blandini Joseph	168	electrician	30	"
	e	Blandini Madeline M—†	168	housewife	25	"
	f	Bartlett Elizabeth M—†	169	at home	57	"
	g	Cronin Eleanor E—†	169	saleswoman	37	"
	h	Cronin Patrick F	169	U S A	37	"
	k	Dolaher Albert J	169	attendant	34	"
	l	Hogan Annie J—†	169	housekeeper	76	"
	m	Silva Alfred F	170	machinist	31	35 Prescott
	n	Silva Constance A—†	170	housewife	27	35 "
	o	*Silva Mary C—†	170	"	56	35 "

Bennington Street—Continued

P	Meaney Alice M—†	170	housewife	54	68 Brooks
R	Meaney John T	170	U S N	21	68 "
S	Meaney Margaret M—†	170	bookkeeper	23	68 "
T	Meaney Thomas	170	laborer	60	68 "
U	Miller Eleanor J—†	170	nurse	24	here
V	Miller Florence C—†	170	housewife	49	"
W	Miller Gladys C—†	170	inspector	23	"
X	Miller James E	170	foreman	51	"
Y	Greene Catherine M—†	173	housewife	39	"
Z	Greene Walter	173	electrician	45	"
	1206				
A	Coriani Louis	173	machinist	43	"
B	Coriani Rita—†	173	housewife	39	"
C	Morgner Rita M—†	174	typist	24	··
D	Murray Dora A—†	174	housewife	60	"
E	Murray Walter T	174	chauffeur	60	"
F	Pitts John E	174	watchman	49	"
G	Barry Catherine A—†	174	at home	73	"
H	Barry Hannah T—†	174	housekeeper	75	"
K	Corkery Louise A—†	174	"	35	··
L	Donovan Timothy F	174	retired	74	
M	*Castagnio Concetta—†	175	housewife	44	"
N	*Castagnio Frank	175	barber	56	··
O	McGuire James	175	U S N	30	"
P	McGuire Jennie—†	175	housewife	29	"
R	Nolan Aaron J	177	laborer	44	
S	*Nolan Anna—†	177	housewife	44	"
T	Nolan Elizabeth—†	177	clerk	20	
V	Curran Bridget—†	178	housewife	74	"
W	Curran Catherine T—†	178	housekeeper	38	"
X	Curran Charles L	178	laborer	39	"
Y	Curran Edward E	178	"	34	
Z	Curran Ethel F—†	178	at home	37	"
	1207				
A	Curran Leo M	178	laborer	40	··
B	Curran Paul P	178	"	35	
C	Curran William H	178	"	44	"
D	Cunha Joseph	178	molder	47	
E	Cunha Lourdes—†	178	housewife	44	"
H	Albano Antonio A	180	U S A	28	
K	Albano Lucia F—†	180	laundress	26	"

5

Page.	Letter.	FULL NAME.	Residence, Jan. 1, 1945.	Occupation.	Supposed Age.	Reported Residence, Jan. 1, 1944. Street and Number.

Bennington Street—Continued

	L	Albano Philomena—†	180	packer	33	here
	M	DeFalco Raffaella A—†	180	stitcher	30	"
	N	*Tortora Gerardo	180	tailor	59	"
	O	Silva Marion—†	181	housekeeper	40	"
	P	DeMarco Mary A—†	182	housewife	21	53 Chelsea
	R	DeMarco Nicholas A	182	shipper	21	Revere
	S	Pace Dominic	182	laborer	50	here
	T	Pace Grace—†	182	dressmaker	20	"
	U	Pace Mary—†	182	housewife	38	"
	V	Ferriero Angelo J	182	fireman	50	
	W	Ferriero Angelo M	182	U S A	22	
	X	Ferriero Maria—†	182	housewife	53	"
	Y	Ferriero Mary G—†	182	stitcher	23	"
	Z	Mora Angelina—†	184	housewife	30	"

1208

	A	Mora Walter J	184	laborer	34	
	B	*Lima Anthony	184	operator	51	"
	C	Lima Jennie M—†	184	housekeeper	27	"
	D	*Lima Mary—†	184	housewife	49	"
	E	Grieco Amando	184	U S N	20	
	F	Grieco John	184	"	23	
	G	Grieco Manuel	184	pressman	57	"
	H	Grieco Margaret—†	184	housewife	49	"
	K	Spallo Mary—†	184	stenographer	25	"
	M	Santaniello Armando	185	mechanic	25	76 Bennington
	N	Santaniello Elvira—†	185	housewife	23	103 Chelsea
	O	Fernandez Adolph	185	engineer	37	here
	P	Fernandez Annie—†	185	housewife	29	"
	R	*Mayo Lucy—†	185	housekeeper	58	"
	S	Mayo Raymond	185	mechanic	20	"
	T	Murray Lillian—†	186	factoryhand	24	"
	U	Graziano Carmello	186	U S A	26	"
	V	Raimondi Mary—†	186	housewife	50	"
	W	Raimondi Peter	186	boilermaker	63	"
	X	DiBaccari Bresci	186	U S A	26	
	Y	DiBaccari Louise—†	186	housewife	20	"
	Z	Granese Mary—†	186	"	55	"

1209

	A	Hannon John D	186	U S A	25	
	B	Hannon Rose—†	186	housewife	22	"
	D	Pina Louis	187	laborer	39	Connecticut

Page	Letter	Full Name.	Residence, Jan. 1, 1945.	Occupation.	Suppressed Age.	Reported Residence, Jan. 1, 1944. Street and Number.

Bennington Street—Continued

	E	Pina May A—†	187	housewife	28	Connecticut
	F	*Rossetti Theresa—†	187	housekeeper	60	here
	K	Sullivan Joseph V	188	chipper	33	"
	L	Sullivan Leah—†	188	housewife	35	"
	M	*LeBlanc Alfred J	188	laborer	47	
	N	*LeBlanc Elizabeth M—†	188	housewife	37	"
	O	*Hazell Agnes E—†	190	"	47	443 Lubec
	P	Lawson Ellis E	190	U S C G	23	Georgia
	R	Lawson Margaret M—†	190	housewife	26	"
	S	DiMinico Louise—†	190	"	24	here
	T	DiMinico Nicholas	190	U S A	24	"
	U	Politano Frank A	190	"	20	"
	V	Politano Guiseppe	190	shipfitter	49	"
	W	Politano Josephine—†	190	housewife	52	"
	X	Bishop Helen—†	190	assembler	26	"
	Y	Bishop Paul	190	U S N	25	
	Z	O'Connor Frank	190	longshoreman	50	"

1210

	A	O'Connor Nora—†	190	housewife	48	"
	B	*Malvey Timothy	192	longshoreman	46	"
	C	*Peddle Mary—†	192	housewife	55	"
	D	Peddle Patrick J	192	fisherman	45	"
	E	Gianino Lena M—†	192	housewife	30	"
	F.	Gianino Ralph J	192	fishcutter	33	"

Bremen Street

	G	Cardarelli Grace—†	236	housewife	37	here
	H	Cardarelli Ralph	236	plumber	36	"
	K	Forgione Joseph	236	chauffeur	43	"
	L	Forgione Rose—†	236	housewife	40	"
	M	*Genzale Carmela—†	236	housekeeper	54	"
	N	Genzale James	236	seaman	20	..
	O	Genzale Rose—†	236	stitcher	27	"
	P	Sollazzo Antonio	238	carpenter	75	"
	R	*Sollazzo Emma—†	238	factoryhand	65	"
	S	Celeste Joseph	238	laborer	33	
	T	Celeste Julia—†	238	housewife	30	"
	U	LoConte Dora—†	238	forewoman	25	"
	V	LoConte John	238	longshoreman	58	"
	W	LoConte John	238	U S A	24	

Page.	Letter.	FULL NAME.	Residence, Jan. 1, 1945.	Occupation.	Supposed Age.	Reported Residence, Jan. 1, 1944. Street and Number.

Bremen Street—Continued

	x	LoConte Lena—†	238	housewife	49	here
	y	LoConte Marion—†	238	stitcher	22	"
	z	*Russo Lucy—†	240	housekeeper	58	"
1211						
	a	Russo Virginia—†	240	inspector	21	"
	b	*Costa Stephen	240	operator	64	"
	c	Cutrona Jennie—†	240	housewife	34	"
	d	Cutrona Peter	240	tailor	41	
	e	Palermo Agrippino	240	shipwright	33	"
	f	Palermo Santina—†	240	housewife	33	"
	g	Capreralla Florence—†	242	"	25	
	h	Capreralla Gerald	242	rigger	27	
	k	Constantine Joseph	242	U S A	23	
	l	Constantine Rose—†	242	housewife	22	"
	m	Izzo Mary—†	242	"	42	
	n	Izzo Nicholas	242	U S A	20	
	o	Izzo Paul	242	laborer	49	"
	p	*Ialuna Agrippina—†	244	housewife	57	"
	r	Ialuna Nazzareno	244	foreman	57	"
	s	Taluna Sarah—†	244	stitcher	21	"
	t	Taluna Angelo J	244	engineer	26	"
	u	Ialuna Concetta—†	244	housewife	27	"
	v	Stella Anna—†	244	"	34	
	w	Stella Joseph	244	gasfitter	39	"
	x	*Cutrona Mary—†	246	at home	71	"
	y	Luongo Charles	246	bartender	49	"
	z	Silva Edmund	246	laborer	34	
1212						
	a	Silva Marie—†	246	stitcher	31	"
	b	Bellitti Frances—†	246	at home	53	"
	c	Bellitti Josephine—†	246	saleswoman	30	"
	d	Bellitti Leonard	246	U S N	24	"
	f	Fucillo Angelo	252	factoryhand	29	"
	g	Fucillo Emanuela—†	252	housewife	27	"
	h	DeVita James	252	clerk	36	"
	k	DeVita Rose—†	252	housewife	37	"
	l	Tamaseo John	252	U S A	23	"
	m	Tamaseo Louis	252	draftsman	20	"
	n	Tamaseo Michael	252	U S A	22	"
	o	Tamaseo Nicholas	252	weaver	50	"
	p	*Tamaseo Sylvia—†	252	housewife	45	"

Bremen Street—Continued

R	Raffaele Jean—†	254	housewife	34	here
S	Raffaele Vincent J	254	brazier	39	"
T	Schraffa Angelo	254	painter	30	"
U	Schraffa Mary—†	254	housewife	29	"
V	Massaro Carlo	254	retired	57	"
W	Massaro Mary—†	254	housewife	57	"
X	Massaro Peter	254	welder	28	

1213

A	Lopilato Arthur	264	U S A	27	::
B	Lopilato George	264	"	34	
C	Lopilato Lucy—†	264	housewife	68	"
D	Lopilato Rose—†	264	saleswoman	40	"
E	Lopilato Vincenzo	264	retired	72	"
F	Pilato Massie	264	painter	43	"
G	*Cali Frank	266	salesman	39	"
H	*Cali Theresa—†	266	housewife	29	"
K	Joy Joseph	268	retired	85	..
L	Kelly Anna—†	268	at home	24	"
M	Sullivan Alice—†	268	waitress	55	"
P	Familiare Augustine—†	284	housewife	59	"
R	Familiare Inez B—†	284	teacher	36	"
S	Rogers Anthony J	284	shipper	57	"
T	Rogers Mary—†	284	seamstress	61	"
V	Zeoli Mary—†	286	housekeeper	39	"
X	Tramonte Albert	290	fishcutter	29	"
Y	Tramonte Yolanda—†	290	housewife	22	"
Z	Nazzaro Eugene	290	laborer	59	

1214

A	Nazzaro Mary—†	290	housewife	47	"
B	Celeste Agnes—†	292	"	21	
C	Celeste Salvatore A	292	U S A	22	
D	*Donnaruma John	292	laborer	52	..
E	*Donnaruma Rose—†	292	housewife	47	"
F	Donnaruma Vincent J	292	U S N	23	"
G	Gagne Edith—†	294	housewife	27	Lynn
H	Gagne Leo	294	electrician	28	"
K	Hollander Catherine—†	294	housewife	26	here
L	Hollander William	294	U S N	28	"
M	Carco Dorothy—†	294	housewife	28	"
N	Carco Louis	294	shipwright	35	"
O	Brigante Augustino	294	U S M C	23	"

Bremen Street—Continued

P	Brigante Joseph	294	carpenter	58	here	
R	Carco Agrippina—†	294	housewife	56	"	
S	Carco John	294	chemist	24	"	
T	Carco Manuel	294	retired	63		
U	Carco Mary—†	294	saleswoman	22	"	
V	LiFave Concetta—†	294	at home	29	"	
Z	Simington Arthur	310	foreman	50	"	

1215

A	Simington Edith—†	310	housewife	50	"	
B	Clark Edna—†	310	"	53		
C	Clark Herbert	310	U S A	23		
D	Marks Frank	310	operator	49	"	
E	Marks Harold F	310	U S N	20	"	
F	Marks Mary G—†	310	housewife	44	"	
G	Powers Anna E—†	312	boxmaker	34	"	
H	*Powers Eva—†	312	at home	72	"	
K	Powers John	312	U S A	28		
M	Lombardi Louis	312	shipfitter	33	"	
N	Powers Anna—†	312	housewife	38	"	
O	Powers Michael	312	millhand	40	"	
P	Powers Joseph	312	"	37		
R	Powers Josephine—†	312	housewife	31	"	

Brooks Street

S	Brady Mary—†	2	packer	53	286 Bremen	
T	Overly Katherine—†	2	housewife	26	286 "	
V	Chianea Jennie—†	2	"	25	here	
W	Chianea Vincent	2	painter	31	10 Cottage	
X	*Festa Gaetano	2	candymaker	67	here	
Y	*DeGregorio Felice—†	4	operator	50	185 Chelsea	
Z	*DeGregorio Frank	4	retired	68	185 "	

1216

A	*Arancio Edward	4	oiler	63	here	
B	*Arancio Margaret—†	4	housewife	56	"	
C	Rezendes Florence—†	4	"	25	Somerville	
D	Rezendes Lebert	4	U S A	25	"	
E	Boncore Charles	6	tailor	55	here	
F	Boncore Louise—†	6	housewife	48	"	
G	Boncore Louise—†	6	stitcher	27	"	

Brooks Street—Continued

H	Garten Mary—†	6	housewife	22	here
K	Garten William K	6	U S N	24	23 Brooks
L	Walsh Edward	6	metalworker	24	here
M	Walsh Phyllis—†	6	housewife	22	"
P	Giarla Anthony M	19	chauffeur	26	"
R	Giarla Josephine—†	19	housewife	27	"
S	Giarla Margaret—†	19	"	53	
T	Giarla Margaret A—†	19	clerk	20	"
U	Giarla Pasquale	19	painter	53	"
V	Bruno Ermenagilda—†	19	teacher	29	"
W	Bruno Maria—†	19	housewife	54	"
X	Bruno Mario A	19	U S A	21	
Y	Bruno Michael	19	barber	54	"
Z	Porazza Michael A	19	U S A	31	165 Cottage

1217

A	Porazza Olga B—†	19	housewife	27	165 "
B	Cappuccio Joseph F	20	U S N	20	here
C	Cappuccio Matilda—†	20	housewife	45	"
D	Cappuccio Nicholas	20	mason	52	"
E	Dobbins James	20	U S A	23	"
F	Dobbins Mary L—†	20	secretary	22	"
G	Albanese Anthony	20	U S A	24	"
H	Albanese Carmella—†	20	clerk	24	
K	Minichiello Christie	20	U S N	22	
L	Minichiello John	20	U S A	32	
M	*Minichiello Rafael	20	rubberworker	64	"
N	*Minichiello Rosa—†	20	housewife	59	"
O	Anzalone Ernest	21	electrician	35	"
P	Anzalone Jennie—†	21	housewife	35	"
R	Anzalone Rose—†	21	"	69	
S	DaVoilio Esther—†	21	packer	34	
T	Manzi Alfonse	21	machinist	64	"
U	Manzi Jean—†	21	inspector	23	"
V	*Manzi Jennie—†	21	housewife	53	"
W	Manzi Salvatore	21	U S A	30	
X	Manzi Theresa—†	21	inspector	22	"
Y	Markovitz Charles	22	proprietor	50	"
Z	Markovitz Eva—†	22	housewife	50	"

1218

A	Markovitz Sarah—†	22	clerk	24	"
B	Rosenthal Celia—†	22	housewife	28	New Jersey

Brooks Street—Continued

	c	DelloRusso Alice—†	22	stitcher	20	here
	d	DelloRusso Carmine	22	laborer	50	"
	e	DelloRusso Matilda—†	22	housewife	50	"
	f	DelloRusso Ralph	22	U S C G	23	"
	g	Falzone Anna—†	22	stitcher	35	"
	h	Falzone Rosario	22	presser	52	"
	k	Falzone Salvatore	22	U S A	22	
	l	Driver Harold	23	engineer	35	"
	m	Driver Stella—†	23	housewife	30	"
	n	Kushner Anna—†	23	"	70	"
	o	Kushner Max	23	U S A	31	"
	p	Richmond Sally—†	23	housewife	28	"
	r	Richmond Theodore	23	salesman	30	"
	s	Gennaco Joseph	23	chauffeur	32	"
	t	Gennaco Pauline—†	23	housewife	29	"
	u	Crowley Albert	25	retired	69	"
	v	Crowley Henry R	25	seaman	32	"
	w	Crowley John K	25	U S N	20	
	x	Crowley Margaret J—†	25	housewife	63	"
	y	Sandler Morris	25	junk dealer	58	"
	z	Sandler Tillie—†	25	clerk	28	
1219						
	a	Gioia John	25	painter	34	
	b	Gioia Josephine—†	25	housewife	33	"
	c	Donahue Helen F—†	26	"	40	
	d	Donahue James E	26	clerk	40	
	e	McDonald Marguerite E—†	26	housewife	44	"
	f	McDonald Marguerite L—†	26	clerk	20	
	g	McDonald Thomas H	26	"	51	
	h	Mogan Joseph F	26	court officer	51	"
	k	Cali Catherine—†	27	housewife	59	"
	l	Cali Joseph	27	rigger	30	"
	m	Cali Michael	27	U S A	26	"
	n	Ciampa Irene—†	27	housewife	25	28 Hull
	o	Ciampa Michael	27	U S N	31	28 "
	p	Palumbo Lorraine—†	27	housewife	48	here
	r	Palumbo Michael	27	machinist	57	"
	s	Palumbo Michael, jr	27	U S A	23	"
	t	Palumbo Rose—†	27	clerk	21	"
	u	Mustone Angelo	27	electrician	43	"
	v	Mustone Rose—†	27	housewife	36	"

Brooks Street—Continued

Y	Donahue Charles A	35	clergyman	56	here
z	McKeon James F	35	"	41	"
1220					
A	O'Donnell Walter J	35	"	39	"
B	Welch James E	35	"	53	Brookline
C	Alisio Benjamin	44	U S N	32	616 Dudley
D	Alisio Catherine—†	44	clerk	29	616 "
E	Recuppero Nicholas	44	mason	63	here
G	Gugluciello Rosalia—†	46	housewife	68	"
H	Bossi Antoinette—†	46	typist	21	"
K	Bossi Fiore	46	U S A	23	342 Princeton
L	*Porcellini Carmella—†	46	housewife	49	here
M	*Porcellini Joseph	46	buyer	53	"
N	Villani Concetta—†	46	housewife	46	"
O	Villani James	46	U S A	21	
P	Villani Nunzio	46	barber	48	
R	*Santosuosso Luigi	48	factoryhand	55	"
S	*Santosuosso Theresa—†	48	stitcher	65	"
T	Ceraso Josephine—†	48	housewife	42	"
U	Ceraso Julius	48	laborer	51	
V	Lepore John	48	foreman	35	"
W	Lepore Phyllis—†	48	housewife	31	"
X	*Cosentino Angelina—†	57	"	62	
Y	Frustaglia Anthony	57	plater	50	
z	Frustaglia Elizabeth—†	57	stitcher	40	"
1221					
A	Femia Mary—†	57	housewife	23	"
B	Preshong Ephraim	59	painter	47	"
C	Preshong Helen—†	59	housewife	37	"
D	*Kirragas Mary—†	59	"	73	
E	Kurgan Anthony J	59	machinist	33	"
F	Karish Alfred	59	"	46	
G	Karish Mary—†	59	housewife	43	"
H	D'Amico Louis	61	U S A	28	
K	D'Amico Mary—†	61	housewife	25	"
L	Moscillo James	61	tailor	41	
M	Moscillo Mary—†	61	housewife	40	"
N	Panzini Josephine—†	61	"	43	
O	Panzini Patrick	61	U S A	22	
P	Panzini Rocco	61	chauffeur	46	"
R	Bruno Anthony	63	student	20	"

Brooks Street—Continued

s	Bruno Eleanor—†	63	housewife	42	here
t	Bruno Ignazio	63	cutter	54	"
u	Baldassarre Anthony	63	teacher	22	"
v	DiNapoli Alfred	63	painter	35	
w	DiNapoli Esther—†	63	housewife	32	"
x	Briana Florence—†	63	"	34	
y	Briana James	63	manager	41	"
z	Barrasso Andrew	65	operator	41	"
	1222				
a	Barrasso Nicoletta—†	65	housewife	37	"
b	*Barrasso Raffaela—†	65	"	65	
c	Sirianni Pasquale	65	marketman	38	"
d	Sirianni Thomasina—†	65	housewife	34	"
f	Hawes Mary—†	77	"	27	"
g	Hawes Thomas M	77	U S N	30	"
h	Doucette Joseph	77	watchman	68	"
k	*Doucette Mary E—†	77	housewife	68	"
l	Doucette Vincent M	77	U S A	25	"
m	Walker Samuel	79	retired	63	3 Saratoga pl
n	*Ippolito Frank	79	shoemaker	61	here
o	Ippolito Grace E—†	79	housewife	50	"
p	D'Agostino Ignazia—†	79	typist	31	"
r	*D'Agostino Jennie—†	79	housewife	58	"
s	D'Agostino Pasquale	79	longshoreman	26	"
t	Cirone Dorothy—†	81	housewife	37	Maine
u	Cirone Walter H	81	U S C G	35	"
v	Insley Aphra	81	seaman	64	here
w	Insley Leonard	81	laborer	24	"
x	Insley Lessie—†	81	housewife	54	"
y	Lombardi Anthony	81	laborer	29	"
z	Lombardi Sabina—†	81	housewife	25	"
	1223				
a	Harris Dorothy—†	83	"	31	126 Marion
b	Harris Earl J	83	cleaner	44	126 "
c	*Duarte Mary R—†	83	housewife	35	242 Paris
d	Gonsalves Eva—†	83	clerk	21	242 "
e	Gonsalves Henry	83	"	23	242 "
f	Fiorentino Anna—†	83	housewife	41	here
g	Fiorentino Charles	83	shipfitter	48	"
h	Marciano John	85	janitor	60	"
k	Pastore Phillip	85	U S A	26	"

Page.	Letter.	FULL NAME.	Residence, Jan. 1, 1945.	Occupation.	Supposed Age.	Reported Residence, Jan. 1, 1944. Street and Number.

Brooks Street—Continued

L	Pastore Rose—†	85	housewife	49	here
M	Pastore Vito M	85	barber	56	"
N	Pastore Vito M, jr	85	metalworker	21	"
O	Marciano Michael	85	packer	32	Somerville
P	Marciano Sophie—†	85	housewife	30	"
R	Carpenito Anthony	87	merchant	42	here
S	Carpenito Mary—†	87	housewife	37	"
V	Cooley Francis	101	baker	29	"
W	Duffy Anna—†	101	housewife	62	"
X	Caggiano James	103	chauffeur	29	"
Y	Caggiano Rose—†	103	housewife	30	"
Z	Ceresi Angelo	103	pressman	59	"
1224					
A	Ceresi Anthony A	103	U S A	30	"
B	Ceresi Justine—†	103	housewife	50	"
C	Ceresi Laura E—†	103	stenographer	24	"
D	Regan Catherine—†	107	housewife	39	"
E	Regan Herbert	107	tester	40	
F	Siracusa Anthony	107	U S A	28	
G	*Siracusa Antoinetta—†	107	housewife	52	"
H	Siracusa Frank	107	cutter	26	"
K	Siracusa Rosario	107	U S A	25	
L	Siracusa Salvatore	107	"	32	
M	Siracusa Sarah—†	107	stitcher	23	"
N	Limole Helen—†	107	housewife	34	"
P	Genualdo Arthur	111	rigger	31	"
R	Genualdo Rose—†	111	housewife	31	"
S	Paolucci Luigi	111	upholsterer	57	"
T	Preziosi Alphonse	113	meatcutter	30	111 Princeton
U	Preziosi Mary—†	113	housewife	23	89 Lexington

Chelsea Street

V	Sciarrillo Lena—†	194	housewife	26	here
W	Sciarrillo Phillip	194	laborer	29	"
X	Salembene Antonia—†	194	housewife	53	"
Y	Salembene Sebastiano	194	attendant	54	"
Z	Amico Bernice—†	194	housewife	28	"
1225					
A	Amico Joseph	194	foreman	32	"
B	Fumicello Jennie—†	196	housewife	38	"

Chelsea Street—Continued

c	Fumicello Joseph	196	painter	45	here
d	Aleo Mary—†	196	housewife	26	"
e	Aleo Philip	196	rigger	29	"
f	*Piermattei Panfilo	196	mason	66	
g	Rizzo Frank	196	retired	92	
h	Rizzo John	196	clerk	61	
k	Rizzo Stella—†	196	housewife	57	"
l	Gagliolo Alfonso	197	laborer	65	"
m	Gagliolo Mary—†	197	housewife	60	"
n	Nurano Alba—†	197	"	48	"
o	Nurano Raymond	197	laborer	22	
p	Nurano Rose—†	197	typist	20	
r	Salamone Anthony	197	U S A	23	
s	Salamone Ignazio	197	"	32	
t	Salamone Joseph	197	"	20	
u	Salamone Luigi	197	shoemaker	63	"
v	Salamone Stella—†	197	housewife	52	"
x	Guerra Alberto	198	U S N	22	"
y	Guerra Luigi	198	carpenter	69	"
z	Guerra Luigi R	198	U S N	27	

1226

a	Grasso Antoinetta—†	198	housewife	27	"
b	Grasso Michael	198	chipper	27	
c	Grasso Ralph	198	watchman	22	"
d	Cormier Gerald	198	U S A	34	
e	Cormier Rose—†	198	housewife	34	"
f	Cioppa Joseph A	199	welder	41	"
g	Cioppa Louise—†	199	housewife	36	"
h	Interbartolo Antoinette—†	199	housekeeper	22	Washington
k	Lopilato Nellie—†	199	housewife	40	here
l	Lopilato Salvatore	199	machinist	50	"
m	Pisano Angela—†	199	housewife	37	"
n	Pisano Nicholas J	199	machinist	37	"
o	Morse Bernard	200	electrician	30	"
p	Morse Mary—†	200	housewife	25	"
r	Walsh Mary—†	200	factoryhand	22	"
s	Walsh Patrick	200	rigger	55	
t	Walsh Theresa—†	200	housewife	55	"
u	Pasquantonio Angelo	200	maintenance	45	"
v	Pasquantonio Margaret—†	200	saleswoman	41	"
w	Sarno Michael	200	laborer	52	"

Chelsea Street—Continued

	x	Perella Esther—†	201	housekeeper	37	here
	y	Perella Pelegrino	201	inspector	64	"
	z	Doucette Peter F	201	machinist	31	"
1227						
	a	Doucette Ruby A—†	201	housewife	26	"
	b	Zaffiro Margaret—†	201	"	38	..
	c	Zaffiro Salvatore	201	machinist	40	"
	d	DeWart Antone	202	fishcutter	43	"
	e	*Cohen Dora—†	202	housewife	55	"
	f	Cohen Isaac	202	U S A	28	
	g	*Cohen Max	202	cooper	62	
	h	Muscarelli Angelina—†	202	factoryhand	23	"
	k	Muscarelli Frances—†	202	housewife	47	"
	l	Muscarelli Salvatore	202	tailor	50	
	m	Muscarelli Vincenza—†	202	factoryhand	21	"
	n	DiGeorgio Anthony	203	U S A	20	
	o	DiGeorgio Dominic	203	laborer	55	"
	p	DiGeorgio Maria—†	203	housewife	50	"
	r	Salerni Angelina—†	203	"	60	
	s	Salerni Santo	203	retired	68	
	t	Lacascia Joseph	203	machinist	41	"
	u	Lacascia Sarah—†	203	stitcher	37	"
	v	Forgione Olympia—†	204	housewife	25	"
	w	Forgione Robert A	204	painter	24	
	x	DelliPriscoli Anthony	204	U S A	21	
	y	DelliPriscoli Geraldine—†	204	factoryhand	24	"
	z	DelliPriscoli Girolamo	204	laborer	55	
1228						
	a	DelliPriscoli Jennie—†	204	factoryhand	26	"
	b	DelliPriscoli Virginia—†	204	housewife	50	"
	c	Yellin Abraham	204	proprietor	42	"
	d	Yellin Lillian—†	204	bookkeeper	23	"
	e	Yellin Rose—†	204	factoryhand	41	"
	f	*Marchetti Jennie—†	205	housewife	41	"
	g	*Marchetti John	205	tailor	45	
	h	*Chianca Carmella—†	205	housewife	57	"
	k	Chianca Pasquale	205	U S A	20	
	l	Gravallese Arthur	205	laborer	28	
	m	Polizzi Angelo	205	U S A	22	
	n	*Polizzi Josephine—†	205	housewife	45	"
	o	Polizzi Phillip	205	laborer	49	

1—12   17

Chelsea Street—Continued

P	Polizzi Salvatore	205	U S A	20	here
R	Cutrone Antonina—†	206	housekeeper	74	"
S	Cutrone Orazio	206	retired	72	"
T	Caprio Louisa—†	206	housewife	37	"
U	Caprio Nicholas	206	clerk	50	
V	*Lampiana Josephine—†	206	housekeeper	68	"
W	Saia Maria—†.	206	"	72	..
X	Amarosi Angelo, jr	207	tailor	32	
Y	Amarosi Mary—†	207	housewife	28	"
Z	Caprigno Louise—†.	207	"	30	

1229

A	*Rosata Marie—†	207	"	56	
B	Rosata Viola—†	207	stitcher	27	"
C	Amorosi Americo	207	"	23	..
D	Amorosi Angelina—†	207	tailor	20	
E	*Amorosi Angelo	207	"	57	
F	Amorosi Carmella—†	207	at home	25	"
G	Amorosi Rose—†	207	housewife	56	"
H	Goudreau John	208	retired	78	
K	Goudreau Marie M—†	208	housewife	80	"
L	*Rena Agostino	208	retired	71	
M	*Rena Josephine—†	208	housewife	70	"
N	Wahlqvist Eva—†	208	"	33	
O	*Wahlqvist Nils	208	engineer	47	"
P	Mugnano Joseph	209	laborer	66	
R	*Mugnano Josephine—†	209	housewife	61	"
S	Torra Catherine—†	209	"	32	
T	Torra Frank	209	proprietor	35	"
U	Mugnano Antoinette—†	209	housewife	28	"
V	Mugnano Charles	209	rigger	36	..
W	Barone John	210	laborer	53	
X	Hassett Agnes C—†	210	housewife	47	"
Y	Hassett Robert J	210	guard	48	

1230

A	DellOrfano Liberata—†	211	housewife	34	"
B	DellOrfano Pasquale	211	checker	37	"
C	Miranda Americo	211	U S A	36	"
D	Miranda Emma—†	211	electrician	23	"
E	Cangiano Lucia—†	211	operator	37	"
F	Cangiano Maria M—†	211	housewife	65	"
G	Cangiano Pasquale	211	welder	33	..

18

Chelsea Street—Continued

H	Cangiano Rose—†	211	tinsmith	31	here
K	Marrocco Carmella—†	211	factoryhand	40	"
L	Ferrera Josephine—†	211	housewife	58	"
M	Ferrera Peter	211	weaver	23	
N	Ferrera Rosalie—†	211	stitcher	33	"
O	Ferrera Samuel J	211	U S A	20	"
P	Minichéllo Louisa—†	212	factoryhand	21	"
R	Minichello Nancy—†	212	housewife	44	"
S	Minichello Pasquale	212	U S A	23	
T	Minichello Ralph	212	U S C G	22	"
U	Minichello Salvatore	212	candymaker	46	"
V	Petrocioni Joseph	212	"	50	
W	Petrocioni Mary—†	212	factoryhand	37	"
X	Petrocioni Theresa—†	212	"	21	
Y	Logiudice Anthony	213	carpenter	58	"
Z	Logiudice Frank	213	U S A	25	"
	1231				
A	Logiudice Ida—†	213	clerk	21	
B	Logiudice Mary—†	213	housewife	48	"
C	Fiandaca Joseph	213	grinder	22	"
D	*Fiandaca Josephine—†	213	housewife	61	"
E	Fiandaca Loretta—†	213	dressmaker	31	"
G	*Berardinelli Cesidino	214	baker	74	"
H	Tracia Anthony	214	factoryhand	34	175 Chelsea
K	Tracia Carmela—†	214	housewife	28	175 "
L	Zecchino Antonio	214	laborer	48	here
M	Zecchino Mary—†	214	saleswoman	20	"
N	Zecchino Raffaela—†	214	housewife	47	"
P	Ferrante Joseph	215	hatter	43	
R	Ferrante Phyllis—†	215	housewife	34	"
S	Ferrante Concetta—†	215	clerk	37	"
T	*Ferrante Florence—†	215	housewife	69	"
U	Ferrante John	215	waiter	33	
V	Ferrante Rose—†	215	packer	41	
W	Brunaccini Charles	215	barber	42	"
X	Brunaccini Josephine—†	215	housewife	43	"
Y	Cassell Ann—†	215	saleswoman	21	"
Z	Santosuosso Angelo	216	clerk	45	
	1232				
A	Santosuosso Frances—†	216	housewife	41	"
B	Caccaviello Joseph P	216	U S A	25	

Chelsea Street—Continued

	c	Caccaviello Leonora—†	216	housewife	24	here
	D	Cericola Thomas	216	tailor	66	"
	F	Zarrella Generoso	217	clerk	45	"
	G	Zarrella Natalie—†	217	housewife	36	"
	H	Phillips Abraham	217	chauffeur	47	"
	K	Phillips Milton	217	U S A	22	
	L	Phillips Sophia—†	217	housewife	44	"
	M	Martucci Augustine	217	engineer	35	"
	N	Martucci Lena—†	217	housewife	35	"
	O	Cuono Allessandra—†	218	"	53	
	P	Cuono Concetta—†	218	factoryhand	26	"
	R	Cuono John	218	U S N	27	
	S	Cuono Luigi	218	factoryhand	55	"
	T	Pittela Joseph	218	operator	49	"
	U	Pittela Miriam—†	218	housewife	44	"
	V	Caprera Antonio	218	fireman	48	"
	W	Caprera Frances—†	218	factoryhand	37	"
	Y	Messina Antoinette—†	219	housewife	29	"
	Z	Messina Frank	219	welder	30	

1233

	A	Ferullo Concetta—†	219	stitcher	36	"
	B	Ferullo Emilio	219	laborer	67	
	C	Ferullo Pasqualina—†	219	stitcher	33	"
	D	Ferullo Ralph	219	shipper	38	
	E	Catanese Joseph	219	buyer	27	"
	F	Catanese Lena—†	219	housewife	26	"
	G	Rodrigues John T	220	U S A	28	
	H	Rodrigues Rose—†	220	housewife	27	"
	L	Carmosino Angelina—†	221	"	30	"
	M	Carmosino Anthony	221	merchant	31	"
	N	Piscitelli Angelina—†	221	dressmaker	35	"
	O	*Piscitelli Lucia—†	221	housewife	74	"
	P	Piscitelli Pasquale	221	U S A	37	"
	R	Ericksen Angelina—†	221	seamstress	36	"
	S	Ericksen Reidar	221	seaman	28	
	T	Freda Leopoldo	221	U S A	37	
	U	*Longo Nicoletta—†	221	housewife	71	"
	V	Correia Charles	223	weaver	32	
	W	Correia Jennie—†	223	housewife	30	"
	X	Crusco Anthony	223	janitor	48	
	Y	Crusco Josephine—†	223	housewife	46	"

20

Page	Letter	Full Name.	Residence, Jan. 1, 1945.	Occupation.	Supposed Age.	Reported Residence, Jan. 1, 1944. Street and Number.

Chelsea Street—Continued

	z	Crusco Nicholas	223	clerk	24	here
1234						
	A	Gatti Daniel	223	foreman	41	New York
	B	Gatti Nanette—†	223	tester	38	"
	C	Panzini Mafalda—†	224	housewife	28	here
	D	Panzini Thomas	224	painter	32	"
	E	DeBenedictis Daniel	224	U S A	25	"
	F	DeBenedictis Jean—†	224	operator	23	"
	G	DeBenedictis Louis	224	U S A	28	
	H	DeBenedictis Vincenzo	224	tailor	53	
	K	Baldini Girio P	224	electrician	31	"
	L	Baldini Palmina A—†	224	housewife	29	"
	M	Marotta Antoinette—†	225	"	28	
	N	Marotta Joseph	225	musician	32	"
	O	Trabucco Albert	225	U S N	21	
	P	Trabucco Anthony	225	bricklayer	54	"
	R	Trabucco Eleanor—†	225	teacher	25	"
	S	Trabucco Theresa—†	225	housewife	54	"
	T	*Mastone Angelina—†	225	"	52	
	U	Mastone Antoinette—†	225	clerk	25	
	V	Mastone Nancia—†	225	stitcher	20	"
	W	Mastone Nicholas	225	laborer	52	"
	X	Mastone Pasquale	225	U S A	29	"
	Y	DiMora Grace—†	226	housewife	39	"
	z	DiMora John	226	metalworker	42	"
1235						
	A	Sclafani Emanuella—†	226	factoryhand	39	83 London
	B	Quartarone John T	227	U S A	32	98 Orient av
	C	Quartarone Mary J—†	227	housewife	25	here
	D	Tavella Rosina—†	227	stitcher	50	"
	E	*Ciccia Emilio	227	"	26	"
	F	Ciccia Millie—†	227	housewife	20	"
	G	Albanese Daisy—†	227	stitcher	36	"
	H	Albanese Michael	227	laborer	39	
	K	Pastore Concetta—†	228	housewife	56	"
	L	Pastore Ousilio	228	factoryhand	56	"
	M	DiNucci Ferdinand	228	clerk	32	"
	N	DiNucci Nancy—†	228	housewife	32	"
	O	Pilato Angelo	229	bartender	42	"
	P	Pilato Josephine—†	229	housewife	37	"
	R	Micciche Andrina—†	229	"	40	"

Page.	Letter.	FULL NAME.	Residence, Jan. 1, 1945.	Occupation.	Supposed Age.	Reported Residence, Jan. 1, 1944. Street and Number.

Chelsea Street—Continued

s	Micciche Rocco	229	chauffeur	42	here
T	Micciche Christina—†	229	housewife	43	"
U	*Micciche Mary—†	229	"	67	"
V	*Micciche Pasquale	229	retired	81	
W	Micciche Pasquale, jr	229	U S A	22	"
X	Micciche Santo	229	shoemaker	48	"
Y	Vertuccio Margaret—†	231	housewife	38	"
z	Vertuccio Nicholas	231	machinist	40	"
	1236				
A	Micciche Damiana—†	231	stitcher	46	238 Marion
B	Micciche Joseph	231	painter	47	238 "
C	Desio Benjamin	231	laborer	50	here
D	Desio Mary—†	231	housewife	43	"
E	Minichino Celia—†	232	factoryhand	22	"
F	Minichino Dominic	232	chauffeur	62	"
G	Minichino Phyllis—†	232	housewife	62	"
H	DePlacido Elizabeth—†	232	"	37	
K	DePlacido Peter	232	tailor	41	
L	DiVingo Flora—†	232	housekeeper	73	"
N	Casaletto Eva—†	233	housewife	33	"
O	Casaletto Joseph	233	millhand	37	"
P	Casaletto Helen—†	233	housewife	28	"
R	Casaletto Gerald	233	laborer	33	"
s	*Casaletto Grace—†	233	housewife	58	"
T	Casaletto John A	233	retired	58	
U	Casaletto Robert	233	U S A	21	"
W	DeNisi Philomena—†	235	housewife	52	231 Chelsea
X	DeNisi Vincent	235	tailor	58	231 "
Y	Fiandaca Margaret—†	235	housewife	29	here
z	Fiandaca Nunzio	235	postal clerk	30	"
	1237				
A	Calistro Angelina—†	235	housewife	52	"
B	Calistro Bruno	235	proprietor	62	"
C	Calistro Frank	235	U S A	20	"
D	Calistro Marion—†	235	stitcher	31	"
E	Palumbo Edward	235	U S A	26	Revere
F	Palumbo Fortunate—†	235	housewife	22	"
H	Dunphy James A	237	U S A	40	72 Sullivan
K	Dunphy John L	237	"	35	72 "
L	Dunphy Sarah—†	237	housewife	68	72 "
M	Tassone Joseph	237	laborer	50	193 London

Chelsea Street—Continued

N	Tassone Mary—†	237	housewife	46	193 London
O	Coleman David B	237	carpenter	48	258 Marion
P	Coleman Marguerite—†	237	housewife	44	258 "
R	McKinley Philomena—†	239	"	37	here
S	McKinley William E	239	pipefitter	33	"
T	Alfonso Joseph	239	janitor	64	"
U	Alfonso Palma—†	239	housewife	60	"
V	Cambria Joseph	239	U S A	25	"
W	Cambria Josephine—†	239	housewife	24	"
X	Aamot Harold	239	welder	42	New York
Y	Aamot Susan—†	239	housewife	36	"
Z	Sanchez Frank G	241	engineer	60	here
	1238				
A	Sanchez Frank T	241	U S A	24	
B	Sanchez Mary R—†	241	housewife	59	"
D	Kootkonety Pola—†	243	housekeeper	56	"
E	LaPusata Alexander	243	laborer	56	"
F	*LaPusata Angelina—†	243	housewife	48	"
G	LaPusata Louis	243	U S N	22	
H	LaPusata Stella—†	243	factoryhand	20	"
K	DeStefano Ella—†	243	housewife	58	"
L	*DeStefano Gerardo	243	laborer	59	
M	DeStefano Linda—†	243	operator	21	"
N	Pezzullo Virginia—†	245	housekeeper	36	"
O	Bozzi Adeline—†	245	tailor	52	"
P	Bozzi Alfred	245	chauffeur	20	"
R	Bozzi Louis	245	tailor	54	
S	Connolly Rose—†	245	housewife	25	"
T	Connolly Thomas	245	U S N	29	
U	Nappa John	247	U S A	24	
V	Nappa Mary—†	247	housewife	56	"
W	Nappa Ralph	247	laborer	66	
X	Vertuccio Pauline—†	247	housewife	29	"
Y	Vertuccio Ralph P	247	operator	27	"
Z	Martori Ida—†	247	housewife	36	"
	1239				
A	Martori Joseph	247	mechanic	37	"
B	Graziano Antoinette—†	249	housewife	53	"
C	Graziano Joseph	249	laborer	44	
D	Graziano Louis	249	U S A	24	
E	Faldetta John	249	"	23	

Chelsea Street—Continued

		FULL NAME.	Residence, Jan. 1, 1945.	Occupation.	Supposed Age.	Reported Residence, Jan. 1, 1944. Street and Number.
F		Faldetta Palma—†	249	assembler	22	here
H		Gubitosi Anna—†	249	housewife	34	"
K		Gubitosi Samuel	249	bookbinder	33	"
G		Olivieri James	249	laborer	27	"
L		Manzi Grace—†	251	saleswoman	30	Medford
M	*Cianculli Mary—†		251	housewife	45	here
N		Cianculli Nicholas	251	laborer	45	"
O	*Capobianco Angelina—†		251	housewife	54	"
P		Capobianco Anthony	251	laborer	59	
R		Capobianco Frederick	251	U S A	30	
S		Montero Anthony P	253	retired	72	
T		Spinazola Guy H	253	candymaker	32	"
U		Spinazola Mary E—†	253	housewife	31	"
V		Stergios James	253	machinist	43	"
W		Stergios Rose—†	253	housewife	35	"
X		Dunbar Anna J—†	253	"	43	
Y		Dunbar George A	253	painter	48	
Z		Young Thomas	253	retired	83	
		1240				
A		Pemintel John	255	painter	54	
B		Pemintel John	255	U S A	35	"
C		Pemintel Mary—†	255	housewife	53	"
D		Falzone Concetta—†	255	factoryhand	26	"
E		Falzone Josephine—†	255	stitcher	24	"
F		Falzone Salvatore	255	U S A	23	
G	*Falzone Theresa—†		255	housewife	56	"
H		Brennan Emily T—†	255	"	66	"
K		Brennan Lillian A—†	255	trimmer	41	"
L		Finelli Dominic	257	laborer	52	
M	*Finelli Marie—†		257	housewife	47	"
N		Venezia Albert R	257	laborer	29	
O		Venezia Rose—†	257	housewife	30	"
P		Pepe John A	257	fireman	32	"
R		Pepe Margaret N—†	257	housewife	29	"
S		Albanese Anthony	259	cutter	61	
T		Albanese Marcia—†	259	housewife	55	"
U		Albanese Raymond A	259	U S A	33	
V		Albanese Richard R	259	U S N	23	
X		Albanese John L	259	machinist	26	"
Y		Albanese Lucy—†	259	housewife	24	"
Z		O'Brien Mary—†	261	"	48	

24

1241
Chelsea Street—Continued

A	O'Brien William	261	chauffeur	60	here
B	Cannella Charles	261	ropemaker	32	"
C	Cannella Domenica—†	261	housewife	30	"
D	Picardi Madeline L—†	261	" .	29	49 Bennington
E	Picardi Pasquale	261	laborer	34	39 Haynes
F	Chambers James	263	pipefitter	21	140 Orleans
H	Messina Alfonso	263	welder	24	here
K	Messina Catherine—†	263	housewife	47	"
G	Messina Charles	263	proprietor	56	"
L	Priore Joseph	263	U S A	27	
M	Priore Lucy—†	263	housewife	26	"
O	Rothwell Alice—†	271	"	61	
P	Rothwell Mitchell	271	laborer	24	"
R	Venezia Irene—†	271	housewife	26	11 Curtis
S	Venezia Michael	271	chauffeur	26	11 "
T	Tango John	271	welder	29	here
U	Tango Margaret—†	271	housewife	27	"
V	*Allen Mary—†	273	"	72	2 Wilbur ct
W	*Bodkins Getel—†	273	at home	73	here
X	Stone Bella—†	273	"	70	"
Y	Albanese Mary—†	273	candymaker	31	"
Z	Torrone Anna—†	275	housewife	27	"

1242

A	Torrone Anthony	275	stitcher	29	"
C	Balbanti Frank	275	pressman	45	"
D	Balbanti Mary—†	275	housewife	62	"
E	Cotreau Albertina—†	276	"	56	
F	Cotreau Roy	276	fishcutter	57	"
G	Tusini Alphonse	276	wireworker	32	"
H	Tusini Rose—†	276	housewife	31	"
K	Costa Lawrence	276	U S N	25	
L	Costa Victoria—†	276	housewife	25	"
M	Mastrangelo Albert	276	U S A	29	
N	Mastrangelo Anthony	276	U S N	27	
O	Mastrangelo Jean—†	276	laundress	20	"
P	Mastrangelo John	276	laborer	68	
R	Mastrangelo Mary—†	276	housewife	60	"
S	Mastrangelo Mary—†	276	clerk	23	
T	Mastrangelo Ralph	276	U S A	36	
U	Walsh James	277	retired	66	

25

Chelsea Street—Continued

v	Walsh Nellie—†	277	housewife	71	here
w	Carvalho Manuel	277	millhand	55	"
x	Carvalho Selstina—†	277	stitcher	25	"
y	*O'Hara Antoinetta—†	277	housewife	21	"
z	O'Hara Hugh J	277	U S A	25	

1243

a	Veglia John	278	longshoreman	29	"
b	Veglia Lillian—†	278	housewife	21	"
d	Ingaciola Anthony	278	U S A	25	
e	Ingaciola Beatrice—†	278	factoryhand	26	"
f	*Ingaciola Marie—†	278	housewife	61	"
g	Ingaciola Nicholas	278	U S A	23	
h	*Ingaciola Pasquale	278	laborer	68	
k	Jordan John W	279	retired	84	
l	Jordan Mabel H—†	279	housekeeper	43	"
m	Lindholm Allen	279	operator	36	Chelsea
n	Lindholm Emily—†	279	housewife	32	"
o	*Jannis Mary—†	279	"	42	147 Princeton
p	Gallo Grace—†	280	operator	22	here
r	Gallo Marie—†	280	housewife	42	"
s	Gallo Pasquale	280	laborer	47	"
t	Stefano Mary—†	280	housewife	38	"
u	Stefano Ralph	280	floorlayer	37	"
v	Accardi Annetta—†	280	dressmaker	32	"
w	*Accardi Joseph	280	retired	71	"
x	*Accardi Marie—†	280	housewife	63	"
y	*Rogowicz Amelia—†	281	"	47	
z	Rogowicz Annie J—†	281	operator	21	"

1244

a	*Rogowicz John	281	baker	54	
c	Mangino Frank	281	toolkeeper	29	"
d	Mangino Stella M—†	281	housewife	26	"
e	Vieira Emilio	282	retired	73	
f	Vieira Emily—†	282	housewife	72	"
g	Francis Anthony	282	U S N	21	"
h	Francis Margaret—†	282	housewife	42	"
k	Oliver James R	282	salesman	33	"
l	Oliver Vera—†	282	housewife	30	"
m	Santosuosso Albert J	283	chauffeur	31	"
n	Santosuosso Theresa M—†	283	housewife	30	"

Chelsea Street—Continued

o	Sonn Joseph A	283	U S A	31	here
p	Boehner Minnie E—†	283	waitress	55	"
r	Mangino Anna M—†	283	housewife	27	"
s	Mangino John A	283	machinist	27	"
t	Alteriso Alexander	284	technician	40	"
u	Alteriso Mary—†	284	housewife	40	"
v	Selvitella Mary—†	284	clerk	21	46 Morris
w	Selvitella Ralph	284	laborer	50	46 "
x	Selvitella Virginia—†	284	housewife	48	46 "
y	Magaletta Mary—†	284	"	34	178 Marion
z	Magaletta Michael	284	longshoreman	27	144 Maverick

1245

a	Ricciardi Alexandria C–†	285	clerk	24	here
b	Ricciardi Concetta—†	285	housewife	50	"
c	Ricciardi Frank	285	packer	55	"
d	Sacco Rose R—†	285	housewife	35	"
e	Sacco Salvatore J	285	boilermaker	45	"
f	Guazzerotti Andrew J	285	seaman	21	
g	Guazzerotti Mary—†	285	housewife	40	"
h	*Cipriano Francesca—†	286	"	81	
k	Cipriano Salvatore	286	retired	83	
l	*Mauro Emelia—†	286	housewife	50	"
m	Mauro Pellegrino	286	tailor	56	
n	Pisano Phililp	286	shoemaker	30	"
o	*Pisano Philomena—†	286	housewife	29	"
r	Trager Frances—†	287	"	32	
s	Trager Louis	287	foreman	38	"
t	Young Anna T—†	287	housewife	56	21 Bennington
u	Young Ethel G—†	287	"	24	21 "
v	Young Frederick A	287	rigger	32	21 "
w	Angelo Catherine—†	288	housewife	46	here
x	Angelo Pasquale	288	laborer	57	"
y	Balletto Carmen	288	"	49	"
z	*Balletto Susie—†	288	housewife	56	"

1246

a	Collicconi Florence—†	288	dressmaker	33	"
b	Terranova Joseph	288	tilesetter	52	"
c	Terranova Josephine—†	288	housewife	42	"
d	Luongo John R	289	U S N	29	
e	Luongo Mary—†	289	housewife	27	"
f	Adelman Bernard H	289	U S A	25	

Page.	Letter.	FULL NAME.	Residence, Jan. 1, 1945.	Occupation.	Supposed Age.	Reported Residence, Jan. 1, 1944. Street and Number.

Chelsea Street—Continued

G	Adelman E Milton	289	U S A	23	here
H	Adelman Jacob	289	carpenter	61	"
K	Adelman Sadie—†	289	housewife	47	"
L	Adelman Shirley D—†	289	secretary	20	"
M	Neidleman Julius	289	U S A	31	..
N	Neidleman Mollie A—†	289	housewife	24	"
O	Cambria Josephine M—†	289	"	26	193 Chelsea
P	Cambria Pasquale B	289	chauffeur	21	165 Putnam
R	Lachiano Fannie—†	290	housewife	23	here
S	Lachiano Peter	290	laborer	32	"
T	Amarena Alma—†	290	housewife	39	"
U	Amarena John	290	laborer	40	"
V	*Muccio Celia—†	290	housewife	33	"
W	Muccio Domenic	290	candymaker	37	"
X	Muccio Olga—†	290	operator	20	"
Y	Sheehan Daniel H	291	inspector	43	"
Z	Sheehan Daniel H, jr	291	U S A	20	

1247

A	Sheehan Mary A—†	291	housewife	41	"
B	Kania Gladys—†	291	at home	23	"
C	Kania Michael J	291	U S A	27	
D	Muise Doris—†	291	at home	20	"
E	*Muise Mary E—†	291	housewife	50	"
F	*Muise Wilfred J	291	carpenter	68	"
G	Velardo Lena—†	292	housewife	23	"
H	Velardo Victor	292	diesetter	26	"
K	Napolitano Frances—†	292	housewife	44	"
L	Napolitano Pasquale	292	laborer	48	
M	*Grasso Mary—†	292	housekeeper	80	"
N	Ruggerio Augustine	292	laborer	51	"
O	Ruggerio Margaret—†	292	housewife	50	"
P	Gauthier Ellen A—†	293	"	73	
R	Gauthier Homer F	293	clerk	36	
S	Gauthier John J	293	longshoreman	33	"
T	LaCortiglia Dominic	294	driller	44	"
U	LaCortiglia Katherine—†	294	housewife	42	"
V	Freda Angeline—†	294	operator	22	"
W	Freda Carmella—†	294	housewife	60	"
X	Freda Pellegrino	294	candymaker	58	"
Y	Guarnacci Agata—†	294	housewife	45	"
Z	Guarnacci Calogero	294	factoryhand	48	"

28

1248

Chelsea Street—Continued

	A	*Pallizzoti Benedetto	296	retired	83	here
	B	*Pallizzoti Gaetana—†	296	housewife	82	"
	C	Bilotta James	296	U S A	27	Weymouth
	D	Bilotta Rose—†	296	housewife	27	"
	E	Murphy Edward	296	U S A	28	here
	F	Murphy Evelyn—†	296	housewife	27	"
	G	Silva William P	298	barber	83	"
	H	Corza Anna—†	298	housekeeper	38	400 Bremen
	K	Fischer Catherine—†	298	stitcher	22	here
	L	Fischer Dorothy—†	298	"	20	"
	M	Fischer Jennie—†	298	"	24	"
	N	Rinaldi Flabia—†	298	housewife	50	"
	O	*Rinaldi Frank	298	baker	52	
	P	*Consolo Bruno	300	fishcutter	52	"
	R	Intraversato Matilda—†	300	housewife	28	31 Chelsea
	S	Intraversato Sabino	300	laborer	29	31 "
	T	Charette Anna—†	300	housewife	26	here
	U	Charette Emile	300	U S A	34	"
	V	Rizzo Palma—†	302	at home	82	374 Bennington
	W	Grieco Felix	302	salesman	63	here
	X	*Grieco Philomena—†	302	housewife	63	"
	Y	Grieco Anna—†	302	tubemaker	26	"
	Z	Grieco Marguerite—†	302	stitcher	27	"

1249

	A	Grieco Pasquale	302	U S A	21	
	C	Russo Nicholas	304	"	25	
	D	Russo Sophie—†	304	housewife	23	"
	E	Fasano Josephine—†	304	"	36	
	F	*Sarmento Fernando	306	retired	77	
	G	LaCerda Frederick	306	operator	32	"
	H	LaCerda Lillian—†	306	housewife	29	"
	K	Rose Evelyn—†	306	operator	33	"
	L	Rose Mary A—†	306	housewife	65	"
	M	Rose Otto	306	carpenter	66	"
	N	Balletto Josephine—†	306	housewife	45	"
	O	Balletto Lena—†	306	operator	21	"
	P	Balletto Mary—†	306	"	21	
	R	Ardita Frank	308	U S A	36	
	S	Ardita Theresa—†	308	housewife	31	"
	T	Incerto Anthony	308	U S A	27	

Page.	Letter.	Full Name.	Residence, Jan. 1, 1945.	Occupation.	Supposed Age.	Reported Residence, Jan. 1, 1944. Street and Number.

Chelsea Street—Continued

u	Incerto Hazel—†	308	housewife	25	Georgia
v	Incerto Josephine—†	308	"	55	here
w	Incerto Rose—†	308	hairdresser	24	"
x	Incerto Vincent	308	candymaker	65	"
y	Marrama Edward	308	U S A	28	148 Everett
z	Marrama Mary—†	308	stitcher	29	here

1250

a	Cammorato Andrew	308	U S A	27	
b	Cammorato Anna—†	308	housewife	48	"
c	Cammorato Gaetano	308	factoryhand	61	"
d	Cammorato Mary—†	308	"	21	
e	Cammorato Pasquale	308	U S A	24	"
f	*Mirisola Giuseppina—†	310	at home	72	"
g	Mirisola Angelina—†	310	housewife	42	"
h	Mirisola Fannie—†	310	tool sharpener	20	"
k	Mirisola Josephine—†	310	stitcher	22	"
l	Mirisola Peter	310	welder	47	
m	Mirisola James	310	"	34	"
n	Mirisola Philomena—†	310	housewife	32	"
o	DeFronzo Clara—†	312	at home	34	"
p	Bohanan Delia—†	312	housewife	55	"
r	Bohanan Pearl—†	312	tel operator	20	"
s	Flynn Frederick P	312	U S A	22	
t	Flynn Helena A—†	312	housekeeper	55	"
u	Movitz Marjorie E—†	312	saleswoman	35	"
v	Movitz Morris	312	U S N	37	
w	Harrison Frederick J	314	deckhand	55	"
x	Harrison Winifred—†	314	housewife	38	"
y	Raia Eva—†	314	saleswoman	22	"
z	Raia Mary—†	314	housewife	43	"

1251

a	Raia Mildred—†	314	clerk	23	

Marion Street

d	Micele Anna—†	230	labeler	23	here
e	Micele John	230	foreman	46	"
f	Micele John A	230	U S A	20	"
g	Micele Mary—†	230	inspector	22	"
h	Micele Minnie—†	230	housewife	42	"
k	*Albanese Cecelia—†	230	"	46	

Marion Street—Continued

L	Albanese Concellatta—†	230	operator	23	here
M	Albanese Pasquale	230	U S A	22	"
N	Albanese Salvatore	230	laborer	50	"
O	Albanese Samuel	230	U S M C	20	"
R	Matarazza Enis	232	etcher	28	..
S	Matarazza Florence—†	232	factoryhand	26	"
T	Matarazza Gabriel	232	"	67	,,
U	Matarazza Joseph	232	U S A	35	
V	*Matarazza Rose—†	232	housewife	65	"
W	DeAngelis Alfred R	232	agent	47	
X	DeAngelis Mollie—†	232	housewife	38	"
Y	*Terlino Frank	234	retired	61	
Z	Terlino Margaret—†	234	stitcher	28	"
	1252				
A	*Terlino Marianna—†	234	housewife.	60	"
B	*Samproni Catherine—†	234	stitcher	45	"
C	*Samproni Frank	234	laborer	57	
D	Samproni Joseph	234	U S A	24	"
E	Samproni Virginia—†	234	stitcher	22	"
F	*Guiffrida Frances—†	234	housekeeper	67	"
G	Sinatra Frances—†	234	factoryhand	20	"
H	Sinatra Joseph	234	U S A	22	"
K	Sinatra Phillip	234	"	21	"
L	Sinatra Sarah—†	234	housewife	41	"
M	*Faraci Phillipa—†	236	stitcher	54	165 Chelsea
N	Faraci Stella—†	236	domestic	24	165 "
O	Faraci Yolanda—†	236	welder	20	165 "
P	Dragani Anthony	236	toolmaker	26	5 North sq
R	Dragani Pauline—†	236	housewife	22	23 Fleet
S	Rotondo Alice—†	236	"	51	here
T	Rotondo Orazio	236	laborer	63	"
U	Rotondo Rose—†	236	stitcher	20	"
V	Fallica Jennie—†	238	clerk	21	
W	Fallica John	238	proprietor	55	"
X	Fallica Lucy—†	238	housewife	45	"
Y	Finocchio Anne—-†	238	housekeeper	53	110 Paris
Z	Finocchio Anne M—†	238	examiner	20	110 "
	1253				
A	Finocchio Anthony	238	chauffeur	29	110 "
B	Finocchio Susan—†	238	operator	23	110 "
D	Interbartolo Charles	252	salesman	38	here

Marion Street—Continued

E	Interbartolo Helen—†	252	housewife	32	here
F	DeGloria Immaculata—†	252	"	54	4 Brooks
G	DeGloria Rosario	252	laborer	54	4 "
H	Forgione Angelo	252	packer	40	here
K	Forgione Battista	252	seaman	62	"
L	Forgione Christina—†	252	housewife	37	"
M	Chiello Angela—†	254	assembler	22	"
N	Chiello Joseph	254	porter	54	
O	Fabello Louis	254	U S A	26	
P	Fabello Marie—†	254	inspector	23	"
R	Pisano Frank	254	finisher	53	"
S	Pisano Louise—†	254	factoryhand	20	"
T	Pisano Palma—†	254	housewife	46	"
U	Burke Joseph J	254	U S N	24	"
V	Burke Mary—†	254	factoryhand	40	"
W	*Chiello Angelo	256	retired	83	
X	*Chiello Mary A—†	256	housewife	83	"
Y	Schepici Andrew	256	bartender	27	264 Paris
Z	Schepici Anne—†	256	housewife	22	264 "

1254

A	Cobino Angelo	256	laborer	50	here
B	*Cobino Erminia—†	256	housewife	40	"
C	Cobino Mary—†	256	factoryhand	21	"
D	Fulginiti Frank	258	chipper	34	471 Col av
E	Fulginiti Ruth—†	258	housewife	37	471 "
F	DiGiroloma Dominica—†	258	"	55	here
G	DiGiroloma Emilio	258	U S A	22	"
H	DiGiroloma Eugene	258	"	26	"
K	DiGiroloma Joseph	258	laborer	57	
L	DiGiroloma Louis	258	U S C G	23	"
M	DiGiroloma Mary—†	258	housewife	31	"
N	DiGiroloma Nicholas	258	U S A	24	"
O	Sacks Rachel—†	258	housekeeper	54	"

Morris Street

P	DiGregorio Angela—†	5	housewife	27	here
R	DiGregorio Armando	5	electrician	27	"
S	Catanese Anthony	5	laborer	35	"
T	Catanese Lena—†	5	housewife	32	"
U	Chiave Josephine—†	5	clerk	20	

Morris Street—Continued

v	Chiave Julia—†	5	housewife	47	here
w	Chiave Mario	5	pressman	54	"
x	Chiave Mario, jr	5	U S A	25	"
y	Chiave Martha—†	5	clerk	23	
z	*Singarella Mario	5	retired	73	
	1255				
A	Mazzarella Anthony J	7	pipecoverer	39	"
B	Mazzarella Mary—†	7	housewife	39	"
c	Capezzuto James	7	metalworker	27	"
D	Capezzuto Mary—†	7	housewife	25	"
E	Capezzuto Grace—†	7	"	29	
F	Capezzuto Nicholas J	7	machinist	31	"
G	Gioiosa Daniel	13	operator	32	"
H	Gioiosa Josephine—†	13	housewife	24	"
K	Giusta Josephine—†	13	clerk	25	
L	*Giusta Phillipa—†	13	housekeeper	54	"
M	Knopp Vincenza G—†	13	clerk	20	"
N	Tornami Angelina—†	13	stitcher	25	"
o	*Tornami Joseph	13	retired	70	
P	Tornami Louis	13	U S A	23	
R	*Tornami Marie—†	13	housewife	60	"
s	Tornami Salvatore	13	U S A	27	"
T	*Avola Michael	15	shoemaker	54	"
U	*Avola Ola—†	15	housewife	54	"
v	Jorgensen Charlotte—†	15	"	31	
w	Jorgensen George	15	seaman	28	"
x	Yancovitz Alice—†	15	clerk	24	
y	Yancovitz Dominic	15	laborer	58	
z	Yancovitz Frank	15	U S N	21	"
	1256				
A	*Yancovitz Monica—†	15	housewife	55	"
B	*Casaccio Angelo	15	proprietor	68	"
c	Casaccio Josephine—†	15	housewife	53	"
D	Nesta Antoinette—†	17	stitcher	21	"
E	Nesta Dominic	17	fishcutter	20	"
F	*Nesta Lena—†	17	sorter	55	
G	Nesta Louis	17	candymaker	55	"
H	Nesta Salvatore	17	U S N	22	"
K	Ottana Joseph	17	policeman	55	"
L	Ottana Katherine—†	17	laundress	23	"
M	Ottana Mary—†	17	housewife	42	"

Morris Street—Continued

N	Ottana Thelma—†	17	laundress	20	here
O	Schena Rose—†	17	clerk	21	"
P	Schena Silverio	17	laborer	49	"
R	Schena Theresa—†	17	housewife	43	"
S	Indorato Filadelfio	19	pipefitter	27	"
T	Indorato Phillipa—†	19	housewife	25	"
U	Minichiello Angelina—†	19	"	26	Everett
V	Minichiello Angelo	19	rigger	34	"
W	Montalto Josephine—†	19	clerk	21	here
X	Montalto Mary—†	19	housewife	39	"
Y	Montalto Nicholas	19	laborer	49	"
Z	Fumicello Concetta—†	20	housewife	36	"
	1257				
A	Fumicello Michael	20	carpenter	39	"
B	Block Grace—†	21	housewife	26	"
C	Fumicello Josephine—†	21	"	38	
D	Fumicello Paul	21	laborer	47	
E	Dinota Andrew	21	"	50	
F	Dinota Angelina—†	21	dressmaker	22	"
G	Dinota Fred	21	U S A	26	
H	Dinota Mary—†	21	housewife	51	"
K	DiMinico Jennie M—†	22	"	42	New Jersey
L	DiMinico John	22	proprietor	39	"
M	Picariello Elisa—†	22	housewife	65	here
N	Picariello Salvatore	22	shoemaker	65	"
O	*Fumicello Philippa—†	23	housekeeper	68	"
R	Milano Lena—†	23	"	51	
S	Benedetti Alfred	24	meatcutter	39	"
T	Benedetti Phyllis—†	24	housewife	36	"
U	Flammia Angelo M	24	U S A	24	
V	Flammia Antonio	24	laborer	49	
W	Flammia Frances L—†	24	clerk	20	"
X	Flammia Lucia—†	24	housewife	47	"
Y	Richard William	25	carpenter	49	477 Meridian
Z	Kinder Ethel—†	25	housekeeper	39	477 "
	1258				
B	Balzano Adeline—†	26	operator	39	here
C	Vertuccio Emelio	27	electroplater	25	81 Brooks
D	Vertuccio Josephine—†	27	housewife	24	81 "
E	*Meloni Amelia—†	27	candymaker	48	here
F	Meloni John	27	machinist	38	"

Page.	Letter.	FULL NAME.	Residence, Jan. 1, 1945.	Occupation.	Supposed Age.	Reported Residence, Jan. 1, 1944. Street and Number.

Morris Street—Continued

G	*Meloni Mary—†	27	housekeeper	72	here
H	Miranda Dionizio	27	machinist	45	"
K	Miranda Enrico	27	U S A	20	"
L	Miranda James	27	"	21	
M	Miranda Mary—†	27	housewife	41	"
N	LaMarca Alfred	28	electrician	33	"
O	LaMarca Mary—†	28	housewife	31	"
P	Parisse Alesio	28	factoryhand	44	"
R	Parisse Mary A—†	28	housewife	37	"
S	Mazza Antoinetta—†	28	"	35	
T	Mazza John	28	laborer	41	"
U	Vaccaro Joseph H	30	U S A	22	244 Havre
V	Vaccaro Mary E—†	30	housewife	20	244 "
W	Casazza Deodato T	30	painter	45	here
X	Casazza Victoria R—†	30	housewife	34	"
Y	Constantine Henry A	30	laborer	33	"
Z	Constantine Louise—†	30	housewife	33	"
	1259				
A	*Cresta Elizabeth M—†	32	"	28	73 Cottage
B	Cresta Gerardo	32	butcher	30	73 "
C	Dushinsky Anna—†	32	housewife	65	here
D	Dushinsky Louis	32	tailor	73	"
E	Gioioso Joseph J	32	laborer	33	"
F	Gioioso Josephine T—†	32	housewife	29	"
G	Mastromarino John	33	U S A	23	··
H	Mastromarino Rose—†	33	housewife	25	"
K	Taurone Angelo	33	laborer	47	
L	Taurone Frank	33	U S M C	21	"
M	*Pittella Victoria—†	33	housewife	38	"
N	Terlino Eleanor—†	34	"	21	
O	Terlino Vincent	34	U S A	23	
P	Aguiar Eleanor—†	34	stitcher	23	··
R	*Gomes Benvinda—†	34	houseworker	44	"
S	Lemmo Joseph	34	rigger	41	
T	Lemmo Phyllis—†	34	housewife	32	"
V	Muldoon Thomas P	36	driller	49	
W	Muldoon Victoria M—†	36	housewife	48	" ·
Y	Pellegrini Rose—†	37	"	25	
Z	Pellegrini Salverino	37	U S A	23	··
	1260				
A	Santaniello Augustine	37	riveter	27	

35

Page.	Letter.	FULL NAME.	Residence, Jan. 1, 1945.	Occupation.	Supposed Age.	Reported Residence, Jan. 1, 1944. Street and Number.

Morris Street—Continued

B	Santaniello Josephine—†	37	housewife	27	here
c	Cagnina Anna—†	37	"	56	"
D	Cagnina Joseph	37	laborer	55	"
E	Cagnina Salvatore	37	U S A	21	..
F	*Bandino Antoinette—†	38	housewife	80	"
G	*Bandino Paul	38	retired	76	
H	*Pimental John	38	painter	41	"
K	Pimental Mary—†	38	housewife	42	"
L	Francis Frank	38	machinist	26	Somerville
M	Francis Margaret—†	·38	housewife	24	"
N	Depari Frank	40	mechanic	32	here
O	Depari Vito	40	retired	65	"
P	Pagliuso Alphonso	40	U S A	28	"
R	Pagliuso Anna—†	40	housewife	25	"
S	Collins Margaret—†	40	assembler	26	"
T	Collins Marie—†	40	waitress	65	"
U	Barone Carmella—†	41	housewife	56	"
V	Barone Vito	41	laborer	66	
W	Polito Gabriel	42	boilermaker	39	"
X	*Polito Theresa—†	42	housewife	68	"
Y	Castelucci Sadie—†	42	stitcher	39	"
Z	Castelucci Samuel	42	laborer	46	
	1261				
A	DiMarino Gerard	42	electrician	31	58 Frankfort
B	DiMarino Pasqualina—†	42·	housewife	60	58 "
C	LaMonica Lawrence	43	machinist	33	here
D	LaMonica Lucy—†	43	housewife	33	"
E	Russo Angelo	43	U S A	35	"
F	Russo Gabriella—†	43	operator	28	"
G	Russo Laura—†	43	housewife	64	"
H	Russo Madeline—†	43	typist	22	
K	Russo Mary—†	43	packer	37	
L	Russo Thomas	43	longshoreman	31	"
M	Incerto Antonio	44	retired	67	..
O	Incerto Florence—†	44	stitcher	23	"
N	Incerto Jennie—†	44	shipper	26	"
P	Griffin Ann F—†	44	housewife	63	Revere
R	DiPlacido Bernardo	44	laborer	54	here
S	DiPlacido Mary—†	44	housewife	46	"
T	Cassia Joseph	45	mechanic	44	"
U	Cassia Mary—†	45	housewife	44	"

Morris Street—Continued

v	Marino Frank	45	operator	50	here
w	*Aliano Concetta—†	45	housekeeper	76	"
x	Aliano Samuel	45	painter	46	"
y	*Lembo Catherine—†	46	housewife	64	13 Havre
z	Lembo Peter	46	potter	64	13 "

1262

a	Vella Josephine—†	46	housewife	31	here
b	Vella Rosario	46	counterman	35	"
c	O'Connell Thomas	46	shipfitter	47	"
e	Viarella Joseph	51	fisherman	36	"
f	Viarella Vita—†	51	housewife	30	"
g	Perrone Angelo	51	U S M C	21	"
h	Perrone Dominic	51	factoryhand	54	"
k	Perrone Jessie—†	41	housewife	50	"
l	*Perrone Susan—†	51	at home	80	"
m	Perrone Susan—†	51	dressmaker	22	"
n	Mancuso Charles	51	laborer	50	"
o	Mancuso Jennie—†	51	housewife	40	"
p	Mancuso Julia—†	51	stitcher	20	"
r	*Perriello Philip	51	retired	78	
s	Mirabella Anthony	65	U S A	29	
t	Mirabella Nora—†	65	housewife	30	"
u	Cella Anthony	65	laborer	34	
v	Cella Elizabeth—†	65	clerk	32	
w	*Guarino Lena—†	65	housewife	44	"
x	Accomando Michael	67	baker	26	
y	Accomando Veronica—†	67	housewife	25	"
z	Ruggiero Diletta—†	67	burner	22	"

1263

a	Ruggiero Fortunato	67	porter	50	
b	Ruggiero Jennie—†	67	housewife	50	"
c	Penta Ernest G	67	operator	31	"
d	Penta Helen—†	67	housewife	28	"
e	DeCristoforo Antonio	69	machinist	33	"
f	DeCristoforo Fannie—†	69	housewife	31	"
g	Levins Joseph	69	presser	21	"
h	Levins Louis	69	tailor	48	
k	Levins Robert	69	instructor	25	"
l	Levins Sarah—†	69	housewife	49	"
m	Gubitosi Joseph	69	binder	35	
n	Gubitosi Philomena—†	69	housewife	34	"

Page:	Letter.	FULL NAME.	Residence, Jan. 1, 1945.	Occupation.	Supposed Age.	Reported Residence, Jan. 1, 1944.
						Street and Number.

Morris Street—Continued

	P	Olivieri Mario	71	longshoreman	23	here
	R	Olivieri Mary—†	71	housewife	25	"
	S	Doucette Charles E	71	U S A	37	"
	T	Doucette Josephine—†	71	operator	33	"
	U	Olivieri John	71	laborer	50	"
	V	Olivieri Mary—†	71	housewife	48	"
	W	Fratto Peter	73	diecutter	35	"
	X	Fratto Rose—†	73	housewife	28	"
	Y	Senese Michael	73	welder	33	36 Morris
	Z	Senese Phyllis—†	73	housewife	35	36 "
1264						
	A	Johnson Ada D—†	73	clerk	25	here
	B	Johnson Joseph B	73	laborer	50	"
	C	Johnson Margaret B—†	73	SPAR	20	"
	D	Johnson Marion F—†	73	clerk	28	"
	E	Johnson Mary F—†	73	housewife	47	"
	F	Sousa Meda—†	75	laundress	44	"
	G	*Molino Charles	75	laborer	56	"
	H	*Molino Rose—†	75	housewife	48	"
	K	Molino Theresa—†	75	SPAR	25	
	L	Stewart Nolen	75	U S A	27	
	M	Stewart Sophie—†	75	clerk	27	
	N	Lettieri Antonio	75	shipper	20	"
	O	Lettieri Joseph	75	laborer	57	
	P	Lettieri Josephine—†	75	housewife	54	"
	R	Lettieri Rosario	75	U S A	25	"
	S	Lettieri Sophie—†	75	packer	21	
	T	*Delsie Antoinette—†	77	housewife	60	"
	U	Delsie John	77	electrician	24	"
	V	Indingaro Rose—†	77	machinist	24	"
	W	Sarro Angelina—†	77	inspector	29	"
	X	Sarro Anthony	77	U S A	25	
	Y	Sarro Elizabeth—†	77	stitcher	22	"
	Z	Sarro Marie—†	77	solderer	20	"
1265						
	A	Sarro Theresa—†	77	housewife	51	"
	B	White Catherine B—†	77	"	73	
	C	White George F	77	checker	41	"
	D	Cocozza Dominic	79	retired	64	"
	E	Cocozza Julia—†	79	sorter	25	"
	F	McGuine James W	79	machinist	59	"

38

Page.	Letter.	Full Name.	Residence, Jan. 1, 1945.	Occupation.	Supposed Age.	Reported Residence, Jan. 1, 1944. Street and Number.

Morris Street—Continued

	G	Sanchez Frank	79	U S A	24	here
	H	Sanchez Lorraine—†	79	housewife	24	"
	K	Cocozza Charles	79	shipper	30	"
	L	Cocozza Theresa—†	79	housewife	29	"
	M	Agre Antonio	81	retired	69	
	N	Agre Frances—†	81	housewife	67	"
	O	Bartolomeo Helen—†	81	"	29	
	P	Bartolomeo Lawrence	81	U S A	29	
	R	Cimino Frances—†	81	boxmaker	21	"
	S	Farulla Candida—†	81	housewife	40	"
	T	Farulla Vincent	81	assembler	49	"
	U	Accomando Fiore	83	laborer	32	
	V	Accomando Madeline—†	83	housewife	30	"
	W	Shapiro Anna—†	83	saleswoman	32	"
	X	Shapiro Minnie—†	83	bookkeeper	27	"
	Y	Shapiro Samuel	83	proprietor	67	"
	Z	Pappalardo Mary—†	83	housewife	47	"

1266

	A	Pappalardo Vincent	83	laborer	56	"
	B	Russo Alma—†	87	housewife	39	"
	C	Russo Anthony	87	machinist	39	"
	D	Indingaro Isabelle—†	87	housewife	64	"
	E	Indingaro Lawrence	87	U S A	36	"
	F	Tavella Catherine—†	89	housewife	22	59 Chelsea
	G	Tavella Frank	89	laborer	23	59 "
	H	Jameson Helen—†	89	housewife	44	here
	K	Jameson John	89	chauffeur	43	"
	L	Napolitano Clement	89	laborer	40	"
	M	Napolitano Ida—†	89	housewife	36	"
	N	Ruggiero Diega—†	90	stitcher	26	"
	O	Ruggiero Joseph	90	U S N	25	
	P	Bratt Gustaf	90	retired	74	"
	R	Hennessey Anna—†	90	assembler	35	"
	S	Hennessey John	90	U S N	37	"
	T	Scarpa Carmen	90	"	28	
	U	Scarpa Margaret—†	90	clerk	26	"
	V	Caccaviello Assunta—†	91	painter	24	"
	W	*Caccaviello Celesta—†	91	housewife	53	"
	X	*Caccaviello Michael	91	laborer	59	
	Y	Caccaviello Michael	91	U S A	23	
	Z	*Caccaviello Peter	91	florist	20	

Page.	Letter.	Full Name.	Residence, Jan. 1, 1945.	Occupation.	Supposed Age.	Reported Residence, Jan. 1, 1944. Street and Number.

1267
Morris Street—Continued

A	Caccaviello Theresa—†	91	stitcher	26	here
B	Ferrante Graziano	91	retired	73	"
C	LaCortiglia Harry	91	laborer	38	"
D	LaCortiglia Louise—†	91	housewife	34	"
E	Genova Anthony	99	U S A	29	
F	Genova Florence—†	99	clerk	24	
G	Genova Pasquale	99	porter	65	
H	*Genova Pasqualina—†	99	housewife	64	"
K	Kavjian Anna—†	99	"	26	52 Saratoga
L	Kavjian Leo	99	conductor	24	52 "
M	Barbanti Alfreda—†	101	housewife	30	here
N	Barbanti John	101	proprietor	36	"
O	Mandella Helen—†	101	housewife	47	"
P	Mandella Patrick	101	laborer	62	
R	Barbanti Antonio	101	retired	78	
S	Barbanti Josephine—†	101	housewife	72	"
U	Lanagan Catherine—†	103	clerk	21	"
V	Lanagan Elizabeth—†	103	housewife	45	"
W	Lanagan Henry J	103	laborer	51	"
X	Napolitano Catherine—†	103	housewife	33	"
Y	Napolitano Michael	103	millhand	48	"
Z	Marino Dora—†	103	housewife	25	"

1268

A	Marino Thomas	103	chauffeur	30	"
B	Porter Christian	106	supervisor	30	"
C	Porter Grace—†	106	housewife	28	"
D	Fine Anna—†	106	secretary	35	"
E	Fine Harry	106	junk dealer	47	"
F	Fine Morris	106	laborer	32	
G	Israel Isabella—†	106	housewife	34	"
H	Lombardo Dario	106	welder	20	
K	Lombardo Helen—†	106	factoryhand	28	"
L	Lombardo Joseph	106	driller	37	
M	Serra Alma—†	106	housewife	34	"
N	Serra Patrick	106	electrician	38	"

Paris Street

P	Pasquantonio Phyllis—†	253	housewife	28	here
R	Pasquantonio William	253	pipefitter	33	"

Paris Street—Continued

s	Lamonica Anthony	253	U S A	24	here
t	Lamonica Antonio	253	presser	52	"
u	Lamonica James	253	U S N	21	"
v	*Lamonica Mary—†	253	housewife	42	"
w	LaGrassa Peter	253	chauffeur	28	"
x	LaGrassa Virginia—†	253	housewife	29	"
y	Cerone Mary—†	255	"	27	420 Chelsea
z	Cerone Sandino	255	clerk	35	420 "

1269

a	Calderone Anthony	255	laborer	48	here
b	Calderone Edward	255	U S A	20	"
c	Calderone Mary—†	255	housewife	41	"
d	Calderone Phyllis—†	255	operator	23	"
e	Calderone Vincent	255	musician	22	"
f	Luciano Joseph	255	U S A	27	
g	Luciano Mary—†	255	dressmaker	20	"
h	Luciano Michael	255	U S N	22	
k	Luciano Theresa—†	255	housekeeper	47	"
l	Pasquantonio Antonio	257	retired	75	
m	*Pasquantonio Jennie—†	257	housewife	68	"
n	Casamassima Dominic	257	shoemaker	41	"
o	Casamassima Emelia—†	257	housekeeper	33	"
p	*Casamassima Gaetana—†	257	housewife	71	"
r	Casamassima Michael	257	clerk	71	
s	Casamassima Rocco	257	U S M C	25	"
t	Lauletta Catherine—†	257	packer	65	
u	Miraglia Vincenzia—†	257	at home	86	"
v	*Albanese Carmella—†	259	housewife	57	"
w	Albanese Frederick	259	electrician	33	"
x	Albanese John	259	operator	29	"
y	Albanese Louis	259	electrician	32	"
z	Siraco Antonio	259	retired	67	"

1270

a	*Siraco Dellarosa—†	259	housewife	63	"
b	Siraco Dominic	259	U S A	24	
c	Cedrone Anne—†	259	clerk	21	"
d	Cedrone Anthony	259	U S N	23	
e	Cedrone Dominic	259	laborer	59	
f	*Cedrone Mary—†	259	housewife	55	"
h	Pazzanese Anna L—†	261	"	26	
k	Pazzanese Frank	261	welder	28	

Page.	Letter.	FULL NAME.	Residence, Jan. 1, 1945.	Occupation.	Supposed Age.	Reported Residence, Jan. 1, 1944. Street and Number.

Paris Street—Continued

	L	Sorrentino Henry	261	electrician	37	here
	M	Sorrentino Josephine—†	261	housewife	34	"
	N	Festa Alfred	263	meatcutter	33	"
	O	Festa Julia—†	263	housewife	34	"
	P	Capezzuto Charles	263	clerk	33	
	R	Capezzuto John	263	retired	56	"
	S	Pazzanese Carmen	263	laborer	58	
	T	*Pazzanese Florence—†	263	housewife	51	"
	U	Pazzanese Joseph	263	U S A	22	
	V	Ventullo Anthony	265	longshoreman	40	"
	W	Ventullo Margaret—†	265	housewife	37	"
	X	*Holden Blanche—†	265	"	33	"
	Y	Holden Frederick	265	machinist	46	"
	Z	Picariello Felix	265	electrician	33	"
		1271				
	A	Picariello Irene—†	265	housewife	29	"
	B	Tannone Andrew J	267	U S A	28	
	C	Tannone Phyllis—†	267	housewife	30	"
	D	Guarino Anthony	267	longshoreman	23	"
	E	Guarino Carmella—†	267	stitcher	25	"
	F	*Guarino Ciriaco	267	retired	66	
	G	*Guarino Mary—†	267	housewife	54	"
	H	Guarino Salvatore	267	U S N	29	
	K	*Hovhanesian Vartan—†	267	packer	58	
	L	Erickson Frank	269	pipefitter	31	"
	M	Erickson Louise—†	269	housewife	27	"
	N	*Bova Christina—†	269	"	66	
	O	*Bova Joseph	269	retired	72	
	P	Letterello Mary—†	269	housewife	29	"
	R	Letterello Nicholas	269	laborer	31	
	S	DiChiaro Alice—†	271	housewife	21	"
	T	DiChiaro Antonio	271	musician	22	"
	U	*DiChiaro Lena—†	271	housekeeper	58	"
	V	Caucci Marion—†	271	housewife	49	"
	W	Caucci Thomas	271	laborer	53	
	X	Caucci William	271	"	27	"
	Y	Curallo Angelina—†	271	housewife	58	170 Putnam
	Z	Curallo Rosario	271	welder	25	170 "
		1272				
	A	Crisione Agrippino	273	laborer	62	here
	B	Spadorcia Dominic	273	pressman	33	"

42

Page.	Letter.	Full Name.	Residence, Jan. 1, 1945.	Occupation.	Supposed Age.	Reported Residence, Jan. 1, 1944. Street and Number.

	c	Spadorcia Palmina—†	273	housewife	33	here
	d	*Matarazzo Clementina-†	273	housekeeper	49	"
	e	Cannon Annie E—†	275	housewife	58	"
	f	Cannon Herbert T	275	U S A	32	
	g	Cannon Joseph J	275	chauffeur	30	"
	h	Cannon Mary A—†	275	housewife	30	"
	k	Cannon Thomas L	275	chauffeur	58	"
	l	DeAcetis Angelina—†	275	housewife	26	"
	m	DeAcetis Luigi	275	welder	24	"
	n	Ricciardi Antoinetta—†	277	housewife	27	"
	o	Ricciardi Battista	277	shipfitter	28	"
	p	Gioioso Frances—†	277	housewife	33	"
	r	Gioioso Patrick	277	clerk	35	"
	s	Mercuri Joseph F	277	musician	32	"
	t	Mercuri Natalie—†	277	housewife	33	"
	u	Dillon Catherine—†	279	at home	68	"
	v	Dillon Francis J	279	chauffeur	32	"
	w	Dillon Olga—†	279	housewife	31	"
	y	Scopa Henry	292	laborer	37	..
	z	Scopa Philomena—†	292	housewife	34	"
1273						
	a	DeRosa Mary F—†	292	"	57	
	b	DeRosa Pasquale	292	laborer	61	"
	c	Gillespie Eleanor—†	292	housewife	43	"
	d	Gillespie Joseph	292	inspector	45	"
	e	Walbourne Lena—†	292	housewife	30	"
	f	Walbourne Leonard	292	U S A	26	"
	g	*Comeau Joseph	294	carpenter	65	149 Marion
	h	Comeau Joseph S	294	"	52	149 "
	m	Mulcahy Albert	296	U S A	30	here
	n	Mulcahy Mary—†	296	housewife	26	"
	o	DiNublia Anthony	296	laborer	29	"
	p	DiNublia Josephine—†	296	housewife	28	"
	r	*Fawcett Irene—†	296	"	37	"
	s	Fawcett Peter	296	shipfitter	37	"
	u	Stella Charles	298	laborer	64	
	v	Stella Dominic	298	U S A	23	
	w	Stella Marie S—†	298	spinner	28	"
	x	Stella Mary—†	298	housewife	65	"
	y	Capozzoli Marie—†	298	"	35	
	z	Capozzoli Robert	298	printer	40	

Page.	Letter.	FULL NAME.	Residence, Jan. 1, 1945.	Occupation.	Supposed Age.	Reported Residence, Jan. 1, 1944. Street and Number.

1274
Paris Street—Continued

A	Cassidy Julia—†	300	housewife	67	here
B	Cassidy Thomas A	300	retired	76	"
C	Digotas Rose—†	300	housewife	29	"
D	Digotas Stanley	300	seaman	25	"
E	LeBlanc George L	300	fishcutter	26	Somerville
F	LeBlanc Josephine—†	300	housewife	29	"
G	Pinkshaw Anna—†	302	at home	36	here
H	Hires Rose—†	302	housewife	36	"
K	Hires William H	302	painter	36	86 Brooks
L	Dicks Elizabeth M—†	302	domestic	42	here
M	Dicks Francis J	302	U S N	40	"
N	Bassett Mary—†	303	teacher	37	Cambridge
O	Brockelbank Agnes—†	303	"	33	Lynn
P	Cadigan Mary—†	303	"	51	here
R	Connolly Mary—†	303	"	28	"
S	Coughlan Mary—†	303	"	43	Wash'n D C
T	Croft Helen—†	303		71	Cambridge
U	Crowley Julia—†	303	"	48	here
V	Dunnigan Anna M—†	303	"	59	"
W	Ford Marion—†	303		40	"
X	*Hogan Marjorie—†	303	"	40	
Y	Hughes Kathryn—†	303	"	40	
Z	Hynes Ann—† .	303		55	"

1275

A	Lafayette Mary J—†	303	"	44	
B	Maurer Catherine—†	303	"	28	
C	Meehan Helen—†	303	"	54	
D	Murphy Catherine—†	303	"	34	
E	Murray Catherine—†	303	"	40	
F	Richards Mary J—†	303	"	42	
G	Scott Mary F—†	303		67	
H	Trant Elizabeth—†	303	"	41	
K	Waraulo Lillian—†	303	housekeeper	52	"
L	Hagan Mary—†	306	"	44	"
M	Pedrazzi Henrietta—†	306	"	65	
N	Pedrazzi Henry	306	pipefitter	33	"
O	Pedrazzi Louis	306	U S A	37	
P	Orso Anthony	308	"	26	"
R	Orso Mary—†	308	housewife	22	"
S	Aquino Annie—†	308	"	43	

Page.	Letter.	FULL NAME.	Residence, Jan. 1, 1945.	Occupation.	Supposed Age.	Reported Residence, Jan. 1, 1944. Street and Number.

Paris Street—Continued

	T	Aquino Carmen	308	laborer	44	here
	U	Hodson Harry R	310	painter	45	"
	V	Doucette Ella M—†	310	housewife	50	"
	W	Doucette Stanley	310	machinist	52	"
	X	Hodson Clara—†	312	housewife	79	"
	Y	Hodson Henry N	312	retired	82	"
	Z	Hodson Margaret M—†	312	housewife	48	"

1276

	A	Hodson William E	312	engraver	50	"
	B	Baker Alfred	315	supt	50	
	C	Baker Jack P	315	welder	45	"
	D	Baker Rebecca A—†	315	housekeeper	70	"
	E	Aptekar Rebecca—†	315	at home	75	"
	F	Gallagher Nora—†	315	"	70	"
	G	Gillar Rose—†	315	housekeeper	46	"
	H	Silva Manuel	317	retired	58	49 Bennington
	K	Donovan Josephine—†	317	housewife	30	here
	L	Donovan Sylvester	317	welder	30	"
	M	Lauria Anna—†	317	housewife	21	306 Saratoga
	N	Lauria Guy	317	chauffeur	23	306 "
	O	Corumbeau Catherine—†	319	housewife	45	here
	P	Corumbeau Dorothea—†	319	student	20	"
	R	D'Angelico Flora—†	319	factoryhand	38	"
	S	D'Angelico Michael	319	repairman	49	"
	T	Campanella Frances—†	319	stenographer	20	"
	U	Campanella Josephine—†	319	stitcher	21	"
	V*	Campanella Mary—†	319	"	24	
	W	Campanella Rocco	319	retired	54	
	X	Campanella Rose—†	319	housewife	43	"
	Y	Daye Ruth—†	321	"	28	"
	Z	Daye Wilfred	321	machinist	44	"

1277

	A	Ricciardi Joseph	321	welder	61	
	B	Ricciardi Mary A—†	321	housewife	44	"
	C	Ricciardi Michelina R—†	321	operator	23	"
	D	Warner William F	325	laborer	60	Chelsea
	F	Bullock Mary E—†	325	housekeeper	72	here
	G	St Croix John W	325	calker	36	"
	H	St Croix Mary E—†	325	housewife	36	"
	K	Oliver Mary—†	325	housekeeper	53	"
	L	Tarentino Hilda—†	325	housewife	22	"

Paris Street—Continued

M	Adams Anthony	325	welder	47	here
N	Adams Elizabeth—†	325	housewife	55	"
O	Donnaruma Benjamin	325	U S A	49	"
P	Donnaruma Victoria—†	325	housewife	33	"
S	Charotas Mary—†	327	"	66	
T	Charotas Stephen	327	laborer	64	
U	*Lawrence Julia—†	327	housekeeper	55	"
V	Indelicato Anna M—†	327	operator	29	"
W	Renoni James	327	laborer	65	
X	Renoni Nicholas	327	U S A	23	"
Y	Renoni Virginia—†	327	housewife	58	"
Z	Scopa Margaret—†	327	at home	27	"
	1278				
B	Gubitore Charles	329	tailor	59	
C	Gubitore Marie—†	329	housewife	61	"
D	Coltraro Anthony	329	clerk	30	
E	Coltraro Josephine—†	329	housewife	29	"
F	Ruggiero Eleanor—†	329	"	25	Revere
G	Ruggiero Frank	329	U S N	26	"
H	Stuppia John	329	U S A	33	here
K	Stuppia Mary—†	329	housewife	53	"
L	Stuppia Michael	329	laborer	65	"
M	Whitehead Bella—†	331	at home	73	"
N	Ligotti Charles	331	attorney	26	"
O	Ligotti Virginia—†	331	housewife	27	"
P	DeRosa Mary—†	331	stenographer	24	Wash'n D C
R	DeRosa Stephen	331	U S A	24	"
S	Ligotte Beatrice—†	331	bookkeeper	22	here
T	*Ligotte Ida—†	331	housekeeper	53	"
U	Ligotte John	331	attorney	28	"
V	Morrison Anna—†	333	housekeeper	74	"
W	Rizzuti Catherine—†	333	housewife	21	114 Cottage
X	Rizzuti Pasquale	333	guard	26	114 "
Y	Francis Elizabeth—†	333	housewife	61	here
Z	Francis John	333	laborer	73	"
	1279				
A	Silva Edward	335	U S N	24	
B	Silva Pauline—†	335	housewife	24	"
C	*Grasso Frank	335	butcher	37	"
D	*Grasso Rose—†	335	housewife	37	"

Page.	Letter.	FULL NAME.	Residence. Jan. 1, 1945.	Occupation.	Supposed Age.	Reported Residence, Jan. 1, 1944. Street and Number.

Princeton Street

	F	Ciampa Guy	137	U S A	26	here
	G	Ciampa Mary—†	137	housewife	49	"
	H	Ciampa William -	137	U S A	22	"
	K	Ciampa William N	137	mason	51	
	L	Indorato Louis J	137	U S A	27	
	M	Indorato Mary C—†	137	housewife	25	"
	N	D'Entremont Alfred E	139	seaman	20	
	O	D'Entremont Joseph A	139	carpenter	64	"
	P	D'Entremont Lester J	139	U S A	25	
	R	D'Entremont Mary H—†	139	housewife	60	"
	S	D'Entremont Phillip A	139	U S A	27	
	T	Godin Elizabeth M—†	139	housewife	23	"
	U	Godin Henry N	139	U S M C	26	"
	V	Carlsen Madeline—†	139	inspector	33	"
	W	Penney Elizabeth J—†	141	at home	68	"
	X	Penney John C	141	retired	35	"
	Y	Nazzaro Rosaria—†	141	at home	74	"
	Z	Arone Joseph A	141	operator	29	108 Bremen
		1280				
	A	Arone Victoria—†	141	housewife	25	Lowell
	B	DeProspero Jennie—†	143	"	33	here
	C	DeProspero Michael D	143	chauffeur	35	"
	D	Boudreau Evangeline—†	143	housewife	36	"
	E	Boudreau George S	143	rigger	42	
	F	Goyetche Anna—†	143	at home	38	"
	G	DelCare Arthur	143	electrician	35	"
	H	DelCare Gertrude—†	143	housewife	33	"
	K	Connell Dennis	145	U S A	23	Chelsea
	M	Carmen Hyman	147	proprietor	58	California
	N	Carmen Tillie—†	147	clerk	50	"
	O	Abbate Christine—†	147	factoryhand	20	96 Chelsea
	P*	Abbate Frances—†	147	housewife	45	96 "
	R	Abbate Louis	147	shipfitter	50	96 "
	S	Sequeira Lillian—†	149	at home	25	232 Lexington
	T	Siraco Frank J	149	U S N	20	here
	U	Siraco Julia F—†	149	clerk	24	"
	V	Siraco Michelena—†	149	"	57	"
	W	Siraco Peter D	149	U S N	22	
	X	Siraco Philomeno	149	grocer	62	··
	Y	Tontodonato Anna—†	149	housewife	35	"

47

Princeton Street—Continued

z	Tontodonato Nicholas	149	welder	38	here
1281						
A	Rizzo Angelo	151	presser	25	
B	Rizzo Jacqueline—†	151	housewife	22	"
C	Tontodonato Antonia—†	151	"	31	
D	Tontodonato John	151	chauffeur	32	"
E	George Edward M	151	shipfitter	36	"
F	George Lillian G—†	151	housewife	32	"
G	Munn Edith M—†	151	baker	35	
H	Leville Alice C—†	153	housewife	34	"
K	Leville William T	153	laborer	36	
L	Barrett Benjamin F	153	seaman	34	
M	Barrett Helen E—†	153	housewife	49	"
N	*Silvey Pauline—†	153	"	29	
O	Silvey William	153	locksmith	31	"
P	Giardini Dante	157	machinist	53	"
R	Giardini Dante, jr	157	U S A	22	
S	Giardini Emelia—†	157	teacher	51	
T	Giardini Gloria—†	157	packer	21	
U	Giardini Salvatore	157	U S A	23	
V	Surrette Elizabeth—†	157	housewife	29	"
W	Surrette Joseph W	157	machinist	32	"
X	Gaeta Edward	157	U S A	28	
Y	Gaeta Fiore	157	salesman	55	"
Z	Gaeta Lucy—†	157	housewife	55	"
1282						
A	Sarrabia Anthony	159	watchman	53	"
B	Pignato James F	159	pedler	33	
C	Pignato Theresa—†	159	housewife	32	"
D	Perrotta Aida—†	159	clerk	20	
E	Perrotta Gaetano	159	laborer	50	
F	Perrotta Olympia—†	159	housewife	46	"
G	Picceo Anna—†	159	stitcher	54	"
H	Picceo Anna—†	159	clerk	23	
K	Picceo Barbara—†	159	"	22	
L	Picceo Dominica—†	159	"	20	"
M	Picceo Margaret—†	159	"	29	
N	Moore Ellen M—†	165	housewife	39	"
O	Moore Henry A	165	factoryhand	41	"
P	Barron Mary—†	165	housewife	40	"
R	Barron Thomas	165	fisherman	42	"

Princeton Street—Continued

s	Sandquist Kathleen—†	165	housewife	29	here
t	Sandquist William O	165	U S N	28	"
u	Cuoco Elvira—†	167	housewife	41	"
v	Cuoco John	167	laborer	47	"
w	Cuoco Michael	167	U S A	20	"
x	Cipriano Carmella—†	167	housewife	32	"
y	Cipriano Pasquale	167	electrician	36	"
z	Bernabi Michael	167	metalworker	34	"
	1283				
a	Bernabi Mildred—†	167	housewife	23	"
b	Mercadante Ethel—†	169	"	36	
c	Mercadante Pasquale	169	buffer	47	
d	Zuccarino Rocco	169	laborer	47	
e	*Zuccarino Thomasina—†	169	housewife	49	"
g	Lane Elizabeth—†	171	packer	66	128 Princeton
h	Lane Frances—†	171	"	40	128 "
k	Lane Joseph	171	retired	78	128 "
l	Petralia Joseph	171	tailor	28	173 "
m	Petralia Josephine—†	171	housewife	31	173 "
n	*Petralia Rosalia—†	171	at home	42	173 "
o	Zafarana Giacomo	173	retired	62	here
p	Zafarana James	173	agent	31	"
r	Casarano Anthony	173	clerk	32	"
s	Casarano Maria—†	173	housewife	32	"
t	Finamore Antoinette—†	173	"	44	
u	Finamore Donald	173	U S A	22	
v	Finamore Gaetano	173	laborer	53	"
w	Finamore Melba—†	173	clerk	20	"
x	Boyan John J	175	supervisor	51	"
y	Boyan Mary A—†	175	at home	73	"
z	Morrissey Elizabeth L–†	175	"	88	
	1284				
a	Malone Harry E	175	retired	37	
b	Malone Hibbard L	175	blockmaker	64	"
c	Malone Lydia—†	175	housewife	56	"
d	Malone Minnie A—†	175	stenographer	24	"
e	Saggese Angelina—†	179	housewife	25	"
f	Saggese Phillip	179	chauffeur	25	"
g	DeBacco Mario	179	woodworker	51	"
h	DeBacco Philomena—†	179	housewife	40	"
k	Vaccaro Antonio	179	machinist	45	"

Princeton Street—Continued

L	Vaccaro Carmella—†	179	tailor	27	here
M	*Vaccaro Giuseppe	179	retired	72	"
N	Vaccaro Maria—†	179	tailor	33	"
O	*LaPòrta Agostino	181	salesman	59	"
P	LaPorta Albert	181	laborer	20	
R	LaPorta Antoinette—†	181	operator	24	"
S	LaPorta Concetta—†	181	"	22	
T	LaPorta Frank	181	U S A	28	"
U	LaPorta Helen—†	181	packer	27	
V	*LaPorta Philomena—†	181	housewife	53	"
W	Zaccaria Antoinette—†	181	tailor	22	
X	Zaccaria Concetta—†	181	factoryhand	20	"
Y	*Zaccaria Esther—†	181	housewife	43	"
Z	Zaccaria Salvatore	181	molder	52	
	1285				
A	Vilkas Cecelia—†	181	housewife	30	5 Prescott
B	Vilkas John	181	laborer	30	5 "
C	Poncia Gino	183	U S A	26	here
D	Poncia Mary—†	183	housewife	25	"
E	Cucchiello Frank	183	laborer	36	"
F	Cucchiello Margaret—†	183	housewife	35	"
G	Beiras Jose	185	machinist	50	"
H	Beiras Pasqualena—†	185	housewife	35	"
K	Ciampa Albert G	185	chauffeur	22	"
L	Ciampa Maria T—†	185	at home	45	"
M	Melino Francesco	187	laborer	52	"
N	*Melino Maria—†	187	housewife	56	"
O	Umberto Pietri	187	painter	43	
P	Simile Anthony	187	chauffeur	47	"
R	Simile Julia—†	187	housewife	37	"
S	Giorgione Lawrence	189	retired	75	
T	Giorgione Marion—†	189	housewife	60	"
U	Alesi Josephine—†	189	"	38	
V	Alesi Vittario	189	social worker	40	"

Putnam Street

Y	Pannesi Dorothy—†	125	housewife	24	here
Z	Pannesi Frank	125	U S A	25	"
	1286				
A	Pannesi Angelina—†	125	clerk	22	"

Putnam Street—Continued

	B	Pannesi David	125	clerk	27	here
	c	Pannesi Mary—†	125	housewife	58	"
	D	Pannesi Pasquale	125	U S A	20	"
	E	Brun Albert C	127	tilesetter	39	"
	F	Brun Albina—†	127	housewife	35	"
	G*	DeMattia Mary—†	127	at home	78	"
	H	Limoli Aggrippino	127	laborer	61	
	K	Limoli Ambrosina—†	127	housewife	60	"
	L	Puccino Edith—†	127	"	21	222 Princeton
	M	Puccino John	127	chauffeur	21	182 Cottage
	N	Damigella Florence—†	129	housewife	57	here
	o	Damigella Joseph	129	machinist	57	"
	P	DeMattia Angelo	129	chauffeur	49	"
	R	DeMattia Grace—†	129	housewife	47	"
	s	Sullo John	129	machinist	37	"
	T	Sullo Louise—†	129	housewife	29	"
	U	Gelormini Emma—†	131	"	38	108 Bennington
	v	Gelormini Louis	131	carpenter	46	108 "
	w	Avola Alexander	131	electrician	31	here
	x	Avola Edith—†	131	housewife	31	"
	Y	Lee James F	131	U S A	20	186 Bennington
	z	Lee Joseph R	131	"	23	186 "
		1287				
	A	Lee Mary—†	131	housewife	56	186 "
	c	Sciacca Frank	133	burner	26	here
	D	Sciacca Mary—†	133	housewife	25	"
	E	Pagano John	133	storekeeper	50	"
	F	Pagano Lena—†	133	housewife	40	"
	G	Pagano Vera—†	133	clerk	20	
	K	LaMonica Aggrippina—†	163	housewife	24	"
	L	LaMonica Vincent	163	manager	24	"
	M	Caponigro Fiore	163	U S A	28	
	N	Caponigro Theresa—†	163	housewife	29	"
	o	Colombo Rose—†	163	"	54	
	P	Colombo Salvatore	163	shoemaker	52	"
	R	Colombo Christopher	163	mechanic	27	"
	s	Colombo Rachael—†	163	housewife	27	"
	T	Nute Chiarina—†	165	"	31	"
	U	Nute George L	165	laborer	31	171 Trenton
	v	Rossetti Mary—†	165	housewife	38	here
	w	Rossetti Ralph	165	electrician	39	"

Page.	Letter.	FULL NAME.	Residence, Jan. 1, 1945.	Occupation.	Supposed Age.	Reported Residence, Jan. 1, 1944. Street and Number.

Putnam Street—Continued

x	*Cambria Joseph	165	weaver	57	here	
y	Cambria Josephine—†	165	clerk	32	"	
z	*Cambria Lillian—†	165	housewife	47	"	
	1288					
a	Azerowicz Henry	167	U S A	34		
b	Azerowicz Mary—†	167	waitress	34	"	
c	Manartto Margaret—†	167	housewife	28	"	
d	Cassaro Theresa—†	167	"	41		
e	Cassaro Vincent	167	salesman	41	"	
f	Schena Gerald	167	U S A	24	"	
g	Schena Lena—†	167	stitcher	23	"	
h	Schena Lucy—†	167	"	21		
k	Schena Michael	167	electrician	50	"	
l	Schena Vinanza—†	167	housewife	48	"	
m	*White James	177	carpenter	63	"	
n	D'Ettore Concetta—†	177	housewife	51	"	
o	D'Ettore Dominic	177	U S A	21		
p	D'Ettore John	177	laborer	56		
r	Cunningham Clara—†	177	housewife	37	"	
s	Cunningham Clifford	177	boilermaker	40	"	
t	Beaupre Alfred J	179	tester	39		
u	Beaupre Caroline—†	179	housewife	31	"	
v	Baglio Joseph	179	inspector	28	"	
w	Baglio Mary—†	179	housewife	28	"	
x	Dellorfano Ann—†	179	at home	20	"	
y	Dellorfano Joseph	179	welder	44	"	
z	Dellorfano Mary—†	179	housewife	38	"	
	1289					
a	Vernacchio Concordia—†	195	"	29	"	
b	Vernacchio Gerald	195	printer	28		
c	Ferrara Antonette—†	195	inspector	25	"	
d	*Ferrara Henry	195	shoemaker	64	"	
e	Ferrara Michael	195	U S A	22		
f	*Ferrara Rosina—†	195	housewife	56	"	
g	Colangelo Anthony	195	laborer	53		
h	Colangelo Palmina—†	195	housewife	44	"	
k	Cotreau Delphine—†	197	packer	38	289 Chelsea	
l	Cotreau John L	197	clerk	39	289 "	
m	Leary Thomas	197	laborer	46	here	
n	Nolan Beatrice—†	197	housewife	33	"	
o	Nolan Herbert	197	chauffeur	30	"	

Page.	Letter.	FULL NAME.	Residence, Jan. 1, 1945.	Occupation.	Supposed Age.	Reported Residence, Jan. 1, 1944. Street and Number.

Putnam Street—Continued

P	Russo Rose—†	197	housewife	33	here
R	DiAngelo Rose—†	199	"	74	"
S	LaSalla Pasquale	199	barber	41	97 Addison
T	Meyers Julian	199	U S A	34	here
U	Meyers Rose—†	199	housewife	34	"
V	Harkins Anna—†	199	"	34	"
W	Harkins William	199	laborer	34	
X	Silva Delphine V—†	199	housewife	63	"
Y	Silva John F	199	machinist	44	"

1290

Saratoga Street

A	Puzzangheria Maria—†	201	stitcher	46	here
B	Puzzangheria Salvatore	201	tailor	48	"
C	Kehoe Lawrence	201	shipper	41	"
D	Kehoe Margaret—†	201	housewife	40	"
F	Donovan Robert V	202	U S A	21	
G	Leddy Francis A	202	machinist	43	"
H	Leddy Laura—†	202	clerk	44	
L	McCormick John G	203	U S N	23	
M	McCormick John M	203	guard	50	
N	McCormick Mary V—†	203	housewife	47	"
O	Moran Francis A	203	driller	38	215 Bennington
P	Moran Irene—†	203	housewife	35	215 "
S	*Sicuranza Angela—†	204	at home	76	95 Princeton
T	Sicuranza Carmelia—†	204	hairdresser	35	95 "
U	Bellabona Flora—†	204	housewife	29	here
V	Bellabona Leo F	204	U S A	31	"
W	DeFilippis Mary C—†	204	housewife	35	"
X	DeFilippis Nicholas	204	candymaker	40	"
Y	Venedan Rose—†	205	housewife	27	"
Z	Venedan Walter	205	U S N	32	

1291

A	Hurley Daniel J	205	laborer	51	"
B	Hurley Florence—†	205	clerk	21	
C	*Hurley Laura M—†	205	housewife	48	"
D	Alfama Asa	205	metalworker	29	"
E	Alfama Elvira—†	205	housewife	27	"
F	DelVisco Ellen M—†	206	"	24	
G	DelVisco Thomas M	206	U S A	24	

Page.	Letter.	FULL NAME.	Residence, Jan. 1, 1945.	Occupation.	Supposed Age.	Reported Residence, Jan. 1, 1944. Street and Number.

Saratoga Street—Continued

H	DelVisco Antonio P	206	laborer	59	here
K	DelVisco Eleanor M—†	206	secretary	21	"
L	*DelVisco Mary A—†	206	housewife	62	"
M	Corbosiero Louis	206	shoeworker	42	"
N	Corbosiero Rose—†	206	housewife	36	"
O	DeLucia Anthony	207	U S A	25	"
P	DeLucia Jennie—†	207	operator	31	"
R	*DeLucia Rose—†	207	housewife	54	"
S	DeLucia Thomas	207	laborer	59	"
T	Vigliotta Anna—†	207	housewife	34	"
U	Vigliotta Biagio	207	laborer	44	"
V	Burke Catherine—†	207	tinknocker	21	238 Havre
W	Burke John	207	U S A	23	238 "
X	Wilson Julia—†	207	housewife	23	238 "
Y	Wilson Samuel A	207	U S A	27	238 "
Z	Fronduto John	208	laborer	52	here

1292

A	*Fronduto Rose—†	208	housewife	52	"
B	Sacco Margaret L—†	208	"	35	..
C	Sacco Marks F	208	tileworker	41	"
D	*Lopes Jean—†	208	housewife	51	250 Princeton
E	Tutela Jennie—†	209	"	37	here
F	Tutela Richard	209	pipefitter	38	"
G	Caggiano Anna—†	209	factoryhand	41	"
H	Caggiano James	209	fireman	48	"
K	Reed Anna—†	209	housewife	23	"
L	Reed Samuel B	209	U S N	30	"
M	O'Keefe Eugene J	210	operator	36	64 Falcon
N	O'Keefe Sarah—†	210	housewife	31	64 "
O	Carey Helen M—†	210	"	43	here
P	Carey William H	210	clerk	44	"
R	O'Connell Margaret M–†	210	housewife	66	"
S	O'Connell Peter H	210	watchman	68	"
T	*Bossi Antoinette—†	210	housewife	36	208 Saratoga
U	Bossi Joseph	210	laborer	36	208 "
V	Pepe Michael	211	machinist	25	200 Brooks
W	Pepe Nicolina—†	211	housewife	26	200 "
X	Mirra Alice M—†	211	dressmaker	42	here
Y	Mirra Anthony	211	tailor	46	"

1293

A	Colantonio Constantino	212	blacksmith	35	"

Saratoga Street—Continued

B	Colantonio Filomena—†	212	housewife	33	here
E	Urresti Alfred	212	U S A	26	"
F*	Urresti Antonia—†	212	housewife	62	"
C	Urresti Mary—→†	212	packer	20	"
D	Urresti Virginia—†	212	clerk	21	"
H	Agrella Frank	214	millhand	59	212 Saratoga
K*	Agrella Rose—†	214	housewife	58	212 "
L	Campos Eva—†	214	millhand	23	212 "
M	Vigila Alda—†	214	"	21	Portugal
O	DeDominicis Alfred	215	chauffeur	36	here
P	DeDominicis Helen E—†	215	housewife	33	"
R	Eriksen Helen—†	215	"	46	"
S	Eriksen William	215	U S N	21	"
T	Missett Helen—†	215	housewife	23	"
U	Missett Joseph	215	U S A	31	"
V	Chekos James	215	"	22	
W	Tsekos Aristomenis	215	manager	52	"
X	Tsekos Pauline—†	215	housewife	46	"
Y	Bombaci Lucy—†	216	WAC	30	211 Saratoga
Z	Bombaci Rose—†	216	housewife	63	211 "
	1294				
A	Bombaci Salvatore	216	U S A	33	211 "
B	DeBonis Antonetta—†	216	fishcutter	26	here
C*	DeBonis Jennie—†	216	housewife	51	"
D	DeBonis Joseph	216	retired	61	"
E	Sanśone Evelyn R—†	216A	housewife	20	"
F	Sansone Paul I	216A	welder	22	"
G	Racchia Evio	216A	watchman	20	130 Orleans
H*	Recchia Helen—†	216A	housewife	46	130 "
K	Recchia Lodovico	216A	foreman	54	130 "
L	Recchia Mario	216A	U S A	26	here
M	Abbatessa Anthony	217	welder	37	"
N	Abbatessa Catherine—†	217	housewife	34	"
O	Canatta Lena—†	217	factoryhand	21	"
P*	Canatta Mary—†	217	housewife	54	"
R*	Canatta Rosario	217	laborer	58	
S	Timbone Angelina—†	217	clerk	26	
T	Timbone Anna—†	217	housewife	47	"
U	Timbone Eugenia—†	217	stenographer	25	"
V	Timbone John	217	U S C G	22	"
W	Timbone Vincent	217	shoeworker	54	"

Saratoga Street—Continued

x	Martorano Concetta—†	218	housewife	38	here
y	Martorano Leon	218	U S A	44	"
z	DeBonis Frank	218	pipefitter	33	"
	1295					
a	DeBonis Mary—†	218	housewife	28	"
b	*Holt Elizabeth—†	218	at home	58	23 White
c	Boudreau Gladys—†	220	housewife	25	here
d	Boudreau Louis E	220	engineer	33	395 Meridian
e	Miller Henry P	220	shipfitter	44	here
f	Miller Mildred—†	220	housewife	34	"
g	Miller Thomas	220	seaman	45	"
h	DeCicco Elizabeth P—†	220	housewife	23	"
k	DeCicco Robert L	220	welder	26	
l	Diaz Francesco	223	U S A	27	"
m	Diaz Josephine—†	223	housewife	27	"
n	Viola Frank	223	finisher	48	"
o	*Viola Mary—†	223	housewife	49	"
p	*Cordovano Jennie—†	223	"	70	
r	Cordovano Salvatore	223	U S A	28	"
s	Cannizzaro Lucy R—†	225	housewife	30	"
t	Cannizzaro Santo	225	burner	31	
u	*Costigan Margaret—†	225	housewife	43	"
v	Costigan Thomas	225	fisherman	47	"
w	Gushue Mary—†	225	cleaner	53	
x	Saia Arthur	225	presser	33	"
y	Saia Rita—†	225	housekeeper	62	"
z	Saia Romeo	225	shipper	27	"
	1296					
a	Saia Yolanda—†	225	dressmaker	21	"
b	*Halstead Mary—†	226	at home	72	"
c	*Hyder Emily—†	226	millhand	50	"
d	*Coilty Natilda—†	226	at home	64	"
e	Coilty William L	226	U S N	30	
f	Haley Regina—†	226	candymaker	38	"
g	Morano Vincenzo	226	pressman	40	309 Sumner
h	Thompson Frederick	226	fisherman	42	here
k	Thompson Gertrude—†	226	housewife	37	"
l	Aleo Alice—†	227	operator	37	"
m	*Aleo Stella—†	227	housewife	65	"
n	LoConte Angelo	227	chauffeur	25	"
o	LoConte Antonio	227	oil dealer	58	"

Saratoga Street—Continued

	P	Letterie Anna—†	227	housewife	22	Florida
	R	Letterie Frank	227	U S A	22	"
	S	Langone Frank	228	printer	30	3 Sumner pl
	T	Langone Mary—†	228	housewife	30	3 "
	U	Antonelli Esther—†	228	"	35	here
	V	Antonelli William	228	shoeworker	37	"
	W	Vernacchio Jennie—†	228	housewife	65	"
	X	Vernacchio Mary—†	228	operator	29	"
	Y	Vernacchio Pasquale	228	ironworker	67	"
1297						
	A	Rossi Theresa—†	229	housekeeper	48	"
	B	Picariello Joseph	230	chauffeur	37	"
	C	Picariello Josephine—†	230	housewife	35	"
	D	Palazzolo Giacamina—†	230	inspector	32	"
	E	Palazzolo Jennie—†	230	housewife	75	"
	F	Palazzolo John T	230	U S A	22	"
	G	Palazzolo Joseph J	230	candymaker	34	"
	H	Palazzolo Paul	230	pipefitter	58	"
	K	Olitsky Abraham	230	junk dealer	68	"
	L	*Olitsky Minnie—†	230	housewife	66	"
	M	*Longo Theresa—†	231	at home	73	"
	N	Minichino Lucian	231	clerk	33	"
	O	Minichino Margaret—†	231	housewife	33	"
	P	*Berimbau Dolores—†	231A	factoryhand	20	"
	R	Berimbau John F	231A	U S A	24	
	S	Silva Anthony	231A	operator	25	"
	T	*Silva Conceicao—†	231A	stitcher	45	"
	U	Silva Ernest	231A	U S A	22	
	V	Silva Manuel C	231A	weaver	47	
	W	Viscio Dominico	231A	retired	62	
	X	Viscio Elvira—†	231A	stitcher	25	"
	Y	Viscio Louisa—†	231A	housewife	60	"
	Z	DiChiara Antoinette—†	232	"	53	"
1298						
	A	DiChiara Generoso	232	U S A	20	
	B	DiChiara Joseph	232	laborer	57	
	C	DiChiara Mary E—†	232	dressmaker	27	"
	D	*Aronson Dora—†	232	at home	71	"
	E	Denehy John	232	longshoreman	40	"
	F	Denehy Mary E—†	232	housewife	42	"
	G	Russo Angelina—†	233	"	24	257 Saratoga

1—12   57

Saratoga Street—Continued

H	Russo Louis	233	pipefitter	25	257 Saratoga	
K	Coppola Gino	233	clerk	20	here	
L	Coppola Mary—†	233	housewife	44	"	
M	Coppola Pasquale	233	bricklayer	45	"	
N	Coppola Ralph R	233	U S A	24	"	
O	Goveia Augustino	233	chauffeur	27	"	
P	Goveia Sarah—†	233	housewife	26	"	
S	Pasquale John	234	chauffeur	32	"	
R	Pasquale Josephine—†	234	housewife	33	"	
T	*Fisher Esther—†	234	"	60		
U	Fisher Samuel	234	retired	60		
V	Fisher Harold	234	chauffeur	43	"	
W	Fisher Ida—†	234	housewife	36	"	
X	Serpone Frank	235	stitcher	30	"	
Y	Serpone Lena—†	235	housewife	31	"	
Z	Alfano Anna—†	235	"	50	"	

1299

A	Alfano Dominic	235	janitor	26	"	
B	Alfano Joseph	235	cableman	52	"	
C	Ruotolo Adeline—†	235	housewife	33	668 Bennington	
D	Ruotolo Gerard D	235	pipefitter	34	668 "	
E	*Corrao Frank	236	millhand	45	here	
F	Corrao Jennie—†	236	housewife	38	"	
G	*Figliolini Antoinette—†	236	"	55	"	
H	Figliolini Dominic	236	operator	24	"	
K	Figliolini Pasquale	236	tailor	53		
L	Rideout Dorothy—†	236	housewife	27	"	
M	Rideout Wallace	236	foreman	25	"	
N	LoConte Dominic	238	shipfitter	39	"	
O	LoConte Mae G—†	238	housewife	39	"	
P	Interbartolo Charles	238	longshoreman	45	"	
R	Interbartolo Ida—†	238	housewife	31	"	
S	Interbartolo Michael	238	electrician	36	"	
T	Interbartolo Charles	238	U S A	23	"	
U	Interbartolo Michael	238	"	20		
V	Interbartolo Peter	238	"	22		
W	Interbartolo Rosario	238	machinist	56	"	
X	Cordovano Charles	242	U S A	25	"	
Y	Cordovano Yolanda M—†	242	housewife	24	"	
Z	Alabiso Angelo	242	musician	24	"	

1299A
Saratoga Street—Continued

A	Alabiso Carmella—†	242	clerk	22	here
B	Alabiso Nora—†	242	housewife	43	"
C	Alabiso Vincent	242	tailor	52	"
D	Damecio Alexandro	242	machinist	53	"
E	Damecio Jennie—†	242	housewife	53	"
F	*Indingaro Louise—†	243	"	31	85 Brooks
G	Indingaro Thomas	243	clerk	31	85 "
H	Foster Joseph R	244	chauffeur	38	here
K	Foster Mildred C—†	244	housewife	36	"
L	Palladino Anne—†	244	packer	29	"
M	Palladino Gerardo	244	retired	82	"
N	Palladino Vito	244	operator	31	"
O	Shannon John B	244	steamfitter	45	"
P	Shannon Theresa—†	244	housewife	40	"
R	Rezendes Eleanor—†	245	"	20	·
S	Rezendes William	245	meatcutter	23	"
T	*Cinardo Camillo	246	retired	69	··
U	Cinardo David	246	U S N	25	"
V	Cinardo Elizabeth—†	246	stitcher	32	"
W	*Cinardo Frances—†	246	housewife	60	" ·
Y	Tramontozzi Antonio	246	machinist	33	"
Z	Tramontozzi Concetta—†	246	housewife	33	"

1299B

A	Leibman Mary—†	247	"	44	
B	Leibman Max	247	student	20	"
C	DiCicco Roy	248	shipfitter	22	236 Orient av
D	Cinardo Florence—†	248	housewife	27	here
E	Cinardo Patrick	248	cutter	30	"
F	Schraffa Margaret F—†	248	housewife	27	"
G	Schraffa Victor E	248	boilermaker	27	"
H	Santaniello Antoinetta—†	249	housewife	28	"
K	Santaniello Dominic N	249	U S M C	28	"
L	Serra Frank	249	laborer	63	
M	Serra Frank, jr	249	U S A	26	
N	Serra John	249	"	36	
O	Serra Ralph	249	"	20	·
P	*Costa John	250	laborer	59	
R	*Costa Josephine—†	250	housewife	52	"
S	*Mello Mary—†	250	factoryhand	59	"

Page.	Letter.	FULL NAME.	Residence, Jan. 1, 1945.	Occupation.	Supposed Age.	Reported Residence, Jan. 1, 1944. Street and Number.

Saratoga Street—Continued

T	Powers John J	250	clerk	36	here
U	Powers Mary A—†	250	housewife	26	"
V	Lynch Marie—†	250	"	63	"
W	Mercurio Anna—†	252	"	45	"
X	Mercurio Dominic	252	U S A	20	"
Y	Mercurio James	252	inspector	51	"
Z	DiNapoli Agnes—†	252	saleswoman	21	"
	1299C				
A	DiNapoli Carmella—†.	252	"	24	
B	DiNapoli Catherine—†	252	housewife	45	"
C	DiNapoli Pasquale	252	welder	51	"
D	Stasio Henry R	254	agent	32	"
E	Stasio Lillian T—†	254	housewife	32	"
F	Silverman Gertrude—†	254	"	55	
G	Silverman Robert	254	laborer	64	"
H	Scaramozzino Jean—†	254	housewife	23	"
K	Scaramozzino Pasquale	254	steamfitter	23	"

Ward 1–Precinct 13

CITY OF BOSTON

LIST OF RESIDENTS
20 YEARS OF AGE AND OVER

(NON-CITIZENS INDICATED BY ASTERISK)
(FEMALES INDICATED BY DAGGER)

AS OF

JANUARY 1, 1945

THOMAS F. SULLIVAN, *Chairman*
FREDERIC E. DOWLING, *Secretary*
WILLIAM A. MOTLEY, JR.
FRANCIS B. McKINNEY
EVERETT R. PROUT
Listing Board.

CITY OF BOSTON ◆ PRINTING DEPARTMENT

1300
Bennington Street

	Letter	Full Name	Res.	Occupation	Age	Reported Residence
	B	Nagle Catherine—†	256	housekeeper	84	here
	C	Cecelia Margaret—†	256	housewife	51	"
	D	Cecelia William	256	electrician	52	"
	F	Mahoney Sarah—†	260	clerk	42	Revere
	G	Muise John	260	"	27	here
	H	Deeran Annie—†	262	stitcher	23	"
	K	Deeran Tarviz—†	262	housekeeper	57	"
	M	McAllister Thomas	266	rigger	48	
	N	*Nunes Louise—†	266	housekeeper	40	"
	V	Quigley Augustine	290	clerk	56	
	W	Quigley Ellen J—†	290	proprietor	57	"
	X	Quigley Margaret M—†	290	housekeeper	59	"

1301

	A	Marshall Elizabeth—†	292	housewife	57	"
	B	Marshall Frank J	292	painter	57	
	C	Marshall Frank W	292	"	37	"
	D	Thornton Gwendolyn—†	293	housewife	22	"
	E	Thornton John	293	deckhand	66	"
	F	Thornton Thomas	293	U S A	31	
	G	Thornton Virginia—†	293	operator	27	"
	H	Umbro Annie—†	293	housewife	32	"
	K	Umbro Anthony	293	longshoreman	33	"
	L	Taylor Gertrude—†	293	housewife	36	"
	M	Taylor William J	293	chauffeur	37	"
	R	Tonelli Alice—†	297	housewife	39	"
	S	Tonelli Angelo	297	laborer	31	
	T	Tonelli Fred	297	"	35	
	U	*Tonelli Lawrence	297	retired	69	
	V	Tonelli Lawrence	297	U S A	33	
	W	Pace Margaret—†	297	saleswoman	21	"
	X	Pace Mildred—†	297	housewife	30	"
	Y	Pace William	297	laborer	47	
	Z	Pace William	297	U S A	20	

1302

	A	Merchant John	301	machinist	24	265 Lexington
	B	Merchant Virginia—†	301	housewife	21	265 "
	C	Barry Bridget—†	301	"	55	11 Maverick sq
	D	Barry John	301	longshoreman	64	11 "
	E	Barry Raymond	301	U S A	22	here
	F	DeWitt Herman	301	custodian	69	"

2

Bennington Street—Continued

G	Dolan Margaret—†	301	inspector	45	here
H	Dolan Thomas	301	U S N	20	"
K	Trayers Katherine—†	301	WAVE	25	"
M	Olivera Carmen	305	salesman	52	90 Chelsea
N	Olivera Enos—†	305	housewife	35	90 "
O	Olivera Sabanio	305	U S A	22	here
P	Olivera Vincent	305	"	23	"
T	Austin Catherine—†	315	housewife	65	"
U	Austin Michael	315	guard	56	··
V	Austin Michael	315	U S A	24	"
X	*DeAngelo Mary—†	319	candymaker	73	"
Y	*DeAngelo Michael	319	retired	69	
Z	Lanzetta Genaro	319	U S A	40	
	1303				
A	Reynolds George R	319	laborer	61	Lynn
B	Reynolds Joanne—†	319	housewife	66	"
E	Florentino Elmer	360	barber	44	397 Chelsea
F	Florentino Ernestine—†	360	housewife	42	397 "
G	Florentino James	360	butcher	21	here
H	Florentino Joseph	360	U S A	23	"
K	Florentino Florentino	360	shipper	20	"

Bremen Street

L	Wecker Charlotte—†	364	housewife	65	here
M	Wecker Myer	364	U S A	38	"
N	Wecker Simon	364	"	32	"
¹N	Wecker Max	364	pedler	75	
O	Wolfson Ida—†	364	at home	39	"
P	Benson Selma—†	364A	housewife	48	"
R	Benson Sven	364A	retired	79	
S	Gallagher Bernice—†	364A	clerk	27	"
T	Gallagher Edward A	364A	U S N	29	"
U	Lynch Leonard P	364A	seaman	24	
V	Greene Theresa—†	364A	housewife	62	"
W	Greene William J	364A	tailor	63	"
X	Dembro Lorraine A—†	366	housewife	23	257 Bennington
Y	Dembro Paul V	366	burner	34	257 "
Z	*Salerenzo Angelina—†	366	housewife	72	here
	1304				
A	LaMonica Charles	368	brazier	24	··

3

Page.	Letter.	FULL NAME.	Residence, Jan. 1, 1945.	Occupation.	Supposed Age.	Reported Residence, Jan. 1, 1944. Street and Number.

Bremen Street—Continued

	B	LaMonica Joseph	368	laborer	52	here
	c	LaMonica Mary—†	368	housewife	21	26 Margaret
	D	Aversa Mary—†	374	"	29	here
	E	Aversa Patrick M	374	fireman	30	"
	F	Rizzo Carmello S	374	U S A	20	"
	G	Rizzo Fannie—†	374	housewife	43	"
	H	French Angelina—†	376	"	28	Revere
	K	French Roy	376	painter	33	"
	L	Caggiano Frank	376	engineer	35	here
	M	Caggiano Rose—†	376	housewife	33	"
	N	Russell James E	398	longshoreman	62	"
	o	Russell James E, jr	398	U S A	25	
	P	Russell Rose C—†	398	housewife	55	"
	R	Russell Ruth—†	398	saleswoman	23	"
	s	Smith John J	398	longshoreman	53	"
	T	Ferriani Lillian—†	400	housewife	34	"
	U	Ferriani William	400	machinist	29	"
	V	Amerena Joseph	400	salesman	60	"
	W	Amerena Mary—†	400	housewife	59	"
	X	Amerena Robert L	400	U S N	22	
	Y	Colangelo Otto J	400	U S A	23	
	z*	Nigro Mary—†	400	housewife	53	"
1305						
	A	Amodeo Anna—†	408	"	40	"
	B	Amodeo Edward	408	painter	52	"
	c	Kelly Cornelius J	412	longshoreman	53	"
	D	Kelly Francis J	412	U S N	20	
	E	Kelly John J	412	U S A	24	
	F	Kelly Mary C—†	412	housewife	51	"
	G	Silva Edna—†	416	operator	24	121 Addison
	H	Turpin Louise—†	416	housewife	59	121 "
	K	Fairchild Bessie—†	416	at home	77	here
	L	Fairchild Charles A	416	electrician	60	"
	M	Aronson George H	452	photographer	44	1513 Wash'n
	N	Lowell Mabel—†	452	housekeeper	50	1513 "

Chelsea Street

	R	Stella John	345	chauffeur	32	here
	s	Stella Josephine—†	345	housewife	28	"
	T	Soo Hoo Deeng Hin	347	laundryman	45	"

Page.	Letter.	FULL NAME.	Residence, Jan. 1, 1945.	Occupation.	Supposed Age.	Reported Residence, Jan. 1, 1944. Street and Number.

u	Yee Shong Loong	347	laundryman	36	here
x	Nealon Leo	351	machinist	38	"
y	Nealon Mildred—†	351	waitress	37	"
z	McGinness Mary E—†	351	housewife	36	"
	1306				
a	McGinness William	351	cutter	36	"
b	DeFurio Fay—†	353	housewife	24	"
c	DeFurio Julio	353	U S C G	25	"
d	Grillo Frank	353	painter	50	"
e	Grillo Mary—†	353	housewife	41	"
f	Taschetti Vita—†	353	factoryhand	49	"
g	Bernazani Ethel M—†	355	housewife	48	"
h	Stevens William H	355	retired	73	"
k	Puopolo Alfred	355	checker	33	"
l	Puopolo Josephine—†	355	housewife	32	"
m	Puopolo Carmella—†	355	factoryhand	50	"
n	Puopolo Pasquale	355	laborer	52	"
o	Manzelli Alfred	357	U S A	24	
p	Manzelli Antonio	357	"	22	"
r	Manzelli Concetta—†	357	factoryhand	27	"
s	Manzelli Mary—†	357	housewife	56	"
t	Manzelli Vincenzo	357	laborer	60	"
u	MacDonald Aylmer	357	"	36	
v	MacDonald Edith—†	357	housewife	31	"
w	LaSalle Anthony	357	U S A	26	
x	LaSalle Christina—†	357	housewife	26	"
	1307				
b	Blevin Mary—†	367	factoryhand	65	"
c*	Silva Manuel D	367	blacksmith	60	"
d	Hancock Charles E	369	U S N	21	
e	Hancock Lucille—†	369	housewife	26	"
f	Mainieri Mary—†	369	"	26	"
g	Mainieri Nicholas	369	pipefitter	27	"
k	Keith Lulu—†	373	housewife	39	"
l	Keith Ralph	373	chipper	38	"
m	Smith James J	373	laborer	46	"
n	Smith Julia M—†	373	housewife	44	"
p	Garron Alfred	376	U S C G	20	Chelsea
r	Garron Lawrence	376	U S A	21	"
s	McAndrew Joseph J	376	chipper	38	Texas
t	McAndrew Myrtle S—†	376	housewife	39	here

Page.	Letter.	FULL NAME.	Residence, Jan. 1, 1945.	Occupation.	Supposed Age.	Reported Residence, Jan. 1, 1944. Street and Number.

Chelsea Street—Continued

w	Bloom Abraham	378	laborer	48	here
x	*Bloom Elizabeth—†	378	housewife	84	"
y	Shore Esther—†	378	"	41	"
z	Shore Samuel	378	merchant	48	"
	1308				
b	Doherty Agnes C—†	380	typist	24	
c	Doherty Catherine T—†	380	housewife	50	"
d	Doherty William F	380	laborer	51	"
e	Fucalaro Anthony	380	chauffeur	21	"
f	Fucalaro Catherine—†	380	saleswoman	23	"
g	*Fucalaro Rose—†	380	housewife	40	"
h	Fucalaro Victor	380	laborer	48	"
k	Rosa Samuel	382	chauffeur	40	"
l	Rosa Theresa—†	382	housewife	35	"
m	Kirk Rubina I—†	382	"	36	"
r	Terranova Carl	390A	pipefitter	21	"
s	Terranova Frances—†	390A	at home	25	"
t	Terranova Natalie—†	390A	inspector	20	"
u	Terranova Nicholina—†	390A	housewife	50	"
v	Foosett Freda—†	390A	"	52	
w	Foosett John	390A	seaman	52	"
x	Jevoli Billie—†	391	housewife	33	"
y	Booth Arthur A	391	mechanic	29	"
z	Booth Pauline E—†	391	housewife	29	"
	1309				
a	Merrigan Edith H—†	391	"	60	
b	Merrigan William H, jr	391	U S M C	22	"
c	Thibodeau Margaret—†	391	factoryhand	46	"
d	Ferriera Antonio	391	laborer	51	"
e	Ferriera Antonio, jr	391	"	28	
f	Ferriera Candida—†	391	housewife	53	"
g	Ferriera Manuel	391	U S N	23	"
h	Musco Carmen	392	barber	58	Quincy
k	Musco Mary—†	392	housewife	56	"
l	Megna Frank F	392	U S N	32	here
m	Megna Grace—†	392	housewife	36	"
n	Clee Arthur L	392	machinist	20	"
o	Clee Hazel E—†	392	bookkeper	32	"
p	Clee Jennie E—†	392	clerk	57	"
r	Clee Walter R	392	U S A	25	
t	Caponigro Liberto	397	bartender	33	"

6

Chelsea Street—Continued

U	Caponigro Ruth—†	397	housewife	31	here
V	O'Rourke Mary F—†	397	housekeeper	29	"
W	Riccioli Aurelia—†	399	dressmaker	23	"
X	Riccioli Pifania—†	399	housewife	61	"
Y	Riccioli Salvatore	399	barber	35	"
Z	Staffieri Carmine	399.	"	44	
	1310				
A	Staffieri Mary—†	399	factoryhand	42	"
B	Minola Charles	399	cabinetmaker	45	"
C	Minola Josephine—†	399	factoryhand	21	"
D	Minola Sarah—†	399	"	44	"
E	Cunningham Elizabeth–†	401	housekeeper	81	"
F	St Croix Jeannette—†	401	housewife	23	"
G	St Croix Joseph	401	U S N	24	"
H	D'Addio Irene—†	403	housewife	31	"
K	D'Addio Vincent	403	mechanic	34	"
L	Nowicki Frank	403	shipfitter	21	"
M	Nowicki Rose—†	403	housewife	21	"
N	Dorio Edith—†	403	"	28	"
O	Dorio Frank	403	riveter	37	"
R	Rotondo Antonio	405	manager	62	"
S	Rotondo Mariannina—†	405	housewife	62	"
U	Gould Mary—†	407	"	35	··
V	Gould Stephen	407	U S C G	37	"
W	Nagle Anna—†	407	housewife	24	"
X	Nagle John	407	shipfitter	27	"
Y	Lightbody Annie—†	407	operator	43	"
Z	Lightbody Catherine—†	407	housewife	77	"
	1311				
A	Lightbody Frederick	407	compositor	41	"
C	Gillespie Dennis	409	retired	74	
D	Gillespie James L	409	typist	30	··
E	Gillespie Margaret—†	409	housewife	75	"
F	Sweeney Margaret—†	409	factoryhand	48	"
G	Sweeney Paul J	409	U S N	22	"
H	Gallo Bernard	409	chauffeur	45	"
K	Burns William H rear	409	painter	44	··
N	O'Regan Joanna—†	413	housewife	73	"
O	O'Regan Mary—†	413	"	80	"
P	Martin Frank.	415	pipefitter	28	534 Saratoga
R	Martin Margaret—†	415	housewife	23	here

Chelsea Street—Continued

u	Moran Helen M—†	417	housewife	40	here
v	Moran Joseph E	417	bartender	49	"
w	DiCesare Emilio	420	candymaker	38	250 E Eagle
x	DiCesare Emily—†	420	housewife	31	250 "
y	Arbia Anthony	420	tailor	54	here
z	Arbia Attilio	420	U S A	20	"
	1312					
A	Arbia Bella—†	420	dressmaker	25	"
B	Arbia Ernest	420	U S A	22	
c	Arbia Joseph	420	"	24	"
D	Arbia Pasquale	420	"	27	
E	Palumbo Antonio	420	machinist	30	"
F	Palumbo Jennie—†	420	housewife	29	"
G	Gordon Ellen P—†	422	technician	27	"
H	Lucius Manuel P	422	shipwright	42	"
K	Lucius Margaret R—†	422	housewife	40	"
L	DeModena Frances—†	422	"	38	
M	DeModena Leo	422	machinist	45	"
N	Bianchino Caroline—†	422	housewife	26	37 Wordsworth
o	Bianchino Ernest	422	machinist	32	37 "
R	DiGiovanni Amedeo	424	proprietor	52	here
s	DiGiovanni Angelina—†	424	stitcher	20	"
T	DiGiovanni Mary—†	424	housewife	48	"
u	Daviaux Elizabeth—†	426	metalworker	23	5 Shelby
v	Daviaux Robert	426	U S N	23	5 "
w	Kinnally Daniel S	426	"	25	5 "
x	Kinnally Margaret—†	426	operator	23	5 "
y	Mecurio Josephine—†	426	housewife	42	5 "
z	Cincotta Philip	426	packer	24	here
	1313					
A	Scarfa Louis F	426	U S A	34	--
B	Scarfa Mary—†	426	housewife	42	"
C	DiForti Carmella—†	426A	"	31	"
D	DiForti Salvatore, jr	426A	leatherwkr	36	"
E	Consolante Anna—†	428	housewife	44	"
F	Consolante Elizabeth—†	428	stitcher	21	"
G	Consolante Peter	428	machinist	47	"
H	DiCesare Concetta—†	428	housewife	36	"
K	DiCesare Fortunato	428	candymaker	42	"
L	DiCesare Nunziata—†	428	housewife	71	"
M	DiCesare Pasquale	428	retired	74	"

Page	Letter	FULL NAME.	Residence, Jan. 1, 1945.	Occupation.	Supposed Age.	Reported Residence, Jan. 1, 1944. Street and Number.

Chelsea Street—Continued

N	Milano Biagio	428	shipfitter	32	here
O	Milano Rose—†	428	housewife	34	"
P	Driscoll John M	430	driller	36	"
R	Driscoll Lawrence P	430	U S A	28	
S	Driscoll Nellie M—†	430	housewife	30	"
T	Toomey Agnes F—†	430	tel operator	21	"
U	Toomey Alice M—†	430	waitress	23	"
V	Toomey Ellen G—†	430	tel operator	20	"
W	Toomey John A	430	asbestos wkr	65	"
X	*Gagliardi George	430	retired	88	
Y	Gagliardi Josephine—†	430	welder	20	
Z	Gagliardi Marie—†	430	housewife	46	"
	1314				
A	Gagliardi Michael J	430	laborer	47	"
B	*Bunucci Ercole	432	salesman	54	82 Montgomery
C	Censabella Charles	432	U S N	49	here
D	Censabella Mary—†	432	laundress	49	"
E	DeSisto Joseph	rear 432	machinist	28	"
F	DeSisto Lillian—†	" 432	housewife	27	"
G	*Fucillo Philomina—†	" 432	at home	72	432 Chelsea
H	Aronson Muriel—†	434	waitress	34	here
K	Aronson Robert	434	retired	76	"
L	Tango Louis	434	brazier	20	"
M	Tango Phyllis—†	434	housewife	53	"
N	Kennedy Ruth M—†	434	at home	30	661 Saratoga

Cleveland Street

P	Monaco Agostino	3	carpenter	47	here
R	Monaco Lena—†	3	housewife	41	"

Eagle Square

S	Cimmino Frances—†	2	stitcher	28	here
T	*Sabatini Carmella—†	2	housewife	59	"
U	Sabatini Ettore	2	retired	61	"

East Eagle Street

W	Dellucci Arthur	325	machinist	23	here
X	Dellucci Rose—†	325	housewife	23	"

East Eagle Street—Continued

Page.	Letter.	Full Name.	Residence, Jan. 1, 1945.	Occupation.	Supposed Age.	Reported Residence, Jan. 1, 1944. Street and Number.
	Y	Pecora Nicholas	325	pipefitter	29	here
	Z	Pecora Rosalie—†	325	housewife	28	"
1315						
	A	McCormick Mary—†	325	"	27	
	B	McCormick Vincent	325	U S N	27	..
	C	Venuti Jennie—†	327	housewife	31	"
	D	Venuti Joseph	327	pipefitter	31	"
	E	Polito Peter	327	shoeworker	61	"
	F	Polito Theresa—†	327.	housewife	61	"
	G	Lauria Peter	327	U S N	30	
	H	Lauria Susan—†	327	housewife	27	"
	K	Smith George E	329	U S A	23	341 E Eagle
	L	Smith Ruth—†	329	housewife	20	341 "
	M	*Romano Antonio	329	laborer	60	here
	N	Romano Gaetano	329	U S A	35	"
	O	Romano Sophie—†	329	cleanser	31	"
	P	Bingle Margaret—†	329	housewife	30	366 Princeton
	R	Love Alice—†	329	cleaner	56	366 "
	S	Love Clarence	329	U S N	25	366 "
	T	Arena Edith—†	331	housewife	33	here
	U	Arena Joseph	331	chauffeur	34	"
	V	Della Sala Attilio	331	merchant	44	"
	W	Della Sala Clara—†	331	housewife	44	"
	X	Mainiero Carmella—†	331	"	42	
	Y	Mainiero Michael	331	barber	44	
	Z	Pope Dorothy—†	333	housewife	21	"
1316						
	A	Pope William	333	U S N	24	"
	B	Walsh Celia—†	333	housewife	29	"
	C	Walsh Patrick J	333	fisherman	31	"
	D	Caponigro George	333	U S N	30	
	E	Caponigro Sally—†	333	housewife	24	"
	F	Maglitta Frederick	335	electrician	41	"
	G	Maglitta Mary—†	335	housewife	36	"
	H	*Giello Lena—†	335	"	42	"
	K	DeStefano Edith—†	335	stitcher	30	"
	L	DeStefano John	335	barber	68	"
	M	DeStefano John, jr	335	welder	34	
	N	DeStefano Josephine—†	335	housewife	62	"
	O	Gallo Ann—†	337	stitcher	24	"
	P	Gallo Benedict	337	U S A	22	

Page.	Letter.	FULL NAME.	Residence, Jan. 1, 1945.	Occupation.	Supposed Age.	Reported Residence, Jan. 1, 1944. Street and Number.

R	McNaught Harold	337	seaman	36	here
s	*McNaught Sarah—†	337	welder	32	"
T	*Thompson Sarah—†	337	at home	55	Canada
U	Interbartolo Marie—†	337	housewife	22	here
V	Interbartolo Michael	337	U S N	24	"
W	StElmo Anna C—†	341	housewife	44	"
X	StElmo Frank	341	welder	50	
Y	Martucci Anthony	341	pressman	33	"
Z	Martucci Mildred—†	341	housewife	34	"

1317

A	Grande Joseph	341	assembler	45	"
B	Grande Pauline—†	341	housewife	44	"
C	Williams Mary—†	341	clerk	20	"
D	Williams Walter J	341	U S N	21	Indiana
E	Balboni Barbara C—†	345	housewife	48	here
F	Balboni John J	345	shipfitter	54	"
G	D'Alelio Anna—†	345	housewife	22	Utah
H	D'Alelio Henry F	345	U S A	28	here
K	Cirrutti Angelina—†	345	housewife	30	"
L	Cirrutti Charles	345	laborer	48	"
M	Carroll Florence—†	347	housewife	36	"
N	Carroll John H	347	mechanic	36	"

Frankfort Street

O	*Faccadio Peter	373	foundryman	45	here
P	*Faccadio Savino	373	retired	73	"
R	Ferrara Anna—†	373	housewife	31	187 Princeton
S	Ferrara Joseph	373	rigger	32	187 "
T	McMahon Agnes I—†	373	housewife	29	337 Wash'n
U	McMahon Leon L	373	U S N	28	California
V	Morris Helen—†	373	waitress	25	337 Wash'n
W	Cardone Philip	375	mechanic	39	here
X	Cardone Virginia—†	375	housewife	33	"
Y	Silva George E	375	seaman	45	"
Z	Silva Philomena—†	375	housewife	44	"

1318

A	Marino Armand	375	shoeworker	48	"
B	Marino Louise—†	375	mechanic	47	"
C	Aragona Fred	377	U S N	35	
D	Aragona Marion—†	377	housewife	36	"

Page	Letter	Full Name.	Residence, Jan. 1, 1945.	Occupation.	Supposed Age.	Reported Residence, Jan. 1, 1944. Street and Number.

Frankfort Street—Continued

	E	Dolimount Dorothy E—†	377	housewife	32	here
	F	Dolimount George I	377	welder	32	"
	G	Minichio Ida—†	377	housewife	24	"
	H	Minichio Michael	377	policeman	25	226 Chelsea
	K	Dore Carmella—†	379	housewife	25	here
	L	Dore Frank	379	U S N	26	"
	M	Scanzillo Anthony	379	"	24	"
	N	Scanzillo Mary J—†	379	housewife	54	"
	O	Scanzillo Michael	379	tailor	58	
	P	Shea Brendan	379	fisherman	36	"
	R	Shea Hilda—†	379	housewife	33	"
	S	Donovan Anna L—†	381	"	29	
	T	Donovan James H	381	driller	32	
	U	Oliveri Anthony	381	pipecoverer	38	"
	V	Oliveri Arduina—†	381	housewife	30	"
	W	Filosa Albert	381	pipecover	37	"
	X	Filosa Elsie—†	381	housewife	36	"
	Y	DeSteffano Albert	383	rigger	40	75 St Andrew rd
	Z	DeSteffano Maria—†	383	housewife	41	75 "
		1319				
	A	DeSteffano Rose—†	383	clerk	58	here
	B	Porzio Constantino	383	diemaker	36	"
	C	Porzio Margaret—†	383	housewife	34	"
	D	Doucette Alice M—†	385	"	55	"
	E	Doucette Henry A	385	rigger	50	
	F	Calello Angelina—†	385	housewife	43	"
	G	Calello Gerald	385	guard	48	"
	H	Calello Marie—†	385	operator	11	"
	K	Polino Carmella—†	385	at home	84	"
	L	*Autori Andreanna—†	385	housewife	53	"
	M	Autori Carmella—†	385	stitcher	28	"
	N	Autori Domenic	385	U S A	30	"
	O	Autori Francisco	385	rigger	57	"
	P	Autori Theresa—†	385	operator	20	"

Lawson Place

	R	*Allie Nellie M—†	1	housewife	38	here
	S	Allie William D	1	millhand	37	"
	T	Alexander Dorothy—†	2	housewife	40	Malden
	U	Alexander Rose—†	2	"	71	"

12

Lawson Place—Continued

v	DeMeo Anthony	3	salesman	46	72 Porter
w	DeMeo Margaret—†	3	housewife	36	72 "
x	DeMeo Rita—†	3	clerk	20	72
y	Lopez Adeline—†	4	welder	20	here
z	Lopez Joseph	4	laborer	59	"

1320

a	*Lopes Lucenda—†	4	housewife	45	"
b	Noble Annie—†	5	"	70	"
c	Noble Florence—†	5	clerk	45	"
d	Goodrow Margaret—†	5	domestic	64	"
e	Goodrow Thomas	5	retired	73	"
f	Leary Catherine—†	5	packer	59	"
g	Frazier Annie J—†	6	at home	78	"
h	Huskins Evelyn—†	6	clerk	23	
k	Johnson Ellen W—†	6	"	42	
l	Frazier Mary E—†	7	housewife	46	"
m	Frazier Peter L	7	operator	53	"
n	Frazier Rita E—†	7	clerk	21	"
o	Gardner Mary E—†	7	housekeeper	23	Florida

Lexington Street

p	Garchinsky Charles	317	machinist	32	here
r	Garchinsky Loretta—†	317	housewife	29	"
s	Garchinsky Anna M—†	317	"	68	"
t	Garchinsky Michael	317	seaman	26	
u	Garchinsky Walter	317	machinist	40	"
v	Farrell Sophie—†	317	brazier	35	"
w	Sperguino Anna—†	317	factoryhand	45	Newton

Lovell Street

x	Cammarano Angelina—†	371	housewife	47	here
y	Cammarano Vito	371	candymaker	51	"
z	Nicoletti Jean—†	371	housewife	24	"

1321

a	Nicoletti Philip	371	electrician	24	"
b	Panatta Carolina—†	371	clerk	36	
c	Burke Frederick J	372	longshoreman	40	"
d	Burke Helen C—†	372	housewife	39	"
e	Zambello Anthony	372	laborer	64	180 Bennington

Lovell Street—Continued

	F	*Zambello Concetta—†	372	housewife	60	180 Bennington
	G	Zambello Michael	372	U S N	22	180 "
	H	Giromini Bruno	372	electrician	34	here
	K	*Giromini Marie—†	372	housewife	60	"
	L	Saggese Helen—†	373	"	26	"
	M	Saggese Lawrence	373	blacksmith	27	"
	N	DeFronzo Louis	373	chauffeur	38	"
	O	DeFronzo Mary—†	373	dipper	36	
	P	DeFronzo Phyllis—†.	373	saleswoman	20	"
	R	DeFronzo Elizabeth—†	373	stitcher	30	"
	S	DeFronzo Margaret—†	373	dressmaker	25	"
	T	DeFronzo Minnie—†	373	housewife	55	"
	U	DeFronzo Nicholas	373	butcher	64	"
	V	DeFronzo Rita—†	373	saleswoman	22	"
	W	DeFronzo Victoria—†	373	clerk	26	
	X	Jeffrey Bertha—†	374	housewife	47	"
	Y	Jeffrey Joseph H	374	chauffeur	54	"
	Z	Trunfio Helen—†	374	housewife	35	"
1322						
	A	Trunfio Michael	374	chauffeur	53	"
	B	Kelly Esther—†	374	machinist	33	"
	C	Kelly James	374	guard	35	
	D	Sartori Brunetta—†	375	housewife	33	"
	E	Sartori James	375	shipfitter	35	"
	F	Amato Frank	375	guard	50	"
	G	*Amato Vincenza—†	375	housewife	43	"
	H	Nigro Mary—†	375	clerk	20	
	K	Luongo Antoinetta—†	375	housewife	51	"
	L	Luongo Dominic	375	laborer	55	
	M	Gallerani Alberto	376	printer	44	
	N	Gallerani James	376	U S N	35	"
	O	*Gallerani Luigi	376	retired	80	"
	P	DeCristoforo Anthony	376	investigator	37	"
	R	DeCristoforo Mary—†	376	housewife	34	"
	S	Cecchino Angelina A—†	376	"	31	
	T	Cecchino Hector J	376	machinist	34	"
	U	DiStafano Theresa—†	377	housewife	28	"
	V	DiStafano Vincent	377	rigger	30	
	W	Donovan John	377	carpenter	64	"
	X	*Donovan Sarah—†	377	housewife	65	"
	Y	*Samone Marie—†	377	"	26	"

14

Page	Letter	Full Name.	Residence, Jan. 1, 1945.	Occupation.	Supposed Age.	Reported Residence, Jan. 1, 1944. Street and Number.

Lovell Street—Continued

	z	Bettini Flora—†	377	housewife	36	here
1323						
	A	Bettini Nicholas	377	shoeworker	39	"
	B	Salerno Anthony	378	salesman	36	"
	c	Salerno Marion—†	378	forewoman	36	"
	D	Ciampa Concetta—†	378	saleswoman	27	"
	E	Ciampa Ernest	378	U S N	27	
	F	Salerno Joseph	378	welder	34	
	G	Salerno Mary—†	378	housewife	63	"
	H	Salerno Pietro	378	retired	65	"
	K	Salimbene Charles	378	machinist	31	"
	L	Salimbene Palmira—†	378	housewife	26	"
	M	Finn Bernard	379	U S A	37	"
	N	Finn Rita—†	379	housewife	30	"
	O	Keough Michael	379	roofer	59	
	P	Keough Nellie—†	379	housewife	64	"
	R	Spordone Phyllis—†	379	"	37	
	s	Spordone Severio	379	shipfitter	37	"
	T	Moreira John	379	U S N	21	
	U	Moreira Louis	379	laborer	46	
	v*	Moreira Mary—†	379	housewife	51	"
	w	Fatch Catherine—†	380	candymaker	27	"
	x	McConnell Edward	380	U S A	23	
	Y	McConnell Nora—†	380	housewife	52	"
	z	Amato Angelina—†	380	"	50	"
1324						
	A	Amato Catherine—†	380	dressmaker	26	"
	B	Martocchio Angelo	380	chauffeur	33	"
	c	Martocchio Ella—†	380	housewife	29	"
	D	Durlong Joseph	381	electrician	38	"
	E	Durlong Pauline—†	381	clerk	35	
	F	Nastari Anna—†	381	housewife	47	"
	G	Nastari Augustino	381	laborer	22	
	H	Nastari Gennaro	381	curator	52	
	K	Nastari Rose—†	381	clerk	25	
	L	Orlando Albert	381	U S N	31	
	M	Orlando Angelo	381	U S M C	26	"
	N	Orlando Josephine—†	381	housewife	59	"
	O	Veposky Albert	381	waiter	33	"
	P	Veposky Anna—†	381	stitcher	37	"
	R	Chappert Mary—†	382	WAC	28	

Lovell Street—Continued

s	Kennedy Edward	382	drawtender	58	here
T	Kennedy Mary E—†	382	housewife	54	"
U	Kennedy Richard	382	U S A	25	"
V	Kennedy Thomas L	382	U S N	21	
W	DeStefano Carmen	382	shoecutter	55	"
X	DeStefano Frances—†	382	housewife	54	"
Y	Ghelfi Louis	382	U S N	33	
z	Ghelfi Madeline—†	382	housewife	30	"

1325

A	Spenazzola Mary—†	383	"	40	
B	Spenazzola Pasquale	383	barber	40	
c	Fuccillo Carmen	383	tailor	46	
D	Fuccillo Carmen, jr	383	U S N	23	"
E	Fuccillo Isabella—†	383	housewife	45	"
F	Fuccillo Pasquale	383	U S C G	24	"
H	Fuccillo Agata—†	383	housewife	43	"
G	Fuccillo Albert	383	retired	47	
K	Fuccillo Cecelia—†	383	dipper	41	
L	Amato Albert	384	U S A	25	
M	Amato Arthur	384	"	20	
N	Amato Frances—†	384	housewife	52	"
O	Amato John J	384	mechanic	29	"
P	Amato Pasquale	384	U S A	27	
R	Searle Bertha—†	384	packer	49	
s	Searle Edwin	384	checker	49	"
T	Moire Annie M—†	384	housewife	64	"
U	Moire James	384	carpenter	54	"

Neptune Road

V	Greene Anne—†	15	housekeeper	70	here
W	Guidara Adeline—†	15	housewife	55	"
X	Guidara Orlando	15	laborer	27	"
Y	Guidara Paul	15	bricklayer	65	"
z	Hochbaum Esther—†	15	housewife	50	"

1326

A	Hochbaum Gustaf	15	clerk	21	
B	Hochbaum Morris	15	proprietor	53	"
c	Hochbaum Raymond	15	stenographer	27	"
D	Hochbaum Rose—†	15	clerk	25	"
E	Costello Bridget—†	17	housewife	72	"

Page.	Letter.	FULL NAME.	Residence, Jan. 1, 1945.	Occupation.	Supposed Age.	Reported Residence, Jan. 1, 1944. Street and Number.

F	Costello Frederick	17	longshoreman	31	here
G	Costello Nicholas	17	"	35	"
H	Greene Elmer	17	welder	43	"
K	Greene Mary T—†	17	housewife	41	"
L	McDonough Elizabeth—†	17	housekeeper	79	"
M	Mantica Leo	17	U S N	30	"
N	Mantica Mary—†	17	housewife	32	"
O	Dempsey Raymond J	19	B F D	40	"
P	Dempsey Sophie W—†	19	housewife	31	"
R	Toohig Warren A	19	B F D	45	"
S	O'Neil Patrick J	19	retired	69	"
T	Schrage Catherine—†	19	housewife	34	"
U	Schrage James R	19	shipfitter	39	"
V	Avellar John F	19	metalworker	40	"
W	Avellar Marie E—†	'19	housewife	41	"
X	Avellar Mary I—†	19	bookkeeper	20	"
Y	Gordon Anthony	19	U S A	20	"
Z	Cotter Charles	21	operator	28	"
	1327				
A	Cotter Marjorie—†	21	housewife	28	"
B	Kelley William	21	laborer	45	
C	Lane Ethel—†	21	housekeeper	48	"
D	Leverone Blanche—†	21	tel operator	44	"
E	Leverone Evelyn—†	21	clerk	30	"
F	Leverone Frank	21	toolkeeper	43	"
G	Leverone Helena—†	21	housewife	69	"
H	Leverone Rose—†	21	folder	37	"
K	Ryan Eugene F	23	pipefitter	39	"
L	Ryan Rose—†	23	housewife	38	"
M	Vieira Georgeana—†	23	housekeeper	73	"
N	Camara Alexander	23	welder	37	
O	Camara Evelyn L—†	23	housewife	30	"
P	Screnci Josephine—†	23	"	24	
R	Screnci Salvatore	23	laborer	27	"
S	Fallon Mildred M—†	25	housewife	28	"
T	Fallon Walter E	25	U S A	21	"
U	McLaren John	25	retired	78	"
V	Thomas William	25	U S A	25	Pennsylvania
W	Murphy Johanna C—†	25	housewife	85	here
X	Murphy Thomas	25	retired	88	"
Y	Cardina Caroline—†	25	housewife	48	"

Page	Letter	Full Name	Residence, Jan. 1, 1945.	Occupation.	Supposed Age.	Reported Residence, Jan. 1, 1944. Street and Number.

Neptune Road—Continued

	Letter	Full Name	Residence, Jan. 1, 1945.	Occupation.	Supposed Age.	Reported Residence
	z	Cardina William	25	laborer	51	here
1328						
	A	Cardina William, jr	25	U S A	25	
	B	Knudsen Anna—†	27	housewife	83	"
	C	Knudsen Anna R—†	27	clerk	45	
	D	Currie John E	27	rigger	60	
	E	Currie Mary E—†	27	housewife	63	"
	F	Kajander Hilda—†	27	"	53	
	G	Kajander John	27	machinist	53	"
	H	Kajander Toivo D	27	"	30	
	K	Fougere Evelyn—†	33	housewife	39	"
	L	Fougere Napoleon	33	laborer	40	..
	M	Correa Antonio	33	"	52	
	N	Correa Dalfina—†	33	housewife	42	"
	o	*Luciana Eugenia—†	33	housekeeper	63	"
	P	Perdigao Manuel R	33	longshoreman	38	"
	R	Perdigao Mary C—†	33	housewife	33	"
	S	Vieira Manuel	35	longshoreman	43	"
	T	Vieira Mary—†	35	housewife	43	"
	U	Henry Emile	35	retired	65	
	V	Popp Raymond	35	U S A	23	
	W	Popp Richard	35	U S N	25	
	X	Popp Virginia—†	35	housewife	52	"
	Y	Vieira Mary—†	35	"	43	
	z	Vieira Matthew	35	laborer	41	
1329						
	A	Crowley Catherine F—†	37	housewife	65	"
	B	Crowley Claire M—†	37	clerk	33	"
	C	Crowley Francis D	37	U S A	30	
	D	Stasio Carlo	37	salesman	42	"
	E	Stasio Helen—†	37	dressmaker	38	"
	F	Stasio Phyllis—†	37	housewife	38	"
	G	Gaeta Alfonso	37	U S A	36	
	H	Gaeta Emily—†	37	operator	26	"
	K	Gaeta Michael	37	instructor	30	"
	L	Gaeta Theresa—†	37	housewife	58	"
	M	Gaeta Theresa—†	37	clerk	20	
	N	*Maglio Irene—†	37	at home	75	"
	o	DeRosa Archie	39	tailor	50	
	P	DeRosa Edward	39	U S M C	27	"
	R	DeRosa John	39	U S N	25	

Neptune Road—Continued

s	DeRosa Margaret—†	39	housewife	48	here
T	DeRosa Stephen	39	U S A	23	"
U	Mascetti Lydia—†	39	operator	26	"
V	Mascetti Mabel—†	39	dressmaker	28	"
w	Mascetti Nicholas	39	pressman	56	"
x	*Mascetti Renata—†	39	housewife	55	"
Y	Mascetti Rose—†	39	"	24	
z	Vitale Dorothea F—†	39	operator	21	"
	1330				
A	Vitale Frances F—†	39	housewife	51	"
B	Vitale Joseph A	39	operator	51	"
c	Vitale Ralph J	39	U S N	25	
D	Lumia Beatrice—†	41	housewife	25	"
E	Lumia James	41	welder	28	"
F	Johnson Anna—†	41	housewife	50	"
G	Johnson James	41	tel worker	49	"
H	Kennedy Anne E—†	41	housewife	83	"
K	Kennedy Edward T	41	U S A	44	
L	Kennedy Thomas J	41	engineer	35	"
M	Cardarelli Arthur	41	U S N	23	"
N	Cardarelli Inez—†	41	clerk	31	"
O	Cardarelli Lawrence	41	shoeworker	50	"
P	Cardarelli Vincenza—†	41	housewife	46	"
s	Miraglia Anthony	45	retired	69	
T	Miraglia Arthur	45	mechanic	38	"
U	Miraglia Eleanor—†	45	housewife	27	"
V	Miraglia Grace—†	45	"	37	
w	Miraglia James	45	attorney	41	"
X	Miraglia Josephine—†	45	bookkeeper	31	"
Y	Miraglia Lorraine—†	45	operator	25	"
z	LaBlanc Louise—†	47	housewife	53	"
	1331				
A	LaBlanc Roy J	47	fisherman	48	"
B	Flaschner Laura—†	47	housewife	22	"
F	Flaschner Leo	47	chauffeur	22	"
D	Shea Bridget—†	47	housewife	60	"
E	Shea Irene—†	47	clerk	47	
F	Shea Raymond	47	laborer	27	"
G	Granara Anne D—†	49	stenographer	26	"
H	Granara Helena G—†	49	housewife	45	"
K	Granara William J	49	operator	52	"

Neptune Road—Continued

L	Oliver Frank R	49	retired	60	here
M	Oliver John F ·	49	U S A	25	"
N	Oliver Mary C—†	49	housewife	62	"
O	Oliver Paul G	49	U S C G	23	"
P	Oliver Phyllis M—†	49	tel operator	20	"
R	Teixeira Phyllis L—†	49	waitress	56	"
S	Angelides Peter	49	fireman	54	"
T	Dafilo Manuel E	49	engineer	65	"
U	Dafilo Sarah J—† ·	49	housewife	65	"
V	Vella Helen W—†	49	mechanic	31	"
W	Vella Joseph, jr	49	engineer	34	"
X	Walker John T	51	salesman ·	33	"
Y	Walker Mary—†	51	housewife	30	"
Z	McWhinnie James R	51	U S N	36	
	1332				
A	McWhinnie Mary P—†	51	typist	34	
B	Acres Charles J	51	painter	36	"
C	Acres Julia P—†	51	housewife	30	"
D	Gomes Charlotte J—†	53	"	41	
E	Gomes George L	53	chauffeur	48	"
F	Landrigan Mary E—†	53	housewife	57	"
G	Landrigan Russell F	53	clerk	29	
H	Landrigan William R	53	plumber	62	"
K	Fiorentini Gene	53	U S A	24	Haverhill
L	Staffier Anthony F	53	draftsman	23	141 Putnam
M	Staffier Christine E—†	53	auditor	24	141 "
N	Staffier Frank J	53	meatcutter	50	141 "
O	Staffier Jennie—†	53	housewife	49	Haverhill
P	Cantalupo Carmen	55	candymaker	58	here
R	Cantalupo Gabrielle—†	55	housewife	54	"
S	Cantalupo Lucy—†	55	clerk	27	"
T	Knox Mary A—†	55	housewife	55	"
U	Knox Paul V	55	U S N	20	··
V	Knox Raymond J	55	seaman	24	
W	Knox Sylvester J	55	printer	55	
X	Pigott Mary A—†	55	operator	28	"
Y	Pigott William J	55	U S A	27	
Z	Johnson Madeline—†	55	at home	63	"
	1333				
A	Ryan Ellen S—†	55	housewife	33	"
B	Ryan John G	55	brakeman	34	"

20

Neptune Road—Continued

c	Ryan Catherine—†	57	housewife	63	here
d	Ryan Nellie—†	57	"	67	"
e	Olson Frank W	57	machinist	50	"
f	Olson Octavous	57	retired	89	
g	Olson Vera C—†	57	bookkeeper	48	"
h	Olson Victoria L—†	57	typist	46	"
k	Connell James H	57	laborer	35	51 McLellan
l	Connell Margaret—†	57	housewife	73	51 "
m	Connell Mary—†	57	hostess	39	51 "
n	Pelham Helen J—†	63	housewife	38	here
o	Pelham Ivan G	63	clerk	45	"
p	*Gonsalves Lucy—†	63	weaver	51	"
r	Mathias Mary—†	63	clerk	22	
s	*Silva Caroline—†	63	housekeeper	83	"
t	Famolare James L	63	chauffeur	34	400 Bennington
u	Famolare Olympia—†	63	housewife	29	400 "
v	Donahue Catherine R—†	65	tel operator	41	here
w	Kelly Angela J—†	65	clerk	40	"
x	Kelly Richard T	65	retired	87	"
y	Pedro Alfred	65	boilermaker	47	"
z	*Pedro Geramena—†	65	housewife	42	"
	1334				
a	Doherty Ethel J—†	65	"	32	
b	Doherty Henry J	65	repairman	39	"
c	Monahan Mary—†	67	housewife	24	"
d	Monahan Patrick	67	shipper	35	"
e	Butler Helen T—†	67	housewife	32	"
f	Butler William E	67	checker	39	"
g	Granara Anna E—†	67	housewife	42	"
h	Granara Richard L	67	chauffeur	43	"
k	Cameron Agnes T—†	69	housewife	68	"
l	Coffin Ruth L—†	69	clerk	29	
m	Coffin William T	69	U S N	28	
n	Conway Eugene P	68	"	20	"
o	Conway Helen M—†	69	housewife	47	"
p	Conway John J	69	letter carrier	51	"
r	Conway John J, jr	69	U S N	21	
s	Lynch Anna A—†	69	housewife	38	"
t	Lynch Edward T	69	B F D	43	
u	Haskins Jean—†	75	housewife	29	"
v	Johnson Charles J	75	carpenter	55	"

Neptune Road—Continued

	Letter	Full Name	Residence	Occupation	Age	Reported Residence
	w	Johnson Maude B—†	75	housewife	52	here
	x	Lamb Maude—†	75	candymaker	32	Burlington
	y	Peterson Carrie—†	75	housewife	32	here
	z	Peterson Oscar	75	brazier	34	"
1335						
	a	Rossano Frank	75	foreman	30	"
	b	Rossano Hazel—†	75	housewife	30	"
	c	Pupa Angelina—†	93	"	38	91 London
	d	Pupa Angelo	93	chauffeur	37	91 "
	e	Pascucci Marguerite—†	93	candymaker	23	here
	f	*Pascucci Mary—†	93	housewife	53	"
	g	Pascucci Rocco	93	millhand	54	"
	h	Goulet Camille	93	chipper	35	"
	k	Goulet Orise—†	93	housewife	32	"
	l	Cianci Anthony M	111	buyer	53	
	m	Cianci Margaret M—†	111	housewife	49	"
	n	Loschi Augustus	111	lawyer	59	"
	o	Loschi Charles A	111	merchant	47	"
	p	Loschi Harriet B—†	111	housewife	47	"
	r	Loschi John	111	retired	67	
	s	Loschi Mary A—†	111	teacher	51	
	t	Loschi Victor	111	musician	55	"
	u	McGurin Beatrice—†	115	inspector	27	45 Faywood av
	v	McGurin John	115	U S N	30	45 "
	w	Tassinari Agnes—†	115	operator	23	here
	x	Tassinari Anna—†	115	tel operator	32	"
	y	*Tassinari Joseph	115	retired	68	"
	z	*Tassinari Josephine—†	115	housewife	62	"
1336						
	a	Tassinari William	115	welder	29	"
	b	Sexton Richard	115	policeman	46	"
	c	Sexton Ruth C—†	115	housewife	44	"
	d	Giggi Henry	115	bricklayer	41	"
	e	Giggi Louise—†	115	housewife	33	"
	f	*Mariotti Carmella—†	131	"	61	
	g	Mariotti Vasco	131	merchant	61	"
	h	Humphrey Annie—†	131	housewife	73	"
	k	Humphrey Harry H	131	retired	76	
	l	Humphrey Maude—†	131	housewife	53	"
	m	Humphrey William L	131	shipper	55	
	n	Mahoney John H	131	U S A	33	"

Page.	Letter.	FULL NAME.	Residence, Jan. 1, 1945.	Occupation.	Supposed Age.	Reported Residence, Jan. 1, 1944. Street and Number.

Prescott Street

R	Marshall Alfred	50	longshoreman	32	Revere
's	Marshall Anna—†	50	housewife	25	"
T	Cavanagh Edward J	50	U S N	38	here
U	Cavanagh Margaret—†	50	housewife	37	"
V	*Monahan Annie B—†	50	cook	59	"
W	Cain Eileen M—†	50	housewife	38	"
X	Cain John G	50	chauffeur	42	"
Y	Vecchio Anthony	62	U S N	20	
Z	Vecchio Costanza	62	laborer	56	"

1337

A	Vecchio Filomena—†	62	housewife	43	"
B	Souza Edward	62A	carpenter	23	"
C	Souza Helen—†	62A	housewife	23	"
D	Jackson Prudence—†	68	"	31	"
E	Jackson Thomas	68	pipefitter	30	"
F	Jackson Agnes—†	70	factoryhand	55	"
G	Jackson Albert	70	clerk	28	
H	Viglione Americo	72	tinsmith	40	"
K	Viglione Jennie—†	72	housewife	37	"
L	*Viglione Rosalina—†	72	"	72	
M	Aloisi Peter	72	U S N	23	
N	Aloisi Rose—†	72	housewife	23	" .
O	Bolino Constantino	72	U S A	22	"
P	Bolino Nicholas	72	chef	49	
R	Bolino Rose—†	72	stitcher	40	"
S	Dodge Emma—†	72	housewife	38	"
T	Dodge Howard T	72	engineer	43	"
U	Brooks Lillian—†	74	housewife	60	"
V	Brooks Robert W	74	seaman	64	"
W	Curtis Ethel—†	74	inspector	31	"
X	Barr Benjamin	74	attendant	30	"
Y	Barr Ruth—†	74	housewife	28	"
Z	Lupu Celia—†	74	"	62	

1338

A	Lupu William	74	grocer	41	"
B	Mulloy Isabella—†	74	housewife	33	Revere
C	Mulloy William F	74	U S M C	31	"
D	O'Neil Jean—†	74	saleswoman	37	here
E	O'Neil Paul W	74	U S A	33	"
F	Swadel Hannah—†	74	housewife	61	"
G	Swadel Isabella—†	74	attendant	66	"

Prescott Street—Continued

H	Riley Janet H—†	90	secretary	36	here
K	Cone Carl	94	painter	42	"
L	Cone Louise—†	94	housewife	38	"
M	Higgins Doris E—†	181	waitress	23	"
N	Higgins Joseph H	181	U S A	27	"
O	Higgins Thomas A	181	"	21	
P	Higgins Thomas H	181	inspector	55	"
R	Higgins Walter E	181	U S A	24	
S	Higgins Zita—†	181	housewife	50	"
T	Duggan John A	181	foreman	55	"
U	Duggan John A, jr	181	U S A	25	"
V	Duggan Ralph E	181	"	24	"
W	Murphy Angela J—†	209	housewife	24	"
X	Murphy Ralph W	209	cutter	27	"
Y	Tucci Angelo M	209	chauffeur	39	"
Z	Tucci Antoinette M—†	209	housewife	38	"
	1339				
A	Champa Anthony	249	U S A	25	
B	Champa Carmella—†	249	clerk	41	"
C	Champa Celia—†	249	housewife	61	"
D	Champa Ignatius	249	clerk	40	"
E	Champa Lena—†	249	"	23	
F	Champa Ralph	249	retired	68	"
G	Champa William	249	mechanic	21	"
H	*Nalli Adolph	249	baker	57	"
K	Nalli Anthony	249	U S A	29	"
L	Nalli Elizabeth—†	249	stitcher	26	"
M	Nalli Louis	249	U S A	23	
N	*Nalli Mary—†	249	housewife	53	"
O	DellaPiana Elisa—†	249	"	53	
P	DellaPiana Ferdinand	249	U S A	29	
R	DellaPiana Frank	249	"	20	"
S	DellaPiana Leandro	249	carpenter	59	"
T	DellaPiana Pasquale	249	U S A	28	"
U	DellaPiana Ralph	249	"	24	"
V	DellaPiana Rose M—†	249	shipper	22	
W	D'Poto Joseph	259	shoeworker	57	"
X	Tecci Anna—†	259	housewife	31	"
Y	Tecci Salvatore	259	carpenter	34	"
Z	Carito Joseph	259	bookbinder	30	"

1340
Prescott Street—Continued

A	Carito Rose—†	259	housewife	30	here
B	DiFlumeri Luigi	259	laborer	61	"
C	*DiFlumeri Mary—†	259	housewife	58	"
D	Forshner Alma M—†	260	"	40	
E	Forshner Edward J	260	U S A	23	"
F	Forshner Harold J	260	metalworker	52	"
G	Forshner Helen B—†	260	housewife	21	"
H	Bruno Dominica—†	260	clerk	29	
K	Bruno John F	260	machinist	26	"
L	Bruno Lena—†	260	housewife	28	"
M	Bruno Vincent J	260	U S N	22	
N	MacKay Daniel A	260	operator	52	"
O	MacKay Louise V—†	260	inspector	23	"
P	MacKay Rebecca M—†	260	housewife	52	"
R	Boland Eleanor P—†	261	WAC	24	
S	Harrington Frederick J	261	U S A	33	
T	Higgins Ellen N—†	261	housewife	63	"
U	Higgins Joseph P	261	meter reader	59	"
V	Greene Patrick J	261	buyer	32	114 St Andrew rd
W	Greene Rita A—†	261	housewife	29	114 "
X	Deprospo Lawrence J	276	sandblaster	37	303 Chelsea
Y	Deprospo Malvine—†	276	housewife	36	303 "
Z	Spence Evelyn R—†	276	"	26	here

1341

A	Spence John S	276	U S N	27	
B	Hanson John J	276	"	35	
C	Hanson Rose C—†	276	housewife	33	"

Princeton Street

D	Lawton Catherine—†	257	housewife	64	here
F	Lawton James F	257	clerk	25	"
E	Lawton Katherine T—†	257	inspector	26	"
G	Lawton Mary E—†	257	clerk	22	"
H	Lawton Patrick	257	retired	70	"
K	Pascone Charlotte T—†	257	manager	34	"
L	Pascone George	257	salesman	38	"
N	McDonald Katherine M—†	259	housewife	33	"
O	Ahern Bertha—†	259	operator	39	"

Princeton Street—Continued

P	Ahern Catherine—†	259	housewife	76	here
R	Ahern Catherine A—†	259	solderer	43	"
S	Ahern William	259	driller	37	"
T	DiFuria Domenic	259	laborer	30	
U	DiFuria Ruth—†	259	housewife	27	"
V	Joyce Edith L—†	261	"	76	"
W	Joyce William L	261	U S A	39	"
X	Falzone Anna M—†	263	housewife	23	"
Y	Falzone Philip	263	painter	28	
Z	Sorzio Assunta—†	263	housewife	52	"
	1342				
A	Sorzio Joseph	263	candymaker	63	"
B	Sorzio Louise—†	263	operator	26	"
C	Corby Alberta L—†	263	waitress	48	"
D	Corby Edwin K	263	U S A	21	
E	Corby Frederick	263	fireman	52	"
F	Bell Annie E—†	265	housewife	69	13 Haviland
G	Cann Jesse C	265	U S A	21	here
H	Cann Rita L—†	265	secretary	31	"
K	Hannon Robert	265	U S A	30	Maine
L	Hannon Ruth—†	265	clerk	30	"
M	MacLaren Jessie M—†	265	housewife	56	here
N	Mannepa John J	265	chauffeur	34	21 Cortes
O	Mannepa Marion W—†	265	housewife	25	21 "
P	Tosto John J	267	rigger	41	here
R	Tosto Lena—†	267	housewife	38	"
S	Rubico Amelia—†	269	"	35	"
T	Rubico Jerome A	269	shoemaker	32	"
U	Vellante Guistino	269	laborer	51	
V	Vellante Ida—†	269	dressmaker	21	"
W	Vellante Joseph A	269	U S C G	24	"
X	Vellante Theresa—†	269	housewife	47	"
Y	Byres Wilfred	271	rigger	37	Michigan
Z	Prudden Clifford E	271	engineer	39	Florida
	1343				
A	Prudden Dorothy E—†	271	housewife	22	"
B	Quarterninn Gino	271	dredgeman	38	Bourne
C	Silva Dorothy—†	271	laborer	21	247 Benningt'n
D	Silva Rose—†	271	housewife	57	247 "
E	Trevor Joseph	271	chauffeur	45	36 Ashley
F	Gorsky Matthew	273	U S C G	25	271 Princeton

Princeton Street—Continued

G	Gorsky Sophie—†	273	housewife	23	271 Princeton
H	Keeley Joseph	273	longshoreman	45	here
K	Keeley Rose A—†	273	housewife	34	"
L	Bahrs Amy M—†	273	"	50	"
M	Bahrs John H	273	painter	65	"
N	Kruse Carl W	273	plumber	49	"
O	Macrina Dominic	277	U S M C	26	"
P	Macrina Joseph	277	U S A	20	"
R	Villani Constantino	277	machinist	57	"
S	Villani Duido	277	U S A	26	
T	Villani Lena—†	277	housewife	47	"
U	Villani Silvio	277	U S M C	20	"
V	McCormack Blair	277	seaman	39	123 Eutaw
W	McCormack Henrietta—†	277	housewife	51	123 "
X	Mitchell Albian	277	machinist	55	here
Y	Mitchell Ida—†	277	housewife	59	"
Z	Follo Anna—†	279	"	29	263 Princeton
	1344				
A	Follo Salvatore	279	laborer	34	263 "
B	Rubbico Mary—†	279	factoryhand	26	415 Frankfort
C	McDonald Domenic	279	machinist	65	here
D	Schifano Anna V—†	279	housewife	34	"
E	Schifano Joseph	279	presser	36	"
F	Wheaton Lorenzo B	281	chauffeur	32	"
G	Wheaton Viola A—†	281	housewife	41	"
H	Huskins Arnold M	281	U S A	26	"
K	Huskins Joseph A	281	fisherman	58	"
L	Huskins Lloyd M	281	"	23	
M	Huskins Margaret E—†	281	housewife	54	"
N	Henricksen Ruth A—†	281	"	47	
O	Henricksen Thomas W	281	machinist	51	"
P	Carney Esther H—†	283	housewife	31	"
R	Carney William F	283	laborer	35	
S	Saveriano Agnes—†	283	housewife	52	"
T	Saveriano Alfred	283	laborer	24	
U	Saveriano Anellio	283	"	58	
V	Saveriano Carmen A	283	U S A	27	
W	Saveriano Henry	283	U S N	22	
X	Saveriano Mary F—†	283	stitcher	26	"
Y	Gallo Eva F—†	283	housewife	29	381 Lovell
Z	Gallo George C	283	U S A	30	381 "

1345
Princeton Street—Continued

A	Gray Beatrice—†	285	housewife	51	here
B	Gray Cecil M	285	printer	48	"
C	Gray James A	285	U S A	21	"
D	Gray Paul E	285	"	22	
E	Blanco Stellario	285	machinist	57	"
F	Ruotolo Christopher	285	U S N	26	"
G	Ruotolo Rose M—†	285	housewife	24	"
H	Ruotolo Lucy—†	285	"	30	"
K	Ruotolo Rocco J	285	U S N	31	"
L	Spina Angelo	301	laborer	27	134 Havre
M	Freda Elizabeth—†	301	checker	23	here
N	Freda Gabriel	301	chauffeur	21	"
O	Freda Rocco	301	sausagemaker	50	"
P	Freda Susie—†	301	housewife	44	"
S	Salerno Americo	303	welder	31	
T	Salerno Mary—†	303	housewife	29	"
U	Volpa Arthur	303	U S A	23	
V	Volpa Speranza—†	303	housewife	59	"
W	*Johnson Toivo	305	ironworker	57	"
X	*Gallagher Jeanette—†	305	housewife	35	"
Y	Gallagher Joseph	305	welder	40	
Z	King Max	305	pharmacist	50	"

1346

A	King Lima—†	305	housewife	47	"
C	Brazzell Walter	336	laborer	64	
D	Laville Ada—†	336	housewife	66	"
E	Laville Joseph	336	longshoreman	36	"
F	King Helen—†	342	packer	21	"
G	Vargus John	342	meatcutter	46	"
H	Vargus Rose—†	342	housewife	51	"
K	Shaw Audrey—†	342	"	24	82 London
L	Shaw Robert	342	U S N	29	Everett
M	McDonough Doris—† rear	342	housewife	24	80 London
N	McDonough Francis "	342	welder	29	80 "
O	Puleo Angelina—† "	342	housewife	33	here
P	Puleo Charles "	342	driller	38	"
R	*Coprini Adele—†	345	housewife	55	"
S	Coprini Dorothy—†	345	shipper	21	"
T	Coprini Joseph	345	laborer	63	"
U	Coprini Nancy—†	345	machinist	23	"

28

Page	Letter	FULL NAME.	Residence, Jan. 1, 1945.	Occupation.	Supposed Age.	Reported Residence, Jan. 1, 1944. Street and Number.

	w	Fabello Americo	347	shipper	22	here
	x	Fabello Eleanor—†	347	housewife	22	"
	y	Ciampa Lena—†	347	"	49	"
	z	Ciampa Michael	347	laborer	55	
		1347				
	a	Salvaggio Philip	347	shipfitter	29	"
	b	Salvaggio Phyllis—†	347	housewife	26	"
	c	*Capo Rose—†	349	housekeeper	69	"
	d	Marzocchi Josephine—†	349	shipper	27	"
	e	Marzocchi Louise—†	349	housewife	25	"
	f	*Marzocchi Màry—†	349	"	44	
	g	Marzocchi Samuel A	349	painter	48	"
	h	Marzocchi Viola—†	349	brazier	21	"
	k	Scorcello Joseph	349	U S N	25	"
	l	D'India Helen—†	352	factoryhand	21	130 Porter
	m	Theodore Michelina—→†	352	housewife	32	168 Sumner
	n	Theodore Nicholas	352	rigger	48	168 "
	p	Caruso Angelo	356	laborer	65	here
	r	Caruso Frances—†	356	stitcher	24	"
	s	Caruso Margaret—†	356	housewife	57	"
	t	Caruso Maria—†	356	"	31	
	u	Gill Edward	356	foreman	37	"
	v	Gill Lillian—†	356	housewife	32	"
	w	Caruso Ignazio	356	brazier	36	"
	x	Caruso Marie—†	356	housewife	28′	"
	y	Corrado Rose—†	357	housekeeper	25	"
	z	D'Alu Anna—†	357	clerk	28	Quincy
		1348				
	a	DiBartolomeo Grace—†	357	housewife	47	here
	b	DiBartolomeo Leo	357	U S A	21	"
	c	DiBartolomeo Leona—†	357	clerk	22	"
	d	DiBartolomeo Luciano	357	U S A	24	
	e	DiBartolomeo Nicholas	357	contractor	53	"
	f	Monahan William	357	laborer	67	"
	g	Lyons Helen—†	358	housewife	30	"
	h	Lyons James	358	longshoreman	34	"
	k	Puopolo Mary—†	358	housekeeper	39	"
	l	Visco Carmella—†	358	clerk	21	"
	m	Visco Rose—†	358	stitcher	40	"
	n	Grasso Linda—†	359	housewife	43	"
	o	Grasso Thomas O	359	machinist	46	"

Princeton Street—Continued

R	Beraldo John	360	machinist	23	here
s*	DeRosa Angelina—†	360	housewife	65	"
T	DeRosa Armando	360	laborer	34	"
U	Ilmonen Ellen—†	360	housewife	59	"
V	Ilmonen Helmi	360	U S N	29	
W	White Maria—†	360	clerk	26	"
X	Bossi Orlando	361	chauffeur	32	"
Y	Bossi Theresa—†	361	housewife	30	"
z*	Blundo Carmella—†	361	"	51	

1349

A	Blundo Joseph	361	laborer	60	
B	Blundo Lawrence	361	U S A	23	"
C	Blundo Michael	361	"	21	
D	LaMarco Anna—†	362	housewife	31	"
E	LaMarco Charles	362	rigger	38	"
F*	Miraldi Bridget—†	362	at home	85	"
G	Miraldi John	362	distiller	39	"
H	Miraldi Theresa—†	362	housewife	33	"
K	Lepore Gerald	362	rigger	25	237 Saratoga
L	Lepore Nellie—†	362	housewife	24	237 "
N*	Chevier Frederick	366	blacksmith	55	307 Havre
o*	Chevier Helen—†	366	housewife	52	307 "
P	Luongo Alfred	368	machinist	31	here
R	Luongo Mary—†	368	plater	24	"
S	Gavin Frank J	368	clerk	52	"
T	Gavin Mary A—†	368	housewife	36	"
U	Gillis Domenic	370	seaman	20	"
V	Gillis Frances—†	370	inspector	26	"
W	Gillis Mary—†	370	housewife	58	"
X	Gillis William	370	retired	56	"
Y	Rich Mary—†	370	housewife	34	"
z	Rich Peter	370	ironworker	34	"

1350

A	Miles Auranus	370	U S A	24	
B	Parsons John	370	painter	38	
C	Parsons Dorothy—†	370	housewife	42	"

Saratoga Street

D	Pavlov David	401	proprietor	60	77 Poplar
E	Bertulli Arthur	401A	gauger	33	here

Page.	Letter.	Full Name.	Residence, Jan. 1, 1945.	Occupation.	Supposed Age.	Reported Residence, Jan. 1, 1944. Street and Number.

Saratoga Street—Continued

	F	Bertulli Catherine—†	401A	housewife	31	here
	G	Fitzgerald Agnes M—†	401A	"	38	51 Prescott
	H	Fitzgerald John R	401A	longshoreman	42	51 "
	K	Fitzgerald Rita E—†	401A	waitress	20	51 "
	L	Nickerson Arthur	402	cook	56	Cambridge
	M	Nickerson Ida—†	402	housewife	43	195 Marion
	N	Neppa Joseph	402	retired	66	here
	O	Neppa Mary—†	402	housewife	65	"
	P	Steph Mary—†	402	inspector	30	294 Paris
	R	Petrozzelli Angelo	403	laborer	42	here
	S	Petrozzelli Anna—†	403	housewife	40	"
	T	Quinn Lillian—†	404	at home	50	"
	U	Walraven Edith—†	404	housewife	57	"
	V	Walraven Marinus	404	laborer	52	"
	W	Eicher James W	404	U S C G	21	California
	X	Eicher Marie—†	404	messenger	24	409 Saratoga
	Y	Petrozzelli Antonio	405	carpenter	30	here
	Z	Petrozzelli Ida—†	405	housewife	29	"
		1351				
	A	Nugent Anna—†	406	"	45	
	B	Nugent William	406	cutter	23	"
	C	Brunaccini Mary—†	406	housewife	46	"
	D	Marcotullio Carmella—†	406	clerk	21	"
	E	Sparaco Frank	406	"	27	"
	F	Sparaco Mary—†	406	housewife	25	"
	G	Leone Amletto	407	painter	30	
	H	Leone Mary—†	407	housewife	27	"
	K	Crockett Emily—†	407	clerk	45	"
	L	Souza Laura—†	407	factoryhand	25	"
	M	Souza Mary—†	407	housewife	50	"
	N	Souza Victor	407	carpenter	54	"
	O	Damato Henry	408	chauffeur	37	"
	P	Damato Theresa—†	408	housewife	34	392 Chelsea
	R	DeBenedictis Claudia—†	408	"	27	here
	S	DeBenedictis Richard	408	candymaker	29	"
	T	Ricciardelli Frederick	408	U S N	27	Tewksbury
	U	Ricciardelli Mary—†	408	housewife	48	"
	V	Ricciardelli Pasquale	408	laborer	51	"
	W	Ricciardelli Theresa—†	408	student	22	"
	X	Rose Isabel—†	409	technician	25	here
	Y	Rose Thomas J	409	machinist	53	"

Saratoga Street—Continued

z	Rose Valentina—†	409	housewife	48	here
	1352				
A	Hansford Mary—†	409	packer	54	
B	*Trainor Bessie—†	409	stitcher	50	"
C	Trainor James H	409	U S A	31	
D	Trainor James P	409	baker	53	
E	Trainor Raymond	409	U S A	28	"
F	McCarthy Edward	410	retired	36	
G	McCarthy Johanna—†	410	at home	71	"
H	McCarthy Joseph	410	laborer	21	"
K	McCarthy Lawrence	410	U S A	34	"
L	Gregory Benjamin	410	coppersmith	31	"
M	Gregory Margaret—†	410	housewife	31	"
N	Mongello Frances—†	410	"	23	
O	Mongello John	410	U S A	26	
P	DeCosta Mary—†	411	housewife	35	"
R	DeCosta Richard	411	candymaker	40	"
S	Marino Samuel	411	retired	67	
T	Pecora Albert	411	chauffeur	20	"
U	*Pecora Barbara—†	411	housewife	54	"
V	Pecora Frank	411	U S A	28	
W	Arena Cosimo C	411	laborer	41	
X	Arena Rose—†	411	housewife	40	"
Y	Pratt Alice—†	412	"	28	
z	Pratt Frank	412	U S N	28	"
	1353				
B	*Cianfracca Assunta—†	412	housewife	51	"
A	Cianfracca Emilio	412	tailor	55	
C	Cianfracca Gilda—†	412	dressmaker	25	"
D	Cianfracca Joseph	412	clerk	27	
E	Monteiro Anthony	412	U S M C	26	"
F	*Monteiro Frank	412	laborer	55	
G	Monteiro Frank, jr	412	"	29	"
H	*Monteiro Marie—†	412	housewife	53	"
K	Kibler Clarence J	413	inspector	61	"
L	Kibler Joseph M	413	U S A	28	
M	Kibler Margaret L—†	413	operator	23	"
N	Kibler Norah E—†	413	housewife	56	"
O	Kibler Ruth M—†	413	operator	26	"
P	*Oliveira Maria R—†	413	at home	69	"
R	Tisi Maria N—†	413	housewife	34	"

Saratoga Street—Continued

s	Tisi Pasquale J	413	machinist	36	here
t	Green Catherine M—†	413	housekeeper	85	"
u	Veiga Marie—†	414	housewife	27	"
v	Veiga Paul	414	electrician	30	"
w	Arsenault Marcella—†	414	at home	47	103 Faywood av
x	Davolio Jeannette—†	414	housewife	21	here
y	Fougere Eva—†	414	"	50	"
z	Fongere Leon	414	laborer	45	"

1354

a	Veiga Domingos	414	janitor	55	
b	Veiga Edward	414	U S A	20	
c	*Veiga Maria—†	414	housewife	51	"
d	Veiga William	414	laborer	27	
e	O'Brien George	416	foreman	44	"
f	O'Brien Mary—†	416	housewife	29	"
g	Nastri Carlo	416	inspector	42	"
h	Nastri Ralph	416	U S A	36	
k	Nastri Stella—†	416	housewife	40	"
l	DiPrizio Margaret—†	416	stitcher	35	"
m	Picardi Albert	416	U S A	28	
n	Picardi Ralph	416	laborer	62	
o	Ferrara Louis	420	roofer	46	
p	Ferrara Margaret—†	420	housewife	44	"
r	*Cascieri Corrado	420	retired	83	
s	*Cascieri Mary—†	420	housewife	78	"
t	Cascieri Mary—†	420	dressmaker	35	"
u	Reardon Frances—†	420	housewife	57	"
v	Riggs Catherine—†	420	"	21	
w	Riggs Charles	420	U S A	27	"
x	*Castro John	421	retired	55	66 Byron
y	Castro John, jr	421	laborer	26	66 "
z	Castro Louis	421	U S A	22	66 "

1355

a	Travers Manuel	421	custodian	59	here
b	*Travers Mary C—†	421	housewife	46	"
c	Hanton Bernadette—†	421	clerk	36	"
d	Hanton Elizabeth F—†	421	housewife	74	"
e	Hanton John R	421	U S A	31	
f	Quartarone John	422	tinsmith	35	"
g	Quartarone Theresa—†	422	housewife	34	"
h	DiLucia Francisco	422	retired	74	

Saratoga Street—Continued

K	DiLucia Joseph	422	U S A	38	here
L	DiLucia Maria—†	422	housewife	69	"
M	Turco Allesandro	422	machinist	45	"
N	Turco Angelina—†	422	housewife	42	"
O	Turco Florence—†	422	clerk	21	
P	Collins Alice F—†	423	housewife	54	"
R	Collins John J	423	contractor	54	"
S	Collins Lawrence F	423	U S A	28	
T	Briana John H	423	"	22	
U	Briana Mary E—†	423	housewife	45	"
• V	Briana Thomas	423	clerk	47	··
W	Briana Thomas F, jr	423	U S A	24	"
X	Amerino George J	423	tailor	44	512 Sumner
Y	Capone Anna—†	423	housewife	42	512 "
Z	Capone Anthony	423	welder	26	512 "
	1356				
B	Ferrioli Salvatore	424	painter	33	here
C	Ferrioli Susan—†	424	housewife	26	"
D	Belgiorno Concetta—†	424	"	59	"
E	Belgiorno Ermanno	424	salesman	30	"
F	Belgiorno Louis	424	U S A	26	
G	Belgiorno Marguerite—†	424	housewife	22	"
H	Belgiorno Pasquale	424	tailor	59	··
K	Coyle John F	425	U S A	28	
L	Coyle John J	425	inkmaker	65	"
M	Coyle Thomas E	425	U S A	23	
N	Hamilton Barbara—†	425	housewife	30	"
O	Hamilton William J	425	U S A	30	
P	Gaik Anna—†	425	housewife	52	"
R	Gaik Regina—†	425	typist	22	
S	Gaik Stella—†	425	supervisor	32	"
T	Gaik Theodore J	425	spinner	57	
U	Giardella Charles	425	U S A	20	
V	Giardella Divina—†	425	housewife	38	"
W	Giardella Joseph	425	carpenter	42	"
X	King Ann—†	426	housewife	23	"
Y	King Charles W	426	U S N	26	"
Z	Rigillo Alice—†	426	housewife	40	216 E Eagle
	1357				
A	Rigillo Joseph	426	welder	43	216 "
B	Sullivan Michael B	rear 426	clerk	45	here

Saratoga Street—Continued

c	Cronin William	rear 426	laborer	64	here
d	Mosher Mary—†	" 426	at home	62	"
e	Mosher Mary F—†	" 426	clerk	22	"
f	McGloan Catherine—†	427	secretary	41	"
g	McGloan Mary E—†	427	housewife	71	"
h	O'Connell Anna T—†	427	nurse	66	"
k	Reardon Alice J—†	427	clerk	60	"
l	Lappen Eugene	427A	U S N	28	Pennsylvania
m	Lappen Mary—†	427A	clerk	28	"
n	Lerro Ernest	427A	U S A	26	here
o	Lerro Stella—†	427A	clerk	24	"
p	Long Margaret—†	427A	housekeeper	52	"
r	McGuire Kenneth	427A	U S A	23	"
s	McGuire Leonora—†	427A	beautician	22	"
t	Veno Irving	427A	U S A	27	
u	Veno Madeline—†	427A	housewife	26	"
v	Romano Paul	428	shoemaker	42	"
w	*Romano Sebastiana—†	428	housewife	38	"
x	Stapleton Lillian—†	428	at home	40	"
y	Stapleton Mary—†	428	tel operator	42	"
z	Petrucci Grace—†	428	operator	28	"
	1358				
a	Petrucci Salvatore	428	U S A	33	
b	Provenzano Frank	428	"	31	
c	Provenzano John	428	oiler	63	
d	Provenzano Mary—†	428	candymaker	57	"
e	Provenzano Philip	428	U S N	30	
f	Hulke Benjamin	429	retired	77	
g	Nickerson Lillian B—†	429	clerk	49	
h	Ducey Agnes—†	429A	factoryhand	37	"
k	Ducey Irene M—†	429A	housewife	23	"
l	Ducey Nicholas	429A	laborer	34	
m	Sexton Ann—†	431	housewife	80	"
n	Sexton Mary T—†	431	clerk	42	
o	Sexton Robert E	431	inspector	61	"
p	Sexton John H	431A	machinist	42	"
r	Sexton Sarah—†	431A	housewife	66	"
s	Sexton William H	431A	engineer	65	"
t	DiNicolantonio Frank	432	pipecoverer	38	"
u	DiNicolantonio Mary—†	432	housewife	32	"
v	Tarquinio Americo	432	U S A	25	

Saratoga Street—Continued

w	*Tarquinio Anthony	432	laborer	73	here
x	*Tarquinio Beatrice—†	432	housewife	73	"
y	LaCortiglia Charles	432	U S N	24	"
z	*LaCortiglia Peter	432	retired	67	

1359

a	*LaCortiglia Rose—†	432	housewife	65	"
b	Sansone Catherine—†	432	clerk	35	
c	DeCosta Joseph	433	fishcutter	31	"
d	DeCosta Lucy—†	433	stitcher	62	"
e	Vieira Adelaide—†	433	housewife	45	"
f	Vieira Anthony J	433	welder	47	"
g	Berardi Dora—†	433	factoryhand	23	"
h	Berardi Gloria—†	433	"	21	
k	Berardi Joseph	433	porter	61	
l	Berardi Panfilio	433	U S A	32	
m	Anthony Edward J	433A	longshoreman	61	"
n	Anthony Edward J	433A	U S A	26	
o	Anthony Lawrence L	433A	"	23	
p	Anthony Mary E—†	433A	housewife	55	"
r	Anthony William F	433A	U S A	21	"
s	Donohue Bridget F—†	433A	presser	54	230 Waldemar av
t	Ottoni Angelo	440	laborer	58	here
u	*Ottoni Anna—†	440	housewife	68	"
v	Ottoni Michael	440	laborer	35	"
w	Ferrara Angelina—†	440	housewife	44	"
x	Ferrara Vincent	440	glazier	45	
y	Sibelian Edward J	440	mechanic	28	"
z	Sibelian Rose—†	440	housewife	21	"

1360

a	Trabucco Carina—†	440	"	57	
b	Trabucco Elizabeth—†	440	WAC	27	
c	Trabucco Gennaro	440	gardener	61	"
d	Trabucco Mary—†	440	at home	29	"
e	Trabucco Paul	440	U S A	22	"
f	Petitpas Eva M—†	442	housewife	39	"
g	Petitpas James H	442	clerk	42	"
h	Argenzio Amelia—†	442	at home	70	"
k	Argenzio Carmella—†	442	housewife	37	"
l	Argenzio Joseph	442	shoeworker	39	"
m	Caponigro Andrew	442	retired	69	"
n	Caponigro Mary—†	442	at home	61	"

Page:	Letter	FULL NAME.	Residence, Jan. 1, 1945.	Occupation.	Supposed Age.	Reported Residence, Jan. 1, 1944. Street and Number.

Saratoga Street—Continued

o	Caponigro Vincent	442	U S A	25	here	
p	DePaola Albert	442	shipper	36	"	
r	DePaola Mary—†	442	housewife	28	"	
s	Favorito Angelina—†	443	"	58	235 Saratoga	
t	Favorito Emilio	443	rigger	48	235 "	
u	Favorito Gerardo	443	U S A	25	here	
v	Favorito Maria—†	443	at home	24	235 Saratoga	
w	Favorito Philip	443	U S A	27	here	
x	Brazil Bernard J	443	longshoreman	42	"	
y	Brazil Mary—†	443	housewife	38	"	
z	Mullowney Theresa C—†	443	inspector	36	"	

1361

a	*Elefterion Elias	445	cook	35		
b	Teris Mary R—†	445	housewife	48	"	
c	Teris Michael J	445	bartender	48	"	
d	Saari Paul	445	engineer	53	"	
e	Saari Saima—†	445	housewife	57	"	
f	Richards Annie—†	445½	at home	71	"	
g	Thibeau Elizabeth—†	447	presser	35		
h	Thibeau James	447	tinsmith	42	"	
k	Marshall Gertrude—†	447½	housewife	35	402 Saratoga	
l	Marshall William H	447½	clerk	35	402 "	
n	Riccobene Ada—†	449	housewife	37	here	
o	Miraglia Mary—†	449	"	23	"	
p	Miraglia Richard	449	electrician	31	"	
r	Bordonaro Incenzio	449	laborer	63		
s	Bordonaro Josephine—†	449	housewife	56	"	
t	Cornetta Mary—†	451	"	46	"	
u	Cornetta Pasquale	451	inspector	47	"	
v	Ricciardi Domenic	451	electrician	33	"	
w	Ricciardi Jennie—†	451	housewife	36	"	
x	Venuti Anthony	451	guard	41		
y	Venuti Margaret—†	451	inspector	38	"	
z	*Damato Alphonse	454	retired	90		

1362

a	Damato Alphonse, jr	454	mechanic	43	"	
b	Damato Josephine—†	454	housewife	37	"	
c	Chafetz Hyman	454	U S A	30		
d	Chafetz Jacob	454	tailor	58		
e	Chafetz Mary—†	454	housewife	58	"	
f	Polito Anna—†	454	stitcher	20	"	

37

Saratoga Street—Continued

G	Polito Anthony	454	shoeworker	63	here	
H	Polito Joseph	454	"	35	"	
K	Polito Louise—†	454	housewife	32	"	
L	Polito Mary—†	454	clerk	33		
M	Polito Philomena—†	454	housewife	55	"	
N	Russo Rose—†	454	stitcher	30	"	
O	Russo Salvatore	454	U S A	30		
P	Mancini John	456	shoemaker	53	"	
R	Mancini Mary—†	456	housewife	45	"	
S	Mancini Rose—†	456	clerk	21	"	
T	Caton John	456	U S N	25	"	
U	Connelly Andrew	456	machinist	49	"	
V	Connelly Edward	456	foreman	43	"	
W	Drinkwater Lawrence	456	guard	39	227 Chelsea	
X	Drinkwater Rose—†	456	housewife	35	227 "	
Y	Privitero Lucy—†	458	packer	38	here	
Z	Privitero Samuel	458	janitor	45	"	
	1363					
A	Scarpa Catherine—†	458	housewife	37	"	
B	Scarpa Rosario	458	carpenter	37	"	
C	Connelly John J	458	boilermaker	54	"	
D	Gayne Barbara M—†	458	at home	59	"	
E	Scanlon Albert A	458	technician	24	"	
F	Scanlon John L	458	brakeman	32	"	
G	Scanlon Marie A—†	458	housewife	32	"	
H	*Lento Angelina—†	460	"	49	"	
K	*Lento Antonio	460	laborer	62	"	
L	Lento Gasper	460	U S A	21	"	
M	Lento Louise—†	460	bookbinder	26	"	
N	Lento Mary—†	460	"	28		
O	Lento Nicholas	460	U S A	23		
P	Faretra Edward	460	U S M C	22	"	
R	Faretra Joseph	460	laborer	51	"	
S	Faretra Rose—†	460	housewife	50	"	
T	Cuozzo Peter	460	shoeworker	41	"	
U	Cuozzo Rose—†	460	housewife	32	"	
V	DeGruttola Ettore	462	machinist	41	"	
W	DeGruttola Ida—†	462	housewife	38	"	
X	Vanadia Cologero	462	laborer	60	"	
Y	Vanadia Maria—†	462	housewife	48	"	
Z	Pescaturo Carl	462	bartender	34	"	

1364
Saratoga Street—Continued

A	*Pescaturo Pasqualina—†	462	at home	65	here
B	Banks Anna L—†	464	housewife	41	"
C	Banks Martin R	464	installer	43	"
D	Pesiri Phyllis—†	464	housekeeper	58	"
E	Pizzolante Domenic	464	laborer	50	
F	Pizzolante Mary E—†	464	housewife	40	"
G	Pizzolante Mary—†	464	"	45	
H	Pizzolante Vincent	464	fireman	55	"
K	*Porter Elizabeth—†	466	housewife	60	395 Meridian
L	Porter Margaret—†	466	clerk	27	395 "
M	Porter Walter	466	U S A	25	395 "
N	Hancock Arthur L	466	U S N	20	here
O	Hancock John W	466	shipfitter	34	"
P	Hancock Julia E—†	466	housewife	58	"
R	Hancock Reuben J	466	brazier	64	
S	DeRosa Louise—†	466	housewife	36	"
T	DeRosa Pasquale	466	chauffeur	39	"
U	Siltanen Amos	468	machinist	49	"
V	*Siltanen Fannie—†	468	housewife	48	"
W	Cormo Adeline J—†	468	"	36	
X	Cormo Edward J	468	coppersmith	39	"
Y	Cormo Robert E	468	U S A	37	
Z	Brennan Catherine L—†	468	housewife	66	"

1365

A	Brennan Joseph F	468	boilermaker	68	"
B	McGee Catherine G—†	468	at home	46	"
C	Angelli Theresa—†	472	housewife	46	"
D	*Vertuccio Felicia—†	472	at home	77	"
E	Allegra Anthony	472	fireman	42	"
F	Allegra Josephine A—†	472	housewife	38	"
H	Gallo Joseph A	474	U S A	27	"
K	Gallo Louise C—†	474	social worker	25	"
L	Gallo Madelena—†	474	housewife	65	"
M	Gallo Madeline R—†	474	bookkeeper	38	"
N	Gallo Mary A—†	474	clerk	44	
O	Gallo Pasquale	474	retired	76	
P	Gallo Rose L—†	474	clerk	36	
R	Gallo Virginia A—†	474	"	22	
S	Guidara Anna E—†	474	housewife	34	"
T	Guidara John J	474	U S N	33	"

Saratoga Street—Continued

u	Silva Blanche—†	474	housewife	32		216 Saratoga
v	Silva John	474	painter	32		216 "
w	Scanzillo Florio	476	machinist	32		here
x	Scanzillo Madeline—†	476	housewife	29		"
y	Gallo Agnes—†	476	"	41		"
z	Gallo Michael	476	machinist	46		"

1366

a	Riggi Leo	476	laborer	57		
b	Riggi Ralph	476	pipefitter	23		"
c	Riggi Salvatore	476	U S A	25		
d	Riggi Theresa—†	476	housewife	51		"
e	Fanale Angela M—†	476	"	37		
f	Fanale Anthony W	476	laundryman	41		"
g	Caponigro Guido	478	U S N	28		"
h	Caponigro Josephine—†	478	housewife	24		"
k	Fusco Mary—†	478	at home	20		"
l	*Fusco Ralph	478	fruit	54		
m	Caponigro Aida—†	478	at home	37		"
n	Caponigro Americo	478	pharmacist	36		"
o	Caponigro Joseph	478	proprietor	38		"
p	Caponigro Salvatore	478	cashier	30		
r	Siraco Michael	480	metalworker	43		"
s	Siraco Philomena—†	480	housewife	38		"
t	Siraco Frank	480	electrician	34		"
u	Siraco Nicholas	480	U S A	26		"
v	Siraco Salvatricia—†	480	housewife	74		"
w	Siraco Stephen	480	chemist	36		"
x	Fowler Alice—†	480	operator	38		"
y	Kirk Elizabeth—†	480	housewife	48		"
z	Kirk James	480	U S A	23		

1367

a	O'Brien Ruth—†	480	housewife	21		"
b	O'Brien William	480	U S A	25		

Shelby Street

e	Aste Louis	4	orderly	59		12 Kingsbury
f	Scozzella Angela—†	4	housewife	31		here
g	Rella Angelina—†	4	"	42		"
h	Rella Pasquale M	4	U S A	21		"
k	Rella Sabino	4	laborer	54		
l	Costello Howard	6	"	29		"

Shelby Street—Continued

	M	Costello Rita—†	6	housewife	30	here
	N	Vertullo Mary M—†	6	shipfitter	34	"
	O	Vertullo Pasquale	6	U S A	27	" .
	P	Vertullo Rose—†	6	millhand	33	"
	R	Lang Carmella—†	6	housewife	29	"
	S	Lang Vincent	6	pipefitter	34	"
	T	Sacco Salvatore E	8	shipfitter	45	"
	U	Lee Carl H	8	painter	34	
	V	Lee Edith M—†	8	housewife	34	"
	W	Morello Dominic	8	painter	31	"
	X	Morello Mary—†	8	housewife	27	"
	Y	Schiappa Anna—†	10	"	29	
	Z	Schiappa Guido	10	milkman	30	"
1368						
	A	Pimentel Anthony	10	electrician	35	"
	B	Pimentel Lena—†	10	housewife	34	"
	C	Pacifico Salvatore	10	electrician	62	"
	D	Pacifico Theresa—†	10	housewife	55	"
	E	DiNitto Eleanor—†	12	"	23	
	F	Miraldi Anna—†	12	"	38	"
	G	DeLuca Anna—†	12	"	39	4 Shelby
	H	DeLuca Carmen	12	janitor	54	4 "
	K	Flood Mary—†	14	at home	73	22 Bennington
	L	Johnson Charles	14	plumber	34	here
	M	Johnson Lucy—†	14	housewife	32	"
	N	*Dalton Hazel E—†	14	"	34	18 Tufts
	O	Dalton William J	14	metalworker	39	18 "
	P	Coviello Nicholas	16	mason	35	here
	R	Coviello Phyllis—†	16	housewife	34	"
	S	LaPlaca Caroline—†	16	"	30	"
	T	LaPlaca Mario	16	cutter	33	
	U	Regan Cecelia—†	16	clerk	34	"
	V	Regan James	16	laborer	34	
	W	Saviano Andrew	18	repairman	23	"
	X	Saviano Aniello	18	proprietor	68	"
	Y	Saviano Joseph	18	U S A	28	
	Z	Saviano Louis	18	U S N	22	
1369						
	A	Saviano Sophie—†	18	housewife	56	"
	B	Saviano Victor	18	U S A	25	
	C	Saviano Angelina—†	18	housewife	30	"
	D	Saviano Stephen	18	laborer	36	

1—13

Shelby Street—Continued

G	Lunetta Mary—†	24	housewife	33	here
H	Lunetta Michael	24	manager	35	"
K	Rizzo Florence—†	24	housewife	20	"
L	Rizzo Martin	24	laborer	47	
M	Cefaioli Frank	26	brazier	30	
N	Cefaioli Helen—†	26	housewife	25	"
O	Corso Catherine—†	26	"	31	
P	Corso Ignatius	26	driller	31	
R	*Zuccala Josephine—†	26	at home	60	"
S	Festa Louis M	26	tailor	40	
T	Festa Mary—†	26	housewife	38	"
V	Bianco Margaret—†	32	factoryhand	42	"
W	Umana Anne—†	32	housewife	55	"
X	Umana Salvatore	32	proprietor	58	"
Y	Luongo Anthony	32	constable	47	"
Z	Luongo Nellie—†	32	housewife	43	"
	1370				
A	Regan Dorothy—†	34	"	36	"
B	Regan Frederick	34	machinist	38	"
C	Costa Joseph	34	trackman	30	"
D	Costa Margaret—†	34	housewife	28	"
E	Velardo Anna—†	34	"	48	
F	Velardo Pasquale	34	chauffeur	58	"

Shrimpton Street

G	Silva Frances—†	21	forewoman	35	here
H	Silva Henry	21	packer	47	"
K	Silva Henry, jr	21	U S N	22	"
L	Pope Annie M—†	21	housekeeper	62	"
M	Govoni John B	22	machinist	64	"
N	Govoni John B	22	U S N	20	"
O	*Govoni Norma—†	22	housewife	60	"
P	Govoni Rose M—†	22	clerk	24	
R	Usseglio John J	24	painter	46	"
S	Usseglio Theresa V—†	24	housewife	39	"
T	Cavagnaro Francis P	24	retired	47	
U	Cavagnaro Peter J	24	bartender	41	"
V	Merullo John J	24	U S N	31	
W	Merullo Mary U—†	24	clerk	31	
X	Marden Lillian M—†	24	cleaner	58	"

Ward 1–Precinct 14

CITY OF BOSTON

LIST OF RESIDENTS
20 YEARS OF AGE AND OVER

(NON-CITIZENS INDICATED BY ASTERISK)
(FEMALES INDICATED BY DAGGER)

AS OF

JANUARY 1, 1945

THOMAS F. SULLIVAN, *Chairman*
FREDERIC E. DOWLING, *Secretary*
WILLIAM A. MOTLEY, Jr.
FRANCIS B. McKINNEY
EVERETT R. PROUT

Listing Board.

CITY OF BOSTON PRINTING DEPARTMENT

1400
Bennington Street

D	Cashin Ellen—†	387	housewife	71	here
E	Cashin Martina—†	387	textilewkr	30	"
F	Cashin Richard	387	engineer	48	"
G	LaTorre Joseph	387	baker	37	
H	LaTorre Mary—†	387	housewife	28	"
K	Velona Antoinette—†	387	packer	24	"
L	Velona Celeste—†	387	stitcher	26	"
M	*Velona Cesira—†	387	housewife	64	"
N	Velona Rocco	387	laborer	60	"
P	Scarafone Genarro	394	weaver	49	"
R	Scarafone Margaret—†	394	housewife	39	"
U	Devizia Edmund	398	welder	35	
V	Devizia Helen—†	398	housewife	36	"
W	Crump Anna—†	398	"	32	
X	Crump Willard	398	welder	36	
Y	Velardo Annetta—†	400	operator	28	"
Z	Velardo Anthony	400	U S A	30	

1401

A	Finneran Alice—†	400	at home	42	"
B	Finneran Bridget—†	400	housewife	78	"
C	Coughlin Susan P—†	402	"	67	
D	Burke Rosamond—†	402	"	31	"
E	Burke William	402	merchant	36	"
G	DePanfilis James	407	carpenter	56	"
H	DePanfilis Mary—†	407	housewife	45	"
K	DePanfilis Christopher	407	U S C G	24	"
L	DePanfilis Julia—†	407	stenographer	20	"
M	Mierzykowski Kazimiera—†	408	housewife	21	"
N	Belinsky Albert	408	U S A	21	"
O	*Belinsky Mary—†	408	housewife	54	"
P	Forlenza Clara S—†	408	"	39	
R	Forlenza Mario	408	electrician	40	"
S	Flanagan Grace—†	412	tel operator	20	"
T	Flanagan Herbert L	412	U S M C	24	"
U	Flanagan Luke A	412	clerk	47	
W	DeMartinis Anna—†	420	housewife	34	"
X	DeMartinis Salvator	420	merchant	47	"
Y	Mazzone Alice—†	420	housewife	53	"
Z	Mazzone James	420	retired	63	"

2

Page.	Letter.	Full Name.	Residence, Jan. 1, 1945.	Occupation.	Supposed Age.	Reported Residence, Jan. 1, 1944. Street and Number.

Bennington Street—Continued

	A	Balboni Gladys—†	423	housewife	46	221 Trenton
	B	Balboni Joseph	423	sorter	40	221 "
	C	Granara Louis	423	chauffeur	48	here
	D	Stevenson Francis	423	"	46	"
	E	Stevenson Marguerite—†	423	housewife	45	"
	F	Diorio Emily—†	423	"	36	
	G	Diorio Nicholas	423	nurse	38	
	H	Collins Dorothy—†	425	housewife	29	"
	K	Collins John	425	druggist	33	"
	L	O'Shea Evelyn—†	425	ropemaker	43	"
	M	O'Shea Patrick	425	printer	53	
	N	McClellan Joseph	430	machinist	55	"
	O	Balboni James J	430	U S N	39	"
	P	Balboni Mary—†	430	housewife	31	"
	R	Reed John	430	U S A	25	..
	S	Reed Rita—†	430	housewife	25	"
	T	Brothers Michael	431	chauffeur	51	423 Bennington
	U	Collins George W	431	operator	24	here
	V	Collins Margaret—†	431	housewife	49	"
	W	Teta Adelaide—†	431	stitcher	20	"
	X	Teta Anthony	431	machinist	24	"
	Y	Teta Antonetta—†	431	housewife	42	"
	Z	Teta Carmen	431	machinist	22	"

	A	Teta Ralph	431	cutter	22	
	B	Teta Stefano	431	molder	49	
	C	Dellazoppa Margaret—†	431	stringer	31	"
	D	Dellazoppa Mary—†	431	packer	37	"
	E	*Dellazoppa Nora—†	431	housewife	75	"
	F	Knox Mary—†	432	"	26	"
	G	Knox Sylvester J	432	U S N	31	
	H	O'Shea Andrew J	432	clerk	51	..
	K	*O'Shea Bridget—†	432	at home	75	"
	L	O'Shea Nora G—†	432	tel operator	45	"
	M	Busquets Antonio	433	machinist	62	"
	N	Busquets Antonio	433	engineer	21	"
	O	Busquets Catalina—†	433	housewife	45	"
	P	Busquets Isabel—†	433	clerk	23	"
	R	Cabral Dorothea—†	433	"	24	"

3

Page.	Letter.	Full Name.	Residence, Jan. 1, 1945.	Occupation.	Supposed Age.	Reported Residence, Jan. 1, 1944. Street and Number.

Bennington Street—Continued

	s	Cabral Rose—†	433	buyer	31	here
	t	McCarthy Mary—†	433	housewife	27	"
	u	McCarthy Walter	433	laborer	32	"
	v	Malinowski Anthony	433	foundryman	52	"
	w	*Wolochka Mary—†	433	millhand	48	"
	x	Wolochka Morris	433	U S A	24	
	y	Saude Edward	437	U S C G	23	"
	z	*Saude Manuel	427	laborer	66	
1404						
	a	Graham Frank	437	barber	47	
	b	Graham Muriel—†	437	packer	44	
	c	Maher Virginia—†	437	"	20	
	d	Viera Arthur	437	chauffeur	26	"
	e	Viera Elvera—†	437	housewife	25	"
	f	Coyle Charles F	439	manager	58	"
	g	Coyle Helen J—†	439	housewife	53	"
	h	Murphy Thomas A	439	drawtender	51	"
	k	Kelly Nora—†	439	clerk	56	
	l	Kidney Ellen—†	439	at home	74	"
	m	Kidney Mary—†	439	"	76	"
	n	McCarthy Annie—†	439	housewife	64	"
	o	Twomey Joseph L	441	clerk	42	
	p	Twomey Monica M—†	441	housewife	40	"
	s	Cashin Mary—†	445	"	73	"
	t	Colbert Edward	445	engineer	29	"
	u	Colbert Ellen—†	445	operator	29	"
	v	McGregor Catherine—†	445	housewife	40	"
	w	McGregor John	445	laborer	40	
	x	McGregor Mary—†	445	clerk	21	
	y	McGregor Theresa—†	445	U S M C	24	"
	z	McNulty Bridget—†	447	clerk	58	
1405						
	a	Twomey Catherine—†	447	"	54	
	b	Shea Dennis F	447	retired	54	
	c	Shea Patrick	447	"	85	
	d	Shea Patrick F	447	laborer	52	
	e	Shea Thomas	447	tel worker	56	"
	f	Hickey Anna—†	449	housewife	48	"
	g	Hickey James	449	laborer	48	
	h	Conlin Esther—†	449	housewife	44	"
	k	Coughlin Elizabeth—†	449	"	75	

Page.	Letter.	FULL NAME.	Residence, Jan. 1, 1945.	Occupation.	Supposed Age.	Reported Residence, Jan. 1, 1944. Street and Number.

Bennington Street—Continued

L	Coughlin Patrick	449	retired	74	here
M	Coughlin Thomas	449	clerk	36	"
N	LeBlanc Alma R—†	451	housewife	49	"
O	LeBlanc Charles L	451	engineer	48	"
P	Barretto Maud E—†	451	housewife	54	"
R	Barretto William A	451	engraver	54	"
T	Day Julia—†	456	laborer	51	"
U	Flanagan Agnes E—†	456	operator	44	"
V	Flanagan Grace J—†	456	secretary	36	"
W	Flanagan John	456	clerk	49	24 Glendon
Y	Flanagan Isabella M—†	460	housewife	43	here
Z	Flanagan Luke A	460	clerk	48	412 Bennington
	1406				
A	Williams William J	460	watchman	48	here
B	Colbert Edward F	460	retired	68	"
C	Colbert Josephine A—†	460	housewife	50	"
D	*Rochini Diomira—†	490	"	59	
E	Rochini Santino	490	U S N	34	"
F	Maloney Mary—†	496	housewife	38	"
G	Maloney Theodore	496	manager	39	"
H	Hardy Doris—†	496	housewife	24	423 Bennington
K	Hardy Warren	496	fireman	25	1 Fourth St pl
L	Murray Bertha B—†	498	housewife	56	here
M	Murray Henry B	498	laborer	62	"
N	Petrillo Lewis	498	painter	43	"
O	Petrillo Lewis C	498	electrician	23	"
P	Petrillo Josephine—†	498	housewife	43	"
R	Hallahan Charles D	504	U S C G	23	"
S	Hallahan James J	504	engineer	66	"
T	Hallahan John J	504	U S A	29	
U	Hallahan Margaret A—†	504	housewife	69	"
V	Maher Bridget—†	506	"	65	
W	Doyle Mary A—†	506	tel operator	44	"
X	Paris Charles A	508	machinist	29	"
Y	Paris Christi C	508	foreman	52	"
Z	Paris Margaret E—†	508	housewife	47	"
	1407				
A	Callahan Francis C	508	U S A	25	
B	Callahan John T	508	gateman	60	"
C	Callahan Joseph T	508	instructor	27	"
D	Callahan Mary J—†	508	housewife	54	"

5

Page.	Letter.	Full Name.	Residence, Jan. 1, 1945.	Occupation.	Supposed Age.	Reported Residence, Jan. 1, 1944. Street and Number.

Bennington Street—Continued

	E	Callahan Robert W	508	U S A	22	here
	F	Maher Estelle—†	510	candymaker	41	"
	G	Powers Helen—†	510	housewife	45	"
	H	Powers John	510	stenographer	26	"
	K	Powers William	510	clerk	20	"
	L	Henderson Cornelius	512	"	41	
	M	Henderson John E	512	retired	72	
	N	Henderson Josephine M—†	512	housewife	71	"
	O	Henderson Mary J—†	512	typist	32	"
	P	Henderson Neil J	512	U S A	45	
	R	Vieira Geneva—†	512	operator	38	"
	S	Murphy Joseph H	516	metalworker	46	"
	T	Murphy Madeline M—†	516	housewife	47	"
	U	Murphy Neil M	516	chauffeur	45	"
	V	Arone Irene—†	524	housewife	28	"
	W	Arone John	524	U S A	28	
	X	Memmolo Anthony	524	chauffeur	30	"
	Y	*Memmolo Mary—†	524	housewife	63	"
	Z	Memmolo Mildred—†	524	clerk	33	"

1408

	A	Memmolo Angelo	524	chauffeur	40	"
	B	Memmolo Phyllis—†	524	housewife	38	"
	C	Hickey Catherine T—†	528	operator	30	"
	D	Hickey Charles W	528	U S N	35	
	E	Hickey Joseph F	528	U S A	33	
	F	Hickey Mary C—†	528	housewife	33	"
	G	Volpini Augusto	528	tilesetter	42	"
	H	Volpini Emma—†	528	housewife	36	"
	L	Avola Alex	532	cleanser	36	"
	M	Avola Jean—†	532	"	34	
	N	Giliberto Agostino	532	joiner	26	
	O	Giliberto Anna—†	532	housewife	24	"
	P	Kondrasky Andrew	534	laborer	50	
	R	Kondrasky Anna—†	534	housewife	49	"
	S	Frazier Alfred	534	retired	83	
	T	Frazier Edmond W	534	bookkeeper	45	"
	U	Frazier George	534	electrician	40	"
	V	Frazier Sara S—†	534	housekeeper	77	"
	W	Burke Lillian M—†	534	at home	74	"
	X	Rutledge Elmira H—†	534	housewife	69	"
	Y	Rutledge Harold B	534	clerk	47	

Bennington Street—Continued

z	Shea Antonette—†	536	housewife	29	here
	1409				
A	Shea Patrick J	536	U S A	33	
B	Mattia Ernest	536	driller	35	
C	Mattia Michelena—†	536	housewife	32	"
D	Carbone Gabriel	536	contractor	40	"
E	Carbone Mary—†	536	housewife	31	"
G	DeLeo Alfred	540	waiter	25	
H	DeLeo Anna—†	540	housewife	25	"
K	Butler James L	540	laborer	34	"
L	Butler Theresa M—†	540	housewife	33	"
M	Dogherty Frances M—†	540	operator	36	Winthrop
N	Robertson Barbara—†	540	cosmetician	30	"
O	Robertson Willard K	540	U S N	30	"
P	Cantalupo Edna—†	544	housewife	23	here
R	Cantalupo Guy	544	U S A	23	"
S	LaCortiglia Anthony	546	painter	37	"
T	LaCortiglia Theresa—†	546	housewife	30	"
U	Cantalupo Florence—†	546	"	39	
V	Cantalupo Mary—†	546	clerk	22	
W	Cantalupo Ottavio	546	storekeeper	50	"
X	Mezzocchi Alfred F	546	chauffeur	34	"
Y	Mezzocchi Anna—†	546	housewife	32	"
Z	Barrasso Lucy—†	548	"	26	
	1410				
A	Barrasso Orazio	548	shipfitter	29	"
B	Tarquinio Clement	548	laborer	42	
C	Tarquinio Pasqualina—†	548	housewife	35	"
D	*Ferrati Barbara—†	548	"	51	
E	Ferrati Catherine—†	548	stitcher	27	"
F	Ferrati Mario	548	operator	60	"

Chaucer Street

K	Olsen Mary—†	3	housewife	41	here
L	Olsen William A	3	cashier	42	"
M	Conway James	3	U S A	36	"
N	Conway Patrick	3	retired	72	"
O	Conway Thomas	3	U S A	35	"
P	Gagliardi Daniel	3	technician	24	169 Orient av
R	Gagliardi Josephine—†	3	housewife	25	169 "

7

Chaucer Street—Continued

s	Weagle Elizabeth—†	5	housewife	48	here
t	Nowosielski Boleslawa—†	5	"	49	"
u	Nowosielski Walery	5	loom fixer	53	"
v	Pare Luciana—†	5	clerk	24	
w	Mierzykowski Arthur	5	U S A	27	
x	Mierzykowski Joseph	5	operator	51	"
y	Mierzykowski Joseph	5	U S A	23	
z	Mierzykowski Mary—†	5	housewife	48	"

1411

a	Bisett Margaret—†	9	clerk	49	
b	Gowdy Blanche—†	9	seamstress	52	"
c	Gowdy Frank	9	steamfitter	62	"
d	Keyes Annie J—†	9	at home	75	"
e	Curran Cecelia—†	9	textilewkr	46	"
f	Curran John J	9	ironworker	51	"
g	Curran Mary A—†	9	housewife	76	"
h	Leonard Annie—†	17	"	51	84 Chelsea
k	Leonard Charles	17	rigger	53	84 "
l	Leonard Charles	17	fireman	22	here
m	Teixeira Edmund	19	laborer	33	"
n	*Teixeira Maria—†	19	housewife	54	"
o	Teixeira Mary—†	19	"	31	
p	Flanagan Beatrice W—†	25	clerk	24	
r	Flanagan Catherine M—†	25	"	26	"
s	Flanagan Delia—†	25	housewife	52	"
t	Flanagan Joseph	25	U S A	21	
u	Flanagan Nicholas	25	clerk	62	"
v	Cavalieri Ella—†	25	housewife	32	Andover
w	Cavalieri James	25	teacher	36	"
x	Mazza Theresa—†	25	housewife	49	here
y	McCarthy Warren	25	burner	31	"
z	McLaughlin Gertrude—†	25	housewife	27	"

1412

a	McLaughlin Hugh	25	U S N	29	
b	Murphy Emma—†	25	at home	75	"
c	Gill Helen T—†	27	housewife	35	"
d	Gill Joseph F	27	policeman	42	"
e	Murphy Mary F—†	27	nurse	35	"
f	Murphy Warren W	27	manager	36	"
g	Hayes Michael	31	seaman	45	"

Chaucer Street—Continued

H	Hayes Ruth—†	31	housewife	25	here
K	Carbon Dorothy—†	31	"	35	"
L	Carbon Warren	31	clerk	37	"
M	McNeil Madeline—†	31	housewife	37	"
N	Clingen Frederick	rear 35	plumber	49	"
O	Clingen Mildred—†	" 35	clerk	33	
P	Clingen Robert	" 55	watchman	68	"
R	Clingen Sadie—†	" 35	housewife	54	"
S	Donovan Dennis	" 35	clerk	67	"
T	Donovan Sarah—†	" 35	at home	56	"
U	Almeida Frank	37	cabinetmaker	58	"
V	Almeida Josephine—†	37	housewife	56	"
W	Furlong Mary M—†	39	domestic	88	"
X	Jensen Susan I—†	39	forewoman	45	"
Y	Thibault Gertrude E—†	39	saleswoman	44	"
Z	Gannon Catherine—†	39	bookkeeper	31	"
	1413				
A	Gannon John	39	engineer	61	"
B	Gannon Mary A—†	39	housewife	60	"
C	Velardo Frances—†	43	domestic	65	"
D	Velardo Guy A	43	painter	32	
E	Werner Harold	47	retired	46	
F	Werner Harold E	47	student	25	"
G	Werner Margaret T—†	47	housewife	48	"
H	Werner Mary V—†	47	clerk	22	..
K	Scofield Lillian M—†	49	domestic	24	"
L	Scofield William H	49	U S A	21	
M	Dunn Harry E	49	electrician	34	"
N	Dunn Ruth E—†	49	housewife	31	"
O	Hurley Daniel F	49	retired	61	
P	Hurley Mary A—†	49	housewife	66	"
R	Hurley William J	49	U S N	29	
S	Martin Edith L—†	53	housewife	51	"
T	Martin Ellsworth J	53	clerk	54	"
U	Carino Ann M—†	55	housewife	30	31 Moore
V	Carino Ernest	55	clerk	36	567 Saratoga
W	Carino Matthew J	55	pharmacist	30	31 Moore
X	DiFazio Anthony	55	U S A	24	here
Y	DiFazio Camilla—†	55	housewife	47	"
Z	DiFazio Camillo	55	tilesetter	46	"

1414

Chelsea Street

A	Busby Ella F—†	429	metalworker	42	here
B	Busby Ella M—†	429	housewife	69	"
C	Busby John W	429	retired	79	"
D	Powers Mary S—†	429	housewife	47	"
E	*Powers Nicholas J	429	laborer	51	
F	Powers Thomas F	429	U S N	20	
G	Brenton Thomas J	429	U S M C	23	"
H	Simington Margaret J—†	429	factoryhand	23	"
K	Simington Odina A—†	429	housewife	46	"
L	Simington Robert B	429	doorman	59	"
M	Simington Robert E	429	U S M C	20	"
N	Tucker Irene E—†	429	welder	44	
O	*Dryden Corabelle—†	431	housewife	72	"
P	Flynn John F	431	bartender	42	"
R	Kehoe William S	431	retired	82	360 Saratoga
S	McCarthy Daniel B	431	wool sorter	62	here
T	Ricciole Grace E—†	435	housewife	30	"
U	Ricciole Joseph A	435	entertainer	32	"
V	Cardinale Carmen	435	U S A	23	
W	Cardinale Frank	435	operator	33	"
X	Cardinale Marie—†	435	housewife	57	"
Y	Cardinale Vincenzo	435	retired	69	
Z	Scarpa Anna A—†	437	housewife	38	"

1415

A	Scarpa Ralph F	437	blueprints	43	"
B	Scarpa Frances—†	437	housewife	73	"
C	Brody Ann—†	439	"	21	
D	Brody Norman	439	U S M C	20	"
E	Sullo Michael	439	U S A	23	"
F	Sullo Nicholas	439	carpenter	64	"
G	Sullo Salvatore	439	U S A	25	"
H	Tassinari Horace V	439	chauffeur	36	301 Bennington
K	Tassinari Marie A—†	439	housewife	31	301 "

Curtis Street

Y	Maguire Florence E—†	8	housewife	45	here
Z	Maguire William J	8	engineer	42	"

1416

A	Fagan Josephine E—†	8	housewife	20	"

10

Page.	Letter.	FULL NAME.	Residence, Jan. 1, 1945.	Occupation.	Supposed Age.	Reported Residence, Jan. 1, 1944. Street and Number.

Curtis Street—Continued

	B	Fagan Mary J—†	8	housewife	52	here
	C	Fagan Mary M—†	8	tel operator	23	"
	D	Fagan Thomas F	8	retired	55	"
	E	McIntyre Alfred R	8	weaver	40	"
	F	McIntyre Annie—†	8	housewife	72	"
	G	Boudreau Lena—†	11	waitress	52	"
	H	Gayhart Harry	11	welder	29	
	K	Gayhart Helen D—†	11	housewife	25	"

Frankfort Street

	L	Norris Mary E—†	404	housewife	43	here
	M	Norris Thomas J	404	laborer	50	"
	N	McGovern Ann—†	404	housewife	58	"
	O	McGovern Patrick	404	janitor	59	
	P	*Sheremeta Andrew	404	foreman	59	"
	S	Sheremeta Boleslawa—†	404	beautician	29	"
	R	*Sheremeta Johanna—†	404	housewife	50	"
	T	Pastore Eugene	406	U S N	28	
	U	Pastore Rita—†	406	housewife	25	"
	V	Sweeney Alice—†	406	clerk	23	"
	W	Avola Alexander	406	"	23	
	X	Avola Mary—†	406	housewife	23	"
	Y	*Pastore Angelo	406	barber	62	
	Z	Pastore Armine	406	"	36	

1417

	A	Pastore Carmine A	406	salesman	33	"
	B	McCarthy Edward W	406	U S N	24	739 Bennington
	C	McCarthy Eileen H—†	406	clerk	21	here
	D	Ronayne Eileen J—†	406	housewife	47	"
	E	Ronayne Robert F	406	machinist	58	"
	F	Ronayne Robert F	406	U S A	26	"
	G	Sweeney James A	406	U S N	22	75 Wadsworth
	H	Sweeney Margaret A—†	406	housewife	24	here
	K	Gubitosi Henry J	409	operator	29	"
	L	Gubitosi Philomena—†	409	cleanser	26	"
	M	D'Addio Francis A	409	U S N	28	
	N	Passaggio Alphonse	409	loom fixer	31	"
	O	Passaggio Nancy—†	409	housewife	31	"
	P	Micarelli Anthony E	409	mechanic	25	521 Bennington
	R	Micarelli Antoinette—†	409	housewife	25	521 "

11

Page.	Letter.	FULL NAME.	Residence, Jan. 1, 1945.	Occupation.	Supposed Age.	Reported Residence, Jan. 1, 1944. Street and Number.

Frankfort Street—Continued

s	Mazzarella Ralph	411	laborer	35	here
t	Mazzarella Rose M—†	411	housewife	35	"
u	Oliveri Catherine R—†	411	"	26	"
v	Oliveri Joseph P	411	shipfitter	29	"
w	Aiello Carmella—†	411	housewife	48	"
x	Aiello Egnazio	411	pressman	50	"
y	Aiello Mary P—†	411	operator	20	"
z	Aiello Peter J	411	U S A	25	
	1418				
a	Aiello Sarah V—†	411	laborer	24	
b	Albano Antonia—†	415	housewife	31	"
c	Albano Joseph	415	U S A	31	
d	Butler Rita E—†	415	stock girl	23	"
e	Butler William F	415	laborer	60	
f	*Mazzarello Columbia—†	415	housewife	58	"
g	Mazzarello Gerard	415	welder	30	
h	*Mazzarello Vincent	415	retired	59	
k	Gallo Anna—†	417	housewife	32	"
l	Gallo Cesare	417	driller	50	"
m	Brown Mabel H—†	417	housewife	32	"
n	Brown William P	417	U S C G	30	"
o	Cullen Mable H—†	417	packer	57	
p	Fairchild Bernard A	417	seaman	36	
r	Connelly Mary F—†	417	housewife	61	"
s	Laundry John C	417	U S A	24	
t	Laundry Ruth—†	417	housewife	21	"
u	Cyr Albert	420	millhand	58	"
v	Cyr Elizabeth—†	420	housewife	53	"
w	Cyr Paul J	420	U S N	23	
x	McGrath Mary E—†	420	housewife	48	"
y	McGrath Paul D	420	fireman	53	"
	1419				
a	Campiglia Anthony	424	joiner	51	
b	Campiglia Giovina—†	424	housewife	46	"
c	Martorana Louis	424	U S N	26	
d	Martorana Marie—†	424	housewife	22	"
e	Ricci Anna—†	424	"	71	"
f	Callidare Alfred	424	U S A	29	"
g	*Callidare Michael	424	chipper	63	"
h	Callidare Rena—†	424	clerk	21	
k	*Callidare Virginia—†	424	housewife	53	"

Frankfort Street—Continued

L	Lawrence Anthony	425	retired	76	here
M	Mosca Achille, jr	426	chauffeur	36	"
N	Mosca Romiloa—†	426	housewife	32	"
O*	Mosca Achille	426	shoemaker	66	"
P	Mosca Concette—†	426	waitress	32	"
R*	Mosca Louise M—†	426	housewife	69	"
S	Marranzini Carmella—†	426	"	46	
T	Marranzini Carmen	426	cobbler	49	"
U	Marranzini Olga—†	426	assembler	22	"
V	Marranzini Rudolph	426	U S M C	21	"
W	Cashin Elizabeth M—†	427	housewife	34	"
X	Cashin Leo F	427	molder	36	
Y	Frati Anthony	428	U S A	37	
Z	Frati Giaccomo	428	retired	72	"
	1420				
A	Frati Mary—†	428	housewife	55	"
B	Surette Eloi J	428	fish handler	47	"
C	Surette Mary L—†	428	housewife	42	"
D	McKurdy Alice L—†	428	"	33	
E	McKurdy William F	428	fireman	34	
F	Mambuca Anthony F	429	U S A	23	"
G	Mambuca Catherine M—†	429	housewife	33	"
H	Mambuca Francis M	429	U S A	29	
K	Mambuca James V	429	laborer	54	"
L	Mambuca Marion J—†	429	welder	25	
M	Mambuca Theresa M—†	429	waitress	21	"
N	Bolivar Helen—†	430	housewife	46	"
O	Bolivar Herbert H	430	carpenter	43	"
R	Flammia Theresa—†	431	machinist	32	209 Saratoga
S	MacDonald Irene K—†	431	waitress	33	118 Moore
T	MacDonald John D	431	U S A	36	118 "
V	Pastore Carmen M	433	butcher	27	here
W	Pastore Yolanda—†	433	housewife	27	"
X	Fariole Angelina M—†	435	"	45	"
Y	Fariole Dorothy L—†	435	typist	20	"
Z	Fariole Robert J	435	electrician	44	"
	1421				
A	Petrillo Lena—†	435	housewife	64	"
B	Petrillo Vito	435	laborer	70	
E	Coleman Louise M—†	447	housewife	27	"
F	Coleman Matthew J	447	plumber	30	"

13

Page.	Letter.	FULL NAME.	Residence, Jan. 1, 1945.	Occupation.	Supposed Age.	Reported Residence, Jan. 1, 1944. Street and Number.

Frankfort Street—Continued

	G	McGrath Margaret A—†	447	housewife	68	here
	H	Costello John H	447	U S N	35	464 Sumner
	K	Costello Mary F—†	447	housewife	32	464 "
	L	Scott William D	447	longshoreman	30	464 "
	M	Liss Elizabeth—†	447	inspector	24	here
	N	Liss George	447	laborer	52	"
	O	Liss Mary—†	447	housewife	48	"
	P	Keane Mary E—†	449	"	29	..
	R	Keane Matthew R	449	manager	31	"
	S	Scopa James A	453	shipfitter	44	"
	T	Scopa Josephine J—†	453	housewife	37	"
	U	Pepicelli Pasquale L	453	shipwright	34	"
	V	Pepicelli Virginia—†	453	housewife	32	"
	W	Pepicelli Antonio	453	shipwright	65	"
	X	Pepicelli Concetta—†	453	housewife	22	Everett
	Y	*Pepicelli Lucia—†	453	"	64	here
	Z	Pepicelli William J	453	letter carrier	28	"
1422						
	A	Lecesse Anthony	455	U S M C	20	"
	B	Lecesse Lazzaro	455	shoemaker	64	"
	C	*Lecesse Rafaele—†	455	housewife	57	"
	D	Sava Agatha—†	455	"	46	
	E	Sava John	455	merchant	47	"
	F	DeCalogero Eleanor L—†	455	housewife	25	"
	G	DeCalogero James V	455	presser	25	"

Lubec Street

	H	LaPage Elizabeth—†	428	housewife	57	here
	K	LaPage William G	428	shoecutter	60	"
	L	DeFrancesco Charles	436	pipefitter	40	"
	M	DeFrancesco Emily—†	436	housewife	37	"
	O	Gibbons Edward F	438	U S N	25	
	P	Gibbons Fannie M—†	438	housewife	51	"
	R	Gibbons Harold J	438	U S N	20	
	S	Gibbons Patrick J	438	laborer	58	..
	U	DeSimone Jennie—†	440	housewife	31	"
	V	DeSimone John	440	rigger	41	
	W	*Clarke Ennis	441	retired	84	
	X	Clarke Ennis	441	photographer	48	"
	Y	Clarke Gertrude—†	441	housewife	71	"

Page.	Letter.	FULL NAME.	Residence, Jan. 1, 1945.	Occupation.	Supposed Age.	Reported Residence, Jan. 1, 1944. Street and Number.

Lubec Street—Continued

	z	Clarke Robert W	441	mechanic	47	here
1423						
	A	Beatrice Annie—†	442	housewife	45	"
	B	Beatrice Marino	442	U S A	22	
	C	Pomodoro Filomena—†	442	housewife	24	"
	D	Pomodoro Salvatore	442	U S N	25	"
	E	Carter Delia L—†	443	housewife	64	"
	F	Carter John M	443	chauffeur	33	"
	G	Hazell Edward J	443	retired	62	
	H	Flynn Mary—†	443	housewife	31	"
	K	Flynn Roland	443	welder	34	"
	L	Jones Earl	446	U S A	37	"
	M	Jones Mary A—†	446	housewife	69	"
	N	Jones Mildred—†	446	inspector	30	"
	O	McArdle Charles J	446	operator	33	"
	P	McArdle Dorothy C—†	446	housewife	33	"

Moore Street

	R	Burnett Mary I—†	30	laundress	61	664 Saratoga
	S	Mosca Barbara E—†	30	housewife	29	here
	T	Mosca Thomas	30	laborer	34	"
	U	Cammarano Mary—†	30	housewife	59	"
	V	Cammarano Matthew	30	laborer	59	
	W	Cammarano Vincent	30	U S A	27	"
	X	Donoghue Anna M—†	36	operator	41	"
	Y	Donoghue Mary G—†	36	machinist	43	"
	Z	Comeau Elizabeth O—†	36	cook	36	
1424						
	A	Gaudet Clarence J	36	machinist	41	"
	B	Gaudet Emil J	36	welder	52	
	C	Gaudet Mary E—†	36	clerk	44	
	E	Battaglia Angelina—†	38	housewife	25	"
	F	Battaglia Charles	38	welder	25	
	G	Vecchio Ernestine—†	38	housewife	28	"
	H	Vecchio Nicholas	38	merchant	41	"
	K	Bonito Eugene T	42	driller	39	658 Saratoga
	L	Bonito Mary M—†	42	housewife	33	658 "
	M	Beck Anna—†	58	teacher	35	here
	N	Caulfield Margaret—†	58	"	34	"
	O	Clifford Elizabeth—†	58	"	38	"

15

Moore Street—Continued

P	Conway Margaret—†	58	housekeeper	52	here
R	Dwyer Anna—†	58	teacher	29	"
S	Flanagan Mary—†	58	"	27	"
T	Fogg Caroline—†	58	"	55	
U	Griffin Dorothy—†	58		35	"
V	Lewis Mary—†	58		58	N Hampshire
W	Maddix Helen—†	58	"	23	here
X	O'Connell Ella—†	58	"	57	N Hampshire
Y	O'Donnell Katherine—†	58	"	47	"
Z	Shane Mary—†	58		36	here

1425

A	Welch Helen—†	58	cook	67	

Neptune Road

B	Ahearn Laurence	4	U S C G	27	here
C	Ahearn Louise—†	4	technician	26	"
D	Burns Edward J	4	welder	49	"
E	Burns Julia M—†	4	housewife	44	"
F	Johnson Christopher	4	U S A	25	
G	Johnson Eleanor—†	4	WAC	21	"
H	Mullen Bernard M	4	manager	64	"
K	Mullen Charles B	4	chauffeur	37	837 Saratoga
L	Mullen Helena A—†	4	housewife	60	here
M	Mullen Herbert F	4	manager	33	"
N	Greeley Ann—†	6	housewife	50	"
O	Greeley Lloyd	6	foreman	26	"
P	Surfin Dorothy—†	6	housewife	24	"
R	Lee Evelyn C—†	6	"	34	
S	Lee Karl B	6	mechanic	33	"
T	Gleason Mary—†	6	housewife	50	"
U	Gleason Mildred—†	6	stenographer	21	"
V	Sampson Raymond A	12	laborer	48	
W	Sampson Violet—†	12	housewife	37	"
X	Coriani Katherine—†	12	"	66	
Y	Coriani Leo	12	watchman	69	"
Z	DeSimone Florence—†	12	housewife	30	"

1426

A	DeSimone Gabriel	12	checker	32	"
B	Chaloner Mary F—†	14	housewife	57	"
C	McIntosh Agnes L—†	14	"	50	

16

Page.	Letter.	FULL NAME.	Residence, Jan. 1, 1945.	Occupation.	Supposed Age.	Reported Residence, Jan. 1, 1944. Street and Number.

Neptune Road—Continued

	D	McIntosh William J	14	operator	51	here
	E	McIntosh William J, jr	14	U S A	23	"
	F	Buno Annette—†	14	clerk	20	"
	G	Buno Joseph	14	marbleworker	48	"
	H	Buno Lavinia—†	14	housewife	48	"
	K	Schwamb Barbara—†	16	packer	22	"
	L	Schwamb Gerald	16	U S A	23	"
	M	Schwamb Joseph	16	guard	49	"
	N	Schwamb Margaret—†	16	housewife	48	"
	O	Grace Clarence	16	checker	41	"
	P	Grace Michael	16	retired	74	"
	R	Marchi Margaret—†	18	packer	23	"
	S	Middleton Arthur F	18	U S A	30	"
	T	Middleton Mary—†	18	housewife	65	"
	U	Grady Lena M—†	18	"	59	619 Saratoga
	V	Grady William J	18	U S N	23	619 "
	W	Wessling Henry B	18	blockmaker	51	619 "
	X	Wessling Herman	18	machinist	57	619 "
	Y	Fucillo Angelo	18	U S N	22	here
	Z	Fucillo John	18	operator	50	"

1427

	A	Fucillo John, jr	18	U S N	24	"
	B	Fucillo Joseph	18	U S A	21	"
	C	Fucillo Julia—†	18	housewife	47	"
	D	Parziale Louis	20	engineer	30	"
	E	Parziale Phyllis—†	20	housewife	26	"
	F	Beninaso Alphonzo	20	tailor	55	"
	G	Beninaso Filomena—†	20	housewife	55	"
	H	Beninaso Vincent J	20	U S A	20	"
	K	Gavegnano John	20	"	23	
	L	Gavegnano Sarah—†	20	housewife	23	"
	M	Garufo Anna—†	20	"	47	"
	N	Garufo Filomena—†	20	welder	22	"
	O	Garufo Joseph	20	pressman	55	"
	P	Garufo Sarah—†	20	clerk	21	"
	R	Ruggiero Bella A—†	22	housewife	29	"
	S	Ruggiero Daniel	22	burner	33	"
	T	Lifave Angelo	22	U S N	35	
	U	*Lifave Pauline—†	22	housewife	62	"
	V	Screnci Elizabeth—†	22	operator	20	"
	W	Screnci Josephine—†	22	housewife	40	"

Neptune Road—Continued

	X	Screnci William	22	tailor	46	here
	Y	Saccardo Adeline—†	24	housewife	64	"
	Z	Tassinari Archetta—†	24	"	29	"
1428						
	A	Tassinari Max	24	welder	34	
	B	Dykstra Harry M	24	rigger	61	
	C	Dykstra Margaret—†	24	housewife	61	"
	D	Struzziero Alex	24	U S N	27	"
	E	Struzziero Erminio	24	laborer	58	"
	F	Struzziero Ernest	24	U S N	20	
	G	Struzziero Esther—†	24	housewife	59	"
	H	Struzziero Mary—†	24	clerk	25	"
	K	Vecchio Louise—†	28	housewife	36	30 Neptune rd
	L	Vecchio Rudolph	28	shoeworker	46	30 "
	M	Martorano Dante	30	chauffeur	21	here
	N	*Martorano Esther—†	30	housekeeper	33	"
	O	Martorano John	30	cobbler	60	"
	P	Martorano Maria—†	30	housewife	59	"
	R	Cappannelli Albert	30	U S A	22	"
	S	Cappannelli Alveria—†	30	housewife	56	"
	T	Cappannelli Ferrero	30	laborer	24	
	U	Cappannelli Sestilio	30	finisher	60	"
	V	Massaro Anthony F	32	tilesetter	43	"
	W	Massaro Fannie—†	32	housewife	41	"
	X	Picardi Celia—†	32	"	64	"
	Y	Picardi Emma—†	32	stitcher	34	"
	Z	Picardi Fred	32	U S A	31	
1429						
	A	Picardi Julis—†	32	stitcher	39	"
	B	Picardi Lillian—†	32	bookbinder	38	"
	C	Picardi Michael	32	retired	74	
	D	Picardi Samuel	32	inspector	36	"
	E	Wirth Mary A—†	32	housewife	65	"
	F	Wirth William R	32	longshoreman	68	"
	G	August Rose—†	34	millhand	40	"
	H	August William	34	longshoreman	50	"
	K	D'Addario Josephine—†	34	housewife	39	"
	L	D'Addario Louis	34	buyer	33	
	M	Toscano Marion—†	34	bookkeeper	22	"
	O	Travers Ida—†	36	housewife	29	"
	P	Travers Joseph	36	clerk	32	

Neptune Road—Continued

		FULL NAME	Residence	Occupation	Age	Reported Residence
R		Forgione Angelina—†	36	housewife	41	here
S		Forgione Mary—†	36	housekeeper	22	"
T		Forgione Salvatore	36	U S A	24	"
U		Forgione Vincent	36	stevedore	49	"
V		Dellazoppa Anthony	36	fisherman	40	431 Bennington
W		Dellazoppa Matilda—†	36	housewife	30	Somerville
X		Howard Charles C	38	clerk	57	here
Y		Howard Helen M—†	38	WAVE	21	"
Z		Howard Margaret—†	38	housewife	52	"
		1430				
A		Scheel Anna M—†	38	"	50	
B		Scheel Carl W	38	foreman	57	"
C		Bennett Margaret—†	38	housewife	24	"
D		Bennett Reed J	38	U S N	29	
E		Lomas Harry	38	policeman	47	"
F		Lomas Harry, jr	38	U S N	22	
G		Lomas Mildred—†	38	housewife	44	"
H		Natalucci Josephine—†	44	"	34	
K		Natalucci Phillip	44	laborer	35	
L	*DiNublia Frank	44	retired	63	"
M	*DiNublia Mary—†	44	housekeeper	39	"
N		DiNublia Rose—†	44	clerk	31	"
O		Taylor Mary—†	44	waitress	35	"
P		Firth Margaret—†	44	housewife	24	"
R		Firth Walter	44	U S N	29	Dedham
S		Scannell Daniel	44	seaman	44	here
T		Scannell Elise—†	44	housewife	46	"
U		Scannell Elizabeth—†	44	clerk	20	"
V		Villani Dorothy—†	46	housewife	26	"
W		Villani Michael	46	manager	36	"
X		Terranova Frank	46	laborer	49	
Y		Terranova Phyllis—†	46	housewife	49	"
Z		Collins Charles H	46	clerk	30	
		1431				
A		Collins Joseph F	46	U S A	24	"
B		Collins Mary—†	46	housewife	58	"
C		Collins Mary I—†	46	clerk	26	
D		Marshall Isabelle—†	48	"	38	
E		Marshall Isabelle—†	48	housewife	74	"
F		Marshall John F	48	retired	75	
K		Fleming Michael	48	"	72	

Neptune Road—Continued

G	Ferry Frank	48	policeman	46	here
H	Ferry Mary—†	48	secretary	26	"
L	Gallison Ann—†	50	housewife	35	"
M	Gallison Charles H	50	painter	39	"
N	Venti Rose—†	50	housewife	34	"
O	Venti Vincent	50	checker	36	"
P	Venti Amelia—†	50	stenographer	29	"
R	Venti Americo	50	mechanic	31	"
S	Venti Bragio	50	laborer	57	"
T	Venti Deno	50	U S A	24	"
U	Venti Jean—†	50	clerk	35	"
V	Venti Nicolena—†	50	housewife	58	"
W	Domenico Anceli	52	chauffeur	48	"
X	Domenico Rose—†	52	housewife	37	"
Y	Domenico Arthur	52	laborer	48	"
Z	Domenico Rose—†	52	housewife	37	"
	1432				
A	Ruggiero Carmine	52	salesman	35	"
B	Ruggiero Josephine—†	52	housewife	34	"
C	Fitzgerald Dorothy M—†	54	"	22	"
D	Fitzgerald Henry	54	U S N	27	Revere
E	Repucci Anna—†	54	housewife	39	here
F	Repucci Anthony	54	contractor	40	"
G	Repucci Pasquale	54	retired	81	"
H	Iandoli Guy	54	jeweler	39	"
K	Iandoli Josephine—†	54	housewife	40	"
L	Murray Catherine—†	56	"	32	"
M	Murray Harold	56	checker	37	"
N	Doherty Margaret R—†	56	clerk	52	
O	Hunter Grace F—†	56	"	22	
P	Hunter John A	56	manager	50	"
R	Hunter Mary A—†	56	housewife	50	"
S	Raymond Carmen	56	tailor	42	
T	Raymond Mary—†	56	housewife	31	"
N	Canavan Margaret—†	60	checker	32	"
V	Mirandi Arthur A	60	"	35	
W	Mirandi Caroline—†	60	housewife	35	"
X	Bulduzzi Rachela—†	62	"	68	
Y	Miranda Ersilia—†	62	"	67	
Z	Miranda Margaret—†	62	clerk	30	"

Neptune Road—Continued

A	Miranda Michael	62	retired	63	here
B	O'Donnell George	62	shipfitter	26	Rhode Island
C	O'Donnell John	62	"	48	"
D	O'Donnell Mary—†	62	housewife	46	"

Orleans Street

F	McGuire Phoebe M—†	505	housewife	25	here
G	McGuire William J	505	shipfitter	27	"
H	Fiatarone Anna—†	505	glazier	29	"
K	Fiatarone Margaret—†	505	housewife	48	"
L	Fiatarone Marie—†	505	clerk	21	
M	Fiatarone Vincent	505	machinist	54	"
N	Caranfa Christine—†	505	housewife	27	"
O	Caranfa Umberto	505	driller	26	
P	Smith Edward E	507	nurse	34	
R	Smith Margaret M—†	507	housewife	31	"
S	Cullen Gertrude B—†	507	attendant	52	"
T	Cullen Mary E—†	507	housewife	67	"
U	Cullen Thomas H	507	laborer	68	"
V	*Borgasano Carmella—†	507	housewife	56	"
W	Borgasano Gaetano	507	U S A	31	"
X	Borgasano Lillian—†	507	stitcher	32	
Y	Boulay Dorothy E—†	509	waitress	33	
Z	Boulay William E	509	musician	35	"
	1434				
A	Buono Domenica—†	511	housewife	31	"
B	Buono Quirino	511	driller	37	
C	Centracchio Cecelia—†	511	housewife	40	"
D	Centracchio John	511	clerk	45	
E	Centracchio John, jr	511	U S A	21	
F	Mazzone James, jr	511	merchant	29	"
G	Mazzone Pauline—†	511	housewife	25	"
H	Baldinelli Albert	513	U S N	23	
K	Baldinelli Alice—†	513	housewife	21	"
L	Baldinelli Angelina—†	513	"	54	
M	Baldinelli Armand	513	seaman	21	
O	Collins Francis L	517	electrician	27	"
P	Collins James J	517	retired	81	"

Page.	Letter.	Full Name.	Residence, Jan. 1, 1945.	Occupation.	Supposed Age.	Reported Residence, Jan. 1, 1944. Street and Number.

Orleans Street—Continued

	R	Collins Mary A—†	517	housewife	72	here
	S	Collins Walter E	517	U S A	31	"
	T	Phillips Helen—†	517	housewife	44	30 Peterboro
	U	Phillips William W	517	shipfitter	40	30 "
	V	Seguin Delia—†	517	housekeeper	69	30 "

Saratoga Street

	W	Overton Albert W	511	U S N	29	N Carolina
	X	Overton Gloria L—†	511	housewife	22	here
	Y	Tassinari Albano C	511	U S A	26	"
	Z	Tassinari Giacondo E	511	technician	24	"
1435
	A	Tassinari Mary L—†	511	housewife	56	"
	C	Elixson Margaret—†	514	"	32	
	D	Elixson Torio	514	foreman	31	"
	E	March Margaret J—†	514	housewife	63	"
	F	Maguire Alice L—†	515	"	46	
	G	Maguire Alice M—†	515	packer	22	
	H	Maguire John J	515	U S A	26	
	K	Stock George T	515	retired	75	
	L	Paull Charles E	515	clerk	59	
	M	Paull Margaret L—†	515	housewife	47	"
	O	Farmer Rose—†	516	"	28	
	N	Farmer Thomas	516	U S N	28	
	P	Giordano Albert	516	laborer	35	"
	R	Giordano Sarah—†	516	operator	34	"
	S	Coon James	516	"	39	
	T	Coon Margaret—†	516	housewife	38	"
	U*	Sartini Caroline—†	518	stitcher	65	"
	V	Sartini Charles	518	U S N	21	"
	W	Graziano Felicia—†	518	housewife	57	"
	X	Graziano Joseph	518	U S A	24	
	Y	Graziano Mary—†	518	operator	22	"
	Z	Graziano Nicolo	518	laborer	56	"
1436
	A	Graziano Nicolo	518	operator	21	"
	C	Kilmartin Bridget—†	520	housewife	65	434 Chelsea
	D	Fenton Bridget—†	520	"	68	here
	E	Fenton Lawrence	520	boilermaker	36	"
	F	Fenton Phillip	520	laborer	37	"

22

Page.	Letter.	FULL NAME.	Residence, Jan. 1, 1945.	Occupation.	Supposed Age.	Reported Residence, Jan. 1, 1944. Street and Number.

Saratoga Street—Continued

	G	Riley Robert	520	U S C G	22	here
	H	Serafin Dorothy—†	520	operator	26	"
	K	Serafin Geroname	520	U S A	28	"
	L	Herrick Charlotte—†	522	housewife	53	"
	M	Herrick Joseph G	522	operator	71	"
	N	Wygnot John	522	baker	53	
	O	O'Donnell Mary A—†	522	saleswoman	28	"
	P	O'Donnell Mary M—†	522	housewife	55	"
	R	O'Donnell William F	522	retired	60	"
	T	Landry Catherine—†	524	clerk	25	
	U	Landry George	524	U S N	25	
	V	Giannattasio Mary—†	524	housewife	28	"
	W	Giannattasio Michael	524	cabinetmaker	32	"
	X	Luciano Angelina—†	524	housewife	33	"
	Y	Luciano Nicholas	524	shipwright	34	"
	Z	Bridgman Margaret—†	526	waitress	21	"
1437						
	A	Dooley Elizabeth—†	526	housewife	74	"
	B	Dair John P	526	U S A	37	
	C	Doherty Bernard	526	rigger	42	
	D	*Doyle Margaret—†	526	housewife	35	"
	E	Collins Dorothy—†	526	"	24	423 Saratoga
	F	Collins James J	526	laborer	26	423 "
	G	Henderson Dorothy—†	534	clerk	21	here
	H	Henderson James	534	longshoreman	43	"
	K	Henderson James	534	U S N	22	"
	L	Henderson Laura—†	534	housewife	39	"
	M	*Gordon Michael	534	laborer	69	"
	N	Portrait Catherine—†	534	housewife	32	"
	R	Maiorano Luigi	538	barber	40	
	S	Maiorano Rose—†	538	housewife	40	"
	T	Mancino Alfred	540	U S C G	21	"
	U	Mancino Carmen	540	laborer	57	
	V	Mancino Joseph	540	U S A	26	
	W	Mancino Mary—†	540	housewife	52	"
	X	Littlejohn Arthur	540	machinist	32	"
	Y	Littlejohn Margaret—†	540	housewife	31	"
	Z	Lawson Edith—†	540	clerk	45	
1438						
	A	Lawson Michael	540	retired	40	
	B	Canty John A	542	laborer	50	

Page:	Letter.	FULL NAME.	Residence, Jan. 1, 1945.	Occupation.	Supposed Age.	Reported Residence, Jan. 1, 1944. Street and Number.

Saratoga Street—Continued

c	Canty Oliver	542	pipecoverer	47	here
d	Canty Florence—†	542	clerk	36	"
e	Canty Margaret E—†	542	housewife	74	"
f	Canty Chester D	542	inspector	52	"
g	Canty Genevieve—†	542	housewife	48	"
h	Gardullo Gertrude—†	544	inspector	31	Everett
k	Pfeil Frank	544	U S N	28	here
l	Pfeil Helen—†	544	housewife	26	"
m	McBournie Mary—†	544	"	26	"
n	McBournie William	544	machinist	27	"
o	Gioioso Anthony	544	guard	28	76 Frankfort
p	Gioioso Julia—†	544	housewife	26	76 "
r	Condon Alice—†	546	"	28	here
s	Condon John	546	chauffeur	33	"
t	Anderson Eleanor R—†	551	housewife	27	"
u	Anderson Joseph B	551	U S A	31	Saugus
v	Granara Elizabeth—†	551	saleswoman	21	here
w	Granara Eugene	551	U S A	24	"
x	Granara Joseph E	551	chauffeur	49	"
y	Granara Joseph E, jr	551	U S N	26	"
z	Granara Nora M—†	551	housewife	44	"
	1439				
a	Cody Dorothy—†	553	"	24	"
b	Cody Herbert T	553	U S A	24	
c	Flynn Mary A—†	553	at home	90	"
d	Goulland Carroll	553	U S A	30	"
f	Trainor George F	559	chauffeur	52	"
g	Trainor Katheryn G—†	559	housewife	46	"
h	Hall Elizabeth—†	559	at home	80	"
k	Hall Frederick O	559	guard	50	
l	Trainor Helen C—†	561	housewife	30	"
m	Trainor Louis J	561	laborer	41	
n	LaGuaglia Agnes R—†	563	housewife	33	"
o	LaGuaglia Joseph J	563	laborer	32	"
p	Hansen Anna E—†	563	housewife	43	"
r	Hansen Ringwell A	563	printer	43	"
s	Kenney Claire A—†	563	packer	20	
t	Kenney George J	563	U S N	22	"
u	Seward Mary—†	563	millhand	34	"
v	Comunale Frank	567	manager	42	"
w	Comunale Mary T—†	567	housewife	39	"

24

Saratoga Street—Continued

x	*Ricci Ippolita—†	567	housewife	81	here
y	Ricci John	567	salesman	41	"
z	Ricci Mary—†	567	housewife	39	"

1440

a	Cecere Edith—†	567	manager	37	Somerville
b	Cecere William	567	shipfitter	36	"
c	Sheehan John L	579	chauffeur	41	here
d	Sheehan Mary M—†	579	housewife	39	"
e	Carideo Amelia G—†	579	"	29	"
f	Carideo Frank S	579	laborer	31	"
g	Morgan Anna M—†	579	cleaner	54	
h	Ranahan Thomas R	579	retired	68	
k	Staff Gertrude F—†	579	housewife	38	"
l	Staff John L	579	welder	39	
m	DelSordo Josephine R—†	585	housewife	25	"
n	DelSordo Ralph J	585	welder	25	
o	Megna Ferdinand	585	printer	43	
p	Megna Marie—†	585	housewife	41	"
r	*Glatis Anna—†	585	"	45	
s	Glatis William D	585	bartender	49	"
t	Quaglioti Angelina—†	587	shoeworker	23	"
u	Quaglioti Nicolo	587	laborer	54	
v	Quaglioti Rose—†	587	shipfitter	21	"
w	Quaglioti Sofie—†	587	housewife	44	"
x	Keohane John J	587	U S A	35	
y	McCarthy Daniel J	587	manager	29	"
z	McCarthy Mildred F—†	587	housewife	28	"

1441

a	Manoli Fay—†	589	housewife	28	"
b	Manoli Martin J	589	mechanic	29	"
c	DiChristoforo John	589	boilermaker	27	"
d	DiChristoforo Mary—†	589	housewife	28	"
e	Abbott Helen—†	591	"	30	
f	Abbott William H	591	chauffeur	35	"
g	Hogan Bridget J—†	591	housewife	61	"
h	Hogan Henry P	591	auditor	33	"
k	Hogan Patricia F—†	591	bookkeeper	20	"
l	Hogan Patrick J	591	stevedore	66	"
m	Fossett John R	593	laborer	47	390A Chelsea
n	Landry Sarah A—†	593	cook	56	here
o	Solstran Florence M—†	593	housewife	28	"

Saratoga Street—Continued

P	Solstran Nicholas	593	fisherman	42	56 Princeton
R	*Palmer Frank	594	storekeeper	60	here
S	*Palmer Rose—†	594	housewife	60	"
T	Foster Evelyn A—†	595	"	28	"
U	Foster George T	595	rigger	27	
V	*Melillo Alphonsine—†	596	housewife	62	"
W	Melillo Charles G	596	U S A	31	
X	Melillo Mary—†	596	housewife	30	"
Y	Brigandi Gaetano	596	U S A	39	
Z	Brigandi Josephine—†	596	packer	35	
	1442				
A	Alcott Andrew A	597	U S N	26	Everett
B	Alcott Barbara V—†	597	housewife	20	"
C	Casey Lenora L—†	597	welder	22	here
D	Musone Leona—†	597	housewife	41	"
E	Musone Peter	597	bricklayer	49	"
F	Musone Vaughn	597	U S N	24	"
H	Belfiglio Daniel	600	painter	20	"
K	*Belfiglio Esilia—†	600	housewife	45	"
L	Belfiglio Peirino	600	operator	51	"
M	Keohane Arthur	602	longshoreman	64	"
N	*Keohane Ellen—†	602	housewife	52	"
O	Kenny John	604	U S A	24	
P	Kenny William	604	operator	60	"
R	Kenny William, jr	604	U S A	26	
S	Pitano Michael	604	machinist	65	"
T	Leno Catherine—†	606	housewife	31	"
U	Leno John	606	U S N	31	
V	Impemba Alfonso	608	retired	66	"
W	Impemba Victor	608	U S A	22	
X	Impemba Victoria—†	608	housewife	57	"
Y	Sanchez Joseph	610	seaman	27	
Z	Sanchez Sarah—†	610	housewife	27	"
	1443				
A	Morante Ralph	612	telegrapher	39	"
B	Morante Rose—†	612	housewife	40	"
C	Malgeri Rocco	614	U S A	23	
D	Malgeri Vincent	614	laborer	50	"
F	Marry Catherine—†	616	housewife	44	"
G	O'Hearn John	616	fisherman	49	"
H	O'Hearn Mary T—†	616	housewife	48	"

Saratoga Street—Continued

K	*Rodophele Jennie—†	618	housewife	60	here
L	Rodophele Joseph	618	pipefitter	24	"
M	Lepore Henry J	619	chauffeur	29	"
N	Lepore Julia A—†	619	housewife	59	"
O	Lepore Peter A	619	machinist	59	"
P	Chiachio Julia A—†	619	housewife	27	Medford
R	Chiachio Peter	619	U S A	25	"
S	Howard Catherine—†	620	housewife	29	65 Joy
T	Howard John C, jr	620	mechanic	33	65 "
V	Velardo Alice—†	624	stitcher	34	here
W	Velardo Dominick	624	U S A	36	"
X	Ristaino Helen—†	624	housewife	24	61 Saratoga
Y	Ristaino Joseph	624	agent	24	61 "
Z	Dennehy James F	625	retired	63	460 Bennington
	1444				
A	Dennehy Sarah A—†	625	housewife	85	460 "
B	*Cavalieri Carmela—†	625	at home	89	here
C	Sortini Adam	625	U S A	23	"
D	Sortini Lena—†	625	burner	44	"
E	Brems Elizabeth E-†	626–28	supervisor	24	"
F	Brems Joseph F	626–28	pipefitter	21	"
G	Brems Lillian—†	626–28	housewife	59	"
H	Brems Phillip E	626–28	U S C G	28	"
K	D'Agostino Filomena—†	626–28	housewife	36	"
L	D'Agostino Pasquale	626–28	machinist	36	"
M	Micarelli John	629	U S N	20	
N	Micarelli Joseph	629	"	23	
O	Micarelli Louis	629	U S A	25	
P	Micrelli Mario	629	"	27	
R	Micarelli Mary—†	629	housewife	53	"
S	Micarelli Nicolo	629	merchant	58	"
T	Micarelli Phyllis—†	629	housewife	25	Texas
U	Cohan Laura C—†	630	"	36	here
V	Cohan William M	630	foreman	36	"
W	Micarelli Catherine—†	631	housewife	38	"
X	Micarelli James	631	meatcutter	32	"
Y	DePaolo Adeline—†	631	housewife	26	"
Z	DePaolo James	631	laborer	27	
	1445				
A	Russo Margaret—†	631	packer	30	"
B	Keith Mary C—†	632	at home	20	643 Saratoga

27

Page.	Letter.	Full Name.	Residence, Jan. 1, 1945.	Occupation.	Supposed Age.	Reported Residence, Jan. 1, 1944. Street and Number.

Saratoga Street—Continued

	c	Ryan Sarah—†	632	housewife	44	here
	d	Ryan Thomas J	632	operator	52	"
	e	DeWolfe Frank	634	laborer	52	"
	f	DeWolfe May—†	634	housewife	48	"
	g	DeWolfe William E	634	U S C G	23	"
	h	Fitzgerald Annie—†	634	housewife	68	"
	k	Fitzgerald Lawrence	634	retired	76	
	l	O'Regan Anna L—†	635	housewife	49	"
	m	O'Regan John P	635	electrician	53	"
	n	O'Regan John P	635	laborer	20	
	o	Dundon Mary C—†	635	clerk	55	
	p	O'Donnell Agnes V—†	636	stripper	44	"
	r	O'Donnell Charles W	636	longshoreman	37	"
	s	DiGenio Annibale	636	pressman	59	"
	t	DiGenio Antonetta—†	636	housewife	47	"
	u	DiGenio Giovanna—†	636	packer	21	"
	v	Ingegneri Peter	637	U S A	25	36 Neptune rd
	w	Ingegneri Rose—†	637	housewife	29	here
	x	Marinelli Joseph	637	retired	65	"
	y	*Marinelli Josephine—†	637	housewife	55	"
	z	DiFronzo Carmela—†	638	"	47	
		1446				
	a	*DiFronzo Concetta—†	638	at home	88	"
	b	DiFronzo Concetta—†	638	clerk	24	
	c	DiFronzo Nicholas	638	U S A	23	
	d	DiFronzo Peter	638	laborer	50	"
	e	Ambrogne Edward	638	chauffeur	53	"
	f	Ambrogne Rose A—†	638	housewife	50	"
	g	Green Ella—†	639	bookkeeper	61	"
	h	Green Mary—†	639	at home	63	"
	k	Martin Ann—†	639	nurse	38	
	l	Conte Giulio	641	laborer	42	"
	m	Conte Grace—†	641	clerk	45	"
	n	Scott Alice—†	643	housewife	23	10 Jeffries
	o	Scott John	643	seaman	34	10 "
	p	Connelly James T	643	welder	31	417 Frankfort
	r	Connelly Mary E—†	643	housewife	26	417 "
	s	Valenti Alfred	643	U S N	22	Medford
	t	Valenti Mary—† •	643	housewife	22	549 Bennington
	u	DiNapoli Gertrude M—†	645	"	28	here
	v	DiNapoli Ralph J	645	clerk	29	"

28

Saratoga Street—Continued

w	Petrillo Carmen P	645	chauffeur	34	here
x	Petrillo Nancy F—†	645	housewife	27	"
z	Holden George	647	laborer	30	"
1447					
A	Holden Julia—†	647	housewife	27	"
B	Lombardo Carmela—†	647	"	40	..
C	Lombardo Nunzio	647	foundryman	53	"
D	Sanfelipe Salvatore	647	laborer	55	::
E	Sanfelipe Tina—†	647	stitcher	41	"
F	Daley Lillian—†.	648	housewife	32	"
G	Daley Michael L	648	clerk	35	..
H	Collins Alma E—†	648	restaurateur	24	"
K	Collins George E	648	U S A	28	..
L	Jones Herman W	648	laborer	52	"
M	Jones Rose M—†	648	housewife	56	"
N	Rogers Silas F	648	U S A	24	Texas
O	Dutra Jerome J	648	machinist	58	here
P	Dutra Mary A—†	648	housewife	61	"
R	Leonard John F	650	timekeeper	45	"
S	Leonard Theresa V—†	650	housewife	44	"
T	Hogan Alexander J	650	printer	45	
U	Hogan Josephine M—†	650	housewife	45	"
V	Kirby John T	650	welder	38	
w	Kirby Mary A—†	650	housewife	38	"
x	McMullen Joseph J	650	watchman	54	"
Y	McMullen Ruth E—†	650	machinist	24	"
z	Henneberry Florence—†	650	clerk	20	57 McClellan H'way
1448					
A	Henneberry Florence M-†	650	housewife	50	57 "
B	Henneberry John T	650	policeman	50	57 "
C	Stanton George A	650	seaman	23	Fitchburg
D	Stanton Madeline M—†	650	operator	23	57 McClellan H'way
E	Spear Louisa—†	652	packer	60	here
F	Dwelley Arthur G	652	electrician	64	"
G	Dwelley Donatella J—†	652	operator	27	"
H	Dwelley Elizabeth F—†	652	housewife	60	"
K	Dwelley George W	652	U S A	31	
L	Bua Angelo	652	electrician	31	"
M	Bua Stella—†	652	housewife	24	"
N	*Medeiros Anthony	653	mechanic	44	"
O	*Medeiros Mary—†	653	housewife	43	"

Page	Letter	Full Name	Residence, Jan. 1, 1945.	Occupation	Supposed Age	Reported Residence, Jan. 1, 1944. Street and Number.

Saratoga Street—Continued

	P	Medeiros Richard	653	U S A	20	here
	R	Gioioso Margaret—†	653	housewife	28	"
	S	Gioioso Michael	653	tester	30	"
	T	Scarafone Anthony	653	U S A	30	
	U	Scarafone Domenic	653	U S N	29	"
	V	Scarafone Francis	653	U S M C	20	"
	W	Scarafone Joseph	653	mechanic	32	"
	X	Scarafone Nicholas	653	U S N	21	
	Y	Scarafone Romeo	653	U S A	26	"
	Z	Joyce John	rear 653	retired	47	
1449						
	A	Joyce Mary—†	" 653	at home	79	"
	B	Joyce William	" 653	engraver	50	Cambridge
	C	Ward Florence—†	" 653	housewife	70	here
	D	Lawrence Clare E	654	U S N	23	"
	E	Lawrence Margaret M—†654		housewife	21	"
	F	Muldoon Edward J	654	U S N	29	196 Falcon
	G	Muldoon Joseph F	654	U S A	30	here
	H	Muldoon Lawrence P	654	"	34	196 Falcon
	K	Sullivan Katherine F—†	654	waitress	43	196 "
	L	Sullo Caroline M—†	654	housewife	31	here
	M	Sullo Marco	654	U S A	31	"
	N	Mambuca Mary—†	654	housewife	35	"
	O	Mambuca Nicholas	654	attendant	31	"
	R	Boyle John J	656	kitchenman	55	301 E Eagle
	S	Ward Katherine G—†	656	housewife	22	here
	T	Ward Richard M	656	blacksmith	29	"
	U	McCarthy Katherine—†	656	housewife	48	"
	V	McCarthy Patrick J	656	longshoreman	48	"
	W	Tierney Bridget A—†	656	housewife	56	"
	X	Tierney Francis J	656	seaman	58	"
	Y	Wilkes Frederick C	658	driller	28	"
	Z	Wilkes Helen—†	658	housewife	26	"
1450						
	A	DiNapoli Martin	658	driller	30	
	B	DiNapoli Ruth—†	658	housewife	27	"
	C	D'Ambrosio Elsie—†	658	operator	26	49 Chelsea
	D	D'Ambrosio Ernesto	658	shoemaker	65	49 "
	E	D'Ambrosio Filomena—†	658	packer	31	49 "
	F	D'Ambrosio Frank	658	laborer	22	49 '
	G	D'Ambrosio John	658	U S A	20	49 '

Saratoga Street—Continued

H	D'Ambrosio Maria—†	658	housewife	63	49 Chelsea
K	D'Ambrosio Rosaria—-†	658	stitcher	30	49 "
L	Candela Emma—†	660	housewife	52	here
M	Candela John	660	fireman	53	"
N	Ruggerio Carmen	660	laborer	51	"
O	Ruggerio Barbara—†	660	housewife	37	"
P	Ruggerio Gennaro	660	rubberworker	40	"
W	DeMarks Mary—†	664	at home	67	"
X	Facey Harriet M—†	664	housekeeper	58	"
Y	*Tsandarnis Nicholas	664	millhand	65	"
Z	Westall Harold A	664	cleaner	62	Brookline
	1451				
B	Coleman Clara—†	665	storekeeper	70	here
C	Gomes Braz	666	oiler	40	"
D	*Santos Francisco F	666	millhand	52	"
E	Benson John A	666	retired	71	
F	Benson Mary N—†	666	housewife	68	"
G	Farmer Beatrice—†	666	"	43	
H	Farmer Edward H	666	printer	43	"
K	White Helen—†	667	stitcher	51	"
L	White William	667	laborer	52	
M	White William	667	U S A	20	"
N	Berry Elizabeth—†	669	housewife	30	235 Webster
O	Berry Frank	669	machinist	31	235 "
P	Conners James	669	U S C G	29	here
R	Conners Martha—†	669	housewife	40	"
S	O'Regan Fred	670	physician	50	"
T	Ahearn Katherine E—†	670	clerk	33	3 Chaucer
U	Ahearn Mary E—†	670	at home	72	3 "
V	Ahearn Mary E—†	670	tel operator	43	3 "
W	Blasetti Angelo	671	laborer	37	here
X	Blasetti Yolanda—†	671	housewife	32	"
T	Romano Antonio	671	U S N	20	"
Z	Romano Carmela—†	671	stitcher	22	"
	1452				
A	*Romano Mary—†	671	housewife	63	"
B	Romano Pasquale	671	seaman	25	"
C	Romano Ralph	671	U S A	27	
D	Romano Rose—†	671	stitcher	29	"
E	Boudreau Delphine—†	673	housewife	68	"
F	Dawber Michael	673	shipfitter	45	"

Saratoga Street—Continued

Page.	Letter.	Full Name.	Residence, Jan. 1, 1945.	Occupation.	Supposed Age.	Reported Residence, Jan. 1, 1944. Street and Number.
	G	Snow Arthur C	673	cook	62	here
	H	Snow Sabina—†	673	housewife	62	"
	K	Cavalieri Nicolo	674	retired	65	"
	L	Cavalieri Rosa—†	674	housewife	70	"
	M	Cavalieri Salvatore	674	boilermaker	40	"
	N	Cavalieri Frank O	674	floorlayer	42	"
	O	Cavalieri Josephine—†	674	housewife	35	"
	P	Nuzzo Elizabeth—†	675	"	34	"
	R	Nuzzo Frank	675	electrician	39	"
	S	Nuzzo Marie—†	675	housewife	74	"
	T	Sturniolo James	675	U S A	26	"
	U	Sturniolo Mary—†	675	electrician	46	"
	V	Sturniolo Rose—†	675	trimmer	23	"
	W	DeMeo Josephine—†	675	electrician	43	"
	X	DeMeo Michael	675	laborer	47	
	Y	DeMeo Michael	675	U S A	25	
	Z	DiNapoli Frank	676	laborer	56	
1453						
	A	DiNapoli Nicholas	676	U S A	26	
	B	*DiNapoli Rose—†	676	housewife	69	"
	C	Powers Anna—†	676	"	32	
	D	*Powers David M	676	printer	31	"
	E	Chase Catherine—†	677	cleaner	34	14 Park
	F	Ruggiero Angelo	677	engineer	21	here
	G	Ruggiero Jennie—†	677	at home	53	"
	H	Stephano Angelina—†	677	housewife	31	"
	K	Stephano Joseph	677	cook	33	
	L	Zitano James	677	foreman	45	"
	M	Giaraffa Gaetano	678	electrician	31	"
	N	Giaraffa Mary—†	678	housewife	29	"
	O	Salamone Dante A	678	U S A	20	"
	P	Salamone Joseph	678	barber	56	"
	R	Salamone Lawrence F	678	U S A	27	"
	S	Salamone Lillian—†	678	housewife	52	"
	T	*Salamone Maria—†	678	at home	78	"
	U	Salamone Virgil J	678	U S A	23	"
	V	Crawford Mary C—†	678	housewife	30	"
	W	Crawford Robert	678	machinist	44	"
	X	Vargus Ethel—†	679	housewife	27	"
	Y	Vargus James	679	assembler	27	"
	Z	Vargus Virginia—†	679	housewife	24	"

1454
Saratoga Street—Continued

A	Vargus William	679	fishcutter	30	here
B	Critch Jennie—†	679	housewife	25	"
C	Critch Richard	679	machinist	28	"
D	Vargus Edmund	680	fishcutter	31	"
E	Vargus Rose—†	680	housewife	26	"
F	Smith Josephine M—†	680	"	30	
G	Smith Wilfred C	680	welder	36	"
H	Davies George	681	clerk	71	
K	Nazzaro Carlo	681	"	26	
L	Nazzaro Louise—†	681	housewife	25	"
M	Saviano Frank	681	shipfitter	34	"
N	Saviano Isabelle—†	681	housewife	26	"
O	Raymond Barbara—†	681	"	40	"
P	Raymond John	681	laborer	44	"
R	Meninno Carmela—†	682	stitcher	48	"
S	Meninno Domenick	682	cutter	52	"
U	Beatrice Alice—†	687	operator	21	"
V	Beatrice Anna—†	687	housewife	46	"
W	Vieira Florence—†	687	"	40	
X	Vieira John	687	mechanic	44	"
Y	Vieira John	687	at home	20	"
Z	Newhook Hester—†	689	housewife	77	"

1455

A	Newhook Joseph	689	retired	35	
B	Newhook Mary—†	689	housewife	35	"
C	Newhook Robert	689	shipfitter	37	"
D	Riley Edwin J	690	policeman	42	"
E	Riley Florence J—†	690	housewife	42	"
F	Turner Margaret—†	691	"	58	"
G	Turner Robert C	691	maintenance	59	"
H	Turner Jean—†	691	packer	53	"
K	Turner Jean L—†	691	stenographer	23	"
L	Watson Agnes L—†	691	saleswoman	49	"
M	Turner Mary D—†	692	housewife	56	"
N	Turner Rose T—†	692	at home	90	"
O	Turner William L	692	engineer	60	"
P	Turner Edwin J	694	U S A	35	
R	Turner Florence M—†	694	secretary	34	"
S	Turner Marie V—†	694	stenographer	38	"
T	Fife Mary—†	696	auditor	67	"

Saratoga Street—Continued

u	DeAngelis Grace—†	696	at home	33	here
v	DeAngelis Joseph	696	optician	41	"
w	Knudson Evelyn—†	696	clerk	36	"
x	Kelley Anna A—†	702	at home	52	"
y	Kelley Dorothy M—†	702	tel operator	28	"
z	Kelley Edmund A	702	U S N	26	
	1456				
a	Zinna Anthony	704	"	25	
b	Zinna Concetta—†	704	operator	30	"
c	Zinna Frances—†	704	"	32	
d	*Zinna Nunzio	704	candymaker	62	"
e	Zinna Vincent	704	U S A	27	
g	Thompson Amelia M—†	710	housewife	44	"
h	Thompson Newell L	710	janitor	44	

William F McClellan Highway

m	Collins James	47	machinist	39	here
n	Collins Lillian—†	47	housewife	34	"
o	Keenan Edward	47	foreman	52	"
p	Keenan Edward J	47	U S N	22	
r	Keenan Mary J—†	47	housewife	43	"
s	Drago Anna—†	47	"	23	252 Marion
t	Drago Charles	47	stitcher	27	134 Chelsea
u	Driscoll Bridget—†	49	housewife	75	here
v	Colarusso Enrico	49	U S A	35	"
w	Colarusso Phyllis—†	49	secretary	32	"
x	Pereira Joaquin	49	weaver	42	"
y	Pereira Marie—†	49	housewife	27	"
z	Puopolo Domenic	51	presser	35	
	1457				
a	Puopolo Mary—†	51	housewife	31	" '
b	Duggan Martin	51	engineer	28	1098 Saratoga
c	Duggan Mary—†	51	housewife	28	1098 "
d	*Santos Albert	51	laborer	40	here
e	*Santos John I	51	fisherman	45	"
f	*Santos Mary—†	51	housewife	54	"
g	Mini Alice—†	53	"	31	
h	Mini William	53	chauffeur	36	"
k	DelBianco Ernest	53	U S N	32	"
l	DelBianco Katherine—†	53	factoryhand	32	"

William F McClellan Highway—Continued

M	*Farro Lena—†	53	housewife	35	305 Saratoga
N	Farro Michael	53	operator	38	305 "
o	Altieri Edith—†	55	housewife	28	here
P	Altieri Frank	55	laborer	30	"
R	Monzo Joseph	55	shipfitter	51	"
s	Paolucci Louis	55	retired	76	
T	O'Connell Anna—†	55	fitter	50	
U	O'Connell Edward	55	calker	26	
V	O'Connell Edward F	55	"	50	
w	O'Connell John	55	U S N	22	"
x	Reilly Catherine—†	57	housewife	33	53 McClellan H'way
Y	Reilly James	57	mechanic	37	53 "
z	Conroy Barbara—†	57	housewife	62	here
	1458				
A	Conroy Bernadette—†	57	clerk	24	"
B	Conroy Joseph	57	U S A	32	"
C	Conroy Mary—†	57	clerk	34	
D	Puleo Blanche—†	57	housewife	37	"
E	Puleo Robert	57	electrician	39	"
G	Zaverson Anna—†	59	clerk	44	
H	Zaverson John	59	tester	42	
K	Gallagher William	59	retired	80	"
L	Gallagher William F	59	U S N	43	
M	Smith Catherine—†	59	housewife	45	"
N	Smith Ethel—†	59	stenographer	29	"

Ward 1–Precinct 15

CITY OF BOSTON

LIST OF RESIDENTS
20 YEARS OF AGE AND OVER

(NON-CITIZENS INDICATED BY ASTERISK)
(FEMALES INDICATED BY DAGGER)

AS OF

JANUARY 1, 1945

THOMAS F. SULLIVAN, *Chairman*
FREDERIC E. DOWLING, *Secretary*
WILLIAM A. MOTLEY, JR.
FRANCIS B. McKINNEY
EVERETT R. PROUT
Listing Board.

CITY OF BOSTON PRINTING DEPARTMENT

1500
Bennington Street

B	Carty Mary—†	519	housewife	50	here	
C	Carty Stephen	519·	operator	53	"	
D	DiBonis Carina—†	521	housewife	36	"	
E	DiBonis Olivio	521	laborer	42		
F	Rothwell Ethel—†	521	housekeeper	44	"	
G	Rothwell Margaret E—†	521	tel operator	21	"	
H	Scaramella Christina—†	523	stitcher	33	"	
K	Scaramella Domenica—†	523	housekeeper	70	..	
M	Marmo Anthony	527	laborer	25		
N	Marmo Antonette—†	527	social worker	22	"	
O	Marmo Jane—†	527	housewife	49	"	
P	Marmo Nicholas	527	bartender	54	"	
R	Traina Angelo	527	U S A	23		
S	Traina Anna—†	527	housekeeper	45	"	
T	Traina Joseph	527	U S A	22	..	
U	Traina Salvatore	527	"	27		
V	Long Bridget—†	527	housewife	55	"	
W	Long Patrick J	527	laborer	64		
X	LeGallo Helen—†	529	housewife	38	"	
Y	LeGallo Joseph	529	agent	38		
Z	Rideout Jane—†	529	housekeeper	64	"	

1501

A	Alterisio Antonio	529	laborer	60		
B	Alterisio Emilia—†	529	housekeeper	38	"	
C	DeBenidetto Pasquale	529	retired	72	..	
D	DeCosta Anna—†	529	housewife	32	"	
E	DeCosta Mario	529	seaman	52		
F	Carino George	531	clerk	34		
G	Carino Goldie	531	housewife	28	"	
H	Gay Anna—†	531	operator	21	"	
K	Gay Francis	531	U S A	20		
L	Gay John	531	"	22		
M	Gay John W	531	chauffeur	51	"	
N	Gay Theresa—†	531	housewife	52	"	
O	Gay Thomas	531	U S A	23	"	
P	Tierney Ann—†	531	housekeeper	51	"	
R	Clemente Louis	531	welder	32	..	
S	Clemente Martha—†	531	housewife	32	"	
T	Gardner Catherine G—†	533	WAC	22	..	
U	Gardner John L	533	laborer	20		

2

Bennington Street—Continued

v	Gardner Lucy—†	533	housekeeper	44	here
w	O'Brien Helen B—†	533	clerk	28	"
x	O'Brien William T	533	U S A	32	"
y	Winston Alma P—†	533	clerk	25	"
z	Winston Edward F	533	shipfitter	59	"
	1502				
a	Winston Edward F, jr	533	U S A	23	
b	Winston Sadie A—†	533	housewife	54	"
c	Winston Thomas A	533	letter carrier	57	"
d	Morse Lillian—†	533	WAVE	21	
e	Morse Mary—†	533	housewife	55	"
f	Morse William	533	laborer	49	
g	Morse William, jr	533	U S M C	20	"
h	Hyland Frank W	537	U S N	26	
k	Hyland Mary A—†	537	housewife	26	"
l	Sands James	537	mechanic	51	"
m	Sands Mary—†	537	housewife	58	"
n	Lewis Miriam C—†	537	clerk	31	
o	Lewis Miriam E—†	537	housewife	53	"
p	Lewis William A	537	inspector	57	"
r	Gundersen Dorothy—†	537	housewife	40	"
s	Gundersen Tallman H	537	weigher	46	"
t	Visconti Anna—†	549	housewife	38	"
u	Visconti Anthony	549	plumber	38	"
v	Guerra Frank	549	laborer	49	
w	Guerra Mary—† .	549	housewife	45	"
x	Guerra Rose—†	549	clerk	21	"
y	Lazzaro Helen—†	549	housewife .	28	"
z	Lazzaro Nicholas	549	plumber	29	"
	1503				
a	Previte Frank	551	chauffeur	53	"
b	Previte Frank, jr	551	U S N	22	
c	Previte Irene—†	551	housewife	46	"
d	Brady Joseph P	553	expressman	28	"
e	Brady Margaret M—†	553	housewife	30	"
f	Hankard Margaret E—†	553	"	38	
g	Hankard Walter J	553	policeman	39	"
h	Hyland Emma I—†	555	housewife	57	"
k	Hyland Frederick D	555	designer	54	"
l	Hyland William J	555	retired	79	
n	Newby Thomas H	557	"	96	

Bennington Street—Continued

o	Budd Emily—†	557	housekeeper	84	here
p	Budd Emily E—†	557	at home	60	"
r	Budd Ruby V—†	557	clerk	44	"
s	Scott George	559	laborer	59	
t	McLaughlin Elizabeth F–†	559	housewife	42	"
u	McLaughlin Joseph	559	laborer	43	
v	DeGregorio Carmella—†	561	housewife	68	"
w	DeGregorio Vincenzo	561	retired	72	
x	DeGregorio Albert A	561	oiler	34	"
y	DeGregorio Natalie V-†	561	housewife	29	"
z	Miraglia Ida—†	561	clerk	24	"
	1504				
a	Donovan James R	563	U S A	24	
b	Donovan Margaret G—†	563	housewife	49	"
c	Donovan Richard D	563	U S A	26	"
d	Donovan Richard J	563	machinist	53	"
e	Donovan Rita M—†	563	secretary	27	"
f	Farmer Hannah F—†	563	housekeeper	57	"
k	Clark Martha—†	569	"	58	
l	McCulpha John H	569	clerk	73	"
m	Hyde Letitia C—†	569	housekeeper	63	"
n	McDonough Bertha G-†	569	clerk	20	"
o	McDonough Catherine-†	569	housewife	38	"
p	McDonough Miles W	569	seaman	38	
r	*Fernandes Antonio	571	carder	57	
s	Fernandes Clementina—†	571	housewife	47	"
t	Sousa Frank	571	grinder	42	
u	Barry Ellen M—†	571	housewife	34	"
v	Barry Lawrence J	571	U S N	37	
w	Warner Ernest C	571	U S A	36	
x	Lyons Gerald	573	U S N	38	"
y	Lyons Ruth—†	573	housewife	36	"
z	Mortimer Catherine G-†	573	clerk	39	
	1505				
a	Mortimer Catherine M-†	573	bookkeeper	24	"
b	Mortimer Mary A—†	573	housekeeper	74	"
c	Mortimer Peter	573	U S A	35	"
d	Burns John J	575	boilermaker	36	"
e	Burns Mary—†	575	housewife	31	"
f	Colletta Antonio	577	cabinetmaker	52	"

Bennington Street—Continued

G	Colletta Joseph	577	U S A	25	here
H	Colletta Nicholas	577	"	24	"
K	Colletta Rudolph	577	"	22	"
L	Colletta Theresa—†	577	housewife	53	"
M	Rosano Frank	579	laborer	62	
N	Rosano Madalena—†	579	housewife	53	"
O	Ambrose Joseph	583	U S N	24	"
P	Ambrose Josephine—†	583	housekeeper	41	"
R	Sullivan Helen C—†	585	bookkeeper	47	"
S	Sullivan Mary E—†	585	housewife	71	"
T	Tasinari Antenori	587	mechanic	28	"
U	Tasinari Doris—†	587	housewife	27	"
V	Naples Elvia—†	589	"	38	
W	Naples Joseph	589	operator	43	"
X	Hamilton Elizabeth—†	591	housewife	42	"
Y	Hamilton John	591	salesman	42	"
Z	Smith Mary—†	593	housewife	55	"
	1506				
A	Smith Michael	593	fireman	60	"
B	Leoshena Alexander	595	machinist	31	"
C	Leoshena Alice—†	595	operator	26	"
D	Leoshena Anne—†	595	housewife	31	"
E	Cassetina Catherine—†	595	"	68	
F	Cassetina Dorothy—†	595	secretary	25	"
G	Cassetina Joseph	595	retired	71	"
H	Gannon Frances R—†	595	housewife	38	"
K	Gannon Mark L	595	retired	50	
L	Allegra Joseph	597	machinist	27	"
M	Allegra Mary—†	597	housewife	27	"
N	Marcella Benedict	597	operator	33	"
O	Marcella Frances—†	597	housewife	29	"
P	Connolly Mary A—†	599	housekeeper	80	"
R	Anderson Mary—†	599	"	55	"
S	McLean Grace E—†	601	housewife	36	"
T	McLean William A	601	policeman	39	"
U	Gormley Catherine E—†	601	saleswoman	54	"
V	Gormley James F	601	B F D	45	
W	Gormley Mary—†	601	housekeeper	83	"
X	Miles Helen—†	603	"	44	"
Y	Wood Laura B—†	603	housewife	48	"

5

Bennington Street—Continued

		FULL NAME.	Residence	Occupation	Age	Reported Residence
	z	Wood Randall E	603	painter	49	here
1507						
	A	McGee Catherine—†	603	housekeeper	40	"
	B	McGee Mary—†	603	at home	42	"
	C	Dorso Angelina—†	605	housewife	31	"
	D	Dorso Anthony	605	longshoreman	35	"
	E	Schieb Margaret—†	605	housewife	40	"
	F	Schieb William	605	electrician	42	"
	G	White Henrietta—†	605	housekeeper	55	"
	H	White James L	605	electrician	21	"
	K	White Lauretta—†	605	at home	25	"
	L	White Rose E—†	605	clerk	23	"
	M	Pepi Ella—†	607	housewife	20	63 Lawrence av
	N	Pepi William	607	artist	26	63 "
	O	Reppendelli Gerald	607	laborer	45	63 "
	P	Butler Florence—†	607	housewife	31	here
	R	Butler John	607	laborer	32	"
	S	Pellegriti Thomas A	609	electrician	24	"
	T	Corresi Catherine—†	611	housewife	40	"
	U	Corresi Nora—†	611	WAVE	23	
	V	Corresi Pasquale	611	shipfitter	40	"
	W	Corresi Phyllis—†	611	operator	21	"
	X	Smith Christina—†	613	housewife	28	"
	Y	Smith William H	613	U S N	32	
	Z	Hill Mary—†	613	housewife	69	"
1508						
	A	Silk Edwin	615	U S A	32	"
	B	Silk Elizabeth—†	615	housewife	32	"
	C	Bois Henry	615	welder	44	"
	D	Bois Madeline—†	615	housewife	44	"
	E	Silk Julia—†	615	"	34	
	F	Silk Walter C	615	assembler	38	"
	G	Howard Joseph J	617	retired	65	"
	H	Melanson Adeline—†	617	housewife	43	"
	K	Melanson Melvin	617	guard	44	
	L	Murray Kathleen—†	617	clerk	38	"
	M	Silva Mary A—†	617	housewife	71	"
	N	Murphy Edward J	617A	clerk	63	
	O	Galzerano Joseph	619	fireman	63	"
	P	Galzerano Nancy—†	619	shipfitter	23	"
	R	Galzerano Samuel	619	U S A	25	

s	Galzerano Viola—†	619	shoeworker	31	here
T	Glennon Adeline—†	619	stenographer	28	"
U	Zocco Nellie—†	619	housewife	43	"
V	Zocco Thomas	619	butcher	43	
W	Trainor Charles H	619	mortician	44	"
X	Trainor Louise G—†	619	housewife	42	"
Z	Karas Frank	633	rigger	46	
	1509				
A	Karas Rose—†	633	housewife	28	"
C	Smith Sarah G—†	635	"	70	
D	Smith William G	635	retired	71	
E	D'Ambrosio Anthony	641	mechanic	36	"
F	D'Ambrosio Jennie—†	641	housewife	35	"
G	D'Ambrosio Alice—†	641A	inspector	34	"
H	D'Ambrosio Amelia—†	641A	housewife	67	"
K	D'Ambrosio Carmen	641A	laborer	67	
L	D'Ambrosio Edward	641A	U S A	22	
M	D'Ambrosio Joseph	641A	"	26	
N	D'Ambrosio Leo	641A	laborer	57	
O	D'Ambrosio Nancy—†	641A	houseworker	28	"
P	D'Ambrosio Susan—†	641A	bookkeeper	32	"
R	Molino Ettore	641A	tailor	50	
S	Molino Gino	641A	U S A	20	
T	Molino Nino	641A	U S N	23	
U	Molino Rose—†	641A	housewife	47	"
V	Errobino Assunta—†	643	cementer	21	"
W	Errobino Mary—†	643	housewife	43	"
X	Errobino Michael	643	U S A	24	
Y	Errobino Pasquale	643	laborer	47	
Z	Picardi Amelia—†	643	houseworker	27	"
	1510				
A	Picardi George	643	foreman	31	
B	Picardi Giacomo	643	retired	82	
C	*Picardi Lucy—†	643	housewife	70	"
D	Santosuosso Evelyn—†	643	"	46	
E	Santosuosso Principio	643	editor	54	
F	Capo Maccio Joseph	645	manager	31	
G	Capo Maccio Laura—†	645	housewife	32	"
H	Skane Margaret—†	645	"	53	
K	Skane Margaret E—†	645	clerk	24	
L	Skane William	645	motorman	53	"

Bennington Street—Continued

	Letter	Full Name	Res.	Occupation	Age	Reported Residence
	M	Skane William J	645	U S A	23	here
	N	Thompson Delia—†	645	housewife	53	"
	O	Thompson Dorothy—†	645	stenographer	22	"
	P	Thompson George H	645	custodian	53	"
	R	Thompson Robert	645	U S A	21	"
	S	Cody Catherine—†	647	housewife	36	"
	T	Cody Joseph	647	burner	43	
	U	Peterson Mary L—†	647	housewife	65	"
	V	Swift Margaret A—†	651	"	58	
	W	Swift Robert	651	boilermaker	58	"
	X	*Minichiello Elizabeth—†	651	housewife	34	"
	Y	Minichiello Gaetano	651	laborer	48	"
	Z	Souza Albert D	651	mechanic	31	"
1511						
	A	Souza Gabrielle A—†	651	housewife	31	"
	C	McDonough Alfred	653	checker	35	"
	D	McDonough Virginia—†	653	housewife	32	"
	E	Sinibaldi Albert J	653	chauffeur	29	43 Saratoga
	F	Sinibaldi Bertine—†	653	housewife	27	43 "
	G	Briscoe Alfred	673	operator	68	here
	H	Briscoe Catherine—†	673	housewife	69	"
	K	DePalma Dorothy M—†	675	"	32	"
	L	DePalma Nicholas J	675	blacksmith	32	"
	M	Hudson Isabelle—†	675	housewife	40	"
	N	Hudson Roy	675	checker	40	"
	O	Donatelli Fernando	675	U S A	30	"
	P	Donatelli Lydia—†	675	housewife	52	"
	R	Donatelli William	675	tailor	52	
	S	Pascucci Emilio	677	plumber	43	"
	T	Pascucci Grace—†	677	housewife	41	"
	U	Sullivan James A	677	seaman	47	
	V	Sullivan Lillian M—†	677	housewife	36	"
	W	Gallagher James	677	U S N	27	
	X	Gallagher Julia—†	677	housewife	23	"
	Y	Castagnola Alfonse F	681	merchant	45	"
	Z	Castagnola Aurelia E—†	681	housewife	45	"
1512						
	A	Sorensen Freda—†	683	"	58	"
	B	Sorensen Herman	683	attorney	35	"
	C	Sorensen John W	683	supervisor	61	"
	D	Sorensen Norman	683	U S A	30	

E	Pinkham Ella B—†	687	housewife	53	here
F	Pinkham Harold A	687	painter	32	"
G	Barron Donald	687	U S N	20	"
H	Uliano Joseph	687	candymaker	61	"
K	Uliano Mary—†	687	housewife	54	"
L	*Gallo Philomena—†	691	"	83	
M	McBride Amelia—†	691	"	26	
N	McBride Earl	691	U S M C	25	"
O	Sena Anna—†	691	assembler	21	"
P	Sena Giocchino	691	laborer	54	
R	Sena Pompelia—†	691	housewife	53	"
S	Sena Rose—†	691	clerk	30	
T	McClements Eva D—†	691	houseworker	63	"
U	Porter Madeline—†	691	waitress	36	
V	Shute Francis J	691	U S A	28	
W	Shute Louise R—†	691	operator	25	
X	Shute Manuel J	691	clerk	66	
Y	Shute Paul J	691	U S N	27	
Z	Cancellieri Blanche—†	691	housewife	32	"
	1513				
A	Cancellieri Joseph	691	clerk	34	
B	Sanford Mary—†	693	at home	74	
C	Sanford Patrick F	693	engineer	69	
D	Trask Charles A	693	"	49	
E	Murphy Jean—†	693	bookkeeper	35	"
F	Murphy Walter	693	laborer	64	
G	Cancellieri Dominic J	693	U S N	26	"
H	Cancellieri Eleanor M—†	693	housewife	30	"
K	Cancellieri Romeo G	693	shipwright	29	"
L	Comeau Marie R—†	695	inspector	38	"
M	Joyce Florence S—†	695	housewife	32	"
N	Joyce John A	695	U S N	30	
O	Boudreau Daniel J	695	U S A	30	"
P	Boudreau Mary E—†	695	housewife	67	"
R	Boudreau Mary M—†	695	librarian	33	"
S	Boudreau William P	695	fireman	68	"
T	Carbon Christine—†	695	housewife	37	"
U	Carbon Francis	695	U S N	39	
V	Mainero Ann—†	697	housewife	28	"
W	Mainero Arthur	697	collector	29	
X	Cosato Anthony	697	U S N	25	

Page.	Letter.	Full Name.	Residence, Jan. 1, 1945.	Occupation.	Supposed Age.	Reported Residence, Jan. 1, 1944. Street and Number.

	Y	Cosato Bernadine—†	697	bookkeeper	27	here
	z	Iapicco Rose—†	697	housewife	53	"
1514						
	A	Iapicco Vincenzo	697	barber	54	
	B	Barnett Jeremiah D	697	U S A	26	"
	C	Barnett Ruth L—†	697	housewife	26	"
	D	Powers Louise E—†	697	"	58	
	E	Powers Patrick J	697	clerk	60	"
	F	Curtin Eileen—†	699	housekeeper	62	"
	G	Curtin John J	699	coppersmith	62	"
	H	Hurley Edward	699	clerk	70	"
	K	Boyle Rose—†	699	"	48	
	L	McCarthy Gerald	699	attorney	50	"
	M	Green Charles E	699	retired	66	
	N	Green Charles E, jr	699	electrician	24	"
	O	Green Elizabeth—†	699	housewife	56	"
	P	Green Rita C—†	699	stenographer	30	"
	R	Kulka Helen—†	699	housewife	23	"
	S	Kulka William	699	U S N	26	
	T	Rockford Doris—†	699	housewife	21	"
	U	Rockford Joseph	699	U S N	21	
	V	Rogers Helen C—†	701	housewife	46	"
	W	Rogers Henry F	701	U S A	21	
	X	Rogers William J	701	motorman	60	"
	Y	Rogers Henry D	701	retired	67	
	z	Rogers Thomas M	701	stereotyper	69	"
1515						
	A	Porter Agnes—†	701	teacher	35	
	B	Porter Helen—†	701	tel operator	25	"
	C	Porter James	701	U S A	30	
	D	Porter Joseph	701	clerk	38	
	E	Porter Margaret—†	701	tel operator	39	"
	F	Amorata Rosina—†	703	factoryhand	52	"
	G	*LaCascia Antonina—†	703	housekeeper	72	"
	H	LaCascia Salvatore	703	laborer	30	"
	K	Campbell Dorothy M—†	703	bookkeeper	34	
	L	Campbell Hugh J	703	U S A	33	
	M	Fitzpatrick Julia T—†	703	housekeeper	64	"
	N	Gasper Edward	703	U S A	26	
	O	Gasper Gertrude—†	703	housewife	26	"
	P	Ciampa Emilio	703	mattressmakr	36	"

Page.	Letter.	FULL NAME.	Residence, Jan. 1, 1945.	Occupation.	Supposed Age.	Reported Residence, Jan. 1. 1944. Street and Number.

Bennington Street—Continued

R	Ciampa Jennie—†	703	housewife	36	here
s	Merlino Angela—†	705	"	41	"
T	Merlino Anthony	705	barber	53	"
U	Pomfrey Jennie—†	705	housewife	33	"
V	Pomfrey Timothy	705	technician	42	"
W	Velardo Catherine—†	705	housewife	67	"
X	Velardo Frank	705	salesman	39	"
Y	Velardo Stephen	705	retired	77	"
z	Testa Anna—†	705	housewife	40	"

1516

A	Testa Frank	705	salesman	40	"
B	Dillon Joseph P	707	letter carrier	37	"
c	Dillon Mildred A—†	707	housewife	35	"
D	McKay Elizabeth—†	707	"	69	
E	McKay Henry F	707	U S N	43	
F	McKay Mathew W	707	manager	38	"
G	McDonald Alma M—†	707	housewife	42	"
H	McDonald Helen A—†	707	factoryhand	21	"
K	McDonald John F	707	machinist	44	"
L	Goss Bridget—†	709	housekeeper	79	"
M	Wickstrom Sarah J—†	709	saleswoman	45	"
N	Boudreau Edna T—†	709	clerk	21	
O	Boudreau Francis H	709	U S M C	22	"
P	Boudreau Helen M—†	709	housewife	45	"
R	Boudreau Richard W	709	U S A	26	
s	Boudreau William T	709	policeman	45	"
T	Boudreau William T	709	U S N	24	
U	Colarusso Helen—†	709	housewife	47	"
V	Colarusso Joseph	709	foreman	54	"
W	Colarusso Joseph J	709	U S A	22	
X	Colarusso Mary—†	709	clerk	25	

Byron Street

Y	Picciuolo Amelia—†	146	housewife	63	here
z	Picciuolo Carmino	146	U S A	39	"

1517

A	Picciuolo Isabella—†	146	clerk	26	
B	Picciuolo Stefano	146	retired	73	
c	Sexton Albert J	150	clerk	55	
D	Sexton Frederick B	150	salesman	45	"

11

Byron Street—Continued

E	Sexton Mary J—†	150	housekeeper	66	here
F	Blaikie Doris—†	163	housewife	22	42 Moore
G	Blaikie George	163	laborer	22	42 "
H	McPhee John J	163	shipfitter	47	here
K	McPhee Joseph H	163	U S A	25	"
L	McPhee Marcella B—†	163	housewife	48	"
M	Fahey Martha—†	163	clerk	35	
N	Gleason John	163	guard	51	"
O	Fennell Catherine—†	165	housekeeper	39	Stoneham
P	Conway Emily—†	165	housewife	23	here
R	Conway Frederick	165	chauffeur	25	"
S	Mattera Frederick	165	foreman	44	"
T	Mattera Louise—†	165	housewife	38	"
U	Mattina Angelina—†	167	"	31	
V	Mattina Joseph	167	welder	31	
W	Sacco Angelo	167A	printer	39	
X	Sacco Mary—†	167A	housewife	31	"
Y	D'India Americo	169	painter	33	"
Z	D'India Phyllis—†	169	housewife	22	"

1518

A	Cutler Mary—†	169A	"	21	
B	Cutler Warren	169A	machinist	23	"
C	Norton Alice C—†	198	clerk	24	
D	Norton Nellie C—†	198	housewife	64	"
E	Norton William F	198	guard	66	"
F	Norton James T	200	retired	68	
G	Norton Mary E—†	201	housewife	66	"
H	Norton Mary E—†	201	teacher	31	"
K	Norton Thomas M	201	retired	76	"
L	Niland Anna M—†	202	at home	76	"
M	Niland Thomas A	202	realtor	71	
N	Lyons Alice M—†	206	housewife	49	"
O	Lyons Charles E	206	electrician	47	"
P	Lyons Charles E, jr	206	U S A	21	
R	Mendoza Bartholomew	206	laborer	74	
S	Mendoza Helen B—†	206	housewife	31	"
T	Mendoza John J	206	machinist	33	"
U	*Mendoza Mary—†	206	housewife	66	"
V	DiNucci Caroline—†	210	"	45	
W	DiNucci Francis	210	U S A	27	
X	DiNucci Harry	210	pipecoverer	55	"

Byron Street—Continued

	Letter	Full Name	Res.	Occupation	Age	Reported Residence
	Y	DiNucci Violanda—†	210	housewife	20	here
	Z	Cahill Herbert J	210	B F D	43	"
1519						
	A	Cahill Mary L—†	210	housewife	43	"
	B	Middleton William J	210	shoeworker	52	"

Coleridge Street

	Letter	Full Name	Res.	Occupation	Age	Reported Residence
	D	Laskey Jerome F	120	policeman	47	here
	E	Laskey Margaret—†	120	housewife	43	"
	F	Hyland Sarah C—†	124	teacher	31	"
	G	Thompson Alice—†	124	clerk	23	
	H	Thompson Mary—†	124	housekeeper	55	"
	K	Thompson Mary F—†	124	chemist	29	"
	L	Thompson Robert E	124	U S C G	32	"
	M	Thompson Winfield S	124	U S A	21	
	N	Page Arthur J	126	retired	85	
	O	Page Dorothy J—†	126	teacher	39	"
	P	Page Muriel M—†	126	"	36	
	R	Page Sarah H—†	126	housewife	81	"
	S	Dower Cecelia—†	130	typist	25	Hawaii
	T	Dower William	130	U S A	26	"
	U	McNabb Hugh	130	retired	47	here
	V	McNabb Madeline—†	130	housewife	45	"
	W	Fairclough Agnes T—†	134	housekeeper	70	"
	X	Lukeman Fergus W	134	supervisor	45	"
	Y	Roche Elizabeth M—†	136	housewife	51	"
	Z	Roche Michael T	136	guard	58	
1520						
	A	Roche Thomas J	136	U S N	20	"
	B	Roche William P	136	U S A	25	"
	C	Boyan Helen—†	138	factoryhand	22	"
	D	Boyan Joseph	138	U S N	23	
	E	Sloan Charles H	138	shipfitter	57	"
	F	Sloan Rose L—†	138	storekeeper	53	"
	G	Rothwell Grace—†	148	housewife	22	90 Sumner
	H	Rothwell Louis	148	machinist	21	90 "
	K	Fenton Marie—†	148	clerk	21	75 Wordsworth
	L	Reilly Dorothy—†	148	housewife	35	75 "
	M	Reilly Maurice	148	pipefitter	43	75 "
	N	Burke Norma—†	148	housewife	25	here

13

Coleridge Street—Continued

o	Burke William	148	U S C G	25	here
p	Connolly Elsie—†	148	housewife	27	"
r	Connolly Lawrence ·	148	U S N	27	"
s	Johannessen Christian	148	machinist	52	"
t	Johannessen Henrietta—†	148	housewife	48	"
u	Scigliano Eugene	149	machinist	28	"
v	Scigliano Joseph	149	U S A	34	
w	*McGonigle Philip	149	retired	62	
x	Seigliano Frances—†	149	housewife	36	"
y	Seigliano Francis	149	manager	40	"
z	Anderson John E	156	mechanic	56	"
	1521				
a	Anderson Lillian—†	156	housewife	51	"
b	Barnard Chester W	156	foreman	53	"
c	Barnard Marian—†	156	housewife	48	"
d	Farnum Gleason	156	U S A	30	"
e	Farnum Ruth W—†	156	housewife	27	"
f	Musil Andrew H	157	retired	64	
g	Musil Letitia—†	157	housewife	58	"
h	Musil Thomas	157	U S A	30	"
k	Buckingham Florence H—†	157	clerk	43	1057 Saratoga
l	Buckingham Gertrude—†	157	housewife	64	1057 "
m	Ballem Evelyn—†	163	factoryhand	40	here
n	Lahey James J	163	electrician	47	"
o	Parker Catherine—†	163	housekeeper	49	"
p	Lampron Mary A—†	165	clerk	33	
r	Nagle Edward J	165	shipper	26	
s	Nagle Hattie B—†	165	housewife	56	"
t	Nagle Horace L	165	shipper	62	
u	Cantwell Benjamin F	167	laborer	66	"
v	Cantwell Rose M—†	167	housewife	65	"
w	Brown Ernest	169	clerk	57	
x	Smith Charles	169	U S A	26	
y	Smith Lillian—†	169	housewife	27	"
z	Scigliano Alfred T	171	attorney	44	"
	1522				
a	Scigliano Anna E—†	171	housewife	40	"
b	Anderson Lillian—†	173	"	40	"
c	Anderson Martin F	173	longshoreman	42	"
d	Anderson Martin F, jr	173	U S N	20	
e	Finch Richard H	173	janitor	74	

F	Finch Thomas	173	mechanic	44	here
G	McIsaac Francis C	175	assembler	48	"
H	McIsaac James	175	U S N	20	"
K	McIsaac Loretta B—†	175	housewife	45	"
L	McIsaac Mary—†	175	clerk	21	
M	Nelson William J	175	U S A	24	
N	McGunigle John E	176	manager	43	"
O	McGunigle Robina—†	176	housewife	37	"
P	Lamb Nina M—†	177	"	60	116 Bennington
R	Lamb Stella M—†	177	"	23	641 Hunt'n av
S	Lamb William	177	boilermaker	64	116 Bennington
T	Lamb William A	177	"	28	641 Hunt'n av

Cowper Street

W	DeBlasio Mildred—†	93	clerk	31	here
X	DeBlasio Samuel	93	U S A	31	"
Y	Donahue Catherine T—†	93	housewife	36	"
Z	Donahue Charles	93	longshoreman	41	"
	1523				
A	Donahue Frederick W	93	U S A	25	
B	Donahue Thomas	93	guard	71	"
C	Fratus Edward	93	U S A	34	
D	Fratus Rita—†	93	clerk	28	"
E	Barron Edward W	93	U S N	22	"
F	Barron Ellen E—†	93	clerk	27	
G	Barron Ellen P—†	93	operator	54	"
H	Barron Pauline M—†	93	"	20	"
K	DeIeso Margaret—†	94	housewife	39	"
L	DeIeso Nicola	94	laborer	49	
M	Roach George H	94	longshoreman	54	"
N	Roach Richard W	94	U S N	26	
O	Roach William A	94	longshoreman	56	"
P	Trunfio Concetta—†	94	housewife	34	"
R	Trunfio Paul	94	retired	48	
S	Balboni John	95	polisher	28	"
T	Balboni Ruth—†	95	housewife	27	"
U	Gagin Henry A	95	clerk	44	
V	Gagin Josephine—†	95	housewife	33	"
W	McDonald Dorothy—†	95	operator	25	"
X	McDonald Edwin	95	U S A	20	

Page.	Letter.	FULL NAME.	Residence, Jan. 1, 1945.	Occupation.	Supposed Age.	Reported Residence, Jan. 1, 1944. Street and Number.

Cowper Street—Continued

	Y	McDonald John	95	retired	63	here
	z	McDonald Margaret—†	95	housewife	60	"
1524						
	A	McDonald William	95	U S A	30	"
	B	Cooper Eva—†	97	waitress	50	"
	c	Cottey Alexander	97	operator	65	"
	D	Trautz Margaret T—†	97	housekeeper	71	"
	E	Trautz John G	97	rigger	41	"
	F	Trautz Mary M—†	97	housewife	40	"
	G	Spadaro George	98	U S A	27	
	H	Spadaro Louise—†	98	housewife	24	"
	K	Torredimare Adeline—†	98	"	46	
	L	Torredimare Anthony	98	U S M C	23	"
	M	Torredimare Frank	98	barber	48	
	N	Torredimare Rose—†	98	teacher	27	"
	o	McWilliams Mary—†	99	at home	76	"
	P	McWilliams Mary A—†	99	operator	36	"
	R	Doherty Anna—†	99	housewife	52	"
	s	Doherty Edward	99	U S A	25	
	T	Doherty John	99	retired	62	"
	U	Doherty Mary—†	99	bookkeeper	21	"
	v	Lowell Ellen—†	99	at home	87	"
	w	Silva Anthony	100	shipfitter	39	"
	x	Silva Kathleen—†	100	housewife	30	"
	Y	Pantos Mary—†	100	"	34	
	z	Pantos Steve	100	driller	43	
1525						
	A	Francis Joseph L	104	U S N	28	
	B	Francis Maria—†	104	housewife	28	"
	c	Williams Agnes M—†	104	"	54	
	D	Williams Anne M—†	104	typist	22	
	E	Williams John A	104	custodian	56	"
	F	Love Merton	106	retired	80	"
	G	Ray Tavia—†	106	housekeeper	72	"
	H	Fowler Edward J	110	U S A	26	"
	K	Fowler Mary C—†	110	housewife	49	"
	L	Fowler William L	110	clerk	28	"
	M	Forshner Mabel B—†	114	housewife	60	"
	N	Osborne Dorothy—†	114	"	36	
	o	Osborne Merrill E	114	clerk	44	
	P	DeCosta Josephine—†	118	at home	83	"

Cowper Street—Continued

R	DeCosta Mary—†	118	at home	63	here
S	Hubbard Josephine—†	118	housekeeper	60	"
T	Bennett Clifford S	118	carpenter	46	"
U	Bennett Jessie I—†	118	housewife	50	"
V	Morgan Edmund	151	inspector	45	"
W	Morgan Edmund, jr	151	U S A	21	
X	Morgan Frances—†	151	housewife	42	"
Y	Gallagher Frederick	151	U S N	28	"
Z	Gallagher Kathryn—†	151	bookkeeper	40	"
	1526				
A	Gallagher Thomas	151	U S A	36	
B	Mahoney Marie—†	151	housewife	32	"
C	McLean Mary—†	155	"	50	
D	McLean Thomas	155	custodian	58	"
E	Molloy John A	155	retired	71	Medford
F	Callahan John F	172	carpenter	37	here
G	Callahan Margaret T—†	172	housewife	34	"
H	Bagley Sarah A—†	174	housekeeper	75	"
K	DuWors Helen A—†	174	housewife	79	"
L	DuWors Robert J	174	retired	79	
M	Bagley Kathryn G—†	176	housewife	67	"
N	Bagley Robert J	176	pipefitter	39	"
O	Moriarty Clarence J	176	welder	32	"
P	Moriarty Kathryn—†	176	housewife	30	"
R	Bagley Richard W	176	attendant	43	"
S	Bagley Ruth F—†	176	housewife	40	"
T	Banks Minnie A—†	177	at home	69	"
U	Hagemeister Frederick C	177	metalworker	57	"
V	Hagemeister Josephine A—†	177	housewife	51	"
W	Hagemeister Thomas D	177	welder	20	"
X	Chase Annie R—†	179	housewife	56	"
Y	Chase Frank	179	laundryman	21	"
Z	Chase Edward	179	U S A	33	"
	1527				
A	Chase George W	179	guard	57	
B	Chase James	179	U S N	29	"
C	Chase John	179	clerk	21	"
D	Shea Eva M—†	181	housewife	38	"
E	Shea William M	181	draftsman	41	"
F	Gayton Clifford	181	carpenter	42	"
G	Gayton Nellie—†	181	packer	43	"

Page.	Letter.	FULL NAME.	Residence, Jan. 1, 1945.	Occupation.	Supposed Age.	Reported Residence, Jan. 1, 1944. Street and Number.

Cowper Street—Continued

	H	Moran Lawrence P	184	U S N	21	here
	K	Moran Mary E—†	184	housewife	54	"
	L	Mullin Sheila M—†	184	operator	23	"
	M	Lombardi George	184	U S N	24	
	N	Ryan Michael J	184	pipefitter	52	"

Homer Street

	O	Shea Francis	58	U S N	23	here
	P	Shea John J ·	58	operator	52	"
	R	Shea Marguerite—†	58	housewife	48	"
	S	Rogan Abbie J—†	58	"	75	
	T	Rogan Abbie J—†	58	clerk	38	"
	U	Rogan Mary A—†	58	operator	35	"
	V	Welch John F.	63	guard	53	
	W	Welch Lillian—†	63	housewife	48	"
	X	Brown Mildred M—†	63	"	20	"
	Y	Johnson Daniel	63	U S N	22	
	Z	Johnson James P	63	seaman	52	
		1528				
	A	Johnson Margaret—†	63	housewife	45	"
	B	Forrest Marjorie M—†	63	"	21	
	C	Kelly Charles J	63	chauffeur	44	"
	D	Kelly Charles J	63	U S A	22	
	E	Kelly Ethel—†	63	housewife	41	"
	F	McLaughlin Edward J	64	retired	66	"
	G	McLaughlin Paul	64	U S N	22	
	H	McLaughlin Philip	64	painter	62	
	K	Thompson Mary—†	66	housewife	45	"
	L	Thompson Richard	66	U S N	21	"
	M	Thompson Richard F	66	fireman	51	"
	N	Gibbons Anna—†	67	housewife	23	Cambridge
	O	Gibbons Joseph	67	U S N	27	"
	P	Potter Alice—†	67	housewife	32	here
	R	Potter Joseph	67	mechanic	31	"
	S	Mealey Francis G	69	clerk	44	"
	T	Mealey Helen—†	69	"	20	
	U	Mealey Mary—†	69	housewife	45	"
	V	Mealey Mary E—†	69	secretary	22	"
	W	Foley Mary—†	69	housewife	60	"
	X	Sabbagh Florence—†	69	"	34	

Page	Letter	Full Name	Residence, Jan. 1, 1945.	Occupation	Supposed Age	Reported Residence, Jan. 1, 1944. Street and Number.

Homer Street—Continued

	Y	Sabbagh George	69	driller	35	here
	z	Purciello Augustine	70	laborer	45	"
1529						
	A	Purciello Edith—†	70	teacher	22	"
	B	Purciello Florence—†	70	housewife	43	"
	c	Purciello Louis	70	U S N	20	"
	D	Najaryan Eleanor—†	71	housewife	23	99 Morris
	E	Najaryan Peter	71	shipper	29	99 "
	F	Cataruzolo Angelina—†	71	housewife	50	here
	G	Cataruzolo Felix	71	laborer	56	"
	H	Cataruzolo Florence—†	71	presser	28	"
	K	Tartoloni Anthony	71	shipper	31	"
	L	Tartoloni Lucy—†	71	housewife	30	"
	M	Bagley Blanche—†	72	"	30	
	N	Bagley Walter	72	foreman	32	"
	o	Hartery Andrew T	72	mechanic	52	"
	P	Hartery Andrew T	72	U S A	23	"
	R	Hartery Eleanor—†	72	housewife	50	"
	s	Hartery William J	72	U S A	21	
	T	O'Hanley Elizabeth—†	73	housewife	45	"
	U	O'Hanley John W	73	laborer	45	"
	v	Brown Sarah—†	73	matron	60	"
	w	Diskin Ellen—†	73	housewife	80	"
	x	Boise Bridget—†	73	"	47	
	Y	Boise Joseph	73	laborer	48	"
	z	Rossano Josephine—†	74	housewife	26	1 Murray ct
1530						
	A	Rossano Louis	74	U S N	27	579 Bennington
	B	Miller Charles, jr	74	U S A	20	here
	c	Miller Charles W	74	mechanic	50	"
	D	Miller Mary J—†	74	housewife	49	"
	E	Hughes Ellen M—†	75	"	51	
	F	Hughes John K	75	U S A	25	
	G	Hughes John W	75	pipefitter	52	"
	H	Hughes Joseph W	75	U S A	21	"
	K	McCormick Eleanor—†	75	operator	29	Winthrop
	L	McCormick Thomas J	75	U S N	30	"
	M	Wren Thomas	75	fireman	62	here
	N	Maggoli Stephen	76	sausagemaker	49	103 Leyden
	o	Maggoli Teresa—†	76	housewife	42	103 "
	P	Pignat John	76	tilelayer	42	103 "

Homer Street—Continued

R	Boyan Mary—†	76	housewife	24	here
s	Boyan Robert	76	U S N	26	"
T	Laskey Helen P—†	78	housewife	42	"
U	Laskey Lloyd	78	policeman	44	"
v	Hartery Elena—†	78	housewife	37	"
w	Hartery William J	78	mechanic	42	"
x	Ricciardi Anna—†	82	housewife	49	"
Y	Ricciardi Antonio	82	retired	49	
z	Ricciardi Samuel	82	laborer	66	
	1531				
A	Goullaud James	82	milkman	32	"
B	Goullaud Martha—†	82	housewife	30	"
c	Picard Jeanne—†	82	at home	55	"
D	Murphy Alfred J	83	U S N	21	"
E	Murphy James P	83	policeman	44	"
F	Murphy Sadie—†	83	housewife	42	"
G	Meuse Alberta—†	83	operator	21	"
H	Meuse Raymond	83	engineer	54	"
K	Meuse Raymond, jr	83	U S A	29	
L	D'Avella Helen—†	83	housewife	29	"
M	D'Avella Vincent	83	operator	31	"
N	Gunderson Christopher	87	retired	82	"
o	Montone Jerry	87	U S A	24	80 Horace
P	Ruggeiro Elvira—†	87	housewife	40	here
R	Ruggeiro Fiontino	87	merchant	49	"
s	Pomer Frank	90	U S A	20	"
T	Pomer Joseph	90	metalworker	47	"
U	Pomer Sadie—†	90	housewife	42	"
v	Camberia Louis	91	laborer	59	
w	Camberia Mary—†	91	housewife	50	"
x	Camberia Peter	91	clerk	32	"
Y	Storin Bertha A—†	91	"	29	
z	Storin George W	91	U S N	26	
	1532				
A	Storin Helen C—†	91	housewife	54.	"
B	Scarnici Ida—†	92	stenographer	21	"
c	Scarnici Jennie—†	92	housewife	47	"
D	Scarnici Philip	92	agent	54	"
E	Scandurra Joseph	93	cabinetmaker	63	"
F	Scandurra Josephine—†	93	housewife	62	"
G	Scandurra Mary—†	93	"	29	

Page.	Letter.	FULL NAME.	Residence, Jan. 1, 1945.	Occupation.	Supposed Age.	Reported Residence, Jan. 1, 1944. Street and Number.

Homer Street—Continued

H	Scandurra Peter	93	barber	30	here	
K	Hoff Karl A	94	foreman	39	"	
L	Hoff Marguerite—†	94	housewife	32	"	
M	Ferry Manuel	94A	laborer	55		
N	Gibbs Anna—†	94A	housewife	44	"	
O	Gibbs Ivy	94A	engineer	43	"	
P	*Doull Mary J—†	95	at home	93	60 London	
R	Locke Lillian F—†	95	housewife.	51	60 "	
S	Manfra Alfred	96	cabinetmaker	44	here	
T	Manfra Philomena—†	96	housewife	35	"	
U	Romano Edmund	96A	chauffeur	30	"	
V	Romano Etta—†	96A	housewife	30	"	
W	Harrington Charlotte—†	97	clerk	23		
X	Harrington Ethel—†	97	welder	20	"	
Y	Harrington Sadie—†	97	housewife	58	"	
Z	McCormick Mary C—†	99	"	60	"	
	1533					
A	McCormick Raymond	99	clerk	38	"	
B	Boudreau Margaret—†	101	housewife	27	"	
C	Boudreau Paul	101	meter reader	34	"	
D	Rowe Frederick	101	repairman	54	"	
E	Leonard Esther J—†	103	housewife	62	"	
F	Leonard Esther J—†	103	librarian	34	"	
G	Leonard Joseph W	103	U S A	24		
H	Leonard Mary M—†	103	clerk	28	"	
K	Leonard Nicholas F	103	manager	63	"	
L	Clayton Charles W	105	retired	72		
M	Clayton Constance M—†	105	clerk	33	"	
N	Clayton Nora M—†	105	housewife	70	"	
O	Regan John	107	machinist	40	"	
P	Regan Joseph	107	"	30	"	
R	McLean Harold	107	U S N	36		
S	Riley Annie T—†	107	housewife	76	"	
T	Riley James J	107	laborer	48	26 Mystic	
U	Riley Loretta—†	107	housewife	36	26 "	
V	Riley William J	107	retired	77	here	

Horace Street

X	Bartlett Ann—†	53	housewife	23	here	
Y	Bartlett Erwin	53	U S N	32	"	

Page.	Letter.	FULL NAME.	Residence, Jan. 1, 1945.	Occupation.	Supposed Age.	Reported Residence, Jan. 1, 1944. Street and Number.

Horace Street—Continued

z	Lane John	57	carpenter	57	here
	1534				
A	Lane Wilfred J	57	seaman	33	
B	Rogers George	59	mechanic	48	"
C	Rogers George J	59	seaman	22	"
D	Rogers Mary A—†	59	housewife	42	"
E	Kelley William E	60	retired	83	"
F	O'Connell Matilda—†	60	housewife	54	"
G	O'Connell Mildred A—†	60	technician	25	"
H	Smith Albert E	63	clerk	65	
K	Smith Alice M—†	63	housewife	62	"
L	Smith Harold E	63	U S A	24	"
M	Smith Helen E—†	63	factoryhand	24	"
N	Carey Katherine L—†	63	nurse	55	
O	Horrigan Michael	63	shipper	67	"
P	Prendergast Helen—†	64	housewife	39	7 Darius
R	Prendergast William E	64	rigger	42	7 "
S	Gillespie Michael F	64	janitor	58	here
T	McHugh Gerald	64	U S N	20	"
U	McHugh James L	64	"	27	"
V	Sullivan Margaret A—†	64	clerk	25	
W	Coughlin Catherine G—†	65	housewife	65	"
X	Coughlin Frank J	65	clerk	44	
Y	Coughlin Helen C—†	65	at home	40	"
Z	Coughlin Mary H—†	65	clerk	27	
	1535				
A	Coughlin Michael F	65	engineer	66	"
B	Gillespie Gertrude M—†	65	clerk	42	
C	Fitzpatrick Anna L—†	67	housewife	50	"
D	Fitzpatrick Evelyn M—†	67	secretary	25	"
E	Fitzpatrick Irene B—†	67	"	20	"
F	Fitzpatrick John H	67	patternmaker	21	"
G	Fitzpatrick Joseph H	67	clerk	55	"
H	Fitzpatrick Joseph H	67	U S N	24	
K	Fitzpatrick Marie A—†	67	secretary	26	"
M	Sullivan Francis J	70	electrician	35	"
N	Sullivan Mary A—†	70	housewife	35	"
O	Parkinson Beatrice B—†	70	"	49	
P	Parkinson John T	70	U S A	24	"
R	Parkinson Robert E	70	repairman	52	"
S	Tierney Margaret E—†	70	clerk	50	"

Horace Street—Continued

u	Gleason Anna M—†	73	housewife	35	here
v	Gleason William D	73	U S A	33	"
w	Hansen Richard C	73	U S N	21	"
x	Joyce Annie M—†	73	housewife	75	"
y	Joyce John F	73	painter	48	"
z	Poirer Sabine R—†	73	seamstress	59	160 Princeton
	1536				
a	Poirier Wilfred M	73	salesman	59	160 "
b	McWilliams Mary M—†	74	housewife	35	here
c	McWilliams Richard	74	clerk	43	"
d	Austin Mary M—†	74	housewife	57	"
e	Austin Richard J	74	guard	57	
f	Berry James J	75	clerk	37	
g	Berry Mary A—†	75	housewife	35	"
h	Parascand Dorothy T—†	75	"	30	Revere
k	Parascand Nicholas A	75	welder	30	"
l	Sweeney Emily M—†	77	housewife	33	here
m	Sweeney Wilfred J	77	letter carrier	34	"
n	Beale Edward A	77	electrician	37	"
o	Beale Mildred L—†	77	housewife	34	"
p	Belton Francis J	77	estimator	47	600 Saratoga
r	Ciampa Anna—†	78	housewife	24	here
s	Ciampa John G	78	shipfitter	29	"
t	Festa Florence—†	78	housewife	44	"
u	Festa Jean—†	78	nurse	23	
v	Festa Joseph	78	mason	55	
w	Festa Yola—†	78	stenographer	20	"
x	Launey Esther—†	78	housewife	22	"
y	Sacco Gerald	78	retired	74	
z	Mortimer Ellen A—†	79	housewife	59	"
	1537				
a	Mortimer John P	79	U S A	20	
b	Mortimer Michael J	79	"	21	
c	O'Donnell Mary C—†	79	at home	47	"
d	O'Donnell Rose—†	79	"	75	"
e	Montone Edward	80	U S A	22	
f	Montone Francesco	80	tailor	53	
g	Montone Teresa—†	80	housewife	46	"
h	Moran John J	80	freighthandler	67	"
k	Moran Joseph F	80	laborer	68	"
l	Moran Mary L—†	80	inspector	63	"

Page.	Letter.	FULL NAME.	Residence, Jan. 1, 1945.	Occupation.	Supposed Age.	Reported Residence, Jan. 1, 1944. Street and Number.

Horace Street—Continued

M	Flanagan Anna M—†	81	housewife	45	here
N	Flanagan John	81	decorator	51	"
O	Travaglini Albert	81	tilesetter	40	"
P	Travaglini Margaret—†	81	housewife	35	"
R	Cunningham Eleanor—†	82	"	47	
S	Cunningham Eleanor M-†	82	operator	22	"
T	Cunningham Terrence	82	U S N	20	"
U	McWilliams John H	82	clerk	38	
V	McWilliams Margaret E-†	82	housewife	33	"
W	Howard Bridget F—†	84	"	55	"
X	Howard Frances M—†	84	WAVE	25	..
Y	Howard John C	84	cable splicer	58	"
Z	Thibeault Dorothea—†	84	housewife	28	"
	1538				
A	Thibeault Leo W	84	U S A	29	"
B	Gallagher Jean E—†	87	machinist	21	"
C	Kelly Beatrice—†	87	housewife	49	"
D	Kelly Richard F	87	custodian	49	"
E	Colucci Helene—†	87	housewife	57	"
F	Colucci Louis	87	tilesetter	57	"
G	Buchanan Solange—†	87	housewife	30	"
H	Buchanan William	87	operator	36	"
K	McGurin Cecelia—†	91	housewife	32	"
L	McGurin Charles	91	repairman	28	"
M	Lewis Eva M—†	91	housewife	44	"
N	Lewis Glenn	91	operator	54	"
O	Ahern Margaret—†	95	housewife	47	"
P	Guglielmo Anthony	97	U S N	30	
R	Guglielmo Florence—†	97	clerk	27	"
S	Romolo John	97	clergyman	59	422 Chelsea
T	Rothwell Louis J	97	repairman	42	here
U	Rothwell Mary—†	97	housewife	41	"
V	Rothwell Robert J	97	U S N	20	"

Milton Street

W	Colosi Frank	30	U S A	20	here
X	Colosi Salvatore	30	shipwright	49	"
Y	LaFay Fred	30	millhand	34	"
Z	*LaFay Thomas	30	laborer	57	"

Page.	Letter.	FULL NAME.	Residence, Jan. 1, 1945.	Occupation.	Supposed Age.	Reported Residence, Jan. 1, 1944. Street and Number.

1539
Milton Street—Continued

A	Wilbur Evelyn—†	30	housewife	25	here
B	Wilbur Fred	30	U S A	33	"
C	Robicheau Dorothy—†	34	housewife	45	"
D	Robicheau Peter	34	laborer	43	
E	Robicheau Peter	34	U S A	22	
F	Robicheau Wilbur	34	U S M C	20	"
G	Marcella Charles	38	painter	40	"
H	Marcella Charlotte—†	38	housewife	39	"
L	Warrino Annariso—†	45	"	38	
M	Warrino Domenic	45	oiler	50	
N	Marotta Pasquale	45	U S A	28	
O	Marotta Ruth—†	45	housewife	25	"
P	Romano Angelina—†	45	stitcher	36	"
R	Romano Salvatore	45	cleaner	53	"
S	Incrovato Frank	45	shipfitter	30	202 Havre
T	Incrovato Mary—†	45	housewife	28	202 "
U	Callahan Catherine—†	134	at home	71	here
V	Flynn Mary—†	134	millhand	44	"
W	Sammon Christopher	137	machinist	42	"
X	Sammon James	137	fireman	51	"
Y	Sammon Joseph	137	operator	48	"
Z	Sammon Mary F—†	137	housewife	78	"

1540   Moore Street

A	Greenwood Mary B—†	73	housekeeper	41	here
B	Shannon Arthur C	73	engineer	35	"
C	Shannon Catherine—†	73	housewife	74	"
D	Shannon Francis T	73	engineer	32	"
E	McCaffrey Annie G—†	75	at home	78	"
F	Rich Evelyn C—†	75	housewife	37	"
G	Rich Frank J	75	contractor	42	"
H	Sheehan James H	75	bookkeeper	44	"
K	Carlton Ellen F—†	76	tel operator	44	"
L	Carlton Mary A—†	76	stenographer	21	"
M	Sullivan Anna M—†	76	at home	31	"
N	Sullivan Florence W	76	pilot	64	
O	Sullivan Margaret H—†	76	at home	33	"
P	Sullivan Mary A—†	76	"	43	
R	Stott Jessie G—†	78	housewife	35	"

Page.	Letter.	FULL NAME.	Residence, Jan. 1, 1945.	Occupation.	Supposed Age.	Reported Residence, Jan. 1, 1944. Street and Number.

Moore Street—Continued

s	Stott John W	78	machinist	37	here
u	Scott Dorothy—†	84	housewife	31	"
v	Scott Herbert	84	machinist	31	"
w	Stott Charlotte E—†	84	housewife	44	"
x	Stott Harry	84	mechanic	65	"
y	Porter Elda F—†	88	housewife	34	"
z	Porter William J	88	chemist	34	"
	1541				
b	Vieira Joseph	91	plumber	42	Saugus
c	Vieira Maria—†	91	housewife	70	"
d	Dimond Daniel L	92	B F D	69	here
e	Dimond Margaret E—†	92	housewife	68	"
f	Curran Edgar L	92	supt	58	"
g	Curran Mary M—†	92	housewife	61	"
h	Carroll Evelyn—†	93	"	24	
k	Carroll James	93	electrician	30	"
l	Coredio Agnes G—†	96	housewife	37	"
m	Coredio Joseph C	96	assembler	39	"
n	Fougere Ethel—†	98	housewife	42	"
o	Fougere Philip A	98	seaman	44	"
p	*Dunn James	106	retired	84	74 Homer
r	*Dunn Josephine—†	106	housewife	67	74 "
s	Riley Helen T—†	106	"	36	here
t	Riley Thomas A, jr	106	machinist	37	"
u	Costa Theresa—†	107	housewife	26	"
v	Costa Vincent	107	fireman	27	"
w	Costa Agnes M—†	107	housewife	48	"
x	Costa John J	107	janitor	56	
y	Costa Manuel	107	retired	58	
z	Costa Richard J	107	U S C G	21	"
	1542				
a	Joyce Marion—†	108	housewife	28	"
b	Joyce Thomas	108	mechanic	27	"
c	Cotte Joseph	108	carpenter	39	"
d	Cotte Julia—†	108	housewife	39	"
e	McCauley John	109	U S A	45	"
f	*McCauley Mary—†	109	housewife	75	"
g	McCauley Mary J—†	109	tel operator	42	"
h	Raymond Ivy—†	109	housewife	41	"
k	Raymond Lyman	109	manager	42	"
l	Gillis Ann—†	110	tel operator	46	"

Moore Street—Continued

M	Gillis Anthony	110	letter carrier	44	here
N	Cerella Ann—†	111	stitcher	31	"
O	Rubino Antonio	111	laborer	55	"
P	Rubino Geraldine—†	111	saleswoman	20	"
R	Rubino Josephine—†	111	operator	22	"
S	*Rubino Philomena—†	111	housewife	63	"
T	Donahue Elizabeth M—†	111	"	42	"
U	Donahue George F	111	engineer	44	"
V	Currie Henry	112	fireman	47	"
W	Currie Mildred E—†	112	housewife	44	"
X	Currie William J	112	engineer	22	"
Y	McClellan Frances—†	113	operator	20	431 Frankfort
Z	McClellan Henry	113	machinist	49	431 "
	1543				
A	Boyd Elizabeth—†	113	matron	52	here
B	Edwards George	114	metalworker	36	"
C	Edwards Jessie—†	114	at home	75	"
D	Edwards Gertrude—†	114	housewife	32	"
E	Edwards Walter	114	U S C G	42	"
F	Holden Michael	114	machinist	27	"
G	Holden William	114	ironworker	25	"
H	Driscoll Nellie—†	115	housewife	67	"
K	Driscoll Timothy J	115	clerk	67	
L	Hawco Angela R—†	115	supervisor	37	"
M	Hawco Mary B—†	115	housewife	73	"
N	Hawco Mary L—†	115	at home	34	"
O	Hawco Thomas	115	fireman	70	"
P	Green Mary—†	116	millhand	51	"
R	Green William F, jr	116	U S A	21	
S	Nickerson Harold L	116	fishcutter	46	"
T	Burns Edward	116	laborer	33	
X	Sullivan Christopher D	120	painter	53	
Y	Sullivan Elizabeth A—†	120	housewife	53	"

1544   Short Street

B	Miles Catherine A—†	4	at home	76	here
C	Miles Ruth E—†	4	nurse	32	"
D	Miles Sylvester C	4	U S A	34	"
E	Shattuck George A	4	seaman	40	"
F	Shattuck Lillian M—†	4	housewife	38	"

Wordsworth Street

G	Benoit Augustus	125	chauffeur	30	here
H	Benoit James	125	U S N	24	"
K	Benoit Joseph	125	operator	61	"
L	Benoit Mary—†	125	housewife	30	"
M	Mottala Angelina—†	125	bookkeeper	26	"
N	Mottala Angeline—†	125	housewife	53	"
O	Mottala Jeremiah	125	shoemaker	53	"
P	Mottala Joseph	125	U S A	23	"
R	Mottala Michael	125	U S N	21	
S	Russo Frank	125	plasterer	49	"
T	Russo Guy	125	U S N	23	"
U	Russo Mary—†	125	housewife	45	"
V	Russo Paul	125	U S N	21	
W	Doyle Alfred F	127	shipfitter	25	"
X	Doyle Anna M—†	127	housewife	30	"
Y	Doyle Eleanor C—†	127	houseworker	22	"
Z	Doyle Joseph	127	carpenter	33	"

1545

A	Doyle Thomas N	127	shipfitter	27	"
B	Gormley John	128	longshoreman	40	"
C	Gormley John, jr	128	clerk	21	
D	Gormley Mary—†	128	housewife	40	"
E	Lupi Adeline—†	128	"	53	
F	Lupi Anthony	128	U S A	32	"
G	Lupi Helen—†	128	housewife	23	"
H	Lupi Henry	128	clerk	25	"
K	Lupi Nicholas	128	shoeworker	56	"
L	Rawson Mildred V—†	130	packer	47	
M	Rawson William J	130	chauffeur	58	"
N	Rawson William J, jr	130	"	20	"
R	Gannon Austin	142	U S A	22	"
S	Gannon Mary—†	142	clerk	49	"
T	Gannon Mary—†	142	checker	20	"
U	Morrison Edward R	142	chipper	38	
V	Morrison Helen M—†	142	housewife	31	"
W	Andrews Ernest	148	carpenter	61	"
X	Andrews Helen—†	148	housewife	47	"
Y	Desautelle Cecil S	148	U S A	30	"
Z	Desautelle Ruby I—†	148	inspector	30	"

1546

A	McCarthy Dennis F	148	retired	73	"

Page.	Letter.	FULL NAME.	Residence, Jan. 1, 1945.	Occupation.	Supposed Age.	Reported Residence, Jan. 1, 1944. Street and Number.

Wordsworth Street—Continued

	B	McCarthy Josephine—†	148	housewife	77	here
	C	Pearson Alice C—†	154	"	46	"
	D	Pearson Arthur	154	bridgetender	46	"
	E	O'Kane James	158	caretaker	72	"
	F	O'Kane Mary—†	158	housewife	69	"
	G	Hagemeister Eleanor G–†	178	"	31	
	H	Hagemeister Frederick J	178	mechanic	31	"
	K	Nutile John R	178	chauffeur	34	"
	L	Nutile Mary F—†	178	housewife	33	"
	M	Potter Edith E—†	182	"	63	
	N	Potter Hannah M—†	182	at home	38	"
	O	Potter Joseph E	182	agent	61	...
	P	Potter William R	182	U S A	25	
	R	Breault John R	185	welder	37	
	S	Breault Phyllis—†	185	housewife	31	"
	T	Maglio Ellen—†	185	clerk	21	..
	U	Maglio Louis	185	barber	29	
	V	Maglio Michael	185	candymaker	56	"
	W	Potter Edith E—†	186	housewife	63	"
	X	Potter Hannah M—†	186	"	38	
	Y	Potter Joseph E	186	agent	61	
	Z	Potter William R	186	U S A	25	
		1547				
	A	Kacos Carl	189	proprietor	40	"
	B	Kacos Louise—†	189	housewife	38	"
	C	Colantino Ann—†	189	"	29	
	D	Colantino John	189	mechanic	34	"

Ward 1–Precinct 16

CITY OF BOSTON

LIST OF RESIDENTS
20 YEARS OF AGE AND OVER

(NON-CITIZENS INDICATED BY ASTERISK)
(FEMALES INDICATED BY DAGGER)

AS OF

JANUARY 1, 1945

THOMAS F. SULLIVAN, *Chairman*
FREDERIC E. DOWLING, *Secretary*
WILLIAM A. MOTLEY, JR.
FRANCIS B. McKINNEY
EVERETT R. PROUT

Listing P d.

CITY OF BOSTON ⬤ PRINTING DEPARTM

1600
Addison Street

B	Fagone Delia—†	81	inspector	36	here
C	Mingotti Frances—†	81	operator	29	"
D	*Mingotti Gilda—†	81	housewife	62	"
E	Mingotti Mary—†	81	clerk	35	
F	*Mikus Emily—†	95–97	weaver	59	
G	*Pontolilo Teufila—†	95–97	"	78	"
H	Higgins George	95–97	laborer	40	
K	Higgins Mary—†	95–97	cleaner	44	''
L	Geremonte Agnes I—†	95–97	housewife	57	"
M	Geremonte Joseph	95–97	guard	57	
N	Biskupek Annie—†	95–97	weaver	51	
O	Biskupek Walter	95–97	welder	53	
P	Biskupek Wanda—†	95–97	beautician	27	"
R	Cross Mary—†	95–97	housewife	23	"
S	Cross Richard	95–97	rigger	30	
T	Suozzo Angela—†	95–97	inspector	41	"
U	Suozzo Anthony	95–97	U S N	21	"
V	Suozzo Jessie—†	95–97	technician	22	"
W	Ulm Phoebe M—†	95–97	housewife	35	Chelsea
X	Ulm William F	95–97	U S N	32	"
Z	Cook Flora—†	95–97	millhand	70	here

1601

A	Cataldo Albert F	95–97	laborer	40	
B	Cataldo Dorothy—†	95–97	housewife	35	"
C	*Brown Alexandra—†	95–97	"	37	
D	Colosi Antoinette—†	95–97	"	42	"
E	Contois Rose—†	95–97	"	23	Lawrence
F	Zebniak Tillie—†	95–97	"	37	here
G	Zebniak Wasel	95–97	millhand	48	"
H	Lynch Lorraine—†	99	clerk	20	"
K	O'Connell Mary—†	99	housewife	33	"
L	O'Connell Peter F	99	machinist	35	"
M	Waterman Ethel—†	101	housewife	50	"
N	Rich Alice—†	103	"	25	Chelsea
O	Rich Robert J	103	molder	29	"
P	*Ferman Helen—†	105	housewife	42	here
R	Ferman William	105	chauffeur	33	"
S	Michalopulos Andrew	113	machinist	51	"
T	Michalopulos Sophie—†	113	housewife	54	"
U	Mason Marie—†	117	weaver	65	"

2

Addison Street—Continued

	w	Lada Stella—†	117	weaver	48	115 Temple
	x	Gatta Evelyn—†	117	waitress	43	here
	y	Silver Harriet—†	121	housewife	32	"
	z	Silver William	121	shipfitter	38	"
1602						
	A	Gilleo Joseph	125	operator	52	"
	B	Gilleo Mary M—†	125	housewife	37	"
	C	Condon Catherine—†	131	cashier	47	"
	D	Condon Elizabeth—†	131	saleswoman	51	"
	E	Condon Joanna—†	131	cashier	49	
	F	Condon Mary—†	131	housewife	66	"
	G	Cox Edward J	135	U S C G	21	"
	H	Cox Estelle R—†	135	housewife	48	"
	K	Cox George L	135	policeman	49	"
	L	Cox George L, jr	135	U S A	20	
	M	Cox Margaret F—†	135	typist	22	

Bennington Street

	P	Calhoun George W	600	U S A	39	here
	R	Calhoun Jean E—†	600	housewife	39	"
	S	McCarthy Francis G	602	U S N	24	"
	T	Milward Anna P—†	602	clerk	28	
	U	Milward Edward M	602	"	52	··
	V	Milward Marcella L—†	602	housewife	61	"
	W	Cestroni Achille	604	carpenter	49	"
	X	Cestroni Concetta—†	604	housewife	41	"
	Y	Ferrari Anthony	604	mason	66	
	Z	Costello Benjamin	606	longshoreman	41	"
1603						
	A	Costello Mary E—†	606	housewife	34	"
	B	Dalton Agnes—†	606	"	32	··
	C	Dalton Edward E	606	U S N	37	
	D	Sullivan Mary A—†	606	housewife	59	"
	E	Ward Albert	606	longshoreman	27	Winthrop
	F	Ward Mary—†	606	housewife	25	"
	G	Sullivan Henry	610	fireman	54	here
	H	Forster Gertrude M—†	610	housewife	26	"
	K	Forster William J	610	U S A	26	"
	L	Vargus Cecilia A—†	610	housewife	43	"
	M	Vargus Joseph G	610	operator	48	"

3

Bennington Street—Continued

N	Cody Lorraine M—†	614	housewife	26	here
O	Cody Walter L	614	machinist	28	"
P	Follo Carlo	614	shipwright	40	"
R	Follo Carmella—†	614	clerk	34	"
S	*Follo Mary—†	614	housewife	68	"
T	Moynihan Cornelius J	614	U S A	24	357 Chelsea
U	Moynihan Elizabeth F—†	614	housewife	52	357 "
V	Moynihan Francis W	614	U S A	22	357 "
Z	Gately George L	624	U S N	48	here

1604

A	Hulke Almeda—†	624	housewife	50	"
B	Hulke Ruth G—†	624	bookkeeper	24	"
C	McGinn Thelma—†	624	WAVE	27	"
D	D'Amico Anna M—†	624	clerk	23	
E	D'Amico Delia—†	624	housewife	47	"
F	D'Amico Pasquale	624	custodian	52	"
G	D'Amico Ralph	624	U S A	24	
H	D'Amico Theresa M—†	624	secretary	21	"
K	Dooley John J	626	burner	45	"
L	Dooley Mary—†	626	housewife	76	"
M	Healy John H	626	metalworker	69	"
N	Healy Mabel—†	626	housewife	57	"
O	Garden Manuel	626	welder	39	
P	Garden Mary—†	626	housewife	28	"
R	Levangie Joseph D	628	salesman	55	"
S	Levangie Margaret A—†	628	housewife	56	"
T	Terrio John	628	operator	51	"
U	Terrio Mary G—†	628	housewife	47	"
V	Lanzilli Frank	628	welder	34	
W	Lanzilli Lucy—†	628	housewife	29	"
X	Whalen Henry J	630	chauffeur	44	"
Y	Whalen Louise—†	630	housewife	43	"
Z	Souza Elizabeth M—†	630	"	24	"

1605

A	Souza Frances K—†	630	clerk	22	"
B	Souza George L	630	longshoreman	49	"
C	Souza Henry T	630	U S A	27	"
D	Souza Mary G—†	630	housewife	48	"
E	Strangie Augustino	630	salesman	31	"
F	Strangie Margaret—†	630	housewife	30	"
G	McHatton Alexander J	632	packer	59	

Bennington Street—Continued

H	McHatton Mary—†	632	housewife	64	here
K	*Korsak Anna—†	632	"	68	"
L	*Korsak Roman	632	tester	68	"
M	Statkum Josephine—†	632	at home	40	"
N	Tracia Charles	632	chauffeur	44	"
O	Tracia Marcella—†	632	housewife	44	"
P	Keane Anna—†	634	"	40	..
R	Keane James D	634	millwright	41	"
S	Flynn Amy—†	634	housewife	36	"
T	Flynn James E	634	starter	43	
U	Livesey Hannah—†	634	housewife	59	"
V	Livesey Robert	634	clerk	59	
X	Hunter David W	656	"	40	
Y	Hunter Mary M—†	656	housewife	40	"
Z	Ferriera Joseph	656	fireman	54	"

1606

A	Ferriera Joseph, jr	656	U S A	21	
B	Ferriera Mary—†	656	housewife	39	"
C	Berube Evelyn—†	656	"	48	
D	Berube Gabrielle—†	656	spinner	20	"
E	Berube Lionel	656	U S A	26	
F	Berube Pierce	656	machinist	48	"
G	Lombardo Theresa—†	656	housekeeper	21	"
H	Mercurio Frederick	656	U S N	24	
K	Mercurio Simone—†	656	housewife	22	"
L	Morrissette Alfred	656	U S A	26	
M	Morrissette Loretta—†	656	clerk	28	
N	Schleicher Carl H	660	retired	76	
O	Schleicher Charlotte R—†	660	clerk	52	"
P	Schleicher Teresa M—†	660	housewife	78	"
R	Schleicher Henry	660	chauffeur	44	"
S	Schleicher Margaret—†	660	housewife	33	"
T	Moran Edmund F	664	physician	63	"
U	Moran Edmund F, jr	664	U S N	26	
V	Moran Grace E—†	664	housewife	49	"
W	Moran Mary B—†	664	student	23	"
X	Stapleton Mary B—†	664	housekeeper	58	"
Y	Adamo Annie—†	666	housewife	53	"
Z	*Adamo Carmen	666	laborer	61	

1607

A	Adamo Marion—†	666	dressmaker	26	"

Page.	Letter.	FULL NAME.	Residence, Jan. 1, 1945.	Occupation.	Supposed Age.	Reported Residence, Jan. 1, 1944. Street and Number.

Bennington Street—Continued

	B	Adamo Peter	666	plumber	31	here
	D	Santamaria Amelia—†	668	housewife	59	"
	E	Santamaria Arthur	668	U S A	30	"
	F	Santamaria Beatrice—†	668	clerk	22	
	C	Santamaria Michael	668	barber	67	"
	G	Bagley Frieda E—†	670	housewife	40	"
	H	Bagley James E, jr	670	attorney	44	"
	K	Gorman Barbara—†	670	at home	31	"
	L	Gorman Peter	670	retired	76	"
	M	Coluntino Helen—†	678	housewife	31	"
	N	Coluntino Ralph P	678	painter	37	"
	O	Frongillo Armando	678	dishwasher	33	"
	P	Frongillo Florence—†	678	stitcher	26	"
	R	De Leo Lena—†	678	housewife	54	"
	S	De Leo Pasquale	678	carpenter	56	"
	T	Fernandez Claire—†	680	clerk	20	
	U	Souza Blanche—†	680	inspector	30	"
	V	Souza Julia—†	680	housewife	57	"
	W	Roach Elizabeth—†	680	"	70	
	X	Roach George	680	carpenter	57	"
	Y	Brock Catherine M—†	680	housewife	24	Winthrop
	Z	Brock Chester D	680	brakeman	30	"
1608						
	A	Currie Lillian—†	682	housewife	31	here
	B	Currie Wallace W	682	policeman	37	"
	C	Edwards Katherine T—†	682	housekeeper	64	"
	D	O'Connell Mary F—†	682	"	68	
	E	Cain Bernard J	684	machinist	52	"
	F	Cain Eileen A—†	684	housewife	42	"
	G	Western Edmund	686	carpenter	67	"
	H	Western Lena—†	686	housewife	70	"
	K	De Rosa Anthony	688	welder	31	
	L	De Rosa Evelyn—†	688	housewife	36	"
	M	Burke John	690	salesman	55	"
	N	*Burke Nora—†	690	housewife	47	"
	O	Burke Thomas J	690	laborer	44	"
	P	Nichols Joseph L	690	chauffeur	50	"
	R	Nichols Kathleen J—†	690	housewife	46	"
	S	Duff James M	692	printer	54	
	T	Duff Sarah J—†	692	housewife	54	"

6

Page.	Letter.	FULL NAME.	Residence, Jan. 1, 1945.	Occupation.	Supposed Age.	Reported Residence, Jan. 1, 1944. Street and Number.

Byron Street

	u	Maggiore Anthony	45	U S A	25	here
	v	Maggiore Antonio	45	tailor	53	"
	w	Maggiore Imprimo	45	U S A	28	"
	x	Maggiore Marie—†	45	teacher	29	"
	y	Maggiore Nellie—†	45	housewife	52	"
	z	Cataldo Charles	48	U S A	35	
1609						
	a	Cataldo Helene—†	48	housewife	34	"
	b	Merullo Attilio	49	painter	37	8 Orient av
	c	Merullo Mercedes—†	49	housewife	31	8 "
	d	*Merullo Angelina—†	49	"	59	here
	e	Merullo Carmen	49	laborer	60	"
	f	Merullo Carmen, jr	49	U S N	21	"
	g	Merullo Jennie—†	49	clerk	25	
	h	Merullo Manuel	49	"	24	..
	k	Carlsen George	52	laborer	42	"
	l	Carlsen Isabella M—†	52	housewife	41	"
	m	*Cataldo Luigo	52	retired	80	
	n	Croce Charles	52	U S A	26	"
	o	Croce June—†	52	housewife	22	"
	p	Cardarelli Giovaninna—†	53	at home	60	"
	r	Giardullo Emma—†	53	housewife	31	"
	s	Giardullo Leo	53	agent	32	
	t	Wilcox Agnes—†	55	housewife	63	"
	u	Wilcox Daniel R	55	U S A	21	
	v	Wilcox Gifford D	55	foreman	62	"
	w	Wilcox Stella M—†	55	packer	26	..
	x	Russo Anna—†	· 56	housewife	33	"
	y	Russo Charles	56	tester	38	..
	z	*Cornetta Mary—†	56	at home	82	"
1610						
	a	Mazza Francis	56	U S A	30	
	b	Mazza Mary—†	56	operator	51	"
	c	Mazza Mary A—†	56	inspector	27	"
	d	Mazza Nicholas	56	U S A	24	
	e	Mazza Rita—†	56	lampmaker	22	"
	f	Alleas John M	57	mechanic	68	"
	g	Alleas Rose—†	57	housewife	65	"
	h	Cahill Herbert C	59	guard	68	
	k	Cahill Rita T—†	59	inspector	22	"

Byron Street—Continued

L	Cahill Sophie M—†	59	housewife	63	here
M	Cahill Thomas L	59	U S N	29	"
N	Cahill William J	59	"	24	"
O	Chase Robert	60	welder	23	
P	Geggis Mary—†	60	housewife	45	"
R	Geggis William	60	pipefitter	53	"
S	Geggis William, jr	60	U S M C	20	"
T	Fennelly Andrew	61	U S A	26	
U	Fennelly Dennis J	61	fisherman	54	"
V	Fennelly Sarah—†	61	inspector	50	"
W	Joy Gerald	61	U S A	24	
X	Joy Margaret—†	61	operator	23	"
Y	Grillo Emily—†	64	housewife	25	"
Z	Grillo Jack	64	U S N	26	

1611

A	Stoia Veronica—†	64	housewife	67	"
B	Stoia William	64	U S A	29	
C	Cabral Francis	64	U S N	25	
D	Cabral Lillian—†	64	housewife	23	"
E	Molino Anna—†	64	shoeworker	24	"
F	Molino Frank	64	"	50	
G	Molino Ida—†	64	housewife	42	"
H	Venezia Edna—†	66	housekeeper	39	"
K	Venezia Mary—†	66	clerk	41	"
L	Venezia Nellie—†	66	stitcher	48	"
M	*Venezia Victoria—†	66	housewife	74	"
N	Mazzola Mary—†	66	"	29	
O	Mazzola Michael	66	laborer	36	
P	Wilkes William J	66	manager	62	"
R	Wright Basil	66	welder	39	"
S	Wright Ruth—†	66	housewife	32	"
T	Marcantonio Dora—†	67	"	57	
U	Marcantonio Gistie	67	U S A	26	"
V	Marcantonio Louis	67	barber	61	"
W	Marcantonio Marguerite—†	67	packer	20	
X	Dirito Dominic	67	U S N	24	"
Y	*Dirito Rose—†	67	wrapper	51	"
Z	Pagliacci Dominic	67	welder	52	

1612

A	*Isasi Antonio	67	repairman	55	"
B	*Isasi Paula—†	67	housewife	40	"

Byron Street—Continued

c	Morse Daniel	68	longshoreman	44	here
d	Morse Mary F—†	68	saleswoman	48	"
e	Barker George H	68	letter carrier	38	"
f	Barker Harry	68	retired	66	
g	Barker Henry R	68	U S A	36	
h	Barker Susan—†	68	housewife	58	"
k	Zeppernick Robert	68	U S C G·	28	"
l	Zeppernick Ruth—†	68	housewife	29	"
m	Wilcox Fannie—†	70	"	26	
n	Wilcox John H	70	driller	32	
o	Dagnelli Dominic	70	mechanic	41	"
p	Dagnelli Mary—†	70	housewife	45	"
r	DiOrio Mary—†	70	at home	77	"
s	Iannone Dominic	70	mason	51	
t	Rutledge Arthur, jr	71	U S A	24	
u	Rutledge Arthur E	71	rigger	50	
v	Rutledge Catherine B—†	71	tel operator	21	"
w	Rutledge Mildred N—†	71	stenographer	23	"
x	Rutledge Nora C—†	71	housewife	47	"
y	Vecchio Josephine—†	72	"	29	
z	Vecchio Vincent A	72	millhand	31	"
	1613				
a	Vecchio John	72	candymaker	53	"
b*	Vecchio Marie—†	72	housewife	53	"
c	Vecchio Susan—†	72	shoeworker	25	"
d	Vecchio Vito H	72	U S A	23	
e	McIntyre Anna W—†	74	housewife	34	"
f	McIntyre John A	74	shipfitter	34	"
g	Jackson John H	74	ironworker	68	"
h*	Jackson Mary L—†	74	housewife	60	"
k	MacLean Arthur F	74	U S A	34	
l	MacLean Eileen M—†	74	clerk	32	"
m	Dorgan Anna—†	76	furrier	60	
n	Flanigan Anna—†	76	housewife	48	"
o	Flanigan Charles	76	plumber	58	"
p	Flanigan Charles H, jr	76	U S N	21	"
r	Flanigan Elinor—†	76	stenographer	24	"
s	Flanigan Laura—†	76	housewife	53	"
t	Belange Anthony	77	plumber	52	"
u	Belange Joseph	77	U S C G	24	"
v	Belange Lucy—†	77	housewife	52	"

Byron Street—Continued

w	Belange Mary—†	77	clerk	26	here
x	Sutton Eleanor—†	77	housewife	20	"
y	Sutton Julius C	77	U S N	24	"
z	Belange John	77	weaver	45	
	1614				
A	Belange Peter P	77	custodian	47	1004 Benningt'n
B	Cardillo Joseph	77	electrician	42	here
c	Cardillo Lucy—†	77	housewife	42	"
D	Maraio Rosalie M—†	77	clerk	23	"
E	Maraio Vincent	77	U S A	24	
F	Necco Annette F—†	79	housewife	58	"
G	Necco Claire E—†	79	"	26	"
H	Necco John, jr	79	policeman	31	"
K	McDuffie Catherine—†	79	nurse	33	
L	McDuffie Daniel B	79	electrician	39	"
M	Mazza Angelina—†	81	weaver	41	
N	Mazza Joseph	81	painter	49	
o	McCormack Laura—†	81	dressmaker	55	"
P	McCormack Mary—†	81	shoeworker	50	"
R	Connelly Anna—†	83	housewife	43	"
s	Connelly Thomas J	83	chauffeur	40	"
T	Lane Frederick J	84	salesman	50	"
U	Lane Helen E—†	84	physician	24	"
v	Lane Dorothy—†	84	secretary	38	"
w	Lane Ella G—†	84	nurse	40	
x	Lane Mary—†	84	clerk	35	"
Y	Lane Mary E—†	84	housewife	75	"
z	Lane Thomas F	84	retired	80	
	1615				
A	Olson Ellen G—†	84	housekeeper	35	"
B	McIntire Alice E—†	85	housewife	40	"
c	McIntire Frank C	85	chauffeur	39	"
D	Lahti Charles A	85	shipper	43	"
E	*Lahti Taimi —†	85	housewife	41	"
F	Bobrek Edward	87	U S A	32	"
G	*Bobrek John	87	laborer	63	"
H	Cronin Ann—†	87	housewife	35	"
K	Cronin John W	87	laborer	37	
L	Bois Ernest	89	pedler	45	"
M	Bois Sarah—†	89	housewife	45	"
N	Bois Louis	89	retired	53	

Byron Street—Continued

	o	Bois Melvina—†	89	weaver	52	here
	p	Gannon Mary—†	90	housewife	38	"
	r	Gannon Robert	90	machinist	43	"
	t	Graves Lester	94	foreman	41	"
	u	Graves Mary I—†	94	housewife	40	"
	v	Abrahams Joseph W	94	longshoreman	52	"
	w	Abrahams Lillian S—†	94	housewife	44	"
	x	DiCicco Anna—†	94	operator	37	"
	y	Madden John	94	longshoreman	28	"
	z	Madden Theresa—†	94	housewife	28	"

1616

	b	Aikens Irene—†	96	"	38	
	c	Aikens Leo	96	manager	40	"
	d	Amirault Cyrus	96	shipworker	50	"
	e	Amirault Gertrude—†	96	housewife	47	"
	f	Amirault Raymond	96	U S N	21	
	g	Amirault Robert	96	"	21	
	h	Amirault Walter	96	"	20	
	k	McNeil Anna—†	96	laundress	50	"
	l	Forrest Edward	96	U S A	26	"
	m	Forrest Frances—†	96	clerk	28	
	n	Powers Christina—†	96	housewife	48	"
	o	Powers Francis	96	retired	60	
	p	Powers Joseph	96	U S A	23	
	r	Powers William	96	"	30^	"
	s	Cuneo Alfred	97	soapmaker	46'	"
	t	Cuneo Alfred, jr	97	U S A	26	
	u	Cuneo Catherine—†	97	clerk	27	"
	v	Cuneo Helen—†	97	housewife	45	"
	w	Cuneo Joseph	97	chauffeur	22	"
	x	O'Donnell Catherine—†	104	housewife	82	"
	y	O'Donnell James F	104	clerk	47	"
	z	Prendergast Frances—†	104	stenographer	44	"

1617

	a	Prendergast Patricia—†	104	at home	22	"
	b	Akins Emma—†	106	operator	28	"
	c	Akins John	106	U S A	25	
	d	Ciarlone Anna—†	106	housewife	33	"
	e	Ciarlone Clara—†	106	at home	20	"
	f	Ciarlone Linda—†	106	housewife	57	"
	g	Ciarlone William	106	clerk	33	

Page:	Letter	FULL NAME.	Residence, Jan. 1, 1945.	Occupation.	Supposed Age.	Reported Residence, Jan. 1, 1944. Street and Number.

Byron Street—Continued

H	Nicewonger Audrey—†	106	secretary	25	here
K	Nicewonger Jack	106	U S A	33	"
L	Daly Emma—†	106	housewife	24	"
M	Demarco Clara—†	106	"	85	
N	Demarco Guido	106	guard	52	"
O	Leone Anthony	108	laborer	55	177 Condor
P	Leone Jennie—†	108	waitress	24	177 "
R	Leone Lena—†	108	housewife	47	177 "
S	Leone Matthew	108	U S N	22	177 "
T	Canavan Catherine—†	112	housewife	49	here
U	Canavan Joseph	112	retired	53	"
V	Canavan Joseph I	112	rigger	27	"
W	Turner Charles	112	accountant	38	"
X	Turner Lillian—†	112	housewife	35	"
Y	Thornton Edwin, jr	114	machinist	22	"
Z	Thornton Edwin J	114	shipfitter	49	"

1618

	Thornton Margaret—†	114	housewife	46	"
A	Morse Mary J—†	114	"	71	"
C	Morse William	114	clerk	46	
D	Impeduglia Carmella—†	127	"	26	
E	Impeduglia Sebastiana—†	127	housewife	72	"
F	Ciampa Helen—†	129	stenographer	33	"
G	Ciampa Jean—†	129	entertainer	23	"
H	Ciampa Jennie—†	129	housewife	63	"
K	Ciampa Rocco	129	retired	73	
L	Ciampa Theresa—†	129	seamstress	31	"
M	Laurano Lillian—†	129	housewife	26	20 Chelsea
N	Laurano Michael A, jr	129	U S N	28	20 "
O	Palozzi Anna—†	129	stitcher	23	here
P	Palozzi Josephine—†	129	housewife	49	"
R	Palozzi Lena—†	129	saleswoman	22	"
S	Palozzi Ralph	129	spinner	55	"
T	Palozzi Victor	129	U S A	26	

Moore Street

U	McDonald Alexander	1	retired	66	here
V	McDonald Emma—†	1	housewife	66	"
W	McDonald Emma T—†	1	clerk	37	"
X	McDonald Joseph R	1	chauffeur	39	"

Moore Street—Continued

Y	McNamara Mary—†	3	clerk	34	here
z	McNamara William E	3	pipefitter	42	"
1619						
A	McNamara William J	3	cook	69	"
B	Mack John T	5	shipfitter	48	742 Bennington
c	Thornton Annie I—†	5	housewife	49	742 "
D	Thornton William H	5	machinist	45	742 "
E	Uliano Helen—†	5	housewife	24	742 "
F	Uliano Joseph, jr	5	machinist	23	742 "
G	Kirby Edward F	5	U S N	23	Malden
H	Kirby Margaret J—†	5	housewife	20	here
K	LeBlanc Doris—†	5	leatherworker	24	"
L	LeBlanc James D	5	painter	54	"
M	LeBlanc Mary C—†	5	housewife	50	"
N	Carroll Genevieve—†	15	"	50	
o	Carroll James	15	engineer	57	"
P	Carroll John A	15	ironworker	59	"
R	Carroll Kenneth J	15	U S A	24	
s	Carroll Walter R	15	metalworker	47	"
T	Gillespie John P	15	forger	59	
U	McAleer Claire M—†	15	mechanic	20	"
w	Gillis Bertha—†	19	at home	75	21 Bullard
X	Lockwood Marie G—†	19	housewife	50	here
Y	Lockwood Ralph F	19	retired	50	"
z	MacMaster Charles H	19	painter	54	"
1620						
A	MacMaster Jane—†	19	milliner	52	"
B	Gleeson Margaret—†	21	tel operator	51	"
c	Gleeson Mary E—†	21	"	21	
D	Sullivan Louise—†	21	"	40	
E	Pike Campbell	25	deckhand	46	"
F*	Pike Mary—†	25	housewife	42	"
G	Gervizzi Pasquale	25	attorney	37	"
H	Cervizzi Thelma—†	25	housewife	31	"
K	Crowley Mary M—†	25	"	57	
L	Crowley Michael A	25	policeman	57	"
M	Flynn Alice C—†	27	housewife	38	"
N	McGeney Anna—†	27	cook	39	
o	McGeney Joseph	27	U S N	20	
P	Crowley Anna—†	27	housewife	52	"
R	Crowley Joseph A	27	U S N	31	

13

Moore Street—Continued

s	Fahey Elizabeth—†	27	clerk	24	New York
u	Doyle Anna—†	31	teacher	50	here
v	Doyle Gertrude—†	31	secretary	48	"
w	Doyle Joseph F	31	carpenter	49	"
x	Doyle Nora—†	31	housewife	79	"
z	Albano Flora—†	35	"	28	91 Moore
	1621				
A	Albano Genaros	35	U S A	31	91 "
B	DeLuca Anthony	35	chauffeur	32	here
C	DeLuca John	35	barber	52	"
D	DeLuca Mario	35	chauffeur	22	"
E	DeLuca Sophie—†	35	housewife	52	"
F	McCarthy Francis X	39	U S A	21	"
G	McCarthy Helen E—†	39	saleswoman	20	"
H	McCarthy Jennie E—†	39	housewife	40	"
K	McCarthy Timothy J	39	custodian	45	"
L	Connolly James E	63	clergyman	27	"
M	Ducie Mary—†	63	maid	48	332 Beacon
N	Flynn Leo	63	clergyman	45	here
O	McCarthy Patrick J	63	"	64	"
P	McDonough Delia—†	63	housekeeper	53	"

Saratoga Street

s	Newhook Arthur	716	engineer	41	here
T	Newhook Thomas	716	U S N	21	"
U	Keating Hattie—†	716	housewife	62	"
v	Keating James P	716	bartender	68	"
w	Galli Philip	718	mechanic	31	"
x	Galli Rita—†	718	saleswoman	28	"
Y	Malloy Anna—†	718	"	34	
z	Malloy John J	718	meatcutter	65	"
	1622				
A	Malloy Joseph	718	U S A	22	
B	Malloy Margaret—†	718	housewife	56	"
C	Malloy William	718	longshoreman	21	"
D	Bibber Caroline—†	718	housewife	59	"
E	Bibber Caroline—†	718	WAVE	22	
F	Bibber Edward	718	U S N	20	
G	Bibber James	718	U S A	27	"
H	Bibber Walter	718	U S C G	23	"

14

Saratoga Street—Continued

K	Ying Soo-Hoo-Moy	720	laundryman	33	here
L	Wing Yee Shun	720	"	38	".
M	Fronduto James	722	attendant	37	"
N	Fronduto Jennie—†	722	housewife	32	"
O	Stasio Annetta—†	722	"	44	
P	Stasio Anthony	722	machinist	20	"
R	Stasio Arthur	722	salesman	44	"
S	Chretien Lillian—†	722	housewife	23	"
T	Chretien Lucien	722	U S N	23	47 Monument
U	Lane John	722	"	27	Somerville
V	Lane Mary—†	722	housewife	27	here
W	Stasio Albert	722	U S N	24	"
X	Stasio Dominic	722	plumber	54	"
Y	Stasio Stella—†	722	housewife	52	"
Z	Hughes Catherine—†	724	"	63	

1623

A	Hughes John	724	millhand	25	"
B	Meehan Mary—†.	724	forewoman	43	"
C	Vitale Emma—†	724	inspector	31	"
D	Pedersen Louis	724	pipefitter	50	"
E	Pedersen Margaret—†	724	housewife	35	"
F	Connolly Mary—†	724	inspector	42	"
G	Young Anna R—†	724	housewife	42	"
H	Young Joseph P	724	shipper	47	"
L	Treanor Alice C—†	728	housekeeper	49	"
M	Gilgan Harriet—†	736	housewife	63	"
N	Gilgan James E	736	retired	67	
O	Lubofsky Julius	736	pipefitter	28	"
P	Lubofsky Louise—†	736	housewife	27	"
R	Rago Oreste	736	U S N	24	
S	Rago Patrick	736	"	28	
T	Rago Rose—†	736	housewife	52	"
V	Kelly Joseph E	740	U S A	23	"
W	Kelly Mary—†	740	stewardess	22	"
X	Kelly Mary E—†.	740	housewife	53	"
Y	Kelly Paul	740	U S A	26	
Z	Kelly William C	740	U S N	25	

1624

A	Hogan Cecilia F—†	740	bookkeeper	20	"
B	Hogan Margaret C—†	740	supervisor	24	"
C	Hogan Mary P—†	740	stenographer	22	"

15

Page.	Letter.	FULL NAME.	Residence, Jan. 1, 1945.	Occupation.	Supposed Age.	Reported Residence, Jan. 1, 1944. Street and Number.

Saratoga Street—Continued

	D	Hogan Mary T—†	740	housewife	49	here
	E	Hogan William T	740	B F D	50	"
	F	O'Brien William L	740	steamfitter	44	"
	G	Cohan Dorothy—†	740	bookkeeper	23	"
	H	Cohan Edna—†	740	"	25	..
	K	Cohan Theresa—†	740	housewife	47	"
	L	Cohan William	740	policeman	49	"
	M	Knox Doris—†	741	bookkeeper	22	"
	N	Rauth Florence—†	741	housewife	57	"
	O	Rauth William	741	operator	60	"
	P	Milward Louis A	742	watchman	61	"
	R	Milward Margaret W—†	742	housewife	51	"
	S	Milward Philip F	742	clerk	24	
	T	Milward William J	742	U S A	22	
	U	Eastwood Harry	745	U S M C	26	"
	V	Eastwood Malcolm	745	"	30	
	W	Byrnes Arthur	745	clerk	46	
	X	Fitzgerald William	745	chauffeur	52	"
	Y	Keenan Hannah—†	745	housewife	72	"
	Z	Keenan James	745	bartender	74	"
1625						
	A	Maher Bridget F—†	745	clerk	71	
	B	*Coscia Aurora—†	746	housewife	59	"
	C	*Coscia Generoso	746	laborer	73	
	D	Giuffre Josephine—†	746	housewife	25	"
	E	Giuffre Peter	746	metalworker	27	"
	F	Young Benjamin J	746	painter	52	
	G	Young Harold J	746	U S A	20	
	H	Young Mary E—†	746	housewife	55	"
	K	Morrison Herbert L	746	policeman	54	"
	L	Morrison Mildred E—†	746	housewife	44	"
	M	McQueeney John	749	retired	70	
	N	McQueeney Margaret—†	749	housewife	62	"
	O	McQueeney Margaret A-†	749	clerk	32	
	P	Crosby Marie—†	749	housewife	45	"
	R	Crosby Robert E	749	inspector	50	"
	S	Crosby Robert E, jr	749	U S A	20	"
	T	Crosby Catherine E—†	749	teacher	46	
	U	McGee Margaret—†	749	housewife	42	"
	V	McGee Michael	749	checker	45	"
	W	Hamilton Amy—†	750	matron	62	

16

Saratoga Street—Continued

x	Havey Helen E—†	750	housewife	31	here
y	Havey Walter	750	longshoreman	36	"
z	Coulombe Edward	750	U S A	34	"
	1626				
a	Coulombe Mary A—†	750	housewife	36	"
b	Hoey Amy M—†	750	"	33	
c	Hoey Matthew T	750	U S A	36	
d	Ackerman Rose—†	753	secretary	21	"
e	Park Mary—†	753	housekeeper	66	"
f	Balboni Fred J	753	policeman	36	"
g	Balboni Margaret—†	753	housewife	31	"
h	Hartnett William A	754	repairman	44	"
k	Spillane Lena—†	754	housekeeper	73	"
l	Pennell Eugene L	754	U S A	21	"
m	Pennell Marie J—†	754	inspector	45	"
n	Duffy Arthur J	754	foreman	61	"
o	Duffy Arthur J	754	U S A	30	
p	Duffy Ellen—†	754	housewife	54	"
r	Duffy James P	754	U S A	25	
s	Duffy Laura E—†	754	tel operator	22	"
t	Nugent Cecelia L—†	755	housewife	28	"
u	Nugent Mansell	755	policeman	27	"
v	Crowell Alfred J	755	U S A	27	756 Saratoga
w	Crowell Eileen W—†	755	clerk	28	756 "
x	Crowell Merle G	755	gardener	60	756 "
y	Crowell Murray A	755	U S A	25	756 '
z	Crowell Myrta E—†	755	housewife	56	756 "
	1627				
a	Berry Bridget—†	755	"	68	here
b	Berry Patrick	755	laborer	65	"
c	Sherwin Anna—†	755	housewife	34	"
d	Sherwin Joseph	755	longshoreman	33	"
e	Keough Mary C—†	756	housekeeper	77	"
f	Sparrow Katherine—†	756	"	63	California
g	Czarnetzki Agnes—†	756	housewife	44	here
h	Czarnetzki Augustine	756	machinist	44	"
k	Murphy Eva L—†	756	candymaker	65	"
l	Murphy Mary A—†	756	housekeeper	68	"
n	Donahue Bridget—†	759	"	80	849 Saratoga
o	Wessling Helen—†	759	housewife	38	849 "
p	Wessling William	759	foreman	44	849 "

Saratoga Street—Continued

R	McRae George	784	accountant	37	here
S	McRae Margaret—†	784	housewife	35	"
T	*Ruggerio Mary—†	784	"	49	"
U	Ruggerio Nicholas	784	laborer	50	
V	Samuelson Harold	784	U S N	26	"
W	Samuelson Lucy—†	784	housewife	24	Lynn
X	Donahue Gerard J	784	U S A	35	here
Y	Donahue Mary M—†	784	housewife	35	"
Z	Duffy Mary C—†	784	housekeeper	64	"

1628

A	Dini Angelo	786	waiter	58	
B	Dini Julia—†	786	housewife	49	"
C	McQueeney John, jr	786	clerk	32	
D	McQueeney Loretta M—†	786	housewife	32	"
E	Montanari Albina—†	786	typist	24	
F	Ortolan Bernard A	786	U S A	24	
G	Ortolan Elvira—†	786	housewife	24	"
H	Ortolan Julius	786	U S A	21	
K	Ortolan Peter	786	baker	49	
L	Donahue Cornelius V	788	foreman	64	"
M	Donahue John F	788	U S A	38	
N	Donahue Julia—†	788	housewife	89	"
O	Donahue Kathryn M—†	788	stenographer	48	"
P	Donahue Mary T—†	788	maid	67	..
R	Toomey Andrew J	788	letter carrier	64	"
S	Twomey Andrew J, jr	788	U S A	24	
T	Twomey Eleanor G—†	788	teacher	30	
U	Twomey Raymond A	788	U S A	28	"
V	Canino Charles	789	"	23	"
W	Canino Lillian—†	789	cleaner	20	"
X	Canino Susan—†	789	housewife	53	"
Y	Canino Thomas	789	shoeworker	53	"
Z	Pezzella Angelina—†	789	bookkeeper	32	"

1629

A	Silano Angelo	789	watchman	69	"
B	Silano Assunta—†	789	housewife	64	" '
C	Silano John	789	chauffeur	55	"
D	Terilli John	789	"	29	
E	Terilli Mary—†	789	housewife	24	"
F	Frazier John W	790	laborer	42	

18

Saratoga Street—Continued

	G	Gillespie John	790	trimmer	41	here
	H	Gillespie Mary L—†	790	housewife	36	"
	K	Gorman James A	790	repairman	59	"
	L	Gorman Louise H—†	790	housewife	58	"
	M	Howard John A	790	operator	50	"
	N	Howard Margaret J—†	790	housewife	33	"
	O	Hesenius Alfreda—†	790	"	27	
	P	Hesenius Lawrence	790	U S A	28	
	R	McCluskey Henry	790	"	34	
	S	McCluskey Rita—†	790	housewife	30	"
	T	O'Connell David	790	U S N	21	
	U	O'Connell Dorothy—†	790	clerk	25	
	V	*O'Connell Mary—†	790	housewife	65	"
	W	O'Connell Mary—†	790	millhand	25	"
	X	Osterhout Edison	790	U S A	33	
	Y	Osterhout Helen—†	790	housewife	33	"
	Z	*Buono Elvira—†	791	"	59	"
		1630				
	A	Buono Gabriel	791	shoeworker	34	"
	B	Buono Margaret—†	791	trimmer	22	"
	C	Buono Mildred—†	791	housewife	32	"
	D	Buono Pasquale	791	manager	37	"
	E	Silvio Guy	791	U S A	26	
	F	Silvio Sarah—†	791	stenographer	27	"
	G	Hourihan Annie—†	792	housewife	39	"
	H	Hourihan Joseph P	792	laborer	40	
	K	McLaughlin Dorothy—†	792	housewife	43	"
	L	McLaughlin Samuel	792	machinist	43	"
	M	Massa Gerado	793	welder	54	
	N	Massa Ida—†	793	housewife	55	"
	O	Massa Ralph	793	U S A	30	
	P	Powers Ellen—†	793	housewife	36	"
	R	Powers Patrck	793	rigger	34	
	S	Finn Margaret—†	794	clerk	60	
	T	Finn Katherine G—†	794	"	54	
	U	Necco Edward	795	operator	26	"
	V	Necco Irene—†	795	housewife	23	"
	W	Cuneo Eva—†	795	"	49	"
	X	Cuneo Frederick	795	operator	61	"
	Y	Cuneo Nellie—†	795	packer	56	

Page.	Letter.	FULL NAME.	Residence, Jan. 1, 1945.	Occupation.	Supposed Age.	Reported Residence, Jan. 1, 1944. Street and Number.

Saratoga Street—Continued

z	Canavan Anna L—†	796	secretary	47	here
	1631				
A	Walsh Mary L—†	796	housewife	54	"
B	Walsh Walter J	796	clerk	62	
C	Richardson Charles	796	foreman	51	"
D	Richardson Hazel—†	796	housewife	48	"
E	Moran Mary—†	797	housekeeper	55	"
F	Burke Eleanor—†	797	housewife	40	"
G	Burke James	797	U S A	20	"
H	*Rockliff Charles	797	retired	78	
L	Walsh Mary—†	799	housewife	37	"
M	Walsh Timothy	799	carpenter	40	"
N	Giardullo Frances—†	799	housewife	41	"
O	Giardullo Maria—†	799	"	72	
P	Giardullo Nazzario	799	operator	45	"
S	Phillips Catherina—†	801	boxmaker	53	"
T	Phillips Ernest	801	chauffeur	34	"
U	McLaughlin George W	801	bartender	48	"
V	Morey Emma G—†	801	clerk	51	
W	Barker Edwin J	801	retired	60	"
X	Barker Lillian G—†	801	housewife	56	"
Z	Barry Marie—†	803	operator	52	"
	1632				
A	Wellings Augustine	803	painter	64	"
B	Wellings Augustine J	803	U S A	23	"
C	Wellings Emily A—†	803	housewife	55	"
D	Wellings Emily P—†	803	WAVE	25	"
E	Wellings Mary—†	803	stenographer	21	"
K	*Capogreco Anna—†	809	housewife	47	"
L	Capogreco Nicodemo	809	carpenter	47	"
M	*Ciccia Angela—†	809	housewife	51	"
N	Ciccia John	809	clerk	22	"
O	Ciccia Nicholas	809	tailor	55	"
P	Bruzzese Filaberto	809	retired	53	
R	*Bruzzese Nancy—†	809	housewife	44	"
S	Scotti Angelina—†	810	"	44	
T	Scotti John	810	painter	45	"
U	Calla George	814	machinist	26	"
V	Calla Theresa—†	814	housewife	21	"
W	DiMinico Mary—†	814	"	37	
X	Haynes Frank	815	printer	51	

20

Page.	Letter.	Full Name.	Residence, Jan. 1, 1945.	Occupation.	Supposed Age.	Reported Residence, Jan. 1, 1944. Street and Number.

	Y	Haynes Margaret—†	815	housewife	50	here
	z	Kiley Bernice—†	815	"	26	"
1633						
	A	Iapicca Augustino	815	shoeworker	70	"
	B	Iapicca Nicholina—†	815	housewife	68	"
	c	Iapicca Samuel	815	barber	45	
	D	Iapicca Tancredi	815	U S A	35	
	E	Iapicca Rocco	815	shoeworker	44	"
	F	Iapicca Theresa—†	815	housewife	41	"
	G	Fleming Eleanor—†	816	"	27	966 Bennington
	H	Fleming John	816	U S A	32	966 "
	K	Rogers Anna—†	816	housewife	42	here
	L	Rogers Florence—†	816	painter	28	"
	M	Rogers Manuel	816	electrician	48	"
	N	Spadaro John	816	U S A	20	"
	o	Sullivan Agnes—†	818	housewife	33	"
	P	Sullivan Francis	818	laborer	39	108 Byron
	R	Smith Margaret Y—†	818	housewife	54	here
	s	Smith Robert C	818	chauffeur	51	"
	T	*Sergi Camilla—†	819	housewife	66	"
	U	Sergi Joseph	819	laborer	64	"
	v	Smith Charles	819	machinist	32	"
	w	Smith Mildred—†	819	housewife	31	"
	x	Silvagni Alexander	819	laborer	43	"
	Y	*Silvagni Ascenzio	819	"	82	"
	z	Silvagni Ascenzio	819	U S N	22	"
1634						
	A	Silvagni Celia—†	819	bookkeeper	23	"
	B	Silvagni Rose—†	819	housewife	42	"
	c	O'Brien Catherine—†	820	"	39	816 Saratoga
	D	O'Brien James H	820	foreman	48	816 "
	E	Berkeley Gertrude—†	820	tel operator	45	44 Russett rd
	F	Doyle Helen—†	820	housewife	56	here
	G	Doyle James J	820	guard	53	"
	H	Jacobsen Elvina—†	820	housewife	70	"
	K	Jacobsen Marie—†	820	bookkeeper	34	"
	L	Jacobsen Walter	820	U S A	32	"
	M	Amoroso Catherine—†	821	housewife	26	"
	N	Amoroso Michael	821	U S N	28	"
	o	Pepi Antonio	821	barber	58	"
	P	Pepi Francis A	821	chiropodist	31	"

Saratoga Street—Continued

R	Pepi John	821	U S A	34	here
S	Pepi Sophie—†	821	housewife	53	"
T	Pepi William	821	mortician	27	"
U	Croce Helen—†	821	saleswoman	34	11 Boardman
V	Croce Mathilda—†	821	housewife	60	11 "
W	Grenier Catherine—†	822	"	48	here
X	Grenier Catherine J—†	822	maid	21	"
Y	Grenier Joseph L	822	loom fixer	59	"
Z	LaCroix Amedee	822	machinist	50	"
	1635				
A	LaCroix Eleanor M—†	822	clerk	28	
B	LaCroix Harold R	822	U S A	20	"
C	LaCroix Rita M—†	822	clerk	26	"
D	LaCroix Stella M—†	822	housewife	50	"
E	LaCroix Thomas F	822	U S N	22	
F	Jacobsen Frank E	822	chauffeur	42	"
G	Jacobsen Rose M—†	822	housewife	44	"
H	Robichaud Eugenia—†	822	stenographer	35	617 Hyde Park av
K	*Tierney Anna—†	823	housewife	40	here
L	Tierney Edward	823	longshoreman	44	"
M	Doyle Arthur	823	U S A	23	"
N	Doyle James	823	retired	62	
O	Doyle Josephine—†	823	housewife	57	"
P	Traveis Florence—†	823	"	52	
R	Traveis Joseph F	823	chauffeur	52	"
S	Traveis Ruth—†	823	clerk	23	
T	Burns Agnes—†	825	housewife	58	"
U	Burns Daniel	825	operator	56	"
V	Byrne Angela—†	825	clerk	26	
W	Byrne Veronica—†	825	nurse	23	"
X	Vieira Doris L—†	825	shipper	23	
Y	Vieira Francis	825	"	30	
Z	Jasus Justin S	825	engineer	43	"
	1636				
A	Vieira Ursula—†	825	housewife	53	"
B	Vieira William A	825	U S A	28	
C	Stokes Madeline—†	827	housewife	42	"
D	Stokes William	827	printer	45	"
E	Stack Agnes—†	827	housekeeper	62	"
F	Brangiforte Philip	827	chauffeur	30	"

Page.	Letter.	FULL NAME.	Residence, Jan. 1, 1945.	Occupation.	Supposed Age.	Reported Residence, Jan. 1, 1944. Street and Number.

	G	Brangiforte Ruth—†	827	housewife	31	here
	H	Greeley Mary K—†	829	secretary	42	"
	K	Kelley Helen J—†	829	"	40	"
	L	Kelley Sarah A—†	829	housewife	73	"
	M	McNabb Cecelia C—†	829	"	45	
	N	O'Hare Alice G—†	829	"	55	
	O	Geer Mary B̄—†	831	"	40	..
	P	Gallagher Edward W	831	U S N	26	"
	R	Gallagher Regina E—†	831	housewife	27	"
	S	McLaughlin John J	831	guard	67	
	T	McLaughlin Mary M—†	831	housewife	64	"
	U	Sprague Dorothy—†	833	waitress	33	Winthrop
	V	Cipoletta Mary H—†	833	housewife	45	here
	W	Cipoletta Nicholas	833	operator	51	"
	X	Cipoletta Nicholas W	833	U S N	22	"
	Y	Ferrante Dominic	833	U S A	26	"
	Z	Ferrante Edward	833	draftsman	24	"
1637						
	A	*Ferrante Rose—†	833	housewife	50	"
	B	Ferrante Sabina A—†	833	clerk	25	"
	C	Fiandaca Charles	835	chauffeur	30	"
	D	Fiandaca Gilda—†	835	boxmaker	27	"
	E	Lupi John C	835	electrician	48	"
	F	Lupi Louise—†	835	housewife	28	"
	G	Sabbag Salemme—†	835	"	52	"
	H	Sabbag Samuel G	835	painter	33	
	K	Sateriale Gaetano	835	chauffeur	50	"
	L	Sateriale John	835	U S A	24	
	M	Sateriale Olympia—†	835	housewife	45	"
	N	Cross David	837	dishwasher	60	"
	O	Gallagher Benjamin F	837	shipfitter	58	"
	P	Gallagher Susan A—†	837	housewife	47	"
	R	Mullen Mabel T—†	837	waitress	31	"
	S	Parker Robert W	837	U S N	23	"
	T	Parker Ruth—†	837	sorter	22	
	U	Coe Janet—†	837	housewife	75	"
	V	Corsetti Leo G	837	valet	30	
	W	Corsetti Virginia H—†	837	housewife	29	"
	X	Hanlon Eva M—†	837	clerk	47	"
	Y	Hanlon William H	837	mechanic	52	"

Page.	Letter.	FULL NAME.	Residence, Jan. 1, 1945.	Occupation.	Supposed Age.	Reported Residence, Jan. 1, 1944. Street and Number.

	z	Ramsay David A	837	printer	62	here
1638						
	A	Ramsay David A, jr	837	clerk	35	
	B	Ramsay George A	837	U S A	25	
	-c	Ramsay Lucy E—†	837	housewife	61	"
	D	Petitpas Bartholomew A	839	laborer	51	
	E	Petitpas Lorraine M—†	839	secretary	20	"
	F	Petitpas Melina M—†	839	housewife	46	"
	G	Cooper Edward L	839	laborer	28	818 Saratoga
	H	Cooper Mary A—†	839	housewife	58	here
	K	Cooper William F	839	laborer	35	"
	L	Veiga Charles P	839	welder	31	"
	M	Veiga Florence G—†	839	housewife	32	"
	N	Cullen Catherine A—†	849	"	55	
	O	Cullen Joseph H	849	guard	65	
	P	Steiner Beatrice M—†	849	tel operator	21	"
	R	Steiner Francis E	849	U S A	30	
	S	Steiner Irene E—†	849	clerk	24	
	T	Steiner Thomas M	849	salesman	55	"
	U	McDonald Ellen F—†	849	housewife	72	21 Ashley
	V	McDonald Florence—†	849	waitress	44	21 "
	W	McDonald James M	849	technician	43	21 "
	X	Mazzarino Joseph	850	chauffeur	27	here
	Y	Mazzarino Mary N—†	850	housewife	24	"
	z	Felzani Ernest N	850	estimator	32	"
1639						
	A	Felzani Lena—†	850	housewife	33	"
	B	Stepankoski Chester	851	U S A	29	
	C	Stepankoski Rita—†	851	housewife	24	"
	D	Coscia Ferdinando	851	pipefitter	30	142 Lexington
	E	Coscia Yolanda—†	851	housewife	23	142 "
	F	Vozzella Joseph	851	shipper	46	here
	G	Vozzella Mary R—†	851	housewife	39	"
	H	Capolupo Gloria—†	852	assembler	22	Newton
	K	Mascis Alice—†	852	"	20	here
	L	Mascis Elsie—†	852	housewife	41	"
	M	Mascis James	852	laborer	37	"
	N	Perry Frederick	852	U S A	22	"
	O	Perry Marion—†	852	stitcher	48	"
	P	Perry Rene	852	guard	45	..

Saratoga Street—Continued

R	Perry Thelma—†	852	stitcher	20	here
s	Case Anthony J	853	assembler	39	"
T	Case Antoinette—†	853	housewife	35	"
U	Cutlip Susan—†	853	"	70	
V	Webber Carl	853	laborer	38	
W	D'Agosta Adéline—†	853	housewife	43	"
X	D'Agosta Frank J	853	electrician	41	"
Y	Polcari Carmen	854	cook	31	"
Z	Polcari Tina M—†	854	housewife	27	"
	1640				
A	Peluso Joseph	854	blacksmith	48	"
B	Peluso Mary—†	854	housewife	43	"
C	Sacco Louise M—†	855	"	33	
D	Sacco Orlando D	855	welder	38	
E	Frattaroli Beatrice—†	855	U S C G	22	"
F	Frattaroli Elvira—†	855	housewife	45	"
G	Frattaroli Olga—†	855	stenographer	21	"
H	DiPietro Felix	855	U S N	21	..
K	DiPietro Marion T—†	855	dressmaker	30	"
L	DiPietro Michalena—†	855	housewife	52	"
M	McNeil Alfred J	856	U S N	29	"
N	McNeil Dorothy—†	856	housewife	26	"
O	Venezia Antoinetta—†	856	assembler	22	"
P	Venezia John	856	laborer	54	
R	Venezia Theresa—†	856	housewife	45	"
S	Wilbanks Esther—†	856	"	20	"
T	Colantuoni Ida—†	857	"	35	269 Lexington
U	Colantuoni Samuel O	857	painter	40	269 "
V	MacCormack Herbert E	857	printer	56	Everett
W	MacCormack Katherine-†857		housewife	56	here
X	MacCormack Robert A	857	U S A	21	"
Y	MacCormack William H	857	U S M C	24	"
Z	MacCormack Daniel A	857	operator	27	"
	1641				
A	MacCormack Margaret-†	857	housewife	25	"
B	Scally Veronica M—†	857	laundress	54	Everett
C	Riley Catherine—†	858	housewife	35	here
D	Riley Henry L	858	chauffeur	40	"
E	Rice Henry L	858	housewife	66	"
F	Rice John	858	finisher	72	"

Saratoga Street—Continued

G	Rice William A	858	U S A	31	here
H	Pacifico Adeline—†	859	housewife	42	"
K	Pacifico Joseph F	859	baker	52	"
L	Santoro Alfred	859	machinist	39	"
M	*Santoro Dominic	859	retired	76	
N	Santoro Harriet C—†	859	housewife	32	"
O	*Santoro Theresa—†	859	"	72	
P	Dalton Elmer D	859	welder	33	
R	Dalton Florence F—†	859	housewife	27	"
S	Piano Donato	860	laborer	58	
T	Piano Josephine—†	860	housewife	55	"
U	McCarthy Callahan	860	chauffeur	49	"
V	McCarthy Mabel M—†	860	housewife	54	"
W	Panora Alfred C	861	U S N	24	
X	Panora Anna—†	861	housewife	46	"
Y	Panora James J	861	laborer	20	
Z	McGloan Dorothy B—†	861	housewife	28	"
	1642				
A	McGloan Jeffrey J	861	electrician	34	"
B	McNeil Francis J	861	chauffeur	53	"
C	McNeil George F	861	U S A	31	
D	McNeil James J	861	machinist	27	"
E	McNeil Mary E—†	861	"	21	
F	McNeil Nellie—†	861	housewife	52	"
G	Sarcia Carmen	862	carpenter	30	"
H	Sarcia Lucy—†	862	housewife	28	"
K	Peterson Albert	862	policeman	43	"
L	Peterson Helen—†	862	housewife	30	"
M	Belmonte Louis	863	machinist	36	"
N	Belmonte Theresa—†	863	housewife	36	"
O	Gross Elizabeth F—†	863	"	29	
P	Gross George H	863	electrician	44	"
R	Memmolo Grace M—†	863	housewife	38	"
S	Memmolo Thomas	863	salesman	38	"
T	*Sepo Salvatore	863	retired	73	
U	Ross Earl M	864	U S A	24	
V	Ross Margaret M—†	864	housewife	28	"
W	*Nucci Divina—†	864	"	60	"
X	Nucci Enos H	864	packer	32	"
Y	Nucci John D	864	U S A	23	"

William E. McClellan Highway

z	English Alice—†	119	housewife	35	here
	1643				
A	English Kenneth E	119	shipfitter	38	"
B	*O'Riordan Ellen—†	121	housewife	70	"
C	*O'Riordan John	121	weaver	72	
D	Greco Delia G—†	121	housewife	30	"
E	Greco William J	121	chauffeur	50	"

Wordsworth Street

F	Marotta John	7	confectioner	50	here
G	Quinn John	7	laundryman	31	"
H	Quinn Mary E—†	7	housewife	55	"
K	Mannix Anna M—†	7	operator	20	
L	Mannix James J	7	U S A	31	
M	Mannix Mary B—†	7	housewife	52	"
N	Mannix Mary M—†	7	welder	22	
O	*O'Hara Henry	9	retired	72	
P	O'Hara John	9	millhand	62	
R	Casaccio Carmella—.†	9	housewife	34	"
S	Casaccio Joseph A	9	longshoreman	36	"
T	Sinclair Margaret E—†	9	millhand	35	
U	Sinclair William J	9	longshoreman	40	"
V	*Halle Mary—†	9A	housewife	54	"
W	Halle Michael	9A	weaver	57	
X	Halle Mitchell J	9A	U S A	24	
Y	Pascucci Anna A—†	9A	housewife	30	"
z	Pascucci Henry A	9A	machinist	30	"
	1644				
A	Guarnera Joseph	9A	photographer	31	"
B	Guarnera Mary M—†	9A	housewife	32	"
C	Corcoran Theresa—†	10	"	38	
D	Corcoran William	10	shipper	41	
E	Campbell Julia—†	10	at home	70	
F	Tomello Evelyn R—†	11	housewife	30	"
G	Tomello Guido J	11	diemaker	35	"
H	Langone Lena—†	11	housewife	31	"
K	Langone Patrick	11	optician	33	
L	Pastore Carmen A	11	driller	31	
M	Pastore Norma E—†	11	housewife	30	"

Page.	Letter.	FULL NAME.	Residence, Jan. 1, 1945.	Occupation.	Supposed Age.	Reported Residence, Jan. 1, 1944. Street and Number.

Wordsworth Street—Continued

	Letter	Full Name	Res.	Occupation	Age	Residence
	N	Layne Alice—†	12	secretary	25	here
	O	Layne Jennie —†	12	housewife	51	"
	P	Layne Warren	12	U S A	23	"
	R	Martin Frank R	12	machinist	53	"
	S	Martin Rose—†	12	housewife	48	"
	T	Mirabile Mary—†	13	"	32	
	U	Mirabile Richard	13	mechanic	36	"
	V	Regan Helen F—†	13	housewife	45	"
	W	Rebak Claudia—†	13	"	44	
	X	Rebak Daniel	13	U S N	20	
	Y	Rebak Evdakin	13	millhand	54	"

1645

	A	Companaro Clara C—†	15	housewife	22	"
	B	Companaro Louis G	15	U S M C	22	"
	C	Tedeschi Amelio	15	tailor	48	
	D	Tedeschi Fortuna—†	15	housewife	45	"
	E	Celia Santa M—†	15	"	30	
	F	Celia William O	15	operator	38	"
	G	Gatti Bruno	16	machinist	49	"
	H	Gatti Coradina—†	16	WAC	21	"
	K	Gatti Gina—†	16	housewife	42	"
	L	Gatti Leo	16	U S A	20	"
	M	Travaglini John	16	upholsterer	35	"
	N	Travaglini Lucy—†	16	housewife	70	"
	O	Camerano Charles C	17	laborer	33	
	P*	Camerano Florence M—†	17	housewife	56	"
	R	Camerano Frank	17	retired	68	
	S	Camerano Matilda E—†	17	factoryhand	21	"
	T	Camerano Philip R	17	welder	25	
	U	MacDonald Bessie E—†	17	housewife	40	"
	V	MacDonald Melvin M	17	policeman	49	"
	W	MacKay Duncan A	17	bookkeeper	64	"
	X	Interbartolo Joseph	17	chauffeur	33	"
	Y	Interbartolo Rose F—†	17	housewife	30	"
	Z	Keenan Mary—†	18	at home	78	"

1646

	B	Martello Peter	19	merchant	54	"
	C	Martello Phyllis—†	19	housewife	31	"
	D	DeSimone Joseph A	19	chauffeur	24	"
	E	DeSimone Philomenia—†	19	housewife	48	"

F	DeSimone Theresa A—†·	19	bookkeeper	20	here
G	Barnes Charlotte—†	19	housewife	57	"
H	Magee George W	19	clerk	39	"
K	Turner Olga—†	20	housewife	34	"
L	Turner Oliver G	20	U S N	36	
M	Seaberg Elfreda—†	20	housewife	61	"
N	Seaberg Gustaf W	20	patternmaker	58	"
O	Ware Doris—†	20	secretary	23	"
P	Ware Robert H	20	U S N	27	,,
R	Chioccola Gaetano	21	brazier	35	"
S	Chioccola Mary—†	21	housewife	33	"
T	Mancuso Frank	21	rubberworker	51	"
U	Mancuso Mary—†	21	housewife	44	"
V	Turco Pasquale	21	draftsman	25	"
W	Turco Philip	21	millhand	56	"
X	*Turco Vincenza—†	21	housewife	51	"
Y	D'Avella Armand	22	U S A	23	
Z	D'Avella Luigi	22	"	31	

1647

A	D'Avella Michelina—†	22	housewife	61	"
B	D'Avella Nicholas	22	laborer	57	
C	Gross Lavinia—†	22	housewife	43	"
D	*Fortino Anna—†	23	"	49	
E	Fortino Antonio	23	fireman	55	
F	Fortino Edmund A	23	U S A	24	..
G	*Moniz Emma—†	23	textileworker	46	"
H	*Moniz John	23	"	42	"
K	Cannata Aurora—†	23	housewife	25	"
L	Cannata Charles	23	U S N	28	"
M	DeLeo Anthony S	25	carpenter	29	47 Leyden
N	DeLeo Mary J—†	25	housewife	27	47 "
O	Caldwell Arthur	25	U S A	26	here
P	Sweeney Edward J	25	painter	46	"
R	Sweeney Esther A—†	25	housewife	44	"
S	Sweeney Florence M—†	25	millhand	21	"
T	Sweeney John E	25	U S N	23	
U	Bruno Libera M—†	25	housewife	38	" .
V	Bruno Pasquale	25	mechanic	39	"
X	Henderson Edith J—†	27	housewife	39	"
Y	Henderson Roderick M	27	laundryman	39	"

Page.	Letter.	Full Name.	Residence, Jan. 1, 1945.	Occupation.	Supposed Age.	Reported Residence, Jan. 1, 1944. Street and Number.

Wordsworth Street—Continued

	z	Ruggiero Helen M—†	29	housewife	30	here
1648						
	A	Ruggiero Joseph	29	fireman	31	
	B	DeGennaro Antoinetta—†	29	housewife	46	"
	C	DeGennaro Peter	29	machinist	56	"
	D	DeGennaro Peter, jr	29	U S A	22	
	E	DeGennaro Stella—†	29	stitcher	20	"
	F	Foster Charles L	30	chauffeur	27	"
	G	Foster Virginia G—†	30	housewife	28	"
	H	McCarthy Charles J	30	U S N	27	
	K	McCarthy Violet E—†	30	conductor	26	"
	L	Ingersoll John W	30	chipper	29	97 Trenton
	M	Ingersoll Lorraine—†	30	housewife	26	97 "
	N	*Adelizzi Jacqueline—†	31	at home	80	here
	O	Adelizzi Pasquale	31	shoeworker	58	"
	P	Adelizzi Susan J—†	31	nurse	20	"
	R	Rosa Anthony J	31	U S N	24	21A Ashley
	S	Rosa Henrietta T—†	31	housewife	24	21A "
	T	DeRosa Alphonsina—†	33	"	50	here
	U	DeRosa Antoinette—†	33	operator	24	"
	V	DeRosa Eleanor--†	33	inspector	26	"
	W	DeRosa Raymond	33	foreman	61	"
	X	Napolitano Margaret—†	33	housewife	23	"
	Y	Kane Daniel J	35	machinist	36	"
	z	Nickley Agnes—†	35	operator	36	"
1649						
	A	Nickley Alice M—†	35	"	47	
	B	Nickley Francis A	35	seaman	34	"
	C	Nickley Joseph F	35	clerk	40	
	D	Nickley Rose V—†	35	operator	38	"
	E	Farro Mary—†	37	housewife	22	"
	F	Sarro George	37	laborer	20	"
	G	Sarro Joseph	37	painter	42	"
	H	Sarro Mary—†	37	housewife	41	"
	K	Grandolfi Cirio A	37	carpenter	34	362 Princeton
	L	Grandolfi Mary—†	37	housewife	31	362 "
	M	Fleming Joseph P	39	foreman	34	here
	N	Fleming Margaret M—†	39	housewife	30	"
	O	Dolan Florence—†	39	clerk	22	"
	P	Mahoney Mary C—†	39	at home	50	"
	R	Mitchell Mary G—†	39	"	75	

Wordsworth Street—Continued

s	Smith Dorothy—†	41	housewife	34	here
t	Smith Edward A	41	tel operator	33	"
u	Puopolo Anthony J	41	operator	44	"
v	Puopolo Francis	41	U S N	20	
w	Puopolo Rose—†	41	housewife	40	"
x	Allie Georgiana—†	41	"	66	
y	Allie Mary—†	41	cashier	33	
z	Hansford Catherine—†	42	housewife	26	"
	1650				
a	Hansford Leonard	42	U S N	28	..
b	Harrington Annie M—†	42	housewife	51	"
c	Harrington George	42	U S N	22	
d	Harrington John	42	guard	24	
e	Aiello Concetta—†	43	housewife	38	' "
f	Aiello Joseph A	43	foundryman	39	"
g	Aiello Leonard	43	mechanic	44	"
h	*Aiello Margaret—†	43	at home	76	"
k	Leclair Ferdinand	45	millhand	65	"
l	Martel Anita—†	45	housewife	38	"
m	Martel Arthur J	45	barber	41	
n	Donahue Catherine T—†	46	clerk	29	
o	Donahue Cornelius	46	policeman	47	"
p	Donahue William E	46	pipefitter	37	"
r	Curry Jane—†	46	housewife	45	"
s	Curry Joseph P	46	drawtender	48	"
t	D'Innocenza Anthony	48	U S A	25	
u	D'Innocenza Leonora—†	48	saleswoman	23	"
v	Giammatteo Anthony	48	retired	64	"
w	Giammatteo Mary—†	48	stitcher	51	"
x	Hansen Charles G	50	teller	44	
y	Hansen Frances H—†	50	housewife	40	"
z	Hanson Annie—†	50	"	71	
	1651				
a	Hanson William	50	policeman	49	"
b	Pinkham Arthur E	51	assembler	40	"
c	Pinkham Hilda—†	51	housewife	36	"
d	Thomas Beatrice H—†	51	saleswoman	31	"
e	McInnis Alice—†	51	housewife	37	"
f	McInnis Herman A	51	metalworker	41	"
g	Cody Jennie—†	51	housewife	47	"
h	Cody Thomas H	51	shipper	49	

Wordsworth Street—Continued

K	Marsh Hazel—†	51	electrician	22	here	
L	Marsh Walter	51	U S A	24	"	
M	Morrison Edith—†	51	housewife	20	"	
N	Morrison Frank	51	U S N	21	716 Saratoga	
O	Houghton Edna—†	52	operator	51	here	
P	Sullivan Dennis B	52	retired	80	"	
R	Sullivan Mildred—†	52	operator	45	"	
S	Amato Anthony	53	machinist	35	"	
T	Amato Gertrude—†	53	housewife	29	"	
U	Ginsti Dante	53	chauffeur	28	"	
V	Ginsti Muriel—†	53	housewife	28	"	
W	Andrade Anthony	53	proprietor	52	"	
X	Andrade Mary—†	53	at home	20	"	
Y	*Andrade Rose—†	53	housewife	44	"	
Z	Burke John P	54	cashier	38		

1652

A	Burke Mary T—†	54	housewife	38	"	
B	Bambrick Henry J	54	chauffeur	43	"	
C	Bambrick Marcella—†	54	housewife	40	"	
D	Iapicca Marion I—†	55	"	28	69 Putnam	
E	Iapicca Rocco A	55	mechanic	28	69 "	
F	DeAngelis Carmella M—†	55	machinist	22	821 Saratoga	
G	DeAngelis Christine J—†	55	operator	24	821 "	
H	DeAngelis Pasquale A	55	chauffeur	51	821 "	
K	DeAngelis Rose—†	55	housewife	46	821 "	
L	Brennan Francis J	56	laborer	60	here	
M	Brennan Nellie—†	56	housewife	64	"	
N	Callaghan Catherine—†	56	"	55	"	
O	Callaghan Catherine P—†	56	clerk	20		
P	Callaghan Mary M—†	56	stenographer	25	"	
R	Callaghan William	56	laborer	63	"	
S	Munroe Helen M—†	57	housewife	40	"	
T	Munroe Joseph	57	U S N	42		
U	Hugye Gustave	57	mechanic	65	"	
V	Hugye Jennie—†	57	housewife	64	"	
W	Bradley Peter	58	retired	82	"	
X	Mills Kathleen—†	58	housewife	47	"	
Y	*Mills William	58	painter	44		
Z	Sullivan Clara R—†	58	housewife	30	"	

1653

A	Sullivan Lawrence J	58	stockman	29	"	

Wordsworth Street—Continued

	B	Bottelsen Olaf	59	retired	69	here
	C	Bottelsen Olaf H	59	operator	39	"
	D	Jensen Agnes E—†	59	housewife	45	"
	E	Jensen William	59	U S N	45	
	F	Jensen William H	59	"	21	
	G	Barry Helen A—†	59	housewife	59	"
	H	Barry Helen F—†	59	stenographer	24	"
	K	Barry Thomas F	59	pharmacist	63	"
	L	Leville Charles	60	clerk	33	
	M	Leville Jennie—†	60	housewife	27	"
	N	Wingard Alice—†	60	"	33	
	O	Wingard William	60	laborer	40	
	P	Mortimer Abraham P	61	salesman	34	"
	R	Mortimer Agnes—†	61	bookkeeper	24	"
	S	Mortimer Thomas J	61	retired	70	..
	T	Smith Herbert	61	machinist	40	"
	U	Shelton Barbara—†	62	housewife	20	1089 Saratoga
	V	Shelton Catherine—†	62	"	43	here
	W	Shelton Franklin	62	U S A	22	"
	X	Shelton George L	62	machinist	47	"
	Y	*Benoit Anna—†	63	housewife	30	"
	Z	Mambuca Domenic	63	laborer	26	
		1654				
		Mambuca Rose—†	63	housewife	26	"
		Moniz Harold	65	U S A	26	..
		Moniz Margaret—†	65	housewife	25	"
		Ramsdell George	65	chauffeur	50	"
		Ramsdell Winifred—†	65	housewife	55	"
		Austin Rita M—†	65	"	21	
	G	Pennell Addie E—†	65	"	51	
	H	Pennell John C	65	foreman	56	"
	K	Yeo Margaret C—†	67	housewife	33	"
	L	Yeo Warren W	67	seaman	31	"
	M	Wingard Carrie—†	67	housewife	62	293 Webster
	N	Wingard Olaf	67	longshoreman	60	here
	O	Olsen Charles E	69	retired	55	"
	P	Olsen Florence D—†	69	housewife	47	"
	R	Olsen Florence D—†	69	clerk	23	
	S	Olsen Frances L—†	69	stenographer	20	"
	T	Olsen Rita E—†	69	"	24	..
	U	Dunbar Frank D	69	U S N	57	

Wordsworth Street—Continued

v	Palazzolo Leo	70	candymaker	37	here
w	Palazzolo Rose—†	70	housewife	33	"
x	*Piano Josephine—†	70	operator	67	"
y	*Piano Patrick	70	candymaker	60	"
z	Dorgan Florence—†	70	housewife	33	"

1655

A	Dorgan James	70	packer	33	"
B	Brindamour Dorothy—†	70	housewife	28	"
C	Brindamour Francis	70	laborer	33	
D	Caturano Dora—†	71	housewife	32	"
E	Caturano James	71	mechanic	31	"
F	Hastings Catherine M—†	71	housewife	62	"
G	Hastings James F	71	shipfitter	39	"
H	Hastings James H	71	laborer	73	
K	Hastings John A	71	welder	40	"
L	Giardiello Anthony F	72	rigger	32	Everett
M	*Giardiello Ida—†	72	stitcher	60	here
N	*Giardiello Joseph	72	candymaker	61	"
O	Molino Enrico	72	shoeworker	49	"
P	Molino Josephine—†	72	"	36	
R	Jameson Evelyn T—†	72	housewife	38	"
S	Jameson Robert J	72	optician	45	"
T	Driscoll John	73	fireman	22	"
U	Driscoll Thomas	73	U S N	34	"
V	Purvitsky Alice—†	73	operator	35	"
W	Purvitsky John	73	U S A	33	Malden
X	Stack John E	73	foreman	33	here
Y	Stack Mary E—†	73	housewife	25	"
Z	Cook Mary—†	74	operator	45	"

1656

A	Gallaway Dorothy—†	74	millhand	22	"
B	Gooby Doris—†	74	U S M C	20	"
C	Gooby Ingham	74	cook	56	
D	Sweeney Gerald C	75	drawtender	45	"
E	Sweeney Susan L—†	75	housewife	45	"
G	Chase Evelyn E—†	78	forewoman	42	"
H	O'Keefe Edward	78	retired	83	"
K	O'Keefe Henry	78	boilermaker	45	"
L	DeSisto Gerald	80	engineer	57	"
M	DeSisto Helen—†	80	housewife	41	"
N	Searle John W	86	U S A	25	

Wordsworth Street—Continued

	o	Searle Mary—†	86	tel operator	26	here
	p	Searle Ruth I—†	86	housewife	22	"
	r	Wilcox Gifford	88	laborer	36	"
	s	Wilcox Mildred—†	88	housewife	30	"
	t	Fennelly Anna M—†	90	"	57	"
	u	Fennelly Canice, jr	90	policeman	53	"
	v	Fennelly Cyril L	90	U S C G	24	"
	w	Harvender William H	92	weaver	29	
	x	Sullivan Agnes E—†	92	housewife	45	"
	y	Sullivan Alexander F	92	clerk	53	
	z	Kelsey Arline—†	96	housewife	31	"
1657						
	a	Kelsey Rosferd	96	machinist	35	"
	b	McMahon Annie—†	96	at home	70	"
	c	Dever Alice L—†	107	operator	20	"
	d	Dever George F	107	custodian	49	"
	e	Dever Mary A—†	107	housewife	49	"
	f	Bernard Catherine—†	109	"	43	"
	g	Bernard Ralph	109	seaman	43	
	h	Cali Mary—†	109	housewife	22	"
	k	Cali Salvatore	109	U S A	27	
	l	Bullock Rose—†	109	forewoman	47	"
	m	Bullock William	109	welder	48	

Ward 1–Precinct 17

CITY OF BOSTON

LIST OF RESIDENTS
20 YEARS OF AGE AND OVER

(NON-CITIZENS INDICATED BY ASTERISK)
(FEMALES INDICATED BY DAGGER)

AS OF

JANUARY 1, 1945

THOMAS F. SULLIVAN, *Chairman*
FREDERIC E. DOWLING, *Secretary*
WILLIAM A. MOTLEY, JR.
FRANCIS B. McKINNEY
EVERETT R. PROUT
Listing Board.

CITY OF BOSTON PRINTING DEPARTMENT

Page.	Letter.	FULL NAME.	Residence, Jan. 1, 1945.	Occupation.	Supposed Age.	Reported Residence, Jan. 1, 1944. Street and Number.

1700
Ashley Street

	A	*Carideo Angelina—†	19	housewife	56	here
	B	Carideo Patrick	19	electrician	30	"
	C	Ryan John	19	engineer	68	"
	D	Ryan Margaret—†	19	saleswoman	54	"
	E	Ryan Mary—†	19	machinist	21	"
	F	Conley Florence—†	19	housewife	35	"
	G	Conley Harry	19	manager	34	"
	H	Campanella Jennie—†	19A	housewife	55	1062 Benningt'n
	K	Campanella John	19A	U S A	22	1062 "
	L	Vadala Diego	19A	fireman	52	1062 "
	M	Marcella Arthur	19A	steamfitter	35	here
	N	*Marcella Nicholina—†	19A	housewife	69	"
	O	Marcella Rachel—†	19A	"	38	"
	P	Castranova Alfred	21	machinist	28	1054 Benningt'n
	R	Castranova Antoinette—†	21	housewife	26	1054 "
	S	Vernarelli Alfred	21	baker	34	154 Cottage
	T	*Vernarelli Giacomo	21	tailor	67	236 Maverick
	U	Vernarelli Grace—†	21	housewife	30	154 Cottage
	V	*Censabella Carmella—†	21A	"	74	here
	W	Censabella Domenic	21A	retired	74	"
	X	Pemberton Mary—†	21A	operator	36	"
	Y	Pemberton Ralph	21A	U S N	37	
	Z	Velardo Frances—†	23	at home	32	"

1701

	A	Velardo Jasper	23	clerk	20	
	B	Velardo Joseph	23	"	36	
	C	Velardo Rose—†	23	housewife	61	"
	D	Mangiaratti Joseph	23A	electrician	35	"
	E	Mangiaratti Phyllis—†	23A	housewife	34	"
	F	Rotondo Letitia—†	23A	"	22	
	G	Rotondo Salvatore	23A	fireman	26	"
	H	DePaolo Margaret—†	23A	housewife	30	137 London
	K	DePaolo Pasquale	23A	shipfitter	33	137 "
	L	Casale Elizabeth—†	25	housewife	39	here
	M	Casale Richard	25	metalworker	42	"
	N	*Munichello Antoinetta—†	27	housewife	43	"
	O	Munichello Raffaele	27	laborer	54	"
	P	Gemelli Giovanna—†	29	clerk	20	"
	R	Gemelli Michael	29	retired	56	
	S	Gemelli Raffaela—†	29	housewife	53	"

2

Page.	Letter.	Full Name.	Residence, Jan. 1, 1945.	Occupation.	Supposed Age.	Reported Residence, Jan. 1, 1944. Street and Number.

Ashley Street—Continued

	T	Cassaro Adeline—†	31	stitcher	21	here
	U	Cassaro Mary—†	31	trimmer	24	"
	V	Cassaro Michael	31	laborer	59	"
	W	Cassaro Sadie—†	31	housewife	47	"
	X	Contardo Joseph	31	electrician	29	"
	Y	Contardo Liboria—†	31	housewife	26	"
1702						
	A	*D'Amelio Carmela—†	35	"	73	
	B	D'Amelio Mary—†	35	clerk	37	"
	C	Gregory Joseph	35	chauffeur	46	"
	D	Gregory Theresa—†	35	housewife	41	"
	E	Giglio Caroline—†	39	dressmaker	47	"
	F	Giglio Domenic	39	boxmaker	46	"
	G	Craviotto Margaret—†	39	housewife	35	"
	H	Craviotto Silvio	39	plumber	37	"
	K	Bellio Angela—†	41	housewife	49	"
	L	Bellio Moses	41	maintenance	51	"
	M	Masone Pasqualina—†	41	housewife	55	"
	N	Masone Raffaele	41	pipefitter	56	"
	O	Roberts John	rear 41	trainman	41	"
	P	Roberts Mildred—†	" 41	housewife	39	"

Beachview Road

	R	Meaney David M	9	policeman	42	here
	S	Meaney Theresa—†	9	housewife	35	"
	T	Meaney William J	9	U S M C	24	"
	U	Saraceno Mary G—†	11	housewife	42	17 Norman
	V	Saraceno Pasquale M	11	shipfitter	42	17 "
	W	Antonucci Ancilla—†	15	housewife	32	here
	X	Antonucci Frank J	15	painter	32	"
	Y	Smith Charles H	15	compositor	63	"
	Z	Groppi Alfred	23	U S C G	22	"
1703						
	A	Groppi Arena—†	23	housewife	65	"
	B	Groppi John	23	U S A	28	
	C	Groppi Joseph	23	carpenter	30	"
	D	Groppi Orestes	23	laborer	74	
	E	Indrisano Margaret—†	23	housewife	39	"
	F	Indrisano Victor	23	cutter	44	"
	G	Guidi Genevieve A—†	23	checker	30	101½ Calumet

3

Beachview Road—Continued

H	Guidi James C	23	foreman	61	456 Saratoga
K	Guidi Louis	23	toolmaker	32	456 "
L	Sardini Ida—†	27	housewife	37	here
M	Sardini John·	27	welder	36	"
N	Antonucci Rose—†	27	housewife	55	"
O	Antonucci Salvatore	27	laborer	57	"
P	Antonucci William	27	U S A	20	"
R	Ford Jennie M—†	30–32	housewife	62	"
S	Nolan Joseph W	30–32	clerk	31	
T	Nolan Ruth H—†	30–32	housewife	27	"
U	Carrigg Margaret T—†	30–32	clerk	33	
V	Ford Charles J	30–32	U S N	31	
W	Ford Mary H—†	30–32	housewife	27	"
X	*Perricotti Cesira—†	31	"	79	
Y	Perricotti Charles ·A	31	operator	35	"
Z	Perricotti John	31	pipefitter	50	"

1704

A	*Rondelli Adolf	31	retired	54	"
B	Rando Antonio	36	operator	52	"
C	Rando Josephine—†	36	dressmaker	23	"
D	Rando Mary—†	36	housewife	55	"
E	Walsh Margaret—†	36	clerk	28	"
F	Velardo Anthony	36	barber	67	"
G	Velardo Josephine—†	36	housewife	59	"
H	Velardo Margaret—†	36	operator	23	"
K	Velardo Natalie—†	36	nurse	27	"
L	Ciampa Frank	36	foreman	43	"
M	Ciampa Laura T—†	36	housewife	36	"
N	*Bondi Elvira—†	47	"	44	
O	Bondi Gino	47	painter	50	"
P	Palladino Joseph	47	rigger	32	
R	Palladino Pauline—†	47	saleswoman	35	"
S	Caizzi Mildred A—†	47	housewife	27	"
T	Caizzi Thomas	47	chauffeur	31	"
U	Pesce Angelo	47	painter	61	"
V	Pesce Anna T—†	47	U S M C	22	"
W	Frederick Marilyn—†	53	housewife	20	"
X	Frederick William R	53	U S N	21	
Y	Hoyt Irving H	53	policeman	53	"
Z	Hoyt Violetta ·T—†	53	housewife	46	"

1705

A	Pollard Leigh	53	operator	32	"

Page.	Letter.	FULL NAME.	Residence, Jan. 1, 1945.	Occupation.	Supposed Age.	Reported Residence, Jan. 1, 1944. Street and Number.

Bennington Street

	B	Venditti Celia—†	1144	housewife	55	here
	C	Venditti Edward	1144	tailor	57	"
	D	Venditti Loretta—†	1144	clerk	27	"
	E	Casaletto Alfred	1144	mason	38	
	F	Casaletto Joseph	1144	clerk	36	
	G	Casaletto Josephine—†	1144	at home	66	"
	H	Casaletto Vincenza—†	1144	housewife	32	"
	K	Caselden Daniel F	1144	policeman	48	"
	L	Caselden Daniel F, jr	1144	U S N	22	
	M	Caselden Margaret E-†	1144	housewife	48	"
	N	Caselden Rita—†	1144	WAVE	20	··
	O	Queenan Agnes M—†	1148	housewife	40	"
	P	Queenan John F	1148	clerk	38	"
	R	Griffin Doris N—†	1148	cashier	25	"
	S	Griffin Elizabeth C—†	1148	housewife	53	"
	T	Griffin John F	1148	cashier	57	
	U	Calledare Antonio	1148	shipfitter	33	"
	V	Calledare Mary—†	1148	housewife	26	"
	W	Savasta Anthony	1150	U S N	23	
	X	Savasta Antonia—†	1150	housewife	57	"
	Y	Savasta Mary—†	1150	packer	33	
	Z	Lanfranchi Antoinetta-†	1150	housewife	43	"
1706						
	A	Lanfranchi John	1150	metalworker	44	"
	B	Lanfranchi Joseph	1150	·U S C G	22	"
	C	Bonanno Leo	1150	carpenter	50	"
	D	Bonanno Mary—†	1150	housewife	44	"
	E	*DeBella Frank	1150	retired	78	"

Breed Street

	F	Ferrara Frances—†	29	operator	24	here
	G	*Ferrara Frank	29	carpenter	65	"
	H	Ferrara Maria—†	29	housewife	62	"
	K	Ferrara Lucy—†	29	"	27	
	L	Ferrara Salvatore	29	chauffeur	27	"
	M	Murphy Elizabeth—†	31	housewife	24	5 Starr King ct
	N	Murphy George	31	mechanic	22	41 Cross
	O	DeSantis Anthony	31	U S A	24	41 "
	P	DeSantis Giulio	31	baker	46	41 "
	R	DeSantis Lucy—†	31	housewife	40	41 "
	S	Mini Andrew	33	U S A	33	here

Breed Street—Continued

T	Mini Lena—†	33	housewife	29	here
U	Smith Alfred H	33	janitor	65	"
V	Smith Alfred H, jr	33	U S M C	32	"
W	DeFrancesco Francis	35	machinist	30	"
X	DeFrancesco Mary—†	35	housewife	24	"
Y	Famolare Celia—†	35	"	34	984 Saratoga
Z	Famolare Manuel	35	chauffeur	37	984 "

1707   Faywood Avenue

B	Labadini Alda—†	31	trimmer	37	here
C	Labadini Ernest G	31	shipfitter	39	"
D	DeSimone Eleanor—†	31	secretary	40	"
E	DeSimone Sarah—†	31	housewife	67	"
F	Grasso Edmund A	31	U S N	28	
G	DiLorenzo George	31	social worker	25	"
H	DiLorenzo Virginia—†	31	housewife	25	"
K	Visco Alphonse	33	accountant	27	544 Saratoga
L	Visco Philomena—†	33	artist	22	544 "
M	Visco Philomeno	33	weaver	50	544 "
N	Visco Susan—†	33	housewife	47	544 "
O	Moran Henry F	33	foreman	44	here
P	Moran Mary J—†	33	housewife	39	"
R	Breau Mary A—†	33	"	65	"
S	Breau Thaddeus	33	retired	74	
T	Crossley Marie E—†	33	housewife	31	"
U	Crossley Robert H	33	U S N	25	Pennsylvania
V	Muse Mary E—†	35	housewife	45	here
W	Muse Wilfred F	35	seaman	52	"
X	Sparco John	35	laborer	47	"
Y	Sparco Lillian—†	35	housewife	48	"
Z	Quinlan Catherine—†	35	"	53	

1708

A	Quinlan John J	35	fisherman	60	"
B	Quinlan Richard J	35	U S N	21	"
C	Wood Bernard B	37	U S C G	28	"
D	Wood Fred S	37	pilot	56	"
E	Wood Mabel—†	37	housewife	55	"
F	Wood Robert S	37	U S A	22	"
G	Butera Jennie—†	37	housewife	42	"
H	Butera Mary—†	37	student	22	"

Faywood Avenue—Continued

K	Butera Rocco	37	hairdresser	45	here
L	Butera Rosario R	37	U S A	24	"
M	Lanzilli Carlo	37	engineer	29	31 Breed
N	Lanzilli Gertrude—†	37	housewife	23	31 "
O	Pesce Edith I—†	43	"	43	here
P	Pesce Geronima—†	43	at home	71	"
R	Pesce Louis E	43	coppersmith	44	"
S	Campatelli Augustus E	45	metalworker	36	"
T	Campatelli Marjorie—†	45	housewife	37	"
U	Cavalucci Joseph S	45	chauffeur	30	80 Frankfort
V	Cavalucci Katherine—†	45	housewife	29	Everett
W	Dundon Cornelius L	48	clerk	63	here
X	Dundon Mary L—†	48	housewife	64	"
Y	Lemos Clarence	51	engraver	51	"
Z	Lemos Margaret—†	51	housewife	42	"

1709

A	Valardi Anthony C	52	policeman	50	"
B	Granato Carmelo	52	U S A	30	
C	*Granato Fannie—†	52	housewife	52	"
D	Granato Joseph	52	candymaker	60	"
E	Granato Rose—†	52	supt	22	"
F	Granato Salvatore	52	U S A	24	"
G	Granato Theresa—†	52	operator	32	"
H	Orlandella Tina—†	52	supt	29	"
K	Doherty Edward N	55	salesman	43	"
L	Doherty Leona—†	55	WAVE	21	"
M	Doherty Louise—†	55	housewife	44	"
N	Kenney Alice K—†	56	"	42	
O	Kenney Nicholas E	56	policeman	49	"
P	Kenney Nicholas N	56	U S A	21	
R	Vincent Catherine I—†	60	housewife	35	"
S	Vincent Robert H	60	dentist	48	
T	Tyrell John A	64	custodian	45	"
U	Tyrell Marguerite M—†	64	housewife	44	"
V	Tyrell Richard S	64	U S A	20	"
W	Stasio Anthony J	67	toolmaker	30	"
X	Stasio Genevieve—†	67	housewife	26	"
Y	DeLeo Gaetano	67	metalworker	57	66 Hunt'n av
Z	Serignano Charles	67	U S N	25	here

1710

A	Serignano Nancy—†	67	housewife	45	"

Faywood Avenue—Continued

	B	Serignano Nancy C—†	67	teacher	23	here
	c	Celia Christopher	68	U S A	24	"
	D	Celia Joseph	68	manager	52	"
	E*	Celia Josephine—†	68	housewife	49	"
	F	Celia Stella—†	68	waitress	22	"
	G	Cappucci Enrico	69	attorney	33	"
	H	Cappucci Virginia—†	69	housewife	27	"
	K	O'Malley Delia A—†	69	"	72	
	L	O'Malley Lillian—†	69	bookkeeper	44	"
	M	Warren Richard F	73	U S A	21	"
	N	Warren Samuel A	73	inspector	51	"
	O	Warren Winifred F—†	73	housewife	50	"
	P	Oresteen Mary A—†	74	at home	71	"
	R	Wright Charles D	74	inspector	51	"
	S	Wright Margaret J—†	74	housewife	47	"
	T	Gahen Catherine—†	76	"	34	
	U	Gahen Frank	76	U S A	38	
	V	Gahen John	76	machinist	44	"
	W	Moran Margaret M—†	76	stenographer	21	"
	X	Moran Marie F—†	76	"	24	"
	S	Moran Thomas J	76	U S A	54	
	Z	Moran Thomas J, jr	76	"	26	
1711						
	A	Tammans Charles N	76	metalworker	44	"
	B	Tammans Margaret N—†	76	housewife	42	"
	C	Newbury Warren C	79	supt	51	"
	D	Williams Catherine N—†	79	clerk	42	"
	E	Cutillo Alice—†	84	housewife	41	"
	F	Cutillo William	84	chauffeur	46	"
	G	Cotreau Delphis N	85	rigger	44	"
	H	Cotreau Julia A—†	85	housewife	42	"
	K	Telese Assunta—†	85	"	40	"
	L	Telese Eugene	85	machinist	45	"
	M	Ferraro Edna—†	87	housewife	24	New York
	N	Ferraro Frank	87	U S A	23	here
	O	Ferraro Henrietta—†	87	housewife	42	"
	P	Ferraro Joseph	87	welder	43	"
	R	Schwarz Beatrice R—†	87	tel operator	35	"
	S	Schwarz Catherine—†	87	housewife	64	"
	T	Schwarz George	87	optician	42	"
	U	Faiella Anna—†	88	housewife	59	"

8

Page.	Letter.	Full Name.	Residence, Jan. 1, 1945.	Occupation.	Supposed Age.	Reported Residence, Jan. 1, 1944. Street and Number.

Faywood Avenue—Continued

	V	Faiella Felix	88	barber	59	here
	W	Faiella John	88	U S A	24	"
	X	Venezia Anthony	88	rigger	43	"
	Y	Venezia Mary A—†	88	housewife	43	"
	Z	Faiella Ralph	88	barber	33	
1712						
	A	Faiella Theresa—†	88	housewife	31	"
	B	Triulzi Josephine—†	92	"	21	26 Bremen
	C	Triulzi Louis	92	watchmaker	21	Murray ct
	D	*DeFelice Leo	92	printer	39	here
	E	DeFelice Millie—†	92	housewife	39	"
	G	Bonito Anna C—†	93	at home	20	"
	H	Bonito Annie—†	93	housewife	56	"
	K	Bonito Joseph	93	U S A	27	
	L	Bonito Louis	93	electrician	34	"
	M	Bonito Mary—†	93	bookkeeper	37	"
	N	Sozio Frederick	95	printer	39	"
	O	Sozio Lucy—†	95	housewife	37	"
	P	DeFelice Clara—†	95	clerk	28	
	R	DeFelice Michael	95	U S A	31	
	S	Lanno Genaro	95	barber	62	
	T	*Lanno Madeline—†	95	housewife	62	"
	U	Lanno Michael P	95	U S A	34	
	V	Osganian George	100	butcher	50	"
	W	Osganian Rose—†	100	housewife	40	"
	X	Thibeault Edward G	103	seaman	57	
	Y	Thibeault Elizabeth A—†	103	housewife	57	"
	Z	Thibeault Mary H—†	103	nurse	33	
1713						
	A	Morelli Caesar	108	machinist	43	"
	B	Morelli Grace—†	108	stitcher	40	"
	C	Tribuna Bartholomew	110	buyer	42	
	D	Tribuna Joseph M	110	U S A	21	"
	E	Tribuna Marion—†	110	housewife	40	"
	F	Capillo Joseph	116	laborer	47	"
	G	Capillo Margaret—†	116	stitcher	52	"
	H	Dato Eleanor—†	116	stringer	25	"
	K	Dato Horace	116	U S A	31	"
	L	Fournier Catherine L—†	124	housewife	31	"
	M	Fournier John L	124	policeman	34	"
	N	Gallo Angelina—†	125	saleswoman	25	"

Faywood Avenue—Continued

o	Gallo Frank	125	U S A	24	here	
p	Gallo Joseph	125	baker	52	"	
r	Gallo Nicholas	125	laborer	22	"	
s	Gallo Thomasina—†	125	housewife	46	"	
t	Bianco Carmen	150	proprietor	32	"	
u	Bianco Ethel—†	150	housewife	33	"	
v	Clarke Richard	150	retired	72		
w	MacNealy Edward	150	chauffeur	45	"	
x	Gillis Dorothy—†	154	housewife	48	"	
y	Gillis Frank	154	letter carrier	52	"	
z	Wilkie William J	154	U S A	27	"	

1714   Gladstone Street

a	Catillo Mary G—†	1	housewife	42	here	
b	Catillo Pasquale	1	shoemaker	44	"	
c	Ciampi Anthony	1	coppersmith	30	"	
d	Ciampi Gennaro	1	retired	74	"	
e	Ciampi Theresa—†	1	dressmaker	36	"	
f	McLeod Eleanor—†	1	housewife	28	"	
g	McLeod Vernon	1	drop forger	32	"	
l	DeWitt Margaret—†	5	tel operator	46	"	
m	Grady Mary E—†	5	housekeeper	45	"	
n	Stevredis Chris	7	fruit	49	"	
o*	Stevredis Viola—†	7	housewife	43	"	
p	Lentini Guy C	7	teacher	36	111 Barnes av	
r	Lentini Rose M—†	8	housewife	32	111 "	
s	Anderson Abbie M—†	9	receptionist	42	here	
t	Anderson Frank E	9	retired	73	"	
u	Anderson Lillian J—†	9	housewife	72	"	
v	Perry Thomas J	9	fisherman	70	"	
w	Goldberg Beatrice—†	9	housewife	31	"	
x	Goldstein Anna—†	9	"	54	"	
y	Goldstein Milton	9	U S A	24		
z	Goldstein Ruth F—†	9	clerk	27		

1715

a	Goldstein Samuel	9	proprietor	58	"	
b	Maffeo Consiglia—†	10	housewife	59	"	
c	Maffeo Eleanor E—†	10	technician	26	"	
d	Maffeo Henry A	10	attorney	29	"	
e	Maffeo Paul	10	florist	59	"	

Gladstone Street—Continued

F	Maffeo Paul D	10	U S A	25	here	
G	Maffeo Peter A	10	"	27	"	
H	Maffeo Sylvia M—†	10	technician	31	"	
K	Krebs John F	12	foreman	43	"	
L	Krebs Joseph F	12	U S N	22	"	
M	Krebs Victoria—†	12	housewife	42	"	
N	*Lovett John	12	retired	80		
O	Lovett Stella—†	12	operator	52	"	
P	Marino Louise—†	12	housewife	48	"	
R	Marino Mary—†	12	stenographer	24	"	
S	*Marino Samuel	12	barber	50	··	
T	Ciampa John B	16	bartender	41	"	
U	Ciampa Mary—†	16	housewife	41	"	
V	D'Amore Anthony	17	U S A	31		
W	D'Amore Nina—†	17	housewife	27	"	
X	Piscopo Concettina—†	17	clerk	58	"	
Y	Monahan Ellen—†	17	at home	60	107 St Andrew	
Z	Monahan Francis	17	U S N	25	107 "	
	1716					
A	Monahan Helen—†	17	tel operator	27	107 "	
B	Gilbrook John F	18	foreman	48	here	
C	Gilbrook Mary J—†	18	housewife	49	"	
D	Gilbrook William F	18	U S M C	22	"	
E	Berg Mabel E—†	18	housewife	50	"	
F	Berg Olaf D	18	painter	55		
G	Grimshaw Cecelia B—†	20	housewife	41	"	
H	Grimshaw James P	20	chauffeur	44	"	
K	Grimshaw James P, jr	20	U S A	21		
L	DeSessa Louis	21	policeman	53	" ·	
M	DeSessa Mary F—†	21	housewife	49	"	
N	Johnston Elizabeth—†	21	"	20	"	
O	Johnston Thomas	21	U S N	21	Arlington	
P	DiLorenzo Mary—†	21	housekeeper	67	here	
R	Zitano Mary—†	21	housewife	39	"	
S	Zitano Peter	21	laborer	42	"	
T	Freeman Agnes L—†	22	housewife	74	"	
U	Freeman James H	22	retired	80		
V	Sullivan Alice M—†	22	teacher	54	"	
W	Sullivan Michael N	22	retired	86		
X	Boushell Irene—†	24	housewife	46	"	
Y	Boushell William	24	mechanic	50	"	

Page.	Letter.	Full Name.	Residence, Jan. 1, 1945.	Occupation.	Supposed Age.	Reported Residence, Jan. 1, 1944. Street and Number.

Gladstone Street—Continued

	z	Sullivan John J	24	reporter	49	here
1717						
	A	Sullivan Margaret E—†	24	housewife	44	"
	B	DeSimone Carl	25	engineer	43	"
	c	DeSimone Michael	25	U S A	24	
	D	Pastore Marciano	25	mechanic	53	"
	E	Pastore Rose—†	25	housewife	52	"
	F	Sacco Angelina—†	25	"	30	
	G	Sacco Ernest T	25	chemist	38	"
	H	Genzale Frances—†	25	saleswoman	32	"
	K	Genzale Ralph	25	U S N	30	"
	L	Granata Flora—†	25	housewife	28	57 Orient av
	M	Granata James	25	salesman	37	57 "
	N	Giarrusso Caroline—†	26	housewife	44	here
	o	Giarrusso James	26	salesman	47	"
	P	Bianco John	26	retired	75	"
	R	Cataldo Annie—†	26	housewife	66	"
	s	Butts Cecelia M—†	26	"	48	
	T	Butts Joseph	26	metalworker	58	"
	U	Belli Angelina—†	33	housewife	51	"
	v	Belli Gilda—†	33	dressmaker	23	"
	w	Belli Luigi	33	rigger	58	"
	x	Mennella Eleanor—†	33	housewife	21	"
	Y	Mennella Randolph, jr	33	U S C G	21	"
	z	Viscione Anna—†	33	housewife	52	169 Orient av
1718						
	A	Viscione Ralph	33	laborer	57	169 "
	B	*Strangie Parmella—†	33	housewife	54	here
	c	Strangie Frank	33	U S N	22	"
	D	Strangie Jennie—†	33	clerk	23	"
	E	Strangie Pasquale	33	U S M C	23	"
	F	Strangie Rose—†	33	stenographer	20	"
	G	DiGregorio Angelina—†	34	housewife	43	"
	H	DiGregorio Rizziero	34	carpenter	49	"
	K	Forster Charles D	37	U S A	20	"
	L	McDonald Mary B—†	37	draftswoman	42	"
	M	Reagan Anna E—†	37	housewife	67	"
	N	Reagan Charles A	37	salesman	66	"
	o	Reagan Charles J	37	U S A	25	"
	P	Caputo Andrew	37	machinist	30	"
	R	Caputo Elizabeth—†	37	housewife	55	"

Page.	Letter.	Full Name.	Residence, Jan. 1, 1945.	Occupation.	Supposed Age.	Reported Residence, Jan. 1, 1944. Street and Number.

	s	Caputo John	37	ironworker	55	here
	t	Consalata Gladys—†	37	clerk	25	"
	u	DeFronzo Angelina—†	37	housewife	31	"
	v	DeFronzo Pasqualino	37	machinist	36	"
	w	Cardinale Eleanor—†	44	stenographer	21	"
	x	Cardinale Mary—†	44	"	28	
	y	Cardinale Nicholas	44	U S N	29	
	z	Cardinale Raffaela—†	44	clerk	26	"
1719						
	a	*Cardinale Tose—†	44	housewife	55	"
	b	Cardinale Vincent	44	U S A	23	
	c	Piscopo Guy	45	attorney	40	"
	d	Piscopo John	45	retired	68	"
	e	Piscopo Lillian—†	45	bookkeeper	45	"
	f	Piscopo Louise—†	45	receptionist	38	"
	g	Piscopo Mary—†	45	at home	41	"
	h	Guerini Olga—†	46	stitcher	22	"
	k	Guerini Oswald	46	U S A	20	
	l	Guerini Purifica—†	46	housewife	57	"
	m	Guerini Joseph	46	U S A	25	
	n	Guerini Mary—†	46	housewife	24	"
	o	Paladino Aimee—†	51	teacher	33	"
	p	Paladino Aldo	51	U S A	30	"
	r	Paladino Marie—†	51	housewife	68	"
	s	Ekholm Charles F	52	retired	70	
	t	Ekholm Helena I—†	52	housewife	64	"
	u	McGinn Helen E—†	52	"	39	
	v	McGinn Joseph G	52	manager	40	"
	w	Cummings Catherine—†	56	housewife	35	"
	x	Cummings William S	56	planner	40	"
	y	Cummings Catherine—†	56	supt	50	
	z	Cummings Edward	56	coppersmith	43	"
1720						
	a	Cummings Ellen—†	56	housewife	72	"
	b	Cummings John	56	plumber	80	"
	c	Cummings Joseph	56	clerk	39	"
	d	Cummings Thomas	56	"	48	
	e	Larkin Mary A—†	57	housekeeper	59	"
	f	McDonald Elias	57	engineer	69	"
	g	McDonald Josephine—†	57	housewife	67	"
	k	Bruno Salvatore	60	storekeeper	27	"

13

Gladstone Street—Continued

L	Bruno Susan—†	60	housewife	28	here
M	Angrisano Anthony	61	musician	27	"
N	Angrisano Josephine—†	61	housewife	26	"
O	Dinarello Mary C—†	61	housekeeper	53	"
P	Zafarana Alfonse	61	U S A	25	..
R	Zafarana Carmella H—†	61	housewife	25	"
S	Bruno Eleanor—†	62	"	30	"
T	Bruno James	62	merchant	28	"
U	Bruno Julia—†	62	"	50	
V	Abruzese Gabriel	65	retired	66	"
W	Abruzese Gertrude—†	65	housewife	26	"
X	Abruzese James	65	driller	36	
Y	Carosella Antonetta—†	65	housewife	49	"
Z	Carosella Pasquale	65	tailor	50	

1721

A	Farley Marie—†	66	housewife	34	"
B	Farley Vincent	66	optician	39	"
C	Reilly Mary A—†	66	housewife	61	"
D	Jennings Mildred—†	69	secretary	26	"
E	Jennings William	69	electrician	30	"
F	Luongo John A	69	cook	31	
G	Luongo Madeline—†	69	housewife	28	"
H	Marino Irene—†	69	"	41	
K	Marino Joseph	69	machinist	43	"
L	Bronzo Anthony	71	U S A	28	
M	Bronzo Casimiro	71	tailor	51	
N	Bronzo Madaline—†	71	housewife	49	"
O	Bronzo Martha—†	71	dressmaker	24	"
P	Bronzo Raymond	71	student	20	".
R	Famolare John	72	chauffeur	46	"
S	Famolare Joseph	72	U S N	20	
T	Famolari Ruth—†	72	housewife	43	"
U	Guptill Louis	72	retired	67	
V	Neff Margaret—†	72	housewife	31	"
W	Neff Robert	72	chemist	32	"
X	O'Hara Dorothy—†	72	housewife	23	"
Y	O'Hara James	72	U S A	24	
Z	Luongo Joseph	73	"	25	

1722

A	Luongo Margaret—†	73	housewife	57	"
B	Luongo Marie—†	73	"	23	818 Harrison av

14

Page.	Letter.	FULL NAME.	Residence, Jan. 1, 1945.	Occupation.	Supposed Age.	Reported Residence, Jan. 1, 1944. Street and Number.

Gladstone Street—Continued

c	Luongo Mary—†	73	clerk	22	here
d	Luongo Michael	73	U S A	27	"
e	Luongo Ralph	73	retired	57	"
f	Martino Alfonzina—†	81	housewife	52	"
g	Martino Eliseo	81	merchant	55	"
h	Martino Gerald	81	U S A	24	
k	Martino Jennie—†	81	stenographer	21	"
l	Patturella Mary—†	81	housekeeper	58	"
m	DeFreitas Clementine—†	81	housewife	30	"
n	DeFreitas Thomas	81	shipfitter	32	"
o	Marino Grace—†	82	clerk	20	
p	Marino John	82	inspector	46	"
r	Marino Rose—†	82	housewife	42	"
s	Briggs Margaret M—†	82	at home	49	260 Everett
t	Lombardi Angelo A	82	contractor	44	4 Winthrop
u	Lombardi Rita B—†	82	housewife	28	260 Everett
v	Marino Delma—†	82	"	36	here
w	Marino Frank	82	merchant	36	"
x	Marino Grace—†	82	at home	75	"
y	Gianturco Angelina—†	85	housewife	29	Chelsea
z	Marino Anthony	85	custodian	53	here
	1723				
a	Marino Flavia—†	85	housewife	50	"
b	Marino Sabastian	85	U S N	21	"
c	Pratt Arthur W	86	retired	68	
d	Pratt Mary—†	86	housewife	70	"
e	Sacco Grace C—†	87-	"	34	
f	Sacco John	87-	mechanic	38	"
g	Bird Mary E—†	88	at home	76	"
h	Bird Sarah L—†	88	"	80	
k	Sampson Blanche—†	89	housekeeper	60	"
l	DeFranco Rosemary—†	90	clerk	23	"
m	Duscio Concetto	90	candymaker	73	"
n	Duscio Mary—†	90	housewife	61	"
o	Rapino Phyllis—†	92	"	29	"
p	Rapino Vincent	92	mortician	32	"
r	Breed Helen—†	93	housewife	31	"
s	Breed James	93	printer	34	"
t	Eramo Fred	93	U S A	37	
u	Eramo George	93	U S N	39	
v	Eramo Guido	93	chauffeur	34	"

15

Page	Letter	Full Name.	Residence, Jan. 1, 1945.	Occupation.	Supposed Age.	Reported Residence, Jan. 1, 1944. Street and Number.

Gladstone Street—Continued

	w	Eramo John	93	machinist	26	here
	x	Eramo Mary—†	93	housewife	60	"
	y	Eramo Vincenzo	93	retired	70	"
	z	Eramo Viola—†	93	clerk	28	
1724						
	a	Bisignani Marie—†	94	housewife	28	Somerville
	b	Bisignani Richard	94	attorney	34	62 Gove
	c	Indegaro Anthony	98	welder	27	here
	d	Indegaro Bertha—†	98	stitcher	23	"
	e	Indegaro Evelyn—†	98	inspector	37	"
	f	Indegaro Margaret—†	98	housewife	57	"
	g	Indegaro Romeo	98	U S A	30	
	h	Merluzzi Carlo	99	retired	65	
	k	Merluzzi Gino U	99	rigger	40	
	l	Merluzzi Ida—†	99	housewife	63	"
	m	Whalen Annie F—†	101	"	72	
	n	Whalen John I	101	retired	76	
	o	Whalen Marion L—†	101	secretary	41	"
	p	Bertagna Euba—†	111	WAVE	30	"
	r	Bertagna Mary—†	111	housewife	26	"
	s	Bertagna Robert B	111	U S N	33	
	t	Bertagna Speranza—†	111	at home	54	"
	u	Santarpio Elizabeth—†	112	housewife	32	"
	v	Santarpio Vincent	112	machinist	33	"
	w	Skehan Alice W—†	112	housewife	55	"
	x	Skehan John J	112	retired	55	
	y	Skehan John J	112	laborer	34	"
	z	Skehan Lucia—†	112	typist	31	
1725						
	a	Consuolo Earl	112	U S A	34	"
	b	Consuolo Lillian—†	112	milliner	32	"
	c	Sacco Frank	114	engineer	48	"
	d	Sacco Mary T—†	114	housewife	48	"
	e	*DeRose Concetta—†	114	"	48	
	f	DeRose Domenic	114	plasterer	55	"
	g	Vozzella Albert	114	electrician	36	"
	h	Vozzella Florindo	114	retired	74	
	k	Vozzella Mildred—†	114	housewife	36	"
	l	Grande Joseph	116	mason	29	
	m	Grande Pauline—†	116	housewife	30	"
	n	Viscione Antoinette—†	116	"	62	..

16

Gladstone Street—Continued

o	Viscione Concetta—†	116	housewife	23	here
p	Viscione Dominick	116	laborer	64	"
r	Viscione Raymond	116	U S N	30	"
s	Santarpio Mary—†	116	housewife	23	"
t	Santarpio Victor	116	machinist	26	"
u	Abbott John	117	USMC	36	
v	Abbott Josephine—†	117	housewife	33	"
w	Allescia Grace—†	117	"	28	"
x	Allescia Louis	117	metalworker	30	"
y	Mastrolia Thelma—†	117	waitress	33	Cambridge
z	Mastrolia William	117	U S N	31	"

1726

a	Pienta Ida—†	118	housewife	23	167 Leyden
b	Pienta Leo	118	shipper	25	167 "
c	Silvia Isabelle—†	118	factoryhand	20	here
d	Silvia Manuel	118	painter	44	"
e	Silvia Shandra—†	118	housewife	43	"
f	Faccini Charles	118	grocer	48	
g	Faccini Ida—†	118	typist	23	
h	Faccini Mary—†	118	saleswoman	20	"
k	Faccini Victoria—†	118	housewife	47	"
l	DeBenedectes Albert	118	U S A	28	
m	DeBenedectes Emma—†	118	housewife	30	"
n	Visconto James	118	longshoreman	52	"
o	Visconto Mary—†	118	housewife	52	"
p	Visconto Vincent	118	U S A	30	
r	Ciriello Carmen	120	laborer	53	
s	Ciriello Esther—†	120	housewife	53	"
t	Silvia August	120	painter	42	"
u	Silvia Mary—†	120	housewife	44	"
v	*Mirro Antoinette—†	120	tailor	36	
w	Mirra Florence—†	120	operator	29	"
x	Mirra Paul	120	U S A	34	
y	Mirra Pedro	120	retired	73	
z	LaRose Margaret—†	120	housewife	53	"

1727

a	LaRose Vincent	120	electrician	53	"
b	Velardo John B	122	mason	33	
c	Velardo Mae—†	122	housewife	21	"
d	Decillio Mary—†	122	"	35	
e	Decillio Raymond	122	laborer	45	

Gladstone Street—Continued

F	Kennedy Annie E—†	122	housewife	34	here
G	Kennedy Matthew H	122	electrician	42	"
H	Irvin Carmella—†	124	housewife	21	"
K	Irvin Robert L	124	U S A	23	
L	Olivieri Agrippina—†	124	housewife	52	"
M	Olivieri Joseph	124	retired	60	..
N	Colucci Margaret—†	124	housewife	33	"
O	Colucci Raymond	124	barber	36	"
P	Nunes Joseph	124	instructor	36	"
R	Nunes Phyllis—†	124	laborer	34	
S	Vitagliano Frank P	126	metalworker	28	"
T	Vitagliano Leo	126	laborer	55	
U	Vitagliano Mary G—†	126	housewife	47	"
V	Richards Fred	128	clerk	31	
W	Richards Grace H—†	128	housewife	30	"
X	Savoia Concetta—†	129	stitcher	22	"
Y	Savoia Domenic	129	bartender	26	"
Z	Savoia Frances—†	129	housekeeper	48	"
	1728				
A	Savoia Phyllis—†	129	stitcher	24	"
B	Sacco Frances—†	137	housewife	43	"
C	Sacco Henry	137	engineer	40	"
D	Sacco Michael	137	retired	70	"
E	Sacco Pasquale	137	counterman	37	"

Leyden Street

H	Gashin Cecelia L—†	150	clerk	25	here
K	Goldstein Benjamin	150	physician	27	"
L	Goldstein Isaac	150	merchant	50	"
M	Goldstein Minnie—†	150	housewife	48	"
N	*Basso Neva—†	150	"	42	
O	Basso William D	150	chef	43	
P	Natale Joseph	150	embosser	23	"
R	Testa Anthony	150	U S A	25	
S	Testa Joseph	150	electrician	57	"
T	Testa Maria—†	150	housewife	53	"
U	Baldassaro Fred	151	pipefitter	26	1109 Saratoga
V	Baldassaro Mary F—†	151	housewife	26	1109 "
W	Vincenti Florence—†	151	stenographer	21	here
X	Vincenti Jean—†	151	"	22	"

Leyden Street—Continued

Y	Ciampa Enrico	151	welder	26	here
Z	Ciampa Mary—†	151	housewife	24	"
	1729				
A	Howell Elsie—†	151	waitress	32	152 Leyden
B	McCarthy Anna—†	151	housewife	33	here
C	McCarthy John J	151	printer	35	"
D	Iovanna Anthony	152	U S A	28	"
E	Iovanna Carmen	152	"	22	"
F	Iovanna Frank	152	bartender	53	"
G	Schepici Josephine—†	152	housewife	24	"
H	Luca Jennie—†	152	"	40	Revere
K	Luca Rocco	152	laborer	45	"
L	Cocchi Aldo	152	stevedore	34	here
M	Cocchi Alice—†	152	housewife	33	"
N	Wolinsky Ethel—†	152	packer	34	"
L	Langone Aurelia—†	153	housewife	69	"
P	Langone Frank J	153	mechanic	49	"
R	Alioto Joseph	153	barber	54	
S	Alioto Marion R—†	153	entertainer	23	"
T	Alioto Mary—†	153	housewife	50	"
U	Alioto Rosa P—†	153	clerk	21	
V	Alioto Anthony	153	chauffeur	45	"
W	Alioto Anthony	153	U S A	20	"
X	Alioto Antoinette—†	153	housewife	45	"
Y	Alioto Frances C—†	153	clerk	22	
Z	LaSpina Lillian M—†	155	housewife	41	"
	1730				
A	LaSpina Paul J	155	compositor	48	"
B	Alioto Ernest	155	manager	49	"
C	Alioto Frances R—†	155	secretary	21	"
D	Alioto May A—†	155	housewife	45	"
E	Sindoni Marion—†	155	nurse	23	
F	Sindoni Mary—†	155	housewife	59	"
G	Sindoni Thomas	155	agent	62	
H	Booth Edward	160	salesman	42	"
K	Booth Helen—†	160	saleswoman	38	"
L	Fitzpatrick Katherine L—†	161	at home	63	"
M	Fitzpatrick Sarah J—†	161	housewife	88	"
N	Grieco Joseph	166	salesman	25	"
O	Grieco Marie—†	166	housewife	25	"
P	McGillvary Grace—†	166	"	28	

Leyden Street—Continued

R	McGillvary Isadore	166	machinist	32	here
S	Schepici Carmella—†	166	housewife	28	"
T	Schepici Mario	166	painter	30	"
U	Rossi Anthony	167	U S N	30	
V	Rossi Eda—†	167	packer	22	
W	Rossi Gus	167	retired	62	
X	Rossi Julia—†	167	packer	29	"
Y	*Rossi Mary—†	167	housewife	48	"
Z	Biagiotti Anthony	167	tester	21	
	1731				
A	*Biagiotti Mary—†	167	housewife	51	"
B	Biagiotti Ralph	167	laborer	51	
C	Cardozzi Leo	167	"	54	
D	Celona Grace—†	168	stitcher	36	"
E	Celona Stephen	168	salesman	40	"
F	Carrideo Augustine—†	168	machinist	27	"
G	Carrideo Carmella—†	168	housewife	45	"
H	Carrideo Frank	168	laborer	24	
K	Carrideo Mary—†	168	clerk	22	
L	Carrideo Samuel	168	shoeworker	52	"
M	Natale Mario	168	millhand	37	"
N	Natale Mary—†	168	housewife	34	"
O	Memmolo Dominic	169	U S A	24	
P	Memmolo Louis	169	U S N	22	
R	Memmolo Nellie—†	169	housewife	48	"
S	Memmolo Ralph	169	mason	50	
T	Felzani Anna—†	172	collector	33	"
U	*Felzani Antoinetta—†	172	housewife	54	"
V	Felzani Dora—†	172	operator	27	"
W	Felzani Joseph	172	U S A	23	
X	Felzani Louis	172	teller	66	
Y	DeCristoforo Carl	174	salesman	39	"
Z	DeCristoforo Carmen	174	retired	72	
	1732				
A	DeCristoforo Dorothy—†	174	housewife	38	"
B	Frassica Mary—†	175	domestic	74	"
C	Farssica Philippa—†	175	stenographer	49	"
D	Forlani Mary—†	175	housewife	46	"
E	DeMayo Alba—†	176	"	26	"
F	DeMayo Charles	176	shipfitter	26	"

Page.	Letter.	Full Name.	Residence, Jan. 1, 1945.	Occupation.	Supposed Age.	Reported Residence, Jan. 1, 1944. Street and Number.

Leyden Street—Continued

	G	Pareschi Celso	176	grocer	58	here
	H	Pareschi John	176	U S A	28	"
	K	Pareschi Mildred—†	176	saleswoman	22	"
	L	Landry Louis	177	fisherman	63	"
	M	McDonald Clement	177	machinist	33	"
	N	McDonald Estelle—†	177	housewife	28	"
	O	Marshall Concetta C—†	177	"	49	
	P	Marshall Joseph A	177	engineer	49	"
	R	Mazzarino Pauline—†	177	finisher	50	
	S	Mazzarino Sebastian	177	operator	54	"
	T	Magnifico Jerome	178	pharmacist	35	"
	U	Magnifico Leonora—†	178	housewife	32	"
	V	Sinatra Carl	180	salesman	33	"
	W	Sinatra Constance—†	180	operator	35	"
	X	Sinatra Josephine—†	180	shoeworker	37	"
	Y	DeGregorio George	180	operator	35	"
	Z	DeGregorio Jean—†	180	housewife	32	"
		1733				
	A	Flaherty Adele M—†	182	tel operator	26	"
	B	Flaherty Catherine C—†	182	WAVE	20	"
	C	Flaherty Catherine M—†	182	housewife	60	"
	D	Flaherty Lawrence J	182	U S A	28	"
	E	Flaherty Mary—†	182	stockwoman	24	"
	F	Flaherty Michael J	182	guard	68	
	G	Lavelle Jeremiah	182	bartender	50	"
	H	Lavelle Mary—†	182	housewife	48	"
	K	Gallagher Frances—†	183	"	27	"
	L	Gallagher Frank	183	chauffeur	32	"
	M	*Grieco Domenic	183	oilman	56	
	N	Grieco Michael	183	U S N	29	
	O	Grieco Nicholas	183	U S A	20	
	P	Grieco Vito	183	"	27	
	R	Sgroi Frances—†	183	housewife	42	"
	S	Sgroi Samuel	183	electrician	49	"
	T	Grieco Joseph	183	U S A	24	
	U	Grieco Josephine—†	183	housewife	46	"
	V	Grieco Mary—†	183	supervisor	27	"
	W	Grieco Michael	183	clerk	52	
	X	Grieco Phyllis—†	183	welder	25	
	Y	Terriciano Angelina—†	186	housewife	41	"

Page	Letter	Full Name.	Residence, Jan. 1, 1945.	Occupation.	Supposed Age.	Reported Residence, Jan. 1, 1944. Street and Number.

Leyden Street—Continued

	z	Terriciano Ann—†	186	clerk	20	here
		1734				
	A	Terriciano Joseph	186	painter	44	"
	B	DeAngelis Florence L—†	186	housewife	43	"
	C	DeAngelia Henry C ،	186	inspector	44	"
	D	Sirignano Luigi	186	retired	83	
	F	Salerno Cecelia—†	188	housewife	34	"
	G	Salerno Gloria C—†.	188	assembler	21	"
	H	Salerno John	188	bartender	35 ·	"
	K	Salerno Peter M	188	waiter	54	"
	L	Salerno Rose—†	188	housewife	53	"
	M	Nason John F	192	operator	37	"
	N	Nason Margaret—†	192	housewife	33	"
	O	Gallagher Frederick	194	U S N	27	212 E Eagle
	P	Gallagher Ruth—†	194	operator	27	212 "
	R	Milroy Albert A	194	"	57	212 "
	S	Milroy Rita—†	194	housewife	49	212 "
	T	Walsh James	194	U S A	33	212 ‘
	U	Walsh Mildred—†	194	housewife	33	212 "
	V	Moltedo Henry P	196	attorney	67	here
	W	Moltedo Kathryn S—†	196	housewife	64	"
	X	Biggi Louis	198	shipper	56	"
	Y	Biggi Mary—†	198	at home	94	"
	z	Christoforo Nellie—†	198	housewife	50	"
		1735				
	A	Christoforo Olga—†	198	clerk	25	
	B	Conway Norma—†	198	"	30	"
	C	Allegra Iola—†	200	housewife	40	"
	D	Allegra Stephen	200	machinist	40	"
	E	Biagi Frances—†	200	housewife	23	472 Saratoga
	F	Biagi Mario	200	U S A	24	472 "
	G	*Maglitta Salvina—†	200	domestic	74	here
	H	Kelly Mary R—†	210	housewife	46	"
	K	Kelly William F	210	clerk	48	"
	L	McIntosh Ruth A—†	210	typist	22	"
	M	McIntosh William J	210	U S A	22	14 Neptune rd
	N	Simbaldi Mary R—†	210	housewife	21	here
	O	Simbaldi Raymond	210	U S A	21	177 Cottage
	P	Cipoletta Anthony	214	electrician	28	here
	R	Cipoletta Josephine—†	214	housewife	51	"
	S	Fraga Elizabeth C—†	226	"	32	"

22

T	Fraga John	226	pipefitter	41	here
U	Turner Catherine—†	226	housewife	73	"
V	Turner Frederick	226	retired	89	"
W	Turner Josephine B—†	226	domestic	55	"
X	Turner Manuel J	226	policeman	53	"
Y	Turner Mary—†	226	housewife	80	"
Z	McEachern Dorothy G-†	226	"	27	
	1736				
A	McEachern James J	226	U S A	27	18 Lexington
B	McRae Anna C—†	226	bookbinder	37	here
C	McRae Mary L—†	226	domestic	60	"
D	McRae Mildred M—†	226	bookbinder	39	"
E	McRae Walter	226	U S N	28	
F	McRae William	226	bookbinder	30	"
G	*Cardinale Raffaela—†	240	housewife	65	"
H	DeAngelico Dominick	240	U S N	27	
K	DeAngelico Mary—†	240	housewife	26	"
L	Schwarz Albert	240	porter	35	
M	Schwarz Julia—†	240	housewife	36	"
N	Capone Margaret—†	240½	"	30	
O	Capone Richard	240½	operator	31	"
P	DeSimone Constance—†	242	housewife	29	"
R	DeSimone Oliver	242	U S A	27	"
S	Lanzilli Leona—†	242	housewife	36	Winthrop
T	Lanzilli Nicholas	242	engineer	37	"
U	Velona Anna—†	242	housewife	34	here
V	Velona Nicholas	242	welder	30	"
W	Deeran Josephine—†	244	housewife	21	"
X	Deeran Sarkis	244	shipfitter	34	"
Y	Corbett Dennis	244	U S A	31	··
Z	Corbett Eleanor—†	244	housewife	29	"
	1737				
A	Bruxelles Agnes E—†	244	"	55	
B	Bruxelles Gloria C—†	244	clerk	20	
C	Bruxelles Gregory W	244	U S A	22	
D	Bruxelles Pasquale	244	woodcarver	53	"
E	Giella Edward	246	shipwright	40	"
F	Giella Ida—†	246	housewife	36	"
G	Cincotta Thomas	246	baker	52	
H	*Zagarri Jennie—†	246	housewife	47	"
K	Zagarri Marie—†	246	stitcher	26	

23

Leyden Street—Continued

L	Zagarri Phillip	246	U S A	20	here
M	Zagarri Salvatore	246	painter	28	"
N	Zagarri Vincenza—†	246	stenographer	23	"
O	Bianco Josephine—†	246	packer	32	"
P	Bianco Mary—†	246	housewife	63	"
R	Sacco Salvatore	246	shoeworker	38	"
S	Cincotta Grace—†	250	housewife	24	"
T	Cincotta Phillip	250	U S A	27	
U	Erickson Eleanor—†	250	housewife	30	"
V	Erickson Henry	250	machinist	31	"
W	Bianco Angelina—†	250	housewife	64	"
X	Bianco Bartholomew	250	laborer	42	
Y	Bianco Lawrence	250	chauffeur	45	"
Z	Grasso Angela—†	250	saleswoman	35	"
	1738				
A	Grasso Clara—†	250	clerk	28	"
B	Grasso Mae—†	250	packer	33	
C*	Grasso Rosemarie—†	250	housewife	70	"
D	Messina Diego R	256	U S A	21	
E	Messina James D	256	agent	43	
F*	Messina Josephine—†	256	housewife	63	"
G	Messina Margaret—†	256	saleswoman	35	"
H	Messina Mary—†	256	stitcher	34	"
K	Mullone Diega—†	256	housewife	43	"
L	Warren Catherine—†	258	"	49	
M	Warren John	258	machinist	57	"
N	O'Brien Edward J	258	longshoreman	32	"
O	O'Brien Florence—†	258	housewife	27	"

Montmorenci Avenue

P	Clark Arthur R	68	milkman	54	here
R	Clark Myrtle—†	68	housewife	51	"
S	Taft Harold L	68	chauffeur	35	"
T	Taft Marie C—†	68	housewife	31	"
U*	Hermanson Hgordis—†	75	"	39	New York
V	Hermanson John	75	foreman	52	"
W	Angelucci Assunto	75	carpenter	50	here
X	Angelucci Gina—†	75	clerk	22	"
Y	Angelucci Maria—†	75	housewife	43	"
Z	Fucile Steven J	75	manager	24	"

24

Page.	Letter.	FULL NAME.	Residence, Jan. 1, 1945.	Occupation.	Supposed Age.	Reported Residence, Jan. 1, 1944. Street and Number.

1739

Montmorenci Avenue—Continued

A	Rejo Ernest	91	agent	38	here
B	Rejo Helen—†	91	housewife	38	"
C	Phillips Anthony L	111	operator	55	"
D	Phillips Edna M—†	111	housewife	51	"
E	Phillips Richard A	111	U S A	25	
F	Canellos Peter L	119	salesman	46	"
G	Canellos Pota—†	119	housewife	33	"

Orient Avenue

H	LeBlanc Joseph R	1	U S N	34	here
K	LeBlanc Margaret—†	1	housewife	33	"
L	Quirck Frances—†	1	"	71	"
M	Quirck Francis	1	shipfitter	43	"
N	Quirck Paul	1	U S A	37	"
O	Quirck William	1	U S N	39	"
P	Greenfield Charles H	1	checker	68	"
R	Greenfield Mary B—†	1	housewife	61	"
S	Greenfield William	1	U S A	38	
T	Laforet Helen—†	1	clerk	20	
U	Laforet Jennette—†	1	U S M C	21	"
V	Johnson Julia—†	3	at home	72	"
W	Johnson Lawrence	3	printer	39	
X	Johnson Mary—†	3	housewife	38	"
Y	McLaughlin John J	3	retired	68	
Z	McLaughlin Mary—†	3	housewife	60	"
	1740					
A	Grant Charles	3	cutter	44	
B	Grant Henry	3	machinist	46	"
C	Matthews Donald L	3	"	43	
D	Matthews Marie—†	3	housewife	36	"
E	Whelan Irene N—†	5	"	35	
F	Whelan John E	5	clerk	39	
G	O'Brien Elizabeth—†	5	housewife	65	"
H	O'Brien James E	5	clerk	40	
K	Sears Margaret W—†	5	housewife	42	"
L	Sears William W	5	chauffeur	44	"
M	Murray George	5	operator	65	"
N	Verry John	5	U S N	38	
O	Verry Pauline—†	5	clerk	35	

Orient Avenue—Continued

P	Balboni Catherine F—†	7	housewife	33	here
R	Balboni Louis A	7	machinist	39	"
S	Pattee Charlotte A—†	7	housewife	33	"
T	Pattee Leon B	7	machinist	34	"
U	Whalen Thomas J	7	chauffeur	26	325 E Eagle
V	Whalen Winifred—†	7	housewife	25	325 "
W	Fiore Phyllis—†	8	"	27	Somerville
X	Fiore Samuel	8	electrician	34	
Y	Zambello Frank	8	storekeeper	55	48 Porter
Z	Zambello Lucy—†	8	housewife	44	48 "
	1741				
A	Maffei Nicholas	11	U S C G	24	here
B	Maffei Reufina—†	11	housewife	64	"
C	Maffei Salvatore	11	guard	61	"
D	Cray Richard S	11	retired	78	
E	Fontes Manuel S	11	chauffeur	46	"
F	Fontes Natalie—†	11	housewife	46	"
G	Fontes Ralph E	11	U S A	23	
H	Fontes Roland	11	seaman	21	"
K	Vitagliano Orlando	12	merchant	37	165 London
L	Vitagliano Philomena—†	12	housewife	37	165 "
M	Smallcomb John P	12	shipfitter	45	here
N	Smallcomb Peter	12	U S N	37	"
O	Thompson Agnes—†	12	operator	37	"
P	Thompson James	12	salesman	28	"
R	Thompson Margaret—†	12	at home	88	"
S	Walsh Bridget—†	12	"	77	
T	Mollerstrom Sophia—†	15	"	81	
U	Rasmussen Charlotte W—†	15	housewife	53	"
V	Rasmussen Robert	15	machinist	57	"
W	Callen Madeline—†	19	clerk	42	
X	Callen Mary—†	19	at home	82	"
Y	Rowe George A, jr	19	U S A	29	
Z	Rowe Margaret A—†	19	housewife	54	"
	1742				
A	O'Donnell Anastasia D—†	21	"	51	
B	O'Donnell Edwin F	21	U S N	27	"
¹B	O'Donnell George D	21	"	29	
C	Adreani Andrew	24	merchant	37	"
D	Adreani Eleanor—†	24	housewife	32	"
E	Lawton Olga—†	24	"	25	..

Page.	Letter.	FULL NAME.	Residence, Jan. 1, 1945.	Occupation.	Supposed Age.	Reported Residence, Jan. 1, 1944. Street and Number.

	F	Trongone Albert	24	U S N	39	here
	G	Trongone Marie—†	24	at home	60	"
	H	Vozella Joseph	24	retired	50	"
	K	McGinn Harold J	27	agent	51	"
	L	McGinn Rose W—†	27	housewife	39	"
	M	Todesca Angelina—†	27	timekeeper	20	152 Leyden
	N	Todesca Artemia—†	27	housewife	44	152 "
	O	Todesca Idalo	27	U S A	22	152 "
	P	Todesca Joseph	27	carpenter	45	152 "
	R	Fiorentino Nicholas	28	U S N	24	here
	S	Fiorentino Pauline B—†	28	housewife	23	"
	T	Pearson Charles	28	janitor	55	"
	U	Pearson Charles	28	U S N	33	
	V	Pearson Henrietta—†	28	housewife	55	"
	W	Landry Margaret W—†	29	"	51	
	X	Landry Walter C	29	B F D	61	
	Y	Bernard Marie P—†	29	waitress	60	"
	Z	Landry Mary B—†	29	saleswoman	38	"
		1743				
	A	Landry Peter E	29	machinist	63	"
	B	Polodec Mary S—†	29	housekeeper	72	"
	C	Merlino Andrew	32	barber	52	"
	D	Merlino Christina—†	32	housewife	45	"
	E	Merlino Frank A	32	U S A	22	
	F	Merlino Nunzia F—†	32	secretary	24	"
	G	Piscitelli Lucia—†	32	housewife	38	"
	H	Piscitelli Salvatore	32	defense wkr	51	"
	K	Santoro Emanuela—†	32	housewife	52	"
	L	Santoro Sabino	32	shoemaker	57	"
	M	Dondero Florence—†	37	clerk	30	
	P	Petrone Frances—†	39	housewife	27	"
	O	Petrone Leonard F	39	chauffeur	33	"
	P	Zambella Anna—†	39	housewife	29	72 Chelsea
	R	Zambella Frank	39	butcher	28	72 "
	S	Boncordo Domenica—†	40	housewife	56	here
	S*	Boncordo Joseph	40	retired	73	"
	U	Vadala Ignazio	40	policeman	52	"
	V	Vadala Rose—†	40	housewife	33	"
	W	Fuccillo Carmen	40	presser	29	
	X	Fuccillo Sadie—†	40	housewife	26	"
	Y	Cohane Virginia—†	41	"	25	1090 Benningt'n

Page.	Letter.	Full Name.	Residence, Jan. 1, 1945.	Occupation.	Supposed Age.	Reported Residence, Jan. 1, 1944. Street and Number.

Orient Avenue—Continued

z	Cohane William	41	welder	25	1090 Benningt'n

1744

A	Campatelli Gino	41	policeman	55	here
B	Campatelli Irene—†	41	typist	20	"
C	Campatelli Natalie—†	41	machinist	24	"
D	Campatelli Robert	41	U S A	21	
E	Campatelli Stella—†	41	housewife	49	"
F	*Gravallese Angelina—†	42	at home	66	"
G	Luongo Elizabeth—†	42	housewife	44	"
H	Luongo John A	42	merchant	52	"
K	Luongo Mary—†	42	secretary	21	"
L	Mastrangelo Charles F	44	physician	50	"
M	Mastrangelo Lillian—†	44	secretary	21	"
N	Mastrangelo Mary—†	44	housewife	46	"
O	Barker Regina B—†	48	"	45	..
P	Barker William H	48	clerk	52	"
R	Testa Eugene F	49	proprietor	75	"
S	Staffier Domenic T	54	physician	39	"
T	Staffier Helen—†	54	housewife	41	"
U	Fiorentino Caroline—†	56	"	50	"
V	Fiorentino Frank S	56	proprietor	54	"
W	Fiorentino Mary R—†	56	teacher	24	"
X	Fiorentino Raffaella—†	56	"	28	"
Y	Bellevia Carmella—†	57	housewife	30	177 Gladstone
z	Bellevia Charles	57	pipefitter	32	177 "

1745

A	Palaza Adam	57	attorney	36	here
B	Palaza Mildred—†	57	teacher	42	"
C	DiMari Mary—†	60	housewife	44	"
D	DiMari Sebastian	60	salesman	48	"
E	DiNunno Maria F—†	62	housewife	33	"
F	DiNunno Vincent	62	secretary	39	"
G	Briganta Lawrence	63	machinist	39	"
H	Pilato Charles J	63	shoemaker	40	"
K	Pilato Rose N—†	63	housewife	37	"
L	Pilato Louise—†	63	"	43	
M	Pilato Michael	63	shoemaker	42	"
N	Leone Amelia—†	68	housewife	44	"
O	Leone Lawrence	68	U S N	22	
P	Leone Patrick	68	pedler	55	
R	Leone Sabina—†	68	clerk	20	

28 .

Orient Avenue—Continued

s	D'Addario Albert	68	laborer	24	here
t	D'Addario Elisa—†	68	housewife	54	"
u	D'Addario Gerald	68	U S A	23	"
v	D'Addario Gilda—†	68	trimmer	27	"
w	D'Addario Ida—†	68	inspector	25	"
x	D'Addario Mario	68	U S A	31	
y	D'Addario Pasquale	68	"	28	
z	Giannattasio Eleanor—†	68	clerk	21	

1746

a	Giannattasio Frank	68	U S A	24	
b	Giannattasio Louise—†	68	clerk	26	
c	Giannattasio Michael A	68	upholsterer	52	"
d	Giannattasio Philomena—†	68	housewife	48	"
e	Giannattasio Phyllis—†	68	clerk	28	
f	Staffier Agnes—†	68	housewife	48	"
g	Staffier Rocco	68	proprietor	47	"
h	Laiacona Guy	72	painter	26	242 Leyden
k	Laiacona Mary—†	72	housewife	26	242 "
l	Tedeschi Concetta—†	72	"	28	here
m	Tedeschi Gerardo	72	realtor	28	"
n	Savasta Joseph	72	supt	29	"
o	Savasta Mafalda—†	72	housewife	26	"
p	Fobert Lillian—†	75	"	32	
r	Fobert Rosario	75	bartender	30	"
s	Eldridge Francis	75	machinist	55	"
t	Eldridge Paul	75	laborer	22	
u	Eldridge Sophia—†	75	housewife	55	"
v	Keleher Albert F	75	U S A	27	
w	Keleher Marie—†	75	saleswoman	25	"
x	McLaughlin Charles	75	B F D	62	"
y	DePaulo Gertrude R—†	76	housewife	39	"
z	DePaulo John C	76	leatherworker	49	"

1747

a	Alessandroni Aldo	76	U S N	29	
b	Alessandroni Anna—†	76	machinist	26	"
c	Alessandroni Edith—†	76	clerk	21	
d	Alessandroni Mary—†	76	housewife	55	"
e	Alessandroni Nora—†	76	clerk	30	
f	Alessandroni Salvatore	76	shoeworker	56	"
g	Mainardi Ettore	80	U S A	21	
h	Selvitella Frances—†	80	typist	20	

Orient Avenue—Continued

K	Selvitella Henry	80	attorney	49	here
L	Selvitella Lena—†	80	housewife	45	"
M	Selvitella George	80	U S A	30	"
N	Selvitella Helen—†	80	waitress	37	"
O	Selvitella Margaret—†	80	machinist	23	"
P	Selvitella Mary—†	80	stenographer	26	"
R	Selvitella Vera—†	80	housekeeper	39	"
S	Masullo Benjamin	81	barber	65	"
T	Masullo Catherine—†	81	housewife	62	"
U	Masullo Dominic	81	barber	35	"
V	Masullo Frank	81	U S A	30	
W	Masullo Amelia—†	83	housewife	34	"
X	Masullo Anthony	83	baker	36	
Y	Campbell Cecil	84	U S N	27	
Z	Campbell Frank	84	retired	54	

1748

A	Grey George	84	U S N	26	"
B	Grey Mary—†	84	housewife	25	"
C	O'Hara Barbara—†	84	"	22	
D	O'Hara George	84	U S A	22	
E	Phelan George	84	"	25	
F	Phelan Rose—†	84	housewife	21	"
G	Merlino Louis	86	proprietor	64	"
H	Merlino Mary—†	86	housewife	61	"
K	Merlino Nunzia—†	86	secretary	26	"
L	Belmonte Concetta—†	87	housewife	43	"
M	Belmonte Frank	87	bartender	22	"
N	Belmonte Vincenzo	87	proprietor	43	"
O	Puleo Frances H—†	89	housewife	46	"
P	Puleo Samuel R	89	chauffeur	51	"
R	Schuster Barbara—†	89	operator	27	"
S	Maida Mary—†	90	housewife	53	"
T	Maida Pasquale	90	clergyman	57	"
U	Maida William	80	U S A	23	
V	DiMella Angelina—†	90	housewife	51	"
W	DiMella Domenic	90	fitter	55	
X	DiMella Josephine—†	90	dressmaker	21	"
Y	DiMella Louise—†	90	clerk	29	
Z	DiMella Nicholas	90	U S A	25	

1749

A	Pinardi Charles F	90	engineer	29	"

Orient Avenue—Continued

	B	Pinardi Pauline P—†	90	housewife	29	here
	C	Marinelli Agostino S	94	policeman	58	"
	D	Marinelli Marguerita—†	94	housewife	50	"
	E	Quartarone John	98	U S A	30	
	F	Quartarone Joseph	98	"	27	
	G	Quartarone Margaret—†	98	housewife	54	"
	H	Quartarone Samuel	98	barber	55	"
	K	Perrier Edna W—†	98	housewife	35	"
	L	Perrier Ralph J	98	U S N	29	"
	M	Lawrence Clifton J	99	salesman	36	Melrose
	N	Lawrence Mary A—†	99	housewife	37	"
	O	Esposito Ellen—†	99	"	42	here
	P	Esposito Peter	99	proprietor	49	"
	R	Visco Carmella—†	99	at home	77	64 W Eagle
	S	Visco Rose—†	99	stitcher	39	64 "
	T	Gallo Anthony	100	butcher	49	here
	U	Gallo Josephine E—†	100	housewife	35	"
	V	Perrier Ruth E—†	112	"	44	"
	W	Perrier Wilfred J	112	U S N	42	
	X	Perrier Delvenia O—†	112	housewife	67	"
	Y	Perrier Evangeline M—†	112	clerk	31	
	Z	Perry Joseph C	112	mariner	40	"
1750						
	B	*Caron Marie A—†	150	secretary	53	Rhode Island
	C	Couture Cecile—†	150	clerk	24	here
	D	*Cyr Yvonne—†	150	housekeeper	25	Rhode Island
	E	DeAngelis Raffaella—†	150	buyer	33	here
	F	*Donovan Mary—†	150	cook	50	"
	G	*Dorion Belzemire—†	150	sacristan	76	"
	H	*Gagne Claire—†	150	caretaker	57	"
	K	Hinchey Irene—†	150	teacher	25	
	L	Jay Lillian—†	150	"	46	"
	M	*LaCroix Eva—†	150	librarian	65	"
	N	Lavigne Nadia—†	150	missionary	44	Rhode Island
	O	*LeStang Blanche—†	150	nurse	66	here
	P	Miller Angela—†	150	teacher	32	"
	R	*Parayre Lucie—†	150	seamstress	59	"
	S	Paulino Clara—†	150	laundress	52	"
	T	*Presseau Marie A—†	150	at home	71	"
	U	Schooley Helen J—†	150	teacher	22	Rhode Island
	V	Talbot Alma—†	150	burser	46	here

Page.	Letter.	FULL NAME.	Residence, Jan. 1. 1945.	Occupation.	Supposed Age.	Reported Residence, Jan. 1, 1944. Street and Number.

Orient Avenue—Continued

	w	Van Reeth Clotilde—†	150	teacher	64	here
	x	Whelan Anna T—†	150	"	25	Fall River

Overlook Street

	y	Larsen Alfred C	14	laborer	29	here
	z	Larsen Anna E—†	14	housewife	72	"
1751						
	A	Larsen Edith E—†	14	auditor	38	
	B	Larsen Hans C	14	foreman	68	"
	c	Larsen Harry O	14	U S C G	41	"
	D	Larsen Louis H	14	chemist	31	"
	E	Nielsen Fredericka—†	18	secretary	35	"
	F	Nielsen Heinrich	18	contractor	68	"
	G	Nielsen Louise—†	18	housewife	70	"
	H	Nielsen Robert	18	accountant	28	"
	K	Cameron Archibald	26	shipfitter	34	"
	L	Cameron Christina—†	26	at home	70	"
	M	Lane Beatrice—†	26	clerk	45	
	N	Lane Henry	26	salesman	54	"

Sea View Avenue

	o	Belmonte Angelina—†	1–3	housewife	40	here
	P	Belmonte Generoso	1–3	bartender	49	"
	R	Lanza Nan G—†	1–3	clerk	42	"
	s	Pinardi Gloria C—†	1–3	"	25	"
	T	Pinardi Raymond A	1–3	U S N	27	"
	U	Pinardi Richard J	1–3	U S A	20	"
	v	Pinardi Rose—†	1–3	housewife	53	"
	w	O'Connor Charles	5–7	clerk	41	
	x	O'Connor Helen—†	5–7	"	40	
	y	Taddonio Joseph	5–7	watchmaker	54	"
	z	Taddonio Joseph, jr	5–7	U S A	23	
1752						
	A	Taddonio Michael J	5–7	clerk	25	
	B	Taddonio Rose—†	5–7	housewife	46	"
	c	Magro Anthony I	9	U S A	21	10 Barnes av
	D	Magro Joseph D	9	manager	42	10 "
	E	Magro Lavinia M—†	9	housewife	39	10 "
	F	Puopolo Esther M—†	11	"	45	here

32

Sea View Avenue—Continued

G	Puopolo Rocco A	11	machinist	47	here
H	*Wallace Mary—†	11	at home	98	"
K	Bennett Beatrice—†	15	housewife	32	"
L	Bennett Walter	15	U S A	36	
M	Cavalieri Frank	15	chauffeur	36	"
N	Cavalieri Jennie—†	15	housewife	24	Chelsea
O	Abate Arthur	19	guard	51	here
P	Abate Marietta—†	19	housewife	47	"
R	Abate Norma—†	19	clerk	23	"
S	Catrone Emma—†	19	housewife	40	"
T	Catrone John	19	student	20	"
U	Catrone Michael J	19	salesman	42	"
V	Berarei Joseph	27	retired	74	
W	Conti Agnes—†	27	housewife	38	"
X	Conti Anthony	27	carpenter	44	"
Y	DeFronzo Alphonse	31	pharmacist	36	"
Z	DeFronzo Rose—†	31	housewife	36	"
¹z	Calla Angia J—†	39	"	47	

1753

A	Calla Edmund	39	U S A	27	"
B	Calla Francis J	39	tailor	50	"
C	Calla Judith—†	39	clerk	21	
D	DePaola Jennie—†	43	housewife	39	"
E	DePaola Ottone	43	agent	39	
F	Caruso Anne L—†	43	housewife	27	"
G	Caruso Carmen A	43	announcer	28	"

Selma Street

H	Cragin Anna E—†	10	housewife	48	here
K	Cragin Thomas E	10	engineer	52	"
L	Hamer Virginia—†	10	housewife	31	"
M	Parker Evelyn—†	10	"	24	"
N	Parker Murray M	10	seaman	24	N Carolina

Tower Street

O	Abate Alfred	30	milkman	53	here
P	Abate Alma—†	30	stenographer	21	"
R	Abate Mary—†	30	housewife	49	"

Waldemar Avenue

s	Boudreau Harold	15	shipfitter	31	here
t	Boudreau Vander L	15	rigger	46	"
u	Boudreau Violette—†	15	housewife	34	"
v	Martell Annie—†	17	"	72	
w	Martell Louis D	17	retired	75	
x	Muise Alice B—†	17	clerk	25	
y	Muise Alice M—†	17	housewife	48	"
z	Muise Francis J	17	seaman	49	

1754

a	Muise Muriel A—†	17	clerk	25	
b	Favello Louis	20	watchman	38	"
c	Favello Pauline—†	20	housewife	35	"
d	Driscoll Arthur G	21	clerk	28	
e	Driscoll Florence J—†	21	tel operator	24	"
f	Driscoll James F	21	U S A	21	"
g	Driscoll John J	21	U S N	35	"
h	Driscoll Margaret T—†	21	housewife	64	"
k	Driscoll Marguerita—†	21	tel operator	26	"
l	Morris Albert N	21	U S N	37	
m	Morris Mary A—†	21	clerk	37	"
n	Fleming Ellen G—†	23	housewife	73	"
o	Fleming George J	23	U S A	32	"
p	Fleming Margaret—†	23	clerk	32	40 Waldemar av
r	Cadigan Alice—†	32	housewife	50	here
s	Cadigan William J	32	steamfitter	50	"
t	Nolan Thomas	32	merchant	54	"
u	Roche John M	32	U S N	23	
v	Magrath Frederick J	36	director	45	"
w	Magrath Mary E—†	36	housewife	41	"
x	Johnson Frank J	37	retired	71	
y	Johnson Mary A—†	37	housewife	68	"
z	Moore John J	40	U S M C	34	"

1755

a	Moore Mary G—†	40	housewife	26	"
b	Murphy Mary M—†	40	at home	69	"
c	Olsen Caroline E—†	40	housewife	47	"
d	Olsen Harold J	40	U S M C	23	"
e	Olsen Harry J	40	fireman	47	"
f	Taylor L Frances—†	44	housekeeper	72	Wakefield
g	Terry David	44	laborer	41	here
h	Balboni Alfred	52	caretaker	36	"

34

Waldemar Avenue—Continued

K	Balboni Annie—†	52	housewife	65	here	
L	Balboni Evo	52	machinist	38	"	
M	Balboni Jean—†	52	housewife	32	"	
N	Fagone Delia—†	52	inspector	36	"	
O	Fagone Stephen	52	U S A	35		
R	Caruso Anthony T	93	farmer	22		
S	Caruso Pasquale	93	"	49		
T	Caruso Peter P	93	U S A	21		
U	Caruso Rose—†	93	housewife	45	"	
V	Brady Austin	116	U S A	24	"	
W	Brady Eleanor—†	116	tel operator	21	"	
X	Vignoli Helen C—†	116	housewife	50	"	
Y	Vignoli John B	116	carpenter	49	"	
Z	Harris James A	166	inspector	52	"	
	1756					
A	Harris Winifred V—†	166	housewife	49	"	
B	Gallagher William	230	boilermaker	45	"	
C	Gallagher Winifred—†	230	housewife	44	"	
D	King Elizabeth—†	230	"	50		
E	King George T	230	inspector	52	"	
F	Thibeault Edward P	254	seaman	29	"	
G	Thibeault Frances M—†	254	housewife	26	"	
H	Gotgart Charles R	254	U S N	25	103 Faywood av	
K	Gotgart Elizabeth V—†	254	housewife	26	103 "	

Walley Street

M	Howard Joseph F	7	coppersmith	30	here	
N	Howard Virginia A—†	7	housewife	27	"	
O	O'Neil Geraldine A—†	7	WAVE	24	"	
P	O'Neil Mary B—†	7	at home	60	"	
R	McGilvery Marian E—†	7	nurse	35		
S	McGilvery Minnie—†	7	at home	58	"	
T	Ciampa Carmella M—†	10	housewife	31	"	
U	Ciampa James G	10	clerk	33		
Y	Cincotti Mary—†	18	housewife	41	"	
Z	Cincotti Vincent	18	baker	49		

Ward 1–Precinct 18

CITY OF BOSTON

LIST OF RESIDENTS
20 YEARS OF AGE AND OVER

(NON-CITIZENS INDICATED BY ASTERISK)
(FEMALES INDICATED BY DAGGER)

AS OF

JANUARY 1, 1945

THOMAS F. SULLIVAN, *Chairman*
FREDERIC E. DOWLING, *Secretary*
WILLIAM A. MOTLEY, JR.
FRANCIS B. McKINNEY
EVERETT R. PROUT
Listing Board.

CITY OF BOSTON PRINTING DEPARTMENT

1800
Barnes Avenue

B	Cochrane Dorothy T—†	6	bookkeeper	20	here
C	Cochrane Edward P	6	electrotypist	46	"
D	Cochrane Elizabeth F—†	6	stenographer	22	"
E	Cochrane Josephine—†	6	housewife	47	"
F	Ford Frances C—†	6	"	26	
G	Ford Jerome J	6	shipfitter	28	"
H	DiSessa Concetta—†	8	at home	73	"
K	DiSessa Peter A	8	policeman	47	"
L	DiSessa Peter G	8	U S N	24	
M	DiSessa Theresa—†	8	housewife	44	"
N	Thornton Frank	8	laborer	41	"
O	Perrone Frances J—†	10	student	26	"
P	Perrone Frank	10	salesman	63	"
R	Perrone Julia—†	10	housewife	57	"
S	Palladino Josephine—†	10	"	28	
T	Palladino Rocco	10	electrician	34	"
U	Crowley Anna A—†	14	housewife	61	"
V	Crowley David J	14	clerk	63	
W	Crowley Marie E—†	14	"	30	
X	McCarthy James J	14	retired	60	
Y	Stewart Grace E—†	17	housewife	62	"
Z	Stewart John A	17	retired	77	"

1801

A	Lambert Charles	18	upholsterer	51	"
B	Lambert Charles, jr	18	U S A	22	
C	Lambert Helen—†	18	clerk	43	
D	Giella Florence L—†	18	housewife	41	"
E	Giella Vincent J	18	shipfitter	41	"
F	Hedrington Alice F—†	18	at home	46	"
G	Hedrington Ellen M—†	18	clerk	45	
H	Curtis John F	18	U S N	36	
K	Curtis Mary M—†	18	housewife	37	"
L	*Cavicchi Adelcisa—†	21	at home	75	"
M	Cavicchi Edward E	21	U S A	35	"
N	Cavicchi Joseph V	21	toolmaker	39	"
P	Barry Mary—†	22	at home	70	"
R	Jackson Anne E—†	22	housewife	28	"
S	Jackson John J	22	shipfitter	30	"
T	*Liberatore Carolina—†	22	housewife	67	"
U	Liberatore Pasquale	22	retired	72	

2

Page.	Letter.	FULL NAME.	Residence, Jan. 1, 1945.	Occupation.	Supposed Age.	Reported Residence, Jan. 1, 1944. Street and Number.

Barnes Avenue—Continued

	v	Lally Julia—†	22	housewife	22	90 Adams
	w	Lally Walter F	22	electrician	37	90 "
	x	Mangini Frederick J	25	liquors	41	here
	y	Mangini Madeline V—†	25	housewife	40	"
	z	Cavicchi John B	25	electrician	39	21 Barnes av
1802						
	a	Cavicchi Louise—†	25	chauffeur	25	here
	b	Piscopo Alice L—†	26	housewife	35	"
	c	Piscopo Thomas J	26	attorney	36	"
	d	Carlson Carl A	26	carpenter	65	"
	e	Carlson Oscar V	26	U S A	32	"
	f	McDonnell Claire C—†	26	housewife	30	Winthrop
	g	McDonnell Harold E	26	longshoreman	29	"
	h	Chisholm Andrew	30	mechanic	61	here
	k	Chisholm Annie—†	30	housewife	54	"
	l	Chisholm Virginia I—†	30	tel operator	27	"
	m	Spinney Anne D—†	30	housewife	35	"
	n	Spinney Leland J	30	clerk	37	
	o	Vega Emelia—†	30	housewife	55	"
	p	Vega Pellegrino	30	laborer	57	
	r	Vega Rose—†	30	clerk	21	
	s	Foley Edward D	34	retired	66	
	t	Regan Arthur W	34	electrician	26	"
	u	Bowen Annie E—†	40	housewife	54	"
	v	Bowen John P	40	foreman	56	"
	w	White Josephine—†	40	clerk	55	
	x	White Nathaniel	40	carpenter	60	"
	y	Repola Angelo	42	machinist	32	"
	z	Repola Jennie—†	42	housewife	33	"
1803						
	a	Indrisano Albert	44	U S A	36	
	c	Indrisano Maria—†	44	housewife	67	"
	d	Indrisano Pasquale	44	machinist	46	"
	e	Indrisano Peter	44	retired	72	
	b	Indrisano Rugero	44	U S A	34	
	f	Celata C Joseph	49	U S N	24	"
	g	Celata Joseph	49	policeman	48	"
	h	Celata Lucy—†	49	clerk	30	
	k	Celata Palmina—†	49	housewife	48	"
	l	Whittington John R	50	retired	73	
	m	McCormick Jessie M—†	50	housewife	63	"

3

Barnes Avenue—Continued

N	McCormick Joseph	50	watchman	64	here
O	Sheedy George	50	operator	42	"
P	Sheedy John	50	painter	40	"
R	Sheedy Lucy—†	50	housewife	38	"
S	Blackwell Louise G—†	54	clerk	34	
T	Blackwell Mary E—†	54	at home	69	"
U	O'Mara Agnes—†	54	boxmaker	66	"
V	*MacCrossen Minnie—†	54	housewife	62	"
W	*MacCrossen Thomas F	54	machinist	62	"
X	McLaughlin Dorothea M–†	54	housewife	29	"
Y	McLaughlin William E	54	boilermaker	29	"
Z	Mucci Giovanni	58	chauffeur	37	"

1804

A	Mucci Maria A—†	58	housewife	33	"
B	Capone Benjamin W·	58	U S N	26	
C	Capone Domenick	58	engineer	33	"
D	Capone Romilda—†	58	at home	58	"
E	Capone William D	58	U S N	27	
F	Mucci Angelina—†	58	housewife	52	"
G	Mucci Antonio	58	retired	66	"
H	Mucci Pasquale	58	kitchenman	63	"
K	Saggese Salvatore	58	U S A	32	
L	Nordby Edith—†	62	housewife	51	"
M	Nordby Sigwald C	62	asbestos wkr	54	"
N	Crocker Ina M—†	62	investigator	34	"
O	Dahl Olaf	62	fisherman	50	"
P	Snow Effa A—†	62	at home	65	"
R	Alla Elena H—†	62	housewife	39	"
S	Alla Vincent	62	mechanic	49	"
U	Heffron Margaret J—†	66·	housewife	25	35 Moore
V	Heffron William J	66	repairman	26	35 "
W	Rezendes Alfred	66	U S N	34	here
X	Rezendes Benjamin	66	cabinetmaker	58	"
Y	Rezendes Evelyn—†	66	clerk	27	"
Z	Rezendes Rita—†	66	housewife	56	"

1805

A	Rezendes Clara—†	66	clerk	30	
B	Rezendes Ernest	66	"	35	"
C	Accetta Alice M—†	69	housewife	62	"
D	Accetta Manfredi	69	clerk	62	
E	Muldoon Loretta E—†	70	housewife	53	"

Barnes Avenue—Continued

F	Muldoon William E	70	cutter	55	here
G	Nugent William B	70	investigator	50	"
H	McCarthy Elizabeth E—†	70	marker	50	"
K	McCarthy John J	70	U S A	21	
L	McCarthy Mary E—†	70	clerk	23	
M	Supple Mary L—†	70	"	46	"
N	Griffin Alice G—†	70	housewife	26	Medford
O	Griffin John P	70	laborer	26	"
P	Fenocketti Alfred	73	blocker	61	here
R	Fenocketti Alma A—†	73	teacher	33	"
S	Fenocketti Mary J—†	73	housewife	60	"
T	Croce Concetta N—†	73	"	26	
U	Croce Frederick	73	engineer	37	"
V	Lovezzola Michael	73	engraver	55	"
W	Lovezzola Michael M	73	U S N	21	
X	Lovezzola Theresa G—†	73	housewife	54	"
Y	Serra Lillian F—†	74	"	33	
Z	Serra Thomas A	74	printer	33	
	1806				
A	Sousa Irene M—†	74	housewife	31	"
B	Sousa Manuel J	74	U S C G	46	"
C	Abbott Mary E—†	74	waitress	32	"
D	O'Connell James J	74	mechanic	64	"
E	O'Connell Margaret A—†	74	housewife	62	"
F	Kelly Florence C—†	78	"	53	
G	Kelly John C	78	custodian	55	"
H	Kelly Michael T	78	guard	53	
K	Fitzpatrick Alice M—†	78	housewife	44	"
L	Fitzpatrick Edward J	78	policeman	44	"
M	Fitzpatrick Edward J, jr	78	U S A	22	
N	Mahoney William J	78	policeman	48	"
O	Daley Anna P—†	78	housewife	57	"
P	Daley Maurice A	78	B F D	57	
R	Daley Mildred P—†	78	clerk	23	"
S	Daley Rose A—†	78	teacher	29	"
T	Pierce Ellen E—†	82	housewife	31	"
U	Pierce Francis R	82	custodian	38	"
V	Sanders William W	82	laborer	58	
W	Williams Katherine L—†	82	housewife	78	"
X	Williams William J	82	watchman	78	"
Y	Mandia Mary C—†	82	supervisor	37	"

Barnes Avenue—Continued

	z	Mandia Winifred V—†	82	at home	57	here
		1807				
	A	Bruce Marie P—†	86	housewife	30	"
	B	Bruce Robert W	86	U S A	28	
	c	Schindhelm Henry J	86	"	37	
	D	Schindhelm Louise M—†	86	telegrapher	45	"
	E	Murray Margaret A—†	86	clerk	60	"
	F	Murray Mary A—†	86	at home	65	"
	G	Brown Sophie E—†	86	housewife	74	"
	H	Brown William M	86	retired	70	
	K	Burns Claire J—†	90	tel operator	38	"
	L	McWilliams Anna L—†	90	at home	49	"
	M	McWilliams Barbara A—†	90	tel operator	20	"
	N	Wilson Alecia F—†	90	"	26	"
	o	Kelley Annie M—†	90	inspector	52	"
	P	Lane David E	90	B F D	43	"
	R	Lane Katherine A—†	90	housewife	43	"
	s	Deagan Ruth M—†	90	clerk	27	"
	T	McEachern Charles L	90	U S C G	47	"
	U	McEachern Jeanette E—†	90	waitress	45	"

Bayswater Street

	v	Landry Clarence	15	machinist	44	here
	w	Landry Mary—†	15	housewife	76	"
	x	Marchand Maud—†	15	"	43	"
	Y	Marchand Narcisse	15	operator	43	"
	z	Basile Lena—†	16	housekeeper	70	"
		1808				
	A	McMorrow May—†	16	housewife	49	"
	B	McMorrow William	16	fireman	47	"
	c	Preble Dorothea—†	16	tel operator	26	"
	D	Andrews Emily—†	16	waitress	55	"
	E	August Mary J—†	16	housekeeper	71	"
	F	Bordman Charles A	16	retired	73	"
	G	Bordman Marion—†	16	maid	64	"
	H	Stearns Katherine—†	21	housewife	44	"
	K	Stearns Morris	21	engraver	42	"
	L	Bianco Alexander F	22	retired	74	
	M	Bianco Jennie M—†	22	housewife	67	"
	N	Cantillo Lena—†	23	"	25	"

6

Page.	Letter.	FULL NAME.	Residence, Jan. 1, 1945.	Occupation.	Supposed Age.	Reported Residence, Jan. 1, 1944. Street and Number.

Bayswater Street—Continued

	o	Cantillo Thomas	23	storekeeper	27	here
	p	D'Avallone Eleanor—†	23	maid	21	"
	r	D'Avallone John	23	U S N	24	"
	s	D'Avallone Mary—†	23	housewife	48	"
	t	D'Avallone Matthew	23	tailor	59	
	u	Keller Andrew J	25	U S A	36	..
	v	Keller Eileen—†	25	maid	41	
	w	Keller John J	25	inspector	48	"
	x	Keller Robert J	25	photographer	47	"
	y	Keller Susan—†	25	at home	82	"
	z	Bowen Margaret J—†	29	housekeeper	60	"

1809

	a	Gibbons Daniel J	31	retired	53	
	b	Gibbons Elizabeth—†	31	housewife	51	"
	c	Zimmerman Frank M	31	U S N	33	
	d	Zimmerman Margaret—†	31	housewife	22	"
	e	Sullivan Charles	33	clerk	37	
	f	Sullivan Mary—†	33	housekeeper	68	"
	g	Driscoll Catherine—†	35	saleswoman	28	"
	h	Driscoll Irene—†	35	housewife	45	"
	k	Driscoll Timothy	35	laborer	50	"
	l	Capezutto Charles	37	tailor	44	
	m	Capezutto Helen—†	37	housewife	39	"
	n	Capezutto Marie—†	37	"	69	"
	o	Bonaccorso Margaret—†	41	"	28	
	p	Bonaccorso Nunzio	41	lawyer	34	
	s	Meloni Charles	45	physician	45	"
	t	Meloni Mary—†	45	housewife	43	"
	u	Barry Helene—†	49	"	39	"
	v	Barry Thomas E	49	inspector	45	"
	w	Lund Hilma E—†	49	housewife	61	"
	x	Spadafora Anthony	49	druggist	38	"
	y	Spadafora Winifred—†	49	housewife	28	"
	z	Dwyer Elizabeth G—†	50	"	72	

1810

	a	Dwyer John J	50	messenger	73	"
	b	Taylor Mary E—†	50	housekeeper	73	Watertown
	c	Leonard Doris M—†	50	"	33	here
	d	Leonard Francis	50	U S A	33	"
	e	Pryor Mathilda E—†	50	housewife	53	"
	f	Pryor Percy J	50	retired	70	

Bayswater Street—Continued

G	O'Connell Daniel J	53	manager	57	here
H	O'Connell Daniel J, jr	53	U S N	26	"
K	O'Connell James S	53	U S A	23	"
L	O'Connell Lillian S—†	53	housewife	49	"
M	Herman Alta—†	54	"	67	
N	Herman Henry C	54	retired	67	
O	Connors Eliza—†	54	housekeeper	60	"
P	McGonigle Anna—†	54	housewife	64	"
R	McGonigle Daniel H	54	U S N	41	"
S	McGonigle George E	54	attorney	45	"
T	McGonigle Madeline—†	54	housewife	35	"
U	McGonigle Mary A—†	54	statistician	43	"
V	Reardon Grace T—†	54	secretary	40	"
W	MacEachern Lottie—†	55	housewife	41	"
X	MacEachern Peter	55	janitor	58	
Y	Evans George E	57	mason	52	
Z	Evans Mary F—†	57	housekeeper	62	"
	1811				
A	Brosnahan Rose H—†	58	housewife	29	"
B	Brosnahan William J	58	U S A	32	"
C	Hicks Alice C—†	58	housewife	27	"
D	Hicks Charles H	58	U S A	31	
E	Solari Louis M	58	laundrywkr	69	"
F	Solari Rose H—†	58	housewife	52	"
H	Keating Alice D—†	66	prob'n officer	51	"
K	Keating Gertrude—†	66	teacher	41	"
L	Keating Kathryn F—†	66	housekeeper	47	"
M	Weafer Leonard E	70	attorney	42	"
N	Weafer Margaret—†	70	housewife	39	"
O	Mullen James H	74	machinist	56	"
P	Queenan Harold R	74	electrician	36	"
R	Queenan Rosanna—†	74	housekeeper	63	"
S	Halbrick Margaret—†	74	"	51	"
T	Tipping Charles	74	U S A	26	
U	Tipping Margaret—†	74	housewife	26	"
V	Grisdale Ada—†	74	housekeeper	76	"
W	White Howard	74	barber	65	

Bennington Street

X	Smith Evelyn—†	715	bookkeeper	21	here
Y	Smith George	715	policeman	49	"

Bennington Street—Continued

z	Smith Irene—†	715	housewife	44	here

1812

A	Healy Edward C	715	U S A	29	
B	Healy Francis P	715	U S N	36	"
C	Healy Irma P—†	715	clerk	21	
D	Healy Margaret T—†	715	housewife	55	"
E	Healy Peter H	715	paymaster	60	"
F	Healy Peter H, jr	715	U S A	32	
G	Healy Warren J	715	".	25	
H	Terry Mary L—†	719	housewife	24	"
K	Terry William J	719	U S N	28	"
L	Lewis Frank	719	manager	37	"
M	Lewis Margaret—†	719	housewife	38	"
N	Shafer Edward J	723	U S A	40	
O	Shafer Henry W	723	U S N	44	
P	Shafer Ruth—†	723	housewife	38	"
R	Nigro Frank	723	blacksmith	70	"
S	Nigro Mary—†	723	housewife	70	"
T	Daniels Charles H, jr	727	laborer	44	
U	Daniels Evelyn J—†	727	housewife	46	"
V	Trevor Francis J	727	laborer	35	
W	Daniels Charles H	727	machinist	65	"
X	Daniels Della—†	727	housewife	64	"
Y	Riley Grace M—†	727	clerk	35	
Z	Riley Lawrence	727	"	35	"

1813

A	Gazzara Joseph	731	mechanic	42	"
B	Gazzara Rita G—†	731	housewife	39	"
C	Burns Helene M—†	731	"	34	
D	Burns Michael L	731	policeman	44	"
E	Dell Grotte Anthony	735	U S A	25	"
F	Dell Grotte Mary—†	735	housewife	25	"
G	Bowles Marion—†	735	"	37	
H	Bowles Richard M	735	seaman	33	
K	Dellano Dominic	735	packer	26	
L	Dellano Florence—†	735	housewife	24	"
M	Magliari Theodore	735	retired	81	
N	Recchia Anthony	735	assembler	29	"
O	Recchia Frank	735	tailor	58	
P	Recchia Mary—†	735	housewife	55	"
R	Recchia Theodore	735	U S A	21	"
S	McCarthy Margaret—†	739	housewife	22	" .

9

Bennington Street—Continued

T	McCarthy Paul J	739	U S C G	28	here
U	McCarthy Annie T—†	739	housewife	52	"
V	McCarthy Catherine G–†	739	student	21	"
W	McCarthy Charles J	739	engraver	53	"
X	McCarthy Charles J, jr	739	U S A	26	
Y	Winston Bernard W	739	custodian	50	"
Z	Winston John J	739	fireman	63	"

1814

A	Bagley Grace E—†	743	housewife	32	"
B	Bagley William M	743	attorney	37	"
C	Curran Barbara—†	743	housewife	57	"
D	Curran Catherine—†	743	tel operator	24	"
E	Curran John	743	U S A	26	"
F	Curran Mary—†	743	bookkeeper	27	"
G	Curran Michael	743	U S A	23	
H	Curran Patrick	743	laborer	65	"
K	Decker Joseph	743	salesman	51	"
L	DeFranco Antonio	747	policeman	53	"
M	DeFranco Matilda—†	747	housewife	50	"
N	Turriello Tina—†	747	housekeeper	23	"
O	Calla Adelina—†	747	housewife	59	"
P	Calla Margaret—†	747	bookkeeper	20	"
R	Calla Nicolino	747	tailor	62	
S	Meyers Frederick	751	electrician	30	"
T	Meyers Helen M—†	751	housewife	41	"
U	McLaughlin Albert J	751	motorman	52	"
V	McLaughlin Katherine–†	751	housewife	80	"
W	McLaughlin Paul	751	machinist	35	"
X	McLaughlin Theresa E–†	751	housewife	47	"
Y	Bradley Elizabeth J—†	755	"	42	
Z	Donovan Susan K—†	755	housekeeper	49	"

1815

A	Ryan Mary A—†	755	"	59	
B	Anderson Agnes T—†	755	nurse	29	"
C	McLaughlin Catherine A—†	755	housekeeper	64	"
D	Wall Agnes T—†	755	housewife	53	"
E	Wall James	755	B F D	57	"
F	Corson Louise—†	759	manager	56	"
G	Brown Annie G—†	759	housekeeper	66	"
H	Stevens Louise M—†	759	"	78	"

10

Bennington Street—Continued

K	Sweeney Lena—†	759	housekeeper	76	here
L	Walker Annie—†	759	"	82	"
Y	Sardina Esther—†	989	housewife	33	"
Z	Sardina Humbert	989	U S N	33	

1816

A	Galiazzo Dominic	989	U S A	28	
B	Galiazzo Florence—†	989	spinner	25	"
C	Bassett Elmer	989	machinist	51	6 Eutaw
D	Bassett Evelyn—†	989	bookkeeper	38	6 "
E	Mora John F	989	operator	42	here
F	Silvia Emma—†	989	housewife	48	"
G	Silvia Mary—†	989	cleaner	22	"
P	Ferrara Dorothy—†	1025	saleswoman	24	"
R	Ferrara Eleanor—†	1025	hairdresser	26	"
S	Ferrara Elizabeth—†	1025	saleswoman	22	"
T	Ferrara Jeanette—†	1025	housewife	50	"
U	Ferrara Peter	1025	agent	50	"
V	Mirabella Mary—†	1025	hairdresser	35	Saugus
W	Mirabella Matthew	1025	U S A	34	"
X	Spadafora Marion—†	1025	housewife	69	here
Y	Spadafora Michael	1025	retired	76	"
Z	Maniglia Caroline—†	1025	finisher	65	"

1817

A	Maniglia Diego	1025	barber	38	
B	Maniglia Rose—†	1025	housewife	37	"
C	Morgner Edward A	1027	machinist	61	"
D	Morgner Mary A—†	1027	housewife	61	"
E	Sasso John A	1027	painter	68	..
F	Sasso Josephine A—†	1027	housewife	58	"
G	Carter George H	1027	retired	75	
H	Carter George H, jr	1027	longshoreman	42	"
K	Carter George H	1027	seaman	21	
L	Carter Rose—†	1027	housewife	39	"
N	Santiano Louis	1065	electrician	22	"
O	Santiano Madeline—†	1065	housewife	42	"
P	Santiano Michael	1065	electrician	42	"
R	Santiano Thomas	1065	U S N	20	
S	Powers Gerard A	1067	clerk	22	
T	Powers Martin J	1067	fireman	51	"
U	Powers Martin J	1067	U S A	21	
V	Powers Mary V—†	1067	housewife	50	"

Bennington Street—Continued

w	Russo Albina—†	1069	housewife	46		here
x	Russo Anna—†	1069	rubberwkr	26		"
y	Russo Elinor—†	1069	clerk	24		"
z	Russo Pauline—†	1069	"	28		
	1818					
a	Nazzaro Clarence	1071	motorman	32		"
b	Nazzaro Mary—†	1071	housewife	30		"
c	Smarrella Anna—†	1073	typist	21		
d	*Smarrella Josephine—†	1073	housewife	59		"
e	Smarrella Peter	1073	tailor	64		"
f	Smarrella Phyllis—†	1073	ropemaker	33		"
g	Smarrella Theresa—†	1073	supervisor	25		"
h	Smarrella Jennie—†	1075	housewife	36		"
k	Smarrella Vincent	1075	optician	36		"
n	Hendricks Albert	1088	printer	54		"
o	Hendricks Florence—†	1088	housewife	65		"
p	Marotta Aurelia—†	1088	"	54		
r	Marotta John M	1088	U S N	21		
s	Marotta Michael A	1088	bartender	54		"
t	Indrisano Anthony	1088	guard	48		
u	Indrisano Lena—†	1088	housewife	44		"
w	Cosgrove James	1092	retired	74		
x	Cosgrove Mary L—†	1092	tel operator	43		"
y	Mullen Argentina V—†	1092	housewife	61		"
z	Mullen William F	1092	retired	67		"
	1819					
a	Casale Gertrude—†	1092	housewife	43		"
b	Casale Herbert	1092	architect	45		"
c	Nastari Albert	1092	U S N	20		415 Chelsea
d	Nastari Gloria—†	1092	housewife	21		here
e	Walsh Edna—†	1092	secretary	34		"
f	Celona Cosimo	1096	finisher	62		"
g	Celona Josephine—†	1096	factoryhand	56		"
h	Celona Geraldine—†	1096	housewife	34		"
k	Celona Joseph	1096	teacher	36		"
l	Celona Florence—†	1096	housewife	39		"
m	Celona Frank	1096	teacher	37		"
n	Giacoppo Anna—†	1098	housewife	50		"
o	Giacoppo Joseph	1098	finisher	57		"
p	Celino Edward	1098	U S A	23		"
r	Celino Lucy—†	1098	housewife	53		"

12

Page.	Letter.	FULL NAME.	Residence, Jan. 1, 1945.	Occupation.	Supposed Age.	Reported Residence, Jan. 1, 1944. Street and Number.

	s	Celino Pasquale	1098	barber	64	here
	T	*Mazzeo Catherine—†	1098	housewife	60	"
	U	Mazzeo Dominick	1098	finisher	62	"
	V	Mazzeo Dominick	1098	U S A	30	
	W	Mazzeo Mary—†	1098	housewife	27	"
	X	Mazzeo Sally—†	1098	tailor	26	"
	Y	Belgiorno Albert J	1100	salesman	31	1102 Benningt'n
	z	Belgiorno Florence—†	1100	housewife	29	1102 "
1820						
	A	Fasano Antoinette—†	1100	"	35	here
	B	Fasano Pasquale	1100	electrician	45	"
	c	Campanella Anna—†	1100	housewife	34	"
	D	*Campanella John	1100	salesman	38	"
	E	Iannetta Jennie—†	1100	housewife	20	"
	F	Iannetta Victor	1100	U S A	26	"
	G	Ferrara Anthony	1102	manager	41	"
	H	Ferrara Olga—†	1102	housewife	40	"
	K	Gozzi Rose—†	1102	"	64	"
	L	Gerrior Annie—†	1102	"	71	112 Orient av
	M	Martell Mary—†	1102		57	27 "
	N	Martell Mary P—†	1102	"	86	27 "
	o	*Merchant Maria—†	1102	"	88	27 "
	P	Benincuore Arcangela–†	1102	clerk	22	9 Breed
	R	Benincuore Nicola	1102	barber	61	9 "
	s	Cosimo Biagio	1106	grocer	58	here
	T	Cosimo Jennie—†	1106	housewife	47	"
	U	*Hopp Richard	1106½	tailor	65	11 Monmouth
	V	Surette Dora—†	1106½	clerk	31	11 "
	W	Surette John	1106½	shipwright	38	11 "
	X	Cunningham Catherine–†1112		housewife	77	here
	Y	Cunningham Catherine–†1112		bookkeeper	41	"
	z	Tyrrell Josephine—†	1114	at home	65	"
1821						
	A	Tyrrell Lillian T—†	1114	dressfitter	52	"
	B	Pitman Lucy E—†	1114	housewife	66	"
	c	Pitman William A	1114	guard	63	
	D	Venezia Mary E—†	1114	auditor	29	"
	E	Venezia Michael J	1114	machinist	30	"
	F	Cowhig Barbara A—†	1114	nurse	21	
	G	Cowhig Charles C	1114	policeman	46	"
	H	Cowhig Charles P	1114	U S A	20	"

Bennington Street—Continued

	Letter	FULL NAME	Residence	Occupation	Age	Reported Residence
	K	Cowhig Margaret M—†	1114	housewife	44	here
	L	White John J, jr	1114	U S A	23	115 Barnes av
	M	White Margaret M—†	1114	artist	22	here
	N	Graham Bertha—†	1118	housewife	37	"
	O	Graham Raymond D	1118	foreman	39	"
	P	Jensen Edward A	1118	switchman	40	989 Benningt'n
	R	Miller Annie C—†	1118	housewife	67	here
	S	Miller Charles W	1118	retired	69	"
	T	Chaison Augustus J	1124	guard	45	"
	U	Chaison Augustus J	1124	U S M C	23	"
	V	Chaison Robert F	1124	U S N	21	
	W	Chaison Ruth M—†	1124	housewife	34	"
	X	Wallace Genevieve—†	1130	clerk	20	
	Y	Wallace John	1130	engraver	49	"
	Z	Wallace Louis	1130	foreman	52	"
1822						
	B	Caputo Gaetanina—†	1183	housewife	50	"
	C	Caputo Michael	1183	ironworker	26	"
	D	Caputo Paul	1183	blacksmith	56	"
	E	Dinarello Mafalda—†	1183	housewife	24	"
	F	Dinarello Victor	1183	machinist	27	"
	G	Moralis Joseph	1183	welder	31	138 Trenton
	H	Moralis Nellie—†	1183	housewife	33	here
	K	*Castagnola Rubina—†	1185	"	87	"
	L	Lombardi Camella—†	1185	"	24	"
	M	Lombardi Maddalena–†	1185	"	62	"
	N	Lombardi Peter	1185	butcher	67	"
	O	Lombardi William G	1185	machinist	27	"
	P	Mennella Florence M–†	1185	"	23	
	R	Mennella Margaret M–†	1185	housewife	43	"
	S	Mennella Randolph	1185	motorman	52	"
	T	Femino Charles	1185	baker	30	102 Marion
	U	Femino Mary—†	1185	factoryhand	34	here
	V	*Femino Minnie—†	1185	housewife	59	"
	W	*Femino Paul	1185	baker	59	"
	X	Ferrara Jennie—†	1185	housewife	31	"
	Y	Ferrara Joseph	1185	carpenter	34	"
	Z	Campatelli Joseph	1189	metalwkr	42	"
1823						
	A	Campatelli Margaret—†	1189	housewife	40	"
	B	Ferrara Ruth L—†	1189	"	35	"

Bennington Street—Continued

c	Ferrara Tony	1189	U S N	35	here
E	Gill Clifton	1193	salesman	43	"
F	*Gill Rita—†	1193	factoryhand	25	"
G	*Lotti Eugenia—†	1193	housewife	51	"
H	Lotti John	1193	cook	51	"
L	Covalucci Alberta—†	1201	housewife	35	115 Leyden
M	Covalucci Mario	1201	rigger	37	here
N	Brown James	1201	retired	76	"
O	Brown Lida—†	1201	housewife	62	"
P	Dibble Tracey A	1201	U S A	21	
R	Flynn Francis W	1201	engineer	40	"
S	Flynn Shirley W—†	1201	housewife	44	"
T	McCormick Harold	1201	electrician	33	"
U	McCormick Mary—†	1201	housewife	32	"
V	*Venza Anna—†	1203	"	43	"
W	Venza Anthony	1203	shipfitter	23	"
X	Venza Giacomo	1203	U S N	21	
Y	Venza Jennie—†	1203	candymaker	26	"
Z	Venza Peter	1203	manager	51	"
	1824				
A	Venza Sebastian	1203	U S N	24	
B	Lanzilli Enis—†	1205	hairdresser	25	"
C	Lanzilli Joseph	1205	inspector	64	"
D	Lanzilli Theresa—†	1205	housewife	60	"
E	Cavalieri Angela—†	1209	"	25	"
F	Cavalieri Lawrence	1209	machinist	27	"
G	Trischitta Bernadina—†	1209	housewife	56	"
H	Trischitta Conchetta—†	1209	hairdresser	31	"
K	Trischitta Roasrio	1209	carpenter	62	"
L	Trischitta Violet—†	1209	stenographer	27	"
M	Trischitta Virginia—†	1209	factoryhand	25	"
N	Lazzari Arela—†	1211	candymaker	20	"
O	*Lazzari Bettina—†	1211	housewife	53	"
P	Lazzari Salvatore	1211	tailor	59	
R	Prochilo Michael	1211	U S A	30	
S	Prochilo Victoria—†	1211	candymaker	27	"
T	Spaziani Patricia—†	1211	"	31	
U	Spaziani Peter	1211	barber	41	
W	Contarino Anthony	1215	storekeeper	41	"
X	*Contarino Frances—†	1215	housewife	69	"
Y	*Contarino Joseph	1215	retired	82	"

Bennington Street—Continued

z	Contarino Mary—†	1215	machinist	35	here
1825					
A	Contarino Ralph	1215	storekeeper	42	"
B	Rosa Charles	1215	baker	50	"
C	Rosa Joseph	1215	U S A	22	
D	Girone Catherine—†	1219	housewife	44	"
E	Girone Frank	1219	U S A	22	
F	Girone John	1219	"	23	"
G	Girone Nicholas	1219	carpenter	63	"
H	Lauricella Anthony	1219	storekeeper	58	"
K	Lauricella Frank	1219	laborer	22	"
L	Lauricella Sarah—†	1219	housewife	52	"
M	*Piloto Grace—†	1219	clerk	35	"
N	Conlon Joseph	1223	electrician	45	114 Elm
O	Conlon Mary—†	1223	housewife	40	114 "
P	Allbee James H	1223	manager	49	here
R	Manfra George J	1223	repairman	22	"
S	Manfra Margaret F—†	1223	housewife	22	"
T	*Buldini Raffaele	1229	sausagemaker	60	"
U	*Buldini Venusta—†	1229	seamstress	55	"
V	Kimble Rena—†	1229	bookkeeper	34	"
W	Fussell Vera—†	1229	housewife	32	"
X	Fussell William R	1229	clerk	34	

Blackinton Street

z	Ratto Ernest A	1	painter	47	here
1826					
A	Ratto Mary L—†	1	tel operator	20	"
B	Ratto Sarah—†	1	housewife	41	"
C	Wyke Elizabeth H—†	3	"	64	
D	Wyke Ernest L	3	laborer	47	"
E	Wyke Jesse	3	machinist	57	"
F	O'Brien Eileen M—†	5	at home	32	"
G	O'Brien John F	5	printer	47	"
H	O'Brien Kathleen G—†	5	clerk	40	
K	O'Brien Margaret—†	5	housewife	70	"
L	O'Brien Mary G—†	5	bookkeeper	42	"
M	O'Brien Maurice T	5	U S N	36	"
N	O'Brien Richard T	5	steamfitter	45	"
O	Lagamasino John	7	machinist	53	"

16

P	Lagamasino Lillian E—†	7	librarian	28	here
R	Lagamasino Merle C—†	7	teacher	26	"
S	Lagamasino Mildred—†	7	housewife	54	"
T	Powell Clarence G	9	shipfitter	29	"
U	Powell Marie B—†	9	housewife	31	"
V	Cianci Aida—†	9	"	43	
W	Cianci Henry	9	optician	43	"
X	Casale Agnes—†	11	typist	47	
Y	Casale Anne—†	11	housewife	69	"
Z	*Cerisola Elsie F—†	11	"	40	Canada

1827

A	Cerisola Joseph J	11	manager	51	"
B	Lavezzo Rose—†	11	wrapper	62	here
C	MacPherson Donald W	11	proprietor	46	"
D	MacPherson Eugenia—†	11	housewife	45	"

Leyden Street

L	Dondero Albert S	215	machinist	41	here
M	Dondero Frank C	215	retired	55	"
N	Dondero Theresa—†	215	housewife	54	"
O	Favello Anthony	215	clerk	67	
P	Favello Nellie—†	215	housewife	65	"
R	Disario Caroline E—†	215	"	58	
S	Disario Paul C	215	inspector	61	"
T	Disario Paul C, jr	215	U S M C	24	"
U	Elwell Henry T	215	U S A	28	
V	Elwell Martha G—†	215	housewife	29	"
W	Vernaglia Beatrice A—†	215	"	32	Rhode Island
X	Dondero Evelyn T—†	215	leatherwkr	42	here
Y	Dondero William H	215	chauffeur	46	"
Z	Solari Mary F—†	215	housewife	70	"

1828

A	Flynn Ruth M—†	219	"	23	Connecticut
B	Flynn William R	219	engineer	36	"
C	Dresser Charles H	219	"	40	here
D	Oblenes Doris P—†	219	housewife	30	"
E	Coggswell Charles L	221	metalwkr	36	"
F	Coggswell Mildred F—†	221	housewife	35	"
G	McMillan Edward A	223	U S A	24	
H	McMillan Mary T—†	223	clerk	30	

Page	Letter	FULL NAME.	Residence, Jan. 1, 1945.	Occupation.	Supposed Age.	Reported Residence, Jan. 1, 1944. Street and Number.

Leyden Street—Continued

	Letter	FULL NAME.	Res.	Occupation.	Age	Residence
	K	McMillan Normon R	223	U S A	22	here
	L	Normile Gertrude—†	223	housewife	26	"
	M	Normile John F	223	U S A	29	"
	N	Courtois Lucille—†	225	housewife	33	"
	O	Courtois Oscar F	225	rigger	34	
	P	Console Anna—†	225	housewife	51	"
	R	Console Antonio	225	barber	53	
	S	Sergi Benjamin A	225	U S A	30	"
	T	Blangiordo Dorothy L—†	225	housewife	33	"
	U	Blangiordo Mariano	225	chipper	34	"
	V	Cross Grace V—†	231	housewife	20	"
	W	Cross James E	231	rigger	27	"
	X	DeNaro Mildred—†	231	welder	30	"
	Y	DeNaro Patricia—†	231	"	26	"
	Z	Marino Florence—†	231	housewife	50	"

1829

	Letter	FULL NAME.	Res.	Occupation.	Age	Residence
	A	Ness Jennie N—†	235	"	59	
	B	Ness Margaret H—†	235	stenographer	25	"
	C	Ness Peter H	235	patternmaker	55	"
	D	Parker Anton D	235	machinist	52	"
	E	Rovatti Fioravante	239	carpenter	50	"
	F	Rovatti Louise—†	239	housewife	49	"
	G	Zermani Andrew J	239	shipwright	33	"
	H	Zermani Lola—†	239	housewife	22	"
	K	Beaton Grace A—†	241	WAVE	22	"
	L	Beaton Helen E—†	241	housewife	55	"
	M	Beaton Hugh F	241	storekeeper	64	"
	N	Beaton John P	241	U S N	20	"
	O	Ponti Guy	249	chef	65	
	P	Lamborghini Alexander	249	machinist	65	"
	R	Lamborghini Elvira—†	249	housewife	58	"
	S	Ivers Angelina—†	249	"	44	"

Saint Andrew Road

	Letter	FULL NAME.	Res.	Occupation.	Age	Residence
	V	Sullivan Mary E—†	2	clerk	44	here
	W	Sullivan William J	2	"	41	"
	Y	Brosnan John J	6	U S N	29	16 Bixley rd
	Z	Brosnan Ruth—†	6	bookkeeper	29	here

1830

	Letter	FULL NAME.	Res.	Occupation.	Age	Residence
	A	Corrigan John J	6	supervisor	56	"

18

Page	Letter	Full Name.	Residence, Jan. 1, 1945.	Occupation.	Supposed Age.	Reported Residence, Jan. 1, 1944. Street and Number.

Saint Andrew Road—Continued

	B	Corrigan Nora F—†	6	housewife	55	here
	C	Shaughnessy Albert L	8	teacher	49	"
	D	Shaughnessy Grace M—†	8	housewife	33	"
	E	Schwartz Lawrence F	10	machinist	29	1024 Benningt'n
	F	Schwartz Thelma M—†	10	housewife	27	1024 "
	G	Sofrine Edward	10	engineer	39	here
	H	Sofrine Eleanor—†	10	housewife	31	"
	K	Sofrine Manuel	10	retired	81	"
	L	Hart Mary A—†	14	housewife	50	"
	M	Hart William J	14	policeman	54	"
	N	Ryan Lawrence J	16	U S A	33	
	O	Ryan Mary A—†	16	housewife	74	"
	P	Short Catherine—†	16	stenographer	34	"
	R	Adams Rose—†	18	housekeeper	70	"
	S	Garbrino Anthony	18	retired	74	..
	T	Hurley Henry A	21	U S A	40	
	U	Hurley Margaret—†	21	housewife	38	"
	V	Roach Eileen—†	21	"	26	
	W	Roach Robert	21	U S N	28	
	X	Wellings Albert A	21	"	38	
	Y	Wellings Augustus J	21	"	48	
	Z	Wellings Gladys D—†	21	teacher	32	"
1831						
	A	Wellings John	21	retired	74	
	B	Wellings Joseph A	21	U S N	42	,,
	C	Wellings Timothy F	21	"	46	
	D	Guarino Frances T—†	24	housewife	38	"
	E	Guarino John	24	architect	39	"
	F	Bonner Catherine A—†	25	housewife	78	"
	G	Bonner William N	25	fireman	55	,,
	H	Morrison Mary L—†	25	teacher	45	"
	K	Morrison Thomas	25	seaman	45	"
	M	McDonald Anthony T	26	fireman	46	70 Barnes av
	N	McDonald James E	26	storekeeper	62	70 "
	O	McGrath Winifred—†	26	tel operator	51	70 "
	P	Scirro Frances—†	29	housewife	41	here
	R	Scirro Ralph	29	chipper	44	"
	S	Tiano Florence—†	29	metalwkr	34	"
	T	*Tiano Jennie—†	29	at home	70	,,
	U	Tiano Samuel	29	engineer	32	"
	V	McInnes Archibald	30	salesman	67	"

Saint Andrew Road—Continued

w	McInnes Ellen E—†	˙30	housewife	59	here
x	McInnes Evelyn—†	30	clerk	37	"
y	McInnes Kathryn E—†	30	"	30	"
z	Rego August	31	assembler	41	"

1832

A	Rego Madeline—†	31	housewife	41	"
B	Scoppettuolo Anthony	31	clerk	72	
C	Scoppettuolo Lena—†	31	stitcher	35	"
D	Sullivan Alice D—†	32	secretary	24	"
E	Sullivan Arthur W	32	registrar	59	"
F	Sullivan Helen J—†	32	housewife	60	"
G	Sullivan Jean M—†	32	secretary	20	"
H	Carcioffo Edward S	33	manager	34	"
K	Mangini Edmund I	33	waiter	34	
¹K	Mangini Madeline—†	33	housewife	35	"
L	Brown Frank P	34	retired	76	"
M	Brown Henry H	34	"	79	
N	Loatz Ada M—†	34	at home	60	"
O	Lawrence Helen—†	37	clerk	36	
P	Lawrence Herbert	37	laborer	65	"
R	Lawrence John	37	pipefitter	39	"
S	Lawrence Sarah—†	37	clerk	37	
T	Ford Clarence P	38	attorney	32	"
U	Ford Helen W—†	38	housewife	29	"
V	Carey Edward L	38	retired	58	"
W	Carey Margaret A—†	38	clerk	53	
X*	Jonasson Sophie—†	39	at home	86	"
Y	Maguire James E	41	attorney	72	"
z	Maguire Katherine K—†	41	housewife	70	"

1833

A	Maguire Richard	41	U S A	31	"
B	Maguire William C	41	attorney	65	"
C	Maguire William C, jr	41	U S A	21	"
D	Millenick George	44	chauffeur	46	"
E	Millenick Isabelle—†	44	housewife	39	"
F	Butler Bride—†	44	"	55	"
G	Butler Edward J	44	pipefitter	33	"
H	Butler Mary H—†	44	social worker	22	"
K	Butler William F	44	inspector	31	"
L	Stevens Joseph P	44	clerk	44	
M	Stevens Margaret E—†	44	housewife	45	"

Saint Edward Road

N	McCarthy James J	32	accountant	25	here
O	McCarthy John	32	manager	30	"
P	McCarthy Margaret M-†	32	housewife	59	"
R	McCarthy Margaret M-†	32	operator	23	
S	Walsh Mary A—†	32	stenographer	29	"
T	Walsh Thomas A	32	U S A	35	..
U	Mullen Anthony	40	machinist	50	"
V	Wilson Ellen—†.	40	at home	76	
X	Wilson George L	40	U S A	28	
W	Wilson George W	40	printer	55	
Y	Wilson John P	40	"	24	
Z	Wilson Katherine L—†	40	clerk	20	
	1834				
A	Wilson Leo J	40	U S A	22	
B	Wilson Mary A—†	40	housewife	55	"
C	*Campbell Alice—†	40	"	45	
D	*Campbell Lillian—†	40	operator	20	"
E	*Campbell William	40	shipper	47	"..
F	Lavezzo Mary F—†	40	housewife	52	"
G	Lavezzo Sylvester	40	bartender	59	"
H	Vieira Frances B—†	40	inspector	25	"
K	DeRosa Lena—†	44	housewife	31	"
L	DeRosa Vito	44	agent	45	
M	DeMatteo Albert	44	U S A	24	
N	DeMatteo Donald	44	operator	50	..
O	DeMatteo Ida—†	44	housewife	45	"
P	Contini Eleanor—†	44	"	39	
R	Contini Paul	44	printer	39	

1835   Saratoga Street

G	Giuliotti Adolph J	1042	policeman	46	here
H	Giuliotti Mary V—†	1042	housewife	40	"
K	Boyd James A	1042	machinist	50	"
L	McDonald Alma E—†	1042	WAC	29	Gardner
M	McDonald Edward T	1042	U S A	24	here
N	McDonald Elizabeth O-†	1042	housewife	46	"
O	McDonald Henry S	1042	retired	46	"
R	Rocciolo Joseph	1044	"	81	
S	Rocciolo Sophia—†	1044	housewife	79	"

21

Saratoga Street—Continued

T	Rocciolo Elva—†	1044	housewife	47	here
U	Rocciolo John	1044	U S A	24	"
V	Rocciolo Joseph	1044	draftsman	25	"
W	Rocciolo Pasquale	1044	musician	51	"
Y	Watchmaker Abraham	1045A	storekeeper	58	"
Z	Watchmaker Lillian E–†	1045A	housewife	55	"

1836

A	Watchmaker Sadie B–†	1045A	factoryhand	29	"
B	Halloran Bridget—†	1046	housewife	41	"
C	Halloran Patrick	1046	manager	42	"
D	Cacchiotti Alice—†	1046	clerk	20	
E	Cacchiotti Louise—†	1046	housewife	45	"
F	Cacchiotti Orazio	1046	tailor	53	
G	Cacchiotti Rose—†	1046	clerk	23	..
H	MacIsaac Anna—†	1047	bookkeeper	40	"
K	MacIsaac Frank	1047	machinist	44	"
L	Muldoon James A	1047	tel splicer	55	"
M	Muldoon Katherine—†	1047	nurse	50	
N	Zielinger Charles	1047	guard	41	
O	Zielinger Christina—†	1047	operator	37	"
P	Zielinger Isabel—†	1047	housewife	67	"
R	Barone Eugene	1048	storekeeper	54	"
S	Barone Palmina—†	1048	housewife	47	"
T	Cutillo Annette—†	1048	at home	35	"
U	*Cutillo Celia—†	1048	housewife	71	"
V	Cutillo John	1048	shoewkr	50	"
W	*Cutillo Joseph	1048	retired	71	
X	Cutillo Richard	1048	U S N	27	"
Z	Pizzano Therese—† rear	1050	candymaker	65	"

1837

A	Petrucci Angelo	1051	laborer	56	"
B	Petrucci Anna—†	1051	stitcher	23	" .
C	Petrucci Elizabeth—†	1051	operator	20	"
D	Petrucci Rose—†	1051	housewife	46	"
E	Ranieri Concetta—†	1051	stitcher	22	"
F	Forgeron Lula—†	1051	housewife	47	"
G	Forgeron Thelma—†	1051	WAVE	22	"
H	Forgeron Theodore	1051	rigger	47	
K	Hicks Grace—†	1051	clerk	28	
L	Gleason Harold	1051	"	46	
M	Gleason Lauretta—†	1051	housewife	35	"

22

Saratoga Street—Continued

N	Keefe Annie—†	1052	housekeeper	56	here
O	Keefe Elizabeth—†	1052	housewife	61	"
P	Keefe Thomas	1052	clerk	58	"
R	Dahnke Caroline—†	1052	housewife	76	"
S	Dahnke Christian	1052	retired	53	
T	Dahnke Frederick	1052	machinist	49	"
U	Haritos Bertha—†	1052	housewife	48	"
V	Haritos Peter	1052	policeman	50	"
W	Morrison Elizabeth—†	1053	housewife	35	"
X	Morrison John	1053	printer	40	
Y	Domenico Josephine—†	1053	housewife	49	"
Z	Domenico Julia J—†	1053	student	20	"

1838

A	Domenico Marie S—†	1053	dressmaker	21	"
B	Domenico Thomas D	1053	steamfitter	52	"
C	Venedam Jean—†	1053	housewife	25	"
D	Venedam Warren	1053	carpenter	29	"
E	Teed Fred	1055	janitor	58	··
F	Teed Fred, jr	1055	U S A	26	
G	Teed Mabel—†	1055	housewife	54	"
H	Anderson Pauline—†	1055	"	37	
K	Anderson Ralph	1055	machinist	47	"
L	Dorgan Charlotte—†	1055	housewife	64	"
M	Dorgan George	1055	U S N	21	
N	Dorgan Michael	1055	retired	72	"
O	Halpin Charlotte—†	1055	housewife	39	7 Antrim
P	Halpin Thomas	1055	U S N	48	7 "
R	McGeney Edward	1055	U S A	34	here
S	McGeney Therese—†	1055	operator	26	"
T	Leigh Annie—†	1057	housewife	77	33 Faywood av
U	Leigh Dorothy—†	1057	stenographer	45	33 "
V	Leigh John	1057	retired	76	33 "
W	Magnasco James	1057	laborer	29	210 Bremen
X	Magnasco Lucy—†	1057	housewife	25	210 "
Y	Georgalos Evangelos	1057	engineer	64	here
Z	Georgalos James	1057	U S A	24	"

1839

A	Georgalos Maria—†	1057	housewife	50	"
B	Georgalos Thomas	1057	engineer	26	"
C	Jeffers Jasper	1059	brazier	42	
D	Jeffers Jennie—†	1059	packer	40	

Saratoga Street—Continued

E	Jeffers Robert	1059	clerk	39	here
F	McGee Frank	1059	retired	78	"
G	Nilson Leslie	1059	upholsterer	51	"
K	Cianci Edwin	1060	electrician	40	"
L	DiMuro Anthony	1060	storekeeper	58	"
M	DiMuro Bernard	1060	U S A	28	"
N	DiMuro Jennie—†	1060	housewife	55	"
O	DiMuro Jerome	1060	U S A	26	
P	Rosenthal Abraham	1060	storekeeper	48	"
R	Rosenthal Sadie—†	1060	housewife	44	"
S	Cianci Josephine—†	1060	"	47	"
T	Cianci Louis	1060	manager	52	"
U	Kirwan Arthur	1061	watchman	46	"
V	Kirwan Rose—†	1061	housewife	37	"
W	McFarlan Joseph J	1061	shipper	47	"
X	Miller John	1061	U S A	31	
Y	Miller Susan—†	1061	clerk	24	
Z	Miller Walter	1061	machinist	56	"
	1840				
A	Miller Winifred—†	1061	housewife	55	"
B	Puzzanghera Joseph	1061	laborer	58	"
C	Puzzanghera Joseph	1061	salesman	27	"
D	Puzzanghera Palma—†	1061	housewife	51	"
E	Graceffa Argentine—†	1062	"	41	
F	Graceffa John	1062	U S N	35	"
G	Santosuosso Doris—†	1062	housewife	35	"
H	Santosuosso Julia—†	1062	operator	38	"
K	Puopolo Joseph	1062	diemaker	29	"
L	Puopolo Nicolina—†	1062	housewife	27	"
M	Conley Gertrude—†	1065	housekeeper	56	"
N	Conley Margaret—†	1065	clerk	50	"
O	Abramo Annette—†	1065	housekeeper	69	"
P	Grady Joseph J	1066	printer	65	"
R	Lombardi Peter	1066	clerk	29	
S	Lombardi Ruth E—†	1066	housewife	29	"
T	Larkin Evelyn—†	1068	"	30	"
U	Larkin Joseph	1068	timekeeper	33	
V	Fiamingo James	1069	retired	65	
W	Fiamingo Lila—†	1069	housewife	60	"
X	Mullane Patrick	1071	lawyer	66	"
Y	Murray Anna J—†	1071	operator	38	"

Saratoga Street—Continued

z	Murray Martin A	1071	teacher	45	here	
	1841					
A	Craviotti Prospero	1072	retired	83		
B	Craviotti Therese—†	1072	housewife	85	"	
C	DeMarchi Mary—†	1072	saleswoman	51	"	
D	Ardini Emma—†	1072	housewife	56	"	
E	Ardini Joseph	1072	steamfitter	67	"	
F	Giacoumis Ethel—†	1072	clerk	25		
G	Giacoumis Joan—†	1072	accountant	27	"	
H	Giacoumis Sophia—†	1072	housewife	50	"	
K	Giacoumis Xenephon	1072	laborer	52		
L	Crovo John	1073	"	45	"	
M	Ingalls Edmond	1073	clerk	29	Winthrop	
N	Ingalls Margaret—†	1073	housewife	50		
O	Kerrigan James J	1073	ironwkr	56	here	
P	Kerrigan John J	1073	clerk	57	"	
R	Kerrigan Margaret V—†	1073	"	50	"	
S	Whelan Edwin	1073	U S A	31	Winthrop	
T	Whelan Martha—†	1073	secretary	27		
U	Matthews Florence—†	1075	teacher	38	here	
V	Riley Arthur	1075	laborer	30	"	
W	Bimber Angelina—†	1075	stitcher	29	"	
X	Bimber Arthur	1075	U S A	34		
Y	Bimber George	1075	machinist	65	"	
Z	Bimber Hilda—†	1075	clerk	22		
	1842					
A	Bimber Madeline—†	1075	housewife	52	"	
B	Bimber Mary—†	1075	"	31		
C	Bimber Octavio	1075	storekeeper	67	"	
E	Sacco Alfred	1078	barber	66	"	
F	Sacco Anna—†	1078	housewife	65	"	
G	Sacco Jennie—†	1078	clerk	43		
H	Sacco Mario	1078	U S A	30		
K	Anderson Dena—†	1078	housewife	56	"	
L	Anderson Edith—†	1078	clerk	30		
M	Merola Domenica—†	1078	housewife	52	"	
N	Merola Guido	1078	tailor	54		
O	Toscano Carmine	1078	"	37		
P	Toscano Mary—†	1078	housewife	26	"	
S	Vivenzio Nicholas	1084	tailor	54		
T	Vivenzio Theresa—†	1084	housewife	50	"	

Saratoga Street—Continued

	U	McGeney Alfred	1084	retired	71	here
	V	McGeney Mary—†	1084	housewife	67	"
	W	Sacco Henry	1084	fireman	31	953 Saratoga
	X	Sacco Mary—†	1084	housewife	31	953 "
	Y	Viscione Frank	rear 1084	candymaker	28	241 Princeton
	Z	Viscione Mildred—†	" 1084	housewife	25	241 "

1843

	B	Bishop Edward	1085	dentist	44	here
	C	Riley Mary F—†	1085	housekeeper	50	"
	D	Riley Rose E—†	1085	"	60	"
	E	Riley William J	1085	dentist	67	
	F	Bucolo Francis	1088	U S A	29	"
	G	*Bucolo Marie—†	1088	housekeeper	66	"
	H	Bucolo Sebastian	1088	U S N	25	..
	K	White Anna—†	1088	housewife	34	"
	L	White Charles	1088	plater	32	
	M	Genoesa Mary—†	1088	housekeeper	40	"

Thurston Street

	P	Cannon John A	2	U S A	31	here
	R	Cannon Mildred R—†	2	housewife	30	"
	S	Guilfoyle Daniel L	2	U S A	35	"
	T	Guilfoyle Mary E—†	2	housewife	35	"
	U	Roddy Gertrude M—†	2	stenographer	37	"
	V	Roddy Helen M—†	2	operator	39	"
	Y	Olpin Elizabeth J—†	3	clerk	62	..
	W	Scott Elizabeth E—†	3	housewife	57	"
	X	Scott James N	3	carpenter	60	"
	Z	Kelly Emmett J	3	assessor	43	"

1844

	A	Kelly Theresa C—†	3	housewife	39	"
	B	Lagamasino Margaret A-†	3	operator	42	"
	C	Anderson Louis A	4	woodwkr	53	"
	D	Anderson Rose—†	4	housewife	51	"
	E	*Silva Gertrude—†	4	at home	75	"
	F	Hollingsworth Daniel J	5	retired	69	
	G	Sweeney Julia F—†	5	clerk	65	
	H	Sweeney Warren F	5	U S A	41	
	K	Callahan Bernard G	5	"	38	
	L	Callahan James D	5	auditor	40	"

Page.	Letter.	FULL NAME:	Residence, Jan. 1, 1945.	Occupation.	Supposed Age.	Reported Residence, Jan. 1, 1944. Street and Number.

Thurston Street—Continued

	M	Callahan James J	5	B F D	70	here
	N	Callahan Joseph F	5	boilermaker	31	"
	O	Callahan Leo B	5	U S A	27	"
	P	Callahan Margaret L—†	5	housewife	66	"
	R	Callahan Margaret L—†	5	clerk	33	
	S	Currier Mary L—†	5	"	35	
	T	Enos Catherine G—†	6	housewife	39	"
	U	Enos Edmund F	6	policeman	48	"
	V	Benker Charles A	7	retired	84	"
	W	Benker Charles W	7	clerk	47	
	X	Benker Jacob J	7	retired	70	
	Y	Benker Rose M—†	7	housewife	34	"
	Z	Benker William A	7	repairman	44	"

1845

	A	Riley Edna E—†	7	housewife	35	"
	B	Riley Edward J	7	planer	35	"
	E	McGunigle Anna M—†	8	clerk	34	
	F	McGunigle John J	8	U S A	35	
	C	O'Connor Bridget A—†	8	at home	76	"
	D	O'Connor Daniel P	8	plasterer	53	"
	G	Vieira Andrew	8	barber	53	
	H	Emery Emerald	8A	policeman	54	"
	K	Mahoney George T	8A	inspector	51	"
	L	Mahoney George T, jr	8A	U S N	24	"
	M	Mahoney Katherine A—†	8A	housewife	48	"
	N	Nolan Mary L—†	10	"	70	"
	O	Powers Carmel—†	10	stenographer	21	Brockton
	P	Turner Mary L—†	10	secretary	40	"
	R	Flood Edward J	10A	salesman	66	here
	S	Flood Margaret C—†	10A	housewife	66	"
	T	Cullinane James F	11	contractor	35	"
	U	Cullinane Rita M—†	11	housewife	29	"
	V	Dunn Barbara A—†	11	secretary	22	"
	W	Dunn Helen N—†	11	housewife	59	"
	X	Sacco Annie—†	11A	at home	64	"
	Y	Sacco Henry	11A	U S A	29	
	Z	Sacco Louise—†	11A	beautician	27	"

1846

	A	Sacco Silvia—†	11A	clerk	22	"
	B	Lopez Frederick	11A	U S N	25	California
	C	Lopez Olga—†	11A	housewife	22	"

27

Page	Letter	Full Name.	Residence, Jan. 1, 1945.	Occupation.	Supposed Age.	Reported Residence, Jan. 1, 1944. Street and Number.

	D	Mahoney Nellie—†	12	at home	55	here
	E	Russell Ann—†	12	housewife	52	"
	F	Russell George	12	clerk	58	"
	G	Crowley Agnes T—†	12	housewife	64	"
	H	Crowley James T	12	watchman	66	"
	K	Cantillo Lucy R—†	14	housewife	34	"
	L	Cantillo Maurice A	14	butcher	34	"
	M	Cantillo Alphonso	14	retired	58	
	N	Cantillo Anna—†	14	clerk	20	
	O	Cantillo Henrietta—†	14	housewife	54	"
	P	Rocco Fiorinda—†	15	at home	73	"
	R	Rocco Josephine—†	15	housewife	45	"
	S	Rocco Louis	15	electrician	50	"
	T	Rocco Michael	15	salesman	48	"
	U	Kincaid Elsie M—†	16	secretary	36	"
	V	Kincaid Mary S—†	16	at home	68	"
	W	Kincaid Sterling J	16	upholsterer	41	"
	X	Murray Catherine E—†	18	statistician	36	"
	Y	Sullivan Mary E—†	18	housewife	61	"
	Z	Calhoun George F	18	retired	80	
1847						
	A	Calhoun Mary—†	18	at home	77	"
	B	Graziano Emilia—†	19	"	68	
	C	Graziano Marie C—†	19	clerk	38	
	D	Spinale Matthew D	19	manager	42	"
	E	Downing Byron D	20	clerk	65	
	F	Downing Hiram A	20	watchman	67	"
	G	Downing Melissa S—†	20	housewife	58	"
	H	Keen Alice R—†	20	at home	30	"
	K	Smith Justina S—†	20	"	80	
	L	Smith Willard M	20	retired	85	
	M	Devlin Louise—†	21	nurse	39	
	N	O'Rourke Helen F—†	21	operator	47	"
	O	O'Rourke Irene—†	21	forewoman	42	"
	P	O'Rourke Mary A—†	21	housewife	71	"
	R	Donavon Arthur J	22	pipecoverer	45	"
	S	Donavon Ellen C—†	22	housewife	43	"
	T	Morrison John P	22	retired	78	"
	U	Morrison Julia F—†	22	teacher	39	"
	V	Morrison Mary E—†	22	operator	50	"
	W	Dobrisky Catherine—†	25	clerk	20	

x	Tigges Catherine—†	25	housewife	46	here
y	Tigges Herman	25	boilermaker	54	"
z	Tigges Walter J	25	machinist	48	"
	1848				
a	Alosa Dina—†	26	housewife	42	"
b	Alosa Umberto	26	manager	43	
c	Rossi Angelo	26	tailor	56	
d	*Rossi Esilda—†	26	housewife	50	"
e	Rossi Guy	26	mechanic	25	"
f	Giordano Antonette—†	26	housewife	36	"
g	Giordano Mario	26	chauffeur	36	"

Ward 1 –Precinct 19

CITY OF BOSTON

LIST OF RESIDENTS
20 YEARS OF AGE AND OVER

(NON-CITIZENS INDICATED BY ASTERISK)
(FEMALES INDICATED BY DAGGER)

AS OF

JANUARY 1, 1945

THOMAS F. SULLIVAN, *Chairman*
FREDERIC E. DOWLING, *Secretary*
WILLIAM A. MOTLEY, JR.
FRANCIS B. McKINNEY
EVERETT R. PROUT

Listing Board.

1900
Annavoy Street

A	Cerullo Crescancio	10	pharmacist	35	here
B	Cerullo Lillian—†	10	housewife	32	"
C	Ruggieri Amelia—†	10	"	58	"
D	Ruggieri Luigi	10	finisher	59	"
E	Bellusci Josephine—†	20	housewife	52	"
F	Bellusci Michael	20	agent	62	
G	Montgomery Edward N	26	B F D	58	
H	Montgomery Helen B—†	26	housewife	54	"

Barnes Avenue

K	MacDonald Clementine B—†	95	secretary	64	here
L	MacDonald Kathryn F—†	95	operator	56	"
M	MacDonald Mary A—†	95	at home	67	"
N	Perrier Albert	95	U S N	35	"
O	Perrier Alice—†	95	housewife	62	"
P	Perrier J Eugene	95	shoeworker	62	"
R	Perrier Leo	95	U S A	37	
S	Riley Irene—†	95	housewife	30	"
T	Riley William	95	engineer	32	"
U	Jannini Alice—†	99	housewife	39	"
V	Jannini Christopher	99	welder	40	"
W	Abate Angelo	99	shoeworker	59	"
X	Abate Frank	99	U S A	34	"
Y	Abate Gloria—†	99	student	22	"
Z	Abate Jeannette—†	99	secretary	32	"

1901

A	Abate Laura—†	99	housewife	52	"
B	Abate Loretta—†	99	stenographer	21	"
C	D'Allesandro Enrico	102	welder	32	Lynn
D	D'Allesandro Lena—†	102	housewife	35	here
E	*D'Allesandro Angelina—†	102	"	56	"
F	D'Allesandro Louis	102	pedler	36	"
G	D'Allesandro Marion—†	102	housewife	32	"
H	Pingaro Edith—†	102	student	20	"
K	*Cleary Ellen—†	103	operator	74	"
L	Fenlon Mary E—†	103	housewife	75	"
M	Fenlon Warren F	103	attorney	46	"
N	Campbell Armina M—†	103	housewife	76	"
O	Campbell John L	103	retired	81	

Barnes Avenue—Continued

P	McDermott Armina M—†	103	housewife	41	here
R	McDermott John L	103	policeman	44	"
S	Shields William J	103	tender	40	"
T	Collins Mary E—†	107	matron	60	
U	Hickey Catherine—†	107	housewife	59	"
V	Hickey Mary E—†	107	tel operator	39	"
W	Mulligan Francis T	107	U S N	39	"
X	Hickey Edward I	107	collector	38	"
Y	Hickey Frances M—†	107	housewife	37	"
Z	Bonugli Anna—†	110	"	49	"

1902

A	Bonugli John	110	operator	53	"
B	Carbone Charles	110	electrician	47	"
C	Carbone Elizabeth—†	110	clerk	50	"
D	McCormick James	110	teacher	32	"
E	McCormick Virginia M—†	110	housewife	26	"
F	Sennett Louise—†	110	housekeeper	47	"
G	Ahern Helen—†	111	saleswoman	53	"
H	Ahern Margaret—†	111	at home	43	"
K	Ahern Nora—†	111	saleswoman	55	"
L	Aylward Alice L—†	111	teacher	23	112 St Andrew rd
M	Aylward Alice R—†	111	housewife	47	112 "
N	Aylward Dorothy R—†	111	clerk	21	112 "
O	Aylward Richard F	111	B F D	51	112 "
P	Hanagan John J	111	"	56	112 "
R	Callanan Pauline A—†	115	housewife	39	here
S	Callanan William A	115	U S A	40	"
T	White John J	115	carpenter	69	"
U	White Mary E—†	115	housewife	63	"
V	White Mary R—†	115	secretary	34	"
W	Lehmann Anton	118	B F D	35	"
X	Lehmann Arthur B	118	printer	52	
Y	Lehmann Dorothy M—†	118	stenographer	32	"
Z	Lehmann Grace A—†	118	timekeeper	31	"

1903

A	Lehmann Lillian A—†	118	housewife	52	"
B	Donovan Florence—†	118	saleswoman	46	"
C	Hart Mary—†	118	supervisor	57	"
D	Lane Alice—†	118	dressmaker	60	"
E	Lane Catherine—†	118	housewife	40	"
F	Lane Helen J—†	118	tel operator	47	"

Barnes Avenue—Continued

G	Lane James	118	metalworker	42	here	
H	Lane John	118	U S A	45	"	
K	Lane Kathryn—†	118	tel operator	43	"	
L	Crawford Mary E—†	126	housekeeper	77	"	
M	Ryan Helen G—†	126	housewife	42	"	
N	Ryan James J	126	supervisor	45	"	
O	Gallagher James F	126	U S A	29		
P	Gallagher Ruth A—†	126	housewife	26	"	
R	Higgins Lillian A—†	126	operator	48	"	
S	Nolan Margaret R—†	126	clerk	52		
T	Shannon Edward	126	chauffeur	44	"	
U	Shannon Elizabeth—†	126	housewife	51	"	
V	Shannon George A	126	U S N	39		
W	Shannon William J	126	"	41		

Bayswater Street

X	Kiley Grace B—†	80	housewife	38	here	
Y	Kiley Henry A	80	clerk	40	"	
Z	Ahearn Bridget—†	82	at home	72	"	
	1904					
A	Recomendes Annie E—†	82	"	70		
B	O'Neil Nellie—†	84	"	73		
C	Keating Regina—†	86	housewife	26	"	
D	Keating William	86	U S A	26	"	
E	McNamee Anna E—†	86	housewife	32	"	
F	McNamee Charles	86	pharmacist	34	"	
G	Engren Theresa—†	88	housewife	52	"	
H	Engren Walter F	88	engineer	48	"	
K	Mullen James	88	retired	86	"	
L	Mullen John J	88	proprietor	48	"	
M	Mullen Marion K—†	88	housewife	42	"	
N	Viglione Anna—†	94	"	44	"	
O	Viglione Marie—†	94	clerk	20		
P	Viglione Pasquale	94	proprietor	42	"	
R	Moschella Anna—†	94	housewife	44	"	
S	Moschella Anthony	94	U S N	22		
T	Moschella Michael	94	proprietor	49	"	
U	Moschella Samuel	94	U S N	23	"	
V	DiNucci Helena—†	98	housewife	31	Lowell	
W	DiNucci Joseph V	98	engineer	34	"	

Page:	Letter.	FULL NAME.	Residence, Jan. 1, 1945.	Occupation.	Supposed Age.	Reported Residence, Jan. 1, 1944. Street and Number.

Bayswater Street—Continued

	x	DiNucci Rose—†	98	clerk	42	here
	y	DiNucci Victoria—†	98	saleswoman	36	"
	z	DiNucci William A	98	U S N	40	"
1905						
	a	Coggiano Evelyn—†	100	housewife	47	"
	b	Coggiano Generoso	100	salesman	49	"
	c	Coggiano Grace—†	100	clerk	22	"
	d	Lavezzo Rose—†	100	at home	87	"
	e	Nutile Edna V—†	102	housewife	48	"
	f	Nutile Thomas	102	realtor	61	
	g	Nutile Thomas A	102	U S A	21	"
	h	Hedrington James V	104	inspector	46	"
	k	Oakes Charles G	104	motorman	47	"
	l	Oakes Henry J	104	retired	82	"
	m	Oakes John L	104	checker	39	"
	n	Oakes Mary E—†	104	clerk	38	"
	o	Chiccarelli Jennie—†	106	stitcher	45	"
	p	Chiccarelli Joseph	106	clerk	46	
	r	Chiccarelli Nardo	106	U S A	22	
	s	Chiccarelli Natalie—†	106	clerk	21	"
	t	Donohue Cornelius	108	plumber	37	"
	u	Donohue Frances—†	108	housewife	36	"
	v	Crowley George	110	supervisor	52	"
	w	Crowley Helen—†	110	housewife	47	"
	x	Swidzinski Anna—†	110	cleaner	47	
	y	Rossetta Angela—†	112	housewife	32	"
	z	Rossetta Anthony	112	rigger	33	
1906						
	a	Mogan Ethel D—†	112	housewife	53	"
	b	Mogan William H	112	realtor	58	"
	c	Alexander William J	114	clerk	55	
	d	Donohue Cornelius J	114	plumber	72	"
	e	Donohue Harriet N—†	114	housewife	67	"
	f	Howard Marie—†	114	"	37	
	g	Howard William	114	policeman	37	"
	h	Walters Rose M—†	114	bookkeeper	57	"
	k	Brown Aimee F—†	116	teacher	35	"
	l	Brown Margaret E—†	116	housewife	60	"
	m	DeSimone Adeline—†	120	"	45	
	n	DeSimone Lena—†	120	clerk	23	
	o	DeSimone Michael	120	chauffeur	47	"

Page.	Letter.	Full Name.	Residence, Jan. 1, 1945.	Occupation.	Supposed Age.	Reported Residence, Jan. 1, 1944. Street and Number.

Bayswater Street—Continued

	P	Lane John A	120	teacher	58	here
	R	Lane Mabel—†	120	clerk	45	"
	S	Pellegrini Helen—†	122	housewife	46	"
	T	Pellegrini Joseph	122	manager	47	"
	U	Cavaliere Anna—†	124	clerk	22	
	V	Cavaliere Carmella—†	124	winder	26	"
	W	Cavaliere Elizabeth—†	124	housewife	49	"
	X	Cavaliere Joseph	124	guard	49	
	Y	Cavaliere Joseph	124	U S A	20	
	Z	Cavaliere Mary—†	124	WAVE	25	"
1907						
	A	Morton Evelyn G—†	126	housewife	40	"
	B	Morton Walter E	126	brakeman	43	"
	C	Morton Walter E, jr	126	fireman	23	"
	D	Digou Agnes I.—†	140	housewife	64	"
	E	Digou Freeman	140	proprietor	67	"
	F	Digou Mary C—†	140	teacher	30	"
	G	Phelan Helen A—†	140	housewife	46	"
	H	Phelan Mary C—†	140	stenographer	21	"
	K	Phelan William M	140	B F D	58	..
	L	Whynot George	144	machinist	63	"
	M	Whynot Lucinda—†	144	housewife	62	"
	N	Silva Anthony	144	proprietor	55	"
	O	Brown Hazel R—†	146	stenographer	28	"
	P	Brown James S	146	electrician	64	"
	R	Burns Clare N—†	146	secretary	30	"
	S	Burns Edward P	146	retired	74	..
	T	Burns Margaret A—†	146	housewife	67	"
	U	Clarke Estelle—†	146	social worker	45	"
	V	Ciampa Elizabeth—†	148	housewife	58	"
	W	Ciampa Rose—†	148	clerk	22	"
	X	Watt John	150	manager	51	"
	Y	Watt Mary—†	150	housewife	50	"
	Z	Montgomery Annie T—†	150	at home	83	"
1908						
	A	Montgomery Hugh J	150	artist	54	"
	B	Montgomery Rose E—†	150	housewife	54	"
	C	Montgomery Claire—†	156	"	45	
	D	Montgomery Eugene	156	jeweler	50	"
	E	Chalmers Hazen A	156	policeman	48	"
	F	Chalmers Julia—†	156	housewife	48	"

6

G	Dolan Frank X	160	inspector	45	here
H	Dolan Margaret—†	160	housewife	41	"
K	O'Brien Catherine—†·	160	at home	75	"
L	Dawley Anastasia—†	160	"	81	
M	Dawley Anna F—†	160	housewife	46	"
N	Dawley William J	160	inspector	48	"
O	Kelly Christopher	160	retired	83	
P	Rosa Albert	164	attorney	36	
R	Rosa Catherine—†	164	clerk	33	
S	Rosa Helen S—·†	164	housewife	38	"
T	Mattola Jennie—†	166	"	61	
U	Mattola Nelson	166	guard	60	
V	Butler Helen—†	168	at home	71	
W	Stenzel Margaret—†	168	nurse	65	"
X	Evans Agnes J—†	170	housewife	39	"
Y	Evans Frances J—†	170	WAC	20	
Z	Evans John	170	machinist	56	"

1909

A	Sablone Albert	172	U S M C	21	"
B	Sablone Alfred	172	U S A	24	
C	Sablone Alice—†	172	supervisor	28	"
D	Sablone Antonio	172	dairyman	51	"
E	Sablone Frank	172	"	26	
F	Sablone Nicoletta—†	172	housewife	54	"
G	Cerulli Ralph F	174	engineer	39	
H	Cerulli Rose M—†	174	housewife	40	"
K	Geuras Peter	174	attorney	35	
L	Geuras Theodora—†	174	housewife	32	"
M	Lowther Anne—†	174A	secretary	38	"
N	Lowther Cecilia—†	174A	housewife	68	"
O	Lowther Frances—†	174A	supervisor	41	"
P	Lowther Grace—†	174A	secretary	35	"
R	Lowther Margaret—†	174A	at home	43	
S	Lafferty Matthew	186	clerk	55	
T	Landry Jeffrey	186	manager	56	"
U	Landry Mary E—†	186	housewife	54	"
V	McLaughlin Frances K-†	186	director	25	"
W	McLaughlin Frances M-†	186	housewife	68	"
X	Mealey Leo	186	clerk	46	
Y	Platt John	186	"	42	
Z	Platt Marion—†	186	housewife	41	"

1910
Bayswater Street—Continued

A	Harkins Celia—†	188	housewife	58	here
B	Harkins Charles J	188	clerk	30	"
C	Harkins John T	188	U S N	29	"
D	Harkins Mary E—†	188	clerk	32	
E	Harkins William J	188	secretary	25	"
F	McGrath James P	188	diemaker	31	"
G	McGrath Ruth—†	188	housewife	28	"
H	Hall Fritz	190	painter	49	"
K	Hall Marion—†	190	housewife	44	"

Lillian Street

O	Harvey Mary M—†	1	clerk	29	here
P	Keleher Dennis J	1	prob'n officer	68	"
R	Keleher Katherine W—†	1	housewife	67	"
S	Penta Joseph J	14	foreman	38	166 Orient av
T	Penta Philomena M—†	14	housewife	31	166 "
U	Zagarella Gemma—†	14	"	47	here
V	Zagarella Joseph S	14	U S A	26	"
W	Zagarelle Salvatore	14	barber	49	"

Nancia Street

X	Heggem Dagny M—†	2	housewife	46	here
Y	Heggem Louis J	2	clergyman	57	"
Z	Heggem Warren L	2	student	21	"

1911

A	Romano Anna L—†	9	housewife	42	"
B	Romano Annetta L—†	9	student	20	"
C	Romano Philip A	9	tailor	46	
D	Treco Louis A	9	electrician	48	"
E	Centracchio Anthony A	10	attorney	38	"
F	Centracchio Lillian E—†	10	housewife	32	"
G	Potito Donald D	14	physician	36	"
H	Potito Leonora—†	14	housewife	28	"

Saint Andrew Road

L	Chiarini Joseph S	50	musician	56	here
M	Chiarini Josephine—†	50	housewife	55	"

8

Saint Andrew Road—Continued

Letter	Full Name	Residence	Occupation	Age	Reported Residence
N	Giuffre Elisa—†	50	beautician	33	here
O	Ciampa Lillian—†	50	housewife	49	"
P	Marsolini Robert	50	U S M C	26	"
R	Massa Ida—†	50	at home	45	"
S	Massa Rose—†	50	"	42	
T	Penta Edith—†	51	stitcher	30	"
U	Penta Marie—†	51	housewife	70	"
V	Penta Theresa—†	51	operator	38	"
W	Lyons Joseph	51	machinist	45	"
X	Lyons Veronica I—†	51	housewife	44	"
Y	Miller John J	51	chauffeur	46	"
Z	Curran Theresa—†	53	housewife	42	"

1912

Letter	Full Name	Residence	Occupation	Age	Reported Residence
A	Curran William C	53	chauffeur	44	"
B	Curran William C	53	U S N	20	
C	Winston James J	53	supervisor	59	"
D	Winston John E	53	statistician	53	"
E	Winston Katherine B—†	53	housewife	46	"
F	Winston Mary F—†	53	"	48	"
G	Watts Gertrude H—†	55	at home	60	"
H	Anderson Christine M—†	55	clerk	43	
K	Anderson Josephine L—†	55	"	45	"
L	Regan Donald A	55	U S N	29	
M	Regan Louise B—†	55	at home	55	"
N	Regan Miriam L—†	55	teacher	24	"
O	Ryan Agnes M—†	56	housewife	43	"
P	Ryan Thomas B	56	electrician	43	"
R	Aronson Harry	57	supervisor	44	"
S	Aronson Margaret—†	57	housewife	35	"
T	Gidney Anna—†	57	bookkeeper	45	"
U	Corrigan Anna—†	57	meteorologist	37	"
V	Corrigan Katherine F—†	57	housewife	68	"
W	Corrigan Robert J	57	U S N	23	
X	McCarthy Harry	57	U S A	25	
Y	Crowley Margaret—†	59	at home	56	"
Z	Sullivan John	59	clerk	20	

1913

Letter	Full Name	Residence	Occupation	Age	Reported Residence
A	Hart Peter	59	printer	44	
B	Hart Susan—†	59	housewife	44	"
C	Sullivan Jane—†	59	nurse	55	"
D	Sullivan Susan—†	59	housewife	78	"

9

Page.	Letter.	FULL NAME.	Residence, Jan. 1, 1945.	Occupation.	Supposed Age.	Reported Residence, Jan. 1, 1944. Street and Number.

Saint Andrew Road—Continued

	E	McLeavey Anna E—†	60	housewife	65	here
	F	McLeavey Patrick	60	retired	76	"
	G	Kane Daniel H	60	U S A	20	"
	H	Plunkett Bernard	60	retired	79	"
	K	Reardon Catherine—†	60	housekeeper	70	"
	L	Kelly John C	61	mortician	54	2 St Andrew rd
	M	Kelly Rose V—†	61	housewife	54	2 "
	N	Gill Mary E—†	61	"	72	here
	O	Gill Richard	61	guard	72	"
	P	Gill Richard M	61	U S A	29	"
	R	Grifone Alice—†	63	housewife	48	"
	S	Grifone Louis P	63	tailor	50	..
	T	Musto Albert S	63	clerk	37	..
	U	Musto Mary A—†	63	housewife	36	"
	V	Yirrell Mary A—†	63	at home	68	"
	W	Murphy Cornelius	63	salesman	33	"
	X	Murphy Ella—†	63	housewife	33	"
	Y	Zalewski Agnes—†	63	"	27	"
	Z	Zalewski Frank C	63	U S A	28	Chelsea
		1914				
	A	Francis Adelaide A—†	64	at home	73	here
	B	Lamb Ethel B—†	64	housewife	49	"
	C	Lamb Frank I	64	policeman	50	"
	D	Haley Susan G—†	65	housewife	60	"
	E	McGovern Margaret A—†	65	inspector	53	"
	F	Amerau Harold	66	draftsman	29	"
	G	Amerau Miriam—†	66	housewife	29	"
	H	Gavagan Ethel—†	66	operator	33	"
	K	Gavagan Helen—†	66	housekeeper	42	"
	L	Gavagan Katherine—†	66	operator	30	"
	M	Gavagan Walter	66	clerk	45	
	N	Carey Alice—†	66	housewife	26	"
	O	Carey Edward	66	tester	32	"
	P	Colbert John J	66	mechanic	52	"
	R	Colbert Nellie—†	66	packer	50	"
	S	McGuigan Ann E—†	68	buyer	22	"
	T	McGuigan Anna—†	68	housewife	54	"
	U	McGuigan Bernard J	68	U S A	28	
	V	McGuigan Mary—†	68	secretary	28	"
	W	Motrone Irene—†	68	clerk	23	..
	X	Motrone Josephine—†	68	housewife	48	"

10

Saint Andrew Road—Continued

	Y	Strong Anne A—†	68	at home	68	here
	Z	Strong Ellen L—†	68	"	70	"

1915

	A	Strong William H	68	dentist	56	"
	B	Hoey Edward	69	treasurer	52	"
	C	Hoey John W	69	retired	55	"
	D	Hoey Mary L—†	69	housewife	50	"
	E	McDonald Dorothy—†	69	social worker	33	"
	F	McDonald Margaret—†	69	housewife	58	"
	G	Leary Helen L—†	69	"	45	
	H	Leary Matthew M	69	retired	68	
	K	Caggiano Arthur	70	U S C G	37	"
	L	Caggiano Florence—†	70	operator	33	"
	M	Caggiano Grace—†	70	housewife	70	"
	N	Caggiano Joseph	70	barber	75	
	O	Schoenfeld Marie—†	70	stenographer	42	"
	P	Caggiano Armand	70	B F D	40	
	R	Caggiano Catherine—†	70	housewife	40	"
	S	Cataldo Chiarina—†	72	at home	73	"
	T	Cataldo Pasquale	72	retired	83	
	U	Zizza Alfred L	72	clerk	41	
	V	Zizza Ermalinda—†	72	housewife	39	"
	W	Belucci Louise—†	72	dressmaker	27	"
	X	Belucci Nicholas	72	U S A	31	
	Y	DiFranzo Michael	72	bartender	60	"
	Z	DiFranzo Philomena—†	72	housewife	65	"

1916

	A	Picardi Louis	72	U S N	27	"
	B	Picardi Rose—†	72	clerk	24	
	C	Duffy Mary M—†	73	housewife	40	"
	D	Duffy Michael H	73	U S N	45	"
	E	Callahan John	73	auditor	55	
	F	Callahan Rose—†	73	housewife	53	"
	G	Dolan Anna L—†	73	at home	61	"
	H	McCarthy Mary F—†	73	"	71	
	K	Carangelo Louise—†	74	teacher	41	"
	L	Miraldi Gerald	74	attorney	42	"
	M	Miraldi Olive—†	74	housewife	39	"
	N	Cohan Alice—†	75	"	66	
	O	Cohan Edward J	75	U S A	23	

Saint Andrew Road—Continued

P	Cohan William	75	laborer	67	here
R	Cerullo Anna—†	75	housewife	65	"
S	Cerullo Sabato	75	laborer	65	"
T	Clague Anna—†	75	housewife	36	Wilmington
U	Clague Daniel, jr	75	surveyor	39	"
V	Pellegrino Adeline—†	76	housewife	36	here
W	Pellegrino Vincent	76	clerk	36	"
X	Calamoneri Domenica—†	77	at home	80	"
Y	Femino Bruno	77	barber	55	"
Z	Femino Jennie—†	77	librarian	29	"

1917

A	Femino John	77	U S N	28	
B	Femino Paul	77	U S A	26	
C	Femino Rose—†	77	housewife	50	"
D	Femino Salvatore	77	U S A	25	"
E	Maresco Helen—†	77	housewife	34	"
F	Maresco Ralph	77	chauffeur	40	"
G	Indrisano Amelio	77	mechanic	31	"
H	Indrisano Mildred—†	77	housewife	31	"
K	McCarthy Helen G—†	77	"	32	
L	McCarthy Joseph L	77	operator	36	"
M	Elmore Joseph F	78	inspector	48	"
N	Elmore Margaret J—†	78	housewife	85	"
O	Elmore Mary G—†	78	clerk	50	
P	McAdams Alfred	78	laborer	50	"
R	McAdams Eleanor—†	78	housewife	48	"
S	Callahan Mary A—†	80	at home	69	"
T	Murphy John D	80	retired	68	"
U	Murphy Margaret L—†	80	housewife	55	"
V	Maffei Marie A—†	81	"	30	
W	Maffei Ralph A	81	pharmacist	34	"
X	Cunningham Mary—†	81	at home	74	"
Y	Drowney Agnes C—†	81	dietitian	64	"
Z	Shaw Henry F	81	broker	54	

1918

A	Shaw Henry F, jr	81	technician	22	"
B	Shaw Marie—†	81	housewife	50	"
C	Lagana Joseph	82	policeman	31	"
D	Lagana Mary—†	82	housewife	31	"
E	Breau Joseph R	82	machinist	29	"
F	Breau Lillian—†	82	housewife	27	"

Saint Andrew Road—Continued

G	DiSessa Alice L—†	82	housewife	26	here
H	DiSessa Peter	82	U S N	29	"
K	Harris James C	83	tender	55	144 St Andrew rd
L	Harris Margaret—†	83	housewife	54	144 "
M	Love Lena R—†	83	clerk	44	here
N	Reardon Catherine M—†	83	housewife	30	"
O	Reardon John J	83	U S A	34	"
P	Labadessa Joseph	85	laborer	64	
R	Labadessa Lucy—†	85	housewife	64	"
S	Arnone Adele—†	86	housekeeper	33	"
T	Arnone Angela—†	86	housewife	57	"
U	Arnone Nicholas J	86	candymaker	59	"
V	Martins Anna—†	86	housewife	52	"
W	Martins John	86	carpenter	50	"
X	Dunn Anne—†	87	housewife	35	"
Y	Dunn Joseph	87	contractor	41	"
Z	DeSimone Joseph	89	proprietor	51	"

1919

A	DeSimone Joseph, jr	89	U S A	22	
B	DeSimone Lena—†	89	clerk	24	..
C	DeSimone Lucas	89	U S A	30	"
D	DeSimone Margaret—†	89	housewife	49	"
E	Collyer Albert J	90	laborer	47	
F	Stoner Beverly—†	90	technician	22	"
G	Stoner Elizabeth E—†	90	housewife	54	"
H	Stoner George H, jr	90	architect	27	"
K	Parrell Catherine L—†	90	housewife	52	25 St Andrew rd
L	Parrell Richard T	90	retired	58	25 "
M	Pendergast Catherine—†	90	housewife	67	here
N	Pendergast Lillian—†	90	operator	44	"
O	McBride Albina—†	91–93	typist	43	"
P	McBride Daniel F	91–93	clerk	48	"
R	McBride Margaret V—†	91–93	housewife	47	"
S	Smith Francis X	91–93	letter carrier	50	"
T	Smith Mary—†	91–93	stitcher	45	"
U	Smith Sarah—†	91–93	housewife	48	"
V	Whaland Helen E—†	92	"	44	
W	Whaland Phillip P	92	policeman	55	"
X	Schlosberg Harold J	94	U S A	23	
Y	Schlosberg Louis H	94	merchant	59	"
Z	Schlosberg Sadie—†	94	housewife	55	"

1920
Saint Andrew Road—Continued

A	Crowley James J	96	U S N	35	here
B	Crowley Sarah H—†	96	housewife	33	"
C	Greer Herbert	98	U S A	28	"
D	Greer Margaret—†	98	housewife	54	"
E	Ryan Nicholas J	98	letter carrier	63	"
F	Kinnaly Ellen—†	100	at home	73	"
G	Kinnaly George	100	clerk	41	
H	Kinnaly Theresa—†	100	housewife	36	"
K	Petrillo Henry	101	tailor	41	"
L	Petrillo Mary—†	101	housewife	43	"
M	Selvitella James	103	proprietor	46	"
N	Selvitella Joseph	103	"	47	
O	Palladino Alphonsina—†	103	housewife	31	"
P	Palladino Anthony	103	proprietor	37	"
R	Corrado John C	104	physician	36	"
S	Corrado Maria—†	104	housewife	33	"
T	Bellavia Mary—†	105	stitcher	55	"
U	D'Amore Marie—†	105	waitress	35	"
V	Vaccaro Rose—†	105	stitcher	37	"
W	Vaccaro Salvatore	105	presser	42	Winthrop
X	Olson Margaret F—†	106	housewife	55	here
Y	Olson Olaf N	106	printer	56	"
Z	Monahan John B	107	collector	33	"

1921

A	Monahan Nora T—†	107	housewife	34	"
B	Valli Blanche M—†	108	"	37	
C	Valli George E	108	proprietor	43	"
D	Calafato Eva—†	109	housewife	32	"
E	Calafato Thomas	109	assembler	35	"
F	Capuana Elizabeth—†	110	housewife	36	"
G	Capuana John	110	U S N	37	"
H	Valli Adele—†	110	housewife	73	"
K	D'Ambrosio Adano	111	U S N	42	
L	D'Ambrosio John	111	agent	37	"
M	D'Ambrosio Josephine—†	111	housewife	33	"
N	D'Ambrosio Maria—†	111	at home	70	"
O	Drew Johanna—†	112	housekeeper	54	9 Seaview av
P	Edwards James W	112	U S C G	29	9 "
R	Edwards Joseph P	112	"	22	9 "
S	Edwards Lawrence J	112	U S N	31	9 "

Saint Andrew Road—Continued

T	Edwards Lillian—†	112	housewife	27	Gloucester
U	Abbruzzese Assunta—†	113	"	40	here
V	Abbruzzese Carlo	113	salesman	40	"
W	Drohan Genevieve—†	114	housewife	42	1124 Saratoga
X	Drohan John F	114	agent	43	1124 "
Y	Drohan John F	114	U S N	22	1124 "
Z	Abbruzzese Edith—†	115	clerk	20	here
	1922				
A	Abbruzzese Louis	115	proprietor	60	"
B	Abbruzzese Patrick	115	U S A	26	
C	Abbruzzese Susan—†	115	at home	29	"
D	Abbruzzese Theresa—†	115	housewife	55	"
E	Carresi Gemma—†	121	"	42	..
F	Carresi Leo	121	electrician	42	"
G	Ciccarelli Michael	121	proprietor	49	"
H	Ciccarelli Rachel—†	121	housewife	42	"
K	Blinn Fred W	123	U S A	23	
L	Blinn Katherine L—†	123	housewife	53	"
M	Blinn Margaret—†	123	"	45	
N	Blinn William	123	seaman	50	..
O	Overlan Leo H	123	finisher	50	"
P	Cianciulli Charles	123	electrician	40	"
R	Cianciulli Mary—†	123	housewife	30	"
S	DiChristoforo Carmelina—†	125	"	38	
T	DiChristoforo Emilio	125	printer	44	"
U	Irwin Cecelia B—†	127	housewife	34	"
V	Irwin Francis W	127	clerk	39	
W	Shanahan James A	127	"	57	"
X	Shanahan James A, jr	127	U S A	22	
Y	Shanahan May E—†	127	housewife	49	"
Z	Breslin Beatrice—†	137	"	26	
	1923				
A	Donovan Daniel J	137	clerk	51	
B	Donovan Daniel J, jr	137	U S N	21	
C	Donovan John J	137	clerk	28	..
D	Donovan Julia A—†	137	housewife	51	"
E	Donovan William F	137	U S A	24	"
F	Ricciardelli John	140	pipefitter	34	"
G	Ricciardelli Rose—†	140	housewife	33	"
H	Kenefick Matthew	140	clerk	57	"
K	Kenefick Violet—†	140	housewife	53	"

Saint Andrew Road—Continued

L	McFarland Mildred—†	140	housewife	32	here
M	McFarland Vincent	140	clerk	32	"
N	Bartlett Catherine M—†	142	housewife	52	"
O	Bartlett John T	142	supt	55	"
P	Bartlett John T	142	U S A	28	
R	Bartlett Robert J	142	"	22	
S	Doherty James P	142	chauffeur	43	"
T	Maffei Grace—†	142	clerk	29	
U	Maffei Rocco	142	representative	29	"
V	Sacco Elizabeth—†	142	stitcher	47	"
W	Sacco Louise—†	142	nurse	20	"
X	Colucci Carl J	144	shipfitter	29	"
Y	Colucci Lillian J—†	144	housewife	26	"
Z	Blangio Albert	144	U S N	34	"
	1924				
A	Blangio Albert J	144	bartender	60	"
B	Blangio Annie—†	144	housewife	51	"
C	Blangio Charles	144	U S A	31	
D	Blangio Dorothy—†	144	clerk	24	
E	Blangio John J	144	U S A	32	
F	Blangio Michael	144	clerk	35	
G	Smith Alice M—†	146	housewife	45	"
H	Smith George H	146	mechanic	49	"
K	Smith William A	146	manager	47	"
L	Smith William A, jr	146	U S A	20	"
M	DeStefano Eleanor—†	146	housewife	43	"
N	DeStefano George	146	shipfitter	46	"
O	DeStefano Katherine—†	146	stitcher	23	"
P	Bacciola Elisa—†	147	buyer	51	
R	Bacciola Emma—†	147	clerk	46	
S	Bacciola Giacomo	147	retired	83	
T	Bacciola Nella—†	147	teacher	43	"
U	Bacciola Theodore P	147	engineer	37	"
V	Arnesano Antonio	148	barber	50	97 Chelsea
W	Arnesano Fannie—†	148	housewife	49	97 "
X	Arnesano Joseph	148	shipfitter	22	97 "
Y	Arnesano Louis	148	accountant	26	97 "
Z	Rapa Anita—†	148	housewife	40	here
	1925				
A	Rapa Fiore	148	manager	44	"
B	Wynters Elmer F	150	U S A	36	"

c	Wynters Henry A	150	chauffeur	39	here
d	Wynters Sylvester J	150	director	65	"
e	Wynters Walter S	150	operator	55	"
f	Cancian Emma—†	150	housewife	46	"
g	Cancian Ottavio	150	contractor	46	"
h	Barnard Warren	152	U S A	26	"
k	Montgomery Cyril	152	policeman	48	"
l	Montgomery Florence—†	152	housewife	40	"
m	Lombardozzi Angelina—†	152	cashier	33	
n	Lombardozzi Mary—†	152	candyworker	43	"
o	Vestute Domenica—†	152	housewife	47	"
p	Vestute Joseph	152	attendant	51	"
r	D'Avalio Angelina—†	154	housewife	41	"
s	D'Avalio Domenic	154	shipfitter	44	"
t	D'Amico Arlene—†	154	housewife	37	"
u	D'Amico Visconte	154	proprietor	42	"

Saint Edward Road

w	Cecero Mary—†	35	housewife	36	here
x	Cecero Nicholas G	35	architect	36	"
y	Lagana Anthony E	35	U S N	24	"
z	Lagana Concetta J—†	35	housewife	52	"
	1926				
a	Lagana Placido F	35	barber	56	
b	Battaglia Frederick	35	"	35	
c	Battaglia Lena—†	35	housewife	32	"
d	Guarino Louise—†	35	"	63	
e	Guarino Raffaele	35	laborer	67	
f	Albano Frederick	37	mechanic	33	"
g	Albano Mary—†	37	housewife	28	"
h	Minichiello Albert A	37	engineer	36	
m	Minichiello Amelio	37	welder	27	
l	Minichiello Elsie L—†	37	housewife	32	"
m	Minichiello Felix	37	retired	75	
n	Albano Felix	37	mechanic	32	"
o	Albano Mary—†	37	housewife	30	"
p	Mauceri Achille	39	retired	71	
r	Mauceri Concettina—†	39	bookkeeper	30	"
s	*Mauceri Corradina—†	39	housewife	70	"

Saint Edward Road—Continued

T	DeLorenzo Anna—†	39	housewife	29	here
U	DeLorenzo Carmine	39	shipfitter	30	"
V	DeLorenzo Rose—†	39	bookkeeper ·	25	"
W	DeLorenzo Stella—†	39	stitcher	31	"
X	DeLorenzo Theresa—†	39	housewife	53	"
Y	Ainola Angelina J—†	39	"	23	Quincy
Z	Ainola Anthony	39	mechanic	24	"
	1927				
A	Bongiovanni Amelia—†	39	housewife	47	here
B	Bongiovanni Anthony	39	shoemaker	53	"
C	Bongiovanni Catherine E–†	39	dressmaker	25	"
D	Bongiovanni Dominic	39	mechanic	27	"
E	Bongiovanni John J ·	39	U S A	20	"
F	Anderson Ellen M—†	41	secretary	39	"
G	Anderson Sarah L—†	41	at home	59	"
H	Lawless Edward F	41	attendant	55	"
K	Sullivan Benjamin F	41	carpenter	39	"
L	Sullivan Theresa M—†	41	housewife	35	"
M	Allavesen George A	41	clerk	49	
N	Allavesen George D	41	laborer	25	"
O	Allavesen Louise—†	41	housekeeper	47	"
P	Sacco Albert	43	B F D	30	"
R	Sacco Helen—†	43	housewife	27	"
S	Babine Benjamin	43	cook	52	"
T	Babine Ella—†	43	housewife	45	".
U	Babine Joseph	43	U S A	20	"
V	Savio Amelia—†	43	WAVE	24	"
W	Savio Domenica—†	43	housewife	54	"
X	Savio Joseph	43	waiter	60	"
Y	Bombaci Carmela—†	45	clerk	28	
Z	Bombaci Leo	45	carpenter	55	"
	1928				
A	Bombaci Peter	45	U S A	23	
B	Bombaci Vera—†	45	housewife	48	"
C	Langana John	45	U S N	29	
D	Langana Stella—†	45	housewife	29	"
E	Boyce Charles H	45	lineman	36	"
F	Boyce Nora—†	45	tel operator	35	"
G	Mortimer Margaret—†	45	"	22	"

Saratoga Street

H	Boudreau Catherine G–†	1093	housekeeper	77	here
K	Boudreau Elizabeth B–†	1093	executive	41	"
L	Boudreau Mary F—†	1093	musician	54	"
M	McDonald Edward	1093	U S M C	26	"
N	McDonald Mary F—†	1093	housewife	54	"
O	McDonald Robert	1093	student	20	"
P	McDonald Thomas E	1093	U S A	24	..
R	McDonald Thomas F	1093	foreman	55	"
S	McDonald Walter	1093	U S A	33	"
U	Seix Marion F—†	1095	bookkeeper	56	"
V	McHugh Edward J	1095	contractor	50	"
W	McHugh Marguerite H–†	1095	housewife	48	"
X	Powell William L	1095	seaman	57	"
Y	Belinsky Madeline—†	1096	housewife	25	561 Saratoga
Z	Belinsky Mitchell	1096	U S N	31	561 "
	1929				
A	Adams Edward W	1096	U S A	40	here
B	Bradley Edna G—†	1096	housewife	42	"
C	Walker Dorothy—†	1097	tel operator	29	"
D	Walker Lillian—†	1097	buyer	27	
E	Geggis Catherine—†	1097	housewife	41	"
F	Geggis Ellen—†	1097	at home	85	"
G	Geggis James S	1097	salesman	48	"
H	Geggis John A	1097	porter	60	..
K	Rego Frances—†	1098	housewife	62	"
L	Karasik Betty S—†	1098	photographer	37	"
M	*Karasik Nathan	1098	shoemaker	67	"
N	Baldassaro Elizabeth—†	1101	housewife	34	"
O	Baldassaro Louis	1101	plumber	39	"
R	LaTorre Frank	1101	realtor	50	
S	LaTorre Marie—†	1101	housewife	45	"
P	Gomes Arthur E	1102	U S A	24	..
T	Gomes Arthur J	1102	pressman	51	"
U	Gomes Madeline—†	1102	housewife	45	"
V	Busalacchi Andrew	1105	U S A	24	
W	Busalacchi Anthony	1105	merchant	62	"
X	Busalacchi Ellen—†	1105	dressmaker	29	"
Y	Busalacchi Josephine—†	1105	housewife	56	"
Z	Busalacchi Julia—†	1105	secretary	26	"

1930
Saratoga Street—Continued

A	Frongillo Adeline—†	1105	housewife	34	here
¹A	Frongillo John	1105	B F D	35	"
B	Cappuci Anthony	1106	waiter	68	"
C	Cappuci Louis	1106	inspector	30	"
D	Cappuci Lucia—†	1106	at home	68	"
E	Morelli Alexander	1106	student	24	"
F	Morelli Angelina—†	1106	housewife	42	"
G	Morelli John	1106	proprietor	48	"
H	Ross Leo	1109	engineer	62	"
K	Ross Mary E—†	1109	housewife	63	"
L	Ross Mary M—†	1109	teacher	35	"
M	Baldassaro Enrico	1109	U S N	22	..
N	Baldassaro Frank	1109	U S A	29	
O	Baldassaro Mary—†	1109	housewife	65	"
P	Baldassaro Pasquale	1109	realtor	66	
R	Fernald Agnes M—†	1110	housewife	59	"
S	Fernald Robert A	1110	dispatcher	59	"
T	Rafuse Gertrude M—†	1110	housewife	23	Reading
U	Rafuse Robert M	1110	machinist	27	"
V	Musto Fortuna—†	1111	housewife	58	here
W	Musto Joseph	1111	machinist	62	"
X	Musto Armand	1111	"	31	"
Y	Musto Linda—†	1111	housewife	30	"
Z	Hazelton James E	1114	engineer	52	"

1931

A	Hazelton James E, jr	1114	U S N	23	
B	Hazelton Mary M—†	1114	housewife	50	"
C	Hazelton Phyllis M—†	1114	secretary	21	"
D	Fouhy Charles J	1114	U S A	60	"
E	Fouhy Mabel C—†	1114	housewife	44	"
F	Cairns James C	1115	printer	57	
G	Cairns Louise M—†	1115	stenographer	25	"
H	Cairns Rosemarie E—†	1115	WAVE	20	"
K	Cairns Theresa L—†	1115	housewife	54	"
L	Buonopane Florence—†	1115	knitter	24	
M	Buonopane Michael	1115	laborer	51	"
N	Buonopane Priscilla—†	1115	housewife	53	"
O	Rauseo Frank	1115	chauffeur	31	"
P	Rauseo Mary—†	1115	housewife	26	"
R	Leary Arthur D	1116	U S A	27	"

Saratoga Street—Continued

s	Leary Sara A—†	1116	housekeeper	63	here
t	Arthur Cathleen M—†	1116	student	20	" .
u	Arthur Joseph L	1116	merchant	49	"
v	Arthur Lawrence L	1116	clerk	45	
w	Arthur Thomas J	1116	"	47	
x	Arthur Veronica C—†	1116	housewife	49	"
y	McGinn Charles E	1116	U S M C	28	"
z	McGinn Josephine—†	1116	housewife	28	"

1932

a	Flynn Anna M—†	1117	clerk	35	
b	Flynn Annie B—†	1117	housewife	65	"
c	Flynn Edna M—†	1117	clerk	34	"
d	Flynn Robert J	1117	U S A	27	
e	Flynn Thomas J	1117	"	33	"
f	Flynn Walter F	1117	carpenter	31	"
g	Russo Angelo M	1117	packer	40	
h	Russo Nancy—†	1117	housewife	34	"
k	Silipigni Grace—†	1117	"	65	
l	Silipigni Lawrence	1117	barber	68	
m	Silipigni Mary—†	1117	clerk	35	
n	Cleary Edward	1118	fisherman	47	"
o	Cleary Margaret—†	1118	housewife	45	"
p	Kelleher Jeremiah J	1118	driller	62	
r	Kelleher John V	1118	watchman	63	"
s	Kelleher Mary M—†	1118	housewife	52	"
t	Kelleher William P	1118	drawtender	57	"
u	Callanan Edward B	1119	U S C G	24	"
v	Callanan Mary A—†	1119	housewife	67	"
w	Sampson Margaret—†	1119	"	50	
x	Sampson Nicholas	1119	fisherman	48	"
y	Jackson Edward	1120	U S N	35	"
z	Jackson Mary—†	1120	tel operator	32	"

1933

a	Bartlett Francis	1120	blacksmith	68	"
b	Bartlett Mary C—†	1120	housewife	62	"
c	Walsh John P	1121	retired	68	
d	Walsh John P, jr	1121	bartender	36	"
e	McCauley Mary B—†	1121	nurse	58	"
f	McCauley Ruth A—†	1121	housekeeper	55	"
g	Bradley Joseph	1122	policeman	48	"

Page.	Letter.	FULL NAME.	Residence, Jan. 1, 1945.	Occupation.	Supposed Age.	Reported Residence, Jan. 1, 1944. Street and Number.

Saratoga Street—Continued

H	Bradley Madeline M—†	1122	housewife	43	here
K	Corbett Mary S—†	1122	bookkeeper	25	"
L	Donoghue Bernadette—†	1122	clerk	21	"
M	Donaghue Daniel J	1122	operator	58	"
N	Donaghue Mary A—†	1122	housewife	58	"
O	DiMartino Frances—†	1123	clerk	34	
P	DiMartino Gusto	1123	U S N	32	"
R	DiMartino Rose—†	1123	housewife	58	"
S	Susi Frances—†	1123	"	47	
T	Susi Frank	1123	candymaker	51	"
U	Susi Rose—†	1123	secretary	26	"
V	Barresi Joseph	1124	shoemaker	48	"
W	Barresi Nicholas	1124	U S A	23	
X	Barressi Sara—†	1124	housewife	45	"
Y	Napier Eleanor—†	1124	"	27	Winthrop
Z	Napier Francis J	1124	electrician	35	"
	1934				
A	Butler Mary—†	1125	at home	60	270 E Eagle
B	Cashman Richard J	1125	foreman	69	here
C	Cashman Susan—†	1125	housewife	52	"
D	Dawes Christopher	1125	carpenter	52	"
E	Dawes Rita—†	1125	housewife	50	"
F	Lenzi Lillian—†	1126	"	42	
G	Lenzi Thomas V	1126	electrician	41	"
H	DeVita Mary—†	1126	housewife	47	"
K	DeVita Michael	1126	printer	49	"
L	Mauceri Helen—†	1127	housewife	29	"
M	Mauceri Joseph	1127	operator	37	"
N	Canney Evelyn—†	1127	housewife	38	"
O	Canney John	1127	U S A	38	
P	Greco Anthony F	1127	inspector	42	"
R	Greco Lucy—†	1127	housewife	38	"
S	Giuffre Carmello	1128	operator	42	"
T	Giuffre Josephine—†	1128	housewife	41	"
U	Barry Janet C—†	1128	"	26	"
V	Barry Joseph F	1128	accountant	30	"
W	Vesce Francis A	1129	salesman	29	"
X	Vesce Joseph A	1129	manager	56	"
Y	Vesce Josephine C—†	1129	housewife	28	"
Z	Vesce Norma T	1129	clerk	27	"

A	Gigliello Domenic	1129	foreman	21	Medford
B	Gigliello Julia—†	1129	housewife	31	7 Antrim
C	DeSimone Armand	1130	realtor	45	here
D	DeSimone Edith—†	1130	housewife	45	"
E	Cogliani Nicholas	1130	laborer	61	"
F	Cogliani Vincenza—†	1130	housewife	58	"
G	Kaddaras George	1130	inspector	32	"
H	Kaddaras Mary—†	1130	housewife	34	"
K	Hazelton Ann L—†	1132	"	35	
L	Hazelton Kenneth C	1132	engineer	35	"
M	Barisano Joseph	1132	U S A	20	
N	Cogliano Antoinette—†	1132	housewife	44	"
O	Cogliano Joseph	1132	chauffeur	54	"
P	Guarino Rafaella—†	1132	hairdresser	24	"
S	Smiddy Kathleen A—†	1141	operator	20	"
T	Smiddy Margaret H—†	1141	housewife	46	"
U	Smiddy Mary R—†	1141	WAVE	24	
V	Smiddy William P	1141	stevedore	50	"
X	Fenlon Ruth C—†	1143	housewife	44	"
Y	Fenlon William	1143	electrician	49	"
Z	Fenlon William F, jr	1143	salesman	25	"

1936

A	Sullivan Stephen C	1143	clerk	55	
B	Rosetti Dorothy—†	1145	saleswoman	24	"
C	Rosetti Frank	1145	printer	47	"
D	Rosetti James	1145	U S M C	22	"
E	Giannotti Aldo	1147	policeman	37	"
F	Giannotti Alice—†	1147	hostess	37	"
G	*Giannotti Anna—†	1147	at home	65	"
H	Crane Joseph A	1149	supervisor	48	"
K	Crane Mary—†	1149	housewife	44	"
L	Wallace Edward F	1149	retired	77	1179 Saratoga
M	DeBeneditto Evelyn—†	1151	housewife	27	here
N	DeBeneditto John	1151	chauffeur	40	"
O	DeBeneditto Pasquale	1151	retired	73	"
P	Casassa Emma—†	1151	housewife	51	"
R	Casassa Stephen	1151	contractor	65	"
S	Spruegel Edith—†	1179	housewife	37	"
T	Spruegel Walter	1179	attorney	39	"

Saratoga Street—Continued

U	Meaney Catherine—†	1179	housewife	38	here
V	Meaney Joseph M	1179	mechanic	39	"
W	Meaney Michael	1179	retired	78	32 Upton
X	Hutchinson Stacia G–†	1181	housewife	40	here
Y	Hutchinson William C	1181	clerk	41	"
Z	Famolare Anthony	1181	barber	38	"

1937

A	Famolare Mary—†	1181	housewife	35	"
B	Hill Charles T	1187	clerk	31	
C	Hill Mary E—†	1187	housewife	32	"
D	Pasillo Anna—†	1187	"	49	
E	Pasillo John	1187	U S A	22	
F	Pasillo Joseph	1187	waiter	54	
G	Ciamma Ida—†	1189	housewife	51	"
H	Ciamma Thomas L	1189	U S A	26	::
K	Gregorie Ada—†	1189	housewife	28	"
L	Gregorie Joseph	1189	U S A	30	"
M	Palladino Dina—†	1189	housewife	24	Revere
N	Palladino Nunzio L	1189	U S N	24	"
O	Pagliarulo Caroline—†	1191	housewife	40	here
P	Pagliarulo Emil	1191	student	22	"
R	Pagliarulo Joseph	1191	salesman	42	"
S	Meoli Antonette—†	1193	housewife	37	"
T	Meoli Guy	1193	manager	49	"
U	DeMild Leonard	1195	machinist	39	"
V	DeMild Thelma—†	1195	housewife	37	"
W	Penta Anthony	1197	glazier	52	30 Maverick
X	Penta John	1197	operator	29	30 "
Y	Penta Joseph	1197	U S A	25	30 "
Z	Penta Mary L—†	1197	housewife	50	30 "

1938

A	Caggiano Jean—†	1199	housewife	43	here
B	Caggiano Michael S	1199	mortician	44	"
C	Sacco Joseph	1201	laborer	53	"
D	Sacco Joseph A	1201	U S N	21	"
E	Sacco Mary A—†	1201	housewife	49	"

Shawsheen Road

G	Driscoll Florence J	30	retired	59	here
H	Shaw Christine M—†	30	housewife	48	"
K	Shaw Francis P	30	merchant	48	"

24

Teregram Street

L	Kirby John F	25	compositor	37	here
M	Kirby Louise—†	25	housewife	37	"
N	Berninger Catherine—†	25	"	54	"
O	Berninger Catherine E–†	25	operator	25	
P	Berninger Claire P—†	25	tel operator	21	"
R	Berninger Jacob	25	B F D	37	"
S	Berninger Mary I—†	25	WAVE	28	
T	Bertolino Gertrude H—†	26	clerk	26	
U	Bertolino Helen—†	26	housewife	52	"
V	Bertolino Nicholas D	26	U S A	31	
W	Bertolino Thomas S	26	U S N	26	
X	Cirasuolo Dorothy—†	26	housewife	22	"
Y	Cirasuolo Pasquale	26	U S N	27	
Z	DiMico John	26	clerk	49	

1939

A	Tiano Dominic W	26	engineer	38	
B	Tiano Helen—†	26	housewife	34	"
C	Kincaid George E	30	U S A	21	
D	Kincaid Grace—†	30	housewife	55	"
E	Kincaid Paul	30	engineer	51	
F	Cicco Grace—†	30	stenographer	21	"
G	Cicco Mary—†	30	housewife	41	"
H	Cicco Michael	30	plumber	46	

Ward 1–Precinct 20

CITY OF BOSTON

LIST OF RESIDENTS
20 YEARS OF AGE AND OVER

(NON-CITIZENS INDICATED BY ASTERISK)
(FEMALES INDICATED BY DAGGER)

AS OF

JANUARY 1, 1945

THOMAS F. SULLIVAN, *Chairman*
FREDERIC E. DOWLING, *Secretary*
WILLIAM A. MOTLEY, JR.
FRANCIS B. McKINNEY
EVERETT R. PROUT

Listing Board.

CITY OF BOSTON PRINTING DEPARTMENT

2000
Castle Court

B	Pepe Joseph	3	laborer	47	here.
c	*Pepe Pasqualina—†	3	housewife	40	"
D	*Pepe Patricia—†	3	housekeeper	69	"
E	Savino Helen—†	3	saleswoman	30	"
F	Severo Fred	5	machinist	21	"
G	Severo Gerald	5	U S C G	23	"
H	Severo Rosa—†	5	housewife	61	"
K	Severo Saverio	5	retired	65	

Cottage Street

M	Lambiasi Nancy—†	115	housewife	42	here
N	Lambiasi Salvatore	115	baker	47	"
O	Collarone Angelo	115	shoewkr	29	"
P	Collarone Lillian—†	115	housewife	30	"
R	DeDonato Mary—†	117	"	29	
S	DeDonato Rocco	117	U S A	32	
T	Grasso Helen—†	117	clerk	20	
U	Grasso Margaret—†	117	housewife	46	"
V	Grasso Michael	117	shoewkr	47	"
W	Bernabei Anna—†	117	housewife	35	"
X	Bernabei Antonio	117	operator	35	"

2001

A	Scalfani Antonio	119	clerk	33	..
B	Scalfani Stella—†	119	housewife	29	"
C	Pascome Ferrara	119	chauffeur	34	"
D	Pascome Rose—†	119	housewife	32	"
E	Ciccone Carmella—†	119	"	46	
F	Ciccone Nicholas	119	laborer	53	
G	Zamponti John N	119	U S A	21	..
H	Zamponti Madalena—†	119	housekeeper	59	"
K	Mazzetti Carmello	119	laborer	43	,,
L	Mazzetti Ernitia—†'	119	housewife	39	"
N	Troiani Elsie—†	119	candymaker	22	"
O	*Troiani Mary—†	119	housewife	51	"
P	Troiani Pasquale	119	laborer	55	
S	DePaolo Antonetta—†	121	housewife	38	"
T	DePaolo Pasquale	121	laborer	40	
U	Prisco Mary—†	121	housekeeper	76	"
V	*Balero Mary—†	121	housewife	38	"

w	Balero Peter	121	laborer	43	here
x	*Pelligritti Angelo	121	"	74	"
y	*Pelligritti Josephine—†	121	housewife	68	"
z	Gallaso Lawrence	121	laborer	64	
	2002				
a	Gallaso Louis	121	U S A	21	"
b	Gallaso Victoria—†	121	housewife	59	"
c	Marrotta Cornelia—†	123	"	41	
d	Marrotta John	123	shoewkr	43	
e	Boschett Amelia—†	123	housewife	43	"
f	Boschetti Antonio	123	metalwkr	42	"
g	Liberatore Olive—†	123	housewife	30	"
h	Liberatore Pompeo	123	shipfitter	34	"
k	Giangregorio Antonio	123	laborer	50	
l	Giangregorio Jennie—†	123	housewife	40	"
m	Palumbo Emma—†	125	stitcher	24	
n	*Palumbo John	125	laborer	62	
o	Palumbo Leonard	125	clerk	27	
p	*Palumbo Rosina—†	125	housewife	59	"
r	Palumbo Salvatore	125	U S A	21	
s	Tedesco Joseph	125	"	27	
t	Tedesco Mary—†	125	housewife	27	"
u	*Riccio Concordia—†	125	"	49	
v	Riccio Domenic	125	laborer	53	
w	Riccio Josephine—†	125	dressmaker	21	"
x	Riccio Nicholas	125	milkman	25	
y	Pellegriti Mary—†	125	housewife	43	"
z	Pellegriti Peter	125	shoewkr	44	"
	2003				
a	Giglio Benjamin	125	laborer	32	
b	Giglio Helen—†	125	housewife	27	"
c	Puleio Joseph	127	chipper	28	
d	Puleio Nancy—†	127	housewife	28	"
e	Nazzaro Alfred	127	U S N	20	
f	Nazzaro Angelina	127	operator	22	
g	Nazzaro Catherine—†	127	candymaker	25	"
h	Nazzaro Jennie—†	127	"	27	
k	Nazzaro Mary—†	127	housewife	60	"
l	Nazzaro Phyllis—†	127	operator	32	"
m	Nazzaro Vincent	127	U S A	24	
n	Butari Angelo	127	"	33	

Cottage Street—Continued

o	Butari Antonetta—†	127	housewife	29	here
p	Butari Americo	127	welder	20	"
r	Butari Assunta—†	127	housekeeper	53	"
s	Butari Frank	127	U S N	24	"
t	Butari Gilda—†	127	clerk	22	"
u	Valletta Rose—†	129	housekeeper	44	"
v	*Rizzo Carmella—†	129	"	61	"
w	Rizzo Mary—†	129	clerk	21	"
x	Saporito Joseph	129	machinist	27	"
y	Saporito Josephine—†	129	housewife	24	"
z	Cianciolo Antonette—†	129	"	23	354 Sumner
	2004				
a	Cianciolo Peter	129	poultry	37	41 Bowdoin
b	Lessa Domenic	129	U S A	22	here
c	Lessa Eleanor—†	129	cutter	24	"
d	Lessa Olga—†	129	housekeeper	26	"
e	Scopa Frank	131	painter	44	"
f	Scopa Rose—†	131	housewife	33	"
g	Scopa Ciriaco	131	fireman	61	
h	Scopa Marion P—†	131	housewife	42	"
k	Giammatteo Anna—†	131	"	21	
l	Giammatteo Frank	131	welder	23	"
m	*Ardagna John	131	salesman	50	"
n	Scopa Elizabeth C—†	131	housewife	64	"
o	Scopa Rosario R	131	electrician	52	"
p	Inglese Grace—†	133	housewife	45	"
r	Inglese Joseph	133	chauffeur	51	"
s	Inglese Luciano	133	U S A	23	
t	Inglese Michael	133	"	21	
u	Centofanti Samuel	133	contractor	58	"
v	Giardina Joseph	133	laborer	35	
w	Giardina Rafaela—†	133	housewife	32	"
x	Sacco Frank	133	U S A	21	
y	Sacco Jennie—†	133	housekeeper	62	"
z	Sacco Pasquale	133	shipfitter	39	"
	2005				
a	Sacco Violanda E—†	133	inspector	24	"
b	Sasso Jennie—†	135	dressmaker	20	"
c	Sasso Joseph	135	shoewkr	45	"
d	*Sasso Mary—†	135	housekeeper	69	"

Cottage Street—Continued

E	Sasso Theresa—†	135	housewife	43	here
F	Beatrice Helen—†	135	instructor	23	"
G	Beatrice John	135	U S A	20	"
H	Beatrice Marsilo	135	laborer	59	
K	Beatrice Philomena—†	135	housewife	52	"
L	DeRocco Louise—†	135	packer	40	
N	Magnanti Enrico	135	U S A	33	"
O	Magnanti Vincenzo	135	shoewkr	72	"
P	*DiPietro Mary—†	137	housekeeper	76	"
R	*Giangregorio Louis	137	retired	68	..
S	Mazzone Assunta—†	137	housewife	46	"
T	Mucci Antonetta—†	137	clerk	26	
U	Mucci Joseph	137	laborer	21	
V	*Mucci Lucy—†	137	housewife	56	"
W	Ferrullo John	137	laborer	38	
X	Ferrullo Mildred—†	137	housewife	35	"
Y	Giangregorio Attillio	137	mechanic	28	"
Z	Giangregorio Mary—†	137	housewife	25	"

2006

A	Cirame Carmella—†	139	millhand	20	"
B	Cirame Joseph	139	machinist	46	"
C	Cirame Mary—†	139	housewife	41	"
D	Iovene Angelo	139	U S A	34	
E	Iovene Susan—†	139	housewife	26	"
F	Rubino Josephine—†	139	"	42	
G	Rubino Louis	139	machinist	52	"
H	Luiso Carmella—†	139	housewife	26	"
K	Luiso Ralph	139	welder	30	
L	Giordano Anthony	139	U S N	26	
M	Giordano Antonette—†	139	housewife	21	"
N	Grieci Angelo	141	shipfitter	39	"
O	Grieci Mary—†	141	housewife	36	"
P	Spataro Joseph	141	laborer	64	
R	*Spataro Stella—†	141	housewife	62	"
S	Moscato Angelo	141	laborer	38	
T	Moscato Rose—†	141	housewife	33	"
U	Fratalia Antonio	141	painter	40	
V	*Fratalia Edith—†	141	housewife	32	"
X	*Giangregorio Carmella—†	143	"	50	
Y	*Giangregorio Lorenzo	143	laborer	67	"

Cottage Street—Continued

z	Giangregorio Sabina—†	143	operator	23	here
	2007				
A	DeLuca Anthony	143	pipefitter	34	"
B	DeLuca Grace—†	143	housewife	32	"
c	Covello Bernardino	143	painter	49	..
D	Covello Matilda—†	143	housewife	46	"
E	Sacco Anthony	143	operator	29	"
F	Sacco Olga—†	143	housewife	22	"
H	Colarusso Anthony	145	operator	65	"
K	*Colarusso Elizabeth—†	145	housewife	55	"
L	Colarusso Dominick	145	carpenter	30	"
M	Colarusso Felix	145	laborer	58	
N	Colarusso Theresa—†	145	inspector	24	"
o	Molinaro Anna—†	145	packer	32	
P	Molinaro Bianca—†	145	operator	26	"
R	Molinaro Pasqualena—†	145	housewife	63	"
s	Molinaro Raffaela—†	145	assembler	23	"
T	Molinaro Thomas	145	operator	65	"
U	Molinaro Yolanda—†	145	"	30	
V	Polsonetti Carmilio	147	carpenter	21	"
W	Polsonetti Joseph	147	boilermaker	55	"
X	Polsonetti Michelina—†	147	housewife	41	"
Y	Palombi Angelo	147	photographer	27	"
z	Palombi Marie—†	147	housewife	32	"
	2008				
A	Molinaro Edith—†	147	packer	39	
B	Molinaro Peter	147	burner	41	"
c	Morello Jennie—†	147	housewife	25	94 Everett
D	Morello Rocco	147	pipefitter	27	28 Prince
E	Bavaro Dominick	147	laborer	33	here
F	Bavaro Virginia—†	147	housewife	32	"
G	Coviello Antonio	149	welder	40	"
H	Coviello Gaitana—†	149	housewife	34	"
K	Guarino Alfred	149	machinist	30	"
L	Guarino Christine—†	149	housewife	29	"
M	DiGenova Phyllis—†	149	"	42	"
N	Coviello Alexander	149	mechanic	28	"
o	Coviello Lillian—†	149	housewife	26	"
P	*Coviello Antonio	149	retired	72	"
R	Coviello Rose—†	149	housewife	72	"
s	Sciarrillo Antonio	151	storekeeper	45	"

T	Sciarrillo Gabriele—†	151	housewife	48	here
U	Sciarrillo Theresa—†	151	beautician	23	"
W	Evangelista Margaret—†	151	housewife	36	"
X	Evangelista Nicola	151	cook	38	"
Y	*Tedescucci Lucia—†	151	housewife	54	164 Gove
Z	Zarlengo Carmen	151	laborer	51	164 "

2009

A	Masiello Frank	151	U S N	21	here
B	Masiello Joseph	151	laborer	50	"
C	Masiello Mary—†	151	stitcher	20	"
D	Cammarata John	151	rigger	27	"
E	Cammaratá Mary—†	151	housewife	28	"
F	Catanzariti Clara—†	152	"	32	
G	Catanzariti Onofrio	152	machinist	37	"
H	*Florio Cecilia—†	152	housewife	76	"
K	*Florio Frank	152	retired	73	
L	Hunter Antoinetta—†	152	bookkeeper	22	"
M	Uva Madeline—†	152	beautician	28	"
N	Uva Nancy—†	152	housewife	49	"
O	Uva Rocco	152	grocer	54	
P	Uva Stanley	152	welder	28	
R	Iannacone Eugenio	152	chef	52	
S	Iannacone Josephine—†	152	housewife	52	"
T	DiBenedetto Eleanor—†	152	"	48	
U	DiBenedetto Thomas	152	tailor	49	
V	Umana Antonette—†	153	storekeeper	56	"
W	Umana Mario	153	U S A	28	"
X	Schittino Frank	154	laborer	47	
Y	Schittino Susan—†	154	housewife	41	"
Z	Schittino Vincent	154	U S A	21	

2010

B	Mercurio Angelina—†	154	housewife	45	"
C	Mercurio Domenic	154	guard	45	
D	Mercurio Thomas	154	U S A	21	"
E	Tramonti Lena—†	154	housewife	30	"
F	Tramonti Oresto	154	guard	49	
G	Fusco Joseph	154	laborer	31	"
H	*Fusco Martha—†	154	at home	58	
K	D'Alto Louisa—†	154	"	61	
L	D'Alto Pasquale	154	retired	65	

Page.	Letter.	FULL NAME.	Residence, Jan. 1, 1945.	Occupation.	Supposed Age.	Reported Residence, Jan. 1, 1944. Street and Number.

Cottage Street—Continued

	N	Ruggiero Anthony	154	shoewkr	42	here
	O	Ruggiero Eva—†	154	housewife	40	"
	R	Peppino Lena—†	155	saleswoman	20	"
	S	*Peppino Mary—†	155	at home	61	"
	T	Peppino Sadie—†	155	shoewkr	38	"
	U	Guzzardi Daniel	155	"	51	
	V	*Guzzardi Gina—†	155	housewife	44	"
	W	Guzzardi Joseph	155	metalwkr	22	"
	X	Guzzardi Salvatore	155	messenger	21	"
	Y	*Vinciguerra Adele—†	155	housewife	56	"
	Z	Vinciguerra Raffael	155	shoewkr	58	"
2011						
	A	Vinciguerra Ralph	155	U S A	24	"
	B	Vinciguerra Theresa—†	155	machinist	23	"
	C	Caporale Carmela—†	155	housewife	41	"
	D	Caporale Peter A	155	shoewkr	42	"
	E	*DeFuria Lucrezia—†	155	housewife	40	"
	F	DeFuria Nicolo	155	shipfitter	49	"
	G	DeMaeio Lena—†	156	at home	69	"
	L	Albaro Josephine—†	156	housewife	34	"
	M	Tramonti Anna—†	156	operator	20	"
	N	Tramonti Ernest	156	laborer	54	"
	O	Tramonti Rose—†	156	housewife	44	"
	P	Gatto Antonio	156	at home	66	"
	R	Gatto Natale	156	U S A	32	
	S	Gatto Natalie—†	156	operator	23	"
	T	Gatto Rose—†	156	shoewkr	25	"
	U	Gatto Vincent	156	at home	69	"
	V	Gatto Carmen	156	rigger	31	
	W	Gatto Mildred—†	156	beautician	27	"
	X	Cioto Frank	157	laborer	63	
	Y	Cioto Gilda—†	157	machinist	31	"
	Z	Cioto Lucy—†	157	checker	23	"
2012						
	A	Cioto Marion—†	157	housewife	57	"
	D	Spaziani Sista—†	157	at home	67	"
	E	Conti Paul	157	packer	46	
	F	Salvi Albert	157	U S N	21	"
	G	Salvi Dominic	157	laborer	50	
	H	Salvi Rosina—†	157	housewife	44	"
	K	*Capuana Agatha—†	158	"	55	"

8

Cottage Street—Continued

L	Capuana Guiseppina—†	158	dressmaker	31	here	
M	Capuana Joseph	158	grocer	59	"	
O	Armato Frank	158	retired	61	"	
P	Armato Louis	158	U S A	36		
R	*Armato Maria—†	158	housewife	62	"	
S	Leone Carmen	158	tailor	53		
T	Leone Julio	158	"	22	..	
U	*Leone Mary—†	158	housewife	52	"	
V	Leone Phyllis—†	158	at home	24	"	
W	Beatrice Alexander	158	shipfitter	28	"	
X	Beatrice Marie—†	158	housewife	29	"	
Y	Castagnozzi Frank	158	U S N	21		
Z	Castagnozzi John	158	chauffeur	22	"	

2013

B	Piscioneri Dominic	158	meatcutter	40	"	
C	Piscioneri Jennie—†	158	housewife	34	"	
D	Ferrantino Benjamin	158	inspector	36	"	
E	Ferrantino Frances—†	158	housewife	30	"	
F	DelGreco John	159	laborer	39		
G	DelGreco Mary—†	159	housewife	35	"	
H	*DelGreco Nicola	159	retired	64	"	
K	Costantini Antonio	159	laborer	51	"	
L	Costantini Lucy—†	159	SPAR	24	..	
M	*Costantini Theodore	159	retired	75		
N	Cocco Maria—†	159	at home	39	"	
O	Mucci Alfred	159	bricklayer	41	"	
P	Mucci Gemma—†	159	housewife	35	"	
R	Luongo Assunta—†	159	"	55		
S	Luongo Giacomo	..159	cleaner	64		
T	Girolamo Frank	159	laborer	49	"	
U	*Girolamo Philomena—†	159	housewife	45	"	
V	Fitzgerald Antoinette—†	159	"	36	"	
W	Fitzgerald Lawrence	159	machinist	35	"	
X	*Cordone Angelina—†	159	housewife	43	173 Cottage	
Y	Cordone Frederick	159	U S N	21	173 "	
Z	Cordone Loretto	159	cleaner	49	173 "	

2014

A	Catanese Anthony	160	U S A	23	here	
B	Catanese Sophie—†	160	stitcher	24	"	
C	Villano Alfred	160	clerk	25	"	
D	*Villano Antoinetta—†	160	at home	60	"	

Cottage Street—Continued

	Letter	FULL NAME	Residence	Occupation	Age	Reported Residence
	E	Villano Eugene	160	rigger	21	here
	F	*Villano Joseph	160	laundrywkr	61	"
	G	Villano Rose—†	160	at home	23	"
	H	Aiello Alvera—†	160	housewife	51	"
	K	Aiello Joseph	160	pressman	57	"
	L	Aiello Joseph	160	U S A	24	"
	M	*Guisti Augusta—†	160	housewife	65	"
	N	Guisti Guiseppe	160	millhand	69	"
	O	*Angelo Guiseppina—†	160	at home	82	"
	P	*Franchina Antonio	160	operator	57	"
	R	*Franchina Vincenza—†	160	housewkr	46	"
	T	Villano Carmen	160	boilermaker	21	258 Marion
	U	Villano Ida—†	160	housewife	22	258 "
	W	Capecci Anthony	161	U S A	23	here
	X	Capecci Mario	161	"	20	"
	Y	Capecci Nicholas	161	dairyman	56	"
	Z	Capecci Nina—†	161	housewife	45	"
2015						
	A	Paolini Henry	161	U S N	33	
	B	*Paolini Marie—†	161	housekeeper	74	"
	C	Paolini Amedio	161	laborer	56	"
	D	Paolini Desolina—†	161	housewife	60	"
	E	Cioto Dominic	161	polisher	30	"
	F	Cioto Rita—†	161	housewife	31	"
	G	DiMarco Antoinette—†	161	"	28	155 Cottage
	H	DiMarco Vincent	161	metalwkr	30	155 "
	K	D'Amico Reginald	161	shipfitter	33	here
	L	D'Amico Rose—†	161	housewife	34	"
	M	Digio Armando	161	metalwkr	24	"
	N	Digio Joseph	161	laborer	61	"
	O	Digio Marion—†	161	housewife	53	"
	P	Lanna Michael	162	shoewkr	45	"
	R	Pagluica Michael	162	painter	45	"
	S	Pagluica Philomena—†	162	housewife	32	"
	T	Sulprizio Bernardino	162	retired	78	
	U	*Sulprizio Theresa—†	162	housewife	77	"
	W	Sulprizio Anthony	162	U S A	20	"
	X	Sulprizio Carmella—†	162	housewife	48	"
	Y	Sulprizio Joseph	162	attendant	55	"
	Z	Sulprizio Bernard	162	U S C G	23	"

2016
Cottage Street—Continued

A	Sulprizio Michelina—†	162	housewife	21	120 Brooks
B	Scannelli Edith—†	162	"	35	here
C	Scannelli Robert	162	chauffeur	32	"
D	Bondanza Gaetano	162	laborer	38	"
E	Bondanza Virginia—†	162	housewife	34	"
F	Del Gaizo Marie—†	163	"	49	"
G	La Corte John B	163	mechanic	42	"
H	La Corte Leona—†	163	housewife	37	"
K	La Corte James	163	laborer	48	"
L	La Corte Jennie—†	163	housewife	29	"
M	La Corte Gaetano	163	laborer	46	
N	La Corte Italia—†	163	housewife	47	"
O	La Corte John	163	electrician	33	"
P	La Corte Mary—†	163	housewife	33	"
R	La Corte Angelina—†	163	seamstress	54	"
S	La Corte Philip	163	retired	60	"
T	Bonanno Nunzio	164	"	62	155 Cottage
U	Camiolo Anthony	164	chauffeur	54	here
V	Camiolo Concetta—†	164	housewife	47	"
W	Camiolo Nunzio	164	U S A	28	"
X	Liberato Nicholas	164	shipfitter	29	Quincy
Y	Liberato Theresa—†	164	housewife	29	"
Z	Dagresto Antonetta—†	164	clerk	32	here

2017

A	Dagresto Carmela—†	164	operator	24	"
B	Dagresto James	164	U S A	28	
C	*Dagresto Liberata—†	164	at home	57	"
D	Dagresto Louis	164	U S A	21	
E	Foti Antonetta—†	164	housewife	23	"
F	Foti Ralph	164	U S N	21	
G	Morelli Luigi	164	laborer	48	
H	*Morelli Philomena—†	164	housewife	43	"
K	De Rosa Angelo	164	rigger	30	
L	De Rosa Theresa—†	164	housewife	25	"
M	Taranti Anthony	164	laborer	30	
N	Taranti Josephine—†	164	operator	27	"
O	Rossetti Josephine—†	165	candymaker	58	"
P	Rossetti Rocco	165	factoryhand	64	"
R	La Monaco Angelo	165	laborer	65	

11

Page.	Letter.	FULL NAME.	Residence, Jan. 1, 1945.	Occupation.	Supposed Age.	Reported Residence, Jan. 1, 1944. Street and Number.

Cottage Street—Continued

	s	La Monaco Joseph	165	laborer	20	here
	t	La Monaco Salvatore	165	welder	23	"
	u	Patuzzi Mary—†	165	housewife	26	170 Cottage
	v	Patuzzi Vito	165	U S A	28	170 "
	w	Deeran Martin	165	"	23	here
	x	Martin Pasqualina—†	165	clerk	22	"
	y	Palmerini Guerino	165	laborer	63	"
	z	Palmerini Santa—†	165	housewife	60	"
2018						
	a	Indelicato John	165	mechanic	26	"
	b	Indelicato Louise—†	165	housewife	25	"
	d	*Pappina Guiseppina—†	166	at home	75	"
	e	Morretti Guiseppe	166	laborer	54	
	f	*Pisano Rose—†	166	at home	48	"
	g	Guerra James	166	laborer	34	
	h	Guerra Jennie—†	166	housewife	35	"
	k	Oppolito Ernest	166	mechanic	35	"
	l	Navarro Celia—†	166	housewife	26	"
	m	Navarro Michael	166	U S M C	30	"
	n	Rauseo Anna—†	166	housewife	28	150 Everett
	o	Rauseo Michael	166	U S N	29	150 "
	p	Gianpapa Josephine—†	166	shoewkr	20	here
	r	*Gianpapa Rosalie—†	166	housewife	45	"
	u	Gianpapa Sando	166	butcher	21	"
	s	*Cammarato Albert	166	operator	50	"
	t	Cammarato Josephine—†	166	"	44	
	v	Vitale Robert	166	U S N	21	"
	w	*Mucci Anthony	167	painter	31	"
	x	Mucci Lena—†	167	housewife	30	"
	y	Morello Augustine	167	boilermaker	33	"
	z	Morello Carmella—†	167	clerk	24	"
2019						
	a	Morello Concetta—†	167	housewife	63	"
	b	Morello Flora—†	167	at home	27	"
	c	Morello Gennaro	167	U S A	39	"
	d	Bolognese Lucy—†	167	housewife	34	"
	e	Bolognese Ottavio	167	laborer	41	
	f	De Frofio Marie—†	167	housewife	75	"
	g	De Frofio Sabatino	167	retired	75	"
	h	Memmolo Edith—†	167	clerk	26	"
	k	Memmolo Louis	167	bartender	51	"

Cottage Street—Continued

L	Memmolo Mary—†	167	seamstress	48	here
M	*D'Amico Adeline—†	167	housewife	66	"
N	D'Amico Edmund	167	timekeeper	23	"
O	D'Amico George	167	laborer	28	..
P	DiFranza Frances—†	167	housewife	40	"
R	DiFranza Paul	167	machinist	45	"
T	Fasciano Guiseppe	168	storekeeper	65	"
U	Fasciano Josephine—†	168	housewife	52	"
V	Cerasa Charles	168	U S N	34	
W	Cerasa Pauline—†	168	housewife	33	"
X	Vinezia Armando	168	U S A	25	
Y	Vinezia Malfalda—†	168	housewife	21	"
Z	Cefaglioli Calisto	168	laborer	66	

2020

A	Incherica Anna—†	168	housewife	22	"
B	Incherica Raymond	168	chauffeur	25	"
C	Angelo Mary—†	168	housewife	51	"
D	Angelo Matteo	168	painter	58	
F	DeBole Pasquale	169	plater	32	
G	DeBole Sally—†	169	housewife	30	"
H	*Salini Vincenza—†	169	"	63	
K	*Salini Vincenzo	169	retired	71	
L	Salini Adriana—†	169	housewife	27	"
M	Salini Leo	169	metalwkr	28	"
N	D'Allesandro Michael	169	laborer	44	
O	D'Allesandro Sarah—†	169	housewife	40	"
P	*Giorgione Carmella—†	169	"	45	
R	Giorgione Ralph	169	oil dealer	43	"
S	Salini Americo	169	pipefitter	32	"
T	Salini Palmina—†	169	housewife	31	"
V	Pinabell Anthony	170	presser	24	62 Everett
W	Pinabell Virginia—†	170	housewife	22	62 "
X	Ragusa Robert	170	clerk	21	163 Cottage
Y	Paolini Domenic	170	U S A	20	here
Z	Paolini Pepina—†	170	housewife	48	"

2021

A	Paolini Umberto	170	laborer	53	"
B	Durbano Angelina—†	170	housewife	31	"
C	*Durbano Giacomo	170	laborer	34	
E	DiGiovanni Domenic	170	U S A	26	..
F	DiGiovanni Dora—†	170	stitcher	30	"

Cottage Street—Continued

	Letter	FULL NAME	Res.	Occupation	Age	Reported Residence
	G	DiGiovanni Gallerana—†	170	housewife	54	here
	H	DiGiovanni Joseph	170	ironwkr	53	"
	K	DiGiovanni Nicholas	170	U S A	28	"
	L	DiGiovanni Susan—†	170	stitcher	22	"
	M	Cappucci Anthony	171	U S N	22	"
	N	Cappucci Elizabeth—†	171	housewife	21	"
	O	Marchese Louisa—†	171	saleswoman	28	"
	P	Marchese Orofio	171	U S A	27	
	R	Mineguzzio Regina—†	171	housewife	66	"
	S	Mineguzzio Ricco	171	U S A	25	"
	U	Ferraro Angelo J	171	laborer	21	"
	V	Ferraro Diodoro	171	storekeeper	52	"
	W	Ferraro Mary—†	171	housewife	49	"
	X	Ferraro Rose M—†	171	clerk	24	
	Y	Carbone Ciriaco	171	retired	78	
	Z	Carbone Ciriaco	171	salesman	32	"
2022						
	A	Carbone Rose—†	171	housewife	30	"
	B	Iacoviello Carmella—†	171	"	42	
	C	Iacoviello Vitantonio	171	engineer	51	"
	D	Grasso Angelo	171	laborer	63	"
	E	*Grasso Jennie—†	171	housewife	63	"
	F	Grasso Nicholas	171	U S A	23	
	G	DiSciscio Sarah—†	172	housewife	23	"
	H	DiSciscio Theodore	172	U S A	26	
	K	Sisto Antonetta—†	172	at home	23	"
	L	Sisto Antonio	172	laborer	58	"
	M	Sisto Lucy—†	172	housewife	47	"
	N	Cieri Domenic	172	U S A	20	
	O	Cieri Elvira—†	172	housewife	51	"
	P	Cieri Frank	172	laborer	57	"
	R	Cieri Helen—†	172	operator	22	"
	S	Cieri Pasqualina—†	172	clerk	28	
	T	Cieri Philomena—†	172	"	30	
	V	DiPietro Elvira—†	172	housewife	26	"
	W	DiPietro Louis	172	brakeman	27	"
	X	Odoardi Antoinetta—†	172	housekeeper	25	"
	Y	Odoardi Emma—†	172	clerk	21	"
	Z	Odoardi Florence—†	172	machinist	22	"
2023						
	A	Odoardi Vincent	172	laborer	45	"

B	Gennari Guido	172	U S A	21	here
C	Gennari James	172	shipfitter	54	"
D	*Gennari Vincenza—†	172	housewife	46	"
E	Lima Lena—†	172	at home	29	"
F	Carnosino John	173	welder	24	
G	Carnosino Louise—†	173	housewife	23	"
H	Iannillo Antonio	173	boilermaker	62	"
K	Iannillo Antonio, jr	173	U S A	23	
L	Iannillo Mary—†	173	housewife	63	"
M	Marotta Angelina—†	173	"	24	64 Lubec
N	Marotta Gasparo	173	welder	25	64 "
O	Carbone Carmella—†	173	housewife	24	here
P	Carbone Ralph	173	rigger	25	"
R	Agnostinelli Arthur	173	machinist	22	"
S	Agnostinelli Lucy—†	173	housewife	52	"
T	Agnostinelli Ralph	173	machinist	20	"
U	Agnostinelli Renaldi	173	laborer	56	
V	May Anita—†	173	housewife	50	"
W	May John	173	U S A	20	..
X	May Louise—†	173	welder	27	
Y	Morelli Nathalina—†	173	clerk	30	
Z	*Patucci Amelia—†	174	housekeeper	70	"
	2024				
A	Gianvitoria Dino	174	musician	26	"
B	Gianvitoria Fiore	174	U S N	24	
C	Gianvitoria Josephine—†	174	seamstress	25	"
D	Gianvitoria Leonora—†	174	factoryhand	22	"
E	Gianvitoria Raphael	174	carpenter	50	"
F	Flammini Anthony	174	operator	23	72 Sullivan
G	Flammini Lillian—†	174	housewife	22	72 "
H	Nappi Isadore	174	dredger	29	here
K	Nappi Levia—†	174	housewife	26	"
L	DiBello Flora—†	174	housekeeper	25	"
M	*Forcellese Bice—†	174	housewife	45	"
N	Forcellese Norma—†	174	clerk	22	
O	Forcellese Peter	174	tailor	47	
P	Forcellese Tito	174	U S A	23	
R	D'Amico Anthony	174	U S N	23	
S	D'Amico Samuel	174	bricklayer	60	"
T	DeLuca Sophie—†	174	housewife	27	93 Webster
U	DeLuca Vito	174	shoewkr	29	93 "

Cottage Street—Continued

v	Grande Flavia—†	174	factoryhand	23	93 Webster
x	Papa Mary—†	175	clerk	28	here
y	Papa Patrick	175	machinist	30	"
z	Mucci Albert	175	clerk	35	"

2025

a	*Mucci Marie—†	175	housewife	70	"
b	*Mucci Pasquale	175	retired	70	
c	Mucci Anna—†	175	seamstress	42	"
d	Mucci Frank	175	candymaker	42	"
e	Mucci Mary—†	175	clerk	20	
g	DiNardo Anna—†	175	stitcher	24	"
h	DiNardo Flaviano	175	laborer	57	
k	DiNardo Joseph	175	"	30	..
l	*DiNardo Pasqua—†	175	housewife	55	"
m	Grasso Liziario	175	rigger	54	"
n	*Grasso Rose—†	175	housewife	55	"
o	Grasso Rose—†	175	presser	27	"
p	Cieri Alfonso	177	clerk	52	
r	Cieri Palmina—†	177	candymaker	50	"
s	Distaula Louis	177	mechanic	32	161 Cottage
t	Distaula Margaret—†	177	housewife	32	161 "
u	Zuzolo Dominic	177	seaman	25	161 "
v	Carbone Carmen	177	maintenance	40	here
w	Carbone Caroline—†	177	housewife	39	"
x	Costa Albert	177	U S A	26	"
y	Costa Josephine—†	177	candymaker	23	"
z	Sinibaldi Angelina—†	177	housewife	63	"

2026

a	Sinibaldi Frank	177	cleaner	65	
b	Sinibaldi Nicholas	177	U S C G	32	"
c	Palmerini Luigi	177	checker	33	161 Cottage
d	Palmerini Mary—†	177	housewife	34	161 "
e	Marmiani Amelio	179	mechanic	35	here
f	Marmiani Eda—†	179	housewife	33	"
g	DiBenedetto Adeline—†	179	"	54	"
h	*DiBenedetto John	179	retired	56	"
k	Placido Remigio E	179	storekeeper	56	"
l	Flammini Ernesto	179	laborer	49	..
m	Flammini Florinda—†	179	housewife	47	"
n	Flammini Victor	179	U S A	22	
o	Carpone Joseph	179	laborer	57	

Cottage Street—Continued

P	*Carpone Paulina—†	179	housewife	55	here
R	Flammini Nancy—†	179	"	23	"
S	Flammini Nicholas	179	clerk	25	"
T	Aceto James	179	laborer	36	58 Lubec
U	Aceto Josephine—†	179	housewife	28	here
W	Battaglia Carmen	181	retired	66	"
X	Battaglia Mary—†	181	housewife	62	"
Y	DiNocco Anna—†	181	"	27	
Z	DiNocco Erminio	181	salesman	33	"

2027

A	Nappi John	181	laborer	65	
B	Nappi Josephine—†	181	saleswoman	20	"
C	Nappi Julia—†	181	housewife	60	"
D	Fiorillo Cosmo	181	U S C G	22	"
E	Fiorillo Florence—†	181	bookkeeper	20	"
F	Fiorillo Joseph	181	laborer	57	"
G	Fiorillo Louise—†	181	housewife	47	"
H	Fiorillo Michael	181	U S A	24	"
K	Marotta Anthony	181	upholsterer	29	"
L	Marotta Charles	181	factoryhand	58	"
M	Marotta Lucy—†	181	candymkr	46	"
N	Marotta Mary—†	181	stitcher	21	"
O	Sarro Charles	181	U S A	24	
P	Sarro Frances—†	181	stitcher	24	"
S	Costra Mary—†	182	at home	42	"
T	*Gaglini Mary—†	182	housekeeper	65	"
U	Mucci Camillo	182	shipfitter	44	"
V	Mucci Laura—†	182	housewife	34	"
W	DiBeneditto Angelo	182	U S A	23	
X	DiBeneditto Enrico	182	chauffeur	48	"
Y	DiBeneditto Laura—†	182	housewife	44	"
Z	DiBeneditto Theresa—†	182	stitcher	22	"

2028

A	Weiner Dorothy—†	182	housewife	26	166 Sumner
B	Weiner Jack	182	riveter	24	166 "
C	Puccino Melindo	182	laborer	45	here
D	Grande Concetta—†	182	housewife	50	"
E	Grande Orlando	182	U S A	21	"
F	Grande Stephen	182	bricklayer	52	"
G	Ciambriello Antonetta—†	182	at home	22	"
H	*Ciambriello Frances—†	182	housewife	48	"

Cottage Street—Continued

K	*Ciambriello Frank	182	laborer	63	here
M	Elwin Edward	184	U S N	30	166 Sumner
N	Elwin Tina—†	184	housewife	25	166 "
O	Weiner Anna—†	184	"	46	166 "
P	Weiner Dorothy—†	184	at home	21	166 "
R	Napolitano Andrew	184	laborer	26	here
S	*Napolitano Assunda—†	184	housewife	56	"
T	Napolitano Ciro	184	clerk	21	"
U	*Napolitano Gerald	184	retired	51	"
V	Giambartolomei Angelina—†	184	factoryhand	20	"
W	Giambartolomei Catherine—†	184	"	22	
X	Giambartolomei Elvira–†	184	housewife	44	"
Y	Giambartolomei John	184	laborer	54	"
Z	Cianciarulo Joseph	184	carpenter	26	"
	2029				
A	Cianciarulo Mary—†	184	housewife	26	"
B	Spagnoli Ivo	184	U S A	22	
C	Spagnoli Louis	184	"	21	
D	Spagnoli Luigi	184	painter	50	"
E	Naso Doris—†	184	housewife	25	"
F	Naso Joseph	184	pipefitter	28	"
G	Guarino Peter	186	laborer	25	"
H	Guarino Rose—†	186	housewife	67	"
L	Fiantaca Angelo	186	U S A	21	
M	Fiantaca Grace—†	186	housewife	57	"
N	Fiantaca Joseph	186	U S A	24	
O	Fiantaca Philip	186	laborer	69	"
P	Fiantaca Philip	186	musician	28	"
R	Fiantaca Salvatore	186	U S A	26	
S	Palombi Loreto	186	carpenter	60	"
T	Pepe Pauline—†	186	housewife	33	"
U	Tritano Anna—†	186	"	38	
V	Iritano Anthony	186	shoewkr	49	"
W	Iritano Catherine—†	186	dressmkr	21	"
X	Iritano Joseph	186	shoewkr	50	"
Y	DiGiampaolo Concetta–†	186	housewife	53	"
Z	DiGiampaolo Dominick	186	U S A	24	
	2030				
A	DiGiampaolo Eda—†	186	attorney	26	"
B	DiGiampaolo Romanina—†	186	operator	22	"

Cottage Street—Continued

c	Ventura Virginia—†	186	housewife	36	here
d	Ciulla Jennie—†	186	typist	26	"
e	Ciulla John	186	U S N	20	"
f	Ciulla Joseph	186	leatherwkr	53	"
g	Ciulla Lena—†	186	housewife	46	"
h	Ciulla Stephen	186	U S A	24	
k	Palumba John	188	machinist	47	"
l	Palumba Mary E—†	188	housewife	46	"
m	Ryan Thomas J	188	factoryhand	49	"
r	Bolognese Dominic	188	pipefitter	54	"
s	Bolognese Frank C	188	U S A	22	
t	Bolognese George A	188	"	20	
u	Bolognese James A	188	welder	24	"
v	Bolognese Lettie E—†	188	housewife	44	"
w	DiNocco Anthony	188	U S A	23	192 Cottage
x	DiNocco Mary N—†	188	at home	23	here
y	Belmonte Christopher A	188	U S A	25	"
z	Belmonte Mary—†	188	housewife	25	"
	2031				
a	Natalucci Lucy—†	188	housewife	66	"
b	Albano Carmen	188	retired	55	
c	Albano Fredrick G	188	U S A	20	
d	Albano Vincenzo	188	"	24	
e	Beatrice Clementina—†	188	factoryhand	25	"
f	Beatrice Helen—†	188	at home	23	"
g	Beatrice Joseph N	188	U S A	21	
h	Beatrice Louis	188	laborer	23	
k	Beatrice Mary—†	188	presser	29	
l	*Beatrice Pasquale	188	laborer	61	
m	Milia Fannie—†	190	housewife	30	"
n	Milia Michael J	190	cleaner	32	
p	Leone Achille	190	laborer	49	
r	Leone Phileomena—†	190	housewife	39	"
s	Forlizzi Antonetta—†	190	housekeeper	28	"
t	Forlizzi John J	190	U S A	22	..
u	Giangregorio Anthony	190	"	22	
v	Giangregorio Caroline—†	190	housewife	54	"
w	*Giangregorio Pasquale	190	laborer	51	"
x	Giangregorio Phyllis—†	190	typist	26	"
y	Giangregorio Ralph	190	U S N	24	

Cottage Street—Continued

z	Giangregorio Vincent	190	U S A	20	here
	2032				
A	*Amada Mary—†	190	housewife	46	"
B	Amada Pasquale	190	laborer	54	"
C	Serrechia Anthony	190	shoewkr	41	"
D	DiNocco Louis	190	joiner	27	
E	DiNocco Margaret M—†	190	housewife	25	"
F	Bellavia Angelo	190	painter	56	"
G	Bellavia Joseph	190	U S A	29	
H	Bellavia Theresa—†	190	housewife	49	"
K	Luciano Augustine	192	pipefitter	51	"
M	Margarone Paul	192	laborer	55	"
N	*Stella Alphonse	192	"	64	273 Maverick
O	Stella Armen—†	192	housewife	43	273 "
P	*Leone Anna—†	192	"	46	here
R	Leone David	192	U S A	24	"
S	Leone Dominic	192	"	21	"
T	Leone Salvatore	192	bricklayer	43	"
U	Fulco Carmen—†	192	housewife	49	"
V	Fulco Calogero	192	laborer	50	"
W	Fulco Charles	192	U S A	20	
X	DiNocco Antonio	192	dishwasher	67	"
Y	DiNocco Donato	192	U S A	21	"
z	DiNocco Frances P—†	192	housewife	29	161 Saratoga
	2033				
A	DiNocco Romeo	192	burner	35	161 "
B	DiNocco Sabatino	192	chauffeur	29	here
C	Cahill Joseph	192	U S A	31	"
D	Cahill Josephine—†	192	clerk	20	"
E	*Dana Joseph	192	laborer	61	"
F	*Dana Josephine—†	192	at home	49	"
G	Marcalde Gabriel	192	U S A	24	"
H	Marcalde Mary—†	192	at home	22	16 Frankfort
K	Cianci Natalie—†	194	housewife	49	here
L	Cianci Pauline—†	194	inspector	29	"
M	Cianci Sebastian	194	laborer	58	"
N	Divona Rocco	194	barber	50	2 Savage ct
O	DeDomenico Antonio	194	laborer	48	here
P	DeDomenico Dominic	194	U S A	23	"
R	*DeDomenico Liberata—†	194	housewife	45	"
S	Vespa Angelo	194	chipper	48	"

T	Vespa Eva—†	194	housewife	31	here
U	Galante Michael M	194	burner	31	"
V	Galante Nellie E—†	194	housewife	23	"

Everett Street

W	Pagliarulo Carmine A	124	metalwkr	28	here
X	Pagliarulo Frances—†	124	housewife	20	Georgia
Y	Pagliarulo Raffaella—†	124	"	64	here
Z	Pagliarulo Vito	124	laborer	63	"
	2034				
A	*Buono Concetta—†	126	housekeeper	60	"
B	D'Andrea Pauline—†	126	clerk	43	"
C	Salamone Frank	126	machinist	26	"
D	Salamone Virginia—†	126	housewife	23	"
E	Pacella Nicholas	128	clerk	65	"
F	Sileno Maria—†	128	housewife	70	"
G	Cogswell Alfred	128	operator	34	73 Grady
H	Cogswell Frances M—†	128	housewife	29	73 "
K	Olsen Frances—†	128	cleaner	64	66 "
L	Martini Gerardo	128	burner	33	here
M	Martini Susan—†	128	factoryhand	30	"
O	Wardell James	134	shipfitter	26	"
R	Leon John	134	clerk	45	"
S	Leon Mary—†	134	housewife	40	"
T	Melchionda Edward	136	welder	31	176 Gove
U	Melchionda Josephine—†	136	housewife	40	176 "
V	Ciampa Angelo	136	burner	27	here
W	Ciampa Ruth—†	136	housewife	21	"
X	Francis Evelyn—†	136	clerk	25	"
Z	D'Amico William	140	shipfitter	44	"
	2035				
A	*Farulla Helen—†	140	housewife	42	"
B	Farulla Julius	140	U S N	24	"
C	*Laicona Frances—†	140	housewife	62	"
D	Laicona Frank	140	U S A	30	
E	Laicona Salvatore	140	laborer	66	"
G	Epps Albert B	142	millhand	25	358 Sumner
H	Epps Charles H	142	bookkeeper	41	358 "
K	Epps Katherine—†	142	housekeeper	61	358 "
L	Luongo Joseph	142	U S A	20	here

Everett Street—Continued

M	Luongo Nicolo	142	laborer	48	here
N	*Luongo Raffaela—†	142	housewife	47	"
O	Rozzi Genevieve—†	142	"	26	73 Cottage
P	Rozzi Vincenzo	142	cook	28	73 "
R	McCarthy Patrick T	144	fishcutter	32	4 Brigham
S	McCarthy Phyllis—†	144	housewife	29	4 "
T	*Famularo Achille	144	laborer	60	here
U	Famularo Elisa—†	144	housewife	55	"
V	Buttero Jean—†	144	"	44	"
W	Buttero Louis	144	U S A	21	
Y	Consalvi Emilio	146	clerk	37	
Z	Consalvi Rose—†	146	housewife	30	"
	2036				
A	D'Eremo Concetta—†	146	"	25	"
B	D'Eremo Robert	146	machinist	31	"
C	Cavino Caroline—†	146	housewife	29	"
D	Cavino James	146	electrician	32	"
E	D'Amelio Carmine	148	fireman	28	"
F	D'Amelio Nancy—†	148	housewife	23	"
G	Briganti Esther—†	148	"	59	
H	Briganti John	148	operator	22	"
K	Briganti Samuel	148	laborer	64	"
L	Marrama Alexander	148	"	28	
M	Marrama Amelia—†	148	housewife	52	"
N	Marrama William	148	laborer	53	"
O	*Rauseo Antonio	150	storekeeper	56	"
P	Rauseo Christina—†	150	housekeeper	25	"
R	Rauseo John	150	U S A	24	"
S	Rauseo Joseph	150	"	27	
T	*Rauseo Katherine—†	150	housewife	57	"
U	Rauseo Michael	150	U S N	30	
Y	Scopa Anthony	153	laborer	50	"
Z	*Scopa Leonarda—†	153	housewife	42	"
	2037				
A	Scopa Ralph	153	U S A	23	
B	Varone Fred	153	painter	28	"
C	Varone Jean—†	153	housewife	25	"
E	Rauseo Anna—†	155	"	32	
F	Rauseo Rocco	155	chauffeur	32	"
G	Salamone Josephine—†	155	housewife	31	"
H	Salamone Peter	155	shoewkr	33	"

22

K	Zeoli Alfred	155	U S A	24	here
L	*Zeoli Clara—†	155	housewife	55	"
M	*Zeoli Domenic	155	tailor	62	"
N	Folino Anna—†	156	housewife	26	164 Everett
O	Folino Joseph	156	laborer	28	164 "
P	Vitale Modestino	156	U S N	23	here
R	Vitale Paul	156	shoewkr	43	"
S	Vitale Philomena—†	156	housewife	43	"
U	*Capadalupo Mary—†	158	housekeeper	67	"
V	Capadalupo Theresa—†	158	clerk	25	"
W	Langlisano Emilio	158	metalwkr	45	"
X	Cerbone Amelia—†	159	beautician	31	"
Y	Cerbone Frank	159	U S A	23	
Z	*Cerbone Josephine—†	159	housewife	61	"

2038

A	Cerbone Mary—†	159	stitcher	25	ˮ
B	Cerbone Peter	159	laborer	65	
C	*Frusciante Angelina—†	160	housewife	55	"
D	Frusciante Anthony	160	laborer	60	
E	Frusciante Joseph	160	U S N	26	
F	Frusciante Ralph	160	U S A	28	
G	Guarino Carmella—†	160	clerk	23	
H	Turco John	160	laborer	47	ˮ
K	Pierro Annamaria—†	160	housekeeper	62	"
L	Pierro Anthony	160	compositor	29	"
M	Vitale Anthony	164	U S A	21	
N	*Vitale Antonetta—†	164	housewife	44	"
O	Vitale Mostino	164	U S M C	20	"
P	Vitale Rocco	164	tailor	46	
S	Coforio Bridget—†	165	housekeeper	69	"
T	Coforio Laura—†	165	clerk	26	ˮ
U	Pauletti Arthur	165	U S A	24	
V	Pauletti Josephine—†	165	stitcher	24	
W	Salamone Josephine—†	165	housekeeper	54	"
X	D'Amato Angelina—†	165	housewife	29	"
Y	D'Amato Ralph	165	shipfitter	28	"
Z	Festa John	166	U S A	22	

2039

A	*Festa Josephine—†	166	housekeeper	60	"
B	Festa Louis	166	laborer	30	ˮ
C	Festa Orlando	166	clerk	24	

23

Page.	Letter.	FULL NAME.	Residence, Jan. 1, 1945.	Occupation.	Supposed Age.	Reported Residence, Jan. 1, 1944.. Street and Number.

Everett Street—Continued

	D	*D'Errico Carmella—†	166	housewife	51	here
	E	D'Errico Domenic	166	U S A	24	"
	F	D'Errico Joseph	166	"	22	"
	M	Fortes Irene—†	171	housewife	22	277 Havre
	N	Fortes John	171	seaman	29	277 "
	O	Correale Carmine	172	electrician	47	here
	P	Correale Mary—†	172	housewife	38	"
	S	*DiMatteo Alfonso	176	retired	85	"
	T	Richardson Florence—†	176	operator	21	"
	U	Richardson William V	176	welder	23	
	V	Clerizuco Antonetta—†	176	stitcher	45	"
	W	Ravagno Alice—†	176	housewife	36	"
	X	Ravagno Salvatore	176	machinist	39	"
	Y	Stella Charles	176	U S A	36	
	Z	Stella Rose—†	176	housekeeper	39	"
		2040				
	A	*Shuntz Eva—†	177	"	74	
	B	Shuntz Helene—†	177	winder	25	"
	C	O'Connell Hilary J	177	U S N	44	
	D	O'Connell Mary—†	177	housewife	42	"
	E	O'Connell Annie—†	177	housekeeper	82	"

Gove Street

	P	*Ricciardi Maria—†	142	housewife	76	here
	R	Cappuccio Carmela—†	142	candymaker	35	"
	S	Cappuccio Chiarina—†	142	housewife	63	"
	T	Cappuccio Virginia—†	142	stitcher	34	"
	U	Puorro Antonette—†	142	housewife	52	"
	V	Puorro Emilio	142	machinist	25	"
	W	Puorro Guy	142	U S A	22	"
	X	Puorro Joseph	142	"	20	
	Y	Puorro Julia—†	142	trimmer	29	"
	Z	Puorro Natalina—†	142	finisher	31	"
		2041				
	B	Liberatore Linda—†	142	housewife	58	"
	C	Liberatore Margaret—†	142	clerk	27	
	D	Liberatore Mario	142	U S A	22	
	E	Liberatore Rocco	142	blacksmith	59	"
	F	Liberatore Rocco, jr	142	U S A	20	
	H	Porfido Margaret—†	146	housewife	41	"

24

K	Porfido Mary—†	146	welder	20	here
L	Pascone Elena—†	146	clerk	21	"
M	Pascone Eustachio	146	carpenter	64	"
N	Pascone Olga—†	146	stitcher	22	
O	Pascone Theresa—†	146	housewife	64	"
P	Pascone Vito	146	laborer	36	
R	Petrillo Columbia—†	146	housewife	39	"
S	Petrillo Henry	146	janitor	37	"
T	Corsano Anna—†	146	housewife	64	"
U	Corsano Nicholas	146	engineer	39	"
V	Scanzillo Angelo	146	laborer	40	
W	Scanzillo Louise—†	146	housewife	37	"
X	DelFraino Antonio	146	laborer	40	
Y	DelFraino Margaret—†	146	spinner	34	
Z	*Sevillatella Lena—†	164	housewife	69	"

2042

A	Lopilato Catherine—†	164	"	66	
B	Lopilato Michael	164	retired	73	
C	Lopilato Anthony	164	machinist	26	"
D	Lopilato Margaret—†	164	housewife	24	"
E	DeFilippo Grace—†	164	"	30	
F	DeFilippo Joseph	164	electrician	32	"
G	Masello Mary—†	164	shoewkr	32	"
H	Leone David	164	U S A	24	
K	Leone Yolanda—†	164	housewife	23	"
L	Danolfo Marian—†	164	"	46	166 Gove
M	Sculfani Frances—†	164	"	28	here
N	Sculfani Frank	164	fishcutter	30	"
O	Gambale Bertha—†	164	housewife	42	"
P	Gambale Geraldine—†	164	stitcher	21	
R	LaVecchio Albert	165	U S A	24	
S	*LaVecchio Angelina—†	165	housewife	64	"
T	*LaVecchio Anthony	165	retired	69	
U	LaVecchio Frank	165	U S A	22	
V	LaVecchio Joseph	165	machinist	29	"
W	LaVecchio Mildred—†	165	inspector	33	"
X	LaVecchio Sarah—†	165	stitcher	30	
Y	Buccillo Carmen	165	laborer	39	
Z	Buccillo Mary—†	165	housewife	30	"

2043

A	Lunetta Eva—†	165	"	37	

25

			Residence, Jan. 1, 1945.		Supposed Age.	Reported Residence, Jan. 1, 1944.
Page.	Letter.	FULL NAME.		Occupation.		Street and Number.

Gove Street—Continued

B	Lunetta Stephen	165	diestamper	.39	here
C	Pepicelli Anthony	165	merchant	40	"
D	Pepicelli Antonette—†	165	housewife	38	"
E	DeFonzo Bernardo	165	laborer	47	"
F	*DeFonzo Marie—†	165	housewife	42	"
G	Genzale Julia—†	165	"	23	
H	Genzale Michael	165	chauffeur	23	"
K	Naples Domenick	165	machinist	45	"
L	Naples Mary—†	165	housewife	39	"
M	LaVecchio Augusta—†	165	"	23	48 Chelsea
N	LaVecchio Augustine	165	buffer	26	here
O	Iannaccone Charles	166	laborer	59	"
P	Iannaccone Cosimo	166	U S N	21	"
R	Iannaccone Eugene	166	at home	27	"
S	Iannaccone Josephine—†	166	housewife	54	"
T	Iannaccone Louis	166	U S A	31	
U	Iannaccone Michael	166	painter	25	"
W	Masillo Pelegrino	166	driller	46	"
X	Masillo Philomena—†	166	housewife	43	"
Z	Masillo Rose—†	166	"	40	"

2044

A	Masillo Tiberio	166	foreman	45	"
B	Mossuto Mary—†	166	housewife	45	63 Lubec
C	Molinaro Albert	166	machinist	34	here
D	Molinaro Elvira—†	166	housewife	29	"
E	Romano Frank	168	laborer	55	"
F	Romano Mary—†	168	housewife	53	"
H	DiGianvittorio Adeline-†	168	at home	66	"
K	*DiGianvittorio Concetta-†	168	housewife	47	"
L	DiGianvittorio Emilio	168	U S A	20	
M	*DiGianvittorio Giovani	168	shoewkr	48	"
N	DeMarco Anthony	168	candymaker	41	"
O	DeMarco Lenora—†	168	housewife	32	"
P	Capuano Lena—†	168	"	40	
R	Capuano Louis	168	shoewkr	44	"
S	Savino John	168	laborer	51	"
T	Savino Regina—†	168	housewife	50	"
U	DeLucia Alfredo	168	laborer	53	"
V	DeLucia Antonio	168	welder	24	"
W	*DeLucia Marie—†	168	housewife	53	"
X	Mondello Elizabeth—†	174	"	29	224 Princeton

Y	Mondello John	174	mechanic	36	224 Princeton
z	Mondello Natale	174	"	50	224 "

2045

A	Giglio Anthony	174	U S N	24	here
B	Giglio Frances—†	174	housewife	51	"
c	Giglio Joseph	174	laborer	55	"
D	Giglio Pauline—†	174	typist	29	
E	Giglio Peter	174	U S N	22	"
F	Giglio Rose—†	174	stitcher	25	"
G	*Antonioli Helen—†	174	housewife	44	"
H	Sinabaldi Joseph	174	laborer	60	
K	Sinabaldi Mary—†	174	housewife	57	"
L	Barrasso Angelina—†	176	packer	29	
M	Lanza Angelo	176	laborer	43	"
N	Lanza Palmina—†	176	housewife	36	"
R	Romano Hermaine—†	176	"	30	Lynn
s	Romano Vincent	176	operator	30	"
T	DiLorenza Edward	176	laborer	70	here
U	DiLorenza Joseph	176	U S N	22	"
V	Romano Josephine—†	176	housewife	68	"
w	Cetrano Biogio	176	laborer	20	
x	Cetrano Julia—†	176	housewife	44	"
Y	Cetrano Tito	176	laborer	51	

Hooten Court

z	Simonelli Josephine—†	1	at home	58	here

2046

A	Fabiano Angelina—†	1	housewife	34	"
B	Fabiano Nicholas	1	welder	40	"
F	*Ciampa Caroline—†	3	at home	53	"
G	*Volpe Leonardo	3	retired	72	15 Lamson ct
H	*Rozzi Antonio	5	laborer	50	here
K	Rozzi Carmella—†	5	clerk	23	"
L	*Rozzi Theresa—†	5	at home	51	"
M	Salamone Benedetto	6	laborer	29	
N	Salamone Josephine—†	6	at home	59	"
o	Salamone Biagio	6	U S A	27	
P	Salamone Liborio	6	"	24	
R	Donovan James	8	retired	69	"
s	Donovan Nora—†	8	at home	73	"

Hooten Court—Continued

T	Laracy Harold J	8	longshoreman	33	here
U	Laracy Herbert	8	U S A	26	"
V	Laracy James F	8	fisherman	40	"
W	Laracy Margaret—†	8	operator	31	"
X	Soldano Antonio	12	laborer	45	
Y	Soldano Ida—†	12	housewife	39	"
Z	Soldano Theresa—†	12	operator	21	"

2047   Lamson Street

A	DeFeo Ralph	19	leatherwkr	32	here
B	DeFeo Vincenza—†	19	housewife	30	"
C	Cacchiotti Anna—†	19	operator	20	"
D	Cacchiotti Antonetta—†	19	housewife	44	"
E	Cacchiotti Carmella—†	19	stitcher	21	"
F	Cacchiotti Costango	19	U S A	23	
G	Cacchiotti Frank	19	laborer	52	
H	Bevere Josephine—†	19	housewife	26	"
K	Bevere Nicholas	19	shipper	30	
L	DiFranza Maria—†	21	machinist	24	"
M	DiFranza Orlando	21	pipefitter	20	"
N	DiFranza Philomena—†	21	housekeeper	54	"
O	Clark Lottie G—†	21	bookkeeper	40	"
P	Clark Margaret L—†	21	clerk	25	"
R	Clark Margaret M—†	21	housekeeper	59	"
S	Fagone Angelina—†	21	housewife	28	"
T	Fagone Michael	21	shipfitter	30	"
U	Mingolelli Carmella-†	rear 21	stitcher	22	"
V	Mingolelli Josephine-†	" 21	housewife	53	"
W	Mingolelli Lena—†	" 21	WAC	30	
X	Mingolelli Michael	" 21	U S M C	24	"
Y	Mingolelli Pasquale	" 21	laborer	56	
Z	Mingolelli Phillip	" 21	U S A	21	"
	2048				
A	Mingolelli Raffaela—†	" 21	buyer	23	
B	Bartolo Catherine—†	35	operator	23	"
C	Bartolo Leonard	35	U S A	24	"
D	Mirabello Anthony	35	"	32	
E	Mirabello Frank S	35	machinist	56	"
F	Mirabello Rose—†	35	housewife	52	"

28

Lamson Street—Continued

Page.	Letter.	FULL NAME.	Residence, Jan. 1, 1945.	Occupation.	Supposed Age.	Reported Residence, Jan. 1, 1944. Street and Number.
	G	Mirabello Ralph	35	guard	29	here
	H	Mirabello Theresa—†	35	housewife	30	"
	K	Albanese Lucy—†	36	at home	24	"
	L	Albanese Raymond	36	U S A	28	"
	M	Petruccelli Frances—†	36	housekeeper	61	"
	N	Petruccelli Josephine—†	36	operator	20	"
	O	Ruggero Gaetano	36	coatmkr	54	"
	P	Ruggero Rose—†	36	inspector	25	"
	R	Bandanza Clara—†	38	housewife	37	"
	S	Bandanza Joseph	38	welder	42	
	T	Morelli Alda—†	38	housekeeper	30	"
	U	Puorro Gerardo	39	storekeeper	50	"
	V	Puorro Mildred—†	39	housewife	39	"
	W	Guarracino Alfred	39	electrician	23	"
	X	Guarracino Bambina—†	39	housekeeper	58	"
	Y	Leone Jean—†	39	stitcher	26	
	Z	DeStefano John	39	watchman	36	
2049						
	A	DeStefano Olympia—†	39	housewife	36	"
	B	Benson Margaret—†	41	mechanic	4'	"
	C	St George Helen—†	41	inspector		
	D	Perry Alton L, jr	41	molder	0	167 Hunt'n av
	E	Price Frank E	41	chauffeur	30	154 Falcon
	F	Price Phyllis M—†	41	housewife	68	154 "
	G	Callanan Nora E—†	43	housekeepr	46	here
	H	Nelson Mary T—†	43	"	29	"
	K	Mirabello Laura—†	45	housewif	30	"
	L	Mirabello William	45	laborer	20	"
	M	Parziale Anthony	45	U S A	47	"
	N	Parziale Emilio	45	laborg	45	"
	O	Parziale Violanda—†	45	hous'	65	"
	P*	Parziale Assunta—†	47	"	35	
	R	Parziale Frank	47	lab	62	
	S	Parziale Joseph	47	r'	25	"
	T	Parziale Joseph J	47	'ekeeper	21	"
	U	Parziale Julia—†	47	'rer	29	
	V	Parziale Vincenzo	47	usekeeper	57	"
	W*	Cieri Mary—†	47	tcher	31	"
	X	D'Argenio Assunta—†	4	hipper	29	"
	Y	D'Argenio Faustino				

Page.	Letter.	FULL NAME.	Residence, Jan. 1, 1945.	Occupation.	Supposed Age.	Reported Residence, Jan. 1, 1944. Street and Number.

Lubec Street

	z	D'Amico Jean C—†	55	clerk	37	142 Gove
		2050				
	A	Rotondo Phillip A	55	U S A	24	here
	B	Rotondo Salvatresa S—†	55	librarian	24	"
	c	Stella Charles, jr	55	electrician	44	"
\	D	Stella Charles W	55	U S A	22	
	E	Stella Ruth M—†	55	housewife	43	"
	F	Corsano Dora M—†	55	"	34	
		Corsano Edmund	55	engineer	37	"
		Caldarelli Armando	57	machinist	25	"
		Caldarelli Marion R—†	57	housewife	21	"
		Zombanti Eleanor—†	57	shoewkr	21	"
		Zombanti Katherine—†	57	at home	22	"
		Zombanti Mary T—†	57	housewife	45	"
		Zombanti Vincenzo	57	painter	54	
	P	DiZio Angelo	57	metalwkr	29	"
	R	DiZio Annie R—†	57	housewife	27	"
	s	DeLafuente Nicola	57	seaman	54	
	T	*Indelicato Carmela—†	57	housewife	53	"
	U	Indelicato Vincenzo	57	retired	68	"
	v	Dattoli Mary—†	57	housewife	37	"
	w	Dattoli Michael	57	shoewkr	44	"
	x	Scrima Generoso	57	U S A	24	
	Y	Scrima Joseph	57	shipfitter	21	"
	z	*Scrima Maria—†	57	housewife	49	"
		2051				
	A	Scrima Pasquale	57	shoewkr	53	"
	D	Mustone Angelo	59	U S A	32	
	E	Mustone Maria—†	59	housewife	28	"
	F	Carangelo Domenick	59	rigger	31	
	G	Carangelo Louise—†	59	housewife	30	"
	H	Gardini Mary—†	59	"	31	
	K	Gardini Samuel	59	shipfitter	29	"
	L	DiFranza Armandò	59	U S A	24	
	M	DiFranza Assunta—†	59	housewife	54	"
	N	DiFranza Carmela—†	59	at home	32	"
	o	DiFranza Leonardo	59	shoecutter	55	"
	P	DiFranza Mary—†	59	typist	30	
	R	DiFranza Olga—†	59	stitcher	21	"
	s	Caruso Josephine—†	61	housewife	23	"
	T	Caruso Nicholas	61	U S A	25	

U	Zichittella Jennie—†	61	stitcher	20	here
V	Zichittella John	61	painter	52	"
W	Zichittella Maria—†	61	housewife	52	"
X	Zichittella Martin	61	welder	25	
Y	Serino Amadeo	61	carpenter	50	"
Z	Serino Joseph	61	machinist	27	"

2052

A	*Serino Theresa—†	61	housewife	48	"
B	D'Angelico Alfred	61	shipfitter	27	"
C	D'Angelico Anita—†	61	housewife	29	"
D	Savino Jennie—†	61	"	24	
E	Savino Nicholas	61	U S A	23	
F	Marcantonio Armando	61	laborer	20	
G	Marcantonio Carmen	61	"	52	"
H	Marcantonio Jean—†	61	stitcher	22	"
K	*Marcantonio Margaret—†	61	housewife	47	"
L	Cibene Anthony	63	shipfitter	27	"
M	Cibene Rose—†	63	housewife	26	"
N	Rizzo Guiseppe	63	laborer	62	..
O	*Rizzo Josephine—†	63	housewife	68	"
P	Trazolini Louis	63	laborer	55	"
R	DePari Pauline—†	63	tailor	32	Dedham
S	Luongo George	63	finisher	42	here
T	Luongo Jennie—†	63	housewife	35	"
U	Ciambriella Domenick	63	garageman	28	"
V	Ciambriella Theresa—†	63	housewife	28	"
W	*Leto Biaga—†	63	at home	63	"
X	Leto Joseph	63	U S A	22	
Y	*Mamucci Masamino	65	retired	70	
Z	*Rizzo Elizabeth—†	65	packer	45	

2053

B	Cucugliato Raimondo	65	storekeeper	55	"
C	Pardo Eleanora—†	65	rubberwkr	25	"
D	Pardo Joseph	65	retired	68	
E	Pardo Santina—†	65	candymaker	55	"
F	Annese Carlo	69	shipper	33	
G	Annese Edith—†	69	housewife	27	"
H	Trdoslavich Francis	69	clerk	26	83 Lubec
K	Trdoslavich Margaret—†	69	housewife	29	83 "
L	*Giordano Angelina—†	69	at home	66	here
M	Giordano Antonette—†	69	stitcher	32	"

Lubec Street—Continued

N	Giordano Assunta—†	69	trimmer	34	here
O	Giordano Caroline—†	69	assembler	38	"
P	Giordano Edith—†	69	stitcher	25	"
R	Giordano Emma M—†	69	assembler	27	"
S	Giordano Helen—†	69	"	32	
T	Giordano Jennie M—†	69	trimmer	40	"
U	Marinelli Amelia—†	69	housewife	38	"
V	Marinelli Joseph	69	electrician	38	"
W	*Nocillo Josephine—†	69	at home	66	"
X	Nocillo Vincenzo	69	foreman	35	"
Y	Pires William	71	seaman	22	2 Wash'n av
Z	Moonagian Lucy—†	71	inspector	23	2 "
	2054				
A	Pires Albert	71	mechanic	45	2 "
B	Pires Marie—†	71	housewife	34	2 "
E	DiLibero Allesandro	71	bricklayer	42	here
F	DiLibero Rose—†	71	housewife	43	"
H	Branciforte Fillipo	73	laborer	58	"
K	Branciforte Joseph	73	U S C G	21	"
L	Branciforte Rosaria—†	73	housewife	48	"
M	Matarazzo Domenick	73	U S A	22	
N	Matarazzo Lucy—†	73	leatherwkr	21	"
O	*Matarazzo Margaret—†	73	at home	40	"
R	Cuillo Josephine—†	73	stitcher	23	"
S	Cuillo Ralph	73	U S N	25	36 Frankfort
T	*D'Amico Antonetta—†	73	at home	54	here
U	Carbone Antonio	73	U S A	34	57 Bremen
V	*Carbone Rosina—†	73	at home	50	57 "
W	*Parelli Annie—†	73	housewife	52	here
X	Parelli Jerry R	73	U S N	22	"
Y	Parelli Mastino	73	clerk	58	"
Z	Parelli Carmella—†	73	operator	20	"
	2055				
A	Siciliano Grecorio	73	tinsmith	61	"
B	Siciliano Raffaela—†	73	packer	57	"
C	Siciliano Salvatore D	73	U S A	23	"
D	*Perrone Antonetta—†	75	housewife	41	54 Chelsea
E	Perrone Frank	75	carpenter	43	54 "
F	Colarusso Carmela—†	75	operator	21	here
G	Colarusso Elvira—†	75	housewife	48	"
H	Colarusso Pellegrino	75	laborer	54	"

Lubec Street—Continued

K	Puccino Carmela—†	75	factoryhand	48	182 Cottage
L	Puccino Carmen	75	U S A	22	182 "
M	Fuccillo Anthony	75	laborer	30	here
N	Fuccillo Michael	75	"	64	"
O	*Fuccillo Nunzia—†	75	housewife	57	"
P	Fuccillo Rose—†	75	stitcher	22	"
R	Polito Bartolo	75	bricklayer	48	"
S	Polito Grace—†	75	tailor	38	"
T	Polito Marco J	75	U S A	20	
U	Zuffante Celia—†	75	housewife	38	"
V	Zuffante Louis	75	laborer	43	
W	Zuffante Saverio	75	"	33	
X	Morgante Margaret—†	75	housewife	22	"
Y	Morgante Pasquale	75	machinist	22	"
Z	*DiMartini Guiseppe	77	baker	64	124 Gove
	2056				
A	*DiMartini Maria—†	77	housewife	64	124 "
B	Straccia Joseph	77	laborer	41	here
C	Straccia Palmina—†	77	housewife	39	"
D	Vigliotta Angela—†	77	at home	26	"
E	Vigliotta Antonio	77	laborer	50	
F	Vigliotta Joseph	77	U S A	23	"
G	Vigliotta Maria—†	77	housewife	49	"
H	Memmolo Louisa—†	77	leatherwkr	23	"
K	Memmolo Marciano	77	laborer	57	
L	*Memmolo Michelina—†	77	housewife	57	"
M	Memmolo Sophie—†	77	stitcher	20	"
N	*Paradiso Anna—†	77	at home	80	"
O	Paulicelli Grace—†	77	clerk	33	
P	Paulicelli Michael	77	laborer	34	
R	*DiFlumeri Maria—†	77	housewife	40	"
S	*DiFlumeri Vincenzo	77	laborer	54	
T	Caldarelli Clara—†	77	at home	31	"
U	Caldarelli Faustino	77	carpenter	60	"
V	Caldarelli Inez—†	77	clerk	21	
W	*Caldarelli Laura—†	77	housewife	61	"
X	Caldarelli Natale	77	U S N	29	
Y	DeFillipo Angelo	77	laborer	49	
Z	DeFillipo Antonetta—†	77	housewife	50	"
	2057				
A	DeFillipo Louise—†	77	operator	25	"

Lubec Street—Continued

Page.	Letter.	Full Name.	Residence, Jan. 1, 1945.	Occupation.	Supposed Age.	Reported Residence, Jan. 1, 1944. Street and Number.
	B	Serina Leonora—†	77	housewife	24	here
	C	Serina Raffaele	77	U S A	24	61 Lubec
	D	*Diotalevi Alessandro	79	laborer	58	here
	E	Diotalevi Dante	79	"	21	"
	F	*Diotalevi Amelia—†	79	housewife	53	"
	G	DiTomasso Joseph	79	chauffeur	37	"
	H	DiTomasso Rose—†	79	housewife	37	"
	K	Arcadipane Andrew	79	pipecoverer	46	"
	L	Arcadipane Grace—†	79	housewife	43	"
	M	Lomuscio Andrew	79	U S A	22	
	N	*Lomuscio Dorothy—†	79	housewife	44	"
	O	Lomuscio Joseph	79	laborer	52	··
	P	Galante Jeanette—†	79	stenographer	25	"
	R	Galante Lena—†	79	candymaker	45	"
	S	DiFlumeri John	79	bricklayer	40	··
	T	DiFlumeri Rose—†	79	housewife	38	"
	U	Grifone Pasquale	79	retired	70	···
	V	Porcelli Peter	79	chipper	27	··
	W	*Porcelli Rachaela—†	79	at home	28	"
	X	Tuttavilla Dora—†	79	housewife	42	"
	Y	Tuttavilla Luigi	79	welder	21	
	Z	Tuttavilla Michael	79	laborer	53	

2058

Page.	Letter.	Full Name.	Residence, Jan. 1, 1945.	Occupation.	Supposed Age.	Reported Residence, Jan. 1, 1944. Street and Number.
	A	Tuttavilla Vincenza—†	79	typist	22	
	B	Nazzaro Raffaella—†	81	stitcher	48	··
	C	Drainoni Gaetano	81	presser	41	··
	D	Drainoni Mary—†	81	at home	36	··
	E	Caso Louis	81	welder	48	"
	F	Caso Theresa—†	81	at home	38	"
	G	Castaldo Christine—†	81	housewife	38	"
	H	Castaldo Ralph	81	laborer	43	"
	K	*Caso Concordia—†	81	at home	82	"
	L	Caso Frank	81	milkman	44	··
	M	DiYess Donato	81	laborer	61	
	N	DiYess George	81	U S A	24	
	O	DiYess Mary—†	81	at home	50	"
	P	DiYess Vincent	81	U S A	26	··
	R	Bernabei Dominick	81	coremaker	64	"
	S	Bernabei Dominick, jr	81	U S N	22	"
	T	Bernabei George	81	"	20	"
	U	Bernabei John	81	"	30	"

Page.	Letter.	FULL NAME.	Residence, Jan. 1, 1945.	Occupation.	Supposed Age.	Reported Residence, Jan. 1, 1944. Street and Number.

Lubec Street—Continued

	v	Bernabei Josephine—†	81	at home	57	here
	w	Pelosi Anna—†	81	"	44	"
	x	Pelosi Augustino	81	U S N	22	"
	y	Pelosi Michael	81	shoewkr	50	"
	z	D'Amico Antonetta—†	83	housewife	21	147 Trenton
2059						
	a	D'Amico William	83	U S A	22	66 Eutaw
	c	Gallo Genarosa—†	83	at home	59	here
	d	Gallo John	83	laborer	62	"
	e	Gallo Pasquale	83	electrician	23	"
	f	Montamino Carmine	83	U S A	26	..
	g	Montamino Joseph	83	clerk	34	
	h	Montamino Michael	83	laborer	64	
	k	Montamino Sadie—†	83	waitress	30	"
	l	Montamino Susan—†	83	checker	24	"
	m	Casciolo Emily—†	83	at home	38	"
	n	Casciolo Joseph	83	shoewkr	42	"
	o	Pellecchia Albert	83	U S N	24	
	p	Pellecchia Dominica—†	83	operator	27	"
	r*	Pellecchia Josephine—†	83	at home	62	"
	s	Colannino Frank	85	U S A	26	..
	t	Colannino Ralph	85	"	23	
	u	Colannino Raphella—†	85	housewife	59	"
	v	Colannino Rosario	85	laborer	60	"
	w	Colannino Joseph	85	rubberwkr	27	"
	x	Colannino Rose—†	85	housewife	·25	"
	y	Sullo Antonio	85	laborer	58	
	z	Sullo Concetta—†	85	ropemaker	23	"
2060						
	a	Sullo Joseph	85	U S A	21	
	b	Sullo Maria—†	85	housewife	50	"
	c	Sullo Nicholas	85	U S A	25	
	d	Ministeri Charles	85	shipfitter	26	"
	e	Ministeri Tina—†	85	housewife	26	"
	f	DeFreitas Louis	85	foreman	34	"
	g	DeFreitas Phyllis—†	85	operator	35	"

Maverick Street

	m	Santarpio Joseph	244	storekeeper	34	here
	n	Santarpio Netta—†	244	housewife	30	"

Page.	Letter.	FULL NAME.	Residence, Jan. 1, 1945.	Occupation.	Supposed Age.	Reported Residence, Jan. 1, 1944. Street and Number.

Maverick Street—Continued

o	Chifino John	244	U S A	26	here
p	Chifino Lena—†	244	candymaker	30	"
r	Chifino Nicolina—†	244	housewife	60	"
s	DiRosa Christopher	244	U S N	35	
t	DiRosa Josephine—†	244	candymaker	35	"
u	Biscotte Mary—†	246	housewife	68	"
v	Rizzo Alfred G	246	machinist	29	"
w	Rizzo Rose—†	246	housewife	28	"
x	Messina Cecelia—†	246	"	26	
y	Messina Edward	246	storekeeper	54	"
z	Messina Edward N	246	U S A	29	..
	2061				
A	Messina Frances—†	246	housewife	47	"
B	Bevilaqua Alfredo	246	U S N	23	
c	Bevilaqua Mario	246	seaman	21	"
D	*Bevilaqua Victoria—†	246	housewife	54	"
E	Campagna Armand	248	metalwkr	32	"
F	Campagna Josephine—†	248	housewife	32	"
G	Scopa Amarosa—†	248	"	37	
H	Scopa John	248	driller	56	·
L	DelPrete Ann—†	250	housewife	22	"
M	*Zuccaro Ernestina—†	250	"	63	
N	Zuccaro John	250	chauffeur	20	"
o	Griffin Katherine—†	250	clerk	39	
p	Grande Christi	250	cutter	30	"
R	Grande Emily—†	250	housewife	29	"
s	Piro John	252	motorman	45	"
t	Piro Josephine—†	252	housewife	42	"
u	DiDonato Joseph	252	welder	47	
v	DiDonato Lydia—†	252	housewife	34	"
w	Coletti Lucy—†	252	factoryhand	40	"
x	Grillo Boldassaro	252	painter	53	"
y	Grillo Carmine—†	252	housewife	63	"
z	D'Agostino Mildred—†	254	"	33	..
	2062				
A	D'Agostino Salvatore	254	chauffeur	37	"
B	Mastascusa Attilio	254	tailor	38	"
c	Mastascusa Clementina-†	254	housewife	65	"
D	Fortunallis Harry	254	chauffeur	26	"
E	Fortunallis Helen—†	254	housewife	26	"

Maverick Street—Continued

F	Kingston Rosalina—†	260	housewife	22	here
G	Kingston Thomas	260	chauffeur	28	"
K	Liberti Angelo	260	physician	54	"
L	Liberti Vincenzo	260	teacher	58	"
M	DiNardo Albert	262	engineer	21	"
N	DiNardo Dominick	262	rigger	52	..
O	DiNardo Lydia—†	262	factoryhand	23	"
P	DiNardo Maria—†	262	housewife	48	"
R	Marmorale Mary—†	262	"	31	
S	Marmorale William	262	U S A	31	
T	Ficcaglia Antonetta—†	262	housewife	52	"
U	Ficcaglia Ugo	262	operator	25	"
V	Rossetti Benjamin	262	chauffeur	31	"
W	Rossetti Mary—†	262	housewife	28	"
X	Pollastrone Mary—†	264	"	39	
Y	Pollastrone Peter	264	ropemaker	48	"
Z	DiBello Catherine—†	264	housewife	55	"
	2063				
A	DiBello Michael	264	tailor	58	,,
B	Stella Carmella—†	264	housewife	63	"
C	Stella Generoso	264	retired	63	
D	Stella Helen—†	264	tailor	31	..
E	Stella Marion—†	264	clerk	21	
F	Stella Patrick	264	U S N	25	,,
G	Gulla Flora—†	266	housewife	29	"
H	Gulla Gregory	266	barber	33	,,
K	DiNush Joseph	266	candymaker	40	"
L	DiNush Mary—†	266	housewife	39	"
M	Tarzia Dominic	266	laborer	57	
N	*Tarzia Palma—†	266	housewife	67	"
O	Tarzia William	266	U S A	28	
P	Cataldo Rose—†	268	housewife	30	"
R	Cataldo Victor	268	clerk	32	
S	Cataldo Generoso	268	laborer	66	
T	Cataldo John	268	seaman	38	
U	Cataldo Lucia—†	268	housewife	63	"
V	Recchia Adeline—†	268	"	34	
W	Recchia Vincent	268	storekeeper	44	,,
X	Sullivan Elizabeth—†	270	housewife	58	"
Y	Sullivan Thomas	270	seaman	65	

Maverick Street—Continued

z	*Hovde Nels	270	watchman	78	here

2064

A	Strand Lina—†	270	at home	63	"
B	O'Keefe Ann—†	270	clerk	52	
C	O'Keefe Margaret—†	270	"	50	"
D	Giordano Frank	276	plumber	48	"
E	Giordano Josephine—†	276	housewife	46	"
F	Giordano Madeline—†	276	stitcher	23	"
G	Giordano Pasquale	276	U S A	20	"
H	Sammartino Anthony	276	shipfitter	32	"
L	Festa Sylvia—†	278	operator	30	"
M	Grillo Frank C	278	accountant	44	"
N	Grillo Jerry	278	retired	73	
O	Grillo Josephine—†	278	housewife	63	"
P	Drago Robert	278	tailor	41	
R	Lewis Edith—†	278	housewife	34	"
S	Lewis John	278	electrician	37	"
T	Zerella Mary—†	278	housewife	40	"
U	Zerella Michael	278	laborer	44	"
V	Zerella Phyllis—†	278	tel operator	20	"
W	Intonti Americo	280	operator	32	"
X	Intonti Jennie—†	280	housewife	31	"
Y	Maddalina Gilda—†	280	"	33	
Z	Maddalina Lucy—†	280	typist	30	

2065

A	Maddalina Theodore	280	machinist	35	"
B	Intonti Angie—†	280	candymaker	34	"
C	Rossi Armando	280	chef	39	152 Bremen
D	Rossi Carmalinda—†	280	housewife	36	152 "
E	Coviello Carmella—†	282	"	64	here
F	Coviello Domenic	282	U S A	25	"
G	Coviello Nicholas	282	foreman	64	"
H	Vitale Edith—†	282	factoryhand	20	"
K	Vitale Jennie—†	282	housewife	56	"
L	Vitale Joseph	282	barber	57	"
M	Schittino Anthony	282	U S A	30	
N	Schittino Nellie—†	282	housewife	53	"
O	Schittino Vincent	282	U S N	23	
P	Spitaleri Frank	282	U S A	32	"
R	Spitaleri Nancy—†	282	housewife	26	"
S	Ravagno Louise—†	284	"	29	206 Maverick

Maverick Street—Continued

T	Ravagno Santo	284	U S A	29		206 Maverick
U	Nyberg Arthur I	284	"	20		here
V	Nyberg Audrey E—†	284	SPAR	22		"
W	Nyberg Mabel F—†	284	housewife	48		"
X	Nyberg Sven	284	machinist	53		"
Y	Assenzo Benjamin	284	rigger	36		
Z	Assenzo Phyllis—†	284	housewife	36		"
	2066					
A	Palmieri Enrico	286	carpenter	35		"
B	Palmieri Lena—†	286	housewife	34		"
C	Palmieri Antonetta—†	286	"	37		
D	Palmieri Frank	286	barber	48		
E*	Palmieri Joseph	286	retired	84		"
F	DelPo Antonio	286	glazier	57		
G	DelPo Carolina—†	286	housewife	50		"
H	DelPo Michael	286	marblewkr	52		"
K	Griffin Mary A—†	296	housewife	55		"
L	Griffin Patrick	296	laborer	55		
M	Marruzzi Angelina—†	296	housewife	46		"
N	Marruzzi Michael	296	proprietor	42		"
O	Marruzzi Pellegrino	296	U S C G	21		"
P	DiSilvio Camillo	296	laborer	64		
R	DiSilvio Dominic	296	clerk	37		
S	DiSilvio Frank	296	U S A	22		
T	DiSilvio Joseph	296	"	24		
U	DiSilvio Nina—†	296	housewife	35		"
V	Porzio Louis	297	U S A	29		
W	Porzio Susan—†	297	housewife	27		"
X	Porzio Antonetta—†	297	dressmaker	23		"
Y	Porzio Henrietta—†	297	housewife	52		"
Z	Porzio John	297	retired	58		
	2067					
A	Porzio Joseph	297	artist	26		"
B	Palmieri Louis	297	shoewkr	44		"
C	Palmieri Rose—†	297	housewife	40		"
D	Gulla Josephine—†	298	"	25		183 Cottage
E	Gulla William	298	laborer	27		183 "
F	Fera Anna M—†	298	housewife	65		here
G	Fera Carolina—†	298	assembler	29		"
H	Fera Frank	298	retired	72		"
K	Fera John J	298	machinist	35		"

Maverick Street—Continued

L	Fiandaca Adeline—†	298	housewife	34	here
M	Fiandaca Pasquale	298	tailor	34	"
N	DeFilippo Anne—†	299	housewife	27	"
O	DeFilippo Arthur	299	U S A	27	
P	DeLucca Amadeo	299	U S N	22	
R	DeLucca Henry	299	chauffeur	23	"
S	LaRossa John	299	carpenter	31	"
T	LaRossa Theresa—†	299	housewife	28	"
U	Rivoire Concetta—†	299	"	60	
V	Rivoire Lamy	299	printer	62	"
W	Russo Albert	300	U S A	22	
X	Russo Joseph	300	salesman	66	"
Y	Russo Susan—†	300	housewife	60	"
Z	Shubert David	300	welder	27	
	2068				
A	Shubert Josephine—†	300	housewife	30	"
B	D'Agostino Irene—†	300	stitcher	25	"
C	D'Agostino Joseph	300	pressman	52	"
D	*D'Agostino Marietta—†	300	housewife	67	"
E	Woodford Anna—†	301	"	32	
F	Woodford William	301	chauffeur	33	"
G	Rowan James P	301	U S N	22	"
H	Rowan Mary J—†	301	housewife	47	"
K	Rowan Mary J—†	301	at home	21	"
L	Lombardi Ralph	301	gluemaker	37	"
M	Lombardi Rose—†	301	housewife	33	"
N	Porzio Alphonso	302	U S N	24	200 Everett
O	Porzio Marie—†	302	housewife	21	200 "
P	Marasca Alfred	302	tailor	68	here
R	Marasca Edith—†	302	stitcher	27	"
S	Marasca Jennie—†	302	housewife	67	"
T	Marasca Joseph	302	U S N	37	
U	Marasca Vincent	302	shipper	32	"
V	Fasano Carl	302	furrier	33	298 Maverick
W	Fasano Eleanor—†	302	housewife	34	298 "
X	Hale Joseph W	303	U S A	38	here
Y	Hale Madeline R—†	303	operator	28	"
Z	Hale Mary—†	303	at home	56	"
	2069				
A	Jackson Mary G—†	303	"	32	"
B	McCarthy James J	303	clerk	70	

Page.	Letter.	FULL NAME.	Residence, Jan. 1, 1945.	Occupation.	Supposed Age.	Reported Residence, Jan. 1, 1944. Street and Number.	

Maverick Street—Continued

c	McCarthy Johanna—†	303	housewife	65	here
d	Jensen Hilda S—†	303	at home	74	"
e	Mattson Eric A	303	machinist	44	"
f	Murdocca Helen—†	304	housewife	29	"
g	Murdocca Peter J	304	electrician	34	"
h	Vigliotta Dominic	304	clerk	29	
k	Vigliotta Eva—†	304	housewife	27	"
l	Murdocca Elizabeth—†	304	stitcher	23	"
m	Murdocca Jennie—†	304	factoryhand	30	"
n	Murdocca Joseph	304	U S A	28	
o	*Murdocca Mary—†	304	housewife	62	"
p	*Murdocca Vincent	304	laborer	67	
s	Savino Liberato ·P	306	welder	40	
t	Savino Yolanda—†	306	housewife	31	"
u	Manuel Armand	306	welder	21	"
v	Manuel Mario	306	U S A	27	
w	*Manuel Mary—†	306	housewife	60	"
x	Manuel Yolanda—†	306	factoryhand	26	"
y	Doyle Margaret—†	307	housewife	37	"
z	Doyle Thomas	307	timekeeper	39	"
	2070				
a	Nelson Bridget—†	307	at home	72	"
b	Gambale Angelina—†	315	stitcher	21	"
c	Gambale Michelina—†	315	housewife	36	"
d	Gambale Nicolo	315	laborer	56	
e	Scarpaci Daniel	315	rubberwkr	35	"
f	Scarpaci Stella—†	315	housewife	30	"
g	Polcari Caroline—†	315	"	44	"
h	Polcari Joseph	315	U S A	21	
k	Polcari Judith—†	315	factoryhand	20	"
l	Polcari Pasquale	315	barber	48	
m	Wardell Mary—†	317	housewife	32	"
n	Wardell Stirling L	317	U S A	34	
o	DiMaro Henry	317	welder	34	
p	DiMaro Susanne—†	317	housewife	25	"
r	Alberto Giovanina—†	319	"	46	
s	Alberto Materio	319	laborer	54	
t	Nicolosi Carmello	319	factoryhand	65	"
v	DiDomenico Concetta—†	321	housewife	49	"
w	DiDomenico Frank	321	machinist	53	"
u	DiDomenico Anthony	321	U S A	21	"

Maverick Street—Continued

x	DiDomenico Joseph	321	U S N	23	here
y	D'Agostino Rose—†	321	housewife	29	"
z	D'Agostino Sabatino	321	presser	29	"

2071

A	Arciero Antonio	323	welder	24	
B	Arciero Jennie—†	323	housewife	27	"
C	Velardo Antonio	323	cleaner	57	"
D	Velardo Guy	323	U S A	26	
E	Velardo Mary—†	323	housewife	56	"
F	Velardo Salvi	323	U S A	25	

Porter Street

G	Temple Anna—†	191	housewife	21	here
H	Temple James	191	U S A	26	"
K	*DeAngelis Carmella—†	191	housewife	68	"
L	DeAngelis Helen—†	191	clerk	29	"
M	Indelicato Alfonso	191	U S N	34	
N	Indelicato Angelina—†	191	candymaker	34	"
O	Arinello Michael	191	mechanic	33	"
P	Arinello Philomena—†	191	housewife	33	"
S	Harvey Jean—†	191	"	22	California
T	Pisani Joseph	191	U S N	24	here
U	Pisani Virginia—†	191	housewife	59	"
V	Magaletta Roberta—†	191	"	28	"
W	Magaletta Vito	191	molder	35	"

Sumner Street

Y	Curran Bridget—†	442	housekeeper	70	here
Z	Santos Hilda—†	442	operator	24	"

2072

A	Santos John	442	laborer	34	"
B	*Santos Josephine—†	442	housewife	52	"
C	Jenkins Charles	442	boilermaker	64	"
D	Jenkins Elizabeth—†	442	clerk	55	"
E	Jenkins John	442	laborer	50	"
F	Jenkins Mary—†	442	candymaker	57	"
G	Welch Charles	444	clerk	52	"

Sumner Street—Continued

H	Welch John F	444	foreman	50	here
K	Burns Jean—†	444	clerk	20	"
L	Burns Julia—†	444	operator	22	"
M	Hearn Annie—†	444	housekeeper	70	"
N	Hearn William H	444	secretary	49	"

Venice Street

P	Thompson Helen—†	1	at home	26	here
R	Verderico Anna—†	1	housekeeper	62	"
S	Verderico George	1	mechanic	31	"
T	Verderico Theresa—†	1	housewife	31	"

Ward 1–Precinct 21

CITY OF BOSTON

LIST OF RESIDENTS
20 YEARS OF AGE AND OVER

(NON-CITIZENS INDICATED BY ASTERISK)
(FEMALES INDICATED BY DAGGER)

AS OF

JANUARY 1, 1945

THOMAS F. SULLIVAN, *Chairman*
FREDERIC E. DOWLING, *Secretary*
WILLIAM A. MOTLEY, JR.
FRANCIS B. McKINNEY
EVERETT R. PROUT
Listing Board.

CITY OF BOSTON PRINTING DEPARTMENT

2100

Bremen Street

A	DiFilippo Joseph	100	laborer	64	here
B	Prisco Stanley	100	longshoreman	46	"
C	Langone Anthony	102	printer	31	"
D	Langone Winifred—†	102	housewife	27	"
E	Moscuzza Josephine—†	102	at home	32	"
F	Ferrera Anna—†	102	housewife	43	"
G	Ferrera Louis	102	roofer	47	
H	Ferrera Louise—†	102	dressmaker	20	"
K	Penta Albina—†	104	housewife	34	"
L	Penta Alfonso	104	guard	61	
M	Cogliano Carmela—†	104	clerk	20	
N	Cogliano Domenic	104	U S A	26	
O´	Cogliano Frank J	104	shipfitter	23	"
P	Cogliano Geriaco	104	retired	68	
R	Cogliano Rita—†	104	housewife	56	"
S	Iasonno Antonetta—†	104	"	70	
T	Iasonno Attillio	104	waiter	38	"
U	Iasonno Salvatore	104	retired	65	
V	Ricupero Arthur	106	laborer	23	"
W	Ricupero Humbert	106	storekeeper	25	"
X	*Ricupero Leonilda—†	106	housekeeper	62	"
Y	Ricupero Angelo	106	salesman	42	"
Z	Ricupero Barbara—†	106	housewife	41	"

2101

A	Ricupero Dennis	106	U S A	20	
B	Ruggiero Blanche—†	106	housewife	24	"
C	Ruggiero Louis	106	machinist	30	"
D	Tremonte Constance—†	108	housewife	23	"
E	Tremonte William H	108	fishcutter	24	"
F	Maratea Elizabeth—†	108	housewife	50	"
G	Maratea Giacomo	108	shoemaker	52	"
H	Maratea Susan—†	108	stitcher	25	"
K	Maratea Venanzio	108	salesman	27	"
L	Arone Angelina—†	108	housewife	53	"
M	Arone Lawrence	108	pressman	55	"
N	Arone Louise—†	108	clerk	25	"
O	*Gaudet Charles	110	retired	77	Belmont
P	Grillo Angela—†	110	housewife	26	300 Chelsea
R	Grillo Santo	110	polisher	32	300 "
S	Nigro Donato	110	candymaker	48	here

Page.	Letter.	FULL NAME.	Residence, Jan. 1, 1945.	Occupation.	Supposed Age.	Reported Residence, Jan. 1, 1944. Street and Number.

Bremen Street—Continued

	T	Nigro Mary—†	110	housewife	50	here
	U	Nigro Rose—†	110	clerk	20	"
	V	Mede Alice—†	112	housewife	38	"
	W	Mede Louis	112	electrician	40	"
	X	Chicariello Anthony	112	retired	79	
	Y	Chicariello John	112	welder	30	
	Z	Chicariello Nancy—†	112	housewife	65	"
2102						
	A	DeMarco Angelina—†	112	"	42	
	B	DeMarco Nicholas	112	stitcher	44	"
	C	Federico Angelina—†	114	housewife	29	"
	D	Federico Joseph	114	U S N	25	..
	E	Braccia Alfred	114	polisher	34	"
	F	Braccia Josephine—†	114	housewife	30	"
	G	*Grillo Angela—†	114	"	58	
	H	*Grillo Frank	114	laundrywkr	62	"
	K	Grillo Joseph	114	U S A	20	
	L	Capozzi Bernard	116	"	23	
	M	Capozzi Irene—†	116	housewife	23	"
	N	*Iannotti Nicholas	116	retired	74	
	O	*Iannotti Pasqualina—†	116	housewife	72	"
	P	Poto Antonetta—†	116	at home	29	"
	R	Poto Vito	116	operator	29	"
	S	*Cicatelli Joseph	118	shoemaker	62	"
	T	*Cicatelli Rose—†	118	housewife	57	"
	U	Cicatelli Susan—†	118	stitcher	20	"
	V	Cicatelli Louise—†	118	clerk	28	"
	W	*Cicatelli Rosario	118	shoemaker	67	"
	X	Birchette Thomas	118	U S N	27	
	Y	Perullo Armando	118	clerk	20	
	Z	*Perullo Louis	118	laundryman	55	"
2103						
	A	*Perullo Mary—†	118	housewife	52	"
	B	Mainiero Alice—†	120	"	34	
	C	Mainiero Fred	120	proprietor	39	"
	D	Mainiero Frank	120	retired	73	
	E	Mainiero Marion—†	120	housewife	39	"
	F	Mainiero Philip	120	retired	44	
	G	Cammarata Baldassaro	122	"	73	
	H	Cammarata Josephine—†	122	housewife	65	"
	K	Bellitti Charles	122	laborer	61	"

3

Bremen Street—Continued

	Letter	Full Name	Residence	Occupation	Age	Reported Residence
	L	Bellitti Frank	122	U S A	25	here
	M	Bellitti Grace—†	122	housewife	48	"
	N	Bellitti Jasper	122	U S N	22	"
	O	Bellitti John	122	U S A	28	
	P	Lanattina Josephine—†	122	housewife	39	"
	R	Lanattina Louis	122	operator	44	"
	S	Reggione Antoinette—†	124	tailor	42	
	T	DelGrosso Lena—†	124	housewife	40	"
	U	DelGrosso Pasquale	124	chauffeur	47	"
	V	Brogna Joseph	124	pipefitter	31	"
	W	Brogna Mary--†	124	housewife	29	"
	X	Patti Catherine—†	126	"	31	
	Y	Patti Joseph	126	barber	33	"
	Z	DeMarco Archangela—†	126	housewife	26	"
2104						
	A	DeMarco Pasquale	126	chauffeur	28	"
	B	Pauletti Adeline—†	126	housewife	55	"
	C	Pauletti Albert	126	U S A	24	"
	D	Pauletti Amelia—†	126	stitcher	27	"
	E	Pauletti Americo	126	U S N	22	
	F	Pauletti Antonio	126	laborer	55	"
	G	Pauletti Gilda—†	126	metalwkr	20	"
	H	DiPasquale Angelo	128	carpenter	33	"
	K	DiPasquale Roslie—†	128	housewife	33	"
	L	DeBlasio Catherine—†	128	"	40	"
	M	DeBlasio Louis	128	U S A	25	
	N	DeBlasio Michael	128	carpenter	48	"
	O	DeBlasio Michael, jr	128	machinist	22	"
	P	DeBlasio Mildred—†	128	stitcher	21	"
	R	Limoli Josephine—†	128	housewife	22	"
	S	Limoli Vincent	128	tailor	22	"
	T	Tedesco Anthony	130	laborer	28	136 Bremen
	U	Tedesco Lucy—†	130	housewife	22	136 "
	V	Tunnera Angelo	130	steamfitter	38	here
	W	Tunnera Jennie—†	130	housewife	35	"
	X	Popolo Joseph	130	fireman	61	"
	Y	Popolo Marie—†	130	housewife	60	"
	Z	Popolo Vincent	130	burner	21	"
2105						
	A	Leone Amelia—†	132	housewife	62	"
	B	Leone Dominic	132	U S A	23	

c	Leone John	132	U S A	24	here
d	Leone Philip	132	laborer	61	"
e	Scimone Mary—†	132	housewife	35	"
f	Scimone Vincenzo	132	musician	35	"
g	*Cecere Elisa—†	132	housewife	66	"
h	Cecere Florence—†	132	housekeeper	30	"
k	Turco Evelyn—†	132	housewife	26	"
l	Giansiracusa Ignazio	136	U S A	31	19 Everett
m	Giansiracusa Violet—†	136	housewife	29	19 "
n	Giansiracusa Anna—†	136	"	55	here
o	Giansiracusa Paul	136	watchman	60	"
p	Giansiracusa Frank	136	machinist	34	"
r	Giansiracusa Mary—†	136	housewife	34	"
s	Petrillo Louis	138	U S A	21	
t	*Petrillo Rose—†	138	housewife	51	"
u	*Petrillo Sabino	138	shipper	51	
v	Albanese Josephine—†	140	housewife	31	"
w	Albanese Louis	140	guard	32	
x	Nocito Pauline—†	140	housewife	34	"
y	Nocito Vincent	140	longshoreman	32	"
z	Collucci Ralph	140	foreman	40	"

2106

a	Collucci Theresa—†	140	housewife	40	"
b	Spelladora John	140	pipefitter	42	"
c	Testa Carmen	142	candymaker	33	"
d	Testa Constantino	142	tinsmith	61	"
e	Testa Gabriel	142	machinist	37	"
f	Testa Parme—†	142	beautician	26	"
g	DiPesa Josephine—†	144	housewife	23	"
h	DiPesa Ralph	144	painter	29	
k	Farro Carmella—†	144	floorwoman	27	"
l	Barrasso Anthony	144	U S A	26	
m	Barrasso Grace—†	144	housewife	23	"
n	DeSteffano Catherine—†	144	stitcher	23	
o	DeSteffano Ralph	144	U S A	20	
p	DeSteffano Theresa—†	144	packer	49	
r	Palermo Carmella—†	144	housewife	33	"
s	Palermo Ignazio E	144	operator	31	"
t	*Constantina Angelina—†	146	housewife	65	"
u	Constantina Mary—†	146	clerk	30	
v	Barker Frank	146	longshoreman	29	"

5

Bremen Street—Continued

	w	Barker James	146	watchman	63	51 Prescott
	x	Barker Mary—†	146	housewife	27	here
	y	Pagliarulo Louis	146	electrician	38	"
	z	Pagliarulo Pauline—†	146	housewife	34	"
2107						
	a	DiGregorio Alfonso	148	laborer	61	71 Lubec
	b	Cattano Louis	148	machinist	35	here
	c	Cattano Mary—†	148	housewife	30	"
	d	Delaia Gaetano	148	laborer	55	"
	e	*Delaia Josephine—†	148	housewife	47	"
	f	Vetrano Dominic	150	shoewkr	36	"
	g	Vetrano Frances—†	150	housewife	36	"
	h	Cheffro Rose—†	150	"	33	"
	k	Cheffro Sylvester	150	shipfitter	33	"
	l	Bellone Anthony	150	baker	32	
	m	Bellone Virginia—†	150	housewife	30	"
	n	Colarusso Anna—†	152	shoewkr	21	Chelsea
	o	Colarusso Samuel	152	"	23	"
	p	Carabis Antonetta—†	152	housewife	49	here
	r	Carabis Carmen	152	laborer	49	"
	s	Storelli Alfonso	152	shoewkr	52	"
	t	Storelli Alfonso, jr	152	U S A	20	
	u	Storelli Thomasina—†	152	shoewkr	42	"
	v	Filadora Louis	154	fireman	37	"
	w	Filadora Rose—†	154	housewife	39	"
	x	Votta Helen—†	154	stitcher	22	"
	y	*Votta Luigi	154	retired	75	
	z	*Votta Theresa—†	154	housewife	69	"
2108						
	a	Martino Anna—†	156	housekeeper	48	158 Bremen
	b	Minichiello Rocco	156	laborer	61	158 "
	c	LaValle Alfred	156	"	54	here
	d	*LaValle Concettina—†	156	housewife	59	"
	e	Troisi Michelina—†	156	stitcher	20	"
	f	Testa Emma—†	156	housewife	32	"
	g	Testa Guy	156	shipfitter	31	"
	k	Lunetta Martina—†	158	housewife	32	"
	l	Lunetta Stephen	158	cabinetmaker	38	"
	m	Scarpa Frank	158	guard	29	
	n	Scarpa Helen—†	158	housewife	26	"
	p	*Baroni Sara—†	160	housekeeper	53	"

Bremen Street—Continued

R	Rizzaro Nicholas	160	laborer	51	here
s	Rizzaro Nicholas, jr	160	U S A	21	"
T	*Rizzaro Nora—†	160	housewife	41	"
U	*Alino Venturo	160	watchman	45	"
v	*Morocini Frank	160	retired	67	..
w	*DeOrio Anna—†	162	housewife	84	"
x	*DeOrio Antonio	162	retired	83	"
Y	Nicosia Angelo	162	"	75	
z	*Nicosia Jennie—†	162	housewife	63	"

2109

D	D'Amico Angelina—†	174	candymaker	35	"
E	Bordonaro Angelo	174	U S N	25	
F	Bordonaro Jennie—†	174	stitcher	23	"
G	*Bordonaro Philip	174	laborer	60	
H	*Bordonaro Rose—†	174	housewife	60	"
K	Frederico Esther—†	174	"	37	"
L	Frederico Joseph	174	painter	35	"
M	Simeone Mary—†	174	operator	23	83 Bremen
o	Nutaro Concetta—†	190	housewife	61	here
P	Nutaro Florence—†	190	nurse	21	"
R	Nutaro Grace—†	190	operator	20	"
s	Nutaro James	190	U S N	23	
T	Meneguzzi Louis	190	shipfitter	38	"
U	Meneguzzi Marion—†	190	housewife	36	"
v	Genualdo Ciro	190	painter	30	"
w	Genualdo Gaetana—†	190	housewife	30	"
Y	Amato Mary—†	192	housekeeper	39	"
z	Ristino Anna—†	192	housewife	30	"

2110

A	Ristino Arthur F	192	machinist	30	"
B	Cianciarulo Anthony	194	tailor	58	
C	Cianciarulo Gabriela—†	194	housewife	56	"
D	Cianciarulo Margaret—†	194	tailor	25	
E	Cianciarulo Mary—†	194	seamstress	31	"
F	Ciccia Elizabeth—†	194	"	30	
G	Ciccia Joseph	194	U S N	32	"
H	Eruzione Eugene	194	U S M C	22	"
K	Eruzione Helen—†	194	clerk	21	
L	Fucillo Henry	194	chauffeur	50	"
M	Fucillo Nancy—†	194	housewife	47	"
N	MacDonald James	196	agent	36	

Page.	Letter.	FULL NAME.	Residence, Jan. 1, 1945.	Occupation.	Supposed Age.	Reported Residence, Jan. 1, 1944. Street and Number.

Bremen Street—Continued

o	MacDonald Stella—†	196	housewife	32	here
p	Margerone Benedict L	196	accountant	22	"
r	Margerone Mary—†	196	housewife	50	"
s	Margerone Peter	196	candymaker	48	"
t	Margerone Rita A—†	196	packer	24	
u	Pascucci Anthony	196	millhand	35	"
v	Pascucci Matilda—†	196	housewife	28	"
w	Mahoney John D	198	U S M C	26	"
x	Mahoney Phyllis—†	198	housewife	26	"
y	*Zaffino Antonette—†	198	"	38	168 Cottage
z	Zaffino Genaro	198	shoemaker	51	168 "
	2111				
a	Giannasoli Andrew	198	laborer	54	here
b	Giannasoli Henry	198	U S A	22	"
c	*Giannasoli Lucy—†	198	housewife	52	"
d	Zambuto Anthony	200	riveter	27	
e	Zambuto Mary—†	200	housewife	26	"
f	LaCava Michael	200	machinist	28	"
g	LaCava Vita—†	200	housewife	29	"
h	LaCava Domenic	200	foreman	50	"
k	LaCava John	200	U S A	24	··
l	LaCava Mary—†	200	housewife	52	"
m	LaCava Thomas	200	U S A	22	
n	*Faraci Catina—†	202	housekeeper	75	"
o	Ferro John	202	pressman	29	"
p	Ferro Mary—†	202	housewife	29	"
r	Chiango Joseph	202	machinist	34	"
s	Chiango Rose—†	202	housewife	35	"
u	Balante Nellie—†	204	"	63	228 Bremen
v	Campochiaro Charles	204	laborer	34	here
w	*Campochiaro Crocifissa-†	204	housewife	60	"
x	Campochiaro Giuseppe	204	laborer	62	"
y	*Radasta Josephine—†	204	housekeeper	85	"
z	Cannarozzo Joseph	204	laborer	51	"
	2112				
a	Cannarozzo Vincenza—†	204	housewife	34	"
b	Fulginiti Delia—†	206	"	34	
c	Fulginiti Joseph	206	seaman	33	"
d	Annastasio Salvatore	206	retired	73	
e	D'Esta Pauline—†	208	housekeeper	67	"
f	Matera Americo	208	U S A	26	"

8

Bremen Street—Continued

	Letter	Full Name	Residence	Occupation	Age	Reported Residence
	G	Matera Anna—†	208	clerk	23	here
	H	Matera Anthony	208	tailor	62	"
	K	Matera Beatrice—†	208	housewife	66	"
	L	Matera Mario C	208	U S A	28	,
	M	Matera James	208	engineer	32	"
	N	Alba Agnes—†	210	housewife	33	"
	O	Alba James	210	metalwkr	39	"
	P	Pandolfo Angela—†	210	housewife	47	185 Havre
	R	Pandolfo Martin	210	laborer	56	185 "
	S	Pandolfo Martin	210	U S A	20	185 "
	T	Szmit Rosalie—†	210	housewife	24	185 "
	U	Szmit Walter	210	U S A	24	Chelsea
	V	Colangia Eugene	210	"	27	Malden
	W	Colangia Vincenzia—†	210	housewife	26	here
	X	Palermo Antoinetta—†	210	"	55	"
	Y	Palermo John	210	welder	59	"
	Z	Palermo Pauline—†	210	beautician	24	"
		2113				
	A	Olivieri Mario	212	shipwright	29	66 Grady ct
	B	Olivieri Mary—†	212	housewife	25	66 "
	C	*DiMarino Anthony	212	laborer	55	here
	D	*DiMarino Antoinetta—†	212	housewife	47	"
	E	*DiMarino Michael	212	laborer	51	"
	F	DiMarino Nicholas	212	U S A	21	..
	G	Calvano Angelina—†	212	clerk	24	
	H	*Calvano Antonetta—†	212	housewife	55	"
	K	Calvano Mary—†	212	stitcher	21	"
	L	Calvano Thomas	212	laborer	50	
	M	Lasofsky Anthony	214	welder	34	
	N	*Lasofsky Michael	214	retired	63	
	O	*Lasofsky Mollie—†	214	housewife	57	"
	P	DeVito Frank	214	calker	31	
	R	DeVito Natalie—†	214	housewife	32	"
	S	Zambella Anna—†	214	"	23	
	T	Zambella Leopoldo	214	U S A	25	"
	U	*Puras Anastasia—†	216	housewife	52	"
	V	*Puras Bernard	216	candymaker	65	"
	W	Puras Josephine—†	216	packer	26	
	X	Sacco Elaine—†	216	housewife	28	"
	Y	Sacco Generoso	216	carpenter	32	"
	Z	Miniscalco Amelia—†	216	housewife	55	"

9

2114
Bremen Street—Continued

A	Miniscalco Frank	216	U S A	22	here
B	Miniscalco Joseph	216	carpenter	60	"
C	Lauria Joseph	218	rigger ·	32	"
D	Lauria Laura M—†	218	housewife	27	"
E	Lauria Agrippino	218	foreman	41	"
F	*Lauria Concetta—†	218	housewife	75	"
G	Barrasso Americo	218	painter	30	70 Chelsea
H	Barrasso Mary—†	218	housewife	29	70 "
K	Lunetta Salvatore	220	machinist	27	here
L	Lunetta Theresa—†	220	housewife	25	"
M	Carco Constantino	220	chipper	47	"
N	Carco Francesco	220	shoemaker	44	"
O	Carco Mary—†	220	housewife	38	"
P	Campagna Edith M—†	220	"	39	
R	Campagna Napoleon L	220	painter	42	"

Chelsea Street

T	Maragioglio Baldasare	55	proprietor	47	here
U	Maragioglio Josephine—†	55	housewife	42	"
V	Sorendino Joseph	55	laborer	30	"
W	Sorendino Lucy—†	55	housewife	26	"
X	Albano Grace—†	57	"	23	
Y	Albano Robert	57	U S N	23	"
Z	Brosca Anthony	57	laborer	50	"
	2115				
A	*Brosca Mary—†	57	housewife	48	"
B	Patti Andrew	57	metalwkr	48	"
C	Patti Grace—†	57	housewife	44	"
D	Patti Joseph	57	U S A	20	
E	Russo Charles	59	laborer	34	"
F	Russo Mary—†	59	housewife	37	"
H	*Macaluso Diana—†	59	"	82	..
K	Macaluso Rosario	59	carpenter	59	"
L	*Macaluso Salvatore	59	retired	86	"
M	Leone Mary—†	61	housewife	45	"
N	Leone Romolo	61	laborer	55	"
O	Tassinari Elizabeth—†	61	housewife	61	"
P	Tassinari Mary—†	61	stenographer	36	"
R	LaMonica Joseph	61	laborer	33	64 Chelsea

s	LaMonica Rose—†	61	housewife	30	64 Chelsea
t	Boitano Loretta—†	63	"	49	here
u	Boitano Robert	63	storekeeper	49	"
v	*Theall Delia—†	63	housekeeper	72	"
w	Guiffreido Anna—†	63	operator	29	"
x	*Guiffreido Antonette—†	63	housewife	65	"
y	Tari Anthony	63	laborer	47	"
z	Tari Bartholomew	63	"	20	"
	2116				
a	Tari Mary—†	63	housewife	40	"
b	Petrillo Amerino	65	U S A	31	
c	Petrillo Concetta—†	65	housewife	58	"
d	Petrillo Gaetano	65	barber	41	
e	Petrillo Grace—†	65	stitcher	28	
f	Petrillo Lena—†	65	clerk	21	
g	Petrillo Palmerino	65	retired	70	"
h	Maffeo Marion—†	65	housewife	67	"
k	Maffeo Pedro	65	retired	68	
l	Langiano Caroline—†	65	candymkr	36	"
m	*Langiano Pasquale	65	laborer	69	
n	Langiano Rose—†	65	operator	35	"
o	*Langiano Thomasino—†	65	housewife	51	"
r	LaConte Gertrude—†	67	"	25	
s	LaConte Joseph	67	U S A	28	
t	Iannuzzi John	67	laborer	49	
u	Iannuzzi Mary—†	67	housewife	37	"
v	Erichiello Donato	67	candymkr	57	"
w	Erichiello Philomena—†	67	housewife	39	"
y	Mustone Crescenzo	69	laborer	47	
z	*Sorrentino Carmella—†	69	housewife	62	"
	2117				
a	Sorrentino Leonardo	69	laborer	62	"
b	Sorrentino Pasquale	69	"	28	
c	Caporale John	69	U S A	21	
d	Caporale Joseph	69	laborer	42	
e	Caporale Julia—†	69	housewife	35	"
f	Tarzia Anthony	69	U S N	22	
g	Tarzia Mary—†	69	housewife	45	"
h	Tarzia Pasquale	69	laborer	52	
k	Mandarano Susan—†	71	housekeeper	34	"
l	*Georgia Fred	71	laborer	69	"

Page.	Letter.	FULL NAME.	Residence, Jan. 1, 1945.	Occupation.	Supposed Age.	Reported Residence, Jan. 1, 1944. Street and Number.

Chelsea Street—Continued

M	Mustone James	71	laborer	65	here
N	*Mustone Marie—†	71	housewife	61	"
O	Accomando Gaetano	71	laborer	45	"
P	Accomando Lucy—†	71	housewife	44	"
R	Accomando Marco	71	U S A	23	
S	Accomando Mary—†	71	operator	22	"
U	Todaro Lucy—†	73	housewife	35	"
V	Todaro Phillip	73	baker	43	"
W	Ippolito Christina—†	73	housewife	22	45 Chelsea
X	Ippolito Peter	73	U S A	24	45 "
Y	*Luca Ida—†	73	housekeeper	53	here
Z	*Simione Anna—†	73	housewife	31	"
	2118				
A	Simione Louis	73	laborer	33	"
B	Iorio Frances—†	75	housewife	49	"
C	Iorio Luciano	75	barber	53	
D	*Guerra Catherine—†	75	housewife	71	"
E	Guerra Mary—†	75	dressmkr	26	"
F	Guerra Salvatore	75	U S A	29	
G	Guerra Teresa—†	75	dressmkr	32	"
H	Paridiso Allesandro	75	presser	45	64 Chelsea
K	*Paridiso Vincenza—†	75	housewife	38	64 "
M	*D'Addona Rafaele	79	laborer	62	here
N	Lombardi Luigi	79	"	59	"
O	*Marrone Marian—†	81	housewife	65	"
P	Marrone Paul	81	U S A	29	"
R	*Ciriello Michele	81	retired	62	
S	Giordani Marie—†	81	operator	27	"
T	Gulla Pantaleone	83	laborer	51	"
U	*Gulla Rose—†	83	housewife	45	"
V	*Gioia Andrew	83	laborer	64	"
W	Gioia Carmella—†	83	rubberwkr	32	"
X	Gioia Edith—†	83	wrapper	21	"
Y	Gioia James	83	laborer	25	"
Z	Gioia Jennie—†	83	wrapper	27	"
	2119				
A	Gioia Joseph	83	foreman	29	"
B	Cioia Mary—†	83	housewife	56	"
C	Spada Bartholomew J	83	U S A	26	"
D	Spada Marie—†	83	housewife	24	"
E	Zito Angelo	83	chauffeur	52	"

12

F	Zito Carmella—†	83	housewife	52	here
G	Zito Joseph	83	U S M C	23	"
H	DiPaulo Anna—†	85	housewife	37	130 Bremen
K	DiPaulo Louis	85	presser	38	130 "
L	Marotta Anna—†	85	housewife	35	here
M	Marotta Louis	85	laborer	40	"
N	DeStefano Alvira—†	85	housewife	23	"
O	DeStefano Vincent	85	U S A	25	
P	*DeChristoforo Susan—†	87	housekeeper	69	"
R	Pesaturo Alfred	87	U S A	21	..
S	Pesaturo Mary—†	87	housewife	42	"
T	Pesaturo Salvatore	87	U S A	22	
U	Pesaturo Vincenzo	87	laborer	50	..
V	Caliccio Celeste—†	87	clerk	25	
W	Caliccio Constantina—†	87	housewife	47	"
X	Caliccio Cosmo	87	barber	52	
Y	Caliccio Frank	87	U S A	22	
Z	DePierro Joseph	87	laborer	44	

2120

A	DePierro Margaret—†	87	housewife	38	"
B	Ferrara James	89	laborer	60	
C	Ferrara Jennie—†	89	housewife	60	"
D	Ferrara Anna—†	89	"	33	
E	Ferrara Arthur	89	electrician	33	"
F	*Farro Andrew	89	laborer	65	
G	Farro John	89	painter	22	"
H	*Farro Rose—†	89	housewife	60	"
K	*Ingala Felecia—†	91	housekeeper	80	"
L	Gurliaccio Concetta—†	91	housewife	50	"
M	Gurliaccio Salvatore	91	laborer	61	
N	Cravotta Joseph	91	"	58	
O	Cravotta Rosaria—†	91	housewife	48	"
P	*Berlingiero Thomas	rear 91	retired	81	"
R	Grieco Alexander	" 91	laborer	20	
S	Grieco Carmella—†	" 91	housewife	36	"
T	Grieco Ercole	" 91	laborer	46	
V	Bua Frank	95	fishcutter	30	"
W	Bua Lena—†	95	housewife	28	"
X	Gaudino Anna—†	95	"	54	
Y	Gaudino Nicholas	95	laborer	64	

Chelsea Street—Continued

z	Gaudino Rose—†	95	shoewkr	30	here	

2121

A	Gaudino Stephen	95	U S A	23		
B	Botte Ernest	95	sander	28	"	
C	Botte Matilda—†	95	housewife	25	"	
E	Smith Benjamin	97	storekeeper	64	"	
F	Smith Eunice—†	97	stenographer	23	"	
G	Smith Evelyn—†	97	"	26		
H	Smith Florence—†	97	artist	32		
M	Cohen Jacob	99	storekeeper	48	"	
N	Cohen Jennie—†	99	housewife	52	"	
O	Ferrara Dominic	99	laborer	64	"	
P	Ferrara Joseph	99	steelwkr	34	"	
R	Ferrara Josephine—†	99	housewife	61	"	
S	Baptista Joseph	101	seaman	32	"	
T	Baptista Lucy—†	101	housewife	26	"	
U	Barbaro Fred	101	janitor	60	"	
V	Spinnazola Christopher	101	U S A	23	"	
W	Spinnazola Louis	101	shoewkr	35	"	
X	*Spinnazola Marie—†	101	housewife	56	"	
Y	Spinnazola Rose—†	101	packer	21	"	
Z	Conti Frank	101	molder	26	"	

2122

A	Conti Theresa—†	101	housewife	24	"	
B	*Monteleone Emmanuel	103	storekeeper	51	"	
C	Monteleone Mary—†	103	housewife	34	"	
D	Sforza Anthony	103	plumber	39	104 Chelsea	
E	Sforza Elvira—†	103	housewife	33	104 "	
F	Principe John	103	U S A	20	here	
G	Principe Joseph	103	shipfitter	26	"	
H	Principe Philomena—†	103	housewife	50	"	
L	Cioffi Esther—†	105	"	34	36 Gove	
M	Cioffi John	105	baker	32	36 "	
N	Trocano James	107	shoewkr	40	here	
O	Trocano Virginia—†	107	housewife	37	"	
P	Gelormini Costantino	107	machinist	47	"	
R	Gelormini Raphaela—†	107	housewife	46	"	
S	Smaldone Catherine—†	107	packer	25	Winchester	
T	*Smaldone Mary—†	107	housewife	65	here	
U	Smaldone Rosario	107	electrician	28	"	
V	Grasso Adeline—†	109	housewife	53	"	

14

Page	Letter	Full Name:	Residence, Jan. 1, 1945,	Occupation:	Supposed Age.	Reported Residence, Jan. 1, 1944. Street and Number:

Chelsea Street—Continued

	w	Grasso Lena—†	109	laundrywkr	22	here
	x	*Grasso Pasquale	109	molder	64	"
	y	Grasso Vincent	109	freighthandl'r	47	"
	z	Bonura Angelo	109	shoewkr	50	"
2123						
	a	Bonura Rose—†	109	stitcher	46	"
	b	DeGloria Joseph	109	U S N	32	
	c	DeGloria Margaret—†	109	housewife	26	"
	e	Cann Geraldine—†	113	welder	20	
	f	Hagstrom Charles	113	seaman	21	"
	g	Hagstrom Oliver	113	shipfitter	55	"
	h	Hagstrom Robert	113	U S A	22	
	k	Suarez Antonette—†	113	housewife	35	"
	l	Suarez Jose	113	machinist	41	"
	m	Lamattina Mary—†	113	housewife	40	"
	n	Lamattina Salvatore	113	mattressmkr	52	"
	o	Lamattina James	113	U S A	21	
	p	Lamattina Rita—†	113	housewife	49	"
	r	Lamattina Rocco	113	laborer	61	
	u	Parziale Carmen	123	electrician	21	"
	v	Parziale Mary—†	123	student	23	"
	w	Parziale Philomena—†	123	housewife	51	"
	x	Parziale Virginia—†	123	"	21	
	y	*Rosso Domenic	123	laborer	58	
	z	Cardinale Domenic	123	retired	67	
2124						
	a	Costanzo Andrew	123	U S A	23	
	b	Costanzo Giacomino—†	123	dressmaker	47	"
	c	Costanzo Placido	123	laborer	48	
	e	Infantino Joseph	125	supervisor	43	"
	f	Infantino Mary—†	125	housewife	44	"
	g	Rosa Theresa—†	125	"	69	
	l	Natali Gene	127	retired	62	
	m	Sgro Anthony	127	U S A	28	
	n	Sgro Joseph	127	storekeeper	60	"
	o	Sgro Rose—†	127	housewife	26	"
	p	Capolupo Concetta—†	127	factoryhand	30	"
	r	Pagliuso Antonette—†	127	"	25	"
	s	*Pagliuso Lucy—†	127	housewife	56	"
	t	Pagliuso Samuel	127	laborer	71	"
	u	*Malino Joseph	129	retired	70	"

Chelsea Street—Continued

v	DeFuria Lorenzo	129	salesman	48	298 Chelsea
w	DeFuria Margaret—†	129	laundrywkr	40	298 "
z	Magalitta Anthony	131	packer	32	here
	2125				
A	*Magalitta Mary—†	131	at home	77	"
B	DeFranzo Otino	131	blacksmith	49	"
c	*DeFranzo Theresa—†	131	housewife	59	"
D	Giacobelli Joseph	131	entertainer	36	"
E	Harrison Annie—†	131	housewife	75	"
F	Harrison Solomon	131	retired	76	
G	Giannusa Benedetto	133	presser	30	"
H	Giannusa Cecilia—†	133	housewife	29	"
K	*DeChristoforo Antonetta—†	133	"	56	
L	DeChristoforo Mary—†	133	packer	29	
M	DeChristoforo Nunzio	133	laborer	59	"
N	Palgia Louis	133	"	55	
o	Martalla Antonette—†	133	packer	29	
P	*Martalla Marie—†	133	housewife	68	"
R	Martalla Michael	133	electrician	28	"
s	*Martalla Nazzaro	133	retired	78	"
T	Palgia Frank	135	laborer	50	Rhode Island
U	Palgia Lena—†	135	housewife	47	"
v	Marro Benjamin	135	laborer	57	186 Paris
w	Marro Rose—†	135	housewife	55	186 "
x	Cefalo Mary—†	135	"	34	128 Chelsea
Y	Cefalo Vincent	135	U S N	32	128 "
z	Botte Elvira—†	137	clerk	20	here
	2126				
A	Botte Frank	137	"	56	
B	Botte Frank	137	U S A	22	
c	Botte Josephine—†	137	stitcher	30	"
D	Botte Matilda—†	137	"	29	
E	Botte Michael	137	U S N	32	
F	Botte Rachael—†	137	housewife	55	"
G	Botte Salvatore	137	U S A	24	"
H	Iarrobino Luigi	137	laborer	46	"
K	Iarrobino Pasqualina—†	137	housewife	40	"
L	Francis Joseph	139	U S A	24	
M	Francis Phyllis—†	139	stenographer	23	"
N	Lalli Concetta—†	139	housewife	47	"
o	Lalli Constantino	139	retired	56	"

P	DeFusco Albert	139	electrician	39	here
R	DeFusco Margaret—†	139	housewife	36	"
S	DeChristoforo Anthony	139	laborer	37	"
T	DeChristoforo Lucy—·†	139	housewife	40	"
U	Ciaburri Elizabeth—†	141	"	40	149 Chelsea
V	Ciaburri Joseph	141	meatcutter	51	here
X	Mari Arthur	141	U S N	25	"
Y	Mari Frank	141	chauffeur	54	"
Z	Mari Lillian—†	141	housewife	54	"

2127

A	Maragarona Rita—†	143	dipper	55	
B	Guiggio Helen—†	143	stitcher	24	" ·
C	Guiggio Joseph	143	laborer	64	"
D	Guiggio Julia—†	143	packer	21	"
E	Guiggio Louise—†	143	housewife	53	"
F	Siciliano Joseph	143	clerk	30	17 Cottage
G	Siciliano Rose—†	143	housewife	31	17 "
K	Briatico Antonio	145	chipper	51	here
L	Briatico Barbara—†	145	stitcher	23	"
M	Briatico Carmella—†	145	housewife	44	"
N	Briatico Vito	145	U S N	21	
O	Capolarello Angelo	145	operator	28	"
R	Stassano Anthony	147	polisher	63	
S	Stassano Dorothy—·†	147	floorwoman	22	"
T	Stassano Joseph	147	bailer	31	
U	Stassano Michael	147	U S A	25	
V	Stassano Leonora—†	147	housewife	31	"
W	Stassano Vito	147	plumber	33	"
X	DiGregorio Carmella—-†	147	stitcher	37	
Y	DiGregorio Joseph	147	laborer	45	

2128

A	Esposito Loretta—†	149	housewife	41	"
B	Esposito Salvatore	149	furrier	51	"
C	Galeota John	149	salesman	21	"
D	Galeota Vito	149	U S N	22	"
E	Gravallese Ida—†	149	housewife	29	132 Paris
F	Gravallese John	149	chauffeur	31	132 "
G	Mastrangelo Angelo	151	laborer	50	184 Marginal
H	*Mastrangelo Antonia—-†	151	housewife	46	184 "
K	*Mastrangelo Michael	151	laborer	24	184 "
L	*Iacomino Antonetta—†	151	housewife	36	59 Havre

1—21 · 17

Chelsea Street—Continued

M	Iacomino John	151	pipefitter	47	59 Havre
N	Silvestri Albert	151	brazier	23	here
O	Silvestri Antonio	151	painter	68	"
P	Silvestri John	151	electrician	21	"
R	*Silvestri Mary—†	151	housewife	65	"
S	Cipriano Annetta—†	153	inspector	25	"
T	Cipriano Armando	153	U S A	27	
U	*Cipriano Michelina—†	153	housewife	49	"
V	Cirpiano Nicholas	153	fireman	59	"
W	Cipriano Olga—†	153	stitcher	21	"
X	Cipriano Philip	153	woolworker	29	"
Y	Cipriano Sylvia—†	153	at home	23	"
Z	Durante Emily—†	155	housewife	34	"
	2129				
A	Durante Pasquale	155	machinist	32	"
B	DeStasi Frances—†	155	housewife	35	"
C	DeStasi Luca	155	clerk	47	
D	Durante Marco	155	laborer	50	"
E	*Durante Theresa—†	155	housewife	45	"
F	Capone Dominic	157	machinist	22	"
G	Capone Jeremiah	157	U S A	24	
H	*Capone Josephine—†	157	housewife	48	"
K	*Indingaro Caroline—†	157	"	74	"
L	Indingaro James	157	U S A	39	"
M	Indingaro Prisco	157	policeman	45	"
N	Constantino Angelina—†	157	housewife	24	"
O	Costantino Antonio	157	U S A	28	"
P	Digiulio Angelo M	157	laborer	59	"
R	Digiulio Anthony	157	U S A	27	"
S	Digiulio Josephine—†	157	shoewkr	20	"
T	Digiulio Michael	157	U S A	21	"
U	Digiulio Rose—†	157	housewife	51	"
V	Digiulio Yolanda—†	157	stitcher	26	"
W	*Weinberg Abraham	159	retired	45	
X	*Weinberg Katie—†	159	housewife	43	"
Y	*Kaplan Ethel—†	159	"	51	...
Z	*Kaplan Max	159	laborer	60	"
	2130				
A	Clayman Harry	159	retired	75	
B	*Clayman Jennie—†	159	housewife	51	"
C	Privitera Charles	161	laborer	63	"

Page.	Letter.	FULL NAME.	Residence, Jan. 1, 1945.	Occupation.	Supposed Age.	Reported Residence, Jan. 1, 1944. Street and Number.

Chelsea Street—Continued

D	Privitera Josephine—†	161	housewife	54	here
E	Privitera Santo	161	laborer	22	"
F	Goldstein Ida—†	161	at home	72	"
G	*Mandel Minnie—†	161	housekeeper	57	"
H	Pitari Catherine—†	161	housewife	59	"
K	Pitari Gabriel	161	retired	67	
L	Pitari Nicholas	161	brazier	25	..
M	Boncore Angelo	163	retired	83	..
N	Boncore Catina—†	163	housewife	73	"
O	Boncore Joseph	163	pressman	32	"
P	Mancuso Phyllis—†	163	stitcher	38	"
R	Boncore Guy	163	merchant	35	"
S	Boncore Josephine—†	163	housewife	33	"
U	Flamburis Annamaria—†	165	"	27	
V	Flamburis Dimitri	165	salesman	34	"
W	Neclette Phillipo	165	cleaner	74	115 Porter
Y	Yorks Abraham	167	plumber	64	here
Z	Yorks Rose—†	167	housewife	63	"
	2131				
C	Anzalone Antonio	169	electrician	29	"
D	Anzalone Carmela—†	169	housewife	25	"
E	Gambardella Carmella—†	169	"	51	165 Chelsea
F	Gambardella Mary—†	169	stitcher	23	here
G	Gambardella William	169	steward	52	165 Chelsea
H	*Giacchetti Joseph	169	shoemaker	43	165 "
L	Previte Antonio	171	retired	56	here
M	Previte Peter	171	U S N	22	"
N	Previte Sarah—†	171	housewife	51	"
O	DeStefano Joseph	171	baker	48	
P	DeStefano Marianna—†	171	housewife	45	"
R	DeStefano Rose—†	171	chauffeur	21	"
S	*Marrone Maria—†	171	at home	78	"
Y	LaRosa Benedecto	175	U S A	21	
Z	LaRosa Lena—†	175	housewife	58	"
	2132				
A	LaRosa Rosario	175	retired	70	"
B	Pungitore John	175	laborer	52	271 Chelsea
C	*Lee Thomas	177	laundrywkr	65	here
D	Vozzella Raffaele	177	laborer	46	"
E	*Eremka Catherine—†	177	housewife	56	"
F	Eremka John	177	pedler	55	

19

Chelsea Street—Continued

G	Lewshuk George	177	laborer	64	here
H	*Mazepa Serge	177	"	55	"
K	Hafey Edward	177	attendant	31	59 Charter
L	Hafey Margaret—†	177	housewife	26	59 "
N	Reece Lillian—†	179	housekeeper	35	here
O	Wood Frederick	179	salesman	50	"
P	Wood Margaret—†	179	at home	79	"
R	Eruzione Anna—†	179	laundrywkr	21	"
S	Eruzione Antonetta—†	179	packer	21	"
T	*Eruzione Concetta—†	179	housewife	59	"
U	Eruzione Eugene	179	U S M C	24	"
V	*Eruzione Michael	179	retired	60	
W	Eruzione Phyllis—†	179	packer	29	
X	Eruzione Vincent	179	U S A	25	
Y	Flynn John J	181	laborer	39	"
Z	O'Connell Clara L—†	181	housekeeper	51	"
	2133				
A	*Cohen Bessie—†	181	housewife	63	"
B	Cohen Celia—†	181	"	31	
C	Cohen Jack	181	printer	33	"
D	Hafey Albert	181	brazier	24	191 Chelsea
E	Hafey Joseph	181	U S A	29	149 Marion
F	Hafey Mabel—†	181	laundrywkr	51	191 Chelsea
G	Hafey Paul	181	U S A	26	149 Marion
H	Hafey Virginia—†	181	inspector	23	191 Chelsea
M	Ginensky Jacob H	183	salesman	59	here
N	Kaplan Jacob H	183	U S A	23	"
O	Kaplan Nellie—†	183	saleswoman	55	"
R	Tasha Catherine—†	185	at home	77	1 Savage ct
S	Iannelli Elaine—†	185	stitcher	25	here
T	Aannelli Ralph	185	U S N	26	"
V	Gorman Mary—†	187	laundrywkr	44	42 Gove
W	Gorman Michael	187	welder	45	42 "
X	Cardinale Antonio	187	U S A	20	here
Y	Cardinale Carmen	187	laborer	52	"
Z	Cardinale John	187	U S N	27	"
	2134				
A	Cardinale Katherine—†	187	at home	21	"
B	Cardinale Philomena—†	187	housewife	54	"
C	*Mondoro Joseph	189	laborer	69	4 Bremen pl
D	*Trepodi Joseph	189	retired	77	here

20

Chelsea Street—Continued

E	Trepodi Teresa—†	189	housewife	55	here
H	Colagioveni Donato	191	shoemaker	53	255 Marion
K	Colagioveni Louise—†	191	housewife	49	255 "
L	Colagioveni Nicholas	191	U S A	20	255 "
N	*Bellitti Catherine—†	193	housewife	45	here
O	Bellitti Mario	193	bottler	29	"
P	Bellitti Mary—†	193	inspector	26	"
S	Cohen Aaron M	195	shipper	20	"
T	Cohen Isadore	195	salesman	57	"
U	Cohen Tillie—†	195	housewife	54	"

Cottage Street

V	Soma John	114	U S A	30	here
W	Soma Michael	114	factoryhand	27	"
X	Soma Raffaelo	114	"	60	"
Y	*Soma Rose—†	114	housewife	60	"
Z	Altavilla John	114	welder	32	
	2135				
A	Altavilla Olympia—†	114	housewife	56	"
B	Altavilla Ralph	114	barber	61	
C	Rizzuti Dominic	114	chauffeur	31	"
D	Rizzuti Sarah—†	114	housewife	34	"
E	Fondini Angelo	114	factoryhand	30	"
F	Fondini Concetta—†	114	housewife	27	"
G	Gulla Mary R—†	114	"	33	
H	Gulla William R	114	brazier	33	

Frankfort Street

O	Stepanian Carmen	12	U S N	24	here
P	Stepanian Mary—†	12	housewife	23	"
R	Venezia Margaret—†	12	"	59	"
S	Venezia Michael A	12	laborer	69	
T	*Stellato Elaine—†	14	housekeeper	41	"
U	*DeMicco Elizabeth—†	14	housewife	41	"
V	DeMicco Gaetano	14	laborer	43	
W	Narda Anna—†	15	housewife	58	"
X	Narda Francezo	15	laborer	76	"
Y	Bartoli Edith—†	15	housewife	29	"
Z	Bartoli Joseph G	15	pedler	31	

2136
Frankfort Street—Continued

	Letter	Full Name	Residence	Occupation	Age	Reported Residence
	A	*Brunette Antonia—†	15	housewife	60	here
	B	Brunette Antonio	15	laborer	60	"
	C	Brunette Baldassare	15	"	25	"
	D	Kelly Lena A—†	15	housewife	23	206 Maverick
	E	Kelly William J	15	U S A	24	206 "
	F	Longo Laura—†	15	housewife	25	67 W Eagle
	G	Longo Louis	15	brazier	27	67 "
	H	Giosa Antonio	16	retired	60	here
	K	*Giosa Mary—†	16	housewife	52	"
	L	Giosa Pasquale	16	U S N	21	"
	M	Metrano Jennie—†	16	housewife	26	"
	N	Metrano Joseph	16	U S A	30	"
	O	Crisafulli Frank E	16	repairman	28	174 Cottage
	P	Crisafulli Josephine—†	16	housewife	25	174 "
	R	*Liberatore Restituta—†	16	housekeeper	56	here
	S	*Forte Josephine—†	16	"	30	193 London
	T	Preveti Angelo	16	U S A	24	193 "
	U	Albo Christaforo	16	retired	67	here
	V	Durante John	17	diesetter	28	"
	W	Durante Mary—†	17	housewife	24	"
	X	Durante Eugene	17	laborer	58	"
	Y	Durante Theresa—†	17	housewife	62	"
	Z	*Martino Frank	17	laborer	65	"

2137

	Letter	Full Name	Residence	Occupation	Age	Reported Residence
	A	Preno George	17	U S A	24	"
	B	Preno Nancy—†	17	housewife	24	"
	C	Mattaroccia Cecil	17	operator	34	"
	D	Mattaroccia Vera—†	17	housewife	28	"
	E	DeSimone Concetta—†	18	"	27	"
	F	DeSimone Fiore	18	candymaker	34	"
	G	Gaeta Adolfo	18	U S A	22	"
	H	Gaeta Matteo	18	laborer	63	"
	K	Gaeta Michael	18	U S A	20	
	L	*Gaeta Michelena—†	18	housewife	53	"
	M	Gaeta Thomas	18	milkman	28	"
	N	Cieri Dominic	18	shipfitter	35	"
	O	Cieri Theresa—†	18	housewife	27	"
	P	Pettine Amilcari	19	retired	84	
	R	Pettine Martha—†	19	housekeeper	48	"
	S	DePari Amelia—†	19	operator	35	"

22

Frankfort Street—Continued

T	Screnci Joseph S	19	chauffeur	27	here
U	Screnci Phyllis—†	19	housewife	27	"
V	*Ranieri Carmella—†	20	housekeeper	54	"
W	DePersis Guido	20	electrician	26	Cambridge
X	DePersis Theresa—†	20	housewife	22	223 Maverick
Y	*DeLorenzo Josephine—†	20	housekeeper	44	here
Z	*D'Amico Madalena—†	20	housewife	44	"
	2138				
A	*D'Amico Vincent	20	laborer	53	
B	LoCalzo Antonio	20	"	52	
C	LoCalzo Carmella—†	20	housewife	42	"
D	Capo Antonio	20	welder	33	
E	Capo Louise—†	20	housewife	31	"
F	DiMarzo Catherine—†	24	"	36	
G	DiMarzo Romolo	24	pipefitter	40	"
H	Fatalo Anthony	24	carpenter	29	"
K	Fatalo Rosaria—†	24	housewife	28	"
L	Giambrone Anthony	24	shoewkr	32	"
M	Giambrone Jennie—†	24	housewife	31	"
N	Giudetta Adeline—†	24	"	34	
O	Giudetta Frank	24	shoewkr	34	"
P	Magliano Rose—†	24	"	35	
R	Mattorocci Antonio	24	laborer	60	
S	Mattorocci Celia—†	24	housewife	54	"
T	Mattorocci Nancy—†	24	clerk	30	"
U	Mattorocci Vito	24	U S N	27	
V	Parisi Joseph	26	metalwkr	38	"
W	Parisi Rocco	26	U S A	32	
X	Sollitto Margaret—†	26	housekeeper	73	"
Y	Belmonte Alexander	26	laborer	50	"
Z	Belmonte Angelina—†	26	housewife	38	"
	2139				
A	Zicconi Frances—†	26	"	59	
B	Zicconi John B	26	retired	72	
C	*Lacoraza Anna—†	26	housewife	70	"
D	*Lacoraza Frank	26	laborer	62	
E	Lacoraza Philomena—†	26	operator	30	"
F	Maglione Frank	26	pressman	36	"
G	Maglione Josephine—†	26	housewife	37	"
K	DeBerto Concetta—†	32	at home	36	"
L	DeBerto Erminia—†	32	housewife	62	"

Frankfort Street—Continued

m	Vaccari Columbia—†	32	packer	39	here
n	Vaccari Lena—†	32	assembler	33	"
o	White Francis J	32	chauffeur	30	"
p	White Gilda—†	32	housewife	29	"
r	Felzani Anna—†	32	"	68	
s	Felzani Joseph	32	tailor	69	"
t	LaGreca Anthony J	32	die sinker	29	Somerville
u	LaGreca Olga E—†	32	housewife	26	"
v	*Fiore Josephine—†	34	"	52	here
w	Fiore Saverio	34	laborer	20	"
x	*Fiore Vincent	34	"	58	"
y	*Rainone Andre	34	retired	75	"
z	Velardo Clementine B—†	34	housewife	41	"
	2140				
a	Velardo Dominic C	34	supt	43	
b	Tamberini Assunta—†	34	housewife	29	"
c	Tamberini James	34	laborer	30	"
d	Venezia Margaret—†	34	housewife	22	"
e	Venezia Ralph	34	U S A	24	..
f	*Cimino Antoinetta—†	36	housewife	70	"
g	*Cimino Simon	36	laundryman	60	"
h	Donatelli Carmillo	36	bricklayer	39	Revere
k	Panasetti Philomena—†	36	housekeeper	62	"
m	Martinoli Emil	36	U S A	39	here
n	Martinoli Ida—†	36	housewife	65	135 Orleans
o	Martinoli Joseph	36	laborer	69	135 "
p	*Antonioli Elizabeth—†	36	housewife	35	here
r	*Antonioli James	36	laborer	42	"
s	Cioffi Anthony	36	"	27	"
t	Cioffi Mary—†	36	housewife	26	"
u	Filippone Antonio	38	laborer	64	"
v	Filippone Benjamin	38	U S A	22	
w	Filippone Samuel	38	mechanic	20	"
x	Filippone Theresa—†	38	housewife	46	"
y	Rossetti Marion—†	38	housekeeper	55	"
z	D'Asto Guido	38	laborer	22	"
	2141				
a	D'Asto Joseph S	38	"	45	
b	D'Asto Louise—†	38	housewife	44	"
c	*Bonanno Anne—†	38	"	64	
d	Bonanno Nicolo	38	retired	67	

Frankfort Street—Continued

	Letter	Full Name	Residence	Occupation	Age	Reported Residence
	E	Oliva Gilda—†	38	housewife	22	here
	F	Oliva Samuel	38	U S A	23	"
	G	Caserta Lena—†	38	housewife	26	"
	H	Caserta Vincent	38	U S A	32	
	K	Colangelo Alfred	40	"	26	
	L	Colangelo Carmella—†	40	housewife	43	"
	M	Calangelo Leonard	40	blacksmith	52	"
	N	Colangelo Mary—†	40	candywkr	23	"
	O	Colangelo Nicholas	40	teacher	27	"
	P	Colangelo Sarah—†	40	candywkr	21	"
	R	*Tontodonato Mary—†	40	housekeeper	70	"
	S	Stallone Giovannina—†	40	housewife	53	"
	T	Stallone Nicolo B	40	tailor	53	141 Cottage
	U	Schettino Angelo	40	cleanser	33	here
	V	Schettino Dorothy—†	40	housewife	27	"
	W	Storniello Mary—†	40	housekeeper	68	"
	X	DeMarco Angelo	42	chauffeur	33	198 Bremen
	Y	DeMarco Mary—†	42	housewife	35	198 "
	Z	D'Amico Anna R—†	42	"	58	here
		2142				
	A	D'Amico Gennaro	42	U S N	26	"
	B	Pisano Jennie—†	42	housewife	25	191 Porter
	C	Pisano Louis	42	shipfitter	27	191 "
	D	Lavognia Marcelino	42	laborer	57	here
	E	Lavognia Mary—†	42	housewife	58	"
	F	Piro Vincent	42	laborer	35	"
	G	Cafarelli Mary—†	44	housewife	33	"
	H	Cafarelli Romeo	44	electrician	37	"
	K	Ranieri Alfred	44	U S A	22	
	L	Ranieri Concetta—†	44	housewife	54	"
	M	Ranieri Jane—†	44	operator	24	"
	N	Ranieri Tito	44	laborer	59	
	O	*Zarrelli Fannie—†	44	housewife	47	"
	P	Zarrelli Paul	44	seaman	65	110 Gove
	R	Ranieri Helen F—†	44	housewife	28	here
	S	Ranieri Oscar	44	millwright	31	"
	T	Zinna Joseph	44	laborer	34	"
	U	Zinna Theresa—†	44	housewife	26	"
	V	Barry Helena—†	48	teacher	44	"
	W	Corcoran Margaret M—†	48	housekeeper	53	"
	X	Duffy Bridget—†	48	teacher	49	"

Page.	Letter.	Full Name.	Residence, Jan. 1, 1945.	Occupation.	Supposed Age.	Reported Residence, Jan. 1, 1944. Street and Number.

Frankfort Street—Continued

	Y	Dunning Mary—†	48	teacher	28	here
	z	Harrington Katherine—†	48	"	38	"
2143						
	A	Mannion Sheila A—†	48	"	44	
	B	McCarthy Mary—†	48	housekeeper	49	"
	C	Murray Margaret—†	48	teacher	34	"
	D	O'Donohue Nora—†	48	"	49	"
	E	Paone Albina—†	48	seamstress	45	"
	F	Ryan Mary J—†	48	teacher	23	"
	G	*Salvatore Maria A—†	48	seamstress	42	"
	H	Yennock Carmela—†	48	teacher	51	"
	L	Gallo Alphonse	56	driller	44	220 Havre
	M	Luongo Carmella—†	56	housewife	46	here
	N	*DelTergo Amelia—†	56	"	46	"
	O	DelTergo Michael	56	laborer	49	"
	P	Caliendo Amelia—†	56	housewife	56	"
	R	Caliendo Charles	56	barber	57	"
	S	*Salvato Amadeo	56	tailor	52	
	T	*Salvato Josephine—†	56	housewife	50	"
	U	Salvato Mary—†	56	WAVE	23	"
	V	*Cuillo Angelina—†	56	housewife	56	"
	W	*Cuillo Gennaro	56	retired	75	
	X	*Franzese Maria—†	58	housewife	66	"
	Y	Sinibaldi Joseph	58	U S N	22	
	z	Sinibaldi Lena—†	58	housewife	21	"
2144						
	A	Russo Anthony	58	laborer	41	"
	B	Russo Julia—†	58	housewife	36	"
	C	Pellecchia Josephine—†	58	"	25	58 Everett
	D	Pellecchia Peter	58	laborer	29	83 Lubec
	E	Celeste Leo	58	chauffeur	25	Winthrop
	F	Celeste Marie—†	58	housewife	22	"...
	G	DiLorenzo Edward	60	clerk	33	here
	H	DiLorenzo Kathleen—†	60	housewife	24	"
	K	Faretra Felicia—†	60	"	57	"
	L	Faretra Nicolo	60	retired	70	"
	M	Laezza John	60	laborer	43	"
	N	Laezza Josephine—†	60	clerk	20	
	O	*Laezza Victoria—†	60	housewife	42	"
	P	Todisco Joseph	60	retired	68	138 Havre
	R	Todisco Achilles	60	tailor	55	here

26

Page.	Letter.	Full Name.	Residence, Jan. 1, 1945.	Occupation.	Supposed Age.	Reported Residence, Jan. 1, 1944. Street and Number.

Frankfort Street—Continued

	s	Todisco Emma—†	60	operator	20	here
	t	*Todisco Fannie—†	60	housewife	52	"
	u	Iannuzzi Mary—†	62	"	33	"
	v	Iannuzzi Vito	62	laborer	36	
	w	Ciardina Biagio	62	operator	65	"
	x	Lopis Esther—†	62	housewife	27	Medford
	y	Lopis Nicholas	62	U S N	28	"
	z	*Porcella Constantina—†	62	housewife	56	here
		2145				
	a	Simole Joseph	62	U S N	27	
	b	Simole Mary—†	62	housewife	25	"
	d	DiGiacomandrea Carmen	63	welder	46	42 Frankfort
	e	DiGiacomandrea Elvira-†	63	housewife	35	42 "
	f	Samms Catherine—†	63	"	23	here
	g	Samms James C	63	electrician	27	"
	h	Samms James	63	retired	51	41 Carney ct
	k	Grillo Anna—†	63	housewife	32	here
	l	Grillo John	63	cutter	41	"
	m	*Paulicelli Emma—†	63	housewife	58	"
	n	Paulicelli John	63	cook	23	
	o	Paulicelli Marie R—†	63	packer	32	
	p	Ruggiero James	64	salesman	45	"
	r	Ruggiero Joseph	64	clerk	21	
	s	Ruggiero Josephine—†	64	housewife	41	"
	t	Ruggiero Mary—†	64	operator	20	"
	u	Ruggiero Nicholas	64	U S A	22	
	v	Jorda Herrico	64	laborer	61	
	w	Jorda Rose—†	64	housewife	59	"
	x	Grifone Mary—†	64	clerk	21	
	y	Grifone Michael	64	repairman	44	"
	z	Grifone Philomena—†	64	housewife	42	"
		2146				
	a	Famiglietti Antonio	64	ironwkr	28	"
	b	Famiglietti Joseph	64	laborer	54	
	c	Famiglietti Maria—†	64	housewife	56	"
	d	Cafazzo Antonio	64	bottler	51	
	e	Cafazzo Mary—†	64	housewife	44	"
	f	Aulino Salvatore	65	foreman	38	"
	g	Aulino Theresa—†	65	housewife	35	"
	h	*Aulino Theresa—†	65	"	62	
	k	Porcaro Antoinette—†	65	"	32	

Page.	Letter.	Full Name.	Residence. Jan. 1, 1945.	Occupation.	Supposed Age.	Reported Residence, Jan. 1, 1944. Street and Number.

Frankfort Street—Continued

	L	Porcaro Emilio	65	U S A	20	here
	M	Shettino Alessandro	65	"	27	"
	N	*Shettino Antonio	65	laborer	55	"
	O	*Shettino Virginia—†	65	housewife	52	"
	P	Bartolo Anna—†	65	"	42	
	R	Bartolo Joseph	65	laborer	45	"
	S	DeNisi Michelena—†	65	housewife	22	"
	T	DeNisi Vincent	65	U S A	22	"
	U	Gangi John	65	cabinetmaker	51	"
	V	Gangi Phyllis—†	65	housewife	41	"
	W	Gangi Rose—†	65	nurse	21	
	X	Giannasoli Jessie—†	66	housewife	24	"
	Y	Giannasoli Santino	66	U S A	25	
	Z	Minichiello Pasquale	66	laborer	56	"
		2147				
	A	Minichiello Rose—†	66	housewife	56	"
	B	Ricatti Jennie—†	66	packer	30	"
	C	*Ricatti Lucy—†	66	housewife	69	"
	D	*Dichio Antoinetta—†	66	"	46	
	E	Dichio Patrick	66	U S N	22	
	F	Mycko Edward	66	U S A	24	
	G	Mycko Lucy—†	66	housewife	25	"
	H	Peluso Raffaela—†	66	"	50	
	K	Peluso Raffaele	66	laborer	54	"
	L	LoConti Angelina—†	66	housewife	38	"
	M	LoConti Carmen	66	musician	21	"
	N	LoConti Frederico	66	presser	39	"
	O	LoConti Raffaele	66	laborer	47	"
	P	*Barrese Ermina—†	67	housekeeper	64	"
	R	DeBellis Helen—†	67	housewife	26	142 Everett
	S	DeBellis Vito	67	carpenter	34	142 "
	T	Ventre Adeline—†	67	housewife	34	here
	U	Ventre Christopher C	67	proprietor	45	"
	V	*Amore Assunta—†	67	housewife	61	"
	W	Amore Joseph	67	U S A	21	"
	X	Amore Matteo	67	laborer	61	"
	Z	Metta Carmella—†	68	housewife	59	"
		2148				
	A	Metta Nicholas	68	U S A	29	"
	B	Metta Samuel	68	laborer	61	"
	C	*Annese Amelia—†	68	housewife	36	"

28

Frankfort Street—Continued

D	Annese Joseph	68	laborer	36	here
E	DiChiara Josephine—†	68	housewife	39	"
F	DiChiara Thomas	68	rigger	42	"
G	Bucci Albert	68	U S A	22	
H	Bucci Antonio	68	laborer	59	
K	Bucci Arnold	68	boilermaker	26	"
L	*Bucci Mary—†	68	housewife	59	"
M	DiSante Helen—†	68	"	27	130 Bremen
N	DiSante Santo	68	presser	33	130 "
O	Monterisi Madelina—†	68	housewife	58	here
P	Bellofatto Concetta—†	69	"	44	"
R	Bellofatto Louis	69	tailor	51	"
S	Bucci Avidio	69	laborer	46	
T	Grasso Delia—†	69	housekeeper	50	"
U	Rizzo Jennie—†	69	housewife	33	"
V	Rizzo Joseph	69	laborer	38	
W	Straccio Ferdinand	69	"	70	
X	Scimone Joseph, jr	69	U S C G	23	"
Y	Scimone Loretta—†	69	housewife	23	"
Z	Matarazzo Amato	70	laborer	45	120 Orleans
	2149				
A	Farinola Ida—†	70	stitcher	23	here
B	Farinola Jennie—†	70	housewife	52	"
C	Farinola Salvatore	70	laborer	61	"
D	Annese Antoinetta—†	70	housewife	38	"
E	Annese Antonio	70	painter	50	
F	Schena Antonio	70	shipfitter	50	"
G	Schena Rose—†	70	housewife	45	"
H	Gasbarro Arthur	70	U S A	24	
K	Gasbarro Dominic	70	finisher	57	"
L	Gasbarro Helen—†	70	clerk	22	
M	Gasbarro Robert	70	U S N	20	"
N	Gasbarro Rubina—†	70	housewife	52	"
O	Bertulli Enzo	70	U S A	23	
P	Bertulli Louise—†	70	housewife	22	"
R	Petrillo Frank	70	laborer	61	
S	Petrillo Rose—†	70	housewife	60	"
T	Mootrey Angelina—†	71	"	35	"
U	Mootrey James	71	operator	38	"
V	Simonelli Angelo	71	guard	63	
W	Simonelli Irene—†	71	stitcher	21	"

Frankfort Street—Continued

x	Simonelli Louise—†	71	stitcher	23	here
y	Simonelli Raphaela—†	71	housewife	57	"
z	*Terino Clementina—†	72	"	82	"

2150

a	*Terino Vincenzo	72	retired	75	
b	*Caso Frances—†	72	housewife	65	"
c	Falanga Clara—†	72	"	29	"
d	Falanga Leo	72	electrician	29	"
e	DellaCroce Amelia—†	72	housewife	51	"
f	DellaCroce Frank	72	welder	20	
g	DellaCroce Gerardo	72	shoewkr	54	"
h	Muino Gerard	72	seaman	43	"
k	Muino Velia—†	72	housewife	32	"
l	Napolitano Antoinetta—†	72	"	48	
m	Napolitano Frank	72	laborer	48	"
p	DeLaglio Joseph	74	U S A	28	"
r	DeLaglio Lucy—†	74	housewife	30	"
n	Ruggiero Frances—†	74	"	65	
o	Ruggiero John	74	U S A	25	
s	Ruggiero Ferdinando	74	shipper	38	"
t	Ruggiero Helen—†	74	housewife	29	"
u	*Dattoli Bella—†	74	"	45	
v	Dattoli John	74	baker	55	
w	Dattoli Marie—†	74	operator	21	"
x	Dattoli Rose—†	74	clerk	22	"
y	Mercurio Antoinetta—†	74	housewife	25	"
z	Mercurio William	74	laborer	29	"

2151

a	Ruggiero Rose—†	74	housewife	26	"
b	Ruggiero Salvatore	74	cutter	30	"
c	Catena Michael	76	retired	70	
d	Piscitelli Angela—†	76	housewife	30	"
e	Piscitelli Michael	76	laborer	39	"
f	Rossetta Elizabeth—†	76	stitcher	20	"
g	Rossetta Mary—†	76	housewife	56	"
h	Rossetta Michael	76	laborer	67	"
k	Sinopoli Mary—†	76	housewife	37	8 Lamson
l	Sinopoli Michael	76	laborer	39	8 "
m	Gaeta Mario	76	cutter	27	here
n	Gaeta Rosa—†	76	housewife	22	"
o	DiTamasso Anthony	76	laborer	27	"
p	DiTamasso Mary—†	76	housewife	26	"

Page:	Letter.	FULL NAME.	Residence, Jan. 1, 1945.	Occupation.	Supposed Age.	Reported Residence, Jan. 1, 1944. Street and Number.

Frankfort Street—Continued

	R	Cérbone Eugene	78	U S N	30	Somerville
	S	Cerbone Hilda—†	78	housewife	27	"
	T	Cafano Mary—†	78	"	47	here
	U	Cafano Peter	78	U S M C	23	"
	V	Basilesco Potenzo	78	tailor	47	"
	W	*Pantuosco Palmera—†	78	housewife	69	"
	X	Pantuosco Peter	78	retired	73	"
	Y	Maniglia Leo	78	barber	42	132 Gove
	Z	Maniglia Rose—†	78	housewife	32	132 "

2152

	A	Scialabba Anthony	78	engineer	33	here
	B	Scialabba Josephine—†	78	housewife	27	"
	C	Carrillo Dominic	78	retired	67	"
	D	Carrillo Veneranda—†	78	housewife	52	"
	E	Polsonetti Augustus	80	welder	23	
	F	Polsonetti Rita—†	80	housewife	23	"
	G	DiGregorio James	80	U S A	27	
	H	DiGregorio Lucille—†	80	housewife	26	"
	K	*Murano Andre	80	retired	63	
	L	Murano Biagio	80	U S A	23	
	M	Murano Mario	80	"	21	
	N	Murano Raymond	80	"	28	
	O	*Murano Susan—†	80	housewife	61	"
	P	Covalucci Americo	80	presser	20	
	R	Covalucci Joseph	80	laborer	59	"
	S	Covalucci Philomena—†	80	stitcher	25	"
	T	Lucibello Andrew	80	baker	42	
	U	Lucibello Philomena—†	80	housewife	48	"
	V	*Caiazza Antonio	80	shoewkr	59	"
	W	*Caiazza Mary—†	80	housewife	52	"
	X	Caiazza Thomas	80	U S A	32	

2153   Gould's Court

	A	Thornton Alice M—†	6	housewife	54	here
	B	Thornton Ruth B—†	6	secretary	24	"
	C	Thornton Thomas	6	boilermaker	69	"

Gove Street

	D	Priore Frank	60	electrician	28	here
	E	Priore Josephine—†	60	housewife	29	"

Gove Street—Continued

F	D'Amico Theresa—†	60	housewife	21	here
G	Morgante Anthony	60	longshoreman	28	"
H	Morgante Josephine—†	60	housewife	25	"
K	Claudio Joseph	62	chauffeur	35	Newton
L	Claudio Justin	62	retired	77	2 Garden Court
M	Filipponi Joseph	62	rigger	29	here
N	Grosso Susan—†	62	housewife	62	"
O	Bisignani Richard.	62	attorney	34	"
P	*Bisignani Rose—†	62	housewife	71	"
R	Lalicata James	64	U S A	20	
S	*Lalicata Paul	64	laborer	61	"
T	*Lalicata Rose—†	64	housewife	52	"
U	Ferragamo Angelo	64	carpenter	33	"
V	Ferragamo Jean—†	64	housewife	26	"
W	Lalicata Josephine—†	64	"	29	
X	Delmuto Alfred	66	U S N	20	
Y	*Delmuto Frank	66	carpenter	51	"
Z	Delmuto Liberato	66	U S A	21	"

2154

A	Delmuto Mary—†	66	clerk	21	"
B	*Delmuto Philomena—†	66	housewife	48	"
C	DiFazio Antonio	66	laborer	65	"
D	DiFazio Peter	66	plumber	38	"
E	Ligiero Marie—†	66	housewife	31	"
F	Ligiero Orlando	66	metalwkr	33	"
G	Bassetti Benjamin	128	clergyman	34	New York
H	Cervone Gerard	128	cook	55	here
K	Cesario Victor.	128	clergyman	30	"
L	Checchia Dominic	128	"	40	"
M	Linkus Louis	128	"	29	Pennsylvania
N	Nix Christopher	128		53	here
O	*Picchisso Guido	128		67	Cambridge
P	Simone Romano	128.	"	62	here
R	Covino Eleanor—†	132	packer	34	"
S	Covino Sabato	132	U S A	35	"
T	Tricomi Jennie—†	132	housewife	50	"
U	Tricomi Josephine—†	132	at home	32	"
V	Tricomi Peter	132	barber	60	
W	Tricomi Sadie—†	132	inspector	22	"
X	Muldoon Eleanor—†	132	housewife	26	"
Y	Muldoon Joseph	132	longshoreman	28	"
Z	Ferraro Angelo	132	U S A	31	"

Page.	Letter.	FULL NAME.	Residence, Jan. 1, 1945.	Occupation.	Supposed Age.	Reported Residence, Jan. 1, 1944. Street and Number.

2155

Gove Street—Continued

A	Ferraro Helen—†	132	housewife	31	here
. B	Danna Concetta D—†	132	"	25	45 Mt Hope
c	Danna James J	132	welder	29	192 Cottage
E	*Simone Jerry	134	retired	72	here
G	Plagenza Frank	134	laborer	60	"
H	Plagenza Girolama—†	134	housewife	52	"
K	*Solazzo Angelina—†	134	"	50	"
L	Solazzo Concetta—†	134	floorwoman	25	"
M	Solazzo Frank	134	U S A	27	
O	Mosca Antonio	134	carpenter	31	"
P	Mosca Lena—†	134	housewife	28	"

Lubec Street

R	DelloRusso Angelina—†	58	housewife	50	here
S	DelloRusso Gaetano	58	proprietor	52	"
T	Intraversato Joseph	58	laborer	68	"
U	*Intraversato Marie—†	58	housewife	64	"
V	Delisio Adelaide—†	58	"	50	
W	Delisio Felice	58	laborer	52	
X	Delisio Nicholas	58	U S A	23	
Y	Ferreira Joseph J, jr	58	"	21	
Z	Ferreira Mary—†	58	stitcher	21	"

2156

A	Errico Edith—†	58	textiles	30	
B	*Errico Marie—†	58	at home	72	"
C	Colarusso Helen—†	58	housewife	35	"
D	Colarusso John	58	longshoreman	38	"
E	Azzelino Frances—†	58	operator	21	"
F	Azzelino Joseph	58	laborer	60	
G	Azzelino Luciano	58	U S A	23	
H	Azzelino Philomena—†	58	trimmer	59	"
K	Riley Bridget—†	60	stitcher	28	184 Cottage
L	Riley John J	60	seaman	28	here
M	Lazzara Carmella—†	60	housewife	63	"
N	Lazzara Joseph	60	laborer	70	"
O	Lazzara Salvatore	60	U S N	26	
P	Badamo Anthony	60	chipper	44	"
R	*Badamo Josephine—†	60	housewife	40	"
S	Rossetti Joseph	60	chauffeur	35	59 Lubec
T	*Rossetti Nancy—†	60	housewife	35	59 "

1—21

33

Lubec Street—Continued

	Letter	Full Name	Residence	Occupation	Age	Reported Residence
	u	Musi Anthony	60	rigger	60	here
	v	*Musi Assunta—†	60	housewife	62	"
	w	Giunta Ida—†	60	"	43	"
	x	Giunta Philip	60	candymkr	50	"
	z	Dellaria Concetta—†	62	housewife	53	"
2157						
	A	Dellaria Jennie—†	62	operator	20	"
	B	Dellaria Vito	62	candy wkr	65	"
	c	Dellaria Vito	62	U S A	22	
	D	*Gambino Anna—†	62	housewife	68	"
	E	Gambino Catherine—†	62	candymaker	34	"
	F	Gambino Louis	62	painter	44	"
	G	LaRosa Benedetto	62	shoewkr	57	"
	H	LaRosa Salvatore	62	U S A	27	
	K	LaRosa Santa—†	62	operator	28	"
	L	Terrazzano Francesco	62	rigger	45	"
	M	Terrazzano Grace—†	62	housewife	30	"
	N	Martin Dorothy—†	62	stitcher	20	"
	O	Martin Joseph	62	foreman	52	"
	P	Martin Mary—†	62	housewife	51	"
	R	Minerva Angelina—†	64	assembler	22	"
	s	*Minerva Caroline—†	64	housewife	48	"
	T	Minerva Joseph	64	U S A	26	..
	U	Minerva Nicholas	64	"	24	
	v	Minerva Nunzio	64	machinist	54	"
	w	LaCorte Carmella—†	64	seamstress	29	146 Gove
	x	LaCorte Patrick	64	electrician	27	163 Cottage
	Y	Barressi Giannino	64	laborer	35	here
	z	Barressi Marie—†	64	housewife	28	"
2158						
	A	DeGregorio Clementina—†	64	"	46	
	B	DeGregorio Vincent	64	glasswkr	50	"
	c	Cibene Anna—†	64	housewife	51	"
	D	Cibene Silvino	64	finisher	54	"
	E	Spitaleri Marie—†	64	winder	23	"
	F	Spitaleri Nicholas	64	U S M D	23	"

Marion Street

	Letter	Full Name	Residence	Occupation	Age	Reported Residence
	G	Silva Mary C—†	247	housewife	65	here
	H	Tassoni Grace—†	247	"	36	"

Marion Street—Continued

K	Tassoni Ventura	247	welder	52	here
L	*Papasodora Catherine—†	247	housewife	65	"
M	Papasodora Lucia—†	247	wrapper	23	"
N	Marmaud Francis W	249	U S A	24	
O	Marmaud Margaret M–†	249	stitcher	20	"
P	Marmaud Marie A—†	249	housewife	44	"
S	Carnabuci Caroline R—†	249	waitress	33	"
T	Carnabuci Jennie—†	249	candywkr	36	"
U	Carnabuci Peter	249	retired	66	
V	Capobianca Ralph	251	clerk	28	
W	Capobianca Raphaela—†	251	housewife	27	"
X	Manna Donaline—†	251	operator	28	"
Y	Manna Joseph	251	laborer	35	
Z	Scherpici Anthony	251	U S A	28	

2159

A	*Schepici Concetta—†	251	housewife	66	"
B	*Schepici Stellario	251	laborer	58	"
C	Interbartolo Anthony G	251	collector	22	"
D	*Interbartolo Rose—†	251	housewife	57	"
E	*Montecalvo Angelina—†	253	"	66	"
F	Montecalvo George	253	U S M C	22	"
G	Montecalvo Josephine—†	253	factoryhand	24	"
H	Simili Angelina—†	253	housewife	44	"
K	Simili Francesco	253	laborer	53	"
L	Montecalvo Angela M—†	253	packer	42	
M	Montecalvo Marciano	253	foreman	45	"
N	Buccheri Mary—†	255	housewife	33	23 Bennington
O	Buccheri Paul	255	welder	33	23 "
P	Falgone Fannie—†	255	stitcher	21	182 "
R	Falgone Michael	255	laborer	49	182 '
S	Falgone Philippa—†	255	housewife	46	182 "
T	Palumbo Mary—†	255	at home	25	182 "
U	Gaudino Anna M—†	255	housewife	24	here
V	Gaudino Jóseph L	255	U S N	25	"

Maverick Street

Z	Martino Dominic	172	tailor	66	here

2160

A	*Martino Mario V	172	"	25	..
B	*Martino Raffaela—†	172	housewife	62	"

Maverick Street—Continued

C	Danna Benjamin	172	U S A	24	here
D	Danna Lillian—†	172	housewife	24	"
E	Giannoccaro Almina—†	172	"	60	"
F	Giannoccaro Antonio	172	mechanic	26	"
G	Giannoccaro Florence—†	172	attendant	28	"
H	Giannoccaro Lola—†	172	saleswoman	21	"
K	Giannoccaro Romeo	172	welder	20	"
L	*Lambiase Henry S	174	photographer	55	"
M	Villalli Theresa—†	174	housewife	58	"
N	Villalli Thomas	174	tailor	62	
O	*Bertuccio Concetta—†	174	housewife	60	"
P	Bertuccio John	174	U S A	20	
R	Bertuccio Rose—†	174	housewife	24	"
S	Bertuccio Salvatore	174	laborer	22	"
U	Cadelo Catherine G—†	178	housewife	71	"
V	Cadelo John	178	framemaker	62	"
W	Falardo Carmen	178	machinist	44	"
X	Falardo Mary—†	178	housewife	41	"
Y	Villella Filomena—†	178	housekeeper	64	"
Z	DiCamillo Dominic	180	laborer	45	131 Orleans

2161

A	Gulla Antonio	180	laborer	58	here
B	Gulla Mary—†	180	operator	22	"
C	Gulla Vincenza—†	180	"	48	"
D	Rizzo Joseph	180	chauffeur	31	"
E	Rizzo Rose—†	180	housewife	30	"
G	LaCorte Angeline—†	186	operator	20	"
H	LaCorte John	186	U S A	24	
K	LaCorte Lucy—†	186	housewife	49	"
L	LaCorte Michael	186	tailor	59	
M	LaCorte Michalina—†	186	inspector	22	"
N	LaCorte Philip	186	U S A	21	
O	DiNuccio Alfonso	186	shoewkr	40	"
P	DiNuccio Eleanor—†	186	housewife	36	"
R	DiSimone Pasqualina—†	186	sorter	40	"
U	Ferrante Gaetano M	188	U S A	23	"
V	*Ferrante Josephine—†	188	housewife	57	"
W	*Ferrante Sebastian	188	laborer	69	"
X	Gusto Joseph D	188	U S A	33	
Y	Ierardi Carmella—†	190	housewife	54	"
Z	Ierardi Dominic	190	engineer	32	"

2162
Maverick Street—Continued

A	Ierardi Joseph	190	musician	35	here
B	Rinaldi Anthony	190	chipper	41	"
C	Rinaldi Bridget—†	190	checker	26	"
D	Rinaldi Lucy—†	190	winder	29	
E	Rinaldi Anthony	190	U S N	21	
F	Rinaldi Antoinette—†	190	housewife	46	"
G	Rinaldi Bridget—†	190	bookkeeper	22	"
H	Rinaldi Dominic A	190	custodian	55	"
L	Capozzi Antonio	192	guard	57	
M	Capozzi Concetta—†	192	housewife	56	"
N	Capozzi Frank	192	U S A	21	
O	Capozzi James	192	"	21	
P	Turco Antonio	192	blacksmith	52	"
R	Turco Elvena—†	192	housewife	49	"
S	Turco Phyllis—†	192	clerk	22	
T	Turco Salvatore	192	U S A	20	
U	Costa Anthony	194	printer	33	
V	Costa Mildred—†	194	housewife	35	"
W	D'Adario Matteo	194	machinist	36	"
X	D'Adario Rose—†	194	housewife	34	"
Y	Argenzio Angelina—†	194	"	39	
Z	Argenzio Louis	194	painter	45	"
	2163				
A	Lena Angelo	rear 194	laborer	55	"
B	Lena Joseph	" 194	polisher	21	"
C	Lena Thomasina—†	" 194	housewife	45	"
D	*Melchionda Carmella—†	196	"	57	
E	Melchionda Florence—†	196	shoewkr	25	"
F	*Melchionda Ralph	196	retired	63	
G	Luongo Alfredo	196	shipper	23	"
H	Luongo Amelia—†	196	housewife	52	"
K	Luongo Antoinetta—†	196	dressmaker	27	"
L	Luongo Carmella—†	196	"	25	
M	Luongo Marino	196	retired	55	
N	Sardellitti Jennie—†	196	housewife	56	"
O	Sardellitti Joseph	196	U S A	27	
P	Sardellitti Louise—†	196	at home	36	"
R	Sardellitti Ralph	196	electrician	26	"
S	Magaletta Albert J	198	longshoreman	26	137 Eutaw
T	Magaletta Edith I—†	198	housewife	26	137 "

Maverick Street—Continued

	U	Carnicelli Anthony	198	presser	25	Winthrop
	V	Carnicelli Sabina—†	198	housewife	23	here
	w	*Nalieri Jennie—†	198	"	52	"
	X	Nalieri Michael	198	laborer	24	"
	Y	Piccarello Andrew	198	"	63	
	Z	Piccarello Bernardo	198	U S A	36	"
2164						
	A	Piccarello Diamante—†	198	clerk	27	..
	B	Piccarello Lena—†	198	"	20	...
	C	Piccarello Mary—†	198	housewife	58	"
	D	Parillo Jennie—†	200	"	41	
	E	Parillo Mary—†	200	inspector	22	"
	F	Tirello Mary—†	200	housewife	41	"
	K	DiPietro Concezio	204	proprietor	60	"
	L	DiPietro Mary—†	204	dressmaker	25	"
	M	DiPietro Ralph	204	U S A	27	"
	N	DiPietro Rose—†	204	housewife	58	"
	O	DiPietro Silvio	204	teacher	31	"
	R	Laulette Raphael	206	retired	87	"
	S	Bonfiglio Santo	206	chipper	62	"
	T	Bonfiglio Vincenza—†	206	housewife	58	"
	U	*Cino Anna—†	206	"	66	"
	V	Cino William	206	laborer	22	"
	W	Diocio Anthony	206	chauffeur	26	"
	X	Diocio Josephine—†	206	housewife	33	"
	Y	D'Agostino Angelo	208	repairman	64	"
	Z	D'Agostino Anthony	208	electrician	31	"
2165						
	A	D'Agostino Gloria—†	208	nurse	22	"
	B	D'Agostino Louise—†	208	stitcher	37	"
	C	D'Agostino Nunciata—†	208	housewife	57	"
	D	Pellecchia Jean—†	208	"	37	"
	E	Pellecchia Joseph	208	driller	38	"
	F	Costanza Mary—†	208	stitcher	42	135 Cottage
	G	Costanza Probei—†	208	shoewkr	21	135 "
	H	Costanza Ralph	208	U S A	20	135 "
	K	Contestabile Attilio	208	machinist	31	here
	L	Contestabile Margaret—†	208	housewife	29	"
	M	Romano Anthony	208	assembler	35	"
	N	Romano Margaret—†	208	housewife	34	"

o	Lawford Fred W	210	chauffeur	52	here
p	Lawford Lillian M—†	210	physician	56	"
r	Vinacci Eleanor—†	210	cook	35	"
s	Vinacci Ferdinando	210	retired	69	
t	Ristaino Lillian—†	210	housewife	23	"
u	Ristaino Michael	210	shipfitter	28	"
v	*Mondina Rose—†	210	housekeeper	62	Woburn
w	Stone Laura—†	210	waitress	38	here
x	Guiffreda Joseph	210	pipefitter	36	"
y	Guiffreda Mary—†	210	packer	29	"
z	Cerulli Nina—†	212	housewife	42	"

2166

a	Cerulli Victor	212	shoewkr	64	"
b	Fulco Antoinetta—†	212	housewife	48	"
c	Fulco John	212	ironwkr	49	"
d	*Conte Jennie—†	212	housewife	67	"
e	Conte Joseph	212	shoemaker	65	"
f	Schiavone Peter	212	U S A	20	
g	*Petrone Celeste—†	212	housewife	60	"
h	*Petrone Luigi	212	candywkr	60	"
k	Finocchio Anna—†	212	housewife	48	"
l	Finocchio Frank	212	laborer	63	"
m	Finocchio Guido	212	U S A	22	"
n	Finocchio Joseph	212	"	21	"
o	Caton Frances—†	226	housewife	42	"
p	Caton Frances M—†	226	operator	21	"
r	Caton Joseph	226	inkmaker	43	"
s	Campiglia Katherine—†	226	milliner	43	
t	DiStasio Louis	226	checker	41	
u	DiStasio Pauline—†	226	housewife	36	"
v	*Lomanno Marie—†	226	at home	80	140 Marginal
w	DeMayo Cassie—†	228	saleswoman	34	here
x	DeMayo Charles	228	proprietor	59	"
y	DeMayo Edward	228	clerk	31	"
z	DeMayo Elizabeth—†	228	housewife	55	"

2167

b	DeDonato Ralph	230	agent	29	
c	DeDonato Theresa—†	230	housewife	27	" '
d	Costa Albert	230	U S N	24	"
e	Costa Andrew	230	draftsman	28	"

Page.	Letter.	FULL NAME.	Residence, Jan. 1, 1945.	Occupation.	Supposed Age.	Reported Residence, Jan. 1, 1944. Street and Number.

Maverick Street—Continued

	F	Costa Jennie—†	230	factoryhand	30	here
	G	Costa Joseph	230	laborer	39	"
	H	Costa Rose—†	230	housewife	66	"
	K	Fuccillo Catherine—†	230	stitcher	35	"
	L	Leonardi Angelina—†	230	housewife	58	"
	M	Leonardi Eugene	230	clerk	22	
	N	Leonardi Nicholas	230	laborer	70	"
	R	Pinto Antonio T	236	salesman	39	"
	S	*Pinto Rose—†	236	housewife	69	"
	T	*Miano Carmella—†	236	"	61	
	U	*Miano Eugene	236	laborer	58	"
	V	*Miano Luigi	236	domestic	65	"
	W	Miano Olga—†	236	stenographer	28	"
	X	LaRaia Frances—†	236	housewife	40	230 Maverick
	Y	Santoro Angelina—†	236	"	25	119 Cottage
	Z	Santoro Bernardino	236	pipefitter	29	119 "

2168

	A	Costanza Katherine—†	238	housewife	46	here
	B	Costanza Pasquale	238	physician	45	"
	C	Costanza Linda—†	238	clerk	33	"
	D	Costanza Mary—†	238	housewife	67	"
	E	Costanza Pasquale A	238	retired	84	"
	F	Giordano Henry	238	pipefitter	42	"
	G	Giordano Rose—†	238	housewife	35	"

McKay Place

	H	DeFlorio Blanche—†	2	housewife	43	here
	K	DeFlorio Joseph	2	laborer	49	"
	L	DeFlorio Phyllis—†	2	beautician	21	"
	N	Terraglia Alfonso	2	rigger	69	
	O	Ferullo Amelia—†	2	housekeeper	81	"
	P	Venezia Anthony	2	laborer	38	"
		Messina Eleanor—†	9	saleswoman	43	"
	S	Messina Peter	9	timekeeper	48	"
	T	Kenneally Anna—†	9	housewife	37	"
	U	Kenneally James F	9	inspector	39	"
	V	Galasso Florence—†	9	saleswoman	35	"
	W	Galasso Joseph	9	metalwkr	36	"
	X	Zicconi Grace—†	9	housewife	30	"
	Y	Zicconi James	9	laborer	34	"

z	DiFlummuri Annette—†	9	housewife	30	150 Putnam
	2169				
A	DiFlummuri Patrick	9	U S N	35	150 "

Orleans Street

B	*Conte Giovanni	101	laborer	64	162 Breman
C	Modugno Carmella—†	101	housewife	36	here
D	Modugno Carmen	101	electrician	44	"
E	Alberti Frances A—†	101	solderer	25	"
F	Alberti Frank P	101	U S A	27	..
G	*Alberti Philip	101	boilermaker	55	"
H	Falanga Joseph	101	proprietor	63	"
K	*Falanga Mary—†	101	housewife	62	"
L	Cuillo Phillip	102	waiter	54	
M	Marcatante Concetta—†	102	housekeeper	53	"
N	Trainer Bertha—†	102	housewife	31	"
O	Trainer Percy	102	pipefitter	47	"
S	Poto James V	103	machinist	46	"
T	Poto Louis D	103	U S A	20	
U	*Poto Mary F—†	103.	housewife	39	"
V	Santoro Madeline C—†	103	"	50	..
W	Santoro Madeline R—†	103	saleswoman	23	"
X	Santoro Nicholas	103	laborer	56	
Y	Santoro Nicholas J	103	U S A	21	
	2170				
D	*Collace Mary—†	106	housekeeper	64	"
E	Braccio Michael	106	laborer	65	..
F	Braccio Philomena—†	106	housewife	57	"
G	Viola Ethel M—†	107	"	28	295 Havre
H	Viola Frank T	107	pipecoverer	32	295 "
K	*DiBenedetta Mary—†	107	packer	64	here
L	Lombardi Joseph A	107	chauffeur	28	"
M	Lombardi Josephine M—†	107	housewife	27	"
P	Denaro Joseph	107	electrician	42	"
R	Denaro Rose—†	107	housewife	31	"
S	Masello Joseph	107	retired	71	
U	Amoroso Louise R—†	107	housewife	38	"
V	Amoroso Rosario	107	painter	49	
W	DiMattia Nove N	107	welder	39	
X	DiMattia Rose M—†	107	housewife	33	"
Y	Teni Vincenzo	107	laborer	51	"

Page	Letter	Full Name	Residence, Jan. 1, 1945.	Occupation	Supposed Age	Reported Residence, Jan. 1, 1944. Street and Number.

Orleans Street—Continued

	z	Terramagra Frank	108A	welder	31	here
2171						
	A	Terramagra Sylvia—†	108A	housewife	30	"
	B	Lespasio Michael	108A	shipfitter	27	"
	C	Lespasio Nicholina—†	108A	housewife	31	"
	D	DeBianco Alfonso	108A	retired	75	
	E	DeBianco Rose—†	108A	housewife	84	"
	F	Melillo Mary—†	108A	"	25	"
	G	Melillo William	108A	U S N	27	
	H	*Miano Rose—†	108A	factoryhand	55	"
	K	Miano Santo	108A	laborer	58	"
	L	Casaburi Addoloratta—†	109	housewife	60	133 Orleans
	M	Casaburi Nicholas	109	laborer	61	133 "
	N	Casaburi Antonio	109	machinist	33	here
	O	Casaburi Florence—†	109	housewife	31	"
	P	Bonasoro Antoinetta J—†	109	"	20	"
	R	Bonasoro Salvatore S	109	electrician	20	"
	S	Cammarata Anthony	111	barber	31	
	T	Cammarata Margaret—†	111	housewife	29	"
	U	Ceruolo Anthony	111	retired	64	"
	V	Ceruolo Arthur	111	U S M C	21	"
	W	Ceruolo John	111	retired	37	
	X	Ceruolo Josephine—†	111	at home	31	"
	Y	Ceruolo Maria—†	111	housewife	60	"
	Z	Ceruolo Ella—†	111	"	27	
2172						
	A	Ceruolo Pasquale	111	welder	25	
	B	Monica Josephine—†	113	housewife	40	"
	C	Monica Sabino F	113	chauffeur	41	"
	D	Martino George F	113	U S A	24	97 Prince
	E	Spera Antoinette—†	113	candywkr	32	97 "
	F	Spera Thomas	113	U S A	35	97 "
	G	LePore John	113	shoemaker	30	here
	H	LePore Viola—†	113	housewife	28	"
	K	Romano Josephine—†	115	stitcher	22	"
	L	Romano Paul R	115	U S N	23	
	M	Siracusa John C	115	U S M C	24	"
	N	*Maggio Vito	115	retired	71	
	O	Tripoli Antonina—†	115	housewife	46	"
	P	Tripoli Frank	115	proprietor	57	"
	R	Tripoli Mary A—†	115	stenographer	28	"

Orleans Street—Continued

	s	Tripoli Mildred V—†	115	beautician	25	here
	T	*Tripoli Salvatore	115	candymaker	55	"
	u	Tripoli Anthony J	115	receiver	20	"
	v	Tripoli Frank C	115	manager	23	"
	w	Federico Josephine—†	115	housewife	27	"
	x	Federico Riziero	115	engineer	25	"
	y	Doria Ralph	115	U S N	21	"
	z	Durante Elizabeth—†	115	housewife	38	"
2173						
	A	Durante Joseph	115	shoewkr	46	"
	B	Durante Salvatore A	115	U S A	22	"
	c	Sotera Salvatore	115	electrician	44	"
	D	Sotera Vita—†	115	housewife	36	"
	E	*Beaulieu Joseph	115	weaver	54	
	F	Hay Albert	115	laborer	43	"
	G	Maggio Anthony L	115	cutter	34	
	H	Maggio Grace—†	115	housewife	30	"
	K	Mancuso Frank	117	retired	75	
	L	*Mancuso Grace—†	117	housewife	59	"
	M	Mancuso Jennie—†	117	dressmaker	23	"
	N	Marotta Joseph	117	laborer	55	
	o	Marotta Luigiano	117	U S A	22	
	P	Marotta Mary—†	117	housewife	27	"
	R	*Marotta Rose—†	117	wrapper	52	"
	s	Marotta Rose A—†	117	nurse	24	
	T	Marotta Samuel	117	U S A	30	
	u	Capone Agnes—†	117	housewife	33	"
	v	Capone Alfred	117	attendant	54	"
	x	Cornacchio Palma—†	117	housewife	54	"
	y	Cornacchio Peter	117	U S A	22	
	z	Cornacchio Tulio	117	laborer	51	
2174						
	A	Lunetta Frances—†	117	housewife	59	"
	B	Lunetta Joseph	117	U S A	26	
	c	Lunetta Salvatore	117	carpenter	61	"
	D	Celata Alfonso	117	pipefitter	41	"
	E	Celata Ernesta—†	117	housewife	42	"
	F	Plunder Albert	117	laborer	29	
	G	Plunder Donald	117	U S M C	21	"
	H	Plunder Gerard	117	painter .	61	
	K	*Plunder Pasqualina—†	117	housewife	62	"

Page.	Letter.	Full Name.	Residence, Jan. 1, 1945.	Occupation.	Supposed Age.	Reported Residence, Jan. 1, 1944. Street and Number.

Orleans Street—Continued

	L	Sandoro Mary—†	117	housewife	27	here
	N	Prezutti Mario	118	tailor	55	"
	O	D'Allesandro Antonio	118	laborer	42	"
	P	D'Allesandro Carmella–†	118	housewife	40	"
	R	*Spinazzola Mary—†	119	packer	56	"
	S	Pepi Lorenzo	119	riveter	29	"
	T	Pepi Phyllis—†	119	housewife	28	"
	U	DeSimone Charles	125	manufacturer	39	"
	V	Magnasco Giovanni S	129	blacksmith	70	"
	W	Magnasco Josephine—†	129	dressmaker	34	"
	X	Magnasco Mary—†	129	operator	28	"
	Y	Magnasco Nicholas	129	U S A	36	
	Z	Magnasco Rose D—†	129	housewife	59	"
		2175				
	A	Magnasco Victor R	129	shipper	25	"
	B	Guinta Angelo S	129	U S A	24	
	C	Guinta Pasqualina M—†	129	housewife	23	"
	D	*Magnasco Florence—†	129	"	55	
	E	Magnasco Georgina—†	129	operator	25	"
	F	Magnasco Jennie—†	129	candymaker	27	"
	G	Magnasco Rosildo	129	shoemaker	64	"
	H	Gallo Margaret—†	129	housewife	30	"
	K	Martinoli Beatrice—†	129	"	23	
	L	Martinoli Octavius	129	musician	27	"
	P	Armata Antonette—†	131	stitcher	26	20 Frankfort
	R	Armata John	131	machinist	27	here
	S	Puzzo Mary—†	131	dipper	59	"
	T	Puzzo Michael	131	laborer	61	"
	U	Siciliano Joseph	131	U S A	33	
	V	Siciliano Josephine—†	131	candymaker	32	"
	W	D'Agresta Angelina—†	131	housewife	47	"
	X	D'Agresta Elizabeth—†	131	operator	20	"
	Y	D'Agresta Gaetano	131	laborer	54	"
	Z	Armata Gasper	131	candymaker	61	"
		2176				
	A	Armata Vincenza—†	131	housewife	59	"
	B	Giardina Angelo	131	machinist	29	"
	C	Giardina Frances—†	131	housewife	36	"
	D	Zona Angelina—†	132	"	47	
	E	Zona Jennie—†	132	beautician	25	"
	F	Zona Philip	132	barber	53	

Page.	Letter.	Full Name.	Residence, Jan. 1, 1945.	Occupation.	Supposed Age.	Reported Residence, Jan. 1, 1944. Street and Number.

Orleans Street—Continued

	G	Zona Concetta—†	132	beautician	22	here
	H	Zona Frank	132	U S A	27	"
	K	LaFaucia Josephine—†	132	factoryhand	55	"
	L	Connors Lillian M—†	133	housekeeper	44	253 Prescott
	M	Trask Austin	133	riveter	44	253 "
	N	Trask Mary—†	133	housewife	35	253 "
	S	Correale Esther—†	133	packer	32	here
	T	Correale James	133	painter	35	"
	V	Messina Carmella—†	135	housewife	34	"
	W	Messina Vincent	135	stitcher	43	"
	X	Marcone Frank	135	cutter	22	
	Y	Marcone Lena—†	135	housewife	23	"
	Z	Marondo Pasquale	135	laborer	50	
2177						
	A	Eppilito Jean—†	135	housewife	26	"
	B	Eppilito Michael	135	welder	29	"
	C	Lunetta Lena—†	135	housewife	21	"
	D	Lunetta Nicholas J	135	carpenter	29	"
	E	Cozzo Helen—†	137	factoryhand	26	"
	F	Cozzo Jennie—†	137	"	40	
	G	Cozzo John	137	retired	75	"
	H	Cozzo Lena—†	137	housewife	67	"
	K	Bonfiglio Carmen	137	electrician	35	"
	L	Bonfiglio Minnie—†	137	housewife	29	"
	M	Mazzoni Nicholas	137	longshoreman	28	"
	N	Mazzoni Rose—†	137	housewife	28	"
	O	Speziale Angelo	137	laborer	60	
	P	Speziale Elvira—†	137	factoryhand	21	"
	R	Speziale Grace—†	137	housewife	48	"
	S	Speziale Pasquale	137	U S A	23	"
	T	Lanzo Concetta—†	137	housewife	31	"
	U	Lanzo Joseph J	137	machinist	35	"

Percival Place

	X	Giaquinto Vincenzo	1	retired	85	240 Bremen
	Y	*Graziano Nicolo	1	"	70	here
	Z	Leone John B	1	laborer	60	92 Bremen
2178						
	A	*Pettenichio Luigi	1	"	61	here
	C	Vertucci Dominic	2	retired	60	"

Percival Place—Continued

D	Butchard Joseph H	2	U S N	31	106 Orleans
E	Butchard Virginia—†	2	housewife	28	106 "
F	Colarusso Frank	2	carpenter	37	here
G	Colarusso Mary—†	2	housewife	37	"
H	*Bisciotti John	3	laborer	60	"
K	*Lespasio Louise—†	3	at home	80	"
L	Lespasio Vito	3	retired	78	
M	Chiardi Valentino	3	laborer	48	"

Porter Street

O	Venuti Frances—†	119	housewife	35	here
P	Venuti Frank	119	carpenter	38	"
R	Damelio Antonio	119	U S A	24	"
S	Damelio Carmella—†	119	housewife	56	"
T	Damelio Dominic	119	U S A	26	
U	Damelio Gennaro	119	laborer	22	"
V	Damelio Joseph	119	U S M C	21	"
W	Damelio Michael	119	laborer	63	"
X	D'India Agatha—†	130	housekeeper	53	"
Y	Porrazzo Edward	134	mechanic	23	286 Sumner
Z	Porrazzo Mary F—†	134	housewife	23	164 Chelsea
	2179				
A	Amesani Frances—†	136	"	39	here
B	Amesani Joseph	136	barber	45	"
C	Quartarella Maria—†	136	housekeeper	29	"
D	Staito Joseph	136	shoemaker	61	"
E	Staito Mary—†	136	housewife	61	"
F	Capozzi Crescenzio	138	U S A	23	
G	Capozzi Nicoletta—†	138	housewife	56	"
H	Capozzi Nicoletta—†	138	factoryhand	25	" .
K	Capozzi Tebia	138	cutter	21	"
L	DeMarco Louis	138	U S A	23	
M	DeMarco Phyllis—†	138	housewife	23	"
N	Nigro Angelina—†	138	factoryhand	21	"
O	Nigro Concetta—†	138	housekeeper	32	"
P	Nigro Nicholina—†	138	housewife	54	"
R	Nigro Rosario	138	laborer	60	"
S	Lonardo John	140	U S A	31	
T	Lonardo Michelina—†	140	housewife	29	"
U	Mannke Josephine—†	140	"	35	

v	Mannke Robert	140	mechanic	40	here
w	Cetrullo Elizabeth—†	142	housewife	45	"
x	Cetrullo Frank	142	laborer	53	"
y	Cetrullo Frank	142	U S N	21	
z	Pastore Americo	142	cashier	21	
	2180				
a	Pastore Lena—†	142	housewife	56	"
b	Pastore Mary—†	142	factoryhand	27	"
c	Pastore Vincent	142	laborer	59	

Ward 1–Precinct 22

CITY OF BOSTON

LIST OF RESIDENTS
20 YEARS OF AGE AND OVER

(NON-CITIZENS INDICATED BY ASTERISK)
(FEMALES INDICATED BY DAGGER)

AS OF

JANUARY 1, 1945

THOMAS F. SULLIVAN, *Chairman*
FREDERIC E. DOWLING, *Secretary*
WILLIAM A. MOTLEY, JR.
FRANCIS B. McKINNEY
EVERETT R. PROUT

Listing Board.

CITY OF BOSTON 〰 PRINTING DEPARTMENT

2200
Antrim Street

A	Colleary James	2	laborer	49	here	
B	Colleary Jessie—†	2	housewife	42	"	
C	Labarge Amos	2	U S A	32	"	
D	Pennell Amelia—†	2	housewife	52	"	
E	Pennell Augustus	2	retired	87		
F	Pennell Orelia—†	2	housewife	79	"	
H	Gagliardi Joseph	5	U S A	28	"	
K	Gagliardi Mary—†	5	housewife	28	"	
L	Gagliardi Mary—†	5	"	48		
M	Gagliardi Salvatore	5	laborer	53	"	
N	Scopa Mary—†	5	housewife	29	"	
O	Scopa Roland	5	chipper	37	"	
P	Martoramo Ernest	7	pipefitter	37	140 Saratoga	
R	Martoramo Gladys—†	7	housewife	30	here	
S	Martoramo Anthony	7	U S A	26	"	
T	Martoramo Elizabeth—†	7	housewife	60	"	
U	Martoramo Jean—†	7	stitcher	24	"	
V	Martoramo Michael	7	retired	74	"	
W	Martoramo Richard	7	U S A	21		
X	Martoramo Sylvia—†	7	factoryhand	29	"	
Y	Maglio Domenic	7	steamfitter	46	"	
Z	Maglio Ida—†	7	housewife	40	"	

2201

A	O'Shea Annie—†	8	"	63		
B	O'Shea Irene—†	8	secretary	29	"	
C	O'Shea James	8	janitor	64	"	
D	Caprio Agnes—†	8	housewife	35	"	
E	Caprio Charles	8	pipefitter	38	"	
F	Donahue David J	8	clerk	45		
G	Sheehan James	8	U S N	39		
H	Weber Anna—†	8	clerk	21		
K	Weber Barbara—†	8	housewife	48	"	
L	Weber Karl	8	machinist	60	"	
M	Zimmerman Agnes—†	9	saleswoman	28	"	
N	Zimmerman Frank	9	U S A	32		
O	Graham John J	9	foreman	54	"	
P	Graham John P	9	machinist	20	"	
R	Graham Theresa—†	9	housewife	54	"	
S	Landrigan Michael J	9	collector	63	"	

Antrim Street—Continued

T	Camacho Louis	9	U S A	29	Winthrop
U	Camacho Theresa—†	9	factoryhand	28	"
V	O'Brien Edith—†	9	"	30	here
W	Celona Frank	10	polisher	57	"
X	Celona Orazio	10	U S A	22	"
Y	*Celona Rosaria—†	10	housewife	55	"
Z	Catapano Antoinette—†	10	"	45	
	2202				
A	Catapano Frank	10	tailor	50	
B	Celona Frank J	10	teacher	32	"
C	*Celona Róse—†	10	housewife	31	"
D	Calicchio Albert	11	carpenter	53	"
E	Calicchio Diana—†	11	spinner	27	
F	*Calicchio Lucy—†	11	housewife	53	"
G	Calicchio Michael	11	seaman	20	
H	DiPesa Alex	11	U S A	28	
K	DiPesa John	11	seaman	25	
L	DiPesa Michael	11	U S A	26	
M	DiPesa Patrick	11	laborer	51	
N	DiPesa Phoebe—†	11	housewife	48	"
O	Silveria Maria—†	11	at home	82	"
P	Powers Dorothy—†	12	clerk	45	
R	Powers Edward	12	inspector	51	"
S	Ford Arthur	12	milkman	47	"
T	Ford Lillian—†	12	housewife	42	"
U	Ford Raymond	12	factoryhand	20	"
V	*Palandro Cecil	12	retired	57	
W	Palandro Esther—†	12	waitress	30	"
X	*Palandro Martha—†	12	housewife	56	"
Y	Palandro Rose—†	12	beautician	26	"
Z	Palandro Ruby—†	12	clerk	21	
	2203				
A	Palandro Ruth—†	12	clerk	22	"
B	DiLorenzo Genaro	14	presser	30	
C	DiLorenzo Mary—†	14	housewife	32	"
D	Martorano Arthur	14	metalwkr	39	"
E	Martorano Edna—†	14	housewife	27	"
F	Blasi Arthur	14	laborer	55	"
G	Blasi Arthur M	14	U S A	22	
H	Blasi Nerina—†	14	clerk	55	

Page.	Letter.	FULL NAME.	Residence, Jan. 1, 1945.	Occupation.	Supposed Age.	Reported Residence, Jan. 1, 1944. Street and Number.

Ashley Street

	Letter.	FULL NAME.	Residence	Occupation.	Age	Reported Residence
	K	DeLaurie Amelia—†	12	housewife	50	here
	¹K	DeLaurie Josephine—†	12	stitcher	20	"
	L	DeLaurie Peter	12	U S N	23	"
	M	Carfagna Helen—†	12	housewife	36	"
	N	Carfagna Henry	12	chauffeur	36	"
	O	Santarpio Edward	18	operator	40	"
	P	Santarpio Theresa—†	18	housewife	38	"
	R	Pucillo Anthony	18	brazier	46	"
	S	Pucillo Elizabeth—†	18	housewife	43	"
	T	Pucillo Gerald	18	U S A	20	
	U	Palladino Antonio	18	U S N	37	"
	V	Palladino Jean—†	18	dressmaker	32	"
	W	*Palladino Joseph	18	laborer	67	"
	X	Palladino Josephine—†	18	clerk	22	
	Y	Palladino Nunzio	18	shipfitter	36	"
	Z	Staffier Anthony	22	auditor	35	"
		2204				
	A	Staffier Jennie—†	22	housewife	33	"
	B	DiLorenzo Jennie—†	22	"	21	223 London
	C	DiLorenzo Lawrence	22	presser	26	here
	D	DiLorenzo Nora—†	22	housewife	57	"
	E	DiLorenzo Thomas	22	tailor	59	"
	F	DiLorenzo Thomas, jr	22	U S A	22	"
	G	Cadden Elizabeth—†	22	shipfitter	22	Natick
	H	O'Brien Cornelius	22	laborer	56	here
	K	O'Brien John J	22	U S A	30	"
	L	O'Brien Margaret—†	22	housewife	55	"
	M	O'Brien Thomas L	22	electrician	24	"
	N	Feinberg Adele—†	26	housewife	30	"
	O	Feinberg Morton	26	chauffeur	30	"
	P	Perrone Ida—†	26	housewife	31	"
	R	Perrone John V	26	foreman	38	"
	S	Spagnolo Anna—†	26	bookkeeper	20	"
	T	Spagnolo Annabil	26	shoemaker	48	"
	U	Spagnolo Dorothy—†	26	housewife	42	"
	V	Smith Frances—†	32	"	22	"
	W	Smith Ralph	32	U S A	23	"
	X	Mandra Joseph	32	bartender	53	"
	Y	Mandra Mary—†	32	housewife	43	"
	Z	Mandra Stephen	32	U S A	24	"

2205

Ashley Street—Continued

A	*Mosarra Anna—†	32	dressmkr	65	here
B	Scalata Angelina—†	32	housewife	39	"
C	Scalata Joseph	32	barber	47	"
D	Cafarelli Frances—†	32	housewife	25	"
E	Cafarelli Louis	32	U S N	26	
F	Messina Jennie—†	32	housewife	52	"
G	Messina Samuel	32	painter	54	
H	Boncordo Joseph	36	machinist	29	"
K	Boncordo Marie—†	36	housewife	28	"
L	Masterangelo Carmella—†	36	"	26	
M	Masterangelo Dominic	36	pipefitter	37	"
N	Trevor Helen—†	36	housewife	42	"
O	Trevor Lawrence	36	steamfitter	49	"
P	Franzese Jennie—†	36	housewife	40	"
R	Franzese William	36	bartender	42	"
S	Capillo Anna—†	40	housewife	38	"
T	Capillo Rosario	40	buyer	38	
U	Capillo Assunta—†	40	florist	26	
V	Capillo Carl	40	accountant	35	"
W	Capillo Pauline—†	40	housewife	60	"
X	Burton Charles F	40	engineer	50	"
Y	Burton Gerald F	40	U S N	21	
Z	Burton Lawrence J	40	U S C G	22	"

2206

A	Burton Margaret E—†	40	housewife	52	"
B	Noonan Margaret—†	40	"	83	
C	Gaglini Angelina—†	44	"	34	
D	Gaglini George F	44	printer	38	
E	Staffieri Angelo	44	tailor	45	"
F	Staffieri Olympia—†	44	housewife	38	"
G	Staffieri Ralph	44	U S A	20	
H	Inello Emily L—†	44	housewife	21	"
K	Inello Frank J	44	U S C G	22	"
L	Vozzella Angelo	44	fabricmaker	26	"
M	Vozzella Antoinetta—†	44	housewife	50	"
N	Vozzella Celestino	44	blacksmith	53	"
O	Statuti John	49	retired	74	"
P	Statuti Louise—†	49	housewife	66	"
R	Statuti Vincent	49	salesman	38	"

Page.	Letter.	FULL NAME.	Residence, Jan. 1, 1945.	Occupation.	Supposed Age.	Reported Residence, Jan. 1, 1944. Street and Number.

Ashley Street—Continued

	s	Maffei Eleanor—†	49	housewife	31	here
	t	Maffei Vincent	49	adjuster	32	"
	u	Siragusa James J	52	physician	49	"
	v	Siragusa K Paula—†	52	housewife	45	"
	w	Sweeney Mary A—†	52	"	74	
	x	Cimmino Emma—†	70	"	41	
	y	Cimmino Joseph	70	chef	49	
	z	Battles Mary E—†	87	teacher	43	"
		2207				
	a	Connolly Helen T—†	87	"	25	"
	b	Demhurst Eileen M—†	87	"	28	Brookline
	c	Finan Dorothy P—†	87	housekeeper	31	here
	d	Kelleher Mary E—†	87	teacher	41	"
	e	McLaughlin Kathleen I—†	87	"	56	"
	f	McMurrer Mary R—†	87	"	48	
	g	Morris Mary F—†	87	"	49	
	h	Murphy Catherine A—†	87	"	39	
	k	Nagle Julia C—†	87	"	53	"
	l	Walsh Agnes D—†	87	"	38	Revere
	m	Donahue Ethel M—†	91	operator	40	here
	n	Malloy William P	91	finisher	54	"
	o	Miller Joseph	91	brakeman	42	"
	p	Miller Mary E—†	91	clerk	45	
	r	Damiano Anna C—†	91	teacher	27	"
	s	Damiano Mary A—†	91	housewife	50	"
	t	Damiano Peter J	91	shoemkr	53	"
	u	Connell Louis	135	chauffeur	58	"
	v	Connell Rose—†	135	housewife	56	"
	w	Bertucelli Jessie—†	135	buttonmkr	37	"
	o	Bertucelli Placido	135	retired	69	"
	p	Bertucelli Vincenza	135	housewife	65	"
	r	l				
	s	S				

Bennington Street

	t	Rich Ardine—†	728	housewife	64	here
	u	**2208**				
	a	Rich Eleanor—†	728	stitcher	37	"
	b	Colatrella Jennie—†	728	housewife	48	"
	c	Colatrella Josephine—†	728	brusher	22	"
	d	Colatrella Marie—†	728	bookkeeper	24	"
	e	Balduzzi Mario	728	mechanic	49	"

6

Page.	Letter.	FULL NAME.	Residence, Jan. 1, 1945.	Occupation.	Supposed Age.	Reported Residence, Jan. 1, 1944. Street and Number.

Bennington Street—Continued

	F	Balduzzi Natalie—†	728	housewife	45	here
	H	*Anzalone Mary—†	732	"	66	"
	K	Anzalone Philip C	732	oiler	75	"
	L	Green Josephine—†	732	stitcher	29	"
	M	Anzalone Filippa—†	732	housewife	49	"
	N	Anzalone Frank	732	stitcher	21	"
	O	Anzalone Joseph	732	U S M C	22	"
	P	Anzalone Placito	732	storekeeper	56	"
	R	Anzalone Charles	732	U S A	24	
	S	Anzalone Frank	732	storekeeper	58	"
	T	Anzalone Joseph	732	chauffeur	26	"
	U	Feeley Claire—†	734	secretary	21	"
	V	Feeley Edward	734	fireman	49	"
	W	Feeley Lorraine—†	734	clerk	25	
	X	Feeley Mary—†	734	housewife	49	"
	Y	Gibson Helen—†	734	"	32	
	Z	Hollander Edna—†	734	stenographer	21	"

2209

	A	Hollander Gertrude—†	734	inspector	24	"
	B	Hollander Helen—†	734	housewife	55	"
	C	Cadigan Catherine—†	734	at home	74	"
	D	Cadigan Hilda—†	734	housewife	28	855 Saratoga
	E	Cadigan John L	734	chauffeur	41	here
	F	Brady John	736	longshoreman	25	"
	G	Brady Mary—†	736	housewife	46	"
	H	Brady Mary A—†	736	bookkeeper	21	"
	K	Doyle Gladys—†	736	housewife	37	"
	L	Doyle Walter	736	foundrywkr	36	"
	M	Calla Concetta—†	736	housewife	24	"
	N	Calla Silvio	736	metalwkr	30	"
	O	*Giannino Lucy—†	736	stitcher	43	"
	P	*Prato Marie—†	736	"	53	
	R	Kingsbury Alice V—†	738	housewife	70	"
	S	Kingsbury Herbert J	738	operator	67	"
	T	Doyle Catherine—†	738	at home	67	"
	U	Doyle Cecile V—†	738	tel operator	44	"
	V	Doyle Edward F	738	retired	50	
	W	Doyle Eleanor D—†	738	secretary	38	"
	X	Sullivan Alyce—†	738	clerk	40	"
	Y	Stewart John J	738	U S N	35	
	Z	Stewart John P	738	engineer	63	"

2210
Bennington Street—Continued

A	Stewart Mary—†	738	housewife	63	here
B	Aloise Domenic	740	pressman	31	"
C	Aloise Rose—†	740	housewife	28	"
D	Delaney Catherine M—†	740	"	47	"
E	Delaney Thomas M	740	checker	47	"
F	Curran Edith C—†	740	housewife	43	"
G	Curran Patrick J	740	metalwkr	44	"
H	Venedam Alice—†	742	housewife	54	1059 Saratoga
K	Venedam Charles W	742	carpenter	54	1059 "
L	Venedam James A	742	U S A	24	1059 "
M	Venedam John R	742	"	26	1059 '
N	Stewart David H	742	"	31	1059 "
O	Venedam Bertha—†	742	housewife	33	Medford
P	Venedam Joseph A	742	engineer	31	"
R	Cook Cecil L	742	shipper	42	here
S	Cook Katherine M—†	742	housewife	38	"
T	Cook Elizabeth—†	744	at home	73	"
U	Cook James J	744	U S A	37	"
V	McAteer Margaret—†	744	housewife	41	"
W	McAteer Thomas	744	laborer	41	"
X	Clogston Abbie L—†	744	housewife	70	"
Y	Clogston Frank A	744	retired	67	"
Z	Monahan Bridget—†	744	housewife	74	"

2211

A	Monahan John J	744	shipfitter	45	"
B	Monahan Richard	744	court officer	46	"
C	Merola Augustine E	746	shoeworker	33	"
D	Merola Clara—†	746	housewife	29	"
E	Beale Benjamin T	746	retired	81	
F	Beale Benjamin T, jr	746	clerk	47	
G	Beale Ellen G—†	746	housewife	72	"
H	Beale Gertrude E—†	746	clerk	44	
K	Beale John F	746	shipfitter	43	"
L	Camarda Alessandra—†	746	at home	20	"
M	Camarda Antoinette M—†	746	cashier	24	"
N	Camarda Jasper F	746	cutter	28	
O	Camarda Louise—†	746	housewife	46	"
P	Camarda Salvatore C	746	U S A	22	
T	Arena Salvatore	960	welder	36	
U	Arena Theresa—†	960	housewife	35	"

Page.	Letter.	FULL NAME.	Residence, Jan. 1, 1945.	Occupation.	Supposed Age.	Reported Residence, Jan. 1, 1944. Street and Number.

	v	Merola Ascanio	960	shoewkr	59	here
	w	Merola Corinne—†	960	inspector	27	"
	x	Merola Elvira—†	960	housewife	55	"
	y	Impeduglia Dora—†	960	"	27	
	z	Impeduglia Salvatore	960	welder	31	
2212						
	a	Dacey Concetta—†	962	operator	34	"
	b	Dacey Timothy	962	repairman	34	"
	c	DiAnni John B	962	foreman	39	"
	d	DiAnni Mary—†	962	housewife	36	"
	e	Albanese Josephine—†	962	"	40	
	f	Albanese Mary—†	962	student	20	"
	g	Albanese Sabino	962	shoemaker	43	"
	h	Polsonetti Augustino	964	foreman	35	"
	k	Polsonetti Ethel—†	964	housewife	33	"
	l	Polsonetti Charles	964	operator	46	"
	m	Polsonetti Fannie—†	964	tailor	38	
	n	Polsonetti Margaret—†	964	housewife	22	"
	o	Polsonetti William	964	U S A	21	
	p	Polsonetti Luigi	964	tailor	59	
	r	Polsonetti Olympai—†	964	housewife	60	"
	s	Burke Catherine—†	966	"	50	"
	t	Burke George F	966	carpenter	61	"
	u	DiFiori Frank	966	barber	56	
	v	Forrey Cathérine—†	966	housewife	78	"
	w	Forrey John	966	retired	78	
	x	Napier Helen—†	966	housewife	52	"
	y	Napier Stephen	966	lineman	56	"
	z	Groppi Anacleto	968	U S A	39	
2213						
	a	Groppi Mildred—†	968	housewife	26	"
	b	Ciccolo Joseph	968	musician	36	"
	c	Ciccolo Providence—†	968	manager	34	"
	d	Ciccolo Santa—†	968	housewife	65	"
	e	Ciccolo Sophie—†	968	operator	30	"
	f	Famolare Anthony	968	U S A	33	
	g	Famolare Mary—†	968	housewife	38	"
	h	Tollo Clara—†	970	"	31	30 Barnes av
	k	Tollo Joseph	970	shipfitter	29	30 "
	l	Iannaccone Louise—†	970	housewife	31	963 Saratoga
	m	Iannaccone Pellegrino	970	machinist	31	963 "

Bennington Street—Continued

N	DeFrancesco Frank	970	barber	55	here
O	DeFrancesco Grace—†	970	housewife	53	"
P*	DeMarco Josephine—†	972	tailor	37	"
R	DeMarco Sabino	972	clerk	39	"
S	Borsa Bridget—†	972	tailor	52	
T	Borsa Frederico	972	"	53	"
U	Fennell Ann—†	972	housewife	26	Cambridge
V	Fennell John	972	U S N	27	"
W	Picardi Aurelio	972	clerk	40	here
X	Picardi Jennie—†	972	housewife	37	"
Z	Indelicato George	976	B F D	37	"
	2214				
A	Indelicato Olympia—†	976	housewife	35	"
B	Frazier Doris—†	976	"	24	
C	Frazier Reed W	976	U S A	26	
D	Lafferty Florence—†	976	secretary	27	"
E	Pescatelli Mabel—†	976	assembler	46	"
F	Pescatelli Norma—†	976	operator	21	"
G	Berretta Theresa—†	976	at home	76	"
H	DeLorenza Louise—†	976	cleaner	50	"
O	Harrington John H	1004	retired	68	
P	Harrington Mary E—†	1004	housewife	57	"
R	Belange Pauline—†	1004	clerk	43	
U	Goulston Louis	1008	dentist	45	"
V*	DiBartolo Maria—†	1008	housewife	65	70 Boardman
W	Sacco Vincent J	1008	electrician	48	here
X	Sozio Anthony	1008	U S N	28	"
Y	Sozio Rose—†	1008	housewife	26	"
Z	DePalma Mary—†	1008	factoryhand	29	"
	2215				
A	DePalma Nancy—†	1008	housewife	58	"
B	Coscia Anthony	1008	electrician	26	"
C	Coscia Ethel—†	1008	housewife	24	"
D	Capillo Dominic V	1008	U S A	31	"
E	Capillo Orietta A—†	1008	operator	29	"
F	DePippo Concetta—†	1008	housewife	56	"
G	Murphy Henry J	1008	brazier	31	64 St Andrew rd
H	Murphy Phyllis—†	1008	housewife	21	84 Faywood av
K	Palladino Edward	1008	U S A	21	here
L	Palladino Josephine—†	1008	housewife	53	92 Faywood av
M	Palladino Rocco L	1008	U S N	24	here

10

Bennington Street—Continued

N	Gundersen Marie—†	1008	waitress	60	here
O	Armeta Anna—†	1008	operator	26	134 Gove
P	Bissett Annette—†	1008	housewife	24	134 "
R	Bissett Charles	1008	U S N	27	here
S	Russo Antonio	1008	laborer	46	"
X	McCarthy Florence A–†	1022	housewife	40	"
Y	McCarthy John L	1022	custodian	52	"
Z	McCarthy John L, jr	1022	U S N	20	
	2216				
A	Lottie Frank	1022	machinist	54	"
B	Lottie Nellie—†	1022	housewife	54	"
E	Bernardi Henry	1024	chauffeur	54	"
F	Buldine Dante	1024	engineer	32	14 Leyden
G	Buldine Florence—†	1024	at home	30	14 "
H	Fennelly Canice J, jr	1024	U S A	26	here
K	Fennelly Norma R—†	1024	at home	25	"
L	Hicks Mary—†	1024	"	53	"
M	Perriore Alphonse	1024	chauffeur	30	"
N	Smith Wilfred	1024	retired	59	27 Orient av
O	Foster Agnes—†	1024	housewife	51	here
P	Foster Joseph	1024	chauffeur	52	"
R	Nugent Forrest	1024	seaman	50	125 Pembroke
¹R	Quartaroni John	1024	storekeeper	52	here
S	Thompson Walter	1024	policeman	60	"
X	Moschella Michael	1046	guard	34	"
Y	Moschella Theresa—†	1046	housewife	34	"
Z	D'Alfonso Cornelia—†	1048	bookbinder	24	"
	2217				
A	D'Alfonso Irma—†	1048	tel operator	21	"
B	D'Alfonso Louise—†	1048	photographer	27	"
C	D'Alfonso Theresa—†	1048	tailor	48	"
D	Grieci Assunta—†	1050	"	36	
E*	Grieci Christine—†	1050	housewife	64	"
F	Grieci Pasquale	1050	retired	72	
G	Fagan Daniel	1052	longshoreman	73	"
H	Fagan Daniel	1052	U S A	29	
K	Fagan Douglas	1052	U S N	27	..
L	Gunn Elizabeth—†	1052	WAC	23	
M	Gunn James P	1052	U S N	20	
N	Gunn Joseph F	1052	clerk	28	
O	Gunn Margaret A—†	1052	"	26	

Bennington Street—Continued

P	Gunn Mary A—†	1052	housewife	56	here
R	Gunn Mary B—†	1052	tel operator	32	"
S	Gallagher Catherine M–†1052		housewife	59	"
T	Gallagher George A	1052	ord'n'nceman	59	"
U	Gallagher William E	1052	electrician	26	"
W	D'Angelico Florence—†	1054	housewife	40	"
X	D'Angelico John	1054	U S A	28	"
V	D'Angelico Leonard	1054	operator	50	"
Y	Ballerini Adelle—†	1054	tel operator	22	"
Z	Ballerini Andrew	1054	machinist	33	"

2218

A	Ballerini Dante	1054	U S A	25	
B	Ballerini Edward	1054	U S N	32	
C	Ballerini Felice—†	1054	retired	68	
D	Ballerini Guy	1054	shipper	38	"
E	Ballerini Rose—†	1054	laundrywrkr	34	"
F	Ferrante Ida—†	1054	housewife	41	"
G	Ferrante John	1054	tailor	51	
H	Damigell Annie—†	1056	housewife	27	"
K	Damigell Thomas	1056	mechanic	29	"
L	Addresi Alice—†	1056	laundress	29	"
M	Addresi Frank	1056	machinist	64	"
N	Addresi Gerard	1056	U S N	20	
O	*Addresi Nora—†	1056	housewife	57	"
P	Addresi Pauline—†	1056	bookkeeper	26	"
R	Hesenius Annie—†	1056	housekeeper	58	"
S	Hesenius Helen—†	1056	clerk	34	"
T	Lawler John J	1056	shipper	50	"
U	Campbell Benjamin	1058	fishcutter	34	"
V	Campbell Mary—†	1058	housewife	29	"
W	Cashman Rita M—†	1058	tel operator	28	"
X	Tosney Frances G—†	1058	clerk	23	"
Y	Tosney John J	1058	"	64	"
Z	Tosney Mary A—†	1058	housewife	60	"

2219

A	Tosney Mary E—†	1058	tel operator	23	"
B	Tosney Christopher J	1058	teacher	34	"
C	Tosney Harriet—†	1058	housewife	35	"
D	Beatrice Charlotte—†	1062	"	28	Winthrop
E	Beatrice Joseph	1062	clerk	30	"
F	Mantica Dominic	1062	carpenter	53	here

Page.	Letter.	FULL NAME.	Residence, Jan. 1, 1945.	Occupation.	Supposed Age.	Reported Residence, Jan. 1, 1944. Street and Number.

Bennington Street—Continued

G	Mantica Mary—†	1062	clerk	23	here
H	Mantica Sarah—†	1062	housewife	52	"
K	Meola Carmen	1062	painter	34	78 Havre
L	Meola Marion—†	1062	housewife	34	78 "
M	Famolare Caroline—†	1064	"	70	here
N	Famolare Dominic	1064	retired	78	"
O	Famolare John	1064	barber	53	"
P	Famolare Paul	1064	shipper	42	..
R	Cappa Ercole	1064	electrician	24	"
S	Cappa Joseph	1064	U S C G	25	"
T	*Cappa Josephine—†	1064	housewife	47	"
U	Cappa Marie P—†	1064	stitcher	24	"
V	Fasolino Elvira—†	1064	housewife	53	"
W	Fasolino Michael	1064	laborer	64	
X	Fronduto Louis A	1066	U S A	26	..
Y	Fronduto Louise—†	1066	assembler	27	"
Z	Polsonetti Filomena—†	1066	housewife	53	"
	2220				
A	Ciafella Carmine	1066	photographer	20	"
B	Ciafella Diego	1066	coppersmith	44	"
C	Ciafella Mary—†	1066	housewife	43	"
D	Polsonetti Anthony	1066	tailor	48	
E	Polsonetti Augustino	1066	U S A	22	
F	Polsonetti Pauline—†	1066	housewife	40	"
G	Bruno Concetta—†	1070	"	50	..
H	Bruno Frank	1070	laborer	55	
K	Hallahan Evelyn—†	1072	housewife	27	"
L	Kennedy Anna—†	1072	"	54	
M	Kennedy Arthur C	1072	U S A	20	"
N	Kennedy John J	1072	inspector	54	"
O	Cuneo Emma—†	1072	housewife	61	"
P	Cuneo John J	1072	U S N	31	
R	Cuneo Mabel L—†	1072	assembler	41	"

Boardman Street

W	Cataldo Alice—†	7	factoryhand	26	here
X	Cataldo Anthony	7	U S N	30	"
Y	*Cataldo Charles	7	retired	60	"
Z	Cataldo Charles	7	U S A	24	

13

2221
Boardman Street—Continued

A	Cataldo Generoso	7	U S A	22	here
B	Cataldo Gloria—†	7	technician	20	"
C	Cataldo Mildred—†	7	secretary	23	"
D	*Cataldo Theresa—†	7	housewife	58	"
E	Baldassaro Benjamin	7	plumber	38	"
F	Baldassaro Esther—†	7	housewife	37	"
G	Palazzo Margaret—†	7	clerk	27	
H	Daquino Mary—†	9	operator	45	"
K	Ferrante Angelina—†	9	housewife	41	"
L	Ferrante Ralph	9	musician	42	"
M	*Iapicca Isabella—†	9	housewife	53	"
N	Iapicca Michael	9	guard	49	"
O	DiLorenzo Carmen	9	shipper	31	"
P	DiLorenzo Gaetano	9	barber	58	"
R	DiLorenzo Madeline—†	9	housewife	54	"
S	DiLorenzo Rose—†	9	operator	23	"
T	Famulari Dominic	11	retired	75	"
U	Famulari Celia—†	11	housewife	23	Chelsea
V	Famulari Frank	11	instructor	25	"
W	Spagnolo Elizabeth—†	11	stitcher	41	here
X	Spagnolo Vincent	11	shoewkr	46	"
Y	Sasso Joseph	11	electrician	55	"
Z	Sasso Mary—†	11	operator	32	"

2222

B	Sousa John	15	maintenance	30	680 Benningt'n
C	Sousa Josephine—†	15	housewife	30	680 "
D	Fischer Minnie—†	15	"	45	here
E	Fischer Robert	15	U S A	21	"
F	Fischer Vincent	15	coppersmith	53	"
G	Lopez John	16	foundrywkr	41	"
H	Lopez Mildred—†	16	housewife	41	"
K	Sacco George	16	U S A	29	"
L	Andersen Arthur	19	electrician	34	"
M	Andersen Margaret—†	19	housewife	30	"
N	Annese Rose—†	19	"	65	157 Cottage
O	Sacco Ralph	19	U S A	33	here
P	Ricci Anna—†	19	clerk	29	"
R	Ricci Louis	19	electrician	42	"
S	Morse Andrew	23	longshoreman	42	"
T	Morse Eva—†	23	housewife	43	"

14

Page.	Letter.	FULL NAME.	Residence, Jan. 1, 1945.	Occupation.	Supposed Age.	Reported Residence, Jan. 1, 1944. Street and Number.

Boardman Street—Continued

	U	Patti Mary—†	23	housewife	33	here
	V	Patti Salvatore	23	machinist	44	"
	W	Raffo George	23	retired	44	"
	X	Raffo John	23	machinist	46	"
	Y	*Raffo Marie—†	23	housewife	79	"
2223						
	A	Vecchio Emily—†	29	"	34	
	B	Vecchio Vito	29	operator	35	"
	C	Capprine Pasquale	31	welder	35	
	D	Capprine Rose—†	31	housewife	30	"
	E	Dente Alphonse	31	pharmacist	32	"
	F	Dente Ida—†	31	housewife	28	"
	G	Reynolds Doris—†	33	clerk	21	
	H	Reynolds Eleanor—†	33	"	45	
	K	Cerullo Antonio	33	laborer	55	"
	L	Cerullo Carmen	33	"	25	
	M	Cerullo Mary—†	33	housewife	50	"
	N	Cerullo Ottavio	33	U S A	23	..
	O	Cerullo Yolanda—†	33	stenographer	21	"
	P	Gravallese Antonio	33	cook	28	"
	R	Gravallese Rose—†	33	housewife	27	"
	S	*Sparaco Briscoe	35	retired	36	
	T	*Sparaco Concetta—†	35	housewife	55	"
	U	Sparaco Melio	35	machinist	35	"
	V	Hanna Galil	35	U S A	32	"
	W	Hanna Marie—†	35	housewife	30	"
	X	Borelli Eleanor—†	41	"	30	
	Y	Borelli Vincenzo	41	laborer	34	"
	Z	DeSimone Anna—†	41	housewife	55	"
2224						
	A	DeSimone Vincenzo	41	laborer	52	
	B	LaVita Leonora—†	41	machinist	26	"
	C	Cotter Clare—†	47	housewife	24	"
	D	Cotter Frederick	47	brazier	30	
	E	Colarusso Palmina—†	49	stitcher	28	"
	F	Cochiarella Giacomo	49	retired	75	
	G	Martiniello Agostino	53	U S A	23	"
	H	Martiniello Francesco	53	laborer	50	"
	K	Martiniello Josephine—†	53	housewife	47	"
	L	Martiniello Rose—†	53	stitcher	22	"
	M	Kaminski Dolores—†	53	housewife	24	"

15

Page.	Letter.	Full Name.	Residence, Jan. 1, 1945.	Occupation.	Supposed Age.	Reported Residence, Jan. 1, 1944. Street and Number.

Boardman Street—Continued

	N	Kaminski John	53	machinist	25	here
	o	*DeLeo Domenic	53	retired	63	"
	T	Ness John H	111	machinist	30	"
	U	Ness Thelma L—†	111	housewife	28	"
	V	Kelleher Charles P	111	electrician	26	"
	W	Kelleher Marion—†	111	housewife	23	"
	X	*Vecchio Guiseppe	162	retired	72	"
	Y	*Vecchio Maria—†	162	housewife	66	"

2225   Breed Street

	G	Boland Evelyn—†	7	housewife	34	here
	H	Boland Thomas J	7	foreman	36	"
	K	Cavagnaro Mary—†	7	housewife	73	"
	L	Cavagnaro Robert	7	U S N	44	"
	M	Romano Louis	7	chauffeur	33	352 Chelsea
	N	Romano Mary—†	7	housewife	29	352 "
	o	Bernardi Isadore	7	laborer	39	here
	P	Bernardi Mary—†	7	housewife	36	"
	R	Garvey Anna—†	7	spinner	33	"
	S	DiFranza John	9	millhand	28	"
	T	DiFranza Vincenza—†	9	housewife	26	"
	U	Coronella Joseph	9	letter carrier	41	1008 Benningt'n
	V	Celia Carmella—†	9	housewife	32	here
	W	Celia Joseph	9	electrician	35	"
	X	Carresi John	10	bartender	44	"
	Y	Carresi Rose—†	10	housewife	43	"
	Z	Rosatto Frank	10	machinist	28	115 Leyden

2226

	E	*Hay Charles	15	laundryman	64	here
	H	DeSimone Joseph	17	retired	65	"
	K	DeSimone Josephine—†	17	clerk	34	"
	L	DeSimone Leonara—†	17	housewife	58	"
	M	DeSimone Rose M—†	17	bookkeeper	24	"
	N	Sirianni John	17	salesman	36	"
	o	Sirianni Rose—†	17	housewife	28	"
	P	Guiffre Joseph	17	salesman	45	"
	R	Guiffre Josephine—†	17	housewife	43	"
	S	London Anna—†	17	at home	66	"
	T	Vitale Guy	20	U S A	26	
	U	Vitale Nicolo	20	retired	71	

Breed Street—Continued

v	Vatalaro Anthony	20	pipefitter	47	here	
w	Vatalaro Marie—†	20	housewife	34	"	
x	Corso Mary—†	20	inspector	28	"	
y	Corso Nazareth	20	U S A	26	"	
z	Patti Anthony	20	retired	68		
	2227					
a	Patti Joseph	20	U S A	26	"	
b	Patti Sebastian	20	salesman	31	"	
d	Kelly Josephine—†	23	housewife	46	"	
e	Kelly William J	23	fireman	48	"	
f	Kelly William J, jr	23	U S A	27		
g	Malatesta Isadore	23	manager	33	"	
h	O'Brien Alma—†	23	housewife	34	"	
k	O'Brien Francis	23	machinist	31	"	
l	Porciello Fiore	23	cutter	49		
m	Porciello Florence—†	23	housewife	54	"	
n	Porciello Gennaro	23	cutter	57		
o	Mangini Albert	23	manager	37	"	
p	*Mangini Angela—†	23	at home	68	"	
r	Culkeen Elizabeth—†	25	housewife	55	"	
s	Culkeen John J	25	broker	59		
t	Culkeen John L	25	U S A	26		
u	Moltedo Aurelia—†	25	at home	52	"	
v	Moltedo Henry R	25	clerk	43	"	
w	Moltedo Mildred B—†	25	manager	56	"	
x	Moltedo Virginia—†	25	at home	77	"	
y	Reidt Mary—†	25	housewife	46	"	
z	Reidt William	25	salesman	52	"	
	2228					
a	Anderson William R	26	clergyman	37	Peabody	
b	Buckley Edmund	26	"	39	here	
c	Cronin Francis	26	"	72	"	
d	Talbot Celeste—†	26	housekeeper	66	"	
e	Fasano Carmella—†	40	dressmaker	40	1100 Benningt'n	
f	Fasano Mildred—†	40	secretary	20	1100 "	
g	Fasano Nicholas	40	shoecutter	48	1100 "	
h	Zucco Grace—†	40	baker	39	here	
k	Zucco Peter	40	"	42	"	
l	Filipponi Emily—†	40	housewife	43	"	
m	Filipponi Pasquale	40	janitor	52		
n	Filipponi Stella—†	40	inspector	21	"	

1—22   17

Page.	Letter.	FULL NAME.	Residence, Jan. 1, 1945.	Occupation.	Supposed Age.	Reported Residence, Jan. 1, 1944. Street and Number.

Breed Street—Continued

	O	Santarpio Francis	42	agent	28	here
	P	Santarpio Marion—†	42	housewife	23	"
	R	Fiorillo Annette—†	42	secretary	32	"
	S	Fischer Joseph F	42	patrolman	46	"
	T	Fischer Josephine—†	42	packer	44	"
	U	Fischer Mary C—†	42	housewife	40	"
	V	Rose Domenica—†	42	"	42	182 Falcon
	W	Rose Frank	42	boilermaker	42	182 "
	Y	Dicenzo Annette—†	46	packer	25	here
	Z	Dicenzo Joseph	46	retired	66	"

2229

	A	Dicenzo Margaret—†	46	housewife	59	"
	B	Meoli Antoinetta—†	46	"	39	
	C	Meoli Felix	46	U S A	24	
	D	Meoli Marino	46	candymaker	50	"
	E	Meoli Michael	46	U S C G	22	"
	F	Tuberosa Lena—†	46	housewife	30	"
	G	Tuberosa Michael	46	U S C G	35	"
	H	Abramovich Basil	56	millwright	56	"
	K	Abramovich Margaret—†	56	housewife	53	"
	L	DeBay Mary—†	56	"	26	53 Horace
	M	DeBay Phillip	56	U S A	35	53 "
	N	Tedesco Anna—†	56	housewife	29	here
	O	Tedesco Anthony	56	chauffeur	31	"
	P	Maio Alice—†	82	housewife	40	"
	R	Maio Joseph	82	machinist	44	"
	S	Wood Alice—†	82	housewife	35	"
	T	Wood Wayman W	82	supt	43	"
	U	Berando Angelina—†	82	housewife	61	"
	V	Berando Anne—†	82	waitress	30	"
	W	Berando Catherine—†	82	clerk	35	
	X	Berando Jules	82	laborer	63	"

2230   Ford Street

	B	Lento Ida—†	4	housewife	37	here
	C	Lento Samuel	4	shoemaker	43	"
	D	Diminico Crescenzo	4	laborer	55	"
	E	*Diminico Vincenza—†	4	housewife	55	"
	F	Marzareci Antonio	6	laborer	55	"
	G	Marzareci Josephine—†	6	supervisor	25	"

18

H	Marzareci Lillian—†	6	housewife	49	here
K	Marzareci Mary—†	6	WAVE	21	"
L	Famolare Joseph	6	U S N	26	"
M	Famolare Mildred—†	6	housewife	23	"
N	Terilli Joseph	6	chauffeur	31	"
O	Terilli Mary—†	6	housewife	26	"
P	Duffy Edward	7	U S A	28	"
R	Duffy Margaret—†	7	housewife	25	"
S	Sullivan Emma—†	7	"	47	
T	Sullivan James A	7	salesman	50	"
U	McDonald Edward	7	chauffeur	45	"
V	McDonald Jeannette—†	7	housewife	37	"
W	Carresi Salvatore	7	clerk	40	
X	Lombard Frank	8	U S N	32	
Y	Lombard Yolande—†	8	clerk	29	
Z	Famolare Concetta—†	8	housewife	29	"

2231

A	Famolare Salvatore	8	chauffeur	31	"
B	Famolare Angelina—†	8	housewife	48	"
C	Famolare Phillip	8	chauffeur	48	"
D	*Sarro Emanuella—†	11	housewife	65	"
E	Sarro Pietro	11	janitor	65	"
F	Abramo Clementina—†	11	stitcher	33	"
G	Abramo Salvatore	11	tailor	38	
H	Pepe Dante S	21	teacher	25	
K	Pepe Jennie—†	21	bookkeeper	22	"
L	Pepe Nicolina—†	21	housewife	52	"
M	Pepe Pasquale	21	U S A	27	
N	Pepe Pasqualina—†	21	housewife	31	"
O	Martucci John	21	laborer	62	
P	*Cataldo Clorinda—†	21	housewife	45	"
R	Cataldo Louis	21	candymaker	50	"
S	Cataldo Phyllis—†	21	"	22	

Gladstone Street

T	O'Leary Catherine T—†	136	cashier	21	here
U	O'Leary Ellen M—†	136	nurse	24	"
V	O'Leary Grace M—†	136	housewife	48	"
W	O'Leary Timothy	136	guard	58	
X	O'Leary William T	136	student	20	

Gladstone Street—Continued

Y	*Marino Genevieve—†	140	housewife	57	here	
Z	Marino Joseph	140	draftsman	36	"	
	2232					
A	Marino Phillip	140	retired	61		
B	Tacelli Susan—†	153	shoewkr	45	"	
C	Tacelli Vincent	153	"	50		
D	DiFronzo Angelo	153	clerk	34	"	
E	DiFronzo Camille—†	153	housewife	31	"	
F	Leccese Inez—†	153	beautician	28	18 Leyden	
G	Leccese Michael	153	U S A	29	18 "	
H	Zito Emily—†	153	housewife	53	here	
K	Zito Marguerite—†	153	beautician	22	"	
L	Zito Vincent	153	contractor	55	"	
M	Megna Joseph	165	U S A	29		
N	Megna Rose—†	165	operator	27	"	
O	*Motta Concetta—†	165	housewife	59	"	
P	Motta Dominic	165	tanner	24		
R	*Motta Mary—†	165	operator	38	"	
S	Bramante Concetta—†	165	stitcher	20	"	
T	Bramante Mary—†	165	at home	21	"	
U	Bramante Sebastian	165	storekeeper	50	"	
W	Zani Adele—†	175	housewife	55	"	
X	Zani Carolyn—†	175	estimator	34	"	
Y	Zani John	175	contractor	62	"	
Z	Zani Joseph P	175	U S A	28	"	
	2233					
A	Massucco Rita—†	176	housewife	39	"	
B	Massucco Robert	176	seaman	41	"	
C	Massucco Ernest	176	chauffeur	31	"	
D	Massucco Helen—†	176	housewife	33	"	
E	Meehan Edward	176	pipefitter	58	"	
F	Meehan Elizabeth—†	176	housewife	58	"	
G	Pochini Albert	176	storekeeper	29	"	
H	Pochini Alma—†	176	housewife	27	"	
K	Beatrice Dorothy—†	183	student	21	"	
L	Beatrice Marie—†	183	clerk	46		
M	Beatrice Peter	183	laborer	48	"	
N	DeRocco Caroline—†	184	factoryhand	40	"	
O	DeRocco Dominic	184	machinist	44	"	
P	Douglas Dorothea A—†	184	operator	35	"	
R	Douglas Frances G—†	184	housewife	66	"	

s	Douglass Genevieve F—†	184	teacher	24	Revere
t	Douglass James A	184	inspector	67	here
u	Douglass John J	184	U S N	23	"
v	Ciriello Leonard	184	plumber	35	"
w	Ciriello Sadie—†	184	housewife	35	"
x	Lombardo Beatrice—†	185	"	34	
y	Lombardo Margheritino	185	shoewkr	43	"
z	Mastrolia Frederick F	185	teacher	32	
	2234				
a	Mastrolia Liberato	185	salesman	62	"
b	Mastrolia Rose—†	185	storekeeper	61	"
c	Benvissuto Euphemia—†	185	housewife	54	"
d	Benvissuto Paul	185	operator	68	"
e	Maggioli Agnes—†	187	housewife	42	"
f	Maggioli Doris—†	187	clerk	22	
g	Maggioli Leo	187	chauffeur	45	"
h	Bergamasco Angelo	189	chemist	25	931 Benningt'n
k	Bergamasco Mary—†	189	clerk	22	here
l	Staffier Angelo	189	tailor	59	"
m	Staffier Concetta—†	189	housewife	22	"
n	Staffier Louis F	189	clerk	37	
o	Staffier Philomena—†	189	housekeeper	30	"
p	Staffier Rocco R	189	U S A	25	"
r	LaGrasta Jennie—†	189	stitcher	48	
s	LaGrasta Sabatino	189	laborer	50	
t	Barbanti Joseph	191	laundryman	40	"
u	Barbanti Rose—†	191	housewife	38	"
v	Sykes Angelina—†	191	"	36	
w	Sykes Walter	191	clerk	42	
x	Bianchi Carlo	192	retired	65	
y	Bianchi Rose—†	192	housewife	65	"
z	Bianchi Stephen	192	clerk	24	"
	2235				
a	Cella Joseph	192	maintenance	32	"
b	Ciullo Michael	192	plumber	32	"
c	Ciullo Philomena—†	192	housewife	30	"
d	Abramo Joseph M	195	metalwkr	43	"
e	Abramo Mary L—†	195	housewife	36	"
f	Ferri Fortunato	195	manufacturer	56	"
g	Ferri Lillian M—†	195	saleswoman	24	"
h	Ferri Marcella I—†	195	housewife	54	"

Gladstone Street—Continued

	K	Uguccioni Attilio	196	laborer	53	here
	L	*Uguccioni Marcella—†	196	housewife	49	"
	M	Gardella Lawrence	196	pressman	43	"
	O	Solari Andrew, jr	196	laundrywkr	21	"
	N	Solari Andrew M	196	chauffeur	45	"
	P	Solari Louis	196	U S A	20	
	R	Solari Mary R—†	196	housewife	45	"
	S	Morris Catherine—†	196	"	47	
	T	*Morris Mary—†	196	at home	76	"
	U	Morris Stanley E	196	U S A	25	
	V	Morris William C	196	pharmacist	43	"
	W	DiCenzo Dena—†	199	housewife	34	"
	X	DiCenzo William	199	electrician	37	"
	Y	Battaini Ambrose	199	U S A	31	
	Z	*Battaini Theresa—†	199	at home	61	"
		2236				
	A	Clark John	199	carpenter	50	"
	B	Columbo Joseph	199	stoneworker	53	"
	C	Lazzari Adaline M—†	203	housewife	47	"
	D	Lazzari Augustus R	203	U S N	23	"
	E	Lazzari Stephen C	203	pressman	48	"
	F	Raffa Yolanda G—†	203	operator	22	"
	G	Vara Alice—†	203	housewife	21	"
	H	Vara Carmen	203	U S C G	25	"
	K	*Carpinella Blanche—†	203	housewife	45	"
	L	Carpinella Dominic	203	furniturewkr	48	"
	M	Carpinella Ralph	203	U S N	27	
	N	Carpinella Silvio	203	shipfitter	21	"
	O	Crovo Herman	204	laborer	40	"
	P	Crovo Mary—†	204	housewife	36	"
	R	Bottini Angelina—†	204	factoryhand	20	"
	S	Bottini Eleanor—†	204	housewife	48	"
	T	Bottini Sebastian	204	carpenter	48	"
	U	Miller Edwin	204	wireman	62	"
	V	Marino Alfonso	207	retired	49	"
	W	Marino Antoinetta—†	207	factoryhand	48	"
	X	Marino Peter	207	clerk	23	
	Y	Robinson James	207	U S A	27	
	Z	Robinson Lena—†	207	housewife	27	"
		2237				
	A	Solari Edmund	207	laundrywkr	39	"

22

Page.	Letter.	FULL NAME.	Residence, Jan. 1, 1945.	Occupation.	Supposed Age.	Reported Residence, Jan. 1, 1944. Street and Number.

Gladstone Street—Continued

B	Solari Nellie—†	207	housewife	31	here	
C	Watson John A	208	electrician	46	"	
D	Watson Martha S—†	208	housewife	78	"	
E	Petrillo Anthony	211	baker	36		
F	Petrillo Concetta—†	211	housewife	31	"	
G	Nasta Alphonso	211	shoewkr	42	"	
H	Nasta Josephine—†	211	operator	35	"	
K	*Nasta Rose—†	211	housewife	48	"	
L	Nasta Salvatore	211	shoewkr	50	"	
M	DeFeo Arthur	215	research wkr	27	"	
N	DeFeo Lena—†	215	bookkeeper	25	"	
O	Sacco Charles	215	mechanic	45	"	
P	Sacco Louise—†	215	housewife	40	"	
R	*Zagarella Josephine—†	219	at home	75	"	
S	Zagarella Mary—†	219	housewife	48	"	
T	Zagarella Peter J	219	machinist	53	"	
U	Veneziano Emma—†	223	housewife	45	"	
V	Veneziano Josephine—†	223	clerk	20		
W	Veneziano Salvatore	223	maintenance	47	"	

Leyden Street

X	Pugliesi Jennie—†	10	housewife	32	here	
Y	*Pugliesi Vincent	10	baker	36	"	
Z	Vecchio Concetta—†	10	housewife	23	"	
	2238					
A	Vecchio William.	10	U S M C	25	"	
B	Catoni Dario	14	waiter	45	Rhode Island	
C	*Catoni Victoria—†	14	housewife	46	"	
D	Morganti Adele—†	14	dressmaker	21	"	
E	Morganti Egidio	14	U S A	23	88 Leydon	
F	Ciriello Alton L	14	electrician	26	here	
G	Ciriello Eleanor—†	14	housewife	24	"	
H	Ricci Anna I—†	15	inspector	24	"	
K	Ricci Sylvio J	15	boilermaker	36	"	
L	Steel Catherine—†	15	clerk	36		
N	Salotti Mary—†	29	laundress	49	"	
O	Bernardi Augustino	29	U S A	30		
P	Bernardi Clara—†	29	operator	31	"	
R	*Bernardi Dino	29	cook	63		
S	*Bernardi Egidia—†	29	housewife	63	"	

Page.	Letter.	FULL NAME.	Residence, Jan. 1, 1945.	Occupation.	Supposed Age.	Reported Residence, Jan. 1, 1944. Street and Number.

Leyden Street—Continued

T	Bernardi Louis J	29	U S N	35	here
U	Bernardi Renaldo	29	U S A	27	"
V	*Donati Marie—†	29	cook	67	"
W	Avolio Anthony A	29	U S A	25	
X	Avolio James V	29	U S N	22	
Y	Avolio John J	29	U S A	20	
Z	*Avolio Marguerite—†	29	housewife	57	"
	2239					
A	Avolio Mary M—†	29	stitcher	22	"
B	Bonugli Dominic L	33	proprietor	56	"
C	Bonugli Jessie M—†	33	housewife	56	"
D	Bonugli Katherine—†	33	factoryhand	20	"
E	Bonugli Madeline A—†	33	clerk	22	
F	Palladino Aldo	33	U S A	29	
G	Palladino Arlene—†	33	clerk	27	"
H	Pedone Anna B—†	35	housewife	31	"
K	Pedone Samuel A	35	manager	30	"
L	Evans Jennie—†	35	housewife	53	"
M	Evans Sigurd G	35	supervisor	41	"
N	Simonini Casmirio	35	butcher	55	"
O	Simonini Esola—†	35	inspector	44	"
P	Simonini George	35	U S A	23	
R	Simonini Joseph	35	U S M C	22	"
S	Simonini Vincent	35	U S A	20	
T	Martini Angelina R—†	35	housewife	34	"
U	Martini Ferdinand R	35	U S A	31	
V	DeMarchi Anna—†	35	candy packer	55	"
W	DeMarchi Frank E	35	machinist	63	"
X	Fitzgerald Elizabeth—†	35	nurse	22	
Y	Martucci Harriet—†	35	"	22	
Z	Sacco Briscoe	35	watchman	56	"
	2240					
A	Sacco Jerome J	35	instructor	28	"
B	Sacco Mary A—†	35	housewife	54	"
C	Sacco Rose F—†	35	inpector	24	"
D	Pasqua Margaret C—†	47	housewife	36	"
E	Pasqua Philip A	47	machinist	42	"
F	Salori Eva—†	49	bookkeeper	55	"
G	Saisi Ella—†	53	housewife	35	88 Leyden
H	Saisi Orlando	53	clerk	38	88 "
K	Capillo Antoinette—†	55	matron	48	59 "

Leyden Street—Continued

M	Colantuone Jennie—†	59	packer	60	61 Leyden
N	Colantuone Paul	59	laborer	63	61 "
O	Celestino Mary—†	59	bookkeeper	22	260 Lexington
P	Celestino Peter	59	machinist	21	105 Liverpool
R	Sarro Anthony	60	laborer	55	here
S	Sarro Joseph	60	U S A	23	"
T	Bacigalupo George	60	U S N	21	"
U	Bacigalupo Joseph	60	U S A	25	
V	Bacigalupo Louis	60	"	31	
W	Bacigalupo Louise—†	60	bookkeeper	30	"
X	Bacigalupo Mary C—†	60	housewife	57	"
Y	Bacigalupo Walter A	60	laborer	60	
Z	Bacigalupo Walter L	60	boilermaker	33	"
	2241				
A	Albanesi Caroline—†	60	housewife	26	190 Paris
B	Albanesi Rocco	60	clerk	34	190 "
C	Brady Donatina—†	61	housewife	30	here
D	Brady Robert T	61	U S N	32	"
E	Serra Natale J	61	U S A	27	"
F	Serra Rose P—†	61	housewife	26	"
G	Sacco Mildred A—†	61	inspector	20	1008 Benningt'n
H	Sozio Anthony	61	U S N	28	1008 "
K	Sozio Rose L—†	61	housewife	26	1008 "
L	Olivieri Angelo	63	laborer	52	862 Saratoga
M	Olivieri Rose—†	63	housewife	49	862 "
N	Carabott Agnes C—†	63	"	25	here
O	Carabott Anthony	63	longshoreman	28	"
P	Rossi Andrew U	65	U S A	31	"
R	Rossi Doris E—†	65	housewife	27	"
S	Amoroso Albert	67	machinist	28	"
T	Amoroso Aniello	67	shoewkr	58	"
U	Amoroso Elizabeth—†	67	stitcher	26	"
V	Amoroso Evelyn M—†	67	housewife	30	"
W	Amoroso John	67	chauffeur	34	"
X	Amoroso Peter	67	longshoreman	32	"
Y	Amoroso Rosina—†	67	housewife	52	"
Z	Palumbo Eugene	67	machinist	28	"
	2242				
A	Palumbo Testa—†	67	housewife	25	"
B	*Christopher Jeremiah	68	shoewkr	62	"
C	Christopher John	68	"	51	

Leyden Street—Continued

D	Christopher Mary R—†	68	clerk	28	here
E	*Christopher Rose—†	68	housekeeper	84	"
F	Hatch Leon	68	driller	23	"
G	Hatch Rose—†	68	housewife	21	"
H	Christopher Dominic	68	pipefitter	40	"
K	Christopher Mary—†	68	housewife	34	"
M	Femia Joseph	70	laborer	50	"
N	Femia Marion—†	70	inspector	21	"
O	Femia Mary—†	70	"	26	
P	Femia Victoria—†	70	housewife	45	"
R	DeStefano Frank	71	metalworker	53	"
S	DeStefano Josephine—†	71	housewife	49	"
T	Massa Amelia—†	71	"	76	
U	Massa Amelia F—†	71	candymaker	50	"
V	Lemos Anne—†	71	"	44	
W	Lemos Lawrence	71	engraver	36	"
X	Lemos Lucinda—†	71	candymaker	40	"
Y	Femia Nicholas	72	coppersmith	28	"
Z	Femia Charles	72	U S N	25	"
	2243				
A	Femia Mary J—†	72	housewife	22	"
B	*Casenza Salvatore	72	retired	83	"
C	Delaney James	74	carpenter	47	"
D	Delaney Robert	74	U S N	22	
E	Delaney Virginia—†	74	housewife	45	"
F	Delaney Virginia—†	74	operator	21	"
G	*Lagamasino Victoria—†	78	housekeeper	78	"
H	Lagamasino Anthony	78	clerk	52	"
K	Lagamasino Eleanor—†	78	housekeeper	38	"
L	Lagamasino Lawrence	78	painter	25	"
M	Lagamasino Louis	78	mechanic	53	"
N	Lagamasino Mary—†	78	housewife	51	"
O	Daloia Carmen	79	pipefitter	37	"
P	Daloia Nerina R—†	79	housewife	30	"
R	Mattera Elizabeth M—†	79	"	28	"
S	Mattera Mario J	79	machinist	28	"
T	Mattera Umberto M	79	die sinker	26	"
U	Dappollonio Arthur	79	U S A	20	
V	Dappollonio Hugh J	79	"	24	
W	Dappollonio Rose G—†	79	housewife	51	"
X	Cook Manuel P	80	guard	59	

Page.	Letter.	FULL NAME.	Residence, Jan. 1, 1945.	Occupation.	Supposed Age.	Reported Residence, Jan. 1, 1944. Street and Number.

Leyden Street—Continued

| Y | Cook Rosa—† | 80 | housewife | 61 | here |
| z | Celona Domenica—† | 80 | " | 54 | " |

2244

A	Celona Josephine—†	80	bookkeeper	21	"
B	Sardina Angelina—†	80	housewife	28	"
c	Sardina Stephen	80	electrician	31	"
D	Bough Annette—†	82	clerk	36	138 Medford
E	Gulla Vera—†	82	housewife	34	here
F	Cicco Alfred	82	welder	30	"
G	Cicco Lena—†	82	housewife	30	"
H	Cicco Catherine—†	82	"	32	"
K	Cicco John	82	pipefitter	37	"
L	*Zozzi Lena—†	83	housewife	54	"
M	Zozzi Mary—†	83	clerk	32	
N	Zozzi Nicholas	83	salesman	57	"
o	Rossi Anna M—†	83	clerk	24	
P	Rossi Joseph G	83	U S A	20	
R	Rossi Mary F—†	83	inspector	22	"
s	*Rossi Natalina—†	83	housewife	55	"
T	*Rossi Ottavio	83	butcher	56	"
u	*Rossi Adaline—†	83	housewife	64	"
v	Rossi Americo	83	inspector	28	"
w	*Rossi Andrew	83	butcher	66	"
x	Rossi Christine—†	83	housewife	29	"
Y	Caradonna Mary V—†	87	"	37	"
z	Caradonna Peter	87	supervisor	39	"

2245

A	*Puzo Frank	87	retired	74	
B	Puzo Lena—†	87	candymaker	35	"
c	*Puzo Mary—†	87	housewife	74	"
D	Puzo Theresa—†	87	typist	26	"
E	Chillemi Grace—†	87	clerk	27	82 Leyden
F	Mayo Emma—†	87	typist	35	here
G	Mayo Frank	87	jeweler	37	"
H	Wainwright Anna—†	88	housewife	26	"
K	Wainwright Charles	88	chauffeur	32	"
L	Bradley Annette—†	88	housewife	30	"
M	Bradley Walter	88	driller	30	
N	*Morganti Georgette—†	88	housewife	58	"
o	Morganti Ralph	88	clerk	59	
P	Morganti Vincenza—†	88	housekeeper	33	"

27

Leyden Street—Continued

R	Murphy Adaline R—†	91	secretary	26	here
s	Murphy Caroline G—†	91	housewife	53	"
T	Murphy James H	91	ordinance	58	"
u	Murphy Kenneth E	91	U S A	20	"
v	Murphy Lawrence T	91	U S N	24	
w	Murphy Pauline L—†	91	WAVE	27	"
x	Murphy Robert H	91	U S A	33	"
y	Carley Mary A—†	91	typist	60	"
z	Guarino Ercolino	96	rigger	40	"

2246

A	Guarino Mary—†	96	housewife	35	"
B	Gaetani Francesco	96	barber	45	
c	Gaetani Margaret—†	96	housewife	41	"
D	Casassa Alfred	100	chauffeur	29	"
E	Casassa Rita—†	100	housekeeper	24	"
F	Muzza Dominic	100	retired	71	"
G	Pochini Michael	100	clerk	68	
H	Mazzarella Margaret—†	101	housewife	34	"
K	Mazzarella Orlando	101	machinist	39	"
L	Kazzarella Albert	101	U S N	27	
M	Mazzarella Ernest	101	"	29	"
N	Mazzarella Leonard	101	machinist	41	— "
o	Mazzarella Mary P—†	101	candymaker	33	"
P.	Mazzarella Philomena—†	101	housewife	66	"
R	Marotta Alfred F	101	U S N	20	
s	Marotta Anthony	101	machinist	40	"
T	Marotta Lena—†	101	housewife	40	" .
u	Saurino Anthony	101	agent	36	"
v	Saurino Margaret—†	101	housewife	30	"
w	Cipoletta Palmina—†	103	shoeworker	30	"
x	Cipoletta William	103	U S N	32	"
y	Colella Bernard	103	candymaker	32	194 Salem
z	Colella Josephine—†	103	housewife	27	194 "

2247

A*	Sozio Angelo	105	retired	67	here
B	Sozio Guy	105	printer	32	"
c*	Sozio Josephine—†	105	housewife	64	"
D	Sozio Pasquale	105	chauffeur	35	"
E	Rosatto Alfred	115	U S N	21	"
F	Rosatto Louis	115	fireman	61	Cambridge

Leyden Street—Continued

	G	*Rosatto Marie—†	115	housewife	49	Cambridge
	H	Church Agnes R—†	115	WAVE	35	here
	K	Church Mary B—†	115	saleswoman	59	"
	L	Fatta Deogrates	125	clergyman	65	"
	M	Toma Louis	125	"	60	"
	N	DiMare Esther—†	126	housewife	35	"
	O	DiMare Santo	126	operator	35	"
	P	Scaramazini Mary—†	126	housewife	51	"
	R	Scaramazini Phillip	126	tailor	59	
	S	Maestri Edmund	126	U S A	31	
	T	*Maestri Louis	126	presser	67	
	U	Maestri Rose—†	126	stitcher	29	"
	V	Maestri Samuel	126	U S A	36	
	W	Colantuone Joseph	128	chauffeur	38	"
	X	Colantuone Rose—†	128	housewife	35	"
	Y	Carideo Charles	129	laborer	39	Dedham
	Z	Carideo Mary—†	129	housewife	30	"
2248						
	A	Nonni Carmella—†	129	"	50	here
	B	Nonni Gennaro	129	U S N	33	"
	C	Nonni Pasquale	129	"	25	"
	D	LaRosa Esther—†	129	housewife	38	"
	E	LaRosa John	129	laborer	39	
	F	DeMarco Anthony	131	"	46	
	G	DeMarco Lillian—†	131	housewife	44	"
	H	Yebba Carmella—†	131	housekeeper	52	"
	K	Garrone Pasquale	131	cook	62	
	L	*Garrone Victoria—†	131	housewife	49	"
	M	Gaeta Anna—†	131	"	29	
	N	Gaeta Giro	131	mechanic	33	"
	O	Curti Edward	135	laborer	33	
	P	Curti Marie—†	135	housewife	29	"
	R	Curti Constantino	135	rigger	66	
	S	Curti Marion—†	135	housewife	67	"
	T	Curti Victor	135	clerk	28	
	U	Colantuoni Alfred	136	stitcher	59	"
	V	Colantuoni Frank	136	U S A	23	
	W	Colantuoni Jennie—†	136	housewife	47	"
	X	Colantuoni Pasquale	136	U S A	25	
	Y	Cariani Eleanor—†	136	housewife	56	"
	Z	Cariani Walter	136	bartender	52	"

2249

Leyden Street—Continued

A	Merola Anna—†	136	housewife	40	here
B	Merola Gerardo	136	boilermaker	53	"
c	*Allegro Maddalena—†	137	housekeeper	74	"
D	Covalucci Rose—†	137	housewife	34	"
E	Covalucci Vito	137	rigger	34	
F	Bray George	137	laborer	45	"
G	Bray Mary—†	137	housewife	40	"
H	Allegra Joseph	137	electrician	44	"
K	Allegra Josephine—†	137	housewife	42	"
L	Visalli Esther—† .	137	housekeeper	74	"
M	Silipigni Ada—†	139	housewife	27	"
N	Silipigni Leo	139	operator	28	"
O	DiTroia Anna—†	139	clerk	20	"
P	DiTroia Mary C—†	139	housewife	42	"
R	DiTroia Peter	139	supt	44	
S	Sullivan Emily—†	140	housewife	38	"
T	Sullivan James	140	rigger	39	
U	Ciampa Bella—†	140	housewife	34	"
V	Ciampa Frank A	140	bartender	37	"
W	Sorace Dominic	142	"	31	
X	Sorace Olive—†	142	housewife	30	"

Montmorenci Avenue

Z	Dinarello Aphrodite—†	2	milliner	24	here
2250					
A	Dinarello Joseph	2	collector	48	"
B	Dinarello Mary—†	2	housewife	42	"
C	Lamborghini Dorothy—†	4	"	34	"
D	Lamborghini Frank	4	shipper	34	"
E	Caruso Jacqueline—†	8	housewife	31	329 Border
F	Caruso Joseph A	8	agent	32	329 "
G	Venuti Josephine—†	12	housewife	28	262 Paris
H	Venuti Vito	12	carpenter	32	262 "
K	Bonanno Carmella—†	16	housewife	29	19 Boardman
L	Bonanno Joseph	16	mortician	27	19 "
M	Berni Lillian—†	24	housewife	36	here
N	Berni Louis	24	mechanic	35	"
O	Rawson Anna M—†	32	housewife	58	"
P	Rawson Robert J	32	U S N	30	..

30

Montmorenci Avenue—Continued

	R	Rawson Thomas R	32	electrician	62	here
	S	McCarthy Mary—†	43	housewife	43	"
	T	McCarthy William	43	foreman	39	"
	U	Censale Domenic	51	U S A	37	"
	V	Censale Iolanda—†	51	storekeeper	30	"
	W	Bradley Barbara C—†	63	clerk	24	
	X	Bradley Carlton J	63	U S A	26	"
	Y	Bradley Hugh H	63	salesman	49	"
	Z	Bradley Mildred C—†	63	housewife	49	"
2251						
	A	Lambert Annette F—†	63	"	28	"
	B	Lambert Louis F	63	U S A	29	

Orient Avenue

	C	Donatelli Jennie—†	162	housewife	44	here
	D	Donatelli Joseph	162	shoemaker	49	"
	E	Donatelli Assunta—†	164	housewife	48	"
	F	Donatelli Augusto	164	tailor	47	
	G	Donatelli Elsa—†	164	stitcher	48	"
	H	Lanza Angelina—†	166	housewife	53	"
	K	Lanza Concetta—†	166	cashier	33	
	L	Lanza Frank	166	U S A	28	
	M	Lanza Louis	166	operator	54	"
	N	LaCascia Anna—†	169	clerk	23	112 London
	O	LaCascia Gaspar	169	baker	50	112 "
	P	LaCascia Mary—†	169	housewife	45	112 "
	R	McKenna Mary A—†	170	at home	69	Cambridge
	S	Watson Mary G—†	170	housewife	69	here
	T	Watson Rudolph	170	guard	70	"
	U	Paterson Charles E	176	treasurer	75	"
	V	Paterson Dorothy L—†	176	housewife	61	"
	W	DeStefano Anthony	190	contractor	45	"
	X	DeStefano Catherine—†	190	housewife	45	"
	Y	DeStefano Ralph A	190	U S N	22	"
	Z	MacLeod Alexander	191	fireman	37	"
2252						
	A	MacLeod Rosalie—†	191	housewife	35	"
	B	Walsh Ella F—†	191	"	68	
	C	Walsh Peter S	191	laborer	68	
	D	Sonego Elmira—†	198	housewife	38	"

Orient Avenue—Continued

E	Sonego Santo	198	foreman	41	here
F	Tarquinio Mary—†	198	housewife	41	"
G	Tarquinio Sabatino	198	machinist	43	"
H	Ruggiero Catherine—†	205	housewife	41	"
K	Ruggiero Guy	205	carpenter	50	"
L	Ruggiero Marie—†	205	designer	22	"
M	Pellegrini Ernest	208	sculptor	56	"
N	Pinardi Mary—†	208	housewife	57	"
O	Carbone Dora—†	216	broker	31	
P	Carbone Judith—†	216	housewife	61	"
R	Carbone Olga—†	216	bookkeeper	31	"
S	Carbone Paul	216	U S A	26	"
T	Carbone Vito	216	agent	61	
U	Palladino Louise—†	232	housewife	39	"
V	Palladino Peter N	232	carpenter	20	"
W	Palladino Rocco	232	proprietor	39	"
X	Interbartolo Louise—†	236	housewife	39	"
Y	Interbartolo Rosario	236	proprietor	36	"
Z	Frederico Angelina—†	240	housewife	46	"
	2253				
A	Frederico Jeannette—†	240	at home	23	"
B	Frederico Paul	240	welder	54	"
C	Frederico Paul J	240	U S N	25	"
D	Bumpus Sarah A—†	244	housewife	39	"
E	Bumpus Warren E	244	teacher	44	"
G	Stone Betty L—†	251	housewife	38	"
H	Stone Julius	251	attorney	43	"
K	Tobia Elvira—†	252	housewife	33	"
L	Tobia Frederico	252	manufacturer	44	"
M	Umana Guy	255	baker	34	
N	Umana Yolanda—†	255	housewife	34	"

Saratoga Street

O	Jackson Gaynell M—†	865	housekeeper	52	here
P	Sacco Edward	869	U S N	28	"
R	Sacco Santa—†	869	housewife	22	"
S	*Santangelo Anna—†	869	"	54	
T	*Santangelo Joseph	869	farmer	55	
U	Santangelo Ralph	869	clerk	20	
V	Sacco George	871	U S N	22	

Saratoga Street—Continued

w	Sacco John	871	foreman	30	here
x	*Sacco Louise—†	871	housewife	54	"
y	Sacco Sabato	871	operator	55	"
z	Martinello Carlo	871	laborer	45	
	2254				
a	Martinello Lucy—†	871	housewife	37	"
b	Durante Armando	873	wool sorter	34	"
c	Durante Virginio	873	cobbler	64	
d	Durante Irene—†	873	housewife	39	"
e	Durante Vincent	873	mechanic	43	"
f	Oliver Ferdinand	875	machinist	42	"
g	Sousa Mary—†	875	housewife	72	"
h	McDonald John	875	laborer	46	
k	McDonald Margaret—†	875	housewife	44	"
l	Buldini Annette—†	877	"	27	
m	Buldini Guido	877	toolmaker	31	"
n	Cognigaro Antonio	877	laborer	57	
o	Cognigaro Concetta—†	877	housewife	54	"
p	Farmer John	879	U S N	26	
r	Farmer Mary E—†	879	housewife	56	"
s	Mastamarino Caroline—†	879A	"	50	
t	Mastamarino Donato	879A	lamplighter	56	"
u	Mastamarino Frederico	879A	U S A	22	"
v	Mastamarino Mary—†	879A	operator	30	"
w	Mastamarino Michael	879A	U S A	28	
x	Joy Edward	897	laborer	21	
y	Joy John	897	U S A	32	
z	Joy Margaret—†	897	operator	26	"
	2255				
a	Joy Mary—†	897	tel operator	27	"
b	Joy Sarah—†	897	housewife	61	"
c	Joy Walter	897	mechanic	28	"
d	Joy Winifred—†	897	operator	25	"
e	Caruso Anthony	898	farmer	31	
f	Caruso Celia—†	898	nurse	29	
g	Caruso Domenic	898	farmer	25	
h	Caruso Gloria—†.	898	beautician	22	"
k	Caruso Patrick G	898	U S A	27	
l	Caruso Ralph	898	"	26	
m	Caruso Rose—†	898	WAC	24	
n	Riccardello Anthony	898	engineer	34	"

Page:	Letter.	FULL NAME.	Residence, Jan. 1, 1945.	Occupation.	Supposed Age.	Reported Residence, Jan. 1, 1944. Street and Number.

o	Riccardello Mary—†	898	housewife	32	here
p	Strati Maria—†	901	"	58	"
r	Strati Paul	901	U S A	20	"
s	Crosby Ann C—†	901	at home	51	"
t	Crosby Catherine F—†	901	sorter	52	
u	Crosby Martin J	901	chauffeur	42	"
v	Crosby Mary I—†	901	operator	48	"
w	Crosby Rose A—†	901	housewife	79	"
x	Malone John E	901	U S A	24	"
y	Malone Margaret—†	901	housewife	21	"
z	Barker Edward J	901	U S A	24	
	2256					
a	Barker Harry L	901	foreman	55	"
b	Barker Margaret E—†	901	housewife	53	"
c	Barker Shirley—†	901	welder	20	
d	Famolare Charles	901	U S N	25	"
e	Famolare Margaret—†	901	housewife	21	"
f	Gylling Selma C—†	903	housekeeper	68	"
g	LaChance Edward	903	foreman	59	"
h	William Albert L	903	decorator	44	"
k	Hansford James	903	U S N	24	
l	Hansford Virginia M—†	903	housewife	20	"
m	Thornton Dorothy—†	903	factoryhand	21	"
n	Thornton George J	903	mechanic	47	"
o	Thornton Mary M—†	903	housewife	46	"
p	Foote Elmer	903	investigator	56	"
r	Pellegrino Frank	903	custodian	57	"
s	Pellegrino Joseph	903	U S A	31	"
t	Pellegrino Nicholas	903	U S N	24	"
u	Pellegrino Philomena—†	903	housewife	51	"
v	Donohue David	905	laborer	58	"
w	Faulkner Grace V—†	905	housewife	42	"
x	Faulkner Joseph R	905	clerk	50	"
y	Duffey Catherine—†	905	housewife	78	"
z	Duffey John	905	U S A	42	"
	2257					
a	Duffey Thomas	905	laborer	75	"
b	Faulkner George	905	clerk	32	"
c	Faulkner Mary M—†	905	housewife	28	"
d	Re Evelyn—†	907	"	29	
e	Re Salvatore	907	welder	28	"

Saratoga Street—Continued

F	Micciche Anne—†	907	housewife	33	here
G	Micciche Santo	907	polisher	45	"
H	Arena Domenic	907	U S A	20	"
K	Arena Gaetano	907	laborer	57	
L	Arena John	907	waiter	27	
M	Arena Josephine—†	907	stitcher	25	"
N	Arena Pauline—†	907	seamstress	28	"
O	Arena Providencia—†	907	housewife	49	"
P	Arena Stefana—†	907	stitcher	22	"
R	*Giodarno Peter	907	gardener	62	"
S	Arrigo George	911	welder	24	"
T	Arrigo Laura—†	911	housewife	22	"
U	Arrigo Canio	911	U S A	21	
V	Arrigo Marie—†	911	housewife	49	"
W	Cosato Anthony	911	U S N	25	
X	Cosato John	911	clerk	29	
Y	Cosato Mary—†	911	housewife	48	"
Z	Cosato Rudolph	911	U S N	22	

2258

A	Cosato Virginio	911	tailor	55	
B	Gravallese Ernest	951	repairman	34	"
C	Gravallese Margaret—†	951	housewife	31	"
D	Maggolli Agrippina—†	951	"	68	
E	Maggolli Emprimo	951	retired	83	
F	Maggolli M Louisa—†	951	secretary	28	"
G	DeSisto Generoso	951	foreman	38	Everett
H	DeSisto Rose M—†	951	housewife	24	"
K	Perrotti Anthony D	953	machinist	25	Beachmont
L	Perrotti Concetta—†	953	housewife	21	"
M	Carrado Mark	953	shoemaker	55	here
N	Carrado Phyllis—†	953	housewife	45	"
O	Scaramozzino Angelo	953	laborer	28	"
P	Scaramozzino Celia—†	953	housewife	25	"
R	McKinnon John	955	salesman	30	"
S	McKinnon Rose—†	955	housewife	25	"
T	Cruccioli Domenic	955	laborer	52	
U	Cruccioli Mario	955	U S A	20	"
V	Cruccioli Pasqualina—†	955	housewife	42	"
W	Giunta Joseph	955	laborer	50	
X	Giunta Margaret—†	955	housewife	49	"
Y	Margarecci Pasquale	955	candymaker	51	"

Saratoga Street—Continued

z	Tannozzini Ido	957	plasterer	58	here
2259						
a	Tannozzini Joseph	957	draft man	28.	"
b	Tannozzini Louis	957	U S A	23	
c	Tannozzini Mabel—†	957	housewife	48	"
d	Pennacchini Frank	957	barber	48	
e	Pennacchini Rose—†	957	housewife	45	"
f	Iannetti Mary—†	957	"	51	
g	Iannetti Raymond	957	electrician	28	"
h	Iannetti Ventorino	957	carpenter	59	"
k	Trigilio Victor	958	chauffeur	21	Revere
l	Biggi Amadeo	958	mechanic	26	"
m	Biggi Eleanor—†	958	housewife	23	"
n	Jefferson Ernest	958	dairyman	32	here
o	Jefferson Madeline—†	958	housewife	34	"
p	Parrelle Catherine—†	958	"	43	"
r	Parrelle Ernest	958	inspector	40	"
s	Campanaro Anna—†	959	receptionist	34	"
t	Campanaro Florence—†	959	secretary	29	"
u	Campanaro Pasqualina—†	959	housewife	69	"
v	Anzalone Mary J—†	959	"	32	"
w	Anzalone Thomas J	959	machinist	43	"
x	Campanaro Anna—†	959	housewife	33	"
y	Campanaro Gabriel	959	electrician	46	"
z	Scarfo Domenic M	960	carpenter	33	409 Frankfort
2260						
a	Scarfo Ida—†	960	housewife	32	409 "
b	Guarino Carlo	960	shipfitter	52	here
c	*Guarino Lucy—†	960	housewife	53	"
d	Sorzio Mario	961	U S A	37	"
e	Sorzio Mary—†	961	housewife	32	"
f	Cesserri George	961	laborer	33	"
g	Cesserri Josephine—†	961	housewife	28	"
h	*Arena Antonio	961	retired	81	"
k	Arena Concetta—†	961	housekeeper	33	"
l	Pino Mary—†	961	housewife	53	"
m	Pino Orazio	961	clerk	58	
n	Richards Edwin	962	machinist	60	"
o	Richards Florence—†	962	housewife	52	"
p	Festa Albert	963	plumber	28	111 Boardman
r	Festa Benita—†	963	housewife	26	here

Saratoga Street—Continued

s	DiTroio Bruno	963	laborer	40	here
t	DiTroio Pia—†	963	housewife	38	"
u	Panaro Concezio	963	tailor	62	"
v	Panaro Edith—†	963	draftswoman	28	"
w	Panaro Olga—†	963	clerk	30	
x	Panaro Olivia—†	963	housewife	66	"
y	DiLegami John	965	barber	53	
z	Scroia Dorothy—†	965	clerk	20	
	2261				
a	Scroia Joseph	965	"	45	
b	Scroia Josephine—†	965	housewife	75	"
c	Mazzapica Anne—†	965	"	48	"
d	Mazzapica Charles	965	barber	52	"
e	Mazzapica Elvira—†	965	clerk	23	
f	Mazzapica Peter	965	U S A	25	
g	Maki Carmella A—†	967	housewife	30	"
h	Maki John	967	U S N	25	
k	Sacco John B	967	retired	57	
l	Sacco Rafaela—†	967	housewife	50	"
m	Carmellieri Millie—†	967	"	30	
n	Carmellieri Victor	967	chauffeur	31	"
o	*Florentino Michael	968	baker	60	967 Saratoga
p	DeLeo Anna—†	968	proprietor	31	Florida
r	DeLeo Joseph	968	waiter	31	
s	Frangos Fannie—†	968	housekeeper	51	here
t	Vasconcellos Frank	968	machinist	36	"
u	Vasconcellos Rita—†	968	housewife	27	"
v	*Strange Frank	968	retired	56	
w	Strange Josephine—†	968	housewife	45	"
z	Vadala Joseph	971	printer	34	
	2262				
a	Vadala Lena—†	971	housewife	28	"
e	Vesce Anthony D	974	proprietor	54	"
f	Vesce Clara C—†	974	housewife	44	"
g	Cianci Dorothy J—†	974	"	42	
h	Cianci William	974	musician	44	"
k	Maniglia Alphonse	974	barber	32	
l	Maniglia Diega—†	974	housewife	28	"
m	DeStefano Etta—†	974	clerk	34	
n	DeStefano Josephine—†	974	at home	71	"
o	DeStefano Lillian—†	974	clerk	36	

Page.	Letter.	FULL NAME.	Residence, Jan. 1, 1945.	Occupation.	Supposed Age.	Reported Residence, Jan. 1, 1944. Street and Number.

Saratoga Street—Continued

P	Wightman Grace—†	974	tel operator	38	here
R	Berry Carmella—†	974	housewife	34	"
S	Berry Lawrence	974	chauffeur	38	"
T	Paci Joseph C	974	shipfitter	32	"
U	Paci Julia—†	974	housewife	30	"

2263

B	Cavagnaro Rose—†	980	housekeeper	65	"
C	Niutta Pietro	980	barber	56	"
D	Depino Grace—†	980	housewife	69	"
E	Depino Mary—†	980	clerk	26	
F	Depino Nicholas	980	electrician	34	"
H	DePino Leo J	984	operator	33	97 Lawrence av
K	DePino Sadie—†	984	housewife	33	97 "
L	Borrelli Eldean—†	984	"	26	here
M	Borrelli Frank	984	electrician	34	"
N	Casella Frank	984	machinist	63	"
O	DeAngelis Eleanor—†	984	bookkeeper	33	"
P*	DeAngelis Josephine—†	984	at home	75	"
R	DeAngelis Robert	984	U S N	31	
T	Capillo Charles	986	laborer	51	"
U	Capillo Esther—†	986	typist	34	
V	Capillo Ethel—†	986	housewife	55	"
W	Cantillo Florence—†	986	"	29	
X	Cantillo James	986	proprietor	33	"

Tower Street

Y	Cotter Margaret M—†	20	housewife	49	here
Z	Cotter William J	20	porter	49	"

2264 ### Trident Street

A	Roskilly Colin	16	woolhandler	67	here
B	Roskilly Josiah	16	metalwkr	62	"

Whitby Street

C	Famolare Joseph	9	retired	72	here
D	Famolare Josephine—†	9	housewife	70	"
E	Famolare Stephen	9	U S A	37	"
F	Famolare Dominic	9	pipefitter	43	"

Page.	Letter.	FULL NAME.	Residence, Jan. 1, 1945.	Occupation.	Supposed Age.	Reported Residence, Jan. 1, 1944. Street and Number.

Whitby Street—Continued

	G	Famolare Elena—†	9	housewife	44	here
	H	Alioto Frank S	9	plumber	26	"
	K	Alioto Lorraine—†	9	housewife	25	"
	L	Santiro Sadie—†	9	matron	60	
	M	Giuffre Anna T—†	10	housewife	32	"
	N	Giuffre John A	10	painter	39	"
	O	DeFrancesco Angelina—†	10	housewife	50	"
	P	DeFrancesco Rose—†	10	at home	29	"
	R	Covino Josephine—†	10	"	25	
	S	Covino Sarah—†	10	housewife	48	"
	T	Schipellite Jennie—†	12	"	34	"
	U	Schipellite Vincent	12	molder	38	
	V	Bartola Lena—†	12	housewife	47	"
	W	Bartola Louis	12	barber	48	
	X	Luongo Helen—†	12	tailor	26	
	Y	Famolare Angelina—†	12	housewife	61	"
	Z	Famolare John	12	laborer	65	"
2265						
	A	Famolare Louis	12	attendant	35	"
	B	Bonugli Mary—†	16	housewife	50	"
	C	Bonugli Rose—†	16	at home	86	"
	D	Ratto Emma—†	16	housewife	46	"
	E	Ratto Joseph	16	clerk	50	
	F	Ratto Mildred—†	16	typist	23	
	G	Luti Annie—†	16	housewife	57	"
	H	Luti Charles	16	metalwkr	36	"
	K	Luti Christina—†	16	"	37	"
	L	Carideo Caroline—†	21	housewife	60	"
	M	Fortunate Ella—†	21	"	40	
	N	Strollo Lillian—†	21	at home	30	"
	O	Carideo Irene—†	21	clerk	42	

Ward 1–Precinct 23

CITY OF BOSTON

LIST OF RESIDENTS
20 YEARS OF AGE AND OVER

(NON-CITIZENS INDICATED BY ASTERISK)
(FEMALES INDICATED BY DAGGER)

AS OF

JANUARY 1, 1945

THOMAS F. SULLIVAN, *Chairman*
FREDERIC E. DOWLING, *Secretary*
WILLIAM A. MOTLEY, JR.
FRANCIS B. McKINNEY
EVERETT R. PROUT

Listing Board.

CITY OF BOSTON PRINTING DEPARTMENT

Page.	Letter.	FULL NAME.	Residence, Jan. 1, 1945.	Occupation.	Supposed Age.	Reported Residence, Jan. 1, 1944. Street and Number.

Cheever Court

F	*Caccaviello Philomena—†	8	housewife	60	here
G	Caccaviello Philomena—†	8	stitcher	23	"
H	*Caccaviello Vincenzo	8	retired	67	"
K	Ruggiero Anna S—†	9	inspector	37	"
L	Ruggiero Dora—†	9	housewife	71	"
M	Ruggiero Frank	9	cable splicer	27	"
N	Ruggiero Joseph	9	retired	72	"
O	DeStefano Josephine—†	10	housekeeper	60	"
P	*George Mary—†	10	housewife	63	"
R	George Susan—†	10	clerk	23	"
S	*Pace Angelina—†	10	housewife	48	"
T	Pace Joseph	10	factoryhand	24	"
U	Pace Phillip	10	U S A	22	
V	Pace Vincenzo	10	painter	56	"
X	Indelicato Charles	12	timekeeper	32	"
Y	Indelicato Rose—†	12	housewife	32	"
Z	Castellano Mary—†	12	at home	32	"

A	Indelicato Catherine—†	12	stitcher	28	"
B	Indelicato Mary—†	12	"	30	
C	Indelicato Michael	12	factoryhand	64	"
D	Indelicato Serafina—†	12	housewife	58	"
E	Castellano Carmella—†	12	"	38	"
F	Castellano Joseph	12	mechanic	43	"

Cottage Street

G	Ciarlone Charles	57	retired	70	here
H	Ciarlone Mary—†	57	housewife	68	"
K	*Marino Charles	57	barber	51	"
L	Marino Concetta—†	57	secretary	22	"
M	Marino Grace—†	57	stitcher	23	"
N	Marino Rose—†	57	housewife	47	"
P	Torregrasso Alfred	59	machinist	31	"
R	Torregrasso Antoinette—†	59	housewife	31	"
S	Simonelli Carmen	59	U S A	23	
T	Simonelli Evelyn—†	59	at home	31	"
U	Simonelli Mary—†	59	housekeeper	22	"
V	Simonelli Reubina—†	59	beautician	28	"
W	Simonelli Samuel	59	barber	63	

Cottage Street—Continued

x	Simonelli Theodore	59	timekeeper	25	here	
z	DeMasellis Louis	61	tailor	45	"	
	2302					
A	DeMasellis Rose—†	61	housewife	40	"	
B	DeMasellis Vincent	61	U S A	21		
C	Selvitelli Carmen	61	proprietor	42	"	
D	Selvitelli Grace—†	61	housewife	52	"	
F	DeMisci Giovanni	67	proprietor	52	"	
G	DeMisci Natalie—†	67	housewife	38	"	
K	Cogliandro Nicholas	68	U S A	24	"	
L	Cogliandro Paola—†	68	housewife	50	"	
M	Cogliandro Saverio	68	proprietor	58	"	
o	*Sharaffa Biagio	69	cabinetmaker	48	"	
P	Sharaffa Mary—†	69	housewife	38	"	
R	Venturelli Josephine—†	69	"	22		
S	Gambardella Carmella—†	69	dressmaker	26	"	
T	Gambardella Dominic	69	seaman	28	"	
U	Gambardella Gaetano	69	proprietor	60	"	
V	Gambardella Lucy—†	69	housewife	61	"	
W	Wardell Joseph F	69	guard	36		
X	Wardell Josephine—†	69	housewife	30	"	
Y	Maglio Frank	70	laborer	33		
z	Maglio Julia—†	70	housewife	33	"	
	2303					
B	Nuccio Rose—†	72	"	29	134 Porter	
C	Nuccio Salvatore	72	salesman	29	134 "	
P	Gravallese John	76	U S A	27	here	
R	Gravallese Louise—†	76	housewife	70	"	
S	Gravallese Michael	76	proprietor	74	"	
V	*Serpentino Antonio	77	retired	73		
z	Brencola Anthony	78	presser	32		
	2304					
A	Brencola Theresa—†	78	housewife	29	"	
B	Galuna James	78	welder	44		
C	Galuna Jennie—†	78	housewife	29	"	
E	Germano Gaetano	79	painter	43		
F	*Tromba Christina—†	79	housewife	57	"	
G	Tromba Pasquale	79	factoryhand	61	"	
H	Tromba Salvatore	79	longshoreman	22	"	
K	Tromba Samuel	79	factoryhand	27	"	
L	Abramo Anita—†	79	housewife	40	"	

3

Page	Letter	Full Name.	Residence, Jan. 1, 1945.	Occupation.	Supposed Age.	Reported Residence, Jan. 1, 1944. Street and Number.

Cottage Street—Continued

	M	Abramo Dominic	79	fisherman	47	here
	O	Picardo Aurelio	80	proprietor	55	"
	P	Picardo Lucy—†	80	housewife	46	"
	R	Picardo Rudolph	80	U S A	22	"
	S	Vigliotte Eleanor—†	80	housekeeper	21	"
	T	Vigliotte Patrick	80	shoewkr	46	"
	U	Vigliotte Rose—†	80	housewife	42	"
	X	*Lania Joseph	81	retired	68	
	Y	*Lania Mary—†	81	housewife	68	"

2305

	B	Mercurio John	87	electrician	35	"
	C	Mercurio Rose—†	87	housewife	32	"
	D	Inzerillo Constance—†	87	operator	35	"
	E	*Inzerillo Mary—†	87	housewife .	62	"
	F	*Inzerillo Sebastiano	87	laundrywkr	72	"
	H	Vazza Americo	88	inspector	40	"
	K	Vazza Clara—†	88	housewife	31	"
	L	*Vazza Emanuela—†	88	housekeeper	78	"
	M	Peppino Ralph	88	machinist	31	258 Lexington
	N	Peppino Rose—†	88	housewife	27	258 "
	O	Raffaele Angelo	88	machinist	35	here
	P	Raffaele Jennie—†	88	housewife	34	"
	S	Ciampa Angelo	89	laborer	65	"
	T	Ciampa Antonetta—†	89	housewife	50	"
	U	Inzirillo Antonio	89	guard	56	
	V	Inzirillo Emily—†	89	clerk	20	
	W	Inzirillo Josephine—†	89	housewife	42	"
	Y	*Rose Dominga—†	90	"	59	
	Z	*Rose Manuel	90	laborer	74	"

2306

	A	Rose Manuel, jr	90	seaman	25	"
	B	Manzione Samuel	90	U S A	33	
	C	Manzione Sarah—†	90	housewife	30	"
	D	Pastore John	90	barber	56	
	E	Pastore Maria—†	90	housewife	50	"
	M	Evangelista Carmen	92	shoewkr	30	"
	N	Evangelista Rose—†	92	housewife	24	"
	O	Pastore Charles	92	engineer	24	"
	P	Pastore Lucy—†	92	housewife	27	"
	S	Quarantello Angelo	93	melter	42	
	T	Quarantello Sarah—†	93	housewife	33	"

Page.	Letter.	FULL NAME.	Residence, Jan. 1, 1945.	Occupation.	Supposed Age.	Reported Residence, Jan. 1, 1944. Street and Number.

Cottage Street—Continued

	U	Barbaro Eugene	93	fish handler	34	here
	V	Barbaro Seraphine—†	93	housewife	28	"
	W	Spinelli Daniel	94	clerk	30	"
	X	Spinelli Mary—†	94	housewife	27	"
2307						
	A	Zeuli Michael	95	shipwkr	28	97 Cottage
	B	Zeuli Nancy—†	95	housewife	26	Quincy
	C	Capobianco Joseph	95	shipwkr	46	here
	D	Capobianco Marie—†	95	housewife	46	"
	G	Rose Victoria—†	96	at home	29	"
	H	Fortes Arthur	96	seaman	25	"
	K	Fortes Mary—†	96	housewife	29	"
	M	Manzione Christine—†	97	housekeeper	26	"
	N	*Manzione Frank	97	retired	65	"
	O	Manzione Rose—†	97	dressmaker	22	"
	P	Manzione Victoria—†	97	factoryhand	24	"
	R	Zeuli Antonio	97	proprietor	58	"
	S	Zeuli Vincenza—†	97	housewife	52	"
	U	Camerlengo Lucy—†	98	housekeeper	50	"
	V	*Laurino Michael	98	watchman	62	"
	W	*Selvitella Carmen	98	retired	78	
	X	*Selvitella Mary—†	98	housewife	72	"
	Y	Colella Dominic	98	U S A	20	
	Z	Colella Philomena—†	98	housewife	46	"
2308						
	A	Chioccola Dominic	99	barber	47	"
	B	Chioccola Anna M—†	99	housewife	46	"
	C	Chioccola Michael	99	shipwkr	23	"
	E	Fiore Madeline—†	100	housewife	28	133 Orleans
	F	Fiore Salvatore	100	packer	26	133 "
	G	Fiorillo Josephine—†	100	stitcher	26	133 "
	H	Petrarca Josephine—†	100	housekeeper	59	133 "
	L	Contestabile Eleanor—†	101	housewife	31	here
	M	Contestabile Louis	101	laborer	34	"
	N	Guercio Angela—†	101	housekeeper	40	"
	O	*Guercio Calogera—†	101	housewife	80	"
	P	Guercio Ida—†	101	factoryhand	38	"
	R	Guercio Marie—†	101	designer	36	"
	U	Cinelli Albert	102	U S A	22	
	V	Cinelli Dominic	102	cutter	58	
	W	Cinelli Rockwood	102	U S A	24	

Cottage Street—Continued

Y	Maiuello Elvira—†	103	housewife	36	306 Maverick
z*	Maiuello Michael	103	baker	45	306 "
	2309				
A	Ardito Anna C—†	103	housewife	56	here
B	Ardito Carmen	103	cutter	58	"
c*	Scolponero John	103	laborer	54	"

Emmet Place

F	Bomba Vincent	2	retired	66	here
G*	Valentino Vincenzo	2	"	83	82 Chelsea
H*	Felucci Pasquale	3	"	83	here

Everett Street

K	Barresi Rosalie—†	4	housewife	26	107 Orleans
L	Barresi Salvatore	4	rigger	32	107 "
M	Cabone Eleanor—†	4	stitcher	21	here
N	Cabone Joseph	4	cutter	49	"
O	Cabone Mary—†	4	housewife	45	"
P	Cabone Mary—†	4	stitcher	24	"
R	Hall Cornelius	4	U S A	23	"
S	Hall Edna—†	4	housewife	20	22 Locke
U	Rinaldi Frank	6	candymaker	44	here
V	Rinaldi Lucy—†	6	housewife	34	"
W	DelSette Anna—†	6	"	63	"
X	DelSette Peter	6	laborer	62	"
Z	Turillo Philomena—†	8	housewife	28	"
	2310				
A	Turillo Serafino	8	chauffeur	29	"
B	Scaramella Dora C—†	8	housewife	40	"
C	Scaramella John C	8	salesman	51	"
E	Maurice Rose—†	11	dipper	41	..
F	Maurice Rose—†	11	stitcher	20	"
G	Frongello Anna—†	11	housewife	47	"
H	Frongello Gaetano	11	carpenter	50	"
K	Frongello Josephine—†	11	bookbinder	21	"
L	Frongello Julia—†	11	factoryhand	22	"
N	Picillo Achille	13	laborer	57	"
O	Picillo Henry	13	attendant	32	"
P	Vitagliano Catherine—†	13	housewife	35	"

6

Everett Street—Continued

Letter	Full Name	Residence	Occupation	Age	Reported Residence
R	Vitagliano Mariano	13	laborer	39	here
S	Barrasso Caroline—†	15	housewife	57	"
T	Barrasso Crescenzo	15	laundrywkr	64	"
U	Barrasso Ernest	15	U S A	27	
V	Falcucci Marion—†	17	housewife	34	"
W	*Falcucci Rocco	17	laborer	44	4 Emmet pl
X	Vitale Ella—†	18	clerk	23	here
Y	Vitale Vincent	18	cutter	27	"
Z	Viscay Elizabeth—†	18	housewife	29	"
	2311				
A	Viscay Richard	18	laborer	30	
C	Todisco Antoinetta—†	19	housewife	44	"
D	Todisco Mario	19	U S A	20	
E	Todisco Pasquale	19	repairman	22	"
F	Grana John	21	electrician	30	"
G	Grana Matilda—†	21	housewife	28	"
H	Ventresca Charles	21	retired	62	
K	Ciampá Carmella—†	21	housewife	29	"
L	Ciampa Joseph	21	welder	30	
M	DeMarco Philip	23	janitor	53	..
N	DeMarco Rose—†	23	housewife	43	"
O	*Riggi Julio	23	chauffeur	31	"
P	Riggi Margaret Y—†	23	housewife	29	"
S	DeRose Anthony	25	laborer	44	
T	DeRose Josephine—†	25	housewife	39	"
U	Discenza Angela—†	27	"	41	"
V	Discenza Louis	27	laborer	43	259 Webster
W	*Giunta Gondolfo	27	retired	73	here
X	*Giunta Lena—†	27	housewife	70	"
Y	Biancucci Albert	28	U S A	23	"
Z	Biancucci David	28	"	25	
	2312				
A	*Biancucci Domenica—†	28	housewife	57	"
B	Biancucci Vincent	28	laborer	27	
C	Pardi Nicholas	28	foreman	58	"
D	DiZio Corradino	29	U S A	23	"
E	DiZio Evelyn—†	29	housewife	52	"
F	DiZio Frances—†	29	"	24	
G	DiZio Renato	29	U S N	21	
H	DiZio Vincenzo	29	laborer	57	
K	Palmerini Diomira—†	31	stitcher	20	"

Everett Street—Continued

L	Palmerini Mary—†	31	stitcher	23	here
M	Testa Antonio	31	laborer	56	"
N	Testa Mary—†	31	housewife	48	"
O	Marciano Gaetano	32	pedler	56	
P	Raso Anthony	33	U S A	23	
R	*Raso Philomena—†	33	housewife	48	"
S	Raso Rocco	33	driller	48	
T	Visconte Rose—†	35	housewife	24	"
U	Visconte Vito	35	laborer	33	"
V	Terrazano Concetta—†	37	housewife	41	"
W	Terrazano Michael	37	U S N	20	
X	Terrazano Pasquale	37	welder	45	"
Y	Sardella Angelo	39	retired	70	"
Z	*Sardella Concetta—†	39	housewife	68	"
	2313				
A	Camplese Arthur	39	U S A	20	
B	Camplese Edward	39	"	22	
C	*Camplese Theresa—†	39	housewife	53	"
D	Ferris Olga—†	39	stitcher	24	"
E	Ferris Shaffe	39	cutter	22	
F	Guarino Antonio	39	U S A	33	
G	Guarino Carmen	39	factoryhand	60	"
H	Guarino Carmen	39	chauffeur	24	"
K	Baptista Carmella—†	42	housewife	37	"
L	Giusto Frank	42	laborer	48	"
M	Giusto John	42	U S A	22	
N	Giusto Joseph	42	clerk	21	
O	*Giusto Teresa—†	42	housewife	48	"
P	Baptista Mario	42	laborer	35	"
R	*Baptista Samuel	42	"	65	
S	*Baptista Teresa—†	42	housewife	65	"
T	Collorone Mary—†	44	"	37	
U	Collorone Michael	44	mechanic	39	"
V	Barrett Mary—†	44	housewife	47	"
W	*Ramano Antoinetta—†	44	"	57	"
X	Ramano Florence—†	44	stitcher	23	"
Y	Ramano Joseph	44	laborer	57	"
Z	DiGiulio Antonio	45	"	41	6 Sumner pl
	2314				
A	Hagstrom Martha—†	45	housekeeper	42	here
B	Sylvester Ernest	45	factoryhand	52	"

Everett Street—Continued

c	Sylvester Mary—†	45	housewife	41	here
d	Pisano Gaspar	45	baker	61	"
e	Pisano Mary—†	45	housewife	52	"
f	Baudanza Samuel	46	laborer	68	
g	Capozzi Mario	46	U S N	34	
h	Capozzi Mary—†	46	beautician	32	"
k	Tango Hugo V	46	painter	42	
l	Tango Mildred—†	46	housewife	35	"
m	DiPietro Ethel—†	48	"	47	,
n	DiPietro Michael	48	pipefitter	46	"
o	Matarazzo Anthony	48	checker	25	"
p	Matarazzo Domenica—†	48	at home	28	"
r	Matarazzo Isabelle—†	48	housewife	64	"
s	Matarazzo Victoria—†	48	stitcher	26	
t	Matarazzo William	48	inspector	68	"
u	Annese Cecilia—†	48	housewife	30	"
v	Annese Joseph	48	metalwkr	33	"
w	Marmiani Alexander	49	U S N	25	
x	Marmiani Helen—†	49	housewife	23	"
y	Provenzano Mary—†	49	factoryhand	25	"
z	Provenzano Philip	49	U S N	28	
	2315				
b	Morello James	49	U S N	36	
c	Morello John	49	supervisor	40	"
d	Morello Peter	49	retired	95	
e	Morello Susan—†	49	housewife	37	"
f	Trevisani Anibale	50	laborer	61	"
g	Trevisani Edward	50	U S A	24	
h	Trevisani Maria—†	50	housewife	60	"
k	Farrara Maria E—†	50	dressmaker	53	"
l	Farrara Nicola P	50	laborer	64	..
m	*Caccamesi Liboria—†	50	stitcher	21	
n	*Caccamesi Mary—†	50	"	28	
o	*Caccamesi Teresa—†	50	housewife	58	"
p	*Caccamesi Tina—†	50	stitcher	21	"
r	DiPietro Amelia—†	51	candymaker	33	"
s	DiPietro Joseph	51	U S A	22	
t	DiPietro Prisco	51	"	26	
u	Beatrice Anthony	51	janitor	38	
v	*Beatrice Martin	51	retired	75	
w	Beatrice Michael	51	clerk	27	

Page.	Letter.	FULL NAME.	Residence, Jan. 1, 1945.	Occupation.	Supposed Age.	Reported Residence, Jan. 1, 1944. Street and Number.

Everett Street—Continued

	x	*Beatrice Philomena—†	51	housewife	64	here
	y	Cardarelli Felicia—†	51	"	50	"
	z	Cardarelli Mary—†	51	clerk	21	"
2316						
	A	Cardarelli Nicholas	51	laborer	52	
	B	Ficarra Joseph	52	U S N	30	
	C	Ficarra Rose—†	52	clerk	24	
	D	Ficarra Vincent	52	laborer	70	"
	E	Santilli Frank	52	chauffeur	27	Everett
	F	Santilli Jenny—†	52	housewife	27	"
	G	Dalelio Josephine—†	52	shipfitter	29	here
	H	Spano Clementina—†	54	housewife	61	"
	K	Spano Pasquale	54	stonecutter	66	"
	L	D'Allesandro Americo	54	shoecutter	36	"
	M	D'Allesandro Eva—†	54	housewife	29	"
	N	Leone Antoinette—†	54	"	36	
	O	Leone Ralph	54	laborer	45	
	S	Salamone Jennie—†	56	housewife	48	"
	T	Salamone Joseph	56	electrician	50	"
	U	Dabene Anthony	58	laborer	64	1 Wilbur ct
	V	Dabene James	58	fishcutter	34	1 "
	W	Dabene Lucy—†	58	housewife	31	1 "
	x	*Dabene Martha—†	58	"	59	1 "
	Y	Simpson Arthur	58	clerk	50	here
	z	Simpson Lillian—†	58	housewife	31	"
2317						
	A	Palazzuolo Anthony	58	laborer	49	
	B	Palazzuolo Constantina—†	58	housewife	50	"
	C	Palazzuolo Lily—†	58	stitcher	24	"
	D	Palazzuolo Philip	58	laborer	20	
	E	Mastrolia Alphonse	60	proprietor	49	"
	F	Mastrolia Amelio	60	U S A	27	
	G	Mastrolia Anna—†	60	checker	26	"
	H	*Mastrolia Lena—†	60	housewife	49	"
	L	Imparato Philip	60	retired	66	
	M	Principato Joseph	60	salesman	39	"
	N	Principato Mary—†	60	housewife	34	"
	O	Metz Rosalie—†	62	"	20	201 Maverick
	P	Metz William	62	U S A	22	201 "
	R	Costello James	62	longshoreman	33	here
	S	Costello Matilda—†	62	housewife	29	"

Everett Street—Continued

T	Veader Angeline—†	62	housewife	35	here
U	Veader Francis	62	shipper	39	"
W	Cinicola Anthony	64	machinist	32	"
X	Cinicola Assunta—†	64	housewife	27	"
Y	Cinicola Joseph	64	U S A	24	
Z	*Cinicola Raphael	64	retired	73	"
	2318				
A	Cinicola Rose—†	64	operator	28	"
B	DelPrato Luigi	64	laborer	56	"
C	*DelPrato Magdalena—†	64	housewife	55	"
D	DelPrato Michael	64	seaman	30	"
E	Scorziello Anna—†	72	housewife	38	"
F	Scorziello Nicholas	72	driller	40	
G	*Fanara Anna—†	72	housekeeper	62	"
K	Chamberlynne Ethel M–†	74	housewife	32	"
L	Chamberlynne Robert	74	chauffeur	34	"
M	DeNisco Henrietta—†	74	housewife	70	"
N	DeNisco Joseph	74	retired	70	
O	DeNisco Olga—†	74	clerk	23	
P	Ciampa Anthony	74	laborer	55	
R	Ciampa Rose—†	74	housewife	47	"
S	Matarazzo Mary—†	74	"	23	
T	Matarazzo Ralph	74	U S A	27	
U	Simonelli Carmen	75	guard	31	
V	Simonelli Catherine—†	75	housewife	27	"
W	Pulicari Angelina—†	75	"	47	
X	Pulicari Joseph	75	proprietor	49	"
Y	Santilli Ida—†	75	housewife	39	"
Z	Santilli Salvatore	75	chauffeur	36	"
	2319				
A	Simonelli John	75	barber	66	
B	Janedy Adeline—†	76	packer	31	
C	*Romano James E	76	machinist	66	"
D	Romano Jennie—†	76	housekeeper	25	"
F	Ferrara Amelia—†	76	welder	24	"
G	Ferrara Taetana—†	76	stitcher	23	"
H	Ferrara Theresa—†	76	housewife	50	"
L	Giacobelli Charles	78	longshoreman	42	"
M	*Giacobelli Mary—†	78	housewife	33	" .en
N	Sorrentino Frances—†	78	"	37	"
O	Sorrentino Frank	78	laborer	36	

Everett Street—Continued

P	Guarino Joseph	83	rigger	41	here	
R	Guarino Turina—†	83	housewife	35	"	
s	*DeMichele Angelina—†	83	"	39	"	
T	DeMichele Crescenzo	83	baker	40		
U	Zuffante Mary—†	83	housewife	39	"	
V	Zuffante Salvatore	83	agent	40	"	
W	Loriso Antoinette—†	84	housewife	23	2 Haynes	
X	Loriso Louis	84	plasterer	23	2 "	
Y	*Sersanti Gervasio	85	retired	75	here	
z	Sersanti Joseph	85	salesman	35	80 Everett	

2320

A	Bagaroza Alberta—†	85	housewife	31	here	
B	Bagaroza Joseph	85	letter carrier	37	"	
c	*Guazzerotti Susan—†	85	housewife	39	"	
D	LoConte Angelina—†	87	factoryhand	25	"	
E	LoConte Carmella—†	87	housewife	48	"	
F	LoConte Carmen	87	shoewkr	60	"	
G	LoConte Mary—†	87	"	22		
H	Mazzarini Anna—†	87	housewife	33	"	
K	*Mazzarini Giacomo	87	painter	46		
L	Pettinicchio Louis	87	rigger	51		
M	*Pettinicchio Mary—†	87	housewife	51	"	
N	Marroni Alfred	88	U S A	24		
O	Marroni Algeri	88	"	26	"	
P	Marroni Amos	88	longshoreman	35	"	
R	Marroni Eliza—†	88	housewife	56	"	
s	Marroni Minnie—†	88	"	31		
T	Marroni Primo	88	laborer	62	"	
U	Guaetta Mary—†	89	housewife	25	"	
V	Guaetta Peter	89	plumber	28	"	
W	Marcucci Margaret—†	89	housewife	49	"	
X	Marcucci Michael	89	butcher	43	"	
Y	Stoia Marion—†	89	housewife	27	"	
z	Stoia Pasquale	89	brazier	27	"	

2321

	~~Frank~~	90	baker	25	"	
	~~a~~—†	90	housewife	26	"	
	~~a~~—†	90	presser	28		
F	~~s~~	90	U S A	25		
R	Co ~~e~~—†	90	housewife	52	"	
s	Coste.	90	laborer	58	"	

12

Everett Street—Continued

G	Guerra Yolanda—†	90	stitcher	20	here
H	Accomando Angelina—†	91	housewife	29	"
K	Accomando Louis	91	machinist	34	"
L	*DeDonato Antoinette—†	91	housewife	43	"
M	DeDonato John	91	laborer	22	
N	DeDonato Lawrence	91	"	48	
O	*Petricca Carmelina—†	91	housewife	37	"
P	Petricca Dominic	91	carpenter	40	"
R	Cogliano Michael	92	laborer	45	..
S	Vitale Pasquale	92	"	60	
T	DiGiulio Assunta—†	92	housewife	44	"
U	DiGiulio Vincent	92	laborer	48	
V	Luisi Egidio	92	"	45	
W	Mangino Gerardo	92	rigger	49	
X	*Arciero Mary—†	93	housewife	39	"
Y	Arciero Michael	93	shoewkr	41	"
Z	Scrima Adele—†	93	housewife	34	"
	2322				
A	Scrima John	93	presser	34	
B	Polino Angelo	93	U S A	22	
C	Polino Louise—†	93	housewife	22	"
D	Mazzuchelli John	94	retired	50	
F	Tiso Annette—†	94	housewife	57	"
G	Tiso Benjamin	94	pipefitter	21	"
H	Tiso Dominic	94	laborer	55	
K	*Amaru Elvira—†	94	housewife	41	"
L	Amaru Salvatore	94	laborer	47	..
M	DiGlory Jennie—†	94	housewife	45	"
N	DiGlory Philip	94	laborer	60	
O	Intraversato Augustino	94	electrician	26	"
P	Intraversato Carmela—†	94	stenographer	22	"
R	Vaccaro Rocco	94	florist	59	"
S	Vaccaro Victoria—†	94	housewife	56	"
T	Ippolito Cosimo	94	laborer	57	
U	Ippolito Josephine—†	94	stitcher	30	..
V	Ippolito Rosaria—†	94	housewife	48	"
Z	Martone Joseph	96	rigger	51	
	2323				
A	Martone Joseph A	96	U S A	20	
B	Martone Mary—†	96	housewife	40	" , den
C	Piazza Charles	96	retired	68	

Everett Street—Continued

D	Piazza Leonard	96	U S A	24	here	
E	Piazza Stephen	96	"	25	"	
F	Cavanaugh Elsie—†	96	housewife	45	"	
G	Cavanaugh Vincent	96	welder	54	54 Rutland sq	
K	Piro Mary—†	96	clerk	46	here	
M	*Bertolino Luigi	97	framemaker	56	"	
N	*Bertolino Raymonda—†	97	housewife	50	"	
O	Marcucci Americo	97	factoryhand	26	"	
P	Marcucci Angela—†	97	housewife	26	"	
R	Bertolino Christopher	97	operator	33	"	
S	Bertolino Theresa—†	97	housewife	30	"	
T	DiFraia Christopher	98	U S A	31	128 Everett	
U	DiFraia Rose—†	98	housewife	26	128 "	
V	*Catalano Frances—†	98	"	55	here	
W	Catalano Joseph	98	retired	65	"	
X	Catalano Joseph	98	U S A	21	"	
Y	Catalano Josephine—†	98	stitcher	23	"	
Z	Catalano Manuel	98	U S A	34		

2324

B	Gilardi Adeline—†	99	housewife	32	98 Everett	
C	Gilardi Frank	99	laborer	32	98 "	
D	Turilli Frances—†	99	housewife	25	298 Sumner	
E	Turilli Raymond	99	painter	28	298 "	
F	Cuzzi Isabelle—†	99	housewife	30	221 Everett	
G	Cuzzi Luigi	99	clerk	28	221 "	
H	Colandrillo Julia—†	100	housekeeper	86	here	
K	Andracchio Frank	100	butcher	38	"	
L	Andracchio Mary—†	100	housewife	33	"	
M	Rigano Anna—†	100	clerk	21		
N	Rigano Letterio	100	carpenter	47	"	
O	Rigano Margaret—†	100	housewife	42	"	
R	Moscato Mary—†	102	"	29	..	
S	Moscato Thomas	102	painter	38	"	
T	Borimano Augustino	102	butcher	55	"	
	Melchione Anthony	102	letter carrier	33	"	
	...one Marie—†	102	housewife	33	"	
		103	proprietor	78	"	
	—†	103	housewife	73	"	
		103	"	44	"	
F		103	factoryhand	54	"	
R	Co					
S	Cost					

14

Everett Street—Continued

Page:	Letter.	Full Name.	Residence, Jan. 1, 1945.	Occupation.	Supposed Age.	Reported Residence, Jan. 1, 1944. Street and Number.
	A	Vaccaro Vito	103	U S N	21	here
	B	Mercurio Alice—†	103	housewife	25	"
	C	Mercurio George	103	welder	31	"
	D	DeAngelis Assunta—†	105	housewife	55	Medford
	E	Musto Louis	105	repairman	30	here
	F	Musto Sophie—†	105	housewife	29	"
	G	Musto Angelo	105	tailor	58	"
	H	Musto Julia—†	105	housewife	56	"
	K	Trapasso Antoinette—†	106	"	54	
	·L	Trapasso Eleanor L—†	106	clerk	21	
	M	Trapasso Joseph A	106	U S A	25	
	N	Trapasso Rose M—†	106	operator	22	"
	O	Trapasso Salvatore L	106	engineer	58	"
	P	Menno Louis R	106	draftsman	30	"
	R	Menno Mary J—†	106	housewife	28	"
	S	Bottaro Frank	106	machinist	53	"
	T	Bottaro Josephine—†	106	welder	24	
	U	Bottaro Theresa—†	106	housewife	45	"
	V	Argenio Carmella—†	107	"	44	
	W	Argenio Joseph	107	laborer	54	
	X	Garadozzi Alfreda—†	107	housewife	25	"
	Y	Garadozzi Robert	107	U S N	28	
	Z	Mastrangelo Amelia—†	107	housewife	30	"
		2326				
	A	Giasello Anthony	110	mechanic	42	"
	B	Giasello Josephine M—†	110	housewife	40	"
	C	Tozza Amato M	110	welder	25	
	D	Tozza Anthony	110	shipper	27	"
	E	Tozza Carmella M—†	110	housewife	21	"
	F	*Tozza Ursula—†	110	"	62	"
	G	Grieco Elizabeth—†	110	stitcher	31	208 Bennington
	H	*Grieco Vincenzo	110	shoemaker	34	208 "
	K	Dionisi Amedeo	111	baker	48	here
	L	Dionisi Inez—†	111	chauffeur	21	"
	M	Dionisi Mary—†	111	housewife	45	"
	N	Dionisi Vincenzo	111	clerk	23	
	O	Dionisi Josephine—†	111	housewife	25	"
	P	Dionisi Philip	111	baker	26	"
	S	Ciampa Guy M	114	U S A	25	151 Leyden

Everett Street—Continued

T	Ciampa Judith—†	114	clerk	22	151 Leyden
U	Ciampa Mary E—†	114	housewife	54	151 "
V	Angelo Joseph	114	tilesetter	49	here
W	Angelo Josephine—†	114	tailor	40	"
X	Angelo Katherine R—†	114	secretary	23	"
Y	D'Italia Angelo R	114	presser	53	
Z	D'Italia Nancy I—†	114	dressmaker	20	"
	2327				
A	D'Italia Pauline M—†	114	housewife	45	"
B	*Micchetti Constantino	115	laborer	38	
C	Calla John	115	U S A	25	
D	Calla Yolanda—†	115	clerk	23	
E	Capoccia Eleanor—†	115	stitcher	54	"
F	Capoccia Veneranda—†	115	stenographer	20	"
G	Faylis Albert	115	U S A	30	Revere
H	Faylis Edna—†	115	housewife	26	"
L	Delcoria Carmen	rear 115	laborer	78	here
N	*Luongo Genarro	" 115	"	77	"
O	*Dambola George	" 115	"	62	"
P	Rinaldi Dante	" 115	"	48	
R	Guerra Frank	" 115	cutter	50	
S	Guerra Josephine—†	" 115	housewife	29	"
T	Maggiore Carmen	116	baker	33	
U	Maggiore Victoria—†	116	housewife	30	"
V	Goarino Guiseppe	116	cabinetmaker	66	"
W	Goarino Jenny—†	116	housekeeper	31	"
X	DiGiorgio John	116	tailor	64	
Y	DiGiorgio John A, jr	116	U S A	23	
Z	*DiGiorgio Lucy—†	116	housewife	57	"
	2328				
A	DiGiorgio Marie—†	116	tailor	33	"
B	Digan Bernardo A	120	motorman	32	"
C	Digan Catherine A—†	120	housewife	32	"
D	*Collins Catherine A—†	120	cleaner	64	
E	Collins Catherine A—†	120	clerk	31	
F	Dello Russo Catherine—†	120	housewife	41	"
G	Dello Russo Harry	120	freighthandler	50	"
H	Dello Russo Joseph G	120	U S A	20	
K	Dello Russo Josephine—†	120	assembler	22	"
L	Savino Margaret J—†	122	"	23	306 Maverick
M	Savino Riccaldo	122	repairman	29	306 "
N	Vitale Felix A	122	barber	44	here

Everett Street—Continued

Letter	Full Name.	Residence, Jan. 1, 1945.	Occupation.	Supposed Age.	Reported Residence, Jan. 1, 1944. Street and Number.
o	Vitale Jenny M—†	122	housewife	38	here
p	Raia Carmella—†	122	"	28	16 Frankfort
r	Raia Matthew I	122	driller	27	16 "
s	Constantino Teresa—†	131	housewife	25	here
t	Constantino Vincenzo	131	fireman	29	"
u	Damato Edith—†	131	stitcher	21	"
v	Damato Mary—†	131	housewife	63	"
w	*Petrivelli Etta—†	131	"	39	
x	Petrivelli Frank	131	U S A	23	
y	*Petrivelli Joseph	131	laborer	48	
z	Petrivelli Mary—†	131	stitcher	21	"
	2329				
a	Bruno Anthony	131	U S A	26	
b	Bruno Carmella—†	131	housewife	49	"
c	Bruno Joseph	131	laborer	61	"
d	Bruno Philip	131	"	22	
e	Bruno Phyllis—†	131	at home	21	"
f	Morella John	133	U S A	24	
g	Morella Ralph	133	laborer	32	"
h	Morella Tosca—†	133	housewife	32	"
k	Morella Virginia—†	133	"	66	
m	Parziale Sabino	137	welder	28	
n	Amico Joseph	137	"	30	
o	Amico Yolanda—†	137	housewife	23	"
r	LaFratta John	139	laborer	31	9 Bowdoin
s	LaFratta Paula—†	139	housewife	24	9 "
t	LaRaia Eleanor—†	141	stitcher	20	here
u	*LaRaia Frances—†	141	housewife	54	"
v	LaRaia Katherine—†	141	stitcher	23	"
w	LaRaia Vincent	141	U S A	25	
x	*Oliviero Concetta—†	141	at home	50	"
y	*Armillo Michael	143	laborer	48	
z	*Armillo Rose—†	143	housewife	45	"
	2330				
a	Olivolo Alfonso	143	laborer	52	
b	Puopolo Carmella—†	143	stitcher	28	"
c	Puopolo Michael	143	laborer	60	
d	Puopolo Ralph	143	"	64	
e	Puopolo Rosa—†	143	housewife	50	"
f	*Rozzo Sabatino	143	retired	78	
g	*Maglio Michael	145	laborer	39	
h	*Maglio Rose—†	145	dipper	35	

1—23

17

Page.	Letter.	FULL NAME.	Residence, Jan. 1, 1945.	Occupation.	Supposed Age.	Reported Residence, Jan. 1, 1944. Street and Number.

Everett Street—Continued

K	Montesanti Dominic	147	shoewkr	64	here
L	Montesanti Dominic	147	laborer	24	"
M	Montesanti Margaret—†	147	stitcher	21	"
N	Montesanti Mary—†	147	housewife	54	"
O	Montesanti Rose—†	147	laundress	31	"
P	Montesanti Elizabeth—†	149	housewife	34	"
R	Montesanti Frank	149	laborer	34	"

Lamson Court

	Cummings James	3	teacher	45	here
	Cummings John	3	longshoreman	43	"
Ŷ	Cummings Richard	3	retired	40	"
Ψ	Johnson Carl	5	"	70	"
Z	Johnson Sophia—†	5	housewife	60	"
	2331				
A	Taconelli Biagio	7	plumber	57	"
B	Taconelli Carmella—†	7	housewife	58	"
C	Taconelli Dominic A	7	bartender	31	106 Appleton
D	Rossi Carlo	9	laborer	41	here
E	Rossi Philomena—†	9	housewife	38	"
G	Tramonte Eleanor—†	10	"	20	3 Airport
H	Tramonte Howard	10	U S A	22	3 "
K	Hall Margaret—†	10	housewife	43	here
L	Hall Thomas J	10	longshoreman	47	3 Airport
M	DelGaudio Carmella—†	10	housewife	53	here
N	DelGaudio Joseph	10	laborer	56	"
O	DelGaudio Samuel	10	U S A	21	"
P	Manganiello Michael	11	"	21	
R	Manganiello Ralph	11	retired	56	
U	Marcantonio Gaetano	17	porter	62	
V	Marcantonio Guy	17	U S A	27	
W	Marcantonio Josephine—†	17	packer	30	"
X	*Marcantonio Vincenza—†	17	housewife	59	"
Y	Marcantonio Yolanda—†	17	inspector	24	"

Lamson Street

Z	Beatrice Frank E	16	U S A	23	here
	2332				
A	Beatrice Lena—†	16	housewife	22	"

Page.	Letter.	FULL NAME.	Residence, Jan. 1, 1945.	Occupation.	Supposed Age.	Reported Residence, Jan. 1, 1944. Street and Number.	

Lamson Street—Continued

B	Licciardi Carmen	16	U S A	20	here
C	Licciardi Mary—†	16	housewife	66	"
D	Licciardi Vincent	16	carpenter	66	"
F	Montesanti Elizabeth—†	26	housewife	34	226 Everett
G	Montesanti Frank	26	shipfitter	34	226 "

Lowland Place

H	Mario Luigi	1	retired	36	here
K	Mario Philomena—†	1	housewife	31	"

Maverick Street

M	*Iocca Pasquale	169	locksmith	53	here
N	*Durante Estella—†	169	at home	70	"
O	Durante Joseph	169	bookbinder	50	"
P	Morelli Ralph	169	mechanic	39	"
R	Morelli Rose—†	169	housewife	35	"
S	*Trocano Joseph	169	retired	80	"
T	*Sica Bruno	171	mattressmkr	53	"
U	*Sica Leonard	171	tinsmith	55	"
V	Addonizio Angelo P	171	U S A	21	
W	*Addonizio Gaetano	171	proprietor	63	"
X	*Addonizio Josephine—†	171	housewife	57	"
Y	Addonizio Mary J—†	171	at home	22	"
Z	Amato Dominic	171	shoemaker	50	"
	2333				
A	Amato Mary—†	171	housewife	49	"
B	Aiello Frank	173	U S A	38	
C	Aiello John	173	porter	45	
D	Aiello Joseph	173	longshoreman	36	"
E	DeAngelis Joseph	173	chauffeur	42	"
F	DeAngelis Santa—†	173	housewife	41	"
G	Spano Angelina—†	173	"	28	
H	Spano Frank	173	mechanic	31	"
L	*DeAngelis Anna—†	175	housewife	66	"
M	Forti Natale—†	175	mechanic	40	"
N	Forti Rose—†	175	housewife	38	"
O	DeAngelis Angelina—†	175	"	40	..
P	DeAngelis Frank	175	baker	40	
R	Otolo Christine—†	177	housewife	31	"

19

Maverick Street—Continued

	Letter	Full Name	Res.	Occupation	Age	Reported Residence
	s	Otolo Joseph	177	proprietor	33	here
	t	Spano Ralph	177	pipecoverer	38	"
	u	Spano Rose C—†	177	housewife	32	"
	y	Arimento Matteo	183	salesman	65	"
	z	Stringi Joseph G	183	U S N	20	
2334						
	a	Stringi Nellie—†	183	housewife	44	"
	b	Valardo Jennie—†	183	"	51	
	d	Blunda Gasper	185	laborer	67	"
	e	Blunda Vincenza—†	185	housewife	63	"
	f	Nicosia Antonina—†	185	"	31	8 Everett
	g	Nicosia Louis	185	painter	40	8 "
	k	*Cataldo Carmella—†	187	packer	47	here
	l	*Cataldo Modestino	187	retired	51	"
	m	Testa Americo	187	candymkr	35	"
	n	Testa Palma—†	187	stitcher	36	"
	r	Rosa Emma—†	191	housewife	39	"
	s	Rosa John	191	baker	46	··
	t	Rosa Salvatore L	191	"	20	
	u	Troisi Giuseppe	191	retired	79	
	v	Troisi Mary—†	191	housewife	68	"
	w	DiCicco Irene—†	191	"	47	
	x	DiCicco Ralph	191	U S A	20	
	y	Bettano John A	191	chauffeur	38	"
	z	Bettano Katherine—†	191	housewife	37	"
2335						
	b	*Bucci Angelo	191	stonecutter	68	"
	c	DeSimone Louis	193	painter	51	"
	d	DeSimone Mary D—†	193	housewife	39	"
	e	Maglio Angelo	193	candymkr	52	"
	f	Maglio Concetta—†	193	housewife	50	"
	g	Maglio Michael	193	U S A	22	"
	h	Guglielmi Angelo	193	engineer	36	"
	k	Guglielmi Mario	193	operator	27	"
	l	Guglielmi William	193	seaman	30	"
	m	Mancini Catherine—†	193	stitcher	58	"
	n	Mancini Eleuterio	193	retired	61	
	o	Packer Dale	193	U S A	22	"
	p	Packer Volandio—†	193	stitcher	25	"
	r	Luti Anna B—†	195	housewife	37	"
	s	Luti Attilio L	195	meatcutter	44	"

Page:	Letter.	FULL NAME.	Residence, Jan. 1, 1945.	Occupation.	Supposed Age.	Reported Residence, Jan. 1, 1944. Street and Number.

	T	Testa Vincenzo	195	candymkr	63	here
	U	Testa Anthony J	195	U S N	39	"
	V	Testa Nancy R—†	195	forewoman	38	"
	X	Guisto Josephine E—†	211	housewife	24	"
	Y	Guisto Pasquale A	211	U S A	24	
	Z	Imbriano Louis A	211	manager	31	"
2336						
	A	Imbriano Viola—†	211	housewife	31	"
	B	Baptista Angelina—†	211	"	33	
	C	Baptista William	211	shoewkr	36	"
	D	Amante Fortunato	213	retired	78	"
	E	Watts Irene V—†	213	inspector	60	"
	F	Mason Alma—†	213	housewife	26	"
	G	Mason Richard	213	mechanic	28	"
	H	Salvo Charles	213	U S A	20	
	K	Salvo Lorenzo	213	"	22	
	L	Salvo Rosaria—†	213	housewife	53	"
	M	Salvo Vita—†	213	stitcher	27	"
	O	DeSimone Frederick C	215	chauffeur	26	"
	P	DeSimone Jilda M—†	215	stitcher	20	"
	R	*DeSimone Marie C—†	215	housewife	53	"
	S	DeSimone Peter	215	proprietor	55	"
	T	DeSimone Rocco	215	mechanic	24	"
	U	Bagnera Anthony	215	rigger	57	
	V	Bagnera Helen L—†	215	operator	30	"
	W	Bagnera Lena—†	215	housewife	54	"
	X	Wilson Antonetta J—†	217	"	23	72 Liverpool
	Y	Wilson Russell E	217	U S A	26	72 "
	Z	*Mercurio Elizabeth—†	217	housewife	56	here
2337						
	A	Mercurio Frank	217	shoewkr	21	"
	B	*Mercurio Joseph	217	retired	60	
	C	Mercurio Salvatore	217	U S A	23	
	D	Conti Carlo	217	laborer	55	
	E	Conti Edith—†	217	clerk	21	
	F	Conti Peter	217	U S A	28	"
	G	*Conti Rose—†	217	housewife	47	"
	H	DeNictolis Anthony G	219	shipfitter	40	"
	M	DeNictolis Mary—†	219	housewife	36	"
	K	DeNictolis Edith—†	219	"	30	
	L	DeNictolis Emelio	219	machinist	34	"

Maverick Street—Continued

N	DeNictolis Vincenzo	219	retired	76	here
O	Santilli Mary—†	219	housewife	34	"
P	Santilli Victor	219	laborer	38	"
R	Cericola Joseph T	223	waiter	31	
S	Cericola Stella C—†	223	housewife	31	"
T	Giello Frances P—†	223	"	60	
U	Giello Nicholas	223	cooper	60	
V	Constanza Jennie—†	223	housewife	51	"
W	Constanza Louis	223	foundrywkr	52	"
X	Constanza Vito	223	U S A	21	"
Y	Battaglia Louis	225	agent	39	
Z	Battaglia Maria A—†	225	housewife	37	"
	2338				
A	Gravallese Anthony	225	milkman	40	"
B	Gravallese Josephine—†	225	housewife	40	"
C	Gravallese Peter A	225	U S N	20	
D	Cieri Thomas	225	U S A	28	"
E	Cieri Virginia V—†	225	housewife	28	"
F	Dente Albert G	225	U S N	24	''
G	Dente Alessio	225	retired	63	
H	Dente Concetta—†	225	housewife	60	"
K	Pigliari Alice M—†	225	"	26	
L	Pigliari Santo A	225	U S N	27	
M	Pirone Dominic	227	U S M C	22	"
N	Pirone Frank	227	"	21	
O	Pirone Josephine—†	227	housewife	50	"
P	Pirone Pasquale	227	shoewkr	53	"
R	Cianfrocca Gustavo	227	tailor	49	
S	Cianfrocca Josephine—†	227	housewife	46	"
T	Cianfrocca Peter	227	chauffeur	21	"
U	Pirone Caroline—†	227	dressmkr	21	"
V	Pirone Gennaro	227	shoewkr	48	"
W	Pirone Philomena—†	227	housewife	40	"
X	Repoli Albina—†	229	"	42	
Y	Repoli Theresa—†	229	stitcher	21	"
Z	Maddalone Carmella—†	229	housewife	30	"
	2339				
A	Maddalone Frank	229	longshoreman	30	"
B	Maddalone Rose—†	229	housewife	68	"
C	Delprete Antoinette—†	229	"	32	
D	Delprete Gennaro	229	candywkr	35	"

22

Maverick Street—Continued

E	Brenna Phyllis—†	231	tavernkeeper	48	here	
	DeAngelis Antonio	231	liquors	56	"	
	Sabia Antonio	231	retired	38	"	
?	Sabia Dora—†	231	housewife	35	"	
K	Sabia Giuseppe	231	proprietor	67	"	
L	Sabia Joseph	231	student	20	"	
M	Sabia Mary—†	231	housewife	35	"	
N	Sabia Peter	231	proprietor	36	"	
O	Sabia Theodora—†	231	housewife	67	"	
P	Collarone Antonio	233	U S A	26		
R	Collarone Josephine—†	233	housewife	57	"	
S	Collarone Richard	233	laborer	67		
T	Gioiosa Charles	237	plumber	45	"	
V	Sabia Marion—†	241	physician	35	"	
W	Sabia Michael	241	proprietor	40	"	
X	Corleto Benjamin	241	retired	73	"	
Y	Maher Mary—†	241	housekeeper	37	"	
Z	Pulicari Josephine—†	247	housewife	22	"	
	2340					
A	Pulicari Mario	247	rigger	27	"	
B	Camuso Amelia—†	247	social worker	26	"	
C	DeBellis Ann—†	247	shoeworker	23	"	
D	DeBellis Benedetto	247	laborer	55		
E	DeBellis Louise—†	247	housewife	44	"	
F	DeBellis Rose—†	247	WAC	24		
G	Leone Dominic	249	laborer	59		
H	Leone Victoria—†	249	housewife	53	"	
K	Leone Lillian—†	249	sprayer	22	"	
L	Leone Louise—†	249	candymaker	29	"	
M	Leone Nicholas	249	U S A	26		
N	Ricco Eugene	249	chauffeur	31	"	
O	Ricco Matilda—†	249	housewife	32	"	
P	Pitto Elizabeth—†	249	"	20		
R	Pitto Manuel	249	U S N	22		
S	DePerri Charles	249	U S A	25	"	
T	DePerri Victoria—†	249	housewife	25	"	
U	Palange Joseph	249	laborer	69		
V	Palange Nicolina—†	249	housewife	64	"	
W	Orlando Liborio	249	U S A	29		
X	Orlando Olga—†	249	housewife	30	"	
Y	Anzalone Josephine—†	249	"	51		

Page	Letter	Full Name	Residence, Jan. 1, 1945.	Occupation	Supposed Age	Reported Residence, Jan. 1, 1944. Street and Number.

Maverick Street—Continued

z	Anzalone Pasquale	249	laborer	63	here
	2341				
A	Santacroce Amando	249	U S N	24	
B	Santacroce Eleanor—†	249	housewife	21	"
C	Carr Mary—†	249	"	29	Pembroke
D	Carr Melvin	249	seaman	30	"
E	Hamel Alphee	249	painter	37	here
F	Hamel Antoinette—†	249	housewife	31	"
G	DeMario John A	249	laborer	54	"
H	DeMario Joseph	249	"	28	
K	DeMario Pasqualina—†	249	housewife	57	"
L	Russo Angelo	249	laborer	38	"
M	Zichella Anthony	249	"	44	"
N	Gigli Leonilda—†	249	housewife	63	"
O	Gigli Nicholas	249	retired	66	"
U	Mesalia Giovanni	273	repairman	55	"
V	Ventre Antonio	273	retired	82	"
X	Lepone Albert	273	U S A	23	
Y	Lepone Anthony	273	manager	30	"
z	*Lepone Joseph	273	retired	61	
	2342				
A	Lepone Mary—†	273	housewife	35	"
B	Santangelo Bambina—†	273	"	49	96 Everett
C	Santangelo Mary—†	273	operator	21	96 "
D	Santangelo Michael	273	retired	59	96 "
E	Santangelo Phillip	273	operator	26	96 "
F	Santangelo Samuel	273	U S A	24	96 "
G	Paolini Anthony	273	operator	20	here
H	*Paolini Ida—†	273	domestic	41	"
K	Scalafani Constance—†	273	housewife	26	16 Auburn
L	Scalafani James	273	cutter	26	16 "

Noble Court

M	Nauman Henry A	4	longshoreman	42	here
N	Nauman Mary A—†	4	clerk	46	"
O	Walter Anna M—†	4	at home	35	"
P	*Arpino Antonio	6	plumber	56	365 Sumner
R	Arpino Concetta—†	6	stitcher	26	365 "
S	*Arpino Lucy—†	6	housewife	50	365 "
T	Politano Elizabeth—†	7	factoryhand	25	here

24

Page.	Letter.	FULL NAME.	Residence, Jan. 1, 1945.	Occupation.	Supposed Age.	Reported Residence, Jun. 1, 1944. Street and Number.

Noble Court—Continued

	U	Politano Evelyn—†	7	factoryhand	24	here
	V	Politano Josephine—†	7	housewife	67	"
	W	Politano Stella—†	7	factoryhand	22	"
	Y	DeFuria Gerald	9	U S C G	21	"
	Z	DeFuria Giacomo	9	laborer	55	

2343

	A	DeFuria Isabella—†	9	housewife	55	"
	B	DeFuria Patrick	9	U S A	21	
	C	DeFuria William	9	factoryhand	24	"
	D	Laracy Clarence	10	U S N	26	
	E	Laracy Ethel P—†	10	bookkeeper	24	"
	F	Laracy Mary J—†	10	housewife	49	"

Orleans Street

	H	Minichiello Josephine—†	80	housewife	28	here
	K	Minichiello Zachary	80	machinist	35	"
	L	*Cincini Gasper	80	plasterer	58	"
	M	*Murano Immaculata—†	80	housewife	56	"
	N	Murano Salvatore	80	U S A	23	
	O	Bonasoro Josephine—†	80	housewife	49	"
	P	Bonasoro Vincent	80	machinist	62	"
	R	Bonasoro Vito	80	U S A	26	
	S	Trocchio Gilda—†	80	factoryhand	35	"
	1s	Trocchio Nicholas	80	operator	66	"
	T	Cammarata Mary—†	80	housewife	28	"
	U	Cammarata Michael	80	shoemaker	27	"
	V	Trippi Giacomo	80	operator	54	"
	W	Trippi Josephine—†	80	housewife	50	"
	X	Trippi Rose—†	80	clerk	26	
	Y	Trippi Virginia—†	80	"	22	
	Z	Spano Carmella—†	80	housewife	29	"

2344

	A	Spano John	80	shoewkr	34	"
	B	Coscia Mary—†	80	housewife	25	36 Coleman
	C	Coscia Ralph	80	bartender	28	36 "
	D	Gulla Anthony	80	"	61	here
	E	Gulla Anthony, jr	80	U S A	29	"
	F	Gulla Grace—†	80	housewife	49	"
	G	Gulla Rose—†	80	shoewkr	23	"
	H	Tosiello Angelina—†	80	housewife	42	"

Orleans Street—Continued

K	Tosiello Joseph	80	laborer	43	here
L	*Tosiello Rosaria—†	80	housewife	66	"
M	Emmett Mary—†	83	"	45	"
N	Emmett Oliver C	83	driller	50	
O	Zarba Christopher R	83	U S A	22	"
P	Zarba Elvira—†	83	housewife	43	"
R	Zarba Joseph	83	carpenter	46	"
S	Coveney Ellen—†	83	housekeeper	62	"
T	Ring Lillian—†	83	teacher	50	"
U	Ring Margaret—†	83	clerk	60	"
V	Autilio Frederico	85	retired	63	
W	Autilio Ralph	85	roofer	27	
X	Autilio Raymond	85	U S A	25	
Y	*Carbone Mary—†	85	candymaker	65	"
Z	Carbone Nicholas	85	U S A	28	
	2345				
A	Chiavuzzi Rocco	85	candymaker	48	"
B	*Candela Jennie—†	87	housewife	65	"
C	*Candela Louis	87	retired	64	"
D	Lauricella Rose—†	87	housekeeper	32	"
E	*Profana Emideo	87	tailor	66	36 Bremen
F	Jacobson John	89	shipfitter	55	here
G	Contreda Adeline—†	89	housewife	45	"
H	Contreda Fiore	89	U S N	21	"
K	Contreda Josephine—†	89	stitcher	23	"
L	Contreda Pasquale	89	painter	49	"
M	Annello Ezio	89	fireman	34	38 Bremen
N	*Annello Joseph	89	retired	70	38 "
O	*Annello Mary—†	89	housewife	57	38 "
R	Grandolfi Angelina—†	93	"	49	here
S	Grandolfi Antonio	93	proprietor	50	"
T	Grandolfi George	93	U S N	21	"
U	Grandolfi Gloria—†	93	buttonmaker	23	"
V	Grandolfi Grace—†	93	clerk	26	
W	Blandini Emma—†	93	housewife	24	"
X	Blandini Rocco	93	welder	27	

Seaver Street

Y	Ciavola John	3	pressman	29	here
Z	*Ciavola Vincenza—†	3	housewife	29	"

Seaver Street—Continued

A	Masala Antoinetta—†		housewife	41 here
B	Masala John		janitor	49 "
C	Celozzi Dora—†		housekeeper	45 "
D	Napier Charles J		baker	34
E	Napier Elvira—†		housewife	32 "
F	D'Amore Frank G		U S N	25 25 Chelsea
G	D'Amore Mary—†		nurse	25 25 "
H	Zichitella James		painter	44 here
K	Zichitella Mildred—†		housewife	40 "
L	*McGowan Margaret—†		"	63 Ireland
M	McGowan Peter	3	janitor	66 here
N	Porrazzo Anna F—†	5A	housewife	29 "
O	Porrazzo Joseph	5A	printer	33 "
P	Mattei Erminia—†	5A	housewife	44 "
R	Mattei Eugene A	5A	machinist	23 "
S	Mattei Mario	5A	"	51

Sumner Place

U	Luongo Edna—†	3	housewife	27 here
V	Luongo Philip	3	U S A	28 "
W	DeBole Angelo	3	welder	20 "
X	DeBole Leo	3	proprietor	57 "
Y	DeBole Leo, jr	3	U S A	29
Z	DeBole Mary—†	3	housewife	54 "

A	Campochiaro Fannie—†	3	"	28 "
B	Campochiaro Guy	3	shoewkr	31
C	Petrucelli Anthony	3	clerk	28
D	Petrucelli Rose—†	3	housewife	28 "
E	O'Connor Charles	3	U S A	29 48 Jeffries
F	O'Connor Rose—†	3	housewife	23 48 "
G	DeBole Joseph	3	pipefitter	30 here
H	DeBole Josephine—†	3	housewife	30 "
K	Del Signore Florence—†	5	"	23 "
L	Del Signore Lawrence	5	salesman	23 "
M	Faiello Arcangelo	5	finisher	69
N	Faiello Christine—†	5	housewife	64 "
O	Faiello Michaelina—†	5	stitcher	20
P	Faiello Orlando	5	shipfitter	36 "

Page:	Letter.	FULL NAME.	Residence, Jan. 1, 1945.	Occupation.	Supposed Age.	Reported Residence, Jan. 1, 1944. Street and Number.

Sumner Place—Continued

T	Zipolo Anna—†	6	attendant	21	here
U	Zipolo Anthony	6	mechanic	43	"
V	Zipolo Sophie—†	6	housewife	41	"
W	Massa Caroline—†	6	"	80	
X	Massa Marciano	6	longshoreman	57	"
Y	Ring Clifford	7	metalwkr	32	"
Z	Ring Musetta—†	7	housewife	26	"
	2348				
A	Falzone Louis	7	mechanic	47	"
B	*Falzone Mary—†	7	housewife	36	"
C	DiRocco Dominic	7	machinist	47	"
D	DiRocco Ida—†	7	housewife	37	"
E	DiRocco Lawrence	7	U S A	21	
L	Thornton Mary J—†	9	housewife	57	"
M	Thornton Mary J—†	9	secretary	36	"
O	Reid L Josephine—†	9	teacher	36	"

Sumner Street

U	DiDonato Phyllis—†	254	housewife	48	here
X	Darcy Matthew J	256	proprietor	60	"
Y	*Fenullo Fortuna—†	256	housewife	50	"
Z	*Fenullo Joseph	256	chef	50	"
	2349				
A	Fenullo Joseph, jr	256	chauffeur	21	"
B	Cipriano Angela—†	256	packer	20	"
C	Cipriano Lena—†	256	housewife	42	"
D	Cipriano Michael	256	waiter	23	"
E	Cipriano Pasquale	256	U S A	23	
F	Cipriano Peter	256	salesman	47	"
G	Cipriano Rose—†	256	stitcher	22	"
K	Gigliello Frank	264	guard	32	6 Wilbur ct
L	Gigliello Mary—†	264	housewife	22	6 "
M	Falzone John	264	U S A	25	here
N	Falzone Lucy—†	264	housewife	23	"
O	Lombardi Albert	264	electrician	21	"
P	*Lombardi Concetta—†	264	housewife	55	"
R	*Lombardi Joseph	264	retired	57	
S	Lombardi Salvatore	264	laborer	25	"
T	Ruggiero Helen—†	264	housewife	29	"
U	Ruggiero Michael	264	painter	27	"

Page.	Letter.	FULL NAME.	Residence, Jan. 1, 1945.	Occupation.	Supposed Age.	Reported Residence, Jan. 1, 1944. Street and Number.

Sumner Street—Continued

x	Culkeen Edward	268	chauffeur	45	here
y	Culkeen Mary—†	268	housewife	31	"
z	Cutrone Jennie—†	268	"	56	"
2350					
a	Cutrone Joseph	268	stitcher	58	"
c	Stellabotta Daniel	270	laborer	22	"
d	Stellabotta Lucy—†	270	housewife	49	"
e	Stellabotta Mary—†	270	packer	24	
f	Lupoli Mary—†	270	housewife	23	"
g	Lupoli Salvatore	270	mechanic	26	"
k	Martucci Carmella—†	272	housewife	52	"
l	Martucci Joseph	272	laborer	59	
m	Martucci Rose—†	272	stitcher	23	"
n	Forcillo Angelo	272	installer	42	"
o	Forcillo Sadie—†	272	housewife	38	"
p	Tentindo Annie—†	274	"	22	103 Bennington
r	Tentindo Ernest	274	printer	24	208 Sumner
s	Nuzzo Americo	274	chauffeur	43	here
t	Nuzzo Marie—†	274	secretary	23	"
u	Nuzzo Virginia—†	274	housewife	40	"
v	Pignato Michael	274	cook	46	
w	Serino Carmine	276	clerk	30	
x	Serino Frances—†	276	housewife	30	"
y	Graziano Antonio	276	technician	32	"
z	Graziano Mary—†	276	housewife	30	"
2351					
a	Armendi Anthony	276	presser	31	274 Sumner
b	Armendi Hilda—†	276	housewife	29	274 "
c	Cantalupo Alessio	278	barber	34	here
d	Cantalupo Jennie—†	278	housewife	29	"
e	Panzini Dominic	278	laborer	45	"
f	Panzini Mary—†	278	housewife	40	"
g	Naumann Delia—†	278	"	40	
h	Naumann Frederick G	278	draftsman	39	"
l	Cervizzi Bernardo	282	proprietor	64	"
m	Cervizzi Eleanor—†	282	beautician	24	"
n	Cervizzi Mary—†	282	housewife	56	"
o	Cervizzi Mary C—†	282	bookkeeper	22	"
p	Cervizzi Victor	282	U S A	25	"
r	Cervizzi Vincent	282	U S N	33	"
s	Palladino Louis	282	operator	39	"

Sumner Street—Continued

T	Palladino Mary—†	282	housewife	33	here
U	Mastrolio Nicholas	284	longshoreman	42	"
V	Panto Elizabeth—†	284	housewife	21	82 Webster
W	Panto Nunzio	284	fisherman	30	82 "
X	Tardo Frank	284	bartender	28	here
Y	Tardo Lillian—†	284	housewife	28	"
Z	DiFlumeri Amelia—†	286	"	43	"
	2352				
A	DiFlumeri Joseph	286	contractor	46	"
B	Sardella Joseph	286	tailor	45	
C	Sardella Mamie—†	286	housewife	40	"
D	Parrazzo Louis	286	laborer	55	"
E	Parrazzo Louise—†	286	stitcher	22	"
F	Parrazzo Mary L—†	286	housewife	54	"
G	King Adeline—†	288	"	20	7 Lamson ct
H	King Donald E	288	painter	27	342 Princeton
K	Rigano Joseph	288	clerk	78	here
L	Mastrangelo Frank	288	retired	69	"
M	Mastrangelo Josephine—†	288	housewife	64	"
N	Mastrangelo Mary—†	288	stitcher	26	"
O	Mastrangelo Michael	288	welder	24	"
P	Denaro Patrick	290	painter	47	47 Maverick sq
R	Denaro Peter	290	retired	86	47 "
S	Denaro Veronica—†	290	housewife	46	47 "
T	Siciliano Frank	292	bartender	67	1 Anthony pl
U	Macrina Phyllis—†	292	dipper	50	here
W	Scaduto John	294	guard	53	"
X	Scaduto Joseph	294	U S A	23	"
Y	Scaduto Lena—†	294	housewife	44	"
Z	Rubano Barbato	300	laborer	60	"
	2353				
A	Rubano Josephine—†	300	housewife	60	"
B	Mercuri Carmella—†	300	"	38	
C	Mercuri George	300	tailor	45	
D	Rubano Frank A	300	electrician	38	"
E	Rubano Helen G—†	300	housewife	33	"
F	Bottaro Anthony	302	laborer	29	"
G	Bottaro John	302	U S A	21	
H	Bottaro Joseph	302	laborer	64	"
K	Bottaro Lillian—†	302	housewife	54	"
L	Bottaro Mario	302	U S A	23	

Page	Letter	Full Name.	Residence, Jan. 1, 1945.	Occupation.	Supposed Age.	Reported Residence, Jan. 1, 1944. Street and Number.
	M	Salerno Joseph P	302	salesman	36	here
	N	Salerno Olga—†	302	housewife	34	"
	O	Dascoli Anthony	302	rigger	37	"
	P	*Marando Joseph	304	barber	53	
	R	*Marando Mary—†	304	housewife	62	"
	S	Russell Itria—†	304	clerk	30	"
	T	Turco Rosina—†	306	at home	60	Walpole
	U	*Longo Adolorata—†	306	"	78	here
	V	Pirroni Frances—†	306	housewife	50	"
	W	Pirroni John	306	shoemaker	61	"
	X	Pirroni Sylvia—†	306	stitcher	21	"
	Y	Ferraro Angelo	306	U S A	28	
	Z	Ferraro Ida—†	306	housewife	26	"
2354						
	A	Dalto Helen—†	308	"	25	
	B	Dalto Michael	308	electrician	29	"
	C	Tentindo Angelo	308	painter	21	"
	D	Tentindo Nunzio	308	carpenter	55	"
	E	Tentindo Rachael—†	308	WAC	20	
	F	Tentindo Theresa—†	308	housewife	47	"
	G	Hock Dorothy B—†	312	clerk	24	
	H	Hock William E	312	cabinetmaker	23	"
	K	Hock William H	312	watchman	61	"
	L	Capone Alfred	312	operator	29	"
	M	Capone Mary—†	312	housewife	25	"
	N	Day Sidney F	314	stockman	62	"
	O	Quinn Lucille—†	314	operator	21	"
	P	Quinn Mary G—†	314	housewife	56	"
	R	Quinn William J	314	freighthandler	52	"
	S	Quinn William R	314	U S A	30	
	T	Verredam Eleanor—†	314	inspector	27	"
	U	Verredam James	314	U S A	24	742 Bennington
	V	Lynch Michael J	314	freighthandler	30	here
	W	Lynch Ruth—†	314	housewife	29	"
	X	Falanga Andrew	318	shoewkr	38	"
	Y	Falanga Mary—†	318	housewife	36	"
	Z	Caprio Adeline—†	318	"	48	
2355						
	A	Caprio Antoinette—†	318	factoryhand	21	"
	B	Caprio John	318	chauffeur	50	"
	C	Caprio Louis	318	U S N	23	

Page.	Letter.	Full Name:	Residence, Jan. 1, 1945.	Occupation:	Supposed Age.	Reported Residence, Jan. 1, 1944. Street and Number:

Sumner Street—Continued

D	Staffieri Celestine—†	318	housewife	20	84 Havre
E	Staffieri Daniel A	318	longshoreman	22	84 "
F	*Frigolini Giuseppe	320	proprietor	68	here
G	Brogna Anthony	320	laborer	67	"
H	Brogna Mary—†	320	stitcher	27	"
K	Brogna Virginia—†	320	housewife	70	"
L	Molea Ignazio	320	fishcutter	36	"
M	Molea Philomena—†	320	housewife	35	"
O	Greco Edith—†	324	bookkeeper	26	"
P	Greco Emily—†	324	clerk	20	"
R	Greco Frances—†	324	housewife	60	"
S	Greco Frank	324	proprietor	65	"
U	Soldani Grace—†	328	housewife	62	"
V	Soldani Josephine—†	328	druggist	41	"
W	Soldani Louis R	328	guard	43	
X	Soldani Michael	328	retired	64	
Y	Soldani Vincenza—†	328	stitcher	43	"
	2356				
A	Chioini Camillo	334	tailor	58	
B	Chioini Mary—†	334	housewife	54	"
C	Finkelstein Anna—†	334	"	55	
D	Finkelstein Morris	334	proprietor	62	"
F	Acone Carmen N—†	336	housewife	20	"
G	Acone Iris M—†	336	machinist	22	"
H	Acone Mary E—†	336	housewife	48	"
K	Acone Ralph	336	druggist	57	"
L	Acone Robert A	336	U S A	24	
M	Scorziello Luigi	344	butcher	58	"
N	*Scorziello Marie A—†	344	housewife	60	"
O	Zollo Anna F—†	344	clerk	25	"
P	Zollo Pellegrino R	344	U S A	27	Revere
R	Capone John A	346	carpenter	28	here
S	Capone Marie C—†	346	housewife	26	"
T	Capone Eda—†	346	"	52	"
U	Capone Joseph L	346	U S N	24	
V	Capone Josephine E—†	346	operator	29	"
W	Capone Norma M—†	346	machinist	21	"
X	Capone Pasquale	346	proprietor	56	"
	2357				
A	Cuozzo Carlo	348	welder	28	
B	Cuozzo Constance—†	348	housewife	28	"

Sumner Street—Continued

c	Magliaro Carmen	348	retired	72	here
d	Yebba Carmen	348	welder	22	"
e	Yebba Julia M—†	348	packer	24	"
f	Yebba Mary—†	348	housewife	49	"
g	Yebba Nicholas	348	laborer	54	
h	Capone Julia—†	348	machinist	38	"
k	Cuozzo Antonio	350	laborer	60	
l	Cuozzo Mario	350	machinist	24	"
m	Picardi Louis A	350	tailor	31	
n	Picardi Philomena—†	350	housewife	32	"
o	Picardi Amato	350	laborer	57	
p	Picardi Anthony	350	U S A	22	
r	Picardi Carlo G	350	"	24	
s	Picardi Gerard I	350	"	20	
t	Picardi Sophia—†	350	housewife	55	"
u	Marmaud Florence—†	351	at home	76	"
v	O'Dea Margaret—†	351	housewife	80	"
w	Aiken Catherine H—†	351	"	52	"
x	Aiken Edna E—†	351	clerk	25	
y	Aiken Edward F	351	laborer	32	
z	Aiken George E	351	boilermaker	54	"
	2358				
a	Aiken George J	351	U S A	21	
b	Aiken Mary—†	351	saleswoman	30	"
c	Incognoli Mary—†	352	housewife	30	"
d	Incognoli Nunzio	352	shoewkr	32	"
e	Magliano Anthony G	352	U S A	26	
f	Magliano Josephine—†	352	housewife	54	"
g	Magliano Nicholas J	352	cooper	20	
h	Magliano Pasquale	352	shipper	65	"
k	Magliano Rose A—†	352	shoewkr	36	"
l	Magliano Vito E	352	U S A	24	
m	Buono Grace M—†	352	trimmer	28	"
n	Buono Michael	352	U S A	30	
o	Rotondo Angelo	353	clerk	46	
p	Rotondo Mary—†	353	housewife	40	"
r	Cuozzo Adele—†	353	beautician	28	"
s	Cuozzo Antonia—†	353	housewife	58	"
t	Cuozzo Antonio	353	laborer	66	
u	Manzoni Leonardo	354	retired	70	
v	*Manzoni Vincenza—†	354	housewife	62	"

1—23

33

Page.	Letter.	FULL NAME.	Residence, Jan. 1, 1945.	Occupation.	Supposed Age.	Reported Residence, Jan. 1, 1944. Street and Number.

Sumner Street—Continued

	w	Iarocci Carmella—†	354	housewife	62	here
	x	*Iarocci Michael A	354	laborer	62	"
	y	Sciaraffa John F	356	counterman	34	"
	z	Sciaraffa Josephine E—†	356	housewife	32	"
2359						
	a	Talieri Anthony	356	timekeeper	36	"
	b	Talieri Jennie—†	356	housewife	37	"
	c	Johnson Anna—†	357	"	26	
	d	*Johnson Beda—†	357	"	57	
	e	Marino Christina—†	357	forewoman	38	"
	f	Marino Louis	357	laborer	41	"
	g	Altri Ida—†	357	housewife	35	"
	h	Altri Joseph	357	U S A	31	"
	k	Steele Mary—†	357	shoewkr	31	California
	l	Colorusso Irene—†	357	housewife	28	56 Mozart
	m	Colorusso Ralph	357	chauffeur	29	here
	n	Angelo Anna—†	358	stitcher	45	"
	o	Angelo Leonardo	358	finisher	56	"
	p	Fiore Charles	358	printer	31	"
	r	Fiore Rose—†	358	housewife	29	"
	s	Contilli Frank	361	electrician	30	"
	t	Contilli Livia—†	361	housewife	30	"
	u	O'Connell Ellen—†	361	"	84	
	v	*Locatelli Alexandre—†	361		69	
	w	Locatelli Frank	361	retired	72	..
	x	Colarusso Eleanor L—†	362	clerk	26	
	y	Colarusso Joseph	362	laborer	65	"
	z	Lovett Margaret T—†	362	clerk	20	
2360						
	a	Pignato Marguerite—†	363	housewife	27	"
	b	Pignato Vincent	363	adjuster	27	"
	c	Galvin John G	363	attendant	44	"
	d	Galvin Julia—†	363	operator	38	"
	e	Locatelli Elizabeth—†	363	housewife	27	"
	f	Locatelli Frank J	363	inspector	30	"
	g	Sarro Frank C	364	chauffeur	46	"
	h	Sarro Josephine—†	364	clerk	45	
	l	Tamberrino John J	365	rigger	33	
	m	Maglio Theresa—†	365	clerk	26	
	n	Rapolla Daniel	365	U S A	22	"
	o	Rapolla Dominic	365	barber	54	

Page.	Letter.	FULL NAME.	Residence, Jan. 1, 1945.	Occupation.	Supposed Age.	Reported Residence, Jan. 1, 1944. Street and Number.

Sumner Street—Continued

	P	Rapolla Mary—†	365	housewife	53	here
	R	Rapolla Ralph	365	accountant	29	"
	s	Gioso Dominic	1st r 365	laborer	59	"
	T	Gioso Mary—†	1st " 365	housewife	53	"
	U	Gioso Rose—†	1st " 365	stitcher	21	"
	v	St John Marie—†	2d " 365	housewife	43	"
	w	Gregorio Agnes—†	2d " 365	"	45	10 Jeffries
	x	Gregorio Cecil	2d " 365	weaver	57	here
	Y	Frazier Mary—†	3d " 365	matron	45	"
	z	Frazier William	3d " 365	packer	21	"

2361

	A	Petrillo Alessandro	3d " 365	painter	47	"
	B	Petrillo Antoinetta-†	3d " 365	housewife	37	"
	c	*DeNajoli Enrico	366	proprietor	76	"
	D	Vassello Joseph	367	shipfitter	22	Everett
	E	Martinello Alexander	367	retired	65	here
	F	Martinello Anna—†	367	at home	32	"
	G	*Martinello Jennie—†	367	housewife	61	"
	H	DeMarco Albert	367	chauffeur	40	"
	K	DeMarco Sylvia—†	367	housewife	34	"
	L	*Hill John	368	laborer	58	2 Brigham
	M	*Hill Olga—†	368	housewife	59	2 "
	N	Matson Aleck	368	laborer	34	2 "
	o	Matson Frederick E	368	fireman	36	2 "
	P	DiNapoli Edward	368	proprietor	76	here
	R	Caprio Catherine C—†	368	housewife	24	"
	s	Caprio Frank P	368	machinist	27	"
	T	Rumley Rose M—†	368	waitress	42	"
	U	West Joseph J	368	U S A	24	
	v	Kirby Mary E—†	368	housewife	21	"
	w	Kirby Robert E	368	timekeeper	27	"
	x	Grella Alfred A	368	shipfitter	31	"
	Y	Grella Edmund J	368	engineer	35	"
	z	Grella Esther M—†	368	housewife	29	"

2362

	A	Grella Margaret M—†	368	clerk	24	
	B	Grella Ralph J	368	U S N	26	
	c	Aceto Anna M—†	368	housewife	28	"
	D	Aceto Louis G	368	tailor	32	
	E	DeFranzo Biase	368	dairyman	36	"
	F	DeFranzo Nicholena G-†	368	housewife	34	"

35

Sumner Street—Continued

G	Mirabile Benjamin	368	mechanic	65	228 Chelsea
H	Spinos Agnes M—†	368	waitress	45	here
K	Dimino Dionisie A—†	368	housewife	22	Swampscott
L	Dimino Ignatius	368	machinist	25	85 Webster
N	Goglia Frank	370	retired	82	here
O	Goglia Louise—†	370	housewife	67	"
P	Hunt Vere	370	guard	70	"
R	*Lupoli Dominic	371	baker	65	
S	Lupoli Samuel	371	"	25	
T	*Lupoli Theresa—†	371	housewife	56	"
U	Colangelo Michael	371	U S A	24	"
V	Colangelo Virginia—†	371	housewife	22	"
W	Iandolfi Dewey	371	painter	38	··
X	Iandolfi Lucy—†	371	housewife	36	"
Y	Repucci Henry	371	chauffeur	48	"
Z	Repucci Mary J—†	371	housewife	49	"
	2363				
A	Buccieri Ann—†	371	housewife	28	"
B	Buccieri Charles	371	shipfitter	37	"
C	Villa Angelina—†	371	housewife	24	21 Salem
D	Villa Frank	371	chauffeur	23	21 "
E	Trunfio Charina—†	372	housewife	51	here
F	Trunfio Pasquale	372	barber	54	"
G	Pingitore Anthony	372	shoemaker	52	"
H	Pingitore Mary A—†	372	dressmaker	47	"
K	DeFilippo Florence—†	372	housewife	36	"
L	DeFilippo Vincent	372	clerk	38	"
N	Edwards Glenn E	376	machinist	23	187 Everett
O	Edwards Olga S—†	376	housewife	21	187 "
P	Giglio Antonio	376	laborer	57	here
R	*Giglio Pompeo	376	housewife	53	"
S	Zirpolo Angelo A	rear 376	shipbuilder	58	"
T	Zirpolo Elizabeth—†	" 376	housewife	49	"
U	Zirpolo Ralph	" 376	U S A	24	
V	Zirpolo Sarah—†	" 376	housewife	23	"
W	*Ryan Mary P—†	" 376	"	81	6 Sumner pl
X	Ryan Thomas F	" 376	laborer	64	6 "
Y	Aiello Gaspero	376	"	54	367 Sumner
	2364				
A	Para Andrew	" 376	engineer	48	here
B	Para Louis	" 376	oiler	52	"
C	*Paraboschi Carolina—†	" 376	housewife	74	"

Sumner Street— Continued

D	*Paraboschi Gaetano	rear 376	retired	87	here
E	Jones Ruth L—†	378	housewife	44	"
F	Jones Thomas R	378	longshoreman	49	"
G	Marino Angela—†	378	housewife	34	"
H	Marino Salvatore	378	fisherman	36	"
M	Seifo Josephine—†	381	housewife	36	"
N	Direnzo Anthony	381	warehouse	45	"
O	Direnzo Concetta—†	381	housewife	43	"
P	Flores Frank	381	U S C G	27	90 Grady ct
R	Flores Mafalda—†	381	housewife	21	90 "
S	Casey Dennis J	382	clerk	68	312 Sumner
T	O'Neil Annie—†	382	housewife	77	here
U	O'Neil Grace M—†	382	laundress	62	"
V	Walsh Richard J	382	longshoreman	65	"
X	Colangelo Carmella—†	387	housewife	49	"
Y	Colangelo Joseph	387	rigger	49	"
Z	Buono Arthur	387	U S N	20	"

2365

A	Buono Fortuna—†	387	housewife	52	"
B	Buono Mildred—†	387	saleswoman	22	"
C	Buono Nicholas	387	laborer	49	
D	Buono Peter	387	rigger	25	
E	Buono Phyllis—†	387	factoryhand	26	"
F	DiCicco Carpina—†	389	housewife	20	"
G	DiCicco Charles	389	U S N	21	
H	DiCicco John	389	guard	46	
K	DiCicco Margaret—†	389	housewife	44	"
L	Little Anna—†	391	clerk	22	
M	Little Delia M—†	391	housewife	60	"
N	Little Philip	391	shipper	24	"
O	Little Valentine	391	laborer	60	
R	Vaccaro Anna—†	406	housewife	49	"
S	Vaccaro Nicholas	406	cook	53	
T	Ferullo Lucy—†	406	housewife	53	"
U	Ferullo Ralph	406	clerk	20	
V	Ferullo Richard	406	waiter	22	
W	Ferullo William	406	laborer	56	
X	Ferullo William	406	longshoreman	24	"
Z	Casey Charles	408	watchman	38	"

2366

A	Casey Gerard	408	engineer	30	"

Sumner Street—Continued

B	Casey Helen B—†	408	housewife	59	here
C	Casey Jeremiah P	408	engineer	64	"
D	Casey Leonard L	408	U S A	22	"
E	Casey Marie—†	408	housewife	35	"
F	Casey Martha—†	408	"	27	"
G	Collotta Mario	410	welder	20	
H	Collotta Samuel	410	U S A	27	"
K	Collotta Albert	410	"	22	
L	Collotta George	410	"	25	
M	Colletta Orazio	410	maintenance	32	"
N	Collotta Tillie—†	410	housewife	29	"
O	Grasso Phyllis—†	412	"	31	
P	Grasso Sylvio	412	clerk	31	
R	Grasso Alfred	412	"	33	"
S	Grasso Americo	412	chauffeur	42	"
T	Grasso Armando	412	clerk	30	
U	Grasso Concetta—†	412	housewife	65	"
V	Bolino Antonio	412	chauffeur	39	"
W	Bolino Elvira—†	412	housewife	38	"
X	Cassetina Alfred	414	clerk	35	
Y	Cassetina Rose—†	414	housewife	30	"
Z	Petitto Ida—†	414	"	28	494 Sumner
	2367				
A	Petitto Samuel	414	welder	31	494 "
B	Bibo Anthony	414	U S A	24	here
C	Bibo Gabriel—†	414	housewife	71	"
D	Bibo John	414	retired	66	"
E	Bibo Joseph	414	U S A	22	
F	Leonard Arthur	414	mechanic	32	"
G	Leonard Dora—†	414	housewife	26	"
H	Ahearn Bridget—†	418	"	84	
K	Ahearn Daniel T	418	shipfitter	44	"
L	Ahearn Joseph B	418	salesman	42	"
M	Ahearn Nora C—†	418	housewife	62	"
N	Ahearn Theresa A—†	418	stenographer	45	"
O	Nee Anne—†	420	housewife	55	"
P	Nee John	420	U S N	20	
R	Nee Thomas	420	shipfitter	55	"
S	Brophy Carolyn—†	420	clerk	47	"
T	Brophy Mae—†	420	"	49	"
U	Castle Arthur	422	retired	70	

Sumner Street—Continued

v	Gillespie Frederick	422	electrician	58	here
w	Griffin Clara—†	422	at home	58	"
x	Griffin Clara—†	422	clerk	21	"

Webster Avenue

z	Leonarda Mary—†	1½	housekeeper	58	5 Brigham
	2368				
a	Scardetta Anthony	1½	warehousem'n	32	here
b	Scardetta Helen—†	1½	housewife	31	"
c	Cirilli Umberto	3	presser	50	130 Webster
d	DiTomaso Nicola	3	laborer	49	here
e	DiTomaso Sylvia—†	3	housewife	48	"
g	*Perito Paul	5	retired	81	"
l	*DiSpirito Antonio	7	"	70	"
m	DiSpirito Mary—†	7	craftwkr	27	"
n	*DiSpirito Robina—†	7	housewife	70	"
r	Misiano Dominic	11	bartender	26	"
s	Misiano Helen—†	11	housewife	23	"
t	Collins Annette—†	15	"	36	
u	Collins James	15	rigger	38	
v	*Colarusso Joseph	15	retired	78	

Webster Street

w	Porcaro Alfred	146	painter	37	here
x	Porcaro Florence L—†	146	housewife	35	"
y	Filippone Frances—†	146	dipper	55	"
z	Filippone Henry C	146	U S A	57	
	2369				
a	Roundy Evelyn—†	146	housewife	29	Maine
b	Roundy Guy A	146	shipfitter	44	"
c	Smith Augustus A	146	operator	24	N Bedford
d	Smith Claire A—†	146	housewife	21	"
e	Balzotti Caesare	148	carpenter	49	here
f	Balzotti Elizabeth—†	148	housewife	39	"
g	Balzotti Dominic	148	laborer	32	"
h	Balzotti Maria—†	148	housewife	62	"
k	Balzotti Michael	148	U S A	24	
l	Balzotti Paul	148	laborer	62	
m	Spinazola Angelina—†	148	stitcher	20	"

Webster Street—Continued

N	*Spinazola Jennie—†	148	housewife	48	here
O	Spinazola Joseph	148	laborer	48	"
P	Spinazola Louise—†	148	welder	27	"
R	Spinazola Mary—†	148	stitcher	22	"
S	*Barbato Antonio	150	pressman	44	"
T	Barbato Louisa—†	150	housewife	36	"
U	Buonopane Angelo	150	laborer	47	"
V	Buonopane Nancy—†	150	housewife	42	"
W	Buonopane Susie—†	150	inspector	20	"
X	Buonopane Ralph	150	U S A	23	
Y	Contestible Antonio	150	retired	66	
Z	Contestible Peter	150	milkman	34	"
	2370				
A	Yacetta Louis	150	barber	33	
B	Yacetta Mildred—†	150	housewife	32	"
C	Salamanca Anna—†	154	clerk	23	
D	Salamanca Mary—†	154	housewife	44	"
E	Salamanca Peter	154	laborer	26	"
F	*Abate Amadeo	154	shoewkr	60	"
G	Abate Jennie—†	154	stenographer	24	"
H	*Abate Mary—†	154	housewife	52	"
K	Occhipinti Adelina—†	154	tinknocker	22	"
L	Occhipinti Anthony	154	rigger	55	
M	Occhipinti Carlo	154	U S N	20	
N	Occhipinti Mary—†	154	housewife	46	"
O	Capone Charles A	156	seaman	21	"
P	Agnew Margaret M—†	156	proprietor	58	"
R	DeAngelis Carmen A	158	chauffeur	24	"
S	DeAngelis Jennie—†	158	housewife	26	"
T	Megliola Edith M—†	158	"	24	Texas
U	St John Blanche D—†	158	secretary	21	here
V	St John Edward J	158	stevedore	61	"
W	St John Mary A—†	158	housewife	62	"
X	St John Mary E—†	158	tel operator	21	"
Y	Hanson Angelia—†	160	housewife	28	"
Z	Hanson James F	160	longshoreman	31	"
	2371				
A	Pesella Assunta—†	160	housewife	60	"
B	Pesella Helen C—†	160	clerk	30	
C	Pesella Pasquale	160	engineer	68	"
D	Pesella Frank	160	burner	36	

Webster Street—Continued

E	Pesella Rose—†	160	operator	32	here
F	Nigro Anne E—†	162	housewife	37	"
G	Nigro Anthony D	162	seaman	39	"
H	Brennan Francis E	162	U S N	48	
K	Brennan Sarah B—†	162	teacher	52	"
L	Brennan William G	162	engineer	54	"
M	Cacici Arthur	166	barber	63	"
N	*Cacici Concetta—†	166	housewife	51	"
O	*Cacici Mario	166	U S C G	21	"
P	Modica Lillian—†	166	housewife	40	"
R	Modica Gioacchino	166	shoemaker	41	"
S	Scire Louis A	166	electrician	35	"
T	Scire Pauline—†	166	housewife	35	"
U	Fratelli Adolph	168	ropemaker	50	"
V	Fratelli Clara—†	168	typist	21	
W	Fratelli Filio	168	foreman	20	"
X	Maragioglio Anthony	168	baker	43	
Y	Maragioglio Eleanor—†	168	housewife	37	"
Z	Martinello Anna—†	172	"	55	
	2372				
A	Martinello Jennie—†	172	at home	29	"
B	Belgiorno Florence—†	172	housewife	33	"
C	Belgiorno John A	172	manager	36	"
D	Delligato Gennaro	174	policeman	36	"
E	Delligato Marie—†	174	housewife	30	" .
F	Pepe Antonio	174	waiter	73	
G	Pepe Louise—†	174	housewife	33	"
H	Pepe Ralph	174	machinist	37	"
K	*Scherma Catherine—†	176	housewife	48	"
L	*Scherma Ciro	176	barber	50	
M	Scherma Joseph	176	U S A	22	
N	DeModena John	176	musician	58	"
O	DeModena Silvio	176	electrician	28	"
R	Santangelo Agatino	178	clerk	48	
S	Santangelo Angelo	178	U S M C	20	"
T	Santangelo Nicholas	178	U S A	23	"
U	Santangelo Rosaria—†	178	housewife	47	"
V	Usseglio Edward	178	meatcutter	37	"
W	Usseglio Mary C—†	178	housewife	34	"
X	*Schifino Angelina—†	178	"	62	
Y	Schifino Antoinetta—†	178	stitcher	23	"

Page.	Letter.	FULL NAME.	Residence, Jan. 1, 1945.	Occupation.	Supposed Age.	Reported Residence, Jan. 1, 1944. Street and Number.

Webster Street—Continued

z	Schifino Carmella M—†	178	cleaner	29	here
	2373				
A	Schifino Gerald	178	U S A	21	
B	Schifino Irene J—†	178	stitcher	31	"
c	*Schifino Michael	178	packer	64	"
E	Knowles Bridget—†	182	housewife	83	"
F	Knowles Mary—†	182	inspector	38	"
G	Knowles Thomas	182	retired	43	
H	DeLuca Rose—†	182	typist	27	
K	Roan Daniel F	182	foreman	57	"
L	Roan John F	182	U S N	28	
M	Roan Rose—†	182	housewife	57	"
N	Tatton Mary—†	182	at home	20	"
o	Shoemaker Clementine—†	184	housewife	30	"
P	Shoemaker George	184	finisher	72	Virginia
R	Shoemaker William M	184	machinist	31	here
s	Ciccia Arthur	184	tailor	24	"
T	Ciccia Rose—†	184	housewife	23	"
U	*Guardabascio Incoronata—†	184	"	48	"
v	*Guardabascio John	184	mechanic	20	"
w	Guardabascio Nicholas	184	tailor	51	
x	Giangregorio Assunta—†	186	housewife	46	"
Y	Giangregorio Carmella—†	186	inspector	21	"
z	Giangregorio John	186	laborer	57	"
	2374				
A	Parente Fannie—†	186	housewife	32	"
B	Parente Fred G	186	agent	40	"
c	*Pingiaro Maria—†	186	housewife	47	516 Sumner
D	*Pingiaro Samuel	186	barber	55	516 "
E	Constantine Elizabeth—†	188	housewife	38	here
F	Constantine William	188	laborer	39	"
G	Acone Benjamin	188	waiter	50	"
H	McIsaac Hilary	188	laborer	49	"
K	McIsaac Sylvester J	188	"	53	"
L	D'Ambrosio Christopher	188	"	48	
M	D'Ambrosio John	188	engineer	52	"
N	*D'Ambrosio Pauline—†	188	housewife	53	"
o	Iorio Jennie S—†	188	"	34	
P	Iorio John	188	barber	37	

Ward 1–Precinct 24

CITY OF BOSTON

LIST OF RESIDENTS
20 YEARS OF AGE AND OVER

(NON-CITIZENS INDICATED BY ASTERISK)
(FEMALES INDICATED BY DAGGER)

AS OF

JANUARY, 1, 1945

THOMAS F. SULLIVAN, *Chairman*
FREDERIC E. DOWLING, *Secretary*
WILLIAM A. MOTLEY, JR.
FRANCIS B. McKINNEY
EVERETT R. PROUT

Listing Board.

CITY OF BOSTON PRINTING DEPARTMENT

2400

Appian Place

A	*Ingala Carmela—†	1	housewife	49	here
B	Ingala Nicholas	1	U S A	22	"
c	*Ingala Salvatore	1	laborer	55	"
D	Ingala Stella—†	1	welder	20	
E	Serino Josephine—†	2	housewife	40	"
F	*Nocilla Cologio	2	retired	82	"
G	*Nocilla Paula—†	2	housewife	73	"
H	Giampietro Amelia—†	3	housekeeper	51	59 Lubec
K	Colito Manuel	3	fireman	43	here
L	Gereno Marie—†	4	housewife	30	"
M	Martell Joseph	4	laborer	67	"
N	Martell Liboria—†	4	housewife	64	"

Bennington Street

V	Murley Alice D—†	89	teacher	46	here
W	Murley Margaret A—†	89	housewife	60	"
X	Gorman Helen—†	90	welder	22	"
Y	Laffey Irene—†	90	housewife	32	"
Z	Laffey John	90	factoryhand	33	"

2401

A	Hegner Edward	90	U S A	33	
B	Hegner Georgia—†	90	housewife	29	"
c	*Theophilos Bessie—†	90	"	56	"
D	Theophilos James	90	laborer	64	"
E	Theophilos Mary—†	90	machinist	23	"
F	Theophilos Spero	90	U S A	26	"
G	Gorman Helen—†	91	clerk	21	90 Bennington
H	Hegner Albert	91	"	31	here
K	Hegner Mary—†	91	housewife	70	"
L	Freitas Augustine	92	laborer	47	"
M	Freitas Mary—†	92	housewife	43	"
N	McGrane Stella—†	92	"	24	"
O	McGrane Thomas A	92	U S A	24	
P	Alves Joseph	92	fireman	72	"
R	Gorge Henrietta—†	92	housewife	53	"
S	Gorge Joaquin	92	U S A	23	
T	Arcaro Nellie—†	94	housewife	41	"
U	Arcaro Pasquale	94	tailor	50	"
V	Arcaro Rose M—†	94	typist	21	

2

Page	Letter	Full Name.	Residence, Jan. 1, 1945.	Occupation.	Supposed Age.	Reported Residence, Jan. 1, 1944. Street and Number.

Bennington Street—Continued

	w	Campana Anthony	94	U S A	24	here
	x	Campana I'elen—†	94	factoryhand	21	"
	y	Campana Louisa—†	94	housewife	53	"
	z	Campana Mary—†	94	dressmaker	25	"
2402						
	a	Campana Phillip	94	chauffeur	53	"
	b	Campana Thomas	94	U S A	27	
	c	Porfido Concetta—†	94	housewife	36	"
	d	Porfido Eugene	94	clerk	40	
	e	Rizzo Fred	95	bartender	42	"
	f	Pomponi Mary—†	95	housewife	40	"
	g	Pomponi Vincent	95	tailor	46	
	h	Leddy Joseph	96	welder	43	
	k	Leddy Julia—†	96	housewife	76	"
	l	Leddy Mary—†	96	factoryhand	40	"
	m	Moran Mary—†	96	housewife	71	"
	n	Farrell Michael	96	retired	70	
	o	Smith Catherine—†	96	housekeeper	70	"
	p	Amelio Concetta—†	97	housewife	30	"
	r	Amelio Michael	97	laborer	39	"
	s	Mirra Carmella—†	97	housewife	76	"
	t	Mirra Martino S	97	stitcher	46	"
	u	Perez Anthony	99	fireman	53	
	v	Perez Anthony	99	electrician	22	"
	w	Perez Armonia—†	99	typist	25	
	x*	Perez Aurora—†	99	at home	65	"
	y	Perez Concha—†	99	housewife	46	"
	z	Perez Frank	99	supt	35	
2403						
	a	Perez Rose—†	99	clerk	27	
	c	Rubin Rose—†	100	housewife	65	"
	d	Rubin Max	100	glazier	65	
	e	Boris Henry	100	shipfitter	54	"
	f	Boris Jennie—†	100	housewife	52	"
	g	Shapleigh George	101	retired	50	Rhode Island
	h	Tolentino Antonio	101	weaver	35	here
	k	Tolentino Louise—†	101	housewife	28	"
	l	Carrozza Anthony	103	electrician	29	"
	m	Carrozza John J	103	U S N	23	"
	n	Carrozza Mario	103	machinist	35	73 Maverick
	o	Carrozza Mary—†	103	housewife	20	here

3

Bennington Street—Continued

P	Carrozza Vincent S	103	U S A	32	here
R	DiMarino Mary—†	104	housewife	32	"
S	DiMarino Vincent	104	laborer	31	"
T	Rizzo Diego	104	presser	53	
U	Rizzo Diego	104	factoryhand	21	"
V	Rizzo Mary—†	104	housewife	53	"
W	Cardone Anthony	104	clerk	28	
X	Cardone John	104	welder	25	"
Y	Cardone Pasquale	104	laborer	55	
Z	Cardone Tomasina—†	104	housewife	55	"

2404

A	Irwin Lillian—†	105	"	25	
B	Irwin Thomas	105	brakeman	28	"
C	McNamara Edna—†	105	housewife	28	"
D	McNamara John	105	shipfitter	28	"
E	Forziati Alphonso	107	chemist	34	"
F	Forziati Edith—†	107	housewife	57	"
G	Forziati Francis	107	tailor	59	"
H	Federico Albert	108	foreman	52	"
K	Federico Jennie—†	108	housewife	50	"
L	Marino Americo	108	laborer	37	"
M	Marino Mary—†	108	housewife	36	"
N	Marino Millie—†	108	factoryhand	38	"
O	Marino Rose—†	108	housewife	77	"
P	Marino Virginia—†	108	stock clerk	34	"
R	Faretra Arthur	108	barber	43	"
S	Faretra Sarah—†	108	housewife	42	"
T	Miccichi John	109	chauffeur	28	"
U	Miccichi Josephine—†	109	housewife	27	"
V	Cipriano Mary L—†	109	bookkeeper	39	"
W	DiAngelis Joseph	109	laborer	63	"
X	DiAngelis Josephine—†	109	packer	26	
Y	DiAngelis Mary G—†	109	housewife	50	"
Z	Viglioni Anthony	110	machinist	38	"

2405

	Viglioni Josephine—†	110	housewife	30	"
	Marino Emelio	110	agent	44	
	Marino Emma—†	110	housewife	44	"
	Rauseo Olga—†	110	"	26	
	Rauseo Vincent	110	rigger	26	"
	Iannello Concetta—†	111	housewife	54	132 Marion

4

Bennington Street—Continued

		FULL NAME.	Res.	Occupation.	Age	Reported Residence
G		Passanello Emilio	111	retired	54	132 Marion
H		Passanello Rocco	111	laborer	20	132 "
K		Passanello Salvatore	111	U S N	22	132 "
L		Russo John	113	printer	37	here
M		Russo Mary—†	113	housewife	36	"
O		Buttiglieri Louis	114	salesman	28	"
P		Buttiglieri Tina—†	114	housewife	28	"
R		Gravallese Alfred E	115	U S N	24	
S		Gravallese Linda H—†	115	housewife	54	"
T		Foley Helen—†	116	"	29	"
U		Foley Joseph	116	shoewkr	32	664 Saratoga
V		Dobbins Ernest A	116	laborer	30	here
W		Dobbins Margaret—†	116	housewife	28	"
X		Russell Florence—†	116	factoryhand	25	"
Y		Russell Joseph	116	clerk	56	"
Z		Russell Katherine—†	116	housewife	58	"
		2406				
A		McNeil Elizabeth F—†	117	housekeeper	65	"
B		Georgia Domenic	118	chef	32	"
C		Georgia Marie—†	118	housewife	30	"
D		Barrett Evelyn R—†	118	cutter	21	
E		Barrett James N	118	U S A	23	
F		Barrett John J	118	foreman	59	"
G		Barrett Margaret A—†	118	housewife	58	"
H		Barrett Mary A—†	118	operator	30	"
K		Barrett William J	118	U S C G	23	"
L		Perroni Clement	118	"	28	
M		Perroni Grace—†	118	housewife	28	"
O		Biancorvi Elizabeth—†	119	"	45	
P		Nadreau Josephine—†	119	tester	22	
R		Nadreau Louis	119	U S A	27	
S		Coelho James	119	"	20	
T		Coelho Ruth—†	119	housewife	44	"
U		Stewart James	119	cutter	83	
V		DiGregorio Pasquale	120	solderer	36	"
W		DiGregorio Rose—†	120	housewife	33	"
X		Masottoli Marie—†	120	"	45	
Y	*Masottoli Oreste.	120	tinsmith	45	"
Z		Miccichi Joseph	120	laborer	60	
		2407				
A		Miccichi Mary—†	120	stitcher	25	"

Page.	Letter.	FULL NAME.	Residence, Jan. 1, 1945.	Occupation.	Supposed Age.	Reported Residence, Jan. 1, 1944. Street and Number.

Bennington Street—Continued

	B	Miccichi Peter	120	U S A	23	here
	C	Miccichi Salvatore	120	U S N	20	"
	D	Miccichi Vincenza—†	120	housewife	60	"
	E	DiGuilio Helen—†	121	"	22	..
	F	DiGuilio Michael	121	U S A	28	
	G	DiStasio Frank	121	bartender	54	"
	H	Hayman Emily—†	123	tester	20	"
	K	Hayman Matthew	123	U S C G	27	Virginia
	L	Marciello Mary—†	123	housewife	38	here
	M	Marciello Phillip	123	salesman	41	" .
	N	Gobez Ronald J	124	shipfitter	30	"
	O	Gobez Sarafina T—†	124	housewife	34	"
	P	Pullo Annie A—†	124	"	66	
	R	Pullo Benedict	124	retired	69	"
	S	Pullo Francis A	124	shipfitter	31	"
	T	Cappucci Joseph	125	inspector	46	"
	U	Cappucci Joseph	125	U S A	20	
	V	Cappucci Lucy—†	125	housewife	45	"
	X	Mazzariello Joseph	128	merchant	55	"
	Y	Mazzariello Mary—†	128	housewife	58	"
	Z	Manfredonia Alvira—†	132	"	49	"
2408						
	A	Manfredonia Leopoldo	132	baker	61	"
	B	Mastrangelo Fannie—†	136	housewife	35	83 Brooks
	C	Mastrangelo Rocco	136	laborer	36	83 "
	E	Chafetz Dora—†	138	housewife	64	here
	F	Chafetz Harry	138	merchant	64	"
	G	Sheehan Gertrude—†	138	machinist	22	"
	H	Sheehan Helen—†	138	operator	20	"
	K	Sheehan Mary—†	138	housewife	50	"
	L	Sheehan William	138	U S A	30	

Brooks Street

	O	Sen James H	52	engineer	31	here
	P	*Sen John	52	retired	69	"
	R	Sen John J	52	U S A	22	"
	S	Sen William J	52	engineer	26	"
	T	Cunningham Mary E—†	52	housewife	63	"

Brooks Street—Continued

	Letter	Full Name	Residence	Occupation	Age	Reported Residence
	u	Cunningham Thomas J	52	shipper	32	here
	v	Sen Blanche V—†	52	bookkeeper	33	"
	w	Sen Mary E—†	52	teacher	35	"
	x	Giarle Loretta M—†	54	housewife	29	"
	y	Giarle Louis A	54	operator	.29	"
	z	Diorio Angelo A	54	U S A	27	
2409						
	a	Diorio Joseph A	54	painter	48	"
	b	Diorio Joseph A	54	U S A	23	
	c	Diorio Minnie M—†	54	housewife	47	"
	d	Ebba Antoinette J—†	54	forewoman	21	"
	e	Ebba Gennaro	54	shipfitter	49	"
	f	Ebba Philomena—†	54	housewife	47	"
	g	Ebba Ralph R	54	U S A	23	
	k	Finno Concetta—†	62	housewife	36	"
	l	Finno Luigi	62	chauffeur	40	"
	m	*Boland Jeremiah	62	fisherman	43	149 Marion
	n	*Boland Violet M—†	62	housewife	40	149 "
	o	Lachiana Luigi	62	laborer	23	here
	p	*Lachiana Mary—†	62	housewife	53	"
	r	Lachiana Pietro	62	laborer	53	"
	s	Ricciardiello Antoinette—†	64	housewife	29	68 Brooks
	t	Ricciardiello Felice—†	64	machinist	28	68 "
	u	Ricciardiello Frederick	64	pipefitter	21	here
	v	Ricciardiello Grace—†	64	stenographer	27	"
	w	Ricciardiello Louise—†	64	teacher	23	"
	x	Ricciardiello Luigi	64	steamfitter	56	"
	y	Orlindino Nicolina—†	68	housewife	25	261 Paris
	z	Orlindino Theodore G	68	chauffeur	27	261 "
2410						
	a	Fatalo Americo J	68	shipfitter	33	17 Havre
	b	Fatalo Ann—†	68	housewife	31	17 "
	c	Bonura Joseph	68	shoemaker	46	here
	d	Bonura Madeline—†	68	seamstress	32	"
	e	D'Agostino Antonio	76	baker	66	"
	f	*D'Agostino Pasqualena—†	76	housewife	64	"
	g	Masiello Josephine—†	76	finisher	40	"
	h	Masiello Rosanne—†	76	domestic	22	"
	k	Masiello Sebastian	76	bartender	45	"
	l	DeFeo Irene—†	78	housewife	34	"

Brooks Street—Continued

M	DeFeo Joseph	78	machinist	33	here
N	Bennett Margaret—†	78	housewife	75	"
O	Nesbitt George A	78	retired	69	"
P	Nesbitt George P	78	U S N	22	
R	Nesbitt Georgina—†	78	housewife	60	"
S	Murphy Lena—†	80	laundress	48	105 Bennington
T	Murphy William	80	clerk	37	15 Meridian
U	Brennan Mary T—†	80	housewife	39	314 "
V	Brennan William	80	electrician	3S	314 "
W	Bouchieri Angelo	80	U S A	24	here
X	Gallo Pauline—†	80	housewife	42	"
Y	Gallo Sabastino	80	mason	52	"
Z	Donners Elizabeth—†	82	at home	81	"

2411

A	Garisto Theresa—†	82	housewife	43	"
B	Murray Alice—†	82	"	27	
C	Murray William	82	chauffeur	28	"
D	Fiore Angelina—†	84	housewife	20	"
E	Fiore Anthony	84	fishcutter	21	"
F	Capezzuto Benjamin	84	painter	50	"
G	Capezzuto Benjamin	84	U S A	21	
H	Capezzuto John	84	"	29	..
K	Capezzuto Joseph	84	optician	23	"
L	Capezzuto Louise—†	84	housewife	48	"
M	Capezzuto Nicholas	84	U S A	25	"
N	Simonelli Anna—†	84	clerk	49	
O	Simonelli Domenic	84	tailor	49	
P	Simonelli Jennie—†	84	housewife	47	"
R	Melanson John	86	seaman	53	306 Meridian
S	Melanson Mary—†	86	stitcher	28	321 Border
T	Melanson Raymond	86	laborer	29	321 "
U	Mastrangelo Margaret—†	86	housewife	46	here
V	Mastrangelo Michael	86	laborer	47	"
W	Celona Frank	86	fisherman	27	Everett
X	Celona Margaret—†	86	housewife	21	"
Z	Dispensiero Charles	88	musician	32	here

2412

A	Dispensiero Emily—†	88	saleswoman	32	"
B	Juliano Angelo	88	U S N	26	..
C	Juliano Sally—†	88	housewife	24	"

Chelsea Street

F	Antonucci Carmela—†	122	stitcher	30	here
G	Frizzi Gaetano	122	painter	55	"
H	Frizzi Jennie—†	122	housewife	54	"
K	Frizzi Mary—†	122	stitcher	21	"
L	Frizzi Victoria	122	"	23	
N	Zaborsky Isaac	124	glazier	65	
O	*Zaborsky Rebecca—†	124	housewife	65	"
S	LaSala Carmela—†	126	"	41	
T	LaSale Louis	126	barber	46	"
U	*DeSimone Nicholas	126	shoewkr	35	"
V	Morico Amelio	126	maintenance	39	"
W	*Morico Louise—†	126	housewife	37	"
Z	Lopez Mary—†	128	operator	40	"

2413

A	Mattivello Albert	128	pipefitter	36	"
B	Mattivello Eleanor—†	128	housewife	33	"
C	Leao Marie R—†	130	"	23	69 Border
D	Leao Orlando A	130	fishcutter	28	69 "
E	Ruivo Carmelana—†	130	operator	22	Portugal
F	Mattivello Joseph	130	mechanic	30	here
G	Mattivello Vera—†	130	housewife	28	"
H	Santos John	130	seaman	27	Cambridge
K	Santos Piededa—†	130	housewife	25	69 Border
L	Belmonte Carmen	132	machinist	33	here
M	Belmonte Patricia—†	132	housewife	33	"
N	Belmonte Peter	132	U S A	21	"
O	*Mattivello Petrina—†	132	housewife	60	"
P	Mattivello Russell	132	pedler	40	
R	Mattivello Salvatore	132	laborer	64	"
S	Mattivello Edna A—†	132	housewife	32	"
T	Mattivello Salvatore	132	shipfitter	31	"
V	Drago Cologero	134	merchant	67	"
W	Drago Joseph W	134	shipper	25	"
X	*Drago Josephine—†	134	housewife	58	"
Y	*Cavallaro Angelina—†	134	"	61	
Z	Cavallaro Charles	134	porter	64	"

2414

A	Cavallaro Josephine S–†	134	stitcher	23	"
C	*Abbisso Crocifissa—†	136	housewife	50	"

Chelsea Street—Continued

D	Abbisso Mary—†	136	stitcher	21	here
E	Abbisso Rocca A	136	U S M C	20	"
F	Abbisso Salvatore	136	retired	59	"
G	Milano Josephine R—†	136	housewife	30	"
H	Milano Pasquale A	136	painter	33	"
K	Matarazzo Antolnette M—†	138	operator	33	"
L	Matarazzo Augustino	138	chauffeur	35	"
M	*Matarazzo Margaret—†	138	housewife	68	"
N	*Matarazzo Raphael	138	retired	71	"
O	Petrola Joseph	138	laborer	21	"
P	Petrola Palamina—†	138	housewife	45	"
R	Petrola Umberto	138	laborer	58	"
S	*Dalia Marie—†	138	at home	51	"
T	Lipizzi Carmela—†	138	stitcher	26	"
U	*Lipizzi Grace—†	138	housewife	51	"
V	Lipizzi Michael	138	laborer	51	"
W	Lipizzi Ralph P	138	U S A	23	
X	Lipizzi Rose G—†	138	clerk	21	
Y	Gallucci Philomena—†	140	housewife	30	"
Z	Gallucci Victor	140	shipwright	30	"

2415

A	Bongiovannl Josephlne A—†	140	stitcher	24	"
B	*Bongiovanni Mariano	140	laborer	63	"
C	Bongiovanni Philip R	140	boilermaker	21	"
D	*Bongiovanni Rose—†	140	housewife	50	"
E	Bongiovanni Vincenza—†	140	stitcher	23	"
F	Cardinale Joseph	140	merchant	58	"
G	*Cardinale Josephine—†	140	housewife	55	"
H	Matarazzo Angelo	142	welder	27	
K	Matarazzo Anna F—†	142	housewife	25	"
L	Matarazzo Antoinette—†	142	leatherwkr	20	"
M	Matarazzo James	142	laborer	60	"
N	Matarazzo Mary—†	142	candymaker	33	"
O	Matarazzo Mary M—†	142	housewife	58	"
P	Marino Marion L—†	142	clerk	23	"
R	*Marino Mary C—†	142	housewife	48	"
S	*Marino Nicholas	142	pedler	53	
T	Marino Theresa—†	142	stitcher	28	"
U	Guglielmo Mary—†	144	housewife	35	12 Frankfort
V	Martori Maria—†	144	"	47	here
W	Martori Vincenzo	144	pressman	60	"

Page.	Letter.	FULL NAME.	Residence, Jan. 1, 1945.	Occupation.	Supposed Age.	Reported Residence, Jan. 1, 1944. Street and Number.

Chelsea Street—Continued

x	Pasciscia Antonio	144	inspector	27	here
y	Pasciscia Giuseppe	144	laborer	58	"
z	Pasciscia Josephine—†	144	housewife	50	"
	2416				
b	Giannetti Anthony J	152	florist	32	
c	Giannetti Florence—†	152	housewife	28	"
d	*Giannetti Frank	152	laborer	67	"
e	Giannetti Jennie—†	152	housewife	59	"
f	Mallardo Margaret M—†	152	"	24	
g	Giullo Joseph F	152	U S N	24	
h	Giullo Virginia—†	152	housewife	25	"
l	Nappi John	154	laborer	61	
m	Nappi Mary—†	154	operator	25	"
n	*Nappi Pauline—†	154	housewife	61	"
o	Nappi Yolanda—†	154	shoewkr	20	"
p	Olivolo Alphonso	154	laborer	49	
r	*Olivolo Carmela—†	154	housewife	52	"
s	DeFronzo Anna M—†	154	"	37	
t	DeFronzo Saverio	154	glazier	35	
v	Manganello Concetta—†	156	housewife	45	"
w	Manganello Genaco	156	laborer	56	
x	Vozella John	156	"	53	
y	Vozella Josephine—†	156	housewife	50	"
z	Vozella Julia—†	156	clerk	20	
	2417				
a	Vozella Theresa—†	156	leatherwkr	22	"
b	Cresta Jennie—†	158	stitcher	22	"
c	*Cresta Maria—†	158	housewife	52	"
d	Cresta Vincenzo J	158	laborer	65	
e	*LaMartina Filippa—†	158	housewife	74	"
f	LaMartina Salvatore	158	retired	78	
g	Pompeo Angelo	158	laundrywkr	52	"
h	*Pompeo Anna—†	158	housewife	44	"
k	Tripoli Lena M—†	158	leatherwkr	20	"
m	Gardina Angelina—†	162	stitcher	20	"
n	Gardina Joseph	162	rigger	47	"
o	Gardina Rose—†	162	housewife	42	127 Paris
p	Marino Giacomo J	162	U S A	20	127 "
r	Scopa Carmine	164	molder	48	here
s	Scopa Laura C—†	164	housewife	50	"
t	Scopa John	164	cutter	46	"

11

Page.	Letter.	Full Name.	Residence, Jan. 1, 1945.	Occupation.	Supposed Age.	Reported Residence, Jan. 1, 1944. Street and Number.

Chelsea Street—Continued

	Letter	Full Name	Res.	Occupation	Age	Reported Residence
	U	Scopa Lucy—†	164	housewife	40	here
	V	Scopa Elizabeth—†	164	"	44	"
	W	Scopa Frances—†	164	at home	77	"
	X	Scopa Ralph A	164	mechanic	44	"
	Y	Pagliarulo Maria—†	164A	housewife	56	"
	Z	Pagliarulo Paul	164A	laborer	57	
2418						
	A	Lucca Leo	164A	guard	40	
	B	Lucca Louise—†	164A	housewife	41	"
	C	Alessandro John	164A	shipfitter	22	"
	D	Alessandro Theresa—†	164A	housewife	21	"
	E	Caggiano Alfred P	166	U S A	22	
	F	Caggiano Amelia—†	166	housewife	53	"
	G	Caggiano Angelo	166	laundryman	53	"
	H	*Clerico Josephine—†	166	housewife	36	"
	K	Clerico Vincent	166	barber	44	"
	L	Perriello Ernest	166	operator	26	Everett
	M	Perriello Ida—†	166	housewife	26	"
	N	Ricci Concetta—†	166A	operator	28	here
	O	Ricci Leo	166A	U S A	31	"
	P	Russo Giovanina J—†	166A	stitcher	21	29 Everett
	R	Russo Joseph	166A	clerk	21	here
	S	Russo Theresa—†	166A	operator	45	"
	T	Gaeta Albert	166A	salesman	31	"
	U	Gaeta Concetta—†	166A	housewife	25	"
	V	DeStefano Angelo	168	merchant	54	"
	W	DeStefano Charles	168	U S A	26	"
	X	DeStefano Maria—†	168	housewife	42	"
	Y	Alberelli Arthur	168	tailor	65	"
	Z	Alberelli Jennie—†	168	at home	59	"
2419						
	A	Celata Bernard	168	electrician	43	"
	B	Celata Josephine—†	168	housewife	38	"
	C	Rubino Florinda D—†	168	operator	27	"
	D	Rubino Frank	168	U S A	25	"
	E	*Rubino Lorenza—†	168	at home	51	"
	F	Rubino Louis	168	U S A	24	
	G	Rubino Rudolph	168	"	22	
	K	Gargiulo Florence—†	170	housewife	38	"
	L	*Gargiulo Giro	170	retired	56	
	M	Spolsino Anthony	170	U S A	23	

12

Chelsea Street—Continued

Page.	Letter.	FULL NAME.	Residence, Jan. 1, 1945.	Occupation.	Supposed Age.	Reported Residence, Jan. 1, 1944. Street and Number.
	N	Spolsino Jennie—†	170	packer	47	here
	O	Spolsino Michael	170	laborer	51	"
	P	Spolsino Nicholas	170	U S A	21	"
	R	Buonopane Generoso	170	operator	50	"
	S	Buonopane Margaret—†	170	housewife	38	"
	T	Sponpinato Antoinetta—†	174	tailor	32	
	U	Sponpinato Joseph	174	painter	36	
	V	Riccio Anna—†	174	clerk	25	
	W	Riccio Antonio	174	laborer	61	
	X	Riccio Carmela—†	174	clerk	20	"
	Y	Riccio John	174	shipfitter	22	"
	Z	Riccio Joseph	174	U S A	26	
2420						
	A	*Riccio Mariana—†	174	housewife	50	"
	B	Riccio Michael	174	U S M C	29	"
	C	Barresi Allesandro	174	laborer	59	
	D	Barresi Antoinetta—†	174	packer	23	
	E	Barresi Frank	174	U S A	28	
	F	Barresi George	174	"	25	
	G	Barresi Helen A—†	174	packer	24	"
	H	Barresi Joseph	174	laborer	32	
	K	Barresi Josephine—†	174	housewife	55	"
	L	*Cataldo Carlo	176	merchant	54	"
	M	Cataldo Louisa—†	176	clerk	42	
	N	Cataldo Maria—†	176	"	21	
	O	Rapino Eleanora D—†	176	typist	20	
	P	Rapino Margaret—†	176	at home	47	"
	R	Rapino Rose M—†	176	metalwkr	22	"
	S	Geraci Benedetto	176	chauffeur	23	"
	T	Geraci Cologero	176	carpenter	54	"
	U	Geraci Columbia—†	176	housewife	54	"
	V	Geraci Gaetano A	176	presser	20	
	W	Geraci Vincent	176	U S N	22	
	X	DiFronzo Giuseppe	180	tailor	67	
	Y	DiFronzo Sarah—†	180	housewife	66	"
	Z	DiFronzo Vincenzo	180	clerk	34	"
2421						
	A	Bruno Alfonse	180	millhand	33	"
	B	Bruno Gabriel	180	chauffeur	53	"
	C	Bruno Henry	180	U S A	21	
	D	*Bruno Maria—†	180	housewife	53	"

Chelsea Street—Continued

E	Addario Josephine—†	180	housewife	32	here
F	Addario Santino	180	salesman	35	"
G	DeStefano Josephine—†	182	housewife	25	"
H	DeStefano Salvatore	182	U S A	24	
K	Petitto Rocco	182	tinsmith	51	
L	Petitto Rosaria—†	182	housewife	46	"
M	Lorina Anthony	182	barber	38	
N	Lorina Josephine—†	182	housewife	38	"
O	Arimento Aida M—†	184	"	26	
P	Arimento Daniel	184	pharmacist	28	"
R	Paterno Angelo	184	painter	44	"
S	Paterno Anna—†	184	housewife	35	"
T	Mari Domenick	184	carpenter	65	"
U	Mari Eugenia—†	184	housewife	61	"
V	Pechner Benjamin	186	U S A	27	
W	Pechner Isaac	186	laborer	60	"
X	Pechner Sarah—†	186	housewife	55	"
Y	Guerriero Christopher	186	shipwright	52	"
Z	Guerriero Florence—†	186	housewife	45	"
	2422				
A	Burke Grace—†	186	"	43	
B	Burke John P	186	foreman	45	"
D	*Santarpio Incoronata—-†	188A	at home	65	"
E	Agri Angelina—†	188A	housewife	32	"
F	Agri Lucio	188A	tailor	35	

Davis Court

G	Faretra Phyllis—†	1	housewife	21	here
H	Faretra Thomas	1	painter	27	"
K	Faretra Concetta—†	1	at home	60	"
L	Faretra Virginia M—†	1	"	30	
M	Tropea Caroline A—†	3	housewife	26	"
N	Tropea Salvatore J	3	U S A	29	"
O	Guerreri Jennie—†	3	stitcher	20	"
P	Guerreri Philip	3	laborer	62	"
R	Guerreri Susie—†	3	housewife	50	"

Havre Street

S	Sardina Carmella—†	174	housewife	62	here
T	Sardina James	174	pedler	48	"

14

Havre Street—Continued

U	Sardina Jerome	174	clerk	40	here
V	*Sardina Joseph	174	pedler	66	"
W	Sardina Joseph	174	U S N	20	"
X	*Dicino Anthony	174	retired	66	"
Y	Dicino Margaret—†	174	housewife	45	175 Havre
Z	Kulbitsky Olympia—†	175	clerk	26	here
2423					
A	Nickerson Clara—†	175	at home	75	"
B	Tremonte Albert	175	laborer	52	
C	Tremonte Nellie—†	175	housewife	49	"
D	Merullo Mary—†	175	at home	30	"
E	Stokes George	176	clerk	43	
F	Stokes John C	176	U S N	39	
G	Stokes Marie E—†	176	housewife	41	"
H	Michaud Adele—†	176	"	45	Chelsea
K	Michaud Fred	176	metalwkr	53	here
L	Salerno Madeline—†	178	housewife	35	"
M	Salerno Michael	178	clerk	30	"
N	Mancuso Grace—†	178	at home	27	"
O	Mancuso Mary—†	178	housewife	52	"
P	Mancuso Peter	178	laborer	63	
R	Gelardi Mary—†	178	stitcher	26	"
S	*Lombardo Joseph	178	laborer	60	
T	*Lombardo Virginia—†	178	housewife	49	"
U	Bertulli Angela—†	179	factoryhand	28	"
V	Bertulli Elvidio	179	U S A	23	
W	Bertulli Elsie—†	179	at home	61	"
X	Bertulli Louise—†	179	factoryhand	34	"
Y	Bertulli Patrick	179	U S A	30	"
Z	Bertulli William	179	"	26	
2424					
B	Salerno Antoinetta—†	179	housewife	54	"
C	Salerno Joseph	179	laborer	50	"
D	Donatelli Celia—†	181	housewife	66	"
E	Donatelli Gaetano	181	retired	69	"
F	Donatelli Maria—†	181	factoryhand	33	"
G	Lightbody Charles	183	laborer	36	"
H	Lightbody Mary—†	183	housewife	38	"
K	Parsons Margaret—†	183	waitress	23	131 Eutaw
L	Deluple Florence—†	183	housewife	39	here
M	Deluple John	183	rigger	44	"
N	Falzone Elsie—†	184	housewife	35	"

Page.	Letter.	FULL NAME.	Residence, Jan. 1, 1945.	Occupation.	Supposed Age.	Reported Residence, Jan. 1, 1944. Street and Number.

Havre Street—Continued

o	Falzone James	184	pedler	36	here
s	Tasha Anthony	185	expressman	52	"
t	Tasha Arthur	185	U S C G	22	"
u	Tasha Dorothy—†	185	shoewkr	26	"
v	Tasha Grace—†	185	housewife	44	"
w	Dellaria Giacomo	185	retired	77	189 Havre
x	Dellaria Rose—†	185	housewife	67	189 "
y	Dellaria Vito	185	salesman	44	189 "
z	Ciarcia Anna—†	185	housewife	44	here
	2425				
a	Ciarcia Manuel	185	molder	21	
b	Ciarcia Michael	185	"	55	
c	Dulcetta Gabriel	186	U S N	23	"
d	*Dulcetta Joseph	186	laborer	59	
e	*Dulcetta Santa—†	186	housewife	57	"
f	Dulcetta Santa J—†	186	stitcher	21	"
g	Sciortino Angelina—†	187	housewife	52	"
h	Sciortino Joseph	187	laborer	52	
k	Sciortino Joseph	187	U S A	21	
l	Sciortino Rose—†	187	shoewkr	25	"
m	Vella Alphonso	187	packer	40	"
n	Vella Rose—†	187	housewife	35	"
o	Lenardi Rose—†	187	at home	59	"
r	Palagreco Filippa—†	189	"	72	"
s	Palagreco Lena—†	189	clerk	32	
t	Palagreco Charles	189	chauffeur	34	"
u	Palagreco Joseph	189	laborer	37	"
v	Palagreco Rose—†	189	housewife	25	"
w	Annese Carmen	194	laborer	53	"
x	Caporale Angeline—†	194	stitcher	24	"
y	Covino James	194	chauffeur	50	"
z	Covino Louis W	194	"	28	
	2426				
a	*Covino Mary—†	194	housewife	61	"
b	*Mazzarella Concetta M—†	195	"	56	"
c	Mazzarella Francisco A	195	shoewkr	64	"
d	Nesbitt Clement	195	operator	31	"
e	Nesbitt Marie—†	195	housewife	27	"
f	Balcom Susie—†	195	"	40	
g	Balcom Thomas	195	retired	76	"
h	Bennett Peter	195	seaman	50	New York

16

Havre Street—Continued

L	Flanagan Gladys—†	196	housekeeper	46	here
M	Nealon Catherine—†	196	"	73	"
N	Pomodoro Josephine—†	197	dressmaker	50	"
O	DiSalvo Maria—†	197	housewife	43	"
P	DiSalvo Michael M	197	merchant.	46	"
R	DiSalvo Paul R	197	U S A	23	"
S	Carfagna Fannie—†	197	housewife	23	176 Paris
T	Carfagna Henry	197	electrician	25	here
U	Quartarone Frank	198	U S A	20	"
V	Quartarone Mario	198	chauffeur	40	"
W	*Quartarone Minnie—†	198	housewife	40	"
X	*Meoli Ernest	198	laborer	47	
Y	*Meoli Mary—†	198	housewife	39	"
Z	Roberts Frank	198	U S A	24	

2427

A	*Roberts Gladys—†	198	housewife	58	"
B	Roberts Joseph	198	laborer	22	
C	Roberts Luigi	198	"	53	
D	Roberts Theresa—†	198	stitcher	20	"
E	Falzarano Andrea	199	painter	27	"
F	*Falzarano Domenic	199	laborer	65	
G	*Falzarano Frances—†	199	housewife	64	"
H	Corsi Angelo	201	laborer	57	"
K	Cuozzo Angelina—†	201	clerk	24	
L	Cuozzo Rose—†	201	housewife	53	"
M	Cuozzo Valentino	201	laborer	57	
N	Cuozzo Viola—†	201	inspector	22	"
O	*Dampolo Mary—†	201	at home	38	"
P	Bruno Aniello	201	shipfitter	49	"
R	Bruno Frank	201	U S A	23	
S	Bruno Helen—†	201	housewife	39	"
T	Bruno Peter	201	U S A	21	"
U	DiGirolamo Anthony	202	laborer	33	"
V	DiGirolamo Josephine—†	202	housewife	29	"
W	Quarantiello Armando	202	U S N	20	
X	*Quarantiello Celia—†	202	housekeeper	50	"
Y	Quarantiello Domenic	202	chauffeur	28	"
Z	Quarantiello Joseph	202	laborer	22	

2428

A	Falzarano Columbia—†	202	housewife	27	"
B	Falzarano Louis	202	rigger	29	

1—24   17

Havre Street—Continued

	Letter	Full Name	Residence	Occupation	Age	Reported Residence
O	c	Riccio Angeline—†	206	housewife	37	here
S	d	Riccio Carmen	206	merchant	46	"
T	e	*Arinella Anna—†	206	housekeeper	54	"
U	f	Arinella John	206	U S A	25	
V	g	Arinella Louis	206	painter	22	"
W	h	Arinella Mary—†	206	beautician	27	"
X	k	Guerra Anthony	206	foreman	34	"
Y	l	Guerra Grace—†	206	housewife	33	"
Z	m	Bowden Herbert	207	engineer	32	"
	n	Bowden Mildred—†	207	housewife	28	"
A	o	Mustone Alfred	208	U S N	30	
B	p	Mustone Christopher	208	"	20	"
C	r	Mustone Eugene	208	chauffeur	24	"
D*	s	Mustone Mary—†	208	housewife	49	"
E*	t	Mustone Samuel	208	laborer	59	"
F	v	*DeFrancesco Frances—†	208	housewife	40	"
G	w	DeFrancesco Frank	208	U S A	34	"
H	x	Ruo Carmine—†	208	inspector	21	"
K	y	Saggese Ferdinand	209	retired	64	"
L	z	Gioioso Phyllis—†	209	housewife	28	"
M		**2429**				
N	a	Gioioso Vincent	209	laborer	32	"
O	b	Greco Catherine—†	209	at home	61	"
R	c	DelloRusso John	rear 209	laborer	52	"
S	d	Camemillo Cologero	" 209	retired	65	207 Chelsea
T	e	*Cerullo Maria—†	" 209	housewife	67	Medford
U	f	*Cerullo Nicolo	" 209	laborer	68	"
V	g	Russo Angelo	210	candymaker	52	here
W	h	Russo Frances—†	210	housewife	45	"
X	k	Russo Philip	210	U S M C	21	"
Y	l	McDonough Alice D—†	211	housewife	31	"
Z	m	McDonough Walter A	211	electrician	41	"
	n	Juliano Joseph	213	laborer	44	"
A*	o	Juliano Lena—†	213	housewife	40	"
B*	p	Alessi Edward	213	retired	76	
C	r	Alessi Eufemia—†	213	housewife	74	"
D	s	Marshall Anna—†	214	housekeeper	65	"
E	t	Lippert Elizabeth—†	214	housewife	54	"
F	u	Lippert Rudolph A	214	repairman	62	"
G	v	Amata Frank	215	cabinetmaker	35	197 Havre
H	w	Amata Marion—†	215	housewife	31	197 "

Havre Street—Continued

x	Casiello Antonio	215	laborer	62	here
y	Casiello John	215	U S A	26	"
z	Piermattei Agnes—†	215	housewife	31	195 Havre
2430					
a	Piermattei Domenic	215	attendant	32	195 "
b	Coliano Florence—†	215	factoryhand	31	here
c	Coliano John	215	U S A	33	"
d	Compana Robert	215	"	21	"
e	Rossetti Jennie—†	215	at home	65	"
f	Rossetti Lenora—†	215	factoryhand	32	"
g	*Bennett Minnie—†	216	housekeeper	53	"
h	Trainor Dorothy—†	216	housewife	34	"
k	Trainor Owen	216	laborer	35	
l	Taft Joseph	216	longshoreman	43	"
m	Taft Margaret—†	216	housewife	37	"
n	Murray Henry	rear 216	painter	34	210 Paris
o	Murray Louise—†	" 216	housewife	33	210 "
p	*Cuscio Michael	217	retired	40	here
r	*Quartarone Frank	217	barber	57	"
s	Quartarone Frank	217	"	20	"
t	*Quartarone Jennie—†	217	housewife	58	"
v	DelloRusso Amedeo	217	laborer	38	
w	*DelloRusso Carlo	217	barber	67	
x	DelloRusso Emelia—†	217	packer	32	
y	DelloRusso Ida—†	217	clerk	22	
z	*DelloRusso Raffaela—†	217	housewife	66	"
2431					
a	DelloRusso Romeo	217	U S A	28	
c	*Crescenzo Biagio	218	millhand	48	"
d	Crescenzo Rose—†	218	housewife	37	"
f	Hudson Eva—†	220	housekeeper	32	"
h	Dionizio Josephine—†	220	housewife	32	185 Marion
k	Dionizio Manuel	220	metalworker	36	185 "
m	Nigro Nicolo	rear 220	laborer	55	here
n	*Cerulli Clementina—†	" 220	housekeeper	52	"
o	Parziale Carmen	" 220	laborer	22	117 Chelsea
p	Parziale Virginia—†	" 220	housewife	21	117 "
r	Finno Virginia—†	" 220	housekeeper	66	here
s	*Amarosa Michael	" 220	laborer	54	"
t	DiSario Frederick	221	"	30	"
u	DiSario Helen—†	221	housewife	28	"

Page.	Letter.	FULL NAME.	Residence, Jan. 1, 1945.	Occupation.	Supposed Age.	Reported Residence, Jan. 1, 1944. Street and Number.

Havre Street—Continued

v	Durante Cecelia—†	221	housewife	62	here
w	Durante Pasquale	221	laborer	53	"
x	Durante Peter A	221	U S N	23	"
y	Colotti Carmen	221	seaman	31	"
z	Colotti Frances—†	221	housewife	25	"
	2432				
B	McMullen Margaret—†	223	at home	57	"
D	Dioguardi Clara—†	226	operator	31	"
E	Dioguardi Louis	226	U S A	27	
F	*Dioguardi Marie—†	226	housewife	74	"
G	Dioguardi Nicholas	226	carpenter	40	"
H	Fucillo Marto	227	chauffeur	47	"
K	Fucillo Ruth—†	227	housewife	49	"
L	Killduff Eleanor—†	227	at home	22	"
M	*Gambino Angelo	228	operator	47	252 Marion
N	Gambino Eva—†	228	housewife	40	252 "
O	Gambino Joseph	228	U S A	21	252 "
P	Carco Agreppino	228	"	25	214 Chelsea
R	Carco Antonio	228	U S N	22	214 "
S	Carco Caruso	228	machinist	41	214 "
T	Carco John	228	U S A	27	214 "
U	Carco Joseph	228	retired	73	214 "
V	Carco Josephine—†	228	housewife	63	214 "
W	Carco Paul	228	laborer	29	214 "
X	Spillman Girolama—†	228	housewife	28	214 "
Y	Spillman John	228	U S A	25	214 "
Z	Risti Achille	228	U S N	21	196 Paris
	2433				
A	Risti Ernest	228	laborer	49	196 "
B	*Risti Jennie—†	228	housewife	49	196 "
C	Bowen Mary—†	229	"	71	here
D	Bowen Patrick	229	laborer	68	"
E	Hazelwood Annie—†	229	housewife	73	"
F	Hazelwood Charles S	229	retired	73	"
G	King Catherine—†	229	housewife	65	"
H	King Thomas	229	longshoreman	66	"
N	Marcoccio Antoinette-†	232	housewife	38	"
O	Marcoccio Domenic	232	pedler	41	"
P	DiOrio John	232	clerk	28	111 Benningt'n
R	DiOrio Mary—†	232	housewife	47	111 "
S	DiOrio Mary—†	232	typist	20	111 "

Page.	Letter.	FULL NAME.	Residence, Jan. 1, 1945.	Occupation.	Supposed Age.	Reported Residence, Jan. 1, 1944. Street and Number.

Havre Street—Continued

т	DiOrio Tobia	232	printer	53	111 Benningt'n
u	Fusco Carmella—†	232	housewife	55	here
v	Fusco Joseph	232	candymaker	60	"
w	Fusco Sylvia—†	232	stitcher	21	"
x	Fusco Vincent	232	U S A	30	
y	Cunha Alfred	236	U S N	37	
z	Cunha Mary—†	236	housewife	67	"
	2434				
b	Donovan Catherine—†	236	housekeeper	72	"
c	Hennessey Catherine—†	236	clerk	42	"
d	Amoroso Anna—†	238	beautician	25	"
e	*Amoroso Catherine—†	238	housewife	49	"
f	Amoroso Phillip	238	laborer	27	
g	Amoroso Salvatore	238	"	58	
h	Amoroso Salvatore	238	U S A	28	
k	Mancuso James	238	chauffeur	22	"
l	*Mancuso Mary—†	238	housewife	44	"
m	*Fulginiti Frances—†	238	"	42	"
n	Fulginiti Jennie—†	238	clerk	20	
o	*Fulginiti Joseph	238	plasterer	45	"
p	Fulginiti Joseph, jr	238	shipfitter	22	"
r	Altri Paul	239	longshoreman	35	"
s	Kelley Delia—†	239	at home	69	"
t	Biancucci Mary—†	239	waitress	30	"
u	*Frizzi Alvira—†	240	housewife	53	"
v	Frizzi Angelo	240	U S A	24	
w	Frizzi Anthony	240	painter	54	
x	Frizzi Cono	240	fireman	21	"
y	Frizzi Victoria—†	240	shoewkr	23	"
z	Kennedy Anna—†	241	at home	76	"
	2435				
a	Melanson Joseph A	241	U S A	28	
b	Melanson Mary—†	241	at home	68	"
d	Sears Mary—†	243	"	75	
e	Reardon Lillian—†	243	"	64	
f	Robbins Evelyn—†	243	housewife	26	"
g	Robbins Llewellyn R	243	U S N	30	"
h	*Gozzo Angelina—†	244	housewife	51	"
k	Gozzo Paul	244	U S N	22	
l	Gozzo Sebastiano	244	laborer	61	"
m	Pannese Donald	244	mechanic	34	Winthrop

Havre Street—Continued

N	Pannese Sadie—†	244	housewife	27	Winthrop
O	Vaccaro Anna—†	244	clerk	26	here
P	*Vaccaro Mary—†	244	housewife	51	"
R	Hurley Blanche—†	244	"	39	"
S	*Hurley Sylvester	244	laundrywkr	37	"
V	Lennon George	245	machinist	27	"
W	Lennon Louise—†	245	housewife	24	"
X	McPhee Catherine—†	245	"	30	
Y	McPhee Joseph L	245	operator	39	"
Z	Nickerson Florence—†	245	housewife	22	245 Saratoga
	2436					
A	Nickerson Ralph	245	rigger	27	245 "
B	Curtis Michael	246	laborer	43	here
C	Curtis Violet—†	246	housewife	42	"
D	Milillo Alvira—†	246	"	53	"
E	Milillo Gaetano	246	laborer	28	...
F	Milillo Pasquale	246	mechanic	24	"
G	Carroll Joseph	247	retired	50	3 Saratoga pl
H	Figueira Boaz S	247	fireman	43	here
K	*Pitta Manuel C	247	weaver	52	"
L	Leman Frederick	247	laborer	51	245 Saratoga
M	Keenan William	247	bartender	35	245 "
N	*Walsh John	247	cutter	28	Maine
O	Puglesi Antoinetta—†	259	housewife	57	here
P	Puglesi Carmello	259	laborer	60	"
R	*Puglesi Laura—†	259	at home	87	"
S	DiLorenzo Frances—†	259	housewife	29	"
T	Fortunato Joseph	259	retired	80	"
U	Grassa Anna—†	259	stitcher	21	139 Paris
V	Grassa Beatrice—†	259	housewife	54	139 "
W	Grassa Mary—†	259	stitcher	24	139 "
X	Grassa Nicholas	259	laborer	55	139 "
Y	Grassa Peter	259	U S A	23	139 "
Z	Pagano Anthony	261	upholsterer	49	here
	2437					
A	Pagano Rose—†	261	housewife	49	"
B	Zona Alvera—†	261	stitcher	28	"
C	Zona Frances—†	261	brushmaker	27	"
D	Zona Grace—†	261	housewife	53	"
E	Zona Grace M—†	261	stitcher	21	"
F	Zona Jennie—†	261	operator	31	"

Havre Street—Continued

G	Zona Josephine—†	261	stitcher	23	here
H	Zona Matthew	261	U S A	25	"
K	Zona Michael	261	guard	57	"
L	Trainor Dorothy E—†	261	inspector	23	"
M	Trainor James	261	U S N	25	
N	Trainor Lawrence	261	"	28	
O	Trainor Mary O—†	261	matron	56	"
P	*Cappuccio Domenic	262	laborer	59	
R	*Cappuccio Rose—†	262	housewife	54	"
S	Battista Felicia—†	262	"	37	
T	Battista Sabatino	262	fireman	39	"
U	Ciulla Lucy—†	262	housewife	24	105 Chelsea
V	Ciulla Michael ·	262	laborer	26	105 "
W	Marino Antonio	263	jeweler	40	here
X	Marino Kathleen—†	263	housewife	32	"
Y	Poirier Edward	263	U S A	24	"
Z	*Poirier Onesime—†	263	housewife	61	"
	2438					
A	Poirier Palma—†	263	waitress	27	"
B	Poirier Rita—†	263	"	22	
C	*Poirier Rosario	263	carpenter	59	"
D	Poirier Viola—†	263	waitress	26	"
E	Melchionna Louis	263	shipfitter	50	7 Chelsea pl
F	Melchionna Nancy—†	263	housewife	36	7 "
G	Lancia Anthony	264	chauffeur	27	82 Porter
H	Lancia Domenic	264	carpenter	63	82 "
K	Pacitta Anthony	264	U S A	40	here
L	Pacitta Louise—†	264	housewife	36	"
M	Sindoni Anthony	264	factoryhand	44	"
N	Sindoni Domenica—†	264	housewife	38	"
O	Guiffrida Grace—†	265	"	35	
P	*Guiffrida Joseph	265	shoewkr	39	"
R	Avola Anna—†	265	housewife	49	"
S	Avola John	265	shoewkr	52	"
T	Styzynski Frances—†	265	housewife	27	59 Webster
U	Styzynski Stanley	265	chauffeur	32	59 "
V	Panzini Domenic	266	candymaker	36	here
W	Panzini Philomena—†	266	housewife	32	"
X	Colotti Geraldine—†	266	stitcher	25	"
Y	Colotti Joseph	266	U S A	21	
Z	Colotti Michael	266	laborer	60	

Page.	Letter.	Full Name.	Residence, Jan. 1, 1945.	Occupation.	Supposed Age.	Reported Residence, Jan. 1, 1944. Street and Number.

Havre Street—Continued

	A	*Colotti Sarah—†	266	housewife	55	here
	B	Maratto Liberio	267	musician	28	"
	C	Maratto Rose—†	267	housewife	27	"
	D	Avola Liberio	267	shoewkr	57	"
	E	Avola Rosalia—†	267	housewife	49	"
	F	Seminatore Joseph	267	seaman	53	"
	G	Seminatore Josephine—†	267	clerk	21	..
	H	Seminatore Philomina—†	267	"	22	
	K	Seminatore Susan—†	267	housewife	43	"
	L	Cordischi Achille	268	millhand	43	"
	M	Cordischi Angelina—†	268	housewife	32	"
	N	DiAngelo Carmen	268	laborer	43	
	O	DiAngelo Vincent	268	"	58	
	P	*Mastrangelo Antoinette—†	270	housewife	49	"
	R	Mastrangelo Mary—†	270	dressmaker	21	"
	S	Mastrangelo Rocco	270	laborer	48	
	T	LaBelle Millie—†	271	housewife	25	"
	U	LaBelle Raymond	271	U S A	31	"
	V	Lindsay Everett T	271	"	27	"
	W	Lindsay Ida—†	271	housewife	23	"
	X	Macrina Amy—†	271	"	33	
	Y	Macrina Anthony	271	clerk	37	"
	Z	Caulfield John T	272	retired	69	

	A	DiTomaso Domenic	273	splicer	41	"
	B	DiTomaso Dora—†	273	housewife	34	"
	C	Murphy Elizabeth—†	274	"	61	
	D	Murphy John H	274	guard	29	
	E	Murphy Richard G	274	U S N	24	
	F	Simone Helen—†	275	stitcher	33	"
	G	Terriciano Marion—†	275	housewife	30	"
	H	Terriciano Salvatore	275	electrician	37	"
	K	Russo George W	275	chipper	35	
	L	Russo Margaret—†	275	housewife	30	"
	M	Battista Amelio	rear 275	laborer	51	"
	N	Battista Rose—†	" 275	housewife	41	"
	O	Pace Anthony	276	laborer	58	
	P	Pace Domenic	276	U S A	23	"
	R	Pace Louisa—†	276	inspector	21	"
	S	Pace Rachel—†	276	housewife	58	"

Page.	Letter.	FULL NAME.	Residence, Jan. 1, 1945.	Occupation.	Supposed Age.	Reported Residence, Jan. 1, 1944. Street and Number.

Havre Street—Continued

	T	Blanchette Joseph E	277	U S A	26	here
	U	Blanchette Pauline—†	277	housewife	28	"
	V	Avila Anna—†	277	"	53	"
	W	Avila Josephine—†	277	stitcher	28	"
	X	Tischetta Carmela—†	277	housewife	27	279 Havre
	Y	Tischetta Joseph	277	pressman	29	353 Chelsea
	Z	Cambria Beatrice—†	278	shoewkr	20	here
2441						
	A	Cambria Joseph	278	laborer	22	
	B	*Cambria Lillian—†	278	housewife	53	"
	C	Cambria Pasquale	278	pedler	62	"
	D	Blanchette Alcide A	279	U S A	28	Medford
	E	Blanchette Antoinette—†	279	housewife	31	"
	F	Stella Angelina—†	279	"	44	here
	G	Stella Charles	279	barber	53	"
	H	Pesce Giuseppe	279	at home	31	"
	K	Pesce Josephine—†	279	housewife	51	"
	L	Pesce Ignazio	279	metalwkr	58	"
	M	Stringi Frank W	280	welder	25	
	N	Stringi Rosanne—†	280	housewife	22	"
	O	Gravallese Charles M	280	plumber	36	"
	P	Gravallese Rose—†	280	housewife	34	"
	S	McDermott Mary M—†	281	"	36	"
	T	McDermott William A	281	inspector	42	Somerville
	U	Carlton Marion A—†	281	entertainer	31	here
	V	Carlton Sarah T—†	281	at home	66	"
	W	Foley William C	283	U S A	22	"
	X	Gessner Bernard H	283	policeman	42	"
	Y	Gessner Mary—†	283	housewife	44	"
	Z	Leddy Mary—†	283	at home	72	"
2442						
	A	Ferguson William	283	mechanic	68	"
	B	Winterson Catherine—†	283	housekeeper	62	"
	C	Harkins Anna L—†	283	at home	46	"
	D	Harkins Annie M—†	283	"	85	
	E	Scolletta Angelina—†	289	housewife	36	"
	F	Scolletta Leonardo	289	laborer	42	
	G	Costello Elizabeth—†	289	housewife	39	"
	H	Costello Valentine	289	laborer	50	
	K	Dione Ethel—†	289	housewife	35	"
	L	Dione Henry	289	U S A	40	

25

Havre Street—Continued

m	Grant James	289	laborer	46	here
n	*Grant Mary—†	289	at home	74	"
o	Fiumara Charles	291	shipfitter	27	"
p	Fiumara Jennie—†	291	housewife	27	"
r	*Reale Joseph	291	laborer	72	
s	*Reale Mary—†	291	housewife	63	"
t	Caldarelli Albert	291	welder	26	
u	Caldarelli Concetta—†	291	housewife	25	"
v	Bucchere Joseph	291	carpenter.	40	"
w	*Bucchere Mary—†	291	housewife	37	"
x	Ventura Anthony	293	laborer	52	New York
y	Ventura Maria D—†	293	housewife	59	here
z	Panzini James	293	U S A	23	"
	2443				
a	Panzini Margaret—†	293	housewife	33	"
b	*Panzini Pasquale	293	retired	71	
c	Panzini Vito	293	laborer	35	"
d	*Nicosia Anna—†	293	at home	70	"
e	Nicosia Grace—†	293	clerk	29	
f	Nicosia Joseph	293	machinist	40	"
g	Nicosia Marie—†	293	clerk	31	
h	DeMarco John	295	chauffeur	27	"
k	DeMarco Nellie—†	295	housewife	25	"
l	DeBella Joseph	295	inspector	29	4 Osborn pl
m	DeBella Louise—†	295	housewife	33	4 "
n	Bruno Felice	295	laborer	69	here
o	Bruno Philomena—†	295	housewife	59	"
p	*Moscritolo Emma—†	297	"	50	"
r	Moscritolo Nicholas J	297	bartender	24	"
s	Moscritolo Pasquale B	297	manager	52	"
t	Moscritolo Yola—†	297	housewife	24	"
v	Mortimer Helen—†	301	"	30	
w	Mortimer John A	301	laborer	33	..
x	Surette Louise—†	301	housewife	27	"
z	Meloni Rose—†	305	"	34	
	2444				
a	Meloni Victor	305	machinist	34	"
b	*Rosa Concetta—†	305	housewife	65	"
c	*Rosa Giuseppe	305	retired	68	"
d	Rosa Roger	305	U S A	23	"
e	Bethel Helen—†	307	housewife	20	Ohio

Page.	Letter.	FULL NAME.	Residence, Jan. 1, 1945.	Occupation.	Supposed Age.	Reported Residence, Jan. 1, 1944. Street and Number.

Havre Street—Continued

	F	Bethel James O	307	chauffeur	23	Ohio
	G	DeStefano Gertrude—†	307	housewife	20	here
	H	DeStefano Joseph	307	laborer	25	"

London Court

	K	Spano Adam	2	laborer	20	here
	L	Spano Frances—†	2	housewife	37	"

London Street

	O	Ferraro Jennie—†	165	housewife	24	here
	P	Ferraro Nunzio	165	welder	30	"
	R	Villa Antoinette—†	165	housewife	25	"
	S	Villa Joseph	165	electrician	24	175 Paris
	T	Tortolano Anna—†	171	dressmaker	38	here
	U	Tortolano Celia D—†	171	embroiderer,	27	"
	V	Tortolano Elvira E—†	171	at home	32	"
	W	Tortolano Mary R—†	171	supervisor	33	"
	X	Tortolano Nancy I—†	171	stitcher	21	Lawrence
	Y	Tortolano William	171	U S A	23	here
	Z	Miano Paul	173	bookkeeper	28	"
2445						
	A	Spadone Josephine—†	173	at home	48	"
	B	Spadone Mary—†	173	stitcher	21	"
	C	Landolfi Anthony	173	U S A	21	
	D	Landolfi Josephine—†	173	presser	23	
	E	Landolfi Lena—†	173	"	22	
	F	Landolfi Maria—†	173	stitcher	49	"
	G	Landolfi Vincenzo	173	laborer	48	"
	H	White Cecelia—†	177	housewife	67	"
	K	White Lawrence P	177	carpenter	67	"
	L	Micciche Jennie—†	177	stitcher	44	"
	M	Micciche Pasquale	177	barber	50	
	N	Emma Phillip	177	operator	41	"
	O	Emma Vincenza—†	177	housewife	36	"
	P	Palladino Frank	179	candywkr	38	"
	R	Palladino Mary—†	179	housewife	29	"
	S	Rosso Anthony	179	shoemaker	54	"
	T	Rosso Carmela—†	179	housewife	46	"
	U	D'Apice Elsie—†	179	tailor	50	"

London Street—Continued

v	Moscatelli Michael	179	shoewkr	58	here	
w	Casaletto James	181	pipefitter	27	"	
x	Casaletto Lillian—†	181	housewife	25	"	
y	Tracia Angelina—†	181	supervisor	32	"	
z	Tracia Louis	181	pipefitter	32	"	
	2446					
a	Casaletto John	181	leatherwkr	35	"	
b	Casaletto Rose—†	181	housewife	31	"	
c	Provanzano Salvatore	183	foreman	31	"	
d	Provanzano Virginia—†	183	housewife	31	"	
e	Gurliaccio Girolama M—†	183	welder	22	"	
f	Gurliaccio Joseph A	183	U S A	25		
g	Gurliaccio Josephine—†	183	housewife	48	"	
h	Gurliaccio Lazzaro	183	laborer	60	"	
k	Gurliaccio Michele	183	electrician	20	"	
l	Gallo Mary—†	183	housewife	29	"	
m	Gallo Salvatore	183	laborer	30		
n	Schieber Ida—†	185	housewife	26	"	
o	Schieber Max	185	U S C G	24	"	
p	Cannata Josephine—†	185	operator	24	"	
r	Cannata Marian—†	185	at home	53	"	
s	Cannata Michael	185	operator	34	"	
t	Cannata Rose A—†	185	housewife	32	"	
v	Dunne James F	187	boilermaker	32	174 Havre	
w	Dunne Rose M—†	187	housewife	29	174 "	
x	Cagnina Mary—†	187	"	32	here	
y	Cagnina Michael	187	shoewkr	39	"	
z	Cagnina Nunzio	187	painter	50	"	
	2447					
a	Johnson Allen W	189	laborer	29		
b	Johnson Amelia—†	189	housewife	27	"	
c	Stornaiuolo Albert	189	retired	72		
d	Stornaiuolo Angelina—†	189	shoewkr	23	"	
e	*Stornaiuolo Jennie—†	189	housewife	66	"	
f	Blair Ernest	189	U S N	27		
g	Blair Lorraine—†	189	housewife	25	"	
h	Mendum Adelaide—†	189	"	50		
k	Mendum Benjamin	189	driller	56	"	
l	Mendum George	189	U S A	27		
m	Cerullo Margaret—†	191	housewife	31	"	
n	Cerullo Marino	191	U S C G	31	"	

Page.	Letter.	FULL NAME.	Residence, Jan. 1, 1945.	Occupation.	Supposed Age.	Reported Residence, Jan. 1, 1944. Street and Number.

London Street—Continued

	o	Grace Emily—†	191	operator	26	here
	p	Grace John	191	U S N	26	Somerville
	r	Rizzuto Anthony	191	guard	32	here
	s	Rizzuto Mary—†	191	operator	51	"
	t	Briana John H	191	U S A	22	432 Saratoga
	u	Briana Mary—†	191	stitcher	24	here
	v	*Buttiglieri Carmella—†	191	at home	67	"
	w	Buttiglieri Carmine	191	U S A	30	"
	x	Buttiglieri Filomena—†	191	candymaker	36	"
	y	Buttiglieri Sarah—†	191	stitcher	22	"
	z	Alu Catina—†	191	candymaker	39	"
2448						
	a	Alu Michael	191	presser	46	
	b	Alu Vincenzo J	191	U S N	20	"
	c	Doherty Mary E—†	193	housewife	70	128 Brooks
	d	Doherty Phillip	193	retired	65	128 "
	e	Canella Alfonse	193	"	67	here
	f	*Canella Antonia—†	193	housewife	59	"
	g	Canella Salvatore	193	laborer	22	"
	h	*Bernhardt Rose—†	193	at home	66	"
	k	Shapiro Jacob	193	retired	71	
	l	Vistola Luigi A	197	laborer	63	
	m	*Vistola Pasqualina—†	197	packer	61	
	n	Ioanna Frank	197	chauffeur	29	"
	o	Ioanna Louise—†	197	housewife	26	"
	p	Corbett Adeline T—†	197	"	24	
	r	Corbett Joseph A	197	shipfitter	26	"
	s	DiPerri Dora—†	199	at home	42	19 Battery
	t	Sarro Angelina—†	199	housewife	77	187 London
	u	Sarro Carmine	199	retired	75	187 "
	v	Storniello Louisa—†	199	housewife	27	here
	w	Storniello Pasquale	199	mechanic	30	"
	x	Stellato Clementina—†	203	housewife	34	"
	y	Stellato Frank	203	painter	33	
	z	Lentine Michael	203	toolmaker	45	"
2449						
	a	Lentini Stephen	203	pharmacist	24	
	b	*Lentini Theresa—†	203	seamstress	30	"
	c	Emma Lucy M—†	203	housewife		"
	d	Emma Phillip	203	rubberwkr		
	e	Robinson Frances—†	203	"		

London Street—Continued

F	Scrima Angelina—†	205	clerk	26	here
G	Scrima Vincenza—†	205	rubberwkr	21	"
H	Santosuosso Henry	205	electrician	38	"
K	Santosuosso Mary—†	205	housewife	29	"
L	*Grimaldi Gloria—†	207	"	60	"
M	Grimaldi Vincenzo J	207	laborer	59	
N	Tropea Margaret—†	207	housewife	25	"
O	Tropea Vincent C	207	coremaker	26	"
P	Marquis John	207	laborer	40	
R	Rossetti Angelo	209	collector	32	"
S	Rossetti Evelyn A—†	209	housewife	32	"
T	Incerto Gennaro	209	electrician	33	"
U	Incerto Nancy—†	209	housewife	33	"
V	Bonniello Cosimo	211	polisher	75	"
W	Salvate Domenic	211	operator	28	"
X	Salvate Frank	211	laborer	59	
Y	Salvate Maria—†	211	housewife	53	"
Z	Lunetta Anthony	211	laborer	25	

2450

A	Lunetta Grace R—†	211	housewife	22	"
B	Lunetta Joseph	211	laborer	72	"
C	*Lunetta Rose—†	211	housewife	62	"
D	Patterson Arthur W	211	U S N	21	W Virginia
F	Sylvestri Helen—†	221	housewife	25	here
G	Sylvestri Joseph	221	brazier	28	"
H	*Adreani Anita—†	221	housewife	59	"
K	Adreani Jennie—†	221	at home	34	"
L	Adreani Lena M—†	221	clerk	24	
M	Adreani Luigi	221	merchant	68	"
N	Luigi William	221	U S A	22	
	Magnanelli Maria C—†	223	typist	28	
R	Magnanelli Peter	223	retired	79	
S	Mella Anna F—†	223	housewife	56	"
T	Mela Anthony	223	operator	55	"
U	Matara Frances P—†	223	buyer	22	
V	Matara Maria—†	223	seamstress	49	"
W	McMahon Michael	223	tailor	50	
X	Merchant Edward L	225	watchman	59	"
Y	Merchant Lu E	225	U S N	33	
Z	Merchant Paul †	225	at home	70	"
	†	225	housewife	32	"

2451
London Street—Continued

A	O'Neill Albert R	225	bartender	35	here
B	O'Neill Harriet J—†	225	housewife	34	"
C	St George Louise—†	227	"	24	"
D	St George Patrick	227	longshoreman	26	"
E	Silvae Emma—†	227	at home	58	"
F	Silvae Louise—†	227	tel operator	28	"
G	Barker Olive—†	227	housewife	26	"
H	Barker William	227	foreman	33	"
K	Cunha Mary—†	227	at home	70	"
L	Hayden Katherine—†	229	"	55	Revere
M	Murphy Grace—†	229	"	38	here
O	Manfrendonia Adelaide E—†	231	inspector	23	"
P	Manfrendonia Giovanna J—†	231	stitcher	21	"
R	Manfrendonia Lepoldo	231	presser	22	
S	Perullo Anthony	231	electrician	25	"
T	Perullo Rose—†	231	housewife	23	"
U	Salvaggio Angelo	231	U S A	21	
V	*Salvaggio Josephine—†	231	housewife	47	"
W	Salvaggio Rocco	231	candymaker	56	"
X	Salvaggio Vincenzo J	231	U S A	26	
Y	Musto Joseph	233	welder	46	
Z	Musto Pasqualina—†	233	housewife	36	"

2452   Marion Street

A	Newhook Charles	156	engineer	52	here
B	Newhook Emma—†	156	housewife	54	"
C	Kraytenberg Ernest B	156	shipper	44	"
D	Kraytenberg Mary L—†	156	packer	35	
E	Proto Alfonso	158	U S A	24	
F	Proto Flora—†	158	stitcher	20	"
G	Proto Salvatore	158	laborer	55	
H	Proto Teresa—†	158	housewife	54	"
K	Nason Margaret—†	158	housekeeper	66	"
L	Crouse Spurgeon	162	clerk	27	"
M	Ivory Eva—†	162	housewife	51	
N	Ivory John	162	laborer	58	
O	Healey Agnes—†	162	clerk	55	
P	Healey Mary—†	162	housewife		
R	Peterson Louise—†	162	operator		

Marion Street—Continued

	s	Starrett Frances J—†	164	clerk	32	here
	t	Prime Mary E—†	166	housewife	36	109 Meridian
	u	Prime Vaughn S	166	U S A	37	109 "
	v	Deveau Mary Z—†	166	housewife	50	here
	w	Deveau Mary Z—†	166	stitcher	25	"
	x	Deveau William	166	U S A	22	"
	y	Hankard James	168	stevedore	23	"
	z	Hankard Mary—†	168	housewife	45	"
2453						
	a	Hankard Thomas	168	stevedore	50	"
	b	Hankard William	168	U S N	20	"
	e	*Budner Bessie—†	172	housewife	68	"
	f	*Budner Harris	172	shoemaker	72	"
	g	Leone Rosaria—†	172	housewife	36	"
	h	*Muselli Carmella—†	174	housekeeper	55	"
	k	*Levenstein Ida—†	174	housewife	67	"
	l	*Levenstein Louis	174	retired	73	
	m	Mangino Caroline—†	174	housewife	45	"
	n	Mangino John	174	candymaker	47	"
	p	Blake Franklin	176	mechanic	63	"
	r	McGowan Catherine—†	176	housewife	69	"
	s	Pinto Marie A—†	176	"	27	
	t	Pinto Nicholas A	176	chauffeur	30	"
	u	Venuti Carmella—†	176	housewife	56	"
	v	Venuti Joseph	176	laborer	60	
	w	Pisco Alfred	178	chauffeur	36	"
	x	Pisco Marie—†	178	housewife	31	"
	y	Misiano Anthony	178	shipfitter	23	Everett
	z	Misiano John	178	laborer	53	"
2454						
		Misiano Mary—†	178	housewife	48	"
	d	racusa Anthony	178	retired	75	here
	e	usa Carmello	178	laborer	43	"
	f	Ehr Lena—†	178	housewife	68	"
	g	Buffa Nicola	178	laborer	32	"
	h	Buffa A—†	179	at home	64	"
	k	Pulio Pet P	179	beautician	36	Brookline
	l	Pulio Rosa	179	housewife	27	"
	m	Papandrea C	179	U S N	22	here
			179	at home	50	"
	†		180	housewife	39	"

32

Page.	Letter.	FULL NAME.	Residence, Jan. 1, 1945.	Occupation.	Supposed Age.	Reported Residence, Jan. 1, 1944. Street and Number.

Marion Street—Continued

N	Papandrea John	180	retired	69	here
O	Papandrea Pasquale	180	U S N	20	"
P	*Pecci Filomena—†	180	housewife	76	"
R	*Pecci Frank	180	retired	78	
S	Pecci Arthur	180	U S A	24	
T	*Pecci Carmella—†	180	housewife	47	"
U	Pecci Edith—†	180	dressmaker	25	"
V	Pecci Leopold	180	shoemaker	52	"
W	Ganno Joseph	181	U S A	24	
X	Ganno Josephine—†	181	housewife	23	"
Y	Pinto Pasquale	181	laborer	24	
Z	Pinto Rita—†	181	housewife	21	"

2455

A	Davola Ann—†	181	operator	27	"
B	Davola Josephine—†	181	"	23	
C	Davola Phillip	181	chipper	53	
D	Davola Stella—†	181	housewife	47	"
E	Anzalone John	182	barber	52	...
F	*Marconi Anna—†	182	housewife	59	"
G	Marconi Geraldo	182	laborer	58	...
H	Marconi Lucy—†	182	clerk	21	
K	Anzalone Anna—†	182	housewife	48	"
L	Anzalone John	182	laborer	22	
M	Anzalone Romeo	182	U S A	20	
O	*D'Angelo Domenico	183	merchant	63	"
P	*D'Angelo Louisa—†	183	housewife	60	"
R	Ciampa Angelo J	183	laundrywkr	24	"
S	Lamonica Catherine—†	184	housewife	49	178 Marion
T	Cassara Mary—†	184	"	67	here
U	Cassara Thomas	184	retired	76	"
V	*Cirello Anthony	184	laborer	59	"
W	*Cirello Mary—†	184	housewife	59	"
X	LaRocca Elizabeth B—†	185	"	33	"
Y	LaRocca Joseph	185	bartender	31	"
Z	LaRocca John	185	operator	32	"
				50	

2456

A	LaRocca Nora—†	185	"	45	
B	*LaRocca Nunzia—†	185	at home	65	"
C	*Dellofano Carmela—†	185	" ...fe	27	"
D	Dellofano Carmen	185	laborer	32	"
E	Dellofano Michele	185	mechanic	29	"

1—24

35

Marion Street—Continued

Letter.	Full Name.	Residence	Occupation	Age	Reported Residence
F	Gianipapa Maria—†	185	at home	63	here
G	Forti Samuel	186	contractor	53	126 Havre
K	Terriciano Benjamin	186	laborer	35	here
L	Terriciano Teresa—†	186	housewife	34	"
M	Renna Frank	187	U S N	26	Revere
N	*Renna Maria—†	187	at home	60	"
O	Fiore Angela A—†	187	housewife	41	here
P	Fiore Maurice	187	electrician	42	"
R	Venuti Joseph, jr	187	U S A	23	Washington
S	Venuti Rosemary—†	187	housewife	20	"
T	Arnella Mary—†	188	sorter	24	Somerville
U	*Texeira John B	188	laborer	45	245 Havre
V	*Texeira Mary—†	188	housewife	53	245 "
W	Serino Anna—†	188	"	37	here
X	Serino Herbert	188	chauffeur	44	"
	2457				
A	Forgione Angelina—†	191	housewife	30	"
B	Forgione Joseph	191	welder	30	"
C	Finamore Angelina—†	191	at home	41	"
D	Finamore Gaetano	191	barber	40	"
E	Finamore Margaret—†	191	cashier	38	"
F	Finamore Maria—†	191	at home	59	"
G	Finamore Romeo	191	laborer	34	"
K	*Binincasa Carmella—†	192	housewife	61	"
L	*Binincasa Carmen	192	shoemaker	70	"
M	Bavaro Anna—†	192	housewife	38	"
N	Bavaro Peter	192	rigger	40	"
O	Miraglia Carmella—†	192	housewife	40	"
	*Miraglia Josephine—†	192	at home	75	"
	Miraglia Rocco	192	shoemaker	49	"
	livan Anna—†	193	housewife	26	"
D	van Thomas	193	fisherman	32	"
E	elico Domenic	193	chauffeur	30	"
F	Elico Rosa—†	193	dressmaker	28	"
G	Buffelico Carl	193A	retired	58	
H	Buffelico Emma—†	193A	housewife	54	"
K	Pulioə Amelio	194	chauffeur	24	"
L	Pulioə Isabella—†	194	housewife	21	"
M	Papar 2458				
	nna—†	194	stitcher	23	"
	omenica—†	194	housewife	29	"

Page	Letter	Full Name	Residence, Jan. 1, 1945.	Occupation.	Supposed Age.	Reported Residence, Jan. 1, 1944. Street and Number.

Marion Street—Continued

	c	Pignato Pasquale	194	U S A	21	here
	d	Pignato Sebastian	194	laborer	56	"
	e	Anzalone Anthony	194	"	24	"
	f	Anzalone Lena—†	194	housewife	21	"
	h	Cammisa Filomena—†	195	welder	25	
	k	Cammisa Frank	195	U S A	26	
	l	Lombardi Anthony	195	shipfitter	55	"
	m	Lombardi Emma—†	195	housewife	49	"
	n	*Amorosa Angelina—†	195	at home	63	"
	o	DellaRusso Natalie—†	195	rubberwkr	27	"
	p	Giglio Antoinette—†	196	housekeeper	61	"
	s	Gangi Lena—†	196	housewife	69	"
	t	Gangi Nicholas	196	laborer	67	"
	u	Maio Joseph	197	storekeeper	52	"
	v	Maio Katherine—†	197	operator	23	"
	w	*Maio Maria—†	197	housewife	44	"
	x	Saetti Albert A	197	machinist	63	"
	y	Saetti Maria—†	197	housewife	48	"

2459

	a	Pulelio Anthony	198	U S N	24	..
	b	Pulelio Lilly—†	198	cook	24	"
	c	Rocco Eleanora—†	198	housewife	41	"
	d	LaFrazia Frank	198	fireman	51	"
	e	LaFrazia Josephine—†	198	housewife	40	"
	g	DeSisto Anthony	199	U S A	22	Revere
	h	DeSisto Sarah—†	199	housewife	23	here
	k	Giambusso Carmella—†	199	"	47	"
	l	Giambusso Charles	199	laborer	57	"
	m	Giambusso Frank	199	presser	21	
	n	Ardito Crocefissa—†	199	housewife	54	"
	o	Ardito John B	199	carpenter	54	"
	p	Pimgitore Rosina M—†	199	at home	45	"
	r	Murphy Francis	200	watchman	26	"
	s	Murphy Mildred—†	200	housewife	24	"
	t	Celesti Angelina—†	200	"	25	
	u	Celesti Gaetano	200	tailor	30	
	v	Cassaro Frances—†	200A	dressmaker	45	"
	w	Cassaro Joseph	200A	laborer	65	
	x	DeCristoforo Eliza—†	201	housewife	27	"
	y	DeCristoforo Joseph	201	pipefitter	32	"
	z	Conti Angelo	201	mechanic	29	"

Page	Letter	Full Name.	Residence, Jan. 1, 1945.	Occupation.	Supposed Age.	Reported Residence, Jan. 1, 1944. Street and Number.

2460

Marion Street—Continued

	Letter	Full Name.	Residence, Jan. 1, 1945.	Occupation.	Supposed Age.	Street and Number.
	A	*Conti Josephine—†	201	at home	59	here
	B	Conti Katherine—†	201	welder	24	"
	C	Conti Margaret—†	201	stitcher	26	"
	D	Conti Ralph	201	carpenter	31	"
	E	Hawes Edward	201	U S A	36	
	F	Hawes Francis	201	laborer	43	..
	G	Hawes James R	201	U S A	32	"
	H	Hawes Margaret—†	201	at home	72	"
	M	D'Angelico Christina—†	205	housewife	29	"
	N	D'Angelico Gaetano	205	laborer	28	"
	O	Freitas Albert J, jr	205	U S A	23	15 Pitts
	P	Freitas Nancy M—†	205	housewife	20	15 "
	R	Rao Frank	205	foreman	33	here
	S	Rao Mary—†	205	housewife	29	"
	T	Rao Nunzio	205	manager	69	"
	U	Cioffi John	206	baker	59	
	V	Cioffi Teresa—†	206	housewife	52	"
	W	Veneziano Catherine—†	206	"	40	
	X	Veneziano Charles	206	presser	50	"
	Z	Cacamesi Angelo	207	shoemaker	26	"

2461

	Letter	Full Name.	Residence, Jan. 1, 1945.	Occupation.	Supposed Age.	Street and Number.
	A	Cacamesi Giacomo	207	retired	69	
	B	Cacamesi Salvatore	207	U S A	24	
	C	*Cacamesi Salvatrice—†	207	housewife	61	"
	D	Chiarenza Charles	207	U S A	24	
	E	*Chiarenza Maria—†	207	housewife	39	"
	F	Chiarenza Vincenzo	207	tailor	48	
	K	Greico Biagio	213	laborer	55	"
	L	Ferrullo Joseph	213	welder	32	
	M	Ferrullo Leda—†	213	packer	28	"
		Ferrullo Joseph	213	welder	45	
	J	Ferrullo Rena—†	213	housewife	34	"
	R	Arnone Elizabeth—†	219	stitcher	26	"
	S	Arnone Nicolena—†	219	rubberwkr	21	"
	T	Arnone Peter	219	laborer	48	..
	U	*Arnone Theresa—†	219	housewife	44	"
	V	Rossetti Fannie—†	219	"	32	
		Rossetti George	219	welder	36	
		'rullo John	221	laborer	30	"
		\llo Mary J—†	221	operator	27	"

36

Page	Letter	Full Name	Residence, Jan. 1, 1945.	Occupation	Supposed Age	Reported Residence, Jan. 1, 1944. Street and Number.
	z	Schraffa Antoinette—†	221	housewife	59	here
2462						
	A	Schraffa Gaetano	221	laborer	61	"
	B	Soldano Angelina—†	221	housewife	50	"
	C	Soldano Frank	221	U S A	22	
	D	Soldano Gabriel	221	ironwkr	51	"
	E	Soldano Rose—†	221	stitcher	24	"
	F	Natola Antonette—† rear	221	housewife	31	"
	G	Natola Frank "	221	candymaker	31	"
	H	*Giardullo Liberato "	221	molder	76	
	K	Giardullo Mary—† "	221	presser	28	
	L	*Giardullo Theresa—† "	221	housewife	64	"
	M	Grande Orlando "	221	U S A	21	182 Cottage
	N	Grande Rose P—† "	221	housewife	22	here
	O	Blundo Angelo	223	laborer	50	"
	P	Blundo Maria A—†	223	housewife	49	"
	R	*Bossi Antonetta—†	223	"	59	
	S	Bossi Domenic	223	U S A	25	
	T	Bossi Frank	223	pedler	59	
	U	Blundo Angelina—†	223	housewife	29	"
	V	Blundo John A	223	welder	24	
	W	*Goldenberg Morris	225	storekeeper	67	"
	X	*Goldenberg Rose—†	225	"	64	"
	Y	Belliveau Louise A—†	225A	housewife	57	"
	z	Belliveau Roger J	225A	cutter	39	
2463						
	A	Addario Carmen	225A	chauffeur	29	"
	B	Addario Mary A—†	225A	housewife	30	"
	C	Rizzo Anthony	227	U S N	20	
	D	Rizzo Elizabeth B—†	227	at home	55	"
	E	Rizzo John F	227	U S C G	23	"
	F	Rizzo Mary G—†	227	stitcher	30	"
	G	Avila Antonio	227	retired	75	
	H	Avila Rosaria—†	227	housewife	64	"
	K	Figliolino Antonio	227	painter	46	
	L	Figliolino Carmela—†	227	housewife	35	"
	M	Vaccaro Frank	229	U S N	21	
	N	Vaccaro John	229	carpenter	56	"
	O	Vaccaro Maria—†	229	packer	47	
	P	Barrasso Laura—†	229	housewife	52	"
	R	Barrasso Pasquale	229	barber	59	

Marion Street—Continued

s	Belgiornio Alberico	229	shoemaker	62	here
T	Belgiornio Anna—†	229	milliner	34	"
U	*Belgiorno Lucy—†	229	housewife	59	"
v	Belgiornio Vincenzo J	229	restaurateur	27	"
w	*Mardus Annie—†	237	storekeeper	65	"
x	*Mardus David	237	retired	73	
Y	Feldman Eva—†	237	housewife	47	"
z	Feldman Hyman H	237	collector	27	"
	2464				
A	*Feldman Max	237	manufacturer	51	"
B	Insano Frank	237	operator	59	"
c	Insano Gaetano	237	U S A	28	
D	Insano Maria C—†	237	housewife	54	"
E	Insano Mary—†	237	rubberwkr	33	"

Paris Street

F	Kaplan Rose—†	163	housewife	58	here
G	Drevitch Bessie—†	163	saleswoman	47	"
H	Drevitch Milton	163	U S A	21	"
K	Drevitch Ruth—†	163	secretary	20	"
L	Drevitch Solomon	163	salesman	50	"
M	*Hoffman Dora—†	163	housewife	72	"
N	Hoffman Philip	163	salesman	38	"
o	Elibero Edward	165	laborer	61	"
P	Elibero Grace—†	165	housewife	58	"
R	Insogna Matthew	165	laborer	26	"
s	Insogna Rose—†	165	housewife	23	"
T	Russo Josephine—†	165	"	26	"
U	Russo Pino	165	machinist	28	"
v	Vecchio Angelina—†	166	housewife	37	"
w	*Vecchio Florence—†	166	at home	70	"
x	Vecchio Michael	166	storekeeper	45	"
Y	Sorrenti Gaetana—†	166	housekeeper	47	"
z	Marsilia Clotuno	166	machinist	20	"
	2465				
A	Marsilia John	166	shoewkr	55	"
B	Marsilia Marie—†	166	housewife	54	"
c	Marsilia Universa—†	166	clerk	21	
D	*Pascarella Leonora—†	167	at home	60	"
E	Alfieri Josephine—†	167	housewife	41	"

Paris Street—Continued

F	Alfieri Louis	167	U S N	24	here
G	Alfieri Thomas	167	operator	22	"
H	Pascarella Louise—†	167	factoryhand	31	"
K	Mascis Angelina—†	167	housewife	26	"
L	Mascis Philip	167	chemist	25	"
M	Marsilia Lillian—†	168	clerk	32	"
N	Palazzolo Joseph	168	U S A	23	"
O	Palazzolo Theresa—†	168	housewife	22	"
P	Fiore Anel A	168	U S A	21	
R	Fiore Filomena—†	168	housewife	43	"
S	Masiello Carlo	168	clerk	48	249 Maverick
T	Masiello Madelina—†	168	housewife	40	249 "
U	Masiello Mary—†	168	clerk	21	249 "
V	Taylor Mary—†	169	housewife	61	here
W	Taylor William	169	agent	53	"
X	Ferreira Joaquin	169	manager	74	"
Y	Fratus Rose—†	169	at home	71	"
Z	Bush Esther—†	169	housewife	36	"
	2466				
A	Bush Henry J	169	clerk	36	
B	Marcandante Celia—†	170	housewife	37	"
C	Marcandante John	170	welder	37	
D	Cogliani Angelina—†	170	at home	25	"
E	Cogliani Anthony	170	U S N	32	
F	*Cogliani Antonetta—†	170	housewife	58	"
G	Cogliani Joseph	170	mechanic	21	"
H	Cogliani Michael	170	custodian	62	"
K	Cogliani Raffaela—†	170	factoryhand	27	"
L	Umbro Anthony	170	U S N	21	
M	Umbro Antonio	170	chef	53	
N	Umbro Elizabeth—†	170	housewife	43	"
O	Hasad Jennie—†	171	"	64	
P	Hasad Wolfe	171	laborer	65	
R	Goldberg Henry	171	U S A	33	
S	*Goldberg Joseph	171	retired	59	
T	Goldberg Louis	171	U S A	22	
U	Goldberg Milton	171	welder	25	
V	Goldberg Shirley—†	171	housewife	22	"
W	Goldberg Solomon	171	U S A	31	
X	Zambello Joseph	172	U S N	22	
Y	Zambello Josephine—†	172	housewife	20	"

Paris Street—Continued

z	Muse Mary—†	172	housewife	35	here
	2467				
A	Muse Philip C	172	pipefitter	36	"
B	Tramontana Maria—†	172	housewife	51	"
C	Tramontana Vincenzo	172	retired	51	
D	DeLeo Giuseppe	173	laborer	51	
E	DeLeo Josephine—†	173	housewife	42	"
F	Dentino Vincent	173	U S M C	20	"
G	Rindone Dianna—†	173	stitcher	29	"
H	*Rindone Josephine—†	173	housewife	65	"
K	Rindone Michael	173	operator	38	"
L	D'Ortono Mary—†	173	housewife	33	"
M	D'Ortono Nicholas	173	shipfitter	35	"
N	Campagna Ernest	174	painter	27	
O	Campagna Rose—†	174	housewife	24	"
P	*Cocca Assunta—†	174	"	47	
R	Cocca Nicolo	174	carpenter	61	"
S	Cocca Pellegrino	174	laborer	55	
T	Arinella Carmen	174	U S A	22	
U	Arinella John J	174	"	23	
V	Arinella Joseph	174	painter	58	
W	Arinella Mary—†	174	housewife	53	"
X	Amorosa Anthony	175	electrician	31	132 Paris
Y	Amorosa Phyllis—†	175	housewife	29	132 "
z	Cigna Catherine—†	175	"	53	here
	2468				
A	Cigna Joseph	175	laborer	54	
B	Cigna Salvatore	175	chiropractor	21	"
C	Noto Anna—†	175	housewife	26	"
D	Noto Salvatore	175	shipfitter	26	"
E	Pascucci Henry	176	electrician	39	"
F	Pascucci Josephine—†	176	housewife	35	"
G	Carfagna Josephine—†	176	"	51	"
H	Carfagna Richard	176	porter	52	
K	Pascucci Antonetta—†	176	nurse	29	
L	Pascucci Ida—†	176	housewife	63	"
M	Pascucci Philip	176	retired	67	
N	Ruo Carmella—†	177	housewife	69	"
O	Ruo Michael	177	retired	69	"
P	Paterna Angelina—†	177	housewife	39	"
R	Paterna Joseph	177	tailor	49	

Paris Street—Continued

	Letter.	FULL NAME.	Residence	Occupation.	Age	Reported Residence
	s	Paterna Josephine—†	177	stitcher	20	here
	t	Kenney Andrew J	177	retired	89	"
	u	Consalvi Anthony J	178	bartender	38	"
	v	Consalvi Mildred—†	178	housewife	34	"
	w	Greco Grace—†	178	housekeeper	44	"
	x	Kaplan Pearl—†	178	housewife	43	"
	y	Kaplan Samuel	178	storekeeper	48	"
	z	Modica Joseph	179	dispatcher	26	"
2469						
	a	Modica Rose—†	179	housewife	24	"
	b	Finamore Arthur	179	pipefitter	37	"
	c	Finamore Mary—†	179	housewife	33	"
	d	Covotta Angelina—†	179	"	70	
	e	Covotta Michael	179	retired	69	
	f	Vella Lucy—†	180	housewife	27	"
	g	Vella Salvatore	180	laborer	30	"
	h	Ferrullo Clara—†	180	housewife	35	214 Saratoga
	k	Ferrullo Michael	180	chauffeur	34	214 "
	l	Capobianco Helen—†	180	operator	20	here
	m	Capobianco John	180	shoemaker	54	"
	n	Capobianco Lucy—†	180	housewife	50	"
	o	Capobianco Pasquale M	180	U S A	27	"
	p	Akell Anna—†	181	housewife	33	"
	r	Akell Harold	181	shipper	32	
	s	Macchione Ernest	181	U S A	29	
	t	*Abramo Grace—†	181	housewife	48	"
	u	Abramo Mary—†	181	stitcher	20	"
	v	*Abramo Natale	181	storekeeper	57	"
	w	Abramo Salvatore	181	U S A	28	
	x	Ferullo Anthony	181	welder	22	
	y	Ferullo John	181	pipefitter	27	"
	z	Ferullo Joseph	181	retired	64	
2470						
	a	Ferullo Mary—†	181	housewife	29	"
	b	Ferullo Susan—†	181	"	56	
	c	Ferullo Viola—†	181	stitcher	21	"
	d	Lombardi Anna—†	182	housewife	28	"
	e	Lombardi Edward	182	laborer	32	
	f	Venuti Anthony	182	welder	38	
	g	Venuti Celia—†	182	housewife	38	"
	h	Calvagno Anthony	182	shipfitter	38	"

Page.	Letter.	FULL NAME.	Residence, Jan. 1, 1945.	Occupation.	Supposed Age.	Reported Residence, Jan. 1, 1944. Street and Number.

Paris Street—Continued

	K	Calvagno Theresa—†	182	housewife	32	here
	N	Ginsburg Albert	183	grocer	65	"
	O	Ginsburg Flora—†	183	housewife	60	"
	P	Ginsburg Ida G—†	183	secretary	40	"
	R	Buck Mary A—†.	183	housewife	62	"
	S	Buck Michael	183	longshoreman	67	"
	T	DeAngelis Mary—†	184	housewife	50	"
	U	DeAngelis Nicholas	184	laborer	52	
	V	DeAngelis Pasquale	184	U S A	23	
	W	DeAngelis Phyllis—†	184	operator	21	"
	X	Adamo Gabriel	184	retired	73	
	Y	Adamo Mary—†	184	housewife	58	"
	Z	*Cosco Andrew	184	retired	81	
		2471				
	A	Pucci Domenic	184	metalwkr	54	"
	B	Pucci Sarah—†	184	housewife	42	"
	C	Cambria Frank	185	laborer	38	"
	D	Cambria Tina—†	185	housewife	38	"
	E	Scarpa Carmella—†	185	"	54	
	F	Scarpa Carmen	185	laborer	58	"
	G	Scarpa Florence—†	185	stitcher	20	"
	H	Scarpa Anthony	185	chipper	32	"
	K	Scarpa Lucy—†	185	housewife	29	"
	L	Caccialino Piro	186	laborer	56	
	M	Pizzoli Rocco	186	blacksmith	44	"
	N	Renna Anna—†	186	housewife	34	"
	O	Renna Paul	186	rigger	39	"
	P	Fiandaca Domenic	186	millhand	57	78 Frankfort
	R	*Fiandaca Pasqualina—†	186	housewife	57	here
	U	Petrone Anthony	190	barber	55	"
	V	Petrone Nancy—†	190	housewife	47	"
	W	D'Agostino Arthur	190	painter	48	
	X	D'Agostino Mary—†	190	saleswoman	22	"
	Y	*D'Agostino Olympia—†	190	housewife	55	"
	Z	DeLorenzo Concetta—†	190	clerk	29	"
		2472				
	A	Mingoria Salvatore	rear 190	porter	50	"
	B	Mingoria Stella—†	" 190	housewife	39	"
	C	Mingoria Stella—†	" 190	clerk	20	"
	D	Diminico Angelina—†	192	stitcher	21	"
	E	Diminico Christopher	192	U S A	20	"

42

Paris Street—Continued

F	Diminico Josephine—†	192	stitcher	26	here
G	Diminico Sabatino	192	laborer	61	"
H	Giunta Beatrice—†	192	housewife	43	"
K	Giunta John	192	U S N	22	
L	Giunta Salvatore	192	laborer	51	"
M	Salamone Angelina—†	192	housewife	48	"
N	Salamone Benedetto	192	laborer	57	
O	Salamone Benedetto, jr	192	"	24	
P	Salamone Maria—†	192	supervisor	21	"
R	Salamone Stella—†	192	stitcher	22	"
S	*Campagna Philomena—†	196	housewife	66	"
T	Campagna Joseph	196	shipper	25	
U	Campagna Robert	196	U S N	22	
V	Fabrizio Antonio	196	retired	57	
W	Fabrizio Carmella—†	196	nurse	30	
X	Fabrizio Pasquale	196	U S A	26	
Y	Fabrizio Tomasina—†	196	housewife	33	"
Z	Vietri Michael	196	laborer	55	

2473

A	DeCristoforo Emilio	196	brazier	38	
B	DeCristoforo Emma—†	196	housewife	37	"
C	LaGrassa Baldasarro	196	mechanic	37	"
D	LaGrassa Mary—†	196	housewife	34	"
E	Bondanza Clara—†	196	at home	26	"
F	*Bondanza Phyllis—†	196	housewife	68	"
G	*Guarino Mary A—†	196	at home	71	"
H	DeLeo Archille	196	laborer	57	
K	DeLeo Archille, jr	196	"	21	
L	DeLeo Guido	196	"	20	
M	DeLeo Julia—†	196	housewife	53	"
N	DeRuosi Angelo	196	laborer	23	
O	DeRuosi Anna—†	196	housewife	20	"
P	Mazzaferra Mary—†	196	"	25	
R	Mazzaferra Rocco	196	U S A	25	
S	Martorana John	196	cutter	28	
T	Martorana Susan—†	196	housewife	26	"
U	DeRosa Rose—†	196	"	35	
W	McDonald Archibald	202	U S A	33	
X	McDonald Claire—†	202	housewife	34	"
Y	Ricupero Erminio H	202	plumber	39	"
Z	Ricupero Marie R—†	202	housewife	24	"

2474

Paris Street—Continued

A	Ricupero Alfonse	202	laborer	27	here
B	Ricupero Elizabeth—†	202	housewife	26	"
C	Chevrie Agnes—†	206	"	70	"
D	Chevrie John	206	retired	73	
E	Luongo Joseph ·	206	laborer	45	
F	Luongo Mamie—†	206	housewife	45	"
G	Lippert Henry	206	U S M C	27	"
H	Lippert Louise—†	206	housewife	26	"
K	Longo Charles	207	U S A	33	
L	Longo Emily—†	207	housewife	26	"
M	Longo Anthony	207	U S A	28	
N	Longo Patrick	207	laborer	65	"
O	*Longo Philomena—†	207	housewife	63	"
P	Longo Joseph	207	laborer	33	
R	Longo Theresa—†	207	housewife	31	"
S	Spina Anthony	209	baker	30	··
T	Spina Laura—†	209	housewife	28	"
U	Dalelio Fiore A	209	gate tender	60	"
V	Dalelio Fiore A, jr	209	electrician	27	"
W	Dalelio Grace—†	209	housewife	60	"
X	Dalelio John J	209	chauffeur	29	"
Y	Dalelio Mary J—†	209	dressmaker	23	"
Z	Dalelio Philomena—†	209	at home	25	"

2475

A	DeSena Mary—†	209	housewife	34	81 Princeton
B	DeSena Paul	209	butcher	40	81 "
C	McKenney Frances—†	210	housekeeper	32	here
D	Hanson Marion—†	210	"	36	"
E	Ryan Daniel J	210	laborer	68	"
F	Ryan Daniel J, jr	210	"	33	
G	Ryan Mary A—†	210	housewife	67	"
H	Shaw J Cameron	210	laborer	56	"
K	Zarrella Mary—†	216	clerk	35	
L	Sugarman Bernard	216	machinist	29	"
M	Sugarman Israel	216	laborer	56	
N	*Sugarman Rose—†	216	housewife	53	"
O	Amando Michael	216	welder	29	"
P	Spolsino Martin	216	laborer	63	
	Spolsino Philomena—†	216	housewife	52	"
	ill Anna T—†	217	"	73	

44

Paris Street—Continued

T	Cahill Frederick C	217	laborer	37	here
U	Cahill Regina E—†	217	waitress	30	"
V	Cahill Robert W	217	cleaner	34	"
W	Johnson Peter J	217	retired	66	
X	D'Argenio Annette—†	218	housewife	27	"
Y	D'Argenio Anthony	218	U S N	29	
Z	*Cecere Carmella—†	218	housewife	57	"

2476

A	Cecere Hilda—†	218	stitcher	22	"
B	Cecere Louis	218	clerk	30	"
C	*Cecere Paul	218	laborer	62	"
D	Venuti Jean—†	218	housewife	30	"
E	Venuti Salvatore	218	laborer	32	
G	Doran Frank	220	fisherman	38	"
H	Doran Rose—†	220	housewife	37	"
K	Spalvero Albert	220	laborer	49	
L	Spalvero Grace—†	220	housewife	36	"
M	Gerace Angelina—†	220	"	28	
N	Gerace Anthony	220	machinist	32	"
O	Indingaro Helen E—†	221	housewife	28	"
P	Indingaro Leo	221	metalwkr	28	"
R	Indingaro Michael	221	shoewkr	54	"
S	Cozzi Gabriella—†	222	housewife	22	"
T	Cozzi Patrick	222	painter	23	
U	DiLorenzo Rose—†	222	housewife	32	"
V	DiLorenzo Vincent	222	painter	31	
W	Meanio Mary—†	222	clerk	23	
X	Peone Alexander	222	salesman	47	"
Y	Peone Ella—†	222	housewife	46	"
Z	Peone Grace—†	222	clerk	22	

2477

A	Cascia Angelina—†	223	stitcher	50	
B	Cascia Angelo	223	laborer	52	
C	Tontadonato Albert	223	clerk	28	
D	Tontadonato Mary—†	223	housewife	31	"
E	Abate Charles	223	U S N	22	
F	Abate Giacomina—†	223	housewife	49	"
G	Abate Joseph	223	presser	61	
H	Sciarappo Angelo	224	laborer	52	
K	Sciarappo Carmella—†	224	housewife	45	"
L	Ryan Larry	224	U S A	29	

Paris Street—Continued

M	Ryan Susan—†	224	housewife	28	here
N	Caccamesi Camilla—†	224	"	28	"
O	Caccamesi Peter	224	shoemaker	33	"
P	Martorano Joseph	225	chauffeur	30	"
R	Martorano Sylvia—†	225	housewife	29	"
S	Alferi Anna—†	225	"	39	..
T	Alferi Gaetano	225	checker	52	"
U	Cinelli Phyllis—†	225	housewife	21	"
V	Cinelli Salvatore	225	laborer	23	"
W	LaVerme John	226	U S N	20	
X	LaVerme Lucy—†	226	housewife	43	"
Y	DiBlasi Anthony	226	storekeeper	55	"
Z	DiBlasi Catherine—†	226	stenographer	20	"

2478

A	DiBlasi Mary—†	226	housewife	50	"
B	*Amari Crucifissa—†	226	"	41	"
C	Amari Josephine—†	226	clerk	20	"
D	Amari Peter	226	laborer	52	"
F	Sgro Anthony	236	plater	29	
G	Sgro Antonina—†	236	storekeeper	33	"
H	*Sgro Marie—†	236	housewife	49	"
K	Antonuccio John	236	U S A	37	
L	Antonuccio John	236	operator	27	"
M	Antonuccio Peter	236	"	55	
N	Antonuccio Roy	236	packer	20	
O	Antonuccio Sara—†	236	housewife	43	"
P	Bollerini Domenic	240	laborer	48	
R	Bollerini Phyllis—†	240	housewife	36	"
S	Hibbard Harry E	242	painter	27	151 Chelsea
T	Hibbard Mary—†	242	housewife	27	151 "
U	Lalicata Joseph	242	brazier	27	147 Trenton
V	Lalicata Phyllis—†	242	housewife	26	147 "
X	Caralino Carl	244	laborer	45	here
Y	Brass Myer	244	collector	67	"
Z	Brass Sarah—†	244	housewife	55	"

2479

A	Mori Girio	244	pipefitter	45	"
	Mori Rose—†	244	housewife	45	"
	ernacchio Frank	252	machinist	36	"
	nacchio Lucy—†	252	housewife	29	"
	ga Joseph	252	U S A	30	

Paris Street—Continued

	Letter	Full Name	Residence	Occupation	Age	Reported Residence
	F	DiTroga Theresa—†	252	housewife	30	here
	G	Sarro Frank	252	painter	21	23 Morris
	H	Sarro Ruth—†	252	housewife	21	23 "
	K	Forgione Alfonso	254	shoewkr	59	here
	L	Forgione George J	254	U S N	22	"
	M	Forgione Vincent	254	U S A	21	"
	P	Palermo Anthony	256	"	24	
	R	Palermo Paul	256	laborer	55	
	S	Palermo Rose—†	256	housewife	54	"
	T	Mangone Anna—†	rear 256	"	37	181 Chelsea
	U	Mangone Michael	" 256	laborer	39	181 "
	V	Blase Emilio	258	"	27	here
	W	Blase Frances—†	258	housewife	27	"
	X	Prudente Anthony	258	longshoreman	40	"
	Y	Prudente Rose—†	258	housewife	41	"
	Z	Cavarretta Mary—†	258	"	51	
2480						
	A	Cavarretta Vincent	258	storekeeper	53	"
	B	LeBlanc John	258	laborer	23	
	C	LeBlanc Josephine—†	258	housewife	21	"
	D	Carr Blanche—†	260	"	32	
	E	Carr Gilman	260	U S N	41	
	F	Francis Anthony	260	woodwkr	55	"
	G	Francis Mary—†	260	housewife	54	
	H	Gill Dennis	260	printer	49	
	K	Littlewood Mary—†	260	housekeeper	80	
	M	Zollo Florence—†	262	housewife		
	N	Zollo James	262	laborer		
	O	Mastromarino John	262	welder		
	P	Mastromarino Margaret—†	262	housewife		
	S	DiLoreto Constance—†	264	"		
	T	DiLoreto Guido	264	chauffe		
	U	Nappi Alphonse	264	"		
	V	Nappi Dora—†	264	hous	29	
	W	Mongiello Angelo	266	we		
	X	Mongiello Concetta—†	266	h	32	
	Y	Chase Eleanora—†	266		40	
	Z	Chase George	266			
2481						
	A	Amico Josephine—†				
	B	Amico Michael				

Page	Letter	Full Name	Residence, Jan. 1, 1945.	Occupation	Supposed Age	Reported Residence, Jan. 1, 1944. Street and Number.

Paris Street—Continued

	c	Fenno Anthony	268	U S M C	28	here
	d	Fenno Louis	268	chauffeur	30	"
	e	Fenno Mildred—†	268	housewife	30	"
	f	Cardinale Joseph	268	shipper	29	"
	g	Cardinale Josephine—†	268	housewife	29	"
	h	Delaney Louise T—†	268	housekeeper	46	"
	l	Barbaro Angelo	276	painter	36	"
	m	Barbaro Jennie—†	276	housewife	34	"
	n	Mazzone Anthony	276	chauffeur	24	Cheslea
	o	Mazzone Joseph	276	laborer	54	here
	p*	Mazzone Mary—†	276	housewife	46	"

Porter Street

z

	a	DiBellato Frances—†	40	nurse	25	here
	b*	DiBellato Pasqualina—†	40	housewife	63	"
	c	Amalimpa Arthur	42	longshoreman	29	"
	d	Amalimpa Rose—†	42	housewife	27	"
	f	Sgrenar Jennie—†	42	housekeeper	25	"
	g	Cardinale Anna—†	46	packer	27	"

2482

	h a	Cardinale Casimo	46	U S C G	23	"
	f b	Cardinale Domiano	46	fisherman	59	"
	c	Cardinale Josephine—†	46	housewife	50	"
	d	Cardinale Peter	46	U S N	21	
	e	Recca Angelo	46	technician	29	"
	f	Recca John	46	factoryhand	25	"
	g	Recca Joseph	46	"	61	
	h	Recca Maria—†	46	housewife	54	"
	l	LaConte Matteo	48	chauffeur	26	"
	m	LaConte Tomasina—†	48	housewife	23	"
	n	Calabro Elizabeth—†	48	"	42	"
	o	Calabro Vincent	48	salesman	49	"
	p*	Attardo Anthony	52	fishcutter	34	"
	r	Attardo Carmella—†	52	housewife	26	"
	u	Napolitano Florence—†	60	housekeeper	29	"
	v	Palosi Betty—†	60	"	25	"
	y	Arinella Anna—†	72	housewife	35	"
		Arinella Edward	72	longshoreman	38	"

2483

| | | rabito Philomena—† | 72 | housewife | 21 | " |

48

Page.	Letter.	Full Name.	Residence, Jan. 1, 1945.	Occupation.	Supposed Age.	Reported Residence, Jan. 1, 1944. Street and Number.

Porter Street—Continued

	B	Morabito William	72	pressman	27	here
	C	Guidara Concetta—†	72	housewife	28	"
	D	Guidara William	72	painter	36	"
	G	*Bawadanza Joseph	72	baker	42	
	F	*Bawadanza Maria—†	72	housewife	67	"
	H	Bawadanza Rose—†	72	factoryhand	44	"
	K	Rao Fannie—†	72	housewife	29	"
	L	Rao Samuel	72	bartender	35	"
	N	*Belardino Concetta—†	76	housewife	59	"
	O	Belardino James	76	guard	33	
	P	*Belardino John	76	retired	69	
	R	Belardino Thomas	76	shoewkr	31	"
	S	DeMarco Carmino	76	laborer	69	
	T	DeMarco Rose—†	76	housewife	68	"
	U	Martorano Antoinette—†	80	"	48	"
	V	Martorano Joseph	80	salesman	55	148 Bremen
	W	Martorano Gaetano	80	shipfitter	27	here
	X	Martorano Lucia—†	80	housewife	22	"
		2484				
	C	Marotta Alfred	84	chemist	34	"
	D	Marotta Rose—†	84	housewife	32	"
	G	Rossi Evelyn—†	86	"	31	
	H	Rossi Michael	86	welder	33	
	K	Puopolo Angelina—†	86	stitcher	27	"
	L	Zarella Consiglia—†	86	housekeeper	62	"
	M	Zarella George	86	U S N	26	
	N	Zarella Ida—†	86	housewife	25	"
	P	DiLuigi Dominic	88	U S N	22	
	R	DiLuigi Frances—†	88	housewife	21	"
	S	DiLuigi Dominica—†	88	"	52	
	T	*DiLuigi Joseph	88	clerk	61	"
	U	DiLuigi Louis	88	U S A	26	
	V	Salabini Elsie—†	88	factoryhand	24	"
		2485				
	A	Lobue Josephine—†	94	clerk	24	
	B	Valanzola Josephine—†	94	at home	74	"
	C	Lobue James	94	clerk	27	
	D	Lobue Josephine—†	94	housewife	45	"
	E	Lobue Luigi	94	storekeeper	47	"
	F	Lobue Salvatore	94	U S A	22	"
	H	Cardarella Joseph	96	laborer	62	

1—24

49

Porter Street—Continued

K	Cardarella Lucia—†	96	housewife	57	here
L	Moscone Anna—†	96	"	39	"
M*	Moscone Fred	96	mason	44	"
N	Moscone Philomena—†	96	factoryhand	21	"
P	Casto Joseph	110	"	53	"
R*	Casto Rosaria—†	110	housewife	43	"
S	DeFreitas Carlo	110	factoryhand	50	"
T	DeFreitas Florence—†	110	housewife	48	"
V	Adierno Assunta—†	112	housekeeper	57	"
W	Adierno Elsie—†	112	welder	31	"
X	Incrovato Anthony	112	foreman	40	"
Y	Incrovato Mary—†	112	housewife	33	"
	2486				
D	Zagorella Joseph	122	pedler	22	
F	Zagorella Leboria—†	122	housewife	44	"
E	Zagorella Phyllis—†	122	factoryhand	21	"
G	Zagorella Rocco	122	fishcutter	53	"

Saratoga Street

A	Ca					
B	Ca					
C	Gehm Gertrude—†	101	housewife	54	here
K	Gehm John	101	custodian	48	"
L	Cowan Emma—†	101	packer	59	"
M	Cowan Lyman W	101	guard	62	
N	Smith Anna F—†	103	housewife	66	"
O	Smith Louis V	103	salesman	66	"
P	DeChristoforo Amedeo	103	laborer	64	
R	DeChristoforo Frederick	103	"	22	
S	DeChristoforo Mary—†	103	housewife	54	"
T	Gardner Helena E—†	105	"	69	"
U	Gardner Joseph E	105	U S A	25	
V	Gardner William B	105	shipper	37	"
W	Moore Alfred L	107	U S A	34	"
X	Moore John A	107	"	30	
Y	Moore Lillian J—†	107	housewife	64	"
Z	Nagle Anna E—†	107	clerk	54	"
	2487				
A	Vose Viola E—†	107	housekeeper	55	Revere
*	Gillberg Axel B	109	laborer	69	here
	Henricksen Charles	109	"	71	"
	lson Hannah—†	109	housewife	86	"

50

Saratoga Street—Continued

E	Morse Edna—†	111	housekeeper	65	here
F	Malfy Anna—†	113	housewife	32	"
G	Malfy Rocco P	113	inspector	32	"
H	Scappato Leo	113	electrician	51	"
K	*Cavalieri Frank	115	guard	69	82 Leverett
L	*Cavalieri Maria—†	115	housewife	56	82 "
M	Daddieco Josephine—†	117	"	59	here
N	Daddieco Louis J	117	policeman	34	"
O	Daddieco Mary—†	117	housewife	34	"
P	Daddieco Ruth—†	117	operator	22	"
R	Lewin Gwendolyn—†	119	clerk	21	
S	MacDonald Abigail—†	119	at home	63	"
T	*MacDonald Catherine—†	119	housewife	73	"
U	MacDonald James G	119	tester	50	
V	MacDonald James J	119	carpenter	81	"
W	MacDonald Margaret—†	119	tel operator	21	"
X	MacDonald William	119	retired	79	
Y	Small Ada—†	121	housewife	37	"
Z	Small George	121	laborer	41	

2488

A	Trask Ada—†	121	at home	70	"
B	Bavaro Anthony J	123	shipper	27	104 Brooks
C	Bavaro Jacqueline—†	123	housewife	20	197 Lexington
D	*Bavaro John A	123	clerk	56	104 Brooks
E	*Bavaro Josephine—†	123	housewife	51	104 "
F	Bavaro Theresa D—†	123	milliner	22	104 "
G	Carter Charles	125	U S A	32	here
H	Carter Margaret F—†	125	housewife	32	"
K	Carter Sylvia—†	125	secretary	24	"
L	Cucugliata Eleanor—†	125	shipper	27	"
M	Cucugliata Grace—†	125	housewife	55	"
N	Pompeo Domenica—†	127	"	47	"
O	Pompeo John	127	shipfitter	53	"
P	Pompeo Livio	127	U S A	21	
R	Barrett Katherine—†	129	domestic	50	"
S	Cheverie Agnes—†	129	clerk	49	Maine
T	Cheverie Frank	129	laborer	55	here
U	Crowley Annie—†	129	housewife	49	"
V	Crowley Michael F	129	carpenter	60	"
W	Jeddy George	129	fishcutter	40	Saugus
X	Magussion Oscar	129	carpenter	60	here

Page.	Letter.	Full Name.	Residence, Jan. 1, 1945.	Occupation.	Supposed Age.	Reported Residence, Jan. 1, 1944. Street and Number.

Saratoga Street—Continued

	Y	Santirocco Dominic	129	laborer	55	217 E Eagle
	z	Sahkarian Thomas	129	storekeeper	55	here
2489						
	A	Andolina Angelo	131	retired	76	
	B	Andolina Charles	131	laborer	46	"
	c	Andolina Josephine—†	131	candymaker	49	"
	D	Andolina Mary G—†	131	clerk	33	
	E	Andolina Rose—†	131	housewife	78	"
	F	Brown Katherine—†	133	domestic	44	"
	G	Terravecchia Anna—†	133	housewife	36	"
	¹G	Terravecchia John	133	laborer	39	"
	H	Pardo Angelo F	135	guard	53	
	K	Pardo Emma G—†	135	housewife	47	"
	L	*Salvaggio Salvatrice—†	137	"	80	
	M	Argentina Minnie—†	137	bookkeeper	29	"
	N	Salvaggio Eleanor—†	137	housewife	33	"
	¹N	Salvaggio Paul	137	manager	49	"
	o	Bates David	139	retired	75	"
	P	Cusack Timothy	139	machinist	38	"
	R	Hayes John	139	fisherman	58	Florida
	s	O'Hearn Michael	139	"	32	here
	T	Swanson Corinne A—†	141	clerk	33	"
	v	Lazzaro Filippa—†	143	housewife	67	"
	w	DiGirolomo Gaetano	143	farmer	32	
	x	DiGirolomo Phyllis—†	143	bookkeeper	30	"
	Y	Gangi Grace—†	143	stitcher	32	"
	z	Gangi Rose—†	143	housewife	61	"
2490						
	A	Gangi Salvatore	143	cabinetmaker	69	"
	B	Gangi Salvatore, jr	143	upholsterer	41	"
	c	Vacchio Carmine—†	145	housewife	46	"
	D	Vacchio Celesta—†	145	inspector	22	"
	E	Vacchio Michael	145	fireman	57	"
	F	Vacchio Rose—†	145	housewife	24	"
		Vacchio Victor	145	U S A	24	
		ley Walter	147	machinist	28	"
		s Thomas P	147	fisherman	40	"
		te Owen	147	rigger	56	Canada
		Anna—†	147	at home	73	here

Letter.	Full Name.	Residence, Jan. 1, 1945.	Occupation.	Supposed Age.	Reported Residence, Jan. 1, 1944. Street and Number.

Saratoga Street—Continued

	Cannata Jennie—†	149	housewife	49	here
	Cannata John	149	candymaker	55	"
s	Cannata Minnie—†	149	machinist	24	"
r	Cannata Phillip	149	metalwkr	20	"
u	*Sombrone Vita—†	149	at home	80	"
v	Vanella Annie—†	149	housewife	45	"
w	Vanella Benjamin	149	chauffeur	48	"
x	Barletta George	149	U S A	34	
y	Zagarella Louise—†	149	housewife	37	"
	2491				
a	Zagarella Peter	149	presser	39	
b	*Reynolds Catherine—†	151	housewife	32	"
c	*Reynolds Thomas	151	fisherman	38	"
d	McNeely Donald W	151	letter carrier	22	"
e	McNeely Madeleine M—†	151	housewife	41	"
f	Hayes James J	151	U S A	24	236
g	*Hayes Mary A—†	151	housewife	64	22
h	*Hayes William	151	fisherman	62	
k	Corbett Florence—†	153	housewife	53	
l	Corbett James H	153	foreman		
m	Consilvio Americo	153	metalwkr		
n	Consilvio Benjamin	153	retired		
o	Consilvio Claire—†	153	tel oper		
p	*Consilvio Concetta—†	153	house		
r	Consilvio Felix J	153	U S		
s	Consilvio John	153	m		
t	Consilvio Nancy—†	153	b		
u	Grella Lorraine—†	153			
v	Grella Susan—†	153			
w	Brizzi Louise—†	15			
x	Ponzo Joseph, jr	15			
y	Ponzo Josephine—†				
z	Flamingo Amelia—				
	2492				
a	Flamingo Leona				
b	Flamingo Rocc				
c	Giusti Hugo				
d	Giusti Marie				
e	Mori Cathe				
f	Mori Jose				
g	Fascia				

reet—Continued

Y	Santirc		housewife	35	here
z	Sahkaria		"	52	"
			perator	58	"
			erk	31	
A	Andolina A		usewife	25	"
B	Andolina Cha		pfitter	36	"
c	Andolina Josep		sewife	35	"
D	Andolina Mary		neer	46	"
E	Andolina Rose—†		visor	40	"
F	Brown Katherine—		eur	27	"
G	Terravecchia Anna—		ife	26	"
¹G	Terravecchia John			60	"
H	Pardo Angelo F			24	"
K	Pardo Emma			22	"
L	*Salvaggio Sa		ith	65	"
M	Argentina				
N	Salvaggic			23	"
¹N	Salvaggic			59	"
o	Bates Da			51	"
P	Cusack T.			50	"
R	Hayes Joh			61	"
s	O'Hearn N			39	"
T	Swanson C			43	"
v	Lazzaro Fi.			42	"
w	DiGirolomc			1	"
x	DiGirolomo				
Y	Gangi Grace				
z	Gangi Rose—				

24

A	Gangi Salvat		laborer	69 9	2 Savage ct
B	Gangi Salvat		retired	4 56	2 "
c	Vacchio Carn		U S N	4 52	here
D	Vacchio Celes	21	sewife	2 56	"
E	Vacchio Mich.	44	spector		
F	Vacchio Rose—	42	fireman		
		45	housewife		
	Vacchio Victor	145	U S A		
	ley Walter	147	machinist		here
	s Thomas P	147	fisherman	40 8	"
	tte Owen	147	rigger	56	"
	Anna—†	147	at home	73	"
	ary—†	147	housewife	60	
	rick	147	fisherman	46	New.

52

Lightning Source UK Ltd.
Milton Keynes UK
UKHW020620241118
332794UK00006B/213/P